Complete Solutions Guide

CALCULUS
SEVENTH EDITION
Larson/Hostetler/Edwards

Volume III
Chapters 10-14
and
Appendix A

Bruce H. Edwards
University of Florida

HOUGHTON MIFFLIN COMPANY   Boston   New York

Editor-in-Chief: Jack Shira
Managing Editor: Cathy Cantin
Development Manager: Maureen Ross
Development Editor: Laura Wheel
Assistant Editor: Rosalind Horn
Supervising Editor: Karen Carter
Project Editor: Patty Bergin
Editorial Assistant: Lindsey Gulden
Production Technology Supervisor: Gary Crespo
Marketing Manager: Michael Busnach
Marketing Assistant: Nicole Mollica
Senior Manufacturing Coordinator: Jane Spelman

Printed in the United States of America

ISBN 0-618-14933-3

456789-VHG-07 06 05 04

Preface

The *Complete Solutions Guide* for *Calculus*, Seventh Edition, is a supplement to the text by Ron Larson, Robert P. Hostetler, and Bruce H. Edwards. Solutions to every exercise in the text are given with all essential algebraic steps included. There are three volumes in the complete set of solutions guides. Volume I contains Chapters P-5, Volume II contains Chapters 6-10, and Volume III contains Chapters 10-14.

I have made every effort to see that the solutions are correct. However, I would appreciate hearing about any errors or other suggestions for improvement.

I would like to thank the staff at Larson Texts, Inc. for their help in the production of this guide.

Bruce H. Edwards
University of Florida
Gainesville, Florida 32611
(be@math.ufl.edu)

CONTENTS

PART I

CHAPTER 10
Vectors and the Geometry of Space

CHAPTER 10
Vectors and the Geometry of Space

Section 10.1   Vectors in the Plane

Solutions to Odd-Numbered Exercises

1. (a) $\mathbf{v} = \langle 5 - 1, 3 - 1 \rangle = \langle 4, 2 \rangle$

(b)

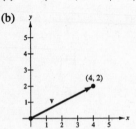

3. (a) $\mathbf{v} = \langle -4 - 3, -2 - (-2) \rangle = \langle -7, 0 \rangle$

(b)

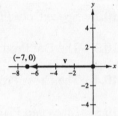

5. $\mathbf{u} = \langle 5 - 3, 6 - 2 \rangle = \langle 2, 4 \rangle$

   $\mathbf{v} = \langle 1 - (-1), 8 - 4 \rangle = \langle 2, 4 \rangle$

   $\mathbf{u} = \mathbf{v}$

7. $\mathbf{u} = \langle 6 - 0, -2 - 3 \rangle = \langle 6, -5 \rangle$

   $\mathbf{v} = \langle 9 - 3, 5 - 10 \rangle = \langle 6, -5 \rangle$

   $\mathbf{u} = \mathbf{v}$

9. (b) $\mathbf{v} = \langle 5 - 1, 5 - 2 \rangle = \langle 4, 3 \rangle$

(a) and (c).

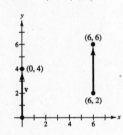

11. (b) $\mathbf{v} = \langle 6 - 10, -1 - 2 \rangle = \langle -4, -3 \rangle$

(a) and (c).

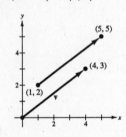

13. (b) $\mathbf{v} = \langle 6 - 6, 6 - 2 \rangle = \langle 0, 4 \rangle$

(a) and (c).

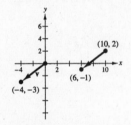

15. (b) $\mathbf{v} = \left\langle \frac{1}{2} - \frac{3}{2}, 3 - \frac{4}{3} \right\rangle = \left\langle -1, \frac{5}{3} \right\rangle$

(a) and (c).

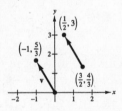

17. (a) $2\mathbf{v} = \langle 4, 6 \rangle$

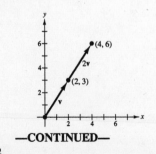

(b) $-3\mathbf{v} = \langle -6, -9 \rangle$

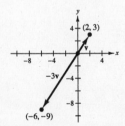

—CONTINUED—

17. **—CONTINUED—**

(c) $\frac{7}{2}\mathbf{v} = \left\langle 7, \frac{21}{2}\right\rangle$

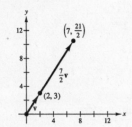

(d) $\frac{2}{3}\mathbf{v} = \left\langle \frac{4}{3}, 2\right\rangle$

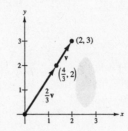

19.

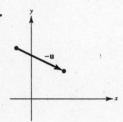

21.

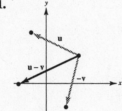

23. (a) $\frac{2}{3}\mathbf{u} = \frac{2}{3}\langle 4, 9\rangle = \left\langle \frac{8}{3}, 6\right\rangle$

(b) $\mathbf{v} - \mathbf{u} = \langle 2, -5\rangle - \langle 4, 9\rangle = \langle -2, -14\rangle$

(c) $2\mathbf{u} + 5\mathbf{v} = 2\langle 4, 9\rangle + 5\langle 2, -5\rangle = \langle 18, -7\rangle$

25. $\mathbf{v} = \frac{3}{2}(2\mathbf{i} - \mathbf{j}) = 3\mathbf{i} - \frac{3}{2}\mathbf{j}$
$$= \left\langle 3, -\frac{3}{2}\right\rangle$$

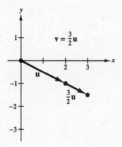

27. $\mathbf{v} = (2\mathbf{i} - \mathbf{j}) + 2(\mathbf{i} + 2\mathbf{j})$
$$= 4\mathbf{i} + 3\mathbf{j} = \langle 4, 3\rangle$$

29. $u_1 - 4 = -1$

$u_2 - 2 = 3$

$u_1 = 3$

$u_2 = 5$

$Q = (3, 5)$

31. $\|\mathbf{v}\| = \sqrt{16 + 9} = 5$

33. $\|\mathbf{v}\| = \sqrt{36 + 25} = \sqrt{61}$

35. $\|\mathbf{v}\| = \sqrt{0 + 16} = 4$

37. $\|\mathbf{u}\| = \sqrt{3^2 + 12^2} = \sqrt{153}$

$\mathbf{v} = \dfrac{\mathbf{u}}{\|\mathbf{u}\|} = \dfrac{\langle 3, 12\rangle}{\sqrt{153}} = \left\langle \dfrac{3}{\sqrt{153}}, \dfrac{12}{\sqrt{153}}\right\rangle$
$$= \left\langle \dfrac{\sqrt{17}}{17}, \dfrac{4\sqrt{17}}{17}\right\rangle \text{ unit vector}$$

39. $\|\mathbf{u}\| = \sqrt{\left(\dfrac{3}{2}\right)^2 + \left(\dfrac{5}{2}\right)^2} = \dfrac{\sqrt{34}}{2}$

$\mathbf{v} = \dfrac{\mathbf{u}}{\|\mathbf{u}\|} = \dfrac{\langle (3/2), (5/2)\rangle}{\sqrt{34}/2} = \left\langle \dfrac{3}{\sqrt{34}}, \dfrac{5}{\sqrt{34}}\right\rangle$
$$= \left\langle \dfrac{3\sqrt{34}}{34}, \dfrac{5\sqrt{34}}{34}\right\rangle \text{ unit vector}$$

41. $\|\mathbf{u}\| = \langle 1, -1 \rangle, \mathbf{v} = \langle -1, 2 \rangle$

(a) $\|\mathbf{u}\| = \sqrt{1+1} = \sqrt{2}$

(b) $\|\mathbf{v}\| = \sqrt{1+4} = \sqrt{5}$

(c) $\mathbf{u} + \mathbf{v} = \langle 0, 1 \rangle$

$\|\mathbf{u} + \mathbf{v}\| = \sqrt{0+1} = 1$

(d) $\dfrac{\mathbf{u}}{\|\mathbf{u}\|} = \dfrac{1}{\sqrt{2}} \langle 1, -1 \rangle$

$\left\| \dfrac{\mathbf{u}}{\|\mathbf{u}\|} \right\| = 1$

(e) $\dfrac{\mathbf{v}}{\|\mathbf{v}\|} = \dfrac{1}{\sqrt{5}} \langle -1, 2 \rangle$

$\left\| \dfrac{\mathbf{v}}{\|\mathbf{v}\|} \right\| = 1$

(f) $\dfrac{\mathbf{u} + \mathbf{v}}{\|\mathbf{u} + \mathbf{v}\|} = \langle 0, 1 \rangle$

$\left\| \dfrac{\mathbf{u} + \mathbf{v}}{\|\mathbf{u} + \mathbf{v}\|} \right\| = 1$

43. $\mathbf{u} = \left\langle 1, \dfrac{1}{2} \right\rangle, \mathbf{v} = \langle 2, 3 \rangle$

(a) $\|\mathbf{u}\| = \sqrt{1 + \dfrac{1}{4}} = \dfrac{\sqrt{5}}{2}$

(b) $\|\mathbf{v}\| = \sqrt{4+9} = \sqrt{13}$

(c) $\mathbf{u} + \mathbf{v} = \left\langle 3, \dfrac{7}{2} \right\rangle$

$\|\mathbf{u} + \mathbf{v}\| = \sqrt{9 + \dfrac{49}{4}} = \dfrac{\sqrt{85}}{2}$

(d) $\dfrac{\mathbf{u}}{\|\mathbf{u}\|} = \dfrac{2}{\sqrt{5}} \left\langle 1, \dfrac{1}{2} \right\rangle$

$\left\| \dfrac{\mathbf{u}}{\|\mathbf{u}\|} \right\| = 1$

(e) $\dfrac{\mathbf{v}}{\|\mathbf{v}\|} = \dfrac{1}{\sqrt{13}} \langle 2, 3 \rangle$

$\left\| \dfrac{\mathbf{v}}{\|\mathbf{v}\|} \right\| = 1$

(f) $\dfrac{\mathbf{u} + \mathbf{v}}{\|\mathbf{u} + \mathbf{v}\|} = \dfrac{2}{\sqrt{85}} \left\langle 3, \dfrac{7}{2} \right\rangle$

$\left\| \dfrac{\mathbf{u} + \mathbf{v}}{\|\mathbf{u} + \mathbf{v}\|} \right\| = 1$

45. $\mathbf{u} = \langle 2, 1 \rangle$

$\|\mathbf{u}\| = \sqrt{5} \approx 2.236$

$\mathbf{v} = \langle 5, 4 \rangle$

$\|\mathbf{v}\| = \sqrt{41} \approx 6.403$

$\mathbf{u} + \mathbf{v} = \langle 7, 5 \rangle$

$\|\mathbf{u} + \mathbf{v}\| = \sqrt{74} \approx 8.602$

$\|\mathbf{u} + \mathbf{v}\| \leq \|\mathbf{u}\| + \|\mathbf{v}\|$

47. $\dfrac{\mathbf{u}}{\|\mathbf{u}\|} = \dfrac{1}{\sqrt{2}} \langle 1, 1 \rangle$

$4\left(\dfrac{\mathbf{u}}{\|\mathbf{u}\|} \right) = 2\sqrt{2} \langle 1, 1 \rangle$

$\mathbf{v} = \langle 2\sqrt{2}, 2\sqrt{2} \rangle$

49. $\dfrac{\mathbf{u}}{\|\mathbf{u}\|} = \dfrac{1}{2\sqrt{3}} \langle \sqrt{3}, 3 \rangle$

$2\left(\dfrac{\mathbf{u}}{\|\mathbf{u}\|} \right) = \dfrac{1}{\sqrt{3}} \langle \sqrt{3}, 3 \rangle$

$\mathbf{v} = \langle 1, \sqrt{3} \rangle$

51. $\mathbf{v} = 3[(\cos 0°)\mathbf{i} + (\sin 0°)\mathbf{j}] = 3\mathbf{i} = \langle 3, 0 \rangle$

53. $\mathbf{v} = 2[(\cos 150°)\mathbf{i} + (\sin 150°)\mathbf{j}]$

$= -\sqrt{3}\mathbf{i} + \mathbf{j} = \langle -\sqrt{3}, 1 \rangle$

55. $\mathbf{u} = \mathbf{i}$

$\mathbf{v} = \dfrac{3\sqrt{2}}{2}\mathbf{i} + \dfrac{3\sqrt{2}}{2}\mathbf{j}$

$\mathbf{u} + \mathbf{v} = \left(\dfrac{2 + 3\sqrt{2}}{2} \right)\mathbf{i} + \dfrac{3\sqrt{2}}{2}\mathbf{j}$

57. $\mathbf{u} = 2(\cos 4)\mathbf{i} + 2(\sin 4)\mathbf{j}$

$\mathbf{v} = (\cos 2)\mathbf{i} + (\sin 2)\mathbf{j}$

$\mathbf{u} + \mathbf{v} = (2\cos 4 + \cos 2)\mathbf{i} + (2\sin 4 + \sin 2)\mathbf{j}$

59. A scalar is a real number. A vector is represented by a directed line segment. A vector has both length and direction.

61. To normalize $\mathbf{v}(\mathbf{v} \neq 0)$, you find a unit vector $\mathbf{u}$ in the direction of $\mathbf{v}$:

$$\mathbf{u} = \frac{\mathbf{v}}{\|\mathbf{v}\|}.$$

For Exercises 63–67, $a\mathbf{u} + b\mathbf{w} = a(\mathbf{i} + 2\mathbf{j}) + b(\mathbf{i} - \mathbf{j}) = (a + b)\mathbf{i} + (2a - b)\mathbf{j}.$

63. $\mathbf{v} = 2\mathbf{i} + \mathbf{j}.$ Therefore, $a + b = 2, 2a - b = 1.$ Solving simultaneously, we have $a = 1, b = 1.$

65. $\mathbf{v} = 3\mathbf{i}.$ Therefore, $a + b = 3, 2a - b = 0.$ Solving simultaneously, we have $a = 1, b = 2.$

67. $\mathbf{v} = \mathbf{i} + \mathbf{j}.$ Therefore, $a + b = 1, 2a - b = 1.$ Solving simultaneously, we have $a = \frac{2}{3}, b = \frac{1}{3}.$

69. $y = x^3, y' = 3x^2 = 3$ at $x = 1.$

(a) $m = 3.$ Let $\mathbf{w} = \langle 1, 3 \rangle,$ then

$$\frac{\mathbf{w}}{\|\mathbf{w}\|} = \pm\frac{1}{\sqrt{10}}\langle 1, 3 \rangle.$$

(b) $m = -\frac{1}{3}.$ Let $\mathbf{w} = \langle 3, -1 \rangle,$ then

$$\frac{\mathbf{w}}{\|\mathbf{w}\|} = \pm\frac{1}{\sqrt{10}}\langle 3, -1 \rangle.$$

71. $f(x) = \sqrt{25 - x^2}$

$$f'(x) = \frac{-x}{\sqrt{25 - x^2}} = \frac{-3}{4} \text{ at } x = 3.$$

(a) $m = -\frac{3}{4}.$ Let $\mathbf{w} = \langle -4, 3 \rangle,$ then

$$\frac{\mathbf{w}}{\|\mathbf{w}\|} = \pm\frac{1}{5}\langle -4, 3 \rangle.$$

(b) $m = \frac{4}{3}.$ Let $\mathbf{w} = \langle 3, 4 \rangle,$ then

$$\frac{\mathbf{w}}{\|\mathbf{w}\|} = \pm\frac{1}{5}\langle 3, 4 \rangle$$

73. $\mathbf{u} = \frac{\sqrt{2}}{2}\mathbf{i} + \frac{\sqrt{2}}{2}\mathbf{j}$

$\mathbf{u} + \mathbf{v} = \sqrt{2}\mathbf{j}$

$\mathbf{v} = (\mathbf{u} + \mathbf{v}) - \mathbf{u} = -\frac{\sqrt{2}}{2}\mathbf{i} + \frac{\sqrt{2}}{2}\mathbf{j}$

75. Programs will vary.

77. $\|\mathbf{F}_1\| = 2, \theta_{\mathbf{F}_1} = 33°$

$\|\mathbf{F}_2\| = 3, \theta_{\mathbf{F}_2} = -125°$

$\|\mathbf{F}_3\| = 2.5, \theta_{\mathbf{F}_3} = 110°$

$\|\mathbf{R}\| = \|\mathbf{F}_1 + \mathbf{F}_2 + \mathbf{F}_3\| \approx 1.33$

$\theta_{\mathbf{R}} = \theta_{\mathbf{F}_1 + \mathbf{F}_2 + \mathbf{F}_3} \approx 132.5°$

79. (a) $180(\cos 30°\mathbf{i} + \sin 30°\mathbf{j}) + 275\mathbf{i} \approx 430.88\mathbf{i} + 90\mathbf{j}$

Direction: $\alpha \approx \arctan\left(\dfrac{90}{430.88}\right) \approx 0.206(\approx 11.8°)$

Magnitude: $\sqrt{430.88^2 + 90^2} \approx 440.18$ newtons

(b) $M = \sqrt{(275 + 180\cos\theta)^2 + (180\sin\theta)^2}$

$\alpha = \arctan\left[\dfrac{180\sin\theta}{275 + 180\cos\theta}\right]$

—CONTINUED—

79. —CONTINUED—

(c)

θ	0°	30°	60°	90°	120°	150°	180°
M	455	440.2	396.9	328.7	241.9	149.3	95
α	0°	11.8°	23.1°	33.2°	40.1°	37.1°	0

(d)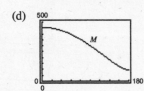

(e) M decreases because the forces change from acting in the same direction to acting in the opposite direction as θ increases from 0° to 180°.

81. $\mathbf{F}_1 + \mathbf{F}_2 + \mathbf{F}_3 = (75\cos 30°\mathbf{i} + 75\sin 30°\mathbf{j}) + (100\cos 45°\mathbf{i} + 100\sin 45°\mathbf{j}) + (125\cos 120°\mathbf{i} + 125\sin 120°\mathbf{j})$

$$= \left(\frac{75}{2}\sqrt{3} + 50\sqrt{2} - \frac{125}{2}\right)\mathbf{i} + \left(\frac{75}{2} + 50\sqrt{2} + \frac{125}{2}\sqrt{3}\right)\mathbf{j}$$

$$\|\mathbf{R}\| = \|\mathbf{F}_1 + \mathbf{F}_2 + \mathbf{F}_3\| \approx 228.5 \text{ lb}$$

$$\theta_{\mathbf{R}} = \theta_{\mathbf{F}_1 + \mathbf{F}_2 + \mathbf{F}_3} \approx 71.3°$$

83. (a) The forces act along the same direction. $\theta = 0°$.

(b) The forces cancel out each other. $\theta = 180°$.

(c) No, the magnitude of the resultant can not be greater than the sum.

85. $(-4, -1), (6, 5), (10, 3)$

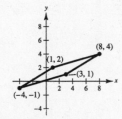
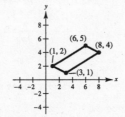
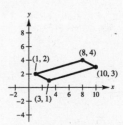

87. $\mathbf{u} = \overrightarrow{CB} = \|\mathbf{u}\|(\cos 30°\,\mathbf{i} + \sin 30°\,\mathbf{j})$

$\mathbf{v} = \overrightarrow{CA} = \|\mathbf{v}\|(\cos 130°\,\mathbf{i} + \sin 130°\,\mathbf{j})$

Vertical components: $\|\mathbf{u}\| \sin 30° + \|\mathbf{v}\| \sin 130° = 2000$

Horizontal components: $\|\mathbf{u}\| \cos 30° + \|\mathbf{v}\| \cos 130° = 0$

Solving this system, you obtain

$\|\mathbf{u}\| \approx 1305.5$ and $\|\mathbf{v}\| \approx 1758.8$.

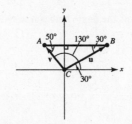

89. Horizontal component $= \|\mathbf{v}\| \cos \theta = 1200 \cos 6° \approx 1193.43$ ft/sec

Vertical component $= \|\mathbf{v}\| \sin \theta = 1200 \sin 6° \approx 125.43$ ft/sec

91. $\mathbf{u} = 900[\cos 148° \,\mathbf{i} + \sin 148° \,\mathbf{j}]$

$\mathbf{v} = 100[\cos 45° \,\mathbf{i} + \sin 45° \,\mathbf{j}]$

$\mathbf{u} + \mathbf{v} = [900 \cos 148° + 100 \cos 45°]\mathbf{i} + [900 \sin 148° + 100 \sin 45°]\mathbf{j}$

$\approx -692.53 \,\mathbf{i} + 547.64 \,\mathbf{j}$

$\theta \approx \arctan\left(\dfrac{547.64}{-692.53}\right) \approx -38.34°. \quad 38.34°$ North of West.

$\|\mathbf{u} + \mathbf{v}\| = \sqrt{(-692.53)^2 + (547.64)^2} \approx 882.9$ km/hr.

93. $\mathbf{F}_1 + \mathbf{F}_2 + \mathbf{F}_3 = \mathbf{0}$

$-3600\mathbf{j} + T_2(\cos 35°\mathbf{i} - \sin 35° \,\mathbf{j}) + T_3(\cos 92°\mathbf{i} + \sin 92°\mathbf{j}) = 0$

$T_2 \cos 35° + T_3 \cos 92° = 0$

$-T_2 \cos 35° + T_3 \sin 92° = 3600$

$T_2 = \dfrac{-T_3 \cos 92°}{\cos 35°} \Longrightarrow \dfrac{T_3 \cos 92°}{\cos 35°} \sin 35° + T_3 \sin 92° = 3600$ and $T_3(0.97495) = 3600 \Longrightarrow T_3 \approx 3692.48$

Finally, $T_2 = 157.32$

95. Let the triangle have vertices at $(0, 0)$, $(a, 0)$, and (b, c). Let $\mathbf{u}$ be the vector joining $(0, 0)$ and (b, c), as indicated in the figure. Then $\mathbf{v}$, the vector joining the midpoints, is

$\mathbf{v} = \left(\dfrac{a + b}{2} - \dfrac{a}{2}\right)\mathbf{i} + \dfrac{c}{2}\mathbf{j}$

$= \dfrac{b}{2}\mathbf{i} + \dfrac{c}{2}\mathbf{j} = \dfrac{1}{2}(b\mathbf{i} + c\mathbf{j}) = \dfrac{1}{2}\mathbf{u}$

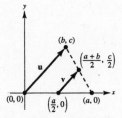

97. $\mathbf{w} = \|\mathbf{u}\|\mathbf{v} + \|\mathbf{v}\|\mathbf{u}$

$= \|\mathbf{u}\|[\|\mathbf{v}\| \cos \theta_v \mathbf{i} + \|\mathbf{v}\| \sin \theta_v \mathbf{j}] + \|\mathbf{v}\|[\|\mathbf{u}\| \cos \theta_u \mathbf{i} + \|\mathbf{u}\| \sin \theta_u \mathbf{j}] = \|\mathbf{u}\|\,\|\mathbf{v}\|[(\cos \theta_u + \cos \theta_v)\mathbf{i} + (\sin \theta_u + \sin \theta_v)\mathbf{j}]$

$= 2\|\mathbf{u}\|\,\|\mathbf{v}\|\left[\cos\left(\dfrac{\theta_u + \theta_v}{2}\right) \cos\left(\dfrac{\theta_u - \theta_v}{2}\right)\mathbf{i} + \sin\left(\dfrac{\theta_u + \theta_v}{2}\right) \cos\left(\dfrac{\theta_u - \theta_v}{2}\right)\mathbf{j}\right]$

$\tan \theta_w = \dfrac{\sin\left(\dfrac{\theta_u + \theta_v}{2}\right) \cos\left(\dfrac{\theta_u - \theta_v}{2}\right)}{\cos\left(\dfrac{\theta_u + \theta_v}{2}\right) \cos\left(\dfrac{\theta_u - \theta_v}{2}\right)} = \tan\left(\dfrac{\theta_u + \theta_v}{2}\right)$

Thus, $\theta_w = (\theta_u + \theta_v)/2$ and $\mathbf{w}$ bisects the angle between $\mathbf{u}$ and $\mathbf{v}$.

99. True   **101.** True   **103.** False

$\|a\mathbf{i} + b\mathbf{j}\| = \sqrt{2}\,|a|$

Section 10.2   Space Coordinates and Vectors in Space

1.

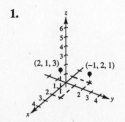

3.

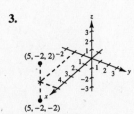

5. $A(2, 3, 4)$

    $B(-1, -2, 2)$

7. $x = -3, y = 4, z = 5$: $(-3, 4, 5)$

9. $y = z = 0, x = 10$: $(10, 0, 0)$

11. The z-coordinate is 0.

13. The point is 6 units above the xy-plane.

15. The point is on the plane parallel to the yz-plane that passes through $x = 4$.

17. The point is to the left of the xz-plane.

19. The point is on or between the planes $y = 3$ and $y = -3$.

21. The point (x, y, z) is 3 units below the xy-plane, and below either quadrant I or III.

23. The point could be above the xy-plane and thus above quadrants II or IV, or below the xy-plane, and thus below quadrants I or III.

25. $d = \sqrt{(5-0)^2 + (2-0)^2 + (6-0)^2}$

    $= \sqrt{25 + 4 + 36} = \sqrt{65}$

27. $d = \sqrt{(6-1)^2 + (-2-(-2))^2 + (-2-4)^2}$

    $= \sqrt{25 + 0 + 36} = \sqrt{61}$

29. $A(0, 0, 0), B(2, 2, 1), C(2, -4, 4)$

    $|AB| = \sqrt{4 + 4 + 1} = 3$

    $|AC| = \sqrt{4 + 16 + 16} = 6$

    $|BC| = \sqrt{0 + 36 + 9} = 3\sqrt{5}$

    $|BC|^2 = |AB|^2 + |AC|^2$

    Right triangle

31. $A(1, -3, -2), B(5, -1, 2), C(-1, 1, 2)$

    $|AB| = \sqrt{16 + 4 + 16} = 6$

    $|AC| = \sqrt{4 + 16 + 16} = 6$

    $|BC| = \sqrt{36 + 4 + 0} = 2\sqrt{10}$

    Since $|AB| = |AC|$, the triangle is isosceles.

33. The z-coordinate is changed by 5 units:

    $(0, 0, 5), (2, 2, 6), (2, -4, 9)$

35. $\left(\dfrac{5+(-2)}{2}, \dfrac{-9+3}{2}, \dfrac{7+3}{2}\right) = \left(\dfrac{3}{2}, -3, 5\right)$

37. Center: $(0, 2, 5)$

    Radius: 2

    $(x-0)^2 + (y-2)^2 + (z-5)^2 = 4$

    $x^2 + y^2 + z^2 - 4y - 10z + 25 = 0$

39. Center: $\dfrac{(2,0,0)+(0,6,0)}{2} = (1, 3, 0)$

    Radius: $\sqrt{10}$

    $(x-1)^2 + (y-3)^2 + (z-0)^2 = 10$

    $x^2 + y^2 + z^2 - 2x - 6y = 0$

41. $x^2 + y^2 + z^2 - 2x + 6y + 8z + 1 = 0$

    $(x^2 - 2x + 1) + (y^2 + 6y + 9) + (z^2 + 8z + 16) = -1 + 1 + 9 + 16$

    $(x-1)^2 + (y+3)^2 + (z+4)^2 = 25$

    Center: $(1, -3, -4)$

    Radius: 5

43. $9x^2 + 9y^2 + 9z^2 - 6x + 18y + 1 = 0$

$$x^2 + y^2 + z^2 - \frac{2}{3}x + 2y + \frac{1}{9} = 0$$

$$\left(x^2 - \frac{2}{3}x + \frac{1}{9}\right) + (y^2 + 2y + 1) + z^2 = -\frac{1}{9} + \frac{1}{9} + 1$$

$$\left(x - \frac{1}{3}\right)^2 + (y + 1)^2 + (z - 0)^2 = 1$$

Center: $\left(\frac{1}{3}, -1, 0\right)$

Radius: 1

45. $x^2 + y^2 + z^2 \le 36$

Solid ball of radius 6 centered at origin.

47. (a) $\mathbf{v} = (2 - 4)\mathbf{i} + (4 - 2)\mathbf{j} + (3 - 1)\mathbf{k}$

$$= -2\mathbf{i} + 2\mathbf{j} + 2\mathbf{k} = \langle -2, 2, 2 \rangle$$

(b)

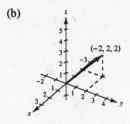

49. (a) $\mathbf{v} = (0 - 3)\mathbf{i} + (3 - 3)\mathbf{j} + (3 - 0)\mathbf{k}$

$$= -3\mathbf{i} + 3\mathbf{k} = \langle -3, 0, 3 \rangle$$

(b)

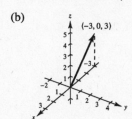

51. $\langle 4 - 3, 1 - 2, 6 - 0 \rangle = \langle 1, -1, 6 \rangle$

$$\|\langle 1, -1, 6 \rangle\| = \sqrt{1 + 1 + 36} = \sqrt{38}$$

Unit vector: $\dfrac{\langle 1, -1, 6 \rangle}{\sqrt{38}} = \left\langle \dfrac{1}{\sqrt{38}}, \dfrac{-1}{\sqrt{38}}, \dfrac{6}{\sqrt{38}} \right\rangle$

53. $\langle -5 - (-4), 3 - 3, 0 - 1 \rangle = \langle -1, 0, -1 \rangle$

$$\|\langle -1, 0, -1 \rangle\| = \sqrt{1 + 1} = \sqrt{2}$$

Unit vector: $\left\langle \dfrac{-1}{\sqrt{2}}, 0, \dfrac{-1}{\sqrt{2}} \right\rangle$

55. (b) $\mathbf{v} = (3 + 1)\mathbf{i} + (3 - 2)\mathbf{j} + (4 - 3)\mathbf{k}$

$$= 4\mathbf{i} + \mathbf{j} + \mathbf{k} = \langle 4, 1, 1 \rangle$$

(a) and (c).

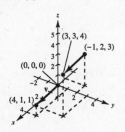

57. $(q_1, q_2, q_3) - (0, 6, 2) = (3, -5, 6)$

$Q = (3, 1, 8)$

59. (a) $2\mathbf{v} = \langle 2, 4, 4 \rangle$

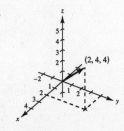

(b) $-\mathbf{v} = \langle -1, -2, -2 \rangle$

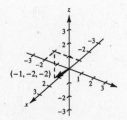

—CONTINUED—

59. —CONTINUED—

(c) $\frac{3}{2}\mathbf{v} = \langle \frac{3}{2}, 3, 3 \rangle$

(d) $0\mathbf{v} = \langle 0, 0, 0 \rangle$

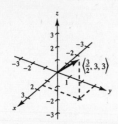

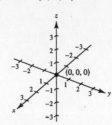

61. $\mathbf{z} = \mathbf{u} - \mathbf{v} = \langle 1, 2, 3 \rangle - \langle 2, 2, -1 \rangle = \langle -1, 0, 4 \rangle$

63. $\mathbf{z} = 2\mathbf{u} + 4\mathbf{v} - \mathbf{w} = \langle 2, 4, 6 \rangle + \langle 8, 8, -4 \rangle - \langle 4, 0, -4 \rangle = \langle 6, 12, 6 \rangle$

65. $2\mathbf{z} - 3\mathbf{u} = 2\langle z_1, z_2, z_3 \rangle - 3\langle 1, 2, 3 \rangle = \langle 4, 0, -4 \rangle$

$2z_1 - 3 = 4 \implies z_1 = \frac{7}{2}$

$2z_2 - 6 = 0 \implies z_2 = 3$

$2z_3 - 9 = -4 \implies z_3 = \frac{5}{2}$

$\mathbf{z} = \langle \frac{7}{2}, 3, \frac{5}{2} \rangle$

67. (a) and (b) are parallel since $\langle -6, -4, 10 \rangle = -2\langle 3, 2, -5 \rangle$ and $\langle 2, \frac{4}{3}, -\frac{10}{3} \rangle = \frac{2}{3}\langle 3, 2, -5 \rangle$.

69. $\mathbf{z} = -3\mathbf{i} + 4\mathbf{j} + 2\mathbf{k}$

(a) is parallel since $-6\mathbf{i} + 8\mathbf{j} + 4\mathbf{k} = 2\mathbf{z}$.

71. $P(0, -2, -5), Q(3, 4, 4), R(2, 2, 1)$

$\overrightarrow{PQ} = \langle 3, 6, 9 \rangle$

$\overrightarrow{PR} = \langle 2, 4, 6 \rangle$

$\langle 3, 6, 9 \rangle = \frac{3}{2}\langle 2, 4, 6 \rangle$

Therefore, $\overrightarrow{PQ}$ and $\overrightarrow{PR}$ are parallel. The points are collinear.

73. $P(1, 2, 4), Q(2, 5, 0), R(0, 1, 5)$

$\overrightarrow{PQ} = \langle 1, 3, -4 \rangle$

$\overrightarrow{PR} = \langle -1, -1, 1 \rangle$

Since $\overrightarrow{PQ}$ and $\overrightarrow{PR}$ are not parallel, the points are not collinear.

75. $A(2, 9, 1), B(3, 11, 4), C(0, 10, 2), D(1, 12, 5)$

$\overrightarrow{AB} = \langle 1, 2, 3 \rangle$

$\overrightarrow{CD} = \langle 1, 2, 3 \rangle$

$\overrightarrow{AC} = \langle -2, 1, 1 \rangle$

$\overrightarrow{BD} = \langle -2, 1, 1 \rangle$

Since $\overrightarrow{AB} = \overrightarrow{CD}$ and $\overrightarrow{AC} = \overrightarrow{BD}$, the given points form the vertices of a parallelogram.

77. $\|\mathbf{v}\| = 0$

79. $\mathbf{v} = \langle 1, -2, -3 \rangle$

$\|\mathbf{v}\| = \sqrt{1 + 4 + 9} = \sqrt{14}$

81. $\mathbf{v} = \langle 0, 3, -5 \rangle$

$\|\mathbf{v}\| = \sqrt{0 + 9 + 25} = \sqrt{34}$

83. $\mathbf{u} = \langle 2, -1, 2 \rangle$

$\|\mathbf{u}\| = \sqrt{4 + 1 + 4} = 3$

(a) $\dfrac{\mathbf{u}}{\|\mathbf{u}\|} = \dfrac{1}{3}\langle 2, -1, 2 \rangle$

(b) $-\dfrac{\mathbf{u}}{\|\mathbf{u}\|} = -\dfrac{1}{3}\langle 2, -1, 2 \rangle$

85. $\mathbf{u} = \langle 3, 2, -5 \rangle$

$\|\mathbf{u}\| = \sqrt{9 + 4 + 25} = \sqrt{38}$

(a) $\dfrac{\mathbf{u}}{\|\mathbf{u}\|} = \dfrac{1}{\sqrt{38}}\langle 3, 2, -5 \rangle$

(b) $-\dfrac{\mathbf{u}}{\|\mathbf{u}\|} = -\dfrac{1}{\sqrt{38}}\langle 3, 2, -5 \rangle$

87. Programs will vary.

89. $c\mathbf{v} = \langle 2c, 2c, -c \rangle$

$\|c\mathbf{v}\| = \sqrt{4c^2 + 4c^2 + c^2} = 5$

$9c^2 = 25$

$c = \pm\dfrac{5}{3}$

91. $\mathbf{v} = 10\dfrac{\mathbf{u}}{\|\mathbf{u}\|} = 10\left\langle 0, \dfrac{1}{\sqrt{2}}, \dfrac{1}{\sqrt{2}} \right\rangle$

$\qquad = \left\langle 0, \dfrac{10}{\sqrt{2}}, \dfrac{10}{\sqrt{2}} \right\rangle$

93. $\mathbf{v} = \dfrac{3}{2}\dfrac{\mathbf{u}}{\|\mathbf{u}\|} = \dfrac{3}{2}\left\langle \dfrac{2}{3}, \dfrac{-2}{3}, \dfrac{1}{3} \right\rangle = \left\langle 1, -1, \dfrac{1}{2} \right\rangle$

95. $\mathbf{v} = 2[\cos(\pm 30°)\mathbf{j} + \sin(\pm 30°)\mathbf{k}]$

$\qquad = \sqrt{3}\mathbf{j} \pm \mathbf{k} = \langle 0, \sqrt{3}, \pm 1 \rangle$

97.

$\mathbf{v} = \langle -3, -6, 3 \rangle$

$\dfrac{2}{3}\mathbf{v} = \langle -2, -4, 2 \rangle$

$(4, 3, 0) + (-2, -4, 2) = (2, -1, 2)$

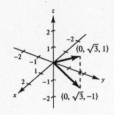

99. (a)

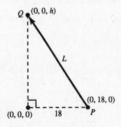

(b) $\mathbf{w} = a\mathbf{u} + b\mathbf{v} = a\mathbf{i} + (a + b)\mathbf{j} + b\mathbf{k} = \mathbf{0}$

$a = 0, a + b = 0, b = 0$

Thus, a and b are both zero.

(c) $a\mathbf{i} + (a + b)\mathbf{j} + b\mathbf{k} = \mathbf{i} + 2\mathbf{j} + \mathbf{k}$

$a = 1, b = 1$

$\mathbf{w} = \mathbf{u} + \mathbf{v}$

(d) $a\mathbf{i} + (a + b)\mathbf{j} + b\mathbf{k} = \mathbf{i} + 2\mathbf{j} + 3\mathbf{k}$

$a = 1, a + b = 2, b = 3$

Not possible

101. $d = \sqrt{(x_2 - x_1)^2 + (y_2 - y_1)^2 + (z_2 - z_1)^2}$

103. Two nonzero vectors $\mathbf{u}$ and $\mathbf{v}$ are parallel if $\mathbf{u} = c\mathbf{v}$ for some scalar c.

105. (a) The height of the right triangle is $h = \sqrt{L^2 - 18^2}$. The vector $\overrightarrow{PQ}$ is given by

$\overrightarrow{PQ} = \langle 0, -18, h \rangle$.

The tension vector $\mathbf{T}$ in each wire is

$\mathbf{T} = c\langle 0, -18, h \rangle$ where $ch = \dfrac{24}{3} = 8$.

Hence, $\mathbf{T} = \dfrac{8}{h}\langle 0, -18, h \rangle$ and

$T = \|\mathbf{T}\| = \dfrac{8}{h}\sqrt{18^2 + h^2} = \dfrac{8}{\sqrt{L^2 - 18^2}}\sqrt{18^2 + (L^2 - 18^2)} = \dfrac{8L}{\sqrt{L^2 - 18^2}}$

(b)

L	20	25	30	35	40	45	50
T	18.4	11.5	10	9.3	9.0	8.7	8.6

—CONTINUED—

105. —CONTINUED—

(c)

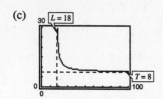

$x = 18$ is a vertical asymptote and $y = 8$ is a horizontal asymptote.

(d) $\displaystyle\lim_{L \to 18^+} \frac{8L}{\sqrt{L^2 - 18^2}} = \infty$

$\displaystyle\lim_{L \to \infty} \frac{8L}{\sqrt{L^2 - 18^2}} = \lim_{L \to \infty} \frac{8}{\sqrt{1 - (18/L)^2}} = 8$

(e) From the table, $T = 10$ implies $L = 30$ inches.

107. Let α be the angle between $\mathbf{v}$ and the coordinate axes.

$$\mathbf{v} = (\cos \alpha)\mathbf{i} + (\cos \alpha)\mathbf{j} + (\cos \alpha)\mathbf{k}$$

$$\|\mathbf{v}\| = \sqrt{3} \cos \alpha = 1$$

$$\cos \alpha = \frac{1}{\sqrt{3}} = \frac{\sqrt{3}}{3}$$

$$\mathbf{v} = \frac{\sqrt{3}}{3}(\mathbf{i} + \mathbf{j} + \mathbf{k}) = \frac{\sqrt{3}}{3}\langle 1, 1, 1 \rangle$$

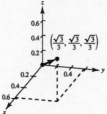

109. $\overrightarrow{AB} = \langle 0, 70, 115 \rangle$, $\mathbf{F}_1 = C_1\langle 0, 70, 115 \rangle$

$\overrightarrow{AC} = \langle -60, 0, 115 \rangle$, $\mathbf{F}_2 = C_2\langle -60, 0, 115 \rangle$

$\overrightarrow{AD} = \langle 45, -65, 115 \rangle$, $\mathbf{F}_3 = C_3\langle 45, -65, 115 \rangle$

$\mathbf{F} = \mathbf{F}_1 + \mathbf{F}_2 + \mathbf{F}_3 = \langle 0, 0, 500 \rangle$

Thus:

$$-60C_2 + 45C_3 = 0$$
$$70C_1 - 65C_3 = 0$$
$$115(C_1 + C_2 + C_3) = 500$$

Solving this system yields $C_1 = \frac{104}{69}$, $C_2 = \frac{28}{23}$, and $C_3 = -\frac{112}{69}$. Thus:

$$\|\mathbf{F}_1\| \approx 202.919N$$
$$\|\mathbf{F}_2\| \approx 157.909N$$
$$\|\mathbf{F}_3\| \approx 226.521N$$

111. $d(AP) = 2d(BP)$

$$\sqrt{x^2 + (y + 1)^2 + (z - 1)^2} = 2\sqrt{(x - 1)^2 + (y - 2)^2 + z^2}$$

$$x^2 + y^2 + z^2 + 2y - 2z + 2 = 4(x^2 + y^2 + z^2 - 2x - 4y + 5)$$

$$0 = 3x^2 + 3y^2 + 3z^2 - 8x - 18y + 2z + 18$$

$$-6 + \frac{16}{9} + 9 + \frac{1}{9} = \left(x^2 - \frac{8}{3}x + \frac{16}{9}\right) + (y^2 - 6y + 9) + \left(z^2 + \frac{2}{3}z + \frac{1}{9}\right)$$

$$\frac{44}{9} = \left(x - \frac{4}{3}\right)^2 + (y - 3)^2 + \left(z + \frac{1}{3}\right)^2$$

Sphere; center: $\left(\frac{4}{3}, 3, -\frac{1}{3}\right)$, radius: $\frac{2\sqrt{11}}{3}$

Section 10.3   The Dot Product of Two Vectors

1. $\mathbf{u} = \langle 3, 4 \rangle$, $\mathbf{v} = \langle 2, -3 \rangle$

(a) $\mathbf{u} \cdot \mathbf{v} = 3(2) + 4(-3) = -6$

(b) $\mathbf{u} \cdot \mathbf{u} = 3(3) + 4(4) = 25$

(c) $\|\mathbf{u}\|^2 = 25$

(d) $(\mathbf{u} \cdot \mathbf{v})\mathbf{v} = -6\langle 2, -3 \rangle = \langle -12, 18 \rangle$

(e) $\mathbf{u} \cdot (2\mathbf{v}) = 2(\mathbf{u} \cdot \mathbf{v}) = 2(-6) = -12$

3. $\mathbf{u} = \langle 2, -3, 4 \rangle$, $\mathbf{v} = \langle 0, 6, 5 \rangle$

(a) $\mathbf{u} \cdot \mathbf{v} = 2(0) + (-3)(6) + (4)(5) = 2$

(b) $\mathbf{u} \cdot \mathbf{u} = 2(2) + (-3)(-3) + 4(4) = 29$

(c) $\|\mathbf{u}\|^2 = 29$

(d) $(\mathbf{u} \cdot \mathbf{v})\mathbf{v} = 2\langle 0, 6, 5 \rangle = \langle 0, 12, 10 \rangle$

(e) $\mathbf{u} \cdot (2\mathbf{v}) = 2(\mathbf{u} \cdot \mathbf{v}) = 2(2) = 4$

5. $\mathbf{u} = 2\mathbf{i} - \mathbf{j} + \mathbf{k}$, $\mathbf{v} = \mathbf{i} - \mathbf{k}$

(a) $\mathbf{u} \cdot \mathbf{v} = 2(1) + (-1)(0) + 1(-1) = 1$

(b) $\mathbf{u} \cdot \mathbf{u} = 2(2) + (-1)(-1) + (1)(1) = 6$

(c) $\|\mathbf{u}\|^2 = 6$

(d) $(\mathbf{u} \cdot \mathbf{v})\mathbf{v} = \mathbf{v} = \mathbf{i} - \mathbf{k}$

(e) $\mathbf{u} \cdot (2\mathbf{v}) = 2(\mathbf{u} \cdot \mathbf{v}) = 2$

7. $\mathbf{u} = \langle 3240, 1450, 2235 \rangle$

   $\mathbf{v} = \langle 2.22, 1.85, 3.25 \rangle$

$\mathbf{u} \cdot \mathbf{v} = \$17,139.05$

This gives the total amount that the person earned on his products.

9. $\dfrac{\mathbf{u} \cdot \mathbf{v}}{\|\mathbf{u}\|\,\|\mathbf{v}\|} = \cos\theta$

$\mathbf{u} \cdot \mathbf{v} = (8)(5)\cos\dfrac{\pi}{3} = 20$

11. $\mathbf{u} = \langle 1, 1 \rangle$, $\mathbf{v} = \langle 2, -2 \rangle$

$\cos\theta = \dfrac{\mathbf{u} \cdot \mathbf{v}}{\|\mathbf{u}\|\,\|\mathbf{v}\|} = \dfrac{0}{\sqrt{2}\sqrt{8}} = 0$

$\theta = \dfrac{\pi}{2}$

13. $\mathbf{u} = 3\mathbf{i} + \mathbf{j}$, $\mathbf{v} = -2\mathbf{i} + 4\mathbf{j}$

$\cos\theta = \dfrac{\mathbf{u} \cdot \mathbf{v}}{\|\mathbf{u}\|\,\|\mathbf{v}\|} = \dfrac{-2}{\sqrt{10}\sqrt{20}} = \dfrac{-1}{5\sqrt{2}}$

$\theta = \arccos\left(-\dfrac{1}{5\sqrt{2}}\right) \approx 98.1°$

15. $\mathbf{u} = \langle 1, 1, 1 \rangle$, $\mathbf{v} = \langle 2, 1, -1 \rangle$

$\cos\theta = \dfrac{\mathbf{u} \cdot \mathbf{v}}{\|\mathbf{u}\|\,\|\mathbf{v}\|} = \dfrac{2}{\sqrt{3}\sqrt{6}} = \dfrac{\sqrt{2}}{3}$

$\theta = \arccos\dfrac{\sqrt{2}}{3} \approx 61.9°$

17. $\mathbf{u} = 3\mathbf{i} + 4\mathbf{j}$, $\mathbf{v} = -2\mathbf{j} + 3\mathbf{k}$

$\cos\theta = \dfrac{\mathbf{u} \cdot \mathbf{v}}{\|\mathbf{u}\|\,\|\mathbf{v}\|} = \dfrac{-8}{5\sqrt{13}} = \dfrac{-8\sqrt{13}}{65}$

$\theta = \arccos\left(-\dfrac{8\sqrt{13}}{65}\right) \approx 116.3°$

19. $\mathbf{u} = \langle 4, 0 \rangle$, $\mathbf{v} = \langle 1, 1 \rangle$

$\mathbf{u} \neq c\mathbf{v} \implies$ not parallel

$\mathbf{u} \cdot \mathbf{v} = 4 \neq 0 \implies$ not orthogonal

Neither

21. $\mathbf{u} = \langle 4, 3 \rangle$, $\mathbf{v} = \left\langle \dfrac{1}{2}, -\dfrac{2}{3} \right\rangle$

$\mathbf{u} \neq c\mathbf{v} \implies$ not parallel

$\mathbf{u} \cdot \mathbf{v} = 0 \implies$ orthogonal

23. $\mathbf{u} = \mathbf{j} + 6\mathbf{k}$, $\mathbf{v} = \mathbf{i} - 2\mathbf{j} - \mathbf{k}$

$\mathbf{u} \neq c\mathbf{v} \implies$ not parallel

$\mathbf{u} \cdot \mathbf{v} = -8 \neq 0 \implies$ not orthogonal

Neither

25. $\mathbf{u} = \langle 2, -3, 1 \rangle$, $\mathbf{v} = \langle -1, -1, -1 \rangle$

$\mathbf{u} \neq c\mathbf{v} \implies$ not parallel

$\mathbf{u} \cdot \mathbf{v} = 0 \implies$ orthogonal

27. $\mathbf{u} = \mathbf{i} + 2\mathbf{j} + 2\mathbf{k}, \|\mathbf{u}\| = 3$

$\cos \alpha = \dfrac{1}{3}$

$\cos \beta = \dfrac{2}{3}$

$\cos \gamma = \dfrac{2}{3}$

$\cos^2 \alpha + \cos^2 \beta + \cos^2 \gamma = \dfrac{1}{9} + \dfrac{4}{9} + \dfrac{4}{9} = 1$

29. $\mathbf{u} = \langle 0, 6, -4 \rangle, \|\mathbf{u}\| = \sqrt{52} = 2\sqrt{13}$

$\cos \alpha = 0$

$\cos \beta = \dfrac{3}{\sqrt{13}}$

$\cos \gamma = -\dfrac{2}{\sqrt{13}}$

$\cos^2 \alpha + \cos^2 \beta + \cos^2 \gamma = 0 + \dfrac{9}{13} + \dfrac{4}{13} = 1$

31. $\mathbf{u} = \langle 3, 2, -2 \rangle \quad \|\mathbf{u}\| = \sqrt{17}$

$\cos \alpha = \dfrac{3}{\sqrt{17}} \Rightarrow \alpha \approx 0.7560 \text{ or } 43.3°$

$\cos \beta = \dfrac{2}{\sqrt{17}} \Rightarrow \beta \approx 1.0644 \text{ or } 61.0°$

$\cos \gamma = \dfrac{-2}{\sqrt{17}} \Rightarrow \gamma \approx 2.0772 \text{ or } 119.0°$

33. $\mathbf{u} = \langle -1, 5, 2 \rangle \quad \|\mathbf{u}\| = \sqrt{30}$

$\cos \alpha = \dfrac{-1}{\sqrt{30}} \Rightarrow \alpha \approx 1.7544 \text{ or } 100.5°$

$\cos \beta = \dfrac{5}{\sqrt{30}} \Rightarrow \beta \approx 0.4205 \text{ or } 24.1°$

$\cos \gamma = \dfrac{2}{\sqrt{30}} \Rightarrow \gamma \approx 1.1970 \text{ or } 68.6°$

35. $\mathbf{F}_1: C_1 = \dfrac{50}{\|\mathbf{F}_1\|} \approx 4.3193$

$\mathbf{F}_2: C_2 = \dfrac{80}{\|\mathbf{F}_2\|} \approx 5.4183$

$\mathbf{F} = \mathbf{F}_1 + \mathbf{F}_2$

$\quad \approx 4.3193 \langle 10, 5, 3 \rangle + 5.4183 \langle 12, 7, -5 \rangle$

$\quad = \langle 108.2126, 59.5246, -14.1336 \rangle$

$\|\mathbf{F}\| \approx 124.310 \text{ lb}$

$\cos \alpha \approx \dfrac{108.2126}{\|\mathbf{F}\|} \Rightarrow \alpha \approx 29.48°$

$\cos \beta \approx \dfrac{59.5246}{\|\mathbf{F}\|} \Rightarrow \beta \approx 61.39°$

$\cos \gamma \approx \dfrac{-14.1336}{\|\mathbf{F}\|} \Rightarrow \gamma \approx 96.53°$

37. Let s = length of a side.

$\mathbf{v} = \langle s, s, s \rangle$

$\|\mathbf{v}\| = s\sqrt{3}$

$\cos \alpha = \cos \beta = \cos \gamma = \dfrac{s}{s\sqrt{3}} = \dfrac{1}{\sqrt{3}}$

$\alpha = \beta = \gamma = \arccos\left(\dfrac{1}{\sqrt{3}}\right) \approx 54.7°$

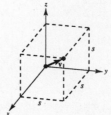

39. $\overrightarrow{OA} = \langle 0, 10, 10 \rangle$

$\cos \alpha = \dfrac{0}{\sqrt{0^2 + 10^2 + 10^2}} = 0 \Rightarrow \alpha = 90°$

$\cos \beta = \cos \gamma = \dfrac{10}{\sqrt{0^2 + 10^2 + 10^2}}$

$\quad = \dfrac{1}{\sqrt{2}} \Rightarrow \beta = \gamma = 45°$

41. $\mathbf{w}_2 = \mathbf{u} - \mathbf{w}_1 = \langle 6, 7 \rangle - \langle 2, 8 \rangle = \langle 4, -1 \rangle$

43. $\mathbf{w}_2 = \mathbf{u} - \mathbf{w}_1 = \langle 0, 3, 3 \rangle - \langle -2, 2, 2 \rangle = \langle 2, 1, 1 \rangle$

45. $\mathbf{u} = \langle 2, 3 \rangle, \mathbf{v} = \langle 5, 1 \rangle$

(a) $\mathbf{w}_1 = \left(\dfrac{\mathbf{u} \cdot \mathbf{v}}{\|\mathbf{v}\|^2}\right)\mathbf{v} = \dfrac{13}{26}\langle 5, 1 \rangle = \left\langle \dfrac{5}{2}, \dfrac{1}{2} \right\rangle$

(b) $\mathbf{w}_2 = \mathbf{u} - \mathbf{w}_1 = \left\langle -\dfrac{1}{2}, \dfrac{5}{2} \right\rangle$

47. $\mathbf{u} = \langle 2, 1, 2 \rangle$, $\mathbf{v} = \langle 0, 3, 4 \rangle$

(a) $\mathbf{w}_1 = \left(\dfrac{\mathbf{u} \cdot \mathbf{v}}{\|\mathbf{v}\|^2} \right) \mathbf{v}$

$\quad = \dfrac{11}{25} \langle 0, 3, 4 \rangle = \left\langle 0, \dfrac{33}{25}, \dfrac{44}{25} \right\rangle$

(b) $\mathbf{w}_2 = \mathbf{u} - \mathbf{w}_1 = \left\langle 2, -\dfrac{8}{25}, \dfrac{6}{25} \right\rangle$

49. $\mathbf{u} \cdot \mathbf{v} = \langle u_1, u_2, u_3 \rangle \cdot \langle v_1, v_2, v_3 \rangle = u_1 v_1 + u_2 v_2 + u_3 v_3$

51. (a) Orthogonal, $\theta = \dfrac{\pi}{2}$ (b) Acute, $0 < \theta < \dfrac{\pi}{2}$ (c) Obtuse, $\dfrac{\pi}{2} < \theta < \pi$

53. See page 738. Direction cosines of $\mathbf{v} = \langle v_1, v_2, v_3 \rangle$ are

$\quad \cos \alpha = \dfrac{v_1}{\|\mathbf{v}\|}, \cos \beta = \dfrac{v_2}{\|\mathbf{v}\|}, \cos \gamma = \dfrac{v_3}{\|\mathbf{v}\|}.$

α, β, and γ are the direction angles. See Figure 10.26.

55. (a) $\left(\dfrac{\mathbf{u} \cdot \mathbf{v}}{\|\mathbf{v}\|^2} \right) \mathbf{v} = \mathbf{u} \implies \mathbf{u} = c\mathbf{v} \implies \mathbf{u}$ and $\mathbf{v}$ are parallel.

(b) $\left(\dfrac{\mathbf{u} \cdot \mathbf{v}}{\|\mathbf{v}\|^2} \right) \mathbf{v} = \mathbf{0} \implies \mathbf{u} \cdot \mathbf{v} = 0 \implies \mathbf{u}$ and $\mathbf{v}$

are orthogonal.

57. Programs will vary.

59. Programs will vary.

61. Because $\mathbf{u}$ appears to be perpendicular to $\mathbf{v}$, the projection of $\mathbf{u}$ onto $\mathbf{v}$ is $\mathbf{0}$. Analytically,

$\quad \text{proj}_\mathbf{v} \mathbf{u} = \dfrac{\mathbf{u} \cdot \mathbf{v}}{\|\mathbf{v}\|^2} \mathbf{v} = \dfrac{\langle 2, -3 \rangle \cdot \langle 6, 4 \rangle}{\|\langle 6, 4 \rangle\|^2} \langle 6, 4 \rangle = 0 \langle 6, 4 \rangle = \mathbf{0}.$

63. $\mathbf{u} = \dfrac{1}{2}\mathbf{i} - \dfrac{2}{3}\mathbf{j}$. Want $\mathbf{u} \cdot \mathbf{v} = 0$.

$\quad \mathbf{v} = 8\mathbf{i} + 6\mathbf{j}$ and $-\mathbf{v} = -8\mathbf{i} - 6\mathbf{j}$ are orthogonal to $\mathbf{u}$.

65. $\mathbf{u} = \langle 3, 1, -2 \rangle$. Want $\mathbf{u} \cdot \mathbf{v} = 0$.

$\quad \mathbf{v} = \langle 0, 2, 1 \rangle$ and $-\mathbf{v} = \langle 0, -2, -1 \rangle$ are orthogonal to $\mathbf{u}$.

67. (a) Gravitational Force $\mathbf{F} = -48,000\,\mathbf{j}$

$\quad \mathbf{v} = \cos 10° \,\mathbf{i} + \sin 10° \,\mathbf{j}$

$\quad \mathbf{w}_1 = \dfrac{\mathbf{F} \cdot \mathbf{v}}{\|\mathbf{v}\|^2} \mathbf{v} = (\mathbf{F} \cdot \mathbf{v})\mathbf{v} = (-48,000)(\sin 10°)\mathbf{v}$

$\quad\quad\quad \approx -8335.1(\cos 10° \,\mathbf{i} + \sin 10° \,\mathbf{j})$

$\quad \|\mathbf{w}_1\| \approx 8335.1 \text{ lb}$

(b) $\mathbf{w}_2 = \mathbf{F} \cdot \mathbf{w}_1 = -48,000\,\mathbf{j} + 8335.1(\cos 10° \,\mathbf{i} + \sin 10° \,\mathbf{j})$

$\quad = 8208.5\,\mathbf{i} - 46,552.6\,\mathbf{j}$

$\quad \|\mathbf{w}_2\| \approx 47,270.8 \text{ lb}$

69. $\mathbf{F} = 85\left(\dfrac{1}{2}\mathbf{i} + \dfrac{\sqrt{3}}{2}\mathbf{j} \right)$

$\quad \mathbf{v} = 10\mathbf{i}$

$\quad W = \mathbf{F} \cdot \mathbf{v} = 425 \text{ ft} \cdot \text{lb}$

71. $\overrightarrow{PQ} = \langle 4, 7, 5 \rangle$

$\quad \mathbf{v} = \langle 1, 4, 8 \rangle$

$\quad W = \overrightarrow{PQ} \cdot \mathbf{v} = 72$

73. False. Let $\mathbf{u} = \langle 2, 4 \rangle$, $\mathbf{v} = \langle 1, 7 \rangle$ and $\mathbf{w} = \langle 5, 5 \rangle$. Then $\mathbf{u} \cdot \mathbf{v} = 2 + 28 = 30$ and $\mathbf{u} \cdot \mathbf{w} = 10 + 20 = 30$.

75. In a rhombus, $\|\mathbf{u}\| = \|\mathbf{v}\|$. The diagonals are $\mathbf{u} + \mathbf{v}$ and $\mathbf{u} - \mathbf{v}$.

$\quad (\mathbf{u} + \mathbf{v}) \cdot (\mathbf{u} - \mathbf{v}) = (\mathbf{u} + \mathbf{v}) \cdot \mathbf{u} - (\mathbf{u} + \mathbf{v}) \cdot \mathbf{v}$

$\quad\quad\quad = \mathbf{u} \cdot \mathbf{u} + \mathbf{v} \cdot \mathbf{u} - \mathbf{u} \cdot \mathbf{v} - \mathbf{v} \cdot \mathbf{v}$

$\quad\quad\quad = \|\mathbf{u}\|^2 - \|\mathbf{v}\|^2 = 0$

Therefore, the diagonals are orthogonal.

77. $\mathbf{u} = \langle \cos \alpha, \sin \alpha, 0 \rangle$, $\mathbf{v} = \langle \cos \beta, \sin \beta, 0 \rangle$

The angle between $\mathbf{u}$ and $\mathbf{v}$ is $\alpha - \beta$. (Assuming that $\alpha > \beta$). Also,

$$\cos(\alpha - \beta) = \frac{\mathbf{u} \cdot \mathbf{v}}{\|\mathbf{u}\| \, \|\mathbf{v}\|} = \frac{\cos \alpha \cos \beta + \sin \alpha \sin \beta}{(1)(1)} = \cos \alpha \cos \beta + \sin \alpha \sin \beta.$$

79. $\|\mathbf{u} - \mathbf{v}\|^2 = (\mathbf{u} - \mathbf{v}) \cdot (\mathbf{u} - \mathbf{v})$

$= (\mathbf{u} - \mathbf{v}) \cdot \mathbf{u} - (\mathbf{u} - \mathbf{v}) \cdot \mathbf{v}$

$= \mathbf{u} \cdot \mathbf{u} - \mathbf{v} \cdot \mathbf{u} - \mathbf{u} \cdot \mathbf{v} + \mathbf{v} \cdot \mathbf{v}$

$= \|\mathbf{u}\|^2 - \mathbf{u} \cdot \mathbf{v} - \mathbf{u} \cdot \mathbf{v} + \|\mathbf{v}\|^2$

$= \|\mathbf{u}\|^2 + \|\mathbf{v}\|^2 - 2\mathbf{u} \cdot \mathbf{v}$

81. $\|\mathbf{u} + \mathbf{v}\|^2 = (\mathbf{u} + \mathbf{v}) \cdot (\mathbf{u} + \mathbf{v})$

$= (\mathbf{u} + \mathbf{v}) \cdot \mathbf{u} + (\mathbf{u} + \mathbf{v}) \cdot \mathbf{v}$

$= \mathbf{u} \cdot \mathbf{u} + \mathbf{v} \cdot \mathbf{u} + \mathbf{u} \cdot \mathbf{v} + \mathbf{v} \cdot \mathbf{v}$

$= \|\mathbf{u}\|^2 + 2\mathbf{u} \cdot \mathbf{v} + \|\mathbf{v}\|^2$

$\leq \|\mathbf{u}\|^2 + 2\|\mathbf{u}\| \, \|\mathbf{v}\| + \|\mathbf{v}\|^2$ from Exercise 66

$\leq (\|\mathbf{u}\| + \|\mathbf{v}\|)^2$

Therefore, $\|\mathbf{u} + \mathbf{v}\| \leq \|\mathbf{u}\| + \|\mathbf{v}\|$.

Section 10.4   The Cross Product of Two Vectors in Space

1. $\mathbf{j} \times \mathbf{i} = \begin{vmatrix} \mathbf{i} & \mathbf{j} & \mathbf{k} \\ 0 & 1 & 0 \\ 1 & 0 & 0 \end{vmatrix} = -\mathbf{k}$

3. $\mathbf{j} \times \mathbf{k} = \begin{vmatrix} \mathbf{i} & \mathbf{j} & \mathbf{k} \\ 0 & 1 & 0 \\ 0 & 0 & 1 \end{vmatrix} = \mathbf{i}$

5. $\mathbf{i} \times \mathbf{k} = \begin{vmatrix} \mathbf{i} & \mathbf{j} & \mathbf{k} \\ 1 & 0 & 0 \\ 0 & 0 & 1 \end{vmatrix} = -\mathbf{j}$

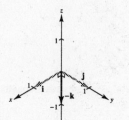

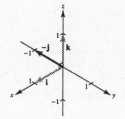

7. (a) $\mathbf{u} \times \mathbf{v} = \begin{vmatrix} \mathbf{i} & \mathbf{j} & \mathbf{k} \\ -2 & 3 & 4 \\ 3 & 7 & 2 \end{vmatrix} = \langle -22, 16, -23 \rangle$

(b) $\mathbf{v} \times \mathbf{u} = -(\mathbf{u} \times \mathbf{v}) = \langle 22, -16, 23 \rangle$

(c) $\mathbf{v} \times \mathbf{v} = \begin{vmatrix} \mathbf{i} & \mathbf{j} & \mathbf{k} \\ 3 & 7 & 2 \\ 3 & 7 & 2 \end{vmatrix} = 0$

9. (a) $\mathbf{u} \times \mathbf{v} = \begin{vmatrix} \mathbf{i} & \mathbf{j} & \mathbf{k} \\ 7 & 3 & 2 \\ 1 & -1 & 5 \end{vmatrix} = \langle 17, -33, -10 \rangle$

(b) $\mathbf{v} \times \mathbf{u} = -(\mathbf{u} \times \mathbf{v}) = \langle -17, 33, 10 \rangle$

(c) $\mathbf{v} \times \mathbf{v} = 0$

11. $\mathbf{u} = \langle 2, -3, 1 \rangle$, $\mathbf{v} = \langle 1, -2, 1 \rangle$

$\mathbf{u} \times \mathbf{v} = \begin{vmatrix} \mathbf{i} & \mathbf{j} & \mathbf{k} \\ 2 & -3 & 1 \\ 1 & -2 & 1 \end{vmatrix} = -\mathbf{i} - \mathbf{j} - \mathbf{k} = \langle -1, -1, -1 \rangle$

$\mathbf{u} \cdot (\mathbf{u} \times \mathbf{v}) = 2(-1) + (-3)(-1) + (1)(-1) = 0 \implies \mathbf{u} \perp \mathbf{u} \times \mathbf{v}$

$\mathbf{v} \cdot (\mathbf{u} \times \mathbf{v}) = 1(-1) + (-2)(-1) + (1)(-1) = 0 \implies \mathbf{v} \perp \mathbf{u} \times \mathbf{v}$

13. $\mathbf{u} = \langle 12, -3, 0 \rangle, \mathbf{v} = \langle -2, 5, 0 \rangle$

$$\mathbf{u} \times \mathbf{v} = \begin{vmatrix} \mathbf{i} & \mathbf{j} & \mathbf{k} \\ 12 & -3 & 0 \\ -2 & 5 & 0 \end{vmatrix} = 54\mathbf{k} = \langle 0, 0, 54 \rangle$$

$\mathbf{u} \cdot (\mathbf{u} \times \mathbf{v}) = 12(0) + (-3)(0) + 0(54)$

$\qquad = 0 \implies \mathbf{u} \perp \mathbf{u} \times \mathbf{v}$

$\mathbf{v} \cdot (\mathbf{u} \times \mathbf{v}) = -2(0) + 5(0) + 0(54)$

$\qquad = 0 \implies \mathbf{v} \perp \mathbf{u} \times \mathbf{v}$

15. $\mathbf{u} = \mathbf{i} + \mathbf{j} + \mathbf{k}, \mathbf{v} = 2\mathbf{i} + \mathbf{j} - \mathbf{k}$

$$\mathbf{u} \times \mathbf{v} = \begin{vmatrix} \mathbf{i} & \mathbf{j} & \mathbf{k} \\ 1 & 1 & 1 \\ 2 & 1 & -1 \end{vmatrix} = -2\mathbf{i} + 3\mathbf{j} - \mathbf{k} = \langle -2, 3, -1 \rangle$$

$\mathbf{u} \cdot (\mathbf{u} \times \mathbf{v}) = 1(-2) + 1(3) + 1(-1)$

$\qquad = 0 \implies \mathbf{u} \perp \mathbf{u} \times \mathbf{v}$

$\mathbf{v} \cdot (\mathbf{u} \times \mathbf{v}) = 2(-2) + 1(3) + (-1)(-1)$

$\qquad = 0 \implies \mathbf{v} \perp \mathbf{u} \times \mathbf{v}$

17.

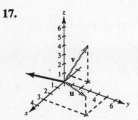

19.

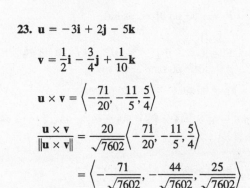

21. $\mathbf{u} = \langle 4, -3.5, 7 \rangle$

$\mathbf{v} = \langle -1, 8, 4 \rangle$

$\mathbf{u} \times \mathbf{v} = \left\langle -70, -23, \dfrac{57}{2} \right\rangle$

$\dfrac{\mathbf{u} \times \mathbf{v}}{\|\mathbf{u} \times \mathbf{v}\|} = \left\langle \dfrac{-140}{\sqrt{24{,}965}}, \dfrac{-46}{\sqrt{24{,}965}}, \dfrac{57}{\sqrt{24{,}965}} \right\rangle$

23. $\mathbf{u} = -3\mathbf{i} + 2\mathbf{j} - 5\mathbf{k}$

$\mathbf{v} = \dfrac{1}{2}\mathbf{i} - \dfrac{3}{4}\mathbf{j} + \dfrac{1}{10}\mathbf{k}$

$\mathbf{u} \times \mathbf{v} = \left\langle -\dfrac{71}{20}, -\dfrac{11}{5}, \dfrac{5}{4} \right\rangle$

$\dfrac{\mathbf{u} \times \mathbf{v}}{\|\mathbf{u} \times \mathbf{v}\|} = \dfrac{20}{\sqrt{7602}}\left\langle -\dfrac{71}{20}, -\dfrac{11}{5}, \dfrac{5}{4} \right\rangle$

$\qquad = \left\langle -\dfrac{71}{\sqrt{7602}}, -\dfrac{44}{\sqrt{7602}}, \dfrac{25}{\sqrt{7602}} \right\rangle$

25. Programs will vary.

27. $\mathbf{u} = \mathbf{j}$

$\mathbf{v} = \mathbf{j} + \mathbf{k}$

$$\mathbf{u} \times \mathbf{v} = \begin{vmatrix} \mathbf{i} & \mathbf{j} & \mathbf{k} \\ 0 & 1 & 0 \\ 0 & 1 & 1 \end{vmatrix} = \mathbf{i}$$

$A = \|\mathbf{u} \times \mathbf{v}\| = \|\mathbf{i}\| = 1$

29. $\mathbf{u} = \langle 3, 2, -1 \rangle$

$\mathbf{v} = \langle 1, 2, 3 \rangle$

$$\mathbf{u} \times \mathbf{v} = \begin{vmatrix} \mathbf{i} & \mathbf{j} & \mathbf{k} \\ 3 & 2 & -1 \\ 1 & 2 & 3 \end{vmatrix} = \langle 8, -10, 4 \rangle$$

$A = \|\mathbf{u} \times \mathbf{v}\| = \|\langle 8, -10, 4 \rangle\| = \sqrt{180} = 6\sqrt{5}$

31. $A(1, 1, 1,), B(2, 3, 4), C(6, 5, 2), D(7, 7, 5)$

$\overrightarrow{AB} = \langle 1, 2, 3 \rangle, \ \overrightarrow{AC} = \langle 5, 4, 1 \rangle, \ \overrightarrow{CD} = \langle 1, 2, 3 \rangle,$
$\overrightarrow{BD} = \langle 5, 4, 1 \rangle$

Since $\overrightarrow{AB} = \overrightarrow{CD}$ and $\overrightarrow{AC} = \overrightarrow{BD}$, the figure is a parallelogram. $\overrightarrow{AB}$ and $\overrightarrow{AC}$ are adjacent sides and

$$\overrightarrow{AB} \times \overrightarrow{AC} = \begin{vmatrix} \mathbf{i} & \mathbf{j} & \mathbf{k} \\ 1 & 2 & 3 \\ 5 & 4 & 1 \end{vmatrix} = -10\mathbf{i} + 14\mathbf{j} - 6\mathbf{k}.$$

$A = \|\overrightarrow{AB} \times \overrightarrow{AC}\| = \sqrt{332} = 2\sqrt{83}$

33. $A(0, 0, 0), B(1, 2, 3), C(-3, 0, 0)$

$\overrightarrow{AB} = \langle 1, 2, 3 \rangle, \overrightarrow{AC} = \langle -3, 0, 0 \rangle$

$$\overrightarrow{AB} \times \overrightarrow{AC} = \begin{vmatrix} \mathbf{i} & \mathbf{j} & \mathbf{k} \\ 1 & 2 & 3 \\ -3 & 0 & 0 \end{vmatrix} = -9\mathbf{j} + 6\mathbf{k}$$

$A = \dfrac{1}{2}\|\overrightarrow{AB} \times \overrightarrow{AC}\| = \dfrac{1}{2}\sqrt{117} = \dfrac{3}{2}\sqrt{13}$

35. $A(2, -7, 3), B(-1, 5, 8), C(4, 6, -1)$

$\overrightarrow{AB} = \langle -3, 12, 5 \rangle, \overrightarrow{AC} = \langle 2, 13, -4 \rangle$

$$\overrightarrow{AB} \times \overrightarrow{AC} = \begin{vmatrix} \mathbf{i} & \mathbf{j} & \mathbf{k} \\ -3 & 12 & 5 \\ 2 & 13 & -4 \end{vmatrix} = \langle -113, -2, -63 \rangle$$

Area $= \dfrac{1}{2} \| \overrightarrow{AB} \times \overrightarrow{AC} \| = \dfrac{1}{2} \sqrt{16{,}742}$

37. $\mathbf{F} = -20\mathbf{k}$

$\overrightarrow{PQ} = \dfrac{1}{2}(\cos 40° \mathbf{j} + \sin 40° \mathbf{k})$

$$\overrightarrow{PQ} \times \mathbf{F} = \begin{vmatrix} \mathbf{i} & \mathbf{j} & \mathbf{k} \\ 0 & \cos 40°/2 & \sin 40°/2 \\ 0 & 0 & -20 \end{vmatrix} = -10 \cos 40° \mathbf{i}$$

$\| \overrightarrow{PQ} \times \mathbf{F} \| = 10 \cos 40° \approx 7.66 \text{ ft} \cdot \text{lb}$

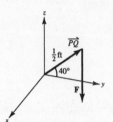

39. (a) $\overrightarrow{OA} = \dfrac{3}{2}\mathbf{k}$

$\mathbf{F} = -60(\sin \theta \mathbf{j} + \cos \theta \mathbf{k})$

$$\overrightarrow{OA} \times \mathbf{F} = \begin{vmatrix} \mathbf{i} & \mathbf{j} & \mathbf{k} \\ 0 & 0 & 3/2 \\ 0 & -60 \sin \theta & -60 \cos \theta \end{vmatrix} = 90 \sin \theta \mathbf{i}$$

$\| \overrightarrow{OA} \times \mathbf{F} \| = 90 \sin \theta$

(b) When $\theta = 45°$: $\| \overrightarrow{OA} \times \mathbf{F} \| = 90\left(\dfrac{\sqrt{2}}{2}\right) = 45\sqrt{2} \approx 63.64.$

(c) Let $T = 90 \sin \theta$.

$\dfrac{dT}{d\theta} = 90 \cos \theta = 0$ when $\theta = 90°$.

This is what we expected. When $\theta = 90°$ the pipe wrench is horizontal.

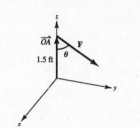

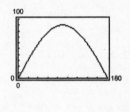

41. $\mathbf{u} \cdot (\mathbf{v} \times \mathbf{w}) = \begin{vmatrix} 1 & 0 & 0 \\ 0 & 1 & 0 \\ 0 & 0 & 1 \end{vmatrix} = 1$

43. $\mathbf{u} \cdot (\mathbf{v} \times \mathbf{w}) = \begin{vmatrix} 2 & 0 & 1 \\ 0 & 3 & 0 \\ 0 & 0 & 1 \end{vmatrix} = 6$

45. $\mathbf{u} \cdot (\mathbf{v} \times \mathbf{w}) = \begin{vmatrix} 1 & 1 & 0 \\ 0 & 1 & 1 \\ 1 & 0 & 1 \end{vmatrix} = 2$

$V = |\mathbf{u} \cdot (\mathbf{v} \times \mathbf{w})| = 2$

47. $\mathbf{u} = \langle 3, 0, 0 \rangle$

$\mathbf{v} = \langle 0, 5, 1 \rangle$

$\mathbf{w} = \langle 2, 0, 5 \rangle$

$\mathbf{u} \cdot (\mathbf{v} \times \mathbf{w}) = \begin{vmatrix} 3 & 0 & 0 \\ 0 & 5 & 1 \\ 2 & 0 & 5 \end{vmatrix} = 75$

$V = |\mathbf{u} \cdot (\mathbf{v} \times \mathbf{w})| = 75$

49. $\mathbf{u} \times \mathbf{v} = \langle u_1, u_2, u_3 \rangle \cdot \langle v_1, v_2, v_3 \rangle = (u_2 v_3 - u_3 v_2)\mathbf{i} - (u_1 v_3 - u_3 v_1)\mathbf{j} + (u_1 v_2 - u_2 v_1)\mathbf{k}$

51. The magnitude of the cross product will increase by a factor of 4.

53. If the vectors are ordered pairs, then the cross product does not exist. False.

55. True

57. $\mathbf{u} = \langle u_1, u_2, u_3 \rangle$, $\mathbf{v} = \langle v_1, v_2, v_3 \rangle$, $\mathbf{w} = \langle w_1, w_2, w_3 \rangle$

$$\mathbf{u} \times (\mathbf{v} + \mathbf{w}) = \begin{vmatrix} \mathbf{i} & \mathbf{j} & \mathbf{k} \\ u_1 & u_2 & u_3 \\ v_1 + w_1 & v_2 + w_2 & v_3 + w_3 \end{vmatrix}$$

$$= [u_2(v_3 + w_3) - u_3(v_2 + w_2)]\mathbf{i} - [u_1(v_3 + w_3) - u_3(v_1 + w_1)]\mathbf{j} + [u_1(v_2 + w_2) - u_2(v_1 + w_1)]\mathbf{k}$$

$$= (u_2 v_3 - u_3 v_2)\mathbf{i} - (u_1 v_3 - u_3 v_1)\mathbf{j} + (u_1 v_2 - u_2 v_1)\mathbf{k} + (u_2 w_3 - u_3 w_2)\mathbf{i} -$$

$$(u_1 w_3 - u_3 w_1)\mathbf{j} + (u_1 w_2 - u_2 w_1)\mathbf{k}$$

$$= (\mathbf{u} \times \mathbf{v}) + (\mathbf{u} \times \mathbf{w})$$

59. $\mathbf{u} = \langle u_1, u_2, u_3 \rangle$

$$\mathbf{u} \times \mathbf{u} = \begin{vmatrix} \mathbf{i} & \mathbf{j} & \mathbf{k} \\ u_1 & u_2 & u_3 \\ u_1 & u_2 & u_3 \end{vmatrix} = (u_2 u_3 - u_3 u_2)\mathbf{i} - (u_1 u_3 - u_3 u_1)\mathbf{j} + (u_1 u_2 - u_2 u_1)\mathbf{k} = \mathbf{0}$$

61. $\mathbf{u} \times \mathbf{v} = (u_2 v_3 - u_3 v_2)\mathbf{i} - (u_1 v_3 - u_3 v_1)\mathbf{j} + (u_1 v_2 - u_2 v_1)\mathbf{k}$

$(\mathbf{u} \times \mathbf{v}) \cdot \mathbf{u} = (u_2 v_3 - u_3 v_2)u_1 + (u_3 v_1 - u_1 v_3)u_2 + (u_1 v_2 - u_2 v_1)u_3 = 0$

$(\mathbf{u} \times \mathbf{v}) \cdot \mathbf{v} = (u_2 v_3 - u_3 v_2)v_1 + (u_3 v_1 - u_1 v_3)v_2 + (u_1 v_2 - u_2 v_1)v_3 = 0$

Thus, $\mathbf{u} \times \mathbf{v} \perp \mathbf{u}$ and $\mathbf{u} \times \mathbf{v} \perp \mathbf{v}$.

63. $\|\mathbf{u} \times \mathbf{v}\| = \|\mathbf{u}\| \, \|\mathbf{v}\| \sin \theta$

If $\mathbf{u}$ and $\mathbf{v}$ are orthogonal, $\theta = \pi/2$ and $\sin \theta = 1$. Therefore, $\|\mathbf{u} \times \mathbf{v}\| = \|\mathbf{u}\| \, \|\mathbf{v}\|$.

Section 10.5   Lines and Planes in Space

1. $x = 1 + 3t,\ y = 2 - t,\ z = 2 + 5t$

(a)

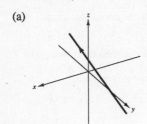

(b) When $t = 0$ we have $P = (1, 2, 2)$. When $t = 3$ we have $Q = (10, -1, 17)$.

$\overrightarrow{PQ} = \langle 9, -3, 15 \rangle$

The components of the vector and the coefficients of t are proportional since the line is parallel to $\overrightarrow{PQ}$.

(c) $y = 0$ when $t = 2$. Thus, $x = 7$ and $z = 12$.
Point: $(7, 0, 12)$

$x = 0$ when $t = -\dfrac{1}{3}$. Point: $\left(0, \dfrac{7}{3}, \dfrac{1}{3}\right)$

$z = 0$ when $t = -\dfrac{2}{5}$. Point: $\left(-\dfrac{1}{5}, \dfrac{12}{5}, 0\right)$

3. Point: $(0, 0, 0)$

Direction vector: $\mathbf{v} = \langle 1, 2, 3 \rangle$

Direction numbers: $1, 2, 3$

(a) Parametric: $x = t,\ y = 2t,\ z = 3t$

(b) Symmetric: $x = \dfrac{y}{2} = \dfrac{z}{3}$

5. Point: $(-2, 0, 3)$

Direction vector: $\mathbf{v} = \langle 2, 4, -2 \rangle$

Direction numbers: $2, 4, -2$

(a) Parametric: $x = -2 + 2t,\ y = 4t,\ z = 3 - 2t$

(b) Symmetric: $\dfrac{x + 2}{2} = \dfrac{y}{4} = \dfrac{z - 3}{-2}$

7. Point: $(1, 0, 1)$

Direction vector: $\mathbf{v} = 3\mathbf{i} - 2\mathbf{j} + \mathbf{k}$

Direction numbers: $3, -2, 1$

(a) Parametric: $x = 1 + 3t, y = -2t, z = 1 + t$

(b) Symmetric: $\dfrac{x - 1}{3} = \dfrac{y}{-2} = \dfrac{z - 1}{1}$

9. Points: $(5, -3, -2), \left(\dfrac{-2}{3}, \dfrac{2}{3}, 1\right)$

Direction vector: $\mathbf{v} = \dfrac{17}{3}\mathbf{i} - \dfrac{11}{3}\mathbf{j} - 3\mathbf{k}$

Direction numbers: $17, -11, -9$

(a) Parametric: $x = 5 + 17t, y = -3 - 11t, z = -2 - 9t$

(b) Symmetric: $\dfrac{x - 5}{17} = \dfrac{y + 3}{-11} = \dfrac{z + 2}{-9}$

11. Points: $(2, 3, 0), (10, 8, 12)$

Direction vector: $\langle 8, 5, 12 \rangle$

Direction numbers: $8, 5, 12$

(a) Parametric: $x = 2 + 8t, y = 3 + 5t, z = 12t$

(b) Symmetric: $\dfrac{x - 2}{8} = \dfrac{y - 3}{5} = \dfrac{z}{12}$

13. Point: $(2, 3, 4)$

Direction vector: $\mathbf{v} = \mathbf{k}$

Direction numbers: $0, 0, 1$

Parametric: $x = 2, y = 3, z = 4 + t$

15. Point: $(-2, 3, 1)$

Direction vector: $\mathbf{v} = 4\mathbf{i} - \mathbf{k}$

Direction numbers: $4, 0, -1$

Parametric: $x = -2 + 4t, y = 3, z = 1 - t$

Symmetric: $\dfrac{x + 2}{4} = \dfrac{z - 1}{-1}, y = 3$

(a) On line

(b) On line

(c) Not on line $(y \neq 3)$

(d) Not on line $\left(\dfrac{6 + 2}{4} \neq \dfrac{-2 - 1}{-1}\right)$

17. L_1: $\mathbf{v} = \langle -3, 2, 4 \rangle$ $(6, -2, 5)$ on line

L_2: $\mathbf{v} = \langle 6, -4, -8 \rangle$ $(6, -2, 5)$ on line

L_3: $\mathbf{v} = \langle -6, 4, 8 \rangle$ $(6, -2, 5)$ not on line

L_4: $\mathbf{v} = \langle 6, 4, -6 \rangle$ not parallel to L_1, L_2, nor L_3

Hence, L_1 and L_2 are identical.

$L_1 = L_2$ and L_3 are parallel.

19. At the point of intersection, the coordinates for one line equal the corresponding coordinates for the other line. Thus,

(i) $4t + 2 = 2s + 2$, (ii) $3 = 2s + 3$, and (iii) $-t + 1 = s + 1$.

From (ii), we find that $s = 0$ and consequently, from (iii), $t = 0$. Letting $s = t = 0$, we see that equation (i) is satisfied and therefore the two lines intersect. Substituting zero for s or for t, we obtain the point $(2, 3, 1)$.

$\mathbf{u} = 4\mathbf{i} - \mathbf{k}$ (First line)

$\mathbf{v} = 2\mathbf{i} + 2\mathbf{j} + \mathbf{k}$ (Second line)

$\cos \theta = \dfrac{|\mathbf{u} \cdot \mathbf{v}|}{\|\mathbf{u}\| \, \|\mathbf{v}\|} = \dfrac{8 - 1}{\sqrt{17}\sqrt{9}} = \dfrac{7}{3\sqrt{17}} = \dfrac{7\sqrt{17}}{51}$

21. Writing the equations of the lines in parametric form we have

$x = 3t$ $y = 2 - t$ $z = -1 + t$

$x = 1 + 4s$ $y = -2 + s$ $z = -3 - 3s$.

For the coordinates to be equal, $3t = 1 + 4s$ and $2 - t = -2 + s$. Solving this system yields $t = \frac{17}{7}$ and $s = \frac{11}{7}$. When using these values for s and t, the z coordinates are not equal. The lines do not intersect.

23. $x = 2t + 3$ $x = -2s + 7$

$y = 5t - 2$ $y = s + 8$

$z = -t + 1$ $z = 2s - 1$

Point of intersection: $(7, 8, -1)$

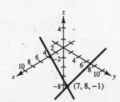

25. $4x - 3y - 6z = 6$

(a) $P = (0, 0, -1)$, $Q = (0, -2, 0)$, $R = (3, 4, -1)$

$\overrightarrow{PQ} = \langle 0, -2, 1 \rangle$, $\overrightarrow{PR} = \langle 3, 4, 0 \rangle$

(b) $\overrightarrow{PQ} \times \overrightarrow{PR} = \begin{vmatrix} \mathbf{i} & \mathbf{j} & \mathbf{k} \\ 0 & -2 & 1 \\ 3 & 4 & 0 \end{vmatrix} = \langle -4, 3, 6 \rangle$

The components of the cross product are proportional to the coefficients of the variables in the equation. The cross product is parallel to the normal vector.

27. Point: $(2, 1, 2)$

$\mathbf{n} = \mathbf{i} = \langle 1, 0, 0 \rangle$

$1(x - 2) + 0(y - 1) + 0(z - 2) = 0$

$x - 2 = 0$

29. Point: $(3, 2, 2)$

Normal vector: $\mathbf{n} = 2\mathbf{i} + 3\mathbf{j} - \mathbf{k}$

$2(x - 3) + 3(y - 2) - 1(z - 2) = 0$

$2x + 3y - z = 10$

31. Point: $(0, 0, 6)$

Normal vector: $\mathbf{n} = -\mathbf{i} + \mathbf{j} - 2\mathbf{k}$

$-1(x - 0) + 1(y - 0) - 2(z - 6) = 0$

$-x + y - 2z + 12 = 0$

$x - y + 2z = 12$

33. Let $\mathbf{u}$ be the vector from $(0, 0, 0)$ to $(1, 2, 3)$:

$\mathbf{u} = \mathbf{i} + 2\mathbf{j} + 3\mathbf{k}$

Let $\mathbf{v}$ be the vector from $(0, 0, 0)$ to $(-2, 3, 3)$:

$\mathbf{v} = -2\mathbf{i} + 3\mathbf{j} + 3\mathbf{k}$

Normal vector: $\mathbf{u} \times \mathbf{v} = \begin{vmatrix} \mathbf{i} & \mathbf{j} & \mathbf{k} \\ 1 & 2 & 3 \\ -2 & 3 & 3 \end{vmatrix}$

$= -3\mathbf{i} + (-9)\mathbf{j} + 7\mathbf{k}$

$-3(x - 0) - 9(y - 0) + 7(z - 0) = 0$

$3x + 9y - 7z = 0$

35. Let $\mathbf{u}$ be the vector from $(1, 2, 3)$ to $(3, 2, 1)$: $\mathbf{u} = 2\mathbf{i} - 2\mathbf{k}$

Let $\mathbf{v}$ be the vector from $(1, 2, 3)$ to $(-1, -2, 2)$: $\mathbf{v} = -2\mathbf{i} - 4\mathbf{j} - \mathbf{k}$

Normal vector: $\left(\frac{1}{2}\mathbf{u}\right) \times (-\mathbf{v}) = \begin{vmatrix} \mathbf{i} & \mathbf{j} & \mathbf{k} \\ 1 & 0 & -1 \\ 2 & 4 & 1 \end{vmatrix} = 4\mathbf{i} - 3\mathbf{j} + 4\mathbf{k}$

$4(x - 1) - 3(y - 2) + 4(z - 3) = 0$

$4x - 3y + 4z = 10$

37. $(1, 2, 3)$, Normal vector: $\mathbf{v} = \mathbf{k}$, $1(z - 3) = 0$, $z = 3$

39. The direction vectors for the lines are $\mathbf{u} = -2\mathbf{i} + \mathbf{j} + \mathbf{k}$, $\mathbf{v} = -3\mathbf{i} + 4\mathbf{j} - \mathbf{k}$.

Normal vector: $\mathbf{u} \times \mathbf{v} = \begin{vmatrix} \mathbf{i} & \mathbf{j} & \mathbf{k} \\ -2 & 1 & 1 \\ -3 & 4 & -1 \end{vmatrix} = -5(\mathbf{i} + \mathbf{j} + \mathbf{k})$

Point of intersection of the lines: $(-1, 5, 1)$

$(x + 1) + (y - 5) + (z - 1) = 0$

$x + y + z = 5$

41. Let $\mathbf{v}$ be the vector from $(-1, 1, -1)$ to $(2, 2, 1)$: $\mathbf{v} = 3\mathbf{i} + \mathbf{j} + 2\mathbf{k}$

Let $\mathbf{n}$ be a vector normal to the plane $2x - 3y + z = 3$: $\mathbf{n} = 2\mathbf{i} - 3\mathbf{j} + \mathbf{k}$

Since v and n both lie in the plane p, the normal vector to p is

$\mathbf{v} \times \mathbf{n} = \begin{vmatrix} \mathbf{i} & \mathbf{j} & \mathbf{k} \\ 3 & 1 & 2 \\ 2 & -3 & 1 \end{vmatrix} = 7\mathbf{i} + \mathbf{j} - 11\mathbf{k}$

$7(x - 2) + 1(y - 2) - 11(z - 1) = 0$

$7x + y - 11z = 5$

43. Let $\mathbf{u} = \mathbf{i}$ and let $\mathbf{v}$ be the vector from $(1, -2, -1)$ to $(2, 5, 6)$: $\mathbf{v} = \mathbf{i} + 7\mathbf{j} + 7\mathbf{k}$

Since $\mathbf{u}$ and $\mathbf{v}$ both lie in the plane P, the normal vector to P is:

$$\mathbf{u} \times \mathbf{v} = \begin{vmatrix} \mathbf{i} & \mathbf{j} & \mathbf{k} \\ 1 & 0 & 0 \\ 1 & 7 & 7 \end{vmatrix} = -7\mathbf{j} + 7\mathbf{k} = -7(\mathbf{j} - \mathbf{k})$$

$$[y - (-2)] - [z - (-1)] = 0$$

$$y - z = -1$$

45. The normal vectors to the planes are

$$\mathbf{n}_1 = \langle 5, -3, 1 \rangle, \mathbf{n}_2 = \langle 1, 4, 7 \rangle, \cos\theta = \frac{|\mathbf{n}_1 \cdot \mathbf{n}_2|}{\|\mathbf{n}_1\| \|\mathbf{n}_2\|} = 0.$$

Thus, $\theta = \pi/2$ and the planes are orthogonal.

47. The normal vectors to the planes are

$$\mathbf{n}_1 = \mathbf{i} - 3\mathbf{j} + 6\mathbf{k}, \; \mathbf{n}_2 = 5\mathbf{i} + \mathbf{j} - \mathbf{k},$$

$$\cos\theta = \frac{|\mathbf{n}_1 \cdot \mathbf{n}_2|}{\|\mathbf{n}_1\| \|\mathbf{n}_2\|} = \frac{|5 - 3 - 6|}{\sqrt{46}\sqrt{27}} = \frac{4\sqrt{138}}{414}.$$

Therefore, $\theta = \arccos\left(\frac{4\sqrt{138}}{414}\right) \approx 83.5°.$

49. The normal vectors to the planes are $\mathbf{n}_1 = \langle 1, -5, -1 \rangle$ and $\mathbf{n}_2 = \langle 5, -25, -5 \rangle$. Since $\mathbf{n}_2 = 5\mathbf{n}_1$, the planes are parallel, but not equal.

51. $4x + 2y + 6z = 12$

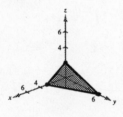

53. $2x - y + 3z = 4$

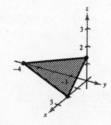

55. $y + z = 5$

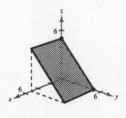

57. $x = 5$

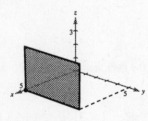

59. $2x + y - z = 6$

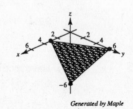

Generated by Maple

61. $-5x + 4y - 6z + 8 = 0$

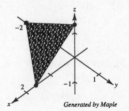

Generated by Maple

63. P_1: $\mathbf{n} = \langle 3, -2, 5 \rangle$ $(1, -1, 1)$ on plane

P_2: $\mathbf{n} = \langle -6, 4, -10 \rangle$ $(1, -1, 1)$ not on plane

P_3: $\mathbf{n} = \langle -3, 2, 5 \rangle$

P_4: $\mathbf{n} = \langle 75, -50, 125 \rangle$ $(1, -1, 1)$ on plane

P_1 and P_4 are identical.

$P_1 = P_4$ is parallel to P_2.

65. Each plane passes through the points

$(c, 0, 0), (0, c, 0),$ and $(0, 0, c)$.

67. The normals to the planes are $\mathbf{n}_1 = 3\mathbf{i} + 2\mathbf{j} - \mathbf{k}$ and $\mathbf{n}_2 = \mathbf{i} - 4\mathbf{j} + 2\mathbf{k}$. The direction vector for the line is

$$\mathbf{n}_2 \times \mathbf{n}_1 = \begin{vmatrix} \mathbf{i} & \mathbf{j} & \mathbf{k} \\ 1 & -4 & 2 \\ 3 & 2 & -1 \end{vmatrix} = 7(\mathbf{j} + 2\mathbf{k}).$$

Now find a point of intersection of the planes.

$$\begin{array}{rcl} 6x + 4y - 2y &=& 14 \\ x - 4y + 2z &=& 0 \\ 7x &=& 14 \\ x &=& 2 \end{array}$$

Substituting 2 for x in the second equation, we have $-4y + 2z = -2$ or $z = 2y - 1$. Letting $y = 1$, a point of intersection is $(2, 1, 1)$.

$$x = 2, y = 1 + t, z = 1 + 2t$$

69. Writing the equation of the line in parametric form and substituting into the equation of the plane we have:

$$x = \frac{1}{2} + t, \ y = \frac{-3}{2} - t, \ z = -1 + 2t$$

$$2\left(\frac{1}{2} + t\right) - 2\left(\frac{-3}{2} - t\right) + (-1 + 2t) = 12, \ t = \frac{3}{2}$$

Substituting $t = 3/2$ into the parametric equations for the line we have the point of intersection $(2, -3, 2)$. The line does not lie in the plane.

71. Writing the equation of the line in parametric form and substituting into the equation of the plane we have:

$$x = 1 + 3t, \ y = -1 - 2t, \ z = 3 + t$$

$$2(1 + 3t) + 3(-1 - 2t) = 10, -1 = 10, \text{ contradiction}$$

Therefore, the line does not intersect the plane.

73. Point: $Q(0, 0, 0)$

Plane: $2x + 3y + z - 12 = 0$

Normal to plane: $\mathbf{n} = \langle 2, 3, 1 \rangle$

Point in plane: $P(6, 0, 0)$

Vector $\overrightarrow{PQ} = \langle -6, 0\ 0 \rangle$

$$D = \frac{|\overrightarrow{PQ} \cdot \mathbf{n}|}{\|\mathbf{n}\|} = \frac{|-12|}{\sqrt{14}} = \frac{6\sqrt{14}}{7}$$

75. Point: $Q(2, 8, 4)$

Plane: $2x + y + z = 5$

Normal to plane: $\mathbf{n} = \langle 2, 1, 1 \rangle$

Point in plane: $P\langle 0, 0, 5 \rangle$

Vector: $\overrightarrow{PQ} = \langle 2, 8, -1 \rangle$

$$D = \frac{|\overrightarrow{PQ} \cdot \mathbf{n}|}{\|\mathbf{n}\|} = \frac{11}{\sqrt{6}} = \frac{11\sqrt{6}}{6}$$

77. The normal vectors to the planes are $\mathbf{n}_1 = \langle 1, -3, 4 \rangle$ and $\mathbf{n}_2 = \langle 1, -3, 4 \rangle$. Since $\mathbf{n}_1 = \mathbf{n}_2$, the planes are parallel. Choose a point in each plane.

$P = (10, 0, 0)$ is a point in $x - 3y + 4z = 10$.
$Q = (6, 0, 0)$ is a point in $x - 3y + 4z = 6$.

$$\overrightarrow{PQ} = \langle -4, 0, 0 \rangle, D = \frac{|\overrightarrow{PQ} \cdot \mathbf{n}_1|}{\|\mathbf{n}_1\|} = \frac{4}{\sqrt{26}} = \frac{2\sqrt{26}}{13}$$

79. The normal vectors to the planes are $\mathbf{n}_1 = \langle -3, 6, 7 \rangle$ and $\mathbf{n}_2 = \langle 6, -12, -14 \rangle$. Since $\mathbf{n}_2 = -2\mathbf{n}_1$, the planes are parallel. Choose a point in each plane.

$P = (0, -1, 1)$ is a point in $-3x + 6y + 7z = 1$.

$Q = \left(\frac{25}{6}, 0, 0\right)$ is a point in $6x - 12y - 14z = 25$.

$$\overrightarrow{PQ} = \left\langle \frac{25}{6}, 1, -1 \right\rangle$$

$$D = \frac{|\overrightarrow{PQ} \cdot \mathbf{n}_1|}{\|\mathbf{n}_1\|} = \frac{|-27/2|}{\sqrt{94}} = \frac{27}{2\sqrt{94}} = \frac{27\sqrt{94}}{188}$$

81. $\mathbf{u} = \langle 4, 0, -1 \rangle$ is the direction vector for the line. $Q(1, 5, -2)$ is the given point, and $P(-2, 3, 1)$ is on the line. Hence, $\overrightarrow{PQ} = \langle 3, 2, -3 \rangle$ and

$$\overrightarrow{PQ} \times \mathbf{u} = \begin{vmatrix} \mathbf{i} & \mathbf{j} & \mathbf{k} \\ 3 & 2 & -3 \\ 4 & 0 & -1 \end{vmatrix} = \langle -2, -9, -8 \rangle$$

$$D = \frac{\|\overrightarrow{PQ} \times \mathbf{u}\|}{\|\mathbf{u}\|} = \frac{\sqrt{149}}{\sqrt{17}} = \frac{\sqrt{2533}}{17}$$

83. The parametric equations of a line L parallel to $\mathbf{v} = \langle a, b, c, \rangle$ and passing through the point $P(x_1, y_1, z_1)$ are

$$x = x_1 + at, y = y_1 + bt, z = z_1 + ct.$$

The symmetric equations are

$$\frac{x - x_1}{a} = \frac{y - y_1}{b} = \frac{z - z_1}{c}.$$

85. Solve the two linear equations representing the planes to find two points of intersection. Then find the line determined by the two points.

87. (a) Sphere

$$(x - 3)^2 + (y + 2)^2 + (z - 5)^2 = 16$$
$$x^2 + y^2 + z^2 - 6x + 4y - 10z + 22 = 0$$

(b) Parallel planes

$$4x - 3y + z = 10 \pm 4\|\mathbf{n}\| = 10 \pm 4\sqrt{26}$$

89. (a) $z = 28.7 - 1.83x - 1.09y$

Year	1980	1985	1990	1994	1995	1996	1997
z (approx.)	16.16	14.23	9.81	8.60	8.42	8.27	8.23

(b) An increase in x or y will cause a decrease in z. In fact, any increase in two variables will cause a decrease in the third.

(c)

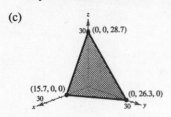

91. True

Section 10.6   Surfaces in Space

1. Ellipsoid

Matches graph (c)

3. Hyperboloid of one sheet

Matches graph (f)

5. Elliptic paraboloid

Matches graph (d)

7. $z = 3$

Plane parallel to the xy-coordinate plane

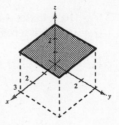

9. $y^2 + z^2 = 9$

The x-coordinate is missing so we have a cylindrical surface with rulings parallel to the x-axis. The generating curve is a circle.

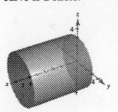

11. $y = x^2$

The z-coordinate is missing so we have a cylindrical surface with rulings parallel to the z-axis. The generating curve is a parabola.

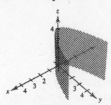

13. $4x^2 + y^2 = 4$

$$\frac{x^2}{1} + \frac{y^2}{4} = 1$$

The z-coordinate is missing so we have a cylindrical surface with rulings parallel to the z-axis. The generating curve is an ellipse.

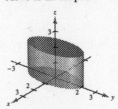

15. $z = \sin y$

The x-coordinate is missing so we have a cylindrical surface with rulings parallel to the x-axis. The generating curve is the sine curve.

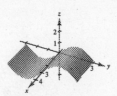

17. $x = x^2 + y^2$

(a) You are viewing the paraboloid from the x-axis: $(20, 0, 0)$

(b) You are viewing the paraboloid from above, but not on the z-axis: $(10, 10, 20)$

(c) You are viewing the paraboloid from the z-axis: $(0, 0, 20)$

(d) You are viewing the paraboloid from the y-axis: $(0, 20, 0)$

19. $\dfrac{x^2}{1} + \dfrac{y^2}{4} + \dfrac{z^2}{1} = 1$

Ellipsoid

xy-trace: $\dfrac{x^2}{1} + \dfrac{y^2}{4} = 1$ ellipse

xz-trace: $x^2 + z^2 = 1$ circle

yz-trace: $\dfrac{y^2}{4} + \dfrac{z^2}{1} = 1$ ellipse

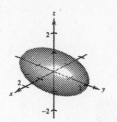

21. $16x^2 - y^2 + 16z^2 = 4$

$4x^2 - \dfrac{y^2}{4} + 4z^2 = 1$

Hyperboloid on one sheet

xy-trace: $4x^2 - \dfrac{y^2}{4} = 1$ hyperbola

xz-trace: $4(x^2 + z^2) = 1$ circle

yz-trace: $\dfrac{-y^2}{4} + 4z^2 = 1$ hyperbola

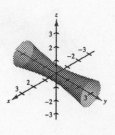

23. $x^2 - y + z^2 = 0$

Elliptic paraboloid

xy-trace: $y = x^2$

xz-trace: $x^2 + z^2 = 0$,

   point $(0, 0, 0)$

yz-trace: $y = z^2$

$y = 1: x^2 + z^2 = 1$

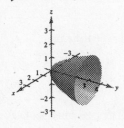

25. $x^2 - y^2 + z = 0$

Hyperbolic paraboloid

xy-trace: $y = \pm x$

xz-trace: $z = -x^2$

yz-trace: $z = y^2$

$y = \pm 1: z = 1 - x^2$

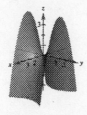

27. $z^2 = x^2 + \dfrac{y^2}{4}$

Elliptic Cone

xy-trace: point $(0, 0, 0)$

xz-trace: $z = \pm x$

yz-trace: $z = \dfrac{\pm 1}{2} y$

$z = \pm 1: x^2 + \dfrac{y^2}{4} = 1$

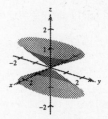

29. $16x^2 + 9y^2 + 16z^2 - 32x - 36y + 36 = 0$

$16(x^2 - 2x + 1) + 9(y^2 - 4y + 4) + 16z^2 = -36 + 16 + 36$

$16(x - 1)^2 + 9(y - 2)^2 + 16z^2 = 16$

$\dfrac{(x - 1)^2}{1} + \dfrac{(y - 2)^2}{16/9} + \dfrac{z^2}{1} = 1$

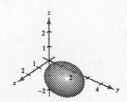

Ellipsoid with center $(1, 2, 0)$.

31. $z = 2 \sin x$

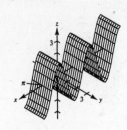

33. $z^2 = x^2 + 4y^2$

$z = \pm\sqrt{x^2 + 4y^2}$

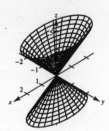

35. $x^2 + y^2 = \left(\dfrac{2}{z}\right)^2$

$y = \pm\sqrt{\dfrac{4}{z^2} - x^2}$

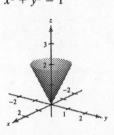

37. $z = 4 - \sqrt{|xy|}$

39. $4x^2 - y^2 + 4z^2 = -16$

$z = \pm\sqrt{\dfrac{y^2}{4} - x^2 - 4}$

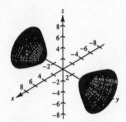

41. $z = 2\sqrt{x^2 + y^2}$

$z = 2$

$2\sqrt{x^2 + y^2} = 2$

$x^2 + y^2 = 1$

43. $x^2 + y^2 = 1$

$x + z = 2$

$z = 0$

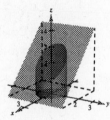

45. $x^2 + z^2 = [r(y)]^2$ and $z = r(y) = \pm 2\sqrt{y}$; therefore,

$x^2 + z^2 = 4y.$

47. $x^2 + y^2 = [r(z)]^2$ and $y = r(z) = \dfrac{z}{2}$; therefore,

$x^2 + y^2 = \dfrac{z^2}{4}, \; 4x^2 + 4y^2 = z^2.$

49. $y^2 + z^2 = [r(x)]^2$ and $y = r(x) = \dfrac{2}{x}$; therefore,

$y^2 + z^2 = \left(\dfrac{2}{x}\right)^2, \; y^2 + z^2 = \dfrac{4}{x^2}.$

51. $x^2 + y^2 - 2z = 0$

$x^2 + y^2 = \left(\sqrt{2z}\right)^2$

Equation of generating curve: $y = \sqrt{2z}$ or $x = \sqrt{2z}$

53. Let C be a curve in a plane and let L be a line not in a parallel plane. The set of all lines parallel to L and intersecting C is called a cylinder.

55. See pages 765 and 766.

57. $V = 2\pi\displaystyle\int_0^4 x(4x - x^2)\,dx$

$= 2\pi\left[\dfrac{4x^3}{3} - \dfrac{x^4}{4}\right]_0^4 = \dfrac{128\pi}{3}$

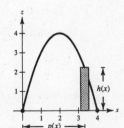

59. $z = \dfrac{x^2}{2} + \dfrac{y^2}{4}$

(a) When $z = 2$ we have $2 = \dfrac{x^2}{2} + \dfrac{y^2}{4}$, or $1 = \dfrac{x^2}{4} + \dfrac{y^2}{8}$

Major axis: $2\sqrt{8} = 4\sqrt{2}$

Minor axis: $2\sqrt{4} = 4$

$c^2 = a^2 - b^2, c^2 = 4, c = 2$

Foci: $(0, \pm 2, 2)$

(b) When $z = 8$ we have $8 = \dfrac{x^2}{2} + \dfrac{y^2}{4}$, or $1 = \dfrac{x^2}{16} + \dfrac{y^2}{32}$.

Major axis: $2\sqrt{32} = 8\sqrt{2}$

Minor axis: $2\sqrt{16} = 8$

$c^2 = 32 - 16 = 16, c = 4$

Foci: $(0, \pm 4, 8)$

61. If (x, y, z) is on the surface, then

$$(y + 2)^2 = x^2 + (y - 2)^2 + z^2$$

$$y^2 + 4y + 4 = x^2 + y^2 - 4y + 4 + z^2$$

$$x^2 + z^2 = 8y$$

Elliptic paraboloid

Traces parallel to xz-plane are circles.

63. $\dfrac{x^2}{3963^2} + \dfrac{y^2}{3963^2} + \dfrac{z^2}{3942^2} = 1$

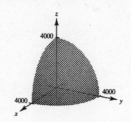

65. $z = \dfrac{y^2}{b^2} - \dfrac{x^2}{a^2}, z = bx + ay$

$$bx + ay = \dfrac{y^2}{b^2} - \dfrac{x^2}{a^2}$$

$$\dfrac{1}{a^2}\left(x^2 + a^2 bx + \dfrac{a^4 b^2}{4}\right) = \dfrac{1}{b^2}\left(y^2 - ab^2 y + \dfrac{a^2 b^4}{4}\right)$$

$$\dfrac{\left(x + \dfrac{a^2 b}{2}\right)^2}{a^2} = \dfrac{\left(y - \dfrac{ab^2}{2}\right)^2}{b^2}$$

$$y = \pm\dfrac{b}{a}\left(x + \dfrac{a^2 b}{2}\right) + \dfrac{ab^2}{2}$$

Letting $x = at$, you obtain the two intersecting lines
$x = at, y = -bt, z = 0$ and $x = at, y = bt + ab^2$
$z = 2abt + a^2 b^2$.

67. The Klein bottle *does not* have both an "inside" and an "outside." It is formed by inserting the small open end through the side of the bottle and making it contiguous with the top of the bottle.

Section 10.7 Cylindrical and Spherical Coordinates

1. $(5, 0, 2)$, cylindrical
$x = 5\cos 0 = 5$
$y = 5\sin 0 = 0$
$z = 2$
$(5, 0, 2)$, rectangular

3. $\left(2, \dfrac{\pi}{3}, 2\right)$, cylindrical
$x = 2\cos\dfrac{\pi}{3} = 1$
$y = 2\sin\dfrac{\pi}{3} = \sqrt{3}$
$z = 2$
$\left(1, \sqrt{3}, 2\right)$, rectangular

5. $\left(4, \dfrac{7\pi}{6}, 3\right)$, cylindrical
$x = 4\cos\dfrac{7\pi}{6} = -2\sqrt{3}$
$y = 4\sin\dfrac{7\pi}{6} = -2$
$z = 3$
$\left(-2\sqrt{3}, -2, 3\right)$, rectangular

7. $(0, 5, 1)$, rectangular

$r = \sqrt{(0)^2 + (5)^2} = 5$

$\theta = \arctan\dfrac{5}{0} = \dfrac{\pi}{2}$

$z = 1$

$\left(5, \dfrac{\pi}{2}, 1\right)$, cylindrical

9. $\left(1, \sqrt{3}, 4\right)$, rectangular

$r = \sqrt{1^2 + \left(\sqrt{3}\right)^2} = 2$

$\theta = \arctan\sqrt{3} = \dfrac{\pi}{3}$

$z = 4$

$\left(2, \dfrac{\pi}{3}, 4\right)$, cylindrical

11. $(2, -2, -4)$, rectangular

$r = \sqrt{2^2 + (-2)^2} = 2\sqrt{2}$

$\theta = \arctan(-1) = -\dfrac{\pi}{4}$

$z = -4$

$\left(2\sqrt{2}, \dfrac{-\pi}{4}, -4\right)$, cylindrical

13. $x^2 + y^2 + z^2 = 10$ rectangular equation

   $r^2 + z^2 = 10$ cylindrical equation

15. $y = x^2$ rectangular equation

$r \sin\theta = (r \cos\theta)^2$

$\sin\theta = r \cos^2\theta$

$r = \sec\theta \cdot \tan\theta$ cylindrical equation

17. $r = 2$

$\sqrt{x^2 + y^2} = 2$

$x^2 + y^2 = 4$

19. $\theta = \dfrac{\pi}{6}$

$\tan\dfrac{\pi}{6} = \dfrac{y}{x}$

$\dfrac{1}{\sqrt{3}} = \dfrac{y}{x}$

$x = \sqrt{3}\,y$

$x - \sqrt{3}\,y = 0$

21. $r = 2 \sin\theta$

$r^2 = 2r \sin\theta$

$x^2 + y^2 = 2y$

$x^2 + y^2 - 2y = 0$

$x^2 + (y - 1)^2 = 1$

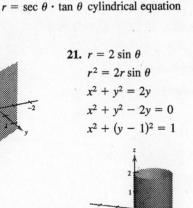

23. $r^2 + z^2 = 4$

$x^2 + y^2 + z^2 = 4$

25. $(4, 0, 0)$, rectangular

$\rho = \sqrt{4^2 + 0^2 + 0^2} = 4$

$\theta = \arctan 0 = 0$

$\phi = \arccos 0 = \dfrac{\pi}{2}$

$\left(4, 0, \dfrac{\pi}{2}\right)$, spherical

27. $\left(-2, 2\sqrt{3}, 4\right)$, rectangular

$\rho = \sqrt{(-2)^2 + \left(2\sqrt{3}\right)^2 + 4^2} = 4\sqrt{2}$

$\theta = \arctan\left(-\sqrt{3}\right) = \dfrac{2\pi}{3}$

$\phi = \arccos\dfrac{1}{\sqrt{2}} = \dfrac{\pi}{4}$

$\left(4\sqrt{2}, \dfrac{2\pi}{3}, \dfrac{\pi}{4}\right)$, spherical

29. $\left(\sqrt{3}, 1, 2\sqrt{3}\right)$, rectangular

$\rho = \sqrt{3 + 1 + 12} = 4$

$\theta = \arctan\dfrac{1}{\sqrt{3}} = \dfrac{\pi}{6}$

$\phi = \arccos\dfrac{\sqrt{3}}{2} = \dfrac{\pi}{6}$

$\left(4, \dfrac{\pi}{6}, \dfrac{\pi}{6}\right)$, spherical

31. $\left(4, \dfrac{\pi}{6}, \dfrac{\pi}{4}\right)$, spherical

$x = 4 \sin \dfrac{\pi}{4} \cos \dfrac{\pi}{6} = \sqrt{6}$

$y = 4 \sin \dfrac{\pi}{4} \sin \dfrac{\pi}{6} = \sqrt{2}$

$z = 4 \cos \dfrac{\pi}{4} = 2\sqrt{2}$

$\left(\sqrt{6}, \sqrt{2}, 2\sqrt{2}\right)$, rectangular

33. $\left(12, \dfrac{-\pi}{4}, 0\right)$, spherical

$x = 12 \sin 0 \cos\left(\dfrac{-\pi}{4}\right) = 0$

$y = 12 \sin 0 \sin\left(\dfrac{-\pi}{4}\right) = 0$

$z = 12 \cos 0 = 12$

$(0, 0, 12)$, rectangular

35. $\left(5, \dfrac{\pi}{4}, \dfrac{3\pi}{4}\right)$, spherical

$x = 5 \sin \dfrac{3\pi}{4} \cos \dfrac{\pi}{4} = \dfrac{5}{2}$

$y = 5 \sin \dfrac{3\pi}{4} \sin \dfrac{\pi}{4} = \dfrac{5}{2}$

$z = 5 \cos \dfrac{3\pi}{4} = -\dfrac{5\sqrt{2}}{2}$

$\left(\dfrac{5}{2}, \dfrac{5}{2}, -\dfrac{5\sqrt{2}}{2}\right)$, rectangular

37. (a) Programs will vary.

(b) $(x, y, z) = (3, -4, 2)$

$(\rho, \theta, \phi) = (5.385, -0.927, 1.190)$

39. $x^2 + y^2 + z^2 = 36$ rectangular equation

$\rho^2 = 36$ spherical equation

41. $x^2 + y^2 = 9$ rectangular equation

$\rho^2 \sin^2 \phi \cos^2 \theta + \rho^2 \sin^2 \phi \sin^2 \theta = 9$

$\rho^2 \sin^2 \phi = 9$

$\rho \sin \phi = 3$

$\rho = 3 \csc \phi$ spherical equation

43. $\rho = 2$

$x^2 + y^2 + z^2 = 4$

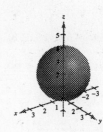

45. $\phi = \dfrac{\pi}{6}$

$\cos \phi = \dfrac{z}{\sqrt{x^2 + y^2 + z^2}}$

$\dfrac{\sqrt{3}}{2} = \dfrac{z}{\sqrt{x^2 + y^2 + z^2}}$

$\dfrac{3}{4} = \dfrac{z^2}{x^2 + y^2 + z^2}$

$3x^2 + 3y^2 - z^2 = 0$

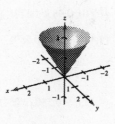

47. $\rho = 4 \cos \phi$

$\sqrt{x^2 + y^2 + z^2} = \dfrac{4z}{\sqrt{x^2 + y^2 + z^2}}$

$x^2 + y^2 + z^2 - 4z = 0$

$x^2 + y^2 + (z - 2)^2 = 4$

49. $\rho = \csc \phi$

$\rho \sin \phi = 1$

$\sqrt{x^2 + y^2} = 1$

$x^2 + y^2 = 1$

51. $\left(4, \dfrac{\pi}{4}, 0\right)$, cylindrical

$\rho = \sqrt{4^2 + 0^2} = 4$

$\theta = \dfrac{\pi}{4}$

$\phi = \arccos 0 = \dfrac{\pi}{2}$

$\left(4, \dfrac{\pi}{4}, \dfrac{\pi}{2}\right)$, spherical

53. $\left(4, \dfrac{\pi}{2}, 4\right)$, cylindrical

$\rho = \sqrt{4^2 + 4^2} = 4\sqrt{2}$

$\theta = \dfrac{\pi}{2}$

$\phi = \arccos\left(\dfrac{4}{4\sqrt{2}}\right) = \dfrac{\pi}{4}$

$\left(4\sqrt{2}, \dfrac{\pi}{2}, \dfrac{\pi}{4}\right)$, spherical

55. $\left(4, \dfrac{-\pi}{6}, 6\right)$, cylindrical

$\rho = \sqrt{4^2 + 6^2} = 2\sqrt{13}$

$\theta = \dfrac{-\pi}{6}$

$\phi = \arccos \dfrac{3}{\sqrt{13}}$

$\left(2\sqrt{13}, \dfrac{-\pi}{6}, \arccos \dfrac{3}{\sqrt{13}}\right)$,
spherical

57. $(12, \pi, 5)$, cylindrical

$\rho = \sqrt{12^2 + 5^2} = 13$

$\theta = \pi$

$\phi = \arccos \dfrac{5}{13}$

$\left(13, \pi, \arccos \dfrac{5}{13}\right)$, spherical

59. $\left(10, \dfrac{\pi}{6}, \dfrac{\pi}{2}\right)$, spherical

$r = 10 \sin \dfrac{\pi}{2} = 10$

$\theta = \dfrac{\pi}{6}$

$z = 10 \cos \dfrac{\pi}{2} = 0$

$\left(10, \dfrac{\pi}{6}, 0\right)$, cylindrical

61. $\left(36, \pi, \dfrac{\pi}{2}\right)$, spherical

$r = \rho \sin \phi = 36 \sin \dfrac{\pi}{2} = 36$

$\theta = \pi$

$z = \rho \cos \phi = 36 \cos \dfrac{\pi}{2} = 0$

$(36, \pi, 0)$, cylindrical

63. $\left(6, -\dfrac{\pi}{6}, \dfrac{\pi}{3}\right)$, spherical

$r = 6 \sin \dfrac{\pi}{3} = 3\sqrt{3}$

$\theta = -\dfrac{\pi}{6}$

$z = 6 \cos \dfrac{\pi}{3} = 3$

$\left(3\sqrt{3}, -\dfrac{\pi}{6}, 3\right)$, cylindrical

65. $\left(8, \dfrac{7\pi}{6}, \dfrac{\pi}{6}\right)$, spherical

$r = 8 \sin \dfrac{\pi}{6} = 4$

$\theta = \dfrac{7\pi}{6}$

$z = 8 \cos \dfrac{\pi}{6} = \dfrac{8\sqrt{3}}{2}$

$\left(4, \dfrac{7\pi}{6}, 4\sqrt{3}\right)$, cylindrical

Rectangular	*Cylindrical*	*Spherical*
67. $(4, 6, 3)$	$(7.211, 0.983, 3)$	$(7.810, 0.983, 1.177)$
69. $(4.698, 1.710, 8)$	$\left(5, \dfrac{\pi}{9}, 8\right)$	$(9.434, 0.349, 0.559)$
71. $(-7.071, 12.247, 14.142)$	$(14.142, 2.094, 14.142)$	$\left(20, \dfrac{2\pi}{3}, \dfrac{\pi}{4}\right)$
73. $(3, -2, 2)$	$(3.606, -0.588, 2)$	$(4.123, -0.588, 1.064)$
75. $\left(\dfrac{5}{2}, \dfrac{4}{3}, \dfrac{-3}{2}\right)$	$(2.833, 0.490, -1.5)$	$(3.206, 0.490, 2.058)$
77. $(-3.536, 3.536, -5)$	$\left(5, \dfrac{3\pi}{4}, -5\right)$	$(7.071, 2.356, 2.356)$
79. $(2.804, -2.095, 6)$	$(-3.5, 2.5, 6)$	$(6.946, 5.642, 0.528)$

[Note: Use the cylindrical coordinates $(3.5, 5.642, 6)$]

81. $r = 5$

Cylinder

Matches graph (d)

83. $\rho = 5$

Sphere

Matches graph (c)

85. $r^2 = z$, $x^2 + y^2 = z$

Paraboloid

Matches graph (f)

87. Rectangular to cylindrical: $r^2 = x^2 + y^2$

$\tan \theta = \dfrac{y}{x}$

$z = z$

Cylindrical to rectangular: $x = r \cos \theta$

$y = r \sin \theta$

$z = z$

89. Rectangular to spherical: $\rho^2 = x^2 + y^2 + z^2$

$\tan \theta = \dfrac{y}{x}$

$\phi = \arccos \left(\dfrac{z}{\sqrt{x^2 + y^2 + z^2}}\right)$

Spherical to rectangular: $x = \rho \sin \phi \cos \theta$

$y = \rho \sin \phi \sin \theta$

$z = \rho \cos \phi$

91. $x^2 + y^2 + z^2 = 16$

  (a) $r^2 + z^2 = 16$

  (b) $\rho^2 = 16, \rho = 4$

93. $x^2 + y^2 + z^2 - 2z = 0$

  (a) $r^2 + z^2 - 2z = 0, r^2 + (z - 1)^2 = 1$

  (b) $\rho^2 - 2\rho \cos \phi = 0, \rho(\rho - 2 \cos \phi) = 0,$

     $\rho = 2 \cos \phi$

95. $x^2 + y^2 = 4y$

  (a) $r^2 = 4r \sin \theta, \ r = 4 \sin \theta$

  (b) $\rho^2 \sin^2 \phi = 4\rho \sin \phi \sin \theta,$

    $\rho \sin \phi (\rho \sin \phi - 4 \sin \theta) = 0,$

    $\rho = \dfrac{4 \sin \theta}{\sin \phi}, \ \rho = 4 \sin \theta \csc \phi$

97. $x^2 - y^2 = 9$

  (a) $r^2 \cos^2 \theta - r^2 \sin^2 \theta = 9,$

    $r^2 = \dfrac{9}{\cos^2 \theta - \sin^2 \theta}$

  (b) $\rho^2 \sin^2 \phi \cos^2 \theta - \rho^2 \sin^2 \phi \sin^2 \theta = 9,$

    $\rho^2 \sin^2 \phi = \dfrac{9}{\cos^2 \theta - \sin^2 \theta},$

    $\rho^2 = \dfrac{9 \csc^2 \phi}{\cos^2 \theta - \sin^2 \theta}$

99. $0 \le \theta \le \dfrac{\pi}{2}$

  $0 \le r \le 2$

  $0 \le z \le 4$

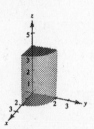

101. $0 \le \theta \le 2\pi$

  $0 \le r \le a$

  $r \le z \le a$

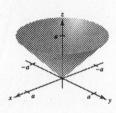

103. $0 \le \theta \le 2\pi$

  $0 \le \phi \le \dfrac{\pi}{6}$

  $0 \le \rho \le a \sec \phi$

105. Rectangular

  $0 \le x \le 10$

  $0 \le y \le 10$

  $0 \le z \le 10$

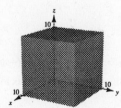

107. Spherical

  $4 \le \rho \le 6$

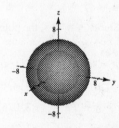

109. $z = \sin \theta, r = 1$

  $z = \dfrac{y}{r} = \dfrac{y}{1} = y$

The curve of intersection is the ellipse formed by the intersection of the plane $z = y$ and the cylinder $r = 1$.

Review Exercises for Chapter 10

1. $P = (1, 2), \ Q = (4, 1), \ R = (5, 4)$

  (a) $\mathbf{u} = \overrightarrow{PQ} = \langle 3, -1 \rangle = 3\mathbf{i} - \mathbf{j},$

    $\mathbf{v} = \overrightarrow{PR} = \langle 4, 2 \rangle = 4\mathbf{i} + 2\mathbf{j}$

  (b) $\|\mathbf{v}\| = \sqrt{4^2 + 2^2} = 2\sqrt{5}$

  (c) $2\mathbf{u} + \mathbf{v} = \langle 6, -2 \rangle + \langle 4, 2 \rangle = \langle 10, 0 \rangle = 10\mathbf{i}$

3. $\mathbf{v} = \|\mathbf{v}\| \cos \theta \, \mathbf{i} + \|\mathbf{v}\| \sin \theta \, \mathbf{j} = 8 \cos 120° \, \mathbf{i} + 8 \sin 120° \, \mathbf{j}$

      $= -4\mathbf{i} + 4\sqrt{3}\mathbf{j}$

5. $120 \cos \theta = 100$

$$\theta = \arccos\!\left(\frac{5}{6}\right)$$

$$\tan \theta = \frac{2}{y} \implies y = \frac{2}{\tan \theta}$$

$$y = \frac{2}{\tan[\arccos(5/6)]} = \frac{2}{\sqrt{11}/5} = \frac{10}{\sqrt{11}} \approx 3.015 \text{ ft}$$

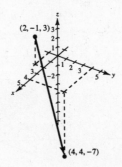

7. $z = 0, \ y = 4, \ x = -5: \ (-5, 4, 0)$

9. Looking down from the positive x-axis towards the yz-plane, the point is either in the first quadrant ($y > 0, z > 0$) or in the third quadrant ($y < 0, z < 0$). The x-coordinate can be any number.

11. $(x - 3)^2 + (y + 2)^2 + (z - 6)^2 = \left(\dfrac{15}{2}\right)^2$

13. $(x^2 - 4x + 4) + (y^2 - 6y + 9) + z^2 = -4 + 4 + 9$

$(x - 2)^2 + (y - 3)^2 + z^2 = 9$

Center: $(2, 3, 0)$

Radius: 3

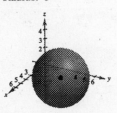

15. $\mathbf{v} = \langle 4 - 2, 4 + 1, -7 - 3 \rangle = \langle 2, 5, -10 \rangle$

17. $\mathbf{v} = \langle -1 - 3, 6 - 4, 9 + 1 \rangle = \langle -4, 2, 10 \rangle$

$\mathbf{w} = \langle 5 - 3, 3 - 4, -6 + 1 \rangle = \langle 2, -1, -5 \rangle$

Since $-2\mathbf{w} = \mathbf{v}$, the points lie in a straight line.

19. Unit vector: $\dfrac{\mathbf{u}}{\|\mathbf{u}\|} = \dfrac{\langle 2, 3, 5 \rangle}{\sqrt{38}} = \left\langle \dfrac{2}{\sqrt{38}}, \dfrac{3}{\sqrt{38}}, \dfrac{5}{\sqrt{38}} \right\rangle$

21. $P = (5, 0, 0), \ Q = (4, 4, 0), \ R = (2, 0, 6)$

  (a) $\mathbf{u} = \overrightarrow{PQ} = \langle -1, 4, 0 \rangle = -\mathbf{i} + 4\mathbf{j}$,

      $\mathbf{v} = \overrightarrow{PR} = \langle -3, 0, 6 \rangle = -3\mathbf{i} + 6\mathbf{k}$

  (b) $\mathbf{u} \cdot \mathbf{v} = (-1)(-3) + 4(0) + 0(6) = 3$

  (c) $\mathbf{v} \cdot \mathbf{v} = 9 + 36 = 45$

23. $\mathbf{u} = \langle 7, -2, 3 \rangle, \ \mathbf{v} = \langle -1, 4, 5 \rangle$

Since $\mathbf{u} \cdot \mathbf{v} = 0$, the vectors are orthogonal.

25. $\mathbf{u} = 5\!\left(\cos \dfrac{3\pi}{4}\mathbf{i} + \sin \dfrac{3\pi}{4}\mathbf{j}\right) = \dfrac{5\sqrt{2}}{2}[-\mathbf{i} + \mathbf{j}]$

$\mathbf{v} = 2\!\left(\cos \dfrac{2\pi}{3}\mathbf{i} + \sin \dfrac{2\pi}{3}\mathbf{j}\right) = -\mathbf{i} + \sqrt{3}\mathbf{j}$

$\mathbf{u} \cdot \mathbf{v} = \dfrac{5\sqrt{2}}{2}\!\left(1 + \sqrt{3}\right)$

$\|\mathbf{u}\| = 5$

$\|\mathbf{v}\| = 2$

$\cos \theta = \dfrac{|\mathbf{u} \cdot \mathbf{v}|}{\|\mathbf{u}\| \, \|\mathbf{v}\|} = \dfrac{\left(5\sqrt{2}/2\right)\!\left(1 + \sqrt{3}\right)}{5(2)} = \dfrac{\sqrt{2} + \sqrt{6}}{4}$

$\theta = \arccos \dfrac{\sqrt{2} + \sqrt{6}}{4} = 15°$

27. $\mathbf{u} = \langle 10, -5, 15 \rangle, \ \mathbf{v} = \langle -2, 1, -3 \rangle$

$\mathbf{u} = -5\mathbf{v} \implies \mathbf{u}$ is parallel to $\mathbf{v}$ and in the opposite direction.

$$\theta = \pi$$

29. There are many correct answers. For example: $v = \pm\langle 6, -5, 0 \rangle$.

In Exercises 31–39, $\mathbf{u} = \langle 3, -2, 1 \rangle$, $\mathbf{v} = \langle 2, -4, -3 \rangle$, $\mathbf{w} = \langle -1, 2, 2 \rangle$.

31. $\mathbf{u} \cdot \mathbf{u} = 3(3) + (-2)(-2) + (1)(1)$

$= 14 = \left(\sqrt{14}\right)^2 = \|\mathbf{u}\|^2$

33. $\text{proj}_{\mathbf{u}}\mathbf{w} = \left(\dfrac{\mathbf{u} \cdot \mathbf{w}}{\|\mathbf{u}\|^2}\right)\mathbf{u}$

$= -\dfrac{5}{14}\langle 3, -2, 1 \rangle$

$= \left\langle -\dfrac{15}{14}, \dfrac{10}{14}, -\dfrac{5}{14} \right\rangle$

$= \left\langle -\dfrac{15}{14}, \dfrac{5}{7}, -\dfrac{5}{14} \right\rangle$

35. $\mathbf{n} = \mathbf{v} \times \mathbf{w} = \begin{vmatrix} \mathbf{i} & \mathbf{j} & \mathbf{k} \\ 2 & -4 & -3 \\ -1 & 2 & 2 \end{vmatrix} = -2\mathbf{i} - \mathbf{j}$

$\|\mathbf{n}\| = \sqrt{5}$

$\dfrac{\mathbf{n}}{\|\mathbf{n}\|} = \dfrac{1}{\sqrt{5}}(-2\mathbf{i} - \mathbf{j})$

37. $V = |\mathbf{u} \cdot (\mathbf{v} \times \mathbf{w})|$

$= |\langle 3, -2, 1 \rangle \cdot \langle -2, -1, 0 \rangle| = |-4| = 4$

39. Area parallelogram $= \|\mathbf{u} \times \mathbf{v}\| = \sqrt{10^2 + 11^2 + (-8)^2}$ (See Exercises 36, 38)

$= \sqrt{285}$

41. $\mathbf{F} = c(\cos 20°\mathbf{j} + \sin 20°\mathbf{k})$

$\overrightarrow{PQ} = 2\mathbf{k}$

$\overrightarrow{PQ} \times \mathbf{F} = \begin{vmatrix} \mathbf{i} & \mathbf{j} & \mathbf{k} \\ 0 & 0 & 2 \\ 0 & c\cos 20° & c\sin 20° \end{vmatrix} = -2c\cos 20°\mathbf{i}$

$200 = \|\overrightarrow{PQ} \times \mathbf{F}\| = 2c\cos 20°$

$c = \dfrac{100}{\cos 20°}$

$\mathbf{F} = \dfrac{100}{\cos 20°}(\cos 20°\mathbf{j} + \sin 20°\mathbf{k}) = 100(\mathbf{j} + \tan 20°\mathbf{k})$

$\|\mathbf{F}\| = 100\sqrt{1 + \tan^2 20°} = 100 \sec 20° \approx 106.4 \text{ lb}$

43. $\mathbf{v} = \mathbf{j}$

(a) $x = 1$, $y = 2 + t$, $z = 3$

(b) None

45. $3x - 3y - 7z = -4$, $x - y + 2z = 3$

Solving simultaneously, we have $z = 1$. Substituting $z = 1$ into the second equation we have $y = x - 1$. Substituting for x in this equation we obtain two points on the line of intersection, $(0, -1, 1)$, $(1, 0, 1)$. The direction vector of the line of intersection is $\mathbf{v} = \mathbf{i} + \mathbf{j}$.

(a) $x = t$, $y = -1 + t$, $z = 1$

(b) $x = y + 1$, $z = 1$

47. The two lines are parallel as they have the same direction numbers, $-2, 1, 1$. Therefore, a vector parallel to the plane is $\mathbf{v} = -2\mathbf{i} + \mathbf{j} + \mathbf{k}$. A point on the first line is $(1, 0, -1)$ and a point on the second line is $(-1, 1, 2)$. The vector $\mathbf{u} = 2\mathbf{i} - \mathbf{j} - 3\mathbf{k}$ connecting these two points is also parallel to the plane. Therefore, a normal to the plane is

$$\mathbf{v} \times \mathbf{u} = \begin{vmatrix} \mathbf{i} & \mathbf{j} & \mathbf{k} \\ -2 & 1 & 1 \\ 2 & -1 & -3 \end{vmatrix}$$

$$= -2\mathbf{i} - 4\mathbf{j} = -2(\mathbf{i} + 2\mathbf{j}).$$

Equation of the plane: $(x - 1) + 2y = 0$

$$x + 2y = 1$$

49. $Q = (1, 0, 2)$

$2x - 3y + 6z = 6$

A point P on the plane is $(3, 0, 0)$.

$$\overrightarrow{PQ} = \langle -2, 0, 2 \rangle$$

$$\mathbf{n} = \langle 2, -3, 6 \rangle$$

$$D = \frac{|\overrightarrow{PQ} \cdot \mathbf{n}|}{\|\mathbf{n}\|} = \frac{8}{7}$$

51. $Q(3, -2, 4)$ point

$P(5, 0, 0)$ point on plane

$\mathbf{n} = \langle 2, -5, 1 \rangle$ normal to plane

$\overrightarrow{PQ} = \langle -2, -2, 4 \rangle$

$$D = \frac{|\overrightarrow{PQ} \cdot \mathbf{n}|}{\|\mathbf{n}\|} = \frac{10}{\sqrt{30}} = \frac{\sqrt{30}}{3}$$

53. $x + 2y + 3z = 6$

Plane

Intercepts: $(6, 0, 0), (0, 3, 0), (0, 0, 2)$

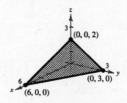

55. $y = \frac{1}{2}z$

Plane with rulings parallel to the x-axis

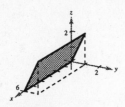

57. $\frac{x^2}{16} + \frac{y^2}{9} + z^2 = 1$

Ellipsoid

xy-trace: $\frac{x^2}{16} + \frac{y^2}{9} = 1$

xz-trace: $\frac{x^2}{16} + z^2 = 1$

yz-trace: $\frac{y^2}{9} + z^2 = 1$

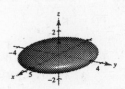

59. $\frac{x^2}{16} - \frac{y^2}{9} + z^2 = -1$

Hyperboloid of two sheets

xy-trace: $\frac{y^2}{4} - \frac{x^2}{16} = 1$

xz-trace: None

yz-trace: $\frac{y^2}{9} - z^2 = 1$

61. (a)
$$x^2 + y^2 = [r(z)]^2$$
$$= \left[\sqrt{2(z-1)}\right]^2$$
$$x^2 + y^2 - 2z + 2 = 0$$

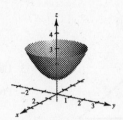

(b) $V = 2\pi \displaystyle\int_0^2 x\left[3 - \left(\frac{1}{2}x^2 + 1\right)\right] dx$

$\quad = 2\pi \displaystyle\int_0^2 \left(2x - \frac{1}{2}x^3\right) dx$

$\quad = 2\pi\left[x^2 - \dfrac{x^4}{8}\right]_0^2$

$\quad = 4\pi \approx 12.6 \text{ cm}^3$

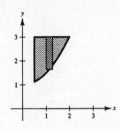

(c) $V = 2\pi \displaystyle\int_{1/2}^2 x\left[3 - \left(\frac{1}{2}x^2 + 1\right)\right] dx$

$\quad = 2\pi \displaystyle\int_{1/2}^2 \left(2x - \frac{1}{2}x^3\right) dx$

$\quad = 2\pi\left[x^2 - \dfrac{x^4}{8}\right]_{1/2}^2$

$\quad = 4\pi - \dfrac{31\pi}{64} = \dfrac{225\pi}{64} \approx 11.04 \text{ cm}^3$

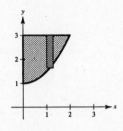

63. $\left(-2\sqrt{2}, 2\sqrt{2}, 2\right)$, rectangular

(a) $r = \sqrt{\left(-2\sqrt{2}\right)^2 + \left(2\sqrt{2}\right)^2} = 4$, $\theta = \arctan(-1) = \dfrac{3\pi}{4}$, $z = 2$, $\left(4, \dfrac{3\pi}{4}, 2\right)$, cylindrical

(b) $\rho = \sqrt{\left(-2\sqrt{2}\right)^2 + \left(2\sqrt{2}\right)^2 + (2)^2} = 2\sqrt{5}$, $\theta = \dfrac{3\pi}{4}$, $\phi = \arccos\dfrac{2}{2\sqrt{5}} = \arccos\dfrac{1}{\sqrt{5}}$, $\left(2\sqrt{5}, \dfrac{3\pi}{4}, \arccos\dfrac{\sqrt{5}}{5}\right)$, spherical

65. $\left(100, -\dfrac{\pi}{6}, 50\right)$, cylindrical

$\rho = \sqrt{100^2 + 50^2} = 50\sqrt{5}$

$\theta = -\dfrac{\pi}{6}$

$\phi = \arccos\left(\dfrac{50}{50\sqrt{5}}\right) = \arccos\left(\dfrac{1}{\sqrt{5}}\right) \approx 63.4°$

$\left(50\sqrt{5}, -\dfrac{\pi}{6}, 63.4°\right)$, spherical

67. $\left(25, -\dfrac{\pi}{4}, \dfrac{3\pi}{4}\right)$, spherical

$r^2 = \left(25\sin\left(\dfrac{3\pi}{4}\right)\right)^2 \Rightarrow r = 25\dfrac{\sqrt{2}}{2}$

$\theta = -\dfrac{\pi}{4}$

$z = \rho\cos\phi - 25\cos\dfrac{3\pi}{4} = -25\dfrac{\sqrt{2}}{2}$

$\left(25\dfrac{\sqrt{2}}{2}, -\dfrac{\pi}{4}, -\dfrac{25\sqrt{2}}{2}\right)$, cylindrical

69. $x^2 - y^2 = 2z$

(a) Cylindrical: $r^2\cos^2\theta - r^2\sin^2\theta = 2z$, $r^2\cos 2\theta = 2z$

(b) Spherical: $\rho^2\sin^2\phi\cos^2\theta - \rho^2\sin^2\phi\sin^2\theta = 2\rho\cos\phi$, $\rho\sin^2\phi\cos 2\theta - 2\cos\phi = 0$, $\rho = 2\sec 2\theta\cos\phi\csc^2\phi$

Problem Solving for Chapter 10

1. $\mathbf{a} + \mathbf{b} + \mathbf{c} = \mathbf{0}$

$\mathbf{b} \times (\mathbf{a} + \mathbf{b} + \mathbf{c}) = \mathbf{0}$

$(\mathbf{b} \times \mathbf{a}) + (\mathbf{b} \times \mathbf{c}) = \mathbf{0}$

$\|\mathbf{a} \times \mathbf{b}\| = \|\mathbf{b} \times \mathbf{c}\|$

$\|\mathbf{b} \times \mathbf{c}\| = \|\mathbf{b}\|\,\|\mathbf{c}\| \sin A$

$\|\mathbf{a} \times \mathbf{b}\| = \|\mathbf{a}\|\,\|\mathbf{b}\| \sin C$

Then,

$$\frac{\sin A}{\|\mathbf{a}\|} = \frac{\|\mathbf{b} \times \mathbf{c}\|}{\|\mathbf{a}\|\,\|\mathbf{b}\|\,\|\mathbf{c}\|}$$

$$= \frac{\|\mathbf{a} \times \mathbf{b}\|}{\|\mathbf{a}\|\,\|\mathbf{b}\|\,\|\mathbf{c}\|}$$

$$= \frac{\sin C}{\|\mathbf{c}\|}.$$

The other case, $\dfrac{\sin A}{\|\mathbf{a}\|} = \dfrac{\sin B}{\|\mathbf{b}\|}$ is similar.

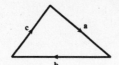

3. Label the figure as indicated.

From the figure, you see that

$$\overrightarrow{SP} = \frac{1}{2}\mathbf{a} - \frac{1}{2}\mathbf{b} = \overrightarrow{RQ} \text{ and}$$

$$\overrightarrow{SR} = \frac{1}{2}\mathbf{a} + \frac{1}{2}\mathbf{b} = \overrightarrow{PQ}.$$

Since $\overrightarrow{SP} = \overrightarrow{RQ}$ and $\overrightarrow{SR} = \overrightarrow{PQ}$, *PSRQ* is a parallelogram.

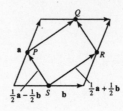

5. (a) $\mathbf{u} = \langle 0, 1, 1 \rangle$ direction vector of line determined by P_1 and P_2.

$$D = \frac{\|\overrightarrow{P_1Q} \times \mathbf{u}\|}{\|\mathbf{u}\|}$$

$$= \frac{\|\langle 2, 0, -1 \rangle \times \langle 0, 1, 1 \rangle\|}{\sqrt{2}}$$

$$= \frac{\|\langle 1, -2, 2 \rangle\|}{\sqrt{2}} = \frac{3}{\sqrt{2}} = \frac{3\sqrt{2}}{2}$$

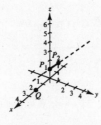

(b) The shortest distance to the line **segment** is $\|P_1Q\| = \|\langle 2, 0, -1 \rangle\| = \sqrt{5}$.

7. (a) $V = \pi \displaystyle\int_0^1 \left(\sqrt{2}\right)^2 dz = \left[\pi \frac{z^2}{2}\right]_0^1 = \frac{1}{2}\pi$

Note: $\dfrac{1}{2}(\text{base})(\text{altitude}) = \dfrac{1}{2}\pi(1) = \dfrac{1}{2}\pi$

(b) $\dfrac{x^2}{a^2} + \dfrac{y^2}{b^2} = z$: (slice at $z = c$)

$$\frac{x^2}{\left(\sqrt{ca}\right)^2} + \frac{y^2}{\left(\sqrt{cb}\right)^2} = 1$$

At $z = c$, figure is ellipse of area

$$\pi\left(\sqrt{ca}\right)\left(\sqrt{cb}\right) = \pi abc.$$

$$V = \int_0^k \pi abc \cdot dc = \left[\frac{\pi abc^2}{2}\right]_0^k = \frac{\pi abk^2}{2}$$

(c) $V = \dfrac{1}{2}(\pi abk)k = \dfrac{1}{2}(\text{base})(\text{height})$

9. (a) $\rho = 2 \sin \phi$

Torus

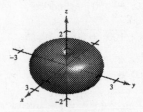

(b) $\rho = 2 \cos \phi$

Sphere

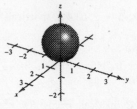

11. From Exercise 64, Section 10.4, $(\mathbf{u} \times \mathbf{v}) \times (\mathbf{w} \times \mathbf{z}) = [(\mathbf{u} \times \mathbf{v}) \cdot \mathbf{z}]\mathbf{w} - [(\mathbf{u} \times \mathbf{v}) \cdot \mathbf{w}]\mathbf{z}$.

13. (a) $\mathbf{u} = \|\mathbf{u}\|(\cos 0\,\mathbf{i} + \sin 0\,\mathbf{j}) = \|\mathbf{u}\|\mathbf{i}$

Downward force $\mathbf{w} = -\mathbf{j}$

$\mathbf{T} = \|\mathbf{T}\|(\cos(90° + \theta)\mathbf{i} + \sin(90° + \theta)\mathbf{j})$

$\quad = \|\mathbf{T}\|(-\sin\theta\,\mathbf{i} + \cos\theta\,\mathbf{j})$

$\mathbf{0} = \mathbf{u} + \mathbf{w} + \mathbf{T} = \|\mathbf{u}\|\mathbf{i} - \mathbf{j} + \|\mathbf{T}\|(-\sin\theta\,\mathbf{i} + \cos\theta\,\mathbf{j})$

$\quad \|\mathbf{u}\| = \sin\theta\,\|\mathbf{T}\|$

$\quad\quad 1 = \cos\theta\,\|\mathbf{T}\|$

If $\theta = 30°$, $\|\mathbf{u}\| = (1/2)\|\mathbf{T}\|$ and $1 = \left(\sqrt{3}/2\right)\|\mathbf{T}\|$

$\Rightarrow \|\mathbf{T}\| = \dfrac{2}{\sqrt{3}} \approx 1.1547$ lb

and

$\|\mathbf{u}\| = \dfrac{1}{2}\left(\dfrac{2}{\sqrt{3}}\right) \approx 0.5774$ lb

(b) From part (a), $\|\mathbf{u}\| = \tan\theta$ and $\|\mathbf{T}\| = \sec\theta$.

Domain: $0 \le \theta \le 90°$

(c)

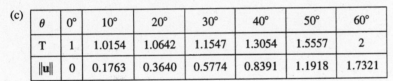

θ	0°	10°	20°	30°	40°	50°	60°
T	1	1.0154	1.0642	1.1547	1.3054	1.5557	2
$\|\mathbf{u}\|$	0	0.1763	0.3640	0.5774	0.8391	1.1918	1.7321

(d)

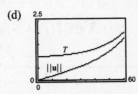

(e) Both are increasing functions.

(f) $\lim\limits_{\theta \to \pi/2^-} T = \infty$ and $\lim\limits_{\theta \to \pi/2^-} \|\mathbf{u}\| = \infty$.

15. Let $\theta = \alpha - \beta$, the angle between $\mathbf{u}$ and $\mathbf{v}$. Then

$\sin(\alpha - \beta) = \dfrac{\|\mathbf{u} \times \mathbf{v}\|}{\|\mathbf{u}\|\,\|\mathbf{v}\|} = \dfrac{\|\mathbf{v} \times \mathbf{u}\|}{\|\mathbf{u}\|\,\|\mathbf{v}\|}.$

For $\mathbf{u} = \langle \cos\alpha, \sin\alpha, 0\rangle$ and $\mathbf{v} = \langle \cos\beta, \sin\beta, 0\rangle$, $\|\mathbf{u}\| = \|\mathbf{v}\| = 1$ and

$\mathbf{v} \times \mathbf{u} = \begin{vmatrix} \mathbf{i} & \mathbf{j} & \mathbf{k} \\ \cos\beta & \sin\beta & 0 \\ \cos\alpha & \sin\alpha & 0 \end{vmatrix} = (\sin\alpha\cos\beta - \cos\alpha\sin\beta)\mathbf{k}.$

Thus, $\sin(\alpha - \beta) = \|\mathbf{v} \times \mathbf{u}\| = \sin\alpha\cos\beta - \cos\alpha\sin\beta$.

17. From Theorem 10.13 and Theorem 10.7 (6) we have

$D = \dfrac{\left|\overrightarrow{PQ} \cdot \mathbf{n}\right|}{\|\mathbf{n}\|}$

$\quad = \dfrac{|\mathbf{w} \cdot (\mathbf{u} \times \mathbf{v})|}{\|\mathbf{u} \times \mathbf{v}\|} = \dfrac{|(\mathbf{u} \times \mathbf{v}) \cdot \mathbf{w}|}{\|\mathbf{u} \times \mathbf{v}\|} = \dfrac{|\mathbf{u} \cdot (\mathbf{v} \times \mathbf{w})|}{\|\mathbf{u} \times \mathbf{v}\|}.$

19. a_1, b_1, c_1, and a_2, b_2, c_2 are two sets of direction numbers for the same line. The line is parallel to both $\mathbf{u} = a_1\mathbf{i} + b_1\mathbf{j} + c_1\mathbf{k}$ and $\mathbf{v} = a_2\mathbf{i} + b_2\mathbf{j} + c_2\mathbf{k}$. Therefore, $\mathbf{u}$ and $\mathbf{v}$ are parallel, and there exists a scalar d such that $\mathbf{u} = d\mathbf{v}$, $a_1\mathbf{i} + b_1\mathbf{j} + c_1\mathbf{k} = d(a_2\mathbf{i} + b_2\mathbf{j} + c_2\mathbf{k})$, $a_1 = a_2d$, $b_1 = b_2d$, $c_1 = c_2d$.

CHAPTER 11
Vector-Valued Functions

CHAPTER 11
Vector-Valued Functions

Section 11.1   Vector-Valued Functions

Solutions to Odd-Numbered Exercises

1. $\mathbf{r}(t) = 5t\mathbf{i} - 4t\mathbf{j} - \dfrac{1}{t}\mathbf{k}$

Component functions: $f(t) = 5t$

$\qquad\qquad\qquad\qquad g(t) = -4t$

$\qquad\qquad\qquad\qquad h(t) = -\dfrac{1}{t}$

Domain: $(-\infty, 0) \cup (0, \infty)$

3. $\mathbf{r}(t) = \ln t\mathbf{i} - e^t\mathbf{j} - t\mathbf{k}$

Component functions: $f(t) = \ln t$

$\qquad\qquad\qquad\qquad g(t) = -e^t$

$\qquad\qquad\qquad\qquad h(t) = -t$

Domain: $(0, \infty)$

5. $\mathbf{r}(t) = \mathbf{F}(t) + \mathbf{G}(t) = \left(\cos t\mathbf{i} - \sin t\mathbf{j} + \sqrt{t}\mathbf{k}\right) + \left(\cos t\mathbf{i} + \sin t\mathbf{j}\right) = 2\cos t\mathbf{i} + \sqrt{t}\mathbf{k}$

Domain: $[0, \infty)$

7. $\mathbf{r}(t) = \mathbf{F}(t) \times \mathbf{G}(t) = \begin{vmatrix} \mathbf{i} & \mathbf{j} & \mathbf{k} \\ \sin t & \cos t & 0 \\ 0 & \sin t & \cos t \end{vmatrix} = \cos^2 t\mathbf{i} - \sin t\cos t\mathbf{j} + \sin^2 t\mathbf{k}$

Domain: $(-\infty, \infty)$

9. $\mathbf{r}(t) = \frac{1}{2}t^2\mathbf{i} - (t - 1)\mathbf{j}$

(a) $\mathbf{r}(1) = \frac{1}{2}\mathbf{i}$

(b) $\mathbf{r}(0) = \mathbf{j}$

(c) $\mathbf{r}(s + 1) = \frac{1}{2}(s + 1)^2\mathbf{i} - (s + 1 - 1)\mathbf{j} = \frac{1}{2}(s + 1)^2\mathbf{i} - s\mathbf{j}$

(d) $\mathbf{r}(2 + \Delta t) - \mathbf{r}(2) = \frac{1}{2}(2 + \Delta t)^2\mathbf{i} - (2 + \Delta t - 1)\mathbf{j} - (2\mathbf{i} - \mathbf{j})$

$\qquad\qquad\qquad\qquad\quad = \left(2 + 2\Delta t + \frac{1}{2}(\Delta t)^2\right)\mathbf{i} - (1 + \Delta t)\mathbf{j} - 2\mathbf{i} + \mathbf{j}$

$\qquad\qquad\qquad\qquad\quad = \left(2\Delta t + \frac{1}{2}(\Delta t)^2\right)\mathbf{i} - (\Delta t)\mathbf{j}$

11. $\mathbf{r}(t) = \ln t\mathbf{i} + \dfrac{1}{t}\mathbf{j} + 3t\mathbf{k}$

(a) $\mathbf{r}(2) = \ln 2\mathbf{i} + \dfrac{1}{2}\mathbf{j} + 6\mathbf{k}$

(b) $\mathbf{r}(-3)$ is not defined. $(\ln(-3)$ does not exist.$)$

(c) $\mathbf{r}(t - 4) = \ln(t - 4)\mathbf{i} + \dfrac{1}{t - 4}\mathbf{j} + 3(t - 4)\mathbf{k}$

(d) $\mathbf{r}(1 + \Delta t) - \mathbf{r}(1) = \ln(1 + \Delta t)\mathbf{i} + \dfrac{1}{1 + \Delta t}\mathbf{j} + 3(1 + \Delta t)\mathbf{k} - (0\mathbf{i} + \mathbf{j} + 3\mathbf{k})$

$\qquad\qquad\qquad\qquad\quad = \ln(1 + \Delta t)\mathbf{i} + \left(\dfrac{1}{1 + \Delta t} - 1\right)\mathbf{j} + (3\Delta t)\mathbf{k}$

13. $\mathbf{r}(t) = \sin 3t\mathbf{i} + \cos 3t\mathbf{j} + t\mathbf{k}$

$\|\mathbf{r}(t)\| = \sqrt{(\sin 3t)^2 + (\cos 3t)^2 + t^2} = \sqrt{1 + t^2}$

15. $\mathbf{r}(t) \cdot \mathbf{u}(t) = (3t - 1)(t^2) + \left(\frac{1}{4}t^3\right)(-8) + 4(t^3)$

$\qquad = 3t^3 - t^2 - 2t^3 + 4t^3 = 5t^3 - t^2$, a scalar.

The dot product is a scalar-valued function.

17. $\mathbf{r}(t) = t\mathbf{i} + 2t\mathbf{j} + t^2\mathbf{k}, -2 \le t \le 2$

$x = t, y = 2t, z = t^2$

Thus, $z = x^2$. Matches (b)

19. $\mathbf{r}(t) = t\mathbf{i} + t^2\mathbf{j} + e^{0.75t}\mathbf{k}, -2 \le t \le 2$

$x = t, y = t^2, z = e^{0.75t}$

Thus, $y = x^2$. Matches (d)

21. (a) View from the negative x-axis: $(-20, 0, 0)$

(c) View from the z-axis: $(0, 0, 20)$

(b) View from above the first octant: $(10, 20, 10)$

(d) View from the positive x-axis: $(20, 0, 0)$

23. $x = 3t$

$y = t - 1$

$y = \dfrac{x}{3} - 1$

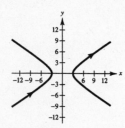

25. $x = t^3, y = t^2$

$y = x^{2/3}$

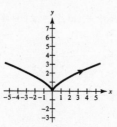

27. $x = \cos \theta, y = 3 \sin \theta$

$x^2 + \dfrac{y^2}{9} = 1$ Ellipse

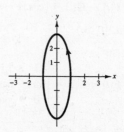

29. $x = 3 \sec \theta, y = 2 \tan \theta$

$\dfrac{x^2}{9} = \dfrac{y^2}{4} + 1$ Hyperbola

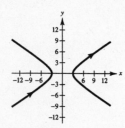

31. $x = -t + 1$

$y = 4t + 2$

$z = 2t + 3$

Line passing through the points:

$(0, 6, 5), \ (1, 2, 3)$

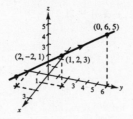

33. $x = 2 \cos t, y = 2 \sin t, z = t$

$\dfrac{x^2}{4} + \dfrac{y^2}{4} = 1$

$z = t$

Circular helix

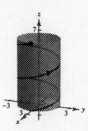

35. $x = 2 \sin t, y = 2 \cos t, z = e^{-t}$

$x^2 + y^2 = 4$

$z = e^{-t}$

37. $x = t, y = t^2, z = \frac{2}{3}t^3$

$y = x^2, z = \frac{2}{3}x^3$

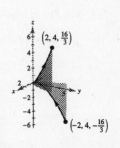

t	-2	-1	0	1	2
x	-2	-1	0	1	2
y	4	1	0	1	4
z	$-\frac{16}{3}$	$-\frac{2}{3}$	0	$\frac{2}{3}$	$\frac{16}{3}$

39. $\mathbf{r}(t) = -\frac{1}{2}t^2\mathbf{i} + t\mathbf{j} - \frac{\sqrt{3}}{2}t^2\mathbf{k}$

Parabola

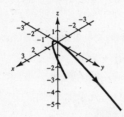

41. $\mathbf{r}(t) = \sin t\mathbf{i} + \left(\frac{\sqrt{3}}{2}\cos t - \frac{1}{2}t\right)\mathbf{j} + \left(\frac{1}{2}\cos t + \frac{\sqrt{3}}{2}\right)\mathbf{k}$

Helix

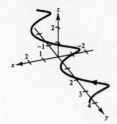

43.

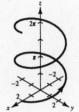

(a)

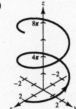

The helix is translated 2 units back on the *x*-axis.

(b)

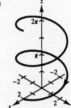

The height of the helix increases at a faster rate.

(c)

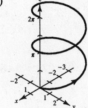

The orientation of the helix is reversed.

(d)

The axis of the helix is the *x*-axis.

(e)

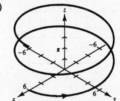

The radius of the helix is increased from 2 to 6.

45. $y = 4 - x$

Let $x = t$, then $y = 4 - t$.

$\mathbf{r}(t) = t\mathbf{i} + (4 - t)\mathbf{j}$

47. $y = (x - 2)^2$

Let $x = t$, then $y = (t - 2)^2$.

$\mathbf{r}(t) = t\mathbf{i} + (t - 2)^2\mathbf{j}$

49. $x^2 + y^2 = 25$

Let $x = 5\cos t$, then $y = 5\sin t$.

$\mathbf{r}(t) = 5\cos t\mathbf{i} + 5\sin t\mathbf{j}$

51. $\frac{x^2}{16} - \frac{y^2}{4} = 1$

Let $x = 4\sec t$, $y = 2\tan t$.

$\mathbf{r}(t) = 4\sec t\mathbf{i} + 2\tan t\mathbf{j}$

53. The parametric equations for the line are

$x = 2 - 2t,\ y = 3 + 5t,\ z = 8t.$

One possible answer is

$\mathbf{r}(t) = (2 - 2t)\mathbf{i} + (3 + 5t)\mathbf{j} + 8t\mathbf{k}.$

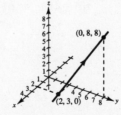

55. $\mathbf{r}_1(t) = t\mathbf{i},\qquad\qquad 0 \le t \le 4\quad (\mathbf{r}_1(0) = \mathbf{0}, \mathbf{r}_1(4) = 4\mathbf{i})$

$\mathbf{r}_2(t) = (4 - 4t)\mathbf{i} + 6t\mathbf{j},\ \ 0 \le t \le 1\quad (\mathbf{r}_2(0) = 4\mathbf{i}, \mathbf{r}_2(1) = 6\mathbf{j})$

$\mathbf{r}_3(t) = (6 - t)\mathbf{j},\qquad\quad 0 \le t \le 6\quad (\mathbf{r}_3(0) = 6\mathbf{j}, \mathbf{r}_3(6) = \mathbf{0})$

(Other answers possible)

57. $\mathbf{r}_1(t) = t\mathbf{i} + t^2\mathbf{j}, \quad 0 \le t \le 2 \ (y = x^2)$

$\mathbf{r}_2(t) = (2 - t)\mathbf{i}, \quad 0 \le t \le 2$

$\mathbf{r}_3(t) = (4 - t)\mathbf{j}, \quad 0 \le t \le 4$

(Other answers possible)

59. $z = x^2 + y^2, \ x + y = 0$

Let $x = t$, then $y = -x = -t$ and $z = x^2 + y^2 = 2t^2$. Therefore,

$$x = t, \ y = -t, \ z = 2t^2.$$

$$\mathbf{r}(t) = t\mathbf{i} - t\mathbf{j} + 2t^2\mathbf{k}$$

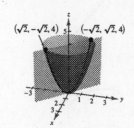

61. $x^2 + y^2 = 4, \ z = x^2$

$x = 2 \sin t, \ y = 2 \cos t$

$z = x^2 = 4 \sin^2 t$

t	0	$\dfrac{\pi}{6}$	$\dfrac{\pi}{4}$	$\dfrac{\pi}{2}$	$\dfrac{3\pi}{4}$	π
x	0	1	$\sqrt{2}$	2	$\sqrt{2}$	0
y	2	$\sqrt{3}$	$\sqrt{2}$	0	$-\sqrt{2}$	-2
z	0	1	2	4	2	0

$$\mathbf{r}(t) = 2 \sin t\mathbf{i} + 2 \cos t\mathbf{j} + 4 \sin^2 t\mathbf{k}$$

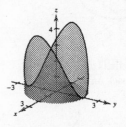

63. $x^2 + y^2 + z^2 = 4, \ x + z = 2$

Let $x = 1 + \sin t$, then $z = 2 - x = 1 - \sin t$ and $x^2 + y^2 + z^2 = 4$.

$$(1 + \sin t)^2 + y^2 + (1 - \sin t)^2 = 2 + 2 \sin^2 t + y^2 = 4$$

$$y^2 = 2 \cos^2 t, \quad y = \pm\sqrt{2} \cos t$$

$$x = 1 + \sin t, \ y = \pm\sqrt{2} \cos t$$

$$z = 1 - \sin t$$

t	$-\dfrac{\pi}{2}$	$-\dfrac{\pi}{6}$	0	$\dfrac{\pi}{6}$	$\dfrac{\pi}{2}$
x	0	$\dfrac{1}{2}$	1	$\dfrac{3}{2}$	2
y	0	$\pm\dfrac{\sqrt{6}}{2}$	$\pm\sqrt{2}$	$\pm\dfrac{\sqrt{6}}{2}$	0
z	2	$\dfrac{3}{2}$	1	$\dfrac{1}{2}$	0

$\mathbf{r}(t) = (1 + \sin t)\mathbf{i} + \sqrt{2} \cos t\mathbf{j} + (1 + \sin t)\mathbf{k}$ and

$\mathbf{r}(t) = (1 + \sin t)\mathbf{i} - \sqrt{2} \cos t\mathbf{j} + (1 - \sin t)\mathbf{k}$

65. $x^2 + z^2 = 4, \ y^2 + z^2 = 4$

Subtracting, we have $x^2 - y^2 = 0$ or $y = \pm x$.

Therefore, in the first octant, if we let $x = t$, then $x = t, \ y = t, \ z = \sqrt{4 - t^2}$.

$$\mathbf{r}(t) = t\mathbf{i} + t\mathbf{j} + \sqrt{4 - t^2}\mathbf{k}$$

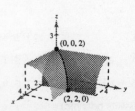

67. $y^2 + z^2 = (2t\cos t)^2 + (2t\sin t)^2 = 4t^2 = 4x^2$

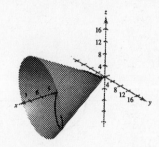

69. $\lim\limits_{t\to 2}\left[t\mathbf{i} + \dfrac{t^2 - 4}{t^2 - 2t}\mathbf{j} + \dfrac{1}{t}\mathbf{k}\right] = 2\mathbf{i} + 2\mathbf{j} + \dfrac{1}{2}\mathbf{k}$

since

$$\lim\limits_{t\to 2}\frac{t^2 - 4}{t^2 - 2t} = \lim\limits_{t\to 2}\frac{2t}{2t - 2} = 2. \quad \text{(L'Hôpital's Rule)}$$

71. $\lim\limits_{t\to 0}\left[t^2\mathbf{i} + 3t\mathbf{j} + \dfrac{1 - \cos t}{t}\mathbf{k}\right] = \mathbf{0}$

since

$$\lim\limits_{t\to 0}\frac{1 - \cos t}{t} = \lim\limits_{t\to 0}\frac{\sin t}{1} = 0. \quad \text{(L'Hôpital's Rule)}$$

73. $\lim\limits_{t\to 0}\left[\dfrac{1}{t}\mathbf{i} + \cos t\mathbf{j} + \sin t\mathbf{k}\right]$

does not exist since $\lim\limits_{t\to 0}\dfrac{1}{t}$ does not exist.

75. $\mathbf{r}(t) = t\mathbf{i} + \dfrac{1}{t}\mathbf{j}$

Continuous on $(-\infty, 0),\ (0, \infty)$

77. $\mathbf{r}(t) = t\mathbf{i} + \arcsin t\mathbf{j} + (t - 1)\mathbf{k}$

Continuous on $[-1, 1]$

79. $\mathbf{r}(t) = \langle e^{-t}, t^2, \tan t\rangle$

Discontinuous at $t = \dfrac{\pi}{2} + n\pi$

Continuous on $\left(-\dfrac{\pi}{2} + n\pi, \dfrac{\pi}{2} + n\pi\right)$

81. See the definition on page 786.

83. $\mathbf{r}(t) = t^2\mathbf{i} + (t - 3)\mathbf{j} + t\mathbf{k}$

(a) $\mathbf{s}(t) = \mathbf{r}(t) + 2\mathbf{k} = t^2\mathbf{i} + (t - 3)\mathbf{j} + (t + 3)\mathbf{k}$

(b) $\mathbf{s}(t) = \mathbf{r}(t) - 2\mathbf{i} = (t^2 - 2)\mathbf{i} + (t - 3)\mathbf{j} + t\mathbf{k}$

(c) $\mathbf{s}(t) = \mathbf{r}(t) + 5\mathbf{j} = t^2\mathbf{i} + (t + 2)\mathbf{j} + t\mathbf{k}$

85. Let $\mathbf{r}(t) = x_1(t) + y_1(t)\mathbf{j} + z_1(t)\mathbf{k}$ and $\mathbf{u}(t) = x_2(t)\mathbf{i} + y_2(t)\mathbf{j} + z_2(t)\mathbf{k}$. Then:

$$\begin{aligned}
\lim\limits_{t\to c}[\mathbf{r}(t) \times \mathbf{u}(t)] &= \lim\limits_{t\to c}\{[y_1(t)z_2(t) - y_2(t)z_1(t)]\mathbf{i} - [x_1(t)z_2(t) - x_2(t)z_1(t)]\mathbf{j} + [x_1(t)y_2(t) - x_2(t)y_1(t)]\mathbf{k}\}\\
&= \left[\lim\limits_{t\to c}y_1(t)\lim\limits_{t\to c}z_2(t) - \lim\limits_{t\to c}y_2(t)\lim\limits_{t\to c}z_1(t)\right]\mathbf{i} - \left[\lim\limits_{t\to c}x_1(t)\lim\limits_{t\to c}z_2(t) - \lim\limits_{t\to c}x_2(t)\lim\limits_{t\to c}z_1(t)\right]\mathbf{j}\\
&\quad + \left[\lim\limits_{t\to c}x_1(t)\lim\limits_{t\to c}y_2(t) - \lim\limits_{t\to c}x_2(t)\lim\limits_{t\to c}y_1(t)\right]\mathbf{k}\\
&= \left[\lim\limits_{t\to c}x_1(t)\mathbf{i} + \lim\limits_{t\to c}y_1(t)\mathbf{j} + \lim\limits_{t\to c}z_1(t)\mathbf{k}\right] \times \left[\lim\limits_{t\to c}x_2(t)\mathbf{i} + \lim\limits_{t\to c}y_2(t)\mathbf{j} + \lim\limits_{t\to c}z_2(t)\mathbf{k}\right]\\
&= \lim\limits_{t\to c}\mathbf{r}(t) \times \lim\limits_{t\to c}\mathbf{u}(t)
\end{aligned}$$

87. Let $\mathbf{r}(t) = x(t)\mathbf{i} + y(t)\mathbf{j} + z(t)\mathbf{k}$. Since $\mathbf{r}$ is continuous at $t = c$, then $\lim\limits_{t\to c}\mathbf{r}(t) = \mathbf{r}(c)$.

$\mathbf{r}(c) = x(c)\mathbf{i} + y(c)\mathbf{j} + z(c)\mathbf{k} \Rightarrow x(c),\ y(c),\ z(c)$

are defined at c.

$$\|\mathbf{r}\| = \sqrt{(x(t))^2 + (y(t))^2 + (z(t))^2}$$

$$\lim\limits_{t\to c}\|\mathbf{r}\| = \sqrt{(x(c))^2 + (y(c))^2 + (z(c))^2} = \|\mathbf{r}(c)\|$$

Therefore, $\|\mathbf{r}\|$ is continuous at c.

89. True

Section 11.2   Differentiation and Integration of Vector-Valued Functions

1. $\mathbf{r}(t) = t^2\mathbf{i} + t\mathbf{j}$, $t_0 = 2$

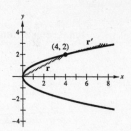

$x(t) = t^2$, $y(t) = t$

$x = y^2$

$\quad \mathbf{r}(2) = 4\mathbf{i} + 2\mathbf{j}$

$\quad \mathbf{r}'(t) = 2t\mathbf{i} + \mathbf{j}$

$\quad \mathbf{r}'(2) = 4\mathbf{i} + \mathbf{j}$

$\mathbf{r}'(t_0)$ is tangent to the curve.

3. $\mathbf{r}(t) = \cos t\mathbf{i} + \sin t\mathbf{j}$, $t_0 = \dfrac{\pi}{2}$

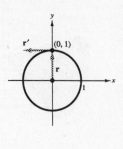

$x(t) = \cos t$, $y(t) = \sin t$

$x^2 + y^2 = 1$

$\quad \mathbf{r}\left(\dfrac{\pi}{2}\right) = \mathbf{j}$

$\quad \mathbf{r}'(t) = -\sin t\mathbf{i} + \cos t\mathbf{j}$

$\quad \mathbf{r}'\left(\dfrac{\pi}{2}\right) = -\mathbf{i}$

$\mathbf{r}'(t_0)$ is tangent to the curve.

5. $\mathbf{r}(t) = t\mathbf{i} + t^2\mathbf{j}$

(a)

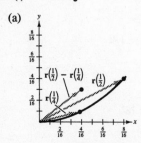

(b) $\qquad \mathbf{r}\left(\dfrac{1}{4}\right) = \dfrac{1}{4}\mathbf{i} + \dfrac{1}{16}\mathbf{j}$

$\qquad\quad \mathbf{r}\left(\dfrac{1}{2}\right) = \dfrac{1}{2}\mathbf{i} + \dfrac{1}{4}\mathbf{j}$

$\qquad \mathbf{r}\left(\dfrac{1}{2}\right) - \mathbf{r}\left(\dfrac{1}{4}\right) = \dfrac{1}{4}\mathbf{i} + \dfrac{3}{16}\mathbf{j}$

(c) $\qquad\qquad \mathbf{r}'(t) = \mathbf{i} + 2t\mathbf{j}$

$\qquad\qquad \mathbf{r}'\left(\dfrac{1}{4}\right) = \mathbf{i} + \dfrac{1}{2}\mathbf{j}$

$\dfrac{\mathbf{r}(1/2) - \mathbf{r}(1/4)}{(1/2) - (1/4)} = \dfrac{(1/4)\mathbf{i} + (3/16)\mathbf{j}}{1/4} = \mathbf{i} + \dfrac{3}{4}\mathbf{j}$

This vector approximates $\mathbf{r}'\left(\tfrac{1}{4}\right)$.

7. $\mathbf{r}(t) = 2\cos t\mathbf{i} + 2\sin t\mathbf{j} + t\mathbf{k}$, $t_0 = \dfrac{3\pi}{2}$

$x^2 + y^2 = 4$, $z = t$

$\quad \mathbf{r}'(t) = -2\sin t\mathbf{i} + 2\cos t\mathbf{j} + \mathbf{k}$

$\quad \mathbf{r}\left(\dfrac{3\pi}{2}\right) = -2\mathbf{j} + \dfrac{3\pi}{2}\mathbf{k}$

$\quad \mathbf{r}'\left(\dfrac{3\pi}{2}\right) = 2\mathbf{i} + \mathbf{k}$

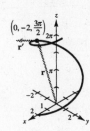

9. $\mathbf{r}(t) = 6t\mathbf{i} - 7t^2\mathbf{j} + t^3\mathbf{k}$

$\quad \mathbf{r}'(t) = 6\mathbf{i} - 14t\mathbf{j} + 3t^2\mathbf{k}$

11. $\mathbf{r}(t) = a\cos^3 t\mathbf{i} + a\sin^3 t\mathbf{j} + \mathbf{k}$

$\quad \mathbf{r}'(t) = -3a\cos^2 t\sin t\mathbf{i} + 3a\sin^2 t\cos t\mathbf{j}$

13. $\mathbf{r}(t) = e^{-t}\mathbf{i} + 4\mathbf{j}$

$\quad \mathbf{r}'(t) = -e^{-t}\mathbf{i}$

15. $\mathbf{r}(t) = \langle t\sin t, t\cos t, t\rangle$

$\quad \mathbf{r}'(t) = \langle \sin t + t\cos t, \cos t - t\sin t, 1\rangle$

17. $\mathbf{r}(t) = t^3\mathbf{i} + \dfrac{1}{2}t^2\mathbf{j}$

(a) $\mathbf{r}'(t) = 3t^2\mathbf{i} + t\mathbf{j}$

$\quad \mathbf{r}''(t) = 6t\mathbf{i} + \mathbf{j}$

(b) $\mathbf{r}'(t) \cdot \mathbf{r}''(t) = 3t^2(6t) + t = 18t^3 + t$

19. $\mathbf{r}(t) = 4\cos t\mathbf{i} + 4\sin t\mathbf{j}$

(a) $\mathbf{r}'(t) = -4\sin t\mathbf{i} + 4\cos t\mathbf{j}$

    $\mathbf{r}''(t) = -4\cos t\mathbf{i} - 4\sin t\mathbf{j}$

(b) $\mathbf{r}'(t) \cdot \mathbf{r}''(t) = (-4\sin t)(-4\cos t) + 4\cos t(-4\sin t)$

                    $= 0$

21. $\mathbf{r}(t) = \frac{1}{2}t^2\mathbf{i} - t\mathbf{j} + \frac{1}{6}t^3\mathbf{k}$

(a) $\mathbf{r}'(t) = t\mathbf{i} - \mathbf{j} + \frac{1}{2}t^2\mathbf{k}$

    $\mathbf{r}''(t) = \mathbf{i} + t\mathbf{k}$

(b) $\mathbf{r}'(t) \cdot \mathbf{r}''(t) = t(1) - 1(0) + \frac{1}{2}t^2(t) = t + \frac{t^3}{2}$

23. $\mathbf{r}(t) = \langle \cos t + t\sin t, \sin t - t\cos t, t \rangle$

(a) $\mathbf{r}'(t) = \langle -\sin t + \sin t + t\cos t, \cos t - \cos t + t\sin t, 1 \rangle$

    $= \langle t\cos t, t\sin t, 1 \rangle$

    $\mathbf{r}''(t) = \langle \cos t - t\sin t, \sin t + t\cos t, 0 \rangle$

(b) $\mathbf{r}'(t) \cdot \mathbf{r}''(t) = (t\cos t)(\cos t - t\sin t) + (t\sin t)(\sin t + t\cos t) = t$

25. $\qquad \mathbf{r}(t) = \cos(\pi t)\mathbf{i} + \sin(\pi t)\mathbf{j} + t^2\mathbf{k}, \ t_0 = -\frac{1}{4}$

$\qquad \mathbf{r}'(t) = -\pi\sin(\pi t)\mathbf{i} + \pi\cos(\pi t)\mathbf{j} + 2t\mathbf{k}$

$\mathbf{r}'\left(-\frac{1}{4}\right) = \frac{\sqrt{2}\pi}{2}\mathbf{i} + \frac{\sqrt{2}\pi}{2}\mathbf{j} - \frac{1}{2}\mathbf{k}$

$\left\|\mathbf{r}'\left(\frac{1}{4}\right)\right\| = \sqrt{\left(\frac{\sqrt{2}\pi}{2}\right)^2 + \left(\frac{\sqrt{2}\pi}{2}\right)^2 + \left(-\frac{1}{2}\right)^2} = \sqrt{\pi^2 + \frac{1}{4}} = \frac{\sqrt{4\pi^2 + 1}}{2}$

$\dfrac{\mathbf{r}'(-1/4)}{\|\mathbf{r}'(-1/4)\|} = \dfrac{1}{\sqrt{4\pi^2 + 1}}(\sqrt{2}\pi\mathbf{i} + \sqrt{2}\pi\mathbf{j} - \mathbf{k})$

$\qquad \mathbf{r}''(t) = -\pi^2\cos(\pi t)\mathbf{i} - \pi^2\sin(\pi t)\mathbf{j} + 2\mathbf{k}$

$\mathbf{r}''\left(-\frac{1}{4}\right) = -\frac{\sqrt{2}\pi^2}{2}\mathbf{i} + \frac{\sqrt{2}\pi^2}{2}\mathbf{j} + 2\mathbf{k}$

$\left\|\mathbf{r}''\left(-\frac{1}{4}\right)\right\| = \sqrt{\left(-\frac{\sqrt{2}\pi^2}{2}\right)^2 + \left(\frac{\sqrt{2}\pi^2}{2}\right)^2 + (2)^2} = \sqrt{\pi^4 + 4}$

$\dfrac{\mathbf{r}''(-1/4)}{\|\mathbf{r}''(-1/4)\|} = \dfrac{1}{2\sqrt{\pi^4 + 4}}(-\sqrt{2}\pi^2\mathbf{i} + \sqrt{2}\pi^2\mathbf{j} + 4\mathbf{k})$

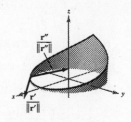

27. $\mathbf{r}(t) = t^2\mathbf{i} + t^3\mathbf{j}$

$\mathbf{r}'(t) = 2t\mathbf{i} + 3t^2\mathbf{j}$

$\mathbf{r}'(0) = \mathbf{0}$

Smooth on $(-\infty, 0), \ (0, \infty)$

29. $\qquad \mathbf{r}(\theta) = 2\cos^3\theta\mathbf{i} + 3\sin^3\theta\mathbf{j}$

$\qquad \mathbf{r}'(\theta) = -6\cos^2\theta\sin\theta\mathbf{i} + 9\sin^2\theta\cos\theta\mathbf{j}$

$\mathbf{r}'\left(\frac{n\pi}{2}\right) = \mathbf{0}$

Smooth on $\left(\frac{n\pi}{2}, \frac{(n+1)\pi}{2}\right)$, n any integer.

31. $\mathbf{r}(\theta) = (\theta - 2\sin\theta)\mathbf{i} + (1 - 2\cos\theta)\mathbf{j}$

$\mathbf{r}'(\theta) = (1 - 2\cos\theta)\mathbf{i} + (1 + 2\sin\theta)\mathbf{j}$

$\mathbf{r}'(\theta) \neq \mathbf{0}$ for any value of θ

Smooth on $(-\infty, \infty)$

33. $\mathbf{r}(t) = (t - 1)\mathbf{i} + \frac{1}{t}\mathbf{j} - t^2\mathbf{k}$

$\mathbf{r}'(t) = \mathbf{i} - \frac{1}{t^2}\mathbf{j} - 2t\mathbf{k} \neq \mathbf{0}$

$\mathbf{r}$ is smooth for all $t \neq 0$: $(-\infty, 0), \cup (0, \infty)$

35. $\mathbf{r}(t) = t\mathbf{i} - 3t\mathbf{j} + \tan t\mathbf{k}$

$\mathbf{r}'(t) = \mathbf{i} - 3\mathbf{j} + \sec^2 t\mathbf{k} \neq \mathbf{0}$

$\mathbf{r}$ is smooth for all $t \neq \dfrac{\pi}{2} + n\pi = \dfrac{2n+1}{2}\pi$.

Smooth on intervals of form $\left(-\dfrac{\pi}{2} + n\pi, \dfrac{\pi}{2} + n\pi\right)$

37. $\mathbf{r}(t) = t\mathbf{i} + 3t\mathbf{j} + t^2\mathbf{k}$, $\mathbf{u}(t) = 4t\mathbf{i} + t^2\mathbf{j} + t^3\mathbf{k}$

(a) $\mathbf{r}'(t) = \mathbf{i} + 3\mathbf{j} + 2t\mathbf{k}$

(b) $\mathbf{r}''(t) = 2\mathbf{k}$

(c) $\mathbf{r}(t) \cdot \mathbf{u}(t) = 4t^2 + 3t^3 + t^5$

$D_t[\mathbf{r}(t) \cdot \mathbf{u}(t)] = 8t + 9t^2 + 5t^4$

(d) $3\mathbf{r}(t) - \mathbf{u}(t) = -t\mathbf{i} + (9t - t^2)\mathbf{j} + (3t^2 - t^3)\mathbf{k}$

$D_t[3\mathbf{r}(t) - \mathbf{u}(t)] = -\mathbf{i} + (9 - 2t)\mathbf{j} + (6t - 3t^2)\mathbf{k}$

(e) $\mathbf{r}(t) \times \mathbf{u}(t) = 2t^4\mathbf{i} - (t^4 - 4t^3)\mathbf{j} + (t^3 - 12t^2)\mathbf{k}$

$D_t[\mathbf{r}(t) \times \mathbf{u}(t)] = 8t^3\mathbf{i} + (12t^2 - 4t^3)\mathbf{j} + (3t^2 - 24t)\mathbf{k}$

(f) $\|\mathbf{r}(t)\| = \sqrt{10t^2 + t^4} = t\sqrt{10 + t^2}$

$D_t[\|\mathbf{r}(t)\|] = \dfrac{10 + 2t^2}{\sqrt{10 + t^2}}$

39. $\mathbf{r}(t) = 3\sin t\mathbf{i} + 4\cos t\mathbf{j}$

$\mathbf{r}'(t) = 3\cos t\mathbf{i} - 4\sin t\mathbf{j}$

$\mathbf{r}(t) \cdot \mathbf{r}'(t) = 9\sin t\cos t - 16\cos t\sin t = -7\sin t\cos t$

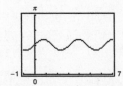

$\cos\theta = \dfrac{\mathbf{r}(t) \cdot \mathbf{r}'(t)}{\|\mathbf{r}(t)\| \, \|\mathbf{r}'(t)\|} = \dfrac{-7\sin t\cos t}{\sqrt{9\sin^2 t + 16\cos^2 t}\sqrt{9\cos^2 t + 16\sin^2 t}}$

$\theta = \arccos\left[\dfrac{-7\sin t\cos t}{\sqrt{(9\sin^2 t + 16\cos^2 t)(9\cos^2 t + 16\sin^2 t)}}\right]$

$\theta = 1.855$ maximum at $t = 3.927\left(\dfrac{5\pi}{4}\right)$ and $t = 0.785\left(\dfrac{\pi}{4}\right)$.

$\theta = 1.287$ minimum at $t = 2.356\left(\dfrac{3\pi}{4}\right)$ and $t = 5.498\left(\dfrac{7\pi}{4}\right)$.

$\theta = \dfrac{\pi}{2}(1.571)$ for $t = n\dfrac{\pi}{2}$, $n = 0, 1, 2, 3, \ldots$

41. $\mathbf{r}'(t) = \displaystyle\lim_{\Delta t \to 0} \dfrac{\mathbf{r}(t + \Delta t) - \mathbf{r}(t)}{\Delta t}$

$= \displaystyle\lim_{\Delta t \to 0} \dfrac{[3(t + \Delta t) + 2]\mathbf{i} + [1 - (t + \Delta t)^2]\mathbf{j} - (3t + 2)\mathbf{i} - (1 - t^2)\mathbf{j}}{\Delta t}$

$= \displaystyle\lim_{\Delta t \to 0} \dfrac{(3\Delta t)\mathbf{i} - (2t(\Delta t) + (\Delta t)^2)\mathbf{j}}{\Delta t}$

$= \displaystyle\lim_{\Delta t \to 0} 3\mathbf{i} - (2t + \Delta t)\mathbf{j} = 3\mathbf{i} - 2t\mathbf{j}$

43. $\displaystyle\int (2t\mathbf{i} + \mathbf{j} + \mathbf{k})\, dt = t^2\mathbf{i} + t\mathbf{j} + t\mathbf{k} + \mathbf{C}$

45. $\displaystyle\int \left(\dfrac{1}{t}\mathbf{i} + \mathbf{j} - t^{3/2}\mathbf{k}\right) dt = \ln t\mathbf{i} + t\mathbf{j} - \dfrac{2}{5}t^{5/2}\mathbf{k} + \mathbf{C}$

47. $\displaystyle\int \left[(2t - 1)\mathbf{i} + 4t^3\mathbf{j} + 3\sqrt{t}\mathbf{k}\right] dt = (t^2 - t)\mathbf{i} + t^4\mathbf{j} + 2t^{3/2}\mathbf{k} + \mathbf{C}$

49. $\displaystyle\int \left[\sec^2 t\mathbf{i} + \dfrac{1}{1 + t^2}\mathbf{j}\right] dt = \tan t\mathbf{i} + \arctan t\mathbf{j} + \mathbf{C}$

51. $\int_0^1 (8t\mathbf{i} + t\mathbf{j} - \mathbf{k})\,dt = \left[4t^2\mathbf{i}\right]_0^1 + \left[\frac{t^2}{2}\mathbf{j}\right]_0^1 - \left[t\mathbf{k}\right]_0^1 = 4\mathbf{i} + \frac{1}{2}\mathbf{j} - \mathbf{k}$

53. $\int_0^{\pi/2} [(a\cos t)\mathbf{i} + (a\sin t)\mathbf{j} + \mathbf{k}]\,dt = \left[a\sin t\mathbf{i}\right]_0^{\pi/2} - \left[a\cos t\mathbf{j}\right]_0^{\pi/2} + \left[t\mathbf{k}\right]_0^{\pi/2} = a\mathbf{i} + a\mathbf{j} + \frac{\pi}{2}\mathbf{k}$

55. $\mathbf{r}(t) = \int (4e^{2t}\mathbf{i} + 3e^t\mathbf{j})\,dt = 2e^{2t}\mathbf{i} + 3e^t\mathbf{j} + \mathbf{C}$

$\mathbf{r}(0) = 2\mathbf{i} + 3\mathbf{j} + \mathbf{C} = 2\mathbf{i} \implies \mathbf{C} = -3\mathbf{j}$

$\mathbf{r}(t) = 2e^{2t}\mathbf{i} + 3(e^t - 1)\mathbf{j}$

57. $\mathbf{r}'(t) = \int -32\mathbf{j}\,dt = -32t\mathbf{j} + \mathbf{C}_1$

$\mathbf{r}'(0) = \mathbf{C}_1 = 600\sqrt{3}\mathbf{i} + 600\mathbf{j}$

$\mathbf{r}'(t) = 600\sqrt{3}\mathbf{i} + (600 - 32t)\mathbf{j}$

$\mathbf{r}(t) = \int \left[600\sqrt{3}\mathbf{i} + (600 - 32t)\mathbf{j}\right]\,dt$

$\quad = 600\sqrt{3}\,t\mathbf{i} + (600t - 16t^2)\mathbf{j} + \mathbf{C}$

$\mathbf{r}(0) = \mathbf{C} = \mathbf{0}$

$\mathbf{r}(t) = 600\sqrt{3}\,t\mathbf{i} + (600t - 16t^2)\mathbf{j}$

59. $\mathbf{r}(t) = \int (te^{-t^2}\mathbf{i} - e^{-t}\mathbf{j} + \mathbf{k})\,dt = -\frac{1}{2}e^{-t^2}\mathbf{i} + e^{-t}\mathbf{j} + t\mathbf{k} + \mathbf{C}$

$\mathbf{r}(0) = -\frac{1}{2}\mathbf{i} + \mathbf{j} + \mathbf{C} = \frac{1}{2}\mathbf{i} - \mathbf{j} + \mathbf{k} \implies \mathbf{C} = \mathbf{i} - 2\mathbf{j} + \mathbf{k}$

$\mathbf{r}(t) = \left(1 - \frac{1}{2}e^{-t^2}\right)\mathbf{i} + (e^{-t} - 2)\mathbf{j} + (t + 1)\mathbf{k} = \left(\frac{2 - e^{-t^2}}{2}\right)\mathbf{i} + (e^{-t} - 2)\mathbf{j} + (t + 1)\mathbf{k}$

61. See "Definition of the Derivative of a Vector-Valued Function" and Figure 11.8 on page 794.

63. At $t = t_0$, the graph of $\mathbf{u}(t)$ is increasing in the x, y, and z directions simultaneously.

65. Let $\mathbf{r}(t) = x(t)\mathbf{i} + y(t)\mathbf{j} + z(t)\mathbf{k}$. Then $c\mathbf{r}(t) = cx(t)\mathbf{i} + cy(t)\mathbf{j} + cz(t)\mathbf{k}$ and

$D_t[c\mathbf{r}(t)] = cx'(t)\mathbf{i} + cy'(t)\mathbf{j} + cz'(t)\mathbf{k}$

$\quad = c[x'(t)\mathbf{i} + y'(t)\mathbf{j} + z'(t)\mathbf{k}] = c\mathbf{r}'(t)$.

67. Let $\mathbf{r}(t) = x(t)\mathbf{i} + y(t)\mathbf{j} + z(t)\mathbf{k}$, then $f(t)\mathbf{r}(t) = f(t)x(t)\mathbf{i} + f(t)y(t)\mathbf{j} + f(t)z(t)\mathbf{k}$.

$D_t[f(t)\mathbf{r}(t)] = [f(t)x'(t) + f'(t)x(t)]\mathbf{i} + [f(t)y'(t) + f'(t)y(t)]\mathbf{j} + [f(t)z'(t) + f'(t)z(t)]\mathbf{k}$

$\quad = f(t)[x'(t)\mathbf{i} + y'(t)\mathbf{j} + z'(t)\mathbf{k}] + f'(t)[x(t)\mathbf{i} + y(t)\mathbf{j} + z(t)\mathbf{k}]$

$\quad = f(t)\mathbf{r}'(t) + f'(t)\mathbf{r}(t)$

69. Let $\mathbf{r}(t) = x(t)\mathbf{i} + y(t)\mathbf{j} + z(t)\mathbf{k}$. Then $\mathbf{r}(f(t)) = x(f(t))\mathbf{i} + y(f(t))\mathbf{j} + z(f(t))\mathbf{k}$ and

$D_t[\mathbf{r}(f(t))] = x'(f(t))f'(t)\mathbf{i} + y'(f(t))f'(t)\mathbf{j} + z'(f(t))f'(t)\mathbf{k}$ \quad (Chain Rule)

$\quad = f'(t)[x'(f(t))\mathbf{i} + y'(f(t))\mathbf{j} + z'(f(t))\mathbf{k}] = f'(t)\mathbf{r}'(f(t))$.

71. Let $\mathbf{r}(t) = x_1(t)\mathbf{i} + y_1(t)\mathbf{j} + z_1(t)\mathbf{k}$, $\mathbf{u}(t) = x_2(t)\mathbf{i} + y_2(t)\mathbf{j} + z_2(t)\mathbf{k}$, and $\mathbf{v}(t) = x_3(t)\mathbf{i} + y_3(t)\mathbf{j} + z_3(t)\mathbf{k}$. Then:

$$\mathbf{r}(t) \cdot [\mathbf{u}(t) \times \mathbf{v}(t)] = x_1(t)[y_2(t)z_3(t) - z_2(t)y_3(t)] - y_1(t)[x_2(t)z_3(t) - z_2(t)x_3(t)] + z_1(t)[x_2(t)y_3(t) - y_2(t)x_3(t)]$$

$$D_t[\mathbf{r}(t) \cdot (\mathbf{u}(t) \times \mathbf{v}(t))] = x_1(t)y_2(t)z_3{}'(t) + x_1(t)y_2{}'(t)z_3(t) + x_1{}'(t)y_2(t)z_3(t) - x_1(t)y_3(t)z_2{}'(t) -$$

$$x_1(t)y_3{}'(t)z_2(t) - x_1{}'(t)y_3(t)z_2(t) - y_1(t)x_2(t)z_3{}'(t) - y_1(t)x_2{}'(t)z_3(t) - y_1{}''(t)x_2(t)z_3(t) +$$

$$y_1(t)z_2(t)x_3{}'(t) + y_1(t)z_2{}'(t)x_3(t) + y_1{}'(t)z_2(t)x_3(t) + z_1(t)x_2(t)y_3{}'(t) + z_1(t)x_2{}'(t)y_3(t) +$$

$$z_1{}'(t)x_2(t)y_3(t) - z_1(t)y_2(t)x_3{}'(t) - z_1(t)y_2{}'(t)x_3(t) - z_1{}'(t)y_2(t)x_3(t)$$

$$= \{x_1{}'(t)[y_2(t)z_3(t) - y_3(t)z_2(t)] + y_1{}'(t)[-x_2(t)z_3(t) + z_2(t)x_3(t)] + z_1{}'(t)[x_2(t)y_3(t) - y_2(t)x_3(t)]\} +$$

$$\{x_1(t)[y_2{}'(t)z_3(t) - y_3(t)z_2{}'(t)] + y_1(t)[-x_2{}'(t)z_3(t) + z_2{}'(t)x_3(t)] + z_1(t)[x_2{}'(t)y_3(t) - y_2{}'(t)x_3(t)]\} +$$

$$\{x_1(t)[y_2(t)z_3{}'(t) - y_3{}'(t)z_2(t)] + y_1(t)[-x_2(t)z_3{}'(t) + z_2(t)x_3{}'(t)] + z_1(t)[x_2(t)y_3{}'(t) - y_2(t)x_3{}'(t)]\}$$

$$= \mathbf{r}'(t) \cdot [\mathbf{u}(t) \times \mathbf{v}(t)] + \mathbf{r}(t) \cdot [\mathbf{u}'(t) \times \mathbf{v}(t)] + \mathbf{r}(t) \cdot [\mathbf{u}(t) \times \mathbf{v}'(t)]$$

73. False. Let $\mathbf{r}(t) = \cos t\mathbf{i} + \sin t\mathbf{j} + \mathbf{k}$.

$$\|\mathbf{r}(t)\| = \sqrt{2}$$

$$\frac{d}{dt}[\|\mathbf{r}(t)\|] = 0$$

$$\mathbf{r}'(t) = -\sin t\mathbf{i} + \cos t\mathbf{j}$$

$$\|\mathbf{r}'(t)\| = 1$$

Section 11.3   Velocity and Acceleration

1. $\mathbf{r}(t) = 3t\mathbf{i} + (t - 1)\mathbf{j}$

$\mathbf{v}(t) = \mathbf{r}'(t) = 3\mathbf{i} + \mathbf{j}$

$\mathbf{a}(t) = \mathbf{r}''(t) = \mathbf{0}$

$x = 3t,\ y = t - 1,\ y = \dfrac{x}{3} - 1$

At $(3, 0)$, $t = 1$.

$\mathbf{v}(1) = 3\mathbf{i} + \mathbf{j},\ \mathbf{a}(1) = \mathbf{0}$

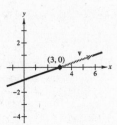

3. $\mathbf{r}(t) = t^2\mathbf{i} + t\mathbf{j}$

$\mathbf{v}(t) = \mathbf{r}'(t) = 2t\mathbf{i} + \mathbf{j}$

$\mathbf{a}(t) = \mathbf{r}''(t) = 2\mathbf{i}$

$x = t^2,\ y = t,\ x = y^2$

At $(4, 2)$, $t = 2$.

$\mathbf{v}(2) = 4\mathbf{i} + \mathbf{j}$

$\mathbf{a}(2) = 2\mathbf{i}$

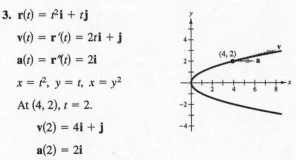

5. $\mathbf{r}(t) = 2\cos t\mathbf{i} + 2\sin t\mathbf{j}$

$\mathbf{v}(t) = \mathbf{r}'(t) = -2\sin t\mathbf{i} + 2\cos t\mathbf{j}$

$\mathbf{a}(t) = \mathbf{r}''(t) = -2\cos t\mathbf{i} - 2\sin t\mathbf{j}$

$x = 2\cos t,\ y = 2\sin t,\ x^2 + y^2 = 4$

At $\left(\sqrt{2}, \sqrt{2}\right)$, $t = \dfrac{\pi}{4}$.

$\mathbf{v}\left(\dfrac{\pi}{4}\right) = -\sqrt{2}\mathbf{i} + \sqrt{2}\mathbf{j}$

$\mathbf{a}\left(\dfrac{\pi}{4}\right) = -\sqrt{2}\mathbf{i} - \sqrt{2}\mathbf{j}$

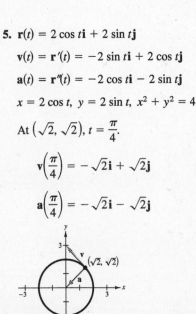

7. $\mathbf{r}(t) = \langle t - \sin t, 1 - \cos t \rangle$

$\mathbf{v}(t) = \mathbf{r}'(t) = \langle 1 - \cos t, \sin t \rangle$

$\mathbf{a}(t) = \mathbf{r}''(t) = \langle \sin t, \cos t \rangle$

$x = t - \sin t,\ y = 1 - \cos t$ (cycloid)

At $(\pi, 2)$, $t = \pi$.

$\mathbf{v}(\pi) = \langle 2, 0 \rangle = 2\mathbf{i}$

$\mathbf{a}(\pi) = \langle 0, -1 \rangle = -\mathbf{j}$

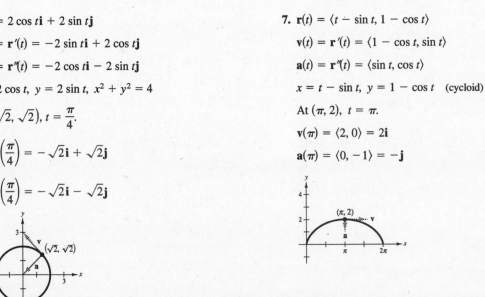

9. $\mathbf{r}(t) = t\mathbf{i} + (2t - 5)\mathbf{j} + 3t\mathbf{k}$

$\mathbf{v}(t) = \mathbf{i} + 2\mathbf{j} + 3\mathbf{k}$

$s(t) = \|\mathbf{v}(t)\| = \sqrt{1 + 4 + 9} = \sqrt{14}$

$\mathbf{a}(t) = \mathbf{0}$

11. $\mathbf{r}(t) = t\mathbf{i} + t^2\mathbf{j} + \dfrac{t^2}{2}\mathbf{k}$

$\mathbf{v}(t) = \mathbf{i} + 2t\mathbf{j} + t\mathbf{k}$

$s(t) = \sqrt{1 + 4t^2 + t^2} = \sqrt{1 + 5t^2}$

$\mathbf{a}(t) = 2\mathbf{j} + \mathbf{k}$

13. $\mathbf{r}(t) = t\mathbf{i} + t\mathbf{j} + \sqrt{9 - t^2}\,\mathbf{k}$

$\mathbf{v}(t) = \mathbf{i} + \mathbf{j} - \dfrac{t}{\sqrt{9 - t^2}}\mathbf{k}$

$s(t) = \sqrt{1 + 1 + \dfrac{t^2}{9 - t^2}} = \sqrt{\dfrac{18 - t^2}{9 - t^2}}$

$\mathbf{a}(t) = -\dfrac{9}{(9 - t^2)^{3/2}}\mathbf{k}$

15. $\mathbf{r}(t) = \langle 4t, 3\cos t, 3\sin t \rangle$

$\mathbf{v}(t) = \langle 4, -3\sin t, 3\cos t \rangle = 4\mathbf{i} - 3\sin t\mathbf{j} + 3\cos t\mathbf{k}$

$s(t) = \sqrt{16 + 9\sin^2 t + 9\cos^2 t} = 5$

$\mathbf{a}(t) = \langle 0, -3\cos t, -3\sin t \rangle = -3\cos t\mathbf{j} - 3\sin t\mathbf{k}$

17. (a) $\mathbf{r}(t) = \left\langle t, -t^2, \dfrac{t^3}{4} \right\rangle, \ t_0 = 1$

$\mathbf{r}'(t) = \left\langle 1, -2t, \dfrac{3t^2}{4} \right\rangle$

$\mathbf{r}'(1) = \left\langle 1, -2, \dfrac{3}{4} \right\rangle$

$x = 1 + t, \ y = -1 - 2t, \ z = \dfrac{1}{4} + \dfrac{3}{4}t$

(b) $\mathbf{r}(1 + 0.1) \approx \left\langle 1 + 0.1, -1 - 2(0.1), \dfrac{1}{4} + \dfrac{3}{4}(0.1) \right\rangle$

$\qquad = \langle 1.100, -1.200, 0.325 \rangle$

19. $\mathbf{a}(t) = \mathbf{i} + \mathbf{j} + \mathbf{k}, \mathbf{v}(0) = \mathbf{0}, \mathbf{r}(0) = \mathbf{0}$

$\mathbf{v}(t) = \int (\mathbf{i} + \mathbf{j} + \mathbf{k})\, dt = t\mathbf{i} + t\mathbf{j} + t\mathbf{k} + \mathbf{C}$

$\mathbf{v}(0) = \mathbf{C} = \mathbf{0}, \mathbf{v}(t) = t\mathbf{i} + t\mathbf{j} + t\mathbf{k}, \mathbf{v}(t) = t(\mathbf{i} + \mathbf{j} + \mathbf{k})$

$\mathbf{r}(t) = \int (t\mathbf{i} + t\mathbf{j} + t\mathbf{k})\, dt = \dfrac{t^2}{2}(\mathbf{i} + \mathbf{j} + \mathbf{k}) + \mathbf{C}$

$\mathbf{r}(0) = \mathbf{C} = \mathbf{0}, \mathbf{r}(t) = \dfrac{t^2}{2}(\mathbf{i} + \mathbf{j} + \mathbf{k}),$

$\mathbf{r}(2) = 2(\mathbf{i} + \mathbf{j} + \mathbf{k}) = 2\mathbf{i} + 2\mathbf{j} + 2\mathbf{k}$

21. $\mathbf{a}(t) = t\mathbf{j} + t\mathbf{k}, \mathbf{v}(1) = 5\mathbf{j}, \mathbf{r}(1) = \mathbf{0}$

$\mathbf{v}(t) = \int (t\mathbf{j} + t\mathbf{k})\, dt = \dfrac{t^2}{2}\mathbf{j} + \dfrac{t^2}{2}\mathbf{k} + \mathbf{C}$

$\mathbf{v}(1) = \dfrac{1}{2}\mathbf{j} + \dfrac{1}{2}\mathbf{k} + \mathbf{C} = 5\mathbf{j} \Rightarrow \mathbf{C} = \dfrac{9}{2}\mathbf{j} - \dfrac{1}{2}\mathbf{k}$

$\mathbf{v}(t) = \left(\dfrac{t^2}{2} + \dfrac{9}{2} \right)\mathbf{j} + \left(\dfrac{t^2}{2} - \dfrac{1}{2} \right)\mathbf{k}$

$\mathbf{r}(t) = \int \left[\left(\dfrac{t^2}{2} + \dfrac{9}{2} \right)\mathbf{j} + \left(\dfrac{t^2}{2} - \dfrac{1}{2} \right)\mathbf{k} \right] dt$

$\qquad = \left(\dfrac{t^3}{6} + \dfrac{9}{2}t \right)\mathbf{j} + \left(\dfrac{t^3}{6} - \dfrac{1}{2}t \right)\mathbf{k} + \mathbf{C}$

$\mathbf{r}(1) = \dfrac{14}{3}\mathbf{j} - \dfrac{1}{3}\mathbf{k} + \mathbf{C} = \mathbf{0} \Rightarrow \mathbf{C} = -\dfrac{14}{3}\mathbf{j} + \dfrac{1}{3}\mathbf{k}$

$\mathbf{r}(t) = \left(\dfrac{t^3}{6} + \dfrac{9}{2}t - \dfrac{14}{3} \right)\mathbf{j} + \left(\dfrac{t^3}{6} - \dfrac{1}{2}t + \dfrac{1}{3} \right)\mathbf{k}$

$\mathbf{r}(2) = \dfrac{17}{3}\mathbf{j} + \dfrac{2}{3}\mathbf{k}$

23. The velocity of an object involves both magnitude and direction of motion, whereas speed involves only magnitude.

25. $\mathbf{r}(t) = (88\cos 30°)t\mathbf{i} + [10 + (88\sin 30°)t - 16t^2]\mathbf{j}$

$\qquad = 44\sqrt{3}\,t\mathbf{i} + (10 + 44t - 16t^2)\mathbf{j}$

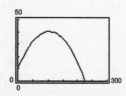

27. $\mathbf{r}(t) = (v_0 \cos\theta)t\mathbf{i} + \left[h + (v_0\sin\theta)t - \frac{1}{2}gt^2\right]\mathbf{j} = \frac{v_0}{\sqrt{2}}t\mathbf{i} + \left(3 + \frac{v_0}{\sqrt{2}}t - 16t^2\right)\mathbf{j}$

$\dfrac{v_0}{\sqrt{2}}t = 300$ when $3 + \dfrac{v_0}{\sqrt{2}}t - 16t^2 = 3$.

$$t = \frac{300\sqrt{2}}{v_0}, \ \frac{v_0}{\sqrt{2}}\left(\frac{300\sqrt{2}}{v_0}\right) - 16\left(\frac{300\sqrt{2}}{v_0}\right)^2 = 0, \ 300 - \frac{300^2(32)}{v_0^2} = 0$$

$$v_0^2 = 300(32), \ v_0 = \sqrt{9600} = 40\sqrt{6}, \ v_0 = 40\sqrt{6} \approx 97.98 \text{ ft/sec}$$

The maximum height is reached when the derivative of the vertical component is zero.

$$y(t) = 3 + \frac{tv_0}{\sqrt{2}} - 16t^2 = 3 + \frac{40\sqrt{6}}{\sqrt{2}}t - 16t^2 = 3 + 40\sqrt{3}t - 16t^2$$

$$y'(t) = 40\sqrt{3} - 32t = 0$$

$$t = \frac{40\sqrt{3}}{32} = \frac{5\sqrt{3}}{4}$$

Maximum height: $y\left(\dfrac{5\sqrt{3}}{4}\right) = 3 + 40\sqrt{3}\left(\dfrac{5\sqrt{3}}{4}\right) - 16\left(\dfrac{5\sqrt{3}}{4}\right)^2 = 78$ feet

29. $x(t) = t(v_0\cos\theta)$ or $t = \dfrac{x}{v_0\cos\theta}$

$y(t) = t(v_0\sin\theta) - 16t^2 + h$

$$y = \frac{x}{v_0\cos\theta}(v_0\sin\theta) - 16\left(\frac{x^2}{v_0^2\cos^2\theta}\right) + h = (\tan\theta)x - \left(\frac{16}{v_0^2}\sec^2\theta\right)x^2 + h$$

31. $\mathbf{r}(t) = t\mathbf{i} + (-0.004t^2 + 0.3667t + 6)\mathbf{j}$, or

(a) $y = -0.004x^2 + 0.3667x + 6$

(b)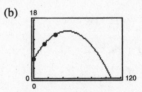

(c) $y' = -0.008x + 0.3667 = 0 \implies x = 45.8375$ and

$y(45.8375) \approx 14.4$ feet.

(d) From Exercise 29,

$\tan\theta = 0.3667 \implies \theta \approx 20.14°$

$$\frac{16\sec^2\theta}{v_0^2} = 0.004 \implies v_0^2 = \frac{16\sec^2\theta}{0.004} = \frac{4000}{\cos^2\theta}$$

$$\implies v_0 \approx 67.4 \text{ ft/sec.}$$

33. $100 \text{ mph} = \left(100\dfrac{\text{miles}}{\text{hr}}\right)\left(5280\dfrac{\text{feet}}{\text{mile}}\right)/(3600 \text{ sec/hour}) = \dfrac{440}{3}$ ft/sec

(a) $\mathbf{r}(t) = \left(\dfrac{440}{3}\cos\theta_0\right)t\mathbf{i} + \left[3 + \left(\dfrac{440}{3}\sin\theta_0\right)t - 16t^2\right]\mathbf{j}$

(b)

Graphing these curves together with $y = 10$ shows that $\theta_0 = 20°$.

—CONTINUED—

33. —CONTINUED—

(c) We want

$$x(t) = \left(\frac{440}{3} \cos \theta\right)t \geq 400 \quad \text{and} \quad y(t) = 3 + \left(\frac{440}{3} \sin \theta\right)t - 16t^2 \geq 10.$$

From $x(t)$, the minimum angle occurs when $t = 30/(11 \cos \theta)$. Substituting this for t in $y(t)$ yields:

$$3 + \left(\frac{440}{3} \sin \theta\right)\left(\frac{30}{11 \cos \theta}\right) - 16\left(\frac{30}{11 \cos \theta}\right)^2 = 10$$

$$400 \tan \theta - \frac{14,400}{121} \sec^2 \theta = 7$$

$$\frac{14,400}{121}(1 + \tan^2 \theta) - 400 \tan \theta + 7 = 0$$

$$14,400 \tan^2 \theta - 48,400 \tan \theta + 15,247 = 0$$

$$\tan \theta = \frac{48,400 \pm \sqrt{48,400^2 - 4(14,400)(15,247)}}{2(14,400)}$$

$$\theta = \tan^{-1}\left(\frac{48,400 - \sqrt{1,464,332,800}}{28,800}\right) \approx 19.38°$$

35. $\mathbf{r}(t) = (v \cos \theta)t\mathbf{i} + [(v \sin \theta)t - 16t^2]\mathbf{j}$

(a) We want to find the minimum initial speed v as a function of the angle θ. Since the bale must be thrown to the position $(16, 8)$, we have

$$16 = (v \cos \theta)t$$

$$8 = (v \sin \theta)t - 16t^2.$$

$t = 16/(v \cos \theta)$ from the first equation. Substituting into the second equation and solving for v, we obtain:

$$8 = (v \sin \theta)\left(\frac{16}{v \cos \theta}\right) - 16\left(\frac{16}{v \cos \theta}\right)^2$$

$$1 = 2\frac{\sin \theta}{\cos \theta} - 512\left(\frac{1}{v^2 \cos^2 \theta}\right)$$

$$512\frac{1}{v^2 \cos^2 \theta} = 2\frac{\sin \theta}{\cos \theta} - 1$$

$$\frac{1}{v^2} = \left(2\frac{\sin \theta}{\cos \theta} - 1\right)\frac{\cos^2 \theta}{512} = \frac{2 \sin \theta \cos \theta - \cos^2 \theta}{512}$$

$$v^2 = \frac{512}{2 \sin \theta \cos \theta - \cos^2 \theta}$$

We minimize $f(\theta) = \dfrac{512}{2 \sin \theta \cos \theta - \cos^2 \theta}$.

$$f'(\theta) = -512\frac{2 \cos^2 \theta - 2 \sin^2 \theta + 2 \sin \theta \cos \theta}{(2 \sin \theta \cos \theta - \cos^2 \theta)^2}$$

$$f'(\theta) = 0 \implies 2 \cos(2\theta) + \sin(2\theta) = 0$$

$$\tan(2\theta) = -2$$

$$\theta \approx 1.01722 \approx 58.28°$$

Substituting into the equation for v, $v \approx 28.78$ feet per second.

(b) If $\theta = 45°$,

$$16 = (v \cos \theta)t = v\frac{\sqrt{2}}{2}t$$

$$8 = (v \sin \theta)t - 16t^2 = v\frac{\sqrt{2}}{2}t - 16t^2$$

From part (a), $v^2 = \dfrac{512}{2(\sqrt{2}/2)(\sqrt{2}/2) - (\sqrt{2}/2)^2} = \dfrac{512}{1/2} = 1024 \implies v = 32$ ft/sec.

37. $\mathbf{r}(t) = (v_0 \cos \theta)t\mathbf{i} + [(v_0 \sin \theta)t - 16t^2]\mathbf{j}$

$(v_0 \sin \theta)t - 16t^2 = 0$ when $t = 0$ and $t = \dfrac{v_0 \sin \theta}{16}$.

The range is

$x = (v_0 \cos \theta)t = (v_0 \cos \theta)\dfrac{v_0 \sin \theta}{16} = \dfrac{v_0^2}{32} \sin 2\theta.$

Hence,

$x = \dfrac{1200^2}{32} \sin(2\theta) = 3000 \Rightarrow \sin 2\theta = \dfrac{1}{15} \Rightarrow \theta \approx 1.91°.$

39. (a) $\theta = 10°$, $v_0 = 66$ ft/sec

$\mathbf{r}(t) = (66 \cos 10°)t\mathbf{i} + [0 + (66 \sin 10°)t - 16t^2]\mathbf{j}$

$\mathbf{r}(t) \approx (65t)\mathbf{i} + (11.46t - 16t^2)\mathbf{j}$

Maximum height: 2.052 feet

Range: 46.557 feet

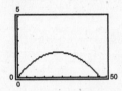

(c) $\theta = 45°$, $v_0 = 66$ ft/sec

$\mathbf{r}(t) = (66 \cos 45°)t\mathbf{i} + [0 + (66 \sin 45°)t - 16t^2]\mathbf{j}$

$\mathbf{r}(t) \approx (46.67t)\mathbf{i} + (46.67t - 16t^2)\mathbf{j}$

Maximum height: 34.031 feet

Range: 136.125 feet

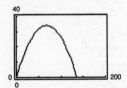

(e) $\theta = 60°$, $v_0 = 66$ ft/sec

$\mathbf{r}(t) = (66 \cos 60°)t\mathbf{i} + [0 + (66 \sin 60°)t - 16t^2]\mathbf{j}$

$\mathbf{r}(t) \approx (33t)\mathbf{i} + (57.16t - 16t^2)\mathbf{j}$

Maximum height: 51.074 feet

Range: 117.888 feet

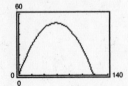

(b) $\theta = 10°$, $v_0 = 146$ ft/sec

$\mathbf{r}(t) = (146 \cos 10°)t\mathbf{i} + [0 + (146 \sin 10°)t - 16t^2]\mathbf{j}$

$\mathbf{r}(t) \approx (143.78t)\mathbf{i} + (25.35t - 16t^2)\mathbf{j}$

Maximum height: 10.043 feet

Range: 227.828 feet

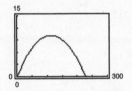

(d) $\theta = 45°$, $v_0 = 146$ ft/sec

$\mathbf{r}(t) = (146 \cos 45°)t\mathbf{i} + [0 + (146 \sin 45°)t - 16t^2]\mathbf{j}$

$\mathbf{r}(t) \approx (103.24t)\mathbf{i} + (103.24t - 16t^2)\mathbf{j}$

Maximum height: 166.531 feet

Range: 666.125 feet

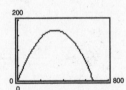

(f) $\theta = 60°$, $v_0 = 146$ ft/sec

$\mathbf{r}(t) = (146 \cos 60°)t\mathbf{i} + [0 + (146 \sin 60°)t - 16t^2]\mathbf{j}$

$\mathbf{r}(t) \approx (73t)\mathbf{i} + (126.44t - 16t^2)\mathbf{j}$

Maximum height: 249.797 feet

Range: 576.881 feet

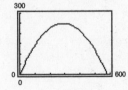

41. $\mathbf{r}(t) = (v_0 \cos \theta)t\mathbf{i} + [h + (v_0 \sin \theta)t - 4.9t^2]\mathbf{j}$

$\qquad = (100 \cos 30°)t\mathbf{i} + [1.5 + (100 \sin 30°)t - 4.9t^2]\mathbf{j}$

The projectile hits the ground when $-4.9t^2 + 100(\frac{1}{2})t + 1.5 = 0 \implies t \approx 10.234$ seconds.

The range is therefore $(100 \cos 30°)(10.234) \approx 886.3$ meters.

The maximum height occurs when $dy/dt = 0$.

$\qquad 100 \sin 30 = 9.8t \implies t \approx 5.102$ sec

The maximum height is

$\qquad y = 1.5 + (100 \sin 30°)(5.102) - 4.9(5.102)^2 \approx 129.1$ meters.

43. $\mathbf{r}(t) = b(\omega t - \sin \omega t)\mathbf{i} + b(1 - \cos \omega t)\mathbf{j}$

$\qquad \mathbf{v}(t) = b(\omega - \omega \cos \omega t)\mathbf{i} + b\omega \sin \omega t\, \mathbf{j} = b\omega(1 - \cos \omega t)\mathbf{i} + b\omega \sin \omega t\mathbf{j}$

$\qquad \mathbf{a}(t) = (b\omega^2 \sin \omega t)\mathbf{i} + (b\omega^2 \cos \omega t)\mathbf{j} = b\omega^2[\sin(\omega t)\mathbf{i} + \cos(\omega t)\mathbf{j}]$

$\qquad \|\mathbf{v}(t)\| = \sqrt{2}\, b\omega \sqrt{1 - \cos(\omega t)}$

$\qquad \|\mathbf{a}(t)\| = b\omega^2$

(a) $\|\mathbf{v}(t)\| = 0$ when $\omega t = 0, 2\pi, 4\pi, \dots$

(b) $\|\mathbf{v}(t)\|$ is maximum when $\omega t = \pi, 3\pi, \dots$, then $\|\mathbf{v}(t)\| = 2b\omega$.

45. $\qquad \mathbf{v}(t) = -b\omega \sin(\omega t)\mathbf{i} + b\omega \cos(\omega t)\mathbf{j}$

$\qquad \mathbf{r}(t) \cdot \mathbf{v}(t) = -b^2\omega \sin(\omega t) \cos(\omega t) + b^2\omega \sin(\omega t) \cos(\omega t) = 0$

Therefore, $\mathbf{r}(t)$ and $\mathbf{v}(t)$ are orthogonal.

47. $\mathbf{a}(t) = -b\omega^2 \cos(\omega t)\mathbf{i} - b\omega^2 \sin(\omega t)\mathbf{j} = -b\omega^2[\cos(\omega t)\mathbf{i} + \sin(\omega t)\mathbf{j}] = -\omega^2 \mathbf{r}(t)$

$\mathbf{a}(t)$ is a negative multiple of a unit vector from $(0, 0)$ to $(\cos \omega t, \sin \omega t)$ and thus $\mathbf{a}(t)$ is directed toward the origin.

49. $\|\mathbf{a}(t)\| = \omega^2 b$

$\qquad 1 = m(32)$

$\qquad F = m(\omega^2 b) = \dfrac{1}{32}(2\omega^2) = 10$

$\qquad \omega = 4\sqrt{10}$ rad/sec

$\qquad \|\mathbf{v}(t)\| = b\omega = 8\sqrt{10}$ ft/sec

51. To find the range, set $y(t) = h + (v_0 \sin \theta)t - \frac{1}{2}gt^2 = 0$ then $0 = (\frac{1}{2}g)t^2 - (v_0 \sin \theta)t - h$.

By the Quadratic Formula, (discount the negative value)

$$t = \frac{v_0 \sin \theta + \sqrt{(-v_0 \sin \theta)^2 - 4[(1/2)g](-h)}}{2[(1/2)g]} = \frac{v_0 \sin \theta + \sqrt{v_0{}^2 \sin^2 \theta + 2gh}}{g}.$$

At this time,

$$\begin{aligned} x(t) &= v_0 \cos \theta \left(\frac{v_0 \sin \theta + \sqrt{v_0{}^2 \sin^2 \theta + 2gh}}{g} \right) = \frac{v_0 \cos \theta}{g}\left(v_0 \sin \theta + \sqrt{v_0{}^2\left(\sin^2 \theta + \frac{2gh}{v_0{}^2} \right)} \right) \\ &= \frac{v_0{}^2 \cos \theta}{g}\left(\sin \theta + \sqrt{\sin^2 \theta + \frac{2gh}{v_0{}^2}} \right). \end{aligned}$$

53. $\mathbf{r}(t) = x(t)\mathbf{i} + y(t)\mathbf{j} + z(t)\mathbf{k}$ Position vector

$\quad \mathbf{v}(t) = x'(t)\mathbf{i} + y'(t)\mathbf{j} + z'(t)\mathbf{k}$ Velocity vector

$\quad \mathbf{a}(t) = x''(t)\mathbf{i} + y''(t)\mathbf{j} + z''(t)\mathbf{k}$ Acceleration vector

$$\text{Speed} = \|\mathbf{v}(t)\| = \sqrt{(x'(t))^2 + y'(t)^2 + z'(t)^2}$$

$$= C, \; C \text{ is a constant.}$$

$$\frac{d}{dt}[x'(t)^2 + y'(t)^2 + z'(t)^2] = 0$$

$$2x'(t)x''(t) + 2y'(t)y''(t) + 2z'(t)z''(t) = 0$$

$$2[x'(t)x''(t) + y'(t)y''(t) + z'(t)z''(t)] = 0$$

$$\mathbf{v}(t) \cdot \mathbf{a}(t) = 0$$

Orthogonal

55. $\mathbf{r}(t) = 6 \cos t\mathbf{i} + 3 \sin t\mathbf{j}$

(a) $\mathbf{v}(t) = \mathbf{r}'(t) = -6 \sin t\mathbf{i} + 3 \cos t\mathbf{j}$

$\qquad \|\mathbf{v}(t)\| = \sqrt{36 \sin^2 t + 9 \cos^2 t}$

$\qquad\qquad = 3\sqrt{4 \sin^2 t + \cos^2 t}$

$\qquad\qquad = 3\sqrt{3 \sin^2 t + 1}$

$\quad \mathbf{a}(t) = \mathbf{v}'(t) = -6 \cos t\mathbf{i} - 3 \sin t\mathbf{j}$

(b)

t	0	$\dfrac{\pi}{4}$	$\dfrac{\pi}{2}$	$\dfrac{2\pi}{3}$	π
Speed	3	$\dfrac{3}{2}\sqrt{10}$	6	$\dfrac{3}{2}\sqrt{13}$	3

(c)

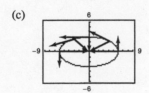

(d) The speed is increasing when the angle between $\mathbf{v}$ and $\mathbf{a}$ is in the interval

$$\left[0, \frac{\pi}{2}\right).$$

The speed is decreasing when the angle is in the interval

$$\left(\frac{\pi}{2}, \pi\right].$$

Section 11.4   Tangent Vectors and Normal Vectors

1. $\mathbf{r}(t) = t^2\mathbf{i} + 2t\mathbf{j}$

$\quad \mathbf{r}'(t) = 2t\mathbf{i} + 2\mathbf{j}, \|\mathbf{r}'(t)\| = \sqrt{4t^2 + 4} = 2\sqrt{t^2 + 1}$

$\quad \mathbf{T}(t) = \dfrac{\mathbf{r}'(t)}{\|\mathbf{r}'(t)\|} = \dfrac{2t\mathbf{i} + 2\mathbf{j}}{2\sqrt{t^2 + 1}} = \dfrac{1}{\sqrt{t^2 + 1}}(t\mathbf{i} + \mathbf{j})$

$\quad \mathbf{T}(1) = \dfrac{1}{\sqrt{2}}(\mathbf{i} + \mathbf{j}) = \dfrac{\sqrt{2}}{2}\mathbf{i} + \dfrac{\sqrt{2}}{2}\mathbf{j}$

3. $\mathbf{r}(t) = 4 \cos t\mathbf{i} + 4 \sin t\mathbf{j}$

$\quad \mathbf{r}'(t) = -4 \sin t\mathbf{i} + 4 \cos t\mathbf{j}$

$\quad \|\mathbf{r}'(t)\| = \sqrt{16 \sin^2 t + 16 \cos^2 t} = 4$

$\quad \mathbf{T}(t) = \dfrac{\mathbf{r}'(t)}{\|\mathbf{r}'(t)\|} = -\sin t\mathbf{i} + \cos t\mathbf{j}$

$\quad \mathbf{T}\left(\dfrac{\pi}{4}\right) = -\dfrac{\sqrt{2}}{2}\mathbf{i} + \dfrac{\sqrt{2}}{2}\mathbf{j}$

5. $\mathbf{r}(t) = t\mathbf{i} + t^2\mathbf{j} + t\mathbf{k}$

$\quad \mathbf{r}'(t) = \mathbf{i} + 2t\mathbf{j} + \mathbf{k}$

$\quad$ When $t = 0$, $\mathbf{r}'(0) = \mathbf{i} + \mathbf{k}$, $[t = 0$ at $(0, 0, 0)]$.

$$\mathbf{T}(0) = \dfrac{\mathbf{r}'(0)}{\|\mathbf{r}'(0)\|} = \dfrac{\sqrt{2}}{2}(\mathbf{i} + \mathbf{k})$$

Direction numbers: $a = 1$, $b = 0$, $c = 1$

Parametric equations: $x = t$, $y = 0$, $z = t$

7. $\mathbf{r}(t) = 2 \cos t\mathbf{i} + 2 \sin t\mathbf{j} + t\mathbf{k}$

$\quad \mathbf{r}'(t) = -2 \sin t\mathbf{i} + 2 \cos t\mathbf{j} + \mathbf{k}$

$\quad$ When $t = 0$, $\mathbf{r}'(0) = 2\mathbf{j} + \mathbf{k}$, $[t = 0$ at $(2, 0, 0)]$.

$$\mathbf{T}(0) = \dfrac{\mathbf{r}'(0)}{\|\mathbf{r}'(0)\|} = \dfrac{\sqrt{5}}{5}(2\mathbf{j} + \mathbf{k})$$

Direction numbers: $a = 0$, $b = 2$, $c = 1$

Parametric equations: $x = 2$, $y = 2t$, $z = t$

9. $\mathbf{r}(t) = \langle 2\cos t, 2\sin t, 4 \rangle$

$\mathbf{r}'(t) = \langle -2\sin t, 2\cos t, 0 \rangle$

When $t = \dfrac{\pi}{4}$, $\mathbf{r}'\!\left(\dfrac{\pi}{4}\right) = \langle -\sqrt{2}, \sqrt{2}, 0 \rangle$, $\left[t = \dfrac{\pi}{4} \text{ at } \left(\sqrt{2}, \sqrt{2}, 4\right) \right]$.

$\mathbf{T}\!\left(\dfrac{\pi}{4}\right) = \dfrac{\mathbf{r}'(\pi/4)}{\|\mathbf{r}'(\pi/4)\|} = \dfrac{1}{2}\langle -\sqrt{2}, \sqrt{2}, 0 \rangle$

Direction numbers: $a = -\sqrt{2}$, $b = \sqrt{2}$, $c = 0$

Parametric equations: $x = -\sqrt{2}\,t + \sqrt{2}$, $y = \sqrt{2}\,t + \sqrt{2}$, $z = 4$

11. $\mathbf{r}(t) = \left\langle t, t^2, \dfrac{2}{3}t^3 \right\rangle$

$\mathbf{r}'(t) = \langle 1, 2t, 2t^2 \rangle$

When $t = 3$, $\mathbf{r}'(3) = \langle 1, 6, 18 \rangle$, $[t = 3$ at $(3, 9, 18)]$.

$\mathbf{T}(3) = \dfrac{\mathbf{r}'(3)}{\|\mathbf{r}'(3)\|} = \dfrac{1}{19}\langle 1, 6, 18 \rangle$

Direction numbers: $a = 1$, $b = 6$, $c = 18$

Parametric equations: $x = t + 3$, $y = 6t + 9$, $z = 18t + 18$

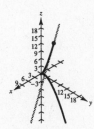

13. $\mathbf{r}(t) = t\mathbf{i} + \ln t\,\mathbf{j} + \sqrt{t}\,\mathbf{k}$, $t_0 = 1$

$\mathbf{r}'(t) = \mathbf{i} + \dfrac{1}{t}\mathbf{j} + \dfrac{1}{2\sqrt{t}}\mathbf{k} \cdot \mathbf{r}'(1) = \mathbf{i} + \mathbf{j} + \dfrac{1}{2}\mathbf{k}$

$\mathbf{T}(1) = \dfrac{\mathbf{r}'(t)}{\|\mathbf{r}'(t)\|} = \dfrac{\mathbf{i} + \mathbf{j} + (1/2)\mathbf{k}}{\sqrt{1 + 1 + (1/4)}} = \dfrac{2}{3}\mathbf{i} + \dfrac{2}{3}\mathbf{j} + \dfrac{1}{3}\mathbf{k}$

Tangent line: $x = 1 + t$, $y = t$, $z = 1 + \dfrac{1}{2}t$

$\mathbf{r}(t_0 + 0.1) = \mathbf{r}(1.1) \approx 1.1\mathbf{i} + 0.1\mathbf{j} + 1.05\mathbf{k}$

$= \langle 1.1, 0.1, 1.05 \rangle$

15. $\mathbf{r}(4) = \langle 2, 16, 2 \rangle$

$\mathbf{u}(8) = \langle 2, 16, 2 \rangle$

Hence the curves intersect.

$\mathbf{r}'(t) = \left\langle 1, 2t, \dfrac{1}{2} \right\rangle$, $\mathbf{r}'(4) = \left\langle 1, 8, \dfrac{1}{2} \right\rangle$

$\mathbf{u}'(s) = \left\langle \dfrac{1}{4}, 2, \dfrac{1}{3}s^{-2/3} \right\rangle$, $\mathbf{u}'(8) = \left\langle \dfrac{1}{4}, 2, \dfrac{1}{12} \right\rangle$

$\cos\theta = \dfrac{\mathbf{r}'(4) \cdot \mathbf{u}'(8)}{\|\mathbf{r}'(4)\|\,\|\mathbf{u}'(8)\|} \approx \dfrac{16.29167}{16.29513} \Rightarrow \theta \approx 1.2^\circ$

17. $\mathbf{r}(t) = t\mathbf{i} + \dfrac{1}{2}t^2\mathbf{j}$, $t = 2$

$\mathbf{r}'(t) = \mathbf{i} + t\mathbf{j}$

$\mathbf{T}(t) = \dfrac{\mathbf{r}'(t)}{\|\mathbf{r}'(t)\|} = \dfrac{\mathbf{i} + t\mathbf{j}}{\sqrt{1 + t^2}}$

$\mathbf{T}'(t) = \dfrac{-t}{(t^2 + 1)^{3/2}}\mathbf{i} + \dfrac{1}{(t^2 + 1)^{3/2}}\mathbf{j}$

$\mathbf{T}'(2) = \dfrac{-2}{5^{3/2}}\mathbf{i} + \dfrac{1}{5^{3/2}}\mathbf{j}$

$\mathbf{N}(2) = \dfrac{\mathbf{T}'(2)}{\|\mathbf{T}'(2)\|} + \dfrac{1}{\sqrt{5}}(-2\mathbf{i} + \mathbf{j}) = \dfrac{-2\sqrt{5}}{5}\mathbf{i} + \dfrac{\sqrt{5}}{5}\mathbf{j}$

19. $\mathbf{r}(t) = 6\cos t\,\mathbf{i} + 6\sin t\,\mathbf{j} + \mathbf{k}$, $t = \dfrac{3\pi}{4}$

$\mathbf{r}'(t) = -6\sin t\,\mathbf{i} + 6\cos t\,\mathbf{j}$

$\mathbf{T}(t) = \dfrac{\mathbf{r}'(t)}{\|\mathbf{r}'(t)\|} = -\sin t\,\mathbf{i} + \cos t\,\mathbf{j}$

$\mathbf{T}'(t) = -\cos t\,\mathbf{i} - \sin t\,\mathbf{j}$, $\|\mathbf{T}(t)\| = 1$

$\mathbf{N}\!\left(\dfrac{3\pi}{4}\right) = \dfrac{\sqrt{2}}{2}\mathbf{i} - \dfrac{\sqrt{2}}{2}\mathbf{j}$

21. $\mathbf{r}(t) = 4t\mathbf{i}$

$\mathbf{v}(t) = 4\mathbf{i}$

$\mathbf{a}(t) = \mathbf{O}$

$\mathbf{T}(t) = \dfrac{\mathbf{v}(t)}{\|\mathbf{v}(t)\|} = \dfrac{4\mathbf{i}}{4} = \mathbf{i}$

$\mathbf{T}'(t) = \mathbf{O}$

$\mathbf{N}(t) = \dfrac{\mathbf{T}'(t)}{\|\mathbf{T}'(t)\|}$ is undefined.

The path is a line and the speed is constant.

23. $\mathbf{r}(t) = 4t^2\mathbf{i}$

$\mathbf{v}(t) = 8t\mathbf{i}$

$\mathbf{a}(t) = 8\mathbf{i}$

$\mathbf{T}(t) = \dfrac{\mathbf{v}(t)}{\|\mathbf{v}(t)\|} = \dfrac{8t\mathbf{i}}{8t} = \mathbf{i}$

$\mathbf{T}'(t) = \mathbf{O}$

$\mathbf{N}(t) = \dfrac{\mathbf{T}'(t)}{\|\mathbf{T}'(t)\|}$ is undefined.

The path is a line and the speed is variable.

25. $\mathbf{r}(t) = t\mathbf{i} + \dfrac{1}{t}\mathbf{j}$, $\mathbf{v}(t) = \mathbf{i} - \dfrac{1}{t^2}\mathbf{j}$, $\mathbf{v}(1) = \mathbf{i} - \mathbf{j}$,

$\mathbf{a}(t) = \dfrac{2}{t^3}\mathbf{j}$, $\mathbf{a}(1) = 2\mathbf{j}$

$\mathbf{T}(t) = \dfrac{\mathbf{v}(t)}{\|\mathbf{v}(t)\|} = \dfrac{t^2}{\sqrt{t^4 + 1}}\left(\mathbf{i} - \dfrac{1}{t^2}\mathbf{j}\right) = \dfrac{1}{\sqrt{t^4 + 1}}(t^2\mathbf{i} - \mathbf{j})$

$\mathbf{T}(1) = \dfrac{1}{\sqrt{2}}(\mathbf{i} - \mathbf{j}) = \dfrac{\sqrt{2}}{2}(\mathbf{i} - \mathbf{j})$

$\mathbf{N}(t) = \dfrac{\mathbf{T}'(t)}{\|\mathbf{T}'(t)\|} = \dfrac{\dfrac{2t}{(t^4 + 1)^{3/2}}\mathbf{i} + \dfrac{2t^3}{(t^4 + 1)^{3/2}}\mathbf{j}}{\dfrac{2t}{(t^4 + 1)}}$

$\qquad = \dfrac{1}{\sqrt{t^4 + 1}}(\mathbf{i} + t^2\mathbf{j})$

$\mathbf{N}(1) = \dfrac{1}{\sqrt{2}}(\mathbf{i} + \mathbf{j}) = \dfrac{\sqrt{2}}{2}(\mathbf{i} + \mathbf{j})$

$a_{\mathbf{T}} = \mathbf{a} \cdot \mathbf{T} = -\sqrt{2}$

$a_{\mathbf{N}} = \mathbf{a} \cdot \mathbf{N} = \sqrt{2}$

27. $\mathbf{r}(t) = (e^t \cos t)\mathbf{i} + (e^t \sin t)\mathbf{j}$

$\mathbf{v}(t) = e^t(\cos t - \sin t)\mathbf{i} + e^t(\cos t + \sin t)\mathbf{j}$

$\mathbf{a}(t) = e^t(-2 \sin t)\mathbf{i} + e^t(2 \cos t)\mathbf{j}$

At $t = \dfrac{\pi}{2}$, $\mathbf{T} = \dfrac{\mathbf{v}}{\|\mathbf{v}\|} = \dfrac{1}{\sqrt{2}}(-\mathbf{i} + \mathbf{j}) = \dfrac{\sqrt{2}}{2}(-\mathbf{i} + \mathbf{j})$.

Motion along $\mathbf{r}$ is counterclockwise. Therefore,

$\mathbf{N} = \dfrac{1}{\sqrt{2}}(-\mathbf{i} - \mathbf{j}) = -\dfrac{\sqrt{2}}{2}(\mathbf{i} + \mathbf{j})$.

$a_{\mathbf{T}} = \mathbf{a} \cdot \mathbf{T} = \sqrt{2}e^{\pi/2}$

$a_{\mathbf{N}} = \mathbf{a} \cdot \mathbf{N} = \sqrt{2}e^{\pi/2}$

29. $\mathbf{r}(t_0) = (\cos \omega t_0 + \omega t_0 \sin \omega t_0)\mathbf{i} + (\sin \omega t_0 - \omega t_0 \cos \omega t_0)\mathbf{j}$

$\mathbf{v}(t_0) = (\omega^2 t_0 \cos \omega t_0)\mathbf{i} + (\omega^2 t_0 \sin \omega t_0)\mathbf{j}$

$\mathbf{a}(t_0) = \omega^2[(\cos \omega t_0 - \omega t_0 \sin \omega t_0)\mathbf{i} + (\omega t_0 \cos \omega t_0 + \sin \omega t_0)\mathbf{j}]$

$\mathbf{T}(t_0) = \dfrac{\mathbf{v}}{\|\mathbf{v}\|} = (\cos \omega t_0)\mathbf{i} + (\sin \omega t_0)\mathbf{j}$

Motion along $\mathbf{r}$ is counterclockwise. Therefore

$\mathbf{N}(t_0) = (-\sin \omega t_0)\mathbf{i} + (\cos \omega t_0)\mathbf{j}$.

$a_{\mathbf{T}} = \mathbf{a} \cdot \mathbf{T} = \omega^2$

$a_{\mathbf{N}} = \mathbf{a} \cdot \mathbf{N} = \omega^2(\omega t_0) = \omega^3 t_0$

31. $\mathbf{r}(t) = a\cos(\omega t)\mathbf{i} + a\sin(\omega t)\mathbf{j}$

$\mathbf{v}(t) = -a\omega\sin(\omega t)\mathbf{i} + a\omega\cos(\omega t)\mathbf{j}$

$\mathbf{a}(t) = -a\omega^2\cos(\omega t)\mathbf{i} - a\omega^2\sin(\omega t)\mathbf{j}$

$\mathbf{T}(t) = \dfrac{\mathbf{v}(t)}{\|\mathbf{v}(t)\|} = -\sin(\omega t)\mathbf{i} + \cos(\omega t)\mathbf{j}$

$\mathbf{N}(t) = \dfrac{\mathbf{T}'(t)}{\|\mathbf{T}'(t)\|} = -\cos(\omega t)\mathbf{i} - \sin(\omega t)\mathbf{j}$

$a_{\mathbf{T}} = \mathbf{a}\cdot\mathbf{T} = 0$

$a_{\mathbf{N}} = \mathbf{a}\cdot\mathbf{N} = a\omega^2$

33. Speed: $\|\mathbf{v}(t)\| = a\omega$

The speed is constant since $a_{\mathbf{T}} = 0$.

35. $\mathbf{r}(t) = t\mathbf{i} + \dfrac{1}{t}\mathbf{j}$, $t_0 = 2$

$x = t, \; y = \dfrac{1}{t} \Rightarrow xy = 1$

$\mathbf{r}'(t) = \mathbf{i} - \dfrac{1}{t^2}\mathbf{j}$

$\mathbf{T}(t) = \dfrac{t^2\mathbf{i} - \mathbf{j}}{\sqrt{t^4 + 1}}$

$\mathbf{N}(t) = \dfrac{\mathbf{i} + t^2\mathbf{j}}{\sqrt{t^4 + 1}}$

$\mathbf{r}(2) = 2\mathbf{i} + \dfrac{1}{2}\mathbf{j}$

$\mathbf{T}(2) = \dfrac{\sqrt{17}}{17}(4\mathbf{i} - \mathbf{j})$

$\mathbf{N}(2) = \dfrac{\sqrt{17}}{17}(\mathbf{i} + 4\mathbf{j})$

37. $\mathbf{r}(t) = t\mathbf{i} + 2t\mathbf{j} - 3t\mathbf{k}$

$\mathbf{v}(t) = \mathbf{i} + 2\mathbf{j} - 3\mathbf{k}$

$\mathbf{a}(t) = \mathbf{0}$

$\mathbf{T}(t) = \dfrac{\mathbf{v}}{\|\mathbf{v}\|} = \dfrac{1}{\sqrt{14}}(\mathbf{i} + 2\mathbf{j} - 3\mathbf{k}) = \dfrac{\sqrt{14}}{14}(\mathbf{i} + 2\mathbf{j} - 3\mathbf{k})$

$\mathbf{N}(t) = \dfrac{\mathbf{T}'}{\|\mathbf{T}'\|}$ is undefined.

$a_{\mathbf{T}}, a_{\mathbf{N}}$ are not defined.

39. $\mathbf{r}(t) = t\mathbf{i} + t^2\mathbf{j} + \dfrac{t^2}{2}\mathbf{k}$

$\mathbf{v}(t) = \mathbf{i} + 2t\mathbf{j} + t\mathbf{k}$

$\mathbf{v}(1) = \mathbf{i} + 2\mathbf{j} + \mathbf{k}$

$\mathbf{a}(t) = 2\mathbf{j} + \mathbf{k}$

$\mathbf{T}(t) = \dfrac{\mathbf{v}}{\|\mathbf{v}\|} = \dfrac{1}{\sqrt{1 + 5t^2}}(\mathbf{i} + 2t\mathbf{j} + t\mathbf{k})$

$\mathbf{T}(1) = \dfrac{\sqrt{6}}{6}(\mathbf{i} + 2\mathbf{j} + \mathbf{k})$

$\mathbf{N}(t) = \dfrac{\mathbf{T}'}{\|\mathbf{T}'\|} = \dfrac{\dfrac{-5t\mathbf{i} + 2\mathbf{j} + \mathbf{k}}{(1 + 5t^2)^{3/2}}}{\dfrac{\sqrt{5}}{1 + 5t^2}} = \dfrac{-5t\mathbf{i} + 2\mathbf{j} + \mathbf{k}}{\sqrt{5}\sqrt{1 + 5t^2}}$

$\mathbf{N}(1) = \dfrac{\sqrt{30}}{30}(-5\mathbf{i} + 2\mathbf{j} + \mathbf{k})$

$a_{\mathbf{T}} = \mathbf{a}\cdot\mathbf{T} = \dfrac{5\sqrt{6}}{6}$

$a_{\mathbf{N}} = \mathbf{a}\cdot\mathbf{N} = \dfrac{\sqrt{30}}{6}$

41. $\mathbf{r}(t) = 4t\mathbf{i} + 3\cos t\mathbf{j} + 3\sin t\mathbf{k}$

$\mathbf{v}(t) = 4\mathbf{i} - 3\sin t\mathbf{j} + 3\cos t\mathbf{k}$

$\mathbf{v}\left(\dfrac{\pi}{2}\right) = 4\mathbf{i} - 3\mathbf{j}$

$\mathbf{a}(t) = -3\cos t\mathbf{j} - 3\sin t\mathbf{k}$

$\mathbf{a}\left(\dfrac{\pi}{2}\right) = -3\mathbf{k}$

$\mathbf{T}(t) = \dfrac{\mathbf{v}}{\|\mathbf{v}\|} = \dfrac{1}{5}(4\mathbf{i} - 3\sin t\mathbf{j} + 3\cos t\mathbf{k})$

$\mathbf{T}\left(\dfrac{\pi}{2}\right) = \dfrac{1}{5}(4\mathbf{i} - 3\mathbf{j})$

$\mathbf{N}(t) = \dfrac{\mathbf{T}'}{\|\mathbf{T}'\|} = -\cos t\mathbf{j} - \sin t\mathbf{k}$

$\mathbf{N}\left(\dfrac{\pi}{2}\right) = -\mathbf{k}$

$a_{\mathbf{T}} = \mathbf{a}\cdot\mathbf{T} = 0$

$a_{\mathbf{N}} = \mathbf{a}\cdot\mathbf{N} = 3$

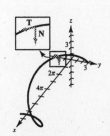

43. $\mathbf{T}(t) = \dfrac{\mathbf{r}'(t)}{\|\mathbf{r}'(t)\|}$

$\mathbf{N}(t) = \dfrac{\mathbf{T}'(t)}{\|\mathbf{T}'(t)\|}$

If $a(t) = a_\mathbf{T}\mathbf{T}(t) + a_\mathbf{N}\mathbf{N}(t)$, then $a_\mathbf{T}$ is the tangential component of acceleration and $a_\mathbf{N}$ is the normal component of acceleration.

45. If $a_\mathbf{N} = 0$, then the motion is in a straight line.

47. $\mathbf{r}(t) = \langle \pi t - \sin \pi t, 1 - \cos \pi t \rangle$

The graph is a cycloid.

(a) $\mathbf{r}(t) = \langle \pi t - \sin \pi t, 1 - \cos \pi t \rangle$

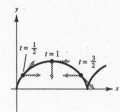

$\mathbf{v}(t) = \langle \pi - \pi \cos \pi t, \pi \sin \pi t \rangle$

$\mathbf{a}(t) = \langle \pi^2 \sin \pi t, \pi^2 \cos \pi t \rangle$

$\mathbf{T}(t) = \dfrac{\mathbf{v}(t)}{\|\mathbf{v}(t)\|} = \dfrac{1}{\sqrt{2(1 - \cos \pi t)}}\langle 1 - \cos \pi t, \sin \pi t \rangle$

$\mathbf{N}(t) = \dfrac{\mathbf{T}'(t)}{\|\mathbf{T}'(t)\|} = \dfrac{1}{\sqrt{2(1 - \cos \pi t)}}\langle \sin \pi t, -1 + \cos \pi t \rangle$

$a_\mathbf{T} = \mathbf{a} \cdot \mathbf{T} = \dfrac{1}{\sqrt{2(1 - \cos \pi t)}}[\pi^2 \sin \pi t(1 - \cos \pi t) + \pi^2 \cos \pi t \sin \pi t] = \dfrac{\pi^2 \sin \pi t}{\sqrt{2(1 - \cos \pi t)}}$

$a_\mathbf{N} = \mathbf{a} \cdot \mathbf{N} = \dfrac{1}{\sqrt{2(1 - \cos \pi t)}}[\pi^2 \sin^2 \pi t + \pi^2 \cos \pi t(-1 + \cos \pi t)] = \dfrac{\pi^2(1 - \cos \pi t)}{\sqrt{2(1 - \cos \pi t)}} = \dfrac{\pi^2\sqrt{2(1 - \cos \pi t)}}{2}$

When $t = \dfrac{1}{2}$: $a_\mathbf{T} = \dfrac{\pi^2}{\sqrt{2}} = \dfrac{\sqrt{2}\pi^2}{2}$, $a_\mathbf{N} = \dfrac{\sqrt{2}\pi^2}{2}$

When $t = 1$: $a_\mathbf{T} = 0$, $a_\mathbf{N} = \pi^2$

When $t = \dfrac{3}{2}$: $a_\mathbf{T} = -\dfrac{\sqrt{2}\pi^2}{2}$, $a_\mathbf{N} = \dfrac{\sqrt{2}\pi^2}{2}$

(b) Speed: $s = \|\mathbf{v}(t)\| = \pi\sqrt{2(1 - \cos \pi t)}$

$\dfrac{ds}{dt} = \dfrac{\pi^2 \sin \pi t}{\sqrt{2(1 - \cos \pi t)}} = a_\mathbf{T}$

When $t = \dfrac{1}{2}$: $a_\mathbf{T} = \dfrac{\sqrt{2}\pi^2}{2} > 0 \implies$ the speed in increasing.

When $t = 1$: $a_\mathbf{T} = 0 \implies$ the height is maximum.

When $t = \dfrac{3}{2}$: $a_\mathbf{T} = -\dfrac{\sqrt{2}\pi^2}{2} < 0 \implies$ the speed is decreasing.

49. $\mathbf{r}(t) = 2\cos t\mathbf{i} + 2\sin t\mathbf{j} + \dfrac{t}{2}\mathbf{k}, \ t_0 = \dfrac{\pi}{2}$

$\mathbf{r}'(t) = -2\sin t\mathbf{i} + 2\cos t\mathbf{j} + \dfrac{1}{2}\mathbf{k}$

$\mathbf{T}(t) = \dfrac{2\sqrt{17}}{17}\left(-2\sin t\mathbf{i} + 2\cos t\mathbf{j} + \dfrac{1}{2}\mathbf{k}\right)$

$\mathbf{N}(t) = -\cos t\mathbf{i} - \sin t\mathbf{j}$

$\mathbf{r}\left(\dfrac{\pi}{2}\right) = 2\mathbf{j} + \dfrac{\pi}{4}\mathbf{k}$

$\mathbf{T}\left(\dfrac{\pi}{2}\right) = \dfrac{2\sqrt{17}}{17}\left(-2\mathbf{i} + \dfrac{1}{2}\mathbf{k}\right) = \dfrac{\sqrt{17}}{17}(-4\mathbf{i} + \mathbf{k})$

$\mathbf{N}\left(\dfrac{\pi}{2}\right) = -\mathbf{j}$

$\mathbf{B}\left(\dfrac{\pi}{2}\right) = \mathbf{T}\left(\dfrac{\pi}{2}\right) \times \mathbf{N}\left(\dfrac{\pi}{2}\right) = \begin{vmatrix} \mathbf{i} & \mathbf{j} & \mathbf{k} \\ -\dfrac{4\sqrt{17}}{17} & 0 & \dfrac{\sqrt{17}}{17} \\ 0 & -1 & 0 \end{vmatrix} = \dfrac{\sqrt{17}}{17}\mathbf{i} + \dfrac{4\sqrt{17}}{17}\mathbf{k} = \dfrac{\sqrt{17}}{17}(\mathbf{i} + 4\mathbf{k})$

51. From Theorem 11.3 we have:

$\mathbf{r}(t) = (v_0 t \cos\theta)\mathbf{i} + (h + v_0 t\sin\theta - 16t^2)\mathbf{j}$

$\mathbf{v}(t) = v_0\cos\theta\mathbf{i} + (v_0\sin\theta - 32t)\mathbf{j}$

$\mathbf{a}(t) = -32\mathbf{j}$

$\mathbf{T}(t) = \dfrac{(v_0\cos\theta)\mathbf{i} + (v_0\sin\theta - 32t)\mathbf{j}}{\sqrt{v_0^2\cos^2\theta + (v_0\sin\theta - 32t)^2}}$

$\mathbf{N}(t) = \dfrac{(v_0\sin\theta - 32t)\mathbf{i} - v_0\cos\theta\mathbf{j}}{\sqrt{v_0^2\cos^2\theta + (v_0\sin\theta - 32t)^2}}$ (Motion is clockwise.)

$a_{\mathbf{T}} = \mathbf{a}\cdot\mathbf{T} = \dfrac{-32(v_0\sin\theta - 32t)}{\sqrt{v_0^2\cos^2\theta + (v_0\sin\theta - 32t)^2}}$

$a_{\mathbf{N}} = \mathbf{a}\cdot\mathbf{N} = \dfrac{32v_0\cos\theta}{\sqrt{v_0^2\cos^2\theta + (v_0\sin\theta - 32t)^2}}$

Maximum height when $v_0\sin\theta - 32t = 0$; (vertical component of velocity)

At maximum height, $a_{\mathbf{T}} = 0$ and $a_{\mathbf{N}} = 32$.

53. $\mathbf{r}(t) = \langle 10\cos 10\pi t, \ 10\sin 10\pi t, \ 4 + 4t \rangle, \ 0 \le t \le \dfrac{1}{20}$

   (a) $\mathbf{r}'(t) = \langle -100\pi\sin(10\pi t), \ 100\pi\cos(10\pi t), \ 4 \rangle$

   $\|\mathbf{r}'(t)\| = \sqrt{(100\pi)^2\sin^2(10\pi t) + (100\pi)^2\cos^2(10\pi t) + 16}$

   $= \sqrt{(100\pi)^2 + 16} = 4\sqrt{625\pi^2 + 1} \approx 314 \text{ mi/hr}$

   (b) $a_{\mathbf{T}} = 0$ and $a_{\mathbf{N}} = 1000\pi^2$

   $a_{\mathbf{T}} = 0$ because the speed is constant.

55. $\mathbf{r}(t) = (a\cos\omega t)\mathbf{i} + (a\sin\omega t)\mathbf{j}$

From Exercise 31, we know $\mathbf{a}\cdot\mathbf{T} = 0$ and $\mathbf{a}\cdot\mathbf{N} = a\omega^2$.

   (a) Let $\omega_0 = 2\omega$. Then

   $\mathbf{a}\cdot\mathbf{N} = a\omega_0^2 = a(2\omega)^2 = 4a\omega^2$

   or the centripetal acceleration is increased by a factor of 4 when the velocity is doubled.

   (b) Let $a_0 = a/2$. Then

   $\mathbf{a}\cdot\mathbf{N} = a_0\omega^2 = \left(\dfrac{a}{2}\right)\omega^2 = \left(\dfrac{1}{2}\right)a\omega^2$

   or the centripetal acceleration is halved when the radius is halved.

57. $v = \sqrt{\dfrac{9.56 \times 10^4}{4100}} \approx 4.83$ mi/sec

59. $v = \sqrt{\dfrac{9.56 \times 10^4}{4385}} \approx 4.67$ mi/sec

61. Let $\mathbf{T}(t) = \cos\phi\,\mathbf{i} + \sin\phi\,\mathbf{j}$ be the unit tangent vector. Then

$$\mathbf{T}'(t) = \frac{d\mathbf{T}}{dt} = \frac{d\mathbf{T}}{d\phi}\frac{d\phi}{dt} = -(\sin\phi\,\mathbf{i} + \cos\phi\,\mathbf{j})\frac{d\phi}{dt} = \mathbf{M}\frac{d\phi}{dt}.$$

$\mathbf{M} = -\sin\phi\,\mathbf{i} + \cos\phi\,\mathbf{j} = \cos[\phi + (\pi/2)]\mathbf{i} + \sin[\phi + (\pi/2)]\mathbf{j}$ and is rotated counterclockwise through an angle of $\pi/2$ from $\mathbf{T}$.

If $d\phi/dt > 0$, then the curve bends to the left and $\mathbf{M}$ has the same direction as $\mathbf{T}'$. Thus, $\mathbf{M}$ has the same direction as

$$\mathbf{N} = \frac{\mathbf{T}'}{\|\mathbf{T}'\|},$$

which is toward the concave side of the curve.

If $d\phi/dt < 0$, then the curve bends to the right and $\mathbf{M}$ has the opposite direction as $\mathbf{T}'$. Thus,

$$\mathbf{N} = \frac{\mathbf{T}'}{\|\mathbf{T}'\|}$$

again points to the concave side of the curve.

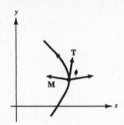

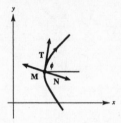

63. Using $\mathbf{a} = a_\mathbf{T}\mathbf{T} + a_\mathbf{N}\mathbf{N}$, $\mathbf{T} \times \mathbf{T} = \mathbf{O}$, and $\|\mathbf{T} \times \mathbf{N}\| = 1$, we have:

$$\mathbf{v} \times \mathbf{a} = \|\mathbf{v}\|\mathbf{T} \times (a_\mathbf{T}\mathbf{T} + a_\mathbf{N}\mathbf{N})$$

$$= \|\mathbf{v}\|a_\mathbf{T}(\mathbf{T} \times \mathbf{T}) + \|\mathbf{v}\|a_\mathbf{N}(\mathbf{T} \times \mathbf{N})$$

$$= \|\mathbf{v}\|a_\mathbf{N}(\mathbf{T} \times \mathbf{N})$$

$$\|\mathbf{v} \times \mathbf{a}\| = \|\mathbf{v}\|a_\mathbf{N}\|\mathbf{T} \times \mathbf{N}\|$$

$$= \|\mathbf{v}\|a_\mathbf{N}$$

Thus, $a_\mathbf{N} = \dfrac{\|\mathbf{v} \times \mathbf{a}\|}{\|\mathbf{v}\|}$.

Section 11.5   Arc Length and Curvature

1. $\mathbf{r}(t) = t\mathbf{i} + 3t\mathbf{j}$

$\dfrac{dx}{dt} = 1,\ \dfrac{dy}{dt} = 3,\ \dfrac{dz}{dt} = 0$

$s = \displaystyle\int_0^4 \sqrt{1 + 9}\,dt$

$= \sqrt{10}\displaystyle\int_0^4 dt$

$= \left[\sqrt{10}\,t\right]_0^4 = 4\sqrt{10}$

3. $\mathbf{r}(t) = a\cos^3 t\,\mathbf{i} + a\sin^3 t\,\mathbf{j}$

$\dfrac{dx}{dt} = -3a\cos^2 t\sin t,\ \dfrac{dy}{dt} = 3a\sin^2 t\cos t$

$s = 4\displaystyle\int_0^{\pi/2} \sqrt{[3a\cos^2 t(-\sin t)]^2 + [3a\sin^2 t\cos t]^2}\,dt$

$= 12a\displaystyle\int_0^{\pi/2} \sin t\cos t\,dt$

$= 3a\displaystyle\int_0^{\pi/2} 2\sin 2t\,dt = \left[-3a\cos 2t\right]_0^{\pi/2} = 6a$

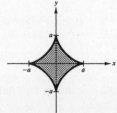

5. (a) $\mathbf{r}(t) = (v_0 \cos \theta)t\mathbf{i} + \left[h + (v_0 \sin \theta)t - \frac{1}{2}gt^2 \right]\mathbf{j}$

$\qquad = (100 \cos 45°)t\mathbf{i} + \left[3 + (100 \sin 45°)t - \frac{1}{2}(32)t^2 \right]\mathbf{j}$

$\qquad = 50\sqrt{2}t\mathbf{i} + \left[3 + 50\sqrt{2}t - 16t^2 \right]\mathbf{j}$

(b) $\mathbf{v}(t) = 50\sqrt{2}\mathbf{i} + \left(50\sqrt{2} - 32t \right)\mathbf{j}$

$\qquad 50\sqrt{2} - 32t = 0 \implies t = \dfrac{25\sqrt{2}}{16}$

$\qquad$ Maximum height: $3 + 50\sqrt{2}\left(\dfrac{25\sqrt{2}}{16} \right) - 16\left(\dfrac{25\sqrt{2}}{16} \right)^2 = 81.125 \text{ ft}$

(c) $3 + 50\sqrt{2}t - 16t^2 = 0 \implies t \approx 4.4614$

$\qquad$ Range: $50\sqrt{2}(4.4614) \approx 315.5 \text{ feet}$

(d) $s = \displaystyle\int_0^{4.4614} \sqrt{\left(50\sqrt{2}\right)^2 + \left(50\sqrt{2} - 32t\right)^2}\, dt \approx 362.9 \text{ feet}$

7. $\mathbf{r}(t) = 2t\mathbf{i} - 3t\mathbf{j} + t\mathbf{k}$

$\dfrac{dx}{dt} = 2 \quad \dfrac{dy}{dt} = -3, \quad \dfrac{dz}{dt} = 1$

$s = \displaystyle\int_0^2 \sqrt{2^2 + (-3)^2 + 1^2}\, dt$

$\quad = \displaystyle\int_0^2 \sqrt{14}\, dt = \left[\sqrt{14}\,t \right]_0^2 = 2\sqrt{14}$

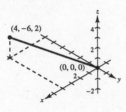

9. $\mathbf{r}(t) = a \cos t\mathbf{i} + a \sin t\mathbf{j} + bt\mathbf{k}$

$\dfrac{dx}{dt} = -a \sin t, \quad \dfrac{dy}{dt} = a \cos t, \quad \dfrac{dz}{dt} = b$

$s = \displaystyle\int_0^{2\pi} \sqrt{a^2 \sin^2 t + a^2 \cos^2 t + b^2}\, dt$

$\quad = \displaystyle\int_0^{2\pi} \sqrt{a^2 + b^2}\, dt = \left[\sqrt{a^2 + b^2}\,t \right]_0^{2\pi} = 2\pi\sqrt{a^2 + b^2}$

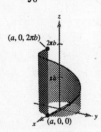

11. $\mathbf{r}(t) = t^2\mathbf{i} + t\mathbf{j} + \ln t\mathbf{k}$

$\dfrac{dx}{dt} = 2t, \quad \dfrac{dy}{dt} = 1, \quad \dfrac{dz}{dt} = \dfrac{1}{t}$

$s = \displaystyle\int_1^3 \sqrt{(2t)^2 + (1)^2 + \left(\dfrac{1}{t} \right)^2}\, dt$

$\quad = \displaystyle\int_1^3 \sqrt{\dfrac{4t^4 + t^2 + 1}{t^2}}\, dt$

$\quad = \displaystyle\int_1^3 \dfrac{\sqrt{4t^4 + t^2 + 1}}{t}\, dt \approx 8.37$

13. $\mathbf{r}(t) = t\mathbf{i} + (4 - t^2)\mathbf{j} + t^3\mathbf{k}, \quad 0 \le t \le 2$

(a) $\mathbf{r}(0) = \langle 0, 4, 0 \rangle, \quad \mathbf{r}(2) = \langle 2, 0, 8 \rangle$

$\qquad$ distance $= \sqrt{2^2 + 4^2 + 8^2} = \sqrt{84} = 2\sqrt{21} \approx 9.165$

—CONTINUED—

13. —CONTINUED—

(b) $\mathbf{r}(0) = \langle 0, 4, 0 \rangle$

$\mathbf{r}(0.5) = \langle 0.5, 3.75, .125 \rangle$

$\mathbf{r}(1) = \langle 1, 3, 1 \rangle$

$\mathbf{r}(1.5) = \langle 1.5, 1.75, 3.375 \rangle$

$\mathbf{r}(2) = \langle 2, 0, 8 \rangle$

distance $\approx \sqrt{(0.5)^2 + (.25)^2 + (.125)^2} + \sqrt{(.5)^2 + (.75)^2 + (.875)^2} + \sqrt{(0.5)^2 + (1.25)^2 + (2.375)^2} +$

$\sqrt{(0.5)^2 + (1.75)^2 + (4.625)^2}$

$\approx 0.5728 + 1.2562 + 2.7300 + 4.9702 \approx 9.529$

(c) Increase the number of line segments.

(d) Using a graphing utility, you obtain 9.57057.

15. $\mathbf{r}(t) = \langle 2 \cos t, 2 \sin t, t \rangle$

(a) $s = \displaystyle\int_0^t \sqrt{[x'(u)]^2 + [y'(u)]^2 + [z'(u)]^2} \, du$

$= \displaystyle\int_0^t \sqrt{(-2 \sin u)^2 + (2 \cos u)^2 + (1)^2} \, du$

$= \displaystyle\int_0^t \sqrt{5} \, du = \left[\sqrt{5} u \right]_0^t = \sqrt{5} t$

(b) $\dfrac{s}{\sqrt{5}} = t$

$x = 2 \cos\left(\dfrac{s}{\sqrt{5}}\right), \ y = 2 \sin\left(\dfrac{s}{\sqrt{5}}\right), \ z = \dfrac{s}{\sqrt{5}}$

$\mathbf{r}(s) = 2 \cos\left(\dfrac{s}{\sqrt{5}}\right)\mathbf{i} + 2 \sin\left(\dfrac{s}{\sqrt{5}}\right)\mathbf{j} + \dfrac{s}{\sqrt{5}}\mathbf{k}$

(c) When $s = \sqrt{5}$: $x = 2 \cos 1 \approx 1.081$

$y = 2 \sin 1 \approx 1.683$

$z = 1$

$(1.081, 1.683, 1.000)$

When $s = 4$: $x = 2 \cos \dfrac{4}{\sqrt{5}} \approx -0.433$

$y = 2 \sin \dfrac{4}{\sqrt{5}} \approx 1.953$

$z = \dfrac{4}{\sqrt{5}} \approx 1.789$

$(-0.433, 1.953, 1.789)$

(d) $\|\mathbf{r}'(s)\| = \sqrt{\left(-\dfrac{2}{\sqrt{5}} \sin\left(\dfrac{s}{\sqrt{5}}\right)\right)^2 + \left(\dfrac{2}{\sqrt{5}} \cos\left(\dfrac{s}{\sqrt{5}}\right)\right)^2 + \left(\dfrac{1}{\sqrt{5}}\right)^2} = \sqrt{\dfrac{4}{5} + \dfrac{1}{5}} = 1$

17. $\mathbf{r}(s) = \left(1 + \dfrac{\sqrt{2}}{2} s\right)\mathbf{i} + \left(1 - \dfrac{\sqrt{2}}{2} s\right)\mathbf{j}$

$\mathbf{r}'(s) = \dfrac{\sqrt{2}}{2}\mathbf{i} - \dfrac{\sqrt{2}}{2}\mathbf{j}$ and $\|\mathbf{r}'(s)\| = \sqrt{\dfrac{1}{2} + \dfrac{1}{2}} = 1$

$\mathbf{T}(s) = \dfrac{\mathbf{r}'(s)}{\|\mathbf{r}'(s)\|} = \mathbf{r}'(s)$

$\mathbf{T}'(s) = \mathbf{0} \implies K = \|\mathbf{T}'(s)\| = 0$ (The curve is a line.)

19. $\mathbf{r}(s) = 2 \cos\left(\dfrac{s}{\sqrt{5}}\right)\mathbf{i} + 2 \sin\left(\dfrac{s}{\sqrt{5}}\right)\mathbf{j} + \dfrac{s}{\sqrt{5}}\mathbf{k}$

$\mathbf{T}(s) = \mathbf{r}'(s) = -\dfrac{2}{\sqrt{5}} \sin\left(\dfrac{s}{\sqrt{5}}\right)\mathbf{i} + \dfrac{2}{\sqrt{5}} \cos\left(\dfrac{s}{\sqrt{5}}\right)\mathbf{j} + \dfrac{1}{\sqrt{5}}\mathbf{k}$

$\mathbf{T}'(s) = -\dfrac{2}{5} \cos\left(\dfrac{s}{\sqrt{5}}\right)\mathbf{i} - \dfrac{2}{5} \sin\left(\dfrac{s}{\sqrt{5}}\right)\mathbf{j}$

$K = \|\mathbf{T}'(s)\| = \dfrac{2}{5}$

21. $\mathbf{r}(t) = 4t\mathbf{i} - 2t\mathbf{j}$

$\mathbf{v}(t) = 4\mathbf{i} - 2\mathbf{j}$

$\mathbf{T}(t) = \dfrac{1}{\sqrt{5}}(2\mathbf{i} - \mathbf{j})$

$\mathbf{T}'(t) = 0$

$K = \dfrac{\|\mathbf{T}'(t)\|}{\|\mathbf{r}'(t)\|} = 0$ (The curve is a line.)

23. $\mathbf{r}(t) = t\mathbf{i} + \dfrac{1}{t}\mathbf{j}$

$\mathbf{v}(t) = \mathbf{i} - \dfrac{1}{t^2}\mathbf{j}$

$\mathbf{v}(1) = \mathbf{i} - \mathbf{j}$

$\mathbf{a}(t) = \dfrac{2}{t^3}\mathbf{j}$

$\mathbf{a}(1) = 2\mathbf{j}$

$\mathbf{T}(t) = \dfrac{t^2\mathbf{i} - \mathbf{j}}{\sqrt{t^4 + 1}}$

$\mathbf{N}(t) = \dfrac{1}{(t^4 + 1)^{1/2}}(\mathbf{i} + t^2\mathbf{j})$

$\mathbf{N}(1) = \dfrac{1}{\sqrt{2}}(\mathbf{i} + \mathbf{j})$

$K = \dfrac{\mathbf{a} \cdot \mathbf{N}}{\|\mathbf{v}\|^2} = \dfrac{\sqrt{2}}{2}$

25. $\mathbf{r}(t) = 4\cos(2\pi t)\mathbf{i} + 4\sin(2\pi t)\mathbf{j}$

$\mathbf{r}'(t) = -8\pi\sin(2\pi t)\mathbf{i} + 8\pi\cos(2\pi t)\mathbf{j}$

$\mathbf{T}(t) = -\sin(2\pi t)\mathbf{i} + \cos(2\pi t)\mathbf{j}$

$\mathbf{T}'(t) = -2\pi\cos(2\pi t)\mathbf{i} - 2\pi\sin(2\pi t)\mathbf{j}$

$K = \dfrac{\|\mathbf{T}'(t)\|}{\|\mathbf{r}'(t)\|} = \dfrac{2\pi}{8\pi} = \dfrac{1}{4}$

27. $\mathbf{r}(t) = a\cos(\omega t)\mathbf{i} + a\sin(\omega t)\mathbf{j}$

$\mathbf{r}'(t) = -a\omega\sin(\omega t)\mathbf{i} + a\omega\cos(\omega t)\mathbf{j}$

$\mathbf{T}(t) = -\sin(\omega t)\mathbf{i} + \cos(\omega t)\mathbf{j}$

$\mathbf{T}'(t) = -\omega\cos(\omega t)\mathbf{i} - \omega\sin(\omega t)\mathbf{j}$

$K = \dfrac{\|\mathbf{T}'(t)\|}{\|\mathbf{r}'(t)\|} = \dfrac{\omega}{a\omega} = \dfrac{1}{a}$

29. $\mathbf{r}(t) = e^t\cos t\,\mathbf{i} + e^t\sin t\,\mathbf{j}$

$\mathbf{r}'(t) = (-e^t\sin t + e^t\cos t)\mathbf{i} + (e^t\cos t + e^t\sin t)\mathbf{j}$

$\mathbf{T}(t) = \dfrac{1}{\sqrt{2}}[(-\sin t + \cos t)\mathbf{i} + (\cos t + \sin t)\mathbf{j}]$

$\mathbf{T}'(t) = \dfrac{1}{\sqrt{2}}[(-\cos t - \sin t)\mathbf{i} + (-\sin t + \cos t)\mathbf{j}]$

$K = \dfrac{\|\mathbf{T}'(t)\|}{\|\mathbf{r}'(t)\|} = \dfrac{1}{\sqrt{2}e^t} = \dfrac{\sqrt{2}}{2}e^{-t}$

31. $\mathbf{r}(t) = \langle\cos\omega t + \omega t\sin\omega t,\ \sin\omega t - \omega t\cos\omega t\rangle$

From Exercise 21, Section 11.4, we have:

$\mathbf{a} \cdot \mathbf{N} = \omega^3 t$

$K = \dfrac{\mathbf{a}(t) \cdot \mathbf{N}(t)}{\|\mathbf{v}\|^2} = \dfrac{\omega^3 t}{\omega^4 t^2} = \dfrac{1}{\omega t}$

33. $\mathbf{r}(t) = t\mathbf{i} + t^2\mathbf{j} + \dfrac{t^2}{2}\mathbf{k}$

$\mathbf{r}'(t) = \mathbf{i} + 2t\mathbf{j} + t\mathbf{k}$

$\mathbf{T}(t) = \dfrac{\mathbf{i} + 2t\mathbf{j} + t\mathbf{k}}{\sqrt{1 + 5t^2}}$

$\mathbf{T}'(t) = \dfrac{-5t\mathbf{i} + 2\mathbf{j} + \mathbf{k}}{(1 + 5t^2)^{3/2}}$

$K = \dfrac{\|\mathbf{T}'(t)\|}{\|\mathbf{r}'(t)\|}$

$= \dfrac{\dfrac{\sqrt{5}}{(1 + 5t^2)}}{\sqrt{1 + 5t^2}} = \dfrac{\sqrt{5}}{(1 + 5t^2)^{3/2}}$

35. $\mathbf{r}(t) = 4t\mathbf{i} + 3\cos t\,\mathbf{j} + 3\sin t\,\mathbf{k}$

$\mathbf{r}'(t) = 4\mathbf{i} - 3\sin t\,\mathbf{j} + 3\cos t\,\mathbf{k}$

$\mathbf{T}(t) = \dfrac{1}{5}[4\mathbf{i} - 3\sin t\,\mathbf{j} + 3\cos t\,\mathbf{k}]$

$\mathbf{T}'(t) = \dfrac{1}{5}[-3\cos t\,\mathbf{j} - 3\sin t\,\mathbf{k}]$

$K = \dfrac{\|\mathbf{T}'(t)\|}{\|\mathbf{r}'(t)\|} = \dfrac{3/5}{5} = \dfrac{3}{25}$

37. $y = 3x - 2$

Since $y'' = 0$, $K = 0$, and the radius of curvature is undefined.

39. $y = 2x^2 + 3$

$y' = 4x$

$y'' = 4$

$K = \dfrac{4}{[1 + (-4)^2]^{3/2}} = \dfrac{4}{17^{3/2}} \approx 0.057$

$\dfrac{1}{K} = \dfrac{17^{3/2}}{4} \approx 17.523$ (radius of curvature)

41. $y = \sqrt{a^2 - x^2}$

$y' = \dfrac{-x}{\sqrt{a^2 - x^2}}$

$y'' = \dfrac{-(2x^2 - a^2)}{(a^2 - x^2)^{3/2}}$

At $x = 0$: $y' = 0$

$y'' = \dfrac{1}{a}$

$K = \dfrac{1/a}{(1 + 0^2)^{3/2}} = \dfrac{1}{a}$

$\dfrac{1}{K} = a$ (radius of curvature)

43. (a) Point on circle: $\left(\dfrac{\pi}{2}, 1\right)$

Center: $\left(\dfrac{\pi}{2}, 0\right)$

Equation: $\left(x - \dfrac{\pi}{2}\right)^2 + y^2 = 1$

(b) The circles have different radii since the curvature is different and

$r = \dfrac{1}{K}$.

45. $y = x + \dfrac{1}{x}, y' = 1 - \dfrac{1}{x^2}, y'' = \dfrac{2}{x^3}$

$K = \dfrac{2}{(1 + 0^2)^{3/2}} = 2$

Radius of curvature $= 1/2$. Since the tangent line is horizontal at $(1, 2)$, the normal line is vertical. The center of the circle is $1/2$ unit above the point $(1, 2)$ at $(1, 5/2)$.

Circle: $(x - 1)^2 + \left(y - \dfrac{5}{2}\right)^2 = \dfrac{1}{4}$

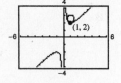

47. $y = e^x,$ $x = 0$

$y' = e^x,$ $y'' = e^x$

$y'(0) = 1,$ $y''(0) = 1$

$K = \dfrac{1}{(1 + 1^2)^{3/2}} = \dfrac{1}{2^{3/2}} = \dfrac{1}{2\sqrt{2}},\ r = \dfrac{1}{K} = 2\sqrt{2}$

The slope of the tangent line at $(0, 1)$ is $y'(0) = 1$.

The slope of the normal line is -1.

Equation of normal line: $y - 1 = -x$ or $y = -x + 1$

The center of the circle is on the normal line $2\sqrt{2}$ units away from the point $(0, 1)$.

$$\sqrt{(0 - x)^2 + (1 - y)^2} = 2\sqrt{2}$$

$$x^2 + x^2 = 8$$

$$x^2 = 4$$

$$x = \pm 2$$

Since the circle is above the curve, $x = -2$ and $y = 3$.

Center of circle: $(-2, 3)$

Equation of circle: $(x + 2)^2 + (y - 3)^2 = 8$

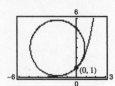

49.

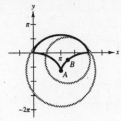

51. $y = (x - 1)^2 + 3$, $y' = 2(x - 1)$, $y'' = 2$

$$K = \frac{2}{(1 + [2(x - 1)]^2)^{3/2}} = \frac{2}{[1 + 4(x - 1)^2]^{3/2}}$$

(a) K is maximum when $x = 1$ or at the vertex $(1, 3)$.

(b) $\lim_{x \to \infty} K = 0$

53. $y = x^{2/3}$, $y' = \dfrac{2}{3}x^{-1/3}$, $y'' = -\dfrac{2}{9}x^{-4/3}$

$$K = \left| \frac{(-2/9)x^{-4/3}}{[1 + (4/9)x^{-2/3}]^{3/2}} \right| = \left| \frac{6}{x^{1/3}(9x^{2/3} + 4)^{3/2}} \right|$$

(a) $K \Rightarrow \infty$ as $x \Rightarrow 0$. No maximum

(b) $\lim_{x \to \infty} K = 0$

55. $y = (x - 1)^3 + 3$

$y' = 3(x - 1)^2$

$y'' = 6(x - 1)$

$$K = \frac{|y''|}{[1 + (y')^2]^{3/2}} = \frac{|6(x - 1)|}{[1 + 9(x - 1)^4]^{3/2}} = 0 \text{ at } x = 1.$$

Curvature is 0 at $(1, 3)$.

57. $K = \dfrac{|y''|}{[1 + (y')^2]^{3/2}}$

The curvature is zero when $y'' = 0$.

59. $s = \displaystyle\int_a^b \|\mathbf{r}'(t)\| \, dt$

61. The curve is a line.

63. Endpoints of the major axis: $(\pm 2, 0)$

Endpoints of the minor axis: $(0, \pm 1)$

$x^2 + 4y^2 = 4$

$2x + 8yy' = 0$

$$y' = -\frac{x}{4y}$$

$$y'' = \frac{(4y)(-1) - (-x)(4y')}{16y^2} = \frac{-4y - (x^2/y)}{16y^2} = \frac{-(4y^2 + x^2)}{16y^3} = \frac{-1}{4y^3}$$

$$K = \frac{|-1/4y^3|}{[1 + (-x/4y)^2]^{3/2}} = \frac{|-16|}{(16y^2 + x^2)^{3/2}} = \frac{16}{(12y^2 + 4)^{3/2}} = \frac{16}{(16 - 3x^2)^{3/2}}$$

Therefore, since $-2 \le x \le 2$, K is largest when $x = \pm 2$ and smallest when $x = 0$.

65. $f(x) = x^4 - x^2$

(a) $K = \dfrac{2|6x^2 - 1|}{[16x^6 - 16x^4 + 4x^2 + 1]^{3/2}}$

(b) For $x = 0$, $K = 2$. $f(0) = 0$. At $(0, 0)$, the circle of curvature has radius $\frac{1}{2}$. Using the symmetry of the graph of f, you obtain

$$x^2 + \left(y + \frac{1}{2}\right)^2 = \frac{1}{4}.$$

For $x = 1$, $K = \left(2\sqrt{5}\right)/5$. $f(1) = 0$. At $(1, 0)$, the circle of curvature has radius

$$\frac{\sqrt{5}}{2} = \frac{1}{K}.$$

Using the graph of f, you see that the center of curvature is $\left(0, \frac{1}{2}\right)$. Thus,

$$x^2 + \left(y - \frac{1}{2}\right)^2 = \frac{5}{4}.$$

To graph these circles, use

$$y = -\frac{1}{2} \pm \sqrt{\frac{1}{4} - x^2} \quad \text{and} \quad y = \frac{1}{2} \pm \sqrt{\frac{5}{4} - x^2}.$$

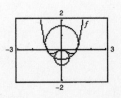

—CONTINUED—

65. **—CONTINUED—**

(c) The curvature tends to be greatest near the extrema of f, and K decreases as $x \to \pm\infty$. However, f and K do not have the same critical numbers.

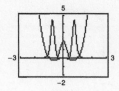

Critical numbers of f: $x = 0, \pm\dfrac{\sqrt{2}}{2} \approx \pm 0.7071$

Critical numbers of K: $x = 0, \pm.7647, \pm 0.4082$

67. (a) Imagine dropping the circle $x^2 + (y - k)^2 = 16$ into the parabola $y = x^2$. The circle will drop to the point where the tangents to the circle and parabola are equal.

$$y = x^2 \quad \text{and} \quad x^2 + (y - k)^2 = 16 \implies x^2 + (x^2 - k)^2 = 16$$

Taking derivatives, $2x + 2(y - k)y' = 0$ and $y' = 2x$. Hence,

$$(y - k)y' = -x \implies y' = \frac{-x}{y - k}.$$

Thus,

$$\frac{-x}{y - k} = 2x \implies -x = 2x(y - k) \implies -1 = 2(x^2 - k) \implies x^2 - k = -\frac{1}{2}.$$

Thus,

$$x^2 + (x^2 - k)^2 = x^2 + \left(-\frac{1}{2}\right)^2 = 16 \implies x^2 = 15.75.$$

Finally, $k = x^2 + \frac{1}{2} = 16.25$, and the center of the circle is 16.25 units from the vertex of the parabola. Since the radius of the circle is 4, the circle is 12.25 units from the vertex.

(b) In 2-space, the parabola $z = y^2$ (or $z = x^2$) has a curvature of $K = 2$ at $(0, 0)$. The radius of the largest sphere that will touch the vertex has radius $= 1/K = \frac{1}{2}$.

69. Given $y = f(x)$: $K = \dfrac{|y''|}{(1 + [y']^2)^{3/2}}$

$$R = \frac{1}{K}$$

The center of the circle is on the normal line at a distance of R from (x, y).

Equation of normal line: $y - y_0 = -\dfrac{1}{y'}(x - x_0)$

$$\sqrt{(x - x_0)^2 + \left[-\frac{1}{y'}(x - x_0)\right]^2} = \frac{(1 + [y']^2)^{3/2}}{|y''|}$$

$$(x - x_0)^2\left[1 + \frac{1}{(y')^2}\right] = \frac{(1 + [y']^2)^3}{(y'')^2}$$

$$(x - x_0)^2 = \frac{(y')^2(1 + [y']^2)^2}{(y'')^2}$$

$$x - x_0 = \frac{y'(1 + [y']^2)}{y''} = y'z$$

$$x_0 = x - y'z$$

$$y - y_0 = -\frac{1}{y'}(x - (x - y'z)) = -z$$

$$y_0 = y + z$$

Thus, $(x_0, y_0) = (x - y'z, y + z)$.

For $y = e^x$, $y' = e^x$, $y'' = e^x$, $z = \dfrac{1 + e^{2x}}{e^x} = e^{-x} + e^x$.

When $x = 0$: $x_0 = x - y'z = 0 - (1)(2) = -2$

$$y_0 = y + z = 1 + 2 = 3$$

Center of curvature: $(-2, 3)$

(See Exercise 47)

71. $r = 1 + \sin\theta$

$r' = \cos\theta$

$r'' = -\sin\theta$

$K = \dfrac{|2(r')^2 - rr'' + r^2|}{[(r')^2 + r^2]^{3/2}}$

$\quad = \dfrac{|2\cos^2\theta - (1 + \sin\theta)(-\sin\theta) + (1 + \sin\theta)^2|}{\sqrt{[\cos^2\theta + (1 + \sin\theta)^2]^3}}$

$\quad = \dfrac{3(1 + \sin\theta)}{\sqrt{8(1 + \sin\theta)^3}} = \dfrac{3}{2\sqrt{2(1 + \sin\theta)}}$

73. $r = a\sin\theta$

$r' = a\cos\theta$

$r'' = -a\sin\theta$

$K = \dfrac{|2(r\omega)^2 - rr'' + r^2|}{[(r')^2 + r^2]^{3/2}}$

$\quad = \dfrac{|2a^2\cos^2\theta + a^2\sin^2\theta + a^2\sin^2\theta|}{\sqrt{[a^2\cos^2\theta + a^2\sin^2\theta]^3}}$

$\quad = \dfrac{2a^2}{a^3} = \dfrac{2}{a}, a > 0$

75. $r = e^{a\theta}, a > 0$

$r' = ae^{a\theta}$

$r'' = a^2 e^{a\theta}$

$K = \dfrac{|2(r')^2 - rr'' + r^2|}{[(r')^2 + r^2]^{3/2}} = \dfrac{|2a^2 e^{2a\theta} - a^2 e^{2a\theta} + e^{2a\theta}|}{[a^2 e^{2a\theta} + e^{2a\theta}]^{3/2}}$

$\quad = \dfrac{1}{e^{a\theta}\sqrt{a^2 + 1}}$

(a) As $\theta \Rightarrow \infty$, $K \Rightarrow 0$.

(b) As $a \Rightarrow \infty$, $K \Rightarrow 0$.

77. $r = 4\sin 2\theta$

$r' = 8\cos 2\theta$

At the pole: $K = \dfrac{2}{|r'(0)|} = \dfrac{2}{8} = \dfrac{1}{4}$

79. $x = f(t)$

$\quad y = g(t)$

$y' = \dfrac{dy}{dx} = \dfrac{\dfrac{dy}{dt}}{\dfrac{dx}{dt}} = \dfrac{g'(t)}{f'(t)}$

$y'' = \dfrac{\dfrac{d}{dt}\left[\dfrac{g'(t)}{f'(t)}\right]}{\dfrac{dx}{dt}} = \dfrac{\dfrac{f'(t)g''(t) - g'(t)f''(t)}{[f'(t)]^2}}{f'(t)}$

$\quad = \dfrac{f'(t)g''(t) - g'(t)f''(t)}{[f'(t)]^3}$

$K = \dfrac{|y''|}{[1 + (y')^2]^{3/2}} = \dfrac{\left|\dfrac{f'(t)g''(t) - g'(t)f''(t)}{[f'(t)]^3}\right|}{\left[1 + \left(\dfrac{g'(t)}{f'(t)}\right)^2\right]^{3/2}}$

$\quad = \dfrac{\left|\dfrac{f'(t)g''(t) - g'(t)f''(t)}{[f'(t)]^3}\right|}{\sqrt{\left\{\dfrac{[f'(t)]^2 + [g'(t)]^2}{[f'(t)]^2}\right\}^3}}$

$\quad = \dfrac{|f'(t)g''(t) - g'(t)f''(t)|}{([f'(t)]^2 + [g'(t)]^2)^{3/2}}$

81. $x(\theta) = a(\theta - \sin\theta)$ $y(\theta) = a(1 - \cos\theta)$

$x'(\theta) = a(1 - \cos\theta)$ $y'(\theta) = a\sin\theta$

$x''(\theta) = a\sin\theta$ $y''(\theta) = a\cos\theta$

$K = \dfrac{|x'(\theta)y''(\theta) - y'(\theta)x''(\theta)|}{[x'(\theta)^2 + y'(\theta)^2]^{3/2}}$

$\quad = \dfrac{|a^2(1 - \cos\theta)\cos\theta - a^2\sin^2\theta|}{[a^2(1 - \cos\theta)^2 + a^2\sin^2\theta]^{3/2}}$

$\quad = \dfrac{1}{a}\dfrac{|\cos\theta - 1|}{[2 - 2\cos\theta]^{3/2}}$

$\quad = \dfrac{1}{a}\dfrac{1 - \cos\theta}{2\sqrt{2}[1 - \cos\theta]^{3/2}}$ $(1 - \cos \geq 0)$

$\quad = \dfrac{1}{2a\sqrt{2 - 2\cos\theta}} = \dfrac{1}{4a}\csc\left(\dfrac{\theta}{2}\right)$

Minimum: $\dfrac{1}{4a}$ $(\theta = \pi)$

Maximum: none $(K \to \infty$ as $\theta \to 0)$

83. $a_N = mK\left(\dfrac{ds}{dt}\right)^2 = \left(\dfrac{5500\text{ lb}}{32\text{ ft/sec}^2}\right)\left(\dfrac{1}{100\text{ ft}}\right)\left(\dfrac{30(5280)\text{ ft}}{3600\text{ sec}}\right)^2 = 3327.5\text{ lb}$

85. Let $\mathbf{r} = x(t)\mathbf{i} + y(t)\mathbf{j} + z(t)\mathbf{k}$. Then $r = \|\mathbf{r}\| = \sqrt{[x(t)]^2 + [y(t)]^2 + [z(t)]^2}$ and $\mathbf{r}' = x'(t)\mathbf{i} + y'(t)\mathbf{j} + z'(t)\mathbf{k}$. Then,

$$r\left(\frac{dr}{dt}\right) = \sqrt{[x(t)]^2 + [y(t)]^2 + [z(t)]^2}\left[\frac{1}{2}\{[x(t)]^2 + [y(t)]^2 + [z(t)]^2\}^{-1/2} \cdot (2x(t)x'(t) + 2y(t)y'(t) + 2z(t)z'(t))\right]$$

$$= x(t)x'(t) + y(t)y'(t) + z(t)z'(t) = \mathbf{r} \cdot \mathbf{r}'.$$

87. Let $\mathbf{r} = x\mathbf{i} + y\mathbf{j} + z\mathbf{k}$ where x, y, and z are functions of t, and $r = \|\mathbf{r}\|$.

$$\frac{d}{dt}\left[\frac{\mathbf{r}}{r}\right] = \frac{r\mathbf{r}' - \mathbf{r}(dr/dt)}{r^2} = \frac{r\mathbf{r}' - \mathbf{r}[(\mathbf{r} \cdot \mathbf{r}')/r]}{r^2} = \frac{r^2\mathbf{r}' - (\mathbf{r} \cdot \mathbf{r}')\mathbf{r}}{r^3} \quad \text{(using Exercise 77)}$$

$$= \frac{(x^2 + y^2 + z^2)(x'\mathbf{i} + y'\mathbf{j} + z'\mathbf{k}) - (xx' + yy' + zz')(x\mathbf{i} + y\mathbf{j} + z\mathbf{k})}{r^3}$$

$$= \frac{1}{r^3}[(x'y^2 + x'z^2 - xyy' - xzz')\mathbf{i} + (x^2y' + z^2y' - xx'y - zz'y)\mathbf{j} + (x^2z' + y^2z' - xx'z - yy'z)\mathbf{k}]$$

$$= \frac{1}{r^3}\begin{vmatrix} \mathbf{i} & \mathbf{j} & \mathbf{k} \\ yz' - y'z & -(xz' - x'z) & xy' - x'y \\ x & y & z \end{vmatrix} = \frac{1}{r^3}\{[\mathbf{r} \times \mathbf{r}'] \times \mathbf{r}\}$$

89. From Exercise 86, we have concluded that planetary motion is planar. Assume that the planet moves in the xy-plane with the sun at the origin. From Exercise 88, we have

$$\mathbf{r}' \times \mathbf{L} = GM\left(\frac{\mathbf{r}}{r} + \mathbf{e}\right).$$

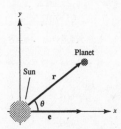

Since $\mathbf{r}' \times \mathbf{L}$ and $\mathbf{r}$ are both perpendicular to $\mathbf{L}$, so is $\mathbf{e}$. Thus, $\mathbf{e}$ lies in the xy-plane. Situate the coordinate system so that $\mathbf{e}$ lies along the positive x-axis and θ is the angle between $\mathbf{e}$ and $\mathbf{r}$. Let $e = \|\mathbf{e}\|$. Then $\mathbf{r} \cdot \mathbf{e} = \|\mathbf{r}\|\,\|\mathbf{e}\|\cos\theta = re\cos\theta$. Also,

$$\|\mathbf{L}\|^2 = \mathbf{L} \cdot \mathbf{L} = (\mathbf{r} \times \mathbf{r}') \cdot \mathbf{L}$$

$$= \mathbf{r} \cdot (\mathbf{r}' \times \mathbf{L}) = \mathbf{r} \cdot \left[GM\left(\mathbf{e} + \frac{\mathbf{r}}{r}\right)\right] = GM\left[\mathbf{r} \cdot \mathbf{e} + \frac{\mathbf{r} \cdot \mathbf{r}}{r}\right] = GM[re\cos\theta + r]$$

Thus,

$$\frac{\|\mathbf{L}\|^2/GM}{1 + e\cos\theta} = r$$

and the planetary motion is a conic section. Since the planet returns to its initial position periodically, the conic is an ellipse.

91. $A = \dfrac{1}{2}\displaystyle\int_{\alpha}^{\beta} r^2\, d\theta$

Thus,

$$\frac{dA}{dt} = \frac{dA}{d\theta}\frac{d\theta}{dt} = \frac{1}{2}r^2\frac{d\theta}{dt} = \frac{1}{2}\|\mathbf{L}\|$$

and $\mathbf{r}$ sweeps out area at a constant rate.

Review Exercises for Chapter 11

1. $\mathbf{r}(t) = t\mathbf{i} + \csc t\mathbf{k}$

   (a) Domain: $t \neq n\pi$, n an integer

   (b) Continuous except at $t = n\pi$, n an integer

3. $\mathbf{r}(t) = \ln t\mathbf{i} + t\mathbf{j} + t\mathbf{k}$

   (a) Domain: $(0, \infty)$

   (b) Continuous for all $t > 0$

5. (a) $\mathbf{r}(0) = \mathbf{i}$

(b) $\mathbf{r}(-2) = -3\mathbf{i} + 4\mathbf{j} + \frac{8}{3}\mathbf{k}$

(c) $\mathbf{r}(c - 1) = (2(c - 1) + 1)\mathbf{i} + (c - 1)^2\mathbf{j} - \frac{1}{3}(c - 1)^3\mathbf{k}$

$\qquad = (2c - 1)\mathbf{i} + (c - 1)^2\mathbf{j} - \frac{1}{3}(c - 1)^3\mathbf{k}$

(d) $\mathbf{r}(1 + \Delta t) - \mathbf{r}(1) = ([2(1 + \Delta t) + 1]\mathbf{i} + [1 + \Delta t]^2\mathbf{j} - \frac{1}{3}[1 + \Delta t]^3\mathbf{k}) - (3\mathbf{i} + \mathbf{j} - \frac{1}{3}\mathbf{k})$

$\qquad = 2\Delta t\mathbf{i} + \Delta t(\Delta t + 2)\mathbf{j} - \frac{1}{3}(\Delta t^3 + 3\Delta t^2 + 3\Delta t)\mathbf{k}$

7. $\mathbf{r}(t) = \cos t\mathbf{i} + 2\sin^2 t\mathbf{j}$

$x(t) = \cos t,\ y(t) = 2\sin^2 t$

$\qquad x^2 + \dfrac{y}{2} = 1$

$\qquad\qquad y = 2(1 - x^2)$

$-1 \leq x \leq 1$

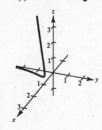

9. $\mathbf{r}(t) = \mathbf{i} + t\mathbf{j} + t^2\mathbf{k}$

$x = 1$

$y = t$

$z = t^2 \Longrightarrow z = y^2$

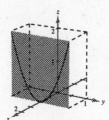

11. $\mathbf{r}(t) = \mathbf{i} + \sin t\mathbf{j} + \mathbf{k}$

$x = 1,\ y = \sin t,\ z = 1$

t	0	$\dfrac{\pi}{2}$	π	$\dfrac{3\pi}{2}$
x	1	1	1	1
y	0	1	0	-1
z	1	1	1	1

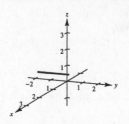

13. $\mathbf{r}(t) = t\mathbf{i} + \ln t\mathbf{j} + \frac{1}{2}t^2\mathbf{k}$

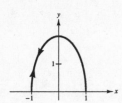

15. One possible answer is:

$\qquad \mathbf{r}_1(t) = 4t\mathbf{i} + 3t\mathbf{j}, \qquad 0 \leq t \leq 1$

$\qquad \mathbf{r}_2(t) = 4\mathbf{i} + (3 - t)\mathbf{j}, \qquad 0 \leq t \leq 3$

$\qquad \mathbf{r}_3(t) = (4 - t)\mathbf{i}, \qquad 0 \leq t \leq 4$

17. The vector joining the points is $\langle 7, 4, -10 \rangle$. One path is

$\qquad \mathbf{r}(t) = \langle -2 + 7t, -3 + 4t, 8 - 10t \rangle$.

19. $z = x^2 + y^2,\ x + y = 0,\ t = x$

$\qquad x = t,\ y = -t,\ z = 2t^2$

$\qquad\qquad \mathbf{r}(t) = t\mathbf{i} - t\mathbf{j} + 2t^2\mathbf{k}$

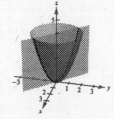

21. $\displaystyle\lim_{t \to 2^-} (t^2\mathbf{i} + \sqrt{4 - t^2}\mathbf{j} + \mathbf{k}) = 4\mathbf{i} + \mathbf{k}$

23. $\mathbf{r}(t) = 3t\mathbf{i} + (t-1)\mathbf{j}$, $\mathbf{u}(t) = t\mathbf{i} + t^2\mathbf{j} + \frac{2}{3}t^3\mathbf{k}$

(a) $\mathbf{r}'(t) = 3\mathbf{i} + \mathbf{j}$

(b) $\mathbf{r}''(t) = \mathbf{0}$

(c) $\mathbf{r}(t) \cdot \mathbf{u}(t) = 3t^2 + t^2(t-1) = t^3 + 2t^2$

$D_t[\mathbf{r}(t) \cdot \mathbf{u}(t)] = 3t^2 + 4t$

(d) $\mathbf{u}(t) - 2\mathbf{r}(t) = -5t\mathbf{i} + (t^2 - 2t + 2)\mathbf{j} + \frac{2}{3}t^3\mathbf{k}$

$D_t[\mathbf{u}(t) - 2\mathbf{r}(t)] = -5\mathbf{i} + (2t - 2)\mathbf{j} + 2t^2\mathbf{k}$

(e) $\|\mathbf{r}(t)\| = \sqrt{10t^2 - 2t + 1}$

$D_t[\|\mathbf{r}(t)\|] = \dfrac{10t - 1}{\sqrt{10t^2 - 2t + 1}}$

(f) $\mathbf{r}(t) \times \mathbf{u}(t) = \frac{2}{3}(t^4 - t^3)\mathbf{i} - 2t^4\mathbf{j} + (3t^3 - t^2 + t)\mathbf{k}$

$D_t[\mathbf{r}(t) \times \mathbf{u}(t)] = \left(\frac{8}{3}t^3 - 2t^2\right)\mathbf{i} - 8t^3\mathbf{j} + (9t^2 - 2t + 1)\mathbf{k}$

25. $x(t)$ and $y(t)$ are increasing functions at $t = t_0$, and $z(t)$ is a decreasing function at $t = t_0$.

27. $\displaystyle\int (\cos t\mathbf{i} + t\cos t\mathbf{j})\, dt = \sin t\mathbf{i} + (t\sin t + \cos t)\mathbf{j} + \mathbf{C}$

29. $\displaystyle\int \|\cos t\mathbf{i} + \sin t\mathbf{j} + t\mathbf{k}\|\, dt = \int \sqrt{1 + t^2}\, dt = \frac{1}{2}\left[t\sqrt{1 + t^2} + \ln|t + \sqrt{1 + t^2}|\right] + \mathbf{C}$

31. $\mathbf{r}(t) = \displaystyle\int (2t\mathbf{i} + e^t\mathbf{j} + e^{-t}\mathbf{k})\, dt = t^2\mathbf{i} + e^t\mathbf{j} - e^{-t}\mathbf{k} + \mathbf{C}$

$\mathbf{r}(0) = \mathbf{j} - \mathbf{k} + \mathbf{C} = \mathbf{i} + 3\mathbf{j} - 5\mathbf{k} \Rightarrow \mathbf{C} = \mathbf{i} + 2\mathbf{j} - 4\mathbf{k}$

$\mathbf{r}(t) = (t^2 + 1)\mathbf{i} + (e^t + 2)\mathbf{j} - (e^{-t} + 4)\mathbf{k}$

33. $\displaystyle\int_{-2}^{2} (3t\mathbf{i} + 2t^2\mathbf{j} - t^3\mathbf{k})\, dt = \left[\frac{3t^2}{2}\mathbf{i} + \frac{2t^3}{3}\mathbf{j} - \frac{t^4}{4}\mathbf{k}\right]_{-2}^{2} = \frac{32}{3}\mathbf{j}$

35. $\displaystyle\int_{0}^{2} (e^{t/2}\mathbf{i} - 3t^2\mathbf{j} - \mathbf{k})\, dt = \left[2e^{t/2}\mathbf{i} - t^3\mathbf{j} - t\mathbf{k}\right]_{0}^{2} = (2e - 2)\mathbf{i} - 8\mathbf{j} - 2\mathbf{k}$

37. $\mathbf{r}(t) = \langle \cos^3 t, \sin^3 t, 3t \rangle$

$\mathbf{v}(t) = \mathbf{r}'(t) = \langle -3\cos^2 t \sin t, 3\sin^2 t \cos t, 3 \rangle$

$\|\mathbf{v}(t)\| = \sqrt{9\cos^4 t \sin^2 t + 9\sin^4 t \cos^2 t + 9}$

$= 3\sqrt{\cos^2 t \sin^2 t(\cos^2 t + \sin^2 t) + 1}$

$= 3\sqrt{\cos^2 t \sin^2 t + 1}$

$\mathbf{a}(t) = \mathbf{v}'(t) = \langle -6\cos t(-\sin^2 t) + (-3\cos^2 t)\cos t,\ 6\sin t \cos^2 t + 3\sin^2 t(-\sin t),\ 0 \rangle$

$= \langle 3\cos t(2\sin^2 t - \cos^2 t),\ 3\sin t(2\cos^2 t - \sin^2 t),\ 0 \rangle$

39. $\mathbf{r}(t) = \left\langle \ln(t - 3), t^2, \frac{1}{2}t \right\rangle$, $t_0 = 4$

$\mathbf{r}'(t) = \left\langle \dfrac{1}{t - 3}, 2t, \dfrac{1}{2} \right\rangle$

$\mathbf{r}'(4) = \left\langle 1, 8, \dfrac{1}{2} \right\rangle$ direction numbers

Since $\mathbf{r}(4) = \langle 0, 16, 2 \rangle$, the parametric equations are

$x = t$, $y = 16 + 8t$, $z = 2 + \frac{1}{2}t$.

$\mathbf{r}(t_0 + 0.1) = \mathbf{r}(4.1) \approx \langle 0.1, 16.8, 2.05 \rangle$

41. Range $= x = \dfrac{v_0^2}{32}\sin 2\theta = \dfrac{(75)^2}{32}\sin 60° \approx 152$ feet

43. Range $= x = \dfrac{v_0^2}{9.8}\sin 2\theta = 80 \Rightarrow v_0 = \sqrt{\dfrac{(80)(9.8)}{\sin 40°}} \approx 34.9$ m/sec

45. $\mathbf{r}(t) = 5t\mathbf{i}$

$\mathbf{v}(t) = 5\mathbf{i}$

$\|\mathbf{v}(t)\| = 5$

$\mathbf{a}(t) = \mathbf{0}$

$\mathbf{T}(t) = \mathbf{i}$

$\mathbf{N}(t)$ does not exist

$\mathbf{a} \cdot \mathbf{T} = 0$

$\mathbf{a} \cdot \mathbf{N}$ does not exist

(The curve is a line.)

47. $\mathbf{r}(t) = t\mathbf{i} + \sqrt{t}\mathbf{j}$

$\mathbf{v}(t) = \mathbf{i} + \dfrac{1}{2\sqrt{t}}\mathbf{j}$

$\|\mathbf{v}(t)\| = \dfrac{\sqrt{4t+1}}{2\sqrt{t}}$

$\mathbf{a}(t) = -\dfrac{1}{4t\sqrt{t}}\mathbf{j}$

$\mathbf{T}(t) = \dfrac{\mathbf{i} + (1/2\sqrt{t})\mathbf{j}}{(\sqrt{4t+1})/2\sqrt{t}} = \dfrac{2\sqrt{t}\mathbf{i} + \mathbf{j}}{\sqrt{4t+1}}$

$\mathbf{N}(t) = \dfrac{\mathbf{i} - 2\sqrt{t}\mathbf{j}}{\sqrt{4t+1}}$

$\mathbf{a} \cdot \mathbf{T} = \dfrac{-1}{4t\sqrt{t}\sqrt{4t+1}}$

$\mathbf{a} \cdot \mathbf{N} = \dfrac{1}{2t\sqrt{4t+1}}$

49. $\mathbf{r}(t) = e^t\mathbf{i} + e^{-t}\mathbf{j}$

$\mathbf{v}(t) = e^t\mathbf{i} - e^{-t}\mathbf{j}$

$\|\mathbf{v}(t)\| = \sqrt{e^{2t} + e^{-2t}}$

$\mathbf{a}(t) = e^t\mathbf{i} + e^{-t}\mathbf{j}$

$\mathbf{T}(t) = \dfrac{e^t\mathbf{i} - e^{-t}\mathbf{j}}{\sqrt{e^{2t} + e^{-2t}}}$

$\mathbf{N}(t) = \dfrac{e^{-t}\mathbf{i} + e^t\mathbf{j}}{\sqrt{e^{2t} + e^{-2t}}}$

$\mathbf{a} \cdot \mathbf{T} = \dfrac{e^{2t} - e^{-2t}}{\sqrt{e^{2t} + e^{-2t}}}$

$\mathbf{a} \cdot \mathbf{N} = \dfrac{2}{\sqrt{e^{2t} + e^{-2t}}}$

51. $\mathbf{r}(t) = t\mathbf{i} + t^2\mathbf{j} + \dfrac{1}{2}t^2\mathbf{k}$

$\mathbf{v}(t) = \mathbf{i} + 2t\mathbf{j} + t\mathbf{k}$

$\|\mathbf{v}\| = \sqrt{1 + 5t^2}$

$\mathbf{a}(t) = 2\mathbf{j} + \mathbf{k}$

$\mathbf{T}(t) = \dfrac{\mathbf{i} + 2t\mathbf{j} + t\mathbf{k}}{\sqrt{1 + 5t^2}}$

$\mathbf{N}(t) = \dfrac{-5t\mathbf{i} + 2\mathbf{j} + \mathbf{k}}{\sqrt{5}\sqrt{1 + 5t^2}}$

$\mathbf{a} \cdot \mathbf{T} = \dfrac{5t}{\sqrt{1 + 5t^2}}$

$\mathbf{a} \cdot \mathbf{N} = \dfrac{5}{\sqrt{5}\sqrt{1 + 5t^2}} = \dfrac{\sqrt{5}}{\sqrt{1 + 5t^2}}$

53. $\mathbf{r}(t) = 2\cos t\mathbf{i} + 2\sin t\mathbf{j} + t\mathbf{k}$, $x = 2\cos t$, $y = 2\sin t$, $z = t$

When $t = \dfrac{3\pi}{4}$, $x = -\sqrt{2}$, $y = \sqrt{2}$, $z = \dfrac{3\pi}{4}$.

$\mathbf{r}'(t) = -2\sin t\mathbf{i} + 2\cos t\mathbf{j} + \mathbf{k}$

Direction numbers when $t = \dfrac{3\pi}{4}$, $a = -\sqrt{2}$, $b = -\sqrt{2}$, $c = 1$

$x = -\sqrt{2}t - \sqrt{2}$, $y = -\sqrt{2}t + \sqrt{2}$, $z = t + \dfrac{3\pi}{4}$

55. $v = \sqrt{\dfrac{9.56 \times 10^4}{4600}} \approx 4.56$ mi/sec

57. $\mathbf{r}(t) = 2t\mathbf{i} - 3t\mathbf{j}$, $0 \le t \le 5$

$\mathbf{r}'(t) = 2\mathbf{i} - 3\mathbf{j}$

$s = \displaystyle\int_a^b \|\mathbf{r}'(t)\| \, dt = \int_0^5 \sqrt{4+9} \, dt$

$= \sqrt{13}\,t \Big]_0^5 = 5\sqrt{13}$

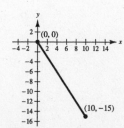

59. $\mathbf{r}(t) = 10 \cos^3 t\mathbf{i} + 10 \sin^3 t\mathbf{j}$

$\mathbf{r}'(t) = -30 \cos^2 t \sin t\mathbf{i} + 30 \sin^2 t \cos t\mathbf{j}$

$\|\mathbf{r}'(t)\| = 30\sqrt{\cos^4 t \sin^2 t + \sin^4 t \cos^2 t}$

$= 30|\cos t \sin t|$

$s = 4\int_0^{\pi/2} 30 \cos t \cdot \sin t \, dt = \left[120\frac{\sin^2 t}{2}\right]_0^{\pi/2} = 60$

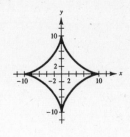

61. $\mathbf{r}(t) = -3t\mathbf{i} + 2t\mathbf{j} + 4t\mathbf{k}, 0 \le t \le 3$

$\mathbf{r}'(t) = -3\mathbf{i} + 2\mathbf{j} + 4\mathbf{k}$

$s = \int_a^b \|\mathbf{r}'(t)\| \, dt = \int_0^3 \sqrt{9 + 4 + 16} \, dt = \int_0^3 \sqrt{29} \, dt = 3\sqrt{29}$

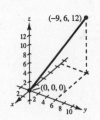

63. $\mathbf{r}(t) = \langle 8 \cos t, 8 \sin t, t \rangle, 0 \le t \le \dfrac{\pi}{2}$

$\mathbf{r}'(t) = \,< -8 \sin t, 8 \cos t, 1 >, \|\mathbf{r}'(t)\| = \sqrt{65}$

$s = \int_a^b \|\mathbf{r}'(t)\| \, dt = \int_0^{\pi/2} \sqrt{65} \, dt = \dfrac{\pi\sqrt{65}}{2}$

65. $\mathbf{r}(t) = \dfrac{1}{2}t\mathbf{i} + \sin t\mathbf{j} + \cos t\mathbf{k}, \quad 0 \le t \le \pi$

$\mathbf{r}'(t) = \dfrac{1}{2}\mathbf{i} + \cos t\mathbf{j} - \sin t\mathbf{k}$

$s = \int_0^\pi \|\mathbf{r}'(t)\| \, dt$

$= \int_0^\pi \sqrt{\dfrac{1}{4} + \cos^2 t + \sin^2 t} \, dt$

$= \dfrac{\sqrt{5}}{2}\int_0^\pi dt = \left[\dfrac{\sqrt{5}}{2}t\right]_0^\pi = \dfrac{\sqrt{5}}{2}\pi$

67. $\mathbf{r}(t) = 3t\mathbf{i} + 2t\mathbf{j}$

Line

$k = 0$

69. $\mathbf{r}(t) = 2t\mathbf{i} + \dfrac{1}{2}t^2\mathbf{j} + t^2\mathbf{k}$

$\mathbf{r}'(t) = 2\mathbf{i} + t\mathbf{j} + 2t\mathbf{k}, \|\mathbf{r}'\| = \sqrt{5t^2 + 4}$

$\mathbf{r}''(t) = \mathbf{j} + 2\mathbf{k}$

$\mathbf{r}' \times \mathbf{r}'' = \begin{vmatrix} \mathbf{i} & \mathbf{j} & \mathbf{k} \\ 2 & t & 2t \\ 0 & 1 & 2 \end{vmatrix} = -4\mathbf{j} + 2\mathbf{k}, \|\mathbf{r}' \times \mathbf{r}''\| = \sqrt{20}$

$K = \dfrac{\|\mathbf{r}' \times \mathbf{r}''\|}{\|\mathbf{r}'\|^3} = \dfrac{\sqrt{20}}{(5t^2 + 4)^{3/2}} = \dfrac{2\sqrt{5}}{(4 + 5t^2)^{3/2}}$

71. $y = \dfrac{1}{2}x^2 + 2$

$y' = x$

$y'' = 1$

$K = \dfrac{|y''|}{[1 + (y')^2]^{3/2}} = \dfrac{1}{(1 + x^2)^{3/2}}$

At $x = 4, K = \dfrac{1}{17^{3/2}}$ and $r = 17^{3/2} = 17\sqrt{17}$.

73. $y = \ln x$

$y' = \dfrac{1}{x}, y'' = -\dfrac{1}{x^2}$

$K = \dfrac{|y''|}{[1 + (y')^2]^{3/2}} = \dfrac{1/x^2}{[1 + (1/x)^2]^{3/2}}$

At $x = 1, K = \dfrac{1}{2^{3/2}} = \dfrac{1}{2\sqrt{2}} = \dfrac{\sqrt{2}}{4}$ and $r = 2\sqrt{2}$.

75. The curvature changes abruptly from zero to a nonzero constant at the points B and C.

Problem Solving for Chapter 11

1. $x(t) = \displaystyle\int_0^t \cos\!\left(\frac{\pi u^2}{2}\right) du, \, y(t) = \int_0^t \sin\!\left(\frac{\pi u^2}{2}\right) du$

$x'(t) = \cos\!\left(\frac{\pi t^2}{2}\right), \, y'(t) = \sin\!\left(\frac{\pi t^2}{2}\right)$

(a) $s = \displaystyle\int_0^a \sqrt{x'(t)^2 + y'(t)^2}\, dt = \int_0^a dt = a$

(b) $x''(t) = -\pi t \sin\!\left(\frac{\pi t^2}{2}\right), \, y''(t) = \pi t \cos\!\left(\frac{\pi t^2}{2}\right)$

$K = \dfrac{\left| \pi t \cos^2\!\left(\frac{\pi t^2}{2}\right) + \pi t \sin^2\!\left(\frac{\pi t^2}{2}\right) \right|}{1} = \pi t$

At $t = a$, $K = \pi a$.

(c) $K = \pi a = \pi(\text{length})$

3. Bomb: $\mathbf{r}_1(t) = \langle 5000 - 400t, 3200 - 16t^2 \rangle$

Projectile: $\mathbf{r}_2(t) = \langle (v_0 \cos\theta)t, \, (v_0 \sin\theta)t - 16t^2 \rangle$

At 1600 feet: Bomb:

$3200 - 16t^2 = 1600 \implies t = 10$ seconds.

Projectile will travel 5 seconds:

$5(v_0 \sin\theta) - 16(25) = 1600$

$v_0 \sin\theta = 400.$

Horizontal position:

At $t = 10$, bomb is at $5000 - 400(10) = 1000$.

At $t = 5$, projectile is at $5v_0 \cos\theta$.

Thus, $v_0 \cos\theta = 200$.

Combining, $\dfrac{v_0 \sin\theta}{v_0 \cos\theta} = \dfrac{400}{200} \implies \tan\theta = 2 \implies \theta \approx 63.4°$.

$v_0 = \dfrac{200}{\cos\theta} \approx 447.2$ ft/sec

5. $x'(\theta) = 1 - \cos\theta, \, y'(\theta) = \sin\theta, \, 0 \le \theta \le 2\pi$

$\sqrt{x'(\theta)^2 + y'(\theta)^2} = \sqrt{(1 - \cos\theta)^2 + \sin^2\theta}$

$= \sqrt{2 - 2\cos\theta} = \sqrt{4\sin^2\frac{\theta}{2}}$

$s(t) = \displaystyle\int_\pi^t 2\sin\frac{\theta}{2}\, d\theta = \left[-4\cos\frac{\theta}{2} \right]_\pi^t = -4\cos\frac{t}{2}$

$x''(\theta) = \sin\theta, \, y''(\theta) = \cos\theta$

$K = \dfrac{1|(1 - \cos\theta)\cos\theta - \sin\theta\sin\theta|}{\left(2\sin\frac{\theta}{2}\right)^3} = \dfrac{|1\cos\theta - 1|}{8\sin^3\frac{\theta}{2}}$

$= \dfrac{1}{4\sin\frac{\theta}{2}}$

Thus, $\rho = \dfrac{1}{K} = 4\sin\frac{t}{2}$ and

$s^2 + \rho^2 = 16\cos^2\!\left(\frac{t}{2}\right) + 16\sin^2\!\left(\frac{t}{2}\right) = 16.$

7. $\|\mathbf{r}^2(t)\| = \mathbf{r}(t) \cdot \mathbf{r}(t)$

$\dfrac{d}{dt}(\|\mathbf{r}(t)\|)^2 = 2\|\mathbf{r}(t)\|\dfrac{d}{dt}\|\mathbf{r}(t)\|$

$= \mathbf{r}(t) \cdot \mathbf{r}'(t) + \mathbf{r}'(t) \cdot \mathbf{r}(t) \implies \dfrac{d}{dt}\|\mathbf{r}(t)\| = \dfrac{\mathbf{r}(t) \cdot \mathbf{r}'(t)}{\|\mathbf{r}(t)\|}$

9. $\mathbf{r}(t) = 4 \cos t\mathbf{i} + 4 \sin t\mathbf{j} + 3t\mathbf{k}, \ t = \dfrac{\pi}{2}$

$\mathbf{r}'(t) = -4 \sin t\mathbf{i} + 4 \cos t\mathbf{j} + 3\mathbf{k}, \ \|\mathbf{r}'(t)\| = 5$

$\mathbf{r}''(t) = -4 \cos t\mathbf{i} - 4 \sin t\mathbf{j}$

$\mathbf{T} = -\dfrac{4}{5} \sin t\mathbf{i} + \dfrac{4}{5} \cos t\mathbf{j} + \dfrac{3}{5}\mathbf{k}$

$\mathbf{T}' = -\dfrac{4}{5} \cos t\mathbf{i} - \dfrac{4}{5} \sin t\mathbf{j}$

$\mathbf{N} = -\cos t\mathbf{i} - \sin t\mathbf{j}$

$\mathbf{B} = \mathbf{T} \times \mathbf{N} = \dfrac{3}{5} \sin t\mathbf{i} - \dfrac{3}{5} \cos t\mathbf{j} + \dfrac{4}{5}\mathbf{k}$

At $t = \dfrac{\pi}{2}, \ \mathbf{T}\left(\dfrac{\pi}{2}\right) = -\dfrac{4}{5}\mathbf{i} + \dfrac{3}{5}\mathbf{k}$

$\mathbf{N}\left(\dfrac{\pi}{2}\right) = -\mathbf{j}$

$\mathbf{B}\left(\dfrac{\pi}{2}\right) = \dfrac{3}{5}\mathbf{i} + \dfrac{4}{5}\mathbf{k}$

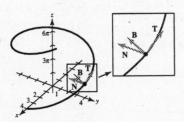

11. (a) $\|\mathbf{B}\| = \|\mathbf{T} \times \mathbf{N}\| = 1$ constant length $\Rightarrow \dfrac{d\mathbf{B}}{ds} \perp \mathbf{B}$

$\dfrac{d\mathbf{B}}{ds} = \dfrac{d}{ds}(\mathbf{T} \times \mathbf{N}) = (\mathbf{T} \times \mathbf{N}') + (\mathbf{T}' \times \mathbf{N})$

$\mathbf{T} \cdot \dfrac{d\mathbf{B}}{ds} = \mathbf{T} \cdot (\mathbf{T} \times \mathbf{N}') + \mathbf{T} \cdot (\mathbf{T}' \times \mathbf{N})$

$= (\mathbf{T} \times \mathbf{T}) \cdot \mathbf{N}' + \mathbf{T} \cdot \left(\mathbf{T}' \times \dfrac{\mathbf{T}'}{\|\mathbf{T}'\|}\right) = 0$

Hence, $\dfrac{d\mathbf{B}}{ds} \perp \mathbf{B}$ and $\dfrac{d\mathbf{B}}{ds} \perp \mathbf{T} \Rightarrow \dfrac{d\mathbf{B}}{ds} = -\tau\mathbf{N}$

for some scalar τ.

(b) $\mathbf{B} = \mathbf{T} \times \mathbf{N}$. Using Exercise 10.3, number 64,

$\mathbf{B} \times \mathbf{N} = (\mathbf{T} \times \mathbf{N}) \times \mathbf{N} = -\mathbf{N} \times (\mathbf{T} \times \mathbf{N})$

$= -[(\mathbf{N} \cdot \mathbf{N})\mathbf{T} - (\mathbf{N} \cdot \mathbf{T})\mathbf{N}]$

$= -\mathbf{T}$

$\mathbf{B} \times \mathbf{T} = (\mathbf{T} \times \mathbf{N}) \times \mathbf{T} = -\mathbf{T} \times (\mathbf{T} \times \mathbf{N})$

$= -[(\mathbf{T} \cdot \mathbf{N})\mathbf{T} - (\mathbf{T} \cdot \mathbf{T})\mathbf{N}]$

$= \mathbf{N}.$

Now, $K\mathbf{N} = \left\|\dfrac{d\mathbf{T}}{ds}\right\| \dfrac{\mathbf{T}'(s)}{\|\mathbf{T}'(s)\|} = \mathbf{T}'(s) = \dfrac{d\mathbf{T}}{ds}.$

Finally,

$\mathbf{N}'(s) = \dfrac{d}{ds}(\mathbf{B} \times \mathbf{T}) = (\mathbf{B} \times \mathbf{T}') + (\mathbf{B}' \times \mathbf{T})$

$= (\mathbf{B} \times K\mathbf{N}) + (-\tau\mathbf{N} \times \mathbf{T})$

$= -K\mathbf{T} + \tau\mathbf{B}.$

13. $\mathbf{r}(t) = \langle t \cos \pi t, t \sin \pi t \rangle, \ 0 \le t \le 2$

(a)

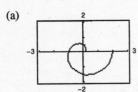

(b) Length $= \displaystyle\int_0^2 \|\mathbf{r}'(t)\| \, dt$

$= \displaystyle\int_0^2 \sqrt{\pi^2 t^2 + 1} \, dt \approx 6.766$ (graphing utility)

(c) $K = \dfrac{\pi(\pi^2 t^2 + 2)}{[\pi^2 t^2 + 1]^{3/2}}$

$K(0) = 2\pi$

$K(1) = \dfrac{\pi(\pi^2 + 2)}{(\pi^2 + 1)^{3/2}} \approx 1.04$

$K(2) \approx 0.51$

(d)

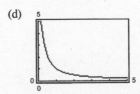

(e) $\displaystyle\lim_{t \to \infty} K = 0$

(f) As $t \to \infty$, the graph spirals outward and the curvature decreases.

C H A P T E R   1 2
Functions of Several Variables

CHAPTER 12
Functions of Several Variables

Section 12.1 Introduction to Functions of Several Variables

Solutions to Odd-Numbered Exercises

1. $x^2z + yz - xy = 10$

$z(x^2 + y) = 10 + xy$

$z = \dfrac{10 + xy}{x^2 + y}$

Yes, z is a function of x and y.

3. $\dfrac{x^2}{4} + \dfrac{y^2}{9} + z^2 = 1$

No, z is not a function of x and y. For example,
$(x, y) = (0, 0)$ corresponds to both $z = \pm 1$.

5. $f(x, y) = \dfrac{x}{y}$

   (a) $f(3, 2) = \dfrac{3}{2}$

   (b) $f(-1, 4) = -\dfrac{1}{4}$

   (c) $f(30, 5) = \dfrac{30}{5} = 6$

   (d) $f(5, y) = \dfrac{5}{y}$

   (e) $f(x, 2) = \dfrac{x}{2}$

   (f) $f(5, t) = \dfrac{5}{t}$

7. $f(x, y) = xe^y$

   (a) $f(5, 0) = 5e^0 = 5$

   (b) $f(3, 2) = 3e^2$

   (c) $f(2, -1) = 2e^{-1} = \dfrac{2}{e}$

   (d) $f(5, y) = 5e^y$

   (e) $f(x, 2) = xe^2$

   (f) $f(t, t) = te^t$

9. $h(x, y, z) = \dfrac{xy}{z}$

   (a) $h(2, 3, 9) = \dfrac{(2)(3)}{9} = \dfrac{2}{3}$

   (b) $h(1, 0, 1) = \dfrac{(1)(0)}{1} = 0$

11. $f(x, y) = x \sin y$

   (a) $f\left(2, \dfrac{\pi}{4}\right) = 2 \sin \dfrac{\pi}{4} = \sqrt{2}$

   (b) $f(3, 1) = 3 \sin 1$

13. $g(x, y) = \displaystyle\int_x^y (2t - 3)\, dt$

   (a) $g(0, 4) = \displaystyle\int_0^4 (2t - 3)\, dt = \left[t^2 - 3t \right]_0^4 = 4$

   (b) $g(1, 4) = \displaystyle\int_1^4 (2t - 3)\, dt = \left[t^2 - 3t \right]_1^4 = 6$

15. $f(x, y) = x^2 - 2y$

   (a) $\dfrac{f(x + \Delta x, y) - f(x, y)}{\Delta x} = \dfrac{[(x + \Delta x)^2 - 2y] - (x^2 - 2y)}{\Delta x}$

$$= \dfrac{x^2 + 2x(\Delta x) + (\Delta x)^2 - 2y - x^2 + 2y}{\Delta x} = \dfrac{\Delta x(2x + \Delta x)}{\Delta x} = 2x + \Delta x,\ \Delta x \neq 0$$

   (b) $\dfrac{f(x, y + \Delta y) - f(x, y)}{\Delta y} = \dfrac{[x^2 - 2(y + \Delta y)] - (x^2 - 2y)}{\Delta y} = \dfrac{x^2 - 2y - 2\Delta y - x^2 + 2y}{\Delta y} = \dfrac{-2\Delta y}{\Delta y} = -2,\ \Delta y \neq 0$

17. $f(x, y) = \sqrt{4 - x^2 - y^2}$

Domain: $4 - x^2 - y^2 \geq 0$

$$x^2 + y^2 \leq 4$$

$$\{(x, y): x^2 + y^2 \leq 4\}$$

Range: $0 \leq z \leq 2$

19. $f(x, y) = \arcsin(x + y)$

Domain:
$\{(x, y): -1 \leq x + y \leq 1\}$

Range: $-\dfrac{\pi}{2} \leq z \leq \dfrac{\pi}{2}$

21. $f(x, y) = \ln(4 - x - y)$

Domain: $4 - x - y > 0$

$$x + y < 4$$

$$\{(x, y): y < -x + 4\}$$

Range: all real numbers

23. $z = \dfrac{x + y}{xy}$

Domain: $\{(x, y): x \neq 0 \text{ and } y \neq 0\}$

Range: all real numbers

25. $f(x, y) = e^{x/y}$

Domain: $\{(x, y): y \neq 0\}$

Range: $z > 0$

27. $g(x, y) = \dfrac{1}{xy}$

Domain: $\{(x, y): x \neq 0 \text{ and } y \neq 0\}$

Range: all real numbers except zero

29. $f(x, y) = \dfrac{-4x}{x^2 + y^2 + 1}$

(a) View from the positive x-axis: $(20, 0, 0)$

(b) View where x is negative, y and z are positive:
$(-15, 10, 20)$

(c) View from the first octant: $(20, 15, 25)$

(d) View from the line $y = x$ in the xy-plane: $(20, 20, 0)$

31. $f(x, y) = 5$

Plane: $z = 5$

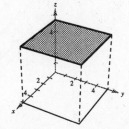

33. $f(x, y) = y^2$

Since the variable x is missing, the surface is a cylinder with rulings parallel to the x-axis. The generating curve is $z = y^2$. The domain is the entire xy-plane and the range is $z \geq 0$.

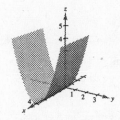

35. $z = 4 - x^2 - y^2$

Paraboloid

Domain: entire xy-plane

Range: $z \leq 4$

37. $f(x, y) = e^{-x}$

Since the variable y is missing, the surface is a cylinder with rulings parallel to the y-axis. The generating curve is $z = e^{-x}$. The domain is the entire xy-plane and the range is $z > 0$.

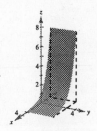

39. $z = y^2 - x^2 + 1$

Hyperbolic paraboloid

Domain: entire xy-plane

Range: $-\infty < z < \infty$

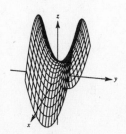

41. $f(x, y) = x^2 e^{(-xy/2)}$

43. $f(x, y) = x^2 + y^2$

(a)

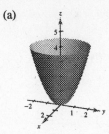

(b) g is a vertical translation of f two units upward

(c) g is a horizontal translation of f two units to the right. The vertex moves from $(0, 0, 0)$ to $(0, 2, 0)$.

(d) g is a reflection of f in the xy-plane followed by a vertical translation 4 units upward.

(e)

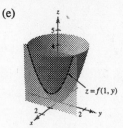 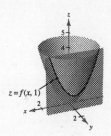

$z = f(1, y)$ $z = f(x, 1)$

45. $z = e^{1-x^2-y^2}$

Level curves:

$$c = e^{1-x^2-y^2}$$

$$\ln c = 1 - x^2 - y^2$$

$$x^2 + y^2 = 1 - \ln c$$

Circles centered at $(0, 0)$

Matches (c)

47. $z = \ln|y - x^2|$

Level curves:

$$c = \ln|y - x^2|$$

$$\pm e^c = y - x^2$$

$$y = x^2 \pm e^c$$

Parabolas

Matches (b)

49. $z = x + y$

Level curves are parallel lines of the form $x + y = c$.

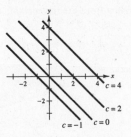

$c = 4$
$c = 2$
$c = 0$
$c = -1$

51. $f(x, y) = \sqrt{25 - x^2 - y^2}$

The level curves are of the form

$$c = \sqrt{25 - x^2 - y^2},$$

$$x^2 + y^2 = 25 - c^2.$$

Thus, the level curves are circles of radius 5 or less, centered at the origin.

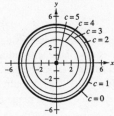

$c = 5$
$c = 4$
$c = 3$
$c = 2$
$c = 1$
$c = 0$

53. $f(x, y) = xy$

The level curves are hyperbolas of the form $xy = c$.

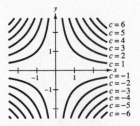

$c = 6$
$c = 5$
$c = 4$
$c = 3$
$c = 2$
$c = 1$
$c = -1$
$c = -2$
$c = -3$
$c = -4$
$c = -5$
$c = -6$

55. $f(x, y) = \dfrac{x}{x^2 + y^2}$

The level curves are of the form

$$c = \frac{x}{x^2 + y^2}$$

$$x^2 - \frac{x}{c} + y^2 = 0$$

$$\left(x - \frac{1}{2c}\right)^2 + y^2 = \left(\frac{1}{2c}\right)^2$$

$c = -\frac{1}{2}$ $c = 1$

$c = -\frac{3}{2}$ $c = 2$

$c = -2$ $c = \frac{3}{2}$

$c = -1$ $c = \frac{1}{2}$

Thus, the level curves are circles passing through the origin and centered at $(1/2c, 0)$.

57. $f(x, y) = x^2 - y^2 + 2$

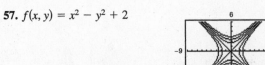

59. $g(x, y) = \dfrac{8}{1 + x^2 + y^2}$

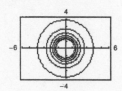

61. See Definition, page 838.

63. No, The following graphs are not hemispheres.

$z = e^{-(x^2 + y^2)}$

$z = x^2 + y^2$

65. The surface is sloped like a saddle. The graph is not unique. Any vertical translation would have the same level curves.

One possible function is

$f(x, y) = x^2 - y^2.$

67. $V(I, R) = 1000 \left[\dfrac{1 + 0.10(1 - R)}{1 + I} \right]^{10}$

	Inflation Rate		
Tax Rate	0	0.03	0.05
0	2593.74	1929.99	1592.33
0.28	2004.23	1491.34	1230.42
0.35	1877.14	1396.77	1152.40

69. $f(x, y, z) = x - 2y + 3z$

$c = 6$

$6 = x - 2y + 3z$

Plane

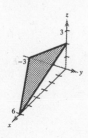

71. $f(x, y, z) = x^2 + y^2 + z^2$

$c = 9$

$9 = x^2 + y^2 + z^2$

Sphere

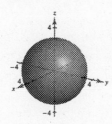

73. $f(x, y, z) = 4x^2 + 4y^2 - z^2$

$c = 0$

$0 = 4x^2 + 4y^2 - z^2$

Elliptic cone

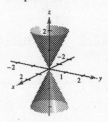

75. $N(d, L) = \left(\dfrac{d - 4}{4} \right)^2 L$

(a) $N(22, 12) = \left(\dfrac{22 - 4}{4} \right)^2 (12) = 243$ board-feet

(b) $N(30, 12) = \left(\dfrac{30 - 4}{4} \right)^2 (12) = 507$ board-feet

77. $T = 600 - 0.75x^2 - 0.75y^2$

The level curves are of the form

$c = 600 - 0.75x^2 - 0.75y^2$

$x^2 + y^2 = \dfrac{600 - c}{0.75}.$

The level curves are circles centered at the origin.

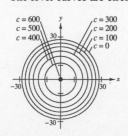

79. $C = 0.75xy + \quad 2(0.40)xz + 2(0.40)yz$

base + front & back + two ends

$= 0.75xy + 0.80(xz + yz)$

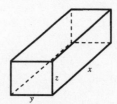

81. $PV = kT,\ 20(2600) = k(300)$

(a) $k = \dfrac{20(2600)}{300} = \dfrac{520}{3}$

(b) $P = \dfrac{kT}{V} = \dfrac{520}{3}\left(\dfrac{T}{V}\right)$

The level curves are of the form: $c = \left(\dfrac{520}{3}\right)\left(\dfrac{T}{V}\right)$

$$V = \frac{520}{3c}T$$

Thus, the level curves are lines through the origin with slope $\dfrac{520}{3c}$.

83. (a) Highest pressure at C

(b) Lowest pressure at A

(c) Highest wind velocity at B

85. (a) The boundaries between colors represent level curves

(b) No, the colors represent intervals of different lengths, as indicated in the box

(c) You could use more colors, which means using smaller intervals

87. False. Let

$$f(x, y) = 2xy$$

$$f(1, 2) = f(2, 1),\ \text{but}\ 1 \neq 2$$

89. False. Let

$$f(x, y) = 5.$$

Then, $f(2x, 2y) = 5 \neq 2^2 f(x, y)$.

Section 12.2 Limits and Continuity

1. Let $\varepsilon > 0$ be given. We need to find $\delta > 0$ such that $|f(x, y) - L| = |y - b| < \varepsilon$ whenever $0 < \sqrt{(x - a)^2 + (y - b)^2} < \delta$. Take $\delta = \varepsilon$.

Then if $0 < \sqrt{(x - a)^2 + (y - b)^2} < \delta = \varepsilon$, we have

$$\sqrt{(y - b)^2} < \varepsilon$$

$$|y - b| < \varepsilon.$$

3. $\displaystyle\lim_{(x, y)\to(a, b)} [f(x, y) - g(x, y)] = \lim_{(x, y)\to(a, b)} f(x, y) - \lim_{(x, y)\to(a, b)} g(x, y) = 5 - 3 = 2$

5. $\displaystyle\lim_{(x, y)\to(a, b)} [f(x, y)g(x, y)] = \left[\lim_{(x, y)\to(a, b)} f(x, y)\right]\left[\lim_{(x, y)\to(a, b)} g(x, y)\right] = 5(3) = 15$

7. $\displaystyle\lim_{(x, y)\to(2, 1)} (x + 3y^2) = 2 + 3(1)^2 = 5$

Continuous everywhere

9. $\displaystyle\lim_{(x, y)\to(2, 4)} \frac{x + y}{x - y} = \frac{2 + 4}{2 - 4} = -3$

Continuous for $x \neq y$

11. $\displaystyle\lim_{(x, y)\to(0, 1)} \frac{\arcsin(x/y)}{1 + xy} = \arcsin 0 = 0$

Continuous for $xy \neq -1,\ y \neq 0,\ |x/y| \leq 1$

13. $\displaystyle\lim_{(x, y)\to(-1, 2)} e^{xy} = e^{-2} = \frac{1}{e^2}$

Continuous everywhere

15. $\displaystyle\lim_{(x, y, z)\to(1, 2, 5)} \sqrt{x + y + z} = \sqrt{8} = 2\sqrt{2}$

Continuous for $x + y + z \geq 0$

17. $\displaystyle\lim_{(x, y)\to(0, 0)} e^{xy} = 1$

Continuous everywhere

19. $\lim\limits_{(x,\,y)\to(0,\,0)} \ln(x^2 + y^2) = \ln(0) = -\infty$

The limit does not exist.

Continuous except at $(0, 0)$

21. $f(x, y) = \dfrac{xy}{x^2 + y^2}$

Continuous except at $(0, 0)$

Path: $y = 0$

(x, y)	$(1, 0)$	$(0.5, 0)$	$(0.1, 0)$	$(0.01, 0)$	$(0.001, 0)$
$f(x, y)$	0	0	0	0	0

Path: $y = x$

(x, y)	$(1, 1)$	$(0.5, 0.5)$	$(0.1, 0.1)$	$(0.01, 0.01)$	$(0.001, 0.001)$
$f(x, y)$	$\frac{1}{2}$	$\frac{1}{2}$	$\frac{1}{2}$	$\frac{1}{2}$	$\frac{1}{2}$

The limit does not exist because along the path $y = 0$ the function equals 0, whereas along the path $y = x$ the function equals $\frac{1}{2}$.

23. $f(x, y) = -\dfrac{xy^2}{x^2 + y^4}$

Continuous except at $(0, 0)$

Path: $x = y^2$

(x, y)	$(1, 1)$	$(0.25, 0.5)$	$(0.01, 0.1)$	$(0.0001, 0.01)$	$(0.000001, 0.001)$
$f(x, y)$	$-\frac{1}{2}$	$-\frac{1}{2}$	$-\frac{1}{2}$	$-\frac{1}{2}$	$-\frac{1}{2}$

Path: $x = -y^2$

(x, y)	$(-1, 1)$	$(-0.25, 0.5)$	$(-0.01, 0.1)$	$(-0.0001, 0.01)$	$(-0.000001, 0.001)$
$f(x, y)$	$\frac{1}{2}$	$\frac{1}{2}$	$\frac{1}{2}$	$\frac{1}{2}$	$\frac{1}{2}$

The limit does not exist because along the path $x = y^2$ the function equals $-\frac{1}{2}$, whereas along the path $x = -y^2$ the function equals $\frac{1}{2}$.

25. $\lim\limits_{(x,\,y)\to(0,\,0)} f(x, y) = \lim\limits_{(x,\,y)\to(0,\,0)} \left(\dfrac{x^2 + 2xy^2 + y^2}{x^2 + y^2} \right)$

$\qquad = \lim\limits_{(x,\,y)\to(0,\,0)} \left(1 + \dfrac{2xy^2}{x^2 + y^2} \right) = 1$

(same limit for g)

Thus, f is not continuous at $(0, 0)$, whereas g is continuous at $(0, 0)$.

27. $\lim\limits_{(x,\,y)\to(0,\,0)} (\sin x + \sin y) = 0$

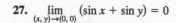
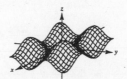

29. $\lim\limits_{(x,\,y)\to(0,\,0)} \dfrac{x^2 y}{x^4 + 4y^2}$

Does not exist

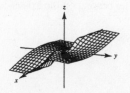

31. $f(x, y) = \dfrac{10xy}{2x^2 + 3y^2}$

The limit does not exist. Use the paths $x = 0$ and $x = y$.

33. $\displaystyle\lim_{(x, y)\to(0, 0)} \frac{\sin(x^2 + y^2)}{x^2 + y^2} = \lim_{r\to 0} \frac{\sin r^2}{r^2} = \lim_{r\to 0} \frac{2r \cos r^2}{2r} = \lim_{r\to 0} \cos r^2 = 1$

35. $\displaystyle\lim_{(x, y)\to(0, 0)} \frac{x^3 + y^3}{x^2 + y^2} = \lim_{r\to 0} \frac{r^3 (\cos^3 \theta + \sin^3 \theta)}{r^2} = \lim_{r\to 0} r(\cos^3 \theta + \sin^3 \theta) = 0$

37. $f(x, y, z) = \dfrac{1}{\sqrt{x^2 + y^2 + z^2}}$

Continuous except at $(0, 0, 0)$

39. $f(x, y, z) = \dfrac{\sin z}{e^x + e^y}$

Continuous everywhere

41. $f(t) = t^2$

$g(x, y) = 3x - 2y$

$\begin{aligned} f(g(x, y)) &= f(3x - 2y) \\ &= (3x - 2y)^2 \\ &= 9x^2 - 12xy + 4y^2 \end{aligned}$

Continuous everywhere

43. $f(t) = \dfrac{1}{t}$

$g(x, y) = 3x - 2y$

$f(g(x, y)) = f(3x - 2y) = \dfrac{1}{3x - 2y}$

Continuous for $y \neq \dfrac{3x}{2}$

45. $f(x, y) = x^2 - 4y$

(a) $\displaystyle\lim_{\Delta x\to 0} \frac{f(x + \Delta x, y) - f(x, y)}{\Delta x} = \lim_{\Delta x\to 0} \frac{[(x + \Delta x)^2 - 4y] - (x^2 - 4y)}{\Delta x}$

$\displaystyle = \lim_{\Delta x\to 0} \frac{2x\Delta x - (\Delta x)^2}{\Delta x} = \lim_{\Delta x\to 0} (2x - \Delta x) = 2x$

(b) $\displaystyle\lim_{\Delta y\to 0} \frac{f(x, y + \Delta y) - f(x, y)}{\Delta y} = \lim_{\Delta y\to 0} \frac{[x^2 - 4(y + \Delta y)] - (x^2 - 4y)}{\Delta y}$

$\displaystyle = \lim_{\Delta y\to 0} \frac{-4\Delta y}{\Delta y} = \lim_{\Delta y\to 0} (-4) = -4$

47. $f(x, y) = 2x + xy - 3y$

(a) $\displaystyle\lim_{\Delta x\to 0} \frac{f(x + \Delta x, y) - f(x, y)}{\Delta x} = \lim_{\Delta x\to 0} \frac{[2(x + \Delta x) + (x + \Delta x)y - 3y] - (2x + xy - 3y)}{\Delta x}$

$\displaystyle = \lim_{\Delta x\to 0} \frac{2\Delta x + \Delta xy}{\Delta x} = \lim_{\Delta x\to 0} (2 + y) = 2 + y$

(b) $\displaystyle\lim_{\Delta y\to 0} \frac{f(x, y + \Delta y) - f(x, y)}{\Delta y} = \lim_{\Delta y\to 0} \frac{[2x + x(y + \Delta y) - 3(y + \Delta y)] - (2x + xy - 3y)}{\Delta y}$

$\displaystyle = \lim_{\Delta y\to 0} \frac{x\Delta y - 3\Delta y}{\Delta y} = \lim_{\Delta y\to 0} (x - 3) = x - 3$

49. See the definition on page 851.

Show that the value of $\displaystyle\lim_{(x, y)\to(x_0, y_0)} f(x, y)$ is not the same

for two different paths to (x_0, y_0).

51. No.

The existence of $f(2, 3)$ has no bearing on the existence of the limit as $(x, y) \to (2, 3)$.

53. Since $\lim\limits_{(x, y)\to(a, b)} f(x, y) = L_1$, then for $\varepsilon/2 > 0$, there corresponds $\delta_1 > 0$ such that $|f(x, y) - L_1| < \varepsilon/2$ whenever

$$0 < \sqrt{(x - a)^2 + (y - b)^2} < \delta_1.$$

Since $\lim\limits_{(x, y)\to(a, b)} g(x, y) = L_2$, then for $\varepsilon/2 > 0$, there corresponds $\delta_2 > 0$ such that $|g(x, y) - L_2| < \varepsilon/2$ whenever

$$0 < \sqrt{(x - a)^2 + (y - b)^2} < \delta_2.$$

Let δ be the smaller of δ_1 and δ_2. By the triangle inequality, whenever $\sqrt{(x - a)^2 + (y - b)^2} < \delta$, we have

$$|f(x, y) + g(x, y) - (L_1 + L_2)| = |(f(x, y) - L_1) + (g(x, y) - L_2)| \le |f(x, y) - L_1| + |g(x, y) - L_2| < \frac{\varepsilon}{2} + \frac{\varepsilon}{2} = \varepsilon.$$

Therefore, $\lim\limits_{(x, y)\to(a, b)} [f(x, y) + g(x, y)] = L_1 + L_2$.

55. True

57. False. Let

$$f(x, y) = \begin{cases} \ln(x^2 + y^2), & (x, y) \ne (0, 0) \\ 0, & x = 0, y = 0 \end{cases}$$

See Exercise 19.

Section 12.3   Partial Derivatives

1. $f_x(4, 1) < 0$

3. $f_y(4, 1) > 0$

5. $f(x, y) = 2x - 3y + 5$

$f_x(x, y) = 2$

$f_y(x, y) = -3$

7. $z = x\sqrt{y}$

$\dfrac{\partial z}{\partial x} = \sqrt{y}$

$\dfrac{\partial z}{\partial y} = \dfrac{x}{2\sqrt{y}}$

9. $z = x^2 - 5xy + 3y^2$

$\dfrac{\partial z}{\partial x} = 2x - 5y$

$\dfrac{\partial z}{\partial y} = -5x + 6y$

11. $z = x^2 e^{2y}$

$\dfrac{\partial z}{\partial x} = 2x e^{2y}$

$\dfrac{\partial z}{\partial y} = 2x^2 e^{2y}$

13. $z = \ln(x^2 + y^2)$

$\dfrac{\partial z}{\partial x} = \dfrac{2x}{x^2 + y^2}$

$\dfrac{\partial z}{\partial y} = \dfrac{2y}{x^2 + y^2}$

15. $z = \ln\left(\dfrac{x + y}{x - y}\right) = \ln(x + y) - \ln(x - y)$

$\dfrac{\partial z}{\partial x} = \dfrac{1}{x + y} - \dfrac{1}{x - y} = -\dfrac{2y}{x^2 - y^2}$

$\dfrac{\partial z}{\partial y} = \dfrac{1}{x + y} + \dfrac{1}{x - y} = \dfrac{2x}{x^2 - y^2}$

17. $z = \dfrac{x^2}{2y} + \dfrac{4y^2}{x}$

$\dfrac{\partial z}{\partial x} = \dfrac{2x}{2y} - \dfrac{4y^2}{x^2} = \dfrac{x^3 - 4y^3}{x^2 y}$

$\dfrac{\partial z}{\partial y} = -\dfrac{x^2}{2y^2} + \dfrac{8y}{x} = \dfrac{-x^3 + 16y^3}{2xy^2}$

19. $h(x, y) = e^{-(x^2 + y^2)}$

$h_x(x, y) = -2x e^{-(x^2 + y^2)}$

$h_y(x, y) = -2y e^{-(x^2 + y^2)}$

21. $f(x, y) = \sqrt{x^2 + y^2}$

$f_x(x, y) = \dfrac{1}{2}(x^2 + y^2)^{-1/2}(2x) = \dfrac{x}{\sqrt{x^2 + y^2}}$

$f_y(x, y) = \dfrac{1}{2}(x^2 + y^2)^{-1/2}(2y) = \dfrac{y}{\sqrt{x^2 + y^2}}$

23. $z = \tan(2x - y)$

$\dfrac{\partial z}{\partial x} = 2 \sec^2(2x - y)$

$\dfrac{\partial z}{\partial y} = -\sec^2(2x - y)$

25. $z = e^y \sin xy$

$\dfrac{\partial z}{\partial x} = ye^y \cos xy$

$\dfrac{\partial z}{\partial y} = e^y \sin xy + xe^y \cos xy$

$\quad = e^y(x \cos xy + \sin xy)$

27. $f(x, y) = \displaystyle\int_x^y (t^2 - 1)\, dt$

$\quad = \left[\dfrac{t^3}{3} - t\right]_x^y = \left(\dfrac{y^3}{3} - y\right) - \left(\dfrac{x^3}{3} - x\right)$

$f_x(x, y) = -x^2 + 1 = 1 - x^2$

$f_y(x, y) = y^2 - 1$

[You could also use the Second Fundamental Theorem of Calculus.]

29. $f(x, y) = 2x + 3y$

$\dfrac{\partial f}{\partial x} = \lim\limits_{\Delta x \to 0} \dfrac{f(x + \Delta x, y) - f(x, y)}{\Delta x} = \lim\limits_{\Delta x \to 0} \dfrac{2(x + \Delta x) + 3y - 2x - 3y}{\Delta x} = \lim\limits_{\Delta x \to 0} \dfrac{2\Delta x}{\Delta x} = 2$

$\dfrac{\partial f}{\partial y} = \lim\limits_{\Delta y \to 0} \dfrac{f(x, y + \Delta y) - f(x, y)}{\Delta y} = \lim\limits_{\Delta y \to 0} \dfrac{2x + 3(y + \Delta y) - 2x - 3y}{\Delta y} = \lim\limits_{\Delta y \to 0} \dfrac{3\Delta y}{\Delta y} = 3$

31. $f(x, y) = \sqrt{x + y}$

$\dfrac{\partial f}{\partial x} = \lim\limits_{\Delta x \to 0} \dfrac{f(x + \Delta x, y) - f(x, y)}{\Delta x} = \lim\limits_{\Delta x \to 0} \dfrac{\sqrt{x + \Delta x + y} - \sqrt{x + y}}{\Delta x}$

$\quad = \lim\limits_{\Delta x \to 0} \dfrac{\left(\sqrt{x + \Delta x + y} - \sqrt{x + y}\right)\left(\sqrt{x + \Delta x + y} + \sqrt{x + y}\right)}{\Delta x\left(\sqrt{x + \Delta x + y} + \sqrt{x + y}\right)}$

$\quad = \lim\limits_{\Delta x \to 0} \dfrac{1}{\sqrt{x + \Delta x + y} + \sqrt{x + y}} = \dfrac{1}{2\sqrt{x + y}}$

$\dfrac{\partial f}{\partial y} = \lim\limits_{\Delta y \to 0} \dfrac{f(x, y + \Delta y) - f(x, y)}{\Delta y} = \lim\limits_{\Delta y \to 0} \dfrac{\sqrt{x + y + \Delta y} - \sqrt{x + y}}{\Delta y}$

$\quad = \lim\limits_{\Delta y \to 0} \dfrac{\left(\sqrt{x + y + \Delta y} - \sqrt{x + y}\right)\left(\sqrt{x + y + \Delta y} + \sqrt{x + y}\right)}{\Delta y\left(\sqrt{x + y + \Delta y} + \sqrt{x + y}\right)}$

$\quad = \lim\limits_{\Delta y \to 0} \dfrac{1}{\sqrt{x + y + \Delta y} + \sqrt{x + y}} = \dfrac{1}{2\sqrt{x + y}}$

33. $g(x, y) = 4 - x^2 - y^2$

$g_x(x, y) = -2x$

At $(1, 1)$: $g_x(1, 1) = -2$

$g_y(x, y) = -2y$

At $(1, 1)$: $g_y(1, 1) = -2$

35. $z = e^{-x} \cos y$

$\dfrac{\partial z}{\partial x} = -e^{-x} \cos y$

At $(0, 0)$: $\dfrac{\partial z}{\partial x} = -1$

$\dfrac{\partial z}{\partial y} = -e^{-x} \sin y$

At $(0, 0)$: $\dfrac{\partial z}{\partial y} = 0$

37. $f(x, y) = \arctan \dfrac{y}{x}$

$f_x(x, y) = \dfrac{1}{1 + (y^2/x^2)}\left(-\dfrac{y}{x^2}\right) = \dfrac{-y}{x^2 + y^2}$

At $(2, -2)$: $f_x(2, -2) = \dfrac{1}{4}$

$f_y(x, y) = \dfrac{1}{1 + (y^2/x^2)}\left(\dfrac{1}{x}\right) = \dfrac{x}{x^2 + y^2}$

At $(2, -2)$: $f_y(2, -2) = \dfrac{1}{4}$

39. $f(x, y) = \dfrac{xy}{x - y}$

$f_x(x, y) = \dfrac{y(x - y) - xy}{(x - y)^2} = \dfrac{-y^2}{(x - y)^2}$

At $(2, -2)$: $f_x(2, -2) = -\dfrac{1}{4}$

$f_y(x, y) = \dfrac{x(x - y) + xy}{(x - y)^2} = \dfrac{x^2}{(x - y)^2}$

At $(2, -2)$: $f_y(2, -2) = \dfrac{1}{4}$

41. $z = \sqrt{49 - x^2 - y^2}$, $x = 2$,
$(2, 3, 6)$

Intersecting curve: $z = \sqrt{45 - y^2}$

$$\frac{\partial z}{\partial y} = \frac{-y}{\sqrt{45 - y^2}}$$

At $(2, 3, 6)$: $\dfrac{\partial z}{\partial y} = \dfrac{-3}{\sqrt{45 - 9}} = -\dfrac{1}{2}$

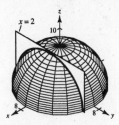

43. $z = 9x^2 - y^2$, $y = 3$, $(1, 3, 0)$

Intersecting curve: $z = 9x^2 - 9$

$$\frac{\partial z}{\partial x} = 18x$$

At $(1, 3, 0)$: $\dfrac{\partial z}{\partial x} = 18(1) = 18$

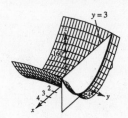

45. $f_x(x, y) = 2x + 4y - 4$, $f_y(x, y) = 4x + 2y + 16$

$f_x = f_y = 0$: $2x + 4y = 4$

$\qquad\qquad\quad 4x + 2y = -16$

Solving for x and y,

$\qquad x = -6$ and $y = 4$.

47. $f_x(x, y) = -\dfrac{1}{x^2} + y$, $f_y(x, y) = -\dfrac{1}{y^2} + x$

$f_x = f_y = 0$: $-\dfrac{1}{x^2} + y = 0$ and $-\dfrac{1}{y^2} + x = 0$

$\qquad\qquad y = \dfrac{1}{x^2}$ and $x = \dfrac{1}{y^2}$

$y = y^4 \implies y = 1 = x$

Points: $(1, 1)$

49. (a) The graph is that of f_y.

    (b) The graph is that of f_x.

51. $w = \sqrt{x^2 + y^2 + z^2}$

$$\frac{\partial w}{\partial x} = \frac{x}{\sqrt{x^2 + y^2 + z^2}}$$

$$\frac{\partial w}{\partial y} = \frac{y}{\sqrt{x^2 + y^2 + z^2}}$$

$$\frac{\partial w}{\partial z} = \frac{z}{\sqrt{x^2 + y^2 + z^2}}$$

53. $F(x, y, z) = \ln \sqrt{x^2 + y^2 + z^2}$

$$= \frac{1}{2}\ln(x^2 + y^2 + z^2)$$

$$F_x(x, y, z) = \frac{x}{x^2 + y^2 + z^2}$$

$$F_y(x, y, z) = \frac{y}{x^2 + y^2 + z^2}$$

$$F_z(x, y, z) = \frac{z}{x^2 + y^2 + z^2}$$

55. $H(x, y, z) = \sin(x + 2y + 3z)$

$H_x(x, y, z) = \cos(x + 2y + 3z)$

$H_y(x, y, z) = 2\cos(x + 2y + 3z)$

$H_z(x, y, z) = 3\cos(x + 2y + 3z)$

57. $z = x^2 - 2xy + 3y^2$

$$\frac{\partial z}{\partial x} = 2x - 2y$$

$$\frac{\partial^2 z}{\partial x^2} = 2$$

$$\frac{\partial^2 z}{\partial y \partial x} = -2$$

$$\frac{\partial z}{\partial y} = -2x + 6y$$

$$\frac{\partial^2 z}{\partial y^2} = 6$$

$$\frac{\partial^2 z}{\partial x \partial y} = -2$$

59. $z = \sqrt{x^2 + y^2}$

$$\frac{\partial z}{\partial x} = \frac{x}{\sqrt{x^2 + y^2}}$$

$$\frac{\partial^2 z}{\partial x^2} = \frac{y^2}{(x^2 + y^2)^{3/2}}$$

$$\frac{\partial^2 z}{\partial y \partial x} = \frac{-xy}{(x^2 + y^2)^{3/2}}$$

$$\frac{\partial z}{\partial y} = \frac{y}{\sqrt{x^2 + y^2}}$$

$$\frac{\partial^2 z}{\partial y^2} = \frac{x^2}{(x^2 + y^2)^{3/2}}$$

$$\frac{\partial^2 z}{\partial x \partial y} = \frac{-xy}{(x^2 + y^2)^{3/2}}$$

61. $z = e^x \tan y$

$$\frac{\partial z}{\partial x} = e^x \tan y$$

$$\frac{\partial^2 z}{\partial x^2} = e^x \tan y$$

$$\frac{\partial^2 z}{\partial y \partial x} = e^x \sec^2 y$$

$$\frac{\partial z}{\partial y} = e^x \sec^2 y$$

$$\frac{\partial^2 z}{\partial y^2} = 2e^x \sec^2 y \tan y$$

$$\frac{\partial^2 z}{\partial x \partial y} = e^x \sec^2 y$$

63. $z = \arctan \dfrac{y}{x}$

$$\frac{\partial z}{\partial x} = \frac{1}{1 + (y^2/x^2)}\left(-\frac{y}{x^2}\right) = \frac{-y}{x^2 + y^2}$$

$$\frac{\partial^2 z}{\partial x^2} = \frac{2xy}{(x^2 + y^2)^2}$$

$$\frac{\partial^2 z}{\partial y \partial x} = \frac{-(x^2 + y^2) + y(2y)}{(x^2 + y^2)^2} = \frac{y^2 - x^2}{(x^2 + y^2)^2}$$

$$\frac{\partial z}{\partial y} = \frac{1}{1 + (y^2/x^2)}\left(\frac{1}{x}\right) = \frac{x}{x^2 + y^2}$$

$$\frac{\partial^2 z}{\partial y^2} = \frac{-2xy}{(x^2 + y^2)^2}$$

$$\frac{\partial^2 z}{\partial x \partial y} = \frac{(x^2 + y^2) - x(2x)}{(x^2 + y^2)^2} = \frac{y^2 - x^2}{(x^2 + y^2)^2}$$

65. $z = x \sec y$

$$\frac{\partial z}{\partial x} = \sec y$$

$$\frac{\partial^2 z}{\partial x^2} = 0$$

$$\frac{\partial^2 z}{\partial y \partial x} = \sec y \tan y$$

$$\frac{\partial z}{\partial y} = x \sec y \tan y$$

$$\frac{\partial^2 z}{\partial y^2} = x \sec y(\sec^2 y + \tan^2 y)$$

$$\frac{\partial^2 z}{\partial x \partial y} = \sec y \tan y$$

Therefore, $\dfrac{\partial^2 z}{\partial y \partial x} = \dfrac{\partial^2 z}{\partial x \partial y}$.

There are no points for which $z_x = 0 = z_y$, because

$$\frac{\partial z}{\partial x} = \sec y \neq 0.$$

67. $z = \ln\left(\dfrac{x}{x^2 + y^2}\right) = \ln x - \ln(x^2 + y^2)$

$$\frac{\partial z}{\partial x} = \frac{1}{x} - \frac{2x}{x^2 + y^2} = \frac{y^2 - x^2}{x(x^2 + y^2)}$$

$$\frac{\partial^2 z}{\partial x^2} = \frac{x^4 - 4x^2y^2 - y^4}{x^2(x^2 + y^2)^2}$$

$$\frac{\partial^2 z}{\partial y \partial x} = \frac{4xy}{(x^2 + y^2)^2}$$

$$\frac{\partial z}{\partial y} = -\frac{2y}{x^2 + y^2}$$

$$\frac{\partial^2 z}{\partial y^2} = \frac{2(y^2 - x^2)}{(x^2 + y^2)^2}$$

$$\frac{\partial^2 z}{\partial x \partial y} = \frac{4xy}{(x^2 + y^2)^2}$$

There are no points for which $z_x = z_y = 0$.

69. $f(x, y, z) = xyz$

$f_x(x, y, z) = yz$

$f_y(x, y, z) = xz$

$f_{yy}(x, y, z) = 0$

$f_{xy}(x, y, z) = z$

$f_{yx}(x, y, z) = z$

$f_{yyx}(x, y, z) = 0$

$f_{xyy}(x, y, z) = 0$

$f_{yxy}(x, y, z) = 0$

Therefore, $f_{xyy} = f_{yxy} = f_{yyx} = 0$.

71. $f(x, y, z) = e^{-x} \sin yz$

$f_x(x, y, z) = -e^{-x} \sin yz$

$f_y(x, y, z) = ze^{-x} \cos yz$

$f_{yy}(x, y, z) = -z^2 e^{-x} \sin yz$

$f_{xy}(x, y, z) = -ze^{-x} \cos yz$

$f_{yx}(x, y, z) = -ze^{-x} \cos yz$

$f_{yyx}(x, y, z) = z^2 e^{-x} \sin yz$

$f_{xyy}(x, y, z) = z^2 e^{-x} \sin yz$

$f_{yxy}(x, y, z) = z^2 e^{-x} \sin yz$

Therefore, $f_{xyy} = f_{yxy} = f_{yyx}$.

73. $z = 5xy$

$$\frac{\partial z}{\partial x} = 5y$$

$$\frac{\partial^2 z}{\partial x^2} = 0$$

$$\frac{\partial z}{\partial y} = 5x$$

$$\frac{\partial^2 z}{\partial y^2} = 0$$

Therefore, $\dfrac{\partial^2 z}{\partial x^2} + \dfrac{\partial^2 z}{\partial y^2} = 0 + 0 = 0.$

75. $z = e^x \sin y$

$\dfrac{\partial z}{\partial x} = e^x \sin y$

$\dfrac{\partial^2 z}{\partial x^2} = e^x \sin y$

$\dfrac{\partial z}{\partial y} = e^x \cos y$

$\dfrac{\partial^2 z}{\partial y^2} = -e^x \sin y$

Therefore, $\dfrac{\partial^2 z}{\partial x^2} + \dfrac{\partial^2 z}{\partial y^2} = e^x \sin y - e^x \sin y = 0.$

77. $z = \sin(x - ct)$

$\dfrac{\partial z}{\partial t} = -c \cos(x - ct)$

$\dfrac{\partial^2 z}{\partial t^2} = -c^2 \sin(x - ct)$

$\dfrac{\partial z}{\partial x} = \cos(x - ct)$

$\dfrac{\partial^2 z}{\partial x^2} = -\sin(x - ct)$

Therefore, $\dfrac{\partial^2 z}{\partial t^2} = c^2 \dfrac{\partial^2 z}{\partial x^2}.$

79. $z = e^{-t} \cos \dfrac{x}{c}$

$\dfrac{\partial z}{\partial t} = -e^{-t} \cos \dfrac{x}{c}$

$\dfrac{\partial z}{\partial x} = -\dfrac{1}{c} e^{-t} \sin \dfrac{x}{c}$

$\dfrac{\partial^2 z}{\partial x^2} = -\dfrac{1}{c^2} e^{-t} \cos \dfrac{x}{c}$

Therefore, $\dfrac{\partial z}{\partial t} = c^2 \dfrac{\partial^2 z}{\partial x^2}.$

81. See the definition on page 859.

83.

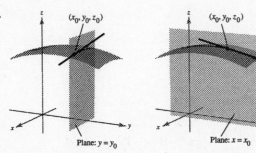

$\dfrac{\partial f}{\partial x}$ denotes the slope of the surface in the *x*-direction.

$\dfrac{\partial f}{\partial y}$ denotes the slope of the surface in the *y*-direction.

85. The plane $z = x + y = f(x, y)$ satisfies

$$\dfrac{\partial f}{\partial x} > 0 \text{ and } \dfrac{\partial f}{\partial y} > 0.$$

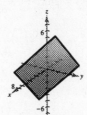

87. (a) $C = 32\sqrt{xy} + 175x + 205y + 1050$

$\dfrac{\partial C}{\partial x} = 16\sqrt{\dfrac{y}{x}} + 175$

$\dfrac{\partial C}{\partial x}\bigg]_{(80,\,20)} = 16\sqrt{\dfrac{1}{4}} + 175 = 183$

$\dfrac{\partial C}{\partial y} = 16\sqrt{\dfrac{x}{y}} + 205$

$\dfrac{\partial C}{\partial y}\bigg]_{(80,\,20)} = 16\sqrt{4} + 205 = 237$

(b) The fireplace-insert stove results in the cost increasing at a faster rate because

$$\dfrac{\partial C}{\partial y} > \dfrac{\partial C}{\partial x}.$$

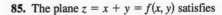

89. An increase in either price will cause a decrease in demand.

91. $T = 500 - 0.6x^2 - 1.5y^2$

$$\frac{\partial T}{\partial x} = -1.2x, \frac{\partial T}{\partial x}(2, 3) = -2.4°/m$$

$$\frac{\partial T}{\partial y} = -3y = \frac{\partial T}{\partial y}(2, 3) = -9°/m$$

93.
$$PV = mRT$$

$$T = \frac{PV}{mR} \Rightarrow \frac{\partial T}{\partial P} = \frac{V}{mR}$$

$$P = \frac{mRT}{V} \Rightarrow \frac{\partial P}{\partial V} = -\frac{mRT}{V^2}$$

$$V = \frac{mRT}{P} \Rightarrow \frac{\partial V}{\partial T} = \frac{mR}{P}$$

$$\frac{\partial T}{\partial P} \cdot \frac{\partial P}{\partial V} \cdot \frac{\partial V}{\partial T} = \left(\frac{V}{mR}\right)\left(-\frac{mRT}{V^2}\right)\left(\frac{mR}{P}\right)$$

$$= -\frac{mRT}{VP} = -\frac{mRT}{mRT} = -1$$

95. (a) $\dfrac{\partial z}{\partial x} = -1.83$

$\dfrac{\partial z}{\partial x} = -1.09$

(b) As the consumption of skim milk (x) increases, the consumption of whole milk (z) decreases.

Similarly, as the consumption of reduced-fat milk (y) increases, the consumption of whole milk (z) decreases.

97. $f(x, y) = \begin{cases} \dfrac{xy(x^2 - y^2)}{x^2 + y^2}, & (x, y) \neq (0, 0) \\ 0, & (x, y) = (0, 0) \end{cases}$

(a) $f_x(x, y) = \dfrac{(x^2 + y^2)(3x^2y - y^3) - (x^3y - xy^3)(2x)}{(x^2 + y^2)^2} = \dfrac{y(x^4 + 4x^2y^2 - y^4)}{(x^2 + y^2)^2}$

$f_y(x, y) = \dfrac{(x^2 + y^2)(x^3 - 3xy^2) - (x^3y - xy^3)(2y)}{(x^2 + y^2)^2} = \dfrac{x(x^4 - 4x^2y^2 - y^4)}{(x^2 + y^2)^2}$

(b) $f_x(0, 0) = \lim\limits_{\Delta x \to 0} \dfrac{f(\Delta x, 0) - f(0, 0)}{\Delta x} = \lim\limits_{\Delta x \to 0} \dfrac{0/[(\Delta x)^2] - 0}{\Delta x} = 0$

$f_y(0, 0) = \lim\limits_{\Delta y \to 0} \dfrac{f(0, \Delta y) - f(0, 0)}{\Delta y} = \lim\limits_{\Delta y \to 0} \dfrac{0/[(\Delta y)^2] - 0}{\Delta y} = 0$

(c) $f_{xy}(0, 0) = \dfrac{\partial}{\partial y}\left(\dfrac{\partial f}{\partial x}\right)\Bigg|_{(0, 0)} = \lim\limits_{\Delta y \to 0} \dfrac{f_x(0, \Delta y) - f_x(0, 0)}{\Delta y} = \lim\limits_{\Delta y \to 0} \dfrac{\Delta y(-(\Delta y)^4)}{((\Delta y)^2)^2(\Delta y)} = \lim\limits_{\Delta y \to 0} (-1) = -1$

$f_{yx}(0, 0) = \dfrac{\partial}{\partial x}\left(\dfrac{\partial f}{\partial y}\right)\Bigg|_{(0, 0)} = \lim\limits_{\Delta x \to 0} \dfrac{f_y(\Delta x, 0) - f_y(0, 0)}{\Delta x} = \lim\limits_{\Delta x \to 0} \dfrac{\Delta x((\Delta x)^4)}{((\Delta x)^2)^2(\Delta x)} = \lim\limits_{\Delta x \to 0} 1 = 1$

(d) f_{yx} or f_{xy} or both are not continuous at $(0, 0)$.

99. True

101. True

Section 12.4   Differentials

1. $z = 3x^2y^3$

$dz = 6xy^3\, dx + 9x^2y^2\, dy$

3. $z = \dfrac{-1}{x^2 + y^2}$

$dz = \dfrac{2x}{(x^2 + y^2)^2}\, dx + \dfrac{2y}{(x^2 + y^2)^2}\, dy$

$= \dfrac{2}{(x^2 + y^2)^2}(x\, dx + y\, dy)$

5. $z = x \cos y - y \cos x$

$dz = (\cos y + y \sin x)\, dx + (-x \sin y - \cos x)\, dy = (\cos y + y \sin x)\, dx - (x \sin y + \cos x)\, dy$

7. $z = e^x \sin y$

$dz = (e^x \sin y)\, dx + (e^x \cos y)\, dy$

9. $w = 2z^3 y \sin x$

$dw = 2z^3 y \cos x\, dx + 2z^3 \sin x\, dy + 6z^2 y \sin x\, dz$

11. (a) $f(1, 2) = 4$

   $f(1.05, 2.1) = 3.4875$

   $\Delta z = f(1.05, 2.1) - f(1, 2) = -0.5125$

   (b) $dz = -2x\, dx - 2y\, dy$

   $= -2(0.05) - 4(0.1) = -0.5$

13. (a) $f(1, 2) = \sin 2$

   $f(1.05, 2.1) = 1.05 \sin 2.1$

   $\Delta z = f(1.05, 2.1) - f(1, 2) \approx -0.00293$

   (b) $dz = \sin y\, dx + x \cos y\, dy$

   $= (\sin 2)(0.05) + (\cos 2)(0.1) \approx 0.00385$

15. (a) $f(1, 2) = -5$

   $f(1.05, 2.1) = -5.25$

   $\Delta z = -0.25$

   (b) $dz = 3\, dx - 4\, dy$

   $= 3(0.05) - 4(0.1) \approx -0.25$

17. Let $z = \sqrt{x^2 + y^2}$, $x = 5$, $y = 3$, $dx = 0.05$, $dy = 0.1$. Then: $dz = \dfrac{x}{\sqrt{x^2 + y^2}}\, dx + \dfrac{y}{\sqrt{x^2 + y^2}}\, dy$

$\sqrt{(5.05)^2 + (3.1)^2} - \sqrt{5^2 + 3^2} \approx \dfrac{5}{\sqrt{5^2 + 3^2}}(0.05) + \dfrac{3}{\sqrt{5^2 + 3^2}}(0.1) = \dfrac{0.55}{\sqrt{34}} \approx 0.094$

19. Let $z = (1 - x^2)/y^2$, $x = 3$, $y = 6$, $dx = 0.05$, $dy = -0.05$. Then: $dz = -\dfrac{2x}{y^2}\, dx + \dfrac{-2(1 - x^2)}{y^3}\, dy$

$\dfrac{1 - (3.05)^2}{(5.95)^2} - \dfrac{1 - 3^2}{6^2} \approx -\dfrac{2(3)}{6^2}(0.05) - \dfrac{2(1 - 3^2)}{6^3}(-0.05) \approx -0.012$

21. See the definition on page 869.

23. The tangent plane to the surface $z = f(x, y)$ at the point P is a linear approximation of z.

25. $A = lh$

$dA = l\, dh + h\, dl$

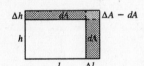

27. $V = \dfrac{\pi r^2 h}{3}$

$r = 3$

$h = 6$

$dV = \dfrac{2\pi rh}{3}\, dr + \dfrac{\pi r^2}{3}\, dh = \dfrac{\pi r}{3}(2h\, dr + r\, dh)$

Δr	Δh	dV	ΔV	$\Delta V - dV$
0.1	0.1	4.7124	4.8391	0.1267
0.1	-0.1	2.8274	2.8264	-0.0010
0.001	0.002	0.0565	0.0566	0.0001
-0.0001	0.0002	-0.0019	-0.0019	0.0000

29. (a) $dz = -1.83\,dx - 1.09\,dy$

(b) $dz = \dfrac{\partial z}{\partial x}\,dx + \dfrac{\partial z}{\partial y}\,dy$

$= -1.83(\pm 0.25) + (-1.09)(\pm 0.25)$

$= \pm 0.73$

Maximum propagated error: ± 0.73

Relative error: $\dfrac{dz}{z} = \dfrac{\pm 0.73}{(-1.83)(7.2) - 1.09(8.5) + 28.7} = \dfrac{\pm 0.73}{6.259} \approx \pm 0.1166 = 11.67\%$

31. $V = \pi r^2 h = dV = (2\pi rh)\,dr + (\pi r^2)\,dh$

$\dfrac{dV}{V} = 2\dfrac{dr}{r} + \dfrac{dh}{h}$

$= 2(0.04) + (0.02) = 0.10 = 10\%$

33. $A = \tfrac{1}{2}ab\sin C$

$dA = \tfrac{1}{2}[(b\sin C)\,da + (a\sin C)\,db + (ab\cos C)\,dC]$

$= \tfrac{1}{2}[4(\sin 45°)(\pm\tfrac{1}{16}) + 3(\sin 45°)(\pm\tfrac{1}{16}) + 12(\cos 45°)(\pm 0.02)] \approx \pm 0.24\text{ in.}^2$

35. (a) $V = \dfrac{1}{2}bhl$

$= \left(18\sin\dfrac{\theta}{2}\right)\left(18\cos\dfrac{\theta}{2}\right)(16)(12)$

$= 31{,}104\sin\theta\text{ in.}^3$

$= 18\sin\theta\text{ ft}^3$

V is maximum when $\sin\theta = 1$ or $\theta = \pi/2$.

(b) $V = \dfrac{s^2}{2}(\sin\theta)l$

$dV = s(\sin\theta)l\,ds + \dfrac{s^2}{2}l(\cos\theta)\,d\theta + \dfrac{s^2}{2}(\sin\theta)\,dl$

$= 18\left(\sin\dfrac{\pi}{2}\right)(16)(12)\left(\dfrac{1}{2}\right) + \dfrac{18^2}{2}(16)(12)\left(\cos\dfrac{\pi}{2}\right)\left(\dfrac{\pi}{90}\right) + \dfrac{18^2}{2}\left(\sin\dfrac{\pi}{2}\right)\left(\dfrac{1}{2}\right)$

$= 1809\text{ in}^3 \approx 1.047\text{ ft}^3$

37. $P = \dfrac{E^2}{R}$

$dP = \dfrac{2E}{R}\,dE - \dfrac{E^2}{R^2}\,dR$

$\dfrac{dP}{P} = 2\dfrac{dE}{E} - \dfrac{dR}{R} = 2(0.02) - (-0.03) = 0.07 = 7\%$

39. $L = 0.00021\left(\ln\frac{2h}{r} - 0.75\right)$

$dL = 0.00021\left[\frac{dh}{h} - \frac{dr}{r}\right] = 0.00021\left[\frac{(\pm 1/100)}{100} - \frac{(\pm 1/16)}{2}\right] \approx (\pm 6.6) \times 10^{-6}$

$L = 0.00021(\ln 100 - 0.75) \approx 8.096 \times 10^{-4} \pm dL = 8.096 \times 10^{-4} \pm 6.6 \times 10^{-6}$ micro–henrys

41. $z = f(x, y) = x^2 - 2x + y$

$\Delta z = f(x + \Delta x, y + \Delta y) - f(x, y)$

$= (x^2 + 2x(\Delta x) + (\Delta x)^2 - 2x - 2(\Delta x) + y + (\Delta y)) - (x^2 - 2x + y)$

$= 2x(\Delta x) + (\Delta x)^2 - 2(\Delta x) + (\Delta y)$

$= (2x - 2)\,\Delta x + \Delta y + \Delta x(\Delta x) + 0(\Delta y)$

$= f_x(x, y)\,\Delta x + f_y(x, y)\,\Delta y + \epsilon_1 \Delta x + \epsilon_2 \Delta y$ where $\epsilon_1 = \Delta x$ and $\epsilon_2 = 0$.

As $(\Delta x, \Delta y) \to (0, 0)$, $\epsilon_1 \to 0$ and $\epsilon_2 \to 0$.

43. $z = f(x, y) = x^2 y$

$\Delta z = f(x + \Delta x,\ y + \Delta y) - f(x, y)$

$= (x^2 + 2x(\Delta x) + (\Delta x)^2)(y + \Delta y) - x^2 y$

$= 2xy(\Delta x) + y(\Delta x)^2 + x^2 \Delta y + 2x(\Delta x)(\Delta y) + (\Delta x)^2\,\Delta y$

$= 2xy(\Delta x) + x^2 \Delta y + (y\Delta x)\,\Delta x + [2x\Delta x + (\Delta x)^2]\,\Delta y$

$= f_x(x, y)\,\Delta x + f_y(x, y)\,\Delta y + \epsilon_1 \Delta x + \epsilon_2 \Delta y$ where $\epsilon_1 = y(\Delta x)$ and $\epsilon_2 = 2x\Delta x + (\Delta x)^2$.

As $(\Delta x, \Delta y) \to (0, 0)$, $\epsilon_1 \to 0$ and $\epsilon_2 \to 0$.

45. $f(x, y) = \begin{cases} \dfrac{3x^2 y}{x^4 + y^2}, & (x, y) \neq (0, 0) \\ 0, & (x, y) = (0, 0) \end{cases}$

(a) $f_x(0, 0) = \lim\limits_{\Delta x \to 0} \dfrac{f(\Delta x, 0) - f(0, 0)}{\Delta x} = \lim\limits_{\Delta x \to 0} \dfrac{\frac{0}{(\Delta x)^4} - 0}{\Delta x} = 0$

$f_y(0, 0) = \lim\limits_{\Delta y \to 0} \dfrac{f(0, \Delta y) - f(0, 0)}{\Delta y} = \lim\limits_{\Delta y \to 0} \dfrac{\frac{0}{(\Delta y)^2} - 0}{\Delta y} = 0$

Thus, the partial derivatives exist at $(0, 0)$.

(b) Along the line $y = x$: $\lim\limits_{(x, y) \to (0, 0)} f(x, y) = \lim\limits_{x \to 0} \dfrac{3x^3}{x^4 + x^2} = \lim\limits_{x \to 0} \dfrac{3x}{x^2 + 1} = 0$

Along the curve $y = x^2$: $\lim\limits_{(x, y) \to (0, 0)} f(x, y) = \dfrac{3x^4}{2x^4} = \dfrac{3}{2}$

f is not continuous at $(0, 0)$. Therefore, f is not differentiable at $(0, 0)$. (See Theroem 12.5)

47. Essay. For example, we can use the equation $F = ma$:

$dF = \dfrac{\partial F}{\partial m}\,dm + \dfrac{\partial F}{\partial a}\,da = a\,dm + m\,da.$

Section 12.5   Chain Rules for Functions of Several Variables

1. $w = x^2 + y^2$

    $x = e^t$

    $y = e^{-t}$

    $\dfrac{dw}{dt} = 2xe^t + 2y(-e^{-t}) = 2(e^{2t} - e^{-2t})$

3. $w = x \sec y$

    $x = e^t$

    $y = \pi - t$

    $\dfrac{dw}{dt} = (\sec y)(e^t) + (x \sec y \tan y)(-1)$

          $= e^t \sec(\pi - t)[1 - \tan(\pi - t)]$

          $= -e^t (\sec t + \sec t \tan t)$

5. $w = xy, \; x = 2 \sin t, \; y = \cos t$

    (a) $\dfrac{dw}{dt} = 2y \cos t + x(-\sin t) = 2y \cos t - x \sin t$

         $= 2(\cos^2 t - \sin^2 t) = 2 \cos 2t$

    (b) $w = 2 \sin t \cos t = \sin 2t, \; \dfrac{dw}{dt} = 2 \cos 2t$

7. $w = x^2 + y^2 + z^2$

    $x = e^t \cos t$

    $y = e^t \sin t$

    $z = e^t$

    (a) $\dfrac{dw}{dt} = 2x(-e^t \sin t + e^t \cos t) + 2y(e^t \cos t + e^t \sin t) + 2ze^t = 4e^{2t}$

    (b) $w = 2e^{2t}, \; \dfrac{dw}{dt} = 4e^{2t}$

9. $w = xy + xz + yz, \; x = t - 1, \; y = t^2 - 1, \; z = t$

    (a) $\dfrac{dw}{dt} = (y + z) = (x + z)(2t) + (x + y)$

         $= (t^2 - 1 + t) + (t - 1 + 1)(2t) + (t - 1 + t^2 - 1) = 3(2t^2 - 1)$

    (b) $w = (t - 1)(t^2 - 1) + (t - 1)t + (t^2 - 1)t$

        $\dfrac{dw}{dt} = 2t(t - 1) + (t^2 - 1) + 2t - 1 + 3t^2 - 1 = 3(2t^2 - 1)$

11.   Distance $= f(t) = \sqrt{(x_1 - x_2)^2 + (y_1 - y_2)^2} = \sqrt{(10 \cos 2t - 7 \cos t)^2 + (6 \sin 2t - 4 \sin t)^2}$

      $f'(t) = \dfrac{1}{2}[(10 \cos 2t - 7 \cos t)^2 + (6 \sin 2t - 4 \sin t)^2]^{-1/2}$

           $[[2(10 \cos 2t - 7 \cos t)(-20 \sin 2t + 7 \sin t)] + [2(6 \sin 2t - 4 \sin t)(12 \cos 2t - 4 \cos t)]]$

      $f'\!\left(\dfrac{\pi}{2}\right) = \dfrac{1}{2}[(-10)^2 + 4^2]^{-1/2}[[2(-10)(7)] + (2(-4)(-12)]$

         $= \dfrac{1}{2}(116)^{-1/2}(-44) = \dfrac{22}{2\sqrt{29}} = \dfrac{-11\sqrt{29}}{20} \approx -2.04$

13. $w = \arctan(2xy)$, $x = \cos t$, $y = \sin t$, $t = 0$

$$\frac{dw}{dt} = \frac{\partial w}{\partial x}\frac{dx}{dt} + \frac{\partial w}{\partial y}\frac{dy}{dt}$$

$$= \frac{2y}{1 + (4x^2y^2)}(-\sin t) + \frac{2x}{1 + (4x^2y^2)}(\cos t)$$

$$= \frac{2\sin t}{1 + 4\cos^2 t \sin^2 t}(-\sin t) + \frac{2\cos t}{1 + 4\cos^2 t \sin^2 t}(\cos t)$$

$$= \frac{2\cos^2 t - 2\sin^2 t}{1 + 4\cos^2 t \sin^2 t}$$

$$\frac{d^2w}{dt^2} = \frac{(1 + 4\cos^2 t \sin^2 t)(-8\cos t \sin t) - (2\cos^2 t - 2\sin^2 t)(8\cos^3 t \sin t - 8\sin^3 t \cos t)}{(1 + 4\cos^2 t \sin^2 t)^2}$$

$$= \frac{-8\cos t \sin t(1 + 2\sin^4 t + 2\cos^4 t)}{(1 + 4\cos^2 t \sin^2 t)^2}$$

At $t = 0$, $\dfrac{d^2w}{dt^2} = 0$.

15. $w = x^2 + y^2$

$x = s + t$

$y = s - t$

$\dfrac{\partial w}{\partial s} = 2x + 2y = 2(x + y) = 4s$

$\dfrac{\partial w}{\partial t} = 2x + 2y(-1) = 2(x - y) = 4t$

When $s = 2$ and $t = -1$,

$\dfrac{\partial w}{\partial s} = 8$ and $\dfrac{\partial w}{\partial t} = -4$.

17. $w = x^2 - y^2$

$x = s\cos t$

$y = s\sin t$

$\dfrac{\partial w}{\partial s} = 2x\cos t - 2y\sin t$

$\qquad = 2s\cos^2 t - 2s\sin^2 t = 2s\cos 2t$

$\dfrac{\partial w}{\partial t} = 2x(-s\sin t) - 2y(s\cos t) = -2s^2\sin 2t$

When $s = 3$ and $t = \dfrac{\pi}{4}$, $\dfrac{\partial w}{\partial s} = 0$ and $\dfrac{\partial w}{\partial t} = -18$.

19. $w = x^2 - 2xy + y^2$, $x = r + \theta$, $y = r - \theta$

(a) $\dfrac{\partial w}{\partial r} = (2x - 2y)(1) + (-2x + 2y)(1) = 0$

$\dfrac{\partial w}{\partial \theta} = (2x - 2y)(1) + (-2x + 2y)(-1)$

$\qquad = 4x - 4y = 4(x - y)$

$\qquad = 4[(r + \theta) - (r - \theta)] = 8\theta$

(b) $w = (r + \theta)^2 - 2(r + \theta)(r - \theta) + (r - \theta)^2$

$\qquad = (r^2 + 2r\theta + \theta^2) - 2(r^2 - \theta^2) + (r^2 - 2r\theta + \theta^2)$

$\qquad = 4\theta^2$

$\dfrac{\partial w}{\partial r} = 0$

$\dfrac{\partial w}{\partial \theta} = 8\theta$

21. $w = \arctan \dfrac{y}{x}$, $x = r \cos \theta$, $y = r \sin \theta$

   (a) $\dfrac{\partial w}{\partial r} = \dfrac{-y}{x^2 + y^2} \cos \theta + \dfrac{x}{x^2 + y^2} \sin \theta = \dfrac{-r \sin \theta \cos \theta}{r^2} + \dfrac{r \cos \theta \sin \theta}{r^2} = 0$

       $\dfrac{\partial w}{\partial \theta} = \dfrac{-y}{x^2 + y^2}(-r \sin \theta) + \dfrac{x}{x^2 + y^2}(r \cos \theta) = \dfrac{-(r \sin \theta)(-r \sin \theta)}{r^2} + \dfrac{(r \cos \theta)(r \cos \theta)}{r^2} = 1$

   (b) $w = \arctan \dfrac{r \sin \theta}{r \cos \theta} = \arctan(\tan \theta) = \theta$

       $\dfrac{\partial w}{\partial r} = 0$

       $\dfrac{\partial w}{\partial \theta} = 1$

23. $w = xyz$, $x = s + t$, $y = s - t$, $z = st^2$

   $\dfrac{\partial w}{\partial s} = yz(1) + xz(1) + xy(t^2)$

      $= (s - t)st^2 + (s + t)st^2 + (s + t)(s - t)t^2$

      $= 2s^2t^2 + s^2t^2 - t^4 = 3s^2t^2 - t^4 = t^2(3s^2 - t^2)$

   $\dfrac{\partial w}{\partial t} = yz(1) + xz(-1) + xy(2st)$

      $= (s - t)st^2 - (s + t)st^2 + (s + t)(s - t)(2st)$

      $= -2st^3 + 2s^3t - 2st^3 = 2s^3t - 4st^3 = 2st(s^2 - 2t^2)$

25. $w = ze^{x/y}$, $x = s - t$, $y = s + t$, $z = st$

   $\dfrac{\partial w}{\partial s} = \dfrac{z}{y}e^{x/y}(1) + -\dfrac{zx}{y^2}e^{x/y}(1) + e^{x/y}(t)$

      $= e^{(s-t/s+t)}\left[\dfrac{st}{s + t} - \dfrac{(s - t)st}{(s + t)^2} + t \right]$

      $= e^{(s-t/s+t)}\left[\dfrac{st(s + t) - s^2t + st^2 + t(s + t)^2}{(s + t)^2} \right]$

      $= e^{(s-t/s+t)}\dfrac{t(s^2 + 4st + t^2)}{(s + t)^2}$

   $\dfrac{\partial w}{\partial t} = \dfrac{z}{y}e^{x/y}(-1) + -\dfrac{zx}{y^2}e^{x/y}(1) + e^{x/y}(s)$

      $= e^{(s-t/s+t)}\left[-\dfrac{st}{s + t} - \dfrac{st(s - t)}{(s + t)^2} + s \right]$

      $= e^{(s-t/s+t)}\left[\dfrac{-st(s + t) - st(s - t) + s(s + t)^2}{(s + t)^2} \right]$

      $= e^{(s-t/s+t)}\dfrac{s(s^2 + t^2)}{(s + t)^2}$

27. $x^2 - 3xy + y^2 - 2x + y - 5 = 0$

   $\dfrac{dy}{dx} = -\dfrac{F_x(x, y)}{F_y(x, y)} = -\dfrac{2x - 3y - 2}{-3x + 2y + 1}$

       $= \dfrac{3y - 2x + 2}{2y - 3x + 1}$

29. $\ln \sqrt{x^2 + y^2} + xy = 4$

   $\dfrac{1}{2}\ln(x^2 + y^2) + xy - 4 = 0$

   $\dfrac{dy}{dx} = -\dfrac{F_x(x, y)}{F_y(x, y)} = -\dfrac{\dfrac{x}{x^2 + y^2} + y}{\dfrac{y}{x^2 + y^2} + x} = -\dfrac{x + x^2y + y^3}{y + xy^2 + x^3}$

31. $F(x, y, z) = x^2 + y^2 + z^2 - 25$

   $F_x = 2x$

   $F_y = 2y$

   $F_z = 2z$

   $\dfrac{\partial z}{\partial x} = -\dfrac{F_x}{F_z} = -\dfrac{x}{z}$

   $\dfrac{\partial z}{\partial y} = -\dfrac{F_y}{F_z} = -\dfrac{y}{z}$

33. $F(x, y, z) = \tan(x + y) + \tan(y + z) - 1$

   $F_x = \sec^2(x + y)$

   $F_y = \sec^2(x + y) + \sec^2(y + z)$

   $F_z = \sec^2(y + z)$

   $\dfrac{\partial z}{\partial x} = -\dfrac{F_x}{F_z} = -\dfrac{\sec^2(x + y)}{\sec^2(y + z)}$

   $\dfrac{\partial z}{\partial y} = -\dfrac{F_y}{F_z} = -\dfrac{\sec^2(x + y) + \sec^2(y + z)}{\sec^2(y + z)}$

       $= -\left(\dfrac{\sec^2(x + y)}{\sec^2(y + z)} + 1 \right)$

35. $x^2 + 2yz + z^2 - 1 = 0$

  (i) $2x + 2y\dfrac{\partial z}{\partial x} + 2z\dfrac{\partial z}{\partial x} = 0$ implies $\dfrac{\partial z}{\partial x} = -\dfrac{x}{y+z}.$

  (ii) $2y\dfrac{\partial z}{\partial y} + 2z + 2z\dfrac{\partial z}{\partial y} = 0$ implies $\dfrac{\partial z}{\partial y} = -\dfrac{z}{y+z}.$

37. $e^{xz} + xy = 0$

$$\frac{\partial z}{\partial x} = -\frac{F_x(x,y,z)}{F_z(x,y,z)} = -\frac{ze^{xz}+y}{xe^{xz}}$$

$$\frac{\partial z}{\partial y} = -\frac{F_y(x,y,z)}{F_z(x,y,z)} = \frac{-x}{xe^{xz}} = \frac{-1}{e^{xz}} = -e^{-xz}$$

39. $F(x,y,z,w) = xyz + xzw - yzw + w^2 - 5$

$$F_x = yz + zw$$
$$F_y = xz - zw$$
$$F_z = xy + xw - yw$$
$$F_w = xz - yz + 2w$$
$$\frac{\partial w}{\partial x} = -\frac{F_x}{F_w} = -\frac{z(y+w)}{xz - yz + 2w}$$
$$\frac{\partial w}{\partial y} = -\frac{F_y}{F_w} = -\frac{z(x-w)}{xz - yz + 2w}$$
$$\frac{\partial w}{\partial z} = -\frac{F_z}{F_w} = -\frac{xy + xw - yw}{xz - yz + 2w}$$

41. $F(x,y,z,w) = \cos xy + \sin yz + wz - 20$

$$\frac{\partial w}{\partial x} = \frac{-F_x}{F_w} = \frac{y\sin xy}{z}$$
$$\frac{\partial w}{\partial y} = \frac{-F_y}{F_w} = \frac{x\sin xy - z\cos yz}{z}$$
$$\frac{\partial w}{\partial z} = \frac{-F_z}{F_w} = -\frac{y\cos zy + w}{z}$$

43. $f(x,y) = \dfrac{xy}{\sqrt{x^2+y^2}}$

$$f(tx,ty) = \frac{(tx)(ty)}{\sqrt{(tx)^2+(ty)^2}} = t\left(\frac{xy}{\sqrt{x^2+y^2}}\right) = tf(x,y)$$

Degree: 1

$$xf_x(x,y) + yf_y(x,y) = x\left(\frac{y^3}{(x^2+y^2)^{3/2}}\right) + y\left(\frac{x^3}{(x^2+y^2)^{3/2}}\right)$$
$$= \frac{xy}{\sqrt{x^2+y^2}} = 1f(x,y)$$

45. $f(x,y) = e^{x/y}$

$$f(tx,ty) = e^{tx/ty} = e^{x/y} = f(x,y)$$

Degree: 0

$$xf_x(x,y) + yf_y(x,y) = x\left(\frac{1}{y}e^{x/y}\right) + y\left(-\frac{x}{y^2}e^{x/y}\right) = 0$$

47. $\dfrac{dw}{dt} = \dfrac{\partial w}{\partial x}\dfrac{dx}{dt} + \dfrac{\partial w}{\partial y}\dfrac{dy}{dt}$ (Page 876)

49. $w = f(x,y)$ is the explicit form of a function of two variables, as in $z = x^2 + y^2$.
The implicit form is of the form $F(x,y,z) = 0$, as in $z - x^2 - y^2 = 0$.

51. $A = \dfrac{1}{2}bh = \left(x\sin\dfrac{\theta}{2}\right)\left(x\cos\dfrac{\theta}{2}\right) = \dfrac{x^2}{2}\sin\theta$

$$\frac{dA}{dt} = x\sin\theta\,\frac{dx}{dt} + \frac{x^2}{2}\cos\theta\,\frac{d\theta}{dt}$$
$$= 6\left(\sin\frac{\pi}{4}\right)\left(\frac{1}{2}\right) + \frac{6^2}{2}\left(\cos\frac{\pi}{4}\right)\left(\frac{\pi}{90}\right) = \frac{3\sqrt{2}}{2} + \frac{\pi\sqrt{2}}{10}\ \text{m}^2/\text{hr}$$

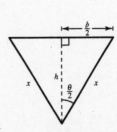

53. (a) $V = \dfrac{1}{3}\pi r^2 h$

$$\frac{dV}{dt} = \frac{1}{3}\pi\left(2rh\frac{dr}{dt} + r^2\frac{dh}{dt}\right) = \frac{1}{3}\pi[2(12)(36)(6) + (12)^2(-4)] = 1536\pi \text{ in.}^3/\text{min}$$

(b) $S = \pi r\sqrt{r^2 + h^2} + \pi r^2$ (Surface area includes base.)

$$\frac{dS}{dt} = \pi\left[\left(\sqrt{r^2 + h^2} + \frac{r^2}{\sqrt{r^2 + h^2}} + 2r\right)\frac{dr}{dt} + \frac{rh}{\sqrt{r^2 + h^2}}\frac{dh}{dt}\right]$$

$$= \pi\left[\left(\sqrt{12^2 + 36^2} + \frac{144}{\sqrt{12^2 + 36^2}} + 2(12)\right)(6) + \frac{36(12)}{\sqrt{12^2 + 36^2}}(-4)\right]$$

$$= \pi\left[\left(12\sqrt{10} + \frac{12}{\sqrt{10}}\right)(6) + 144 + \frac{36}{\sqrt{10}}(-4)\right]$$

$$= \frac{648\pi}{\sqrt{10}} + 144\pi \text{ in.}^2/\text{min} = \frac{36\pi}{5}\left(20 + 9\sqrt{10}\right) \text{ in.}^2/\text{min}$$

55. $I = \dfrac{1}{2}m(r_1{}^2 + r_2{}^2)$

$$\frac{dI}{dt} = \frac{1}{2}m\left[2r_1\frac{dr_1}{dt} + 2r_2\frac{dr_2}{dt}\right] = m[(6)(2) + (8)(2)] = 28m \text{ cm}^2/\text{sec}$$

57. (a)

$$\tan\phi = \frac{2}{x}$$

$$\tan(\theta + \phi) = \frac{4}{x}$$

$$\frac{\tan\theta + \tan\phi}{1 - \tan\theta\tan\phi} = \frac{4}{x}$$

$$\frac{\tan\theta + (2/x)}{1 - (2/x)\tan\theta} = \frac{4}{x}$$

$$x\tan\theta + 2 = 4 - \frac{8}{x}\tan\theta$$

$$x^2\tan\theta - 2x + 8\tan\theta = 0$$

(b) $F(x, \theta) = (x^2 + 8)\tan\theta - 2x = 0$

$$\frac{d\theta}{dx} = -\frac{F_x}{F_\theta} = -\frac{2x\tan\theta - 2}{\sec^2\theta(x^2 + 8)} = \frac{2\cos^2\theta - 2x\sin\theta\cos\theta}{x^2 + 8}$$

(c) $\dfrac{d\theta}{dx} = 0 \Rightarrow 2\cos^2\theta = 2x\sin\theta\cos\theta \Rightarrow \cos\theta = x\sin\theta \Rightarrow \tan\theta = \dfrac{1}{x}$

Thus, $x^2\left(\dfrac{1}{x}\right) - 2x + 8\left(\dfrac{1}{x}\right) = 0 \Rightarrow \dfrac{8}{x} = x \Rightarrow x = 2\sqrt{2}$ ft.

59.

$$w = f(x, y)$$

$$x = u - v$$

$$y = v - u$$

$$\frac{\partial w}{\partial u} = \frac{\partial w}{\partial x}\frac{dx}{du} + \frac{\partial w}{\partial y}\frac{dy}{du} = \frac{\partial w}{\partial x} - \frac{\partial w}{\partial y}$$

$$\frac{\partial w}{\partial v} = \frac{\partial w}{\partial x}\frac{dx}{dv} + \frac{\partial w}{\partial y}\frac{dy}{dv} = -\frac{\partial w}{\partial x} + \frac{\partial w}{\partial y}$$

$$\frac{\partial w}{\partial u} + \frac{\partial w}{\partial v} = 0$$

61. $w = f(x, y)$, $x = r \cos \theta$, $y = r \sin \theta$

$$\frac{\partial w}{\partial r} = \frac{\partial w}{\partial x} \cos \theta + \frac{\partial w}{\partial y} \sin \theta$$

$$\frac{\partial w}{\partial \theta} = \frac{\partial w}{\partial x}(-r \sin \theta) + \frac{\partial w}{\partial y}(r \cos \theta)$$

(a)
$$r \cos \theta \frac{\partial w}{\partial r} = \frac{\partial w}{\partial x} r \cos^2 \theta + \frac{\partial w}{\partial y} r \sin \theta \cos \theta$$

$$-\sin \theta \frac{\partial w}{\partial \theta} = \frac{\partial w}{\partial x}(r \sin^2 \theta) - \frac{\partial w}{\partial x} r \sin \theta \cos \theta$$

$$r \cos \theta \frac{\partial w}{\partial r} - \sin \theta \frac{\partial w}{\partial \theta} = \frac{\partial w}{\partial x}(r \cos^2 \theta + r \sin^2 \theta)$$

$$r \frac{\partial w}{\partial x} = \frac{\partial w}{\partial r}(r \cos \theta) - \frac{\partial w}{\partial \theta} \sin \theta$$

$$\frac{\partial w}{\partial x} = \frac{\partial w}{\partial r} \cos \theta - \frac{\partial w}{\partial \theta} \frac{\sin \theta}{r}$$

$$r \sin \theta \frac{\partial w}{\partial r} = \frac{\partial w}{\partial x} r \sin \theta \cos \theta + \frac{\partial w}{\partial y} r \sin^2 \theta$$

$$\cos \theta \frac{\partial w}{\partial \theta} = \frac{\partial w}{\partial x}(-r \sin \theta \cos \theta) + \frac{\partial w}{\partial y}(r \cos^2 \theta)$$

$$r \sin \theta \frac{\partial w}{\partial r} + \cos \theta \frac{\partial w}{\partial \theta} = \frac{\partial w}{\partial y}(r \sin^2 \theta + r \cos^2 \theta)$$

$$r \frac{\partial w}{\partial y} = \frac{\partial w}{\partial r} r \sin \theta + \frac{\partial w}{\partial \theta} \cos \theta$$

$$\frac{\partial w}{\partial y} = \frac{\partial w}{\partial r} \sin \theta + \frac{\partial w}{\partial \theta} \frac{\cos \theta}{r}$$

(b) $\left(\dfrac{\partial w}{\partial r}\right)^2 + \dfrac{1}{r^2}\left(\dfrac{\partial w}{\partial \theta}\right)^2 = \left(\dfrac{\partial w}{\partial x}\right)^2 \cos^2 \theta + 2 \dfrac{\partial w}{\partial x} \dfrac{\partial w}{\partial y} \sin \theta \cos \theta + \left(\dfrac{\partial w}{\partial y}\right)^2 \sin^2 \theta + \left(\dfrac{\partial w}{\partial x}\right)^2 \sin^2 \theta -$

$$2 \frac{\partial w}{\partial x} \frac{\partial w}{\partial y} \sin \theta \cos \theta + \left(\frac{\partial w}{\partial y}\right)^2 \cos^2 \theta = \left(\frac{\partial w}{\partial x}\right)^2 + \left(\frac{\partial w}{\partial y}\right)^2$$

63. Given $\dfrac{\partial u}{\partial x} = \dfrac{\partial v}{\partial y}$ and $\dfrac{\partial u}{\partial y} = -\dfrac{\partial v}{\partial x}$, $x = r \cos \theta$ and $y = r \sin \theta$.

$$\frac{\partial u}{\partial r} = \frac{\partial u}{\partial x} \cos \theta + \frac{\partial u}{\partial y} \sin \theta = \frac{\partial v}{\partial y} \cos \theta - \frac{\partial v}{\partial x} \sin \theta$$

$$\frac{\partial v}{\partial \theta} = \frac{\partial v}{\partial x}(-r \sin \theta) + \frac{\partial v}{\partial y}(r \cos \theta) = r\left[\frac{\partial v}{\partial y} \cos \theta - \frac{\partial v}{\partial x} \sin \theta\right]$$

Therefore, $\dfrac{\partial u}{\partial r} = \dfrac{1}{r} \dfrac{\partial v}{\partial \theta}$.

$$\frac{\partial v}{\partial r} = \frac{\partial v}{\partial x} \cos \theta + \frac{\partial v}{\partial y} \sin \theta = -\frac{\partial u}{\partial y} \cos \theta + \frac{\partial u}{\partial x} \sin \theta$$

$$\frac{\partial u}{\partial \theta} = \frac{\partial u}{\partial x}(-r \sin \theta) + \frac{\partial u}{\partial y}(r \cos \theta) = -r\left[-\frac{\partial u}{\partial y} \cos \theta + \frac{\partial u}{\partial x} \sin \theta\right]$$

Therefore, $\dfrac{\partial v}{\partial r} = -\dfrac{1}{r} \dfrac{\partial u}{\partial \theta}$.

Section 12.6 Directional Derivatives and Gradients

1. $f(x, y) = 3x - 4xy + 5y$

$$v = \frac{1}{2}(i + \sqrt{3}j)$$

$$\nabla f(x, y) = (3 - 4y)i + (-4x + 5)j$$

$$\nabla f(1, 2) = -5i + j$$

$$u = \frac{v}{\|v\|} = \frac{1}{2}i + \frac{\sqrt{3}}{2}j$$

$$D_u f(1, 2) = \nabla f(1, 2) \cdot u = \frac{1}{2}(-5 + \sqrt{3})$$

3. $f(x, y) = xy$

$$v = i + j$$

$$\nabla f(x, y) = yi + xj$$

$$\nabla f(2, 3) = 3i + 2j$$

$$u = \frac{v}{\|v\|} = \frac{\sqrt{2}}{2}i + \frac{\sqrt{2}}{2}j$$

$$D_u f(2, 3) = \nabla f(2, 3) \cdot u = \frac{5\sqrt{2}}{2}$$

5. $g(x, y) = \sqrt{x^2 + y^2}$

$$v = 3i - 4j$$

$$\nabla g = \frac{x}{\sqrt{x^2 + y^2}}i + \frac{y}{\sqrt{x^2 + y^2}}j$$

$$\nabla g(3, 4) = \frac{3}{5}i + \frac{4}{5}j$$

$$u = \frac{v}{\|v\|} = \frac{3}{5}i - \frac{4}{5}j$$

$$D_u g(3, 4) = \nabla g(3, 4) \cdot u = -\frac{7}{25}$$

7. $h(x, y) = e^x \sin y$

$$v = -i$$

$$\nabla h = e^x \sin yi + e^x \cos yj$$

$$h\left(1, \frac{\pi}{2}\right) = ei$$

$$u = \frac{v}{\|v\|} = -i$$

$$D_u h\left(1, \frac{\pi}{2}\right) = \nabla h\left(1, \frac{\pi}{2}\right) \cdot u = -e$$

9. $f(x, y, z) = xy + yz + xz$

$$v = 2i + j - k$$

$$\nabla f(x, y, z) = (y + z)i + (x + z)j + (x + y)k$$

$$\nabla f(1, 1, 1) = 2i + 2j + 2k$$

$$u = \frac{v}{\|v\|} = \frac{\sqrt{6}}{3}i + \frac{\sqrt{6}}{6}j - \frac{\sqrt{6}}{6}k$$

$$D_u f(1, 1, 1) = \nabla f(1, 1, 1) \cdot u = \frac{2\sqrt{6}}{3}$$

11. $h(x, y, z) = x \arctan yz$

$$v = \langle 1, 2, -1 \rangle$$

$$\nabla h(x, y, z) = \arctan yzi + \frac{xz}{1 + (yz)^2}j + \frac{xy}{1 + (yz)^2}k$$

$$\nabla h(4, 1, 1) = \frac{\pi}{4}i + 2j + 2k$$

$$u = \frac{v}{\|v\|} = \left\langle \frac{1}{\sqrt{6}}, \frac{2}{\sqrt{6}}, -\frac{1}{\sqrt{6}} \right\rangle$$

$$D_u h(4, 1, 1) = \nabla h(4, 1, 1) \cdot u = \frac{\pi + 8}{4\sqrt{6}} = \frac{(\pi + 8)\sqrt{6}}{24}$$

13. $f(x, y) = x^2 + y^2$

$$u = \frac{1}{\sqrt{2}}i + \frac{1}{\sqrt{2}}j$$

$$\nabla f = 2xi + 2yj$$

$$D_u f = \nabla f \cdot u = \frac{2}{\sqrt{2}}x + \frac{2}{\sqrt{2}}y = \sqrt{2}(x + y)$$

15. $f(x, y) = \sin(2x - y)$

$$u = \frac{1}{2}i - \frac{\sqrt{3}}{2}j$$

$$\nabla f = 2\cos(2x - y)i - \cos(2x - y)j$$

$$D_u f = \nabla f \cdot u = \cos(2x - y) + \frac{\sqrt{3}}{2}\cos(2x - y)$$

$$= \left(\frac{2 + \sqrt{3}}{2}\right)\cos(2x - y)$$

17. $f(x, y) = x^2 + 4y^2$

$\mathbf{v} = -2\mathbf{i} - 2\mathbf{j}$

$\nabla f = 2x\mathbf{i} + 8y\mathbf{j}$

$\mathbf{u} = \dfrac{\mathbf{v}}{\|\mathbf{v}\|} = -\dfrac{1}{\sqrt{2}}\mathbf{i} - \dfrac{1}{\sqrt{2}}\mathbf{j}$

$D_{\mathbf{u}}f = -\dfrac{2}{\sqrt{2}}x - \dfrac{8}{\sqrt{2}}y = -\sqrt{2}(x + 4y)$

At $P = (3, 1)$, $D_{\mathbf{u}}f = -7\sqrt{2}$.

19. $h(x, y, z) = \ln(x + y + z)$

$\mathbf{v} = 3\mathbf{i} + 3\mathbf{j} + \mathbf{k}$

$\nabla h = \dfrac{1}{x + y + z}(\mathbf{i} + \mathbf{j} + \mathbf{k})$

At $(1, 0, 0)$, $\nabla h = \mathbf{i} + \mathbf{j} + \mathbf{k}$.

$\mathbf{u} = \dfrac{\mathbf{v}}{\|\mathbf{v}\|} = \dfrac{1}{\sqrt{19}}(3\mathbf{i} + 3\mathbf{j} + \mathbf{k})$

$D_{\mathbf{u}}h = \nabla h \cdot \mathbf{u} = \dfrac{7}{\sqrt{19}} = \dfrac{7\sqrt{19}}{19}$

21. $f(x, y) = 3x - 5y^2 + 10$

$\nabla f(x, y) = 3\mathbf{i} - 10y\mathbf{j}$

$\nabla f(2, 1) = 3\mathbf{i} - 10\mathbf{j}$

23. $z = \cos(x^2 + y^2)$

$\nabla z(x, y) = -2x\sin(x^2 + y^2)\mathbf{i} - 2y\sin(x^2 + y^2)\mathbf{j}$

$\nabla z(3, -4) = -6\sin 25\mathbf{i} + 8\sin 25\mathbf{j} \approx 0.7941\mathbf{i} - 1.0588\mathbf{j}$

25. $w = 3x^2y - 5yz + z^2$

$\nabla w(x, y, z) = 6xy\mathbf{i} + (3x^2 - 5z)\mathbf{j} + (2z - 5y)\mathbf{k}$

$\nabla w(1, 1, -2) = 6\mathbf{i} + 13\mathbf{j} - 9\mathbf{k}$

27. $\overrightarrow{PQ} = 2\mathbf{i} + 4\mathbf{j}$, $\mathbf{u} = \dfrac{1}{\sqrt{5}}\mathbf{i} = \dfrac{2}{\sqrt{5}}\mathbf{j}$

$\nabla g(x, y) = 2x\mathbf{i} + 2y\mathbf{j}$, $\nabla g(1, 2) = 2\mathbf{i} + 4\mathbf{j}$

$D_{\mathbf{u}}g = \nabla g \cdot \mathbf{u} = \dfrac{2}{\sqrt{5}} + \dfrac{8}{\sqrt{5}} = \dfrac{10}{\sqrt{5}} = 2\sqrt{5}$

29. $\overrightarrow{PQ} = 2\mathbf{i} + \mathbf{j}$, $\mathbf{u} = \dfrac{2}{\sqrt{5}}\mathbf{i} + \dfrac{1}{\sqrt{5}}\mathbf{j}$

$\nabla f(x, y) = -e^{-x}\cos y\mathbf{i} - e^{-x}\sin y\mathbf{j}$

$\nabla f(0, 0) = -\mathbf{i}$

$D_{\mathbf{u}}f = \nabla f \cdot \mathbf{u} = -\dfrac{2}{\sqrt{5}} = -\dfrac{2\sqrt{5}}{5}$

31. $h(x, y) = x\tan y$

$\nabla h(x, y) = \tan y\mathbf{i} + x\sec^2 y\mathbf{j}$

$\nabla h\left(2, \dfrac{\pi}{4}\right) = \mathbf{i} + 4\mathbf{j}$

$\left\|\nabla h\left(2, \dfrac{\pi}{4}\right)\right\| = \sqrt{17}$

33. $g(x, y) = \ln\sqrt[3]{x^2 + y^2} = \dfrac{1}{3}\ln(x^2 + y^2)$

$\nabla g(x, y) = \dfrac{1}{3}\left[\dfrac{2x}{x^2 + y^2}\mathbf{i} + \dfrac{2y}{x^2 + y^2}\mathbf{j}\right]$

$\nabla g(1, 2) = \dfrac{1}{3}\left(\dfrac{2}{5}\mathbf{i} + \dfrac{4}{5}\mathbf{j}\right) = \dfrac{2}{15}(\mathbf{i} + 2\mathbf{j})$

$\|\nabla g(1, 2)\| = \dfrac{2\sqrt{5}}{15}$

35. $f(x, y, z) = \sqrt{x^2 + y^2 + z^2}$

$\nabla f(x, y, z) = \dfrac{1}{\sqrt{x^2 + y^2 + z^2}}(x\mathbf{i} + y\mathbf{j} + z\mathbf{k})$

$\nabla f(1, 4, 2) = \dfrac{1}{\sqrt{21}}(\mathbf{i} + 4\mathbf{j} + 2\mathbf{k})$

$\|\nabla f(1, 4, 2)\| = 1$

37. $f(x, y, z) = xe^{yz}$

$\nabla f(x, y, z) = e^{yz}\mathbf{i} + xze^{yz}\mathbf{j} + xye^{yz}\mathbf{k}$

$\nabla f(2, 0, -4) = \mathbf{i} - 8\mathbf{j}$

$\|\nabla f(2, 0, -4)\| = \sqrt{65}$

For Exercises 39–45, $f(x, y) = 3 - \dfrac{x}{3} - \dfrac{y}{2}$ and $D_\theta f(x, y) = -\left(\dfrac{1}{3}\right)\cos\theta - \left(\dfrac{1}{2}\right)\sin\theta.$

39. $f(x, y) = 3 - \dfrac{x}{3} - \dfrac{y}{2}$

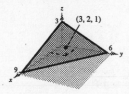

41. (a) $D_{4\pi/3} f(3, 2) = -\left(\dfrac{1}{3}\right)\left(-\dfrac{1}{2}\right) - \left(\dfrac{1}{2}\right)\left(-\dfrac{\sqrt{3}}{2}\right)$

$$= \frac{2 + 3\sqrt{3}}{12}$$

(b) $D_{-\pi/6} f(3, 2) = -\left(\dfrac{1}{3}\right)\left(\dfrac{\sqrt{3}}{2}\right) - \left(\dfrac{1}{2}\right)\left(-\dfrac{1}{2}\right)$

$$= \frac{3 - 2\sqrt{3}}{12}$$

43. (a) $\mathbf{v} = -3\mathbf{i} + 4\mathbf{j}$

$\|\mathbf{v}\| = \sqrt{9 + 16} = 5$

$\mathbf{u} = -\dfrac{3}{5}\mathbf{i} + \dfrac{4}{5}\mathbf{j}$

$D_\mathbf{u} f = \nabla f \cdot \mathbf{u} = \dfrac{1}{5} - \dfrac{2}{5} = -\dfrac{1}{5}$

(b) $\mathbf{v} = \mathbf{i} + 3\mathbf{j}$

$\|\mathbf{v}\| = \sqrt{10}$

$\mathbf{u} = \dfrac{1}{\sqrt{10}}\mathbf{i} + \dfrac{3}{\sqrt{10}}\mathbf{j}$

$D_\mathbf{u} f = \nabla f \cdot \mathbf{u} = \dfrac{-11}{6\sqrt{10}} = -\dfrac{11\sqrt{10}}{60}$

45. $\|\nabla f\| = \sqrt{\dfrac{1}{9} + \dfrac{1}{4}} = \dfrac{1}{6}\sqrt{13}$

For Exercises 47 and 49, $f(x, y) = 9 - x^2 - y^2$ and $D_\theta f(x, y) = -2x\cos\theta - 2y\sin\theta = -2(x\cos\theta + y\sin\theta).$

47. $f(x, y) = 9 - x^2 - y^2$

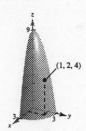

49. $\nabla f(1, 2) = -2\mathbf{i} - 4\mathbf{j}$

$\|\nabla f(1, 2)\| = \sqrt{4 + 16} = \sqrt{20} = 2\sqrt{5}$

51. (a) In the direction of the vector $-4\mathbf{i} + \mathbf{j}$.

(b) $\nabla f = \dfrac{1}{10}(2x - 3y)\mathbf{i} + \dfrac{1}{10}(-3x + 2y)\mathbf{j}$

$\nabla f(1, 2) = \dfrac{1}{10}(-4)\mathbf{i} + \dfrac{1}{10}(1)\mathbf{j} = -\dfrac{2}{5}\mathbf{i} + \dfrac{1}{10}\mathbf{j}$

(Same direction as in part (a).)

(c) $-\nabla f = \dfrac{2}{5}\mathbf{i} - \dfrac{1}{10}\mathbf{j}$, the direction opposite that of the gradient.

53. $f(x, y) = x^2 - y^2, \quad (4, -3, 7)$

(a)

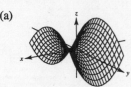

—**CONTINUED**—

53. —CONTINUED—

(b) $D_{\mathbf{u}} f(x, y) = \nabla f(x, y) \cdot \mathbf{u} = 2x \cos \theta - 2y \sin \theta$

$D_{\mathbf{u}} f(4, -3) = 8 \cos \theta + 6 \sin \theta$

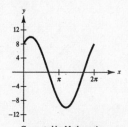

Generated by Mathematica

(c) Zeros: $\theta \approx 2.21, 5.36$

These are the angles θ for which $D_{\mathbf{u}} f(4, 3)$ equals zero.

(d) $g(\theta) = D_{\mathbf{u}} f(4, -3) = 8 \cos \theta + 6 \sin \theta$

$g'(\theta) = -8 \sin \theta + 6 \cos \theta$

Critical numbers: $\theta \approx 0.64, 3.79$

These are the angles for which $D_{\mathbf{u}} f(4, -3)$ is a maximum (0.64) and minimum (3.79).

(e) $\|\nabla f(4, -3)\| = \|2(4)\mathbf{i} - 2(3)\mathbf{j}\| = \sqrt{64 + 36} = 10$, the maximum value of $D_{\mathbf{u}} f(4, -3)$, at $\theta = 0.64$.

(f) $f(x, y) = x^2 - y^2 = 7$

$\nabla f(4, -3) = 8\mathbf{i} + 6\mathbf{j}$ is perpendicular to the level curve at $(4, -3)$.

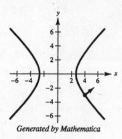

Generated by Mathematica

55. $f(x, y) = x^2 + y^2$

$c = 25, \ P = (3, 4)$

$\nabla f(x, y) = 2x\mathbf{i} + 2y\mathbf{j}$

$x^2 + y^2 = 25$

$\nabla f(3, 4) = 6\mathbf{i} + 8\mathbf{j}$

57. $f(x, y) = \dfrac{x}{x^2 + y^2}$

$c = \dfrac{1}{2}, \ P = (1, 1)$

$\nabla f(x, y) = \dfrac{y^2 - x^2}{(x^2 + y^2)^2}\mathbf{i} - \dfrac{2xy}{(x^2 + y^2)^2}\mathbf{j}$

$\dfrac{x}{x^2 + y^2} = \dfrac{1}{2}$

$x^2 + y^2 - 2x = 0$

$\nabla f(1, 1) = -\dfrac{1}{2}\mathbf{j}$

59. $4x^2 - y = 6$

$f(x, y) = 4x^2 - y$

$\nabla f(x, y) = 8x\mathbf{i} - \mathbf{j}$

$\nabla f(2, 10) = 16\mathbf{i} - \mathbf{j}$

$\dfrac{\nabla f(2, 10)}{\|\nabla f(2, 10)\|} = \dfrac{1}{\sqrt{257}}(16\mathbf{i} - \mathbf{j})$

$= \dfrac{\sqrt{257}}{257}(16\mathbf{i} - \mathbf{j})$

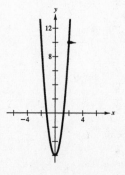

61. $9x^2 + 4y^2 = 40$

$f(x, y) = 9x^2 + 4y^2$

$\nabla f(x, y) = 18x\mathbf{i} + 8y\mathbf{j}$

$\nabla f(2, -1) = 36\mathbf{i} - 8\mathbf{j}$

$\dfrac{\nabla f(2, -1)}{\|\nabla f(2, -1)\|} = \dfrac{1}{\sqrt{85}}(9\mathbf{i} - 2\mathbf{j})$

$= \dfrac{\sqrt{85}}{85}(9\mathbf{i} - 2\mathbf{j})$

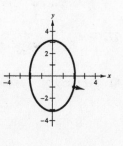

63. $T = \dfrac{x}{x^2 + y^2}$

$$\nabla T = \dfrac{y^2 - x^2}{(x^2 + y^2)^2}\mathbf{i} - \dfrac{2xy}{(x^2 + y^2)^2}\mathbf{j}$$

$$\nabla T(3, 4) = \dfrac{7}{625}\mathbf{i} - \dfrac{24}{625}\mathbf{j} = \dfrac{1}{625}(7\mathbf{i} - 24\mathbf{j})$$

65. See the definition, page 885.

67. Let $f(x, y)$ be a function of two variables and $\mathbf{u} = \cos\theta\mathbf{i} + \sin\theta\mathbf{j}$ a unit vector.

    (a) If $\theta = 0°$, then $D_{\mathbf{u}}f = \dfrac{\partial f}{\partial x}$.

    (b) If $\theta = 90°$, then $D_{\mathbf{u}}f = \dfrac{\partial f}{\partial y}$.

69.

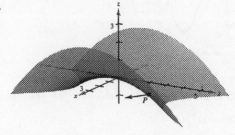

71.

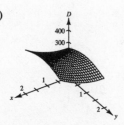

73. $T(x, y) = 400 - 2x^2 - y^2, \qquad P = (10, 10)$

$$\dfrac{dx}{dt} = -4x \qquad\qquad \dfrac{dy}{dt} = -2y$$

$$x(t) = C_1 e^{-4t} \qquad\qquad y(t) = C_2 e^{-2t}$$

$$10 = x(0) = C_1 \qquad\qquad 10 = y(0) = C_2$$

$$x(t) = 10e^{-4t} \qquad\qquad y(t) = 10e^{-2t}$$

$$x = \dfrac{y^2}{10} \qquad\qquad y^2(t) = 100e^{-4t}$$

$$y^2 = 10x$$

75. (a)

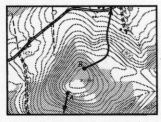

    (b) The graph of $-D = -250 - 30x^2 - 50\sin(\pi y/2)$ would model the ocean floor.

    (c) $D(1, 0.5) = 250 + 30(1) + 50\sin\dfrac{\pi}{4} \approx 315.4$ ft

    (d) $\dfrac{\partial D}{\partial x} = 60x$ and $\dfrac{\partial D}{\partial x}(1, 0.5) = 60$

    (e) $\dfrac{\partial D}{\partial y} = 25\pi\cos\dfrac{\pi y}{2}$ and $\dfrac{\partial D}{\partial y}(1, 0.5) = 25\pi\cos\dfrac{\pi}{4} \approx 55.5$

    (f) $\nabla D = 60x\mathbf{i} + 25\pi\cos\left(\dfrac{\pi y}{2}\right)\mathbf{j}$

        $\nabla D(1, 0.5) = 60\mathbf{i} + 55.5\mathbf{j}$

77. True

79. True

81. Let $f(x, y, z) = e^x\cos y + \dfrac{z^2}{2} + C$. Then $\nabla f(x, y, z) = e^x\cos y\mathbf{i} - e^x\sin y\mathbf{j} + z\mathbf{k}$.

Section 12.7   Tangent Planes and Normal Lines

1. $F(x, y, z) = 3x - 5y + 3z - 15 = 0$

$\quad 3x - 5y + 3z = 15$ Plane

3. $F(x, y, z) = 4x^2 + 9y^2 - 4z^2 = 0$

$\quad 4x^2 + 9y^2 = 4z^2$ Elliptic cone

5. $F(x, y, z) = x + y + z - 4$

$\quad \nabla F = \mathbf{i} + \mathbf{j} + \mathbf{k}$

$\quad \mathbf{n} = \dfrac{\nabla F}{\|\nabla F\|} = \dfrac{1}{\sqrt{3}}(\mathbf{i} + \mathbf{j} + \mathbf{k})$

$\qquad = \dfrac{\sqrt{3}}{3}(\mathbf{i} + \mathbf{j} + \mathbf{k})$

7. $F(x, y, z) = \sqrt{x^2 + y^2} - z$

$\quad \nabla F(x, y, z) = \dfrac{x}{\sqrt{x^2 + y^2}}\mathbf{i} + \dfrac{y}{\sqrt{x^2 + y^2}}\mathbf{j} - \mathbf{k}$

$\quad \nabla F(3, 4, 5) = \dfrac{3}{5}\mathbf{i} + \dfrac{4}{5}\mathbf{j} - \mathbf{k}$

$\quad \mathbf{n} = \dfrac{\nabla F}{\|\nabla F\|} = \dfrac{5}{5\sqrt{2}}\left(\dfrac{3}{5}\mathbf{i} + \dfrac{4}{5}\mathbf{j} - \mathbf{k}\right)$

$\qquad = \dfrac{1}{5\sqrt{2}}(3\mathbf{i} + 4\mathbf{j} - 5\mathbf{k})$

$\qquad = \dfrac{\sqrt{2}}{10}(3\mathbf{i} + 4\mathbf{j} - 5\mathbf{k})$

9. $F(x, y, z) = x^2y^4 - z$

$\quad \nabla F(x, y, z) = 2xy^4\mathbf{i} + 4x^2y^3\mathbf{j} - \mathbf{k}$

$\quad \nabla F(1, 2, 16) = 32\mathbf{i} + 32\mathbf{j} - \mathbf{k}$

$\quad \mathbf{n} = \dfrac{\nabla F}{\|\nabla F\|} = \dfrac{1}{\sqrt{2049}}(32\mathbf{i} + 32\mathbf{j} - \mathbf{k})$

$\qquad = \dfrac{\sqrt{2049}}{2049}(32\mathbf{i} + 32\mathbf{j} - \mathbf{k})$

11. $F(x, y, z) = \ln\left(\dfrac{x}{y - z}\right) = \ln x - \ln(y - z)$

$\quad \nabla F(x, y, z) = \dfrac{1}{x}\mathbf{i} - \dfrac{1}{y - z}\mathbf{j} + \dfrac{1}{y - z}\mathbf{k}$

$\quad \nabla F(1, 4, 3) = \mathbf{i} - \mathbf{j} + \mathbf{k}$

$\quad \mathbf{n} = \dfrac{\nabla F}{\|\nabla F\|} = \dfrac{1}{\sqrt{3}}(\mathbf{i} - \mathbf{j} + \mathbf{k})$

$\qquad = \dfrac{\sqrt{3}}{3}(\mathbf{i} - \mathbf{j} + \mathbf{k})$

13. $F(x, y, z) = -x \sin y + z - 4$

$\quad \nabla F(x, y, z) = -\sin y\,\mathbf{i} - x \cos y\,\mathbf{j} + \mathbf{k}$

$\quad \nabla F\left(6, \dfrac{\pi}{6}, 7\right) = -\dfrac{1}{2}\mathbf{i} - 3\sqrt{3}\mathbf{j} + \mathbf{k}$

$\quad \mathbf{n} = \dfrac{\nabla F}{\|\nabla F\|} = \dfrac{2}{\sqrt{113}}\left(-\dfrac{1}{2}\mathbf{i} - 3\sqrt{3}\mathbf{j} + \mathbf{k}\right)$

$\qquad = \dfrac{1}{\sqrt{113}}(-\mathbf{i} - 6\sqrt{3}\mathbf{j} + 2\mathbf{k})$

$\qquad = \dfrac{\sqrt{113}}{113}(-\mathbf{i} - 6\sqrt{3}\mathbf{j} + 2\mathbf{k})$

15. $f(x, y) = 25 - x^2 - y^2,\ (3, 1, 15)$

$\quad F(x, y, z) = 25 - x^2 - y^2 - z$

$\quad F_x(x, y, z) = -2x \qquad F_y(x, y, z) = -2y \qquad F_z(x, y, z) = -1$

$\quad F_x(3, 1, 15) = -6 \qquad F_y(3, 1, 15) = -2 \qquad F_z(3, 1, 15) = -1$

$\quad -6(x - 3) - 2(y - 1) - (z - 15) = 0$

$\qquad\qquad 0 = 6x + 2y + z - 35$

$\qquad\qquad 6x + 2y + z = 35$

17. $f(x, y) = \sqrt{x^2 + y^2}, (3, 4, 5)$

$F(x, y, z) = \sqrt{x^2 + y^2} - z$

$F_x(x, y, z) = \dfrac{x}{\sqrt{x^2 + y^2}}$ $F_y(x, y, z) = \dfrac{y}{\sqrt{x^2 + y^2}}$ $F_z(x, y, z) = -1$

$F_x(3, 4, 5) = \dfrac{3}{5}$ $F_y(3, 4, 5) = \dfrac{4}{5}$ $F_z(3, 4, 5) = -1$

$\dfrac{3}{5}(x - 3) + \dfrac{4}{5}(y - 4) - (z - 5) = 0$

$3(x - 3) + 4(y - 4) - 5(z - 5) = 0$

$3x + 4y - 5z = 0$

19. $g(x, y) = x^2 - y^2, (5, 4, 9)$

$G(x, y, z) = x^2 - y^2 - z$

$G_x(x, y, z) = 2x$ $G_y(x, y, z) = -2y$ $G_z(x, y, z) = -1$

$G_x(5, 4, 9) = 10$ $G_y(5, 4, 9) = -8$ $G_z(5, 4, 9) = -1$

$10(x - 5) - 8(y - 4) - (z - 9) = 0$

$10x - 8y - z = 9$

21. $z = e^x(\sin y + 1), \left(0, \dfrac{\pi}{2}, 2\right)$

$F(x, y, z) = e^x(\sin y + 1) - z$

$F_x(x, y, z) = e^x(\sin y + 1)$ $F_y(x, y, z) = e^x \cos y$ $F_z(x, y, z) = -1$

$F_x\left(0, \dfrac{\pi}{2}, 2\right) = 2$ $F_y\left(0, \dfrac{\pi}{2}, 2\right) = 0$ $F_z\left(0, \dfrac{\pi}{2}, 2\right) = -1$

$2x - z = -2$

23. $h(x, y) = \ln \sqrt{x^2 + y^2}, (3, 4, \ln 5)$

$H(x, y, z) = \ln \sqrt{x^2 + y^2} - z = \dfrac{1}{2} \ln(x^2 + y^2) - z$

$H_x(x, y, z) = \dfrac{x}{x^2 + y^2}$ $H_y(x, y, z) = \dfrac{y}{x^2 + y^2}$ $H_z(x, y, z) = -1$

$H_x(3, 4, \ln 5) = \dfrac{3}{25}$ $H_y(3, 4, \ln 5) = \dfrac{4}{25}$ $H_z(3, 4, \ln 5) = -1$

$\dfrac{3}{25}(x - 3) + \dfrac{4}{25}(y - 4) - (z - \ln 5) = 0$

$3(x - 3) + 4(y - 4) - 25(z - \ln 5) = 0$

$3x + 4y - 25z = 25(1 - \ln 5)$

25. $x^2 + 4y^2 + z^2 = 36, (2, -2, 4)$

$F(x, y, z) = x^2 + 4y^2 + z^2 - 36$

$F_x(x, y, z) = 2x$ $F_y(x, y, z) = 8y$ $F_z(x, y, z) = 2z$

$F_x(2, -2, 4) = 4$ $F_y(2, -2, 4) = -16$ $F_z(2, -2, 4) = 8$

$4(x - 2) - 16(y + 2) + 8(z - 4) = 0$

$(x - 2) - 4(y + 2) + 2(z - 4) = 0$

$x - 4y + 2z = 18$

27. $xy^2 + 3x - z^2 = 4$, $(2, 1, -2)$

$F(x, y, z) = xy^2 + 3x - z^2 - 4$

$F_x(x, y, z) = y^2 + 3$ $F_y(x, y, z) = 2xy$ $F_z(x, y, z) = -2z$

$F_x(2, 1, -2) = 4$ $F_y(2, 1, -2) = 4$ $F_Z(2, 1, -2) = 4$

$4(x - 2) + 4(y - 1) + 4(z + 2) = 0$

$$x + y + z = 1$$

29. $x^2 + y^2 + z = 9$, $(1, 2, 4)$

$F(x, y, z) = x^2 + y^2 + z - 9$

$F_x(x, y, z) = 2x$ $F_y(x, y, z) = 2y$ $F_z(x, y, z) = 1$

$F_x(1, 2, 4) = 2$ $F_y(1, 2, 4) = 4$ $F_z(1, 2, 4) = 1$

Direction numbers: $2, 4, 1$

Plane: $2(x - 1) + 4(y - 2) + (z - 4) = 0$, $2x + 4y + z = 14$

Line: $\dfrac{x - 1}{2} = \dfrac{y - 2}{4} = \dfrac{z - 4}{1}$

31. $xy - z = 0$, $(-2, -3, 6)$

$F(x, y, z) = xy - z$

$F_x(x, y, z) = y$ $F_y(x, y, z) = x$ $F_z(x, y, z) = -1$

$F_x(-2, -3, 6) = -3$ $F_y(-2, -3, 6) = -2$ $F_z(-2, -3, 6) = -1$

Direction numbers: $3, 2, 1$

Plane: $3(x + 2) + 2(y + 3) + (z - 6) = 0$, $3x + 2y + z = -6$

Line: $\dfrac{x + 2}{3} = \dfrac{y + 3}{2} = \dfrac{z - 6}{1}$

33. $z = \arctan\dfrac{y}{x}$, $\left(1, 1, \dfrac{\pi}{4}\right)$

$F(x, y, z) = \arctan\dfrac{y}{x} - z$

$F_x(x, y, z) = \dfrac{-y}{x^2 + y^2}$ $F_y(x, y, z) = \dfrac{x}{x^2 + y^2}$ $F_z(x, y, z) = -1$

$F_x\left(1, 1, \dfrac{\pi}{4}\right) = -\dfrac{1}{2}$ $F_y\left(1, 1, \dfrac{\pi}{4}\right) = \dfrac{1}{2}$ $F_z\left(1, 1, \dfrac{\pi}{4}\right) = -1$

Direction numbers: $1, -1, 2$

Plane: $(x - 1) - (y - 1) + 2\left(z - \dfrac{\pi}{4}\right) = 0$, $x - y + 2z = \dfrac{\pi}{2}$

Line: $\dfrac{x - 1}{1} = \dfrac{y - 1}{-1} = \dfrac{z - (\pi/4)}{2}$

35. $z = f(x, y) = \dfrac{4xy}{(x^2 + 1)(y^2 + 1)}, \quad -2 \le x \le z, \; 0 \le y \le 3$

(a) Let $F(x, y, z) = \dfrac{4xy}{(x^2 + 1)(y^2 + 1)} - z$

$$\nabla F(x, y, z) = \frac{4y}{y^2 + 1}\left(\frac{x^2 + 1 - 2x^2}{(x^2 + 1)^2}\right)\mathbf{i} + \frac{4x}{x^2 + 1}\left(\frac{y^2 + 1 - 2y^2}{(y^2 + 1)^2}\right)\mathbf{j} - \mathbf{k}$$

$$= \frac{4y(1 - x^2)}{(y^2 + 1)(x^2 + 1)^2}\mathbf{i} + \frac{4x(1 - y^2)}{(x^2 + 1)(y^2 + 1)^2}\mathbf{j} - \mathbf{k}$$

$\nabla F(1, 1, 1) = -\mathbf{k}.$

Direction numbers: $0, 0, -1$.

Line: $x = 1, \; y = 1, \; z = 1 - t$

Tangent plane: $0(x - 1) + 0(y - 1) - 1(z - 1) = 0 \implies z = 1$

(b) $\nabla F\left(-1, 2, -\dfrac{4}{5}\right) = 0\mathbf{i} + \dfrac{-4(-3)}{(2)(5)^2}\mathbf{j} - \mathbf{k} = \dfrac{6}{25}\mathbf{j} - \mathbf{k}$

Line: $x = -1, \; y = 2 + \dfrac{6}{25}t, \; z = -\dfrac{4}{5} - t$

Plane: $0(x + 1) + \dfrac{6}{25}(y - 2) - 1\left(z + \dfrac{4}{5}\right) = 0$

$$6y - 12 - 25z - 20 = 0$$

$$6y - 25z - 32 = 0$$

(c)

 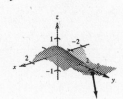

(d) At $(1, 1, 1)$, the tangent plane is parallel to the xy-plane, implying that the surface is level there. At $\left(-1, 2, -\dfrac{4}{5}\right)$, the function does not change in the x-direction.

37. $F_x(x_0, y_0, z_0)(x - x_0) + F_y(x_0, y_0, z_0)(y - y_0) + F_z(x_0, y_0, z_0)(z - z_0) = 0$

(Theorem 12.13)

39. $F(x, y, z) = x^2 + y^2 - 5 \qquad G(x, y, z) = x - z$

$\nabla F(x, y, z) = 2x\mathbf{i} + 2y\mathbf{j} \qquad \nabla G(x, y, z) = \mathbf{i} - \mathbf{k}$

$\nabla F(2, 1, 2) = 4\mathbf{i} + 2\mathbf{j} \qquad \nabla G(2, 1, 2) = \mathbf{i} - \mathbf{k}$

(a) $\nabla F \times \nabla G = \begin{vmatrix} \mathbf{i} & \mathbf{j} & \mathbf{k} \\ 4 & 2 & 0 \\ 1 & 0 & -1 \end{vmatrix} = -2\mathbf{i} + 4\mathbf{j} - 2\mathbf{k} = -2(\mathbf{i} - 2\mathbf{j} + \mathbf{k})$

Direction numbers: $1, -2, 1, \; \dfrac{x - 2}{1} = \dfrac{y - 1}{-2} = \dfrac{z - 2}{1}$

(b) $\cos \theta = \dfrac{|\nabla F \cdot \nabla G|}{\|\nabla F\| \|\nabla G\|} = \dfrac{4}{\sqrt{20}\sqrt{2}} = \dfrac{2}{\sqrt{10}} = \dfrac{\sqrt{10}}{5}$; not orthogonal

41. $F(x, y, z) = x^2 + z^2 - 25 \qquad G(x, y, z) = y^2 + z^2 - 25$

$\nabla F = 2x\mathbf{i} + 2z\mathbf{k} \qquad \nabla G = 2y\mathbf{j} + 2z\mathbf{k}$

$\nabla F(3, 3, 4) = 6\mathbf{i} + 8\mathbf{k} \qquad \nabla G(3, 3, 4) = 6\mathbf{j} + 8\mathbf{k}$

—CONTINUED—

41. —CONTINUED—

(a) $\nabla F \times \nabla G = \begin{vmatrix} \mathbf{i} & \mathbf{j} & \mathbf{k} \\ 6 & 0 & 8 \\ 0 & 6 & 8 \end{vmatrix} = -48\mathbf{i} - 48\mathbf{j} + 36\mathbf{k} = -12(4\mathbf{i} + 4\mathbf{j} - 3\mathbf{k})$

Direction numbers: $4, 4, -3,$ $\dfrac{x-3}{4} = \dfrac{y-3}{4} = \dfrac{z-4}{-3}$

(b) $\cos\theta = \dfrac{|\nabla F \cdot \nabla G|}{\|\nabla F\| \, \|\nabla G\|} = \dfrac{64}{(10)(10)} = \dfrac{16}{25}$; not orthogonal

43. $F(x, y, z) = x^2 + y^2 + z^2 - 6 \qquad\qquad G(x, y, z) = x - y - z$

$\nabla F(x, y, z) = 2x\mathbf{i} + 2y\mathbf{j} + 2z\mathbf{k} \qquad \nabla G(x, y, z) = \mathbf{i} - \mathbf{j} - \mathbf{k}$

$\nabla F(2, 1, 1) = 4\mathbf{i} + 2\mathbf{j} + 2\mathbf{k} \qquad \nabla G(2, 1, 1) = \mathbf{i} - \mathbf{j} - \mathbf{k}$

(a) $\nabla F \times \nabla G = \begin{vmatrix} \mathbf{i} & \mathbf{j} & \mathbf{k} \\ 4 & 2 & 2 \\ 1 & -1 & -1 \end{vmatrix} = 6\mathbf{j} - 6\mathbf{k} = 6(\mathbf{j} - \mathbf{k})$ (b) $\cos\theta = \dfrac{|\nabla F \cdot \nabla G|}{\|\nabla F\| \, \|\nabla G\|} = 0$; orthogonal

Direction numbers: $0, 1, -1, x = 2, \dfrac{y-1}{1} = \dfrac{z-1}{-1}$

45. $f(x, y) = 6 - x^2 - \dfrac{y^2}{4},\ g(x, y) = 2x + y$

(a) $F(x, y, z) = z + x^2 + \dfrac{y^2}{4} - 6$

$\nabla F(x, y, z) = 2x\mathbf{i} + \dfrac{1}{2}y\mathbf{j} + \mathbf{k}$ $G(x, y, z) = z - 2x - y$

$\nabla G(x, y, z) = -2\mathbf{i} - \mathbf{j} + \mathbf{k}$

$\nabla F(1, 2, 4) = 2\mathbf{i} + \mathbf{j} + \mathbf{k}$ $\nabla G(1, 2, 4) = -2\mathbf{i} - \mathbf{j} + \mathbf{k}$

The cross product of these gradients is parallel to the curve of intersection.

$\nabla F(1, 2, 4) \times \nabla G(1, 2, 4) = \begin{vmatrix} \mathbf{i} & \mathbf{j} & \mathbf{k} \\ 2 & 1 & 1 \\ -2 & -1 & 1 \end{vmatrix} = 2\mathbf{i} - 4\mathbf{j}$

Using direction numbers $1, -2, 0$, you get $x = 1 + t,\ y = 2 - 2t,\ z = 4$.

$\cos\theta = \dfrac{\nabla F \cdot \nabla G}{\|\nabla F\| \, \|\nabla G\|} = \dfrac{-4 - 1 + 1}{\sqrt{6}\,\sqrt{6}} = \dfrac{-4}{6} \implies \theta \approx 48.2°$

(b)

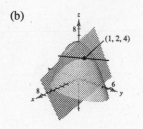

47. $F(x, y, z) = 3x^2 + 2y^2 - z - 15,\ (2, 2, 5)$

$\nabla F(x, y, z) = 6x\mathbf{i} + 4y\mathbf{j} - \mathbf{k}$

$\nabla F(2, 2, 5) = 12\mathbf{i} + 8\mathbf{j} - \mathbf{k}$

$\cos\theta = \dfrac{|\nabla F(2, 2, 5) \cdot \mathbf{k}|}{\|\nabla F(2, 2, 5)\|} = \dfrac{1}{\sqrt{209}}$

$\theta = \arccos\left(\dfrac{1}{\sqrt{209}}\right) \approx 86.03°$

49. $F(x, y, z) = x^2 - y^2 + z,\ (1, 2, 3)$

$\nabla F(x, y, z) = 2x\mathbf{i} - 2y\mathbf{j} + \mathbf{k}$

$\nabla F(1, 2, 3) = 2\mathbf{i} - 4\mathbf{j} + \mathbf{k}$

$\cos\theta = \dfrac{|\nabla F(1, 2, 3) \cdot \mathbf{k}|}{\|\nabla F(1, 2, 3)\|} = \dfrac{1}{\sqrt{21}}$

$\theta = \arccos \dfrac{1}{\sqrt{21}} \approx 77.40°$

51. $F(x, y, z) = 3 - x^2 - y^2 + 6y - z$

$\nabla F(x, y, z) = -2x\mathbf{i} + (-2y + 6)\mathbf{j} - \mathbf{k}$

$-2x = 0, \ x = 0$

$-2y + 6 = 0, \ y = 3$

$z = 3 - 0^2 - 3^2 + 6(3) = 12$

$(0, 3, 12)$ (vertex of paraboloid)

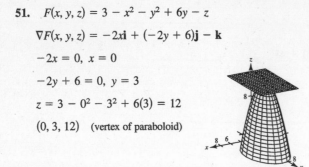

53. $T(x, y, z) = 400 - 2x^2 - y^2 - 4z^2, \ (4, 3, 10)$

$$\frac{dx}{dt} = -4kx \qquad \frac{dy}{dt} = -2ky \qquad \frac{dz}{dt} = -8kz$$

$$x(t) = C_1 e^{-4kt} \qquad y(t) = C_2 e^{-2kt} \qquad z(t) = C_3 e^{-8kt}$$

$$x(0) = C_1 = 4 \qquad y(0) = C_2 = 3 \qquad z(0) = C_3 = 10$$

$$x = 4e^{-4kt} \qquad y = 3e^{-2kt} \qquad z = 10e^{-8kt}$$

55. $F(x, y, z) = \dfrac{x^2}{a^2} + \dfrac{y^2}{b^2} + \dfrac{z^2}{c^2} - 1$

$F_x(x, y, z) = \dfrac{2x}{a^2}$

$F_y(x, y, z) = \dfrac{2y}{b^2}$

$F_z(x, y, z) = \dfrac{2z}{c^2}$

Plane: $\dfrac{2x_0}{a^2}(x - x_0) + \dfrac{2y_0}{b^2}(y - y_0) + \dfrac{2z_0}{c^2}(z - z_0) = 0$

$\dfrac{x_0 x}{a^2} + \dfrac{y_0 y}{b^2} + \dfrac{z_0 z}{c^2} = \dfrac{x_0^2}{a^2} + \dfrac{y_0^2}{b^2} + \dfrac{z_0^2}{c^2} = 1$

57. $F(x, y, z) = a^2 x^2 + b^2 y^2 - z^2$

$F_x(x, y, z) = 2a^2 x$

$F_y(x, y, z) = 2b^2 y$

$F_z(x, y, z) = -2z$

Plane: $2a^2 x_0(x - x_0) + 2b^2 y_0(y - y_0) - 2z_0(z - z_0) = 0$

$a^2 x_0 x + b^2 y_0 y - z_0 z = a^2 x_0^2 + b^2 y_0^2 - z_0^2 = 0$

Hence, the plane passes through the origin.

59. $f(x, y) = e^{x-y}$

$f_x(x, y) = e^{x-y}, \qquad f_y(x, y) = -e^{x-y}$

$f_{xx}(x, y) = e^{x-y}, \qquad f_{yy}(x, y) = e^{x-y}, \qquad\qquad\qquad f_{xy}(x, y) = -e^{x-y}$

(a) $P_1(x, y) \approx f(0, 0) + f_x(0, 0)x + f_y(0, 0)y = 1 + x - y$

(b) $P_2(x, y) \approx f(0, 0) + f_x(0, 0)x + f_y(0,0)y + \frac{1}{2}f_{xx}(0, 0)x^2 + f_{xy}(0, 0)xy + \frac{1}{2}f_{yy}(0, 0)y^2$

$\qquad = 1 + x - y + \frac{1}{2}x^2 - xy + \frac{1}{2}y^2$

(c) If $x = 0$, $P_2(0, y) = 1 - y + \frac{1}{2}y^2$. This is the second–degree Taylor polynomial for e^{-y}.

If $y = 0$, $P_2(x, 0) = 1 + x + \frac{1}{2}x^2$. This is the second–degree Taylor polynomial for e^x.

(d)

x	y	$f(x, y)$	$P_1(x, y)$	$P_2(x, y)$
0	0	1	1	1
0	0	0.9048	0.9000	0.9050
0.2	0.1	1.1052	1.1000	1.1050
0.2	0.5	0.7408	0.7000	0.7450
1	0.5	1.6487	1.5000	1.6250

(e)

61. Given $w = F(x, y, z)$ where F is differentiable at

(x_0, y_0, z_0) and $\nabla F(x_0, y_0, z_0) \neq \mathbf{0}$,

the level surface of F at (x_0, y_0, z_0) is of the form $F(x, y, z) = C$ for some constant C. Let

$G(x, y, z) = F(x, y, z) - C = 0$.

Then $\nabla G(x_0, y_0, z_0) = \nabla F(x_0, y_0, z_0)$ where $\nabla G(x_0, y_0, z_0)$ is normal to $F(x_0, y_0, z_0) - C = 0$.

Therefore, $\nabla F(x_0, y_0 z_0)$ is normal to $F(x_0, y_0, z_0) = C$.

Section 12.8   Extrema of Functions of Two Variables

1. $g(x, y) = (x - 1)^2 + (y - 3)^2 \geq 0$

Relative minimum: $(1, 3, 0)$

$g_x = 2(x - 1) = 0 \Rightarrow x = 1$

$g_y = 2(y - 3) = 0 \Rightarrow y = 3$

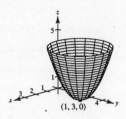

3. $f(x, y) = \sqrt{x^2 + y^2 + 1} \geq 1$

Relative minimum: $(0, 0, 1)$

Check: $f_x = \dfrac{x}{\sqrt{x^2 + y^2 + 1}} = 0 \Rightarrow x = 0$

$f_y = \dfrac{y}{\sqrt{x^2 + y^2 + 1}} = 0 \Rightarrow y = 0$

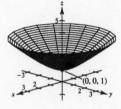

$f_{xx} = \dfrac{y^2 + 1}{(x^2 + y^2 + 1)^{3/2}}, \; f_{yy} = \dfrac{x^2 + 1}{(x^2 + y^2 + 1)^{3/2}}, \; f_{xy} = \dfrac{-xy}{(x^2 + y^2 + 1)^{3/2}}$

At the critical point $(0, 0)$, $f_{xx} > 0$ and $f_{xx} f_{yy} - (f_{xy})^2 > 0$. Therefore, $(0, 0, 1)$ is a relative minimum.

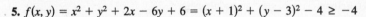

5. $f(x, y) = x^2 + y^2 + 2x - 6y + 6 = (x + 1)^2 + (y - 3)^2 - 4 \geq -4$

Relative minimum: $(-1, 3, -4)$

Check: $f_x = 2x + 2 = 0 \Rightarrow x = -1$

$f_y = 2y - 6 = 0 \Rightarrow y = 3$

$f_{xx} = 2, \; f_{yy} = 2, \; f_{xy} = 0$

At the critical point $(-1, 3)$, $f_{xx} > 0$ and $f_{xx} f_{yy} - (f_{xy})^2 > 0$. Therefore, $(-1, 3, -4)$ is a relative minimum.

7. $f(x, y) = 2x^2 + 2xy + y^2 + 2x - 3$

$\left.\begin{array}{l} f_x = 4x + 2y + 2 = 0 \\ f_y = 2x + 2y = 0 \end{array}\right\}$ Solving simultaneously yields $x = -1$ and $y = 1$.

$f_{xx} = 4, \; f_{yy} = 2, \; f_{xy} = 2$

At the critical point $(-1, 1)$, $f_{xx} > 0$ and $f_{xx} f_{yy} - (f_{xy})^2 > 0$. Therefore, $(-1, 1, -4)$ is a relative minimum.

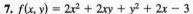

9. $f(x, y) = -5x^2 + 4xy - y^2 + 16x + 10$

$\left.\begin{array}{l} f_x = -10x + 4y + 16 = 0 \\ f_y = 4x - 2y = 0 \end{array}\right\}$ Solving simultaneously yields $x = 8$ and $y = 16$.

$f_{xx} = -10, \; f_{yy} = -2, \; f_{xy} = 4$

At the critical point $(8, 16)$, $f_{xx} < 0$ and $f_{xx} f_{yy} - (f_{xy})^2 > 0$. Therefore, $(8, 16, 74)$ is a relative maximum.

11. $f(x, y) = 2x^2 + 3y^2 - 4x - 12y + 13$

$f_x = 4x - 4 = 4(x - 1) = 0$ when $x = 1$.

$f_y = 6y - 12 = 6(y - 2) = 0$ when $y = 2$.

$f_{xx} = 4, \; f_{yy} = 6, \; f_{xy} = 0$

At the critical point $(1, 2)$, $f_{xx} > 0$ and $f_{xx} f_{yy} - (f_{xy})^2 > 0$. Therefore, $(1, 2, -1)$ is a relative minimum.

13. $f(x, y) = 2\sqrt{x^2 + y^2} + 3$

$\left.\begin{array}{l} f_x = \dfrac{2x}{\sqrt{x^2 + y^2}} = 0 \\ f_y = \dfrac{2y}{\sqrt{x^2 + y^2}} = 0 \end{array}\right\}$ $x = 0, y = 0$

Since $f(x, y) \geq 3$ for all (x, y), $(0, 0, 3)$ is relative minimum.

15. $g(x, y) = 4 - |x| - |y|$

$(0, 0)$ is the only critical point. Since $g(x, y) \leq 4$ for all (x, y), $(0, 0, 4)$ is relative maximum.

17. $z = \dfrac{-4x}{x^2 + y^2 + 1}$

Relative minimum: $(1, 0, -2)$

Relative maximum: $(-1, 0, 2)$

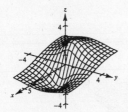

19. $z = (x^2 + 4y^2)e^{1-x^2-y^2}$

Relative minimum: $(0, 0, 0)$

Relative maxima: $(0, \pm 1, 4)$

Saddle points: $(\pm 1, 0, 1)$

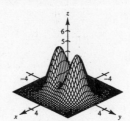

21. $h(x, y) = x^2 - y^2 - 2x - 4y - 4$

$h_x = 2x - 2 = 2(x - 1) = 0$ when $x = 1$.

$h_y = -2y - 4 = -2(y + 2) = 0$ when $y = -2$.

$h_{xx} = 2$, $h_{yy} = -2$, $h_{xy} = 0$

At the critical point $(1, -2)$, $h_{xx} h_{yy} - (h_{xy})^2 < 0$. Therefore, $(1, -2, -1)$ is a saddle point.

23. $h(x, y) = x^2 - 3xy - y^2$

$\left. \begin{array}{l} h_x = 2x - 3y = 0 \\ h_y = -3x - 2y = 0 \end{array} \right\}$ Solving simultaneously yields $x = 0$ and $y = 0$.

$h_{xx} = 2$, $h_{yy} = -2$, $h_{xy} = -3$

At the critical point $(0, 0)$, $h_{xx} h_{yy} - (h_{xy})^2 < 0$. Therefore, $(0, 0, 0)$ is a saddle point.

25. $f(x, y) = x^3 - 3xy + y^3$

$\left. \begin{array}{l} f_x = 3(x^2 - y) = 0 \\ f_y = 3(-x + y^2) = 0 \end{array} \right\}$ Solving by substitution yields two critical points $(0, 0)$ and $(1, 1)$.

$f_{xx} = 6x$, $f_{yy} = 6y$, $f_{xy} = -3$

At the critical point $(0, 0)$, $f_{xx} f_{yy} - (f_{xy})^2 < 0$. Therefore, $(0, 0, 0)$ is a saddle point. At the critical point $(1, 1)$, $f_{xx} = 6 > 0$ and $f_{xx} f_{yy} - (f_{xy})^2 > 0$. Therefore, $(1, 1, -1)$ is a relative minimum.

27. $f(x, y) = e^{-x} \sin y$

$\left. \begin{array}{l} f_x = -e^{-x} \sin y = 0 \\ f_y = e^{-x} \cos y = 0 \end{array} \right\}$ Since $e^{-x} > 0$ for all x and $\sin y$ and $\cos y$ are never both zero for a given value of y, there are no critical points.

29. $z = \dfrac{(x - y)^4}{x^2 + y^2} \geq 0$. $z = 0$ if $x = y \neq 0$.

Relative minimum at all points (x, x), $x \neq 0$.

31. $f_{xx}f_{yy} - (f_{xy})^2 = (9)(4) - 6^2 = 0$

Insufficient information.

33. $f_{xx}f_{yy} - (f_{xy})^2 = (-9)(6) - 10^2 < 0$

f has a saddle point at (x_0, y_0).

35. (a) The function f defined on a region R containing (x_0, y_0) has a relative minimum at (x_0, y_0) if $f(x, y) \geq f(x_0, y_0)$ for all (x, y) in R.

(b) The function f defined on a region R containing (x_0, y_0) has a relative maximum at (x_0, y_0) if $f(x, y) \leq f(x_0, y_0)$ for all (x, y) in R.

(c) A saddle point is a critical point which is not a relative extremum.

(d) See definition page 906.

37. 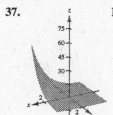 No extrema

39. 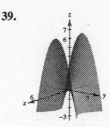 Saddle point

41. In this case, the point A will be a saddle point. The function could be

$$f(x, y) = xy.$$

43. $d = f_{xx}f_{yy} - f_{xy}{}^2 = (2)(8) - f_{xy}{}^2 = 16 - f_{xy}{}^2 > 0$

$\Rightarrow f_{xy}{}^2 < 16 \Rightarrow -4 < f_{xy} < 4$

45. $f(x, y) = x^3 + y^3$

$\left. \begin{array}{l} f_x = 3x^2 = 0 \\ f_y = 3y^2 = 0 \end{array} \right\}$ Solving yields $x = y = 0$

$f_{xx} = 6x, \ f_{yy} = 6y, \ f_{xy} = 0$

At $(0, 0), f_{xx}f_{yy} - (f_{xy})^2 = 0$ and the test fails. $(0, 0, 0)$ is a saddle point.

47. $f(x, y) = (x - 1)^2(y + 4)^2 \geq 0$

$\left. \begin{array}{l} f_x = 2(x - 1)(y + 4)^2 = 0 \\ f_y = 2(x - 1)^2(y + 4) = 0 \end{array} \right\}$ Solving yields the critical points $(1, a)$ and $(b, -4)$.

$f_{xx} = 2(y + 4)^2, f_{yy} = 2(x - 1)^2, f_{xy} = 4(x - 1)(y + 4)$

At both $(1, a)$ and $(b, -4), f_{xx}f_{yy} - (f_{xy})^2 = 0$ and the test fails.

Absolute minima: $(1, a, 0)$ and $(b, -4, 0)$

49. $f(x, y) = x^{2/3} + y^{2/3} \geq 0$

$\left. \begin{array}{l} f_x = \dfrac{2}{3\sqrt[3]{x}} \\[2mm] f_y = \dfrac{2}{3\sqrt[3]{y}} \end{array} \right\}$ f_x and f_y are undefined at $x = 0, y = 0$. The critical point is $(0, 0)$.

$f_{xx} = -\dfrac{2}{9x\sqrt[3]{x}}, f_{yy} = -\dfrac{2}{9y\sqrt[3]{y}}, f_{xy} = 0$

At $(0, 0), f_{xx}f_{yy} - (f_{xy})^2$ is undefined and the test fails.

Absolute minimum: 0 at $(0, 0)$

51. $f(x, y, z) = x^2 + (y - 3)^2 + (z + 1)^2 \geq 0$

$\left. \begin{array}{l} f_x = 2x = 0 \\ f_y = 2(y - 3) = 0 \\ f_z = 2(z + 1) = 0 \end{array} \right\}$ Solving yields the critical point $(0, 3, -1)$.

Absolute minimum: 0 at $(0, 3, -1)$

53. $f(x, y) = 12 - 3x - 2y$ has no critical points. On the line $y = x + 1, 0 \le x \le 1$,

$$f(x, y) = f(x) = 12 - 3x - 2(x + 1) = -5x + 10$$

and the maximum is 10, the minimum is 5. On the line $y = -2x + 4, 1 \le x \le 2$,

$$f(x, y) = f(x) = 12 - 3x - 2(-2x + 4) = x + 4$$

and the maximum is 6, the minimum is 5. On the line $y = -\frac{1}{2}x + 1, 0 \le x \le 2$,

$$f(x, y) = f(x) = 12 - 3x - 2\left(-\frac{1}{2}x + 1\right) = -2x + 10$$

and the maximum is 10, the minimum is 6.

Absolute maximum: 10 at $(0, 1)$

Absolute minimum: 5 at $(1, 2)$

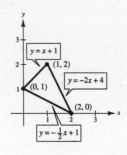

55. $f(x, y) = 3x^2 + 2y^2 - 4y$

$\left. \begin{array}{l} f_x = 6x = 0 \quad \Rightarrow x = 0 \\ f_y = 4y - 4 = 0 \Rightarrow y = 1 \end{array} \right\} f(0, 1) = -2$

On the line $y = 4, -2 \le x \le 2$,

$$f(x, y) = f(x) = 3x^2 + 32 - 16 = 3x^2 + 16$$

and the maximum is 28, the minimum is 16. On the curve $y = x^2, -2 \le x \le 2$,

$$f(x, y) = f(x) = 3x^2 + 2(x^2)^2 - 4x^2 = 2x^4 - x^2 = x^2(2x^2 - 1)$$

and the maximum is 28, the minimum is $-\frac{1}{8}$.

Absolute maximum: 28 at $(\pm 2, 4)$

Absolute minimum: -2 at $(0, 1)$

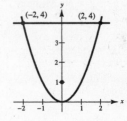

57. $f(x, y) = x^2 + xy, R = \{(x, y): |x| \le 2, |y| \le 1\}$

$\left. \begin{array}{l} f_x = 2x + y = 0 \\ f_y = x = 0 \end{array} \right\} x = y = 0$

$f(0, 0) = 0$

Along $y = 1, -2 \le x \le 2, f = x^2 + x, f' = 2x + 1 = 0 \Rightarrow x = -\frac{1}{2}$.

Thus, $f(-2, 1) = 2, f\left(-\frac{1}{2}, 1\right) = -\frac{1}{4}$ and $f(2, 1) = 6$.

Along $y = -1, -2 \le x \le 2, f = x^2 - x, f' = 2x - 1 = 0 \Rightarrow x = \frac{1}{2}$.

Thus, $f(-2, -1) = 6, f\left(\frac{1}{2}, -1\right) = -\frac{1}{4}, f(2, -1) = 2$.

Along $x = 2, -1 \le y \le 1, f = 4 + 2y \Rightarrow f' = 2 \ne 0$.

Along $x = -2, -1 \le y \le 1, f = 4 - 2y \Rightarrow f' = -2 \ne 0$.

Thus, the maxima are $f(2, 1) = 6$ and $f(-2, -1) = 6$ and the minima are $f\left(-\frac{1}{2}, 1\right) = -\frac{1}{4}$ and $f\left(\frac{1}{2}, -1\right) = -\frac{1}{4}$.

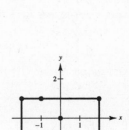

59. $f(x, y) = x^2 + 2xy + y^2, R = \{(x, y): x^2 + y^2 \le 8\}$

$\left. \begin{array}{l} f_x = 2x + 2y = 0 \\ f_y = 2x + 2y = 0 \end{array} \right\} y = -x$

$f(x, -x) = x^2 - 2x^2 + x^2 = 0$

On the boundary $x^2 + y^2 = 8$, we have $y^2 = 8 - x^2$ and $y = \pm\sqrt{8 - x^2}$. Thus,

$$f = x^2 \pm 2x\sqrt{8 - x^2} + (8 - x^2) = 8 \pm 2x\sqrt{8 - x^2}$$

$$f' = \pm(8 - x^2)^{-1/2}(-2x) + 2(8 - x^2)^{1/2}) = \pm\frac{16 - 4x^2}{\sqrt{8 - x^2}}.$$

Then, $f' = 0$ implies $16 = 4x^2$ or $x = \pm 2$.

$$f(2, 2) = f(-2, -2) = 16 \quad \text{and} \quad f(2, -2) = f(-2, 2) = 0$$

Thus, the maxima are $f(2, 2) = 16$ and $f(-2, -2) = 16$, and the minima are $f(x, -x) = 0, |x| \le 2$.

61. $f(x, y) = \dfrac{4xy}{(x^2 + 1)(y^2 + 1)}, R = \{(x, y): 0 \le x \le 1, 0 \le y \le 1\}$

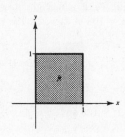

$f_x = \dfrac{4(1 - x^2)y}{(y^2 + 1)(x^2 + 1)} = 0 \implies x = 1 \text{ or } y = 0$

$f_y = \dfrac{4(1 - y^2)x}{(x^2 + 1)(y^2 + 1)^2} \implies x = 0 \text{ or } y = 1$

For $x = 0, y = 0$, also, and $f(0, 0) = 0$.

For $x = 1, y = 1, f(1, 1) = 1$.

The absolute maximum is $1 = f(1, 1)$.

The absolute minimum is $0 = f(0, 0)$. (In fact, $f(0, y) = f(x, 0) = 0$)

63. False

Let $f(x, y) = |1 - x - y|$.

$(0, 0, 1)$ is a relative maximum, but $f_x(0, 0)$ and $f_y(0, 0)$ do not exist.

Section 12.9   Applications of Extrema of Functions of Two Variables

1. A point on the plane is given by $(x, y, 12 - 2x - 3y)$. The square of the distance from the origin to this point is

$S = x^2 + y^2 + (12 - 2x - 3y)^2$

$S_x = 2x + 2(12 - 2x - 3y)(-2)$

$S_y = 2y + 2(12 - 2x - 3y)(-3)$

From the equations $S_x = 0$ and $S_y = 0$, we obtain the system

$5x + 6y = 24$

$3x + 5y = 18.$

Solving simultaneously, we have $x = \frac{12}{7}, y = \frac{18}{7}$

$z = 12 - \frac{24}{7} - \frac{54}{7} = \frac{6}{7}$. Therefore, the distance from the origin to $\left(\frac{12}{7}, \frac{18}{7}, \frac{6}{7}\right)$ is

$$\sqrt{\left(\frac{12}{7}\right)^2 + \left(\frac{18}{7}\right)^2 + \left(\frac{6}{7}\right)^2} = \frac{6\sqrt{14}}{7}.$$

3. A point on the paraboloid is given by $(x, y, x^2 + y^2)$. The square of the distance from $(5, 5, 0)$ to a point on the paraboloid is given by

$S = (x - 5)^2 + (y - 5)^2 + (x^2 + y^2)^2$

$S_x = 2(x - 5) + 4x(x^2 + y^2) = 0$

$S_y = 2(y - 5) + 4y(x^2 + y^2) = 0.$

From the equations $S_x = 0$ and $S_y = 0$, we obtain the system

$2x^3 + 2xy^2 + x - 5 = 0$

$2y^3 + 2x^2y + y - 5 = 0$

Multiply the first equation by y and the second equation by x, and subtract to obtain $x = y$. Then, we have $x = 1$, $y = 1, z = 2$ and the distance is

$\sqrt{(1 - 5)^2 + (1 - 5)^2 + (2 - 0)^2} = 6.$

5. Let x, y and z be the numbers. Since $x + y + z = 30, z = 30 - x - y$.

$P = xyz = 30xy - x^2y - xy^2$

$P_x = 30y - 2xy - y^2 = y(30 - 2x - y) = 0 \left.\right] 2x + y = 30$

$P_y = 30x - x^2 - 2xy = x(30 - x - 2y) = 0 \left.\right] x + 2y = 30$

Solving simultaneously yields $x = 10, y = 10$, and $z = 10$.

7. Let x, y, and z be the numbers and let $S = x^2 + y^2 + z^2$. Since $x + y + z = 30$, we have

$S = x^2 + y^2 + (30 - x - y)^2$

$S_x = 2x + 2(30 - x - y)(-1) = 0 \left.\right] 2x + y = 30$

$S_y = 2y + 2(30 - x - y)(-1) = 0 \left.\right] x + 2y = 30.$

Solving simultaneously yields $x = 10, y = 10$, and $z = 10$.

9. Let x, y, and z be the length, width, and height, respectively. Then the sum of the length and girth is given by $x + (2y + 2z) = 108$ or $x = 108 - 2y - 2z$. The volume is given by

$$V = xyz = 108zy - 2zy^2 - 2yz^2$$

$$V_y = 108z - 4yz - 2z^2 = z(108 - 4y - 2z) = 0$$

$$V_z = 108y - 2y^2 - 4yz = y(108 - 2y - 4z) = 0.$$

Solving the system $4y + 2z = 108$ and $2y + 4z = 108$, we obtain the solution $x = 36$ inches, $y = 18$ inches, and $z = 18$ inches.

11. Let $a + b + c = k$. Then

$$V = \frac{4\pi\,abc}{3} = \frac{4}{3}\,\pi\,ab(k - a - b)$$

$$= \frac{4}{3}\,\pi(kab - a^2b - ab^2)$$

$$V_a = \frac{4\pi}{3}(kb - 2ab - b^2) = 0 \left.\right] kb - 2ab - b^2 = 0$$

$$V_b = \frac{4\pi}{3}(ka - a^2 - 2ab) = 0 \left.\right] ka - a^2 - 2ab = 0.$$

Solving this system simultaneously yields $a = b$ and substitution yields $b = k/3$. Therefore, the solution is $a = b = c = k/3$.

13. Let x, y, and z be the length, width, and height, respectively and let V_0 be the given volume.

Then $V_0 = xyz$ and $z = V_0/xy$. The surface area is

$$S = 2xy + 2yz + 2xz = 2\left(xy + \frac{V_0}{x} + \frac{V_0}{y}\right)$$

$$S_x = 2\left(y - \frac{V_0}{x^2}\right) = 0 \left.\right] x^2y - V_0 = 0$$

$$S_y = 2\left(x - \frac{V_0}{y^2}\right) = 0 \left.\right] xy^2 - V_0 = 0.$$

Solving simultaneously yields $x = \sqrt[3]{V_0}$, $y = \sqrt[3]{V_0}$, and $z = \sqrt[3]{V_0}$.

15. The distance from P to Q is $\sqrt{x^2 + 4}$. The distance from Q to R is $\sqrt{(y - x)^2 + 1}$. The distance from R to S is $10 - y$.

$$C = 3k\sqrt{x^2 + 4} + 2k\sqrt{(y - x)^2 + 1} + k(10 - y)$$

$$C_x = 3k\left(\frac{x}{\sqrt{x^2 + 4}}\right) + 2k\left(\frac{-(y - x)}{\sqrt{(y - x)^2 + 1}}\right) = 0$$

$$C_y = 2k\left(\frac{y - x}{\sqrt{(y - x)^2 + 1}}\right) - k = 0 \implies \frac{y - x}{\sqrt{(y - x)^2 + 1}} = \frac{1}{2}$$

$$3k\left(\frac{x}{\sqrt{x^2 + 4}}\right) + 2k\left(-\frac{1}{2}\right) = 0$$

$$\frac{x}{\sqrt{x^2 + 4}} = \frac{1}{3}$$

$$3x = \sqrt{x^2 + 4}$$

$$9x^2 = x^2 + 4$$

$$x^2 = \frac{1}{2}$$

$$x = \frac{\sqrt{2}}{2}$$

$$2(y - x) = \sqrt{(y - x)^2 + 1}$$

$$4(y - x)^2 = (y - x)^2 + 1$$

$$(y - x)^2 = \frac{1}{3}$$

$$y = \frac{1}{\sqrt{3}} + \frac{1}{\sqrt{2}} = \frac{2\sqrt{3} + 3\sqrt{2}}{6}$$

Therefore, $x = \frac{\sqrt{2}}{2} \approx 0.707$ km and $y = \frac{2\sqrt{3} + 3\sqrt{2}}{6} \approx 1.284$ kms.

17. Let h be the height of the trough and r the length of the slanted sides. We observe that the area of a trapezoidal cross section is given by

$$A = h\left[\frac{(w - 2r) + [(w - 2r) + 2x]}{2}\right] = (w - 2r + x)h$$

where $x = r\cos\theta$ and $h = r\sin\theta$. Substituting these expressions for x and h, we have

$$A(r, \theta) = (w - 2r + r\cos\theta)(r\sin\theta) = wr\sin\theta - 2r^2\sin\theta + r^2\sin\theta\cos\theta$$

Now

$$A_r(r, \theta) = w\sin\theta - 4r\sin\theta + 2r\sin\theta\cos\theta = \sin\theta(w - 4r + 2r\cos\theta) = 0 \implies w = r(4 - 2\cos\theta)$$

$$A_\theta(r, \theta) = wr\cos\theta - 2r^2\cos\theta + r^2\cos 2\theta = 0.$$

Substituting the expression for w from $A_r(r, \theta) = 0$ into the equation $A_\theta(r, \theta) = 0$, we have

$$r^2(4 - 2\cos\theta)\cos\theta - 2r^2\cos\theta + r^2(2\cos^2\theta - 1) = 0$$

$$r^2(2\cos\theta - 1) = 0 \text{ or } \cos\theta = \frac{1}{2}.$$

Therefore, the first partial derivatives are zero when $\theta = \pi/3$ and $r = w/3$. (Ignore the solution $r = \theta = 0$.) Thus, the trapezoid of maximum area occurs when each edge of width $w/3$ is turned up 60° from the horizontal.

19. $R(x_1, x_2) = -5x_1{}^2 - 8x_2{}^2 - 2x_1x_2 + 42x_1 + 102x_2$

$R_{x_1} = -10x_1 - 2x_2 + 42 = 0, \ 5x_1 + x_2 = 21$

$R_{x_2} = -16x_2 - 2x_1 + 102 = 0, \ x_1 + 8x_2 = 51$

Solving this system yields $x_1 = 3$ and $x_2 = 6$.

$R_{x_1x_1} = -10$

$R_{x_1x_2} = -2$

$R_{x_2x_2} = -16$

$R_{x_1x_1} < 0$ and $R_{x_1x_1}R_{x_2x_2} - (R_{x_1x_2})^2 > 0$

Thus, revenue is maximized when $x_1 = 3$ and $x_2 = 6$.

21. $P(x_1, x_2) = 15(x_1 + x_2) - C_1 - C_2$

$$= 15x_1 + 15x_2 - (0.02x_1{}^2 + 4x_1 + 500) - (0.05x_2{}^2 + 4x_2 + 275)$$

$$= -0.02x_1{}^2 - 0.05x_2{}^2 + 11x_1 + 11x_2 - 775$$

$P_{x_1} = -0.04x_1 + 11 = 0, \ x_1 = 275$

$P_{x_2} = -0.10x_2 + 11 = 0, \ x_2 = 110$

$P_{x_1x_1} = -0.04$

$P_{x_1x_2} = 0$

$P_{x_2x_2} = -0.10$

$P_{x_1x_1} < 0$ and $P_{x_1x_1}P_{x_2x_2} - (P_{x_1x_2})^2 > 0$

Therefore, profit is maximized when $x_1 = 275$ and $x_2 = 110$.

23. (a) $S(x, y) = d_1 + d_2 + d_3$

$$= \sqrt{(x - 0)^2 + (y - 0)^2} + \sqrt{(x + 2)^2 + (y - 2)^2} + \sqrt{(x - 4)^2 + (y - 2)^2}$$

$$= \sqrt{x^2 + y^2} + \sqrt{(x + 2)^2 + (y - 2)^2} + \sqrt{(x - 4)^2 + (y - 2)^2}$$

From the graph we see that the surface has a minimum.

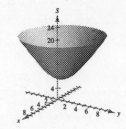

(b) $S_x(x, y) = \dfrac{x}{\sqrt{x^2 + y^2}} + \dfrac{x + 2}{\sqrt{(x + 2)^2 + (y - 2)^2}} + \dfrac{x - 4}{\sqrt{(x - 4)^2 + (y - 2)^2}}$

$S_y(x, y) = \dfrac{y}{\sqrt{x^2 + y^2}} + \dfrac{y - 2}{\sqrt{(x + 2)^2 + (y - 2)^2}} + \dfrac{y - 2}{\sqrt{(x - 4)^2 + (y - 2)^2}}$

(c) $-\nabla S(1, 1) = -S_x(1, 1)\mathbf{i} - S_y(1, 1)\mathbf{j} = -\dfrac{1}{\sqrt{2}}\mathbf{i} - \left(\dfrac{1}{\sqrt{2}} - \dfrac{2}{\sqrt{10}}\right)\mathbf{j}$

$\tan\theta = \dfrac{(2/\sqrt{10}) - (1/\sqrt{2})}{-1/\sqrt{2}} = 1 - \dfrac{2}{\sqrt{5}} \implies \theta \approx 186.027°$

(d) $(x_2, y_2) = (x_1 - S_x(x_1, y_1)t, y_1 - S_y(x_1, y_1)t) = \left(1 - \dfrac{1}{\sqrt{2}}t, 1 + \left(\dfrac{2}{\sqrt{10}} - \dfrac{1}{\sqrt{2}}\right)t\right)$

$$S\left(1 - \dfrac{1}{\sqrt{2}}t, 1 + \left(\dfrac{2}{\sqrt{10}} - \dfrac{1}{\sqrt{2}}\right)t\right) = \sqrt{2 + \left(\dfrac{2\sqrt{10}}{5} - 2\sqrt{2}\right)t + \left(1 - \dfrac{2\sqrt{5}}{5} + \dfrac{2}{5}\right)t^2}$$

$$+ \sqrt{10 - \left(\dfrac{2\sqrt{10}}{5} + 2\sqrt{2}\right)t + \left(1 - \dfrac{2\sqrt{5}}{5} + \dfrac{2}{5}\right)t^2}$$

$$+ \sqrt{10 - \left(\dfrac{2\sqrt{10}}{5} - 4\sqrt{2}\right)t + \left(1 - \dfrac{2\sqrt{5}}{5} + \dfrac{2}{5}\right)t^2}$$

Using a computer algebra system, we find that the minimum occurs when $t \approx 1.344$. Thus, $(x_2, y_2) \approx (0.05, 0.90)$.

(e) $(x_3, y_3) = (x_2 - S_x(x_2, y_2)t, y_2 - S_y(x_2, y_2)t) \approx (0.05 + 0.03t, 0.90 - 0.26t)$

$S(0.05 + 0.03t, 0.90 - 0.26t) = \sqrt{(0.05 + 0.03t)^2 + (0.90 - 0.26t)^2} + \sqrt{(2.05 + 0.03t)^2 + (-1.10 - 0.26t)^2}$

$$+ \sqrt{(-3.95 + 0.03t)^2 + (-1.10 - 0.26t)^2}$$

Using a computer algebra system, we find that the minimum occurs when $t \approx 1.78$. Thus $(x_3, y_3) \approx (0.10, 0.44)$.

$(x_4, y_4) = (x_3 - S_x(x_3, y_3)t, y_3 - S_y(x_3, y_3)t) \approx (0.10 - 0.09t, 0.44 - 0.01t)$

$S(0.10 - 0.09t, 0.45 - 0.01t) = \sqrt{(0.10 - 0.09t)^2 + (0.45 - 0.01t)^2} + \sqrt{(2.10 - 0.09t)^2 + (-1.55 - 0.01t)^2}$

$$+ \sqrt{(-3.90 - 0.09t)^2 + (-1.55 - 0.01t)^2}$$

Using a computer algebra system, we find that the minimum occurs when $t \approx 0.44$. Thus, $(x_4, y_4) \approx (0.06, 0.44)$.

Note: The minimum occurs at $(x, y) = (0.0555, 0.3992)$

(f) $-\nabla S(x, y)$ points in the direction that S *decreases* most rapidly. You would use $\nabla S(x, y)$ for maximization problems.

25. Write the equation to be maximized or minimized as a function of two variables. Set the partial derivatives equal to zero (or undefined) to obtain the critical points. Use the Second Partials Test to test for relative extrema using the critical points. Check the boundary points, too.

27. (a)

x	y	xy	x^2
-2	0	0	4
0	1	0	0
2	3	6	4
$\sum x_i = 0$	$\sum y_i = 4$	$\sum x_i y_i = 6$	$\sum x_i^2 = 8$

$$a = \frac{3(6) - 0(4)}{3(8) - 0^2} = \frac{3}{4}, \quad b = \frac{1}{3}\left[4 - \frac{3}{4}(0)\right] = \frac{4}{3},$$

$$y = \frac{3}{4}x + \frac{4}{3}$$

(b) $S = \left(-\frac{3}{2} + \frac{4}{3} - 0\right)^2 + \left(\frac{4}{3} - 1\right)^2 + \left(\frac{3}{2} + \frac{4}{3} - 3\right)^2$

$$= \frac{1}{6}$$

29. (a)

x	y	xy	x^2
0	4	0	0
1	3	3	1
1	1	1	1
2	0	0	4
$\sum x_i = 4$	$\sum y_i = 8$	$\sum x_i y_i = 4$	$\sum x_i^2 = 6$

$$a = \frac{4(4) - 4(8)}{4(6) - 4^2} = -2, \quad b = \frac{1}{4}[8 + 2(4)] = 4,$$

$$y = -2x + 4$$

(b) $S = (4 - 4)^2 + (2 - 3)^2 + (2 - 1)^2 + (0 - 0)^2 = 2$

31. $(0, 0), (1, 1), (3, 4), (4, 2), (5, 5)$

$$\sum x_i = 13, \qquad \sum y_i = 12,$$
$$\sum x_i y_i = 46, \qquad \sum x_i^2 = 51$$
$$a = \frac{5(46) - 13(12)}{5(51) - (13)^2} = \frac{74}{86} = \frac{37}{43}$$
$$b = \frac{1}{5}\left[12 - \frac{37}{43}(13)\right] = \frac{7}{43}$$
$$y = \frac{37}{43}x + \frac{7}{43}$$

33. $(0, 6), (4, 3), (5, 0), (8, -4), (10, -5)$

$$\sum x_i = 27, \qquad \sum y_i = 0,$$
$$\sum x_i y_i = -70, \qquad \sum x_i^2 = 205$$
$$a = \frac{5(-70) - (27)(0)}{5(205) - (27)^2} = \frac{-350}{296} = -\frac{175}{148}$$
$$b = \frac{1}{5}\left[0 - \left(-\frac{175}{148}\right)(27)\right] = \frac{945}{148}$$
$$y = -\frac{175}{148}x + \frac{945}{148}$$

35. (a) $y = 1.7236x + 79.7334$

(b)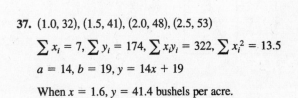

(c) For each one-year increase in age, the pressure changes by 1.7236 (slope of line).

37. $(1.0, 32), (1.5, 41), (2.0, 48), (2.5, 53)$

$$\sum x_i = 7, \sum y_i = 174, \sum x_i y_i = 322, \sum x_i^2 = 13.5$$
$$a = 14, b = 19, y = 14x + 19$$

When $x = 1.6$, $y = 41.4$ bushels per acre.

39. $S(a, b, c) = \displaystyle\sum_{i=1}^{n} (y_i - ax_i^2 - bx_i - c)^2$

$\dfrac{\partial S}{\partial a} = \displaystyle\sum_{i=1}^{n} -2x_i^2(y_i - ax_i^2 - bx_i - c) = 0$

$\dfrac{\partial S}{\partial b} = \displaystyle\sum_{i=1}^{n} -2x_i(y_i - ax_i^2 - bx_i - c) = 0$

$\dfrac{\partial S}{\partial c} = -2\displaystyle\sum_{i=1}^{n} (y_i - ax_i^2 - bx_i - c) = 0$

$a\displaystyle\sum_{i=1}^{n} x_i^4 + b\sum_{i=1}^{n} x_i^3 + c\sum_{i=1}^{n} x_i^2 = \sum_{i=1}^{n} x_i^2 y_i$

$a\displaystyle\sum_{i=1}^{n} x_i^3 + b\sum_{i=1}^{n} x_i^2 + c\sum_{i=1}^{n} x_i = \sum_{i=1}^{n} x_i y_i$

$a\displaystyle\sum_{i=1}^{n} x_i^2 + b\sum_{i=1}^{n} x_i + cn = \sum_{i=1}^{n} y_i$

41. $(-2, 0), (-1, 0), (0, 1), (1, 2), (2, 5)$

$\displaystyle\sum x_i = 0$

$\displaystyle\sum y_i = 8$

$\displaystyle\sum x_i^2 = 10$

$\displaystyle\sum x_i^3 = 0$

$\displaystyle\sum x_i^4 = 34$

$\displaystyle\sum x_i y_i = 12$

$\displaystyle\sum x_i^2 y_i = 22$

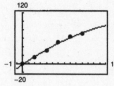

$34a + 10c = 22, \quad 10b = 12, \quad 10a + 5c = 8$

$a = \frac{3}{7}, \; b = \frac{6}{5}, \; c = \frac{26}{35}, \; y = \frac{3}{7}x^2 + \frac{6}{5}x + \frac{26}{35}$

43. $(0, 0), (2, 2), (3, 6), (4, 12)$

$\displaystyle\sum x_i = 9$

$\displaystyle\sum y_i = 20$

$\displaystyle\sum x_i^2 = 29$

$\displaystyle\sum x_i^3 = 99$

$\displaystyle\sum x_i^4 = 353$

$\displaystyle\sum x_i y_i = 70$

$\displaystyle\sum x_i^2 y_i = 254$

$353a + 99b + 29c = 254$

$99a + 29b + 9c = 70$

$29a + 9b + 4c = 20$

$a = 1, \; b = -1, \; c = 0, \; y = x^2 - x$

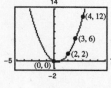

45. $(0, 0), (2, 15), (4, 30), (6, 50), (8, 65), (10, 70)$

$\displaystyle\sum x_i = 30,$

$\displaystyle\sum y_i = 230,$

$\displaystyle\sum x_i^2 = 220,$

$\displaystyle\sum x_i^3 = 1,800,$

$\displaystyle\sum x_i^4 = 15,664,$

$\displaystyle\sum x_i y_i = 1,670,$

$\displaystyle\sum x_i^2 y_i = 13,500$

$15,664a + 1,800b + 220c = 13,500$

$1,800a + 220b + 30c = 1,670$

$220a + 30b + 6c = 230$

$y = -\frac{25}{112}x^2 + \frac{541}{56}x - \frac{25}{14} \approx -0.22x^2 + 9.66x - 1.79$

47. (a) $\ln P = -0.1499h + 9.3018$

(b) $\ln P = -0.1499h + 9.3018$

$P = e^{-0.1499h + 9.3018} = 10{,}957.7e^{-0.1499h}$

(c)

(d) Same answers.

Section 12.10   Lagrange Multipliers

1. Maximize $f(x, y) = xy$.

Constraint: $x + y = 10$

$\nabla f = \lambda \nabla g$

$y\mathbf{i} + x\mathbf{j} = \lambda(\mathbf{i} + \mathbf{j})$

$\left. \begin{array}{l} y = \lambda \\ x = \lambda \end{array} \right\} x = y$

$x + y = 10 = \implies x = y = 5$

$f(5, 5) = 25$

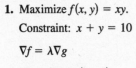

3. Minimize $f(x, y) = x^2 + y^2$.

Constraint: $x + y = 4$

$\nabla f = \lambda \nabla g$

$2x\mathbf{i} + 2y\mathbf{j} = \lambda\mathbf{i} + \lambda\mathbf{j}$

$\left. \begin{array}{l} 2x = \lambda \\ 2y = \lambda \end{array} \right\} x = y$

$x + y = 4 \implies x = y = 2$

$f(2, 2) = 8$

5. Minimize $f(x, y) = x^2 - y^2$.

Constraint: $x - 2y = -6$

$\nabla f = \lambda \nabla g$

$2x\mathbf{i} - 2y\mathbf{j} = \lambda\mathbf{i} - 2\lambda\mathbf{j}$

$2x = \lambda \implies x = \dfrac{\lambda}{2}$

$-2y = -2\lambda \implies y = \lambda$

$x - 2y = -6 \implies -\dfrac{3}{2}\lambda = -6$

$\qquad\qquad \lambda = 4, \ x = 2, \ y = 4$

$f(2, 4) = -12$

7. Maximize $f(x, y) = 2x + 2xy + y$.

Constraint: $2x + y = 100$

$\nabla f = \lambda \nabla g$

$(2 + 2y)\mathbf{i} + (2x + 1)\mathbf{j} = 2\lambda\mathbf{i} + \lambda\mathbf{j}$

$\left. \begin{array}{l} 2 + 2y = 2\lambda \implies y = \lambda - 1 \\ 2x + 1 = \lambda \ \implies x = \dfrac{\lambda - 1}{2} \end{array} \right\} y = 2x$

$2x + y = 100 \implies 4x = 100$

$\qquad\qquad\qquad x = 25, \ y = 50$

$f(25, 50) = 2600$

9. Note: $f(x, y) = \sqrt{6 - x^2 - y^2}$ is maximum when $g(x, y)$ is maximum.

Maximize $g(x, y) = 6 - x^2 - y^2$.

Constraint: $x + y = 2$

$\left. \begin{array}{l} -2x = \lambda \\ -2y = \lambda \end{array} \right\} x = y$

$x + y = 2 \implies x = y = 1$

$f(1, 1) = \sqrt{g(1, 1)} = 2$

11. Maximize $f(x, y) = e^{xy}$.

Constraint: $x^2 + y^2 = 8$

$\left. \begin{array}{l} ye^{xy} = 2x\lambda \\ xe^{xy} = 2y\lambda \end{array} \right\} x = y$

$x^2 + y^2 = 8 \implies 2x^2 = 8$

$\qquad\qquad\qquad x = y = 2$

$f(2, 2) = e^4$

13. Maximize or minimize $f(x, y) = x^2 + 3xy + y^2$.

Constraint: $x^2 + y^2 \le 1$

Case 1: On the circle $x^2 + y^2 = 1$

$\left. \begin{array}{l} 2x + 3y = 2x\lambda \\ 3x + 2y = 2y\lambda \end{array} \right\} x^2 = y^2$

$x^2 + y^2 = 1 \implies x = \pm\dfrac{\sqrt{2}}{2}, y = \pm\dfrac{\sqrt{2}}{2}$

Maxima: $f\left(\pm\dfrac{\sqrt{2}}{2}, \pm\dfrac{\sqrt{2}}{2}\right) = \dfrac{5}{2}$

Minima: $f\left(\pm\dfrac{\sqrt{2}}{2}, \mp\dfrac{\sqrt{2}}{2}\right) = -\dfrac{1}{2}$

Case 2: Inside the circle

$\left. \begin{array}{l} f_x = 2x + 3y = 0 \\ f_y = 3x + 2y = 0 \end{array} \right\} x = y = 0$

$f_{xx} = 2, f_{yy} = 2, f_{xy} = 3, f_{xx}f_{yy} - (f_{xy})^2 \le 0$

Saddle point: $f(0, 0) = 0$

By combining these two cases, we have a maximum of $\dfrac{5}{2}$ at

$\left(\pm\dfrac{\sqrt{2}}{2}, \pm\dfrac{\sqrt{2}}{2}\right)$

and a minimum of $-\dfrac{1}{2}$ at

$\left(\pm\dfrac{\sqrt{2}}{2}, \mp\dfrac{\sqrt{2}}{2}\right)$.

15. Minimize $f(x, y, z) = x^2 + y^2 + z^2$.

Constraint: $x + y + z = 6$

$$\left. \begin{array}{l} 2x = \lambda \\ 2y = \lambda \\ 2z = \lambda \end{array} \right\} x = y = z$$

$x + y + z = 6 \implies x = y = z = 2$

$f(2, 2, 2) = 12$

17. Minimize $f(x, y, z) = x^2 + y^2 + z^2$.

Constraint: $x + y + z = 1$

$$\left. \begin{array}{l} 2x = \lambda \\ 2y = \lambda \\ 2z = \lambda \end{array} \right\} x = y = z$$

$x + y + z = 1 \implies x = y = z = \frac{1}{3}$

$f\left(\frac{1}{3}, \frac{1}{3}, \frac{1}{3}\right) = \frac{1}{3}$

19. Maximize $f(x, y, z) = xyz$.

Constraints: $x + y + z = 32$

$\qquad\qquad x - y + z = 0$

$\nabla f = \lambda \nabla g + \mu \nabla h$

$yz\mathbf{i} + xz\mathbf{j} + xy\mathbf{k} = \lambda(\mathbf{i} + \mathbf{j} + \mathbf{k}) + \mu(\mathbf{i} - \mathbf{j} + \mathbf{k})$

$$\left. \begin{array}{l} yz = \lambda + \mu \\ xz = \lambda - \mu \\ xy = \lambda + \mu \end{array} \right\} yz = xy \implies x = z$$

$$\left. \begin{array}{l} x + y + z = 32 \\ x - y + z = 0 \end{array} \right\} 2x + 2z = 32 \implies x = z = 8$$

$\qquad\qquad\qquad\qquad\qquad y = 16$

$f(8, 16, 8) = 1024$

21. Maximize $f(x, y, z) = xy + yz$.

Constraints: $x + 2y = 6$

$\qquad\qquad x - 3z = 0$

$\nabla f = \lambda \nabla g + \mu \nabla h$

$y\mathbf{i} + (x + z)\mathbf{j} + y\mathbf{k} = \lambda(\mathbf{i} + 2\mathbf{j}) + \mu(\mathbf{i} - 3\mathbf{k})$

$$\left. \begin{array}{l} y = \lambda + \mu \\ x + z = 2\lambda \\ y = -3\mu \end{array} \right\} y = \frac{3}{4}\lambda \implies x + z = \frac{8}{3}y$$

$x + 2y = 6 \implies y = 3 - \frac{x}{2}$

$x - 3z = 0 \implies z = \frac{x}{3}$

$$x + \frac{x}{3} = \frac{8}{3}\left(3 - \frac{x}{2}\right)$$

$$x = 3, y = \frac{3}{2}, z = 1$$

$f\left(3, \frac{3}{2}, 1\right) = 6$

23. Minimize the square of the distance $f(x, y) = x^2 + y^2$ subject to the constraint $2x + 3y = -1$.

$$\left. \begin{array}{l} 2x = 2\lambda \\ 2y = 3\lambda \end{array} \right\} y = \frac{3x}{2}$$

$2x + 3y = -1 \implies x = -\frac{2}{13}, y = -\frac{3}{13}$

The point on the line is $\left(-\frac{2}{13}, -\frac{3}{13}\right)$ and the desired distance is

$$d = \sqrt{\left(-\frac{2}{13}\right)^2 + \left(-\frac{3}{13}\right)^2} = \frac{\sqrt{13}}{13}.$$

25. Minimize the square of the distance

$$f(x, y, z) = (x - 2)^2 + (y - 1)^2 + (z - 1)^2$$

subject to the constraint $x + y + z = 1$.

$$\left. \begin{array}{l} 2(x - 2) = \lambda \\ 2(y - 1) = \lambda \\ 2(z - 1) = \lambda \end{array} \right\} y = z \text{ and } y = x - 1$$

$x + y + z = 1 \implies x + 2(x - 1) = 1$

$\qquad\qquad\qquad\qquad x = 1, y = z = 0$

The point on the plane is $(1, 0, 0)$ and the desired distance is

$$d = \sqrt{(1 - 2)^2 + (0 - 1)^2 + (0 - 1)^2} = \sqrt{3}.$$

27. Maximize $f(x, y, z) = z$ subject to the constraints
$x^2 + y^2 + z^2 = 36$ and $2x + y - z = 2$.

$$\left.\begin{array}{l} 0 = 2x\lambda + 2\mu \\ 0 = 2y\lambda + \mu \\ 1 = 2z\lambda - \mu \end{array}\right\} x = 2y$$

$$x^2 + y^2 + z^2 = 36$$

$$2x + y - z = 2 \implies z = 2x + y - 2 = 5y - 2$$

$$(2y)^2 + y^2 + (5y - 2)^2 = 36$$

$$30y^2 - 20y - 32 = 0$$

$$15y^2 - 10y - 16 = 0$$

$$y = \frac{5 \pm \sqrt{265}}{15}$$

Choosing the positive value for y we have the point

$$\left(\frac{10 + 2\sqrt{265}}{15}, \frac{5 + \sqrt{265}}{15}, \frac{-1 + \sqrt{265}}{3}\right).$$

29. Optimization problems that have restrictions or contstraints on the values that can be used to produce the optimal solution are called contrained optimization problems.

31. Maximize $V(x, y, z) = xyz$ subject to the constraint $x + 2y + 2z = 108$.

$$\left.\begin{array}{l} yz = \lambda \\ xz = 2\lambda \\ xy = 2\lambda \end{array}\right\} y = z \text{ and } x = 2y$$

$$x + 2y + 2z = 108 \implies 6y = 108, y = 18$$

$$x = 36, y = z = 18$$

Volume is maximum when the dimensions are
$36 \times 18 \times 18$ inches

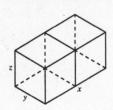

33. Minimize $C(x, y, z) = 5xy + 3(2xz + 2yz + xy)$ subject to the constraint $xyz = 480$.

$$\left.\begin{array}{l} 8y + 6z = yz\lambda \\ 8x + 6z = xz\lambda \\ 6x + 6y = xy\lambda \end{array}\right\} x = y, 4y = 3z$$

$$xyz = 480 \implies \tfrac{4}{3}y^3 = 480$$

$$x = y = \sqrt[3]{360}, z = \tfrac{4}{3}\sqrt[3]{360}$$

Dimensions: $\sqrt[3]{360} \times \sqrt[3]{360} \times \tfrac{4}{3}\sqrt[3]{360}$ feet

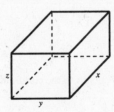

35. Maximize $V(x, y, z) = (2x)(2y)(2z) = 8xyz$ subject to the constraint $\dfrac{x^2}{a^2} + \dfrac{y^2}{b^2} + \dfrac{z^2}{c^2} = 1$.

$$\left.\begin{array}{l} 8yz = \dfrac{2x}{a^2}\lambda \\[2mm] 8xz = \dfrac{2y}{b^2}\lambda \\[2mm] 8xy = \dfrac{2z}{c^2}\lambda \end{array}\right\} \dfrac{x^2}{a^2} = \dfrac{y^2}{b^2} = \dfrac{z^2}{c^2}$$

$$\frac{x^2}{a^2} + \frac{y^2}{b^2} + \frac{z^2}{c^2} = 1 \implies \frac{3x^2}{a^2} = 1, \frac{3y^2}{b^2} = 1, \frac{3z^2}{c^2} = 1$$

$$x = \frac{a}{\sqrt{3}}, y = \frac{b}{\sqrt{3}}, z = \frac{c}{\sqrt{3}}$$

Therefore, the dimensions of the box are $\dfrac{2\sqrt{3}a}{3} \times \dfrac{2\sqrt{3}b}{3} \times \dfrac{2\sqrt{3}c}{3}$.

37. Using the formula Time $= \dfrac{\text{Distance}}{\text{Rate}}$, minimize $T(x, y) = \dfrac{\sqrt{d_1^2 + x^2}}{v_1} + \dfrac{\sqrt{d_2^2 + y^2}}{v_2}$ subject to the constraint $x + y = a$.

$$\left.\begin{array}{l} \dfrac{x}{v_1\sqrt{d_2^2 + x^2}} = \lambda \\[2mm] \dfrac{y}{v_2\sqrt{d_2^2 + y^2}} = \lambda \end{array}\right\} \quad \dfrac{x}{v_1\sqrt{d_1^2 + x^2}} = \dfrac{y}{v_2\sqrt{d_2^2 + y^2}}$$

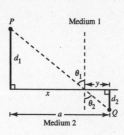

$x + y = a$

Since $\sin \theta_1 = \dfrac{x}{\sqrt{d_1^2 + x^2}}$ and $\sin \theta_2 = \dfrac{y}{\sqrt{d_2^2 + y^2}}$, we have

$$\dfrac{x/\sqrt{d_1^2 + x^2}}{v_1} = \dfrac{y/\sqrt{d_2^2 + y^2}}{v_2} \quad \text{or} \quad \dfrac{\sin \theta_1}{v_1} = \dfrac{\sin \theta_2}{v_2}.$$

39. Maximize $P(p, q, r) = 2pq + 2pr + 2qr$.

Constraint: $p + q + r = 1$

$\nabla P = \lambda \nabla g$

$$\left.\begin{array}{l} 2q + 2r = \lambda \\ 2p + 2r = \lambda \\ 2p + 2q = \lambda \end{array}\right\} \Longrightarrow 3\lambda = 4(p + q + r) = 4(1) \\ \Longrightarrow \lambda = \tfrac{4}{3}$$

$p + q + r = 1$

$$\left.\begin{array}{l} q + r = \tfrac{2}{3} \\ p + q + r = 1 \end{array}\right\} \Longrightarrow p = \tfrac{1}{3}, q = \tfrac{1}{3}, r = \tfrac{1}{3}$$

$P\left(\tfrac{1}{3}, \tfrac{1}{3}, \tfrac{1}{3}\right) = 2\left(\tfrac{1}{3}\right)\left(\tfrac{1}{3}\right) + 2\left(\tfrac{1}{3}\right)\left(\tfrac{1}{3}\right) + 2\left(\tfrac{1}{3}\right)\left(\tfrac{1}{3}\right) = \tfrac{2}{3}$.

41. Maximize $P(x, y) = 100x^{0.25}y^{0.75}$

subject to the constraint $48x + 36y = 100,000$.

$$25x^{-0.75}y^{0.75} = 48\lambda \implies \left(\dfrac{y}{x}\right)^{0.75} = \dfrac{48\lambda}{25}$$

$$75x^{0.25}y^{-0.25} = 36\lambda \implies \left(\dfrac{x}{y}\right)^{0.25} = \dfrac{36\lambda}{75}$$

$$\left(\dfrac{y}{x}\right)^{0.75}\left(\dfrac{y}{x}\right)^{0.25} = \left(\dfrac{48\lambda}{25}\right)\left(\dfrac{75}{36\lambda}\right)$$

$$\dfrac{y}{x} = 4$$

$$y = 4x$$

$48x + 36y = 100,000 \implies 192x = 100,000$

$$x = \dfrac{3125}{6}, y = \dfrac{6250}{3}$$

Therefore, $P\left(\dfrac{3125}{6}, \dfrac{6250}{3}\right) \approx 147,314$.

43. Minimize $C(x, y) = 48x + 36y$ subject to the constraint $100x^{0.25}y^{0.75} = 20,000$.

$$48 = 25x^{-0.75}y^{0.75}\lambda \implies \left(\dfrac{y}{x}\right)^{0.75} = \dfrac{48}{25\lambda}$$

$$36 = 75x^{0.25}y^{-0.25}\lambda \implies \left(\dfrac{x}{y}\right)^{0.25} = \dfrac{36}{75\lambda}$$

$$\left(\dfrac{y}{x}\right)^{0.75}\left(\dfrac{y}{x}\right)^{0.25} = \left(\dfrac{48}{25\lambda}\right)\left(\dfrac{75\lambda}{36}\right)$$

$$\dfrac{y}{x} = 4 \implies y = 4x$$

$100x^{0.25}y^{0.75} = 20,000 \implies x^{0.25}(4x)^{0.75} = 200$

$$x = \dfrac{200}{4^{0.75}} = \dfrac{200}{2\sqrt{2}} = 50\sqrt{2}$$

$$y = 4x = 200\sqrt{2}$$

Therefore, $C\left(50\sqrt{2}, 200\sqrt{2}\right) \approx \$13,576.45$.

45. (a) Maximize $g(\alpha, \beta, \gamma) = \cos\alpha\cos\beta\cos\gamma$ subject to the constraint $\alpha + \beta + \gamma = \pi$.

$$\left.\begin{array}{c} -\sin\alpha\cos\beta\cos\gamma = \lambda \\ -\cos\alpha\sin\beta\cos\gamma = \lambda \\ -\cos\alpha\cos\beta\sin\gamma = \lambda \end{array}\right\} \tan\alpha = \tan\beta = \tan\gamma \Rightarrow \alpha = \beta = \gamma$$

$$\alpha + \beta + \gamma = \pi \Rightarrow \alpha = \beta = \gamma = \frac{\pi}{3}$$

$$g\left(\frac{\pi}{3}, \frac{\pi}{3}, \frac{\pi}{3}\right) = \frac{1}{8}$$

(b) $\alpha + \beta + \gamma = \pi \Rightarrow \gamma = \pi - (\alpha + \beta)$

$$g(\alpha + \beta) = \cos\alpha\cos\beta\cos(\pi - (\alpha + \beta))$$

$$= \cos\alpha\cos\beta[\cos\pi\cos(\alpha + \beta) + \sin\pi\sin(\alpha + \beta)]$$

$$= -\cos\alpha\cos\beta\cos(\alpha + \beta)$$

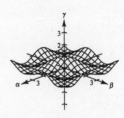

Review Exercises for Chapter 12

1. No, it is not the graph of a function.

3. $f(x, y) = e^{x^2 + y^2}$

The level curves are of the form

$$c = e^{x^2 + y^2}$$

$$\ln c = x^2 + y^2.$$

The level curves are circles centered at the origin.

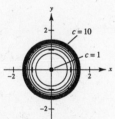

Generated by Mathematica

5. $f(x, y) = x^2 - y^2$

The level curves are of the form

$$c = x^2 - y^2$$

$$1 = \frac{x^2}{c} - \frac{y^2}{c}.$$

The level curves are hyperbolas.

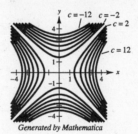

Generated by Mathematica

7. $f(x, y) = e^{-(x^2 + y^2)}$

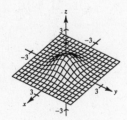

9. $f(x, y, z) = x^2 - y + z^2 = 1$

$$y = x^2 + z^2 - 1$$

Elliptic paraboloid

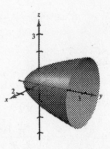

11. $\displaystyle\lim_{(x, y)\to(1, 1)} \frac{xy}{x^2 + y^2} = \frac{1}{2}$

Continuous except at $(0, 0)$.

13. $\displaystyle\lim_{(x, y)\to(0, 0)} \frac{-4x^2 y}{x^4 + y^2}$

For $y = x^2$, $\dfrac{-4x^2 y}{x^4 + y^2} = \dfrac{-4x^4}{x^4 + x^4} = -2$, for $x \neq 0$

For $y = 0$, $\dfrac{-4x^2 y}{x^4 + y^2} = 0$, for $x \neq 0$

Thus, the limit does not exist. Continuous except at $(0, 0)$.

15. $f(x, y) = e^x \cos y$

$f_x = e^x \cos y$

$f_y = -e^x \sin y$

17. $z = xe^y + ye^x$

$\dfrac{\partial z}{\partial x} = e^y + ye^x$

$\dfrac{\partial z}{\partial y} = xe^y + e^x$

19. $g(x, y) = \dfrac{xy}{x^2 + y^2}$

$g_x = \dfrac{y(x^2 + y^2) - xy(2x)}{(x^2 + y^2)^2} = \dfrac{y(y^2 - x^2)}{(x^2 + y^2)^2}$

$g_y = \dfrac{x(x^2 - y^2)}{(x^2 + y^2)^2}$

21. $f(x, y, z) = z \arctan \dfrac{y}{x}$

$f_x = \dfrac{z}{1 + (y^2/x^2)}\left(-\dfrac{y}{x^2}\right) = \dfrac{-yz}{x^2 + y^2}$

$f_y = \dfrac{z}{1 + (y^2/x^2)}\left(\dfrac{1}{x}\right) = \dfrac{xz}{x^2 + y^2}$

$f_z = \arctan \dfrac{y}{x}$

23. $u(x, t) = ce^{-n^2 t} \sin(nx)$

$\dfrac{\partial u}{\partial x} = cne^{-n^2 t} \cos(nx)$

$\dfrac{\partial u}{\partial t} = -cn^2 e^{-n^2 t} \sin(nx)$

25.

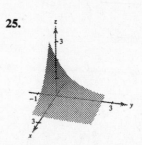

27. $f(x, y) = 3x^2 - xy + 2y^3$

$f_x = 6x - y$

$f_y = -x + 6y^2$

$f_{xx} = 6$

$f_{yy} = 12y$

$f_{xy} = -1$

$f_{yx} = -1$

29. $h(x, y) = x \sin y + y \cos x$

$h_x = \sin y - y \sin x$

$h_y = x \cos y + \cos x$

$h_{xx} = -y \cos x$

$h_{yy} = -x \sin y$

$h_{xy} = \cos y - \sin x$

$h_{yx} = \cos y - \sin x$

31. $z = x^2 - y^2$

$\dfrac{\partial z}{\partial x} = 2x$

$\dfrac{\partial^2 z}{\partial x^2} = 2$

$\dfrac{\partial z}{\partial y} = -2y$

$\dfrac{\partial^2 z}{\partial y^2} = -2$

Therefore, $\dfrac{\partial^2 z}{\partial x^2} + \dfrac{\partial^2 z}{\partial y^2} = 0.$

33. $z = \dfrac{y}{x^2 + y^2}$

$\dfrac{\partial z}{\partial x} = \dfrac{-2xy}{(x^2 + y^2)^2}$

$\dfrac{\partial^2 z}{\partial x^2} = -2y\left[\dfrac{-4x^2}{(x^2 + y^2)^3} + \dfrac{1}{(x^2 + y^2)^2}\right] = 2y\dfrac{3x^2 - y^2}{(x^2 + y^2)^3}$

$\dfrac{\partial z}{\partial y} = \dfrac{(x^2 + y^2) - 2y}{(x^2 + y^2)^2} = \dfrac{x^2 - y^2}{(x^2 + y^2)^2}$

$\dfrac{\partial^2 z}{\partial y^2} = \dfrac{(x^2 + y^2)^2(-2y) - 2(x^2 - y^2)(x^2 + y^2)(2y)}{(x^2 + y^2)^4}$

$= -2y\dfrac{3x^2 - y^2}{(x^2 + y^2)^3}$

Therefore, $\dfrac{\partial^2 z}{\partial x^2} + \dfrac{\partial^2 z}{\partial y^2} = 0.$

35. $z = x \sin \dfrac{y}{x}$

$dz = \dfrac{\partial z}{\partial x}\,dx + \dfrac{\partial z}{\partial y}\,dy = \left(\sin \dfrac{y}{x} - \dfrac{y}{x} \cos \dfrac{y}{x}\right) dx + \left(\cos \dfrac{y}{x}\right) dy$

37. $z^2 = x^2 + y^2$

$2z\,dx = 2x\,dx + 2y\,dy$

$dz = \dfrac{x}{z}dx + \dfrac{y}{z}dy = \dfrac{5}{13}\left(\dfrac{1}{2}\right) + \dfrac{12}{13}\left(\dfrac{1}{2}\right) = \dfrac{17}{26} \approx 0.654 \text{ cm}$

Percentage error: $\dfrac{dz}{z} = \dfrac{17/26}{13} \approx 0.0503 \approx 5\%$

39. $V = \frac{1}{3}\pi r^2 h$

$dV = \frac{2}{3}\pi r h\,dr + \frac{1}{3}\pi r^2\,dh = \frac{2}{3}\pi(2)(5)\left(\pm\frac{1}{8}\right) + \frac{1}{3}\pi(2)^2\left(\pm\frac{1}{8}\right)$

$\qquad = \pm\frac{5}{6}\pi \pm \frac{1}{6}\pi = \pm\pi \text{ in.}^3$

41. $w = \ln(x^2 + y^2)$, $x = 2t + 3$, $y = 4 - t$

Chain Rule: $\dfrac{dw}{dt} = \dfrac{\partial w}{\partial x}\dfrac{dx}{dt} + \dfrac{\partial w}{\partial y}\dfrac{dy}{dt}$

$\qquad = \dfrac{2x}{x^2 + y^2}(2) + \dfrac{2y}{x^2 + y^2}(-1)$

$\qquad = \dfrac{2(2t + 3)2}{(2t + 3)^2 + (4 - t)^2} - \dfrac{2(4 - t)}{(2t + 3)^2 + (4 - t)^2}$

$\qquad = \dfrac{10t + 4}{5t^2 + 4t + 25}$

Substitution: $w = \ln(x^2 + y^2) = \ln[(2t + 3)^2 + (4 - t)^2]$

$\dfrac{dw}{dt} = \dfrac{2(2t + 3)(2) - 2(4 - t)}{(2t + 3)^2 + (4 - t)^2} = \dfrac{10t + 4}{5t^2 + 4t + 25}$

43. $u = x^2 + y^2 + z^2$, $x = r\cos t$, $y = r\sin t$, $z = t$

Chain Rule: $\dfrac{\partial u}{\partial r} = \dfrac{\partial u}{\partial x}\dfrac{\partial x}{\partial r} + \dfrac{\partial u}{\partial y}\dfrac{\partial y}{\partial r} + \dfrac{\partial u}{\partial z}\dfrac{\partial z}{\partial r}$

$\qquad = 2x\cos t + 2y\sin t + 2z(0)$

$\qquad = 2(r\cos^2 t + r\sin^2 t) = 2r$

$\dfrac{\partial u}{\partial t} = \dfrac{\partial u}{\partial x}\dfrac{\partial x}{\partial t} + \dfrac{\partial u}{\partial y}\dfrac{\partial y}{\partial t} + \dfrac{\partial u}{\partial z}\dfrac{\partial z}{\partial t}$

$\qquad = 2x(-r\sin t) + 2y(r\cos t) + 2z$

$\qquad = 2(-r^2\sin t\cos t + r^2\sin t\cos t) + 2t$

$\qquad = 2t$

Substitution: $u(r, t) = r^2\cos^2 t + r^2\sin^2 t + t^2 = r^2 + t^2$

$\qquad \dfrac{\partial u}{\partial r} = 2r$

$\qquad \dfrac{\partial u}{\partial t} = 2t$

45. $\qquad x^2 y - 2yz - xz - z^2 = 0$

$2xy - 2y\dfrac{\partial z}{\partial x} - x\dfrac{\partial z}{\partial x} - z - 2z\dfrac{\partial z}{\partial x} = 0$

$\qquad\qquad \dfrac{\partial z}{\partial x} = \dfrac{-2xy + z}{-2y - x - 2z} = \dfrac{2xy - z}{x + 2y + 2z}$

$x^2 - 2y\dfrac{\partial z}{\partial y} - 2z - x\dfrac{\partial z}{\partial y} - 2z\dfrac{\partial z}{\partial y} = 0$

$\qquad\qquad \dfrac{\partial z}{\partial y} = \dfrac{-x^2 + 2z}{-2y - x - 2z} = \dfrac{x^2 - 2z}{x + 2y + 2z}$

47. $f(x, y) = x^2 y$

$\nabla f = 2xy\mathbf{i} + x^2\mathbf{j}$

$\nabla f(2, 1) = 4\mathbf{i} + 4\mathbf{j}$

$\mathbf{u} = \dfrac{1}{\sqrt{2}}\mathbf{v} = \dfrac{\sqrt{2}}{2}\mathbf{i} - \dfrac{\sqrt{2}}{2}\mathbf{j}$

$D_{\mathbf{u}}f(2, 1) = \nabla f(2, 1) \cdot \mathbf{u} = 2\sqrt{2} - 2\sqrt{2} = 0$

49. $w = y^2 + xz$

$\nabla w = z\mathbf{i} + 2y\mathbf{j} + x\mathbf{k}$

$\nabla w(1, 2, 2) = 2\mathbf{i} + 4\mathbf{j} + \mathbf{k}$

$\mathbf{u} = \dfrac{1}{3}\mathbf{v} = \dfrac{2}{3}\mathbf{i} - \dfrac{1}{3}\mathbf{j} + \dfrac{2}{3}\mathbf{k}$

$D_{\mathbf{u}}w(1, 2, 2) = \nabla w(1, 2, 2) \cdot \mathbf{u} = \dfrac{4}{3} - \dfrac{4}{3} + \dfrac{2}{3} = \dfrac{2}{3}$

51. $z = \dfrac{y}{x^2 + y^2}$

$\nabla z = -\dfrac{2xy}{(x^2 + y^2)^2}\mathbf{i} + \dfrac{x^2 - y^2}{(x^2 + y^2)^2}\mathbf{j}$

$\nabla z(1, 1) = -\dfrac{1}{2}\mathbf{i} = \left\langle -\dfrac{1}{2}, 0 \right\rangle$

$\|\nabla z(1, 1)\| = \dfrac{1}{2}$

53. $z = e^{-x}\cos y$

$\nabla z = -e^{-x}\cos y\mathbf{i} - e^{-x}\sin y\mathbf{j}$

$\nabla z\left(0, \dfrac{\pi}{4}\right) = -\dfrac{\sqrt{2}}{2}\mathbf{i} - \dfrac{\sqrt{2}}{2}\mathbf{j} = \left\langle -\dfrac{\sqrt{2}}{2}, -\dfrac{\sqrt{2}}{2} \right\rangle$

$\left\| \nabla z\left(0, \dfrac{\pi}{4}\right) \right\| = 1$

55. $9x^2 - 4y^2 = 65$

$f(x, y) = 9x^2 - 4y^2$

$\nabla f(x, y) = 18x\mathbf{i} + 8y\mathbf{j}$

$\nabla f(3, 2) = 54\mathbf{i} - 16\mathbf{j}$

Unit normal: $\dfrac{54\mathbf{i} - 16\mathbf{j}}{\|54\mathbf{i} - 16\mathbf{j}\|} = \dfrac{1}{\sqrt{793}}(27\mathbf{i} - 8\mathbf{j})$

57. $F(x, y, z) = x^2 y - z = 0$

$\nabla F = 2xy\mathbf{i} + x^2\mathbf{j} - \mathbf{k}$

$\nabla F(2, 1, 4) = 4\mathbf{i} + 4\mathbf{j} - \mathbf{k}$

Therefore, the equation of the tangent plane is

$4(x - 2) + 4(y - 1) - (z - 4) = 0$ or

$4x + 4y - z = 8,$

and the equation of the normal line is

$\dfrac{x - 2}{4} = \dfrac{y - 1}{4} = \dfrac{z - 4}{-1}.$

59. $F(x, y, z) = x^2 + y^2 - 4x + 6y + z + 9 = 0$

$\nabla F = (2x - 4)\mathbf{i} + (2y + 6)\mathbf{j} + \mathbf{k}$

$\nabla F(2, -3, 4) = \mathbf{k}$

Therefore, the equation of the tangent plane is

$z - 4 = 0$ or $z = 4,$

and the equation of the normal line is

$x = 2,\ y = -3,\ z = 4 + t.$

61. $F(x, y, z) = x^2 - y^2 - z = 0$

$G(x, y, z) = 3 - z = 0$

$\nabla F = 2x\mathbf{i} - 2y\mathbf{j} - \mathbf{k}$

$\nabla G = -\mathbf{k}$

$\nabla F(2, 1, 3) = 4\mathbf{i} - 2\mathbf{j} - \mathbf{k}$

$\nabla F \times \nabla G = \begin{vmatrix} \mathbf{i} & \mathbf{j} & \mathbf{k} \\ 4 & -2 & -1 \\ 0 & 0 & -1 \end{vmatrix} = 2(\mathbf{i} + 2\mathbf{j})$

Therefore, the equation of the tangent line is

$\dfrac{x - 2}{1} = \dfrac{y - 1}{2},\ z = 3.$

63. $f(x, y, z) = x^2 + y^2 + z^2 - 14$

$\nabla f(x, y, z) = 2x\mathbf{i} + 2y\mathbf{j} + 2z\mathbf{k}$

$\nabla f(2, 1, 3) = 4\mathbf{i} + 2\mathbf{j} + 6\mathbf{k}$ Normal vector to plane.

$\cos\theta = \dfrac{|\mathbf{n} \cdot \mathbf{k}|}{\|\mathbf{n}\|} = \dfrac{6}{\sqrt{56}} = \dfrac{3\sqrt{14}}{14}$

$\theta = 36.7°$

65. $f(x, y) = x^3 - 3xy + y^2$

$$f_x = 3x^2 - 3y = 3(x^2 - y) = 0$$

$$f_y = -3x + 2y = 0$$

$$f_{xx} = 6x$$

$$f_{yy} = 2$$

$$f_{xy} = -3$$

From $f_x = 0$, we have $y = x^2$. Substituting this into $f_y = 0$, we have $-3x + 2x^2 = x(2x - 3) = 0$. Thus, $x = 0$ or $\frac{3}{2}$.

At the critical point $(0, 0)$, $f_{xx}f_{yy} - (f_{xy})^2 < 0$. Therefore, $(0, 0, 0)$ is a saddle point.

At the critical point $\left(\frac{3}{2}, \frac{9}{4}\right)$, $f_{xx}f_{yy} - (f_{xy})^2 > 0$ and $f_{xx} > 0$. Therefore, $\left(\frac{3}{2}, \frac{9}{4}, -\frac{27}{16}\right)$ is a relative minimum.

67. $f(x, y) = xy + \dfrac{1}{x} + \dfrac{1}{y}$

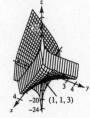

$$f_x = y - \frac{1}{x^2} = 0, \ x^2 y = 1$$

$$f_y = x - \frac{1}{y^2} = 0, \ xy^2 = 1$$

Thus, $x^2 y = xy^2$ or $x = y$ and substitution yields the critical point $(1, 1)$.

$$f_{xx} = \frac{2}{x^3}$$

$$f_{xy} = 1$$

$$f_{yy} = \frac{2}{y^3}$$

At the critical point $(1, 1)$, $f_{xx} = 2 > 0$ and $f_{xx}f_{yy} - (f_{xy})^2 = 3 > 0$. Thus, $(1, 1, 3)$ is a relative minimum.

69. The level curves are hyperbolas. There is a critical point at $(0, 0)$, but there are no relative extrema. The gradient is normal to the level curve at any given point at (x_0, y_0).

71. $P(x_1, x_2) = R - C_1 - C_2$

$$= [225 - 0.4(x_1 + x_2)](x_1 + x_2) - (0.05x_1^2 + 15x_1 + 5400) - (0.03x_2^2 + 15x_2 + 6100)$$

$$= -0.45x_1^2 - 0.43x_2^2 - 0.8x_1x_2 + 210x_1 + 210x_2 - 11,500$$

$$P_{x_1} = -0.9x_1 - 0.8x_2 + 210 = 0$$

$$0.9x_1 + 0.8x_2 = 210$$

$$P_{x_2} = -0.86x_2 - 0.8x_1 + 210 = 0$$

$$0.8x_1 + 0.86x_2 = 210$$

Solving this system yields $x_1 \approx 94$ and $x_2 \approx 157$.

$$P_{x_1x_1} = -0.9$$

$$P_{x_1x_2} = -0.8$$

$$P_{x_2x_2} = -0.86$$

$$P_{x_1x_1} < 0$$

$$P_{x_1x_1}P_{x_2x_2} - (P_{x_1x_2})^2 > 0$$

Therefore, profit is maximum when $x_1 \approx 94$ and $x_2 \approx 157$.

73. Maximize $f(x, y) = 4x + xy + 2y$ subject to the constraint $20x + 4y = 2000$.

$$\left.\begin{array}{l} 4 + y = 20\lambda \\ x + 2 = 4\lambda \end{array}\right\} 5x - y = -6$$

$$20x + 4y = 2000 \implies \quad 5x + y = 500$$

$$\frac{5x - y = -6}{10x = 494}$$

$$x = 49.4$$

$$y = 253$$

$$f(49.4, 253) = 13{,}201.8$$

75. (a) $y = 2.29t + 2.34$

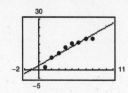

(b)

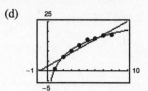

Yes, the data appears more linear.

(c) $y = 8.37 \ln t + 1.54$

(d)

The logarithmic model is a better fit.

77. Optimize $f(x, y, z) = xy + yz + xz$ subject to the constraint $x + y + z = 1$.

$$\left.\begin{array}{l} y + z = \lambda \\ x + z = \lambda \\ x + y = \lambda \end{array}\right\} x = y = z$$

$$x + y + z = 1 \implies x = y = z = \frac{1}{3}$$

Maximum: $f\left(\frac{1}{3}, \frac{1}{3}, \frac{1}{3}\right) = \frac{1}{3}$

79. $PQ = \sqrt{x^2 + 4}, QR = \sqrt{y^2 + 1}, RS = z; x + y + z = 10$

$$C = 3\sqrt{x^2 + 4} + 2\sqrt{y^2 + 1} + 2$$

Constraint: $x + y + z = 10$

$$\nabla C = \lambda \nabla g$$

$$\frac{3x}{\sqrt{x^2 + 4}}\mathbf{i} + \frac{2y}{\sqrt{y^2 + 1}}\mathbf{j} + \mathbf{k} = \lambda[\mathbf{i} + \mathbf{j} + \mathbf{k}]$$

$$3x = \lambda\sqrt{x^2 + 4}$$

$$2y = \lambda\sqrt{y^2 + 1}$$

$$1 = \lambda$$

$$9x^2 = x^2 + 4 \implies x^2 = \frac{1}{2}$$

$$4y^2 = y^2 + 1 \implies y^2 = \frac{1}{3}$$

Hence, $x = \dfrac{\sqrt{2}}{2}, y = \dfrac{\sqrt{3}}{3}, z = 10 - \dfrac{\sqrt{2}}{2} - \dfrac{\sqrt{3}}{3} \approx 8.716$ m.

Problem Solving for Chapter 12

1. (a) The three sides have lengths 5, 6, and 5.

Thus, $s = \frac{16}{2} = 8$ and $A = \sqrt{8(3)(2)(3)} = 12$

(b) Let $f(a, b, c) = (\text{area})^2 = s(s - a)(s - b)(s - c)$, subject to the constraint $a + b + c = \text{constant (perimeter)}$.

Using Lagrange multipliers,

$-s(s - b)(s - c) = \lambda$

$-s(s - a)(s - c) = \lambda$

$-s(s - b)(s - b) = \lambda$

From the first 2 equations $s - b = s - a \Rightarrow a = b$.

Similarly, $b = c$ and hence $a = b = c$ which is an equilateral triangle.

(c) Let $f(a, b, c) = a + b + c$, subject to $(\text{Area})^2 = s(s - a)(s - b)(s - c)$ constant.

Using Lagrange multipliers,

$1 = -\lambda s(s - b)(s - c)$

$1 = -\lambda s(s - a)(s - c)$

$1 = -\lambda s(s - a)(s - b)$

Hence, $s - a = s - b \Rightarrow a = b$ and $a = b = c$.

3. (a) $F(x, y, z) = xyz - 1 = 0$

$F_x = yz, F_y = xz, F_z = xy$

Tangent plane:

$y_0 z_0(x - x_0) + x_0 z_0(y - y_0) + x_0 y_0(z - z_0) = 0$

$y_0 z_0 x + x_0 z_0 y + x_0 y_0 z = 3x_0 y_0 z_0 = 3$

(b) $V = \frac{1}{3}(\text{base})(\text{height})$

$= \frac{1}{3}\left(\frac{1}{2}\frac{3}{y_0 z_0}\frac{3}{x_0 z_0}\right)\left(\frac{3}{x_0 y_0}\right) = \frac{9}{2}$

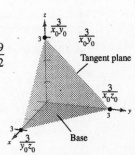

5. We cannot use Theorem 12.9 since f is not a differentiable function of x and y. Hence, we use the definition of directional derivatives.

$$D_{\mathbf{u}} f(x, y) = \lim_{t \to 0} \frac{f(x + t\cos\theta, y + t\sin\theta) - f(x, y)}{t}$$

$$D_{\mathbf{u}} f(0, 0) = \lim_{t \to 0} \frac{f\left[0 + \left(\frac{t}{\sqrt{2}}\right), 0 + \left(\frac{t}{\sqrt{2}}\right)\right] - f(0, 0)}{t}$$

$$= \lim_{t \to 0} \frac{1}{t}\left[\frac{4\left(\frac{t}{\sqrt{2}}\right)\left(\frac{t}{\sqrt{2}}\right)}{\left(\frac{t^2}{2}\right) + \left(\frac{t^2}{2}\right)}\right] = \lim_{t \to 0} \frac{1}{t}\left[\frac{2t^2}{t^2}\right] = \lim_{t \to 0} \frac{2}{t} \text{ which does not exist.}$$

If $f(0, 0) = 2$, then

$$D_{\mathbf{u}} f(0, 0) = \lim_{t \to 0} \frac{f\left(0 + \frac{t}{\sqrt{2}}, 0 + \frac{t}{\sqrt{2}}\right) - 2}{t} = \lim_{t \to 0} \frac{1}{t}\left[\frac{2t^2}{t^2} - 2\right] = 0$$

which implies that the directional derivative exists.

7. $H = k(5xy + 6xz + 6yz)$

$z = \dfrac{1000}{xy} \implies H = k\left(5xy + \dfrac{6000}{y} + \dfrac{6000}{x}\right).$

$H_x = 5y - \dfrac{6000}{x^2} = 0 \implies 5yx^2 = 6000$

By symmetry, $x = y \implies x^3 = y^3 = 1200.$

Thus, $x = y = 2\sqrt[3]{150}$ and $z = \dfrac{5}{3}\sqrt[3]{150}.$

9. (a) $\dfrac{\partial f}{\partial x} = Cax^{a-1}y^{1-a}, \dfrac{\partial f}{\partial y} = C(1-a)x^a y^{-a}$

$x\dfrac{\partial f}{\partial x} + y\dfrac{\partial f}{\partial y} = Cax^a y^{1-a} + C(1-a)x^a y^{1-a}$

$\qquad\qquad = [Ca + C(1-a)]x^a y^{1-a}$

$\qquad\qquad = Cx^a y^{1-a} = f$

(b) $f(tx, ty) = C(tx)^a (ty)^{1-a} = Ct^a x^a t^{1-a}y^{1-a}$

$\qquad\qquad = Cx^a y^{1-a}(t) = tf(x, y)$

11. (a) $x = 64(\cos 45°)t = 32\sqrt{2}\,t$

$\qquad y = 64(\sin 45°)t - 16t^2 = 32\sqrt{2}\,t - 16t^2$

(b) $\tan\alpha = \dfrac{y}{x + 50}$

$\qquad \alpha = \arctan\left(\dfrac{y}{x+50}\right) = \arctan\left(\dfrac{32\sqrt{2}\,t - 16t^2}{32\sqrt{2}\,t + 50}\right)$

(c) $\dfrac{d\alpha}{dt} = \dfrac{1}{1 + \left(\dfrac{32\sqrt{2}\,t - 16t^2}{32\sqrt{2}\,t + 50}\right)^2} \cdot \dfrac{-64\left(8\sqrt{2}\,t^2 + 25t - 25\sqrt{2}\right)}{\left(32\sqrt{2}\,t + 50\right)^2} = \dfrac{-16\left(8\sqrt{2}\,t^2 + 25t - 25\sqrt{2}\right)}{64t^4 - 256\sqrt{2}\,t^3 + 1024t^2 + 800\sqrt{2}\,t + 625}$

(d)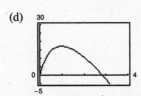

No. The rate of change of α is greatest when the projectile is closest to the camera.

(e) $\dfrac{d\alpha}{dt} = 0$ when

$\qquad 8\sqrt{2}\,t^2 + 25t - 25\sqrt{2} = 0$

$\qquad\qquad t = \dfrac{-25 + \sqrt{25^2 - 4\left(8\sqrt{2}\right)\left(-25\sqrt{2}\right)}}{2\left(8\sqrt{2}\right)} \approx 0.98 \text{ second.}$

No, the projectile is at its maximum height when $dy/dt = 32\sqrt{2} - 32t = 0$ or $t = \sqrt{2} \approx 1.41$ seconds.

13. (a) There is a minimum at $(0, 0, 0)$, maxima at $(0, \pm 1, 2/e)$ and saddle point at $(\pm 1, 0, 1/e)$:

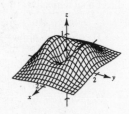

$\qquad f_x = (x^2 + 2y^2)e^{-(x^2+y^2)}(-2x) + (2x)e^{-(x^2+y^2)}$

$\qquad\quad = e^{-(x^2+y^2)}[(x^2 + 2y^2)(-2x) + 2x]$

$\qquad\quad = e^{-(x^2+y^2)}[-2x^3 + 4xy^2 + 2x] = 0 \implies x^3 + 2xy^2 - x = 0$

$\qquad f_y = (x^2 + 2y^2)e^{-(x^2+y^2)}(-2y) + (4y)e^{-(x^2+y^2)}$

$\qquad\quad = e^{-(x^2+y^2)}[(x^2 + 2y^2)(-2y) + 4y]$

$\qquad\quad = e^{-(x^2+y^2)}[-4y^3 - 2x^2y + 4y] = 0 \implies 2y^3 + x^2y - 2y = 0$

Solving the two equations $x^3 + 2xy^2 - x = 0$ and $2y^3 + x^2y - 2y = 0$, you obtain the following critical points: $(0, \pm 1)$, $(\pm 1, 0)$, $(0, 0)$. Using the second derivative test, you obtain the results above.

—CONTINUED—

13. **—CONTINUED—**

(b) As in part (a), you obtain

$$f_x = e^{-(x^2+y^2)}[2x(x^2 - 1 - 2y^2)]$$
$$f_y = e^{-(x^2+y^2)}[2y(2 + x^2 - 2y^2)]$$

The critical numbers are $(0, 0)$, $(0, \pm 1)$, $(\pm 1, 0)$.
These yield

$(\pm 1, 0, -1/e)$ minima
$(0, \pm 1, 2/e)$ maxima
$(0, 0, 0)$ saddle

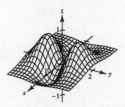

(c) In general, for $\alpha > 0$ you obtain

$(0, 0, 0)$ minimum

$(0, \pm 1, \beta/e)$ maxima

$(\pm 1, 0, \alpha/e)$ saddle

For $\alpha < 0$, you obtain

$(\pm 1, 0, \alpha/e)$ minima

$(0, \pm 1, \beta/e)$ maxima

$(0, 0, 0)$ saddle

15. (a)

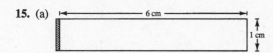

(b)

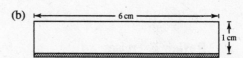

(c) The height has more effect since the shaded region in (b) is larger than the shaded region in (a).

(d) $A = hl \implies dA = l\,dh + h\,dl$

If $dl = 0.01$ and $dh = 0$, then $dA = 1(0.01) = 0.01$.
If $dh = 0.01$ and $dl = 0$, then $dA = 6(0.01) = 0.06$.

17. Essay

19. $u(x, t) = \frac{1}{2}[f(x - ct) + f(x + ct)]$

Let $r = x - ct$ and $s = x + ct$. Then $u(r, s) = \frac{1}{2}[f(r) + f(s)]$.

$$\frac{\partial u}{\partial t} = \frac{\partial u}{\partial r}\frac{\partial r}{\partial t} + \frac{\partial u}{\partial s}\frac{\partial s}{\partial t} = \frac{1}{2}\frac{df}{dr}(-c) + \frac{1}{2}\frac{df}{ds}(c)$$

$$\frac{\partial^2 u}{\partial t^2} = \frac{1}{2}\frac{d^2f}{dr^2}(-c)^2 + \frac{1}{2}\frac{d^2f}{ds^2}(c)^2 = \frac{c^2}{2}\left[\frac{d^2f}{dr^2} + \frac{d^2f}{ds^2}\right]$$

$$\frac{\partial u}{\partial x} = \frac{\partial u}{\partial r}\frac{\partial r}{\partial x} + \frac{\partial u}{\partial s}\frac{\partial s}{\partial x} = \frac{1}{2}\frac{df}{dr}(1) + \frac{1}{2}\frac{df}{ds}(1)$$

$$\frac{\partial^2 u}{\partial x^2} = \frac{1}{2}\frac{d^2f}{dr^2}(1)^2 + \frac{1}{2}\frac{d^2f}{ds^2}(1)^2 = \frac{1}{2}\left[\frac{d^2f}{dr^2} + \frac{d^2f}{ds^2}\right]$$

Thus, $\dfrac{\partial^2 u}{\partial t^2} = c^2 \dfrac{\partial^2 u}{\partial x^2}$.

CHAPTER 13
Multiple Integration

CHAPTER 13
Multiple Integration

Section 13.1 Iterated Integrals and Area in the Plane
Solutions to Odd-Numbered Exercises

1. $\displaystyle\int_0^x (2x - y)\,dy = \left[2xy - \frac{1}{2}y^2\right]_0^x = \frac{3}{2}x^2$

3. $\displaystyle\int_1^{2y} \frac{y}{x}\,dx = \left[y \ln x\right]_1^{2y} = y \ln 2y - 0 = y \ln 2y$

5. $\displaystyle\int_0^{\sqrt{4-x^2}} x^2 y\,dy = \left[\frac{1}{2}x^2 y^2\right]_0^{\sqrt{4-x^2}} = \frac{4x^2 - x^4}{2}$

7. $\displaystyle\int_{e^y}^{y} \frac{y \ln x}{x}\,dx = \left[\frac{1}{2}y \ln^2 x\right]_{e^y}^{y} = \frac{1}{2}y[\ln^2 y - \ln^2 e^y] = \frac{y}{2}[(\ln y)^2 - y^2]$

9. $\displaystyle\int_0^{x^3} ye^{-y/x}\,dy = \left[-xye^{-y/x}\right]_0^{x^3} + x\int_0^{x^3} e^{-y/x}\,dy = -x^4 e^{-x^2} - \left[x^2 e^{-y/x}\right]_0^{x^3} = x^2(1 - e^{-x^2} - x^2 e^{-x^2})$

$u = y,\ du = dy,\ dv = e^{-y/x}\,dy,\ v = -xe^{-y/x}$

11. $\displaystyle\int_0^1\int_0^2 (x + y)\,dy\,dx = \int_0^1 \left[xy + \frac{1}{2}y^2\right]_0^2 dx = \int_0^1 (2x + 2)\,dx = \left[x^2 + 2x\right]_0^1 = 3$

13. $\displaystyle\int_0^1\int_0^x \sqrt{1 - x^2}\,dy\,dx = \int_0^1 \left[y\sqrt{1 - x^2}\right]_0^x dx = \int_0^1 x\sqrt{1 - x^2}\,dx = \left[-\frac{1}{2}\left(\frac{2}{3}\right)(1 - x^2)^{3/2}\right]_0^1 = \frac{1}{3}$

15. $\displaystyle\int_1^2\int_0^4 (x^2 - 2y^2 + 1)\,dx\,dy = \int_1^2 \left[\frac{1}{3}x^3 - 2xy^2 + x\right]_0^4 dy$

$\displaystyle = \int_1^2 \left(\frac{64}{3} - 8y^2 + 4\right) dy = \frac{4}{3}\int_1^2 (19 - 6y^2)\,dy = \left[\frac{4}{3}(19y - 2y^3)\right]_1^2 = \frac{20}{3}$

17. $\displaystyle\int_0^1\int_0^{\sqrt{1-y^2}} (x + y)\,dx\,dy = \int_0^1 \left[\frac{1}{2}x^2 + xy\right]_0^{\sqrt{1-y^2}} dy$

$\displaystyle = \int_0^1 \left[\frac{1}{2}(1 - y^2) + y\sqrt{1 - y^2}\right] dy = \left[\frac{1}{2}y - \frac{1}{6}y^3 - \frac{1}{2}\left(\frac{2}{3}\right)(1 - y^2)^{3/2}\right]_0^1 = \frac{2}{3}$

19. $\displaystyle\int_0^2\int_0^{\sqrt{4-y^2}} \frac{2}{\sqrt{4 - y^2}}\,dx\,dy = \int_0^2 \left[\frac{2x}{\sqrt{4 - y^2}}\right]_0^{\sqrt{4-y^2}} dy = \int_0^2 2\,dy = \left[2y\right]_0^2 = 4$

21. $\displaystyle\int_0^{\pi/2}\int_0^{\sin\theta} \theta r\,dr\,d\theta = \int_0^{\pi/2} \left[\theta \frac{r^2}{2}\right]_0^{\sin\theta} d\theta = \int_0^{\pi/2} \frac{1}{2}\theta \sin^2\theta\,d\theta$

$\displaystyle = \frac{1}{4}\int_0^{\pi/2} (\theta - \theta\cos 2\theta)\,d\theta = \frac{1}{4}\left[\frac{\theta^2}{2} - \left(\frac{1}{4}\cos 2\theta + \frac{\theta}{2}\sin 2\theta\right)\right]_0^{\pi/2} = \frac{\pi^2}{32} + \frac{1}{8}$

23. $\int_1^\infty \int_0^{1/x} y\,dy\,dx = \int_1^\infty \left[\frac{y^2}{2}\right]_0^{1/x} dx = \frac{1}{2}\int_1^\infty \frac{1}{x^2}\,dx = \left[-\frac{1}{2x}\right]_1^\infty = 0 + \frac{1}{2} = \frac{1}{2}$

25. $\int_1^\infty \int_1^\infty \frac{1}{xy}\,dx\,dy = \int_1^\infty \left[\frac{1}{y}\ln x\right]_1^\infty dy = \int_1^\infty \left[\frac{1}{y}(\infty) - \frac{1}{y}(0)\right] dy$

Diverges

27. $A = \int_0^8 \int_0^3 dy\,dx = \int_0^8 \left[y\right]_0^3 dx = \int_0^8 3\,dx = \left[3x\right]_0^8 = 24$

$A = \int_0^3 \int_0^8 dx\,dy = \int_0^3 \left[x\right]_0^8 dy = \int_0^3 8\,dy = \left[8y\right]_0^3 = 24$

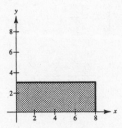

29. $A = \int_0^2 \int_0^{4-x^2} dy\,dx = \int_0^2 \left[y\right]_0^{4-x^2} dx$

$= \int_0^2 (4 - x^2)\,dx$

$= \left[4x - \frac{x^3}{3}\right]_0^2 = \frac{16}{3}$

$A = \int_0^4 \int_0^{\sqrt{4-y}} dx\,dy$

$= \int_0^4 \left[x\right]_0^{\sqrt{4-y}} dy = \int_0^4 \sqrt{4-y}\,dy = -\int_0^4 (4-y)^{1/2}(-1)\,dy = \left[-\frac{2}{3}(4-y)^{3/2}\right]_0^4 = \frac{2}{3}(8) = \frac{16}{3}$

31. $A = \int_{-2}^1 \int_{x+2}^{4-x^2} dy\,dx$

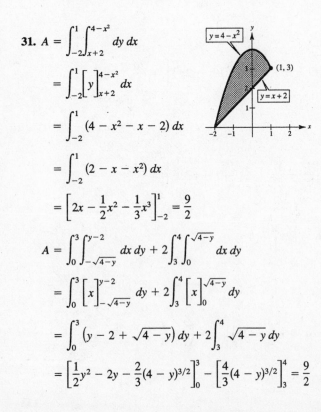

$= \int_{-2}^1 \left[y\right]_{x+2}^{4-x^2} dx$

$= \int_{-2}^1 (4 - x^2 - x - 2)\,dx$

$= \int_{-2}^1 (2 - x - x^2)\,dx$

$= \left[2x - \frac{1}{2}x^2 - \frac{1}{3}x^3\right]_{-2}^1 = \frac{9}{2}$

$A = \int_0^3 \int_{-\sqrt{4-y}}^{y-2} dx\,dy + 2\int_3^4 \int_0^{\sqrt{4-y}} dx\,dy$

$= \int_0^3 \left[x\right]_{-\sqrt{4-y}}^{y-2} dy + 2\int_3^4 \left[x\right]_0^{\sqrt{4-y}} dy$

$= \int_0^3 \left(y - 2 + \sqrt{4-y}\right) dy + 2\int_3^4 \sqrt{4-y}\,dy$

$= \left[\frac{1}{2}y^2 - 2y - \frac{2}{3}(4-y)^{3/2}\right]_0^3 - \left[\frac{4}{3}(4-y)^{3/2}\right]_3^4 = \frac{9}{2}$

33. $\int_0^4 \int_0^{(2-\sqrt{x})^2} dy\,dx = \int_0^4 \left[y\right]_0^{(2-\sqrt{x})^2} dx$

$= \int_0^4 \left(4 - 4\sqrt{x} + x\right) dx$

$= \left[4x - \frac{8}{3}x\sqrt{x} + \frac{x^2}{2}\right]_0^4 = \frac{8}{3}$

$\int_0^4 \int_0^{(2-\sqrt{y})^2} dx\,dy = \frac{8}{3}$

Integration steps are similar to those above.

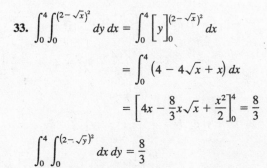

35. $A = \int_0^3 \int_0^{2x/3} dy\, dx + \int_3^5 \int_0^{5-x} dy\, dx$

$= \int_0^3 \left[y \right]_0^{2x/3} dx + \int_3^5 \left[y \right]_0^{5-x} dx$

$= \int_0^3 \frac{2x}{3}\, dx + \int_3^5 (5 - x)\, dx$

$= \left[\frac{1}{3}x^2 \right]_0^3 + \left[5x - \frac{1}{2}x^2 \right]_3^5 = 5$

$A = \int_0^2 \int_{3y/2}^{5-y} dx\, dy$

$= \int_0^2 \left[x \right]_{3y/2}^{5-y} dy$

$= \int_0^2 \left(5 - y - \frac{3y}{2} \right) dy$

$= \int_2^2 \left(5 - \frac{5y}{2} \right) dy = \left[5y - \frac{5}{4}y^2 \right]_0^2 = 5$

37. $\frac{A}{4} = \int_0^a \int_0^{(b/a)\sqrt{a^2-x^2}} dy\, dx = \int_0^a \left[y \right]_0^{(b/a)\sqrt{a^2-x^2}} dx$

$= \frac{b}{a}\int_0^a \sqrt{a^2 - x^2}\, dx = ab\int_0^{\pi/2} \cos^2\theta\, d\theta$

$(x = a\sin\theta,\, dx = a\cos\theta\, d\theta)$

$= \frac{ab}{2}\int_0^{\pi/2} (1 + \cos 2\theta)\, d\theta = \left[\frac{ab}{2}\left(\theta + \frac{1}{2}\sin 2\theta \right) \right]_0^{\pi/2}$

$= \frac{\pi ab}{4}$

Therefore, $A = \pi ab$.

$\frac{A}{4} = \int_0^b \int_0^{(a/b)\sqrt{b^2-y^2}} dx\, dy = \frac{\pi ab}{4}$

Therefore, $A = \pi ab$. Integration steps are similar to those above.

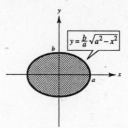

39. $\int_0^4 \int_0^y f(x, y)\, dx\, dy,\, 0 \le x \le y,\, 0 \le y \le 4$

$= \int_0^4 \int_x^4 f(x, y)\, dy\, dx$

41. $\int_{-2}^2 \int_0^{\sqrt{4-x^2}} f(x, y)\, dy\, dx,\, 0 \le y \le \sqrt{4 - x^2},\, -2 \le x \le 2$

$= \int_0^2 \int_{-\sqrt{4-y^2}}^{\sqrt{4-y^2}} dx\, dy$

43. $\int_1^{10} \int_0^{\ln y} f(x, y)\, dx\, dy,\, 0 \le x \le \ln y,\, 1 \le y \le 10$

$= \int_0^{\ln 10} \int_{e^x}^{10} f(x, y)\, dy\, dx$

45. $\int_{-1}^1 \int_{x^2}^1 f(x, y)\, dy\, dx,\, x^2 \le y \le 1,\, 1 \le x \le 1$

$= \int_0^1 \int_{-\sqrt{y}}^{\sqrt{y}} f(x, y)\, dx\, dy$

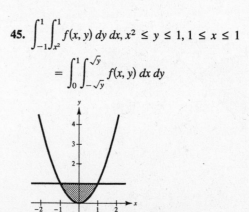

47. $\displaystyle\int_0^1\int_0^2 dy\,dx = \int_0^2\int_0^1 dx\,dy = 2$

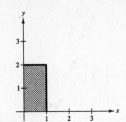

49. $\displaystyle\int_0^1\int_{-\sqrt{1-y^2}}^{\sqrt{1-y^2}} dx\,dy = \int_{-1}^1\int_0^{\sqrt{1-x^2}} dy\,dx = \frac{\pi}{2}$

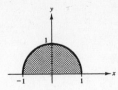

51. $\displaystyle\int_0^2\int_0^x dy\,dx + \int_2^4\int_0^{4-x} dy\,dx = \int_0^2\int_y^{4-y} dx\,dy = 4$

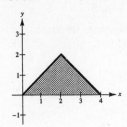

53. $\displaystyle\int_0^2\int_{x/2}^1 dy\,dx = \int_0^1\int_0^{2y} dx\,dy = 1$

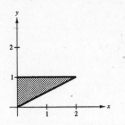

55. $\displaystyle\int_0^1\int_{y^2}^{\sqrt[3]{y}} dx\,dy = \int_0^1\int_{x^3}^{\sqrt{x}} dy\,dx = \frac{5}{12}$

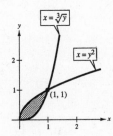

57. The first integral arises using vertical representative rectangles. The second two integrals arise using horizontal representative rectangles.

$$\int_0^5\int_x^{\sqrt{50-x^2}} x^2y^2\,dy\,dx = \int_0^5\left[\frac{1}{3}x^2(50-x^2)^{3/2} - \frac{1}{3}x^5\right] dx$$

$$= \frac{15625}{24}\pi$$

$$\int_0^5\int_0^y x^2y^2\,dx\,dy + \int_5^{5\sqrt{2}}\int_0^{\sqrt{50-y^2}} x^2y^2\,dx\,dy = \int_0^5\frac{1}{3}y^5\,dy + \int_5^{5\sqrt{2}}\frac{1}{3}(50-y^2)^{3/2}\,y^2\,dy = \frac{15625}{18} + \left(\frac{15625}{18}\pi - \frac{15625}{18}\right)$$

$$= \frac{15625}{24}\pi$$

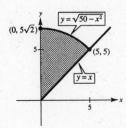

59. $\int_0^2 \int_x^2 x\sqrt{1+y^3}\, dy\, dx = \int_0^2 \int_0^y x\sqrt{1+y^3}\, dx\, dy = \int_0^2 \left[\sqrt{1+y^3} \cdot \frac{x^2}{2} \right]_0^y dy$

$$= \frac{1}{2}\int_0^2 \sqrt{1+y^3}\, y^2\, dy = \left[\frac{1}{2}\cdot\frac{1}{3}\cdot\frac{2}{3}(1+y^3)^{3/2} \right]_0^2 = \frac{1}{9}(27) - \frac{1}{9}(1) = \frac{26}{9}$$

61. $\int_0^1 \int_y^1 \sin(x^2)\, dx\, dy = \int_0^1 \int_0^x \sin(x^2)\, dy\, dx = \int_0^1 \left[y\sin(x^2) \right]_0^x dx$

$$= \int_0^1 x\sin(x^2)\, dx = \left[-\frac{1}{2}\cos(x^2) \right]_0^1 = -\frac{1}{2}\cos 1 + \frac{1}{2}(1) = \frac{1}{2}(1-\cos 1) \approx 0.2298$$

63. $\int_0^2 \int_{x^2}^{2x} (x^3 + 3y^2)\, dy\, dx = \frac{1664}{105} \approx 15.848$

65. $\int_0^4 \int_0^y \frac{2}{(x+1)(y+1)}\, dx\, dy = (\ln 5)^2 \approx 2.590$

67. (a) $x = y^3 \iff y = x^{1/3}$

$x = 4\sqrt{2y} \iff x^2 = 32y \iff y = \frac{x^2}{32}$

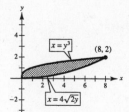

(b) $\int_0^8 \int_{x^2/32}^{x^{1/3}} (x^2 y - xy^2)\, dy\, dx$

(c) Both integrals equal $67520/693 \approx 97.43$

69. $\int_0^2 \int_0^{4-x^2} e^{xy}\, dy\, dx \approx 20.5648$

71. $\int_0^{2\pi} \int_0^{1+\cos\theta} 6r^2 \cos\theta\, dr\, d\theta = \frac{15\pi}{2}$

73. An iterated integral is a double integral of a function of two variables. First integrate with respect to one variable while holding the other variable constant. Then integrate with respect to the second variable.

75. The region is a rectangle.

77. True

Section 13.2   Double Integrals and Volume

For Exercise 1–3, $\Delta x_i = \Delta y_i = 1$ and the midpoints of the squares are

$\left(\frac{1}{2}, \frac{1}{2}\right)$, $\left(\frac{3}{2}, \frac{1}{2}\right)$, $\left(\frac{5}{2}, \frac{1}{2}\right)$, $\left(\frac{7}{2}, \frac{1}{2}\right)$, $\left(\frac{1}{2}, \frac{3}{2}\right)$, $\left(\frac{3}{2}, \frac{3}{2}\right)$, $\left(\frac{5}{2}, \frac{3}{2}\right)$, $\left(\frac{7}{2}, \frac{3}{2}\right)$.

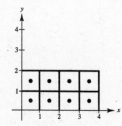

1. $f(x, y) = x + y$

$$\sum_{i=1}^8 f(x_i, y_i)\,\Delta x_i \Delta y_i = 1 + 2 + 3 + 4 + 2 + 3 + 4 + 5 = 24$$

$$\int_0^4 \int_0^2 (x+y)\, dy\, dx = \int_0^4 \left[xy + \frac{y^2}{2} \right]_0^2 dx = \int_0^4 (2x+2)\, dx = \left[x^2 + 2x \right]_0^4 = 24$$

3. $f(x, y) = x^2 + y^2$

$$\sum_{i=1}^{8} f(x_i, y_i)\, \Delta x_i\, \Delta y_i = \frac{2}{4} + \frac{10}{4} + \frac{26}{4} + \frac{50}{4} + \frac{10}{4} + \frac{18}{4} + \frac{34}{4} + \frac{58}{4} = 52$$

$$\int_0^4 \int_0^2 (x^2 + y^2)\, dy\, dx = \int_0^4 \left[x^2 y + \frac{y^3}{3} \right]_0^2 dx = \int_0^4 \left(2x^2 + \frac{8}{3} \right) dx = \left[\frac{2x^3}{3} + \frac{8x}{3} \right]_0^4 = \frac{160}{3}$$

5. $\int_0^4 \int_0^4 f(x, y)\, dy\, dx \approx (32 + 31 + 28 + 23) + (31 + 30 + 27 + 22) + (28 + 27 + 24 + 19) + (23 + 22 + 19 + 14)$

$$= 400$$

Using the corner of the ith square furthest from the origin, you obtain 272.

7. $\int_0^2 \int_0^1 (1 + 2x + 2y)\, dy\, dx = \int_0^2 \left[y + 2xy + y^2 \right]_0^1 dx$

$$= \int_0^2 (2 + 2x)\, dx$$

$$= \left[2x + x^2 \right]_0^2$$

$$= 8$$

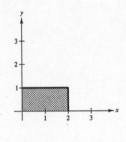

9. $\int_0^6 \int_{y/2}^3 (x + y)\, dx\, dy = \int_0^6 \left[\frac{1}{2} x^2 + xy \right]_{y/2}^3 dy$

$$= \int_0^6 \left(\frac{9}{2} + 3y - \frac{5}{8} y^2 \right) dy$$

$$= \left[\frac{9}{2} y + \frac{3}{2} y^2 - \frac{5}{24} y^3 \right]_0^6$$

$$= 36$$

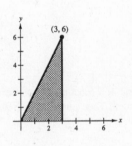

11. $\int_{-a}^a \int_{-\sqrt{a^2 - x^2}}^{\sqrt{a^2 - x^2}} (x + y)\, dy\, dx = \int_{-a}^a \left[xy + \frac{1}{2} y^2 \right]_{-\sqrt{a^2 - x^2}}^{\sqrt{a^2 - x^2}} dx$

$$= \int_{-a}^a 2x\sqrt{a^2 - x^2}\, dx$$

$$= \left[-\frac{2}{3}(a^2 - x^2)^{3/2} \right]_{-a}^a = 0$$

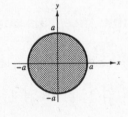

13. $\int_0^5 \int_0^3 xy\, dx\, dy = \int_0^3 \int_0^5 xy\, dy\, dx$

$$= \int_0^3 \left[\frac{1}{2} xy^2 \right]_0^5 dx$$

$$= \frac{25}{2} \int_0^3 x\, dx$$

$$= \left[\frac{25}{4} x^2 \right]_0^3 = \frac{225}{4}$$

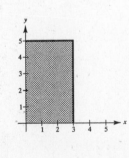

15. $\displaystyle\int_0^2\int_{y/2}^{y}\frac{y}{x^2+y^2}\,dx\,dy + \int_2^4\int_{y/2}^2\frac{y}{x^2+y^2}\,dx\,dy = \int_0^2\int_x^{2x}\frac{y}{x^2+y^2}\,dy\,dx$

$\displaystyle\qquad\qquad = \frac{1}{2}\int_0^2\Big[\ln(x^2+y^2)\Big]_x^{2x}\,dx$

$\displaystyle\qquad\qquad = \frac{1}{2}\int_0^2(\ln 5x^2 - \ln 2x^2)\,dx$

$\displaystyle\qquad\qquad = \frac{1}{2}\ln\frac{5}{2}\int_0^2 dx$

$\displaystyle\qquad\qquad = \left[\frac{1}{2}\Big(\ln\frac{5}{2}\Big)x\right]_0^2 = \ln\frac{5}{2}$

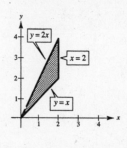

17. $\displaystyle\int_3^4\int_{4-y}^{\sqrt{4-y}}-2y\ln x\,dx\,dy = \int_0^1\int_{4-x}^{4-x^2}-2y\ln x\,dy\,dx$

$\displaystyle\qquad\qquad = -\int_0^1\Big[\ln x\cdot y^2\Big]_{4-x}^{4-x^2}\,dx$

$\displaystyle\qquad\qquad = -\int_0^1[\ln x[(4-x^2)^2-(4-x)^2]]\,dx$

$\displaystyle\qquad\qquad = \frac{26}{25}$

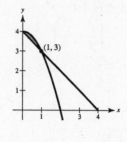

19. $\displaystyle\int_0^4\int_0^{3x/4}x\,dy\,dx + \int_4^5\int_0^{\sqrt{25-x^2}}x\,dy\,dx = \int_0^3\int_{4y/3}^{\sqrt{25-y^2}}x\,dx\,dy$

$\displaystyle\qquad\qquad = \int_0^3\left[\frac{1}{2}x^2\right]_{4y/3}^{\sqrt{25-y^2}}\,dy$

$\displaystyle\qquad\qquad = \frac{25}{18}\int_0^3(9-y^2)\,dy$

$\displaystyle\qquad\qquad = \left[\frac{25}{18}\Big(9y-\frac{1}{3}y^3\Big)\right]_0^3 = 25$

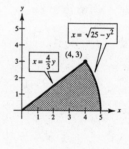

21. $\displaystyle\int_0^4\int_0^2\frac{y}{2}\,dy\,dx = \int_0^4\left[\frac{y^2}{4}\right]_0^2\,dx$

$\displaystyle\qquad\quad = \int_0^4 dx = 4$

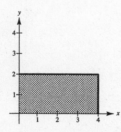

23. $\displaystyle\int_0^2\int_0^y(4-x-y)\,dx\,dy = \int_0^2\left[4x-\frac{x^2}{2}-xy\right]_0^y\,dy$

$\displaystyle\qquad\qquad = \int_0^2\Big(4y-\frac{y^2}{2}-y^2\Big)\,dy$

$\displaystyle\qquad\qquad = \left[2y^2-\frac{y^3}{6}-\frac{y^3}{3}\right]_0^2$

$\displaystyle\qquad\qquad = 8-\frac{8}{6}-\frac{8}{3} = 4$

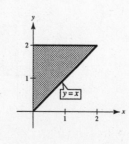

25. $\displaystyle\int_0^6 \int_0^{(-2/3)x+4} \left(\frac{12 - 2x - 3y}{4} \right) dy\, dx = \int_0^6 \left[\frac{1}{4}\left(12y - 2xy - \frac{3}{2}y^2 \right) \right]_0^{(-2/3)x+4} dx$

$\displaystyle = \int_0^6 \left(\frac{1}{6}x^2 - 2x + 6 \right) dx$

$\displaystyle = \left[\frac{1}{18}x^3 - x^2 + 6x \right]_0^6$

$\displaystyle = 12$

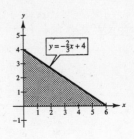

27. $\displaystyle\int_0^1 \int_0^y (1 - xy)\, dx\, dy = \int_0^1 \left[x - \frac{x^2 y}{2} \right]_0^y dy$

$\displaystyle = \int_0^1 \left(y - \frac{y^3}{2} \right) dy$

$\displaystyle = \left[\frac{y^2}{2} - \frac{y^4}{8} \right]_0^1$

$\displaystyle = \frac{3}{8}$

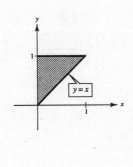

29. $\displaystyle\int_0^\infty \int_0^\infty \frac{1}{(x+1)^2(y+1)^2}\, dy\, dx = \int_0^\infty \left[-\frac{1}{(x+1)^2(y+1)} \right]_0^\infty dx = \int_0^\infty \frac{1}{(x+1)^2}\, dx = \left[-\frac{1}{(x+1)} \right]_0^\infty = 1$

31. $\displaystyle 4\int_0^2 \int_0^{\sqrt{4-x^2}} (4 - x^2 - y^2)\, dy\, dx = 8\pi$

33. $V = \displaystyle\int_0^1 \int_0^x xy\, dy\, dx$

$\displaystyle = \int_0^1 \left[\frac{1}{2}xy^2 \right]_0^x dx = \frac{1}{2}\int_0^1 x^3\, dx$

$\displaystyle = \left[\frac{1}{8}x^4 \right]_0^1 = \frac{1}{8}$

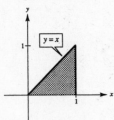

35. $V = \displaystyle\int_0^2 \int_0^4 x^2\, dy\, dx$

$\displaystyle = \int_0^2 \left[x^2 y \right]_0^4 dx = \int_0^2 4x^2\, dx$

$\displaystyle = \left[\frac{4x^3}{3} \right]_0^2 = \frac{32}{3}$

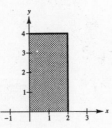

37. Divide the solid into two equal parts.

$V = \displaystyle 2\int_0^1 \int_0^x \sqrt{1 - x^2}\, dy\, dx$

$\displaystyle = 2\int_0^1 \left[y\sqrt{1 - x^2} \right]_0^x dx$

$\displaystyle = 2\int_0^1 x\sqrt{1 - x^2}\, dx$

$\displaystyle = \left[-\frac{2}{3}(1 - x^2)^{3/2} \right]_0^1 = \frac{2}{3}$

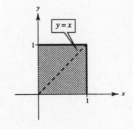

39. $V = \int_0^2 \int_0^{\sqrt{4-x^2}} (x + y) \, dy \, dx$

$= \int_0^2 \left[xy + \frac{1}{2}y^2 \right]_0^{\sqrt{4-x^2}} dx$

$= \int_0^2 \left(x\sqrt{4 - x^2} + 2 - \frac{1}{2}x^2 \right) dx$

$= \left[-\frac{1}{3}(4 - x^2)^{3/2} + 2x - \frac{1}{6}x^3 \right]_0^2 = \frac{16}{3}$

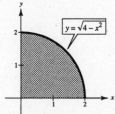

41. $V = 4 \int_0^2 \int_0^{\sqrt{4-x^2}} (x^2 + y^2) \, dy \, dx$

$= 4 \int_0^2 \left[x^2\sqrt{4 - x^2} + \frac{1}{3}(4 - x^2)^{3/2} \right] dx, \quad x = 2 \sin \theta$

$= 4 \int_0^{\pi/2} \left(16 \cos^2 \theta - \frac{32}{3} \cos^4 \theta \right) d\theta$

$= 4 \left[16 \left(\frac{\pi}{4} \right) - \frac{32}{3} \left(\frac{3\pi}{16} \right) \right]$

$= 8\pi$

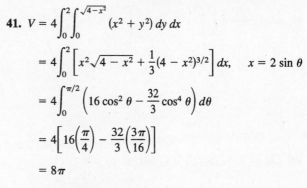

43. $V = 4 \int_0^2 \int_0^{\sqrt{4-x^2}} (4 - x^2 - y^2) \, dy \, dx = 8\pi$

45. $V = \int_0^2 \int_0^{-0.5x+1} \frac{2}{1 + x^2 + y^2} \, dy \, dx \approx 1.2315$

47. f is a continuous function such that $0 \le f(x, y) \le 1$ over a region R of area 1. Let $f(m, n) = $ the minimum value of f over R and $f(M, N) = $ the maximum value of f over R. Then

$$f(m, n) \int_R \int dA \le \int_R \int f(x, y) \, dA \le f(M, N) \int_R \int dA.$$

Since $\int_R \int dA = 1$ and $0 \le f(m, n) \le f(M, N) \le 1$, we have $0 \le f(m, n)(1) \le \int_R \int f(x, y) \, dA \le f(M, N)(1) \le 1$.

Therefore, $0 \le \int_R \int f(x, y) \, dA \le 1$.

49. $\int_0^1 \int_{y/2}^{1/2} e^{-x^2} \, dx \, dy = \int_0^{1/2} \int_0^{2x} e^{-x^2} \, dy \, dx$

$= \int_0^{1/2} 2xe^{-x^2} \, dx$

$= \left[-e^{-x^2} \right]_0^{1/2}$

$= -e^{-1/4} + 1$

$= 1 - e^{-1/4} \approx 0.221$

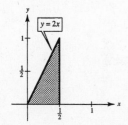

51. $\int_0^1 \int_0^{\arccos y} \sin x \sqrt{1 + \sin^2 x} \, dx \, dy$

$= \int_0^{\pi/2} \int_0^{\cos x} \sin x \sqrt{1 + \sin^2 x} \, dy \, dx$

$= \int_0^{\pi/2} (1 + \sin^2 x)^{1/2} \sin x \cos x \, dx$

$= \left[\frac{1}{2} \cdot \frac{2}{3}(1 + \sin^2 x)^{3/2} \right]_0^{\pi/2} = \frac{1}{3} \left[2\sqrt{2} - 1 \right]$

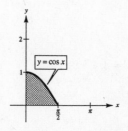

53. Average $= \dfrac{1}{8} \displaystyle\int_0^4 \int_0^2 x \, dy \, dx = \dfrac{1}{8} \int_0^4 2x \, dx = \left[\dfrac{x^2}{8} \right]_0^4 = 2$

55. Average $= \dfrac{1}{4} \displaystyle\int_0^2 \int_0^2 (x^2 + y^2) \, dx \, dy$

$$= \dfrac{1}{4} \int_0^2 \left[\dfrac{x^3}{3} + xy^2 \right]_0^2 dy = \dfrac{1}{4} \int_0^2 \left(\dfrac{8}{3} + 2y^2 \right) dy$$

$$= \left[\dfrac{1}{4}\left(\dfrac{8}{3}y + \dfrac{2}{3}y^3 \right) \right]_0^2 = \dfrac{8}{3}$$

57. See the definition on page 946.

59. The value of $\displaystyle\int_R \int f(x, y) \, dA$ would be kB.

61. Average $= \dfrac{1}{1250} \displaystyle\int_{300}^{325} \int_{200}^{250} 100x^{0.6}y^{0.4} \, dx \, dy$

$$= \dfrac{1}{1250} \int_{300}^{325} \left[(100y^{0.4}) \dfrac{x^{1.6}}{1.6} \right]_{200}^{250} dy = \dfrac{128{,}844.1}{1250} \int_{300}^{325} y^{0.4} \, dy = 103.0753 \left[\dfrac{y^{1.4}}{1.4} \right]_{300}^{325} \approx 25{,}645.24$$

63. $f(x, y) \geq 0$ for all (x, y) and

$$\int_{-\infty}^{\infty} \int_{-\infty}^{\infty} f(x, y) \, dA = \int_0^5 \int_0^2 \dfrac{1}{10} \, dy \, dx = \int_0^5 \dfrac{1}{5} \, dx = 1$$

$$P(0 \leq x \leq 2, 1 \leq y \leq 2) = \int_0^2 \int_1^2 \dfrac{1}{10} \, dy \, dx = \int_0^2 \dfrac{1}{10} \, dx = \dfrac{1}{5}.$$

65. $f(x, y) \geq 0$ for all (x, y) and

$$\int_{-\infty}^{\infty} \int_{-\infty}^{\infty} f(x, y) \, dA = \int_0^3 \int_3^6 \dfrac{1}{27}(9 - x - y) \, dy \, dx$$

$$= \int_0^3 \dfrac{1}{27}\left[9y - xy - \dfrac{y^2}{2} \right]_3^6 dx = \int_0^3 \left(\dfrac{1}{2} - \dfrac{1}{9}x \right) dx = \left[\dfrac{x}{2} - \dfrac{x^2}{18} \right]_0^3 = 1$$

$$P(0 \leq x \leq 1, 4 \leq y \leq 6) = \int_0^1 \int_4^6 \dfrac{1}{27}(9 - x - y) \, dy \, dx = \int_0^1 \dfrac{2}{27}(4 - x) \, dx = \dfrac{7}{27}.$$

67. Divide the base into six squares, and assume the height at the center of each square is the height of the entire square.

Thus,

$$V \approx (4 + 3 + 6 + 7 + 3 + 2)(100) = 2500m^3.$$

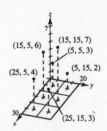

69. $\displaystyle\int_0^1 \int_0^2 \sin\sqrt{x + y} \, dy \, dx \quad m = 4, n = 8$

  (a) 1.78435

  (b) 1.7879

71. $\displaystyle\int_4^6 \int_0^2 y \cos\sqrt{x} \, dx \, dy \quad m = 4, n = 8$

  (a) 11.0571

  (b) 11.0414

73. $V \approx 125$

Matches d.

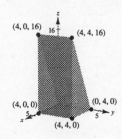

75. False

$$V = 8 \int_0^1 \int_0^{\sqrt{1-y^2}} \sqrt{1 - x^2 - y^2} \, dx \, dy$$

77. Average $= \int_0^1 f(x) \, dx = \int_0^1 \int_1^x e^{t^2} \, dt \, dx = -\int_0^1 \int_x^1 e^{t^2} \, dt \, dx$

$$= -\int_0^1 \int_0^t e^{t^2} \, dx \, dt = -\int_0^1 t e^{t^2} \, dt$$

$$= \left[-\frac{1}{2} e^{t^2} \right]_0^1 = -\frac{1}{2}(e - 1) = \frac{1}{2}(1 - e)$$

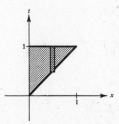

Section 13.3   Change of Variables: Polar Coordinates

1. Rectangular coordinates

3. Polar coordinates

5. $R = \{(r, \theta): 0 \leq r \leq 8, 0 \leq \theta \leq \pi\}$

7. $R = \{(r, \theta): 0 \leq r \leq 3 + 3 \sin \theta, 0 \leq \theta \leq 2\pi\}$ Cardioid

9. $\int_0^{2\pi} \int_0^6 3r^2 \sin \theta \, dr \, d\theta = \int_0^{2\pi} \left[r^3 \sin \theta \right]_0^6 \, d\theta$

$$= \int_0^{2\pi} 216 \sin \theta \, d\theta$$

$$= \left[-216 \cos \theta \right]_0^{2\pi} = 0$$

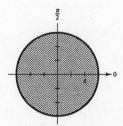

11. $\int_0^{\pi/2} \int_2^3 \sqrt{9 - r^2} \, r \, dr \, d\theta = \int_0^{\pi/2} \left[-\frac{1}{3}(9 - r^2)^{3/2} \right]_2^3 \, d\theta$

$$= \left[\frac{5\sqrt{5}}{3} \theta \right]_0^{\pi/2}$$

$$= \frac{5\sqrt{5}\pi}{6}$$

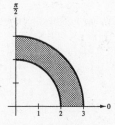

13. $\int_0^{\pi/2} \int_0^{1 + \sin \theta} \theta r \, dr \, d\theta = \int_0^{\pi/2} \left[\frac{\theta r^2}{2} \right]_0^{1 + \sin \theta} \, d\theta$

$$= \int_0^{\pi/2} \frac{1}{2} \theta (1 + \sin \theta)^2 \, d\theta$$

$$= \left[\frac{1}{8} \theta^2 + \sin \theta - \theta \cos \theta + \frac{1}{2} \theta \left(-\frac{1}{2} \cos \theta \cdot \sin \theta + \frac{1}{2} \theta \right) + \frac{1}{8} \sin^2 \theta \right]_0^{\pi/2}$$

$$= \frac{3}{32} \pi^2 + \frac{9}{8}$$

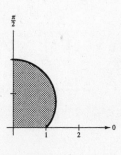

15. $\displaystyle\int_0^a \int_0^{\sqrt{a^2-y^2}} y \, dx \, dy = \int_0^{\pi/2} \int_0^a r^2 \sin\theta \, dr \, d\theta = \frac{a^3}{3} \int_0^{\pi/2} \sin\theta \, d\theta = \left[\frac{a^3}{3}(-\cos\theta) \right]_0^{\pi/2} = \frac{a^3}{3}$

17. $\displaystyle\int_0^3 \int_0^{\sqrt{9-x^2}} (x^2 + y^2)^{3/2} \, dy \, dx = \int_0^{\pi/2} \int_0^3 r^4 \, dr \, d\theta = \frac{243}{5} \int_0^{\pi/2} d\theta = \frac{243\pi}{10}$

19. $\displaystyle\int_0^2 \int_0^{\sqrt{2x-x^2}} xy \, dy \, dx = \int_0^{\pi/2} \int_0^{2\cos\theta} r^3 \cos\theta \sin\theta \, dr \, d\theta = 4\int_0^{\pi/2} \cos^5\theta \sin\theta \, d\theta = \left[-\frac{4\cos^6\theta}{6} \right]_0^{\pi/2} = \frac{2}{3}$

21. $\displaystyle\int_0^2 \int_0^x \sqrt{x^2 + y^2} \, dy \, dx + \int_2^{2\sqrt{2}} \int_0^{\sqrt{8-x^2}} \sqrt{x^2 + y^2} \, dy \, dx = \int_0^{\pi/4} \int_0^{2\sqrt{2}} r^2 \, dr \, d\theta$

$$= \int_0^{\pi/4} \frac{16\sqrt{2}}{3} \, d\theta$$

$$= \frac{4\sqrt{2}\pi}{3}$$

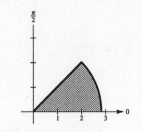

23. $\displaystyle\int_0^2 \int_0^{\sqrt{4-x^2}} (x + y) \, dy \, dx = \int_0^{\pi/2} \int_0^2 (r\cos\theta + r\sin\theta)r \, dr \, d\theta = \int_0^{\pi/2} \int_0^2 (\cos\theta + \sin\theta)r^2 \, dr \, d\theta$

$$= \frac{8}{3} \int_0^{\pi/2} (\cos\theta + \sin\theta) \, d\theta = \left[\frac{8}{3}(\sin\theta - \cos\theta) \right]_0^{\pi/2} = \frac{16}{3}$$

25. $\displaystyle\int_0^{1/\sqrt{2}} \int_{\sqrt{1-y^2}}^{\sqrt{4-y^2}} \arctan\frac{y}{x} \, dx \, dy + \int_{1/\sqrt{2}}^{\sqrt{2}} \int_y^{\sqrt{4-y^2}} \arctan\frac{y}{x} \, dx \, dy$

$$= \int_0^{\pi/4} \int_1^2 \theta r \, dr \, d\theta$$

$$= \int_0^{\pi/4} \frac{3}{2}\theta \, d\theta = \left[\frac{3\theta^2}{4} \right]_0^{\pi/4} = \frac{3\pi^2}{64}$$

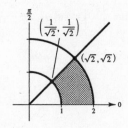

27. $\displaystyle V = \int_0^{\pi/2} \int_0^1 (r\cos\theta)(r\sin\theta)r \, dr \, d\theta$

$$= \frac{1}{2}\int_0^{\pi/2} \int_0^1 r^3 \sin 2\theta \, dr \, d\theta = \frac{1}{8}\int_0^{\pi/2} \sin 2\theta \, d\theta = \left[-\frac{1}{16}\cos 2\theta \right]_0^{\pi/2} = \frac{1}{8}$$

29. $\displaystyle V = \int_0^{2\pi} \int_0^5 r^2 \, dr \, d\theta = \frac{250\pi}{3}$

31. $\displaystyle V = 2\int_0^{\pi/2} \int_0^{4\cos\theta} \sqrt{16 - r^2}\, r \, dr \, d\theta = 2\int_0^{\pi/2} \left[-\frac{1}{3}\left(\sqrt{16 - r^2}\right)^3 \right]_0^{4\cos\theta} d\theta = -\frac{2}{3}\int_0^{\pi/2} (64\sin^3\theta - 64) \, d\theta$

$$= \frac{128}{3}\int_0^{\pi/2} [1 - \sin\theta(1 - \cos^2\theta)] \, d\theta = \frac{128}{3}\left[\theta + \cos\theta - \frac{\cos^3\theta}{3} \right]_0^{\pi/2} = \frac{64}{9}(3\pi - 4)$$

33. $V = \int_0^{2\pi} \int_a^4 \sqrt{16 - r^2}\, r\, dr\, d\theta = \int_0^{2\pi} \left[-\frac{1}{3}\left(\sqrt{16 - r^2}\right)^3 \right]_a^4 d\theta = \frac{1}{3}\left(\sqrt{16 - a^2}\right)^3 (2\pi)$

One-half the volume of the hemisphere is $(64\pi)/3$.

$$\frac{2\pi}{3}(16 - a^2)^{3/2} = \frac{64\pi}{3}$$

$$(16 - a^2)^{3/2} = 32$$

$$16 - a^2 = 32^{2/3}$$

$$a^2 = 16 - 32^{2/3} = 16 - 8\sqrt[3]{2}$$

$$a = \sqrt{4\left(4 - 2\sqrt[3]{2}\right)} = 2\sqrt{4 - 2\sqrt[3]{2}} \approx 2.4332$$

35. Total Volume $= V = \int_0^{2\pi} \int_0^4 25 e^{-r^2/4}\, r\, dr\, d\theta$

$$= \int_0^{2\pi} \left[-50 e^{-r^2/4} \right]_0^4 d\theta$$

$$= \int_0^{2\pi} -50(e^{-4} - 1)\, d\theta$$

$$= (1 - e^{-4})\, 100\pi \approx 308.40524$$

Let c be the radius of the hole that is removed.

$$\frac{1}{10} V = \int_0^{2\pi} \int_0^c 25 e^{-r^2/4}\, r\, dr\, d\theta = \int_0^{2\pi} \left[-50 e^{-r^2/4} \right]_0^c d\theta$$

$$= \int_0^{2\pi} -50(e^{-c^2/4} - 1)\, d\theta \Rightarrow 30.84052 = 100\pi(1 - e^{-c^2/4})$$

$$\Rightarrow e^{-c^2/4} = 0.90183$$

$$-\frac{c^2}{4} = -0.10333$$

$$c^2 = 0.41331$$

$$c = 0.6429$$

$$\Rightarrow \text{diameter} = 2c = 1.2858$$

37. $A = \int_0^\pi \int_0^{6\cos\theta} r\, dr\, d\theta = \int_0^\pi 18 \cos^2\theta\, d\theta = 9 \int_0^\pi (1 + \cos 2\theta)\, d\theta = \left[9\left(\theta + \frac{1}{2}\sin 2\theta\right) \right]_0^\pi = 9\pi$

39. $\int_0^{2\pi} \int_0^{1+\cos\theta} r\, dr\, d\theta = \frac{1}{2} \int_0^{2\pi} (1 + 2\cos\theta + \cos^2\theta)\, d\theta$

$$= \frac{1}{2} \int_0^{2\pi} \left(1 + 2\cos\theta + \frac{1 + \cos 2\theta}{2} \right) d\theta = \frac{1}{2} \left[\theta + 2\sin\theta + \frac{1}{2}\left(\theta + \frac{1}{2}\sin 2\theta\right) \right]_0^{2\pi} = \frac{3\pi}{2}$$

41. $3 \int_0^{\pi/3} \int_0^{2\sin 3\theta} r\, dr\, d\theta = \frac{3}{2} \int_0^{\pi/3} 4 \sin^2 3\theta\, d\theta = 3 \int_0^{\pi/3} (1 - \cos 6\theta)\, d\theta = 3\left[\theta - \frac{1}{6}\sin 6\theta \right]_0^{\pi/3} = \pi$

43. Let R be a region bounded by the graphs of $r = g_1(\theta)$ and $r = g_2(\theta)$, and the lines $\theta = a$ and $\theta = b$.

When using polar coordinates to evaluate a double integral over R, R can be partitioned into small polar sectors.

45. r-simple regions have fixed bounds for θ.

θ-simple regions have fixed bounds for r.

47. You would need to insert a factor of r because of the $r\,dr\,d\theta$ nature of polar coordinate integrals. The plane regions would be sectors of circles.

49. $\displaystyle\int_{\pi/4}^{\pi/2}\int_{0}^{5} r\sqrt{1+r^3}\,\sin\sqrt{\theta}\,dr\,d\theta \approx 56.051$

$\left[\textbf{Note: } \text{This integral equals } \left(\displaystyle\int_{\pi/4}^{\pi/2}\sin\sqrt{\theta}\,d\theta\right)\!\left(\displaystyle\int_{0}^{5} r\sqrt{1+r^3}\,dr\right)\right]$

51. Volume = base × height

$\approx 8\pi \times 12 \approx 300$

Answer (c)

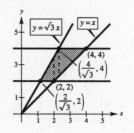

53. False

Let $f(r,\theta) = r - 1$ where R is the circular sector $0 \le r \le 6$ and $0 \le \theta \le \pi$. Then,

$\displaystyle\int_{R}\int (r-1)\,dA > 0 \quad \text{but} \quad r - 1 \ngtr 0 \text{ for all } r.$

55. (a) $\displaystyle I^2 = \int_{-\infty}^{\infty}\int_{-\infty}^{\infty} e^{-(x^2+y^2)/2}\,dA = 4\int_{0}^{\pi/2}\int_{0}^{\infty} e^{-r^2/2}\,r\,dr\,d\theta = 4\int_{0}^{\pi/2}\left[-e^{-r^2/2}\right]_{0}^{\infty}d\theta = 4\int_{0}^{\pi/2}d\theta = 2\pi$

(b) Therefore, $I = \sqrt{2\pi}$.

57. $\displaystyle\int_{-7}^{7}\int_{-\sqrt{49-x^2}}^{\sqrt{49-x^2}} 4000e^{-0.01(x^2+y^2)}\,dy\,dx = \int_{0}^{2\pi}\int_{0}^{7} 4000e^{-0.01r^2}\,r\,dr\,d\theta = \int_{0}^{2\pi}\left[-200{,}000e^{-0.01r^2}\right]_{0}^{7}d\theta$

$= 2\pi(-200{,}000)(e^{-0.49}-1) = 400{,}000\pi(1-e^{-0.49}) \approx 486{,}788$

59. (a) $\displaystyle\int_{2}^{4}\int_{y/\sqrt{3}}^{y} f\,dx\,dy$

(b) $\displaystyle\int_{2/\sqrt{3}}^{2}\int_{2}^{\sqrt{3}x} f\,dy\,dx + \int_{2}^{4/\sqrt{3}}\int_{x}^{\sqrt{3}x} f\,dy\,dx + \int_{4/\sqrt{3}}^{4}\int_{x}^{4} f\,dy\,dx$

(c) $\displaystyle\int_{\pi/4}^{\pi/3}\int_{2\csc\theta}^{4\csc\theta} fr\,dr\,d\theta$

61. $A = \dfrac{\Delta\theta r_2^{\,2}}{2} - \dfrac{\Delta\theta r_1^{\,2}}{2} = \Delta\theta\left(\dfrac{r_1+r_2}{2}\right)(r_2-r_1) = r\,\Delta r\,\Delta\theta$

Section 13.4   Center of Mass and Moments of Inertia

1. $\displaystyle m = \int_{0}^{4}\int_{0}^{3} xy\,dy\,dx = \int_{0}^{4}\left[\dfrac{xy^2}{2}\right]_{0}^{3}dx = \int_{0}^{4}\dfrac{9}{2}x\,dx = \left[\dfrac{9x^2}{4}\right]_{0}^{4} = 36$

3. $\displaystyle m = \int_{0}^{\pi/2}\int_{0}^{2} (r\cos\theta)(r\sin\theta)r\,dr\,d\theta = \int_{0}^{\pi/2}\int_{0}^{2}\cos\theta\sin\theta\cdot r^3\,dr\,d\theta$

$= \displaystyle\int_{0}^{\pi/2} 4\cos\theta\sin\theta\,d\theta$

$= \left[4\dfrac{\sin^2\theta}{2}\right]_{0}^{\pi/2} = 2$

5. (a) $m = \int_0^a \int_0^b k \, dy \, dx = kab$

$M_x = \int_0^a \int_0^b ky \, dy \, dx = \dfrac{kab^2}{2}$

$M_y = \int_0^a \int_0^b kx \, dy \, dx = \dfrac{ka^2b}{2}$

$\bar{x} = \dfrac{M_y}{m} = \dfrac{ka^2b/2}{kab} = \dfrac{a}{2}$

$\bar{y} = \dfrac{M_x}{m} = \dfrac{kab^2/2}{kab} = \dfrac{b}{2}$

$(\bar{x}, \bar{y}) = \left(\dfrac{a}{2}, \dfrac{b}{2}\right)$

(b) $m = \int_0^a \int_0^b ky \, dy \, dx = \dfrac{kab^2}{2}$

$M_x = \int_0^a \int_0^b ky^2 \, dy \, dx = \dfrac{kab^3}{3}$

$M_y = \int_0^a \int_0^b kxy \, dy \, dx = \dfrac{ka^2b^2}{4}$

$\bar{x} = \dfrac{M_y}{m} = \dfrac{ka^2b^2/4}{kab^2/2} = \dfrac{a}{2}$

$\bar{y} = \dfrac{M_x}{m} = \dfrac{kab^3/3}{kab^2/2} = \dfrac{2}{3}b$

$(\bar{x}, \bar{y}) = \left(\dfrac{a}{2}, \dfrac{2}{3}b\right)$

(c) $m = \int_0^a \int_0^b kx \, dy \, dx = k\int_0^a xb \, dx = \dfrac{1}{2}ka^2b$

$M_x = \int_0^a \int_0^b kxy \, dy \, dx = \dfrac{ka^2b^2}{4}$

$M_y = \int_0^a \int_0^b kx^2 \, dy \, dx = \dfrac{ka^3b}{3}$

$\bar{x} = \dfrac{M_y}{m} = \dfrac{ka^3b/3}{ka^2b/2} = \dfrac{2}{3}a$

$\bar{y} = \dfrac{M_x}{m} = \dfrac{ka^2b^2/4}{ka^2b/2} = \dfrac{b}{2}$

$(\bar{x}, \bar{y}) = \left(\dfrac{2}{3}a, \dfrac{b}{2}\right)$

7. (a) $m = \dfrac{k}{2}bh$

$\bar{x} = \dfrac{b}{2}$ by symmetry

$M_x = \int_0^{b/2} \int_0^{2hx/b} ky \, dy \, dx + \int_{b/2}^{b} \int_0^{-2h(x-b)/b} ky \, dy \, dx$

$= \dfrac{kbh^2}{12} + \dfrac{kbh^2}{12} = \dfrac{kbh^2}{6}$

$\bar{y} = \dfrac{M_x}{m} = \dfrac{kbh^2/6}{kbh/2} = \dfrac{h}{3}$

$(\bar{x}, \bar{y}) = \left(\dfrac{b}{2}, \dfrac{h}{3}\right)$

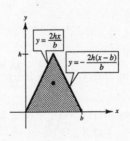

—CONTINUED—

7. —CONTINUED—

(b) $m = \int_0^{b/2} \int_0^{2hx/b} ky \, dy \, dx + \int_{b/2}^b \int_0^{-2h(x-b)/b} ky \, dy \, dx = \dfrac{kbh^2}{6}$

$M_x = \int_0^{b/2} \int_0^{2hx/b} ky^2 \, dy \, dx + \int_{b/2}^b \int_0^{-2h(x-b)/b} ky^2 \, dy \, dx = \dfrac{kbh^3}{12}$

$M_y = \int_0^{b/2} \int_0^{2hx/b} kxy \, dy \, dx + \int_{b/2}^b \int_0^{-2h(x-b)/b} kxy \, dy \, dx = \dfrac{kb^2h^2}{12}$

$\bar{x} = \dfrac{M_y}{m} = \dfrac{kb^2h^2/12}{kbh^2/6} = \dfrac{b}{2}$

$\bar{y} = \dfrac{M_x}{m} = \dfrac{kbh^3/12}{kbh^2/6} = \dfrac{h}{2}$

(c) $m = \int_0^{b/2} \int_0^{2hx/b} kx \, dy \, dx + \int_{b/2}^b \int_0^{-2h(x-b)/b} kx \, dy \, dx$

$= \dfrac{1}{12}kb^2h + \dfrac{1}{6}kb^2h = \dfrac{1}{4}kb^2h$

$M_x = \int_0^{b/2} \int_0^{2hx/b} kxy \, dy \, dx + \int_{b/2}^b \int_0^{-2h(x-b)/b} kxy \, dy \, dx$

$= \dfrac{1}{32}kh^2b^2 + \dfrac{5}{96}kh^2b^2 = \dfrac{1}{12}kh^2b^2$

$M_y = \int_0^{b/2} \int_0^{2hx/b} kx^2 \, dy \, dx + \int_{b/2}^b \int_0^{-2h(x-b)/b} kx^2 \, dy \, dx$

$= \dfrac{1}{32}kb^3h + \dfrac{11}{96}kb^3h = \dfrac{7}{48}kb^3h$

$\bar{x} = \dfrac{M_y}{m} = \dfrac{7kb^3h/48}{kb^2h/4} = \dfrac{7}{12}b$

$\bar{y} = \dfrac{M_x}{m} = \dfrac{kh^2b^2/12}{kb^2h/4} = \dfrac{h}{3}$

9. (a) The x-coordinate changes by 5: $(\bar{x}, \bar{y}) = \left(\dfrac{a}{2} + 5, \dfrac{b}{2}\right)$

(b) The x-coordinate changes by 5: $(\bar{x}, \bar{y}) = \left(\dfrac{a}{2} + 5, \dfrac{2b}{3}\right)$

(c) $m = \int_5^{a+5} \int_0^b kx \, dy \, dx = \dfrac{1}{2}k(a+5)^2 b - \dfrac{25}{2}kb$

$M_x = \int_5^{a+5} \int_0^b kxy \, dy \, dx = \dfrac{1}{4}k(a+5)^2 b^2 - \dfrac{25}{4}kb^2$

$M_y = \int_5^{a+5} \int_0^b kx^2 \, dy \, dx = \dfrac{1}{3}k(a+5)^3 b - \dfrac{125}{3}kb$

$\bar{x} = \dfrac{M_y}{m} = \dfrac{2(a^2 + 15a + 75)}{3(a + 10)}$

$\bar{y} = \dfrac{M_x}{m} = \dfrac{b}{2}$

11. (a) $\bar{x} = 0$ by symmetry

$m = \dfrac{\pi a^2 k}{2}$

$M_x = \int_{-a}^a \int_0^{\sqrt{a^2 - x^2}} yk \, dy \, dx = \dfrac{2a^3 k}{3}$

$\bar{y} = \dfrac{M_x}{m} = \dfrac{2a^3 k}{3} \cdot \dfrac{2}{\pi a^2 k} = \dfrac{4a}{3\pi}$

(b) $m = \int_{-a}^a \int_0^{\sqrt{a^2 - x^2}} k(a - y) y \, dy \, dx = \dfrac{a^4 k}{24}(16 - 3\pi)$

$M_x = \int_{-a}^a \int_0^{\sqrt{a^2 - x^2}} k(a - y) y^2 \, dy \, dx = \dfrac{a^5 k}{120}(15\pi - 32)$

$M_y = \int_{-a}^a \int_0^{\sqrt{a^2 - x^2}} kx(a - y) y \, dy \, dx = 0$

$\bar{x} = \dfrac{M_y}{m} = 0$

$\bar{y} = \dfrac{M_x}{m} = \dfrac{a}{5}\left[\dfrac{15\pi - 32}{16 - 3\pi}\right]$

13. $m = \int_0^4 \int_0^{\sqrt{x}} kxy\,dy\,dx = \dfrac{32k}{3}$

$M_x = \int_0^4 \int_0^{\sqrt{x}} kxy^2\,dy\,dx = \dfrac{256k}{21}$

$M_y = \int_0^4 \int_0^{\sqrt{x}} kx^2y\,dy\,dx = 32k$

$\bar{x} = \dfrac{M_y}{m} = \dfrac{32k}{1} \cdot \dfrac{3}{32k} = 3$

$\bar{y} = \dfrac{M_x}{m} = \dfrac{256k}{21} \cdot \dfrac{3}{32k} = \dfrac{8}{7}$

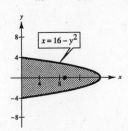

15. $\bar{x} = 0$ by symmetry

$m = \int_{-1}^1 \int_0^{1/(1+x^2)} k\,dy\,dx = \dfrac{k\pi}{2}$

$M_x = \int_{-1}^1 \int_0^{1/(1+x^2)} ky\,dy\,dx = \dfrac{k}{8}(2 + \pi)$

$\bar{y} = \dfrac{M_x}{m} = \dfrac{k}{8}(2 + \pi) \cdot \dfrac{2}{k\pi} = \dfrac{2 + \pi}{4\pi}$

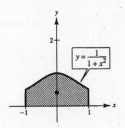

17. $\bar{y} = 0$ by symmetry

$m = \int_{-4}^4 \int_0^{16-y^2} kx\,dx\,dy = \dfrac{8192k}{15}$

$M_y = \int_{-4}^4 \int_0^{16-y^2} kx^2\,dx\,dy = \dfrac{524{,}288k}{105}$

$\bar{x} = \dfrac{M_y}{m} = \dfrac{524{,}288k}{105} \cdot \dfrac{15}{8192k} = \dfrac{64}{7}$

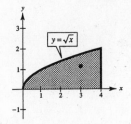

19. $\bar{x} = \dfrac{L}{2}$ by symmetry

$m = \int_0^L \int_0^{\sin \pi x/L} ky\,dy\,dx = \dfrac{kL}{4}$

$M_x = \int_0^L \int_0^{\sin \pi x/L} ky^2\,dy\,dx = \dfrac{4kL}{9\pi}$

$\bar{y} = \dfrac{M_x}{m} = \dfrac{4kL}{9\pi} \cdot \dfrac{4}{kL} = \dfrac{16}{9\pi}$

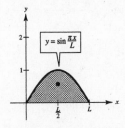

21. $m = \dfrac{\pi a^2 k}{8}$

$M_x = \int\int_R ky\,dA = \int_0^{\pi/4} \int_0^a kr^2 \sin\theta\,dr\,d\theta = \dfrac{ka^3(2 - \sqrt{2})}{6}$

$M_y = \int\int_R kx\,dA = \int_0^{\pi/4} \int_0^a kr^2 \cos\theta\,dr\,d\theta = \dfrac{ka^3\sqrt{2}}{6}$

$\bar{x} = \dfrac{M_y}{m} = \dfrac{ka^3\sqrt{2}}{6} \cdot \dfrac{8}{\pi a^2 k} = \dfrac{4a\sqrt{2}}{3\pi}$

$\bar{y} = \dfrac{M_x}{m} = \dfrac{ka^3(2 - \sqrt{2})}{6} \cdot \dfrac{8}{\pi a^2 k} = \dfrac{4a(2 - \sqrt{2})}{3\pi}$

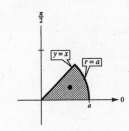

23. $m = \int_0^2 \int_0^{e^{-x}} ky\,dy\,dx = \frac{k}{4}(1 - e^{-4})$

$M_x = \int_0^2 \int_0^{e^{-x}} ky^2\,dy\,dx = \frac{k}{9}(1 - e^{-6})$

$M_y = \int_0^2 \int_0^{e^{-x}} kxy\,dy\,dx = \frac{k(1 - 5e^{-4})}{8}$

$\bar{x} = \frac{M_y}{m} = \frac{k(e^4 - 5)}{8e^4} \cdot \frac{4e^4}{k(e^4 - 1)} = \frac{e^4 - 5}{2(e^4 - 1)} \approx 0.46$

$\bar{y} = \frac{M_x}{m} = \frac{k(e^6 - 1)}{9e^6} \cdot \frac{4e^4}{k(e^4 - 1)} = \frac{4}{9}\left[\frac{e^6 - 1}{e^6 - e^2}\right] \approx 0.45$

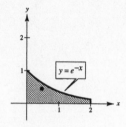

25. $\bar{y} = 0$ by symmetry

$m = \iint_R k\,dA = \int_{-\pi/6}^{\pi/6} \int_0^{2\cos 3\theta} kr\,dr\,d\theta = \frac{k\pi}{3}$

$M_y = \iint_R kx\,dA$

$\quad = \int_{-\pi/6}^{\pi/6} \int_0^{2\cos 3\theta} kr^2\cos\theta\,dr\,d\theta \approx 1.17k$

$\bar{x} = \frac{M_y}{m} \approx 1.17k\left(\frac{3}{\pi k}\right) \approx 1.12$

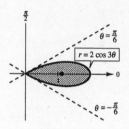

27. $m = bh$

$I_x = \int_0^b \int_0^h y^2\,dy\,dx = \frac{bh^3}{3}$

$I_y = \int_0^b \int_0^h x^2\,dy\,dx = \frac{b^3 h}{3}$

$\bar{\bar{x}} = \sqrt{\frac{I_y}{m}} = \sqrt{\frac{b^3 h}{3} \cdot \frac{1}{bh}} = \sqrt{\frac{b^2}{3}} = \frac{b}{\sqrt{3}} = \frac{\sqrt{3}}{3}b$

$\bar{\bar{y}} = \sqrt{\frac{I_x}{m}} = \sqrt{\frac{bh^3}{3} \cdot \frac{1}{bh}} = \sqrt{\frac{h^2}{3}} = \frac{h}{\sqrt{3}} = \frac{\sqrt{3}}{3}h$

29. $m = \pi a^2$

$I_x = \iint_R y^2\,dA = \int_0^{2\pi} \int_0^a r^3\sin^2\theta\,dr\,d\theta = \frac{a^4\pi}{4}$

$I_y = \iint_R x^2\,dA = \int_0^{2\pi} \int_0^a r^3\cos^2\theta\,dr\,d\theta = \frac{a^4\pi}{4}$

$I_0 = I_x + I_y = \frac{a^4\pi}{4} + \frac{a^4\pi}{4} = \frac{a^4\pi}{2}$

$\bar{\bar{x}} = \bar{\bar{y}} = \sqrt{\frac{I_x}{m}} = \sqrt{\frac{a^4\pi}{4} \cdot \frac{1}{\pi a^2}} = \frac{a}{2}$

31. $m = \frac{\pi a^2}{4}$

$I_x = \iint_R y^2\,dA = \int_0^{\pi/2} \int_0^a r^3\sin^2\theta\,dr\,d\theta = \frac{\pi a^4}{16}$

$I_y = \iint_R x^2\,dA = \int_0^{\pi/2} \int_0^a r^3\cos^2\theta\,dr\,d\theta = \frac{\pi a^4}{16}$

$I_0 = I_x + I_y = \frac{\pi a^4}{16} + \frac{\pi a^4}{16} = \frac{\pi a^4}{8}$

$\bar{\bar{x}} = \bar{\bar{y}} = \sqrt{\frac{I_x}{m}} = \sqrt{\frac{\pi a^4}{16} \cdot \frac{4}{\pi a^2}} = \frac{a}{2}$

33. $\rho = ky$

$m = k\int_0^a \int_0^b y\,dy\,dx = \frac{kab^2}{2}$

$I_x = k\int_0^a \int_0^b y^3\,dy\,dx = \frac{kab^4}{4}$

$I_y = k\int_0^a \int_0^b x^2 y\,dy\,dx = \frac{ka^3 b^2}{6}$

$I_0 = I_x + I_y = \frac{3kab^4 + 2kb^2 a^3}{12}$

$\bar{\bar{x}} = \sqrt{\frac{I_y}{m}} = \sqrt{\frac{ka^3 b^2/6}{kab^2/2}} = \sqrt{\frac{a^2}{3}} = \frac{a}{\sqrt{3}} = \frac{\sqrt{3}}{3}a$

$\bar{\bar{y}} = \sqrt{\frac{I_x}{m}} = \sqrt{\frac{kab^4/4}{kab^2/2}} = \sqrt{\frac{b^2}{2}} = \frac{b}{\sqrt{2}} = \frac{\sqrt{2}}{2}b$

35. $\rho = kx$

$$m = k\int_0^2 \int_0^{4-x^2} x \, dy \, dx = 4k$$

$$I_x = k\int_0^2 \int_0^{4-x^2} xy^2 \, dy \, dx = \frac{32k}{3}$$

$$I_y = k\int_0^2 \int_0^{4-x^2} x^3 \, dy \, dx = \frac{16k}{3}$$

$$I_0 = I_x + I_y = 16k$$

$$\bar{\bar{x}} = \sqrt{\frac{I_y}{m}} = \sqrt{\frac{16k/3}{4k}} = \sqrt{\frac{4}{3}} = \frac{2}{\sqrt{3}} = \frac{2\sqrt{3}}{3}$$

$$\bar{\bar{y}} = \sqrt{\frac{I_x}{m}} = \sqrt{\frac{32k/3}{4k}} = \sqrt{\frac{8}{3}} = \frac{4}{\sqrt{6}} = \frac{2\sqrt{6}}{3}$$

37. $\rho = kxy$

$$m = \int_0^4 \int_0^{\sqrt{x}} kxy \, dy \, dx = \frac{32k}{3}$$

$$I_x = \int_0^4 \int_0^{\sqrt{x}} kxy^3 \, dy \, dx = 16k$$

$$I_y = \int_0^4 \int_0^{\sqrt{x}} kx^3 y \, dy \, dx = \frac{512k}{5}$$

$$I_0 = I_x + I_y = \frac{592k}{5}$$

$$\bar{\bar{x}} = \sqrt{\frac{I_y}{m}} = \sqrt{\frac{512k}{5} \cdot \frac{3}{32k}} = \sqrt{\frac{48}{5}} = \frac{4\sqrt{15}}{5}$$

$$\bar{\bar{y}} = \sqrt{\frac{I_x}{m}} = \sqrt{\frac{16k}{1} \cdot \frac{3}{32k}} = \sqrt{\frac{3}{2}} = \frac{\sqrt{6}}{2}$$

39. $\rho = kx$

$$m = \int_0^1 \int_{x^2}^{\sqrt{x}} kx \, dy \, dx = \frac{3k}{20}$$

$$I_x = \int_0^1 \int_{x^2}^{\sqrt{x}} kxy^2 \, dy \, dx = \frac{3k}{56}$$

$$I_y = \int_0^1 \int_{x^2}^{\sqrt{x}} kx^3 \, dy \, dx = \frac{k}{18}$$

$$I_0 = I_x + I_y = \frac{55k}{504}$$

$$\bar{\bar{x}} = \sqrt{\frac{I_y}{m}} = \sqrt{\frac{k}{18} \cdot \frac{20}{3k}} = \frac{\sqrt{30}}{9}$$

$$\bar{\bar{y}} = \sqrt{\frac{I_x}{m}} = \sqrt{\frac{3k}{56} \cdot \frac{20}{3k}} = \frac{\sqrt{70}}{14}$$

41. $I = 2k\int_{-b}^{b} \int_0^{\sqrt{b^2-x^2}} (x-a)^2 \, dy \, dx = 2k\int_{-b}^{b} (x-a)^2 \sqrt{b^2-x^2} \, dx$

$$= 2k\left[\int_{-b}^{b} x^2 \sqrt{b^2-x^2} \, dx - 2a\int_{-b}^{b} x\sqrt{b^2-x^2} \, dx + a^2\int_{-b}^{b} \sqrt{b^2-x^2} \, dx \right]$$

$$= 2k\left[\frac{\pi b^4}{8} + 0 + \frac{\pi a^2 b^2}{2} \right] = \frac{k\pi b^2}{4}(b^2 + 4a^2)$$

43. $I = \int_0^4 \int_0^{\sqrt{x}} kx(x-6)^2 \, dy \, dx = \int_0^4 kx\sqrt{x}(x^2 - 12x + 36) \, dx = k\left[\frac{2}{9}x^{9/2} - \frac{24}{7}x^{7/2} + \frac{72}{5}x^{5/2} \right]_0^4 = \frac{42{,}752k}{315}$

45. $I = \int_0^a \int_0^{\sqrt{a^2-x^2}} k(a-y)(y-a)^2 \, dy \, dx = \int_0^a \int_0^{\sqrt{a^2-x^2}} k(a-y)^3 \, dy \, dx = \int_0^a \left[-\frac{k}{4}(a-y)^4 \right]_0^{\sqrt{a^2-x^2}} dx$

$= -\frac{k}{4} \int_0^a \left[a^4 - 4a^3 y + 6a^2 y^2 - 4ay^3 + y^4 \right]_0^{\sqrt{a^2-x^2}} dx$

$= -\frac{k}{4} \int_0^a \left[a^4 - 4a^3\sqrt{a^2-x^2} + 6a^2(a^2-x^2) - 4a(a^2-x^2)\sqrt{a^2-x^2} + (a^4 - 2a^2x^2 + x^4) - a^4 \right] dx$

$= -\frac{k}{4} \int_0^a \left[7a^4 - 8a^2x^2 + x^4 - 8a^3\sqrt{a^2-x^2} + 4ax^2\sqrt{a^2-x^2} \right] dx$

$= -\frac{k}{4} \left[7a^4 x - \frac{8a^2}{3}x^3 + \frac{x^5}{5} - 4a^3\left(x\sqrt{a^2-x^2} + a^2 \arcsin\frac{x}{a} \right) + \frac{a}{2}\left(x(2x^2-a^2)\sqrt{a^2-x^2} + a^4 \arcsin\frac{x}{a} \right) \right]_0^a$

$= -\frac{k}{4}\left(7a^5 - \frac{8}{3}a^5 + \frac{1}{5}a^5 - 2a^5\pi + \frac{1}{4}a^5\pi \right) = a^5 k\left(\frac{7\pi}{16} - \frac{17}{15} \right)$

47. $\rho(x,y) = ky$. $\bar{y}$ will increase

49. $\rho(x,y) = kxy$.

Both $\bar{x}$ and $\bar{y}$ will increase

51. Let $\rho(x,y)$ be a continuous density function on the planar lamina R.

The movements of mass with respect to the x- and y-axes are

$$M_x = \int_R \int y \, \rho(x,y) dA \text{ and } M_y = \int_R \int x \, \rho(x,y) \, dA.$$

If m is the mass of the lamina, then the center of mass is

$$(\bar{x}, \bar{y}) = \left(\frac{M_y}{m}, \frac{M_x}{m} \right).$$

53. See the definition on page 968

55. $\bar{y} = \frac{L}{2}, A = bL, h = \frac{L}{2}$

$I_{\bar{y}} = \int_0^b \int_0^L \left(y - \frac{L}{2} \right)^2 dy \, dx$

$= \int_0^b \left[\frac{[y-(L/2)]^3}{3} \right]_0^L dx = \frac{L^3 b}{12}$

$y_a = \bar{y} - \frac{I_{\bar{y}}}{hA} = \frac{L}{2} - \frac{L^3 b/12}{(L/2)(bL)} = \frac{L}{3}$

57. $\bar{y} = \frac{2L}{3}. A = \frac{bL}{2}, h = \frac{L}{3}$

$I_{\bar{y}} = 2\int_0^{b/2} \int_{2Lx/b}^L \left(y - \frac{2L}{3} \right)^2 dy \, dx$

$= \frac{2}{3} \int_0^{b/2} \left[\left(y - \frac{2L}{3} \right)^3 \right]_{2Lx/b}^L dx$

$= \frac{2}{3} \int_0^{b/2} \left[\frac{L}{27} - \left(\frac{2Lx}{b} - \frac{2L}{3} \right)^3 \right] dx$

$= \frac{2}{3} \left[\frac{L^3 x}{27} - \frac{b}{8L}\left(\frac{2Lx}{b} - \frac{2L}{3} \right)^4 \right]_0^{b/2} = \frac{L^3 b}{36}$

$y_a = \frac{2L}{3} - \frac{L^3 b/36}{L^2 b/6} = \frac{L}{2}$

Section 13.5   Surface Area

1. $f(x, y) = 2x + 2y$

R = triangle with vertices $(0, 0)$, $(2, 0)$, $(0, 2)$

$f_x = 2, f_y = 2$

$\sqrt{1 + (f_x)^2 + (f_y)^2} = 3$

$S = \displaystyle\int_0^2 \int_0^{2-x} 3 \, dy \, dx = 3 \int_0^2 (2 - x) \, dx$

$= \left[3\left(2x - \dfrac{x^2}{2}\right) \right]_0^2 = 6$

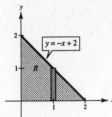

3. $f(x, y) = 8 + 2x + 2y$

$R = \{(x, y): x^2 + y^2 \le 4\}$

$f_x = 2, f_y = 2$

$\sqrt{1 + (f_x)^2 + (f_y)^2} = 3$

$S = \displaystyle\int_{-2}^2 \int_{-\sqrt{4-x^2}}^{\sqrt{4-x^2}} 3 \, dy \, dx = \int_0^{2\pi} \int_0^2 3r \, dr \, d\theta = 12\pi$

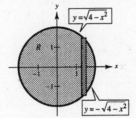

5. $f(x, y) = 9 - x^2$

R = square with vertices, $(0, 0)$, $(3, 0)$, $(0, 3)$, $(3, 3)$

$f_x = -2x, f_y = 0$

$\sqrt{1 + (f_x)^2 + (f_y)^2} = \sqrt{1 + 4x^2}$

$S = \displaystyle\int_0^3 \int_0^3 \sqrt{1 + 4x^2} \, dy \, dx = \int_0^3 3\sqrt{1 + 4x^2} \, dx$

$= \left[\dfrac{3}{4}\left(2x\sqrt{1 + 4x^2} + \ln\left|2x + \sqrt{1 + 4x^2}\right|\right) \right]_0^3 = \dfrac{3}{4}\left(6\sqrt{37} + \ln\left|6 + \sqrt{37}\right|\right)$

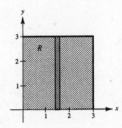

7. $f(x, y) = 2 + x^{3/2}$

R = rectangle with vertices $(0, 0)$, $(0, 4)$, $(3, 4)$, $(3, 0)$

$f_x = \dfrac{3}{2}x^{1/2}, f_y = 0$

$\sqrt{1 + (f_x)^2 + (f_y)^2} = \sqrt{1 + \left(\dfrac{9}{4}\right)x} = \dfrac{\sqrt{4 + 9x}}{2}$

$S = \displaystyle\int_0^3 \int_0^4 \dfrac{\sqrt{4 + 9x}}{2} \, dy \, dx = \int_0^3 4\left(\dfrac{\sqrt{4 + 9x}}{2}\right) dx$

$= \left[\dfrac{4}{27}(4 + 9x)^{3/2} \right]_0^3 = \dfrac{4}{27}\left(31\sqrt{31} - 8\right)$

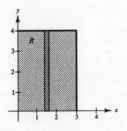

9. $f(x, y) = \ln|\sec x|$

$R = \left\{(x, y): 0 \le x \le \dfrac{\pi}{4}, \ 0 \le y \le \tan x\right\}$

$f_x = \tan x, f_y = 0$

$\sqrt{1 + (f_x)^2 + (f_y)^2} = \sqrt{1 + \tan^2 x} = \sec x$

$S = \displaystyle\int_0^{\pi/4} \int_0^{\tan x} \sec x \, dy \, dx = \int_0^{\pi/4} \sec x \tan x \, dx = \left[\sec x \right]_0^{\pi/4} = \sqrt{2} - 1$

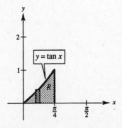

11. $f(x, y) = \sqrt{x^2 + y^2}$

$R = \{(x, y): 0 \leq f(x, y) \leq 1\}$

$0 \leq \sqrt{x^2 + y^2} \leq 1, \ x^2 + y^2 \leq 1$

$f_x = \dfrac{x}{\sqrt{x^2 + y^2}}, \ f_y = \dfrac{y}{\sqrt{x^2 + y^2}}$

$\sqrt{1 + (f_x)^2 + (f_y)^2} = \sqrt{1 + \dfrac{x^2}{x^2 + y^2} + \dfrac{y^2}{x^2 + y^2}} = \sqrt{2}$

$S = \displaystyle\int_{-1}^{1}\int_{-\sqrt{1-x^2}}^{\sqrt{1-x^2}} \sqrt{2} \, dy \, dx = \int_{0}^{2\pi}\int_{0}^{1} \sqrt{2} \, r \, dr \, d\theta = \sqrt{2}\pi$

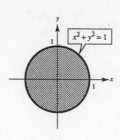

13. $f(x, y) = \sqrt{a^2 - x^2 - y^2}$

$R = \{(x, y): x^2 + y^2 \leq b^2, b < a\}$

$f_x = \dfrac{-x}{\sqrt{a^2 - x^2 - y^2}}, \ f_y = \dfrac{-y}{\sqrt{a^2 - x^2 - y^2}}$

$\sqrt{1 + (f_x)^2 + (f_y)^2} = \sqrt{1 + \dfrac{x^2}{a^2 - x^2 - y^2} + \dfrac{y^2}{a^2 - x^2 - y^2}} = \dfrac{a}{\sqrt{a^2 - x^2 - y^2}}$

$S = \displaystyle\int_{-b}^{b}\int_{-\sqrt{b^2-x^2}}^{\sqrt{b^2-x^2}} \dfrac{a}{\sqrt{a^2 - x^2 - y^2}} \, dy \, dx = \int_{0}^{2\pi}\int_{0}^{b} \dfrac{a}{\sqrt{a^2 - r^2}} \, r \, dr \, d\theta = 2\pi a\left(a - \sqrt{a^2 - b^2}\right)$

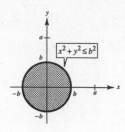

15. $z = 24 - 3x - 2y$

$\sqrt{1 + (f_x)^2 + (f_y)^2} = \sqrt{14}$

$S = \displaystyle\int_{0}^{8}\int_{0}^{-(3/2)x + 12} \sqrt{14} \, dy \, dx = 48\sqrt{14}$

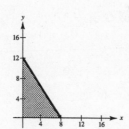

17. $z = \sqrt{25 - x^2 - y^2}$

$\sqrt{1 + (f_x)^2 + (f_y)^2} = \sqrt{1 + \dfrac{x^2}{25 - x^2 - y^2} + \dfrac{y^2}{25 - x^2 - y^2}} = \dfrac{5}{\sqrt{25 - x^2 - y^2}}$

$S = 2\displaystyle\int_{-3}^{3}\int_{-\sqrt{9-x^2}}^{\sqrt{9-x^2}} \dfrac{5}{\sqrt{25 - (x^2 + y^2)}} \, dy \, dx$

$= 2\displaystyle\int_{0}^{2\pi}\int_{0}^{3} \dfrac{5}{\sqrt{25 - r^2}} \, r \, dr \, d\theta = 20\pi$

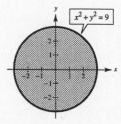

19. $f(x, y) = 2y + x^2$

$R = $ triangle with vertices $(0, 0), (1, 0), (1, 1)$

$\sqrt{1 + (f_x)^2 + (f_y)^2} = \sqrt{5 + 4x^2}$

$S = \displaystyle\int_{0}^{1}\int_{0}^{x} \sqrt{5 + 4x^2} \, dy \, dx = \dfrac{1}{12}\left(27 - 5\sqrt{5}\right)$

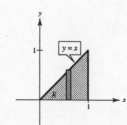

21. $f(x, y) = 4 - x^2 - y^2$

$R = \{(x, y): 0 \le f(x, y)\}$

$0 \le 4 - x^2 - y^2,\ x^2 + y^2 \le 4$

$f_x = -2x,\ f_y = -2y$

$\sqrt{1 + (f_x)^2 + (f_y)^2} = \sqrt{1 + 4x^2 + 4y^2}$

$S = \displaystyle\int_{-2}^{2}\int_{-\sqrt{4-x^2}}^{\sqrt{4-x^2}} \sqrt{1 + 4x^2 + 4y^2}\, dy\, dx$

$= \displaystyle\int_{0}^{2\pi}\int_{0}^{2} \sqrt{1 + 4r^2}\, r\, dr\, d\theta = \dfrac{(17\sqrt{17} - 1)\pi}{6}$

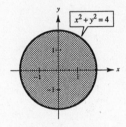

23. $f(x, y) = 4 - x^2 - y^2$

$R = \{(x, y): 0 \le x \le 1,\ 0 \le y \le 1\}$

$f_x = -2x,\ f_y = -2y$

$\sqrt{1 + (f_x)^2 + (f_y)^2} = \sqrt{1 + 4x^2 + 4y^2}$

$S = \displaystyle\int_{0}^{1}\int_{0}^{1} \sqrt{(1 + 4x^2) + 4y^2}\, dy\, dx \approx 1.8616$

25. Surface area $> (4) \cdot (6) = 24$.

Matches (e)

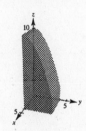

27. $f(x, y) = e^x$

$R = \{(x, y): 0 \le x \le 1,\ 0 \le y \le 1\}$

$f_x = e^x,\ f_y = 0$

$\sqrt{1 + (f_x)^2 + (f_y)^2} = \sqrt{1 + e^{2x}}$

$S = \displaystyle\int_{0}^{1}\int_{0}^{1} \sqrt{1 + e^{2x}}\, dy\, dx$

$= \displaystyle\int_{0}^{1} \sqrt{1 + e^{2x}} \approx 2.0035$

29. $f(x, y) = x^3 - 3xy + y^3$

$R = $ square with vertices $(1, 1),\ (-1, 1),\ (-1, -1),\ (1, -1)$

$f_x = 3x^2 - 3y = 3(x^2 - y),\ f_y = -3x + 3y^2 = 3(y^2 - x)$

$S = \displaystyle\int_{-1}^{1}\int_{-1}^{1} \sqrt{1 + 9(x^2 - y)^2 + 9(y^2 - x)^2}\, dy\, dx$

31. $f(x, y) = e^{-x} \sin y$

$f_x = -e^{-x} \sin y,\ f_y = e^{-x} \cos y$

$\sqrt{1 + f_x^2 + f_y^2} = \sqrt{1 + e^{-2x} \sin^2 y + e^{-2x} \cos^2 y}$

$= \sqrt{1 + e^{-2x}}$

$S = \displaystyle\int_{-2}^{2}\int_{-\sqrt{4-x^2}}^{\sqrt{4-x^2}} \sqrt{1 + e^{-2x}}\, dy\, dx$

33. $f(x, y) = e^{xy}$

$R = \{(x, y): 0 \le x \le 4,\ 0 \le y \le 10\}$

$f_x = ye^{xy},\ f_y = xe^{xy}$

$\sqrt{1 + (f_x)^2 + (f_y)^2} = \sqrt{1 + y^2 e^{2xy} + x^2 e^{2xy}} = \sqrt{1 + e^{2xy}(x^2 + y^2)}$

$S = \displaystyle\int_{0}^{4}\int_{0}^{10} \sqrt{1 + e^{2xy}(x^2 + y^2)}\, dy\, dx$

35. See the definition on page 972.

37. $f(x, y) = \sqrt{1 - x^2}; f_x = \dfrac{-x}{\sqrt{1^2 - x^2}}, f_y = 0$

$$S = \iint_R \sqrt{1 + f_x^2 + f_y^2}\, dA$$

$$= 16 \int_0^1 \int_0^x \frac{1}{\sqrt{1 - x^2}}\, dy\, dx$$

$$= 16 \int_0^1 \frac{x}{\sqrt{1 - x^2}}\, dx = \left[-16(1 - x^2)^{1/2} \right]_0^1 = 16$$

39. (a) $V = \displaystyle\int_0^{50} \int_0^{\sqrt{50^2 - x^2}} \left(20 + \frac{xy}{100} - \frac{x + y}{5} \right) dy\, dx$

$$= \int_0^{50} \left[20\sqrt{50^2 - x^2} + \frac{x}{200}(50^2 - x^2) - \frac{x}{5}\sqrt{50^2 - x^2} - \frac{50^2 - x^2}{10} \right] dy$$

$$= \left[10\left(x\sqrt{50 - x^2} + 50^2 \arcsin \frac{x}{50} \right) + \frac{25}{4}x^2 - \frac{x^4}{800} + \frac{1}{15}(50^2 - x^2)^{3/2} - 250x + \frac{x^3}{30} \right]_0^{50}$$

$$\approx 30{,}415.74 \text{ ft}^3$$

(b) $z = 20 + \dfrac{xy}{100}$

$$\sqrt{1 + (f_x)^2 + (f_y)^2} = \sqrt{1 + \frac{y^2}{100^2} + \frac{x^2}{100^2}} = \frac{\sqrt{100^2 + x^2 + y^2}}{100}$$

$$S = \frac{1}{100} \int_0^{50} \int_0^{\sqrt{50^2 - x^2}} \sqrt{100^2 + x^2 + y^2}\, dy\, dx$$

$$= \frac{1}{100} \int_0^{\pi/2} \int_0^{50} \sqrt{100^2 + r^2}\, r\, dr\, d\theta \approx 2081.53 \text{ ft}^2$$

41. (a) $V = \displaystyle\iint_R f(x, y)$

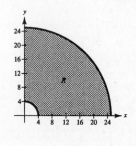

$$= 8 \iint_R \sqrt{625 - x^2 - y^2}\, dA \qquad \text{where } R \text{ is the region in the first quadrant}$$

$$= 8 \int_0^{\pi/2} \int_4^{25} \sqrt{625 - r^2}\, r\, dr\, d\theta$$

$$= -4 \int_0^{\pi/2} \left[\frac{2}{3}(625 - r^2)^{3/2} \right]_4^{25} d\theta$$

$$= -\frac{8}{3}\left[0 - 609\sqrt{609} \right] \cdot \frac{\pi}{2}$$

$$= 812\pi\sqrt{609} \text{ cm}^3$$

(b) $A = \displaystyle\iint_R \sqrt{1 + (f_x)^2 + (f_y)^2}\, dA = 8 \iint_R \sqrt{1 + \frac{x^2}{625 - x^2 - y^2} + \frac{y^2}{625 - x^2 - y^2}}\, dA$

$$= 8 \iint_R \frac{25}{\sqrt{625 - x^2 - y^2}}\, dA = 8 \int_0^{\pi/2} \int_4^{25} \frac{25}{\sqrt{625 - r^2}}\, r\, dr\, d\theta$$

$$= \lim_{b \to 25^-} \left[-200\sqrt{625 - r^2} \right]_4^b \cdot \frac{\pi}{2} = 100\pi\sqrt{609} \text{ cm}^2$$

Section 13.6   Triple Integrals and Applications

1. $\displaystyle\int_0^3\int_0^2\int_0^1 (x+y+z)\,dx\,dy\,dx = \int_0^3\int_0^2\left[\frac{1}{2}x^2+xy+xz\right]_0^1 dy\,dx$

$$= \int_0^3\int_0^2\left(\frac{1}{2}+y+z\right)dy\,dz = \int_0^3\left[\frac{1}{2}y+\frac{1}{2}y^2+yz\right]_0^2 dz = \left[3z+z^2\right]_0^3 = 18$$

3. $\displaystyle\int_0^1\int_0^x\int_0^{xy} x\,dz\,dy\,dx = \int_0^1\int_0^x\left[xz\right]_0^{xy} dy\,dx$

$$= \int_0^1\int_0^x x^2y\,dy\,dx = \int_0^1\left[\frac{x^2y^2}{2}\right]_0^x dx = \int_0^1\frac{x^4}{2}\,dx = \left[\frac{x^5}{10}\right]_0^1 = \frac{1}{10}$$

5. $\displaystyle\int_1^4\int_0^1\int_0^x 2ze^{-x^2}\,dy\,dx\,dz = \int_1^4\int_0^1\left[(2ze^{-x^2})y\right]_0^x dx\,dz = \int_1^4\int_0^1 2zxe^{-x^2}\,dx\,dz$

$$= \int_1^4\left[-ze^{-x^2}\right]_0^1 dz = \int_1^4 z(1-e^{-1})\,dz = \left[(1-e^{-1})\frac{z^2}{2}\right]_1^4 = \frac{15}{2}\left(1-\frac{1}{e}\right)$$

7. $\displaystyle\int_0^4\int_0^{\pi/2}\int_0^{1-x} x\cos y\,dz\,dy\,dx = \int_0^4\int_0^{\pi/2}\left[(x\cos y)z\right]_0^{1-x} dy\,dx = \int_0^4\int_0^{\pi/2} x(1-x)\cos y\,dy\,dx$

$$= \int_0^4\left[x(1-x)\sin y\right]_0^{\pi/2} dx = \int_0^4 x(1-x)\,dx = \left[\frac{x^2}{2}-\frac{x^3}{3}\right]_0^4 = 8-\frac{64}{3} = \frac{-40}{3}$$

9. $\displaystyle\int_0^2\int_{-\sqrt{4-x^2}}^{\sqrt{4-x^2}}\int_0^{x^2} x\,dz\,dy\,dx = \int_0^2\int_{-\sqrt{4-x^2}}^{\sqrt{4-x^2}} x^3\,dy\,dx = \frac{128}{15}$

11. $\displaystyle\int_0^2\int_0^{\sqrt{4-x^2}}\int_1^4 \frac{x^2\sin y}{z}\,dz\,dy\,dx = \int_0^2\int_0^{\sqrt{4-x^2}}\left[x^2\sin y\ln|z|\right]_1^4 dy\,dx$

$$= \int_0^2\left[x^2\ln4(-\cos y)\right]_0^{\sqrt{4-x^2}} dx = \int_0^2 x^2\ln4\left[1-\cos\sqrt{4-x^2}\right]dx \approx 2.44167$$

13. $\displaystyle\int_0^4\int_0^{4-x}\int_0^{4-x-y} dz\,dy\,dx$

15. $\displaystyle\int_{-3}^3\int_{-\sqrt{9-x^2}}^{\sqrt{9-x^2}}\int_0^{9-x^2-y^2} dz\,dy\,dx$

17. $\displaystyle\int_{-2}^2\int_0^{4-y^2}\int_0^x dz\,dx\,dy = \int_{-2}^2\int_0^{4-y^2} x\,dx\,dy$

$$= \frac{1}{2}\int_{-2}^2 (4-y^2)^2\,dy = \int_0^2 (16-8y^2+y^4)\,dy = \left[16y-\frac{8}{3}y^3+\frac{1}{5}y^5\right]_0^2 = \frac{256}{15}$$

19. $\displaystyle 8\int_0^a\int_0^{\sqrt{a^2-x^2}}\int_0^{\sqrt{a^2-x^2-y^2}} dz\,dy\,dx = 8\int_0^a\int_0^{\sqrt{a^2-x^2}}\sqrt{a^2-x^2-y^2}\,dy\,dx$

$$= 4\int_0^a\left[y\sqrt{a^2-x^2-y^2}+(a^2-x^2)\arcsin\left(\frac{y}{\sqrt{a^2-x^2}}\right)\right]_0^{\sqrt{a^2-x^2}} dx$$

$$= 4\left(\frac{\pi}{2}\right)\int_0^a (a^2-x^2)\,dx = \left[2\pi\left(a^2x-\frac{1}{3}x^3\right)\right]_0^a = \frac{4}{3}\pi a^3$$

21. $\displaystyle\int_0^2 \int_0^{4-x^2} \int_0^{4-x^2} dz\, dy\, dx = \int_0^2 (4-x^2)^2\, dx = \int_0^2 (16 - 8x^2 + x^4)\, dx = \left[16x - \frac{8}{3}x^3 + \frac{1}{5}x^5\right]_0^2 = \frac{256}{15}$

23. Plane: $3x + 6y + 4z = 12$

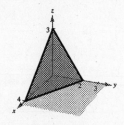

$$\int_0^3 \int_0^{(12-4z)/3} \int_0^{(12-4z-3x)/6} dy\, dx\, dz$$

25. Top cylinder: $y^2 + z^2 = 1$

Side plane: $x = y$

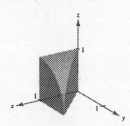

$$\int_0^1 \int_0^x \int_0^{\sqrt{1-y^2}} dz\, dy\, dx$$

27. $Q = \{(x, y, z): 0 \le x \le 1, 0 \le y \le x, 0 \le z \le 3\}$

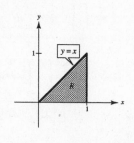

$$\iiint_Q xyz\, dV = \int_0^3 \int_0^1 \int_y^1 xyz\, dx\, dy\, dz = \int_0^3 \int_0^1 \int_0^x xyz\, dy\, dx\, dz$$

$$= \int_0^1 \int_0^3 \int_y^1 xyz\, dx\, dz\, dy$$

$$= \int_0^1 \int_0^3 \int_0^x xyz\, dy\, dz\, dx$$

$$= \int_0^1 \int_y^1 \int_0^3 xyz\, dz\, dx\, dy$$

$$= \int_0^1 \int_0^x \int_0^3 xyz\, dz\, dy\, dx \left(= \frac{9}{16}\right)$$

29. $Q = \{(x, y, z): x^2 + y^2 \le 9, 0 \le z \le 4\}$

$$\iiint_Q xyz\, dV = \int_0^4 \int_{-3}^3 \int_{-\sqrt{9-x^2}}^{\sqrt{9-x^2}} xyz\, dy\, dx\, dz$$

$$= \int_0^4 \int_{-3}^3 \int_{-\sqrt{9-y^2}}^{\sqrt{9-y^2}} xyz\, dx\, dy\, dz$$

$$= \int_{-3}^3 \int_0^4 \int_{-\sqrt{9-y^2}}^{\sqrt{9-y^2}} xyz\, dx\, dz\, dy$$

$$= \int_{-3}^3 \int_{-\sqrt{9-y^2}}^{\sqrt{9-y^2}} \int_0^4 xyz\, dz\, dx\, dy$$

$$= \int_{-3}^3 \int_0^4 \int_{-\sqrt{9-x^2}}^{\sqrt{9-x^2}} xyz\, dy\, dz\, dx$$

$$= \int_{-3}^3 \int_{-\sqrt{9-x^2}}^{\sqrt{9-x^2}} \int_0^4 xyz\, dz\, dy\, dx \ \ (= 0)$$

31. $m = k\displaystyle\int_0^6\int_0^{4-(2x/3)}\int_0^{2-(y/2)-(x/3)} dz\,dy\,dx$

$= 8k$

$M_{yz} = k\displaystyle\int_0^6\int_0^{4-(2x/3)}\int_0^{2-(y/2)-(x/3)} x\,dz\,dy\,dx$

$= 12k$

$\bar{x} = \dfrac{M_{yz}}{m} = \dfrac{12k}{8k} = \dfrac{3}{2}$

33. $m = k\displaystyle\int_0^4\int_0^4\int_0^{4-x} x\,dz\,dy\,dx = k\int_0^4\int_0^4 x(4-x)\,dy\,dx$

$= 4k\displaystyle\int_0^4 (4x - x^2)\,dx = \dfrac{128k}{3}$

$M_{xy} = k\displaystyle\int_0^4\int_0^4\int_0^{4-x} xz\,dz\,dy\,dx = k\int_0^4\int_0^4 x\dfrac{(4-x)^2}{2}\,dy\,dx$

$= 2k\displaystyle\int_0^4 (16x - 8x^2 + x^3)\,dx = \dfrac{128k}{3}$

$\bar{z} = \dfrac{M_{xy}}{m} = 1$

35. $m = k\displaystyle\int_0^b\int_0^b\int_0^b xy\,dz\,dy\,dx = \dfrac{kb^5}{4}$

$M_{yz} = k\displaystyle\int_0^b\int_0^b\int_0^b x^2y\,dz\,dy\,dx = \dfrac{kb^6}{6}$

$M_{xz} = k\displaystyle\int_0^b\int_0^b\int_0^b xy^2\,dz\,dy\,dx = \dfrac{kb^6}{6}$

$M_{xy} = k\displaystyle\int_0^b\int_0^b\int_0^b xyz\,dz\,dy\,dx = \dfrac{kb^6}{8}$

$\bar{x} = \dfrac{M_{yz}}{m} = \dfrac{kb^6/6}{kb^5/4} = \dfrac{2b}{3}$

$\bar{y} = \dfrac{M_{xz}}{m} = \dfrac{kb^6/6}{kb^5/4} = \dfrac{2b}{3}$

$\bar{z} = \dfrac{M_{xy}}{m} = \dfrac{kb^6/8}{kb^5/4} = \dfrac{b}{2}$

37. $\bar{x}$ will be greater than 2, whereas $\bar{y}$ and $\bar{z}$ will be unchanged.

39. $\bar{y}$ will be greater than 0, whereas $\bar{x}$ and $\bar{z}$ will be unchanged.

41. $m = \dfrac{1}{3}k\pi r^2 h$

$\bar{x} = \bar{y} = 0$ by symmetry

$M_{xy} = 4k\displaystyle\int_0^r\int_0^{\sqrt{r^2-x^2}}\int_{h\sqrt{x^2+y^2}/r}^h z\,dz\,dy\,dx$

$= \dfrac{3kh^2}{r^2}\displaystyle\int_0^r\int_0^{\sqrt{r^2-x^2}} (r^2 - x^2 - y^2)\,dy\,dx$

$= \dfrac{4kh^2}{3r^2}\displaystyle\int_0^r (r^2 - x^2)^{3/2}\,dx$

$= \dfrac{k\pi r^2 h^2}{4}$

$\bar{z} = \dfrac{M_{xy}}{m} = \dfrac{k\pi r^2 h^2/4}{k\pi r^2 h/3} = \dfrac{3h}{4}$

43. $m = \dfrac{128k\pi}{3}$

$\bar{x} = \bar{y} = 0$ by symmetry

$z = \sqrt{4^2 - x^2 - y^2}$

$M_{xy} = 4k \displaystyle\int_0^4 \int_0^{\sqrt{4^2-x^2}} \int_0^{\sqrt{4^2-x^2-y^2}} z \, dz \, dy \, dx$

$\quad = 2k \displaystyle\int_0^4 \int_0^{\sqrt{4^2-x^2}} (4^2 - x^2 - y^2) \, dy \, dx = 2k \int_0^4 \left[16y - x^2 y - \frac{1}{3}y^3 \right]_0^{\sqrt{4^2-x^2}} dx = \frac{4k}{3} \int_0^4 (4^2 - x^2)^{3/2} \, dx$

$\quad = \dfrac{1024k}{3} \displaystyle\int_0^{\pi/2} \cos^4 \theta \, d\theta \qquad (\text{let } x = 4 \sin \theta)$

$\quad = 64\pi k \qquad$ by Wallis's Formula

$\bar{z} = \dfrac{M_{xy}}{m} = \dfrac{64k\pi}{1} \cdot \dfrac{3}{128k\pi} = \dfrac{3}{2}$

45. $f(x, y) = \dfrac{5}{12}y$

$m = k \displaystyle\int_0^{20} \int_0^{-(3/5)x+12} \int_0^{(5/12)y} dz \, dy \, dx = 200k$

$M_{yz} = k \displaystyle\int_0^{20} \int_0^{-(3/5)x+12} \int_0^{(5/12)y} x \, dz \, dy \, dx = 1000k$

$M_{xz} = k \displaystyle\int_0^{20} \int_0^{-(3/5)+x+12} \int_0^{(5/12)y} y \, dz \, dy \, dx = 1200k$

$M_{xy} = k \displaystyle\int_0^{20} \int_0^{-(3/5)x+12} \int_0^{(5/12)y} z \, dz \, dy \, dx = 250k$

$\bar{x} = \dfrac{M_{yz}}{m} = \dfrac{1000k}{200k} = 5$

$\bar{y} = \dfrac{M_{xz}}{m} = \dfrac{1200k}{200k} = 6$

$\bar{z} = \dfrac{M_{xy}}{m} = \dfrac{250k}{200k} = \dfrac{5}{4}$

$y = -\dfrac{3}{5}x + 12$

47. (a) $I_x = k \displaystyle\int_0^a \int_0^a \int_0^a (y^2 + z^2) \, dx \, dy \, dz = ka \int_0^a \int_0^a (y^2 + z^2) \, dy \, dz$

$\quad = ka \displaystyle\int_0^a \left[\frac{1}{3}y^3 + z^2 y \right]_0^a dz = ka \int_0^a \left(\frac{1}{3}a^3 + az^2 \right) dz = \left[ka\left(\frac{1}{3}a^3 z + \frac{1}{3}az^3 \right) \right]_0^a = \frac{2ka^5}{3}$

$I_x = I_y = I_z = \dfrac{2ka^5}{3}$ by symmetry

(b) $I_x = k \displaystyle\int_0^a \int_0^a \int_0^a (y^2 + z^2)xyz \, dx \, dy \, dz = \frac{ka^2}{2} \int_0^a \int_0^a (y^3 z + yz^3) \, dy \, dz$

$\quad = \dfrac{ka^2}{2} \displaystyle\int_0^a \left[\frac{y^4 z}{4} + \frac{y^2 z^3}{2} \right]_0^a dz = \frac{ka^4}{8} \int_0^a (a^2 z + 2z^3) \, dz = \left[\frac{ka^4}{8}\left(\frac{a^2 z^2}{2} + \frac{2z^4}{4} \right) \right]_0^a = \frac{ka^8}{8}$

$I_x = I_y = I_z = \dfrac{ka^8}{8}$ by symmetry

49. (a) $I_x = k\displaystyle\int_0^4\int_0^4\int_0^{4-x}(y^2+z^2)\,dz\,dy\,dx = k\int_0^4\int_0^4\left[y^2(4-x)+\frac{1}{3}(4-x)^3\right]dy\,dx$

$\qquad = k\displaystyle\int_0^4\left[\frac{y^3}{3}(4-x)+\frac{y}{3}(4-x)^3\right]_0^4 dx = k\int_0^4\left[\frac{64}{3}(4-x)+\frac{4}{3}(4-x)^3\right]dx$

$\qquad = k\left[-\dfrac{32}{3}(4-x)^2 - \dfrac{1}{3}(4-x)^4\right]_0^4 = 256k$

$I_y = k\displaystyle\int_0^4\int_0^4\int_0^{4-x}(x^2+z^2)\,dz\,dy\,dx = k\int_0^4\int_0^4\left[x^2(4-x)+\frac{1}{3}(4-x)^3\right]dy\,dx$

$\qquad = 4k\displaystyle\int_0^4\left[4x^2-x^3+\frac{1}{3}(4-x)^3\right]dx = 4k\left[\frac{4}{3}x^3-\frac{1}{4}x^4-\frac{1}{12}(4-x)^4\right]_0^4 = \frac{512k}{3}$

$I_z = k\displaystyle\int_0^4\int_0^4\int_0^{4-x}(x^2+y^2)\,dz\,dy\,dx = k\int_0^4\int_0^4(x^2+y^2)(4-x)\,dy\,dx$

$\qquad = k\displaystyle\int_0^4\left[\left(x^2y+\frac{y^3}{3}\right)(4-x)\right]_0^4 dx = k\int_0^4\left(4x^2+\frac{64}{3}\right)(4-x)\,dx = 256k$

(b) $I_x = k\displaystyle\int_0^4\int_0^4\int_0^{4-x}y(y^2+z^2)\,dz\,dy\,dx = k\int_0^4\int_0^4\left[y^3(4-x)+\frac{1}{3}y(4-x)^3\right]dy\,dx$

$\qquad = k\displaystyle\int_0^4\left[\frac{y^4}{4}(4-x)+\frac{y^2}{6}(4-x)^3\right]_0^4 dx = k\int_0^4\left[64(4-x)+\frac{8}{3}(4-x)^3\right]dx$

$\qquad = k\left[-32(4-x)^2 - \dfrac{2}{3}(4-x)^4\right]_0^4 = \dfrac{2048k}{3}$

$I_y = k\displaystyle\int_0^4\int_0^4\int_0^{4-x}y(x^2+z^2)\,dz\,dy\,dx = k\int_0^4\int_0^4\left[x^2y(4-x)+\frac{1}{3}y(4-x)^3\right]dy\,dx$

$\qquad = 8k\displaystyle\int_0^4\left[4x^2-x^3+\frac{1}{3}(4-x)^3\right]dx = 8k\left[\frac{4}{3}x^3-\frac{1}{4}x^4-\frac{1}{12}(4-x)^4\right]_0^4 = \frac{1024k}{3}$

$I_z = k\displaystyle\int_0^4\int_0^4\int_0^{4-x}y(x^2+y^2)\,dz\,dy\,dx = k\int_0^4\int_0^4(x^2y+y^3)(4-x)\,dx$

$\qquad = k\displaystyle\int_0^4\left[\left(\frac{x^2y^2}{2}+\frac{y^4}{4}\right)(4-x)\right]_0^4 dx = k\int_0^4(8x^2+64)(4-x)\,dx$

$\qquad = 8k\displaystyle\int_0^4(32-8x+4x^2-x^3)\,dx = \left[8k\left(32x-4x^2+\frac{4}{3}x^3-\frac{1}{4}x^4\right)\right]_0^4 = \frac{2048k}{3}$

51. $I_{xy} = k\displaystyle\int_{-L/2}^{L/2}\int_{-a}^{a}\int_{-\sqrt{a^2-x^2}}^{\sqrt{a^2-x^2}}z^2\,dz\,dx\,dy = k\int_{-L/2}^{L/2}\int_{-a}^{a}\frac{2}{3}(a^2-x^2)\sqrt{a^2-x^2}\,dx\,dy$

$\qquad = \dfrac{2}{3}\displaystyle\int_{-L/2}^{L/2}k\left[\frac{a^2}{2}\left(x\sqrt{a^2-x^2}+a^2\arcsin\frac{x}{a}\right)-\frac{1}{8}\left(x(2x^2-a^2)\sqrt{x^2-a^2}+a^4\arcsin\frac{x}{a}\right)\right]_{-a}^{a} dy$

$\qquad = \dfrac{2k}{3}\displaystyle\int_{-L/2}^{L/2}2\left(\frac{a^4\pi}{4}-\frac{a^4\pi}{16}\right)dy = \frac{a^4\pi L k}{4}$

Since $m = \pi a^2 L k$, $I_{xy} = ma^2/4$.

—CONTINUED—

51. —CONTINUED—

$$I_{xz} = k \int_{-L/2}^{L/2} \int_{-a}^{a} \int_{-\sqrt{a^2-x^2}}^{\sqrt{a^2-x^2}} y^2 \, dz \, dx \, dy = 2k \int_{-L/2}^{L/2} \int_{-a}^{a} y^2 \sqrt{a^2 - x^2} \, dx \, dy$$

$$= 2k \int_{-L/2}^{L/2} \left[\frac{y^2}{2} \left(x\sqrt{a^2 - x^2} + a^2 \arcsin \frac{x}{a} \right) \right]_{-a}^{a} dy = k\pi a^2 \int_{-L/2}^{L/2} y^2 \, dy = \frac{2k\pi a^2}{3} \left(\frac{L^3}{8} \right) = \frac{1}{12} mL^2$$

$$I_{yz} = k \int_{-L/2}^{L/2} \int_{-a}^{a} \int_{-\sqrt{a^2-x^2}}^{\sqrt{a^2-x^2}} x^2 \, dz \, dx \, dy = 2k \int_{-L/2}^{L/2} \int_{-a}^{a} x^2 \sqrt{a^2 - x^2} \, dx \, dy$$

$$= 2k \int_{-L/2}^{L/2} \frac{1}{8} \left[x(2x^2 - a^2)\sqrt{a^2 - x^2} + a^4 \arcsin \frac{x}{a} \right]_{-a}^{a} dy = \frac{ka^4\pi}{4} \int_{-L/2}^{L/2} dy = \frac{ka^4\pi L}{4} = \frac{ma^2}{4}$$

$$I_x = I_{xy} + I_{xz} = \frac{ma^2}{4} + \frac{mL^2}{12} = \frac{m}{12}(3a^2 + L^2)$$

$$I_y = I_{xy} + I_{yz} = \frac{ma^2}{4} + \frac{ma^2}{4} = \frac{ma^2}{2}$$

$$I_z = I_{xz} + I_{yz} = \frac{mL^2}{12} + \frac{ma^2}{4} = \frac{m}{12}(3a^2 + L^2)$$

53. $\int_{-1}^{1} \int_{-1}^{1} \int_{0}^{1-x} (x^2 + y^2)\sqrt{x^2 + y^2 + z^2} \, dz \, dy \, dx$

55. See the definition, page 978.

See Theorem 13.4, page 979.

57. (a) The annular solid on the right has the greater density.

(b) The annular solid on the right has the greater movement of inertia.

(c) The solid on the left will reach the bottom first. The solid on the right has a greater resistance to rotational motion.

Section 13.7   Triple Integrals in Cylindrical and Spherical Coordinates

1. $\int_{0}^{4} \int_{0}^{\pi/2} \int_{0}^{2} r \cos \theta \, dr \, d\theta \, dz = \int_{0}^{4} \int_{0}^{\pi/2} \left[\frac{r^2}{2} \cos \theta \right]_{0}^{2} d\theta \, dz$

$$= \int_{0}^{4} \int_{0}^{\pi/2} 2 \cos \theta \, d\theta \, dz = \int_{0}^{4} \left[2 \sin \theta \right]_{0}^{\pi/2} dz = \int_{0}^{4} 2 \, dz = 8$$

3. $\int_{0}^{\pi/2} \int_{0}^{2\cos^2 \theta} \int_{0}^{4-r^2} r \sin \theta \, dz \, dr \, d\theta = \int_{0}^{\pi/2} \int_{0}^{2\cos^2 \theta} r(4 - r^2)\sin \theta \, dr \, d\theta = \int_{0}^{\pi/2} \left[\left(2r^2 - \frac{r^4}{4} \right) \sin \theta \right]_{0}^{2\cos^2 \theta} d\theta$

$$= \int_{0}^{\pi/2} [8 \cos^4 \theta - 4 \cos^8 \theta]\sin \theta \, d\theta = \left[-\frac{8 \cos^5 \theta}{5} + \frac{4 \cos^9 \theta}{9} \right]_{0}^{\pi/2} = \frac{52}{45}$$

5. $\int_{0}^{2\pi} \int_{0}^{\pi/4} \int_{0}^{\cos \phi} \rho^2 \sin \phi \, d\rho \, d\phi \, d\theta = \frac{1}{3} \int_{0}^{2\pi} \int_{0}^{\pi/4} \cos^3 \phi \sin \phi \, d\phi \, d\theta = -\frac{1}{12} \int_{0}^{2\pi} \left[\cos^4 \phi \right]_{0}^{\pi/4} d\theta = \frac{\pi}{8}$

7. $\int_{0}^{4} \int_{0}^{z} \int_{0}^{\pi/2} re^r \, d\theta \, dr \, dz = \pi(e^4 + 3)$

9. $\displaystyle\int_0^{\pi/2}\int_0^3\int_0^{e^{-r^2}} r\,dz\,dr\,d\theta = \int_0^{\pi/2}\int_0^3 re^{-r^2}\,dr\,d\theta$

$$= \int_0^{\pi/2}\left[-\frac{1}{2}e^{-r^2}\right]_0^3 d\theta$$

$$= \int_0^{\pi/2}\frac{1}{2}(1-e^{-9})d\theta$$

$$= \frac{\pi}{4}(1-e^{-9})$$

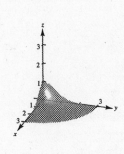

11. $\displaystyle\int_0^{2\pi}\int_{\pi/6}^{\pi/2}\int_0^4 \rho^2\sin\phi\,d\rho\,d\phi\,d\theta = \frac{64}{3}\int_0^{2\pi}\int_{\pi/6}^{\pi/2}\sin\phi\,d\phi\,d\theta$

$$= \frac{64}{3}\int_0^{2\pi}\left[-\cos\phi\right]_{\pi/6}^{\pi/2} d\theta$$

$$= \frac{32\sqrt{3}}{3}\int_0^{2\pi} d\theta$$

$$= \frac{64\sqrt{3}\,\pi}{3}$$

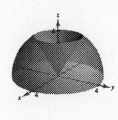

13. (a) $\displaystyle\int_0^{2\pi}\int_0^2\int_{r^2}^4 r^2\cos\theta\,dz\,dr\,d\theta = 0$

(b) $\displaystyle\int_0^{2\pi}\int_0^{\arctan(1/2)}\int_0^{4\sec\phi} \rho^3\sin^2\phi\cos\theta\,d\rho\,d\phi\,d\theta + \int_0^{2\pi}\int_{\arctan(1/2)}^{\pi/2}\int_0^{\cot\phi\csc\phi} \rho^3\sin^2\phi\cos\theta\,d\rho\,d\phi\,d\theta = 0$

15. (a) $\displaystyle\int_0^{2\pi}\int_0^a\int_a^{a+\sqrt{a^2-r^2}} r^2\cos\theta\,dz\,dr\,d\theta = 0$

(b) $\displaystyle\int_0^{\pi/4}\int_0^{2\pi}\int_{a\sec\phi}^{2a\cos\phi} \rho^3\sin^2\phi\cos\theta\,d\rho\,d\theta\,d\phi = 0$

17. $V = 4\displaystyle\int_0^{\pi/2}\int_0^{a\cos\theta}\int_0^{\sqrt{a^2-r^2}} r\,dz\,dr\,d\theta = 4\int_0^{\pi/2}\int_0^{a\cos\theta} r\sqrt{a^2-r^2}\,dr\,d\theta$

$$= \frac{4}{3}a^3\int_0^{\pi/2}(1-\sin^3\theta)\,d\theta = \frac{4}{3}a^3\left[\theta+\frac{1}{3}\cos\theta(\sin^2\theta+2)\right]_0^{\pi/2} = \frac{4}{3}a^3\left(\frac{\pi}{2}-\frac{2}{3}\right) = \frac{2a^3}{9}(3\pi-4)$$

19. $V = 2\displaystyle\int_0^{\pi}\int_0^{a\cos\theta}\int_0^{\sqrt{a^2-r^2}} r\,dz\,dr\,d\theta$

$$= 2\int_0^{\pi}\int_0^{a\cos\theta} r\sqrt{a^2-r^2}\,dr\,d\theta$$

$$= 2\int_0^{\pi}\left[-\frac{1}{3}(a^2-r^2)^{3/2}\right]_0^{a\cos\theta} d\theta$$

$$= \frac{2a^3}{3}\int_0^{\pi}(1-\sin^3\theta)\,d\theta$$

$$= \frac{2a^3}{3}\left[\theta+\cos\theta-\frac{\cos^3\theta}{3}\right]_0^{\pi}$$

$$= \frac{2a^3}{9}(3\pi-4)$$

21. $m = \displaystyle\int_0^{2\pi}\int_0^2\int_0^{9-r\cos\theta-2r\sin\theta} (kr)r\,dz\,dr\,d\theta$

$$= \int_0^{2\pi}\int_0^2 kr^2(9-r\cos\theta-2r\sin\theta)\,dr\,d\theta$$

$$= \int_0^{2\pi} k\left[3r^3-\frac{r^4}{4}\cos\theta-\frac{r^4}{2}\sin\theta\right]_0^2 d\theta$$

$$= \int_0^{2\pi} k[24-4\cos\theta-8\sin\theta]\,d\theta$$

$$= k\left[24\theta-4\sin\theta+8\cos\theta\right]_0^{2\pi}$$

$$= k[48\pi+8-8] = 48k\pi$$

23. $z = h - \dfrac{h}{r_0}\sqrt{x^2 + y^2} = \dfrac{h}{r_0}(r_0 - r)$

$$V = 4\int_0^{\pi/2}\int_0^{r_0}\int_0^{h(r_0-r)/r_0} r\, dz\, dr\, d\theta$$

$$= \frac{4h}{r_0}\int_0^{\pi/2}\int_0^{r_0}(r_0 r - r^2)\, dr\, d\theta$$

$$= \frac{4h}{r_0}\int_0^{\pi/2}\frac{r_0^3}{6}\, d\theta$$

$$= \frac{4h}{r_0}\left(\frac{r_0^3}{6}\right)\left(\frac{\pi}{2}\right) = \frac{1}{3}\pi r_0^2 h$$

25. $\rho = k\sqrt{x^2 + y^2} = kr$

$\bar{x} = \bar{y} = 0$ by symmetry

$$m = 4k\int_0^{\pi/2}\int_0^{r_0}\int_0^{h(r_0-r)/r_0} r^2\, dz\, dr\, d\theta$$

$$= \frac{1}{6}k\pi r_0^3 h$$

$$M_{xy} = 4k\int_0^{\pi/2}\int_0^{r_0}\int_0^{h(r_0-r)/r_0} r^2 z\, dz\, dr\, d\theta$$

$$= \frac{1}{30}k\pi r_0^3 h^2$$

$$\bar{z} = \frac{M_{xy}}{m} = \frac{k\pi r_0^3 h^2/30}{k\pi r_0^3 h/6} = \frac{h}{5}$$

27. $I_z = 4k\displaystyle\int_0^{\pi/2}\int_0^{r_0}\int_0^{h(r_0-r)/r_0} r^3\, dz\, dr\, d\theta$

$$= \frac{4kh}{r_0}\int_0^{\pi/2}\int_0^{r_0}(r_0 r^3 - r^4)\, dr\, d\theta$$

$$= \frac{4kh}{r_0}\left(\frac{r_0^5}{20}\right)\left(\frac{\pi}{2}\right)$$

$$= \frac{1}{10}k\pi r_0^4 h$$

Since the mass of the core is $m = kV = k\left(\frac{1}{3}\pi r_0^2 h\right)$ from Exercise 23, we have $k = 3m/\pi r_0^2 h$. Thus,

$$I_z = \frac{1}{10}k\pi r_0^4 h$$

$$= \frac{1}{10}\left(\frac{3m}{\pi r_0^2 h}\right)\pi r_0^4 h$$

$$= \frac{3}{10}m r_0^2$$

29. $m = k(\pi b^2 h - \pi a^2 h) = k\pi h(b^2 - a^2)$

$$I_z = 4k\int_0^{\pi/2}\int_a^b\int_0^h r^3\, dz\, dr\, d\theta$$

$$= 4kh\int_0^{\pi/2}\int_a^b r^3\, dr\, d\theta$$

$$= kh\int_0^{\pi/2}(b^4 - a^4)\, d\theta$$

$$= \frac{k\pi(b^4 - a^4)h}{2}$$

$$= \frac{k\pi(b^2 - a^2)(b^2 + a^2)h}{2}$$

$$= \frac{1}{2}m(a^2 + b^2)$$

31. $V = \displaystyle\int_0^{2\pi}\int_0^{\pi}\int_0^{4\sin\phi} \rho^2 \sin\phi\, d\rho\, d\phi\, d\theta = 16\pi^2$

33. $m = 8k\displaystyle\int_0^{\pi/2}\int_0^{\pi/2}\int_0^a \rho^3 \sin\phi\, d\rho\, d\theta\, d\phi$

$$= 2ka^4\int_0^{\pi/2}\int_0^{\pi/2}\sin\phi\, d\theta\, d\phi$$

$$= k\pi a^4\int_0^{\pi/2}\sin\phi\, d\phi$$

$$= \left[k\pi a^4(-\cos\phi)\right]_0^{\pi/2}$$

$$= k\pi a^4$$

35. $m = \dfrac{2}{3}k\pi r^3$

$\bar{x} = \bar{y} = 0$ by symmetry

$$M_{xy} = 4k\int_0^{\pi/2}\int_0^{\pi/2}\int_0^r \rho^3 \cos\phi\sin\phi\, d\rho\, d\theta\, d\phi$$

$$= \frac{1}{2}kr^4\int_0^{\pi/2}\int_0^{\pi/2}\sin 2\phi\, d\theta\, d\phi$$

$$= \frac{kr^4\pi}{4}\int_0^{\pi/2}\sin 2\phi\, d\phi$$

$$= \left[-\frac{1}{8}k\pi r^4\cos 2\phi\right]_0^{\pi/2} = \frac{1}{4}k\pi r^4$$

$$\bar{z} = \frac{M_{xy}}{m} = \frac{k\pi r^4/4}{2k\pi r^3/3} = \frac{3r}{8}$$

37. $I_z = 4k\int_{\pi/4}^{\pi/2}\int_0^{\pi/2}\int_0^{\cos\phi} \rho^4\sin^3\phi\, d\rho\, d\theta\, d\phi$

$$= \frac{4}{5}k\int_{\pi/4}^{\pi/2}\int_0^{\pi/2}\cos^5\phi\sin^3\phi\, d\theta\, d\phi$$

$$= \frac{2}{5}k\pi\int_{\pi/4}^{\pi/2}\cos^5\phi(1-\cos^2\phi)\sin\phi\, d\phi$$

$$= \left[\frac{2}{5}k\pi\left(-\frac{1}{6}\cos^6\phi + \frac{1}{8}\cos^8\phi\right)\right]_{\pi/4}^{\pi/2}$$

$$= \frac{k\pi}{192}$$

39. $x = r\cos\theta$ $\qquad x^2 + y^2 = r^2$

$y = r\sin\theta$ $\qquad \tan\theta = \dfrac{y}{x}$

$z = z$ $\qquad\qquad z = z$

41. $\displaystyle\int_{\theta_1}^{\theta_2}\int_{g_1(\theta)}^{g_2(\theta)}\int_{h_1(r\cos\theta,\, r\sin\theta)}^{h_2(r\cos\theta,\, r\sin\theta)} f(r\cos\theta,\, r\sin\theta,\, z)r\, dz\, dr\, d\theta$

43. (a) $r = r_0$: right circular cylinder about z-axis

$\quad\theta = \theta_0$: plane parallel to z-axis

$\quad z = z_0$: plane parallel to xy-plane

(b) $\rho = \rho_0$: sphere of radius ρ_0

$\quad\theta = \theta_0$: plane parallel to z-axis

$\quad\phi = \phi_0$: cone

45. $16\displaystyle\int_0^a\int_0^{\sqrt{a^2-x^2}}\int_0^{\sqrt{a^2-x^2-y^2}}\int_0^{\sqrt{a^2-x^2-y^2-z^2}} dw\, dz\, dy\, dx$

$$= 16\int_0^a\int_0^{\sqrt{a^2-x^2}}\int_0^{\sqrt{a^2-x^2-y^2}}\sqrt{a^2-x^2-y^2-z^2}\, dz\, dy\, dx$$

$$= 16\int_0^{\pi/2}\int_0^a\int_0^{\sqrt{a^2-r^2}}\sqrt{(a^2-r^2)-z^2}\, dz(r\, dr\, d\theta)$$

$$= 16\int_0^{\pi/2}\int_0^a \frac{1}{2}\left[z\sqrt{(a^2-r^2)-z^2} + (a^2-r^2)\arcsin\frac{z}{\sqrt{a^2-r^2}}\right]_0^{\sqrt{a^2-r^2}} r\, dr\, d\theta$$

$$= 8\int_0^{\pi/2}\int_0^a \frac{\pi}{2}(a^2-r^2)r\, dr\, d\theta$$

$$= 4\pi\int_0^{\pi/2}\left[\frac{a^2r^2}{2} - \frac{r^4}{4}\right]_0^a d\theta$$

$$= a^4\pi\int_0^{\pi/2} d\theta = \frac{a^4\pi^2}{2}$$

Section 13.8   Change of Variables: Jacobians

1. $x = -\dfrac{1}{2}(u - v)$

$y = \dfrac{1}{2}(u + v)$

$\dfrac{\partial x}{\partial u}\dfrac{\partial y}{\partial v} - \dfrac{\partial y}{\partial u}\dfrac{\partial x}{\partial v} = \left(-\dfrac{1}{2}\right)\left(\dfrac{1}{2}\right) - \left(\dfrac{1}{2}\right)\left(\dfrac{1}{2}\right)$

$\qquad = -\dfrac{1}{2}$

3. $x = u - v^2$

$y = u + v$

$\dfrac{\partial x}{\partial u}\dfrac{\partial y}{\partial v} - \dfrac{\partial y}{\partial u}\dfrac{\partial x}{\partial v} = (1)(1) - (1)(-2v) = 1 + 2v$

5. $x = u\cos\theta - v\sin\theta$

$y = u\sin\theta + v\cos\theta$

$\dfrac{\partial x}{\partial u}\dfrac{\partial y}{\partial v} - \dfrac{\partial y}{\partial u}\dfrac{\partial x}{\partial v} = \cos^2\theta + \sin^2\theta = 1$

7. $x = e^u\sin v$

$y = e^u\cos v$

$\dfrac{\partial x}{\partial u}\dfrac{\partial y}{\partial v} - \dfrac{\partial y}{\partial u}\dfrac{\partial x}{\partial v} = (e^u\sin v)(-e^u\sin v) - (e^u\cos v)(e^u\cos v) = -e^{2u}$

9. $x = 3u + 2v$

$y = 3v$

$v = \dfrac{y}{3}$

$u = \dfrac{x - 2v}{3} = \dfrac{x - 2(y/3)}{3}$

$\quad = \dfrac{x}{3} - \dfrac{2y}{9}$

(x, y)	(u, v)
$(0, 0)$	$(0, 0)$
$(3, 0)$	$(1, 0)$
$(2, 3)$	$(0, 1)$

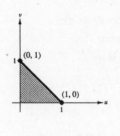

11. $x = \dfrac{1}{2}(u + v)$

$y = \dfrac{1}{2}(u - v)$

$\dfrac{\partial x}{\partial u}\dfrac{\partial y}{\partial v} - \dfrac{\partial y}{\partial u}\dfrac{\partial x}{\partial v} = \left(\dfrac{1}{2}\right)\left(-\dfrac{1}{2}\right) - \left(\dfrac{1}{2}\right)\left(\dfrac{1}{2}\right) = -\dfrac{1}{2}$

$\displaystyle\int_R\!\!\int 4(x^2 + y^2)\,dA = \int_{-1}^{1}\int_{-1}^{1} 4\left[\dfrac{1}{4}(u + v)^2 + \dfrac{1}{4}(u - v)^2\right]\left(\dfrac{1}{2}\right)dv\,du$

$\qquad = \int_{-1}^{1}\int_{-1}^{1}(u^2 + v^2)\,dv\,du = \int_{-1}^{1}2\left(u^2 + \dfrac{1}{3}\right)du = \left[2\left(\dfrac{u^3}{3} + \dfrac{u}{3}\right)\right]_{-1}^{1} = \dfrac{8}{3}$

13. $x = u + v$

$y = u$

$\dfrac{\partial x}{\partial u}\dfrac{\partial y}{\partial v} - \dfrac{\partial y}{\partial u}\dfrac{\partial x}{\partial v} = (1)(0) - (1)(1) = -1$

$\displaystyle\int_R\!\!\int y(x - y)\,dA = \int_0^3\int_0^4 uv(1)\,dv\,du = \int_0^3 8u\,du = 36$

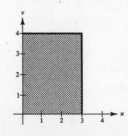

15. $\displaystyle\int_R\!\!\int e^{-xy/2}\,dA$

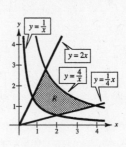

$R:\ y=\dfrac{x}{4},\ y=2x,\ y=\dfrac{1}{x},\ y=\dfrac{4}{x}$

$x=\sqrt{v/u},\ y=\sqrt{uv}\ \Rightarrow\ u=\dfrac{y}{x},\ v=xy$

$$\frac{\partial(x,y)}{\partial(u,v)}=\begin{vmatrix}\dfrac{\partial x}{\partial u}&\dfrac{\partial x}{\partial v}\\[2mm]\dfrac{\partial y}{\partial u}&\dfrac{\partial y}{\partial v}\end{vmatrix}=\begin{vmatrix}-\dfrac{1}{2}\dfrac{v^{1/2}}{u^{3/2}}&\dfrac{1}{2}\dfrac{1}{u^{1/2}v^{1/2}}\\[2mm]\dfrac{1}{2}\dfrac{v^{1/2}}{u^{1/2}}&\dfrac{1}{2}\dfrac{u^{1/2}}{v^{1/2}}\end{vmatrix}=-\frac{1}{4}\left(\frac{1}{u}+\frac{1}{u}\right)=-\frac{1}{2u}$$

Transformed Region:

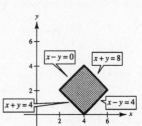

$y=\dfrac{1}{x}\ \Rightarrow\ yx=1\ \Rightarrow\ v=1$

$y=\dfrac{4}{x}\ \Rightarrow\ yx=4\ \Rightarrow\ v=4$

$y=2x\ \Rightarrow\ \dfrac{y}{x}=2\ \Rightarrow\ u=2$

$y=\dfrac{x}{4}\ \Rightarrow\ \dfrac{y}{x}=\dfrac{1}{4}\ \Rightarrow\ u=\dfrac{1}{4}$

$$\int_R\!\!\int e^{-xy/2}\,dA=\int_{1/4}^{2}\!\!\int_{1}^{4}e^{-v/2}\left(\frac{1}{2u}\right)dv\,du=-\int_{1/4}^{2}\left[\frac{e^{-v/2}}{u}\right]_{1}^{4}du=-\int_{1/4}^{2}(e^{-2}-e^{-1/2})\frac{1}{u}\,du$$

$$=-\Big[(e^{-2}-e^{-1/2})\ln u\Big]_{1/4}^{2}=-(e^{-2}-e^{-1/2})\left(\ln 2-\ln\frac{1}{4}\right)=(e^{-1/2}-e^{-2})\ln 8\approx 0.9798$$

17. $u=x+y=4,\qquad v=x-y=0$

$u=x+y=8,\qquad v=x-y=4$

$x=\dfrac{1}{2}(u+v)\qquad y=\dfrac{1}{2}(u-v)$

$\dfrac{\partial(x,y)}{\partial(u,v)}=-\dfrac{1}{2}$

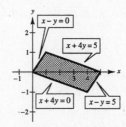

$$\int_R\!\!\int (x+y)e^{x-y}\,dA=\int_{4}^{8}\!\!\int_{0}^{4}ue^{v}\left(\frac{1}{2}\right)dv\,du$$

$$=\frac{1}{2}\int_{4}^{8}u(e^{4}-1)\,du=\left[\frac{1}{4}u^{2}(e^{4}-1)\right]_{4}^{8}=12(e^{4}-1)$$

19. $u=x+4y=0,\qquad v=x-y=0$

$u=x+4y=5,\qquad v=x-y=5$

$x=\dfrac{1}{5}(u+4v),\qquad y=\dfrac{1}{5}(u-v)$

$\dfrac{\partial x}{\partial u}\dfrac{\partial y}{\partial v}-\dfrac{\partial y}{\partial u}\dfrac{\partial x}{\partial v}=\left(\frac{1}{5}\right)\left(-\frac{1}{5}\right)-\left(\frac{1}{5}\right)\left(\frac{4}{5}\right)=-\frac{1}{5}$

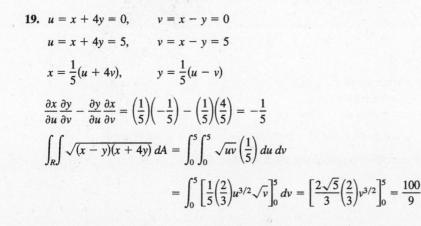

$$\int_R\!\!\int\sqrt{(x-y)(x+4y)}\,dA=\int_{0}^{5}\!\!\int_{0}^{5}\sqrt{uv}\left(\frac{1}{5}\right)du\,dv$$

$$=\int_{0}^{5}\left[\frac{1}{5}\left(\frac{2}{3}\right)u^{3/2}\sqrt{v}\right]_{0}^{5}dv=\left[\frac{2\sqrt{5}}{3}\left(\frac{2}{3}\right)v^{3/2}\right]_{0}^{5}=\frac{100}{9}$$

21. $u = x + y, v = x - y, x = \frac{1}{2}(u + v), y = \frac{1}{2}(u - v)$

$$\frac{\partial x}{\partial u}\frac{\partial y}{\partial v} - \frac{\partial y}{\partial u}\frac{\partial x}{\partial v} = -\frac{1}{2}$$

$$\int\!\!\int_R \sqrt{x + y}\, dA = \int_0^a \int_{-u}^u \sqrt{u}\left(\frac{1}{2}\right) dv\, du = \int_0^a u\sqrt{u}\, du = \left[\frac{2}{5}u^{5/2}\right]_0^a = \frac{2}{5}a^{5/2}$$

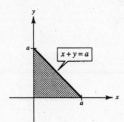 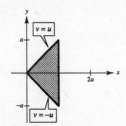

23. $\dfrac{x^2}{a^2} + \dfrac{y^2}{b^2} = 1, x = au, y = bv$ (a) $\dfrac{x^2}{a^2} + \dfrac{y^2}{b^2} = 1$ $u^2 + v^2 = 1$

$$\frac{(au)^2}{a^2} + \frac{(bv)^2}{b^2} = 1$$

$$u^2 + v^2 = 1$$

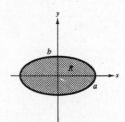 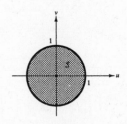

(b) $\dfrac{\partial(x, y)}{\partial(u, v)} = \dfrac{\partial x}{\partial u}\dfrac{\partial y}{\partial v} - \dfrac{\partial y}{\partial u}\dfrac{\partial x}{\partial v}$

$$= (a)(b) - (0)(0) = ab$$

(c) $A = \displaystyle\int\!\!\int_S ab\, dS$

$$= ab(\pi(1)^2) = \pi ab$$

25. Jacobian $= \dfrac{\partial(x, y)}{\partial(u, v)} = \dfrac{\partial x}{\partial u}\dfrac{\partial y}{\partial v} - \dfrac{\partial y}{\partial u}\dfrac{\partial x}{\partial v}$

27. $x = u(1 - v), \ y = uv(1 - w), \ z = uvw$

$$\frac{\partial(x, y, z)}{\partial(u, v, w)} = \begin{vmatrix} 1 - v & -u & 0 \\ v(1 - w) & u(1 - w) & -uv \\ vw & uw & uv \end{vmatrix} = (1 - v)[u^2v(1 - w) + u^2vw] + u[uv^2(1 - w) + uv^2w]$$

$$= (1 - v)(u^2v) + u(uv^2)$$

$$= u^2v$$

29. $x = \rho \sin\phi\cos\theta, \ y = \rho\sin\phi\sin\theta, \ z = \rho\cos\phi$

$$\frac{\partial(x, y, z)}{\partial(\rho, \theta, \phi)} = \begin{vmatrix} \sin\phi\cos\theta & -\rho\sin\phi\sin\theta & \rho\cos\phi\cos\theta \\ \sin\phi\sin\theta & \rho\sin\phi\cos\theta & \rho\cos\phi\sin\theta \\ \cos\phi & 0 & -\rho\sin\phi \end{vmatrix}$$

$$= \cos\phi[-\rho^2\sin\phi\cos\phi\sin^2\theta - \rho^2\sin\phi\cos\phi\cos^2\theta] - \rho\sin\phi[\rho\sin^2\phi\cos^2\theta + \rho\sin^2\phi\sin^2\theta]$$

$$= \cos\phi[-\rho^2\sin\phi\cos\phi(\sin^2\theta + \cos^2\theta)] - \rho\sin\phi[\rho\sin^2\phi(\cos^2\theta + \sin^2\theta)]$$

$$= -\rho^2\sin\phi\cos^2\phi - \rho^2\sin^3\phi$$

$$= -\rho^2\sin\phi(\cos^2\phi + \sin^2\phi)$$

$$= -\rho^2\sin\phi$$

Review Exercises for Chapter 13

1. $\displaystyle\int_1^{x^2} x \ln y \, dy = \left[xy(-1 + \ln y) \right]_1^{x^2} = x^3(-1 + \ln x^2) + x = x - x^3 + x^3 \ln x^2$

3. $\displaystyle\int_0^1 \int_0^{1+x} (3x + 2y) \, dy \, dx = \int_0^1 \left[3xy + y^2 \right]_0^{1+x} dx = \int_0^1 (4x^2 + 5x + 1) \, dx = \left[\frac{4}{3}x^3 + \frac{5}{2}x^2 + x \right]_0^1 = \frac{29}{6}$

5. $\displaystyle\int_0^3 \int_0^{\sqrt{9-x^2}} 4x \, dy \, dx = \int_0^3 4x\sqrt{9 - x^2} \, dx = \left[-\frac{4}{3}(9 - x^2)^{3/2} \right]_0^3 = 36$

7. $\displaystyle\int_0^3 \int_0^{(3-x)/3} dy \, dx = \int_0^1 \int_0^{3-3y} dx \, dy$

$\displaystyle A = \int_0^1 \int_0^{3-3y} dx \, dy = \int_0^1 (3 - 3y) \, dy = \left[3y - \frac{3}{2}y^2 \right]_0^1 = \frac{3}{2}$

9. $\displaystyle\int_{-5}^3 \int_{-\sqrt{25-x^2}}^{\sqrt{25-x^2}} dy \, dx = \int_{-5}^{-4} \int_{-\sqrt{25-y^2}}^{\sqrt{25-y^2}} dx \, dy + \int_{-4}^4 \int_{-\sqrt{25-y^2}}^3 dx \, dy + \int_4^5 \int_{-\sqrt{25-y^2}}^{\sqrt{25-y^2}} dx \, dy$

$\displaystyle A = 2\int_{-5}^3 \int_0^{\sqrt{25-x^2}} dy \, dx = 2\int_{-5}^3 \sqrt{25 - x^2} \, dx = \left[x\sqrt{25 - x^2} + 25 \arcsin \frac{x}{5} \right]_{-5}^3 = \frac{25\pi}{2} + 12 + 25 \arcsin \frac{3}{5} \approx 67.36$

11. $\displaystyle A = 4\int_0^1 \int_0^{x\sqrt{1-x^2}} dy \, dx = 4\int_0^1 x\sqrt{1 - x^2} \, dx = \left[-\frac{4}{3}(1 - x^2)^{3/2} \right]_0^1 = \frac{4}{3}$

$\displaystyle A = 4\int_0^{1/2} \int_{\sqrt{(1-\sqrt{1-4y^2})/2}}^{\sqrt{(1+\sqrt{1-4y^2})/2}} dx \, dy$

13. $\displaystyle A = \int_2^5 \int_{x-3}^{\sqrt{x-1}} dy \, dx + 2\int_1^2 \int_0^{\sqrt{x-1}} dy \, dx = \int_{-1}^2 \int_{y^2+1}^{y+3} dx \, dy = \frac{9}{2}$

15. Both integrations are over the common region R shown in the figure. Analytically,

$\displaystyle\int_0^1 \int_{2y}^{2\sqrt{2-y^2}} (x + y) \, dx \, dy = \frac{4}{3} + \frac{4}{3}\sqrt{2}$

$\displaystyle\int_0^2 \int_0^{x/2} (x + y) \, dy \, dx + \int_2^{2\sqrt{2}} \int_0^{\sqrt{8-x^2}/2} (x + y) \, dy \, dx = \frac{5}{3} + \left(\frac{4}{3}\sqrt{2} - \frac{1}{3} \right) = \frac{4}{3} + \frac{4}{3}\sqrt{2}$

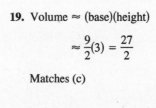

17. $\displaystyle V = \int_0^4 \int_0^{x^2+4} (x^2 - y + 4) \, dy \, dx$

$\displaystyle = \int_0^4 \left[x^2y - \frac{1}{2}y^2 + 4y \right]_0^{x^2+4} dx$

$\displaystyle = \int_0^4 \left(\frac{1}{2}x^4 + 4x^2 + 8 \right) dx$

$\displaystyle = \left[\frac{1}{10}x^5 + \frac{4}{3}x^3 + 8x \right]_0^4 = \frac{3296}{15}$

19. Volume $\approx$ (base)(height)

$\displaystyle \approx \frac{9}{2}(3) = \frac{27}{2}$

Matches (c)

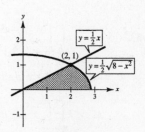

21. $\int_0^\infty \int_0^\infty kxye^{-(x+y)} \, dy \, dx = \int_0^\infty \left[-kxe^{-(x+y)}(y+1) \right]_0^\infty dx = \int_0^\infty kxe^{-x} \, dx = \left[-k(x+1)e^{-x} \right]_0^\infty = k$

Therefore, $k = 1$.

$$P = \int_0^1 \int_0^1 xye^{-(x+y)} \, dy \, dx \approx 0.070$$

23. True

25. True

27. $\int_0^h \int_0^x \sqrt{x^2 + y^2} \, dy \, dx = \int_0^{\pi/4} \int_0^{h\sec\theta} r^2 \, dr \, d\theta$

$$= \frac{h^3}{3} \int_0^{\pi/4} \sec^3\theta \, d\theta = \frac{h^3}{6} \left[\sec\theta\tan\theta + \ln|\sec\theta + \tan\theta| \right]_0^{\pi/4} = \frac{h^3}{6}\left[\sqrt{2} + \ln\left(\sqrt{2} + 1\right) \right]$$

29. $V = 4\int_0^h \int_0^{\pi/2} \int_1^{\sqrt{1+z^2}} r \, dr \, d\theta \, dz$

$= 2\int_0^h \int_0^{\pi/2} (1 + z^2 - 1) \, d\theta \, dz$

$= \pi \int_0^h z^2 \, dz$

$= \left[\pi\left(\frac{1}{3}z^3\right) \right]_0^h = \frac{\pi h^3}{3}$

31. (a) $(x^2 + y^2)^2 = 9(x^2 - y^2)$

$(r^2)^2 = 9(r^2\cos^2\theta - r^2\sin^2\theta)$

$r^2 = 9(\cos^2\theta - \sin^2\theta) = 9\cos 2\theta$

$r = 3\sqrt{\cos 2\theta}$

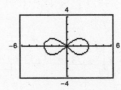

(b) $A = 4\int_0^{\pi/4} \int_0^{3\sqrt{\cos 2\theta}} r \, dr \, d\theta = 9$

(c) $V = 4\int_0^{\pi/4} \int_0^{3\sqrt{\cos 2\theta}} \sqrt{9 - r^2} \, r \, dr \, d\theta \approx 20.392$

33. (a) $m = k\int_0^1 \int_{2x^3}^{2x} xy \, dy \, dx = \frac{k}{4}$

$M_x = k\int_0^1 \int_{2x^3}^{2x} xy^2 \, dy \, dx = \frac{16k}{55}$

$M_y = k\int_0^1 \int_{2x^3}^{2x} x^2 y \, dy \, dx = \frac{8k}{45}$

$\bar{x} = \frac{M_y}{m} = \frac{32}{45}$

$\bar{y} = \frac{M_x}{m} = \frac{64}{55}$

(b) $m = k\int_0^1 \int_{2x^3}^{2x} (x^2 + y^2) \, dy \, dx = \frac{17k}{30}$

$M_x = k\int_0^1 \int_{2x^3}^{2x} y(x^2 + y^2) \, dy \, dx = \frac{392k}{585}$

$M_y = k\int_0^1 \int_{2x^3}^{2x} x(x^2 + y^2) \, dy \, dx = \frac{156k}{385}$

$\bar{x} = \frac{M_y}{m} = \frac{936}{1309}$

$\bar{y} = \frac{M_x}{m} = \frac{784}{663}$

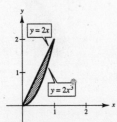

35. $I_x = \int_R\!\!\int y^2\, \rho(x, y)\, dA = \int_0^a \int_0^b kxy^2\, dy\, dx = \frac{1}{6}kb^3a^2$

$I_y = \int_R\!\!\int x^2\, \rho(x, y)\, dA = \int_0^a \int_0^b kx^3\, dy\, dx = \frac{1}{4}kba^4$

$I_0 = I_x + I_y = \frac{1}{6}kb^3a^2 + \frac{1}{4}kba^4 = \frac{ka^2b}{12}(2b^2 + 3a^2)$

$m = \int_R\!\!\int \rho(x, y)\, dA = \int_0^a \int_0^b kx\, dy\, dx = \frac{1}{2}kba^2$

$\overline{\overline{x}} = \sqrt{\dfrac{I_y}{m}} = \sqrt{\dfrac{(1/4)kba^4}{(1/2)kba^2}} = \sqrt{\dfrac{a^2}{2}} = \dfrac{a\sqrt{2}}{2}$

$\overline{\overline{y}} = \sqrt{\dfrac{I_x}{m}} = \sqrt{\dfrac{(1/6)kb^3a^2}{(1/2)kba^2}} = \sqrt{\dfrac{b^2}{3}} = \dfrac{b\sqrt{3}}{3}$

37. $S = \int_R\!\!\int \sqrt{1 + (f_x)^2 + (f_y)^2}\, dA$

$= 4\int_0^4 \int_0^{\sqrt{16-x^2}} \sqrt{1 + 4x^2 + 4y^2}\, dy\, dx$

$= 4\int_0^{\pi/2} \int_0^4 \sqrt{1 + 4r^2}\, r\, dr\, d\theta$

$= \left[\frac{1}{3}(65^{3/2} - 1)\theta\right]_0^{\pi/2} = \frac{\pi}{6}\left(65\sqrt{65} - 1\right)$

39. $f(x, y) = 9 - y^2$

$f_x = 0,\ f_y = -2y$

$S = \int_R\!\!\int \sqrt{1 + f_x^2 + f_y^2}\, dA$

$= \int_0^3 \int_{-y}^y \sqrt{1 + 4y^2}\, dx\, dy$

$= \int_0^3 \left[\sqrt{1 + 4y^2}\, x\right]_{-y}^y dy$

$= \int_0^3 2\sqrt{1 + 4y^2}\, dy = \frac{1}{4}\frac{2}{3}(1 + 4y^2)^{3/2}\Big]_0^3 = \frac{1}{6}[(37)^{3/2} - 1]$

41. $\displaystyle\int_{-3}^3 \int_{-\sqrt{9-x^2}}^{\sqrt{9-x^2}} \int_{x^2+y^2}^9 \sqrt{x^2 + y^2}\, dz\, dy\, dx = \int_0^{2\pi} \int_0^3 \int_{r^2}^9 r^2\, dz\, dr\, d\theta$

$= \int_0^{2\pi} \int_0^3 (9r^2 - r^4)\, dr\, d\theta = \int_0^{2\pi}\left[3r^3 - \frac{r^5}{5}\right]_0^3 d\theta = \frac{162}{5}\int_0^{2\pi} d\theta = \frac{324\pi}{5}$

43. $\displaystyle\int_0^a \int_0^b \int_0^c (x^2 + y^2 + z^2)\, dx\, dy\, dz = \int_0^a \int_0^b \left(\frac{1}{3}c^3 + cy^2 + cz^2\right) dy\, dz$

$= \int_0^a \left(\frac{1}{3}bc^3 + \frac{1}{3}b^3c + bcz^2\right) dz = \frac{1}{3}abc^3 + \frac{1}{3}ab^3c + \frac{1}{3}a^3bc = \frac{1}{3}abc(a^2 + b^2 + c^2)$

45. $\displaystyle\int_{-1}^1 \int_{-\sqrt{1-x^2}}^{\sqrt{1-x^2}} \int_{-\sqrt{1-x^2-y^2}}^{\sqrt{1-x^2-y^2}} (x^2 + y^2)\, dz\, dy\, dx = \int_0^{2\pi} \int_0^1 \int_{-\sqrt{1-r^2}}^{\sqrt{1-r^2}} r^3\, dz\, dr\, d\theta = \frac{8\pi}{15}$

47. $V = 4\displaystyle\int_0^{\pi/2}\int_0^{2\cos\theta}\int_0^{\sqrt{4-r^2}} r\,dz\,dr\,d\theta$

$= 4\displaystyle\int_0^{\pi/2}\int_0^{2\cos\theta} r\sqrt{4-r^2}\,dr\,d\theta$

$= -\displaystyle\int_0^{\pi/2}\left[\frac{4}{3}(4-r^2)^{3/2}\right]_0^{2\cos\theta} d\theta$

$= \frac{32}{3}\displaystyle\int_0^{\pi/2}(1-\sin^3\theta)\,d\theta$

$= \frac{32}{3}\left[\theta + \cos\theta - \frac{1}{3}\cos^3\theta\right]_0^{\pi/2} = \frac{32}{3}\left(\frac{\pi}{2}-\frac{2}{3}\right)$

49. $m = 4k\displaystyle\int_{\pi/4}^{\pi/2}\int_0^{\pi/2}\int_0^{\cos\phi} \rho^2 \sin\phi\,d\rho\,d\theta\,d\phi$

$= \frac{4}{3}k\displaystyle\int_{\pi/4}^{\pi/2}\int_0^{\pi/2}\cos^3\phi\sin\phi\,d\theta\,d\phi = \frac{2}{3}k\pi\int_{\pi/4}^{\pi/2}\cos^3\phi\sin\phi\,d\phi = \left[-\frac{2}{3}k\pi\left(\frac{1}{4}\cos^4\phi\right)\right]_{\pi/4}^{\pi/2} = \frac{k\pi}{24}$

$M_{xy} = 4k\displaystyle\int_{\pi/4}^{\pi/2}\int_0^{\pi/2}\int_0^{\cos\phi} \rho^3\cos\phi\sin\phi\,d\rho\,d\theta\,d\phi$

$= k\displaystyle\int_{\pi/4}^{\pi/2}\int_0^{\pi/2}\cos^5\phi\sin\phi\,d\theta\,d\phi = \frac{1}{2}k\pi\int_{\pi/4}^{\pi/2}\cos^5\phi\sin\phi\,d\phi = \left[-\frac{1}{12}k\pi\cos^6\phi\right]_{\pi/4}^{\pi/2} = \frac{k\pi}{96}$

$\bar{z} = \dfrac{M_{xy}}{m} = \dfrac{k\pi/96}{k\pi/24} = \dfrac{1}{4}$

$\bar{x} = \bar{y} = 0$ by symmetry

51. $m = k\displaystyle\int_0^{\pi/2}\int_0^{\pi/2}\int_0^{a} \rho^2\sin\phi\,d\rho\,d\theta\,d\phi = \frac{k\pi a^3}{6}$

$M_{xy} = k\displaystyle\int_0^{\pi/2}\int_0^{\pi/2}\int_0^{a} (\rho\cos\phi)\rho^2\sin\phi\,d\rho\,d\theta\,d\phi = \frac{k\pi a^4}{16}$

$\bar{x} = \bar{y} = \bar{z} = \dfrac{M_{xy}}{m} = \dfrac{k\pi a^4}{16}\left(\dfrac{6}{k\pi a^3}\right) = \dfrac{3a}{8}$

53. $I_z = 4k\displaystyle\int_0^{\pi/2}\int_3^{4}\int_0^{16-r^2} r^3\,dz\,dr\,d\theta$

$= 4k\displaystyle\int_0^{\pi/2}\int_3^{4}(16r^3 - r^5)\,dr\,d\theta = \frac{833\pi k}{3}$

55. $z = f(x,y) = \sqrt{a^2 - x^2 - y^2}$

$\qquad\qquad = \sqrt{a^2 - r^2}$

$0 \le r \le \sqrt{2ah - h^2}$

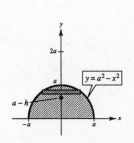

(a) Disc Method

$V = \pi\displaystyle\int_{a-h}^{a}(a^2 - y^2)\,dy$

$= \pi\left[a^2 y - \dfrac{y^3}{3}\right]_{a-h}^{a} = \pi\left[\left(a^3 - \dfrac{a^3}{3}\right) - \left(a^2(a-h) - \dfrac{(a-h)^3}{3}\right)\right]$

$= \pi\left[a^3 - \dfrac{a^3}{3} - a^3 + a^2 h + \dfrac{a^3}{3} - a^2 h + ah^2 - \dfrac{h^3}{3}\right] = \pi\left[ah^2 - \dfrac{h^3}{3}\right] = \dfrac{1}{3}\pi h^2[3a - h]$

Equivalently, use spherical coordinates

$V = \displaystyle\int_0^{2\pi}\int_0^{\cos^{-1}(a-h/a)}\int_{(a-h)\sec\phi}^{a} \rho^2\sin\phi\,d\rho\,d\phi\,d\theta$

—CONTINUED—

55. —CONTINUED—

(b) $M_{xy} = \int_0^{2\pi} \int_0^{\cos^{-1}(a-h/a)} \int_{(a-h)\sec \phi}^{a} (\rho \cos \phi)\rho^2 \sin \phi \, d\rho \, d\phi \, d\theta$

$\quad\quad = \frac{1}{4}h^2\pi(2a - h)^2$

$\bar{z} = \dfrac{M_{xy}}{V} = \dfrac{\frac{1}{4}h^2\pi(2a-h)^2}{\frac{1}{3}h^2\pi(3a-h)} = \dfrac{3}{4}\dfrac{(2a-h)^2}{3a-h}$

centroid: $\left(0, 0, \dfrac{3(2a-h)^2}{4(3a-h)}\right)$

(c) If $h = a$, $\bar{z} = \dfrac{3(a)^2}{4(2a)} = \dfrac{3}{8}a$

centroid of hemisphere: $\left(0, 0, \dfrac{3}{8}a\right)$

(d) $\lim\limits_{h \to 0} \bar{z} = \lim\limits_{h \to 0} \dfrac{3(2a-h)^2}{4(3a-h)} = \dfrac{3(4a^2)}{12a} = a$

(e) $x^2 + y^2 = \rho^2 \sin^2 \phi$

$I_z = \int_0^{2\pi} \int_0^{\cos^{-1}(a-h/a)} \int_{(a-h)\sec \phi}^{a} (\rho^2 \sin^2 \phi)\rho^2 \sin \phi \, d\rho \, d\phi \, d\theta$

$\quad = \dfrac{h^3}{30}(20a^2 - 15ah + 3h^2)\pi$

(f) If $h = a$, $I_z = \dfrac{a^3\pi}{30}(20a^2 - 15a^2 + 3a^2) = \dfrac{4}{15}a^5\pi$

57. $\int_0^{2\pi} \int_0^{\pi} \int_0^{6 \sin \phi} \rho^2 \sin \phi \, d\rho \, d\phi \, d\theta$

Since $\rho = 6 \sin \phi$ represents (in the yz-plane) a circle of radius 3 centered at $(0, 3, 0)$, the integral represents the volume of the torus formed by revolving $(0 < \theta < 2\pi)$ this circle about the z-axis.

59. $\dfrac{\partial(x, y)}{\partial(u, v)} = \dfrac{\partial x}{\partial u}\dfrac{\partial y}{\partial v} - \dfrac{\partial y}{\partial u}\dfrac{\partial x}{\partial v}$

$\quad = 1(-3) - 2(3) = -9$

61. $\dfrac{\partial(x, y)}{\partial(u, v)} = \dfrac{\partial x}{\partial u}\dfrac{\partial y}{\partial v} - \dfrac{\partial x}{\partial v}\dfrac{\partial y}{\partial u} = \dfrac{1}{2}\left(-\dfrac{1}{2}\right) - \dfrac{1}{2}\left(\dfrac{1}{2}\right) = -\dfrac{1}{2}$

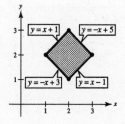

$x = \dfrac{1}{2}(u + v), y = \dfrac{1}{2}(u - v) \implies u = x + y, v = x - y$

Boundaries in xy-plane	Boundaries in uv-plane
$x + y = 3$	$u = 3$
$x + y = 5$	$u = 5$
$x - y = -1$	$v = -1$
$x - y = 1$	$v = 1$

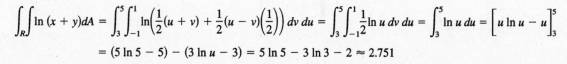

$\displaystyle \int_R\int \ln (x + y)\,dA = \int_3^5 \int_{-1}^1 \ln\left(\dfrac{1}{2}(u + v) + \dfrac{1}{2}(u - v)\left(\dfrac{1}{2}\right)\right) dv \, du = \int_3^5 \int_{-1}^1 \dfrac{1}{2}\ln u \, dv \, du = \int_3^5 \ln u \, du = \Big[u \ln u - u \Big]_3^5$

$\quad = (5 \ln 5 - 5) - (3 \ln u - 3) = 5 \ln 5 - 3 \ln 3 - 2 \approx 2.751$

Problem Solving for Chapter 13

1. (a) $V = 16 \int_R \int \sqrt{1 - x^2} \, dA$

$$= 16 \int_0^{\pi/4} \int_0^1 \sqrt{1 - r^2 \cos^2 \theta} \, r \, dr \, d\theta$$

$$= -\frac{16}{3} \int_0^{\pi/4} \frac{1}{\cos^2 \theta} \left[(1 - \cos^2 \theta)^{3/2} - 1 \right] d\theta$$

$$= -\frac{16}{3} \left[\sec \theta + \cos \theta - \tan \theta \right]_0^{\pi/4}$$

$$= 8(2 - \sqrt{2}) \approx 4.6863$$

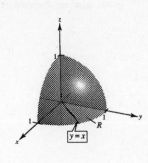

(b) Programs will vary.

3. (a) $\int \dfrac{du}{a^2 + u^2} = \dfrac{1}{a} \arctan \dfrac{u}{a} + c$. Let $a^2 = 2 - u^2$, $u = v$.

Then $\int \dfrac{1}{(2 - u^2) + v^2} \, dv = \dfrac{1}{\sqrt{2 - u^2}} \arctan \dfrac{v}{\sqrt{2 - u^2}} + C$.

(b) $I_1 = \displaystyle\int_0^{\sqrt{2}/2} \left[\dfrac{2}{\sqrt{2 - u^2}} \arctan \dfrac{v}{\sqrt{2 - u^2}} \right]_{-u}^{u} du$

$$= \int_0^{\sqrt{2}/2} \dfrac{2}{\sqrt{2 - u^2}} \left(\arctan \dfrac{u}{\sqrt{2 - u^2}} - \arctan \dfrac{-u}{\sqrt{2 - u^2}} \right) du$$

$$= \int_0^{\sqrt{2}/2} \dfrac{4}{\sqrt{2 - u^2}} \arctan \dfrac{u}{\sqrt{2 - u^2}} \, du$$

Let $u = \sqrt{2} \sin \theta$, $du = \sqrt{2} \cos \theta \, d\theta$, $2 - u^2 = 2 - 2 \sin^2 \theta = 2 \cos^2 \theta$.

$$I_1 = 4 \int_0^{\pi/6} \dfrac{1}{\sqrt{2} \cos \theta} \arctan \left(\dfrac{\sqrt{2} \sin \theta}{\sqrt{2} \cos \theta} \right) \cdot \sqrt{2} \cos \theta \, d\theta$$

$$= 4 \int_0^{\pi/6} \arctan(\tan \theta) d\theta = \dfrac{4\theta^2}{2} \bigg]_0^{\pi/6} = 2 \left(\dfrac{\pi}{6} \right)^2 = \dfrac{\pi^2}{18}$$

(c) $I_2 = \displaystyle\int_{\sqrt{2}/2}^{\sqrt{2}} \left[\dfrac{2}{\sqrt{2 - u^2}} \arctan \dfrac{v}{\sqrt{2 - u^2}} \right]_{u - \sqrt{2}}^{-u + \sqrt{2}} du$

$$= \int_{\sqrt{2}/2}^{\sqrt{2}} \dfrac{2}{\sqrt{2 - u^2}} \left[\arctan \left(\dfrac{-u + \sqrt{2}}{\sqrt{2 - u^2}} \right) - \arctan \left(\dfrac{u - \sqrt{2}}{\sqrt{2 - u^2}} \right) \right] du$$

$$= \int_{\sqrt{2}/2}^{\sqrt{2}} \dfrac{4}{\sqrt{2 - u^2}} \arctan \left(\dfrac{\sqrt{2} - u}{\sqrt{2 - u^2}} \right) du$$

Let $u = \sqrt{2} \sin \theta$.

$$I_2 = 4 \int_{\pi/6}^{\pi/2} \dfrac{1}{\sqrt{2} \cos \theta} \arctan \left(\dfrac{\sqrt{2} - \sqrt{2} \sin \theta}{\sqrt{2} \cos \theta} \right) \cdot \sqrt{2} \cos \theta \, d\theta$$

$$= 4 \int_{\pi/6}^{\pi/2} \arctan \left(\dfrac{1 - \sin \theta}{\cos \theta} \right) d\theta$$

—CONTINUED—

3. —CONTINUED—

(d) $\tan\left(\dfrac{1}{2}\left(\dfrac{\pi}{2} - \theta\right)\right) = \sqrt{\dfrac{1 - \cos((\pi/2) - \theta)}{1 + \cos((\pi/2) - \theta)}} = \sqrt{\dfrac{1 - \sin\theta}{1 + \sin\theta}}$

$\qquad\qquad\qquad\quad = \sqrt{\dfrac{(1 - \sin\theta)^2}{(1 + \sin\theta)(1 - \sin\theta)}} = \sqrt{\dfrac{(1 - \sin\theta)^2}{\cos^2\theta}} = \dfrac{1 - \sin\theta}{\cos\theta}$

(e) $I_2 = 4\displaystyle\int_{\pi/6}^{\pi/2} \arctan\left(\dfrac{1 - \sin\theta}{\cos\theta}\right) d\theta = 4\int_{\pi/6}^{\pi/2} \arctan\left(\tan\left(\dfrac{1}{2}\left(\dfrac{\pi}{2} - \theta\right)\right)\right) d\theta$

$\qquad = 4\displaystyle\int_{\pi/6}^{\pi/2} \dfrac{1}{2}\left(\dfrac{\pi}{2} - \theta\right) d\theta = 2\int_{\pi/6}^{\pi/2}\left(\dfrac{\pi}{2} - \theta\right) d\theta$

$\qquad = 2\left[\dfrac{\pi}{2}\theta - \dfrac{\theta^2}{2}\right]_{\pi/6}^{\pi/2} = 2\left[\left(\dfrac{\pi^2}{4} - \dfrac{\pi^2}{8}\right) - \left(\dfrac{\pi^2}{12} - \dfrac{\pi^2}{72}\right)\right]$

$\qquad = 2\left[\dfrac{18 - 9 - 6 + 1}{72}\pi^2\right] = \dfrac{4}{36}\pi^2 = \dfrac{\pi^2}{9}$

(f) $\dfrac{1}{1 - xy} = 1 + (xy) + (xy)^2 + \cdots \qquad |xy| < 1$

$\displaystyle\int_0^1\int_0^1 \dfrac{1}{1 - xy}\,dx\,dy = \int_0^1\int_0^1 [1 + (xy) + (xy)^2 + \cdots]\,dx\,dy$

$\qquad\qquad\qquad\quad = \displaystyle\int_0^1\int_0^1 \sum_{K=0}^{\infty} (xy)^K\,dx\,dy = \sum_{K=0}^{\infty}\int_0^1 \dfrac{x^{K+1}y^K}{K+1}\bigg|_0^1\,dy$

$\qquad\qquad\qquad\quad = \displaystyle\sum_{K=0}^{\infty}\int_0^1 \dfrac{y^K}{K+1}\,dy = \sum_{K=0}^{\infty}\dfrac{y^{K+1}}{(K+1)^2}\bigg|_0^1$

$\qquad\qquad\qquad\quad = \displaystyle\sum_{K=0}^{\infty}\dfrac{1}{(K+1)^2} = \sum_{n=1}^{\infty}\dfrac{1}{n^2}$

(g) $u = \dfrac{x + y}{\sqrt{2}}, v = \dfrac{y - x}{\sqrt{2}}$

$u - v = \dfrac{2x}{\sqrt{2}} \Rightarrow x = \dfrac{u - v}{\sqrt{2}}$

$u + v = \dfrac{2y}{\sqrt{2}} \Rightarrow y = \dfrac{u + v}{\sqrt{2}}$

$\dfrac{\partial(x, y)}{\partial(u, v)} = \begin{vmatrix} 1/\sqrt{2} & -1/\sqrt{2} \\ 1/\sqrt{2} & 1/\sqrt{2} \end{vmatrix} = 1$

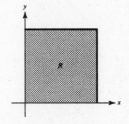

$\underline{R} \qquad \underline{S}$

$(0, 0) \leftrightarrow (0, 0)$

$(1, 0) \leftrightarrow \left(\dfrac{1}{\sqrt{2}}, -\dfrac{1}{\sqrt{2}}\right)$

$(0, 1) \leftrightarrow \left(\dfrac{1}{\sqrt{2}}, \dfrac{1}{\sqrt{2}}\right)$

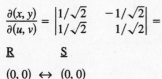

$(1, 1) \leftrightarrow \left(\sqrt{2}, 0\right)$

$\displaystyle\int_0^1\int_0^1 \dfrac{1}{1 - xy}\,dx\,dy = \int_0^{\sqrt{2}/2}\int_{-u}^{u} \dfrac{1}{1 - \dfrac{u^2}{2} + \dfrac{v^2}{2}}\,dv\,du + \int_{\sqrt{2}/2}^{\sqrt{2}}\int_{u-\sqrt{2}}^{-u+\sqrt{2}} \dfrac{1}{1 - \dfrac{u^2}{2} + \dfrac{v^2}{2}}\,dv\,du$

$\qquad\qquad\qquad\qquad = I_1 + I_2 = \dfrac{\pi^2}{18} + \dfrac{\pi^2}{9} = \dfrac{\pi^2}{6}$

5.

Boundary in xy-plane	Boundary in uv-plane
$y = \sqrt{x}$	$u = 1$
$y = \sqrt{2x}$	$u = 2$
$y = \dfrac{1}{3}x^2$	$v = 3$
$y = \dfrac{1}{4}x^2$	$v = 4$

$$\frac{\partial(x, y)}{\partial(u, v)} = \begin{vmatrix} \dfrac{1}{3}\left(\dfrac{v}{u}\right)^{2/3} & \dfrac{2}{3}\left(\dfrac{u}{v}\right)^{1/3} \\ \dfrac{2}{3}\left(\dfrac{v}{u}\right)^{1/3} & \dfrac{1}{3}\left(\dfrac{u}{v}\right)^{2/3} \end{vmatrix} = -\frac{1}{3}$$

$$A = \int_R\!\!\int 1\, dA = \int_S\!\!\int 1\left|\frac{\partial(x, y)}{\partial(u, v)}\right| dA = \frac{1}{3}$$

7.

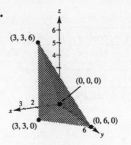

$$V = \int_0^3 \int_0^{2x} \int_x^{6-x} dy\, dz\, dx = 18$$

9. From Exercise 55, Section 13.3,

$$\int_{-\infty}^{\infty} e^{-x^2/2}\, dx = \sqrt{2\pi}$$

Thus, $\displaystyle\int_0^{\infty} e^{-x^2/2}\, dx = \frac{\sqrt{2\pi}}{2}$ and $\displaystyle\int_0^{\infty} e^{-x^2}\, dx = \frac{\sqrt{\pi}}{2}$

$$\int_0^{\infty} x^2 e^{-x^2}\, dx = \left[-\frac{1}{2}x e^{-x^2}\right]_0^{\infty} + \frac{1}{2}\int_0^{\infty} e^{-x^2}\, dx = \frac{1}{2}\frac{\sqrt{\pi}}{2} = \frac{\sqrt{\pi}}{4}$$

11. $f(x, y) = \begin{cases} ke^{-(x+y)/a} & x \geq 0, y \geq 0 \\ 0 & \text{elsewhere} \end{cases}$

$$\int_{-\infty}^{\infty}\int_{-\infty}^{\infty} f(x, y)\, dA = \int_0^{\infty}\int_0^{\infty} ke^{-(x+y)/a}\, dx\, dy$$

$$= k\int_0^{\infty} e^{-x/a}\, dx \cdot \int_0^{\infty} e^{-y/a}\, dy$$

These two integrals are equal to

$$\int_0^{\infty} e^{-x/a}\, dx = \lim_{b \to \infty}\left[(-a)e^{-x/a}\right]_0^b = a.$$

Hence, assuming $a, k > 0$, you obtain

$$1 = ka^2 \quad \text{or} \quad a = \frac{1}{\sqrt{k}}.$$

13. $A = l \cdot w = \left(\dfrac{\Delta x}{\cos\theta}\right)\Delta y = \sec\theta\,\Delta x\,\Delta y$

Area in xy-plane: $\Delta x\,\Delta y$

C H A P T E R 14
Vector Analysis

CHAPTER 14
Vector Analysis

Section 14.1   Vector Fields

Solutions to Odd-Numbered Exercises

1. All vectors are parallel to y-axis.

Matches (c)

3. All vectors point outward.

Matches (b)

5. Vectors are parallel to x-axis for $y = n\pi$.

Matches (a)

7. $\mathbf{F}(x, y) = \mathbf{i} + \mathbf{j}$

$\|\mathbf{F}\| = \sqrt{2}$

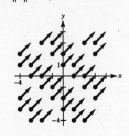

9. $\mathbf{F}(x, y) = x\mathbf{i} + y\mathbf{j}$

$\|\mathbf{F}\| = \sqrt{x^2 + y^2} = c$

$x^2 + y^2 = c^2$

11. $\mathbf{F}(x, y, z) = 3y\mathbf{j}$

$\|\mathbf{F}\| = 3|y| = c$

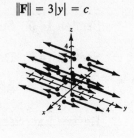

13. $\mathbf{F}(x, y) = 4x\mathbf{i} + y\mathbf{j}$

$\|\mathbf{F}\| = \sqrt{16x^2 + y^2} = c$

$\dfrac{x^2}{c^2/16} + \dfrac{y^2}{c^2} = 1$

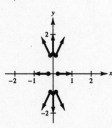

15. $\mathbf{F}(x, y, z) = \mathbf{i} + \mathbf{j} + \mathbf{k}$

$\|\mathbf{F}\| = \sqrt{3}$

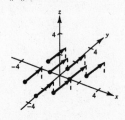

17.

19.

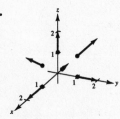

21. $f(x, y) = 5x^2 + 3xy + 10y^2$

$f_x(x, y) = 10x + 3y$

$f_y(x, y) = 3x + 20y$

$\mathbf{F}(x, y) = (10x + 3y)\mathbf{i} + (3x + 20y)\mathbf{j}$

23. $f(x, y, z) = z - ye^{x^2}$

$f_x(x, y, z) = -2xye^{x^2}$

$f_y(x, y, z) = -e^{x^2}$

$f_z = 1$

$\mathbf{F}(x, y, z) = -2xye^{x^2}\mathbf{i} - e^{x^2}\mathbf{j} + \mathbf{k}$

25. $g(x, y, z) = xy \ln(x + y)$

$$g_x(x, y, z) = y \ln(x + y) + \frac{xy}{x + y}$$

$$g_y(x, y, z) = x \ln(x + y) + \frac{xy}{x + y}$$

$$g_z(x, y, z) = 0$$

$$\mathbf{G}(x, y, z) = \left[\frac{xy}{x + y} + y \ln(x + y) \right] \mathbf{i} + \left[\frac{xy}{x + y} + x \ln(x + y) \right] \mathbf{j}$$

27. $\mathbf{F}(x, y) = 12xy\mathbf{i} + 6(x^2 + y)\mathbf{j}$

$M = 12xy$ and $N = 6(x^2 + y)$ have continuous first partial derivatives.

$$\frac{\partial N}{\partial x} = 12x = \frac{\partial M}{\partial y} \implies \mathbf{F} \text{ is conservative.}$$

29. $\mathbf{F}(x, y) = \sin y\mathbf{i} + x \cos y\mathbf{j}$

$M = \sin y$ and $N = x \cos y$ have continuous first partial derivatives.

$$\frac{\partial N}{\partial x} = \cos y = \frac{\partial M}{\partial y} \implies \mathbf{F} \text{ is conservative.}$$

31. $M = 15y^3, N = -5xy^2$

$$\frac{\partial N}{\partial x} = -5y^2 \neq \frac{\partial M}{\partial y} = 45y^2 \implies \text{Not conservative}$$

33. $M = \frac{2}{y}e^{2x/y}, N = \frac{-2x}{y^2}e^{2x/y}$

$$\frac{\partial N}{\partial x} = \frac{-2(y + 2x)}{y^3}e^{2x/y} = \frac{\partial M}{\partial y} \implies \text{Conservative}$$

35. $\mathbf{F}(x, y) = 2xy\mathbf{i} + x^2\mathbf{j}$

$$\frac{\partial}{\partial y}[2xy] = 2x$$

$$\frac{\partial}{\partial x}[x^2] = 2x$$

Conservative

$$f_x(x, y) = 2xy$$

$$f_y(x, y) = x^2$$

$$f(x, y) = x^2y + K$$

37. $\mathbf{F}(x, y) = xe^{x^2y}(2y\mathbf{i} + x\mathbf{j})$

$$\frac{\partial}{\partial y}[2xye^{x^2y}] = 2xe^{x^2y} + 2x^3ye^{x^2y}$$

$$\frac{\partial}{\partial x}[x^2e^{x^2y}] = 2xe^{x^2y} + 2x^3ye^{x^2y}$$

Conservative

$$f_x(x, y) = 2xye^{x^2y}$$

$$f_y(x, y) = x^2e^{x^2y}$$

$$f(x, y) = e^{x^2y} + K$$

39. $\mathbf{F}(x, y) = \frac{x}{x^2 + y^2}\mathbf{i} + \frac{y}{x^2 + y^2}\mathbf{j}$

$$\frac{\partial}{\partial y}\left[\frac{x}{x^2 + y^2}\right] = -\frac{2xy}{(x^2 + y^2)^2}$$

$$\frac{\partial}{\partial x}\left[\frac{y}{x^2 + y^2}\right] = -\frac{2xy}{(x^2 + y^2)^2}$$

Conservative

$$f_x(x, y) = \frac{x}{x^2 + y^2}$$

$$f_y(x, y) = \frac{y}{x^2 + y^2}$$

$$f(x, y) = \frac{1}{2}\ln(x^2 + y^2) + K$$

41. $\mathbf{F}(x, y) = e^x(\cos y\mathbf{i} + \sin y\mathbf{j})$

$$\frac{\partial}{\partial y}[e^x \cos y] = -e^x \sin y$$

$$\frac{\partial}{\partial x}[e^x \sin y] = e^x \sin y$$

Not conservative

43. $\mathbf{F}(x, y, z) = xyz\mathbf{i} + y\mathbf{j} + z\mathbf{k}, \ (1, 2, 1)$

$$\text{curl } \mathbf{F} = \begin{vmatrix} \mathbf{i} & \mathbf{j} & \mathbf{k} \\ \dfrac{\partial}{\partial x} & \dfrac{\partial}{\partial y} & \dfrac{\partial}{\partial z} \\ xyz & y & z \end{vmatrix} = xy\mathbf{j} - xz\mathbf{k}$$

$$\text{curl } \mathbf{F}\,(1, 2, 1) = 2\mathbf{j} - \mathbf{k}$$

45. $\mathbf{F}(x, y, z) = e^x \sin y\mathbf{i} - e^x \cos y\mathbf{j}, \ (0, 0, 3)$

$$\text{curl } \mathbf{F} = \begin{vmatrix} \mathbf{i} & \mathbf{j} & \mathbf{k} \\ \dfrac{\partial}{\partial x} & \dfrac{\partial}{\partial y} & \dfrac{\partial}{\partial z} \\ e^x \sin y & -e^x \cos y & 0 \end{vmatrix} = -2e^x \cos y\mathbf{k}$$

$$\text{curl } \mathbf{F}\,(0, 0, 3) = -2\mathbf{k}$$

47. $\mathbf{F}(x, y, z) = \arctan\left(\dfrac{x}{y}\right)\mathbf{i} + \ln\sqrt{x^2 + y^2}\,\mathbf{j} + \mathbf{k}$

$$\text{curl } \mathbf{F} = \begin{vmatrix} \mathbf{i} & \mathbf{j} & \mathbf{k} \\ \dfrac{\partial}{\partial x} & \dfrac{\partial}{\partial y} & \dfrac{\partial}{\partial z} \\ \arctan\left(\dfrac{x}{y}\right) & \dfrac{1}{2}\ln(x^2 + y^2) & 1 \end{vmatrix} = \left[\dfrac{x}{x^2 + y^2} - \dfrac{(-x/y^2)}{1 + (x/y)^2}\right]\mathbf{k} = \dfrac{2x}{x^2 + y^2}\mathbf{k}$$

49. $\mathbf{F}(x, y, z) = \sin(x - y)\mathbf{i} + \sin(y - z)\mathbf{j} + \sin(z - x)\mathbf{k}$

$$\text{curl } \mathbf{F} = \begin{vmatrix} \mathbf{i} & \mathbf{j} & \mathbf{k} \\ \dfrac{\partial}{\partial x} & \dfrac{\partial}{\partial y} & \dfrac{\partial}{\partial z} \\ \sin(x - y) & \sin(y - z) & \sin(z - x) \end{vmatrix} = \cos(y - z)\mathbf{i} + \cos(z - x)\mathbf{j} + \cos(x - y)\mathbf{k}$$

51. $\mathbf{F}(x, y, z) = \sin y\,\mathbf{i} - x\cos y\,\mathbf{j} + \mathbf{k}$

$$\text{curl } \mathbf{F} = \begin{vmatrix} \mathbf{i} & \mathbf{j} & \mathbf{k} \\ \dfrac{\partial}{\partial x} & \dfrac{\partial}{\partial y} & \dfrac{\partial}{\partial z} \\ \sin y & -x\cos y & 1 \end{vmatrix} = -2\cos y\,\mathbf{k} \neq \mathbf{0}$$

Not conservative

53. $\mathbf{F}(x, y, z) = e^z(y\mathbf{i} + x\mathbf{j} + xy\mathbf{k})$

$$\text{curl } \mathbf{F} = \begin{vmatrix} \mathbf{i} & \mathbf{j} & \mathbf{k} \\ \dfrac{\partial}{\partial x} & \dfrac{\partial}{\partial y} & \dfrac{\partial}{\partial z} \\ ye^z & xe^z & xye^z \end{vmatrix} = \mathbf{0}$$

Conservative

$$f_x(x, y, z) = ye^z$$
$$f_y(x, y, z) = xe^z$$
$$f_z(x, y, z) = xye^z$$
$$f(x, y, z) = xye^z + K$$

55. $\mathbf{F}(x, y, z) = \dfrac{1}{y}\mathbf{i} - \dfrac{x}{y^2}\mathbf{j} + (2z - 1)\mathbf{k}$

$$\text{curl } \mathbf{F} = \begin{vmatrix} \mathbf{i} & \mathbf{j} & \mathbf{k} \\ \dfrac{\partial}{\partial x} & \dfrac{\partial}{\partial y} & \dfrac{\partial}{\partial z} \\ \dfrac{1}{y} & -\dfrac{x}{y^2} & 2z - 1 \end{vmatrix} = \mathbf{0}$$

Conservative

$$f_x(x, y, z) = \dfrac{1}{y}$$

$$f_y(x, y, z) = -\dfrac{x}{y^2}$$

$$f_z(x, y, z) = 2z - 1$$

$$f(x, y, z) = \int \dfrac{1}{y}\,dx = \dfrac{x}{y} + g(y, z) + K_1$$

$$f(x, y, z) = \int -\dfrac{x}{y^2}\,dy = \dfrac{x}{y} + h(x, z) + K_2$$

$$f(x, y, z) = \int (2z - 1)\,dz$$

$$= z^2 - z + p(x, y) + K_3$$

$$f(x, y, z) = \dfrac{x}{y} + z^2 - z + K$$

57. $\mathbf{F}(x, y) = 6x^2\mathbf{i} - xy^2\mathbf{j}$

$$\text{div } \mathbf{F}(x, y) = \dfrac{\partial}{\partial x}[6x^2] + \dfrac{\partial}{\partial y}[-xy^2]$$

$$= 12x - 2xy$$

59. $\mathbf{F}(x, y, z) = \sin x \, \mathbf{i} + \cos y \, \mathbf{j} + z^2 \mathbf{k}$

$\operatorname{div} \mathbf{F}(x, y, z) = \dfrac{\partial}{\partial x}[\sin x] + \dfrac{\partial}{\partial y}[\cos y] + \dfrac{\partial}{\partial z}[z^2] = \cos x - \sin y + 2z$

61. $\mathbf{F}(x, y, z) = xyz\mathbf{i} + y\mathbf{j} + z\mathbf{k}$

$\operatorname{div} \mathbf{F}(x, y, z) = yz + 1 + 1 = yz + 2$

$\operatorname{div} \mathbf{F}(1, 2, 1) = 4$

63. $\mathbf{F}(x, y, z) = e^x \sin y \, \mathbf{i} - e^x \cos y \, \mathbf{j}$

$\operatorname{div} \mathbf{F}(x, y, z) = e^x \sin y + e^x \sin y$

$\operatorname{div} \mathbf{F}(0, 0, 3) = 0$

65. See the definition, page 1008. Examples include velocity fields, gravitational fields and magnetic fields.

67. See the definition on page 1014.

69. $\mathbf{F}(x, y, z) = \mathbf{i} + 2x\mathbf{j} + 3y\mathbf{k}$

$\mathbf{G}(x, y, z) = x\mathbf{i} - y\mathbf{j} + z\mathbf{k}$

$\mathbf{F} \times \mathbf{G} \begin{vmatrix} \mathbf{i} & \mathbf{j} & \mathbf{k} \\ 1 & 2x & 3y \\ x & -y & z \end{vmatrix} = (2xz + 3y^2)\mathbf{i} - (z - 3xy)\mathbf{j} + (-y - 2x^2)\mathbf{k}$

$\operatorname{curl} (\mathbf{F} \times \mathbf{G}) = \begin{vmatrix} \mathbf{i} & \mathbf{j} & \mathbf{k} \\ \dfrac{\partial}{\partial x} & \dfrac{\partial}{\partial y} & \dfrac{\partial}{\partial z} \\ 2xz + 3y^2 & 3xy - z & -y - 2x^2 \end{vmatrix} = (-1 + 1)\mathbf{i} - (-4x - 2x)\mathbf{j} + (3y - 6y)\mathbf{k} = 6x\mathbf{j} - 3y\mathbf{k}$

71. $\mathbf{F}(x, y, z) = xyz\mathbf{i} + y\mathbf{j} + z\mathbf{k}$

$\operatorname{curl} \mathbf{F} = \begin{vmatrix} \mathbf{i} & \mathbf{j} & \mathbf{k} \\ \dfrac{\partial}{\partial x} & \dfrac{\partial}{\partial y} & \dfrac{\partial}{\partial z} \\ xyz & y & z \end{vmatrix} = xy\mathbf{j} - xz\mathbf{k}$

$\operatorname{curl}(\operatorname{curl} \mathbf{F}) = \begin{vmatrix} \mathbf{i} & \mathbf{j} & \mathbf{k} \\ \dfrac{\partial}{\partial x} & \dfrac{\partial}{\partial y} & \dfrac{\partial}{\partial z} \\ 0 & xy & -xz \end{vmatrix} = z\mathbf{j} + y\mathbf{k}$

73. $\mathbf{F}(x, y, z) = \mathbf{i} + 2x\mathbf{j} + 3y\mathbf{k}$

$\mathbf{G}(x, y, z) = x\mathbf{i} - y\mathbf{j} + z\mathbf{k}$

$\mathbf{F} \times \mathbf{G} = \begin{vmatrix} \mathbf{i} & \mathbf{j} & \mathbf{k} \\ 1 & 2x & 3y \\ x & -y & z \end{vmatrix}$

$= (2xz + 3y^2)\mathbf{i} - (z - 3xy)\mathbf{j} + (-y - 2x^2)\mathbf{k}$

$\operatorname{div}(\mathbf{F} \times \mathbf{G}) = 2z + 3x$

75. $\mathbf{F}(x, y, z) = xyz\mathbf{i} + y\mathbf{j} + z\mathbf{k}$

$\operatorname{curl} \mathbf{F} = \begin{vmatrix} \mathbf{i} & \mathbf{j} & \mathbf{k} \\ \dfrac{\partial}{\partial x} & \dfrac{\partial}{\partial y} & \dfrac{\partial}{\partial z} \\ xyz & y & z \end{vmatrix} = xy\mathbf{j} - xz\mathbf{k}$

$\operatorname{div}(\operatorname{curl} \mathbf{F}) = x - x = 0$

77. Let $\mathbf{F} = M\mathbf{i} + N\mathbf{j} + P\mathbf{k}$ and $\mathbf{G} = Q\mathbf{i} + R\mathbf{j} + S\mathbf{k}$ where M, N, P, Q, R, and S have continuous partial derivatives.

$\mathbf{F} + \mathbf{G} = (M + Q)\mathbf{i} + (N + R)\mathbf{j} + (P + S)\mathbf{k}$

$\operatorname{curl}(\mathbf{F} + \mathbf{G}) = \begin{vmatrix} \mathbf{i} & \mathbf{j} & \mathbf{k} \\ \dfrac{\partial}{\partial x} & \dfrac{\partial}{\partial y} & \dfrac{\partial}{\partial z} \\ M + Q & N + R & P + S \end{vmatrix}$

$= \left[\dfrac{\partial}{\partial y}(P + S) - \dfrac{\partial}{\partial z}(N + R)\right]\mathbf{i} - \left[\dfrac{\partial}{\partial x}(P + S) - \dfrac{\partial}{\partial z}(M + Q)\right]\mathbf{j} + \left[\dfrac{\partial}{\partial x}(N + R) - \dfrac{\partial}{\partial y}(M + Q)\right]\mathbf{k}$

$= \left(\dfrac{\partial P}{\partial y} - \dfrac{\partial N}{\partial z}\right)\mathbf{i} - \left(\dfrac{\partial P}{\partial x} - \dfrac{\partial M}{\partial z}\right)\mathbf{j} + \left(\dfrac{\partial N}{\partial x} - \dfrac{\partial M}{\partial y}\right)\mathbf{k} + \left(\dfrac{\partial S}{\partial y} - \dfrac{\partial R}{\partial z}\right)\mathbf{i} - \left(\dfrac{\partial S}{\partial x} - \dfrac{\partial Q}{\partial z}\right)\mathbf{j} + \left(\dfrac{\partial R}{\partial x} - \dfrac{\partial Q}{\partial y}\right)\mathbf{k}$

$= \operatorname{curl} \mathbf{F} + \operatorname{curl} \mathbf{G}$

79. Let $\mathbf{F} = M\mathbf{i} + N\mathbf{j} + P\mathbf{k}$ and $\mathbf{G} = R\mathbf{i} + S\mathbf{j} + T\mathbf{k}$.

$$\text{div}(\mathbf{F} + \mathbf{G}) = \frac{\partial}{\partial x}(M + R) + \frac{\partial}{\partial y}(N + S) + \frac{\partial}{\partial z}(P + T) = \frac{\partial M}{\partial x} + \frac{\partial R}{\partial x} + \frac{\partial N}{\partial y} + \frac{\partial S}{\partial y} + \frac{\partial P}{\partial z} + \frac{\partial T}{\partial z}$$

$$= \left[\frac{\partial M}{\partial x} + \frac{\partial N}{\partial y} + \frac{\partial P}{\partial z} \right] + \left[\frac{\partial R}{\partial x} + \frac{\partial S}{\partial y} + \frac{\partial T}{\partial z} \right]$$

$$= \text{div}\,\mathbf{F} + \text{div}\,\mathbf{G}$$

81. $\mathbf{F} = M\mathbf{i} + N\mathbf{j} + P\mathbf{k}$

$$\nabla \times [\nabla f + (\nabla \times \mathbf{F})] = \mathbf{curl}(\nabla f + (\nabla \times \mathbf{F}))$$

$$= \mathbf{curl}(\nabla f) + \mathbf{curl}(\nabla \times \mathbf{F}) \quad \text{(Exercise 77)}$$

$$= \mathbf{curl}(\nabla \times \mathbf{F}) \quad \text{(Exercise 78)}$$

$$= \nabla \times (\nabla \times \mathbf{F})$$

83. Let $\mathbf{F} = M\mathbf{i} + N\mathbf{j} + P\mathbf{k}$, then $f\mathbf{F} = fM\mathbf{i} + fN\mathbf{j} + fP\mathbf{k}$.

$$\text{div}(f\mathbf{F}) = \frac{\partial}{\partial x}(fM) + \frac{\partial}{\partial y}(fN) + \frac{\partial}{\partial z}(fP) = f\frac{\partial M}{\partial x} + M\frac{\partial f}{\partial x} + f\frac{\partial N}{\partial y} + N\frac{\partial f}{\partial y} + f\frac{\partial P}{\partial z} + P\frac{\partial f}{\partial z}$$

$$= f\left(\frac{\partial M}{\partial x} + \frac{\partial N}{\partial y} + \frac{\partial N}{\partial z} \right) + \left(\frac{\partial f}{\partial x}M + \frac{\partial f}{\partial y}N + \frac{\partial f}{\partial z}P \right)$$

$$= f\,\text{div}\,\mathbf{F} + \nabla f \cdot \mathbf{F}$$

In Exercises 85 and 87, $\mathbf{F}(x, y, z) = x\mathbf{i} + y\mathbf{j} + z\mathbf{k}$ and $f(x, y, z) = \|\mathbf{F}(x, y, z)\| = \sqrt{x^2 + y^2 + z^2}$.

85. $\quad \ln f = \frac{1}{2}\ln(x^2 + y^2 + z^2)$

$$\nabla(\ln f) = \frac{x}{x^2 + y^2 + z^2}\mathbf{i} + \frac{y}{x^2 + y^2 + z^2}\mathbf{j} + \frac{z}{x^2 + y^2 + z^2}\mathbf{k} = \frac{x\mathbf{i} + y\mathbf{j} + z\mathbf{k}}{x^2 + y^2 + z^2} = \frac{\mathbf{F}}{f^2}$$

87. $f^n = \left(\sqrt{x^2 + y^2 + z^2} \right)^n$

$$\nabla f^n = n\left(\sqrt{x^2 + y^2 + z^2} \right)^{n-1} \frac{x}{\sqrt{x^2 + y^2 + z^2}}\mathbf{i} + n\left(\sqrt{x^2 + y^2 + z^2} \right)^{n-1} \frac{y}{\sqrt{x^2 + y^2 + z^2}}\mathbf{j}$$

$$+ n\left(\sqrt{x^2 + y^2 + z^2} \right)^{n-1} \frac{z}{\sqrt{x^2 + y^2 + z^2}}\mathbf{k}$$

$$= n\left(\sqrt{x^2 + y^2 + z^2} \right)^{n-2}(x\mathbf{i} + y\mathbf{j} + z\mathbf{k}) = nf^{n-2}\mathbf{F}$$

89. The winds are stronger over Phoenix. Although the winds over both cities are northeasterly, they are more towards the east over Atlanta.

Section 14.2   Line Integrals

1. $x^2 + y^2 = 9$

$\dfrac{x^2}{9} + \dfrac{y^2}{9} = 1$

$\cos^2 t + \sin^2 t = 1$

$\cos^2 t = \dfrac{x^2}{9}$

$\sin^2 t = \dfrac{y^2}{9}$

$x = 3\cos t$

$y = 3\sin t$

$\mathbf{r}(t) = 3\cos t\,\mathbf{i} + 3\sin t\,\mathbf{j}$

$0 \le t \le 2\pi$

3. $\mathbf{r}(t) = \begin{cases} t\mathbf{i}, & 0 \le t \le 3 \\ 3\mathbf{i} + (t-3)\mathbf{j}, & 3 \le t \le 6 \\ (9-t)\mathbf{i} + 3\mathbf{j}, & 6 \le t \le 9 \\ (12-t)\mathbf{j}, & 9 \le t \le 12 \end{cases}$

5. $\mathbf{r}(t) = \begin{cases} t\mathbf{i} + \sqrt{t}\,\mathbf{j}, & 0 \le t \le 1 \\ (2-t)\mathbf{i} + (2-t)\mathbf{j}, & 1 \le t \le 2 \end{cases}$

7. $\mathbf{r}(t) = 4t\mathbf{i} + 3t\mathbf{j},\ 0 \le t \le 2;\ \mathbf{r}'(t) = 4\mathbf{i} + 3\mathbf{j}$

$\displaystyle\int_C (x - y)\,ds = \int_0^2 (4t - 3t)\sqrt{(4)^2 + (3)^2}\,dt = \int_0^2 5t\,dt = \left[\dfrac{5t^2}{2}\right]_0^2 = 10$

9. $\mathbf{r}(t) = \sin t\,\mathbf{i} + \cos t\,\mathbf{j} + 8t\mathbf{k},\ 0 \le t \le \dfrac{\pi}{2};\ \mathbf{r}'(t) = \cos t\,\mathbf{i} - \sin t\,\mathbf{j} + 8\mathbf{k}$

$\displaystyle\int_C (x^2 + y^2 + z^2)\,ds = \int_0^{\pi/2} (\sin^2 t + \cos^2 t + 64t^2)\sqrt{(\cos t)^2 + (-\sin t)^2 + 64}\,dt$

$\displaystyle = \int_0^{\pi/2} \sqrt{65}(1 + 64t^2)\,dt = \left[\sqrt{65}\left(t + \dfrac{64t^3}{3}\right)\right]_0^{\pi/2} = \sqrt{65}\left(\dfrac{\pi}{2} + \dfrac{8\pi^3}{3}\right) = \dfrac{\sqrt{65}\,\pi}{6}(3 + 16\pi^2)$

11. $\mathbf{r}(t) = t\mathbf{i},\ 0 \le t \le 3$

$\displaystyle\int_C (x^2 + y^2)\,ds = \int_0^3 [t^2 + 0^2]\sqrt{1 + 0}\,dt$

$\displaystyle = \int_0^3 t^2\,dt$

$\displaystyle = \left[\dfrac{1}{3}t^3\right]_0^3 = 9$

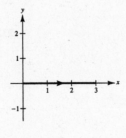

13. $\mathbf{r}(t) = \cos t\,\mathbf{i} + \sin t\,\mathbf{j},\ 0 \le t \le \dfrac{\pi}{2}$

$\displaystyle\int_C (x^2 + y^2)\,ds = \int_0^{\pi/2} [\cos^2 t + \sin^2 t]\sqrt{(-\sin t)^2 + (\cos t)^2}\,dt$

$\displaystyle = \int_0^{\pi/2} dt = \dfrac{\pi}{2}$

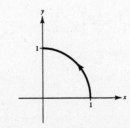

15. $\mathbf{r}(t) = t\mathbf{i} + t\mathbf{j}, \ 0 \leq t \leq 1$

$$\int_C \left(x + 4\sqrt{y}\right) ds = \int_0^1 \left(t + 4\sqrt{t}\right)\sqrt{1 + 1} \, dt$$

$$= \left[\sqrt{2}\left(\frac{t^2}{2} + \frac{8}{3}t^{3/2}\right)\right]_0^1 = \frac{19\sqrt{2}}{6}$$

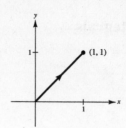

17. $\mathbf{r}(t) = \begin{cases} t\mathbf{i}, & 0 \leq t \leq 1 \\ (2-t)\mathbf{i} + (t-1)\mathbf{j}, & 1 \leq t \leq 2 \\ (3-t)\mathbf{j}, & 2 \leq t \leq 3 \end{cases}$

$$\int_{C_1} \left(x + 4\sqrt{y}\right) ds = \int_0^1 t \, dt = \frac{1}{2}$$

$$\int_{C_2} \left(x + 4\sqrt{y}\right) ds = \int_1^2 \left[(2-t) + 4\sqrt{t-1}\right]\sqrt{1+1} \, dt$$

$$= \sqrt{2}\left[2t - \frac{t^2}{2} + \frac{8}{3}(t-1)^{3/2}\right]_1^2 = \frac{19\sqrt{2}}{6}$$

$$\int_{C_3} \left(x + 4\sqrt{y}\right) ds = \int_2^3 4\sqrt{3-t} \, dt = \left[-\frac{8}{3}(3-t)^{3/2}\right]_2^3 = \frac{8}{3}$$

$$\int_C \left(x + 4\sqrt{y}\right) ds = \frac{1}{2} + \frac{19\sqrt{2}}{6} + \frac{8}{3} = \frac{19 + 19\sqrt{2}}{6} = \frac{19\left(1 + \sqrt{2}\right)}{6}$$

19. $\rho(x, y, z) = \frac{1}{2}(x^2 + y^2 + z^2)$

$\mathbf{r}(t) = 3\cos t\mathbf{i} + 3\sin t\mathbf{j} + 2t\mathbf{k}, \ 0 \leq t \leq 4\pi$

$\mathbf{r}'(t) = -3\sin t\mathbf{i} + 3\cos t\mathbf{j} + 2\mathbf{k}$

$\|\mathbf{r}'(t)\| = \sqrt{(-3\sin t)^2 + (3\cos t)^2 + (2)^2} = \sqrt{13}$

$$\text{Mass} = \int_C \rho(x, y, z) \, ds = \int_0^{4\pi} \frac{1}{2}\left[(3\cos t)^2 + (3\sin t)^2 + (2t)^2\right]\sqrt{13} \, dt$$

$$= \frac{\sqrt{13}}{2}\int_0^{4\pi} (9 + 4t^2) \, dt = \left[\frac{\sqrt{13}}{2}\left(9t + \frac{4t^3}{3}\right)\right]_0^{4\pi}$$

$$= \frac{2\sqrt{13}\pi}{3}(27 + 64\pi^2) \approx 4973.8$$

21. $\mathbf{F}(x, y) = xy\mathbf{i} + y\mathbf{j}$

$C: \mathbf{r}(t) = 4t\mathbf{i} + t\mathbf{j}, \ 0 \leq t \leq 1$

$\mathbf{F}(t) = 4t^2\mathbf{i} + t\mathbf{j}$

$\mathbf{r}'(t) = 4\mathbf{i} + \mathbf{j}$

$$\int_C \mathbf{F} \cdot d\mathbf{r} = \int_0^1 (16t^2 + t) \, dt$$

$$= \left[\frac{16}{3}t^3 + \frac{1}{2}t^2\right]_0^1 = \frac{35}{6}$$

23. $\mathbf{F}(x, y) = 3x\mathbf{i} + 4y\mathbf{i}$

$C: \mathbf{r}(t) = 2\cos t\mathbf{i} + 2\sin t\mathbf{j}, \ 0 \leq t \leq \frac{\pi}{2}$

$\mathbf{F}(t) = 6\cos t\mathbf{i} + 8\sin t\mathbf{j}$

$\mathbf{r}'(t) = -2\sin t\mathbf{i} + 2\cos t\mathbf{j}$

$$\int_C \mathbf{F} \cdot d\mathbf{r} = \int_0^{\pi/2} (-12\sin t\cos t + 16\sin t\cos t) \, dt$$

$$= \left[2\sin^2 t\right]_0^{\pi/2} = 2$$

25. $\mathbf{F}(x, y, z) = x^2 y\mathbf{i} + (x - z)\mathbf{j} + xyz\mathbf{k}$

$C:\ \mathbf{r}(t) = t\mathbf{i} + t^2\mathbf{j} + 2\mathbf{k},\ 0 \le t \le 1$

$\mathbf{F}(t) = t^4\mathbf{i} + (t - 2)\mathbf{j} + 2t^3\mathbf{k}$

$\mathbf{r}'(t) = \mathbf{i} + 2t\mathbf{j}$

$$\int_C \mathbf{F} \cdot d\mathbf{r} = \int_0^1 \left[t^4 + 2t(t - 2)\right] dt$$

$$= \left[\frac{t^5}{5} + \frac{2t^3}{3} - 2t^2\right]_0^1 = -\frac{17}{15}$$

27. $\mathbf{F}(x, y, z) = x^2 z\mathbf{i} + 6y\mathbf{j} + yz^2\mathbf{k}$

$\mathbf{r}(t) = t\mathbf{i} + t^2\mathbf{j} + \ln t\mathbf{k},\ 1 \le t \le 3$

$\mathbf{F}(t) = t^2 \ln t\mathbf{i} + 6t^2\mathbf{j} + t^2 \ln^2 t\mathbf{k}$

$d\mathbf{r} = \left(\mathbf{i} + 2t\mathbf{j} + \frac{1}{t}\mathbf{k}\right) dt$

$$\int_C \mathbf{F} \cdot d\mathbf{r} = \int_1^3 \left[t^2 \ln t + 12t^3 + t(\ln t)^2\right] dt$$

$$\approx 249.49$$

29. $\mathbf{F}(x, y) = -x\mathbf{i} - 2y\mathbf{j}$

$C:\ y = x^3$ from $(0, 0)$ to $(2, 8)$

$\mathbf{r}(t) = t\mathbf{i} + t^3\mathbf{j},\ 0 \le t \le 2$

$\mathbf{r}'(t) = \mathbf{i} + 3t^2\mathbf{j}$

$\mathbf{F}(t) = -t\mathbf{i} - 2t^3\mathbf{j}$

$\mathbf{F} \cdot \mathbf{r}' = -t - 6t^5$

$\text{Work} = \displaystyle\int_C \mathbf{F} \cdot d\mathbf{r} = \int_0^2 (-t - 6t^5)\, dt = \left[-\frac{1}{2}t^2 - t^6\right]_0^2 = -66$

31. $\mathbf{F}(x, y) = 2x\mathbf{i} + y\mathbf{j}$

$C:$ counterclockwise around the triangle whose vertices are $(0, 0)$, $(1, 0)$, $(1, 1)$

$\mathbf{r}(t) = \begin{cases} t\mathbf{i}, & 0 \le t \le 1 \\ \mathbf{i} + (t - 1)\mathbf{j}, & 1 \le t \le 2 \\ (3 - t)\mathbf{i} + (3 - t)\mathbf{j}, & 2 \le t \le 3 \end{cases}$

On C_1: $\mathbf{F}(t) = 2t\mathbf{i},\ \mathbf{r}'(t) = \mathbf{i}$

$\text{Work} = \displaystyle\int_{C_1} \mathbf{F} \cdot d\mathbf{r} = \int_0^1 2t\, dt = 1$

On C_2: $\mathbf{F}(t) = 2\mathbf{i} + (t - 1)\mathbf{j},\ \mathbf{r}'(t) = \mathbf{j}$

$\text{Work} = \displaystyle\int_{C_2} \mathbf{F} \cdot d\mathbf{r} = \int_1^2 (t - 1)\, dt = \frac{1}{2}$

On C_3: $\mathbf{F}(t) = 2(3 - t)\mathbf{i} + (3 - t)\mathbf{j},\ \mathbf{r}'(t) = -\mathbf{i} - \mathbf{j}$

$\text{Work} = \displaystyle\int_{C_3} \mathbf{F} \cdot d\mathbf{r} = \int_2^3 \left[-2(3 - t) - (3 - t)\right] dt = -\frac{3}{2}$

$\text{Total work} = \displaystyle\int_C \mathbf{F} \cdot d\mathbf{r} = 1 + \frac{1}{2} - \frac{3}{2} = 0$

33. $\mathbf{F}(x, y, z) = x\mathbf{i} + y\mathbf{j} - 5z\mathbf{k}$

$C:\ \mathbf{r}(t) = 2\cos t\mathbf{i} + 2\sin t\mathbf{j} + t\mathbf{k},\ 0 \le t \le 2\pi$

$\mathbf{r}'(t) = -2\sin t\mathbf{i} + 2\cos t\mathbf{j} + \mathbf{k}$

$\mathbf{F}(t) = 2\cos t\mathbf{i} + 2\sin t\mathbf{j} - 5t\mathbf{k}$

$\mathbf{F} \cdot \mathbf{r}' = -5t$

$\text{Work} = \displaystyle\int_C \mathbf{F} \cdot d\mathbf{r} = \int_0^{2\pi} -5t\, dt = -10\pi^2$

35. $\mathbf{r}(t) = 3\sin t\mathbf{i} + 3\cos t\mathbf{j} + \dfrac{10}{2\pi}t\mathbf{k},\ 0 \le t \le 2\pi$

$\mathbf{F} = 150\mathbf{k}$

$d\mathbf{r} = \left(3\cos t\mathbf{i} - 3\sin t\mathbf{j} + \frac{10}{2\pi}\mathbf{k}\right) dt$

$$\int_C \mathbf{F} \cdot d\mathbf{r} = \int_0^{2\pi} \frac{1500}{2\pi}\, dt = \left[\frac{1500}{2\pi}t\right]_0^{2\pi} = 1500 \text{ ft} \cdot \text{lb}$$

37. $\mathbf{F}(x, y) = x^2\mathbf{i} + xy\mathbf{j}$

(a) $\mathbf{r}_1(t) = 2t\mathbf{i} + (t-1)\mathbf{j}, 1 \le t \le 3$

$\mathbf{r}_1{}'(t) = 2\mathbf{i} + \mathbf{j}$

$\mathbf{F}(t) = 4t^2\mathbf{i} + 2t(t-1)\mathbf{j}$

$\displaystyle\int_{C_1}\mathbf{F}\cdot d\mathbf{r} = \int_1^3 (8t^2 + 2t(t-1))\, dt = \frac{236}{3}$

Both paths join $(2, 0)$ and $(6, 2)$. The integrals are negatives of each other because the orientations are different.

(b) $\mathbf{r}_2(t) = 2(3-t)\mathbf{i} + (2-t)\mathbf{j}, 0 \le t \le 2$

$\mathbf{r}_2{}'(t) = -2\mathbf{i} - \mathbf{j}$

$\mathbf{F}(t) = 4(3-t)^2\mathbf{i} + 2(3-t)(2-t)\mathbf{j}$

$\displaystyle\int_{C_2}\mathbf{F}\cdot d\mathbf{r} = \int_0^2 [-8(3-t)^2 - 2(3-t)(2-t)]\, dt$

$= -\dfrac{236}{3}$

39. $\mathbf{F}(x, y) = y\mathbf{i} - x\mathbf{j}$

$C:\ \mathbf{r}(t) = t\mathbf{i} - 2t\mathbf{j}$

$\mathbf{r}'(t) = \mathbf{i} - 2\mathbf{j}$

$\mathbf{F}(t) = -2t\mathbf{i} - t\mathbf{j}$

$\mathbf{F}\cdot\mathbf{r}' = -2t + 2t = 0$

Thus, $\displaystyle\int_C \mathbf{F}\cdot d\mathbf{r} = 0.$

41. $\mathbf{F}(x, y) = (x^3 - 2x^2)\mathbf{i} + \left(x - \dfrac{y}{2}\right)\mathbf{j}$

$C:\ \mathbf{r}(t) = t\mathbf{i} + t^2\mathbf{j}$

$\mathbf{r}'(t) = \mathbf{i} + 2t\mathbf{j}$

$\mathbf{F}(t) = (t^3 - 2t^2)\mathbf{i} + \left(t - \dfrac{t^2}{2}\right)\mathbf{j}$

$\mathbf{F}\cdot\mathbf{r}' = (t^3 - 2t^2) + 2t\left(t - \dfrac{t^2}{2}\right) = 0$

Thus, $\displaystyle\int_C \mathbf{F}\cdot d\mathbf{r} = 0.$

43. $x = 2t,\ y = 10t,\ 0 \le t \le 1 \implies y = 5x$ or $x = \dfrac{y}{5},\ 0 \le y \le 10$

$\displaystyle\int_C (x + 3y^2)\, dy = \int_0^{10}\left(\frac{y}{5} + 3y^2\right)dy = \left[\frac{y^2}{10} + y^3\right]_0^{10} = 1010$

45. $x = 2t,\ y = 10t,\ 0 \le t \le 1 \implies x = \dfrac{y}{5},\ 0 \le y \le 10,\ dx = \dfrac{1}{5}\, dy$

$\displaystyle\int_C xy\, dx + y\, dy = \int_0^{10}\left(\frac{y^2}{25} + y\right)dy = \left[\frac{y^3}{75} + \frac{y^2}{2}\right]_0^{10} = \frac{190}{3}$ **OR**

$y = 5x,\ dy = 5\, dx,\ 0 \le x \le 2$

$\displaystyle\int_C xy\, dx + y\, dy = \int_0^2 (5x^2 + 25x)\, dx = \left[\frac{5x^3}{3} + \frac{25x^2}{2}\right]_0^2 = \frac{190}{3}$

47. $\mathbf{r}(t) = t\mathbf{i},\ 0 \le t \le 5$

$x(t) = t,\ \ y(t) = 0$

$dx = dt,\ \ dy = 0$

$\displaystyle\int_C (2x - y)\, dx + (x + 3y)\, dy = \int_0^5 2t\, dt = 25$

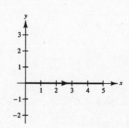

49. $\mathbf{r}(t) = \begin{cases} t\mathbf{i}, & 0 \le t \le 3 \\ 3\mathbf{i} + (t-3)\mathbf{j}, & 3 \le t \le 6 \end{cases}$

C_1: $x(t) = t,\ y(t) = 0,$

     $dx = dt,\ dy = 0$

$$\int_{C_1} (2x - y)\,dx + (x + 3y)\,dy = \int_0^3 2t\,dt = 9$$

C_2: $x(t) = 3,\ y(t) = t - 3$

     $dx = 0,\ dy = dt$

$$\int_{C_2} (2x - y)\,dx + (x + 3y)\,dy = \int_3^6 [3 + 3(t-3)]\,dt = \left[\frac{3t^2}{2} - 6t\right]_3^6 = \frac{45}{2}$$

$$\int_C (2x - y)\,dx + (x + 3y)\,dy = 9 + \frac{45}{2} = \frac{63}{2}$$

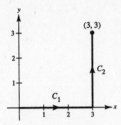

51. $x(t) = t,\ y(t) = 1 - t^2,\ 0 \le t \le 1,\ dx = dt,\ dy = -2t\,dt$

$$\int_C (2x - y)\,dx + (x + 3y)\,dy = \int_0^1 \left[(2t - 1 + t^2) + (t + 3 - 3t^2)(-2t)\right]dt$$

$$= \int_0^1 (6t^3 - t^2 - 4t - 1)\,dt = \left[\frac{3t^4}{2} - \frac{t^3}{3} - 2t^2 - t\right]_0^1 = -\frac{11}{6}$$

53. $x(t) = t,\ y(t) = 2t^2,\ 0 \le t \le 2$

   $dx = dt,\ dy = 4t\,dt$

$$\int_C (2x - y)\,dx + (x + 3y)\,dy = \int_0^2 (2t - 2t^2)\,dt + (t + 6t^2)4t\,dt$$

$$= \int_0^2 (24t^3 + 2t^2 + 2t)\,dt = \left[6t^4 + \frac{2}{3}t^3 + t^2\right]_0^2 = \frac{316}{3}$$

55. $f(x, y) = h$

   C: line from $(0, 0)$ to $(3, 4)$

     $\mathbf{r} = 3t\mathbf{i} + 4t\mathbf{j},\ 0 \le t \le 1$

     $\mathbf{r}'(t) = 3\mathbf{i} + 4\mathbf{j}$

     $\|\mathbf{r}'(t)\| = 5$

   Lateral surface area:

$$\int_C f(x, y)\,ds = \int_0^1 5h\,dt = 5h$$

57. $f(x, y) = xy$

   C: $x^2 + y^2 = 1$ from $(1, 0)$ to $(0, 1)$

     $\mathbf{r}(t) = \cos t\mathbf{i} + \sin t\mathbf{j},\ 0 \le t \le \dfrac{\pi}{2}$

     $\mathbf{r}'(t) = -\sin t\mathbf{i} + \cos t\mathbf{j}$

     $\|\mathbf{r}'(t)\| = 1$

   Lateral surface area:

$$\int_C f(x, y)\,ds = \int_0^{\pi/2} \cos t \sin t\,dt$$

$$= \left[\frac{\sin^2 t}{2}\right]_0^{\pi/2} = \frac{1}{2}$$

59. $f(x, y) = h$

  $C:$ $y = 1 - x^2$ from $(1, 0)$ to $(0, 1)$

$$\mathbf{r}(t) = (1 - t)\mathbf{i} + [1 - (1 - t)^2]\mathbf{j}, \ 0 \le t \le 1$$

$$\mathbf{r}'(t) = -\mathbf{i} + 2(1 - t)\mathbf{j}$$

$$\|\mathbf{r}'(t)\| = \sqrt{1 + 4(1 - t)^2}$$

Lateral surface area:

$$\int_C f(x, y)\, ds = \int_0^1 h\sqrt{1 + 4(1 - t)^2}\, dt$$

$$= -\frac{h}{4}\Big[2(1 - t)\sqrt{1 + 4(1 - t)^2} + \ln|2(1 - t) + \sqrt{1 + 4(1 - t)^2}|\Big]_0^1$$

$$= \frac{h}{4}\big[2\sqrt{5} + \ln(2 + \sqrt{5})\big] \approx 1.4789h$$

61. $f(x, y) = xy$

  $C:$ $y = 1 - x^2$ from $(1, 0)$ to $(0, 1)$

You could parameterize the curve C as in Exercises 59 and 60. Alternatively, let $x = \cos t$, then:

$$y = 1 - \cos^2 t = \sin^2 t$$

$$\mathbf{r}(t) = \cos t\mathbf{i} + \sin^2 t\mathbf{j}, \ 0 \le t \le \frac{\pi}{2}$$

$$\mathbf{r}'(t) = -\sin t\mathbf{i} + 2 \sin t \cos t\mathbf{j}$$

$$\|\mathbf{r}'(t)\| = \sqrt{\sin^2 t + 4 \sin^2 t \cos^2 t} = \sin t\sqrt{1 + 4 \cos^2 t}$$

Lateral surface area:

$$\int_C f(x, y)\, ds = \int_0^{\pi/2} \cos t \sin^2 t\big(\sin t\sqrt{1 + 4 \cos^2 t}\big)\, dt = \int_0^{\pi/2} \sin^2 t[(1 + 4 \cos^2 t)^{1/2} \sin t \cos t]\, dt$$

Let $u = \sin^2 t$ and $dv = (1 + 4 \cos^2 t)^{1/2} \sin t \cos t$, then $du = 2 \sin t \cos t\, dt$ and $v = -\frac{1}{12}(1 + 4 \cos^2 t)^{3/2}$.

$$\int_C f(x, y)\, ds = \Big[-\frac{1}{12} \sin^2 t(1 + 4 \cos^2 t)^{3/2}\Big]_0^{\pi/2} + \frac{1}{6}\int_0^{\pi/2} (1 + 4 \cos^2 t)^{3/2} \sin t \cos t\, dt$$

$$= \Big[-\frac{1}{12} \sin^2 t(1 + 4 \cos^2 t)^{3/2} - \frac{1}{120}(1 + 4 \cos^2 t)^{5/2}\Big]_0^{\pi/2}$$

$$= \Big(-\frac{1}{12} - \frac{1}{120}\Big) + \frac{1}{120}(5)^{5/2} = \frac{1}{120}\big(25\sqrt{5} - 11\big) \approx 0.3742$$

63. (a) $f(x, y) = 1 + y^2$

$$\mathbf{r}(t) = 2 \cos t\mathbf{i} + 2 \sin t\mathbf{j}, \ 0 \le t \le 2\pi$$

$$\mathbf{r}'(t) = -2 \sin t\mathbf{i} + 2 \cos t\mathbf{j}$$

$$\|\mathbf{r}'(t)\| = 2$$

$$S = \int_C f(x, y)\, ds = \int_0^{2\pi} (1 + 4 \sin^2 t)(2)\, dt$$

$$= \Big[2t + 4(t - \sin t \cos t)\Big]_0^{2\pi} = 12\pi \approx 37.70 \ \text{cm}^2$$

(c)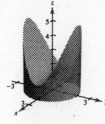

(b) $0.2(12\pi) = \dfrac{12\pi}{5} \approx 7.54 \ \text{cm}^3$

65. $S \approx 25$

Matches b

67. (a) Graph of: $\mathbf{r}(t) = 3 \cos t\mathbf{i} + 3 \sin t\mathbf{j} + (1 + \sin^2 2t)\mathbf{k}$ $0 \le t \le 2\pi$

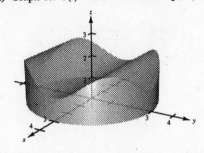

(b) Consider the portion of the surface in the first quadrant. The curve $z = 1 + \sin^2 2t$ is over the curve $\mathbf{r}_1(t) = 3 \cos t\mathbf{i} + 3 \sin t\mathbf{j}$, $0 \le t \le \pi/2$. Hence, the total lateral surface area is

$$4 \int_C f(x, y) \, ds = 4 \int_0^{\pi/2} (1 + \sin^2 2t)3 \, dt = 12\left(\frac{3\pi}{4}\right) = 9\pi \text{ sq. cm}$$

(c) The cross sections parallel to the xz-plane are rectangles of height $1 + 4(y/3)^2(1 - y^2/9)$ and base $2\sqrt{9 - y^2}$. Hence,

$$\text{Volume} = 2 \int_0^3 2\sqrt{9 - y^2}\left(1 + 4\frac{y^2}{9}\left(1 - \frac{y^2}{9}\right)\right) dy \approx 42.412 \text{ cm}^3$$

69. See the definition of Line Integral, page 1020.

See Theorem 14.4.

71. The greater the height of the surface over the curve, the greater the lateral surface area. Hence,

$$z_3 < z_1 < z_2 < z_4.$$

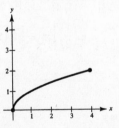

73. False

$$\int_C xy \, ds = \sqrt{2} \int_0^1 t^2 \, dt$$

75. False, the orientations are different.

Section 14.3 Conservative Vector Fields and Independence of Path

1. $\mathbf{F}(x, y) = x^2\mathbf{i} + xy\mathbf{j}$

(a) $\mathbf{r}_1(t) = t\mathbf{i} + t^2\mathbf{j}, \ 0 \le t \le 1$

$\mathbf{r}_1'(t) = \mathbf{i} + 2t\mathbf{j}$

$\mathbf{F}(t) = t^2\mathbf{i} + t^3\mathbf{j}$

$\displaystyle\int_C \mathbf{F} \cdot d\mathbf{r} = \int_0^1 (t^2 + 2t^4)\, dt = \frac{11}{15}$

(b) $\mathbf{r}_2(\theta) = \sin\theta\mathbf{i} + \sin^2\theta\mathbf{j}, \ 0 \le \theta \le \dfrac{\pi}{2}$

$\mathbf{r}_2'(\theta) = \cos\theta\mathbf{i} + 2\sin\theta\cos\theta\mathbf{j}$

$\mathbf{F}(t) = \sin^2\theta\mathbf{i} + \sin^3\theta\mathbf{j}$

$\displaystyle\int_C \mathbf{F} \cdot d\mathbf{r} = \int_0^{\pi/2} (\sin^2\theta\cos\theta + 2\sin^4\theta\cos\theta)\, d\theta$

$\displaystyle = \left[\frac{\sin^3\theta}{3} + \frac{2\sin^5\theta}{5}\right]_0^{\pi/2} = \frac{11}{15}$

3. $\mathbf{F}(x, y) = y\mathbf{i} - x\mathbf{j}$

(a) $\mathbf{r}_1(\theta) = \sec\theta\mathbf{i} + \tan\theta\mathbf{j}, \ 0 \le \theta \le \dfrac{\pi}{3}$

$\mathbf{r}_1'(\theta) = \sec\theta\tan\theta\mathbf{i} + \sec^2\theta\mathbf{j}$

$\mathbf{F}(\theta) = \tan\theta\mathbf{i} - \sec\theta\mathbf{j}$

$\displaystyle\int_C \mathbf{F} \cdot d\mathbf{r} = \int_0^{\pi/3} (\sec\theta\tan^2\theta - \sec^3\theta)\, d\theta = \int_0^{\pi/3} [\sec\theta(\sec^2\theta - 1) - \sec^3\theta]\, d\theta$

$\displaystyle = -\int_0^{\pi/3} \sec\theta\, d\theta = \left[-\ln|\sec\theta + \tan\theta|\right]_0^{\pi/3} = -\ln(2 + \sqrt{3}) \approx -1.317$

(b) $\mathbf{r}_2(t) = \sqrt{t + 1}\,\mathbf{i} + \sqrt{t}\,\mathbf{j}, \quad 0 \le t \le 3$

$\mathbf{r}_2'(t) = \dfrac{1}{2\sqrt{t + 1}}\mathbf{i} + \dfrac{1}{2\sqrt{t}}\mathbf{j}$

$\mathbf{F}(t) = \sqrt{t}\,\mathbf{i} - \sqrt{t + 1}\,\mathbf{j}$

$\displaystyle\int_C \mathbf{F} \cdot d\mathbf{r} = \int_0^3 \left[\frac{\sqrt{t}}{2\sqrt{t + 1}} - \frac{\sqrt{t + 1}}{2\sqrt{t}}\right] dt = -\frac{1}{2}\int_0^3 \frac{1}{\sqrt{t}\sqrt{t + 1}}\, dt = -\frac{1}{2}\int_0^3 \frac{1}{\sqrt{t^2 + t + (1/4) - (1/4)}}\, dt$

$\displaystyle = -\frac{1}{2}\int_0^3 \frac{1}{\sqrt{[t + (1/2)]^2 - (1/4)}}\, dt = \left[-\frac{1}{2}\ln\left|\left(t + \frac{1}{2}\right) + \sqrt{t^2 + t}\right|\right]_0^3$

$\displaystyle = -\frac{1}{2}\left[\ln\left(\frac{7}{2} + 2\sqrt{3}\right) - \ln\left(\frac{1}{2}\right)\right] = -\frac{1}{2}\ln(7 + 4\sqrt{3}) \approx -1.317$

5. $\mathbf{F}(x, y) = e^x \sin y\mathbf{i} + e^x \cos y\mathbf{j}$

$\dfrac{\partial N}{\partial x} = e^x \cos y \qquad \dfrac{\partial M}{\partial y} = e^x \cos y$

Since $\dfrac{\partial N}{\partial x} = \dfrac{\partial M}{\partial y}$, $\mathbf{F}$ is conservative.

7. $\mathbf{F}(x, y) = \dfrac{1}{y}\mathbf{i} + \dfrac{x}{y^2}\mathbf{j}$

$\dfrac{\partial N}{\partial x} = \dfrac{1}{y^2} \qquad \dfrac{\partial M}{\partial y} = -\dfrac{1}{y^2}$

Since $\dfrac{\partial N}{\partial x} \ne \dfrac{\partial M}{\partial y}$, $\mathbf{F}$ is not conservative.

9. $\mathbf{F}(x, y, z) = y^2z\mathbf{i} + 2xyz\mathbf{j} + xy^2\mathbf{k}$

$\mathbf{curl\ F} = \mathbf{0} \implies \mathbf{F}$ is conservative.

11. $\mathbf{F}(x, y) = 2xy\mathbf{i} + x^2\mathbf{j}$

(a) $\mathbf{r}_1(t) = t\mathbf{i} + t^2\mathbf{j}, \ 0 \le t \le 1$

     $\mathbf{r}_1'(t) = \mathbf{i} + 2t\mathbf{j}$

     $\mathbf{F}(t) = 2t^3\mathbf{i} + t^2\mathbf{j}$

     $\displaystyle\int_C \mathbf{F} \cdot d\mathbf{r} = \int_0^1 4t^3 \, dt = 1$

(b) $\mathbf{r}_2(t) = t\mathbf{i} + t^3\mathbf{j}, \ 0 \le t \le 1$

     $\mathbf{r}_2'(t) = \mathbf{i} + 3t^2\mathbf{j}$

     $\mathbf{F}(t) = 2t^4\mathbf{i} + t^2\mathbf{j}$

     $\displaystyle\int_C \mathbf{F} \cdot d\mathbf{r} = \int_0^1 5t^4 \, dt = 1$

13. $\mathbf{F}(x, y) = y\mathbf{i} - x\mathbf{j}$

(a) $\mathbf{r}_1(t) = t\mathbf{i} + t\mathbf{j}, \ 0 \le t \le 1$

     $\mathbf{r}_1'(t) = \mathbf{i} + \mathbf{j}$

     $\mathbf{F}(t) = t\mathbf{i} - t\mathbf{j}$

     $\displaystyle\int_C \mathbf{F} \cdot d\mathbf{r} = 0$

(b) $\mathbf{r}_2(t) = t\mathbf{i} + t^2\mathbf{j}, \ 0 \le t \le 1$

     $\mathbf{r}_2'(t) = \mathbf{i} + 2t\mathbf{j}$

     $\mathbf{F}(t) = t^2\mathbf{i} - t\mathbf{j}$

     $\displaystyle\int_C \mathbf{F} \cdot d\mathbf{r} = \int_0^1 -t^2 \, dt = -\frac{1}{3}$

(c) $\mathbf{r}_3(t) = t\mathbf{i} + t^3\mathbf{j}, \ 0 \le t \le 1$

     $\mathbf{r}_3'(t) = \mathbf{i} + 3t^2\mathbf{j}$

     $\mathbf{F}(t) = t^3\mathbf{i} - t\mathbf{j}$

     $\displaystyle\int_C \mathbf{F} \cdot d\mathbf{r} = \int_0^1 -2t^3 \, dt = -\frac{1}{2}$

15. $\displaystyle\int_C y^2 \, dx + 2xy \, dy$

Since $\partial M / \partial y = \partial N / \partial x = 2y$, $\mathbf{F}(x, y) = y^2\mathbf{i} + 2xy\mathbf{j}$ is conservative. The potential function is $f(x, y) = xy^2 + k$. Therefore, we can use the Fundamental Theorem of Line Integrals.

(a) $\displaystyle\int_C y^2 \, dx + 2xy \, dy = \left[x^2 y\right]_{(0,0)}^{(4,4)} = 64$

(b) $\displaystyle\int_C y^2 \, dx + 2xy \, dy = \left[x^2 y\right]_{(-1,0)}^{(1,0)} = 0$

(c) and (d) Since C is a closed curve, $\displaystyle\int_C y^2 \, dx + 2xy \, dy = 0$.

17. $\displaystyle\int_C 2xy \, dx + (x^2 + y^2) \, dy$

Since $\partial M / \partial y = \partial N / \partial x = 2x$,

     $\mathbf{F}(x, y) = 2xy\mathbf{i} + (x^2 + y^2)\mathbf{j}$ is conservative.

The potential function is $f(x, y) = x^2 y + \dfrac{y^3}{3} + k$.

(a) $\displaystyle\int_C 2xy \, dx + (x^2 + y^2) \, dy = \left[x^2 y + \frac{y^3}{3}\right]_{(5,0)}^{(0,4)} = \frac{64}{3}$

(b) $\displaystyle\int_C 2xy \, dx + (x^2 + y^2) \, dy = \left[x^2 y + \frac{y^3}{3}\right]_{(2,0)}^{(0,4)} = \frac{64}{3}$

19. $\mathbf{F}(x, y, z) = yz\mathbf{i} + xz\mathbf{j} + xy\mathbf{k}$

Since $\mathbf{curl} \ \mathbf{F} = \mathbf{0}$, $\mathbf{F}(x, y, z)$ is conservative. The potential function is $f(x, y, z) = xyz + k$.

(a) $\mathbf{r}_1(t) = t\mathbf{i} + 2\mathbf{j} + t\mathbf{k}, \ 0 \le t \le 4$

     $\displaystyle\int_C \mathbf{F} \cdot d\mathbf{r} = \left[xyz\right]_{(0,2,0)}^{(4,2,4)} = 32$

(b) $\mathbf{r}_2(t) = t^2\mathbf{i} + t\mathbf{j} + t^2\mathbf{k}, \ 0 \le t \le 2$

     $\displaystyle\int_C \mathbf{F} \cdot d\mathbf{r} = \left[xyz\right]_{(0,0,0)}^{(4,2,4)} = 32$

21. $\mathbf{F}(x, y, z) = (2y + x)\mathbf{i} + (x^2 - z)\mathbf{j} + (2y - 4z)\mathbf{k}$

$\mathbf{F}(x, y, z)$ is not conservative.

(a) $\mathbf{r}_1(t) = t\mathbf{i} + t^2\mathbf{j} + \mathbf{k}, \ 0 \le t \le 1$

     $\mathbf{r}_1'(t) = \mathbf{i} + 2t\mathbf{j}$

     $\mathbf{F}(t) = (2t^2 + t)\mathbf{i} + (t^2 - 1)\mathbf{j} + (2t^2 - 4)\mathbf{k}$

     $\displaystyle\int_C \mathbf{F} \cdot d\mathbf{r} = \int_0^1 (2t^3 + 2t^2 - t) \, dt = \frac{2}{3}$

—CONTINUED—

21. —CONTINUED—

(b) $\mathbf{r}_2(t) = t\mathbf{i} + t\mathbf{j} + (2t - 1)^2\mathbf{k},\ 0 \le t \le 1$

$\mathbf{r}_2'(t) = \mathbf{i} + \mathbf{j} + 4(2t - 1)\mathbf{k}$

$\mathbf{F}(t) = 3t\mathbf{i} + [t^2 - (2t - 1)^2]\mathbf{j} + [2t - 4(2t - 1)^2]\mathbf{k}$

$$\int_C \mathbf{F} \cdot d\mathbf{r} = \int_0^1 [3t + t^2 - (2t - 1)^2 + 8t(2t - 1) - 16(2t - 1)^3]\,dt$$

$$= \int_0^1 [17t^2 - 5t - (2t - 1)^2 - 16(2t - 1)^3]\,dt = \left[\frac{17t^3}{3} - \frac{5t^2}{2} - \frac{(2t - 1)^3}{6} - 2(2t - 1)^4\right]_0^1 = \frac{17}{6}$$

23. $\mathbf{F}(x, y, z) = e^z(y\mathbf{i} + x\mathbf{j} + xy\mathbf{k})$

$\mathbf{F}(x, y, z)$ is conservative. The potential function is
$f(x, y, z) = xye^z + k.$

(a) $\mathbf{r}_1(t) = 4 \cos t\mathbf{i} + 4 \sin t\mathbf{j} + 3\mathbf{k},\ 0 \le t \le \pi$

$$\int_C \mathbf{F} \cdot d\mathbf{r} = \left[xye^z\right]_{(4, 0, 3)}^{(-4, 0, 3)} = 0$$

(b) $\mathbf{r}_2(t) = (4 - 8t)\mathbf{i} + 3\mathbf{k},\ 0 \le t \le 1$

$$\int_C \mathbf{F} \cdot d\mathbf{r} = \left[xye^z\right]_{(4, 0, 3)}^{(-4, 0, 3)} = 0$$

25. $\displaystyle\int_C (y\mathbf{i} + x\mathbf{j}) \cdot d\mathbf{r} = \left[xy\right]_{(0, 0)}^{(3, 8)} = 24$

27. $\displaystyle\int_C \cos x \sin y\,dx + \sin x \cos y\,dy = \left[\sin x \sin y\right]_{(0, -\pi)}^{(3\pi/2,\ \pi/2)} = -1$

29. $\displaystyle\int_C e^x \sin y\,dx + e^x \cos y\,dy = \left[e^x \sin y\right]_{(0, 0)}^{(2\pi, 0)} = 0$

31. $\displaystyle\int_C (y + 2z)\,dx + (x - 3z)\,dy + (2x - 3y)\,dz$

$\mathbf{F}(x, y, z)$ is conservative and the potential function is $f(x, y, z) = xy - 3yz + 2xz.$

(a) $\left[xy - 3yz + 2xz\right]_{(0, 0, 0)}^{(1, 1, 1)} = 0 - 0 = 0$

(b) $\left[xy - 3yz + 2xz\right]_{(0, 0, 0)}^{(0, 0, 1)} + \left[xy - 3yz + 2xz\right]_{(0, 0, 1)}^{(1, 1, 1)} = 0 + 0 = 0$

(c) $\left[xy - 3yz + 2xz\right]_{(0, 0, 0)}^{(1, 0, 0)} + \left[xy - 3yz + 2xz\right]_{(1, 0, 0)}^{(1, 1, 0)} + \left[xy - 3yz + 2xz\right]_{(1, 1, 0)}^{(1, 1, 1)} = 0 + 1 + (-1) = 0$

33. $\displaystyle\int_C -\sin x\,dx + z\,dy + y\,dz = \left[\cos x + yz\right]_{(0, 0, 0)}^{(\pi/2, 3, 4)} = 12 - 1 = 11$

35. $\mathbf{F}(x, y) = 9x^2y^2\mathbf{i} + (6x^3y - 1)\mathbf{j}$ is conservative.

$\text{Work} = \left[3x^3y^2 - y\right]_{(0, 0)}^{(5, 9)} = 30{,}366$

37. $\mathbf{r}(t) = 2 \cos 2\pi t \mathbf{i} + 2 \sin 2\pi t \mathbf{j}$

$\mathbf{r}'(t) = -4\pi \sin 2\pi t \mathbf{i} + 4\pi \cos 2\pi t \mathbf{j}$

$\mathbf{a}(t) = -8\pi^2 \cos 2\pi t \mathbf{i} - 8\pi^2 \sin 2\pi t \mathbf{j}$

$\mathbf{F}(t) = m \cdot \mathbf{a}(t) = \dfrac{1}{32}\mathbf{a}(t) = -\dfrac{\pi^2}{4}(\cos 2\pi t \mathbf{i} + \sin 2\pi t \mathbf{j})$

$$W = \int_C \mathbf{F} \cdot d\mathbf{r} = \int_C -\frac{\pi^2}{4}(\cos 2\pi t \mathbf{i} + \sin 2\pi t \mathbf{j}) \cdot 4\pi(-\sin 2\pi t \mathbf{i} + \cos 2\pi t \mathbf{j})\, dt = -\pi^3 \int_C 0\, dt = 0$$

39. Since the sum of the potential and kinetic energies remains constant from point to point, if the kinetic energy is decreasing at a rate of 10 units per minute, then the potential energy is increasing at a rate of 10 units per minute.

41. No. The force field is conservative.   **43.** See Theorem 14.5, page 1033.

45. (a) The direct path along the line segment joining $(-4, 0)$ to $(3, 4)$ requires less work than the path going from $(-4, 0)$ to $(-4, 4)$ and then to $(3, 4)$.

  (b) The closed curve given by the line segments joining $(-4, 0)$, $(-4, 4)$, $(3, 4)$, and $(-4, 0)$ satisfies $\displaystyle\int_C \mathbf{F} \cdot d\mathbf{r} \ne 0$.

47. False, it would be true if $\mathbf{F}$ were conservative.   **49.** True

51. Let

$$\mathbf{F} = M\mathbf{i} + N\mathbf{j} = \frac{\partial f}{\partial y}\mathbf{i} - \frac{\partial f}{\partial x}\mathbf{j}.$$

Then $\dfrac{\partial M}{\partial y} = \dfrac{\partial}{\partial y}\left(\dfrac{\partial f}{\partial y}\right) = \dfrac{\partial^2 f}{\partial y^2}$ and $\dfrac{\partial N}{\partial x} = \dfrac{\partial}{\partial x}\left(-\dfrac{\partial f}{\partial x}\right) = -\dfrac{\partial^2 f}{\partial x^2}$. Since

$\dfrac{\partial^2 f}{\partial x^2} + \dfrac{\partial^2 f}{\partial y^2} = 0$ we have $\dfrac{\partial M}{\partial y} = \dfrac{\partial N}{\partial x}$.

Thus, $\mathbf{F}$ is conservative. Therefore, by Theorem 14.7, we have

$$\int_C \left(\frac{\partial f}{\partial y}\, dx - \frac{\partial f}{\partial x}\, dy\right) = \int_C (M\, dx + N\, dy) = \int_C \mathbf{F} \cdot d\mathbf{r} = 0$$

for every closed curve in the plane.

Section 14.4   Green's Theorem

1. $\mathbf{r}(t) = \begin{cases} t\mathbf{i}, & 0 \le t \le 4 \\ 4\mathbf{i} + (t-4)\mathbf{j}, & 4 \le t \le 8 \\ (12-t)\mathbf{i} + 4\mathbf{j}, & 8 \le t \le 12 \\ (16-t)\mathbf{j}, & 12 \le t \le 16 \end{cases}$

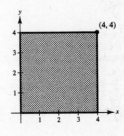

$$\int_C y^2\, dx + x^2\, dy = \int_0^4 [0\, dt + t^2(0)] + \int_4^8 [(t-4)^2(0) + 16\, dt]$$

$$+ \int_8^{12} [16(-dt) + (12-t)^2(0)] + \int_{12}^{16} [(16-t)^2(0) + 0(-dt)]$$

$$= 0 + 64 - 64 + 0 = 0$$

By Green's Theorem, $\displaystyle\iint_R \left(\frac{\partial N}{\partial x} - \frac{\partial M}{\partial y}\right) dA = \int_0^4 \int_0^4 (2x - 2y)\, dy\, dx = \int_0^4 (8x - 16)\, dx = 0.$

3. $\mathbf{r}(t) = \begin{cases} t\mathbf{i} + t^2/4\mathbf{j}, & 0 \le t \le 4 \\ (8-t)\mathbf{i} + (8-t)\mathbf{j}, & 4 \le t \le 8 \end{cases}$

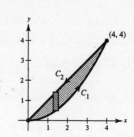

$$\int_C y^2\,dx + x^2\,dy = \int_0^4 \left[\frac{t^4}{16}(dt) + t^2\left(\frac{t}{2}\,dt\right)\right] + \int_4^8 \left[(8-t)^2(-dt) + (8-t)^2(-dt)\right]$$

$$= \int_0^4 \left[\frac{t^4}{16} + \frac{t^3}{2}\right]dt + \int_4^8 -2(8-t)^2\,dt = \frac{224}{5} - \frac{128}{3} = \frac{32}{15}$$

By Green's Theorem,

$$\int\int_R \left(\frac{\partial N}{\partial x} - \frac{\partial M}{\partial y}\right)dA = \int_0^4 \int_{x^2/4}^x (2x - 2y)\,dy\,dx = \int_0^4 \left(x^2 - \frac{x^3}{2} + \frac{x^4}{16}\right)dx = \frac{32}{15}.$$

5. $C: x^2 + y^2 = 4$

Let $x = 2\cos t$ and $y = 2\sin t$, $0 \le t \le 2\pi$.

$$\int_C xe^y\,dx + e^x\,dy = \int_0^{2\pi} \left[2\cos t\, e^{2\sin t}(-2\sin t) + e^{2\cos t}(2\cos t)\right]dt \approx 19.99$$

$$\int\int_R \left(\frac{\partial N}{\partial x} - \frac{\partial M}{\partial y}\right)dA = \int_{-2}^2 \int_{-\sqrt{4-x^2}}^{\sqrt{4-x^2}} (e^x - xe^y)\,dy\,dx = \int_{-2}^2 \left[2\sqrt{4-x^2}\,e^x - xe^{\sqrt{4-x^2}} + xe^{-\sqrt{4-x^2}}\right]dx \approx 19.99$$

In Exercises 7 and 9, $\dfrac{\partial N}{\partial x} - \dfrac{\partial M}{\partial y} = 1.$

7. $\displaystyle\int_C (y-x)\,dx + (2x-y)\,dy = \int_0^2 \int_{x^2-x}^x dy\,dx$

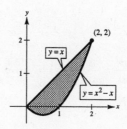

$$= \int_0^2 (2x - x^2)\,dx$$

$$= \frac{4}{3}$$

9. From the accompanying figure, we see that R is the shaded region. Thus, Green's Theorem yields

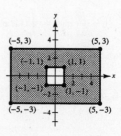

$$\int_C (y-x)\,dx + (2x-y)\,dy = \int\int_R 1\,dA$$

$$= \text{Area of } R$$

$$= 6(10) - 2(2)$$

$$= 56.$$

11. Since the curves $y = 0$ and $y = 4 - x^2$ intersect at $(-2, 0)$ and $(2, 0)$, Green's Theorem yields

$$\int_C 2xy\,dx + (x+y)\,dy = \int\int_R (1 - 2x)\,dA = \int_{-2}^2 \int_0^{4-x^2} (1 - 2x)\,dy\,dx$$

$$= \int_{-2}^2 \left[y - 2xy\right]_0^{4-x^2} dx$$

$$= \int_{-2}^2 (4 - 8x - x^2 + 2x^3)\,dx$$

$$= \left[4x - 4x^2 - \frac{x^3}{3} + \frac{x^4}{2}\right]_{-2}^2$$

$$= -\frac{8}{3} - \frac{8}{3} + 16 = \frac{32}{3}.$$

13. Since R is the interior of the circle $x^2 + y^2 = a^2$, Green's Theorem yields

$$\int_C (x^2 - y^2)\, dx + 2xy\, dy = \iint_R (2y + 2y)\, dA$$

$$= \int_{-a}^{a} \int_{-\sqrt{a^2 - x^2}}^{\sqrt{a^2 - x^2}} 4y\, dy\, dx = 4 \int_{-a}^{a} 0\, dx = 0.$$

15. Since $\dfrac{\partial M}{\partial y} = \dfrac{2x}{x^2 + y^2} = \dfrac{\partial N}{\partial x}$,

we have path independence and

$$\iint_R \left(\frac{\partial N}{\partial x} - \frac{\partial M}{\partial y} \right) dA = 0.$$

17. By Green's Theorem,

$$\int_C \sin x \cos y\, dx + (xy + \cos x \sin y)\, dy = \iint_R [(y - \sin x \sin y) - (-\sin x \sin y)]\, dA$$

$$= \int_0^1 \int_x^{\sqrt{x}} y\, dy\, dx = \frac{1}{2} \int_0^1 (x - x^2)\, dx = \frac{1}{2} \left[\frac{x^2}{2} - \frac{x^3}{3} \right]_0^1 = \frac{1}{12}.$$

19. By Green's Theorem,

$$\int_C xy\, dx + (x + y)\, dy = \iint_R (1 - x)\, dA$$

$$= \int_0^{2\pi} \int_1^3 (1 - r\cos\theta) r\, dr\, d\theta = \int_0^{2\pi} \left(4 - \frac{26}{3}\cos\theta \right) d\theta = 8\pi.$$

21. $\mathbf{F}(x, y) = xy\mathbf{i} + (x + y)\mathbf{j}$

$C: x^2 + y^2 = 4$

$$\text{Work} = \int_C xy\, dx + (x + y)\, dy = \iint_R (1 - x)\, dA = \int_0^{2\pi} \int_0^2 (1 - r\cos\theta) r\, dr\, d\theta = \int_0^{2\pi} \left(2 - \frac{8}{3}\cos\theta \right) d\theta = 4\pi$$

23. $\mathbf{F}(x, y) = (x^{3/2} - 3y)\mathbf{i} + (6x + 5\sqrt{y})\mathbf{j}$

$C:$ boundary of the triangle with vertices $(0, 0), (5, 0), (0, 5)$

$$\text{Work} = \int_C (x^{3/2} - 3y)\, dx + \left(6x + 5\sqrt{y} \right) dy = \iint_R 9\, dA = 9\left(\tfrac{1}{2}\right)(5)(5) = \tfrac{225}{2}$$

25. $C:$ let $x = a\cos t,\ y = a\sin t,\ 0 \le t \le 2\pi$. By Theorem 14.9, we have

$$A = \frac{1}{2} \int_C x\, dy - y\, dx = \frac{1}{2} \int_0^{2\pi} [a\cos t(a\cos t) - a\sin t(-a\sin t)]\, dt = \frac{1}{2} \int_0^{2\pi} a^2\, dt = \left[\frac{a^2}{2} t \right]_0^{2\pi} = \pi a^2.$$

27. From the accompanying figure we see that

C_1: $y = 2x + 1$, $dy = 2\,dx$

C_2: $y = 4 - x^2$, $dy = -2x\,dx$.

Thus, by Theorem 14.9, we have

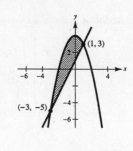

$$A = \frac{1}{2}\int_{-3}^{1}\left[x(2) - (2x + 1)\right]dx + \frac{1}{2}\int_{1}^{-3}\left[x(-2x) - (4 - x^2)\right]dx$$

$$= \frac{1}{2}\int_{-3}^{1}(-1)\,dx + \frac{1}{2}\int_{1}^{-3}(-x^2 - 4)\,dx$$

$$= \frac{1}{2}\int_{-3}^{1}(-1)\,dx + \frac{1}{2}\int_{-3}^{1}(x^2 + 4)\,dx = \frac{1}{2}\int_{-3}^{1}(3 + x^2)\,dx = \frac{1}{2}\left[3x + \frac{x^3}{3}\right]_{-3}^{1} = \frac{32}{3}.$$

29. See Theorem 14.8, page 1042.

31. Answers will vary.

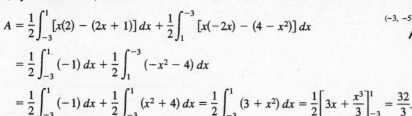

$$\mathbf{F}_1(x, y) = y\mathbf{i} + x\mathbf{j}$$

$$\mathbf{F}_2(x, y) = x^2\mathbf{i} + y^2\mathbf{j}$$

$$\mathbf{F}_3(x, y) = 2xy\mathbf{i} + x^2\mathbf{j}$$

33. $A = \displaystyle\int_{-2}^{2}(4 - x^2)\,dx = \left[4x - \frac{x^3}{3}\right]_{-2}^{2} = \frac{32}{3}$

$\bar{x} = \dfrac{1}{2A}\displaystyle\int_{C_1}x^2\,dy + \dfrac{1}{2A}\int_{C_2}x^2\,dy$

For C_1, $dy = -2x\,dx$ and for C_2, $dy = 0$. Thus,

$$\bar{x} = \frac{1}{2(32/3)}\int_{2}^{-2}x^2(-2x\,dx) = \left[\frac{3}{64}\left(-\frac{x^4}{2}\right)\right]_{2}^{-2} = 0.$$

To calculate $\bar{y}$, note that $y = 0$ along C_2. Thus,

$$\bar{y} = \frac{-1}{2(32/3)}\int_{2}^{-2}(4 - x^2)^2\,dx = \frac{3}{64}\int_{-2}^{2}(16 - 8x^2 + x^4)\,dx = \frac{3}{64}\left[16x - \frac{8x^3}{3} + \frac{x^5}{5}\right]_{-2}^{2} = \frac{8}{5}.$$

$$(\bar{x}, \bar{y}) = \left(0, \frac{8}{5}\right)$$

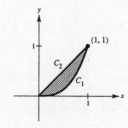

35. Since $A = \displaystyle\int_{0}^{1}(x - x^3)\,dx = \left[\frac{x^2}{2} - \frac{x^4}{4}\right]_{0}^{1} = \frac{1}{4}$, we have $\dfrac{1}{2A} = 2$. On C_1 we have $y = x^3$, $dy = 3x^2\,dx$ and on C_2 we have

$y = x$, $dy = dx$. Thus,

$$\bar{x} = 2\int_{C}x^2\,dy = 2\int_{C_1}x^2(3x^2\,dx) + 2\int_{C_2}x^2\,dx$$

$$= 6\int_{0}^{1}x^4\,dx + 2\int_{1}^{0}x^2\,dx = \frac{6}{5} - \frac{2}{3} = \frac{8}{15}$$

$$\bar{y} = -2\int_{C}y^2\,dx$$

$$= -2\int_{0}^{1}x^6\,dx - 2\int_{1}^{0}x^2\,dx = -\frac{2}{7} + \frac{2}{3} = \frac{8}{21}.$$

$$(\bar{x}, \bar{y}) = \left(\frac{8}{15}, \frac{8}{21}\right)$$

37. $A = \dfrac{1}{2} \displaystyle\int_0^{2\pi} a^2 (1 - \cos\theta)^2 \, d\theta$

$$= \frac{a^2}{2} \int_0^{2\pi} \left(1 - 2\cos\theta + \frac{1}{2} + \frac{\cos 2\theta}{2} \right) d\theta = \frac{a^2}{2}\left[\frac{3\theta}{2} - 2\sin\theta + \frac{1}{4}\sin 2\theta \right]_0^{2\pi} = \frac{a^2}{2}(3\pi) = \frac{3\pi a^2}{2}$$

39. In this case the inner loop has domain $\dfrac{2\pi}{3} \le \theta \le \dfrac{4\pi}{3}$. Thus,

$$A = \frac{1}{2} \int_{2\pi/3}^{4\pi/3} (1 + 4\cos\theta + 4\cos^2\theta) \, d\theta$$

$$= \frac{1}{2} \int_{2\pi/3}^{4\pi/3} (3 + 4\cos\theta + 2\cos 2\theta) \, d\theta = \frac{1}{2}\left[3\theta + 4\sin\theta + \sin 2\theta \right]_{2\pi/3}^{4\pi/3} = \pi - \frac{3\sqrt{3}}{2}.$$

41. $I = \displaystyle\int_C \dfrac{y\,dx - x\,dy}{x^2 + y^2}$

(a) Let $\mathbf{F} = \dfrac{y}{x^2 + y^2}\mathbf{i} - \dfrac{x}{x^2 + y^2}\mathbf{j}$.

F is conservative since $\dfrac{\partial N}{\partial x} = \dfrac{\partial M}{\partial y} = \dfrac{x^2 - y^2}{(x^2 + y^2)^2}$.

F is defined and has continuous first partials everywhere except at the origin. If C is a circle (a closed path) that does not contain the origin, then

$$\int_C \mathbf{F} \cdot d\mathbf{r} = \int_C M\,dx + N\,dy = \iint_R \left(\frac{\partial N}{\partial x} - \frac{\partial M}{\partial y} \right) dA = 0.$$

(b) Let $\mathbf{r} = a\cos t\mathbf{i} - a\sin t\mathbf{j}$, $0 \le t \le 2\pi$ be a circle C_1 oriented clockwise inside C (see figure). Introduce line segments C_2 and C_3 as illustrated in Example 6 of this section in the text. For the region inside C and outside C_1, Green's Theorem applies. Note that since C_2 and C_3 have opposite orientations, the line integrals over them cancel. Thus, $C_4 = C_1 + C_2 + C + C_3$ and

$$\int_{C_4} \mathbf{F} \cdot d\mathbf{r} = \int_{C_1} \mathbf{F} \cdot d\mathbf{r} + \int_C \mathbf{F} \cdot d\mathbf{r} = 0.$$

But,

$$\int_{C_1} \mathbf{F} \cdot d\mathbf{r} = \int_0^{2\pi} \left[\frac{(-a\sin t)(-a\sin t)}{a^2\cos^2 t + a^2\sin^2 t} + \frac{(-a\cos t)(-a\cos t)}{a^2\cos^2 t + a^2\sin^2 t} \right] dt$$

$$= \int_0^{2\pi} (\sin^2 t + \cos^2 t) \, dt = \Big[t \Big]_0^{2\pi} = 2\pi.$$

Finally, $\displaystyle\int_C \mathbf{F} \cdot d\mathbf{r} = -\int_{C_1} \mathbf{F} \cdot d\mathbf{r} = -2\pi.$

Note: If C were orientated clockwise, then the answer would have been 2π.

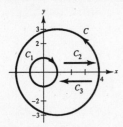

43. Pentagon: $(0, 0), (2, 0), (3, 2), (1, 4), (-1, 1)$

$A = \frac{1}{2}[(0 - 0) + (4 - 0) + (12 - 2) + (1 + 4) + (0 - 0)] = \frac{19}{2}$

45. $\int_C y^n \, dx + x^n \, dy = \int_R \int \left(\frac{\partial N}{\partial x} - \frac{\partial M}{\partial y} \right) dA$

For the line integral, use the two paths

C_1: $\mathbf{r}_1(x) = x\mathbf{i}, \ -a \le x \le a$

C_2: $\mathbf{r}_2(x) = x\mathbf{i} + \sqrt{a^2 - x^2}\mathbf{j}, \ x = a$ to $x = -a$

$\int_{C_1} y^n \, dx + x^n \, dy = 0$

$\int_{C_2} y^n \, dx + x^n \, dy = \int_a^{-a} \left[(a^2 - x^2)^{n/2} + x^n \frac{-x}{\sqrt{a^2 - x^2}} \right] dx$

$\int_R \int \left(\frac{\partial N}{\partial x} - \frac{\partial M}{\partial y} \right) dA = \int_{-a}^a \int_0^{\sqrt{a^2 - x^2}} \left[nx^{n-1} - ny^{n-1} \right] dy \, dx$

(a) For $n = 1, 3, 5, 7$, both integrals give 0.

(b) For n even, you obtain

$n = 2 : -\frac{4}{3}a^3 \qquad n = 4 : -\frac{16}{15}a^5 \qquad n = 6 : -\frac{32}{35}a^7 \qquad n = 8 : -\frac{256}{315}a^9$

(c) If n is odd and $0 < a < 1$, then the integral equals 0.

47. $\int_C (fD_N g - gD_N f) \, ds = \int_C fD_N g \, ds - \int_C gD_N f \, ds$

$= \int_R \int (f\nabla^2 g + \nabla f \cdot \nabla g) \, dA - \int_R \int (g\nabla^2 f + \nabla g \cdot \nabla f) \, dA = \int_R \int (f\nabla^2 g - g\nabla^2 f) \, dA$

49. $\mathbf{F} = M\mathbf{i} + N\mathbf{j}$

$\frac{\partial N}{\partial x} = \frac{\partial M}{\partial y} = 0 \implies \frac{\partial N}{\partial x} - \frac{\partial M}{\partial y} = 0.$

$\int_C \mathbf{F} \cdot d\mathbf{r} = \int_C M \, dx + N \, dy = \int_R \int \left(\frac{\partial N}{\partial x} - \frac{\partial M}{\partial y} \right) dA = \int_R \int (0) \, dA = 0$

Section 14.5   Parametric Surfaces

1. $\mathbf{r}(u, v) = u\mathbf{i} + v\mathbf{j} + uv\mathbf{k}$

$z = xy$

Matches c.

3. $\mathbf{r}(u, v) = 2 \cos v \cos u\mathbf{i} + 2 \cos v \sin u\mathbf{j} + 2 \sin v\mathbf{k}$

$x^2 + y^2 + z^2 = 4$

Matches b.

5. $\mathbf{r}(u, v) = u\mathbf{i} + v\mathbf{j} + \frac{v}{2}\mathbf{k}$

$y - 2z = 0$

Plane

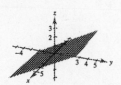

7. $\mathbf{r}(u, v) = 2 \cos u\mathbf{i} + v\mathbf{j} + 2 \sin u\mathbf{k}$

$x^2 + z^2 = 4$

Cylinder

For Exercises 9 and 11,

$$\mathbf{r}(u, v) = u \cos v\mathbf{i} + u \sin v\mathbf{j} + u^2\mathbf{k}, \ 0 \le u \le 2, \ 0 \le v \le 2\pi.$$

Eliminating the parameter yields

$$z = x^2 + y^2, \ 0 \le z \le 4.$$

9. $\mathbf{s}(u, v) = u \cos v\mathbf{i} + u \sin v\mathbf{j} - u^2\mathbf{k}, \ 0 \le u \le 2, \ 0 \le v \le 2\pi$

$z = -(x^2 + y^2)$

The paraboloid is reflected (inverted) through the *xy*-plane.

11. $\mathbf{s}(u, v) = u \cos v\mathbf{i} - u \sin v\mathbf{j} + u^2\mathbf{k}, \ 0 \le u \le 3, \ 0 \le v \le 2\pi$

The height of the paraboloid is increased from 4 to 9.

13. $\mathbf{r}(u, v) = 2u \cos v\mathbf{i} + 2u \sin v\mathbf{j} + u^4\mathbf{k},$

$0 \le u \le 1, \ 0 \le v \le 2\pi$

$z = \dfrac{(x^2 + y^2)^2}{16}$

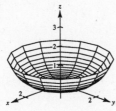

15. $\mathbf{r}(u, v) = 2 \sinh u \cos v\mathbf{i} + \sinh u \sin v\mathbf{j} + \cosh u\mathbf{k},$

$0 \le u \le 2, \ 0 \le v \le 2\pi$

$\dfrac{z^2}{1} - \dfrac{x^2}{4} - \dfrac{y^2}{1} = 1$

17. $\mathbf{r}(u, v) = (u - \sin u) \cos v\mathbf{i} + (1 - \cos u) \sin v\mathbf{j} + u\mathbf{k},$

$0 \le u \le \pi, \ 0 \le v \le 2\pi$

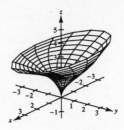

19. $z = y$

$\mathbf{r}(u, v) = u\mathbf{i} + v\mathbf{j} + v\mathbf{k}$

21. $x^2 + y^2 = 16$

$\mathbf{r}(u, v) = 4 \cos u\mathbf{i} + 4 \sin u\mathbf{j} + v\mathbf{k}$

23. $z = x^2$

$\mathbf{r}(u, v) = u\mathbf{i} + v\mathbf{j} + u^2\mathbf{k}$

25. $z = 4$ inside $x^2 + y^2 = 9.$

$\mathbf{r}(u, v) = v \cos u\mathbf{i} + v \sin u\mathbf{j} + 4\mathbf{k}, \ 0 \le v \le 3$

27. Function: $y = \dfrac{x}{2}, \ 0 \le x \le 6$

Axis of revolution: *x*-axis

$x = u, \ y = \dfrac{u}{2} \cos v, \ z = \dfrac{u}{2} \sin v$

$0 \le u \le 6, \ 0 \le v \le 2\pi$

29. Function: $x = \sin z, \ 0 \le z \le \pi$

Axis of revolution: *z*-axis

$x = \sin u \cos v, \ y = \sin u \sin v, \ z = u$

$0 \le u \le \pi, \ 0 \le v \le 2\pi$

31. $\mathbf{r}(u, v) = (u + v)\mathbf{i} + (u - v)\mathbf{j} + v\mathbf{k}, \ (1, -1, 1)$

$\mathbf{r}_u(u, v) = \mathbf{i} + \mathbf{j}, \ \mathbf{r}_v(u, v) = \mathbf{i} - \mathbf{j} + \mathbf{k}$

At $(1, -1, 1), \ u = 0$ and $v = 1.$

$\mathbf{r}_u(0, 1) = \mathbf{i} + \mathbf{j}, \ \mathbf{r}_v(0, 1) = \mathbf{i} - \mathbf{j} + \mathbf{k}$

$N = \mathbf{r}_u(0, 1) \times \mathbf{r}_v(0, 1) = \begin{vmatrix} \mathbf{i} & \mathbf{j} & \mathbf{k} \\ 1 & 1 & 0 \\ 1 & -1 & 1 \end{vmatrix} = \mathbf{i} - \mathbf{j} - 2\mathbf{k}$

Tangent plane: $(x - 1) - (y + 1) - 2(z - 1) = 0$

$$x - y - 2z = 0$$

(The original plane!)

33. $\mathbf{r}(u, v) = 2u \cos v\mathbf{i} + 3u \sin v\mathbf{j} + u^2\mathbf{k}, \ (0, 6, 4)$

$\mathbf{r}_u(u, v) = 2 \cos v\mathbf{i} + 3 \sin v\mathbf{j} + 2u\mathbf{k}$

$\mathbf{r}_v(u, v) = -2u \sin v\mathbf{i} + 3u \cos v\mathbf{j}$

At $(0, 6, 4), \ u = 2$ and $v = \pi/2.$

$\mathbf{r}_u\left(2, \dfrac{\pi}{2}\right) = 3\mathbf{j} + 4\mathbf{k}, \ \mathbf{r}_v\left(2, \dfrac{\pi}{2}\right) = -4\mathbf{i}$

$N = \mathbf{r}_u\left(2, \dfrac{\pi}{2}\right) \times \mathbf{r}_v\left(2, \dfrac{\pi}{2}\right)$

$= \begin{vmatrix} \mathbf{i} & \mathbf{j} & \mathbf{k} \\ 0 & 3 & 4 \\ -4 & 0 & 0 \end{vmatrix} = -16\mathbf{j} + 12\mathbf{k}$

Direction numbers: $0, 4, -3$

Tangent plane: $4(y - 6) - 3(z - 4) = 0$

$$4y - 3z = 12$$

35. $\mathbf{r}(u, v) = 2u\mathbf{i} - \dfrac{v}{2}\mathbf{j} + \dfrac{v}{2}\mathbf{k}, \ 0 \le u \le 2, \ 0 \le v \le 1$

$\mathbf{r}_u(u, v) = 2\mathbf{i}, \ \mathbf{r}_v(u, v) = -\dfrac{1}{2}\mathbf{j} + \dfrac{1}{2}\mathbf{k}$

$\mathbf{r}_u \times \mathbf{r}_v = \begin{vmatrix} \mathbf{i} & \mathbf{j} & \mathbf{k} \\ 2 & 0 & 0 \\ 0 & -\frac{1}{2} & \frac{1}{2} \end{vmatrix} = -\mathbf{j} - \mathbf{k}$

$\|\mathbf{r}_u \times \mathbf{r}_v\| = \sqrt{2}$

$A = \displaystyle\int_0^1 \int_0^2 \sqrt{2} \, du \, dv = 2\sqrt{2}$

37. $\mathbf{r}(u, v) = a \cos u\mathbf{i} + a \sin u\mathbf{j} + v\mathbf{k}, \ 0 \le u \le 2\pi, \ 0 \le v \le b$

$\mathbf{r}_u(u, v) = -a \sin u\mathbf{i} + a \cos u\mathbf{j}$

$\mathbf{r}_v(u, v) = \mathbf{k}$

$\mathbf{r}_u \times \mathbf{r}_v = \begin{vmatrix} \mathbf{i} & \mathbf{j} & \mathbf{k} \\ -a \sin u & a \cos u & 0 \\ 0 & 0 & 1 \end{vmatrix} = a \cos u\mathbf{i} + a \sin u\mathbf{j}$

$\|\mathbf{r}_u \times \mathbf{r}_v\| = a$

$A = \displaystyle\int_0^b \int_0^{2\pi} a \, du \, dv = 2\pi ab$

39. $\mathbf{r}(u, v) = au \cos v\mathbf{i} + au \sin v\mathbf{j} + u\mathbf{k}, \ 0 \le u \le b, \ 0 \le v \le 2\pi$

$\mathbf{r}_u(u, v) = a \cos v\mathbf{i} + a \sin v\mathbf{j} + \mathbf{k}$

$\mathbf{r}_v(u, v) = -au \sin v\mathbf{i} + au \cos v\mathbf{j}$

$\mathbf{r}_u \times \mathbf{r}_v = \begin{vmatrix} \mathbf{i} & \mathbf{j} & \mathbf{k} \\ a \cos v & a \sin v & 1 \\ -au \sin v & au \cos v & 0 \end{vmatrix} = -au \cos v\mathbf{i} - au \sin v\mathbf{j} + a^2u\mathbf{k}$

$\|\mathbf{r}_u \times \mathbf{r}_v\| = au\sqrt{1 + a^2}$

$A = \displaystyle\int_0^{2\pi} \int_0^b a\sqrt{1 + a^2}\, u \, du \, dv = \pi ab^2\sqrt{1 + a^2}$

41. $\mathbf{r}(u, v) = \sqrt{u}\cos v\mathbf{i} + \sqrt{u}\sin v\mathbf{j} + u\mathbf{k}$, $0 \le u \le 4$, $0 \le v \le 2\pi$

$\mathbf{r}_u(u, v) = \dfrac{\cos v}{2\sqrt{u}}\mathbf{i} + \dfrac{\sin v}{2\sqrt{u}}\mathbf{j} + \mathbf{k}$

$\mathbf{r}_v(u, v) = -\sqrt{u}\sin v\mathbf{i} + \sqrt{u}\cos v\mathbf{j}$

$\mathbf{r}_u \times \mathbf{r}_v = \begin{vmatrix} \mathbf{i} & \mathbf{j} & \mathbf{k} \\ \dfrac{\cos v}{2\sqrt{u}} & \dfrac{\sin v}{2\sqrt{u}} & 1 \\ -\sqrt{u}\sin v & \sqrt{u}\cos v & 0 \end{vmatrix} = -\sqrt{u}\cos v\mathbf{i} - \sqrt{u}\sin v\mathbf{j} + \dfrac{1}{2}\mathbf{k}$

$\|\mathbf{r}_u \times \mathbf{r}_v\| = \sqrt{u + \dfrac{1}{4}}$

$A = \displaystyle\int_0^{2\pi}\int_0^4 \sqrt{u + \dfrac{1}{4}}\, du\, dv = \dfrac{\pi}{6}\left(17\sqrt{17} - 1\right) \approx 36.177$

43. See the definition, page 1051.

45. (a) From $(-10, 10, 0)$

  (b) From $(10, 10, 10)$

  (c) From $(0, 10, 0)$

  (d) From $(10, 0, 0)$

47. (a) $\mathbf{r}(u, v) = (4 + \cos v)\cos u\mathbf{i} +$
  $(4 + \cos v)\sin u\mathbf{j} + \sin v\mathbf{k}$,
  $0 \le u \le 2\pi$, $0 \le v \le 2\pi$

(b) $\mathbf{r}(u, v) = (4 + 2\cos v)\cos u\mathbf{i} +$
  $(4 + 2\cos v)\sin u\mathbf{j} + 2\sin v\mathbf{k}$,
  $0 \le u \le 2\pi$, $0 \le v \le 2\pi$

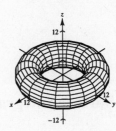

(c) $\mathbf{r}(u, v) = (8 + \cos v)\cos u\mathbf{i} +$
  $(8 + \cos v)\sin u\mathbf{j} + \sin v\mathbf{k}$,
  $0 \le u \le 2\pi$, $0 \le v \le 2\pi$

(d) $\mathbf{r}(u, v) = (8 + 3\cos v)\cos u\mathbf{i} +$
  $(8 + 3\cos v)\sin u\mathbf{j} + 3\sin v\mathbf{k}$,
  $0 \le u \le 2\pi$, $0 \le v \le 2\pi$

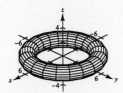

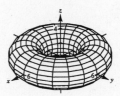

The radius of the generating circle that is revolved about the z-axis is b, and its center is a units from the axis of revolution.

49. $\mathbf{r}(u, v) = 20 \sin u \cos v\mathbf{i} + 20 \sin u \sin v\mathbf{j} + 20 \cos u\mathbf{k} \quad 0 \le u \le \pi/3, \ 0 \le v \le 2\pi$

$\mathbf{r}_u = 20 \cos u \cos v\mathbf{i} + 20 \cos u \sin v\mathbf{j} - 20 \sin u\mathbf{k}$

$\mathbf{r}_v = -20 \sin u \sin v\mathbf{i} + 20 \sin u \cos v\mathbf{j}$

$$\mathbf{r}_u \times \mathbf{r}_v = \begin{vmatrix} \mathbf{i} & \mathbf{j} & \mathbf{k} \\ 20 \cos u \cos v & 20 \cos u \sin v & -20 \sin u \\ -20 \sin u \sin v & 20 \sin u \cos v & 0 \end{vmatrix}$$

$$= 400 \sin^2 u \cos v\mathbf{i} + 400 \sin^2 u \sin v\mathbf{j} + 400(\cos u \sin u \cos^2 v + \cos u \sin u \sin^2 v)\mathbf{k}$$

$$= 400[\sin^2 u \cos v\mathbf{i} + \sin^2 u \sin v\mathbf{j} + \cos u \sin u\mathbf{k}]$$

$$\|\mathbf{r}_u \times \mathbf{r}_v\| = 400\sqrt{\sin^4 u \cos^2 v + \sin^4 u \sin^2 v + \cos^2 u \sin^2 u}$$

$$= 400\sqrt{\sin^4 u + \cos^2 u \sin^2 u}$$

$$= 400\sqrt{\sin^2 u} = 400 \sin u$$

$$S = \iint_S dS = \int_0^{2\pi} \int_0^{\pi/3} 400 \sin u \, du \, dv = \int_0^{2\pi} \left[-400 \cos u \right]_0^{\pi/3} dv$$

$$= \int_0^{2\pi} 200 \, dv = 400\pi \text{ m}^2$$

51. $\mathbf{r}(u, v) = u \cos v\mathbf{i} + u \sin v\mathbf{j} + 2v\mathbf{k}, \ 0 \le u \le 3, \ 0 \le v \le 2\pi$

$\mathbf{r}_u(u, v) = \cos v\mathbf{i} + \sin v\mathbf{j}$

$\mathbf{r}_v(u, v) = -u \sin v\mathbf{i} + u \cos v\mathbf{j} + 2\mathbf{k}$

$$\mathbf{r}_u \times \mathbf{r}_v = \begin{vmatrix} \mathbf{i} & \mathbf{j} & \mathbf{k} \\ \cos v & \sin v & 0 \\ -u \sin v & u \cos v & 2 \end{vmatrix} = 2 \sin v\mathbf{i} - 2 \cos v\mathbf{j} + u\mathbf{k}$$

$$\|\mathbf{r}_u \times \mathbf{r}_v\| = \sqrt{4 + u^2}$$

$$A = \int_0^{2\pi} \int_0^3 \sqrt{4 + u^2} \, du \, dv = \pi \left[3\sqrt{13} + 4 \ln\left(\frac{3 + \sqrt{13}}{2} \right) \right]$$

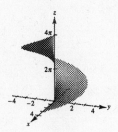

53. Essay

Section 14.6 Surface Integrals

1. S: $z = 4 - x, \ 0 \le x \le 4, \ 0 \le y \le 4, \ \dfrac{\partial z}{\partial x} = -1, \ \dfrac{\partial z}{\partial y} = 0$

$$\iint_S (x - 2y + z) \, dS = \int_0^4 \int_0^4 (x - 2y + 4 - x)\sqrt{1 + (-1)^2 + (0)^2} \, dy \, dx$$

$$= \sqrt{2} \int_0^4 \int_0^4 (4 - 2y) \, dy \, dx = 0$$

3. S: $z = 10$, $x^2 + y^2 \le 1$, $\dfrac{\partial z}{\partial x} = \dfrac{\partial z}{\partial y} = 0$

$$\iint_S (x - 2y + z)\, dS = \int_{-1}^{1} \int_{-\sqrt{1-x^2}}^{\sqrt{1-x^2}} (x - 2y + 10)\sqrt{1 + (0)^2 + (0)^2}\, dy\, dx$$

$$= \int_0^{2\pi} \int_0^1 (r\cos\theta - 2r\sin\theta + 10) r\, dr\, d\theta$$

$$= \int_0^{2\pi} \left(\frac{1}{3}\cos\theta - \frac{2}{3}\sin\theta + 5 \right) d\theta$$

$$= \left[\frac{1}{3}\sin\theta + \frac{2}{3}\cos\theta + 5\theta \right]_0^{2\pi} = 10\pi$$

5. S: $z = 6 - x - 2y$, (first octant) $\dfrac{\partial z}{\partial x} = -1$, $\dfrac{\partial z}{\partial y} = -2$

$$\iint_S xy\, dS = \int_0^6 \int_0^{3-(x/2)} xy\sqrt{1 + (-1)^2 + (-2)^2}\, dy\, dx$$

$$= \sqrt{6} \int_0^6 \left[\frac{xy^2}{2} \right]_0^{3-(x/2)} dx$$

$$= \frac{\sqrt{6}}{2} \int_0^6 x\left(9 - 3x + \frac{1}{4}x^2 \right) dx$$

$$= \frac{\sqrt{6}}{2} \left[\frac{9x^2}{2} - x^3 + \frac{x^4}{16} \right]_0^6 = \frac{27\sqrt{6}}{2}$$

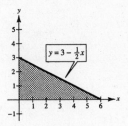

7. S: $z = 9 - x^2$, $0 \le x \le 2$, $0 \le y \le x$,

$\dfrac{\partial z}{\partial x} = -2x$, $\dfrac{\partial z}{\partial y} = 0$

$$\iint_S xy\, dS = \int_0^2 \int_y^2 xy\sqrt{1 + 4x^2}\, dx\, dy = \frac{391\sqrt{17} + 1}{240}$$

9. S: $z = 10 - x^2 - y^2$, $0 \le x \le 2$, $0 \le y \le 2$

$$\iint_S (x^2 - 2xy)\, dS = \int_0^2 \int_0^2 (x^2 - 2xy)\sqrt{1 + 4x^2 + 4y^2}\, dy\, dx \approx -11.47$$

11. S: $2x + 3y + 6z = 12$ (first octant) $\Rightarrow z = 2 - \dfrac{1}{3}x - \dfrac{1}{2}y$

$\rho(x, y, z) = x^2 + y^2$

$$m = \iint_R (x^2 + y^2)\sqrt{1 + \left(-\frac{1}{3}\right)^2 + \left(-\frac{1}{2}\right)^2}\, dA$$

$$= \frac{7}{6} \int_0^6 \int_0^{4-(2x/3)} (x^2 + y^2)\, dy\, dx$$

$$= \frac{7}{6} \int_0^6 \left[x^2\left(4 - \frac{2}{3}x \right) + \frac{1}{3}\left(4 - \frac{2}{3}x \right)^3 \right] dx = \frac{7}{6}\left[\frac{4}{3}x^3 - \frac{1}{6}x^4 - \frac{1}{8}\left(4 - \frac{2}{3}x \right)^4 \right]_0^6 = \frac{364}{3}$$

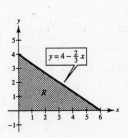

13. S: $\mathbf{r}(u, v) = u\mathbf{i} + v\mathbf{j} + \dfrac{v}{2}\mathbf{k}$, $0 \le u \le 1$, $0 \le v \le 2$

$$\|\mathbf{r}_u \times \mathbf{r}_v\| = \left\| -\frac{1}{2}\mathbf{j} + \mathbf{k} \right\| = \frac{\sqrt{5}}{2}$$

$$\iint_S (y + 5)\, dS = \int_0^2 \int_0^1 (v + 5)\frac{\sqrt{5}}{2}\, du\, dv = 6\sqrt{5}$$

15. S: $\mathbf{r}(u, v) = 2\cos u\mathbf{i} + 2\sin u\mathbf{j} + v\mathbf{k}$, $0 \le u \le \dfrac{\pi}{2}$, $0 \le v \le 2$

$$\|\mathbf{r}_u \times \mathbf{r}_v\| = \|2\cos u\mathbf{i} + 2\sin u\mathbf{j}\| = 2$$

$$\iint_S xy\, dS = \int_0^2 \int_0^{\pi/2} 8\cos u \sin u\, du\, dv = 8$$

17. $f(x, y, z) = x^2 + y^2 + z^2$

S: $z = x + 2$, $x^2 + y^2 \le 1$

$$\iint_S f(x, y, z)\, dS = \int_{-1}^1 \int_{-\sqrt{1-x^2}}^{\sqrt{1-x^2}} [x^2 + y^2 + (x+2)^2]\sqrt{1 + (1)^2 + (0)^2}\, dy\, dx$$

$$= \sqrt{2} \int_0^{2\pi} \int_0^1 [r^2 + (r\cos\theta + 2)^2]r\, dr\, d\theta$$

$$= \sqrt{2} \int_0^{2\pi} \int_0^1 [r^2 + r^2 \cos^2\theta + 4r\cos\theta + 4]r\, dr\, d\theta$$

$$= \sqrt{2} \int_0^{2\pi} \left[\frac{r^4}{4} + \frac{r^4}{4}\cos^2\theta + \frac{4r^3}{3}\cos\theta + 2r^2\right]_0^1 d\theta$$

$$= \sqrt{2} \int_0^{2\pi} \left[\frac{9}{4} + \left(\frac{1}{4}\right)\frac{1 + \cos 2\theta}{2} + \frac{4}{3}\cos\theta\right] d\theta$$

$$= \sqrt{2}\left[\frac{9}{4}\theta + \frac{1}{8}\left(\theta + \frac{1}{2}\sin 2\theta\right) + \frac{4}{3}\sin\theta\right]_0^{2\pi} = \sqrt{2}\left[\frac{18\pi}{4} + \frac{\pi}{4}\right] = \frac{19\sqrt{2}\pi}{4}$$

19. $f(x, y, z) = \sqrt{x^2 + y^2 + z^2}$

S: $z = \sqrt{x^2 + y^2}$, $x^2 + y^2 \le 4$

$$\iint_S f(x, y, z)\, dS = \int_{-2}^2 \int_{-\sqrt{4-x^2}}^{\sqrt{4-x^2}} \sqrt{x^2 + y^2 + \left(\sqrt{x^2 + y^2}\right)^2}\, \sqrt{1 + \left(\frac{x}{\sqrt{x^2 + y^2}}\right)^2 + \left(\frac{y}{\sqrt{x^2 + y^2}}\right)^2}\, dy\, dx$$

$$= \sqrt{2}\int_{-2}^2 \int_{-\sqrt{4-x^2}}^{\sqrt{4-x^2}} \sqrt{x^2 + y^2}\, \sqrt{\frac{x^2 + y^2 + x^2 + y^2}{x^2 + y^2}}\, dy\, dx$$

$$= 2\int_{-2}^2 \int_{-\sqrt{4-x^2}}^{\sqrt{4-x^2}} \sqrt{x^2 + y^2}\, dy\, dx$$

$$= 2\int_0^{2\pi} \int_0^2 r^2\, dr\, d\theta = 2\int_0^{2\pi} \left[\frac{r^3}{3}\right]_0^2 d\theta = \left[\frac{16}{3}\theta\right]_0^{2\pi} = \frac{32\pi}{3}$$

21. $f(x, y, z) = x^2 + y^2 + z^2$

$S: x^2 + y^2 = 9, \ 0 \le x \le 3, \ 0 \le y \le 3, \ 0 \le z \le 9$

Project the solid onto the yz-plane; $x = \sqrt{9 - y^2}, \ 0 \le y \le 3, \ 0 \le z \le 9.$

$$\iint_S f(x, y, z) \, dS = \int_0^3 \int_0^9 [(9 - y^2) + y^2 + z^2] \sqrt{1 + \left(\frac{y}{\sqrt{9 - y^2}}\right)^2 + (0)^2} \, dz \, dy$$

$$= \int_0^3 \int_0^9 (9 + z^2) \frac{3}{\sqrt{9 - y^2}} \, dz \, dy = \int_0^3 \left[\frac{3}{\sqrt{9 - y^2}}\left(9z + \frac{z^3}{3}\right)\right]_0^9 dy$$

$$= 324 \int_0^3 \frac{3}{\sqrt{9 - y^2}} \, dy = \left[972 \arcsin\left(\frac{y}{3}\right)\right]_0^3 = 972\left(\frac{\pi}{2} - 0\right) = 486\pi$$

23. $\mathbf{F}(x, y, z) = 3z\mathbf{i} - 4\mathbf{j} + y\mathbf{k}$

$S: x + y + z = 1$ (first octant)

$G(x, y, z) = x + y + z - 1$

$\nabla G(x, y, z) = \mathbf{i} + \mathbf{j} + \mathbf{k}$

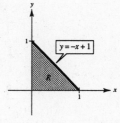

$$\iint_S \mathbf{F} \cdot \mathbf{N} \, dS = \iint_R \mathbf{F} \cdot \nabla G \, dA = \int_0^1 \int_0^{1-x} (3z - 4 + y) \, dy \, dx$$

$$= \int_0^1 \int_0^{1-x} [3(1 - x - y) - 4 + y] \, dy \, dx$$

$$= \int_0^1 \int_0^{1-x} (-1 - 3x - 2y) \, dy \, dx$$

$$= \int_0^1 \left[-y - 3xy - y^2\right]_0^{1-x} dx$$

$$= -\int_0^1 [(1 - x) + 3x(1 - x) + (1 - x)^2] \, dx$$

$$= -\int_0^1 (2 - 2x^2) \, dx = -\frac{4}{3}$$

25. $\mathbf{F}(x, y, z) = x\mathbf{i} + y\mathbf{j} + z\mathbf{k}$

$S: z = 9 - x^2 - y^2, \ 0 \le z$

$G(x, y, z) = x^2 + y^2 + z - 9$

$\nabla G(x, y, z) = 2x\mathbf{i} + 2y\mathbf{j} + \mathbf{k}$

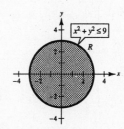

$$\iint_S \mathbf{F} \cdot \mathbf{N} \, dS = \iint_R \mathbf{F} \cdot \nabla G \, dA = \iint_R (2x^2 + 2y^2 + z) \, dA$$

$$= \iint_R [2x^2 + 2y^2 + (9 - x^2 - y^2)] \, dA$$

$$= \iint_R (x^2 + y^2 + 9) \, dA$$

$$= \int_0^{2\pi} \int_0^3 (r^2 + 9)r \, dr \, d\theta$$

$$= \int_0^{2\pi} \left[\frac{r^4}{4} + \frac{9r^2}{2}\right]_0^3 d\theta = \frac{243\pi}{2}$$

27. $\mathbf{F}(x, y, z) = 4\mathbf{i} - 3\mathbf{j} + 5\mathbf{k}$

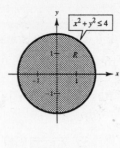

$S: z = x^2 + y^2, \ x^2 + y^2 \le 4$

$G(x, y, z) = -x^2 - y^2 + z$

$\nabla G(x, y, z) = -2x\mathbf{i} - 2y\mathbf{j} + \mathbf{k}$

$$\iint_S \mathbf{F} \cdot \mathbf{N} \, dS = \iint_R \mathbf{F} \cdot \nabla G \, dA = \iint_R (-8x + 6y + 5) \, dA$$

$$= \int_0^{2\pi} \int_0^2 [-8r\cos\theta + 6r\sin\theta + 5] r \, dr \, d\theta$$

$$= \int_0^{2\pi} \left[-\frac{8}{3}r^3 \cos\theta + 2r^3 \sin\theta + \frac{5}{2}r^2 \right]_0^2 d\theta$$

$$= \int_0^{2\pi} \left[-\frac{64}{3} \cos\theta + 16 \sin\theta + 10 \right] d\theta$$

$$= \left[-\frac{64}{3} \sin\theta - 16 \cos\theta + 10\theta \right]_0^{2\pi} = 20\pi$$

29. $\mathbf{F}(x, y, z) = 4xy\mathbf{i} + z^2\mathbf{j} + yz\mathbf{k}$

S: unit cube bounded by $x = 0$, $x = 1$, $y = 0$, $y = 1$, $z = 0$, $z = 1$

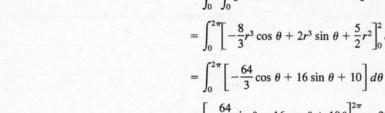

S_1: The top of the cube

$\mathbf{N} = \mathbf{k}, \ z = 1$

$$\iint_{S_1} \mathbf{F} \cdot \mathbf{N} \, dS = \int_0^1 \int_0^1 y(1) \, dy \, dx = \frac{1}{2}$$

S_2: The bottom of the cube

$\mathbf{N} = -\mathbf{k}, \ z = 0$

$$\iint_{S_2} \mathbf{F} \cdot \mathbf{N} \, dS = \int_0^1 \int_0^1 -y(0) \, dy \, dx = 0$$

S_3: The front of the cube

$\mathbf{N} = \mathbf{i}, \ x = 1$

$$\iint_{S_3} \mathbf{F} \cdot \mathbf{N} \, dS = \int_0^1 \int_0^1 4(1)y \, dy \, dz = 2$$

S_4: The back of the cube

$\mathbf{N} = -\mathbf{i}, \ x = 0$

$$\iint_{S_4} \mathbf{F} \cdot \mathbf{N} \, dS = \int_0^1 \int_0^1 -4(0)y \, dy \, dx = 0$$

S_5: The right side of the cube

$\mathbf{N} = \mathbf{j}, \ y = 1$

$$\iint_{S_5} \mathbf{F} \cdot \mathbf{N} \, dS = \int_0^1 \int_0^1 z^2 \, dz \, dx = \frac{1}{3}$$

S_6: The left side of the cube

$\mathbf{N} = -\mathbf{j}, \ y = 0$

$$\iint_{S_6} \mathbf{F} \cdot \mathbf{N} \, dS = \int_0^1 \int_0^1 -z^2 \, dz \, dx = -\frac{1}{3}$$

Therefore,

$$\iint_S \mathbf{F} \cdot \mathbf{N} \, dS = \frac{1}{2} + 0 + 2 + 0 + \frac{1}{3} - \frac{1}{3} = \frac{5}{2}.$$

31. The surface integral of f over a surface S, where S is given by $z = g(x, y)$, is defined as

$$\iint_S f(x, y, z) \, dS = \lim_{\|\Delta\| \to 0} \sum_{i=1}^n f(x_i, y_i, z_i) \Delta S_i. \ \text{(page 1061)}$$

See Theorem 14.10, page 1061.

33. See the definition, page 1067.

See Theorem 14.11, page 1067.

35. (a)

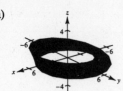

(b) If a normal vector at a point P on the surface is moved around the Möbius strip once, it will point in the opposite direction.

(c) $\mathbf{r}(u, 0) = 4\cos(2u)\mathbf{i} + 4\sin(2u)\mathbf{j}$

This is a circle.

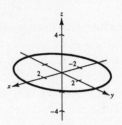

(d) (construction)

(e) You obtain a strip with a double twist and twice as long as the original Möbius strip.

37. $z = \sqrt{x^2 + y^2},\ 0 \le z \le a$

$$m = \iint_S k\, dS = k\iint_R \sqrt{1 + \left(\frac{x}{\sqrt{x^2+y^2}}\right)^2 + \left(\frac{y}{\sqrt{x^2+y^2}}\right)^2}\, dA = k\iint_R \sqrt{2}\, dA = \sqrt{2}\, k\pi a^2$$

$$I_z = \iint_S k(x^2 + y^2)\, dS = \iint_R k(x^2 + y^2)\sqrt{2}\, dA$$

$$= \sqrt{2}\,k\int_0^{2\pi}\int_0^a r^3\, dr\, d\theta = \frac{\sqrt{2}\,ka^4}{4}(2\pi)$$

$$= \frac{\sqrt{2}\,k\pi a^4}{2} = \frac{a^2}{2}\left(\sqrt{2}\,k\pi a^2\right) = \frac{a^2 m}{2}$$

39. $x^2 + y^2 = a^2,\ 0 \le z \le h$

$\rho(x, y, z) = 1$

$y = \pm\sqrt{a^2 - x^2}$

Project the solid onto the xz-plane.

$$I_z = 4\iint_S (x^2 + y^2)(1)\, dS$$

$$= 4\int_0^h\int_0^a [x^2 + (a^2 - x^2)]\sqrt{1 + \left(\frac{-x}{\sqrt{a^2-x^2}}\right)^2 + (0)^2}\, dx\, dz$$

$$= 4a^3\int_0^h\int_0^a \frac{1}{\sqrt{a^2-x^2}}\, dx\, dz$$

$$= 4a^3\int_0^h\left[\arcsin\frac{x}{a}\right]_0^a dz = 4a^3\left(\frac{\pi}{2}\right)(h) = 2\pi a^3 h$$

41. $S:\ z = 16 - x^2 - y^2,\ z \ge 0$

$\mathbf{F}(x, y, z) = 0.5z\mathbf{k}$

$$\iint_S \rho\mathbf{F} \cdot \mathbf{N}\, dS = \iint_R \rho\mathbf{F} \cdot (-g_x(x, y)\mathbf{i} - g_y(x, y)\mathbf{j} + \mathbf{k})\, dA = \iint_R 0.5\rho z\mathbf{k} \cdot (2x\mathbf{i} + 2y\mathbf{j} + \mathbf{k})\, dA$$

$$= \iint_R 0.5\rho z\, dA = \iint_R 0.5\rho(16 - x^2 - y^2)\, dA$$

$$= 0.5\rho\int_0^{2\pi}\int_0^4 (16 - r^2)r\, dr\, d\theta = 0.5\rho\int_0^{2\pi} 64\, d\theta = 64\pi\rho$$

Section 14.7 Divergence Theorem

1. **Surface Integral:** There are six surfaces to the cube, each with $dS = \sqrt{1}\, dA$.

$$z = 0, \quad \mathbf{N} = -\mathbf{k}, \quad \mathbf{F} \cdot \mathbf{N} = -z^2, \quad \int_{S_1}\!\!\int 0\, dA = 0$$

$$z = a, \quad \mathbf{N} = \mathbf{k}, \quad \mathbf{F} \cdot \mathbf{N} = z^2, \quad \int_{S_2}\!\!\int a^2\, dA = \int_0^a \int_0^a a^2\, dx\, dy = a^4$$

$$x = 0, \quad \mathbf{N} = -\mathbf{i}, \quad \mathbf{F} \cdot \mathbf{N} = -2x, \quad \int_{S_3}\!\!\int 0\, dA = 0$$

$$x = a, \quad \mathbf{N} = \mathbf{i}, \quad \mathbf{F} \cdot \mathbf{N} = 2x, \quad \int_{S_4}\!\!\int 2a\, dy\, dz = \int_0^a \int_0^a 2a\, dy\, dz = 2a^3$$

$$y = 0, \quad \mathbf{N} = -\mathbf{j}, \quad \mathbf{F} \cdot \mathbf{N} = 2y, \quad \int_{S_5}\!\!\int 0\, dA = 0$$

$$y = a, \quad \mathbf{N} = \mathbf{j}, \quad \mathbf{F} \cdot \mathbf{N} = -2y, \quad \int_{S_6}\!\!\int -2a\, dA = \int_0^a \int_0^a -2a\, dz\, dx = -2a^3$$

Therefore, $\displaystyle\int_{S}\!\!\int \mathbf{F} \cdot \mathbf{N}\, dS = a^4 + 2a^3 - 2a^3 = a^4$.

Divergence Theorem: Since div $\mathbf{F} = 2z$, the Divergence Theorem yields

$$\int\!\!\int_{Q}\!\!\int \operatorname{div} \mathbf{F}\, dV = \int_0^a \int_0^a \int_0^a 2z\, dz\, dy\, dx = \int_0^a \int_0^a a^2\, dy\, dx = a^4.$$

3. **Surface Integral:** There are four surfaces to this solid.

$z = 0,\ \mathbf{N} = -\mathbf{k},\ \mathbf{F} \cdot \mathbf{N} = -z$

$$\int_{S_1}\!\!\int 0\, dS = 0$$

$y = 0,\ \mathbf{N} = -\mathbf{j},\ \mathbf{F} \cdot \mathbf{N} = 2y - z,\ dS = dA = dx\, dz$

$$\int_{S_2}\!\!\int -z\, dS = \int_0^6 \int_0^{6-z} -z\, dx\, dz = \int_0^6 (z^2 - 6z)\, dz = -36$$

$x = 0,\ \mathbf{N} = -\mathbf{i},\ \mathbf{F} \cdot \mathbf{N} = y - 2x,\ dS = dA = dz\, dy$

$$\int_{S_3}\!\!\int y\, dS = \int_0^3 \int_0^{6-2y} y\, dz\, dy = \int_0^3 (6y - 2y^2)\, dy = 9$$

$x + 2y + z = 6,\ \mathbf{N} = \dfrac{\mathbf{i} + 2\mathbf{j} + \mathbf{k}}{\sqrt{6}},\ \mathbf{F} \cdot \mathbf{N} = \dfrac{2x - 5y + 3z}{\sqrt{6}},\ dS = \sqrt{6}\, dA$

$$\int_{S_4}\!\!\int (2x - 5y + 3z)\, dz\, dy = \int_0^3 \int_0^{6-2y} (18 - x - 11y)\, dx\, dy = \int_0^3 (90 - 90y + 20y^2)\, dy = 45$$

Therefore, $\displaystyle\int_{S}\!\!\int \mathbf{F} \cdot \mathbf{N}\, dS = 0 - 36 + 9 + 45 = 18$.

Divergence Theorem: Since div $\mathbf{F} = 1$, we have

$$\int\!\!\int_{Q}\!\!\int dV = (\text{Volume of solid}) = \frac{1}{3}(\text{Area of base}) \times (\text{Height}) = \frac{1}{3}(9)(6) = 18.$$

5. Since div $\mathbf{F} = 2x + 2y + 2z$, we have

$$\iiint_Q \text{div } \mathbf{F} \, dV = \int_0^a \int_0^a \int_0^a (2x + 2y + 2z) \, dz \, dy \, dx$$

$$= \int_0^a \int_0^a (2ax + 2ay + a^2) \, dy \, dx = \int_0^a (2a^2 x + 2a^3) \, dx = \left[a^2 x^2 + 2a^3 x \right]_0^a = 3a^4.$$

7. Since div $\mathbf{F} = 2x - 2x + 2xyz = 2xyz$

$$\iiint_Q \text{div } \mathbf{F} \, dV = \iiint_Q 2xyz \, dV = \int_0^a \int_0^{2\pi} \int_0^{\pi/2} 2(\rho \sin \phi \cos \theta)(\rho \sin \phi \sin \theta)(\rho \cos \phi)\rho^2 \sin \phi \, d\phi \, d\theta \, d\rho$$

$$= \int_0^a \int_0^{2\pi} \int_0^{\pi/2} 2\rho^5 (\sin \theta \cos \theta)(\sin^3 \phi \cos \phi) \, d\phi \, d\theta \, d\rho$$

$$= \int_0^a \int_0^{2\pi} \frac{1}{2}\rho^5 \sin \theta \cos \theta \, d\theta \, d\rho = \int_0^a \left[\left(\frac{\rho^5}{2} \right) \frac{\sin^2 \theta}{2} \right]_0^{2\pi} d\rho = 0.$$

9. Since div $\mathbf{F} = 3$, we have

$$\iiint_Q 3 \, dV = 3(\text{Volume of sphere}) = 3 \left[\frac{4}{3}\pi(2)^3 \right] = 32\pi.$$

11. Since div $\mathbf{F} = 1 + 2y - 1 = 2y$, we have

$$\iiint_Q 2y \, dV = \int_0^4 \int_{-3}^3 \int_{-\sqrt{9-y^2}}^{\sqrt{9-y^2}} 2y \, dx \, dy \, dz = \int_0^4 \int_{-3}^3 4y\sqrt{9 - y^2} \, dy \, dz = \int_0^4 \left[-\frac{4}{3}(9 - y^2)^{3/2} \right]_{-3}^3 dz = 0.$$

13. Since div $\mathbf{F} = 3x^2 + x^2 + 0 = 4x^2$, we have

$$\iiint_Q 4x^2 \, dV = \int_0^6 \int_0^4 \int_0^{4-y} 4x^2 \, dz \, dy \, dx = \int_0^6 \int_0^4 4x^2(4 - y) \, dy \, dx = \int_0^6 32x^2 \, dx = 2304.$$

15. $\mathbf{F}(x, y, z) = xy\mathbf{i} + 4y\mathbf{j} + xz\mathbf{k}$

div $\mathbf{F} = y + 4 + x$

$$\iint_S \mathbf{F} \cdot \mathbf{N} \, dS = \iiint_Q \text{div } \mathbf{F} \, dV = \iiint_Q (y + x + 4) \, dV$$

$$= \int_0^3 \int_0^{\pi} \int_0^{2\pi} (\rho \sin \phi \sin \theta + \rho \sin \phi \cos \theta + 4)\rho^2 \sin \phi \, d\theta \, d\phi \, d\rho$$

$$= \int_0^3 \int_0^{\pi} \int_0^{2\pi} [\rho^3 \sin^2 \phi \sin \theta + \rho^3 \sin^2 \phi \cos \theta + 4\rho^2 \sin \phi] \, d\theta \, d\phi \, d\rho$$

$$= \int_0^3 \int_0^{\pi} \left[-\rho^3 \sin^2 \phi \cos \theta + \rho^3 \sin^2 \phi \sin \theta + 4\rho^2 \sin \phi \cdot \theta \right]_0^{2\pi} d\phi \, d\rho$$

$$= \int_0^3 \int_0^{\pi} 8\pi\rho^2 \sin \phi \, d\phi \, d\rho$$

$$= \int_0^3 \left[-8\pi\rho^2 \cos \phi \right]_0^{\pi} d\rho$$

$$= \int_0^3 16\pi\rho^2 \, d\rho = \left[\frac{16\pi\rho^3}{3} \right]_0^3 = 144\pi.$$

17. Using the Divergence Theorem, we have

$$\iint_S \text{curl } \mathbf{F} \cdot \mathbf{N} \, dS = \iiint_Q \text{div (curlF)} \, dV$$

$$\text{curl } \mathbf{F}(x, y, z) = \begin{vmatrix} \mathbf{i} & \mathbf{j} & \mathbf{k} \\ \dfrac{\partial}{\partial x} & \dfrac{\partial}{\partial y} & \dfrac{\partial}{\partial z} \\ 4xy + z^2 & 2x^2 + 6yz & 2xz \end{vmatrix} = -6y\mathbf{i} - (2z - 2z)\mathbf{j} + (4x - 4x)\mathbf{k} = -6y\mathbf{i}$$

$$\text{div (curl } \mathbf{F}) = 0.$$

Therefore, $\displaystyle\iiint_Q \text{div (curl } \mathbf{F}) \, dV = 0.$

19. See Theorem 14.12, page 1073.

21. Using the triple integral to find volume, we need $\mathbf{F}$ so that

$$\text{div } \mathbf{F} = \frac{\partial M}{\partial x} + \frac{\partial N}{\partial y} + \frac{\partial P}{\partial z} = 1.$$

Hence, we could have $\mathbf{F} = x\mathbf{i}$, $\mathbf{F} = y\mathbf{j}$, or $\mathbf{F} = z\mathbf{k}$.

For $dA = dy \, dz$ consider $\mathbf{F} = x\mathbf{i}$, $x = f(y, z)$, then $\mathbf{N} = \dfrac{\mathbf{i} + f_y\mathbf{j} + f_z\mathbf{k}}{\sqrt{1 + f_y^2 + f_z^2}}$ and $dS = \sqrt{1 + f_y^2 + f_z^2} \, dy \, dz$.

For $dA = dz \, dx$ consider $\mathbf{F} = y\mathbf{j}$, $y = f(x, z)$, then $\mathbf{N} = \dfrac{f_x\mathbf{i} + \mathbf{j} + f_z\mathbf{k}}{\sqrt{1 + f_x^2 + f_z^2}}$ and $dS = \sqrt{1 + f_x^2 + f_z^2} \, dz \, dx$.

For $dA = dx \, dy$ consider $\mathbf{F} = z\mathbf{k}$, $z = f(x, y)$, then $\mathbf{N} = \dfrac{f_x\mathbf{i} + f_y\mathbf{j} + \mathbf{k}}{\sqrt{1 + f_x^2 + f_y^2}}$ and $dS = \sqrt{1 + f_x^2 + f_y^2} \, dx \, dy$.

Correspondingly, we then have $\displaystyle V = \iint_S \mathbf{F} \cdot \mathbf{N} \, dS = \iint_S x \, dy \, dz = \iint_S y \, dz \, dx = \iint_S z \, dx \, dy.$

23. Using the Divergence Theorem, we have $\displaystyle\iint_S \text{curl } \mathbf{F} \cdot \mathbf{N} \, dS = \iiint_Q \text{div (curl } \mathbf{F}) \, dV.$ Let

$$\mathbf{F}(x, y, z) = M\mathbf{i} + N\mathbf{j} + P\mathbf{k}$$

$$\text{curl } \mathbf{F} = \left(\frac{\partial P}{\partial y} - \frac{\partial N}{\partial z}\right)\mathbf{i} - \left(\frac{\partial P}{\partial x} - \frac{\partial M}{\partial z}\right)\mathbf{j} + \left(\frac{\partial N}{\partial x} - \frac{\partial M}{\partial y}\right)\mathbf{k}$$

$$\text{div (curl } \mathbf{F}) = \frac{\partial^2 P}{\partial x \partial y} - \frac{\partial^2 N}{\partial x \partial z} - \frac{\partial^2 P}{\partial y \partial x} + \frac{\partial^2 M}{\partial y \partial z} + \frac{\partial^2 N}{\partial z \partial x} - \frac{\partial^2 M}{\partial z \partial y} = 0.$$

Therefore, $\displaystyle\iint_S \text{curl } \mathbf{F} \cdot \mathbf{N} \, dS = \iiint_Q 0 \, dV = 0.$

25. If $\mathbf{F}(x, y, z) = x\mathbf{i} + y\mathbf{j} + z\mathbf{k}$, then div $\mathbf{F} = 3$.

$$\iint_S \mathbf{F} \cdot \mathbf{N} \, dS = \iiint_Q \text{div } \mathbf{F} \, dV = \iiint_Q 3 \, dV = 3V.$$

27. $\displaystyle\iint_S f D_\mathbf{N} g \, dS = \iint_S f \nabla g \cdot \mathbf{N} \, dS$

$$= \iiint_Q \text{div } (f \nabla g) \, dV = \iiint_Q (f \, \text{div } \nabla g + \nabla f \cdot \nabla g) \, dV = \iiint_Q (f \nabla^2 g + \nabla f \cdot \nabla g) \, dV$$

Section 14.8   Stokes's Theorem

1. $\mathbf{F}(x, y, z) = (2y - z)\mathbf{i} + xyz\mathbf{j} + e^z\mathbf{k}$

$$\mathbf{curl\ F} = \begin{vmatrix} \mathbf{i} & \mathbf{j} & \mathbf{k} \\ \dfrac{\partial}{\partial x} & \dfrac{\partial}{\partial y} & \dfrac{\partial}{\partial z} \\ 2y - z & xyz & e^z \end{vmatrix} = -xy\mathbf{i} - \mathbf{j} + (yz - 2)\mathbf{k}$$

3. $\mathbf{F}(x, y, z) = 2z\mathbf{i} - 4x^2\mathbf{j} + \arctan x\mathbf{k}$

$$\mathbf{curl\ F} = \begin{vmatrix} \mathbf{i} & \mathbf{j} & \mathbf{k} \\ \dfrac{\partial}{\partial x} & \dfrac{\partial}{\partial y} & \dfrac{\partial}{\partial z} \\ 2z & -4x^2 & \arctan x \end{vmatrix} = \left(2 - \dfrac{1}{1 + x^2}\right)\mathbf{j} - 8x\mathbf{k}$$

5. $\mathbf{F}(x, y, z) = e^{x^2 + y^2}\mathbf{i} + e^{y^2 + z^2}\mathbf{j} + xyz\mathbf{k}$

$$\mathbf{curl\ F} = \begin{vmatrix} \mathbf{i} & \mathbf{j} & \mathbf{k} \\ \dfrac{\partial}{\partial x} & \dfrac{\partial}{\partial y} & \dfrac{\partial}{\partial z} \\ e^{x^2 + y^2} & e^{y^2 + z^2} & xyz \end{vmatrix}$$

$$= (xz - 2ze^{y^2 + z^2})\mathbf{i} - yz\mathbf{j} - 2ye^{x^2 + y^2}\mathbf{k}$$

$$= z(x - 2e^{y^2 + z^2})\mathbf{i} - yz\mathbf{j} - 2ye^{x^2 + y^2}\mathbf{k}$$

7. In this case, $M = -y + z$, $N = x - z$, $P = x - y$ and C is the circle $x^2 + y^2 = 1$, $z = 0$, $dz = 0$.

Line Integral: $\displaystyle\int_C \mathbf{F} \cdot d\mathbf{r} = \int_C -y\,dx + x\,dy$

Letting $x = \cos t$, $y = \sin t$, we have $dx = -\sin t\,dt$, $dy = \cos t\,dt$ and

$$\int_C -y\,dx + x\,dy = \int_0^{2\pi} (\sin^2 t + \cos^2 t)dt = 2\pi.$$

Double Integral: Consider $F(x, y, z) = x^2 + y^2 + z^2 - 1$.

Then

$$\mathbf{N} = \dfrac{\nabla F}{\|\nabla F\|} = \dfrac{2x\mathbf{i} + 2y\mathbf{j} + 2z\mathbf{k}}{2\sqrt{x^2 + y^2 + z^2}} = x\mathbf{i} + y\mathbf{j} + z\mathbf{k}.$$

Since

$$z^2 = 1 - x^2 - y^2,\ z_x = \dfrac{-2x}{2z} = \dfrac{-x}{z},\ \text{and}\ z_y = \dfrac{-y}{z},\ dS = \sqrt{1 + \dfrac{x^2}{z^2} + \dfrac{y^2}{z^2}}dA = \dfrac{1}{z}dA.$$

Now, since $\mathbf{curl\ F} = 2\mathbf{k}$, we have

$$\int_S\int (\mathbf{curl\ F}) \cdot \mathbf{N}\,dS = \int_R\int 2z\left(\dfrac{1}{z}\right)dA = \int_R\int 2\,dA = 2(\text{Area of circle of radius } 1) = 2\pi.$$

9. Line Integral: From the accompanying figure we see that for

$C_1: z = 0, \ dz = 0$

$C_2: x = 0, \ dx = 0$

$C_3: y = 0, \ dy = 0.$

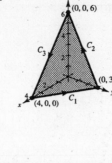

Hence, $\displaystyle\int_C \mathbf{F} \cdot d\mathbf{r} = \int_C xyz \, dx + y \, dy + z \, dz$

$$= \int_{C_1} y \, dy + \int_{C_2} y \, dy + z \, dz + \int_{C_3} z \, dz$$

$$= \int_0^3 y \, dy + \int_3^0 y \, dy + \int_0^6 z \, dz + \int_6^0 z \, dz = 0.$$

Double Integral: $\mathbf{curl \ F} = xy\mathbf{j} - xz\mathbf{k}$

Considering $F(x, y, z) = 3x + 4y + 2z - 12$, then

$$\mathbf{N} = \frac{\nabla F}{\|\nabla F\|} = \frac{3\mathbf{i} + 4\mathbf{j} + 2\mathbf{k}}{\sqrt{29}} \text{ and } dS = \sqrt{29} \, dA.$$

Thus,

$$\int_S\int (\mathbf{curl \ F}) \cdot \mathbf{N} \, dS = \int_R\int (4xy - 2xz) \, dy \, dx$$

$$= \int_0^4 \int_0^{(-3x+12)/4} \left[4xy - 2x\left(6 - 2y - \frac{3}{2}x\right)\right] dy \, dx$$

$$= \int_0^4 \int_0^{(12-3x)/4} (8xy + 3x^2 - 12x) \, dy \, dx$$

$$= \int_0^4 0 \, dx = 0.$$

11. Let $A = (0, 0, 0)$, $B = (1, 1, 1)$ and $C = (0, 2, 0)$. Then $\mathbf{U} = \overrightarrow{AB} = \mathbf{i} + \mathbf{j} + \mathbf{k}$ and $\mathbf{V} = \overrightarrow{AC} = 2\mathbf{j}$. Thus,

$$\mathbf{N} = \frac{\mathbf{U} \times \mathbf{V}}{\|\mathbf{U} \times \mathbf{V}\|} = \frac{-2\mathbf{i} + 2\mathbf{k}}{2\sqrt{2}} = \frac{-\mathbf{i} + \mathbf{k}}{\sqrt{2}}.$$

Surface S has direction numbers $-1, 0, 1$, with equation $z - x = 0$ and $dS = \sqrt{2} \, dA$. Since $\mathbf{curl \ F} = -3\mathbf{i} + \mathbf{j} - 2\mathbf{k}$, we have

$$\int_S\int (\mathbf{curl \ F}) \cdot \mathbf{N} \, dS = \int_R\int \frac{1}{\sqrt{2}}(\sqrt{2}) \, dA = \int_R\int dA = (\text{Area of triangle with } a = 1, b = 2) = 1.$$

13. $\mathbf{F}(x, y, z) = z^2\mathbf{i} + x^2\mathbf{j} + y^2\mathbf{k}$, $S: z = 4 - x^2 - y^2$, $0 \le z$

$$\mathbf{curl \ F} = \begin{vmatrix} \mathbf{i} & \mathbf{j} & \mathbf{k} \\ \frac{\partial}{\partial x} & \frac{\partial}{\partial y} & \frac{\partial}{\partial z} \\ z^2 & x^2 & y^2 \end{vmatrix} = 2y\mathbf{i} + 2z\mathbf{j} + 2x\mathbf{k}$$

$G(x, y, z) = x^2 + y^2 + z - 4$

$\nabla G(x, y, z) = 2x\mathbf{i} + 2y\mathbf{j} + \mathbf{k}$

$$\int_S\int (\mathbf{curl \ F}) \cdot \mathbf{N} \, dS = \int_R\int (4xy + 4yz + 2x) \, dA = \int_{-2}^2 \int_{-\sqrt{4-x^2}}^{\sqrt{4-x^2}} [4xy + 4y(4 - x^2 - y^2) + 2x] \, dy \, dx$$

$$= \int_{-2}^2 \int_{-\sqrt{4-x^2}}^{\sqrt{4-x^2}} [4xy + 16y - 4x^2y - 4y^3 + 2x] \, dy \, dx$$

$$= \int_{-2}^2 4x\sqrt{4 - x^2} \, dx = 0$$

15. $\mathbf{F}(x, y, z) = z^2\mathbf{i} + y\mathbf{j} + xz\mathbf{k}$, $S: z = \sqrt{4 - x^2 - y^2}$

$$\mathbf{curl\ F} = \begin{vmatrix} \mathbf{i} & \mathbf{j} & \mathbf{k} \\ \dfrac{\partial}{\partial x} & \dfrac{\partial}{\partial y} & \dfrac{\partial}{\partial z} \\ z^2 & y & xz \end{vmatrix} = z\mathbf{j}$$

$$G(x, y, z) = z - \sqrt{4 - x^2 - y^2}$$

$$\nabla G(x, y, z) = \frac{x}{\sqrt{4 - x^2 - y^2}}\mathbf{i} + \frac{y}{\sqrt{4 - x^2 - y^2}}\mathbf{j} + \mathbf{k}$$

$$\int_S\!\!\int (\mathbf{curl\ F}) \cdot \mathbf{F}\, dS = \int_R\!\!\int \frac{yz}{\sqrt{4 - x^2 - y^2}}\, dA = \int_R\!\!\int \frac{y\sqrt{4 - x^2 - y^2}}{\sqrt{4 - x^2 - y^2}}\, dA = \int_{-2}^{2}\int_{-\sqrt{4-x^2}}^{\sqrt{4-x^2}} y\, dy\, dx = 0$$

17. $\mathbf{F}(x, y, z) = -\ln\sqrt{x^2 + y^2}\,\mathbf{i} + \arctan\dfrac{x}{y}\mathbf{j} + \mathbf{k}$

$$\mathbf{curl\ F} = \begin{vmatrix} \mathbf{i} & \mathbf{j} & \mathbf{k} \\ \dfrac{\partial}{\partial x} & \dfrac{\partial}{\partial y} & \dfrac{\partial}{\partial z} \\ -1/2\ln(x^2 + y^2) & \arctan x/y & 1 \end{vmatrix} = \left[\frac{(1/y)}{1 + (x^2/y^2)} + \frac{y}{x^2 + y^2}\right]\mathbf{k} = \left[\frac{2y}{x^2 + y^2}\right]\mathbf{k}$$

$S: z = 9 - 2x - 3y$ over one petal of $r = 2\sin 2\theta$ in the first octant.

$$G(x, y, z) = 2x + 3y + z - 9$$

$$\nabla G(x, y, z) = 2\mathbf{i} + 3\mathbf{j} + \mathbf{k}$$

$$\begin{aligned}
\int_S\!\!\int (\mathbf{curl\ F}) \cdot \mathbf{N}\, dS &= \int_R\!\!\int \frac{2y}{x^2 + y^2}\, dA \\
&= \int_0^{\pi/2}\int_0^{2\sin 2\theta} \frac{2r\sin\theta}{r^2} r\, dr\, d\theta \\
&= \int_0^{\pi/2}\int_0^{4\sin\theta\cos\theta} 2\sin\theta\, dr\, d\theta \\
&= \int_0^{\pi/2} 8\sin^2\theta\cos\theta\, d\theta = \left[\frac{8\sin^3\theta}{3}\right]_0^{\pi/2} = \frac{8}{3}
\end{aligned}$$

19. From Exercise 10, we have $\mathbf{N} = \dfrac{2x\mathbf{i} - \mathbf{k}}{\sqrt{1 + 4x^2}}$ and $dS = \sqrt{1 + 4x^2}\, dA$. Since $\mathbf{curl\ F} = xy\mathbf{j} - xz\mathbf{k}$, we have

$$\int_S\!\!\int (\mathbf{curl\ F}) \cdot \mathbf{N}\, dS = \int_R\!\!\int xz\, dA = \int_0^a\int_0^a x^3\, dy\, dx = \int_0^a ax^3\, dx = \left[\frac{ax^4}{4}\right]_0^a = \frac{a^5}{4}.$$

21. $\mathbf{F}(x, y, z) = \mathbf{i} + \mathbf{j} - 2\mathbf{k}$ **23.** See Theorem 14.13, page 1081.

$$\mathbf{curl\ F} = \begin{vmatrix} \mathbf{i} & \mathbf{j} & \mathbf{k} \\ \dfrac{\partial}{\partial x} & \dfrac{\partial}{\partial y} & \dfrac{\partial}{\partial z} \\ 1 & 1 & -2 \end{vmatrix} = \mathbf{0}$$

Letting $\mathbf{N} = \mathbf{k}$, we have $\displaystyle\int_S\!\!\int (\mathbf{curl\ F}) \cdot \mathbf{N}\, dS = 0.$

25. (a) $\displaystyle\int_C f\nabla g \cdot d\mathbf{r} = \iint_S \mathbf{curl}[f\nabla g] \cdot \mathbf{N}\, dS$ (Stoke's Theorem)

$$f\nabla g = f\frac{\partial g}{\partial x}\mathbf{i} + f\frac{\partial g}{\partial y}\mathbf{j} + f\frac{\partial g}{\partial z}\mathbf{k}$$

$$\mathbf{curl}\,(f\nabla g) = \begin{vmatrix} \mathbf{i} & \mathbf{j} & \mathbf{k} \\ \dfrac{\partial}{\partial x} & \dfrac{\partial}{\partial y} & \dfrac{\partial}{\partial z} \\ f(\partial g/\partial x) & f(\partial g/\partial y) & f(\partial g/\partial z) \end{vmatrix}$$

$$= \left[\left[f\left(\frac{\partial^2 g}{\partial y\partial z}\right) + \left(\frac{\partial f}{\partial y}\right)\left(\frac{\partial g}{\partial z}\right)\right] - \left[f\left(\frac{\partial^2 g}{\partial z\partial y}\right) + \left(\frac{\partial f}{\partial z}\right)\left(\frac{\partial g}{\partial y}\right)\right]\right]\mathbf{i}$$

$$\quad - \left[\left[f\left(\frac{\partial^2 g}{\partial x\partial z}\right) + \left(\frac{\partial f}{\partial x}\right)\left(\frac{\partial g}{\partial z}\right)\right] - \left[f\left(\frac{\partial^2 g}{\partial z\partial x}\right) + \left(\frac{\partial f}{\partial z}\right)\left(\frac{\partial g}{\partial x}\right)\right]\right]\mathbf{j}$$

$$\quad + \left[\left[f\left(\frac{\partial^2 g}{\partial x\partial y}\right) + \left(\frac{\partial f}{\partial x}\right)\left(\frac{\partial g}{\partial y}\right)\right] - \left[f\left(\frac{\partial^2 g}{\partial y\partial x}\right) + \left(\frac{\partial f}{\partial y}\right)\left(\frac{\partial g}{\partial x}\right)\right]\right]\mathbf{k}$$

$$= \left[\left(\frac{\partial f}{\partial y}\right)\left(\frac{\partial g}{\partial z}\right) - \left(\frac{\partial f}{\partial z}\right)\left(\frac{\partial g}{\partial y}\right)\right]\mathbf{i} - \left[\left(\frac{\partial f}{\partial x}\right)\left(\frac{\partial g}{\partial z}\right) - \left(\frac{\partial f}{\partial z}\right)\left(\frac{\partial g}{\partial x}\right)\right]\mathbf{j} + \left[\left(\frac{\partial f}{\partial x}\right)\left(\frac{\partial g}{\partial y}\right) - \left(\frac{\partial f}{\partial y}\right)\left(\frac{\partial g}{\partial x}\right)\right]\mathbf{k}$$

$$= \begin{vmatrix} \mathbf{i} & \mathbf{j} & \mathbf{k} \\ \dfrac{\partial f}{\partial x} & \dfrac{\partial f}{\partial y} & \dfrac{\partial f}{\partial z} \\ \dfrac{\partial g}{\partial x} & \dfrac{\partial g}{\partial y} & \dfrac{\partial g}{\partial z} \end{vmatrix} = \nabla f \times \nabla g$$

Therefore, $\displaystyle\int_C f\nabla g \cdot d\mathbf{r} = \iint_S \mathbf{curl}[f\nabla g] \cdot \mathbf{N}\, dS = \iint_S [\nabla f \times \nabla g] \cdot \mathbf{N}\, dS.$

(b) $\displaystyle\int_C (f\nabla f) \cdot d\mathbf{r} = \iint_S (\nabla f \times \nabla f) \cdot \mathbf{N}\, dS$ (using part a.)

$$= 0 \text{ since } \nabla f \times \nabla f = 0.$$

(c) $\displaystyle\int_C (f\nabla g + g\nabla f) \cdot d\mathbf{r} = \int_C (f\nabla g)\cdot d\mathbf{r} + \int_C (g\nabla f)\cdot d\mathbf{r}$

$$= \iint_S (\nabla f \times \nabla g) \cdot \mathbf{N}\, dS + \iint_S (\nabla g \times \nabla f) \cdot \mathbf{N}\, dS \quad \text{(using part a.)}$$

$$= \iint_S (\nabla f \times \nabla g) \cdot \mathbf{N}\, dS + \iint_S -(\nabla f \times \nabla g) \cdot \mathbf{N}\, dS = 0$$

27. Let $\mathbf{C} = a\mathbf{i} + b\mathbf{j} + c\mathbf{k}$, then

$$\frac{1}{2}\int_C (\mathbf{C} \times \mathbf{r}) \cdot d\mathbf{r} = \frac{1}{2}\iint_S \mathbf{curl}\,(\mathbf{C} \times \mathbf{r}) \cdot \mathbf{N}\, dS = \frac{1}{2}\iint_S 2\mathbf{C} \cdot \mathbf{N}\, dS = \iint_S \mathbf{C} \cdot \mathbf{N}\, dS$$

since

$$\mathbf{C} \times \mathbf{r} = \begin{vmatrix} \mathbf{i} & \mathbf{j} & \mathbf{k} \\ a & b & c \\ x & y & z \end{vmatrix} = (bz - cy)\mathbf{i} - (az - cx)\mathbf{j} + (ay - bx)\mathbf{k}$$

and

$$\mathbf{curl}(\mathbf{C} \times \mathbf{r}) = \begin{vmatrix} \mathbf{i} & \mathbf{j} & \mathbf{k} \\ \dfrac{\partial}{\partial x} & \dfrac{\partial}{\partial y} & \dfrac{\partial}{\partial z} \\ bz - cy & cx - az & ay - bx \end{vmatrix} = 2(a\mathbf{i} + b\mathbf{j} + c\mathbf{k}) = 2\mathbf{C}.$$

Review Exercises for Chapter 14

1. $\mathbf{F}(x, y, z) = x\mathbf{i} + \mathbf{j} + 2\mathbf{k}$

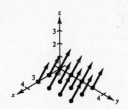

3. $f(x, y, z) = 8x^2 + xy + z^2$

$$\mathbf{F}(x, y, z) = (16x + y)\mathbf{i} + x\mathbf{j} + 2z\mathbf{k}$$

5. Since $\partial M/\partial y = -1/y^2 \neq \partial N/\partial x$, $\mathbf{F}$ is not conservative.

7. Since $\partial M/\partial y = 12xy = \partial N/\partial x$, $\mathbf{F}$ is conservative. From $M = \partial U/\partial x = 6xy^2 - 3x^2$ and $N = \partial U/\partial y = 6x^2y + 3y^2 - 7$, partial integration yields $U = 3x^2y^2 - x^3 + h(y)$ and $U = 3x^2y^2 + y^3 - 7y + g(x)$ which suggests $h(y) = y^3 - 7y$, $g(x) = -x^3$, and $U(x, y) = 3x^2y^2 - x^3 + y^3 - 7y + C$.

9. Since

$$\frac{\partial M}{\partial y} = 4x = \frac{\partial N}{\partial x},$$

$$\frac{\partial M}{\partial z} = 1 \neq \frac{\partial P}{\partial x}.$$

$\mathbf{F}$ is not conservative.

11. Since

$$\frac{\partial M}{\partial y} = \frac{-1}{y^2z} = \frac{\partial N}{\partial x}, \quad \frac{\partial M}{\partial z} = \frac{-1}{yz^2} = \frac{\partial P}{\partial x}, \quad \frac{\partial N}{\partial z} = \frac{x}{y^2z^2} = \frac{\partial P}{\partial y},$$

$\mathbf{F}$ is conservative. From

$$M = \frac{\partial U}{\partial x} = \frac{1}{yz}, \quad N = \frac{\partial U}{\partial y} = \frac{-x}{y^2z}, \quad P = \frac{\partial U}{\partial z} = \frac{-x}{yz^2}$$

we obtain

$$U = \frac{x}{yz} + f(y, z), \quad U = \frac{x}{yz} + g(x, z), \quad U = \frac{x}{yz} + h(x, y) \implies f(x, y, z) = \frac{x}{yz} + K$$

13. Since $\mathbf{F} = x^2\mathbf{i} + y^2\mathbf{j} + z^2\mathbf{k}$:

(a) div $\mathbf{F} = 2x + 2y + 2z$

(b) **curl** $\mathbf{F} = \left(\frac{\partial P}{\partial y} - \frac{\partial N}{\partial z}\right)\mathbf{i} - \left(\frac{\partial P}{\partial x} - \frac{\partial M}{\partial z}\right)\mathbf{j} + \left(\frac{\partial N}{\partial x} - \frac{\partial M}{\partial y}\right)\mathbf{k} = 0\mathbf{i} - 0\mathbf{j} + 0\mathbf{k} = \mathbf{0}$

15. Since $\mathbf{F} = (\cos y + y\cos x)\mathbf{i} + (\sin x - x\sin y)\mathbf{j} + xyz\mathbf{k}$:

(a) div $\mathbf{F} = -y\sin x - x\cos y + xy$

(b) **curl** $\mathbf{F} = xz\mathbf{i} - yz\mathbf{j} + (\cos x - \sin y + \sin y - \cos x)\mathbf{k} = xz\mathbf{i} - yz\mathbf{j}$

17. Since $\mathbf{F} = \arcsin x\mathbf{i} + xy^2\mathbf{j} + yz^2\mathbf{k}$:

(a) $\text{div } \mathbf{F} = \dfrac{1}{\sqrt{1 - x^2}} + 2xy + 2yz$

(b) $\text{curl } \mathbf{F} = z^2\mathbf{i} + y^2\mathbf{k}$

19. Since $\mathbf{F} = \ln(x^2 + y^2)\mathbf{i} + \ln(x^2 + y^2)\mathbf{j} + z\mathbf{k}$:

(a) $\text{div } \mathbf{F} = \dfrac{2x}{x^2 + y^2} + \dfrac{2y}{x^2 + y^2} + 1$

$\qquad = \dfrac{2x + 2y}{x^2 + y^2} + 1$

(b) $\text{curl } \mathbf{F} = \dfrac{2x - 2y}{x^2 + y^2}\mathbf{k}$

21. (a) Let $x = t$, $y = t$, $-1 \le t \le 2$, then $ds = \sqrt{2}\, dt$.

$$\int_C (x^2 + y^2)\, ds = \int_{-1}^2 2t^2\sqrt{2}\, dt = \left[2\sqrt{2}\left(\frac{t^3}{3}\right)\right]_{-1}^2 = 6\sqrt{2}$$

(b) Let $x = 4\cos t$, $y = 4\sin t$, $0 \le t \le 2\pi$, then $ds = 4\, dt$.

$$\int_C (x^2 + y^2)\, ds = \int_0^{2\pi} 16(4\, dt) = 128\pi$$

23. $x = \cos t + t\sin t$, $y = \sin t - t\cos t$, $0 \le t \le 2\pi$, $\dfrac{dx}{dt} = t\cos t$, $\dfrac{dy}{dt} = t\sin t$

$$\int_C (x^2 + y^2)\, ds = \int_0^{2\pi} [(\cos t + t\sin t)^2 + (\sin t - t\cos t)^2]\sqrt{t^2\cos^2 t + t^2\sin^2 t}\, dt = \int_0^{2\pi} [t^3 + t]\, dt$$

$$= 2\pi^2(1 + 2\pi^2)$$

25. (a) Let $x = 2t$, $y = -3t$, $0 \le t \le 1$

$$\int_C (2x - y)\, dx + (x + 3y)\, dy = \int_0^1 [7t(2) + (-7t)(-3)]\, dt = \int_0^1 35t\, dt = \frac{35}{2}$$

(b) $x = 3\cos t$, $y = 3\sin t$, $dx = -3\sin t\, dt$, $dy = 3\cos t\, dt$, $0 \le t \le 2\pi$

$$\int_C (2x - y)\, dx + (x + 3y)\, dy = \int_0^{2\pi} (9 + 9\sin t\cos t)\, dt = 18\pi$$

27. $\displaystyle\int_C (2x + y)\, ds$, $\mathbf{r}(t) = a\cos^3 t\mathbf{i} + a\sin^3 t\mathbf{j}$, $0 \le t \le \dfrac{\pi}{2}$

$x'(t) = -3a \cdot \cos^2 t\sin t$

$y'(t) = 3a \cdot \sin^2 t\cos t$

$$\int_C (2x + y)\, ds = \int_0^{\pi/2} (2(a \cdot \cos^3 t) + a \cdot \sin^3 t)\sqrt{x'(t)^2 + y'(t)^2}\, dt = \frac{9a^2}{5}$$

29. $f(x, y) = 5 + \sin(x + y)$

$C: y = 3x$ from $(0, 0)$ to $(2, 6)$

$\mathbf{r}(t) = t\mathbf{i} + 3t\mathbf{j}$, $0 \le t \le 2$

$\mathbf{r}'(t) = \mathbf{i} + 3\mathbf{j}$

$\|\mathbf{r}'(t)\| = \sqrt{10}$

Lateral surface area:

$$\int_{C_2} f(x, y)\, ds = \int_0^2 [5 + \sin(t + 3t)]\sqrt{10}\, dt = \sqrt{10}\int_0^2 (5 + \sin 4t)\, dt = \frac{\sqrt{10}}{4}(41 - \cos 8) \approx 32.528$$

31. $d\mathbf{r} = (2t\mathbf{i} + 3t^2\mathbf{j})\,dt$

$\mathbf{F} = t^5\mathbf{i} + t^4\mathbf{j}, 0 \le t \le 1$

$\displaystyle\int_C \mathbf{F} \cdot d\mathbf{r} = \int_0^1 5t^6\,dt = \frac{5}{7}$

33. $d\mathbf{r} = [(-2 \sin t)\mathbf{i} + (2 \cos t)\mathbf{j} + \mathbf{k}]\,dt$

$\mathbf{F} = (2 \cos t)\mathbf{i} + (2 \sin t)\mathbf{j} + t\mathbf{k}, 0 \le t \le 2\pi$

$\displaystyle\int_C \mathbf{F} \cdot d\mathbf{r} = \int_0^{2\pi} t\,dt = 2\pi^2$

35. Let $x = t, y = -t, z = 2t^2, -2 \le t \le 2, d\mathbf{r} = [\mathbf{i} - \mathbf{j} + 4t\mathbf{k}]\,dt$.

$\mathbf{F} = (-t - 2t^2)\mathbf{i} + (2t^2 - t)\mathbf{j} + (2t)\mathbf{k}$

$\displaystyle\int_C \mathbf{F} \cdot d\mathbf{r} = \int_{-2}^2 4t^2\,dt = \left[\frac{4t^3}{3}\right]_{-2}^2 = \frac{64}{3}$

37. For $y = x^2$, $\mathbf{r}_1(t) = t\mathbf{i} + t^2\mathbf{j}, 0 \le t \le 2$

For $y = 2x$, $\mathbf{r}_2(t) = (2 - t)\mathbf{i} + (4 - 2t)\mathbf{j}, 0 \le t \le 2$

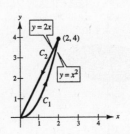

$\displaystyle\int_C xy\,dx + (x^2 + y^2)\,dy = \int_{C_1} xy\,dx + (x^2 + y^2)\,dy + \int_{C_2} xy\,dx + (x^2 + y^2)\,dy$

$\displaystyle = \frac{100}{3} + (-32) = \frac{4}{3}$

39. $\mathbf{F} = x\mathbf{i} - \sqrt{y}\,\mathbf{j}$ is conservative.

Work $= \left[\dfrac{1}{2}x^2 - \dfrac{2}{3}y^{3/2}\right]_{(0,0)}^{(4,8)} = \dfrac{1}{2}(16) - \left(\dfrac{2}{3}\right)8^{3/2} = \dfrac{8}{3}\left(3 - 4\sqrt{2}\right)$

41. $\displaystyle\int_C 2xyz\,dx + x^2z\,dy + x^2y\,dz = \left[x^2yz\right]_{(0,0,0)}^{(1,4,3)} = 12$

43. (a) $\displaystyle\int_C y^2\,dx + 2xy\,dy = \int_0^1 \left[(1 + t)^2(3) + 2(1 + 3t)(1 + t)\right]dt$

$\displaystyle = \int_0^1 3(t^2 + 2t + 1) + 2(3t^2 + 4t + 1)]\,dt$

$\displaystyle = \int_0^1 (9t^2 + 14t + 5)\,dt$

$\displaystyle = \left[3t^3 + 7t^2 + 5t\right]_0^1 = 15$

(b) $\displaystyle\int_C y^2\,dx + 2xy\,dy = \int_1^4 \left[t(1) + 2(t)(\sqrt{t})\frac{1}{2\sqrt{t}}\right]dt$

$\displaystyle = \int_1^4 (t + t)\,dt$

$\displaystyle = \left[t^2\right]_1^4 = 15$

(c) $\mathbf{F}(x, y) = y^2\mathbf{i} + 2xy\,\mathbf{j} = \nabla f$ where $f(x, y) = xy^2$.

Hence,

$\displaystyle\int_C \mathbf{F} \cdot d\mathbf{r} = 4(2)^2 - 1(1)^2 = 15$

45. $\displaystyle\int_C y\,dx + 2x\,dy = \int_0^2\int_0^2 (2 - 1)\,dy\,dx = \int_0^2 2\,dx = 4$

47. $\displaystyle\int_C xy^2\,dx + x^2y\,dy = \int_R\int (2xy - 2xy)\,dA = 0$

49. $\displaystyle\int_C xy\,dx + x^2\,dy = \int_0^1 \int_{x^2}^x x\,dy\,dx = \int_0^1 (x^2 - x^3)\,dx = \frac{1}{12}$

51. $\mathbf{r}(u, v) = \sec u \cos v\,\mathbf{i} + (1 + 2\tan u)\sin v\,\mathbf{j} + 2u\,\mathbf{k}$

$0 \le u \le \dfrac{\pi}{3}, \quad 0 \le v \le 2\pi$

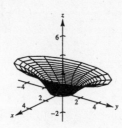

53. (a)

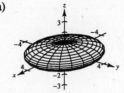

(b)

(c)

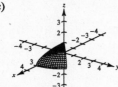

(d)

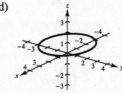

The space curve is a circle:

$\mathbf{r}\left(u, \dfrac{\pi}{4}\right) = \dfrac{3\sqrt{2}}{2}\cos u\,\mathbf{i} + \dfrac{3\sqrt{2}}{2}\sin u\,\mathbf{j} + \dfrac{\sqrt{2}}{2}\mathbf{k}$

(e) $\mathbf{r}_u = -3\cos v \sin u\,\mathbf{i} + 3\cos v \cos u\,\mathbf{j}$

$\mathbf{r}_v = -3\sin v \cos u\,\mathbf{i} - 3\sin v \sin u\,\mathbf{j} + \cos v\,\mathbf{k}$

$\mathbf{r}_u \times \mathbf{r}_v = \begin{vmatrix} \mathbf{i} & \mathbf{j} & \mathbf{k} \\ -3\cos v \sin u & 3\cos v \cos u & 0 \\ -3\sin v \cos u & -3\sin v \sin u & \cos v \end{vmatrix}$

$= (3\cos^2 v \cos u)\mathbf{i} + (3\cos^2 v \sin u)\mathbf{j} + (9\cos v \sin v \sin^2 u + 9\cos v \sin v \cos^2 u)\mathbf{k}$

$= (3\cos^2 v \cos u)\mathbf{i} + (3\cos^2 v \sin u)\mathbf{j} + (9\cos v \sin v)\mathbf{k}$

$\|\mathbf{r}_u \times \mathbf{r}_v\| = \sqrt{9\cos^4 v \cos^2 u + 9\cos^4 v \sin^2 u + 81\cos^2 v \sin^2 v}$

$= \sqrt{9\cos^4 v + 81\cos^2 v \sin^2 v}$

Using a Symbolic integration utility,

$\displaystyle\int_{\pi/4}^{\pi/2} \int_0^{2\pi} \|\mathbf{r}_u \times \mathbf{r}_v\|\,du\,dv \approx 14.44$

(f) Similarly,

$\displaystyle\int_0^{\pi/4} \int_0^{\pi/2} \|\mathbf{r}_u \times \mathbf{r}_v\|\,dv\,du \approx 4.27$

55. $S: \mathbf{r}(u, v) = u\cos v\mathbf{i} + u\sin v\mathbf{j} + (u - 1)(2 - u)\mathbf{k}, \quad 0 \leq u \leq 2, 0 \leq v \leq 2\pi$

$\mathbf{r}_u(u, v) = \cos v\mathbf{i} + \sin v\mathbf{j} + (3 - 2u)\mathbf{k}$

$\mathbf{r}_v(u, v) = -u\sin v\mathbf{i} + u\cos v\mathbf{j}$

$\mathbf{r}_u \times \mathbf{r}_u = \begin{vmatrix} \mathbf{i} & \mathbf{j} & \mathbf{k} \\ \cos v & \sin v & 3 - 2u \\ -u\sin v & u\cos v & 0 \end{vmatrix} = (2u - 3)u\cos v\mathbf{i} + (2u - 3)u\sin v\mathbf{j} + u\mathbf{k}$

$\|\mathbf{r}_u \times \mathbf{r}_v\| = u\sqrt{(2u - 3)^2 + 1}$

$$\iint_S (x + y)\, dS = \int_0^{2\pi} \int_0^2 (u\cos v + u\sin v)\, u\sqrt{(2u - 3)^2 + 1}\, du\, dv$$

$$= \int_0^2 \int_0^{2\pi} (\cos v + \sin v)u^2\sqrt{(2u - 3)^2 + 1}\, dv\, du = 0$$

57. $\mathbf{F}(x, y, z) = x^2\mathbf{i} + xy\mathbf{j} + z\mathbf{k}$

Q: solid region bounded by the coordinates planes and the plane $2x + 3y + 4z = 12$

Surface Integral: There are four surfaces for this solid.

$$z = 0 \quad \mathbf{N} = -\mathbf{k}, \quad \mathbf{F} \cdot \mathbf{N} = -z, \quad \iint_{S_1} 0\, dS = 0$$

$$y = 0, \quad \mathbf{N} = -\mathbf{j}, \quad \mathbf{F} \cdot \mathbf{N} = -xy, \quad \iint_{S_2} 0\, dS = 0$$

$$x = 0, \quad \mathbf{N} = -\mathbf{i}, \quad \mathbf{F} \cdot \mathbf{N} = -x^2, \quad \iint_{S_3} 0\, dS = 0$$

$$2x + 3y + 4z = 12, \mathbf{N} = \frac{2\mathbf{i} + 3\mathbf{j} + 4\mathbf{k}}{\sqrt{29}}, dS = \sqrt{1 + \left(\frac{1}{4}\right) + \left(\frac{9}{16}\right)}dA = \frac{\sqrt{29}}{4}\, dA$$

$$\iint_{S_4} \mathbf{F} \cdot \mathbf{N}\, dS = \frac{1}{4}\iint_R (2x^2 + 3xy + 4z)\, dA$$

$$= \frac{1}{4}\int_0^6 \int_0^{4-(2x/3)} (2x^2 + 3xy + 12 - 2x - 3y)\, dy\, dx$$

$$= \frac{1}{4}\int_0^6 \left[2x^2\left(\frac{12 - 2x}{3}\right) + \frac{3x}{2}\left(\frac{12 - 2x}{3}\right)^2 + 12\left(\frac{12 - 2x}{3}\right) - 2x\left(\frac{12 - 2x}{3}\right) - \frac{3}{2}\left(\frac{12 - 2x}{3}\right)^2\right] dx$$

$$= \frac{1}{6}\int_0^6 (-x^3 + x^2 + 24x + 36)\, dx = \frac{1}{6}\left[-\frac{x^4}{4} + \frac{x^3}{3} + 12x^2 + 36x\right]_0^6 = 66$$

Divergence Theorem: Since div $\mathbf{F} = 2x + x + 1 = 3x + 1$, Divergence Theorem yields

$$\iiint_Q \text{div } \mathbf{F}\, dV = \int_0^6 \int_0^{(12-2x)/3} \int_0^{(12-2x-3y)/4} (3x + 1)\, dz\, dy\, dx$$

$$= \int_0^6 \int_0^{(12-2x)/3} (3x + 1)\left(\frac{12 - 2x - 3y}{4}\right) dy\, dx$$

$$= \frac{1}{4}\int_0^6 (3x + 1)\left[12y - 2xy - \frac{3}{2}y^2\right]_0^{(12-2x)/3} dx$$

$$= \frac{1}{4}\int_0^6 (3x + 1)\left[4(12 - 2x) - 2x\left(\frac{12 - 2x}{3}\right) - \frac{3}{2}\left(\frac{12 - 2x}{3}\right)^2\right] dx$$

$$= \frac{1}{4}\int_0^6 \frac{2}{3}(3x^3 - 35x^2 + 96x + 36)\, dx = \frac{1}{6}\left[\frac{3x^4}{4} - \frac{35x^3}{3} + 48x^2 + 36x\right]_0^6 = 66.$$

59. $\mathbf{F}(x, y, z) = (\cos y + y \cos x)\mathbf{i} + (\sin x - x \sin y)\mathbf{j} + xyz\mathbf{k}$

S: portion of $z = y^2$ over the square in the xy-plane with vertices $(0, 0)$, $(a, 0)$, (a, a), $(0, a)$

Line Integral: Using the line integral we have:

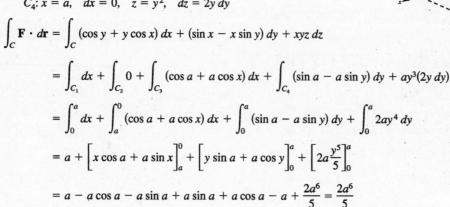

$C_1: y = 0, \quad dy = 0$

$C_2: x = 0, \quad dx = 0, \quad z = y^2, \quad dz = 2y\,dy$

$C_3: y = a, \quad dy = 0, \quad z = a^2, \quad dz = 0$

$C_4: x = a, \quad dx = 0, \quad z = y^2, \quad dz = 2y\,dy$

$$\int_C \mathbf{F} \cdot d\mathbf{r} = \int_C (\cos y + y \cos x)\,dx + (\sin x - x \sin y)\,dy + xyz\,dz$$

$$= \int_{C_1} dx + \int_{C_2} 0 + \int_{C_3} (\cos a + a \cos x)\,dx + \int_{C_4} (\sin a - a \sin y)\,dy + ay^3(2y\,dy)$$

$$= \int_0^a dx + \int_a^0 (\cos a + a \cos x)\,dx + \int_0^a (\sin a - a \sin y)\,dy + \int_0^a 2ay^4\,dy$$

$$= a + \left[x \cos a + a \sin x \right]_a^0 + \left[y \sin a + a \cos y \right]_0^a + \left[2a\frac{y^5}{5} \right]_0^a$$

$$= a - a \cos a - a \sin a + a \sin a + a \cos a - a + \frac{2a^6}{5} = \frac{2a^6}{5}$$

Double Integral: Considering $f(x, y, z) = z - y^2$, we have:

$$\mathbf{N} = \frac{\nabla f}{\|\nabla f\|} = \frac{-2y\mathbf{j} + \mathbf{k}}{\sqrt{1 + 4y^2}}, \quad dS = \sqrt{1 + 4y^2}\,dA, \text{ and } \mathbf{curl\,F} = xz\mathbf{i} - yz\mathbf{j}.$$

Hence,

$$\iint_S (\mathbf{curl\,F}) \cdot \mathbf{N}\,dS = \int_0^a \int_0^a 2y^2z\,dy\,dx = \int_0^a \int_0^a 2y^4\,dy\,dx = \int_0^a \frac{2a^5}{5}\,dx = \frac{2a^6}{5}.$$

Problem Solving for Chapter 14

1. (a) $\nabla T = \dfrac{-25}{(x^2 + y^2 + z^2)^{3/2}}[x\mathbf{i} + y\mathbf{i} + z\mathbf{k}]$

$\mathbf{N} = x\mathbf{i} + \sqrt{1 - x^2}\,\mathbf{k}$

$dS = \dfrac{1}{\sqrt{1 - x^2}}\,dy\,dx$

$\text{Flux} = \iint_S -k\nabla T \cdot \mathbf{N}\,dS$

$$= 25k \iint_R \left[\frac{x^2}{(x^2 + y^2 + z^2)^{3/2}(1 - x^2)^{1/2}} + \frac{z}{(x^2 + y^2 + z^2)^{3/2}} \right] dA$$

$$= 25k \int_{-1/2}^{1/2} \int_0^1 \left[\frac{x^2}{(x^2 + y^2 + z^2)^{3/2}(1 - x^2)^{1/2}} + \frac{1 - x^2}{(x^2 + y^2 + z^2)^{3/2}(1 - x^2)^{1/2}} \right] dy\,dx$$

$$= 25k \int_{-1/2}^{1/2} \int_0^1 \frac{1}{(1 + y^2)^{3/2}(1 - x^2)^{1/2}}\,dy\,dx$$

$$= 25k \int_0^1 \frac{1}{(1 + y^2)^{3/2}}\,dy \int_{-1/2}^{1/2} \frac{1}{(1 - x^2)^{1/2}}\,dx$$

$$= 25k\left(\frac{\sqrt{2}}{2}\right)\left(\frac{\pi}{3}\right) = 25k\frac{\sqrt{2}\pi}{6}$$

—CONTINUED—

1. **—CONTINUED—**

(b) $\mathbf{r}(u, v) = \langle \cos u, v, \sin u \rangle$

$\mathbf{r}_u = \langle -\sin u, 0, \cos u \rangle, \mathbf{r}_v = \langle 0, 1, 0 \rangle$

$\mathbf{r}_u \times \mathbf{r}_v = \langle -\cos u, 0, -\sin u \rangle$

$\nabla T = \dfrac{-25}{(x^2 + y^2 + z^2)^{3/2}}[x\mathbf{i} + y\mathbf{j} + z\mathbf{k}]$

$\quad = \dfrac{-25}{(v^2 + 1)^{3/2}}[\cos u\mathbf{i} + v\mathbf{j} + \sin u\mathbf{k}]$

$\nabla T \cdot (\mathbf{r}_u \times \mathbf{r}_v) = \dfrac{-25}{(v^2 + 1)^{3/2}}(-\cos^2 u - \sin^2 u) = \dfrac{25}{(v^2 + 1)^{3/2}}$

$\text{Flux} = \displaystyle\int_0^1 \int_{\pi/3}^{2\pi/3} \dfrac{25k}{(v^2 + 1)^{3/2}} \, du \, dv = 25k\dfrac{\sqrt{2}\pi}{6}$

3. $\mathbf{r}(t) = \langle 3 \cos t, 3 \sin t, 2t \rangle$

$\mathbf{r}'(t) = \langle -3 \sin t, 3 \cos t, 2 \rangle, \|\mathbf{r}'(t)\| = \sqrt{13}$

$I_x = \displaystyle\int_C (y^2 + z^2)\rho \, ds = \int_0^{2\pi} (9 \sin^2 t + 4t^2)\sqrt{13} \, dt = \dfrac{1}{3}\sqrt{13}\pi(32\pi^2 + 27)$

$I_y = \displaystyle\int_C (x^2 + z^2)\rho \, ds = \int_0^{2\pi} (9 \cos^2 t + 4t^2)\sqrt{13} \, dt = \dfrac{1}{3}\sqrt{13}\pi(32\pi^2 + 27)$

$I_z = \displaystyle\int_C (x^2 + y^2)\rho \, ds = \int_0^{2\pi} (9 \cos^2 t + 9 \sin^2 t)\sqrt{13} \, dt = 18\pi\sqrt{13}$

5. $\dfrac{1}{2}\displaystyle\int_C x \, dy - y \, dx = \dfrac{1}{2}\int_0^{2\pi} [a(\theta - \sin \theta)(a \sin \theta) \, d\theta - a(1 - \cos \theta)(a(1 - \cos \theta)) \, d\theta]$

$\quad = \dfrac{1}{2}a^2 \displaystyle\int_0^{2\pi} [\theta \sin \theta - \sin^2 \theta - 1 + 2 \cos \theta - \cos^2 \theta] \, d\theta$

$\quad = \dfrac{1}{2}a^2 \displaystyle\int_0^{2\pi} (\theta \sin \theta + 2 \cos \theta - 2) \, d\theta$

$\quad = -3\pi a^2$

Hence, the area is $3\pi a^2$.

7. (a) $\mathbf{r}(t) = t\mathbf{j}, 0 \le t \le 1$

$\mathbf{r}'(t) = \mathbf{j}$

$W = \displaystyle\int_C \mathbf{F} \cdot d\mathbf{r} = \int_0^1 (t\mathbf{i} + \mathbf{j}) \cdot \mathbf{j} \, dt = \int_0^1 dt = 1$

(b) $\mathbf{r}(t) = (t - t^2)\mathbf{i} + t\mathbf{j}, 0 \le t \le 1$

$\mathbf{r}'(t) = (1 - 2t)\mathbf{i} + \mathbf{j}$

$W = \mathbf{F} \cdot d\mathbf{r} = \displaystyle\int_0^1 ((2t - t^2)\mathbf{i} + [(t - t^2)^2 + 1]\mathbf{j}) \cdot ((1 - 2t)\mathbf{i} + \mathbf{j}) \, dt$

$\quad = \displaystyle\int_0^1 [(1 - 2t)(2t - t^2) + (t^4 - 2t^3 + t^2 + 1)] \, dt$

$\quad = \displaystyle\int_0^1 (t^4 - 4t^2 + 2t + 1) \, dt = \dfrac{13}{15}$

—CONTINUED—

7. —CONTINUED—

(c) $\mathbf{r}(t) = c(t - t^2)\mathbf{i} + t\mathbf{j}, 0 \le t \le 1$

$\mathbf{r}'(t) = c(1 - 2t)\mathbf{i} + \mathbf{j}$

$\mathbf{F} \cdot d\mathbf{r} = (c(t - t^2) + t)(c(1 - 2t)) + (c^2(t - t^2)^2 + 1)(1)$

$\qquad = c^2t^4 - 2c^2t^2 + c^2t - 2ct^2 + ct + 1$

$W = \int_C \mathbf{F} \cdot d\mathbf{r} = \frac{1}{30}c^2 - \frac{1}{6}c + 1$

$\dfrac{dW}{dc} = \dfrac{1}{15}c - \dfrac{1}{6} = 0 \implies c = \dfrac{5}{2}$

$\dfrac{d^2W}{dc^2} = \dfrac{1}{15} > 0 \quad c = \dfrac{5}{2}$ minimum.

9. $\mathbf{v} \times \mathbf{r} = \langle a_1, a_2, a_3 \rangle \times \langle x, y, z \rangle$

$\qquad = \langle a_2z - a_3y, -a_1z + a_3x, a_1y - a_2x \rangle$

$\mathbf{curl}(\mathbf{v} \times \mathbf{r}) = \langle 2a_1, 2a_2, 2a_3 \rangle = 2\mathbf{v}$

By Stoke's Theorem,

$$\int_C (\mathbf{v} \times \mathbf{r})\, d\mathbf{r} = \int_S\int \mathbf{curl}(\mathbf{v} \times \mathbf{r}) \cdot \mathbf{N}\, dS$$

$$= \int_S\int 2\mathbf{v} \cdot N\, dS.$$

11. $\mathbf{F}(x, y) = M(x, y)\mathbf{i} + N(x, y)\mathbf{j} = \dfrac{m}{(x^2 + y^2)^{5/2}}[3xy\mathbf{i} + (2y^2 - x^2)\mathbf{j}]$

$M = \dfrac{3mxy}{(x^2 + y^2)^{5/2}} = 3mxy(x^2 + y^2)^{-5/2}$

$\dfrac{\partial M}{\partial y} = 3mxy\left[-\dfrac{5}{2}(x^2 + y^2)^{-7/2}(2y)\right] + (x^2 + y^2)^{-5/2}(3mx)$

$\qquad = 3mx(x^2 + y^2)^{-7/2}[-5y^2 + (x^2 + y^2)] = \dfrac{3mx(x^2 - 4y^2)}{(x^2 + y^2)^{7/2}}$

$N = \dfrac{m(2y^2 - x^2)}{(x^2 + y^2)^{5/2}} = m(2y^2 - x^2)(x^2 + y^2)^{-5/2}$

$\dfrac{\partial N}{\partial x} = m(2y^2 - x^2)\left[-\dfrac{5}{2}(x^2 + y^2)^{-7/2}(2x)\right] + (x^2 + y^2)^{-5/2}(-2mx)$

$\qquad = mx(x^2 + y^2)^{-7/2}[(2y^2 - x^2)(-5) + (x^2 + y^2)(-2)]$

$\qquad = mx(x^2 + y^2)^{-7/2}(3x^2 - 12y^2) = \dfrac{3mx(x^2 - 4y^2)}{(x^2 + y^2)^{7/2}}$

Therefore, $\dfrac{\partial N}{\partial x} = \dfrac{\partial M}{\partial y}$ and $\mathbf{F}$ is conservative.

APPENDIX A

Appendix A.1   Additional Topics in Differential Equations

Solutions to Odd-Numbered Exercises

1.

x	-4	-2	0	2	4	8
y	2	0	4	4	6	8
dy/dx	-2	Undef.	0	$\frac{1}{2}$	$\frac{2}{3}$	1

$\dfrac{dy}{dx} = \dfrac{x}{y}$. For $(x, y) = (-4, 2)$, $\dfrac{dy}{dx} = \dfrac{-4}{2} = -2$.

3. (a), (c)

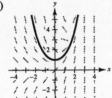

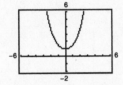

(b) $\dfrac{dy}{dx} = e^x - y$

$\dfrac{dy}{dx} + y = e^x$ Integrating factor: $e^{\int dx} = e^x$

$e^x y' + e^x y = e^{2x}$

$(ye^x) = \displaystyle\int e^{2x}\, dx$

$ye^x = \dfrac{1}{2}e^{2x} + C$

$y(0) = 1 \Rightarrow 1 = \dfrac{1}{2} + C \Rightarrow C = \dfrac{1}{2}$

$ye^x = \dfrac{1}{2}e^{2x} + \dfrac{1}{2}$

$y = \dfrac{1}{2}e^x + \dfrac{1}{2}e^{-x} = \dfrac{1}{2}(e^x + e^{-x})$

5. (a), (c)

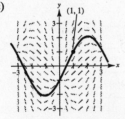

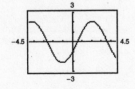

(b) $\dfrac{dy}{dx} = \csc x + y \cot x$

$\dfrac{dy}{dx} - (\cot x)y = \csc x$

Integrating factor: $e^{\int -\cot x\, dx} = e^{-\ln|\sin x|} = \csc x$

$\csc x \cdot y' - \csc x \cot x \cdot y = \csc^2 x$

$(y \csc x)' = \csc^2 x$

$y \csc x = \displaystyle\int \csc^2 x\, dx = -\cot x + C$

$y = -\cos x + C \sin x$

$y(1) = 1 \Rightarrow 1 = -\cos 1 + C \sin 1 \Rightarrow C = \dfrac{1 + \cos 1}{\sin 1}$

≈ 1.83

7.

9. $y' = x + y$, $\quad y(0) = 2$, $\quad n = 10$, $\quad h = 0.1$

$y_1 = y_0 + hF(x_0, y_0) = 2 + (0.1)(0 + 2) = 2.2$

$y_2 = y_1 + hF(x_1, y_1) = 2.2 + (0.1)(0.1 + 2.2) = 2.43$, etc.

n	0	1	2	3	4	5	6	7	8	9	10
x_n	0	0.1	0.2	0.3	0.4	0.5	0.6	0.7	0.8	0.9	1.0
y_n	2	2.2	2.43	2.693	2.992	3.332	3.715	4.146	4.631	5.174	5.781

11. $y' = 3x - 2y$, $\quad y(0) = 3$, $\quad n = 10$, $\quad h = 0.05$

$y_1 = y_0 + hF(x_0, y_0) = 3 + (0.05)(3(0) - 2(3)) = 2.7$

$y_2 = y_1 + hF(x_1, y_1) = 2.7 + (0.05)(3(0.05) - 2(2.7)) = 2.4375$, etc.

n	0	1	2	3	4	5	6	7	8	9	10
x_n	0	0.05	0.1	0.15	0.2	0.25	0.3	0.35	0.4	0.45	0.5
y_n	3	2.7	2.438	2.209	2.010	1.839	1.693	1.569	1.464	1.378	1.308

13. $y' = e^{xy}$, $\quad y(0) = 1$, $\quad n = 10$, $\quad h = 0.1$

$y_1 = y_0 + hF(x_0, y_0) = 1 + (0.1)e^{0(1)} = 1.1$

$y_2 = y_1 + hF(x_1, y_1) = 1.1 + (0.1)e^{(0.1)(1.1)} \approx 1.2116$, etc.

n	0	1	2	3	4	5	6	7	8	9	10
x_n	0	0.1	0.2	0.3	0.4	0.5	0.6	0.7	0.8	0.9	1.0
y_n	1	1.1	1.212	1.339	1.488	1.670	1.900	2.213	2.684	3.540	5.958

15. False

$y' + xy = x^2$ is first-order linear.

17. $\dfrac{dy}{dx} + \left(\dfrac{1}{x}\right)y = 3x + 4$

Integrating factor: $e^{\int (1/x)\,dx} = e^{\ln x} = x$

$xy = \displaystyle\int x(3x + 4)\,dx = x^3 + 2x^2 + C$

$y = x^2 + 2x + \dfrac{C}{x}$

19. $\dfrac{dy}{dx} - 3x^2 y = e^{x^3}$

Integrating factor: $e^{-\int 3x^2\,dx} = e^{-x^3}$

$ye^{-x^3} = \displaystyle\int dx$

$ye^{-x^3} = x + C$

$y = (x + C)e^{x^3}$

21. $y' - y = \cos x$

Integrating factor: $e^{\int -1 \, dx} = e^{-x}$

$ye^{-x} = \int e^{-x} \cos x \, dx$

$= \frac{1}{2}e^{-x}(-\cos x + \sin x) + C$

$y = \frac{1}{2}(\sin x - \cos x) + Ce^x$

23. $\dfrac{dy}{dx} = \dfrac{x + y}{x} = \dfrac{y}{x} + 1$

$y' - \dfrac{1}{x}y = 1$

Integrating factor: $e^{-\int 1/x \, dx} = e^{-\ln x} = 1/x$

$\dfrac{1}{x}y' - \dfrac{1}{x^2}y = 1/x$

$\left(\dfrac{1}{x}y\right)' = 1/x$

$\dfrac{1}{x}y = \int \dfrac{1}{x} dx = \ln|x| + C$

$y = x \ln|x| + Cx$

25. $(3y + \sin 2x) \, dx - dy = 0$

$y' - 3y = \sin 2x$

Integrating factor: $e^{\int -3 \, dx} = e^{-3x}$

$ye^{-3x} = \int e^{-3x} \sin 2x \, dx$

$= \frac{1}{13}e^{-3x}(-3 \sin 2x - 2 \cos 2x) + C$

$y = -\frac{1}{13}(3 \sin 2x + 2 \cos 2x) + Ce^{3x}$

27. $(x - 1)y' + y = x^2 - 1$

$y' + \left(\dfrac{1}{x - 1}\right)y = x + 1$

Integrating factor: $e^{\int [1/(x-1)] \, dx} = e^{\ln|x-1|} = x - 1$

$y(x - 1) = \int (x^2 - 1) \, dx = \frac{1}{3}x^3 - x + C_1$

$y = \dfrac{x^3 - 3x + C}{3(x - 1)}$

29. $dy = (y \tan x + 2e^x) \, dx$

$\dfrac{dy}{dx} - (\tan x)y = 2e^x$

Integrating factor: $e^{-\int \tan x \, dx} = e^{\ln|\cos x|} = \cos x$

$y \cos x = \int 2e^x \cos x \, dx = e^x(\cos x + \sin x) + C$

$y = e^x(1 + \tan x) + C \sec x$

31. $y' - \left(\dfrac{a}{x}\right)y = bx^3$

Integrating factor: $e^{-\int (a/x) \, dx} = e^{-a \ln x} = x^{-a}$

$yx^{-a} = \int bx^3(x^{-a}) \, dx = \dfrac{b}{4 - a}x^{4-a} + C$

$y = \dfrac{bx^4}{4 - a} + Cx^a$

33. $y' \cos^2 x + y - 1 = 0$

$y' + (\sec^2 x)y = \sec^2 x$

Integrating factor: $e^{\int \sec^2 x \, dx} = e^{\tan x}$

$ye^{\tan x} = \int \sec^2 x e^{\tan x} \, dx = e^{\tan x} + C$

$y = 1 + Ce^{-\tan x}$

Initial condition: $y(0) = 5, C = 4$

Particular solution: $y = 1 + 4e^{-\tan x}$

35. $y' + y \tan x = \sec x + \cos x$

Integrating factor: $e^{\int \tan x \, dx} = e^{\ln|\sec x|} = \sec x$

$y \sec x = \int \sec x(\sec x + \cos x) \, dx = \tan x + x + C$

$y = \sin x + x \cos x + C \cos x$

Initial condition: $y(0) = 1, 1 = C$

Particular solution: $y = \sin x + (x + 1) \cos x$

37. $y' + \left(\dfrac{1}{x}\right)y = 0$

Integrating factor: $e^{\int (1/x)\,dx} = e^{\ln|x|} = x$

Separation of variables:

$$\frac{dy}{dx} = -\frac{y}{x}$$

$$\int \frac{1}{y}\,dy = \int -\frac{1}{x}\,dx$$

$$\ln y = -\ln x + \ln C$$

$$\ln xy = \ln C$$

$$xy = C$$

Initial condition: $y(2) = 2$, $C = 4$

Particular solution: $xy = 4$

39. $\qquad x\,dy = (x + y + 2)\,dx$

$$\frac{dy}{dx} - \left(\frac{1}{x}\right)y = \frac{x+2}{x}$$

Integrating factor: $e^{\int -(1/x)\,dx} = e^{-\ln|x|} = \dfrac{1}{x}$

$$y\left(\frac{1}{x}\right) = \int \frac{x+2}{x^2}\,dx = \ln|x| - \frac{2}{x} + C$$

$$y = x\ln|x| - 2 + Cx$$

Initial condition: $y(1) = 10$

$$10 = -2 + C \implies C = 12$$

Particular solution: $y = x\ln|x| - 2 + 12x$

41. (a)

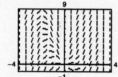

(b) $\dfrac{dy}{dx} - \dfrac{1}{x}y = x^2$

Integrating factor $e^{-1/x\,dx} = e^{-\ln x} = \dfrac{1}{x}$

$$\frac{1}{x}y' - \frac{1}{x^2}y = x$$

$$\left(\frac{1}{x}y\right) = \int x\,dx = \frac{x^2}{2} + C$$

$$y = \frac{x^3}{2} + Cx$$

$(-2, 4)$: $4 = \dfrac{-8}{2} - 2C \implies C = -4 \implies y = \dfrac{x^3}{2} - 4x = \dfrac{1}{2}x(x^2 - 8)$

$(2, 8)$: $8 = \dfrac{8}{2} + 2C \implies C = 2 \implies y = \dfrac{x^3}{2} + 2x = \dfrac{1}{2}x(x^2 + 4)$

(c)

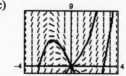

43. $L\dfrac{dI}{dt} + RI = E_0$, $I' + \dfrac{R}{L}I = \dfrac{E_0}{L}$

Integrating factor: $e^{\int (R/L)\,dt} = e^{Rt/L}$

$$I\,e^{Rt/L} = \int \frac{E_0}{L}e^{Rt/L}\,dt = \frac{E_0}{R}e^{Rt/L} + C$$

$$I = \frac{E_0}{R} + Ce^{-Rt/L}$$

45. $L\dfrac{dI}{dt} + RI = E_0 \sin \omega t$

$\dfrac{dI}{dt} + \dfrac{R}{L}I = \dfrac{E_0}{L} \sin \omega t$

Integrating factor: $e^{\int (R/L)\, dt} = e^{Rt/L}$

$Ie^{Rt/L} = \displaystyle\int \dfrac{E_0}{L} e^{Rt/L} \sin \omega t\, dt$

$\qquad = \dfrac{E_0}{L}\left[\dfrac{L^2 e^{Rt/L}}{R^2 + L^2\omega^2}\left(\dfrac{R}{L}\sin \omega t - \omega \cos \omega t\right)\right] + C = \dfrac{E_0 e^{Rt/L}}{R^2 + \omega^2 L^2}(R \sin \omega t - \omega L \cos \omega t) + C$

$\qquad I = \dfrac{E_0}{R^2 + \omega^2 L^2}(R \sin \omega t - \omega L \cos \omega t) + Ce^{-Rt/L}$

47. $\qquad \dfrac{dP}{dt} = kP + N, \; N \text{ constant}$

$\dfrac{dP}{kP + N} = dt$

$\displaystyle\int \dfrac{1}{kP + N}\, dP = \int dt$

$\dfrac{1}{k}\ln(kP + N) = t + C_1$

$\ln(kP + N) = kt + C_2$

$kP + N = e^{kt + C_2}$

$\qquad P = \dfrac{C_3 e^{kt} - N}{k}$

$\qquad P = Ce^{kt} - \dfrac{N}{k}$

When $t = 0$: $P = P_0$

$P_0 = C - \dfrac{N}{k} \implies C = P_0 + \dfrac{N}{k}$

$P = \left(P_0 + \dfrac{N}{k}\right)e^{kt} - \dfrac{N}{k}$

49. (a) $A = \dfrac{P}{r}(e^{rt} - 1)$

$A = \dfrac{100{,}000}{0.06}(e^{0.06(5)} - 1) \approx 583{,}098.01$

(b) $A = \dfrac{250{,}000}{0.05}(e^{0.05(10)} - 1) \approx 3{,}243{,}606.35$

51. $\dfrac{dA}{dt} - rA = -P$

For this linear differential equation, we have $P(t) = -r$ and $Q(t) = -P$. Therefore, the integrating factor is

$u(x) = e^{\int -r\, dt} = e^{-rt}$ and the solution is

$A = e^{rt}\displaystyle\int -Pe^{-rt}\, dt = e^{rt}\left(\dfrac{P}{r}e^{-rt} + C\right) = \dfrac{P}{r} + Ce^{rt}.$

Since $A = A_0$ when $t = 0$, we have $C = A_0 - (P/r)$ which implies that

$A = \dfrac{P}{r} + \left(A_0 - \dfrac{P}{r}\right)e^{rt}.$

53. (a) $\dfrac{dQ}{dt} = q - kQ$, q constant

(b) $Q' + kQ = q$

Let $P(t) = k$, $Q(t) = q$, then the integrating factor is $u(t) = e^{kt}$.

$$Q = e^{-kt} \int q e^{kt}\, dt = e^{-kt}\left(\frac{q}{k}e^{kt} + C\right) = \frac{q}{k} + Ce^{-kt}$$

When $t = 0$: $Q = Q_0$

$$Q_0 = \frac{q}{k} + C \Rightarrow C = Q_0 - \frac{q}{k}$$

$$Q = \frac{q}{k} + \left(Q_0 - \frac{q}{k}\right)e^{-kt}$$

(c) $\displaystyle\lim_{t\to\infty} Q = \frac{q}{k}$

55. $y' - 2x = 0$

$$\int dy = \int 2x\, dx$$

$$y = x^2 + C$$

Matches c.

57. $y' - 2xy = 0$

$$\int \frac{dy}{y} = \int 2x\, dx$$

$$\ln y = x^2 + C_1$$

$$y = Ce^{x^2}$$

Matches a.

PART II

CHAPTER 10
Vectors and the Geometry of Space

CHAPTER 10
Vectors and the Geometry of Space

Section 10.1   Vectors in the Plane

Solutions to Even-Numbered Exercises

2. (a) $\mathbf{v} = \langle 3 - 3, -2 - 4 \rangle = \langle 0, -6 \rangle$

(b)

4. (a) $\mathbf{v} = \langle -1 - 2, 3 - 1 \rangle = \langle -3, 2 \rangle$

(b)

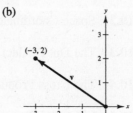

6. $\mathbf{u} = \langle 1 - (-4), 8 - 0 \rangle = \langle 5, 8 \rangle$

$\mathbf{v} = \langle 7 - 2, 7 - (-1) \rangle = \langle 5, 8 \rangle$

$\mathbf{u} = \mathbf{v}$

8. $\mathbf{u} = \langle 11 - (-4), -4 - (-1) \rangle = \langle 15, -3 \rangle$

$\mathbf{v} = \langle 25 - 0, 10 - 13 \rangle = \langle 15, -3 \rangle$

$\mathbf{u} = \mathbf{v}$

10. (b) $\mathbf{v} = \langle 3 - 2, 6 - (-6) \rangle = \langle 1, 12 \rangle$

(a) and (c).

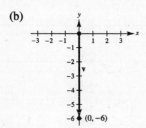

12. (b) $\mathbf{v} = \langle -5 - 0, -1 - (-4) \rangle = \langle -5, 3 \rangle$

(a) and (c).

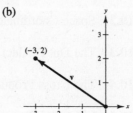

14. (b) $\mathbf{v} = \langle -3 - 7, -1 - (-1) \rangle = \langle -10, 0 \rangle$

(a) and (c).

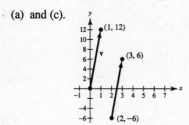

16. (b) $\mathbf{v} = \langle 0.84 - 0.12, 1.25 - 0.60 \rangle = \langle 0.72, 0.65 \rangle$

(a) and (c).

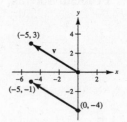

18. (a) $4\mathbf{v} = \langle -4, 20 \rangle$

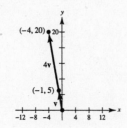

(b) $-\frac{1}{2}\mathbf{v} = \langle \frac{1}{2}, -\frac{5}{2} \rangle$

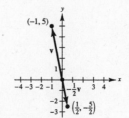

—CONTINUED—

18. **—CONTINUED—**

(c) $0\mathbf{v} = \langle 0, 0 \rangle$

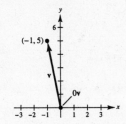

(d) $-6\mathbf{v} = \langle 6, -30 \rangle$

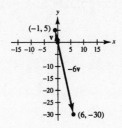

20. Twice as long as given vector **u**.

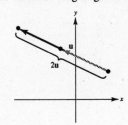

22.

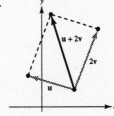

24. (a) $\frac{2}{3}\mathbf{u} = \frac{2}{3}\langle -3, -8 \rangle = \langle -2, -\frac{16}{3} \rangle$

(b) $\mathbf{v} - \mathbf{u} = \langle 8, 25 \rangle - \langle -3, -8 \rangle = \langle 11, 33 \rangle$

(c) $2\mathbf{u} + 5\mathbf{v} = 2\langle -3, -8 \rangle + 5\langle 8, 25 \rangle = \langle 34, 109 \rangle$

26. $\mathbf{v} = (2\mathbf{i} - \mathbf{j}) + (\mathbf{i} + 2\mathbf{j})$

$= 3\mathbf{i} + \mathbf{j} = \langle 3, 1 \rangle$

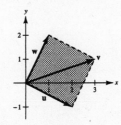

28. $\mathbf{v} = 5\mathbf{u} - 3\mathbf{w} = 5\langle 2, -1 \rangle - 3\langle 1, 2 \rangle = \langle 7, -11 \rangle$

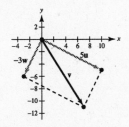

30. $u_1 - 3 = 4$

$u_2 - 2 = -9$

$u_1 = 7$

$u_2 = -7$

$Q = (7, -7)$

32. $\|\mathbf{v}\| = \sqrt{144 + 25} = 13$

34. $\|\mathbf{v}\| = \sqrt{100 + 9} = \sqrt{109}$

36. $\|\mathbf{v}\| = \sqrt{1 + 1} = \sqrt{2}$

38. $\|\mathbf{u}\| = \sqrt{5^2 + 15^2} = \sqrt{250} = 5\sqrt{10}$

$\mathbf{v} = \dfrac{\mathbf{u}}{\|\mathbf{u}\|} = \dfrac{\langle 5, 15 \rangle}{5\sqrt{10}} = \left\langle \dfrac{1}{\sqrt{10}}, \dfrac{3}{\sqrt{10}} \right\rangle$ unit vector

40. $\|\mathbf{u}\| = \sqrt{(-6.2)^2 + (3.4)^2} = \sqrt{50} = 5\sqrt{2}$

$\mathbf{v} = \dfrac{\mathbf{u}}{\|\mathbf{u}\|} = \dfrac{\langle -6.2, 3.4 \rangle}{5\sqrt{2}} = \left\langle \dfrac{-1.24}{\sqrt{2}}, \dfrac{0.68}{\sqrt{2}} \right\rangle$ unit vector

42. $\mathbf{u} = \langle 0, 1 \rangle$, $\mathbf{v} = \langle 3, -3 \rangle$

    (a) $\|\mathbf{u}\| = \sqrt{0 + 1} = 1$

    (b) $\|\mathbf{v}\| = \sqrt{9 + 9} = 3\sqrt{2}$

    (c) $\mathbf{u} + \mathbf{v} = \langle 3, -2 \rangle$

        $\|\mathbf{u} + \mathbf{v}\| = \sqrt{9 + 4} = \sqrt{13}$

    (d) $\dfrac{\mathbf{u}}{\|\mathbf{u}\|} = \langle 0, 1 \rangle$

        $\left\| \dfrac{\mathbf{u}}{\|\mathbf{u}\|} \right\| = 1$

    (e) $\dfrac{\mathbf{v}}{\|\mathbf{v}\|} = \dfrac{1}{3\sqrt{2}} \langle 3, -3 \rangle$

        $\left\| \dfrac{\mathbf{v}}{\|\mathbf{v}\|} \right\| = 1$

    (f) $\dfrac{\mathbf{u} + \mathbf{v}}{\|\mathbf{u} + \mathbf{v}\|} = \dfrac{1}{\sqrt{13}} \langle 3, -2 \rangle$

        $\left\| \dfrac{\mathbf{u} + \mathbf{v}}{\|\mathbf{u} + \mathbf{v}\|} \right\| = 1$

44. $\mathbf{u} = \langle 2, -4 \rangle$, $\mathbf{v} = \langle 5, 5 \rangle$

    (a) $\|\mathbf{u}\| = \sqrt{4 + 16} = 2\sqrt{5}$

    (b) $\|\mathbf{v}\| = \sqrt{25 + 25} = 5\sqrt{2}$

    (c) $\mathbf{u} + \mathbf{v} = \langle 7, 1 \rangle$

        $\|\mathbf{u} + \mathbf{v}\| = \sqrt{49 + 1} = 5\sqrt{2}$

    (d) $\dfrac{\mathbf{u}}{\|\mathbf{u}\|} = \dfrac{1}{2\sqrt{5}} \langle 2, -4 \rangle$

        $\left\| \dfrac{\mathbf{u}}{\|\mathbf{u}\|} \right\| = 1$

    (e) $\dfrac{\mathbf{v}}{\|\mathbf{v}\|} = \dfrac{1}{5\sqrt{2}} \langle 5, 5 \rangle$

        $\left\| \dfrac{\mathbf{v}}{\|\mathbf{v}\|} \right\| = 1$

    (f) $\dfrac{\mathbf{u} + \mathbf{v}}{\|\mathbf{u} + \mathbf{v}\|} = \dfrac{1}{5\sqrt{2}} \langle 7, 1 \rangle$

        $\left\| \dfrac{\mathbf{u} + \mathbf{v}}{\|\mathbf{u} + \mathbf{v}\|} \right\| = 1$

46. $\mathbf{u} = \langle -3, 2 \rangle$

    $\|\mathbf{u}\| = \sqrt{13} \approx 3.606$

    $\mathbf{v} = \langle 1, -2 \rangle$

    $\|\mathbf{v}\| = \sqrt{5} \approx 2.236$

    $\mathbf{u} + \mathbf{v} = \langle -2, 0 \rangle$

    $\|\mathbf{u} + \mathbf{v}\| = 2$

    $\|\mathbf{u} + \mathbf{v}\| \le \|\mathbf{u}\| + \|\mathbf{v}\|$

48. $\dfrac{\mathbf{u}}{\|\mathbf{u}\|} = \dfrac{1}{\sqrt{2}} \langle -1, 1 \rangle$

    $4 \left(\dfrac{\mathbf{u}}{\|\mathbf{u}\|} \right) = 2\sqrt{2} \langle -1, 1 \rangle$

    $\mathbf{v} = \langle -2\sqrt{2}, 2\sqrt{2} \rangle$

50. $\dfrac{\mathbf{u}}{\|\mathbf{u}\|} = \dfrac{1}{3} \langle 0, 3 \rangle$

    $3 \left(\dfrac{\mathbf{u}}{\|\mathbf{u}\|} \right) = \langle 0, 3 \rangle$

    $\mathbf{v} = \langle 0, 3 \rangle$

52. $\mathbf{v} = 5[(\cos 120°)\mathbf{i} + (\sin 120°)\mathbf{j}]$

    $= -\dfrac{5}{2}\mathbf{i} + \dfrac{5\sqrt{3}}{2}\mathbf{j}$

54. $\mathbf{v} = (\cos 3.5°)\mathbf{i} + (\sin 3.5°)\mathbf{j}$

    $\approx 0.9981\mathbf{i} + 0.0610\mathbf{j} = \langle 0.9981, 0.0610 \rangle$

56. $\mathbf{u} = 4\mathbf{i}$

    $\mathbf{v} = \mathbf{i} + \sqrt{3}\mathbf{j}$

    $\mathbf{u} + \mathbf{v} = 5\mathbf{i} + \sqrt{3}\mathbf{j}$

58. $\mathbf{u} = 5[\cos(-0.5)]\mathbf{i} + 5[\sin(-0.5)]\mathbf{j}$

    $= 5[\cos(0.5)]\mathbf{i} - 5[\sin(0.5)]\mathbf{j}$

    $\mathbf{v} = 5[\cos(0.5)]\mathbf{i} + 5[\sin(0.5)]\mathbf{j}$

    $\mathbf{u} + \mathbf{v} = 10[\cos(0.5)]\mathbf{i}$

60. See page 718:

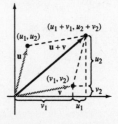
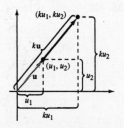

62. See Theorem 10.1, page 719.

For Exercises 64–68, $a\mathbf{u} + b\mathbf{w} = a(\mathbf{i} + 2\mathbf{j}) + b(\mathbf{i} - \mathbf{j}) = (a + b)\mathbf{i} + (2a - b)\mathbf{j}.$

64. $\mathbf{v} = 3\mathbf{j}$. Therefore, $a + b = 0, 2a - b = 3$. Solving simultaneously, we have $a = 1, b = -1$.

66. $\mathbf{v} = 3\mathbf{i} + 3\mathbf{j}$. Therefore, $a + b = 3, 2a - b = 3$. Solving simultaneously, we have $a = 2, b = 1$.

68. $\mathbf{v} = -\mathbf{i} + 7\mathbf{j}$. Therefore, $a + b = -1, 2a - b = 7$. Solving simultaneously, we have $a = 2, b = -3$.

70. $y = x^3, y' = 3x^2 = 12$ at $x = -2$.

(a) $m = 12$. Let $\mathbf{w} = \langle 1, 12 \rangle$, then
$$\frac{\mathbf{w}}{\|\mathbf{w}\|} = \pm \frac{1}{\sqrt{145}} \langle 1, 12 \rangle.$$

(b) $m = -\frac{1}{12}$. Let $\mathbf{w} = \langle 12, -1 \rangle$, then
$$\frac{\mathbf{w}}{\|\mathbf{w}\|} = \pm \frac{1}{\sqrt{145}} \langle 12, -1 \rangle.$$

72. $f(x) = \tan x$
$$f'(x) = \sec^2 x = 2 \text{ at } x = \frac{\pi}{4}.$$

(a) $m = 2$. Let $\mathbf{w} = \langle 1, 2 \rangle$, then
$$\frac{\mathbf{w}}{\|\mathbf{w}\|} = \pm \frac{1}{\sqrt{5}} \langle 1, 2 \rangle.$$

(b) $m = -\frac{1}{2}$. Let $\mathbf{w} = \langle -2, 1 \rangle$, then
$$\frac{\mathbf{w}}{\|\mathbf{w}\|} = \pm \frac{1}{\sqrt{5}} \langle -2, 1 \rangle.$$

74. $\mathbf{u} = 2\sqrt{3}\mathbf{i} + 2\mathbf{j}$
$$\mathbf{u} + \mathbf{v} = -3\mathbf{i} + 3\sqrt{3}\mathbf{j}$$
$$\mathbf{v} = (\mathbf{u} + \mathbf{v}) - \mathbf{u} = \left(-3 - 2\sqrt{3}\right)\mathbf{i} + \left(3\sqrt{3} - 2\right)\mathbf{j}$$

76. magnitude ≈ 63.5
direction $\approx -8.26°$

78. $\|\mathbf{F}_1\| = 2, \theta_{\mathbf{F}_1} = -10°$
$\|\mathbf{F}_2\| = 4, \theta_{\mathbf{F}_2} = 140°$
$\|\mathbf{F}_3\| = 3, \theta_{\mathbf{F}_3} = 200°$
$\|\mathbf{R}\| = \|\mathbf{F}_1 + \mathbf{F}_2 + \mathbf{F}_3\| \approx 4.09$
$\theta_{\mathbf{R}} = \theta_{\mathbf{F}_1 + \mathbf{F}_2 + \mathbf{F}_3} \approx 163.0°$

80. $\mathbf{F}_1 + \mathbf{F}_2 = (500\cos 30°\mathbf{i} + 500 \sin 30°\mathbf{j}) + (200 \cos(-45°)\mathbf{i} + 200 \sin(-45°)\mathbf{j})$
$$= \left(250\sqrt{3} + 100\sqrt{2}\right)\mathbf{i} + \left(250 - 100\sqrt{2}\right)\mathbf{j}$$
$$\|\mathbf{F}_1 + \mathbf{F}_2\| = \sqrt{\left(250\sqrt{3} + 100\sqrt{2}\right)^2 + \left(250 - 100\sqrt{2}\right)^2} \approx 584.6 \text{ lb}$$
$$\tan \theta = \frac{250 - 100\sqrt{2}}{250\sqrt{3} + 100\sqrt{2}} \Rightarrow \theta \approx 10.7°$$

82. $\mathbf{F}_1 + \mathbf{F}_2 + \mathbf{F}_3 = [400(\cos(-30°)\mathbf{i} + \sin(-30°)\mathbf{j})] + [280(\cos(45°)\mathbf{i} + \sin(45°)\mathbf{j})] + [350(\cos(135°)\mathbf{i} + \sin(135°)\mathbf{j})]$
$$= \left[200\sqrt{3} + 140\sqrt{2} - 175\sqrt{2}\right]\mathbf{i} + \left[-200 + 140\sqrt{2} + 175\sqrt{2}\right]\mathbf{j}$$
$$\|\mathbf{R}\| = \sqrt{\left(200\sqrt{3} - 35\sqrt{2}\right)^2 + \left(-200 + 315\sqrt{2}\right)^2} \approx 385.2483 \text{ newtons}$$
$$\theta_{\mathbf{R}} = \arctan\left(\frac{-200 + 315\sqrt{2}}{200\sqrt{3} - 35\sqrt{2}}\right) \approx 0.6908 \approx 39.6°$$

84. $\mathbf{F}_1 = \langle 20, 0 \rangle$, $\mathbf{F}_2 = 10\langle \cos\theta, \sin\theta \rangle$

(a) $\|\mathbf{F}_1 + \mathbf{F}_2\| = \|\langle 20 + 10\cos\theta, 10\sin\theta \rangle\|$

$\quad\quad\quad\quad = \sqrt{400 + 400\cos\theta + 100\cos^2\theta + 100\sin^2\theta}$

$\quad\quad\quad\quad = \sqrt{500 + 400\cos\theta}$

(b)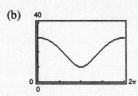

(c) The range is $10 \leq \|\mathbf{F}_1 + \mathbf{F}_2\| \leq 30$.

The maximum is 30, which occur at $\theta = 0$ and $\theta = 2\pi$.

The minimum is 10 at $\theta = \pi$.

(d) The minimum of the resultant is 10.

86. $\mathbf{u} = \langle 7 - 1, 5 - 2 \rangle = \langle 6, 3 \rangle$

$\dfrac{1}{3}\mathbf{u} = \langle 2, 1 \rangle$

$P_1 = (1, 2) + (2, 1) = (3, 3)$

$P_2 = (1, 2) + 2(2, 1) = (5, 4)$

88. $\theta_1 = \arctan\left(\dfrac{24}{20}\right) \approx 0.8761$ or $50.2°$

$\theta_2 = \arctan\left(\dfrac{24}{-10}\right) + \pi \approx 1.9656$ or $112.6°$

$\mathbf{u} = \|\mathbf{u}\|(\cos\theta_1\,\mathbf{i} + \sin\theta_1\,\mathbf{j})$

$\mathbf{v} = \|\mathbf{v}\|(\cos\theta_2\,\mathbf{i} + \sin\theta_2\,\mathbf{j})$

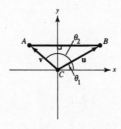

Vertical components: $\|\mathbf{u}\|\sin\theta_1 + \|\mathbf{v}\|\sin\theta_2 = 5000$

Horizontal components: $\|\mathbf{u}\|\cos\theta_1 + \|\mathbf{v}\|\cos\theta_2 = 0$

Solving this system, you obtain

$\|\mathbf{u}\| \approx 2169.4$ and $\|\mathbf{v}\| \approx 3611.2$.

90. To lift the weight vertically, the sum of the vertical components of $\mathbf{u}$ and $\mathbf{v}$ must be 100 and the sum of the horizontal components must be 0.

$\mathbf{u} = \|\mathbf{u}\|(\cos 60°\mathbf{i} + \sin 60°\mathbf{j})$

$\mathbf{v} = \|\mathbf{v}\|(\cos 110°\mathbf{i} + \sin 110°\mathbf{j})$

Thus, $\|\mathbf{u}\|\sin 60° + \|\mathbf{v}\|\sin 110° = 100$, or

$\|\mathbf{u}\|\left(\dfrac{\sqrt{3}}{2}\right) + \|\mathbf{v}\|\sin 110° = 100$.

And $\|\mathbf{u}\|\cos 60° + \|\mathbf{v}\|\cos 110° = 0$ or

$\|\mathbf{u}\|\left(\dfrac{1}{2}\right) + \|\mathbf{v}\|\cos 110° = 0$

Multiplying the last equation by $\left(\sqrt{3}\right)$ and adding to the first equation gives

$\|\mathbf{u}\|(\sin 110° - \sqrt{3}\cos 110°) = 100 \implies \|\mathbf{v}\| \approx 65.27$ lb.

Then, $\|\mathbf{u}\|\left(\dfrac{1}{2}\right) + 65.27\cos 110° = 0$ gives

$\|\mathbf{u}\| \approx 44.65$ lb.

(a) The tension in each rope: $\|\mathbf{u}\| = 44.65$ lb, $\|\mathbf{v}\| = 65.27$ lb.

(b) Vertical components: $\|\mathbf{u}\|\sin 60° \approx 38.67$ lb.

$\quad\quad\quad\quad\quad\quad \|\mathbf{v}\|\sin 110° \approx 61.33$ lb.

92. $\mathbf{u} = 400\mathbf{i}$ (plane)

$\mathbf{v} = 50(\cos 135°\mathbf{i} + \sin 135°\mathbf{j}) = -25\sqrt{2}\mathbf{i} + 25\sqrt{2}\mathbf{j}$ (wind)

$\mathbf{u} + \mathbf{v} = \left(400 - 25\sqrt{2}\right)\mathbf{i} + 25\sqrt{2}\mathbf{j} \approx 364.64\mathbf{i} + 35.36\mathbf{j}$

$\tan\theta = \dfrac{35.36}{364.64} \implies \theta \approx 5.54°$

Direction North of East: $\approx$ N 84.46° E

Speed: ≈ 336.35 mph

94. $\|\mathbf{u}\| = \sqrt{\cos^2\theta + \sin^2\theta} = 1,$

$\|\mathbf{v}\| = \sqrt{\sin^2\theta + \cos^2\theta} = 1$

96. Let $\mathbf{u}$ and $\mathbf{v}$ be the vectors that determine the parallelogram, as indicated in the figure.
The two diagonals are $\mathbf{u} + \mathbf{v}$ and $\mathbf{v} - \mathbf{u}$. Therefore, $\mathbf{r} = x(\mathbf{u} + \mathbf{v})$, $\mathbf{s} = y(\mathbf{v} - \mathbf{u})$. But,

$\mathbf{u} = \mathbf{r} - \mathbf{s}$

$= x(\mathbf{u} + \mathbf{v}) - y(\mathbf{v} - \mathbf{u}) = (x + y)\mathbf{u} + (x - y)\mathbf{v}.$

Therefore, $x + y = 1$ and $x - y = 0$. Solving we have $x = y = \frac{1}{2}$.

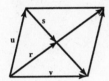

98. The set is a circle of radius 5, centered at the origin.

$\|\mathbf{u}\| = \|\langle x, y\rangle\| = \sqrt{x^2 + y^2} = 5 \implies x^2 + y^2 = 25$

100. True

102. False

$a = b = 0$

104. True

Section 10.2   Space Coordinates and Vectors in Space

2.

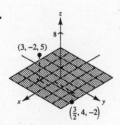

4.

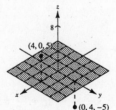

6. $A(2, -3, -1)$

$B(-3, 1, 4)$

8. $x = 7, y = -2, z = -1$:

$(7, -2, -1)$

10. $x = 0, y = 3, z = 2$: $(0, 3, 2)$

12. The x-coordinate is 0.

14. The point is 2 units in front of the xz-plane.

16. The point is on the plane $z = -3$.

18. The point is behind the yz-plane.

20. The point is in front of the plane $x = 4$.

22. The point (x, y, z) is 4 units above the xy-plane, and above either quadrant II or IV.

24. The point could be above the xy-plane, and thus above quadrants I or III, or below the xy-plane, and thus below quadrants II or IV.

26. $d = \sqrt{(2 - (-2))^2 + (-5 - 3)^2 + (-2 - 2)^2}$

$\quad = \sqrt{16 + 64 + 16} = \sqrt{96} = 4\sqrt{6}$

28. $d = \sqrt{(4 - 2)^2 + (-5 - 2)^2 + (6 - 3)^2}$

$\quad = \sqrt{4 + 49 + 9} = \sqrt{62}$

30. $A(5, 3, 4), B(7, 1, 3), C(3, 5, 3)$

$|AB| = \sqrt{4 + 4 + 1} = 3$

$|AC| = \sqrt{4 + 4 + 1} = 3$

$|BC| = \sqrt{16 + 16 + 0} = 4\sqrt{2}$

Since $|AB| = |AC|$, the triangle is isosceles.

32. $A(5, 0, 0), B(0, 2, 0), C(0, 0, -3)$

$|AB| = \sqrt{25 + 4 + 0} = \sqrt{29}$

$|AC| = \sqrt{25 + 0 + 9} = \sqrt{34}$

$|BC| = \sqrt{0 + 4 + 9} = \sqrt{13}$

Neither

34. The y-coordinate is changed by 3 units:

$(5, 6, 4), (7, 4, 3), (3, 8, 3)$

36. $\left(\dfrac{4 + 8}{2}, \dfrac{0 + 8}{2}, \dfrac{-6 + 20}{2} \right) = (6, 4, 7)$

38. Center: $(4, -1, 1)$

Radius: 5

$(x - 4)^2 + (y + 1)^2 + (z - 1)^2 = 25$

$x^2 + y^2 + z^2 - 8x + 2y - 2z - 7 = 0$

40. Center: $(-3, 2, 4)$

$r = 3$

(tangent to yz-plane)

$(x + 3)^2 + (y - 2)^2 + (z - 4)^2 = 9$

42. $\qquad\qquad x^2 + y^2 + z^2 + 9x - 2y + 10z + 19 = 0$

$\left(x^2 + 9x + \dfrac{81}{4} \right) + (y^2 - 2y + 1) + (z^2 + 10z + 25) = -19 + \dfrac{81}{4} + 1 + 25$

$\qquad\qquad \left(x + \dfrac{9}{2} \right)^2 + (y - 1)^2 + (z + 5)^2 = \dfrac{109}{4}$

Center: $\left(-\dfrac{9}{2}, 1, -5 \right)$

Radius: $\dfrac{\sqrt{109}}{2}$

44. $\qquad\qquad 4x^2 + 4y^2 + 4z^2 - 4x - 32y + 8z + 33 = 0$

$\qquad\qquad x^2 + y^2 + z^2 - x - 8y + 2z + \dfrac{33}{4} = 0$

$\left(x^2 - x + \dfrac{1}{4} \right) + (y^2 - 8y + 16) + (z^2 + 2z + 1) = -\dfrac{33}{4} + \dfrac{1}{4} + 16 + 1$

$\qquad\qquad \left(x - \dfrac{1}{2} \right)^2 + (y - 4)^2 + (z + 1)^2 = 9$

Center: $\left(\dfrac{1}{2}, 4, -1 \right)$

Radius: 3

46.
$$x^2 + y^2 + z^2 < 4x - 6y + 8z - 13$$
$$(x^2 - 4x + 4) + (y^2 + 6y + 9) + (z^2 - 8z + 16) < 4 + 9 + 16 - 13$$
$$(x - 2)^2 + (y + 3)^2 + (z - 4)^2 < 16$$

Interior of sphere of radius 4 centered at $(2, -3, 4)$.

48. (a) $\mathbf{v} = (4 - 0)\mathbf{i} + (0 - 5)\mathbf{j} + (3 - 1)\mathbf{k}$

$= 4\mathbf{i} - 5\mathbf{j} + 2\mathbf{k} = \langle 4, -5, 2 \rangle$

(b)

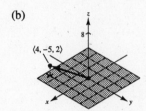

50. (a) $\mathbf{v} = (2 - 2)\mathbf{i} + (3 - 3)\mathbf{j} + (4 - 0)\mathbf{k}$

$= 4\mathbf{k} = \langle 0, 0, 4 \rangle$

(b)

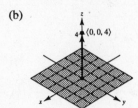

52. $\langle -1 - 4, 7 - (-5), -3 - 2 \rangle = \langle -5, 12, -5 \rangle$

$\|\langle -5, 12, -5 \rangle\| = \sqrt{25 + 144 + 25} = \sqrt{194}$

Unit vector: $\dfrac{\langle -5, 12, -5 \rangle}{\sqrt{194}} = \left\langle \dfrac{-5}{\sqrt{194}}, \dfrac{12}{\sqrt{194}}, \dfrac{-5}{\sqrt{194}} \right\rangle$

54. $\langle 2 - 1, 4 - (-2), -2 - 4 \rangle = \langle 1, 6, -6 \rangle$

$\|\langle 1, 6, -6 \rangle\| = \sqrt{1 + 36 + 36} = \sqrt{73}$

Unit vector: $\left\langle \dfrac{1}{\sqrt{73}}, \dfrac{6}{\sqrt{73}}, \dfrac{-6}{\sqrt{73}} \right\rangle$

56. (b) $\mathbf{v} = (-4 - 2)\mathbf{i} + (3 + 1)\mathbf{j} + (7 + 2)\mathbf{k}$

$= -6\mathbf{i} + 4\mathbf{j} + 9\mathbf{k} = \langle -6, 4, 9 \rangle$

(a) and (c).

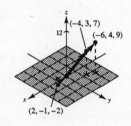

58. $(q_1, q_2, q_3) - \left(0, 2, \dfrac{5}{2}\right) = \left(1, -\dfrac{2}{3}, \dfrac{1}{2}\right)$

$Q = \left(1, -\dfrac{8}{3}, 3\right)$

60. (a) $-\mathbf{v} = \langle -2, 2, -1 \rangle$

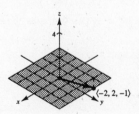

(b) $2\mathbf{v} = \langle 4, -4, 2 \rangle$

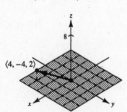

(c) $\dfrac{1}{2}\mathbf{v} = \left\langle 1, -1, \dfrac{1}{2} \right\rangle$

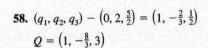

(d) $\dfrac{5}{2}\mathbf{v} = \left\langle 5, -5, \dfrac{5}{2} \right\rangle$

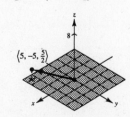

62. $z = u - v + 2w = \langle 1, 2, 3 \rangle - \langle 2, 2, -1 \rangle + \langle 8, 0, -8 \rangle = \langle 7, 0, -4 \rangle$

64. $z = 5u - 3v - \frac{1}{2}w = \langle 5, 10, 15 \rangle - \langle 6, 6, -3 \rangle - \langle 2, 0, -2 \rangle = \langle -3, 4, 20 \rangle$

66. $2u + v - w + 3z = 2\langle 1, 2, 3 \rangle + \langle 2, 2, -1 \rangle - \langle 4, 0, -4 \rangle + 3\langle z_1, z_2, z_3 \rangle = \langle 0, 0, 0 \rangle$

$\langle 0, 6, 9 \rangle + \langle 3z_1, 3z_2, 3z_3 \rangle = \langle 0, 0, 0 \rangle$

$0 + 3z_1 = 0 \implies z_1 = 0$

$6 + 3z_2 = 0 \implies z_2 = -2$

$9 + 3z_3 = 0 \implies z_3 = -3$

$z = \langle 0, -2, -3 \rangle$

68. (b) and (d) are parallel since $-i + \frac{4}{3}j - \frac{3}{2}k = -2\left(\frac{1}{2}i - \frac{2}{3}j + \frac{3}{4}k\right)$ and $\frac{3}{4}i - j + \frac{9}{8}k = \frac{3}{2}\left(\frac{1}{2}i - \frac{2}{3}j + \frac{3}{4}k\right)$.

70. $z = \langle -7, -8, 3 \rangle$

(b) is parallel since $(-z)z = \langle 14, 16, -6 \rangle$.

72. $P(4, -2, 7), Q(-2, 0, 3), R(7, -3, 9)$

$\overrightarrow{PQ} = \langle -6, 2, -4 \rangle$

$\overrightarrow{PR} = \langle 3, -1, 2 \rangle$

$\langle 3, -1, 2 \rangle = -\frac{1}{2}\langle -6, 2, -4 \rangle$

Therefore, $\overrightarrow{PQ}$ and $\overrightarrow{PR}$ are parallel.

The points are collinear.

74. $P(0, 0, 0), Q(1, 3, -2), R(2, -6, 4)$

$\overrightarrow{PQ} = \langle 1, 3, -2 \rangle$

$\overrightarrow{PR} = \langle 2, -6, 4 \rangle$

Since $\overrightarrow{PQ}$ and $\overrightarrow{PR}$ are not parallel, the points are not collinear.

76. $A(1, 1, 3), B(9, -1, -2), C(11, 2, -9), D(3, 4, -4)$

$\overrightarrow{AB} = \langle 8, -2, -5 \rangle$

$\overrightarrow{DC} = \langle 8, -2, -5 \rangle$

$\overrightarrow{AD} = \langle 2, 3, -7 \rangle$

$\overrightarrow{BC} = \langle 2, 3, -7 \rangle$

Since $\overrightarrow{AB} = \overrightarrow{DC}$ and $\overrightarrow{AD} = \overrightarrow{BC}$, the given points form the vertices of a parallelogram.

78. $\|v\| = \sqrt{1 + 0 + 9} = \sqrt{10}$

80. $v = \langle -4, 3, 7 \rangle$

$\|v\| = \sqrt{16 + 9 + 49} = \sqrt{74}$

82. $v = \langle 1, 3, -2 \rangle$

$\|v\| = \sqrt{1 + 9 + 4} = \sqrt{14}$

84. $u = \langle 6, 0, 8 \rangle$

$\|u\| = \sqrt{36 + 0 + 64} = 10$

(a) $\dfrac{u}{\|u\|} = \dfrac{1}{10}\langle 6, 0, 8 \rangle$

(b) $-\dfrac{u}{\|u\|} = -\dfrac{1}{10}\langle 6, 0, 8 \rangle$

86. $u = \langle 8, 0, 0 \rangle$

$\|u\| = 8$

(a) $\dfrac{u}{\|u\|} = \langle 1, 0, 0 \rangle$

(b) $-\dfrac{u}{\|u\|} = \langle -1, 0, 0 \rangle$

88. (a) $u + v = \langle 4, 7.5, -2 \rangle$

(b) $\|u + v\| \approx 8.732$

(c) $\|u\| \approx 5.099$

(d) $\|v\| \approx 9.014$

90. $cu = \langle c, 2c, 3c \rangle$

$\|cu\| = \sqrt{c^2 + 4c^2 + 9c^2} = 3$

$14c^2 = 9$

$c = \pm\dfrac{3\sqrt{14}}{14}$

92. $\mathbf{v} = 3\dfrac{\mathbf{u}}{\|\mathbf{u}\|} = 3\left\langle \dfrac{1}{\sqrt{3}}, \dfrac{1}{\sqrt{3}}, \dfrac{1}{\sqrt{3}} \right\rangle = \left\langle \dfrac{3}{\sqrt{3}}, \dfrac{3}{\sqrt{3}}, \dfrac{3}{\sqrt{3}} \right\rangle$

94. $\mathbf{v} = \sqrt{5}\dfrac{\mathbf{u}}{\|\mathbf{u}\|} = \sqrt{5}\left\langle \dfrac{-2}{\sqrt{14}}, \dfrac{3}{\sqrt{14}}, \dfrac{1}{\sqrt{14}} \right\rangle$

$$= \left\langle \dfrac{-\sqrt{70}}{7}, \dfrac{3\sqrt{70}}{14}, \dfrac{\sqrt{70}}{14} \right\rangle$$

96. $\mathbf{v} = 5(\cos 45^\circ \mathbf{i} + \sin 45^\circ \mathbf{k}) = \dfrac{5\sqrt{2}}{2}(\mathbf{i} + \mathbf{k})$ or

$\mathbf{v} = 5(\cos 135^\circ \mathbf{i} + \sin 135^\circ \mathbf{k}) = \dfrac{5\sqrt{2}}{2}(-i + k)$

98.
$$\mathbf{v} = \langle 5, 6, -3 \rangle$$
$$\tfrac{2}{3}\mathbf{v} = \left\langle \tfrac{10}{3}, 4, -2 \right\rangle$$
$$(1, 2, 5) + \left(\tfrac{10}{3}, 4, -2\right) = \left(\tfrac{13}{3}, 6, 3\right)$$

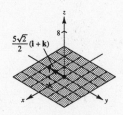

100. x_0 is directed distance to yz-plane.

y_0 is directed distance to xz-plane.

z_0 is directed distance to xy-plane.

102. $(x - x_0)^2 + (y - y_0)^2 + (z - z_0)^2 = r^2$

104. A sphere of radius 4 centered at (x_1, y_1, z_1).

$\|\mathbf{v}\| = \|\langle x - x_2, y - y_1, z - z_1 \rangle\|$

$\qquad = \sqrt{(x - x_1)^2 + (y - y_1)^2 + (z - z_1)^2} = 4$

$(x - x_1)^2 + (y - y_1)^2 + (z - z_1)^2 = 16$ sphere

106. As in Exercise 105(c), $x = a$ will be a vertical asymptote. Hence, $\lim\limits_{r_0 \to a^-} T = \infty.$

108. $\qquad 550 = \|c(75\mathbf{i} - 50\mathbf{j} - 100\mathbf{k})\|$

$302{,}500 = 18{,}125c^2$

$\qquad c^2 = 16.689655$

$\qquad c \approx 4.085$

$\qquad \mathbf{F} \approx 4.085(75\mathbf{i} - 50\mathbf{j} - 100\mathbf{k})$

$\qquad\quad \approx 306\mathbf{i} - 204\mathbf{j} - 409\mathbf{k}$

110. Let A lie on the y-axis and the wall on the x-axis. Then

$A = (0, 10, 0)$, $B = (8, 0, 6)$, $C = (-10, 0, 6)$ and

$\overrightarrow{AB} = \langle 8, -10, 6 \rangle$, $\overrightarrow{AC} = \langle -10, -10, 6 \rangle$.

$\|\overrightarrow{AB}\| = 10\sqrt{2}$, $\|\overrightarrow{AC}\| = 2\sqrt{59}$

Thus, $\mathbf{F}_1 = 420\dfrac{\overrightarrow{AB}}{\|\overrightarrow{AB}\|}$, $\mathbf{F}_2 = 650\dfrac{\overrightarrow{AC}}{\|\overrightarrow{AC}\|}$

$\mathbf{F} = \mathbf{F}_1 + \mathbf{F}_2 \approx \langle 237.6, -297.0, 178.2 \rangle$

$\qquad\qquad\qquad + \langle -423.1, -423.1, 253.9 \rangle$

$\qquad\qquad \approx \langle -185.5, -720.1, 432.1 \rangle$

$\|\mathbf{F}\| \approx 860.0$ lb

Section 10.3   The Dot Product of Two Vectors

2. $\mathbf{u} = \langle 4, 10 \rangle$, $\mathbf{v} = \langle -2, 3 \rangle$

   (a) $\mathbf{u} \cdot \mathbf{v} = 4(-2) + 10(3) = 22$

   (b) $\mathbf{u} \cdot \mathbf{u} = 4(4) + 10(10) = 116$

   (c) $\|\mathbf{u}\|^2 = 116$

   (d) $(\mathbf{u} \cdot \mathbf{v})\mathbf{v} = 22\langle -2, 3 \rangle = \langle -44, 66 \rangle$

   (e) $\mathbf{u} \cdot (2\mathbf{v}) = 2(\mathbf{u} \cdot \mathbf{v}) = 2(22) = 44$

4. $\mathbf{u} = \mathbf{i}$, $\mathbf{v} = \mathbf{i}$

   (a) $\mathbf{u} \cdot \mathbf{v} = 1$

   (b) $\mathbf{u} \cdot \mathbf{u} = 1$

   (c) $\|\mathbf{u}\|^2 = 1$

   (d) $(\mathbf{u} \cdot \mathbf{v})\mathbf{v} = \mathbf{i}$

   (e) $\mathbf{u} \cdot (2\mathbf{v}) = 2(\mathbf{u} \cdot \mathbf{v}) = 2$

6. $\mathbf{u} = 2\mathbf{i} + \mathbf{j} - 2\mathbf{k}, \mathbf{v} = \mathbf{i} - 3\mathbf{j} + 2\mathbf{k}$

(a) $\mathbf{u} \cdot \mathbf{v} = 2(1) + 1(-3) + (-2)(2) = -5$

(b) $\mathbf{u} \cdot \mathbf{u} = 2(2) + 1(1) + (-2)(-2) = 9$

(c) $\|\mathbf{u}\|^2 = 9$

(d) $(\mathbf{u} \cdot \mathbf{v})\mathbf{v} = -5(\mathbf{i} - 3\mathbf{j} + 2\mathbf{k}) = -5\mathbf{i} + 15\mathbf{j} - 10\mathbf{k}$

(e) $\mathbf{u} \cdot (2\mathbf{v}) = 2(\mathbf{u} \cdot \mathbf{v}) = 2(-5) = -10$

8. $\mathbf{u} = \langle 3240, 1450, 2235 \rangle$

$\mathbf{v} = \langle 2.22, 1.85, 3.25 \rangle$

Increase prices by 4%: $1.04\langle 2.22, 1.85, 3.25 \rangle$.

New total amount: $1.04(\mathbf{u} \cdot \mathbf{v}) = 1.04(17,139.05)$

$$= \$17,824.61$$

10. $\dfrac{\mathbf{u} \cdot \mathbf{v}}{\|\mathbf{u}\| \, \|\mathbf{v}\|} = \cos\theta$

$\mathbf{u} \cdot \mathbf{v} = (40)(25)\cos\dfrac{5\pi}{6} = -500\sqrt{3}$

12. $\mathbf{u} = \langle 3, 1 \rangle, \mathbf{v} = \langle 2, -1 \rangle$

$\cos\theta = \dfrac{\mathbf{u} \cdot \mathbf{v}}{\|\mathbf{u}\| \, \|\mathbf{v}\|} = \dfrac{5}{\sqrt{10}\sqrt{5}} = \dfrac{1}{\sqrt{2}}$

$\theta = \dfrac{\pi}{4}$

14. $\mathbf{u} = \cos\left(\dfrac{\pi}{6}\right)\mathbf{i} + \sin\left(\dfrac{\pi}{6}\right)\mathbf{j} = \dfrac{\sqrt{3}}{2}\mathbf{i} + \dfrac{1}{2}\mathbf{j}$

$\mathbf{v} = \cos\left(\dfrac{3\pi}{4}\right)\mathbf{i} + \sin\left(\dfrac{3\pi}{4}\right)\mathbf{j} = -\dfrac{\sqrt{2}}{2}\mathbf{i} + \dfrac{\sqrt{2}}{2}\mathbf{j}$

$\cos\theta = \dfrac{\mathbf{u} \cdot \mathbf{v}}{\|\mathbf{u}\| \, \|\mathbf{v}\|}$

$= \dfrac{\sqrt{3}}{2}\left(-\dfrac{\sqrt{2}}{2}\right) + \dfrac{1}{2}\left(\dfrac{\sqrt{2}}{2}\right) = \dfrac{\sqrt{2}}{4}\left(1 - \sqrt{3}\right)$

$\theta = \arccos\left[\dfrac{\sqrt{2}}{4}\left(1 - \sqrt{3}\right)\right] = 105°$

16. $\mathbf{u} = 3\mathbf{i} + 2\mathbf{j} + \mathbf{k}, \mathbf{v} = 2\mathbf{i} - 3\mathbf{j}$

$\cos\theta = \dfrac{\mathbf{u} \cdot \mathbf{v}}{\|\mathbf{u}\| \, \|\mathbf{v}\|} = \dfrac{3(2) + 2(-3) + 0}{\|\mathbf{u}\| \, \|\mathbf{v}\|} = 0$

$\theta = \dfrac{\pi}{2}$

18. $\mathbf{u} = 2\mathbf{i} - 3\mathbf{j} + \mathbf{k}, \mathbf{v} = \mathbf{i} - 2\mathbf{j} + \mathbf{k}$

$\cos\theta = \dfrac{\mathbf{u} \cdot \mathbf{v}}{\|\mathbf{u}\| \, \|\mathbf{v}\|}$

$= \dfrac{9}{\sqrt{14}\sqrt{6}} = \dfrac{9}{2\sqrt{21}} = \dfrac{3\sqrt{21}}{14}$

$\theta = \arccos\left(\dfrac{3\sqrt{21}}{14}\right) \approx 10.9°$

20. $\mathbf{u} = \langle 2, 18 \rangle, \mathbf{v} = \left\langle \dfrac{3}{2}, -\dfrac{1}{6} \right\rangle$

$\mathbf{u} \ne c\mathbf{v} \implies$ not parallel

$\mathbf{u} \cdot \mathbf{v} = 0 \implies$ orthogonal

22. $\mathbf{u} = -\dfrac{1}{3}(\mathbf{i} - 2\mathbf{j}), \mathbf{v} = 2\mathbf{i} - 4\mathbf{j}$

$\mathbf{u} = -\dfrac{1}{6}\mathbf{v} \implies$ parallel

24. $\mathbf{u} = -2\mathbf{i} + 3\mathbf{j} - \mathbf{k}, \mathbf{v} = 2\mathbf{i} + \mathbf{j} - \mathbf{k}$

$\mathbf{u} \ne c\mathbf{v} \implies$ not parallel

$\mathbf{u} \cdot \mathbf{v} = 0 \implies$ orthogonal

26. $\mathbf{u} = \langle \cos\theta, \sin\theta, -1 \rangle$,

$\mathbf{v} = \langle \sin\theta, -\cos\theta, 0 \rangle$

$\mathbf{u} \ne c\mathbf{v} \implies$ not parallel

$\mathbf{u} \cdot \mathbf{v} = 0 \implies$ orthogonal

28. $\mathbf{u} = \langle 5, 3, -1 \rangle \quad \|\mathbf{u}\| = \sqrt{35}$

$\cos\alpha = \dfrac{5}{\sqrt{35}}$

$\cos\beta = \dfrac{3}{\sqrt{35}}$

$\cos\gamma = \dfrac{-1}{\sqrt{35}}$

$\cos^2\alpha + \cos^2\beta + \cos^2\gamma = \dfrac{25}{35} + \dfrac{9}{35} + \dfrac{1}{35} = 1$

30. $\mathbf{u} = \langle a, b, c \rangle$, $\|\mathbf{u}\| = \sqrt{a^2 + b^2 + c^2}$

$$\cos \alpha = \frac{a}{\sqrt{a^2 + b^2 + c^2}}$$

$$\cos \beta = \frac{b}{\sqrt{a^2 + b^2 + c^2}}$$

$$\cos \gamma = \frac{c}{\sqrt{a^2 + b^2 + c^2}}$$

$$\cos^2 \alpha + \cos^2 \beta + \cos^2 \gamma = \frac{a^2}{a^2 + b^2 + c^2} + \frac{b^2}{a^2 + b^2 + c^2} + \frac{c^2}{a^2 + b^2 + c^2} = 1$$

32. $\mathbf{u} = \langle -4, 3, 5 \rangle$ $\|\mathbf{u}\| = \sqrt{50} = 5\sqrt{2}$

$$\cos \alpha = \frac{-4}{5\sqrt{2}} \qquad \Rightarrow \alpha \approx 2.1721 \text{ or } 124.4°$$

$$\cos \beta = \frac{3}{5\sqrt{2}} \qquad \Rightarrow \beta \approx 1.1326 \text{ or } 64.9°$$

$$\cos \gamma = \frac{5}{5\sqrt{2}} = \frac{1}{\sqrt{2}} \Rightarrow \gamma \approx \frac{\pi}{4} \text{ or } 45°$$

34. $\mathbf{u} = \langle -2, 6, 1 \rangle$ $\|\mathbf{u}\| = \sqrt{41}$

$$\cos \alpha = \frac{-2}{\sqrt{41}} \Rightarrow \alpha \approx 1.8885 \text{ or } 108.2°$$

$$\cos \beta = \frac{6}{\sqrt{41}} \Rightarrow \alpha \approx 0.3567 \text{ or } 20.4°$$

$$\cos \gamma = \frac{1}{\sqrt{41}} \Rightarrow \alpha \approx 1.4140 \text{ or } 81.0°$$

36. $\mathbf{F}_1$: $C_1 = \dfrac{300}{\|\mathbf{F}_1\|} \approx 13.0931$

$\mathbf{F}_2$: $C_2 = \dfrac{100}{\|\mathbf{F}_2\|} \approx 6.3246$

$\mathbf{F} = \mathbf{F}_1 + \mathbf{F}_2$

$\approx 13.0931 \langle -20, -10, 5 \rangle + 6.3246 \langle 5, 15, 0 \rangle$

$= \langle -230.239, -36.062, 65.4655 \rangle$

$\|\mathbf{F}\| \approx 242.067 \text{ lb}$

$\cos \alpha \approx \dfrac{-230.239}{\|\mathbf{F}\|} \Rightarrow \alpha \approx 162.02°$

$\cos \beta \approx \dfrac{-36.062}{\|\mathbf{F}\|} \Rightarrow \beta \approx 98.57°$

$\cos \gamma \approx \dfrac{65.4655}{\|\mathbf{F}\|} \Rightarrow \gamma \approx 74.31°$

38. $\mathbf{v}_1 = \langle s, s, s \rangle$

$\|\mathbf{v}_1\| = s\sqrt{3}$

$\mathbf{v}_2 = \langle s, s, 0 \rangle$

$\|\mathbf{v}_2\| = s\sqrt{2}$

$\cos \theta = \dfrac{s\sqrt{2}}{s\sqrt{3}} = \dfrac{\sqrt{6}}{3}$

$\theta = \arccos \dfrac{\sqrt{6}}{3} \approx 35.26°$

40. $\mathbf{F}_1 = C_1(0, 10, 10)$. $\|\mathbf{F}_1\| = 200 = C_1 10\sqrt{2} \Rightarrow C_1 = 10\sqrt{2}$

and $\mathbf{F}_1 = \langle 0, 100\sqrt{2}, 100\sqrt{2} \rangle$

$\mathbf{F}_2 = C_2 \langle -4, -6, 10 \rangle$

$\mathbf{F}_2 = C_3 \langle 4, -6, 10 \rangle$

$\mathbf{F} = \langle 0, 0, w \rangle$

$\mathbf{F} + \mathbf{F}_1 + \mathbf{F}_2 + \mathbf{F}_3 = 0$

$-4C_2 + 4C_3 = 0 \Rightarrow C_2 = C_3$

$100\sqrt{2} - 6C_2 - 6C_3 = 0 \Rightarrow C_2 = C_3 = \dfrac{25\sqrt{2}}{3} N$

42. $\mathbf{w}_2 = \mathbf{u} - \mathbf{w}_1 = \langle 9, 7 \rangle - \langle 3, 9 \rangle = \langle 6, -2 \rangle$

44. $\mathbf{w}_2 = \mathbf{u} - \mathbf{w}_1 = \langle 8, 2, 0 \rangle - \langle 6, 3, -3 \rangle = \langle 2, -1, 3 \rangle$

46. $\mathbf{u} = \langle 2, -3 \rangle$, $\mathbf{v} = \langle 3, 2 \rangle$

(a) $\mathbf{w}_1 = \left(\dfrac{\mathbf{u} \cdot \mathbf{v}}{\|\mathbf{v}\|^2} \right) \mathbf{v} = 0\mathbf{v} = \langle 0, 0 \rangle$

(b) $\mathbf{w}_2 = \mathbf{u} - \mathbf{w}_1 = \langle 2, -3 \rangle$

48. $\mathbf{u} = \langle 1, 0, 4 \rangle$, $\mathbf{v} = \langle 3, 0, 2 \rangle$

(a) $\mathbf{w}_1 = \left(\dfrac{\mathbf{u} \cdot \mathbf{v}}{\|\mathbf{v}\|^2} \right) \mathbf{v} = \dfrac{11}{13} \langle 3, 0, 2 \rangle = \left\langle \dfrac{33}{13}, 0, \dfrac{22}{13} \right\rangle$

(b) $\mathbf{w}_2 = \mathbf{u} - \mathbf{w}_1 = \langle 1, 0, 4 \rangle - \left\langle \dfrac{33}{13}, 0, \dfrac{22}{13} \right\rangle$

$$= \left\langle -\dfrac{20}{13}, 0, \dfrac{30}{13} \right\rangle$$

50. The vectors $\mathbf{u}$ and $\mathbf{v}$ are orthogonal if $\mathbf{u} \cdot \mathbf{v} = 0$.

The angle θ between $\mathbf{u}$ and $\mathbf{v}$ is given by

$$\cos \theta = \dfrac{\mathbf{u} \cdot \mathbf{v}}{\|\mathbf{u}\| \, \|\mathbf{v}\|}.$$

52. (a) and (b) are defined.

54. See figure 10.29, page 739.

56. Yes, $\left\| \dfrac{\mathbf{u} \cdot \mathbf{v}}{\|\mathbf{v}\|^2} \mathbf{v} \right\| = \left\| \dfrac{\mathbf{v} \cdot \mathbf{u}}{\|\mathbf{u}\|^2} \mathbf{u} \right\|$

$|\mathbf{u} \cdot \mathbf{v}| \dfrac{\|\mathbf{v}\|}{\|\mathbf{v}\|^2} = |\mathbf{v} \cdot \mathbf{u}| \dfrac{\|\mathbf{u}\|}{\|\mathbf{u}\|^2}$

$\dfrac{1}{\|\mathbf{v}\|} = \dfrac{1}{\|\mathbf{u}\|}$

$\|\mathbf{u}\| = \|\mathbf{v}\|$

58. (a) $\|\mathbf{u}\| = 5$, $\|\mathbf{v}\| \approx 8.602$, $\theta \approx 91.33°$

(b) $\|\mathbf{u}\| \approx 9.165$, $\|\mathbf{v}\| \approx 5.745$, $\theta = 90°$

60. (a) $\left\langle \dfrac{64}{17}, \dfrac{16}{17} \right\rangle$

(b) $\left\langle -\dfrac{21}{26}, \dfrac{63}{26}, \dfrac{42}{13} \right\rangle$

62. Because $\mathbf{u}$ appears to be a multiple of $\mathbf{v}$, the projection of $\mathbf{u}$ onto $\mathbf{v}$ is $\mathbf{u}$. Analytically,

$$\text{proj}_{\mathbf{v}} \mathbf{u} = \dfrac{\mathbf{u} \cdot \mathbf{v}}{\|\mathbf{v}\|^2} \mathbf{v} = \dfrac{\langle -3, -2 \rangle \cdot \langle 6, 4 \rangle}{\langle 6, 4 \rangle \cdot \langle 6, 4 \rangle} \langle 6, 4 \rangle$$

$$= \dfrac{-26}{52} \langle 6, 4 \rangle = \langle -3, -2 \rangle = \mathbf{u}.$$

64. $\mathbf{u} = -8\mathbf{i} + 3\mathbf{j}$. Want $\mathbf{u} \cdot \mathbf{v} = 0$.

$\mathbf{v} = 3\mathbf{i} + 8\mathbf{j}$ and $-\mathbf{v} = -3\mathbf{i} - 8\mathbf{j}$ are orthogonal to $\mathbf{u}$.

66. $\mathbf{u} = \langle 0, -3, 6 \rangle$. Want $\mathbf{u} \cdot \mathbf{v} = 0$.

$\mathbf{v} = \langle 0, 6, 3 \rangle$ and $-\mathbf{v} = \langle 0, -6, -3 \rangle$ are orthogonal to $\mathbf{u}$.

68. $\overrightarrow{OA} = \langle 10, 5, 20 \rangle$, $\mathbf{v} = \langle 0, 0, 1 \rangle$

$\text{proj}_{\mathbf{v}} \overrightarrow{OA} = \dfrac{20}{1^2} \langle 0, 0, 1 \rangle = \langle 0, 0, 20 \rangle$

$\|\text{proj}_{\mathbf{v}} \overrightarrow{OA}\| = 20$

70. $\mathbf{F} = 25(\cos 20°\mathbf{i} + \sin 20°\mathbf{j})$

$\mathbf{v} = 50\mathbf{i}$

$W = \mathbf{F} \cdot \mathbf{v} = 1250 \cos 20° \approx 1174.6 \text{ ft} \cdot \text{lb}$

72. $\overrightarrow{PQ} = \langle -4, 2, 10 \rangle$

$\vec{V} = \langle -2, 3, 6 \rangle$

$W = \overrightarrow{PQ} \cdot \vec{V} = 74$

74. True

$\mathbf{w} \cdot (\mathbf{u} + \mathbf{v}) = \mathbf{w} \cdot \mathbf{u} + \mathbf{w} \cdot \mathbf{v}$

$\qquad\qquad = 0 + 0 = 0 \implies \mathbf{w}$

and $\mathbf{u} + \mathbf{v}$ are orthogonal.

76. (a)

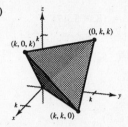

(b) Length of each edge:

$$\sqrt{k^2 + k^2 + 0^2} = k\sqrt{2}$$

(c) $\cos\theta = \dfrac{k^2}{\left(k\sqrt{2}\right)\left(k\sqrt{2}\right)} = \dfrac{1}{2}$

$\theta = \arccos\left(\dfrac{1}{2}\right) = 60°$

(d) $\vec{r_1} = \langle k, k, 0 \rangle - \left\langle \dfrac{k}{2}, \dfrac{k}{2}, \dfrac{k}{2} \right\rangle = \left\langle \dfrac{k}{2}, \dfrac{k}{2}, -\dfrac{k}{2} \right\rangle$

$\vec{r_2} = \langle 0, 0, 0 \rangle - \left\langle \dfrac{k}{2}, \dfrac{k}{2}, \dfrac{k}{2} \right\rangle = \left\langle -\dfrac{k}{2}, -\dfrac{k}{2}, -\dfrac{k}{2} \right\rangle$

$$\cos\theta = \dfrac{-\dfrac{k^2}{4}}{\left(\dfrac{k}{2}\right)^2 \cdot 3} = -\dfrac{1}{3}$$

$\theta = 109.5°$

78. The curves $y_1 = x^2$ and $y_2 = x^{1/3}$ intersect at $(0, 0)$ and at $(1, 1)$.

At $(0, 0)$: $\langle 1, 0 \rangle$ is tangent to y_1 and $\langle 0, 1 \rangle$ is tangent to y_2. The angle between these vectors is $90°$.

At $(1, 1)$: $\left(1/\sqrt{5}\right)\langle 1, 2 \rangle$ is tangent to y_1 and $\left(3/\sqrt{10}\right)\langle 1, 1/3 \rangle = \left(1/\sqrt{10}\right)\langle 3, 1 \rangle$ is tangent to y_2. To find the angle between these vectors,

$$\cos\theta = \dfrac{1}{\sqrt{5}}\dfrac{1}{\sqrt{10}}(3 + 2) = \dfrac{1}{\sqrt{2}} \Rightarrow \theta = 45°.$$

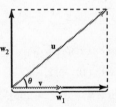

80. $\mathbf{u} \cdot \mathbf{v} = \|\mathbf{u}\| \|\mathbf{v}\| \cos\theta$

$|\mathbf{u} \cdot \mathbf{v}| = \left| \|\mathbf{u}\| \|\mathbf{v}\| \cos\theta \right|$

$\qquad = \|\mathbf{u}\| \|\mathbf{v}\| |\cos\theta|$

$\qquad \leq \|\mathbf{u}\| \|\mathbf{v}\|$ since $|\cos\theta| \leq 1$.

82. Let $\mathbf{w}_1 = \text{proj}_{\mathbf{v}}\mathbf{u}$, as indicated in the figure. Because $\mathbf{w}_1$ is a scalar multiple of $\mathbf{v}$, you can write

$\mathbf{u} = \mathbf{w}_1 + \mathbf{w}_2 = c\mathbf{v} + \mathbf{w}_2.$

Taking the dot product of both sides with $\mathbf{v}$ produces

$\mathbf{u} \cdot \mathbf{v} = (c\mathbf{v} + \mathbf{w}_2) \cdot \mathbf{v} = c\mathbf{v} \cdot \mathbf{v} + \mathbf{w}_2 \cdot \mathbf{v}$

$\qquad = c\|\mathbf{v}\|^2$, since $\mathbf{w}_2$ and $\mathbf{v}$ are orthogonol.

Thus, $\mathbf{u} \cdot \mathbf{v} = c\|\mathbf{v}\|^2 \Rightarrow c = \dfrac{\mathbf{u} \cdot \mathbf{v}}{\|\mathbf{v}\|^2}$ and $\mathbf{w}_1 = \text{proj}_{\mathbf{v}}\mathbf{u} = c\mathbf{v} = \dfrac{\mathbf{u} \cdot \mathbf{v}}{\|\mathbf{v}\|^2}\mathbf{v}.$

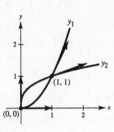

Section 10.4   The Cross Product of Two Vectors in Space

2. $\mathbf{i} \times \mathbf{j} = \begin{vmatrix} \mathbf{i} & \mathbf{j} & \mathbf{k} \\ 1 & 0 & 0 \\ 0 & 1 & 0 \end{vmatrix} = \mathbf{k}$

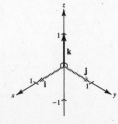

4. $\mathbf{k} \times \mathbf{j} = \begin{vmatrix} \mathbf{i} & \mathbf{j} & \mathbf{k} \\ 0 & 0 & 1 \\ 0 & 1 & 0 \end{vmatrix} = -\mathbf{i}$

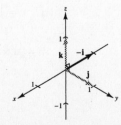

6. $\mathbf{k} \times \mathbf{i} = \begin{vmatrix} \mathbf{i} & \mathbf{j} & \mathbf{k} \\ 0 & 0 & 1 \\ 1 & 0 & 0 \end{vmatrix} = \mathbf{j}$

8. (a) $\mathbf{u} \times \mathbf{v} = \begin{vmatrix} \mathbf{i} & \mathbf{j} & \mathbf{k} \\ 3 & 0 & 5 \\ 2 & 3 & -2 \end{vmatrix} = \langle -15, 16, 9 \rangle$

(b) $\mathbf{v} \times \mathbf{u} = -(\mathbf{u} \times \mathbf{v}) = \langle 15, -16, -9 \rangle$

(c) $\mathbf{v} \times \mathbf{v} = 0$

10. (a) $\mathbf{u} \times \mathbf{v} = \begin{vmatrix} \mathbf{i} & \mathbf{j} & \mathbf{k} \\ 3 & -2 & -2 \\ 1 & 5 & 1 \end{vmatrix} = \langle 8, -5, 17 \rangle$

(b) $\mathbf{v} \times \mathbf{u} = -(\mathbf{u} \times \mathbf{v}) = \langle -8, 5, -17 \rangle$

(c) $\mathbf{v} \times \mathbf{v} = 0$

12. $\mathbf{u} = \langle -1, 1, 2 \rangle, \mathbf{v} = \langle 0, 1, 0 \rangle$

$\mathbf{u} \times \mathbf{v} = \begin{vmatrix} \mathbf{i} & \mathbf{j} & \mathbf{k} \\ -1 & 1 & 2 \\ 0 & 1 & 0 \end{vmatrix} = -2\mathbf{i} - \mathbf{k} = \langle -2, 0, -1 \rangle$

$\mathbf{u} \cdot (\mathbf{u} \times \mathbf{v}) = (-1)(-2) + (1)(0) + (2)(-1)$

$\quad = 0 \Rightarrow \mathbf{u} \perp \mathbf{u} \times \mathbf{v}$

$\mathbf{v} \cdot (\mathbf{u} \times \mathbf{v}) = (0)(-2) + (1)(0) + (0)(-1)$

$\quad = 0 \Rightarrow \mathbf{v} \perp \mathbf{u} \times \mathbf{v}$

14. $\mathbf{u} = \langle -10, 0, 6 \rangle, \mathbf{v} = \langle 7, 0, 0 \rangle$

$\mathbf{u} \times \mathbf{v} = \begin{vmatrix} \mathbf{i} & \mathbf{j} & \mathbf{k} \\ -10 & 0 & 6 \\ 7 & 0 & 0 \end{vmatrix} = 42\mathbf{j} = \langle 0, 42, 0 \rangle$

$\mathbf{u} \cdot (\mathbf{u} \times \mathbf{v}) = (-10)(0) + (0)(42) + 6(0)$

$\quad = 0 \Rightarrow \mathbf{u} \perp \mathbf{u} \times \mathbf{v}$

$\mathbf{v} \cdot (\mathbf{u} \times \mathbf{v}) = 7(0) + (0)(42) + (0)(0)$

$\quad = 0 \Rightarrow \mathbf{v} \perp \mathbf{u} \times \mathbf{v}$

16. $\mathbf{u} \times \mathbf{v} = \begin{vmatrix} \mathbf{i} & \mathbf{j} & \mathbf{k} \\ 1 & 6 & 0 \\ -2 & 1 & 1 \end{vmatrix} = 6\mathbf{i} - \mathbf{j} + 13\mathbf{k}$

$\mathbf{u} \cdot (\mathbf{u} \times \mathbf{v}) = 1(6) + 6(-1) = 0 \Rightarrow \mathbf{u} \perp (\mathbf{u} \times \mathbf{v})$

$\mathbf{v} \cdot (\mathbf{u} \times \mathbf{v}) = -2(6) + 1(-1) + 1(13) = 0 \Rightarrow \mathbf{v} \perp (\mathbf{u} \times \mathbf{v})$

18.

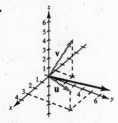

20.

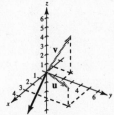

22. $\mathbf{u} = \langle -8, -6, 4 \rangle$

$\mathbf{v} = \langle 10, -12, -2 \rangle$

$\mathbf{u} \times \mathbf{v} = \langle 60, 24, 156 \rangle$

$\dfrac{\mathbf{u} \times \mathbf{v}}{\|\mathbf{u} \times \mathbf{v}\|} = \dfrac{1}{36\sqrt{22}} \langle 60, 24, 156 \rangle$

$\quad = \left\langle \dfrac{5}{3\sqrt{22}}, \dfrac{2}{3\sqrt{22}}, \dfrac{13}{3\sqrt{22}} \right\rangle$

24. $\mathbf{u} = \dfrac{2}{3}\mathbf{k}$

$\mathbf{v} = \dfrac{1}{2}\mathbf{i} + 6\mathbf{k}$

$\mathbf{u} \times \mathbf{v} = \left\langle 0, \dfrac{1}{3}, 0 \right\rangle$

$\dfrac{\mathbf{u} \times \mathbf{v}}{\|\mathbf{u} \times \mathbf{v}\|} = \langle 0, 1, 0 \rangle$

26. (a) $\mathbf{u} \times \mathbf{v} = \langle -18, -12, 48 \rangle$

$\|\mathbf{u} \times \mathbf{v}\| \approx 52.650$

(b) $\mathbf{u} \times \mathbf{v} = \langle -50, 40, -34 \rangle$

$\|\mathbf{u} \times \mathbf{v}\| \approx 72.498$

28. $\mathbf{u} = \mathbf{i} + \mathbf{j} + \mathbf{k}$

$\mathbf{v} = \mathbf{j} + \mathbf{k}$

$\mathbf{u} \times \mathbf{v} = \begin{vmatrix} \mathbf{i} & \mathbf{j} & \mathbf{k} \\ 1 & 1 & 1 \\ 0 & 1 & 1 \end{vmatrix} = -\mathbf{j} + \mathbf{k}$

$A = \|\mathbf{u} \times \mathbf{v}\| = \|-\mathbf{j} + \mathbf{k}\| = \sqrt{2}$

30. $\mathbf{u} = \langle 2, -1, 0 \rangle$

$\mathbf{v} = \langle -1, 2, 0 \rangle$

$$\mathbf{u} \times \mathbf{v} = \begin{vmatrix} \mathbf{i} & \mathbf{j} & \mathbf{k} \\ 2 & -1 & 0 \\ -1 & 2 & 0 \end{vmatrix} = \langle 0, 0, 3 \rangle$$

$A = \|\mathbf{u} \times \mathbf{v}\| = \|\langle 0, 0, 3 \rangle\| = 3$

32. $A(2, -3, 1), B(6, 5, -1), C(3, -6, 4), D(7, 2, 2)$

$\overrightarrow{AB} = \langle 4, 8, -2 \rangle, \overrightarrow{AC} = \langle 1, -3, 3 \rangle, \overrightarrow{CD} = \langle 4, 8, -2 \rangle, \overrightarrow{BD} = \langle 1, -3, 3 \rangle$

Since $\overrightarrow{AB} = \overrightarrow{CD}$ and $\overrightarrow{AC} = \overrightarrow{BD}$, the figure is a parallelogram.

$\overrightarrow{AB}$ and $\overrightarrow{AC}$ are adjacent sides and

$$\overrightarrow{AB} \times \overrightarrow{AC} = \begin{vmatrix} \mathbf{i} & \mathbf{j} & \mathbf{k} \\ 4 & 8 & -2 \\ 1 & -3 & 3 \end{vmatrix} = \langle 18, -14, -20 \rangle.$$

Area $= \|\overrightarrow{AB} \times \overrightarrow{AC}\| = \sqrt{920} = 2\sqrt{230}$

34. $A(2, -3, 4), B(0, 1, 2), C(-1, 2, 0)$

$\overrightarrow{AB} = \langle -2, 4, -2 \rangle, \overrightarrow{AC} = \langle -3, 5, -4 \rangle$

$$\overrightarrow{AB} \times \overrightarrow{AC} = \begin{vmatrix} \mathbf{i} & \mathbf{j} & \mathbf{k} \\ -2 & 4 & -2 \\ -3 & 5 & -4 \end{vmatrix} = -6\mathbf{i} - 2\mathbf{j} + 2\mathbf{k}$$

$A = \dfrac{1}{2}\|\overrightarrow{AB} \times \overrightarrow{AC}\| = \dfrac{1}{2}\sqrt{44} = \sqrt{11}$

36. $A(1, 2, 0), B(-2, 1, 0), C(0, 0, 0)$

$\overrightarrow{AB} = \langle -3, -1, 0 \rangle, \overrightarrow{AC} = \langle -1, -2, 0 \rangle$

$$\overrightarrow{AB} \times \overrightarrow{AC} = \begin{vmatrix} \mathbf{i} & \mathbf{j} & \mathbf{k} \\ -3 & -1 & 0 \\ -1 & -2 & 0 \end{vmatrix} = 5\mathbf{k}$$

$A = \dfrac{1}{2}\|\overrightarrow{AB} \times \overrightarrow{AC}\| = \dfrac{5}{2}$

38. $\mathbf{F} = -2000(\cos 30°\mathbf{j} + \sin 30°\mathbf{k}) = -1000\sqrt{3}\mathbf{j} - 1000\mathbf{k}$

$\overrightarrow{PQ} = 0.16\mathbf{k}$

$$\overrightarrow{PQ} \times \mathbf{F} = \begin{vmatrix} \mathbf{i} & \mathbf{j} & \mathbf{k} \\ 0 & 0 & 0.16 \\ 0 & -1000\sqrt{3} & -1000 \end{vmatrix} = 160\sqrt{3}\mathbf{i}$$

$\|\overrightarrow{PQ} \times \mathbf{F}\| = 160\sqrt{3}$ ft · lb

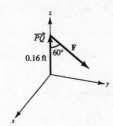

40. (a) B is $-\dfrac{15}{12} = -\dfrac{5}{4}$ to the left of A, and one foot upwards:

$\overrightarrow{AB} = \dfrac{-5}{4}\mathbf{j} + \mathbf{k}$

$\mathbf{F} = -200(\cos \theta\mathbf{j} + \sin \theta\mathbf{k})$

(b) $\overrightarrow{AB} \times \mathbf{F} = \begin{vmatrix} \mathbf{i} & \mathbf{j} & \mathbf{k} \\ 0 & -5/4 & 1 \\ 0 & -200\cos \theta & -200\sin \theta \end{vmatrix}$

$= (250\sin \theta + 200\cos \theta)\mathbf{i}$

$\|\overrightarrow{AB} \times \mathbf{F}\| = |250\sin \theta + 200\cos \theta|$

$= 25(10\sin \theta + 8\cos \theta)$

(c) For $\theta = 30°$,

$\|\overrightarrow{AB} \times \mathbf{F}\| = 25\left(10\left(\dfrac{1}{2}\right) + 8\left(\dfrac{\sqrt{3}}{2}\right)\right)$

$= 25\left(5 + 4\sqrt{3}\right) \approx 298.2.$

(d) If $T = \|\overrightarrow{AB} \times \mathbf{F}\|$,

$\dfrac{dT}{d\theta} = 25(10\cos \theta - 8\sin \theta) = 0 \implies \tan \theta = \dfrac{5}{4}$

$\implies \theta \approx 51.34°.$

The vectors are orthogonal.

(e) The zero is $\theta \approx 141.34°$, the angle making $\overrightarrow{AB}$ parallel to $\mathbf{F}$.

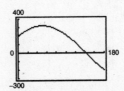

42. $\mathbf{u} \cdot (\mathbf{v} \times \mathbf{w}) = \begin{vmatrix} 1 & 1 & 1 \\ 2 & 1 & 0 \\ 0 & 0 & 1 \end{vmatrix} = -1$

44. $\mathbf{u} \cdot (\mathbf{v} \times \mathbf{w}) = \begin{vmatrix} 2 & 0 & 0 \\ 1 & 1 & 1 \\ 0 & 2 & 2 \end{vmatrix} = 0$

46. $\mathbf{u} \cdot (\mathbf{v} \times \mathbf{w}) = \begin{vmatrix} 1 & 3 & 1 \\ 0 & 6 & 6 \\ -4 & 0 & -4 \end{vmatrix} = -72$

$V = |\mathbf{u} \cdot (\mathbf{v} \times \mathbf{w})| = 72$

48. $\mathbf{u} = \langle 1, 1, 0 \rangle$

$\mathbf{v} = \langle 1, 0, 2 \rangle$

$\mathbf{w} = \langle 0, 1, 1 \rangle$

$\mathbf{u} \cdot (\mathbf{v} \times \mathbf{w}) = \begin{vmatrix} 1 & 1 & 0 \\ 1 & 0 & 2 \\ 0 & 1 & 1 \end{vmatrix} = -3$

$V = |\mathbf{u} \cdot (\mathbf{v} \times \mathbf{w})| = 3$

50. See Theorem 10.8, page 746.

52. Form the vectors for two sides of the triangle, and compute their cross product:

$$\langle x_2 - x_1, y_2 - y_1, z_2 - z_1 \rangle \times \langle x_3 - x_1, y_3 - y_1, z_3 - z_1 \rangle$$

54. False, let $\mathbf{u} = \langle 1, 0, 0 \rangle$, $\mathbf{v} = \langle 1, 0, 0 \rangle$, $\mathbf{w} = \langle -1, 0, 0 \rangle$.

Then,

$$\mathbf{u} \times \mathbf{v} = \mathbf{u} \times \mathbf{w} = \mathbf{0}, \text{ but } \mathbf{v} \neq \mathbf{w}.$$

56. $\mathbf{u} = \langle u_1, u_2, u_3 \rangle$, $\mathbf{v} = \langle v_1, v_2, v_3 \rangle$, $\mathbf{w} = \langle w_1, w_2, w_3 \rangle$

$\mathbf{u} = u_1\mathbf{i} + u_2\mathbf{j} + u_3\mathbf{k}$

$\mathbf{v} \times \mathbf{w} = (v_2 w_3 - v_3 w_2)\mathbf{i} - (v_1 w_3 - v_3 w_1)\mathbf{j} + (v_1 w_2 - v_2 w_1)\mathbf{k}$

$\mathbf{u} \cdot (\mathbf{v} + \mathbf{w}) = u_1(v_2 w_3 - v_3 w_2) - u_2(v_1 w_3 - v_3 w_1) + u_3(v_1 w_2 - v_2 w_1) = \begin{vmatrix} u_1 & u_2 & u_3 \\ v_1 & v_2 & v_3 \\ w_1 & w_2 & w_3 \end{vmatrix}$

58. $\mathbf{u} = \langle u_1, u_2, u_3 \rangle$, $\mathbf{v} = \langle v_1, v_2, v_3 \rangle$, c is a scalar.

$(c\mathbf{u}) \times \mathbf{v} = \begin{vmatrix} \mathbf{i} & \mathbf{j} & \mathbf{k} \\ cu_1 & cu_2 & cu_3 \\ v_1 & v_2 & v_3 \end{vmatrix}$

$\qquad = (cu_2 v_3 - cu_3 v_2)\mathbf{i} - (cu_1 v_3 - cu_3 v_1)\mathbf{j} + (cu_1 v_2 - cu_2 v_1)\mathbf{k}$

$\qquad = c[(u_2 v_3 - u_3 v_2)\mathbf{i} - (u_1 v_3 - u_3 v_1)\mathbf{j} + (u_1 v_2 - u_2 v_1)\mathbf{k}] = c(\mathbf{u} \times \mathbf{v})$

60. $\mathbf{u} \cdot (\mathbf{v} \times \mathbf{w}) = \begin{vmatrix} u_1 & u_2 & u_3 \\ v_1 & v_2 & v_3 \\ w_1 & w_2 & w_3 \end{vmatrix}$

$(\mathbf{u} \times \mathbf{v}) \cdot \mathbf{w} = \mathbf{w} \cdot (\mathbf{u} \times \mathbf{v}) = \begin{vmatrix} w_1 & w_2 & w_3 \\ u_1 & u_2 & u_3 \\ v_1 & v_2 & v_3 \end{vmatrix}$

$\qquad = w_1(u_2 v_3 - v_2 u_3) - w_2(u_1 v_3 - v_1 u_3) + w_3(u_1 v_2 - v_1 u_2)$

$\qquad = u_1(v_2 w_3 - w_2 v_3) - u_2(v_1 w_3 - w_1 v_3) + u_3(v_1 w_2 - w_1 v_2)$

$\qquad = \mathbf{u} \cdot (\mathbf{v} \times \mathbf{w})$

62. If **u** and **v** are scalar multiples of each other, **u** = c**v** for some scalar c.

$$\mathbf{u} \times \mathbf{v} = (c\mathbf{v}) \times \mathbf{v} = c(\mathbf{v} \times \mathbf{v}) = c(\mathbf{0}) = \mathbf{0}$$

If **u** × **v** = **0**, then $\|\mathbf{u}\| \, \|\mathbf{v}\| \sin \theta = 0$. (Assume **u** ≠ **0**, **v** ≠ **0**.) Thus, $\sin \theta = 0$, $\theta = 0$, and **u** and **v** are parallel. Therefore,

u = c**v** for some scalar c.

64. $\mathbf{u} = \langle a_1, b_1, c_1 \rangle$, $\mathbf{v} = \langle a_2, b_2, c_2 \rangle$, $\mathbf{w} = \langle a_3, b_3, c_3 \rangle$

$$\mathbf{v} \times \mathbf{w} = \begin{vmatrix} \mathbf{i} & \mathbf{j} & \mathbf{k} \\ a_2 & b_2 & c_2 \\ a_3 & b_3 & c_3 \end{vmatrix} = (b_2 c_3 - b_3 c_2)\mathbf{i} - (a_2 c_3 - a_3 c_2)\mathbf{j} + (a_2 b_3 - a_3 b_2)\mathbf{k}$$

$$\mathbf{u} \times (\mathbf{v} \times \mathbf{w}) = \begin{vmatrix} \mathbf{i} & \mathbf{j} & \mathbf{k} \\ a_1 & b_1 & c_1 \\ (b_2 c_3 - b_3 c_2) & (a_3 c_2 - a_2 c_3) & (a_2 b_3 - a_3 b_2) \end{vmatrix}$$

$$\mathbf{u} \times (\mathbf{v} \times \mathbf{w}) = [b_1(a_2 b_3 - a_3 b_2) - c_1(a_3 c_2 - a_2 c_3)]\mathbf{i} - [a_1(a_2 b_3 - a_3 b_2) - c_1(b_2 c_3 - b_3 c_2)]\mathbf{j} +$$

$$[a_1(a_3 c_2 - a_2 c_3) - b_1(b_2 c_3 - b_3 c_2)]\mathbf{k}$$

$$= [a_2(a_1 a_3 + b_1 b_3 + c_1 c_3) - a_3(a_1 a_2 + b_1 b_2 + c_1 c_2)]\mathbf{i} +$$

$$[b_2(a_1 a_3 + b_1 b_3 + c_1 c_3) - b_3(a_1 a_2 + b_1 b_2 + c_1 c_2)]\mathbf{j} +$$

$$[c_2(a_1 a_3 + b_1 b_3 + c_1 c_3) - c_3(a_1 a_2 + b_1 b_2 + c_1 c_2)]\mathbf{k}$$

$$= (a_1 a_3 + b_1 b_3 + c_1 c_3)\langle a_2, b_2, c_2 \rangle - (a_1 a_2 + b_1 b_2 + c_1 c_2)\langle a_3, b_3, c_3 \rangle$$

$$= (\mathbf{u} \cdot \mathbf{w})\mathbf{v} - (\mathbf{u} \cdot \mathbf{v})\mathbf{w}$$

Section 10.5   Lines and Planes in Space

2. $x = 2 - 3t$, $y = 2$, $z = 1 - t$

(a)

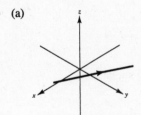

(b) When $t = 0$ we have $P = (2, 2, 1)$. When $t = 2$ we have $Q = (-4, 2, -1)$.

$$\overrightarrow{PQ} = \langle -6, 0, -2 \rangle$$

The components of the vector and the coefficients of t are proportional since the line is parallel to $\overrightarrow{PQ}$.

(c) $z = 0$ when $t = 1$. Thus, $x = -1$ and $y = 2$.

Point: $(-1, 2, 0)$

$x = 0$ when $t = \frac{2}{3}$. Point: $\left(0, 2, \frac{1}{3}\right)$

4. Point: $(0, 0, 0)$

Direction vector: $\mathbf{v} = \left\langle -2, \frac{5}{2}, 1 \right\rangle$

Direction numbers: $-4, 5, 2$

(a) Parametric: $x = -4t$, $y = 5t$, $z = 2t$

(b) Symmetric: $\dfrac{x}{-4} = \dfrac{y}{5} = \dfrac{z}{2}$

6. Point: $(-3, 0, 2)$

Direction vector: $\mathbf{v} = \langle 0, 6, 3 \rangle$

Direction numbers: $0, 2, 1$

(a) Parametric: $x = -3$, $y = 2t$, $z = 2 + t$

(b) Symmetric: $\dfrac{y}{2} = z - 2$, $x = -3$

8. Point: $(-3, 5, 4)$

Directions numbers: $3, -2, 1$

(a) Parametric: $x = -3 + 3t, y = 5 - 2t, z = 4 + t$

(b) Symmetric: $\dfrac{x + 3}{3} = \dfrac{y - 5}{-2} = z - 4$

10. Points: $(2, 0, 2), (1, 4, -3)$

Direction vector: $\langle 1, -4, 5 \rangle$

Direction numbers: $1, -4, 5$

(a) Parametric: $x = 2 + t, y = -4t, z = 2 + 5t$

(b) Symmetric: $x - 2 = \dfrac{y}{-4} = \dfrac{z - 2}{5}$

12. Points: $(0, 0, 25), (10, 10, 0)$

Direction vector: $\langle 10, 10, -25 \rangle$

Direction numbers: $2, 2, -5$

(a) Parametric: $x = 2t, y = 2t, z = 25 - 5t$

(b) Symmetric: $\dfrac{x}{2} = \dfrac{y}{2} = \dfrac{z - 25}{-5}$

14. Point: $(2, 3, 4)$

Direction vector: $\mathbf{v} = 3\mathbf{i} + 2\mathbf{j} - \mathbf{k}$

Direction numbers: $3, 2, -1$

Parametric: $x = 2 + 3t, y = 3 + 2t, z = 4 - t$

16. Points: $(2, 0, -3), (4, 2, -2)$

Direction vector: $\mathbf{v} = 2\mathbf{i} + 2\mathbf{j} + \mathbf{k}$

Direction numbers: $2, 2, 1$

Parametric: $x = 2 + 2t, y = 2t, z = -3 + t$

Symmetric: $\dfrac{x - 2}{2} = \dfrac{y}{2} = \dfrac{z + 3}{1}$

(a) Not on line $\left(1 \neq \dfrac{1}{2} \neq 1 \right)$

(b) On line

(c) Not on line $\left(\dfrac{-3}{2} = \dfrac{-3}{2} \neq -1 \right)$

18. L_1: $\mathbf{v} = \langle 4, -2, 3 \rangle$ $\qquad (8, -5, -9)$ on line

L_2: $\mathbf{v} = \langle 2, 1, 5 \rangle$

L_3: $\mathbf{v} = \langle -8, 4, -6 \rangle$ $\qquad (8, -5, -9)$ on line

L_4: $\mathbf{v} = \langle -2, 1, 1.5 \rangle$

L_1 and L_2 are identical.

20. By equating like variables, we have

(i) $-3t + 1 = 3s + 1$, (ii) $4t + 1 = 2s + 4$, and (iii) $2t + 4 = -s + 1$.

From (i) we have $s = -t$, and consequently from (ii), $t = \frac{1}{2}$ and from (iii), $t = -3$. The lines do not intersect.

22. Writing the equations of the lines in parametric form we have

$x = 2 - 3t \qquad y = 2 + 6t \qquad z = 3 + t$

$x = 3 + 2s \qquad y = -5 + s \qquad z = -2 + 4s.$

By equating like variables, we have $2 - 3t = 3 + 2s$, $2 + 6t = -5 + s$, $3 + t = -2 + 4s$. Thus, $t = -1$, $s = 1$ and the point of intersection is $(5, -4, 2)$.

$\mathbf{u} = \langle -3, 6, 1 \rangle \qquad$ (First line)

$\mathbf{v} = \langle 2, 1, 4 \rangle \qquad$ (Second line)

$\cos \theta = \dfrac{|\mathbf{u} \cdot \mathbf{v}|}{\|\mathbf{u}\| \, \|\mathbf{v}\|} = \dfrac{4}{\sqrt{46}\sqrt{21}} = \dfrac{4}{\sqrt{966}} = \dfrac{2\sqrt{966}}{483}$

24. $x = 2t - 1 \qquad x = -5s - 12$

$y = -4t + 10 \qquad y = 3s + 11$

$z = t \qquad z = -2s - 4$

Point of intersection: $(3, 2, 2)$

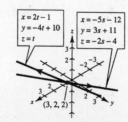

26. $2x + 3y + 4z = 4$

$P = (0, 0, 1), Q = (2, 0, 0), R = (3, 2, -2)$

(a) $\overrightarrow{PQ} = \langle 2, 0, -1 \rangle, \overrightarrow{PR} = \langle 3, 2, -3 \rangle$

(b) $\overrightarrow{PQ} \times \overrightarrow{PR} = \begin{vmatrix} \mathbf{i} & \mathbf{j} & \mathbf{k} \\ 2 & 0 & -1 \\ 3 & 2 & -3 \end{vmatrix} = \langle 2, 3, 4 \rangle$

The components of the cross product are proportional (for this choice of P, Q, and R, they are the same) to the coefficients of the variables in the equation. The cross product is parallel to the normal vector.

28. Point: $(1, 0, -3)$

$\mathbf{n} = \mathbf{k} = \langle 0, 0, 1 \rangle$

$0(x - 1) + 0(y - 0) + 1[z - (-3)] = 0$

$z + 3 = 0$

30. Point: $(0, 0, 0)$

Normal vector: $\mathbf{n} = -3\mathbf{i} + 2\mathbf{k}$

$-3(x - 0) + 0(y - 0) + 2(z - 0) = 0$

$-3x + 2z = 0$

32. Point: $(3, 2, 2)$

Normal vector: $\mathbf{v} = 4\mathbf{i} + \mathbf{j} - 3\mathbf{k}$

$4(x - 3) + (y - 2) - 3(z - 2) = 0$

$4x + y - 3z = 8$

34. Let $\mathbf{u}$ be vector from $(2, 3, -2)$ to $(3, 4, 2)$: $\langle 1, 1, 4 \rangle$.

Let $\mathbf{v}$ be vector from $(2, 3, -2)$ to $(1, -1, 0)$: $\langle -1, -4, 2 \rangle$.

Normal vector: $\mathbf{u} \times \mathbf{v} = \begin{vmatrix} \mathbf{i} & \mathbf{j} & \mathbf{k} \\ 1 & 1 & 4 \\ -1 & -4 & 2 \end{vmatrix} = \langle 18, -6, -3 \rangle$

$= -3\langle -6, 2, 1 \rangle$

$-6(x - 2) + 2(y - 3) + 1(z + 2) = 0$

$-6x + 2y + z = -8$

36. $(1, 2, 3)$, Normal vector: $\mathbf{v} = \mathbf{i}, 1(x - 1) = 0, x = 1$

38. The plane passes through the three points $(0, 0, 0)$, $(0, 1, 0) \left(\sqrt{3}, 0, 1 \right)$.

The vector from $(0, 0, 0)$ to $(0, 1, 0)$: $\mathbf{u} = \mathbf{j}$

The vector from $(0, 0, 0)$ to $\left(\sqrt{3}, 0, 1 \right)$: $\mathbf{v} = \sqrt{3}\mathbf{i} + \mathbf{k}$

Normal vector: $\mathbf{u} \times \mathbf{v} = \begin{vmatrix} \mathbf{i} & \mathbf{j} & \mathbf{k} \\ 0 & 1 & 0 \\ \sqrt{3} & 0 & 1 \end{vmatrix} = \mathbf{i} - \sqrt{3}\mathbf{k}$

$x - \sqrt{3}z = 0$

40. The direction of the line is $\mathbf{u} = 2\mathbf{i} - \mathbf{j} + \mathbf{k}$. Choose any point on the line, $[(0, 4, 0)$, for example], and let $\mathbf{v}$ be the vector from $(0, 4, 0)$ to the given point $(2, 2, 1)$:

$\mathbf{v} = 2\mathbf{i} - 2\mathbf{j} + \mathbf{k}$

Normal vector: $\mathbf{u} \times \mathbf{v} = \begin{vmatrix} \mathbf{i} & \mathbf{j} & \mathbf{k} \\ 2 & -1 & 1 \\ 2 & -2 & 1 \end{vmatrix} = \mathbf{i} - 2\mathbf{k}$

$(x - 2) - 2(z - 1) = 0$

$x - 2z = 0$

42. Let $\mathbf{v}$ be the vector from $(3, 2, 1)$ to $(3, 1, -5)$:

$\mathbf{v} = -\mathbf{j} - 6\mathbf{k}$

Let $\mathbf{n}$ be the normal to the given plane: $\mathbf{n} = 6\mathbf{i} + 7\mathbf{j} + 2\mathbf{k}$

Since $\mathbf{v}$ and $\mathbf{n}$ both lie in the plane P, the normal vector to P is:

$\mathbf{v} \times \mathbf{n} = \begin{vmatrix} \mathbf{i} & \mathbf{j} & \mathbf{k} \\ 0 & -1 & -6 \\ 6 & 7 & 2 \end{vmatrix} = 40\mathbf{i} - 36\mathbf{j} + 6\mathbf{k}$

$= 2(20\mathbf{i} - 18\mathbf{j} + 3\mathbf{k})$

$20(x - 3) - 18(y - 2) + 3(z - 1) = 0$

$20x - 18y + 3z = 27$

44. Let $\mathbf{u} = \mathbf{k}$ and let $\mathbf{v}$ be the vector from $(4, 2, 1)$ to $(-3, 5, 7)$: $\mathbf{v} = -7\mathbf{i} + 3\mathbf{j} + 6\mathbf{k}$

Since $\mathbf{u}$ and $\mathbf{v}$ both lie in the plane P, the normal vector to P is:

$\mathbf{u} \times \mathbf{v} = \begin{vmatrix} \mathbf{i} & \mathbf{j} & \mathbf{k} \\ 0 & 0 & 1 \\ -7 & 3 & 6 \end{vmatrix} = -3\mathbf{i} - 7\mathbf{j} = -(3\mathbf{i} + 7\mathbf{j})$

$3(x - 4) + 7(y - 2) = 0$

$3x + 7y = 26$

46. The normal vectors to the planes are $\mathbf{n}_1 = \langle 3, 1, -4 \rangle$, $\mathbf{n}_2 = \langle -9, -3, 12 \rangle$. Since $\mathbf{n}_2 = -3\mathbf{n}_1$, the planes are parallel, but not equal

48. The normal vectors to the planes are

$$\mathbf{n}_1 = 3\mathbf{i} + 2\mathbf{j} - \mathbf{k}, \quad \mathbf{n}_2 = \mathbf{i} - 4\mathbf{j} + 2\mathbf{k},$$

$$\cos \theta = \frac{|\mathbf{n}_1 \cdot \mathbf{n}_2|}{\|\mathbf{n}_1\| \|\mathbf{n}_2\|} = \frac{|3 - 8 - 2|}{\sqrt{14}\sqrt{21}} = \frac{1}{\sqrt{6}}.$$

Therefore, $\theta = \arccos\left(\dfrac{1}{\sqrt{6}}\right) \approx 65.9°.$

50. The normal vectors to the planes are

$$\mathbf{n}_1 = \langle 2, 0, -1 \rangle, \quad \mathbf{n}_2 = \langle 4, 1, 8 \rangle,$$

$$\cos \theta = \frac{|\mathbf{n}_1 \cdot \mathbf{n}_2|}{\|\mathbf{n}_1\| \|\mathbf{n}_2\|} = 0.$$

Thus, $\theta = \dfrac{\pi}{2}$ and the planes are orthogonal.

52. $3x + 6y + 2z = 6$

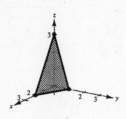

54. $2x - y + z = 4$

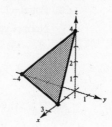

56. $x + 2y = 4$

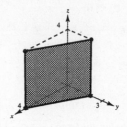

58. $z = 8$

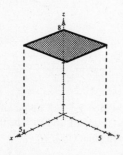

60. $x - 3z = 3$

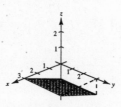

Generated by Mathematica

62. $2.1x - 4.7y - z + 3 = 0$

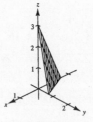

Generated by Mathematica

64. P_1: $\mathbf{n} = \langle -60, 90, 30 \rangle$ or $\langle -2, 3, 1 \rangle$ $\quad \left(0, 0, \frac{9}{10}\right)$ on plane

P_2: $\mathbf{n} = \langle 6, -9, -3 \rangle$ or $\langle -2, 3, 1 \rangle$ $\quad \left(0, 0, -\frac{2}{3}\right)$ on plane

P_3: $\mathbf{n} = \langle -20, 30, 10 \rangle$ or $\langle -2, 3, 1 \rangle$ $\quad \left(0, 0, \frac{5}{6}\right)$ on plane

P_4: $\mathbf{n} = \langle 12, -18, 6 \rangle$ or $\langle -2, 3, -1 \rangle$

$P_1, P_2,$ and P_3 are parallel.

66. If $c = 0, z = 0$ is xy-plane.

If $c \neq 0, cy + z = 0 \implies y = \dfrac{-1}{c}z$ is a plane parallel to x-axis and passing through the points $(0, 0, 0)$ and $(0, 1, -c)$.

68. The normals to the planes are $\mathbf{n}_1 = \langle 6, -3, 1 \rangle$. and $\mathbf{n}_2 = \langle -1, 1, 5 \rangle$.

The direction vector for the line is

$$\mathbf{n}_1 \times \mathbf{n}_2 = \begin{vmatrix} \mathbf{i} & \mathbf{j} & \mathbf{k} \\ 6 & -3 & 1 \\ -1 & 1 & 5 \end{vmatrix} = \langle -16, -31, 3 \rangle.$$

Now find a point of intersection of the planes.

$$\begin{array}{rcl} 6x - 3y + z = 5 & \implies & 6x - 3y + z = 5 \\ -x + y + 5z = 5 & \implies & \underline{-6x + 6y + 30z = 30} \\ & & 3y + 31z = 35 \end{array}$$

Let $y = -9, z = 2 \implies x = -4 \implies (-4, -9, 2)$.

$$x = -4 - 16t, y = -9 - 31t, z = 2 + 3t$$

70. Writing the equation of the line in parametric form and substituting into the equation of the plane we have:

$$x = 1 + 4t, \ y = 2t, \ z = 3 + 6t$$

$$2(1 + 4t) + 3(2t) = -5, \ t = \frac{-1}{2}$$

Substituting $t = -\frac{1}{2}$ into the parametric equations for the line we have the point of intersection $(-1, -1, 0)$. The line does not lie in the plane.

72. Writing the equation of the line in parametric form and substituting into the equation of the plane we have:

$$x = 4 + 2t, \ y = -1 - 3t, \ z = -2 + 5t$$

$$5(4 + 2t) + 3(-1 - 3t) = 17, \ t = 0$$

Substituting $t = 0$ into the parametric equations for the line we have the point of intersection $(4, -1, -2)$. The line does not lie in the plane.

74. Point: $Q(0, 0, 0)$

Plane: $8x - 4y + z = 8$

Normal to plane: $\mathbf{n} = \langle 8, -4, 1 \rangle$

Point in plane: $P\langle 1, 0, 0 \rangle$

Vector: $\vec{PQ} = \langle -1, 0, 0 \rangle$

$$D = \frac{|\vec{PQ} \cdot \mathbf{n}|}{\|\mathbf{n}\|} = \frac{|-8|}{\sqrt{81}} = \frac{8}{9}$$

76. Point: $Q(3, 2, 1)$

Plane: $x - y + 2z = 4$

Normal to plane: $\mathbf{n} = \langle 1, -1, 2 \rangle$

Point in plane: $P\langle 4, 0, 0 \rangle$

Vector: $\vec{PQ} = \langle -1, 2, 1 \rangle$

$$D = \frac{|\vec{PQ} \cdot \mathbf{n}|}{\|\mathbf{n}\|} = \frac{|-1|}{\sqrt{6}} = \frac{1}{\sqrt{6}} = \frac{\sqrt{6}}{6}$$

78. The normal vectors to the planes are $\mathbf{n}_1 = \langle 4, -4, 9 \rangle$ and $\mathbf{n}_2 = \langle 4, -4, 9 \rangle$. Since $\mathbf{n}_1 = \mathbf{n}_2$, the planes are parallel. Choose a point in each plane.

$P = (-5, 0, 3)$ is a point in $4x - 4y + 9z = 7$.

$Q = (0, 0, 2)$ is a point in $4x - 4y + 9z = 18$.

$\vec{PQ} = \langle 5, 0, -1 \rangle$

$$D = \frac{|\vec{PQ} \cdot \mathbf{n}_1|}{\|\mathbf{n}_1\|} = \frac{11}{\sqrt{113}} = \frac{11\sqrt{113}}{113}$$

80. The normal vectors to the planes are $\mathbf{n}_1 = \langle 2, 0, -4 \rangle$ and $\mathbf{n}_2 = \langle 2, 0, -4 \rangle$. Since $\mathbf{n}_1 = \mathbf{n}_2$, the planes are parallel. Choose a point in each plane.

$P = (2, 0, 0)$ is a point in $2x - 4z = 4$. $Q = (5, 0, 0)$ is a point in $2x - 4z = 10$.

$$\vec{PQ} = \langle 3, 0, 0 \rangle, \ D = \frac{|\vec{PQ} \cdot \mathbf{n}_1|}{\|\mathbf{n}_1\|} = \frac{6}{\sqrt{20}} = \frac{3\sqrt{5}}{5}$$

82. $\mathbf{u} = \langle 2, 1, 2 \rangle$ is the direction vector for the line.

$P = \langle 0, -3, 2 \rangle$ is a point on the line (let $t = 0$).

$\vec{PQ} = \langle 1, 1, 2 \rangle$

$$\vec{PQ} \times \mathbf{u} = \begin{vmatrix} \mathbf{i} & \mathbf{j} & \mathbf{k} \\ 1 & 1 & 2 \\ 2 & 1 & 2 \end{vmatrix} = \langle 0, 2, -1 \rangle$$

$$D = \frac{\|\vec{PQ} \times \mathbf{u}\|}{\|\mathbf{u}\|} = \frac{\sqrt{5}}{\sqrt{9}} = \frac{\sqrt{5}}{3}$$

84. The equation of the plane containing $P(x_1, y_1, z_1)$ and having normal vector $\mathbf{n} = \langle a, b, c \rangle$ is

$$a(x - x_1) + b(y - y_1) + c(z - z_1) = 0.$$

You need $\mathbf{n}$ and P to find the equation.

86. $x = a$: plane parallel to yz-plane containing $(a, 0, 0)$

$y = b$: plane parallel to xz-plane containing $(0, b, 0)$

$z = c$: plane parallel to xy-plane containing $(0, 0, c)$

88. (a) $t\mathbf{v}$ represents a line parallel to $\mathbf{v}$.

(b) $\mathbf{u} + t\mathbf{v}$ represents a line through the terminal point of $\mathbf{u}$ parallel to $\mathbf{v}$.

(c) $s\mathbf{u} + t\mathbf{v}$ represent the plane containing $\mathbf{u}$ and $\mathbf{v}$.

90. On one side we have the points $(0, 0, 0)$, $(6, 0, 0)$, and $(-1, -1, 8)$.

$$\mathbf{n}_1 = \begin{vmatrix} \mathbf{i} & \mathbf{j} & \mathbf{k} \\ 6 & 0 & 0 \\ -1 & -1 & 8 \end{vmatrix} = -48\mathbf{j} - 6\mathbf{k}$$

On the adjacent side we have the points $(0, 0, 0)$, $(0, 6, 0)$, and $(-1, -1, 8)$.

$$\mathbf{n}_2 = \begin{vmatrix} \mathbf{i} & \mathbf{j} & \mathbf{k} \\ 0 & 6 & 0 \\ -1 & -1 & 8 \end{vmatrix} = 48\mathbf{i} + 6\mathbf{k}$$

$$\cos \theta = \frac{|\mathbf{n}_1 \cdot \mathbf{n}_2|}{\|\mathbf{n}_1\| \|\mathbf{n}_2\|} = \frac{36}{2340} = \frac{1}{65}$$

$$\theta = \arccos\frac{1}{65} \approx 89.1°$$

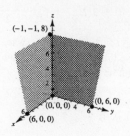

92. False. They may be skew lines. (See Section Project)

Section 10.6   Surfaces in Space

2. Hyperboloid of two sheets

Matches graph (e)

4. Elliptic cone

Matches graph (b)

6. Hyperbolic paraboloid

Matches graph (a)

8. $x = 4$

Plane parallel to the
yz-coordinate plane

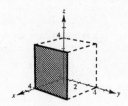

10. $x^2 + z^2 = 25$

The y-coordinate is missing so we have a cylindrical surface with rulings parallel to the y-axis. The generating curve is a circle.

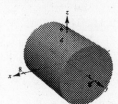

12. $z = 4 - y^2$

The x-coordinate is missing so we have a cylindrical surface with rulings parallel to the x-axis. The generating curve is a parabola.

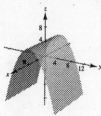

14. $y^2 - z^2 = 4$

$$\frac{y^2}{4} - \frac{z^2}{4} = 1$$

The x-coordinate is missing so we have a cylindrical surface with rulings parallel to the x-axis. The generating curve is a hyperbola.

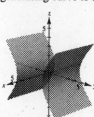

16. $z = e^y$

The x-coordinate is missing so we have a cylindrical surface with rulings parallel to the x-axis. The generating curve is the exponential curve.

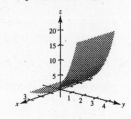

18. $y^2 + z^2 = 4$

(a) From (10, 0, 0):

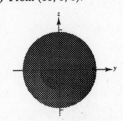

(b) From (0, 10, 0):

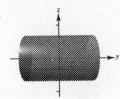

(c) From (10, 10, 10):

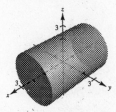

20. $\dfrac{x^2}{16} + \dfrac{y^2}{25} + \dfrac{z^2}{25} = 1$

Ellipsoid

xy-trace: $\dfrac{x^2}{16} + \dfrac{y^2}{25} = 1$ ellipse

xz-trace: $\dfrac{x^2}{16} + \dfrac{z^2}{25} = 1$ ellipse

yz-trace: $y^2 + z^2 = 25$ circle

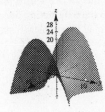

22. $z^2 - x^2 - \dfrac{y^2}{4} = 1$

Hyperboloid of two sheets

xy-trace: none

xz-trace: $z^2 - x^2 = 1$ hyperbola

yz-trace: $z^2 - \dfrac{y^2}{4} = 1$ hyperbola

$z = \pm\sqrt{10}:\ \dfrac{x^2}{9} + \dfrac{y^2}{36} = 1$ ellipse

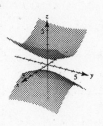

24. $z = x^2 + 4y^2$

Elliptic paraboloid

xy-trace: point $(0, 0, 0)$

xz-trace: $z = x^2$ parabola

yz-trace: $z = 4y^2$ parabola

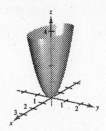

26. $3z = -y^2 + x^2$

Hyperbolic paraboloid

xy-trace: $y = \pm x$

xz-trace: $z = \frac{1}{3}x^2$

yz-trace: $z = -\frac{1}{3}y^2$

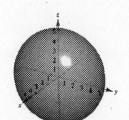

28. $x^2 = 2y^2 + 2z^2$

Elliptic Cone

xy-trace: $x = \pm\sqrt{2}\,y$

xz-trace: $x = \pm\sqrt{2}\,z$

yz-trace: point: $(0, 0, 0)$

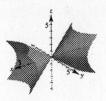

30.

$$9x^2 + y^2 - 9z^2 - 54x - 4y - 54z + 4 = 0$$

$$9(x^2 - 6x + 9) + (y^2 - 4y + 4) - 9(z^2 + 6z + 9) = 81 + 4 - 81$$

$$9(x - 3)^2 + (y - 2)^2 - 9(z + 3)^2 = 4$$

$$\dfrac{(x - 3)^2}{4/9} + \dfrac{(y - 2)^2}{4} - \dfrac{(z + 3)^2}{4/9} = 1$$

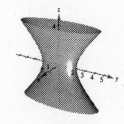

Hyperboloid of one sheet with center $(3, 2, -3)$.

32. $z = x^2 + 0.5y^2$

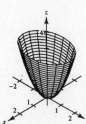

34. $z^2 = 4y - x^2$

$z = \pm\sqrt{4y - x^2}$

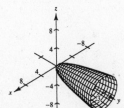

36. $x^2 + y^2 = e^{-z}$

$-\ln(x^2 + y^2) = z$

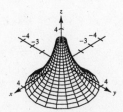

38. $z = \dfrac{-x}{8 + x^2 + y^2}$

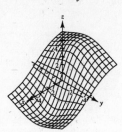

40. $9x^2 + 4y^2 - 8z^2 = 72$

$$z = \pm\sqrt{\dfrac{9}{8}x^2 + \dfrac{1}{2}y^2 - 9}$$

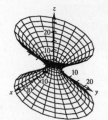

42. $z = \sqrt{4 - x^2}$

$y = \sqrt{4 - x^2}$

$x = 0, y = 0, z = 0$

44. $z = \sqrt{4 - x^2 - y^2}$

$y = 2z$

$z = 0$

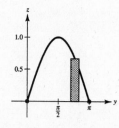

46. $x^2 + z^2 = [r(y)]^2$ and $z = r(y) = 3y$; therefore,

$$x^2 + z^2 = 9y^2.$$

48. $y^2 + z^2 = [r(x)]^2$ and $z = r(x) = \dfrac{1}{2}\sqrt{4 - x^2}$; therefore,

$$y^2 + z^2 = \dfrac{1}{4}(4 - x^2), \ x^2 + 4y^2 + 4z^2 = 4.$$

50. $x^2 + y^2 = [r(z)]^2$ and $y = r(z) = e^z$; therefore,

$$x^2 + y^2 = e^{2z}.$$

52. $x^2 + z^2 = \cos^2 y$

Equation of generating curve:

$x = \cos y$ or $z = \cos y$

54. The trace of a surface is the intersection of the surface with a plane. You find a trace by setting one variable equal to a constant, such as $x = 0$ or $z = 2$.

56. About x-axis: $y^2 + z^2 = [r(x)]^2$

About y-axis: $x^2 + z^2 = [r(y)]^2$

About z-axis: $x^2 + y^2 = [r(z)]^2$

58. $V = 2\pi\displaystyle\int_0^\pi y \sin y \, dy$

$$= 2\pi\Big[\sin y - y \cos y\Big]_0^\pi = 2\pi^2$$

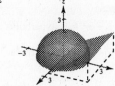

60. $z = \dfrac{x^2}{2} + \dfrac{y^2}{4}$

(a) When $y = 4$ we have $z = \dfrac{x^2}{2} + 4, \ 4\left(\dfrac{1}{2}\right)(z - 4) = x^2$.

Focus: $\left(0, 4, \dfrac{9}{2}\right)$

(b) When $x = 2$ we have

$$z = 2 + \dfrac{y^2}{4}, \ 4(z - 2) = y^2.$$

Focus: $(2, 0, 3)$

62. If (x, y, z) is on the surface, then

$$z^2 = x^2 + y^2 + (z - 4)^2$$

$$z^2 = x^2 + y^2 + z^2 - 8z + 16$$

$$8z = x^2 + y^2 + 16 \Longrightarrow z = \dfrac{x^2}{8} + \dfrac{y^2}{8} + 2$$

Elliptic paraboloid shifted up 2 units. Traces parallel to xy-plane are circles.

64. $z = -0.775x^2 + 0.007y^2 + 22.15x - 0.54y - 45.4$

(a)

Year	1980	1985	1990	1995	1996	1997
z	37.5	72.2	111.5	185.2	200.1	214.6
Model	37.8	72.0	112.2	185.8	204.5	214.7

(b)

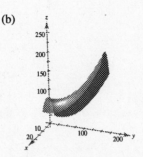

(c) For y constant, the traces parallel to the xz-plane are concave downward. That is, for fixed y (public assistance), the rate of increase of z (Medicare) is decreasing with respect to x (worker's compensation).

(d) The traces parallel to the yz-plane (x constant) are concave upward. That is, for fixed x (worker's compensation), the rate of increase of z (Medicare) is increasing with respect to y (public assistance).

66. Equating twice the first equation with the second equation,

$$2x^2 + 6y^2 - 4z^2 + 4y - 8 = 2x^2 + 6y^2 - 4z^2 - 3x - 2$$

$$4y - 8 = -3x - 2$$

$$3x + 4y = 6, \text{ a plane}$$

Section 10.7   Cylindrical and Spherical Coordinates

2. $\left(4, \dfrac{\pi}{2}, -2\right)$, cylindrical

$x = 4\cos\dfrac{\pi}{2} = 0$

$y = 4\sin\dfrac{\pi}{2} = 4$

$z = -2$

$(0, 4, -2)$, rectangular

4. $\left(6, -\dfrac{\pi}{4}, 2\right)$, cylindrical

$x = 6\cos\left(-\dfrac{\pi}{4}\right) = 3\sqrt{2}$

$y = 6\sin\left(-\dfrac{\pi}{4}\right) = -3\sqrt{2}$

$z = 2$

$\left(3\sqrt{2}, -3\sqrt{2}, 2\right)$

6. $\left(1, \dfrac{3\pi}{2}, 1\right)$, cylindrical

$x = \cos\dfrac{3\pi}{2} = 0$

$y = \sin\dfrac{3\pi}{2} = -1$

$z = 1$

$(0, -1, 1)$, rectangular

8. $\left(2\sqrt{2}, -2\sqrt{2}, 4\right)$, rectangular

$r = \sqrt{(2\sqrt{2})^2 + (-2\sqrt{2})^2} = 4$

$\theta = \arctan(-1) = -\dfrac{\pi}{4}$

$z = 4$

$\left(4, -\dfrac{\pi}{4}, 4\right)$, cylindrical

10. $\left(2\sqrt{3}, -2, 6\right)$, rectangular

$r = \sqrt{12 + 4} = 4$

$\theta = \arctan\left(-\dfrac{1}{\sqrt{3}}\right) = \dfrac{5\pi}{6}$

$z = 1$

$\left(4, -\dfrac{\pi}{6}, 1\right)$, cylindrical

12. $(-3, 2, -1)$, rectangular

$r = \sqrt{(-3)^2 + 2^2} = \sqrt{13}$

$\theta = \arctan\left(\dfrac{-2}{3}\right) = -\arctan\dfrac{2}{3}$

$z = -1$

$\left(\sqrt{13}, -\arctan\dfrac{2}{3}, -1\right)$, cylindrical

14. $z = x^2 + y^2 - 2$ rectangular equation

$z = r^2 - 2$ cylindrical equation

16. $x^2 + y^2 = 8x$ rectangular equation

$r^2 = 8r\cos\theta$

$r = 8\cos\theta$ cylindrical equation

18. $z = 2$

Same

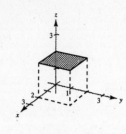

20. $r = \dfrac{z}{2}$

$$\sqrt{x^2 + y^2} = \dfrac{z}{2}$$

$$x^2 + y^2 - \dfrac{z^2}{4} = 0$$

22. $r = 2 \cos \theta$

$$r^2 = 2r \cos \theta$$

$$x^2 + y^2 = 2x$$

$$x^2 + y^2 - 2x = 0$$

$$(x - 1)^2 + y^2 = 1$$

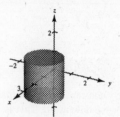

24. $z = r^2 \cos^2 \theta$

$z = x^2$

26. $(1, 1, 1)$, rectangular

$$\rho = \sqrt{1^2 + 1^2 + 1^2} = \sqrt{3}$$

$$\theta = \arctan 1 = \dfrac{\pi}{4}$$

$$\phi = \arccos \dfrac{1}{\sqrt{3}}$$

$\left(\sqrt{3}, \dfrac{\pi}{4}, \arccos \dfrac{1}{\sqrt{3}} \right)$, spherical

28. $\left(2, 2, 4\sqrt{2} \right)$, rectangular

$$\rho = \sqrt{2^2 + 2^2 + \left(4\sqrt{2}\right)^2} = 2\sqrt{10}$$

$$\theta = \arctan 1 = \dfrac{\pi}{4}$$

$$\phi = \arccos \dfrac{2}{\sqrt{5}}$$

$\left(2\sqrt{10}, \dfrac{\pi}{4}, \arccos \dfrac{2}{\sqrt{5}} \right)$, spherical

30. $(-4, 0, 0)$, rectangular

$$\rho = \sqrt{(-4)^2 + 0^2 + 0^2} = 4$$

$$\theta = \pi$$

$$\phi = \arccos 0 = \dfrac{\pi}{2}$$

$\left(4, \pi, \dfrac{\pi}{2} \right)$, spherical

32. $\left(12, \dfrac{3\pi}{4}, \dfrac{\pi}{9} \right)$, spherical

$$x = 12 \sin \dfrac{\pi}{9} \cos \dfrac{3\pi}{4} \approx -2.902$$

$$y = 12 \sin \dfrac{\pi}{9} \sin \dfrac{3\pi}{4} \approx 2.902$$

$$z = 12 \cos \dfrac{\pi}{9} \approx 11.276$$

$(-2.902, 2.902, 11.276)$, rectangular

34. $\left(9, \dfrac{\pi}{4}, \pi \right)$, spherical

$$x = 9 \sin \pi \cos \dfrac{\pi}{4} = 0$$

$$y = 9 \sin \pi \sin \dfrac{\pi}{4} = 0$$

$$z = 9 \cos \pi = -9$$

$(0, 0, -9)$, rectangular

36. $\left(6, \pi, \dfrac{\pi}{2} \right)$, spherical

$$x = 6 \sin \dfrac{\pi}{2} \cos \pi = -6$$

$$y = 6 \sin \dfrac{\pi}{2} \sin \pi = 0$$

$$z = 6 \cos \dfrac{\pi}{2} = 0$$

$(-6, 0, 0)$, rectangular

38. (a) Programs will vary.

(b) $(\rho, \theta, \phi) = (5, 1, 0.5)$

$(x, y, z) = (1.295, 2.017, 4.388)$

40. $x^2 + y^2 - 3z^2 = 0$ rectangular equation

$x^2 + y^2 + z^2 = 4z^2$

$\rho^2 = 4\rho^2 \cos^2 \phi$

$1 = 4\cos^2 \phi$

$\cos \phi = \dfrac{1}{2}$

$\phi = \dfrac{\pi}{3}$ (cone) spherical equation

42. $x = 10$ rectangular equation

$\rho \sin \phi \cos \theta = 10$

$\rho = 10 \csc \phi \sec \theta$ spherical equation

44. $\theta = \dfrac{3\pi}{4}$

$\tan \theta = \dfrac{y}{x}$

$-1 = \dfrac{y}{x}$

$x + y = 0$

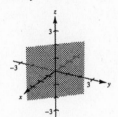

46. $\phi = \dfrac{\pi}{2}$

$\cos \phi = \dfrac{z}{\sqrt{x^2 + y^2 + z^2}}$

$0 = \dfrac{z}{\sqrt{x^2 + y^2 + z^2}}$

$z = 0$

xy-plane

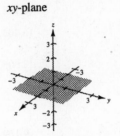

48. $\rho = 2 \sec \phi$

$\rho \cos \phi = 2$

$z = 2$

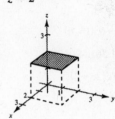

50. $\rho = 4 \csc \phi \sec \phi$

$\quad = \dfrac{4}{\sin \phi \cos \theta}$

$\rho \sin \phi \cos \theta = 4$

$x = 4$

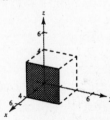

52. $\left(3, -\dfrac{\pi}{4}, 0\right)$, cylindrical

$\rho = \sqrt{3^2 + 0^2} = 3$

$\theta = -\dfrac{\pi}{4}$

$\phi = \arccos\left(\dfrac{0}{9}\right) = \dfrac{\pi}{2}$

$\left(3, -\dfrac{\pi}{4}, \dfrac{\pi}{2}\right)$, spherical

54. $\left(2, \dfrac{2\pi}{3}, -2\right)$, cylindrical

$\rho = \sqrt{2^2 + (-2)^2} = 2\sqrt{2}$

$\theta = \dfrac{2\pi}{3}$

$\phi = \arccos\left(\dfrac{-1}{\sqrt{2}}\right) = \dfrac{3\pi}{4}$

$\left(2\sqrt{2}, \dfrac{2\pi}{3}, \dfrac{3\pi}{4}\right)$, spherical

56. $\left(-4, \dfrac{\pi}{3}, 4\right)$, cylindrical

$\rho = \sqrt{(-4)^2 + 4^2} = 4\sqrt{2}$

$\theta = \dfrac{\pi}{3}$

$\phi = \arccos\dfrac{1}{\sqrt{2}} = \dfrac{\pi}{4}$

$\left(4\sqrt{2}, \dfrac{\pi}{3}, \dfrac{\pi}{4}\right)$, spherical

58. $\left(4, \dfrac{\pi}{2}, 3\right)$, cylindrical

$\rho = \sqrt{4^2 + 3^2} = 5$

$\theta = \dfrac{\pi}{2}$

$\phi = \arccos\dfrac{3}{5}$

$\left(5, \dfrac{\pi}{2}, \arccos\dfrac{3}{5}\right)$, spherical

60. $\left(4, \dfrac{\pi}{18}, \dfrac{\pi}{2}\right)$, spherical

$r = 4 \sin\dfrac{\pi}{2} = 4$

$\theta = \dfrac{\pi}{18}$

$z = 4 \cos\dfrac{\pi}{2} = 0$

$\left(4, \dfrac{\pi}{18}, 0\right)$, cylindrical

62. $\left(18, \frac{\pi}{3}, \frac{\pi}{3}\right)$, spherical

$r = \rho \sin \phi = 18 \sin \frac{\pi}{3} = 9$

$\theta = \frac{\pi}{3}$

$z = \rho \cos \phi = 18 \cos \frac{\pi}{3} = 9\sqrt{3}$

$\left(9, \frac{\pi}{3}, 9\sqrt{3}\right)$, cylindrical

64. $\left(5, -\frac{5\pi}{6}, \pi\right)$, spherical

$r = 5 \sin \pi = 0$

$\theta = -\frac{5\pi}{6}$

$z = 5 \cos \pi = -5$

$\left(0, -\frac{5\pi}{6}, -5\right)$, cylindrical

66. $\left(7, \frac{\pi}{4}, \frac{3\pi}{4}\right)$, spherical

$r = 7 \sin \frac{3\pi}{4} = \frac{7\sqrt{2}}{2}$

$\theta = \frac{\pi}{4}$

$z = 7 \cos \frac{3\pi}{4} = -\frac{7\sqrt{2}}{2}$

$\left(\frac{7\sqrt{2}}{2}, \frac{\pi}{4}, -\frac{7\sqrt{2}}{2}\right)$, cylindrical

	Rectangular	_Cylindrical_	_Spherical_
68.	$(6, -2, -3)$	$(6.325, -0.322, -3)$	$(7.000, -0.322, 2.014)$
70.	$(7.317, -6.816, 6)$	$(10, -0.75, 6)$	$(11.662, -0.750, 1.030)$
72.	$(6.115, 1.561, 4.052)$	$(6.311, 0.25, 4.052)$	$(7.5, 0.25, 1)$
74.	$\left(3\sqrt{2}, 3\sqrt{2}, -3\right)$	$(6, 0.785, -3)$	$(6.708, 0.785, 2.034)$
76.	$(0, -5, 4)$	$(5, -1.571, 4)$	$(6.403, -1.571, 0.896)$
78.	$(-1.732, 1, 3)$	$\left(-2, \frac{11\pi}{6}, 3\right)$	$(3.606, 2.618, 0.588)$

$\left[\text{Note: Use the cylindrical coordinate } \left(2, \frac{5\pi}{6}, 3\right)\right]$

| **80.** | $(2.207, 7.949, -4)$ | $(8.25, 1.3, -4)$ | $(9.169, 1.3, 2.022)$ |

82. $\theta = \frac{\pi}{4}$

Plane

Matches graph (e)

84. $\phi = \frac{\pi}{4}$

Cone

Matches graph (a)

86. $\rho = 4 \sec \phi, z = \rho \cos \phi = 4$

Plane

Matches graph (b)

88. $r = a$ Cylinder with z-axis symmetry

$\theta = b$ Plane perpendicular to xy-plane

$z = c$ Plane parallel to xy-plane

90. $\rho = a$ Sphere

$\theta = b$ Vertical half-plane

$\phi = c$ Half-cone

92. $4(x^2 + y^2) = z^2$

(a) $4r^2 = z^2, 2r = z$

(b) $4(\rho^2 \sin^2 \phi \cos^2 \theta + \rho^2 \sin^2 \phi \sin^2 \theta) = \rho^2 \cos^2 \phi,$

$4 \sin^2 \phi = \cos^2 \phi, \tan^2 \phi = \frac{1}{4},$

$\tan \phi = \frac{1}{2}, \phi = \arctan \frac{1}{2}$

94. $x^2 + y^2 = z$

(a) $r^2 = z$

(b) $\rho^2 \sin^2 \phi = \rho \cos \phi, \rho \sin^2 \phi = \cos \phi,$

$\rho = \frac{\cos \phi}{\sin^2 \phi}, \rho = \csc \phi \cot \phi$

96. $x^2 + y^2 = 16$

(a) $r^2 = 16, r = 4$

(b) $\rho^2 \sin^2 \phi = 16, \rho^2 \sin^2 \phi - 16 = 0,$
$(\rho \sin \phi - 4)(\rho \sin \phi + 4) = 0, \rho = 4 \csc \phi$

98. $y = 4$

(a) $r \sin \theta = 4, r = 4 \csc \theta$

(b) $\rho \sin \phi \sin \theta = 4, \rho = 4 \csc \phi \csc \theta$

100. $-\dfrac{\pi}{2} \le \theta \le \dfrac{\pi}{2}$

$0 \le r \le 3$

$0 \le z \le r \cos \theta$

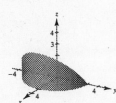

102. $0 \le \theta \le 2\pi$

$2 \le r \le 4$

$z^2 \le -r^2 + 6r - 8$

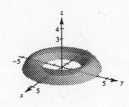

104. $0 \le \theta \le 2\pi$

$\dfrac{\pi}{4} \le \phi \le \dfrac{\pi}{2}$

$0 \le \rho \le 1$

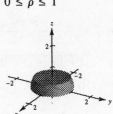

106. Cylindrical: $0.75 \le r \le 1.25, z = 8$

108. Cylindrical

$\dfrac{1}{2} \le r \le 3$

$0 \le \theta \le 2\pi$

$-\sqrt{9 - r^2} \le z \le \sqrt{9 - r^2}$

110. $\rho = 2 \sec \phi \Rightarrow \rho \cos \phi = 2 \Rightarrow z = 2$ plane

$\rho = 4$ sphere

The intersection of the plane and the sphere is a circle.

Review Exercises for Chapter 10

2. $P = (-2, -1), \ Q = (5, -1) \ R = (2, 4)$

(a) $\mathbf{u} = \overrightarrow{PQ} = \langle 7, 0 \rangle = 7\mathbf{i}, \ \mathbf{v} = \overrightarrow{PR} = \langle 4, 5 \rangle = 4\mathbf{i} + 5\mathbf{j}$

(b) $\|\mathbf{v}\| = \sqrt{4^2 + 5^2} = \sqrt{41}$

(c) $2\mathbf{u} + \mathbf{v} = 14\mathbf{i} + (4\mathbf{i} + 5\mathbf{j}) = 18\mathbf{i} + 5\mathbf{j}$

4. $\mathbf{v} = \|\mathbf{v}\| \cos \theta \, \mathbf{i} + \|\mathbf{v}\| \sin \theta \, \mathbf{j} = \dfrac{1}{2} \cos 225° \, \mathbf{i} + \dfrac{1}{2} \sin 225° \, \mathbf{j}$

$= -\dfrac{\sqrt{2}}{4}\mathbf{i} + \dfrac{\sqrt{2}}{4}\mathbf{j}$

6. (a) The length of cable POQ is L.

$\overrightarrow{OQ} = 9\mathbf{i} - y\mathbf{j}$

$L = 2\sqrt{9^2 + y^2} \Rightarrow \sqrt{\dfrac{L^2}{4} - 81} = y$

Tension: $T = c\|\overrightarrow{OQ}\| = c\sqrt{81 + y^2}$

Also,

$cy = 250 \Rightarrow T = \dfrac{250}{y}\sqrt{81 + y^2} \Rightarrow T = \dfrac{250}{\sqrt{(L^2/4) - 81}} \cdot \dfrac{L}{2} = \dfrac{250L}{\sqrt{L^2 - 324}}$

Domain: $L > 18$ inches

(b)

L	19	20	21	22	23	24	25
T	780.9	573.54	485.36	434.81	401.60	377.96	360.24

(c)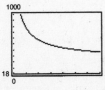

(d) The line $T = 400$ intersects the curve at

$L = 23.06$ inches.

(e) $\displaystyle\lim_{L \to \infty} T = 250$

The maximum tension is 250 pounds in each side of the cable since the total weight is 500 pounds.

8. $x = z = 0$, $y = -7$: $(0, -7, 0)$

10. Looking towards the xy-plane from the positive z-axis. The point is either in the second quadrant ($x < 0$, $y > 0$) or in the fourth quadrant ($x > 0$, $y < 0$). The z-coordinate can be any number.

12. Center: $\left(\dfrac{0 + 4}{2}, \dfrac{0 + 6}{2}, \dfrac{4 + 0}{2}\right) = (2, 3, 2)$

Radius: $\sqrt{(2 - 0)^2 + (3 - 0)^2 + (2 - 4)^2} = \sqrt{4 + 9 + 4} = \sqrt{17}$

$(x - 2)^2 + (y - 3)^2 + (z - 2)^2 = 17$

14. $(x^2 - 10x + 25) + (y^2 + 6y + 9) + (z^2 - 4z + 4) = -34 + 25 + 9 + 4$

$(x - 5)^2 + (y + 3)^2 + (z - 2)^2 = 4$

Center: $(5, -3, 2)$

Radius: 2

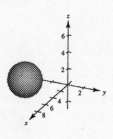

16. $\mathbf{v} = \langle 3 - 6, -3 - 2, 8 - 0 \rangle = \langle -3, -5, 8 \rangle$

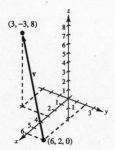

18. $\mathbf{v} = \langle 8 - 5, -5 + 4, 5 - 7 \rangle = \langle 3, -1, -2 \rangle$

$\mathbf{w} = \langle 11 - 5, 6 + 4, 3 - 7 \rangle = \langle 6, 10, -4 \rangle$

Since $\mathbf{v}$ and $\mathbf{w}$ are not parallel, the points do not lie in a straight line.

20. $8\dfrac{\langle 6, -3, 2 \rangle}{\sqrt{49}} = \dfrac{8}{7}\langle 6, -3, 2 \rangle = \left\langle \dfrac{48}{7}, -\dfrac{24}{7}, \dfrac{16}{7} \right\rangle$

22. $P = (2, -1, 3)$, $Q = (0, 5, 1)$, $R = (5, 5, 0)$

(a) $\mathbf{u} = \overrightarrow{PQ} = \langle -2, 6, -2 \rangle = -2\mathbf{i} + 6\mathbf{j} - 2\mathbf{k}$,

$\mathbf{v} = \overrightarrow{PR} = \langle 3, 6, -3 \rangle = 3\mathbf{i} + 6\mathbf{j} - 3\mathbf{k}$

(b) $\mathbf{u} \cdot \mathbf{v} = (-2)(3) + (6)(6) + (-2)(-3) = 36$

(c) $\mathbf{v} \cdot \mathbf{v} = 9 + 36 + 9 = 54$

24. $\mathbf{u} = \langle -4, 3, -6 \rangle$, $\mathbf{v} = \langle 16, -12, 24 \rangle$

Since $\mathbf{v} = -4\mathbf{u}$, the vectors are parallel.

26. $\mathbf{u} = \langle 4, -1, 5 \rangle$, $\mathbf{v} = \langle 3, 2, -2 \rangle$

$\mathbf{u} \cdot \mathbf{v} = 0 \implies$ is orthogonal to $\mathbf{v}$.

$$\theta = \frac{\pi}{2}$$

28. $\mathbf{u} = \langle 1, 0, -3 \rangle$

$\mathbf{v} = \langle 2, -2, 1 \rangle$

$\mathbf{u} \cdot \mathbf{v} = -1$

$\|\mathbf{u}\| = \sqrt{10}$

$\|\mathbf{v}\| = 3$

$\cos \theta = \dfrac{|\mathbf{u} \cdot \mathbf{v}|}{\|\mathbf{u}\| \, \|\mathbf{v}\|} = \dfrac{1}{3\sqrt{10}}$

$\theta \approx 83.9°$

30. $W = \mathbf{F} \cdot \overrightarrow{PQ} = \|\mathbf{F}\| \, \|\overrightarrow{PQ}\| \cos \theta = (75)(8)\cos 30°$

$= 300\sqrt{3}$ ft $\cdot$ lb

In Exercises 32–40, u $= \langle 3, -2, 1 \rangle$, **v** $= \langle 2, -4, -3 \rangle$, **w** $= \langle -1, 2, 2 \rangle$.

32. $\cos \theta = \dfrac{|\mathbf{u} \cdot \mathbf{v}|}{\|\mathbf{u}\| \, \|\mathbf{v}\|} = \dfrac{11}{\sqrt{14}\sqrt{29}}$

$\theta = \arccos\left(\dfrac{11}{\sqrt{14}\sqrt{29}}\right) \approx 56.9°$

34. Work $= |\mathbf{u} \cdot \mathbf{w}| = |-3 - 4 + 2| = 5$

36. $\mathbf{u} \times \mathbf{v} = \begin{vmatrix} \mathbf{i} & \mathbf{j} & \mathbf{k} \\ 3 & -2 & 1 \\ 2 & -4 & -3 \end{vmatrix} = 10\mathbf{i} + 11\mathbf{j} - 8\mathbf{k}$

$\mathbf{v} \times \mathbf{u} = \begin{vmatrix} \mathbf{i} & \mathbf{j} & \mathbf{k} \\ 2 & -4 & -3 \\ 3 & -2 & 1 \end{vmatrix} = -10\mathbf{i} - 11\mathbf{j} + 8\mathbf{k}$

Thus, $\mathbf{u} \times \mathbf{v} = -(\mathbf{v} \times \mathbf{u})$.

38. $\mathbf{u} \times (\mathbf{v} + \mathbf{w}) = \langle 3, -2, 1 \rangle \times \langle 1, -2, -1 \rangle = \begin{vmatrix} \mathbf{i} & \mathbf{j} & \mathbf{k} \\ 3 & -2 & 1 \\ 1 & -2 & -1 \end{vmatrix} = 4\mathbf{i} + 4\mathbf{j} - 4\mathbf{k}$

$\mathbf{u} \times \mathbf{v} = \begin{vmatrix} \mathbf{i} & \mathbf{j} & \mathbf{k} \\ 3 & -2 & 1 \\ 2 & -4 & -3 \end{vmatrix} = 10\mathbf{i} + 11\mathbf{j} - 8\mathbf{k}$

$\mathbf{u} \times \mathbf{w} = \begin{vmatrix} \mathbf{i} & \mathbf{j} & \mathbf{k} \\ 3 & -2 & 1 \\ -1 & 2 & 2 \end{vmatrix} = -6\mathbf{i} - 7\mathbf{j} + 4\mathbf{k}$

$(\mathbf{u} \times \mathbf{v}) + (\mathbf{u} \times \mathbf{w}) = 4\mathbf{i} + 4\mathbf{j} - 4\mathbf{k} = \mathbf{u} \times (\mathbf{v} + \mathbf{w})$

40. Area triangle $= \dfrac{1}{2}\|\mathbf{v} \times \mathbf{w}\| = \dfrac{1}{2}\sqrt{(-2)^2 + (-1)^2} = \dfrac{\sqrt{5}}{2}$ (See Exercise 35)

42. $V = |\mathbf{u} \cdot (\mathbf{v} \times \mathbf{w})| = \begin{vmatrix} 2 & 1 & 0 \\ 0 & 2 & 1 \\ 0 & -1 & 2 \end{vmatrix} = 2(5) = 10$

44. Direction numbers: $1, 1, 1$

(a) $x = 1 + t$, $y = 2 + t$, $z = 3 + t$

(b) $x - 1 = y - 2 = z - 3$

46. $\mathbf{u} \times \mathbf{v} = \begin{vmatrix} \mathbf{i} & \mathbf{j} & \mathbf{k} \\ 2 & -5 & 1 \\ -3 & 1 & 4 \end{vmatrix} = -21\mathbf{i} - 11\mathbf{j} - 13\mathbf{k}$

Direction numbers: $21, 11, 13$

(a) $x = 21t$, $y = 1 + 11t$, $z = 4 + 13t$

(b) $\dfrac{x}{21} = \dfrac{y - 1}{11} = \dfrac{z - 4}{13}$

48. $P = (-3, -4, 2)$, $Q = (-3, 4, 1)$, $R = (1, 1, -2)$

$\overrightarrow{PQ} = \langle 0, 8, -1 \rangle$, $\overrightarrow{PR} = \langle 4, 5, -4 \rangle$

$\mathbf{n} = \overrightarrow{PQ} \times \overrightarrow{PR} = \begin{vmatrix} \mathbf{i} & \mathbf{j} & \mathbf{k} \\ 0 & 8 & -1 \\ 4 & 5 & -4 \end{vmatrix} = -27\mathbf{i} - 4\mathbf{j} - 32\mathbf{k}$

$-27(x + 3) - 4(y + 4) - 32(z - 2) = 0$

$27x + 4y + 32z = -33$

50. The normal vectors to the planes are the same,

$$\mathbf{n} = \langle 5, -3, 1 \rangle.$$

Choose a point in the first plane, $P = (0, 0, 2)$. Choose a point in the second plane, $Q = (0, 0, -3)$.

$$\overrightarrow{PQ} = \langle 0, 0, -5 \rangle$$

$$D = \frac{|\overrightarrow{PQ} \cdot \mathbf{n}|}{\|\mathbf{n}\|} = \frac{|-5|}{\sqrt{35}} = \frac{5}{\sqrt{35}} = \frac{\sqrt{35}}{7}$$

52. $Q(-5, 1, 3)$ point

$\mathbf{u} = \langle 1, -2, -1 \rangle$ direction vector

$P = (1, 3, 5)$ point on line

$\overrightarrow{PQ} = \langle -6, -2, -2 \rangle$

$$\overrightarrow{PQ} \times \mathbf{u} = \begin{vmatrix} \mathbf{i} & \mathbf{j} & \mathbf{k} \\ -6 & -2 & -2 \\ 1 & -2 & -1 \end{vmatrix} = \langle -2, -8, 14 \rangle$$

$$D = \frac{\|\overrightarrow{PQ} \times \mathbf{u}\|}{\|\mathbf{u}\|} = \frac{\sqrt{264}}{\sqrt{6}} = 2\sqrt{11}$$

54. $y = z^2$

Since the x-coordinate is missing, we have a cylindrical surface with rulings parallel to the x-axis. The generating curve is a parabola in the yz-coordinate plane.

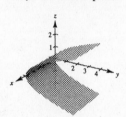

56. $y = \cos z$

Since the x-coordinate is missing, we have a cylindrical surface with rulings parallel to the x-axis. The generating curve is $y = \cos z$.

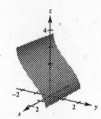

58. $16x^2 + 16y^2 - 9z^2 = 0$

Cone

xy-trace: point $(0, 0, 0)$

xz-trace: $z = \pm\dfrac{4x}{3}$

yz-trace: $z = \pm\dfrac{4y}{3}$

$z = 4, \ x^2 + y^2 = 9$

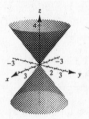

60. $\dfrac{x^2}{25} + \dfrac{y^2}{4} - \dfrac{z^2}{100} = 1$

Hyperboloid of one sheet

xy-trace: $\dfrac{x^2}{25} + \dfrac{y^2}{4} = 1$

xz-trace: $\dfrac{x^2}{25} - \dfrac{z^2}{100} = 1$

yz-trace: $\dfrac{y^2}{4} - \dfrac{z^2}{100} = 1$

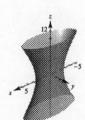

62. Let $y = r(x) = 2\sqrt{x}$ and revolve the curve about the x-axis.

64. $\left(\dfrac{\sqrt{3}}{4}, \dfrac{3}{4}, \dfrac{3\sqrt{3}}{2} \right)$, rectangular

(a) $r = \sqrt{\left(\dfrac{\sqrt{3}}{4} \right)^2 + \left(\dfrac{3}{4} \right)^2} = \dfrac{\sqrt{3}}{2}$, $\theta = \arctan\sqrt{3} = \dfrac{\pi}{3}$, $z = \dfrac{3\sqrt{3}}{2}$, $\left(\dfrac{\sqrt{3}}{2}, \dfrac{\pi}{3}, \dfrac{3\sqrt{3}}{2} \right)$, cylindrical

(b) $\rho = \sqrt{\left(\dfrac{\sqrt{3}}{4} \right)^2 + \left(\dfrac{3}{4} \right)^2 + \left(\dfrac{3\sqrt{3}}{2} \right)^2} = \dfrac{\sqrt{30}}{2}$, $\theta = \dfrac{\pi}{3}$, $\phi = \arccos\dfrac{3}{\sqrt{10}}$, $\left(\dfrac{\sqrt{30}}{2}, \dfrac{\pi}{3}, \arccos\dfrac{3}{\sqrt{10}} \right)$, spherical

66. $\left(81, -\dfrac{5\pi}{6}, 27\sqrt{3}\right)$, cylindrical

$\rho = \sqrt{6561 + 2187} = 54\sqrt{3}$

$\theta = -\dfrac{5\pi}{6}$

$\phi = \arccos\left(\dfrac{27\sqrt{3}}{54\sqrt{3}}\right) = \arccos\dfrac{1}{2} = \dfrac{\pi}{3}$

$\left(54\sqrt{3}, -\dfrac{5\pi}{6}, \dfrac{\pi}{3}\right)$, spherical

68. $\left(12, -\dfrac{\pi}{2}, \dfrac{2\pi}{3}\right)$, spherical

$r^2 = \left(12 \sin\left(\dfrac{2\pi}{3}\right)\right)^2 \Rightarrow r = 6\sqrt{3}$

$\theta = -\dfrac{\pi}{2}$

$z = \rho \cos\phi = 12 \cos\left(\dfrac{2\pi}{3}\right) = -6$

$\left(6\sqrt{3}, -\dfrac{\pi}{2}, -6\right)$, cylindrical

70. $x^2 + y^2 + z^2 = 16$

   (a) Cylindrical: $r^2 + z^2 = 16$

   (b) Spherical: $\rho = 4$

Problem Solving for Chapter 10

2. $f(x) = \displaystyle\int_0^x \sqrt{t^4 + 1}\, dt$

   (a)

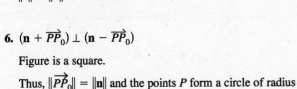

   (c) $\pm\left\langle \dfrac{\sqrt{2}}{2}, -\dfrac{\sqrt{2}}{2} \right\rangle$

   (b) $f'(x) = \sqrt{x^4 + 1}$

   $f'(0) = 1 = \tan\theta$

   $\theta = \dfrac{\pi}{4}$

   $\mathbf{u} = \dfrac{1}{\sqrt{2}}(\mathbf{i} + \mathbf{j}) = \left\langle \dfrac{\sqrt{2}}{2}, \dfrac{\sqrt{2}}{2} \right\rangle$

   (d) The line is $y = x$: $x = t, y = t$.

4. Label the figure as indicated.

$\overrightarrow{PR} = \mathbf{a} + \mathbf{b}$

$\overrightarrow{SQ} = \mathbf{b} - \mathbf{a}$

$(\mathbf{a} + \mathbf{b}) \cdot (\mathbf{b} - \mathbf{a}) = \|\mathbf{b}\|^2 - \|\mathbf{a}\|^2 = 0$, because

$\|\mathbf{a}\| = \|\mathbf{b}\|$ in a rhombus.

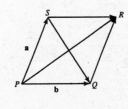

6. $(\mathbf{n} + \overrightarrow{PP_0}) \perp (\mathbf{n} - \overrightarrow{PP_0})$

Figure is a square.

Thus, $\|\overrightarrow{PP_0}\| = \|\mathbf{n}\|$ and the points P form a circle of radius $\|\mathbf{n}\|$ in the plane with center at P.

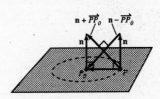

8. (a) $V = 2 \int_0^r \pi(r^2 - x^2)\, dx = 2\pi \left[r^2 x - \dfrac{x^3}{3} \right]_0^r = \dfrac{4}{3}\pi r^3$

(b) At height $z = d > 0$,

$$\frac{x^2}{a^2} + \frac{y^2}{b^2} + \frac{d^2}{c^2} = 1$$

$$\frac{x^2}{a^2} + \frac{y^2}{b^2} = 1 - \frac{d^2}{c^2} = \frac{c^2 - d^2}{c^2}$$

$$\frac{x^2}{\dfrac{a^2(c^2 - d^2)}{c^2}} + \frac{y^2}{\dfrac{b^2(c^2 - d^2)}{c^2}} = 1.$$

$$\text{Area} = \pi \sqrt{\left(\frac{a^2(c^2 - d^2)}{c^2} \right)\left(\frac{b^2(c^2 - d^2)}{c^2} \right)} = \frac{\pi ab}{c^2}(c^2 - d^2)$$

$$V = 2 \int_0^c \frac{\pi ab}{c^2}(c^2 - d^2)\, dd$$

$$= \frac{2\pi ab}{c^2} \left[c^2 d - \frac{d^3}{3} \right]_0^c$$

$$= \frac{4}{3}\pi abc$$

10. (a) $r = 2\cos\theta$

Cylinder

(b) $z = r^2 \cos 2\theta$

$z^2 = x^2 - y^2$

Hyperbolic paraboloid

12. $x = -t + 3,\ y = \dfrac{1}{2}t + 1,\ z = 2t - 1;\ Q = (4, 3, s)$

(a) $\mathbf{u} = \langle -2, 1, 4 \rangle$ direction vector for line

$P = (3, 1, -1)$ point on line

$\overrightarrow{PQ} = \langle 1, 2, s + 1 \rangle$

$$\overrightarrow{PQ} \times \mathbf{u} = \begin{vmatrix} \mathbf{i} & \mathbf{j} & \mathbf{k} \\ 1 & 2 & s + 1 \\ -2 & 1 & 4 \end{vmatrix} = (7 - s)\mathbf{i} + (-6 - 2s)\mathbf{j} + 5\mathbf{k}$$

$$D = \frac{\|\overrightarrow{PQ} \times \mathbf{u}\|}{\|\mathbf{u}\|} = \frac{\sqrt{(7 - s)^2 + (-6 - 2s)^2 + 25}}{\sqrt{21}}$$

(b)

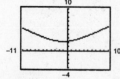

The minimum is $D \approx 2.2361$ at $s = -1$.

(c) Yes, there are slant asymptotes. Using $s = x$, we have

$$D(s) = \frac{1}{\sqrt{21}}\sqrt{5x^2 + 10x + 110} = \frac{\sqrt{5}}{\sqrt{21}}\sqrt{x^2 + 2x + 22}$$

$$= \frac{\sqrt{5}}{\sqrt{21}}\sqrt{(x + 1)^2 + 21} \ \rightarrow\ \pm\sqrt{\frac{5}{21}}(x + 1)$$

$$y = \pm\frac{\sqrt{105}}{21}(s + 1) \ \text{slant asymptotes.}$$

14. (a) The tension T is the same in each tow line.

$6000\mathbf{i} = T(\cos 20° + \cos(-20))\mathbf{i} + T(\sin 20° + \sin(-20°))\mathbf{j}$

$\qquad = 2T\cos 20°\mathbf{i}$

$\Rightarrow T = \dfrac{6000}{2\cos 20°} \approx 3192.5$ lbs

(b) As in part (a), $6000\mathbf{i} = 2T\cos\theta$

$\qquad \Rightarrow T = \dfrac{3000}{\cos\theta}$

Domain: $0 < \theta < 90°$

(c)

θ	10°	20°	30°	40°	50°	60°
T	3046.3	3192.5	3464.1	3916.2	4667.2	6000.0

(d)

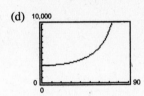

(e) As θ increases, there is less force applied in the direction of motion.

16. (a) Los Angeles: $(4000, -118.24°, 55.95°)$

Rio de Janeiro: $(4000, -43.22°, 112.90°)$

(b) Los Angeles: $x = 4000\sin 55.95°\cos(-118.24°)$

$\qquad\qquad\qquad y = 4000\sin 55.95°\sin(-118.24°)$

$\qquad\qquad\qquad z = 4000\cos 55.95°$

$\qquad\qquad\qquad (-1568.2, -2919.7, 2239.7)$

Rio de Janeiro: $x = (4000\sin 112.90°\cos(-43.22°)$

$\qquad\qquad\qquad y = 4000\sin 112.90°\sin(-43.22°)$

$\qquad\qquad\qquad z = 4000\cos 112.90°$

$\qquad\qquad\qquad (2685.2, -2523.3, -1556.5)$

(c) $\cos\theta = \dfrac{\mathbf{u}\cdot\mathbf{v}}{\|\mathbf{u}\|\,\|\mathbf{v}\|} = \dfrac{(-1568.2)(2685.2) + (-2919.7)(-2523.3) + (2239.7)(-1556.5)}{(4000)(4000)}$

$\qquad \theta \approx 91.18° \approx 1.59$ radians

(d) $s = 4000(1.59) \approx 6366$ miles

—CONTINUED—

16. **—CONTINUED—**

(e) For Boston and Honolulu:

    a. Boston: $(4000, -71.06°, 47.64°)$

       Honolulu: $(4000, -157.86°, 68.69°)$

    b. Boston: $x = 4000 \sin 47.64° \cos(-71.06°)$

$$y = 4000 \sin 47.64° \sin(-71.06°)$$

$$z = 4000 \cos 47.64°$$

$$(959.4, -2795.7, 2695.1)$$

       Honolulu: $x = (4000 \sin 68.69° \cos(-157.86°)$

$$y = 4000 \sin 68.69° \sin(-157.86°)$$

$$z = 4000 \cos 68.69°$$

$$(-3451.7, -1404.4, 1453.7)$$

(f) $\cos \theta = \dfrac{\mathbf{u} \cdot \mathbf{v}}{\|\mathbf{u}\| \|\mathbf{v}\|} = \dfrac{(959.4)(-3451.7) + (-2795.7)(-1404.4) + (2695.1)(1453.7)}{(4000)(4000)}$

$$\theta \approx 73.5° \approx 1.28 \text{ radians}$$

(g) $s = 4000(1.28) \approx 5120$ miles

18. Assume one of $a, b, c,$ is not zero, say a. Choose a point in the first plane such as $(-d_1/a, 0, 0)$. The distance between this point and the second plane is

$$D = \frac{|a(-d_1/a) + b(0) + c(0) + d_2|}{\sqrt{a^2 + b^2 + c^2}}$$

$$= \frac{|-d_1 + d_2|}{\sqrt{a^2 + b^2 + c^2}} = \frac{|d_1 - d_2|}{\sqrt{a^2 + b^2 + c^2}}.$$

20. Essay.

C H A P T E R   11
Vector-Valued Functions

CHAPTER 11
Vector-Valued Functions

Section 11.1   Vector-Valued Functions

Solutions to Even-Numbered Exercises

2. $\mathbf{r}(t) = \sqrt{4 - t^2}\mathbf{i} + t^2\mathbf{j} - 6t\mathbf{k}$

Component functions: $f(t) = \sqrt{4 - t^2}$

$$g(t) = t^2$$

$$h(t) = -6t$$

Domain: $[-2, 2]$

4. $\mathbf{r}(t) = \sin t\mathbf{i} + 4 \cos t\mathbf{j} + t\mathbf{k}$

Component functions: $f(t) = \sin t$

$$g(t) = 4 \cos t$$

$$h(t) = t$$

Domain: $(-\infty, \infty)$

6. $\mathbf{r}(t) = \mathbf{F}(t) - \mathbf{G}(t) = (\ln t\mathbf{i} + 5t\mathbf{j} - 3t^2\mathbf{k}) - (\mathbf{i} + 4t\mathbf{j} - 3t^2\mathbf{k})$

$$= (\ln t - 1)\mathbf{i} + (5t - 4t)\mathbf{j} + (-3t^2 + 3t^2)\mathbf{k}$$

$$= (\ln t - 1)\mathbf{i} + t\mathbf{j}$$

Domain: $(0, \infty)$

8. $\mathbf{r}(t) = \mathbf{F}(t) \times \mathbf{G}(t) = \begin{vmatrix} \mathbf{i} & \mathbf{j} & \mathbf{k} \\ t^3 & -t & t \\ \sqrt[3]{t} & \frac{1}{t+1} & t+2 \end{vmatrix} = \left(-t(t+2) - \frac{t}{t+1}\right)\mathbf{i} - \left(t^3(t+2) - t\sqrt[3]{t}\right)\mathbf{j} + \left(\frac{t^3}{t+1} + t\sqrt[3]{t}\right)\mathbf{k}$

Domain: $(-\infty, -1), (-1, \infty)$

10. $\mathbf{r}(t) = \cos t\mathbf{i} + 2 \sin t\mathbf{j}$

(a) $\mathbf{r}(0) = \mathbf{i}$

(b) $\mathbf{r}\left(\dfrac{\pi}{4}\right) = \dfrac{\sqrt{2}}{2}\mathbf{i} + \sqrt{2}\mathbf{j}$

(c) $\mathbf{r}(\theta - \pi) = \cos(\theta - \pi)\mathbf{i} + 2 \sin(\theta - \pi)\mathbf{j} = -\cos \theta\mathbf{i} - 2 \sin \theta\mathbf{j}$

(d) $\mathbf{r}\left(\dfrac{\pi}{6} + \Delta t\right) - \mathbf{r}\left(\dfrac{\pi}{6}\right) = \cos\left(\dfrac{\pi}{6} + \Delta t\right)\mathbf{i} + 2 \sin\left(\dfrac{\pi}{6} + \Delta t\right)\mathbf{j} - \left(\cos\left(\dfrac{\pi}{6}\right)\mathbf{i} + 2 \sin \dfrac{\pi}{6}\mathbf{j}\right)$

12. $\mathbf{r}(t) = \sqrt{t}\mathbf{i} + t^{3/2}\mathbf{j} + e^{-t/4}\mathbf{k}$

(a) $\mathbf{r}(0) = \mathbf{k}$

(b) $\mathbf{r}(4) = 2\mathbf{i} + 8\mathbf{j} + e^{-1}\mathbf{k}$

(c) $\mathbf{r}(c + 2) = \sqrt{c + 2}\mathbf{i} + (c + 2)^{3/2}\mathbf{j} + e^{-[(c+2)/4]}\mathbf{k}$

(d) $\mathbf{r}(9 + \Delta t) - \mathbf{r}(9) = \left(\sqrt{9 + \Delta t}\right)\mathbf{i} + (9 + \Delta t)^{3/2}\mathbf{j} + e^{-[(9+\Delta t)/4]}\mathbf{k} - (3\mathbf{i} + 27\mathbf{j} + e^{-9/4}\mathbf{k})$

$$= \left(\sqrt{9 + \Delta t} - 3\right)\mathbf{i} + ((9 + \Delta t)^{3/2} - 27)\mathbf{j} + (e^{-[(9+\Delta t)/4]} - e^{-9/4})\mathbf{k}$$

14. $\mathbf{r}(t) = \sqrt{t}\mathbf{i} + 3t\mathbf{j} - 4t\mathbf{k}$

$$\|\mathbf{r}(t)\| = \sqrt{\left(\sqrt{t}\right)^2 + (3t)^2 + (-4t)^2}$$

$$= \sqrt{t + 9t^2 + 16t^2} = \sqrt{t(1 + 25t)}$$

16. $\mathbf{r}(t) \cdot \mathbf{u}(t) = (3\cos t)(4\sin t) + (2\sin t)(-6\cos t) + (t-2)(t^2) = t^3 - 2t^2$, a scalar.

The dot product is a scalar-valued function.

18. $\mathbf{r}(t) = \cos(\pi t)\mathbf{i} + \sin(\pi t)\mathbf{j} + t^2\mathbf{k}, \; -1 \le t \le 1$

$x = \cos(\pi t), \; y = \sin(\pi t), \; z = t^2$

Thus, $x^2 + y^2 = 1$. Matches (c)

20. $\mathbf{r}(t) = t\mathbf{i} + \ln t\mathbf{j} + \dfrac{2t}{3}\mathbf{k}, \; 0.1 \le t \le 5$

$x = t, \; y = \ln t, \; z = \dfrac{2t}{3}$

Thus, $z = \tfrac{2}{3}x$ and $y = \ln x$. Matches (a)

22. $\mathbf{r}(t) = t\mathbf{i} + t\mathbf{j} + 2\mathbf{k}$

$x = t, y = t, z = 2 \implies x = y$

(a) $(0, 0, 20)$

(b) $(10, 0, 0)$

(c) $(5, 5, 5)$

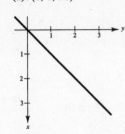

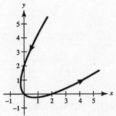

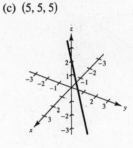

24. $x = 1 - t, y = \sqrt{t}$

$y = \sqrt{1 - x}$

Domain: $t \ge 0$

26. $x = t^2 + t, \; y = t^2 - t$

28. $x = 2\cos t$

$y = 2\sin t$

$x^2 + y^2 = 4$

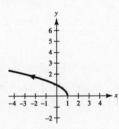

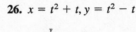

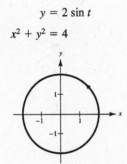

30. $x = 2\cos^3 t, \; y = 2\sin^3 t$

$\left(\dfrac{x}{2}\right)^{2/3} + \left(\dfrac{y}{2}\right)^{2/3} = \cos^2 t + \sin^2 t$

$\qquad\qquad\qquad = 1$

$x^{2/3} + y^{2/3} = 2^{2/3}$

32. $x = t$

$y = 2t - 5$

$y = 3t$

Line passing through the points:

$(0, -5, 0), \left(\dfrac{5}{2}, 0, \dfrac{15}{2}\right)$

34. $x = 3\cos t, \; y = 4\sin t, \; z = \dfrac{t}{2}$

$\dfrac{x^2}{9} + \dfrac{y^2}{16} = 1$

$z = \dfrac{t}{2}$

Elliptic helix

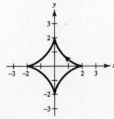

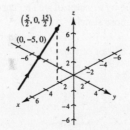

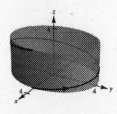

36. $x = t^2, y = 2t, z = \frac{3}{2}t$

$x = \frac{y^2}{4}, z = \frac{3}{4}y$

t	-2	-1	0	1	2
x	4	1	0	1	4
y	-4	-2	0	2	4
z	-3	$-\frac{3}{2}$	0	$\frac{3}{2}$	3

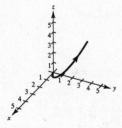

38. $x = \cos t + t \sin t$

$y = \sin t - t \cos t$

$z = t$

$x^2 + y^2 = 1 + t^2 = 1 + z^2$ or $x^2 + y^2 - z^2 = 1$

$z = t$

Helix along a hyperboloid of one sheet

40. $\mathbf{r}(t) = t\mathbf{i} - \frac{\sqrt{3}}{2}t^2\mathbf{j} + \frac{1}{2}t^2\mathbf{k}$

Parabola

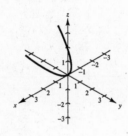

42. $\mathbf{r}(t) = -\sqrt{2} \sin t\mathbf{i} + 2 \cos t\mathbf{j} + \sqrt{2} \sin t\mathbf{k}$

Ellipse

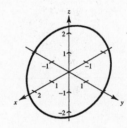

44. $r(t) = t\mathbf{i} + t^2\mathbf{j} + \frac{1}{2}t^3\mathbf{h}$

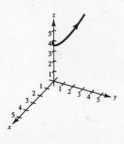

(a) $\mathbf{u}(t) = \mathbf{r}(t) - 2\mathbf{j}$ is a translation 2 units to the left along the y-axis.

(b) $\mathbf{u}(t) = t^2\mathbf{i} + t\mathbf{j} + \frac{1}{2}t^3\mathbf{k}$ has the roles of x and y interchanged. The graph is a reflection in the plane $x = y$.

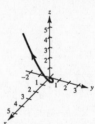

(c) $\mathbf{u}(t) = \mathbf{r}(t) + 4\mathbf{k}$ is an upward shift 4 units.

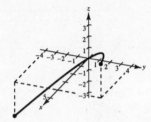

(d) $\mathbf{u}(t) = t\mathbf{i} + t^2\mathbf{j} + \frac{1}{8}t^3\mathbf{k}$ shrinks the z-value by a factor of 4. The curve rises more slowly.

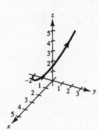

(e) $\mathbf{u}(t) = \mathbf{r}(-t)$ reverses the orientation.

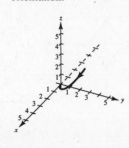

46. $2x - 3y + 5 = 0$

Let $x = t$, then $y = \frac{1}{3}(2t + 5)$.

$$\mathbf{r}(t) = t\mathbf{i} + \frac{1}{3}(2t + 5)\mathbf{j}$$

48. $y = 4 - x^2$

Let $x = t$, then $y = 4 - t^2$.

$$\mathbf{r}(t) = t\mathbf{i} + (4 - t^2)\mathbf{j}$$

50. $(x - 2)^2 + y^2 = 4$

Let $x - 2 = 2 \cos t, y = 2 \sin t$.

$$\mathbf{r}(t) = (2 + 2 \cos t)\mathbf{i} + 2 \sin t\,\mathbf{j}$$

52. $\dfrac{x^2}{16} + \dfrac{y^2}{9} = 1$

Let $x = 4 \cos t, y = 3 \sin t$.

$$\mathbf{r}(t) = 4 \cos t\mathbf{i} + 3 \sin t\mathbf{j}$$

54. One possible answer is

$$\mathbf{r}(t) = 1.5 \cos t\mathbf{i} + 1.5 \sin t\mathbf{j} + \frac{1}{\pi}t\mathbf{k}, \ 0 \le t \le 2\pi$$

Note that $\mathbf{r}(2\pi) = 1.5\mathbf{i} + 2\mathbf{k}$.

56. $\mathbf{r}_1(t) = t\mathbf{i}, \ \ 0 \le t \le 10 \ \ (\mathbf{r}_1(0) = \mathbf{0}, \mathbf{r}_1(10) = 10\mathbf{i})$

$\mathbf{r}_2(t) = 10(\cos t\mathbf{i} + \sin t\mathbf{j}), \ \ 0 \le t \le \dfrac{\pi}{4} \ \ \left(\mathbf{r}_2(0) = 10\mathbf{i}, \mathbf{r}_2\!\left(\dfrac{\pi}{4}\right) = 5\sqrt{2}\mathbf{i} + 5\sqrt{2}\mathbf{j}\right)$

$\mathbf{r}_3(t) = 5\sqrt{2}(1 - t)\mathbf{i} + 5\sqrt{2}(1 - t)\mathbf{j}, \ \ 0 \le t \le 1 \ \ (\mathbf{r}_3(0) = 5\sqrt{2}\mathbf{i} + 5\sqrt{2}\mathbf{j}, \mathbf{r}_3(1) = \mathbf{0})$

(Other answers possible)

58. $\mathbf{r}_1(t) = t\mathbf{i} + \sqrt{t}\mathbf{j}, \ \ 0 \le t \le 1 \ \left(y = \sqrt{x}\right)$

$\mathbf{r}_2(t) = (1 - t)\mathbf{i} + (1 - t)\mathbf{j}, \ \ 0 \le t \le 1 \ (y = x)$

(Other answers possible)

60. $z = x^2 + y^2, z = 4$

Therefore, $x^2 + y^2 = 4$ or

$x = 2 \cos t, y = 2 \sin t, z = 4$.

$\mathbf{r}(t) = 2 \cos t\mathbf{i} + 2\sin t\mathbf{j} + 4\mathbf{k}$

62. $4x^2 + 4y^2 + z^2 = 16, x = z^2$

If $z = t$, then $x = t^2$ and $y = \dfrac{1}{2}\sqrt{16 - 4t^4 - t^2}$.

t	-1.3	-1.2	-1	0	1	1.2
x	1.69	1.44	1	0	1	1.44
y	0.85	1.25	1.66	2	1.66	1.25
z	-1.3	-1.2	-1	0	1	1.2

$\mathbf{r}(t) = t^2\mathbf{i} + \dfrac{1}{2}\sqrt{16 - 4t^4 - t^2}\mathbf{j} + t\mathbf{k}$

64. $x^2 + y^2 + z^2 = 10,\ x + y = 4$

Let $x = 2 + \sin t$, then $y = 2 - \sin t$ and $z = \sqrt{2(1 - \sin^2 t)} = \sqrt{2}\cos t$.

t	$-\dfrac{\pi}{2}$	$-\dfrac{\pi}{6}$	0	$\dfrac{\pi}{6}$	$\dfrac{\pi}{2}$	π
x	1	$\dfrac{3}{2}$	2	$\dfrac{5}{2}$	3	2
y	3	$\dfrac{5}{2}$	2	$\dfrac{3}{2}$	1	2
z	0	$\dfrac{\sqrt{6}}{2}$	$\sqrt{2}$	$\dfrac{\sqrt{6}}{2}$	0	$-\sqrt{2}$

$$\mathbf{r}(t) = (2 + \sin t)\mathbf{i} + (2 - \sin t)\mathbf{j} + \sqrt{2}\cos t\,\mathbf{k}$$

66. $x^2 + y^2 + z^2 = 16,\ xy = 4$ (first octant)

Let $x = t$, then

$$y = \frac{4}{t} \quad \text{and} \quad x^2 + y^2 + z^2 = t^2 + \frac{16}{t^2} + z^2 = 16.$$

$$z = \frac{1}{t}\sqrt{-t^4 + 16t^2 - 16}$$

$$\left(\sqrt{8 - 4\sqrt{3}} \le t \le \sqrt{8 + 4\sqrt{3}}\right)$$

t	$\sqrt{8 + 4\sqrt{3}}$	1.5	2	2.5	3.0	3.5	$\sqrt{8 + 4\sqrt{3}}$
x	1.0	1.5	2	2.5	3.0	3.5	3.9
y	3.9	2.7	2	1.6	1.3	1.1	1.0
z	0	2.6	2.8	2.7	2.3	1.6	0

$$\mathbf{r}(t) = t\mathbf{i} + \frac{4}{t}\mathbf{j} + \frac{1}{t}\sqrt{-t^4 + 16t^2 - 16}\,\mathbf{k}$$

68. $x^2 + y^2 = (e^{-t}\cos t)^2 + (e^{-t}\sin t)^2 = e^{-2t} = z^2$

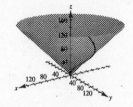

70. $\displaystyle\lim_{t \to 0}\left[e^t\mathbf{i} + \frac{\sin t}{t}\mathbf{j} + e^{-t}\mathbf{k}\right] = \mathbf{i} + \mathbf{j} + \mathbf{k}$

since

$$\lim_{t \to 0}\frac{\sin t}{t} = \lim_{t \to 0}\frac{\cos t}{1} = 1 \quad \text{(L'Hôpital's Rule)}$$

72. $\displaystyle\lim_{t \to 1}\left[\sqrt{t}\,\mathbf{i} + \frac{\ln t}{t^2 - 1}\mathbf{j} + 2t^2\mathbf{k}\right] = \mathbf{i} + \frac{1}{2}\mathbf{j} + 2\mathbf{k}$

since

$$\lim_{t \to 1}\frac{\ln t}{t^2 - 1} = \lim_{t \to 1}\frac{1/t}{2t} = \frac{1}{2}. \quad \text{(L'Hôpital's Rule)}$$

74. $\displaystyle\lim_{t \to \infty}\left[e^{-t}\mathbf{i} + \frac{1}{t}\mathbf{j} + \frac{t}{t^2 + 1}\mathbf{k}\right] = \mathbf{0}$

since

$$\lim_{t \to \infty}e^{-t} = 0, \ \lim_{t \to \infty}\frac{1}{t} = 0, \text{ and } \lim_{t \to \infty}\frac{t}{t^2 + 1} = 0.$$

76. $\mathbf{r}(t) = \sqrt{t}\mathbf{i} + \sqrt{t-1}\mathbf{j}$

Continuous on $[1, \infty)$

78. $\mathbf{r}(t) = \langle 2e^{-t}, e^{-t}, \ln(t-1) \rangle$

Continuous on $t - 1 > 0$ or $t > 1$: $(1, \infty)$.

80. $\mathbf{r}(t) = \langle 8, \sqrt{t}, \sqrt[3]{t} \rangle$

Continuous on $[0, \infty)$

82. No. The graph is the same because $\mathbf{r}(t) = \mathbf{u}(t + 2)$.
For example, if $\mathbf{r}(0)$ is on the graph of $\mathbf{r}$, then $\mathbf{u}(2)$ is the
same point.

84. A vector-valued function $\mathbf{r}$ is continuous at $t = a$ if
the limit of $\mathbf{r}(t)$ exists as $t \to a$ and

$$\lim_{t \to a} \mathbf{r}(t) = \mathbf{r}(a).$$

The function $\mathbf{r}(t) = \begin{cases} \mathbf{i} + \mathbf{j} & t \geq 0 \\ -\mathbf{i} + \mathbf{j} & t < 0 \end{cases}$ is not continuous at $t = 0$.

86. Let $\mathbf{r}(t) = x_1(t)\mathbf{i} + y_1(t)\mathbf{j} + z_1(t)\mathbf{k}$ and $\mathbf{u}(t) = x_2(t)\mathbf{i} + y_2(t)\mathbf{j} + z_2(t)\mathbf{k}$. Then:

$$\lim_{t \to c} [\mathbf{r}(t) \cdot \mathbf{u}(t)] = \lim_{t \to c} [x_1(t)x_2(t) + y_1(t)y_2(t) + z_1(t)z_2(t)]$$

$$= \lim_{t \to c} x_1(t) \lim_{t \to c} x_2(t) + \lim_{t \to c} y_1(t) \lim_{t \to c} y_2(t) + \lim_{t \to c} z_1(t) \lim_{t \to c} z_2(t)$$

$$= \left[\lim_{t \to c} x_1(t)\mathbf{i} + \lim_{t \to c} y_1(t)\mathbf{j} + \lim_{t \to c} z_1(t)\mathbf{k} \right] \cdot \left[\lim_{t \to c} x_2(t)\mathbf{i} + \lim_{t \to c} y_2(t)\mathbf{j} + \lim_{t \to c} z_2(t)\mathbf{k} \right]$$

$$= \lim_{t \to c} \mathbf{r}(t) \cdot \lim_{t \to c} \mathbf{u}(t)$$

88. Let

$$f(t) = \begin{cases} 1, & \text{if } t \geq 0 \\ -1, & \text{if } t < 0 \end{cases}$$

and $\mathbf{r}(t) = f(t)\mathbf{i}$. Then $\mathbf{r}$ is not continuous at $c = 0$,
whereas, $\|\mathbf{r}\| = 1$ is continuous for all t.

90. False. The graph of $x = y = z = t^3$ represents a line.

Section 11.2   Differentiation and Integration of Vector-Valued Functions

2. $\mathbf{r}(t) = t\mathbf{i} + t^3\mathbf{j}, \ t_0 = 1$

$x(t) = t, \ y(t) = t^3$

$y = x^3$

$\mathbf{r}(1) = \mathbf{i} + \mathbf{j}$

$\mathbf{r}'(t) = \mathbf{i} + 3t^2\mathbf{j}$

$\mathbf{r}'(1) = \mathbf{i} + 3\mathbf{j}$

$\mathbf{r}'(t_0)$ is tangent to the curve.

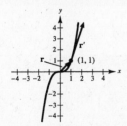

4. $\mathbf{r}(t) = t^2\mathbf{i} + \dfrac{1}{t}\mathbf{j}, \ t_0 = 2$

$x(t) = t^2, \ y(t) = \dfrac{1}{t}$

$x = \dfrac{1}{y^2}$

$\mathbf{r}(2) = 4\mathbf{i} + \dfrac{1}{2}\mathbf{j}$

$\mathbf{r}'(t) = 2t\mathbf{i} - \dfrac{1}{t^2}\mathbf{j}$

$\mathbf{r}'(2) = 4\mathbf{i} - \dfrac{1}{4}\mathbf{j}$

$\mathbf{r}'(t_0)$ is tangent to the curve.

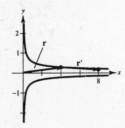

6. $\mathbf{r}(t) = t\mathbf{i} + (4 - t^2)\mathbf{j}$

(a)

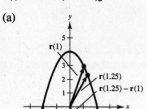

(b) $\mathbf{r}(1) = \mathbf{i} + 3\mathbf{j}$

$\mathbf{r}(1.25) = 1.25\mathbf{i} + 2.4375\mathbf{j}$

$\mathbf{r}(1.25) - \mathbf{r}(1) = 0.25\mathbf{i} - 0.5625\mathbf{j}$

(c) $\mathbf{r}'(t) = \mathbf{i} - 2t\mathbf{j}$

$\mathbf{r}'(1) = \mathbf{i} - 2\mathbf{j}$

$$\frac{\mathbf{r}(1.25) - \mathbf{r}(1)}{1.25 - 1} = \frac{0.25\mathbf{i} - 0.5625\mathbf{j}}{0.25} = \mathbf{i} - 2.25\mathbf{j}$$

This vector approximates $\mathbf{r}'(1)$.

8. $\mathbf{r}(t) = t\mathbf{i} + t^2\mathbf{j} + \frac{3}{2}\mathbf{k}, \ t_0 = 2$

$$y = x^2, \ z = \frac{3}{2}$$

$$\mathbf{r}'(t) = \mathbf{i} + 2t\mathbf{j}$$

$$\mathbf{r}(2) = 2\mathbf{i} + 4\mathbf{j} + \frac{3}{2}\mathbf{k}$$

$$\mathbf{r}'(2) = \mathbf{i} + 4\mathbf{j}$$

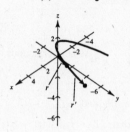

10. $\mathbf{r}(t) = \frac{1}{t}\mathbf{i} + 16t\mathbf{j} + \frac{t^2}{2}\mathbf{k}$

$\mathbf{r}'(t) = -\frac{1}{t^2}\mathbf{i} + 16\mathbf{j} + t\mathbf{k}$

12. $\mathbf{r}(t) = 4\sqrt{t}\mathbf{i} + t^2\sqrt{t}\mathbf{j} + \ln t^2\mathbf{k}$

$\mathbf{r}'(t) = \frac{2}{\sqrt{t}}\mathbf{i} + \left(2t\sqrt{t} + \frac{t^2}{2\sqrt{t}}\right)\mathbf{j} + \frac{2}{t}\mathbf{k}$

14. $\mathbf{r}(t) = \langle \sin t - t\cos t, \cos t + t\sin t, t^2 \rangle$

$\mathbf{r}'(t) = \langle t\sin t, t\cos t, 2t \rangle$

16. $\mathbf{r}(t) = \langle \arcsin t, \arccos t, 0 \rangle$

$\mathbf{r}'(t) = \left\langle \frac{1}{\sqrt{1 - t^2}}, -\frac{1}{\sqrt{1 - t^2}}, 0 \right\rangle$

18. $\mathbf{r}(t) = (t^2 + t)\mathbf{i} + (t^2 - t)\mathbf{j}$

(a) $\mathbf{r}'(t) = (2t + 1)\mathbf{i} + (2t - 1)\mathbf{j}$

$\mathbf{r}''(t) = 2\mathbf{i} + 2\mathbf{j}$

(b) $\mathbf{r}'(t) \cdot \mathbf{r}''(t) = (2t + 1)(2) + (2t - 1)(2) = 8t$

20. $\mathbf{r}(t) = 8\cos t\mathbf{i} + 3\sin t\mathbf{j}$

(a) $\mathbf{r}'(t) = -8\sin t\mathbf{i} + 3\cos t\mathbf{j}$

$\mathbf{r}''(t) = -8\cos t\mathbf{i} - 3\sin t\mathbf{j}$

(b) $\mathbf{r}'(t) \cdot \mathbf{r}''(t) = (-8\sin t)(-8\cos t) + 3\cos t(-3\sin t)$

$= 55\sin t\cos t$

22. $\mathbf{r}(t) = t\mathbf{i} + (2t + 3)\mathbf{j} + (3t - 5)\mathbf{k}$

(a) $\mathbf{r}'(t) = \mathbf{i} + 2\mathbf{j} + 3\mathbf{k}$

$\mathbf{r}''(t) = 0$

(b) $\mathbf{r}'(t) \cdot \mathbf{r}''(t) = 0$

24. $\mathbf{r}(t) = \langle e^{-t}, t^2, \tan(t) \rangle$

(a) $\mathbf{r}'(t) = \langle -e^{-t}, 2t, \sec^2 t \rangle$

$\mathbf{r}''(t) = \langle e^{-t}, 2, 2\sec^2 t\tan t \rangle$

(b) $\mathbf{r}'(t) \cdot \mathbf{r}''(t) = -e^{-2t} + 4t + 2\sec^4 t\tan t$

26. $r(t) = t\mathbf{i} + t^2\mathbf{j} + e^{0.75t}\mathbf{k}, \ t_0 = \dfrac{1}{4}$

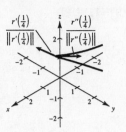

$r'(t) = \mathbf{i} + 2t\mathbf{j} + 0.75e^{0.75t}\mathbf{k}$

$r'\!\left(\dfrac{1}{4}\right) = \mathbf{i} + \dfrac{1}{2}\mathbf{j} + 0.75e^{0.1875}\mathbf{k} = \mathbf{i} + \dfrac{1}{2}\mathbf{j} + \dfrac{3}{4}e^{3/16}\mathbf{k}$

$\left\| r'\!\left(\dfrac{1}{4}\right) \right\| = \sqrt{1^2 + \left(\dfrac{1}{2}\right)^2 + \left(\dfrac{3}{4}e^{3/16}\right)^2} = \sqrt{\dfrac{5}{4} + \dfrac{9}{16}e^{3/8}} = \dfrac{\sqrt{20 + 9e^{3/8}}}{4}$

$\dfrac{r'(1/4)}{\|r'(1/4)\|} = \dfrac{1}{\sqrt{20 + 9e^{3/8}}}(4\mathbf{i} + 2\mathbf{j} + 3e^{3/16}\mathbf{k})$

$r''(t) = 2\mathbf{i} + \dfrac{9}{16}e^{0.75t}\mathbf{k}$

$r''\!\left(\dfrac{1}{4}\right) = 2\mathbf{i} + \dfrac{9}{16}e^{3/16}\mathbf{k}$

$\left\| r''\!\left(\dfrac{1}{4}\right) \right\| = \sqrt{2^2 + \left(\dfrac{9}{16}e^{3/16}\right)^2} = \sqrt{4 + \dfrac{81}{256}e^{3/8}} = \dfrac{\sqrt{1024 + 81e^{3/8}}}{16}$

$\dfrac{r''(1/4)}{\|r'(1/4)\|} = \dfrac{1}{\sqrt{1024 + 81e^{3/8}}}(32\mathbf{j} + 9e^{3/16}\mathbf{k})$

28. $r(t) = \dfrac{1}{t-1}\mathbf{i} + 3t\mathbf{j}$

$r'(t) = -\dfrac{1}{(t-1)^2}\mathbf{i} + 3\mathbf{j}$

Not continuous when $t = 1$

Smooth on $(-\infty, 1), \ (1, \infty)$

30. $r(\theta) = (\theta + \sin\theta)\mathbf{i} + (1 - \cos\theta)\mathbf{j}$

$r'(\theta) = (1 + \cos\theta)\mathbf{i} + \sin\theta\mathbf{j}$

$r'((2n-1)\pi) = \mathbf{0}, n$ any integer

Smooth on $((2n-1)\pi, (2n+1)\pi)$

32. $r(t) = \dfrac{2t}{8+t^3}\mathbf{i} + \dfrac{2t^2}{8+t^3}\mathbf{j}$

$r'(t) = \dfrac{16 - 4t^3}{(t^3+8)^2}\mathbf{i} + \dfrac{32t - 2t^4}{(t^3+8)^2}\mathbf{j}$

$r'(t) \neq \mathbf{0}$ for any value of t.

r is not continuous when $t = -2$.

Smooth on $(-\infty, -2), (-2, \infty)$.

34. $r(t) = e^t\mathbf{i} - e^{-t}\mathbf{j} + 3t\mathbf{k}$

$r'(t) = e^t\mathbf{i} + e^{-t}\mathbf{j} + 3\mathbf{k} \neq \mathbf{0}$

r is smooth for all t: $(-\infty, \infty)$

36. $r(t) = \sqrt{t}\,\mathbf{i} + (t^2 - 1)\mathbf{j} + \dfrac{1}{4}t\mathbf{k}$

$r'(t) = \dfrac{1}{2\sqrt{t}}\mathbf{i} + 2t\mathbf{j} + \dfrac{1}{4}\mathbf{k} \neq \mathbf{0}$

r is smooth for all $t > 0$: $(0, \infty)$

38. $r(t) = t\mathbf{i} + 2\sin t\mathbf{j} + 2\cos t\mathbf{k}$

$u(t) = \dfrac{1}{t}\mathbf{i} + 2\sin t\mathbf{j} + 2\cos t\mathbf{k}$

(a) $r'(t) = \mathbf{i} + 2\cos t\mathbf{j} - 2\sin t\mathbf{k}$

(b) $r''(t) = -2\sin t\mathbf{j} - 2\cos t\mathbf{k}$

(c) $r(t) \cdot u(t) = 1 + 4\sin^2 t + 4\cos^2 t = 5$

$D_t[r(t) \cdot u(t)] = 0, t \neq 0$

(d) $3r(t) - u(t) = \left(3t - \dfrac{1}{t}\right)\mathbf{i} + 4\sin t\mathbf{j} + 4\cos t\mathbf{k}$

$D_t[3r(t) - u(t)] = \left(3 - \dfrac{1}{t^2}\right)\mathbf{i} + 4\cos t\mathbf{j} - 4\sin t\mathbf{k}$

—CONTINUED—

38. —CONTINUED—

(e) $\mathbf{r}(t) \times \mathbf{u}(t) = \begin{vmatrix} \mathbf{i} & \mathbf{j} & \mathbf{k} \\ t & 2\sin t & 2\cos t \\ 1/t & 2\sin t & 2\cos t \end{vmatrix}$

$$= 2\cos t\left(\frac{1}{t} - t\right)\mathbf{j} + 2\sin t\left(t - \frac{1}{t}\right)\mathbf{k}$$

$$D_t[\mathbf{r}(t) - \mathbf{u}(t)] = \left[-2\sin t\left(\frac{1}{t} - t\right) + 2\cos t\left(-\frac{1}{t^2} - 1\right)\right]\mathbf{j}$$

$$+ \left[2\cos t\left(t - \frac{1}{t}\right) + 2\sin t\left(1 + \frac{1}{t^2}\right)\right]\mathbf{k}$$

(f) $\|\mathbf{r}(t)\| = \sqrt{t^2 + 4}$

$$D_t(\|\mathbf{r}(t)\|) = \frac{1}{2}(t^2 + 4)^{-1/2}(2t) = \frac{t}{\sqrt{t^2 + 4}}$$

40. $\mathbf{r}(t) = t^2\mathbf{i} + t\mathbf{j}$

$\mathbf{r}'(t) = 2t\mathbf{i} + \mathbf{j}$

$\mathbf{r}(t) \cdot \mathbf{r}'(t) = 2t^3 + t$

$\|\mathbf{r}(t)\| = \sqrt{t^4 + t^2}, \ \|\mathbf{r}'(t)\| = \sqrt{4t^2 + 1}$

$\cos\theta = \dfrac{2t^3 + t}{\sqrt{t^4 + t^2}\sqrt{4t^2 + 1}}$

$\theta = \arccos\dfrac{2t^3 + t}{\sqrt{t^4 + t^2}\sqrt{4t^2 + 1}}$

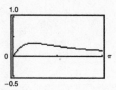

$\theta = 0.340 \ (\approx 19.47°)$ maximum at $t = 0.707 \left(\dfrac{\sqrt{2}}{2}\right)$.

$\theta \neq \dfrac{\pi}{2}$ for any t.

42. $\mathbf{r}'(t) = \lim\limits_{\Delta t \to 0} \dfrac{\mathbf{r}(t + \Delta t) - \mathbf{r}(t)}{\Delta t}$

$$= \lim\limits_{\Delta t \to 0} \frac{\left[\sqrt{t + \Delta t}\,\mathbf{i} + \dfrac{3}{t + \Delta t}\mathbf{j} - 2(t + \Delta t)\mathbf{k}\right] - \left[\sqrt{t}\,\mathbf{i} + \dfrac{3}{t}\mathbf{j} - 2t\mathbf{k}\right]}{\Delta t}$$

$$= \lim\limits_{\Delta t \to 0} \left[\frac{\sqrt{t + \Delta t} - \sqrt{t}}{\Delta t}\mathbf{i} + \frac{\dfrac{3}{t + \Delta t} - \dfrac{3}{t}}{\Delta t}\mathbf{j} - 2\mathbf{k}\right]$$

$$= \lim\limits_{\Delta t \to 0} \left[\frac{\Delta t}{\Delta t\left(\sqrt{t + \Delta t} + \sqrt{t}\right)}\mathbf{i} + \frac{-3\Delta t}{(t + \Delta t)t(\Delta t)}\mathbf{j} - 2\mathbf{k}\right]$$

$$= \lim\limits_{\Delta t \to 0} \left[\frac{1}{\sqrt{t + \Delta t} + \sqrt{t}}\mathbf{i} - \frac{3}{(t + \Delta t)t}\mathbf{j} - 2\mathbf{k}\right]$$

$$= \frac{1}{2\sqrt{t}}\mathbf{i} - \frac{3}{t^2}\mathbf{j} - 2\mathbf{k}$$

44. $\displaystyle\int \left(4t^3\mathbf{i} + 6t\mathbf{j} - 4\sqrt{t}\mathbf{k}\right) dt = t^4\mathbf{i} + 3t^2\mathbf{j} - \frac{8}{3}t^{3/2}\mathbf{k} + \mathbf{C}$

46. $\displaystyle\int \left[\ln t\,\mathbf{i} + \frac{1}{t}\mathbf{j} + \mathbf{k}\right] dt = (t\ln t - t)\mathbf{i} + \ln t\,\mathbf{j} + t\mathbf{k} + \mathbf{C}$

(Integration by parts)

48. $\displaystyle\int \left[e^t\mathbf{i} + \sin t\,\mathbf{j} + \cos t\,\mathbf{k}\right] dt = e^t\mathbf{i} - \cos t\,\mathbf{j} + \sin t\,\mathbf{k} + \mathbf{C}$

50. $\int [e^{-t}\sin t\mathbf{i} + e^{-t}\cos t\mathbf{j}]\,dt = \dfrac{e^{-t}}{2}(-\sin t - \cos t)\mathbf{i} + \dfrac{e^{-t}}{2}(-\cos t + \sin t)\mathbf{j} + \mathbf{C}$

52. $\int_{-1}^{1}\left(t\mathbf{i} + t^3\mathbf{j} + \sqrt[3]{t}\,\mathbf{k}\right)dt = \left[\dfrac{t^2}{2}\mathbf{i}\right]_{-1}^{1} + \left[\dfrac{t^4}{4}\mathbf{j}\right]_{-1}^{1} + \left[\dfrac{3}{4}t^{4/3}\mathbf{k}\right]_{-1}^{1} = \mathbf{0}$

54. $\int_{0}^{2}(t\mathbf{i} + e^{t}\mathbf{j} - te^{t}\mathbf{k})\,dt = \left[\dfrac{t^2}{2}\mathbf{i}\right]_{0}^{2} + \left[e^{t}\mathbf{j}\right]_{0}^{2} - \left[(t-1)e^{t}\mathbf{k}\right]_{0}^{2}$

$\qquad\qquad = 2\mathbf{i} + (e^2 - 1)\mathbf{j} - (e^2 + 1)\mathbf{k}$

56. $\mathbf{r}(t) = \int\left(3t^2\mathbf{j} + 6\sqrt{t}\,\mathbf{k}\right)dt = t^3\mathbf{j} + 4t^{3/2}\mathbf{k} + \mathbf{C}$

$\qquad \mathbf{r}(0) = \mathbf{C} = \mathbf{i} + 2\mathbf{j}$

$\qquad \mathbf{r}(t) = \mathbf{i} + (2 + t^3)\mathbf{j} + 4t^{3/2}\mathbf{k}$

58. $\mathbf{r}''(t) = -4\cos t\mathbf{i} - 3\sin t\mathbf{k}$

$\qquad \mathbf{r}'(t) = -4\sin t\mathbf{i} + 3\cos t\mathbf{k} + \mathbf{C}_1$

$\qquad \mathbf{r}'(0) = 3\mathbf{k} = 3\mathbf{k} + \mathbf{C}_1 \Rightarrow \mathbf{C}_1 = \mathbf{0}$

$\qquad \mathbf{r}(t) = 4\cos t\mathbf{i} + 3\sin t\mathbf{k} + \mathbf{C}_2$

$\qquad \mathbf{r}(0) = 4\mathbf{i} + \mathbf{C}_2 = 4\mathbf{j} \Rightarrow \mathbf{C}_2 = 4\mathbf{j} - 4\mathbf{i}$

$\qquad \mathbf{r}(t) = (4\cos t - 4)\mathbf{i} + 4\mathbf{j} + 3\sin t\mathbf{k}$

60. $\mathbf{r}(t) = \int\left[\dfrac{1}{1 + t^2}\mathbf{i} + \dfrac{1}{t^2}\mathbf{j} + \dfrac{1}{t}\mathbf{k}\right]dt = \arctan t\mathbf{i} - \dfrac{1}{t}\mathbf{j} + \ln t\mathbf{k} + \mathbf{C}$

$\qquad \mathbf{r}(1) = \dfrac{\pi}{4}\mathbf{i} - \mathbf{j} + \mathbf{C} = 2\mathbf{i} \Rightarrow \mathbf{C} = \left(2 - \dfrac{\pi}{4}\right)\mathbf{i} + \mathbf{j}$

$\qquad \mathbf{r}(t) = \left[2 - \dfrac{\pi}{4} + \arctan t\right]\mathbf{i} + \left(1 - \dfrac{1}{t}\right)\mathbf{j} + \ln t\mathbf{k}$

62. To find the integral of a vector-valued function, you integrate each component function separately. The constant of integration $\mathbf{C}$ is a constant vector.

64. The graph of $\mathbf{u}(t)$ does not change position relative to the xy-plane.

66. Let $\mathbf{r}(t) = x_1(t)\mathbf{i} + y_1(t)\mathbf{j} + z_1(t)\mathbf{k}$ and $\mathbf{u}(t) = x_2(t)\mathbf{i} + y_2(t)\mathbf{j} + z_2(t)\mathbf{k}$.

$\qquad \mathbf{r}(t) \pm \mathbf{u}(t) = [x_1(t) \pm x_2(t)]\mathbf{i} + [y_1(t) \pm y_2(t)]\mathbf{j} + [z_1(t) \pm z_2(t)]\mathbf{k}$

$\qquad D_t[\mathbf{r}(t) \pm \mathbf{u}(t)] = [x_1'(t) \pm x_2'(t)]\mathbf{i} + [y_1'(t) \pm y_2'(t)]\mathbf{j} + [z_1'(t) \pm z_2'(t)]\mathbf{k}$

$\qquad\qquad\qquad = [x_1'(t)\mathbf{i} + y_1'(t)\mathbf{j} + z_1'(t)\mathbf{k}] \pm [x_2'(t)\mathbf{i} + y_2'(t)\mathbf{j} + z_2'(t)\mathbf{k}]$

$\qquad\qquad\qquad = \mathbf{r}'(t) \pm \mathbf{u}'(t)$

68. Let $\mathbf{r}(t) = x_1(t)\mathbf{i} + y_1(t)\mathbf{j} + z_1(t)\mathbf{k}$ and $\mathbf{u}(t) = x_2(t)\mathbf{i} + y_2(t)\mathbf{j} + z_2(t)\mathbf{k}$.

$\qquad \mathbf{r}(t) \times \mathbf{u}(t) = [y_1(t)z_2(t) - z_1(t)y_2(t)]\mathbf{i} - [x_1(t)z_2(t) - z_1(t)x_2(t)]\mathbf{j} + [x_1(t)y_2(t) - y_1(t)x_2(t)]\mathbf{k}$

$\qquad D_t[\mathbf{r}(t) \times \mathbf{u}(t)] = [y_1(t)z_2'(t) + y_1'(t)z_2(t) - z_1(t)y_2'(t) - z_1'(t)y_2(t)]\mathbf{i} - [x_1(t)z_2'(t) + x_1'(t)z_2(t) - z_1(t)x_2'(t) - z_1'(t)x_2(t)]\mathbf{j} +$

$\qquad\qquad\qquad [x_1(t)y_2'(t) + x_1'(t)y_2(t) - y_1(t)x_2'(t) - y_1'(t)x_2(t)]\mathbf{k}$

$\qquad\qquad\quad = \{[y_1(t)z_2'(t) - z_1(t)y_2'(t)]\mathbf{i} - [x_1(t)z_2'(t) - z_1(t)x_2'(t)]\mathbf{j} + [x_1(t)y_2'(t) - y_1(t)x_2'(t)]\mathbf{k}\} +$

$\qquad\qquad\qquad \{[y_1'(t)z_2(t) - z_1'(t)y_2(t)]\mathbf{i} - [x_1'(t)z_2(t) - z_1'(t)x_2(t)]\mathbf{j} + [x_1'(t)y_2(t) - y_1'(t)x_2(t)]\mathbf{k}\}$

$\qquad\qquad\quad = \mathbf{r}(t) \times \mathbf{u}'(t) + \mathbf{r}'(t) \times \mathbf{u}(t)$

70. Let $\mathbf{r}(t) = x(t)\mathbf{i} + y(t)\mathbf{j} + z(t)\mathbf{k}$. Then $\mathbf{r}'(t) = x'(t)\mathbf{i} + y'(t)\mathbf{j} + z'(t)\mathbf{k}$.

$$\mathbf{r}(t) \times \mathbf{r}'(t) = [y(t)z'(t) - z(t)y'(t)]\mathbf{i} - [x(t)z'(t) - z(t)x'(t)]\mathbf{j} + [x(t)y'(t) - y(t)x'(t)]\mathbf{k}$$

$$D_t[\mathbf{r}(t) \times \mathbf{r}'(t)] = [y(t)z''(t) + y'(t)z'(t) - z(t)y''(t) - z'(t)y'(t)]\mathbf{i} - [x(t)z''(t) + x'(t)z'(t) - z(t)x''(t) - z'(t)x'(t)]\mathbf{j} +$$

$$[x(t)y''(t) + x'(t)y'(t) - y(t)x''(t) - y'(t)x'(t)]\mathbf{k}$$

$$= [y(t)z''(t) - z(t)y''(t)]\mathbf{i} - [x(t)z''(t) - z(t)x''(t)]\mathbf{j} + [x(t)y''(t) - y(t)x''(t)]\mathbf{k} = \mathbf{r}(t) \times \mathbf{r}''(t)$$

72. Let $\mathbf{r}(t) = x(t)\mathbf{i} + y(t)\mathbf{j} + z(t)\mathbf{k}$. If $\mathbf{r}(t) \cdot \mathbf{r}(t)$ is constant, then:

$$x^2(t) + y^2(t) + z^2(t) = C$$

$$D_t[x^2(t) + y^2(t) + z^2(t)] = D_t[C]$$

$$2x(t)x'(t) + 2y(t)y'(t) + 2z(t)z'(t) = 0$$

$$2[x(t)x'(t) + y(t)y'(t) + z(t)z'(t)] = 0$$

$$2[\mathbf{r}(t) \cdot \mathbf{r}'(t)] = 0$$

Therefore, $\mathbf{r}(t) \cdot \mathbf{r}'(t) = 0$.

74. False

$$D_t[\mathbf{r}(t) \cdot \mathbf{u}(t)] = \mathbf{r}(t) \cdot \mathbf{u}'(t) + \mathbf{r}'(t) \cdot \mathbf{u}(t)$$

(See Theorem 11.2, part 4)

Section 11.3   Velocity and Acceleration

2. $\mathbf{r}(t) = (6 - t)\mathbf{i} + t\mathbf{j}$

$\mathbf{v}(t) = \mathbf{r}'(t) = -\mathbf{i} + \mathbf{j}$

$\mathbf{a}(t) = \mathbf{r}''(t) = \mathbf{0}$

$x = 6 - t, \ y = t, \ y = 6 - x$

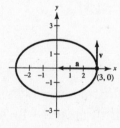

4. $\mathbf{r}(t) = t^2\mathbf{i} + t^3\mathbf{j}$

$\mathbf{v}(t) = \mathbf{r}'(t) = 2t\mathbf{i} + 3t^2\mathbf{j}$

$\mathbf{a}(t) = \mathbf{r}''(t) = 2\mathbf{i} + 6t\mathbf{j}$

$x = t^2, \ y = t^3 \quad x = y^{2/3}$

At $(1, 1), t = 1$.

$\mathbf{v}(1) = 2\mathbf{i} + 3\mathbf{j}$

$\mathbf{a}(1) = 2\mathbf{i} + 6\mathbf{j}$

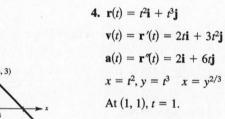

6. $\mathbf{r}(t) = 3\cos t\mathbf{i} + 2\sin t\mathbf{j}$

$\mathbf{v}(t) = -3\sin t\mathbf{i} + 2\cos t\mathbf{j}$

$\mathbf{a}(t) = -3\cos t\mathbf{i} - 2\sin t\mathbf{j}$

$x = 3\cos t, \ y = 2\sin t, \ \dfrac{x^2}{9} + \dfrac{y^2}{4} = 1$ Ellipse

At $(3, 0), t = 0$.

$\mathbf{v}(0) = 2\mathbf{j}$

$\mathbf{a}(0) = -3\mathbf{i}$

8. $\mathbf{r}(t) = \langle e^{-t}, e^t \rangle$

$\mathbf{v}(t) = \mathbf{r}'(t) = \langle -e^{-t}, e^t \rangle$

$\mathbf{a}(t) = \mathbf{r}''(t) = \langle e^{-t}, e^t \rangle$

$x = e^{-t} = \dfrac{1}{e^t}, \ y = e^t, \ y = \dfrac{1}{x}$

At $(1, 1), \ t = 0$.

$\mathbf{v}(0) = \langle -1, 1 \rangle = -\mathbf{i} + \mathbf{j}$

$\mathbf{a}(0) = \langle 1, 1 \rangle = \mathbf{i} + \mathbf{j}$

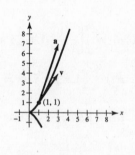

10. $\mathbf{r}(t) = 4t\mathbf{i} + 4t\mathbf{j} + 2t\mathbf{k}$

$\mathbf{v}(t) = 4\mathbf{i} + 4\mathbf{j} + 2\mathbf{k}$

$s(t) = \|\mathbf{v}(t)\| = \sqrt{16 + 16 + 4} = 6$

$\mathbf{a}(t) = \mathbf{0}$

12. $\mathbf{r}(t) = 3t\mathbf{i} + t\mathbf{j} + \dfrac{1}{4}t^2\mathbf{k}$

$\mathbf{v}(t) = 3\mathbf{i} + \mathbf{j} + \dfrac{1}{2}t\mathbf{k}$

$s(t) = \sqrt{9 + 1 + \dfrac{1}{4}t^2} = \sqrt{10 + \dfrac{1}{4}t^2}$

$\mathbf{a}(t) = \dfrac{1}{2}\mathbf{k}$

14. $\mathbf{r}(t) = t^2\mathbf{i} + t\mathbf{j} + 2t^{3/2}\mathbf{k}$

$\mathbf{v}(t) = 2t\mathbf{i} + \mathbf{j} + 3\sqrt{t}\,\mathbf{k}$

$s(t) = \sqrt{4t^2 + 1 + 9t} = \sqrt{4t^2 + 9t + 1}$

$\mathbf{a}(t) = 2\mathbf{i} + \dfrac{3}{2\sqrt{t}}\mathbf{k}$

16. $\mathbf{r}(t) = \langle e^t \cos t,\ e^t \sin t,\ e^t \rangle$

$\mathbf{v}(t) = (e^t \cos t - e^t \sin t)\mathbf{i} + (e^t \sin t + e^t \cos t)\mathbf{j} + e^t\mathbf{k}$

$s(t) = \sqrt{e^{2t}(\cos t - \sin t)^2 + e^{2t}(\cos t + \sin t)^2 + e^{2t}}$

$\quad = e^t\sqrt{3}$

$\mathbf{a}(t) = -2e^t \sin t\mathbf{i} + 2e^t \cos t\mathbf{j} + e^t\mathbf{k}$

18. (a) $\mathbf{r}(t) = \left\langle t,\ \sqrt{25 - t^2},\ \sqrt{25 - t^2} \right\rangle,\ t_0 = 3$

$\mathbf{r}'(t) = \left\langle 1,\ \dfrac{-t}{\sqrt{25 - t^2}},\ \dfrac{-t}{\sqrt{25 - t^2}} \right\rangle$

$\mathbf{r}'(3) = \left\langle 1,\ -\dfrac{3}{4},\ -\dfrac{3}{4} \right\rangle$

$x = 3 + t,\ y = z = 4 - \dfrac{3}{4}t$

(b) $\mathbf{r}(3 + 0.1) \approx \left\langle 3 + 0.1,\ 4 - \dfrac{3}{4}(0.1),\ 4 - \dfrac{3}{4}(0.1) \right\rangle$

$\quad = \langle 3.100,\ 3.925,\ 3.925 \rangle$

20. $\mathbf{a}(t) = 2\mathbf{i} + 3\mathbf{k}$

$\mathbf{v}(t) = \displaystyle\int (2\mathbf{i} + 3\mathbf{k})\,dt = 2t\mathbf{i} + 3t\mathbf{k} + \mathbf{C}$

$\mathbf{v}(0) = \mathbf{C} = 4\mathbf{j} \implies \mathbf{v}(t) = 2t\mathbf{i} + 4\mathbf{j} + 3t\mathbf{k}$

$\mathbf{r}(t) = \displaystyle\int (2t\mathbf{i} + 4\mathbf{j} + 3t\mathbf{k})\,dt = t^2\mathbf{i} + 4t\mathbf{j} + \dfrac{3}{2}t^2\mathbf{k} + \mathbf{C}$

$\mathbf{r}(0) = \mathbf{C} = 0 \implies \mathbf{r}(t) = t^2\mathbf{i} + 4t\mathbf{j} + \dfrac{3}{2}t^2\mathbf{k}$

$\mathbf{r}(2) = 4\mathbf{i} + 8\mathbf{j} + 6\mathbf{k}$

22. $\mathbf{a}(t) = -\cos t\mathbf{i} - \sin t\mathbf{j},\ \mathbf{v}(0) = \mathbf{j} + \mathbf{k},\ \mathbf{r}(0) = \mathbf{i}$

$\mathbf{v}(t) = \displaystyle\int (-\cos t\mathbf{i} - \sin t\mathbf{j})\,dt = -\sin t\mathbf{i} + \cos t\mathbf{j} + \mathbf{C}$

$\mathbf{v}(0) = \mathbf{j} + \mathbf{C} = \mathbf{j} + \mathbf{k} \implies \mathbf{C} = \mathbf{k}$

$\mathbf{v}(t) = -\sin t\mathbf{i} + \cos t\mathbf{j} + \mathbf{k}$

$\mathbf{r}(t) = \displaystyle\int (-\sin t\mathbf{i} + \cos t\mathbf{j} + \mathbf{k})\,dt$

$\quad = \cos t\mathbf{i} + \sin t\mathbf{j} + t\mathbf{k} + \mathbf{C}$

$\mathbf{r}(0) = \mathbf{i} + \mathbf{C} = \mathbf{i} \implies \mathbf{C} = 0$

$\mathbf{r}(t) = \cos t\mathbf{i} + \sin t\mathbf{j} + t\mathbf{k}$

$\mathbf{r}(2) = (\cos 2)\mathbf{i} + (\sin 2)\mathbf{j} + 2\mathbf{k}$

24. (a) The speed is increasing.

(b) The speed is decreasing.

26. $\mathbf{r}(t) = (900 \cos 45°)t\mathbf{i} + [3 + (900 \sin 45°)t - 16t^2]\mathbf{j}$

$\quad = 450\sqrt{2}t\mathbf{i} + (3 + 450\sqrt{2}t - 16t^2)\mathbf{j}$

The maximum height occurs when $y'(t) = 450\sqrt{2} - 32t = 0$, which implies that $t = (225\sqrt{2})/16$.
The maximum height reached by the projectile is

$$y = 3 + 450\sqrt{2}\left(\frac{225\sqrt{2}}{16}\right) - 16\left(\frac{225\sqrt{2}}{16}\right)^2 = \frac{50{,}649}{8} = 6331.125 \text{ feet.}$$

The range is determined by setting $y(t) = 3 + 450\sqrt{2}t - 16t^2 = 0$ which implies that

$$t = \frac{-450\sqrt{2} - \sqrt{405{,}192}}{-32} \approx 39.779 \text{ seconds.}$$

Range: $x = 450\sqrt{2}\left(\dfrac{-450\sqrt{2} - \sqrt{405{,}192}}{-32}\right) \approx 25{,}315.500$ feet

28. $50 \text{ mph} = \dfrac{220}{3} \text{ ft/sec}$

$$\mathbf{r}(t) = \left(\dfrac{220}{3} \cos 15°\right)t\mathbf{i} + \left[5 + \left(\dfrac{220}{3} \sin 15°\right)t - 16t^2\right]\mathbf{j}$$

The ball is 90 feet from where it is thrown when

$$x = \dfrac{220}{3} \cos 15° t = 90 \implies t = \dfrac{27}{22 \cos 15°} \approx 1.2706 \text{ seconds.}$$

The height of the ball at this time is

$$y = 5 + \left(\dfrac{220}{3} \sin 15°\right)\left(\dfrac{27}{22 \cos 15°}\right) - 16\left(\dfrac{27}{22 \cos 15°}\right)^2 \approx 3.286 \text{ feet.}$$

30. $y = x - 0.005x^2$

From Exercise 29 we know that $\tan \theta$ is the coefficient of x. Therefore, $\tan \theta = 1$, $\theta = (\pi/4) \text{ rad} = 45°$. Also

$$\dfrac{16}{v_0^2} \sec^2 \theta = \text{negative of coefficient of } x^2$$

$$\dfrac{16}{v_0^2}(2) = 0.005 \text{ or } v_0 = 80 \text{ ft/sec}$$

$$\mathbf{r}(t) = \left(40\sqrt{2}t\right)\mathbf{i} + \left(40\sqrt{2}t - 16t^2\right)\mathbf{j}. \text{ Position function.}$$

When $40\sqrt{2}t = 60$,

$$t = \dfrac{60}{40\sqrt{2}} = \dfrac{3\sqrt{2}}{4}$$

$$\mathbf{v}(t) = 40\sqrt{2}\mathbf{i} + \left(40\sqrt{2} - 32t\right)\mathbf{j}$$

$$\mathbf{v}\left(\dfrac{3\sqrt{2}}{4}\right) = 40\sqrt{2}\mathbf{i} + \left(40\sqrt{2} - 24\sqrt{2}\right)\mathbf{j} = 8\sqrt{2}(5\mathbf{i} + 2\mathbf{j}) \quad \text{direction}$$

$$\text{Speed} = \left\|\mathbf{v}\left(\dfrac{3\sqrt{2}}{4}\right)\right\| = 8\sqrt{2}\sqrt{25 + 4} = 8\sqrt{58} \text{ ft/sec}$$

32. Wind: $8 \text{ mph} = \dfrac{176}{15} \text{ ft/sec}$

$$\mathbf{r}(t) = \left(140(\cos 22°)t - \dfrac{176}{15}\right)\mathbf{i} + (2.5 + (140 \sin 22°)t - 16t^2)\mathbf{j}$$

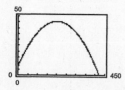

When $x = 375$, $t \approx 2.98$ and $y \approx 16.7$ feet.

Thus, the ball clears the 10-foot fence.

34. $h = 7$ feet, $\theta = 35°$, 30 yards = 90 feet

$$\mathbf{r}(t) = (v_0 \cos 35°)t\mathbf{i} + [7 + (v_0 \sin 35°)t - 16t^2]\mathbf{j}$$

(a) $v_0 \cos 35° t = 90$ when $7 + (v_0 \sin 35°)t - 16t^2 = 4$

$$t = \frac{90}{v_0 \cos 35°}$$

$$7 + (v_0 \sin 35°)\left(\frac{90}{v_0 \cos 35°}\right) - 16\left(\frac{90}{v_0 \cos 35°}\right)^2 = 4$$

$$90 \tan 35° + 3 = \frac{129{,}600}{v_0^2 \cos^2 35°}$$

$$v_0^2 = \frac{129{,}600}{\cos^2 35°(90 \tan 35° + 3)}$$

$$v_0 \approx 54.088 \text{ feet per second}$$

(b) The maximum height occurs when

$$y'(t) = v_0 \sin 35° - 32t = 0.$$

$$t = \frac{v_0 \sin 35°}{32} \approx 0.969 \text{ second}$$

At this time, the height is $y(0.969) \approx 22.0$ feet.

(c) $x(t) = 90 \implies (v_0 \cos 35°)t = 90$

$$t = \frac{90}{54.088 \cos 35°} \approx 2.0 \text{ seconds}$$

36. Place the origin directly below the plane. Then $\theta = 0$, $v_0 = 792$ and

$$\mathbf{r}(t) = (v_0 \cos \theta)t\mathbf{i} + (30{,}000 + (v_0 \sin \theta)t - 16t^2)\mathbf{j}$$

$$= 792t\mathbf{i} + (30{,}000 - 16t^2)\mathbf{j}$$

$$\mathbf{v}(t) = 792\mathbf{i} - 32t\mathbf{j}.$$

At time of impact, $30{,}000 - 16t^2 = 0 \implies t^2 = 1875 \implies t \approx 43.3$ seconds.

$$\mathbf{r}(43.3) = 34{,}294.6\mathbf{i}$$

$$\mathbf{v}(43.3) = 792\mathbf{i} - 1385.6\mathbf{j}$$

$$\|\mathbf{v}(43.3)\| = 1596 \text{ ft/sec} = 1088 \text{ mph}$$

$$\tan \alpha = \frac{30{,}000}{34{,}294.6} \approx 0.8748 \implies \alpha \approx 0.7187(41.18°)$$

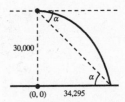

38. From Exercise 37, the range is

$$x = \frac{v_0^2}{32} \sin 2\theta.$$

Hence, $x = 150 = \dfrac{v_0^2}{32} \sin(24°) \implies v_0^2 = \dfrac{4800}{\sin 24°} \implies v_0 \approx 108.6$ ft/sec.

40. (a) $\mathbf{r}(t) = t(v_0 \cos \theta)\mathbf{i} + (tv_0 \sin \theta - 16t^2)\mathbf{j}$

$$t(v_0 \sin \theta - 16t) = 0 \text{ when } t = \frac{v_0 \sin \theta}{16}.$$

Range: $\quad x = v_0 \cos \theta\left(\dfrac{v_0 \sin \theta}{32}\right) = \left(\dfrac{v_0^2}{32}\right) \sin 2\theta$

The range will be maximum when

$$\frac{dx}{dt} = \left(\frac{v_0^2}{32}\right)2 \cos 2\theta = 0$$

or

$$2\theta = \frac{\pi}{2}, \quad \theta = \frac{\pi}{4} \text{ rad.}$$

(b) $y(t) = tv_0 \sin \theta - 16t^2$

$$\frac{dy}{dt} = v_0 \sin \theta - 32t = 0 \text{ when } t = \frac{v_0 \sin \theta}{32}.$$

Maximum height:

$$y\left(\frac{v_0 \sin \theta}{32}\right) = \frac{v_0^2 \sin^2 \theta}{32} - 16\frac{v_0^2 \sin^2 \theta}{32^2} = \frac{v_0^2 \sin^2 \theta}{64}$$

Minimum height when $\sin \theta = 1$, or $\theta = \dfrac{\pi}{2}$.

42. $\mathbf{r}(t) = (v_0 \cos \theta)t\mathbf{i} + [h + (v_0 \sin \theta)t - 4.9t^2]\mathbf{j}$

$\quad\quad = (v_0 \cos 8°)t\mathbf{i} + [(v_0 \sin 8°)t - 4.9t^2]\mathbf{j}$

$x = 50$ when $(v_0 \cos 8°)t = 50 \implies t = \dfrac{50}{v_0 \cos 8°}$. For this value of t, $y = 0$:

$$(v_0 \sin 8°)\left(\frac{50}{v_0 \cos 8°}\right) - 4.9\left(\frac{50}{v_0 \cos 8°}\right)^2 = 0$$

$$50 \tan 8° = \frac{(4.9)(2500)}{v_0^2 \cos^2 8°} \implies v_0^2 = \frac{(4.9)50}{\tan 8° \cos^2 8°} \approx 1777.698$$

$$\implies v_0 \approx 42.2 \text{ m/sec}$$

44. $\mathbf{r}(t) = b(\omega t - \sin \omega t)\mathbf{i} + b(1 - \cos \omega t)\mathbf{j}$

$\quad \mathbf{v}(t) = b\omega[(1 - \cos \omega t)\mathbf{i} + (\sin \omega t)\mathbf{j}]$

$\quad$ Speed $= \|\mathbf{v}(t)\| = \sqrt{2}b\omega\sqrt{1 - \cos \omega t}$ and has a maximum value of $2b\omega$ when $\omega t = \pi, 3\pi, \ldots$.

$\quad\quad$ 55 mph $= 80.67$ ft/sec $= 80.67$ rad/sec $= \omega$ since (since $b = 1$)

$\quad$ Therefore, the maximum speed of a point on the tire is twice the speed of the car:

$\quad\quad 2(80.67)$ ft/sec $= 110$ mph

46. (a) Speed $= \|\mathbf{v}\| = \sqrt{b^2\omega^2 \sin^2(\omega t) + b^2\omega^2 \cos^2(\omega t)}$

$\quad\quad\quad\quad\quad\quad = \sqrt{b^2\omega^2[\sin^2(\omega t) + \cos^2(\omega t)]} = b\omega$

(b)

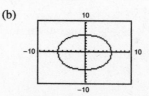

The graphing utility draws the circle faster for greater values of ω.

48. $\|\mathbf{a}(t)\| = b\omega^2\|\cos(\omega t)\mathbf{i} + \sin(\omega t)\mathbf{j}\| = b\omega^2$

50. $\|\mathbf{v}(t)\| = 30$ mph $= 44$ ft/sec

$\quad \omega = \dfrac{\|\mathbf{v}(t)\|}{b} = \dfrac{44}{300}$ rad/sec

$\quad \|\mathbf{a}(t)\| = b\omega^2$

$\quad F = m(b\omega^2) = \dfrac{3000}{32}(300)\left(\dfrac{44}{300}\right)^2 = 605$ lb

Let $\mathbf{n}$ be normal to the road.

$\quad \|\mathbf{n}\| \cos \theta = 3000$

$\quad \|\mathbf{n}\| \sin \theta = 605$

Dividing the second equation by the first:

$\quad \tan \theta = \dfrac{605}{3000}$

$\quad\quad \theta = \arctan\left(\dfrac{605}{3000}\right) \approx 11.4°.$

52. $h = 6$ feet, $v_0 = 45$ feet per second, $\theta = 42.5°$. From Exercise 47,

$$t = \frac{45 \sin 42.5° + \sqrt{(45)^2 \sin^2 42.5° + 2(32)(6)}}{32} \approx 2.08 \text{ seconds.}$$

At this time, $x(t) \approx 69.02$ feet.

54. $\mathbf{r}(t) = x(t)\mathbf{i} + y(t)\mathbf{j}$

$y(t) = m(x(t)) + b$, m and b are constants.

$\mathbf{r}(t) = x(t)\mathbf{i} + [m(x(t)) + b]\mathbf{j}$

$\mathbf{v}(t) = x'(t)\mathbf{i} + mx'(t)\mathbf{j}$

$s(t) = \sqrt{[x'(t)]^2 + [mx'(t)]^2} = C$, C is a constant.

Thus, $x'(t) = \dfrac{C}{\sqrt{1 + m^2}}$

$x''(t) = 0$

$\mathbf{a}(t) = x''(t)\mathbf{i} + mx''(t)\mathbf{j} = \mathbf{0}$.

56. $\mathbf{r}_1(t) = x(t)\mathbf{i} + y(t)\mathbf{j} + z(t)\mathbf{k}$

$\mathbf{r}_2(t) = \mathbf{r}_1(2t)$

Velocity: $\mathbf{r}_2'(t) = 2\mathbf{r}_1'(2t)$

Acceleration: $\mathbf{r}_2''(t) = 4\mathbf{r}_1''(2t)$

In general, if $\mathbf{r}_3(t) = \mathbf{r}_1(\omega t)$, then:

Velocity: $\mathbf{r}_3'(t) = \omega\mathbf{r}_1'(\omega t)$

Acceleration: $\mathbf{r}_3''(t) = \omega^2\mathbf{r}_1''(\omega t)$

Section 11.4   Tangent Vectors and Normal Vectors

2. $\mathbf{r}(t) = t^3\mathbf{i} + 2t^2\mathbf{j}$

$\mathbf{r}'(t) = 3t^2\mathbf{i} + 4t\mathbf{j}$

$\|\mathbf{r}'(t)\| = \sqrt{9t^4 + 16t^2}$

$\mathbf{T}(t) = \dfrac{\mathbf{r}'(t)}{\|\mathbf{r}'(t)\|} = \dfrac{1}{\sqrt{9t^4 + 16t^2}}(3t^2\mathbf{i} + 4t\mathbf{j})$

$\mathbf{T}(1) = \dfrac{1}{\sqrt{9 + 16}}(3\mathbf{i} + 4\mathbf{j}) = \dfrac{3}{5}\mathbf{i} + \dfrac{4}{5}\mathbf{j}$

4. $\mathbf{r}(t) = 6\cos t\,\mathbf{i} + 2\sin t\,\mathbf{j}$

$\mathbf{r}'(t) = -6\sin t\,\mathbf{i} + 2\cos t\,\mathbf{j}$

$\|\mathbf{r}'(t)\| = \sqrt{36\sin^2 t + 4\cos^2 t}$

$\mathbf{T}(t) = \dfrac{\mathbf{r}'(t)}{\|\mathbf{r}'(t)\|} = \dfrac{-6\sin t\,\mathbf{i} + 2\cos t\,\mathbf{j}}{\sqrt{36\sin^2 t + 4\cos^2 t}}$

$\mathbf{T}\left(\dfrac{\pi}{3}\right) = \dfrac{-3\sqrt{3}\mathbf{i} + \mathbf{j}}{\sqrt{36(3/4) + (1/4)}} = \dfrac{1}{\sqrt{28}}(-3\sqrt{3}\mathbf{i} + \mathbf{j})$

6. $\mathbf{r}(t) = t^2\mathbf{i} + t\mathbf{j} + \dfrac{4}{3}\mathbf{k}$

$\mathbf{r}'(t) = 2t\mathbf{i} + \mathbf{j}$

When $t = 1$, $\mathbf{r}'(t) = \mathbf{r}'(1) = 2\mathbf{i} + \mathbf{j}$ $\left[t = 1 \text{ at } \left(1, 1, \dfrac{4}{3}\right)\right]$.

$\mathbf{T}(1) = \dfrac{\mathbf{r}'(1)}{\|\mathbf{r}'(1)\|} = \dfrac{2\mathbf{i} + \mathbf{j}}{\sqrt{5}} = \dfrac{\sqrt{5}}{5}(2\mathbf{i} + \mathbf{j})$

Direction numbers: $a = 2$, $b = 1$, $c = 0$

Parametric equations: $x = 2t + 1$, $y = t + 1$, $z = \dfrac{4}{3}$

8. $\mathbf{r}(t) = \left\langle t, t, \sqrt{4 - t^2}\right\rangle$

$\mathbf{r}'(t) = \left\langle 1, 1, -\dfrac{t}{\sqrt{4 - t^2}}\right\rangle$

When $t = 1$, $\mathbf{r}'(1) = \left\langle 1, 1, -\dfrac{1}{\sqrt{3}}\right\rangle$, $\left[t = 1 \text{ at } \left(1, 1, \sqrt{3}\right)\right]$.

$\mathbf{T}(1) = \dfrac{\mathbf{r}'(1)}{\|\mathbf{r}'(1)\|} = \dfrac{\sqrt{21}}{7}\left\langle 1, 1, -\dfrac{1}{\sqrt{3}}\right\rangle$

Direction numbers: $a = 1$, $b = 1$, $c = -\dfrac{1}{\sqrt{3}}$

Parametric equations: $x = t + 1$, $y = t + 1$,

$z = -\dfrac{1}{\sqrt{3}}t + \sqrt{3}$

10. $\mathbf{r}(t) = \left\langle 2\sin t, 2\cos t, 4\sin^2 t\right\rangle$

$\mathbf{r}'(t) = \left\langle 2\cos t, -2\sin t, 8\sin t\cos t\right\rangle$

When $t = \dfrac{\pi}{6}$, $\mathbf{r}\left(\dfrac{\pi}{6}\right) = \left\langle \sqrt{3}, -1, 2\sqrt{3}\right\rangle$, $\left[t = \dfrac{\pi}{6} \text{ at } \left(1, \sqrt{3}, 1\right)\right]$.

$\mathbf{T}\left(\dfrac{\pi}{6}\right) = \dfrac{\mathbf{r}'(\pi/6)}{\|\mathbf{r}'(\pi/6)\|} = \dfrac{1}{4}\left\langle \sqrt{3}, -1, 2\sqrt{3}\right\rangle$

Direction numbers: $a = \sqrt{3}$, $b = -1$, $c = 2\sqrt{3}$

Parametric equations: $x = \sqrt{3}t + 1$, $y = -t + \sqrt{3}$, $z = 2\sqrt{3}t + 1$

12. $\mathbf{r}(t) = 3\cos t\mathbf{i} + 4\sin t\mathbf{j} + \frac{1}{2}\mathbf{k}$

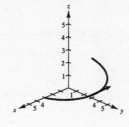

$\mathbf{r}'(t) = -3\sin t\mathbf{i} + 4\cos t\mathbf{j} + \frac{1}{2}\mathbf{k}$

When $t = \frac{\pi}{2}$, $\mathbf{r}'\left(\frac{\pi}{2}\right) = -3\mathbf{i} + \frac{1}{2}\mathbf{k}$, $\left[t = \frac{\pi}{2} \text{ at } \left(0, 4, \frac{\pi}{4}\right)\right]$.

$\mathbf{T}\left(\frac{\pi}{2}\right) = \frac{\mathbf{r}'(\pi/2)}{\|\mathbf{r}'(\pi/2)\|} = \frac{2}{\sqrt{37}}\left(-3\mathbf{i} + \frac{1}{2}\mathbf{k}\right) = \frac{1}{\sqrt{37}}(-6\mathbf{i} + \mathbf{k})$

Direction numbers: $a = -6$, $b = 0$, $c = 1$

Parametric equations: $x = -6t$, $y = 4$, $z = t + \frac{\pi}{4}$

14. $\mathbf{r}(t) = e^{-t}\mathbf{i} + 2\cos t\mathbf{j} + 2\sin t\mathbf{k}$, $t_0 = 0$

$\mathbf{r}'(t) = -e^{-t}\mathbf{i} - 2\sin t\mathbf{j} + 2\cos t\mathbf{k}$

$\mathbf{r}(0) = \mathbf{i} + 2\mathbf{j}$, $\mathbf{r}'(0) = -\mathbf{i} + 2\mathbf{k}$, $\|\mathbf{r}'(0)\| = \sqrt{5}$

$\mathbf{T}(0) = \frac{\mathbf{r}'(0)}{\|\mathbf{r}'(0)\|} = \frac{-\mathbf{i} + 2\mathbf{k}}{\sqrt{5}}$

Parametric equations: $x(s) = 1 - s$, $y(s) = 2$, $z(s) = 2s$

$\mathbf{r}(t_0 + 0.1) = \mathbf{r}(0 + 0.1) \approx \langle 1 - 0.1, 2, 2(0.1)\rangle$

$= \langle 0.9, 2, 0.2 \rangle$

16. $\mathbf{r}(0) = \langle 0, 1, 0 \rangle$

$\mathbf{u}(0) = \langle 0, 1, 0 \rangle$

Hence the curves intersect.

$\mathbf{r}'(t) = \langle 1, -\sin t, \cos t\rangle$, $\mathbf{r}'(0) = \langle 1, 0, 1\rangle$

$\mathbf{u}'(s) = \left\langle -\sin s\cos s - \cos s, -\sin s\cos s - \cos s, \frac{1}{2}\cos 2s + \frac{1}{2}\right\rangle$

$\mathbf{u}'(0) = \langle -1, 0, 1\rangle$

$\cos\theta = \frac{\mathbf{r}'(0) \cdot \mathbf{u}'(0)}{\|\mathbf{r}'(0)\|\,\|\mathbf{u}'(0)\|} = 0 \implies \theta = \frac{\pi}{2}$

18. $\mathbf{r}(t) = t\mathbf{i} + \frac{6}{t}\mathbf{j}$, $t = 3$

$\mathbf{r}'(t) = \mathbf{i} - \frac{6}{t^2}\mathbf{j}$

$\mathbf{T}(t) = \frac{\mathbf{r}'(t)}{\|\mathbf{r}'(t)\|} = \frac{1}{\sqrt{1 + (36/t^4)}}\left(\mathbf{i} - \frac{6}{t^2}\mathbf{j}\right)$

$= \frac{t^2}{\sqrt{t^4 + 36}}\left(\mathbf{i} - \frac{6}{t^2}\mathbf{j}\right)$

$\mathbf{T}'(t) = \frac{72t}{(t^4 + 36)^{3/2}}\mathbf{i} + \frac{12t^3}{(t^4 + 36)^{3/2}}\mathbf{j}$

$\mathbf{N}(2) = \frac{\mathbf{T}'(2)}{\|\mathbf{T}'(2)\|} + \frac{1}{\sqrt{13}}(3\mathbf{i} + 2\mathbf{j})$

20. $\mathbf{r}(t) = \cos t\mathbf{i} + 2\sin t\mathbf{j} + \mathbf{k}$, $t = -\frac{\pi}{4}$

$\mathbf{r}'(t) = -\sin t\mathbf{i} + 2\cos t\mathbf{j}$

$\mathbf{T}(t) = \frac{\mathbf{r}'(t)}{\|\mathbf{r}'(t)\|} = \frac{-\sin t\mathbf{i} + 2\cos t\mathbf{j}}{\sqrt{\sin^2 t + 4\cos^2 t}}$

The unit normal vector is perpendicular to this vector and points toward the z-axis:

$\mathbf{N}(t) = \frac{-2\cos t\mathbf{i} - \sin t\mathbf{j}}{\sqrt{\sin^2 t + 4\cos^2 t}}.$

22. $\mathbf{r}(t) = 4t\mathbf{i} - 2t\mathbf{j}$

$\mathbf{v}(t) = 4\mathbf{i} - 2\mathbf{j}$

$\mathbf{a}(t) = \mathbf{O}$

$\mathbf{T}(t) = \dfrac{\mathbf{v}(t)}{\|\mathbf{v}(t)\|} = \dfrac{1}{\sqrt{5}}(2\mathbf{i} - \mathbf{j})$

$\mathbf{T}'(t) = \mathbf{O}$

$\mathbf{N}(t) = \dfrac{\mathbf{T}'(t)}{\|\mathbf{T}'(t)\|}$ is undefined.

The path is a line and the speed is constant.

24. $\mathbf{r}(t) = t^2\mathbf{j} + \mathbf{k}$

$\mathbf{v}(t) = 2t\mathbf{j}$

$\mathbf{a}(t) = 2\mathbf{j}$

$\mathbf{T}(t) = \dfrac{\mathbf{v}(t)}{\|\mathbf{v}(t)\|} = \dfrac{2t\mathbf{j}}{2t} = \mathbf{j}$

$\mathbf{T}'(t) = \mathbf{O}$

$\mathbf{N}(t) = \dfrac{\mathbf{T}'(t)}{\|\mathbf{T}'(t)\|}$ is undefined.

The path is a line and the speed is variable.

26. $\mathbf{r}(t) = t^2\mathbf{i} + 2t\mathbf{j}, t = 1$

$\mathbf{v}(t) = 2t\mathbf{i} + 2\mathbf{j}, \mathbf{v}(1) = 2\mathbf{i} + 2\mathbf{j}$

$\mathbf{a}(t) = 2\mathbf{i}, \mathbf{a}(1) = 2\mathbf{i}$

$\mathbf{T}(t) = \dfrac{\mathbf{v}(t)}{\|\mathbf{v}(t)\|} = \dfrac{1}{\sqrt{4t^2 + 4}}(2t\mathbf{i} + 2\mathbf{j}) = \dfrac{1}{\sqrt{t^2 + 1}}(t\mathbf{i} + \mathbf{j})$

$\mathbf{T}(1) = \dfrac{1}{\sqrt{2}}(\mathbf{i} + \mathbf{j}) = \dfrac{\sqrt{2}}{2}\mathbf{i} + \dfrac{\sqrt{2}}{2}\mathbf{j}$

$\mathbf{N}(t) = \dfrac{\mathbf{T}'(t)}{\|\mathbf{T}'(t)\|} = \dfrac{\dfrac{1}{(t^2 + 1)^{3/2}}\mathbf{i} + \dfrac{-t}{(t^2 + 1)^{3/2}}\mathbf{j}}{\dfrac{1}{t^2 + 1}}$

$\qquad = \dfrac{1}{\sqrt{t^2 + 1}}(\mathbf{i} + t\mathbf{j})$

$\mathbf{N}(1) = \dfrac{\sqrt{2}}{2}\mathbf{i} - \dfrac{\sqrt{2}}{2}\mathbf{j}$

$a_\mathbf{T} = \mathbf{a} \cdot \mathbf{T} = \sqrt{2}$

$a_\mathbf{N} = \mathbf{a} \cdot \mathbf{N} = \sqrt{2}$

28. $\mathbf{r}(t) = a\cos(\omega t)\mathbf{i} + b\sin(\omega t)\mathbf{j}$

$\mathbf{v}(t) = -a\omega\sin(\omega t)\mathbf{i} + b\omega\cos(\omega t)\mathbf{j}$

$\mathbf{v}(0) = b\omega\mathbf{j}$

$\mathbf{a}(t) = -a\omega^2\cos(\omega t)\mathbf{i} - b\omega^2\sin(\omega t)\mathbf{j}$

$\mathbf{a}(0) = -a\omega^2\mathbf{i}$

$\mathbf{T}(0) = \dfrac{\mathbf{v}(0)}{\|\mathbf{v}(0)\|} = \mathbf{j}$

Motion along $\mathbf{r}(t)$ is counterclockwise. Therefore,

$\mathbf{N}(0) = -\mathbf{i}.$

$a_\mathbf{T} = \mathbf{a} \cdot \mathbf{T} = 0$

$a_\mathbf{N} = \mathbf{a} \cdot \mathbf{N} = a\omega^2$

30. $\mathbf{r}(t_0) = (\omega t_0 - \sin\omega t_0)\mathbf{i} + (1 - \cos\omega t_0)\mathbf{j}$

$\mathbf{v}(t_0) = \omega[(1 - \cos\omega t_0)\mathbf{i} + (\sin\omega t_0)\mathbf{j}]$

$\mathbf{a}(t_0) = \omega^2[(\sin\omega t_0)\mathbf{i} + (\cos\omega t_0)\mathbf{j}]$

$\mathbf{T} = \dfrac{\mathbf{v}}{\|\mathbf{v}\|} = \dfrac{(1 - \cos\omega t_0)\mathbf{i} + (\sin\omega t_0)\mathbf{j}}{\sqrt{2}\sqrt{1 - \cos\omega t_0}}$

Motion along $\mathbf{r}$ is clockwise. Therefore, $\mathbf{N} = \dfrac{(\sin\omega t_0)\mathbf{i} - (1 - \cos\omega t_0)\mathbf{j}}{\sqrt{2}\sqrt{1 - \cos\omega t_0}}$.

$a_\mathbf{T} = \mathbf{a} \cdot \mathbf{T} = \dfrac{\omega^2\sin\omega t_0}{\sqrt{2}\sqrt{1 - \cos\omega t_0}} = \dfrac{\omega^2}{\sqrt{2}}\sqrt{1 + \cos\omega t_0}$

$a_\mathbf{N} = \mathbf{a} \cdot \mathbf{N} = \dfrac{\omega^2}{\sqrt{2}}\sqrt{1 - \cos\omega t_0}$

32. $\mathbf{T}(t)$ points in the direction that $\mathbf{r}$ is moving. $\mathbf{N}(t)$ points in the direction that $\mathbf{r}$ is turning, toward the concave side of the curve.

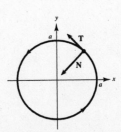

34. If the angular velocity ω is halved,

$$a_N = a\left(\frac{\omega}{2}\right)^2 = \frac{a\omega^2}{4}.$$

a_N is changed by a factor of $\frac{1}{4}$.

36. $\mathbf{r}(t) = 2\cos t\mathbf{i} + 2\sin t\mathbf{j}, \; t_0 = \dfrac{\pi}{4}$

$x = 2\cos t, \; y = 2\sin t \Rightarrow x^2 + y^2 = 4$

$\mathbf{r}'(t) = -2\sin t\mathbf{i} + 2\cos t\mathbf{j}$

$\mathbf{T}(t) = \dfrac{1}{2}(-2\sin t\mathbf{i} + 2\cos t\mathbf{j}) = -\sin t\mathbf{i} + \cos t\mathbf{j}$

$\mathbf{N}(t) = -\cos t\mathbf{i} - \sin t\mathbf{j}$

$\mathbf{r}\left(\dfrac{\pi}{4}\right) = \sqrt{2}\mathbf{i} + \sqrt{2}\mathbf{j}$

$\mathbf{T}\left(\dfrac{\pi}{4}\right) = \dfrac{\sqrt{2}}{2}(-\mathbf{i} + \mathbf{j})$

$\mathbf{N}\left(\dfrac{\pi}{4}\right) = \dfrac{\sqrt{2}}{2}(-\mathbf{i} - \mathbf{j})$

38. $\mathbf{r}(t) = 4t\mathbf{i} - 4t\mathbf{j} + 2t\mathbf{k}$

$\mathbf{v}(t) = 4\mathbf{i} - 4\mathbf{j} + 2\mathbf{k}$

$\mathbf{a}(t) = \mathbf{0}$

$\mathbf{T}(t) = \dfrac{\mathbf{v}}{\|\mathbf{v}\|} = \dfrac{1}{3}(2\mathbf{i} - 2\mathbf{j} + \mathbf{k})$

$\mathbf{N}(t) = \dfrac{\mathbf{T}'}{\|\mathbf{T}'\|}$ is undefined.

a_T, a_N are not defined.

40. $\mathbf{r}(t) = e^t\sin t\,\mathbf{i} + e^t\cos t\,\mathbf{j} + e^t\mathbf{k}$

$\mathbf{v}(t) = (e^t\cos t + e^t\sin t)\mathbf{i} + (-e^t\sin t + e^t\cos t)\mathbf{j} + e^t\mathbf{k}$

$\mathbf{v}(0) = \mathbf{i} + \mathbf{j} + \mathbf{k}$

$\mathbf{a}(t) = 2e^t\cos t\,\mathbf{i} - 2e^t\sin t\,\mathbf{j} + e^t\mathbf{k}$

$\mathbf{a}(0) = 2\mathbf{i} + \mathbf{k}$

$\mathbf{T}(t) = \dfrac{\mathbf{v}}{\|\mathbf{v}\|} = \dfrac{1}{\sqrt{3}}[(\cos t + \sin t)\mathbf{i} + (-\sin t + \cos t)\mathbf{j} + \mathbf{k}]$

$\mathbf{T}(0) = \dfrac{1}{\sqrt{3}}[\mathbf{i} + \mathbf{j} + \mathbf{k}]$

$\mathbf{N}(t) = \dfrac{1}{\sqrt{2}}[(-\sin t + \cos t)\mathbf{i} + (-\cos t - \sin t)\mathbf{j}]$

$\mathbf{N}(0) = \dfrac{\sqrt{2}}{2}\mathbf{i} - \dfrac{\sqrt{2}}{2}\mathbf{j}$

$a_T = \mathbf{a} \cdot \mathbf{T} = \sqrt{3}$

$a_N = \mathbf{a} \cdot \mathbf{N} = \sqrt{2}$

42. $\mathbf{r}(t) = t\mathbf{i} + 3t^2\mathbf{j} + \dfrac{t^2}{2}\mathbf{k}$

$\mathbf{v}(t) = \mathbf{i} + 6t\mathbf{j} + t\mathbf{k}$

$\mathbf{v}(2) = \mathbf{i} + 12\mathbf{j} + 2\mathbf{k}$

$\mathbf{a}(t) = 6\mathbf{j} + \mathbf{k}$

$\mathbf{T}(t) = \dfrac{\mathbf{v}}{\|\mathbf{v}\|} = \dfrac{1}{\sqrt{1 + 37t^2}}(\mathbf{i} + 6t\mathbf{j} + t\mathbf{k})$

$\mathbf{T}(2) = \dfrac{1}{\sqrt{149}}(\mathbf{i} + 12\mathbf{j} + 2\mathbf{k})$

$\mathbf{N}(t) = \dfrac{\mathbf{T}'}{\|\mathbf{T}'\|} = \dfrac{\dfrac{1}{(1 + 37t^2)^{3/2}}[-37t\mathbf{i} + 6\mathbf{j} + \mathbf{k}]}{\dfrac{\sqrt{37}}{1 + 37t^2}}$

$= \dfrac{1}{\sqrt{37}\sqrt{1 + 37t^2}}[-37t\mathbf{i} + 6\mathbf{j} + \mathbf{k}]$

$\mathbf{N}(2) = \dfrac{1}{\sqrt{37}\sqrt{149}}[-74\mathbf{i} + 6\mathbf{j} + \mathbf{k}]$

$= \dfrac{1}{\sqrt{5513}}(-74\mathbf{i} + 6\mathbf{j} + \mathbf{k})$

$a_T = \mathbf{a} \cdot \mathbf{T} = \dfrac{74}{\sqrt{149}}$

$a_N = \mathbf{a} \cdot \mathbf{N} = \dfrac{37}{\sqrt{5513}} = \dfrac{\sqrt{37}}{\sqrt{149}}$

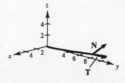

44. The unit tangent vector points in the direction of motion.

46. If $a_T = 0$, then the speed is constant.

48. (a) $\mathbf{r}(t) = \langle \cos \pi t + \pi t \sin \pi t, \ \sin \pi t - \pi t \cos \pi t \rangle$

$\mathbf{v}(t) = \langle -\pi \sin \pi t + \pi \sin \pi t + \pi^2 t \cos \pi t, \ \pi \cos \pi t - \pi \cos \pi t + \pi^2 t \sin \pi t \rangle = \langle \pi^2 t \cos \pi t, \ \pi^2 t \sin \pi t \rangle$

$\mathbf{a}(t) = \langle \pi^2 \cos \pi t - \pi^3 t \sin \pi t, \ \pi^2 \sin \pi t + \pi^3 t \cos \pi t \rangle$

$\mathbf{T}(t) = \dfrac{\mathbf{v}(t)}{\|\mathbf{v}(t)\|} = \langle \cos \pi t, \ \sin \pi t \rangle$

$a_T = \mathbf{a} \cdot \mathbf{T} = \cos \pi t (\pi^2 \cos \pi t - \pi^3 t \sin \pi t) + \sin \pi t (\pi^2 \sin \pi t + \pi^3 t \cos \pi t) = \pi^2$

$a_N = \sqrt{\|\mathbf{a}\|^2 - a_T{}^2} = \sqrt{\pi^4(1 + \pi^2 t^2) - \pi^4} = \pi^3 t$

When $t = 1$, $a_T = \pi^2$, $a_N = \pi^3$. When $t = 2$, $a_T = \pi^2$, $a_N = 2\pi^3$.

(b) Since $a_T = \pi^2 > 0$ for all values of t, the speed is increasing when $t = 1$ and $t = 2$.

50. $\mathbf{r}(t) = t\mathbf{i} + t^2\mathbf{j} + \dfrac{t^3}{3}\mathbf{k}$, $t_0 = 1$

$\mathbf{r}'(t) = \mathbf{i} + 2t\mathbf{j} + t^2\mathbf{k}$

$\mathbf{T}(t) = \dfrac{1}{\sqrt{1 + 4t^2 + t^4}}(\mathbf{i} + 2t\mathbf{j} + t^2\mathbf{k})$

$\mathbf{N}(t) = \dfrac{1}{\sqrt{1 + 4t^2 + t^4}\sqrt{1 + t^2 + t^4}}[(-2t - t^3)\mathbf{i} + (1 - t^4)\mathbf{j} + (t + 2t^3)\mathbf{k}]$

$\mathbf{r}(1) = \mathbf{i} + \mathbf{j} + \dfrac{1}{3}\mathbf{k}$

$\mathbf{T}(1) = \dfrac{1}{\sqrt{6}}(\mathbf{i} + 2\mathbf{j} + \mathbf{k})$

$\mathbf{N}(1) = \dfrac{1}{\sqrt{6}\sqrt{3}}(-3\mathbf{i} + 3\mathbf{k}) = \dfrac{\sqrt{2}}{2}(-\mathbf{i} + \mathbf{k})$

$\mathbf{B}(1) = \mathbf{T}(1) \times \mathbf{N}(1) = \begin{vmatrix} \mathbf{i} & \mathbf{j} & \mathbf{k} \\ \dfrac{\sqrt{6}}{6} & \dfrac{\sqrt{6}}{3} & \dfrac{\sqrt{6}}{6} \\ -\dfrac{\sqrt{2}}{2} & 0 & \dfrac{\sqrt{2}}{2} \end{vmatrix} = \dfrac{\sqrt{3}}{3}\mathbf{i} - \dfrac{\sqrt{3}}{3}\mathbf{j} + \dfrac{\sqrt{3}}{3}\mathbf{k} = \dfrac{\sqrt{3}}{3}(\mathbf{i} - \mathbf{j} + \mathbf{k})$

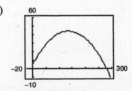

52. (a) $\mathbf{r}(t) = (v_0 \cos \theta)t\mathbf{i} + \left[h + (v_0 \sin \theta)t - \dfrac{1}{2}gt^2 \right]\mathbf{j}$

$= (100 \cos 30°)t\mathbf{i} + [5 + (100 \sin 30°)t - 16t^2]\mathbf{j}$

$= 50\sqrt{3}\,t\mathbf{i} + [5 + 50t - 16t^2]\mathbf{j}$

(b)

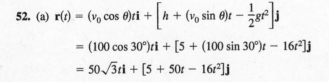

Maximum height ≈ 44.0625

Range ≈ 279.0325

(c) $\mathbf{v}(t) = 50\sqrt{3}\mathbf{i} + (50 - 32t)\mathbf{j}$

Speed $= \|\mathbf{v}(t)\| = \sqrt{2500(3) + (50 - 32t)^2}$

$= 4\sqrt{64t^2 - 200t + 625}\quad \mathbf{a}(t) = -32\mathbf{j}$

(d)

t	0.5	1.0	1.5	2.0	2.5	3.0
Speed	93.04	88.45	86.63	87.73	91.65	98.06

—CONTINUED—

52. —CONTINUED—

(e)
$$T(t) = \frac{25\sqrt{3}\mathbf{i} + (25 - 16t)\mathbf{j}}{2\sqrt{64t^2 - 200t + 625}}$$

$$N(t) = \frac{(25 - 16t)\mathbf{i} - 25\sqrt{3}}{2\sqrt{64t^2 - 200t + 625}}$$

$$a_T = \mathbf{a} \cdot T = \frac{16(16t - 25)}{\sqrt{64t^2 - 200t + 625}}$$

$$a_N = \mathbf{a} \cdot N = \frac{400\sqrt{3}}{\sqrt{64t^2 - 200t + 625}}$$

$$a_T T + a_N N = -32\mathbf{j}$$

(f)
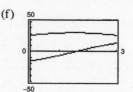

The speed is increasing when a_T and a_N have opposite signs.

54. 600 mph = 880 ft/sec

$$\mathbf{r}(t) = 880t\mathbf{i} + (-16t^2 + 36{,}000)\mathbf{j}$$

$$\mathbf{v}(t) = 880\mathbf{i} - 32t\mathbf{j}$$

$$\mathbf{a}(t) = -32\mathbf{j}$$

$$T(t) = \frac{880\mathbf{i} - 32t\mathbf{j}}{16\sqrt{4t^2 + 3025}} = \frac{55\mathbf{i} - 2t\mathbf{j}}{\sqrt{4t^2 + 3025}}$$

Motion along **r** is clockwise, therefore

$$N(t) = \frac{-2t\mathbf{i} - 55\mathbf{j}}{\sqrt{4t^2 + 3025}}$$

$$a_T = \mathbf{a} \cdot T = \frac{64t}{\sqrt{4t^2 + 3025}}$$

$$a_N = \mathbf{a} \cdot N = \frac{1760}{\sqrt{4t^2 + 3025}}$$

56.
$$\mathbf{r}(t) = (r\cos\omega t)\mathbf{i} + (r\sin\omega t)\mathbf{j}$$

$$\mathbf{v}(t) = (-r\omega\sin\omega t)\mathbf{i} + (r\omega\cos\omega t)\mathbf{j}$$

$$\|\mathbf{v}(t)\| = r\omega\sqrt{1} = r\omega = v$$

$$\mathbf{a}(t) = (-r\omega^2\cos\omega t)\mathbf{i} - (r\omega^2\sin\omega t)\mathbf{j}$$

$$\|\mathbf{a}(t)\| = r\omega^2$$

(a) $F = m\|\mathbf{a}(t)\| = m(r\omega^2) = \dfrac{m}{r}(r^2\omega^2) = \dfrac{mv^2}{r}$

(b) By Newton's Law:

$$\frac{mv^2}{r} = \frac{GMm}{r^2}, \quad v^2 = \frac{GM}{r}, \quad v = \sqrt{\frac{GM}{r}}$$

58. $v = \sqrt{\dfrac{9.56 \times 10^4}{4200}} \approx 4.77$ mi/sec

60. Let x = distance from the satellite to the center of the earth ($x = r + 4000$). Then:

$$v = \frac{2\pi x}{t} = \frac{2\pi x}{24(3600)} = \sqrt{\frac{9.56 \times 10^4}{x}}$$

$$\frac{4\pi^2 x^2}{(24)^2(3600)^2} = \frac{9.56 \times 10^4}{x}$$

$$x^3 = \frac{(9.56 \times 10^4)(24)^2(3600)^2}{4\pi^2} \implies x \approx 26{,}245 \text{ mi}$$

$$v \approx \frac{2\pi(26{,}245)}{24(3600)} \approx 1.92 \text{ mi/sec} \approx 6871 \text{ mph}$$

62. $\mathbf{r}(t) = x(t)\mathbf{i} + y(t)\mathbf{j}$

$y(t) = m(x(t)) + b$, m and b are constants.

$\mathbf{r}(t) = x(t)\mathbf{i} + [m(x(t)) + b]\mathbf{j}$

$\mathbf{v}(t) = x'(t)\mathbf{i} + mx'(t)\mathbf{j}$

$\|\mathbf{v}(t)\| = \sqrt{[x'(t)]^2 + [mx'(t)]^2} = |x'(t)|\sqrt{1 + m^2}$

$T(t) = \dfrac{\mathbf{v}(t)}{\|\mathbf{v}(t)\|} = \dfrac{\pm(\mathbf{i} + m\mathbf{j})}{\sqrt{1 + m^2}}$, constant

Hence, $T'(t) = \mathbf{0}$.

64. $\|\mathbf{a}\|^2 = \mathbf{a} \cdot \mathbf{a}$

$= (a_T T + a_N N) \cdot (a_T T + a_N N)$

$= a_T^2\|T\|^2 + 2a_T a_N T \cdot N + a_N^2\|N\|^2$

$= a_T^2 + a_N^2$

$a_N^2 = \|\mathbf{a}\|^2 - a_T^2$

Since $a_N > 0$, we have $a_N = \sqrt{\|\mathbf{a}\|^2 - a_T^2}$.

Section 11.5   Arc Length and Curvature

2. $\mathbf{r}(t) = t\mathbf{i} + t^2\mathbf{k}$

$$\frac{dx}{dt} = 1, \; \frac{dy}{dt} = 0, \; \frac{dz}{dt} = 2t$$

$$s = \int_0^4 \sqrt{1 + 4t^2} \, dt$$

$$= \frac{1}{4}\left[2t\sqrt{1 + 4t^2} + \ln|2t + \sqrt{1 + 4t}| \right]_0^4$$

$$= \frac{1}{4}\left[8\sqrt{65} + \ln\left(8 + \sqrt{65} \right) \right] \approx 16.819$$

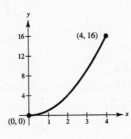

4. $\mathbf{r}(t) = a\cos t\mathbf{i} + a\sin t\mathbf{j}$

$$\frac{dx}{dt} = -a\sin t, \; \frac{dy}{dt} = a\cos t$$

$$s = \int_0^{2\pi} \sqrt{a^2 \sin^2 t + a^2 \cos^2 t} \, dt$$

$$= \int_0^{2\pi} a \, dt = \left[at \right]_0^{2\pi} = 2\pi a$$

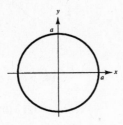

6. (a) $\mathbf{r}(t) = (v_0 \cos\theta)t\mathbf{i} + \left[(v_0 \sin\theta)t - \frac{1}{2}gt^2 \right]\mathbf{j}$

$$y(t) = (v_0 \sin\theta)t - \frac{1}{2}gt^2$$

$$y'(t) = v_0 \sin\theta - gt = 0 \text{ when } t = \frac{v_0 \sin\theta}{g}.$$

Maximum height when $\sin\theta = 1$, or $\theta = \frac{\pi}{2}$.

(b) $y(t) = (v_0 \sin\theta)t - \frac{1}{2}gt^2 = 0 \Rightarrow t = \frac{2v_0 \sin\theta}{g}$

Range: $x(t) = (v_0 \cos\theta)\left(\dfrac{2v_0 \sin\theta}{g} \right) = \dfrac{v_0^2}{g}\sin^2\theta$

The range $x(t)$ is a maximum for $\sin 2\theta = 1$, or $\theta = \dfrac{\pi}{4}$.

(c) $x'(t) = v_0 \cos\theta$

$$y'(t) = v_0 \sin\theta - gt$$

$$x'(t)^2 + y'(t)^2 = v_0^2 \cos^2\theta + (v_0 \sin\theta - gt)^2$$

$$= v_0^2 \cos^2\theta + v_0^2 \sin^2\theta - 2v_0^2 g \sin\theta t + g^2 t^2$$

$$= v_0^2 - 2v_0 g \sin\theta t + g^2 t^2$$

$$s(\theta) = \int_0^{2v_0 \sin\theta / g} \left[v_0^2 - 2v_0 g \sin\theta t + g^2 t^2 \right]^{1/2} dt$$

Since $v_0 = 96$ ft/sec, we have

$$s(\theta) = \int_0^{6\sin\theta} \left[96^2 - (6144 \sin\theta)t + 1024t^2 \right]^{1/2} dt.$$

Using a computer algebra system, $s(\theta)$ is a maximum for $\theta \approx 0.9855 \approx 56.5°$.

8. $\mathbf{r}(t) = \langle 3t, 2\cos t, 2\sin t \rangle$

$$\frac{dx}{dt} = 3, \frac{dy}{dt} = -2\sin t, \frac{dz}{dt} = 2\cos t$$

$$s = \int_0^{\pi/2} \sqrt{3^2 + (-2\sin t)^2 + (2\cos t)^2}\, dt$$

$$= \int_0^{\pi/2} \sqrt{13}\, dt = \sqrt{13}\, t\Big]_0^{\pi/2} = \frac{\sqrt{13}\pi}{2}$$

12. $\mathbf{r}(t) = \sin \pi t\mathbf{i} + \cos \pi t\mathbf{j} + t^3\mathbf{k}$

$$\frac{dx}{dt} = \pi\cos \pi t, \frac{dy}{dt} = -\pi\sin \pi t, \frac{dz}{dt} = 3t^2$$

$$s = \int_0^2 \sqrt{(\pi\cos \pi t)^2 + (-\pi\sin \pi t)^2 + (3t^2)^2}\, dt$$

$$= \int_0^2 \sqrt{\pi^2 + 9t^4}\, dt \approx 11.15$$

10. $\mathbf{r}(t) = \langle \cos t + t\sin t, \sin t - t\cos t, t^2 \rangle$

$$\frac{dx}{dt} = t\cos t, \frac{dy}{dt} = t\sin t, \frac{dz}{dt} = 2t$$

$$s = \int_0^{\pi/2} \sqrt{(t\cos t)^2 + (t\sin t)^2 + (2t)^2}\, dt$$

$$= \int_0^{\pi/2} \sqrt{5t^2}\, dt = \sqrt{5}\frac{t^2}{2}\Big]_0^{\pi/2} = \frac{\sqrt{5}\pi^2}{8}$$

14. $\mathbf{r}(t) = 6\cos\left(\frac{\pi t}{4}\right)\mathbf{i} + 2\sin\left(\frac{\pi t}{4}\right)\mathbf{j} + t\mathbf{k},\ 0 \le t \le 2$

(a) $\mathbf{r}(0) = 6\mathbf{i} = \langle 6, 0, 0 \rangle$

$\mathbf{r}(2) = 2\mathbf{j} + 2\mathbf{k} = \langle 0, 2, 2 \rangle$

distance $= \sqrt{6^2 + 2^2 + 2^2} = \sqrt{44} = 2\sqrt{11} \approx 6.633$

(b) $\mathbf{r}(0) = \langle 6, 0, 0 \rangle$

$\mathbf{r}(0.5) = \langle 5.543, 0.765, 0.5 \rangle$

$\mathbf{r}(1.0) = \langle 4.243, 1.414, 1.0 \rangle$

$\mathbf{r}(1.5) = \langle 2.296, 1.848, 1.5 \rangle$

$\mathbf{r}(2.0) = \langle 0, 2, 2 \rangle$

(c) Increase the number of line segments.

(d) Using a graphing utility, you obtain

$$s = \int_0^2 \|\mathbf{r}'(t)\|\, dt \approx 7.0105.$$

16. $\mathbf{r}(t) = \left\langle 4(\sin t - t\cos t), 4(\cos t + t\sin t), \frac{3}{2}t^2 \right\rangle$

(a) $s = \int_0^t \sqrt{[x'(u)]^2 + [y'(u)]^2 + [z'(u)]^2}\, du$

$$= \int_0^t \sqrt{(4u\sin u)^2 + (4u\cos u)^2 + (3u)^2}\, du = \int_0^t \sqrt{16u + 9u^2}\, du = \int_0^t 5u\, du = \frac{5}{2}t^2$$

—CONTINUED—

16. —CONTINUED—

(b) $t = \sqrt{\dfrac{2s}{5}}$

$$x = 4\left(\sin\sqrt{\dfrac{2s}{5}} - \sqrt{\dfrac{2s}{5}}\cos\sqrt{\dfrac{2s}{5}}\right)$$

$$y = 4\left(\cos\sqrt{\dfrac{2s}{5}} + \sqrt{\dfrac{2s}{5}}\sin\sqrt{\dfrac{2s}{5}}\right)$$

$$z = \dfrac{3}{2}\left(\sqrt{\dfrac{2s}{5}}\right)^2 = \dfrac{3s}{5}$$

$$\mathbf{r}(s) = 4\left(\sin\sqrt{\dfrac{2s}{5}} - \sqrt{\dfrac{2s}{5}}\cos\sqrt{\dfrac{2s}{5}}\right)\mathbf{i} + 4\left(\cos\sqrt{\dfrac{2s}{5}} + \sqrt{\dfrac{2s}{5}}\sin\sqrt{\dfrac{2s}{5}}\right)\mathbf{j} + \dfrac{3s}{5}\mathbf{k}$$

(c) When $s = \sqrt{5}$:

$$x = 4\left(\sin\sqrt{\dfrac{2\sqrt{5}}{5}} - \sqrt{\dfrac{2\sqrt{5}}{5}}\cos\sqrt{\dfrac{2\sqrt{5}}{5}}\right) \approx -6.956$$

$$y = 4\left(\cos\sqrt{\dfrac{2\sqrt{5}}{5}} + \sqrt{\dfrac{2\sqrt{5}}{5}}\sin\sqrt{\dfrac{2\sqrt{5}}{5}}\right) \approx 14.169$$

$$z = \dfrac{3\sqrt{5}}{5} \approx 1.342$$

$(-6.956,\ 14.169,\ 1.342)$

When $s = 4$:

$$x = 4\left(\sin\sqrt{\dfrac{8}{5}} - \sqrt{\dfrac{8}{5}}\cos\sqrt{\dfrac{8}{5}}\right) \approx 2.291$$

$$y = 4\left(\cos\sqrt{\dfrac{8}{5}} + \sqrt{\dfrac{8}{5}}\sin\sqrt{\dfrac{8}{5}}\right) \approx 6.029$$

$$z = \dfrac{12}{5} = 2.4$$

$(2.291,\ 6.029,\ 2.400)$

(d) $\|\mathbf{r}'(s)\| = \sqrt{\left(\dfrac{4}{5}\sin\sqrt{\dfrac{2s}{5}}\right)^2 + \left(\dfrac{4}{5}\cos\sqrt{\dfrac{2s}{5}}\right)^2 + \left(\dfrac{3}{5}\right)^2} = \sqrt{\dfrac{16}{25} + \dfrac{9}{25}} = 1$

18. $\mathbf{r}(s) = (3 + s)\mathbf{i} + \mathbf{j}$

$\mathbf{r}'(s) = \mathbf{i}$ and $\|\mathbf{r}'(s)\| = 1$

$\mathbf{T}(s) = \mathbf{r}'(s)$

$\mathbf{T}'(s) = \mathbf{0} \implies K = \|\mathbf{T}'(s)\| = 0$ (The curve is a line.)

20. $\mathbf{r}(s) = 4\left(\sin\sqrt{\dfrac{2s}{5}} - \sqrt{\dfrac{2s}{5}}\cos\sqrt{\dfrac{2s}{5}}\right)\mathbf{i} + 4\left(\cos\sqrt{\dfrac{2s}{5}} + \sqrt{\dfrac{2s}{5}}\sin\sqrt{\dfrac{2s}{5}}\right)\mathbf{j} + \dfrac{3s}{5}\mathbf{k}$

$\mathbf{T}(s) = \mathbf{r}'(s) = \dfrac{4}{5}\sin\sqrt{\dfrac{2s}{5}}\mathbf{i} + \dfrac{4}{5}\cos\sqrt{\dfrac{2s}{5}}\mathbf{j} + \dfrac{3}{5}\mathbf{k}$

$\mathbf{T}'(s) = \dfrac{4}{25}\sqrt{\dfrac{5}{2s}}\cos\sqrt{\dfrac{2s}{5}}\mathbf{i} - \dfrac{4}{25}\sqrt{\dfrac{5}{2s}}\sin\sqrt{\dfrac{2s}{5}}\mathbf{j}$

$K = \|\mathbf{T}'(s)\| = \dfrac{4}{25}\sqrt{\dfrac{5}{2s}} = \dfrac{2\sqrt{10s}}{25s}$

22. $\mathbf{r}(t) = t^2\mathbf{j} + \mathbf{k}$

$\mathbf{v}(t) = 2t\mathbf{j}$

$\mathbf{T}(t) = \mathbf{j}$

$\mathbf{T}'(t) = 0$

$K = \dfrac{\|\mathbf{T}'(t)\|}{\|\mathbf{r}'(t)\|} = 0$

24. $\mathbf{r}(t) = t\mathbf{i} + t^2\mathbf{j}$

$\mathbf{v}(t) = \mathbf{i} + 2t\mathbf{j}$

$\mathbf{v}(1) = \mathbf{i} + 2\mathbf{j}$

$\mathbf{a}(t) = 2\mathbf{j}$

$\mathbf{a}(1) = 2\mathbf{j}$

$\mathbf{T}(t) = \dfrac{\mathbf{i} + 2t\mathbf{j}}{\sqrt{1 + 4t^2}}$

$\mathbf{N}(t) = \dfrac{1}{\sqrt{1 + 4t^2}}(-2t\mathbf{i} + \mathbf{j})$

$\mathbf{N}(1) = \dfrac{1}{\sqrt{5}}(-2\mathbf{i} + \mathbf{j})$

$K = \dfrac{\mathbf{a} \cdot \mathbf{N}}{\|\mathbf{v}\|^2} = \dfrac{2}{5\sqrt{5}}$

26. $\mathbf{r}(t) = 2\cos \pi t\mathbf{i} + \sin \pi t\mathbf{j}$

$\mathbf{r}\,'(t) = -2\pi \sin \pi t\mathbf{i} + \pi \cos \pi t\mathbf{j}$

$\|\mathbf{r}\,'(t)\| = \pi\sqrt{4\sin^2 \pi t + \cos^2 \pi t}$

$\mathbf{T}(t) = \dfrac{-2\sin \pi t\mathbf{i} + \cos \pi t\mathbf{j}}{\sqrt{4\sin^2 \pi t + \cos^2 \pi t}}$

$\mathbf{T}\,'(t) = \dfrac{-2\pi \cos \pi t\mathbf{i} - 4\pi \sin \pi t\mathbf{j}}{(4\sin^2 \pi t + \cos^2 \pi t)^{3/2}}$

$K = \dfrac{\|\mathbf{T}\,'(t)\|}{\|\mathbf{r}\,'(t)\|} = \dfrac{\dfrac{2\pi}{4\sin^2 \pi t + \cos^2 \pi t}}{\pi\sqrt{4\sin^2 \pi t + \cos^2 \pi t}}$

$= \dfrac{2}{(4\sin^2 \pi t + \cos^2 \pi t)^{3/2}}$

28. $\mathbf{r}(t) = a\cos(\omega t)\mathbf{i} + b\sin(\omega t)\mathbf{j}$

$\mathbf{r}\,'(t) = -a\omega \sin(\omega t)\mathbf{i} + b\omega \cos(\omega t)\mathbf{j}$

$\mathbf{T}(t) = \dfrac{-a\sin(\omega t)\mathbf{i} + b\cos(\omega t)\mathbf{j}}{\sqrt{a^2\sin^2(\omega t) + b^2\cos^2(\omega t)}}$

$\mathbf{T}\,'(t) = \dfrac{-ab^2\omega \cos(\omega t)\mathbf{i} - a^2b\omega \sin(\omega t)\mathbf{j}}{[a^2\sin^2(\omega t) + b^2\cos^2(\omega t)]^{3/2}}$

$K = \dfrac{\|\mathbf{T}\,'(t)\|}{\|\mathbf{r}\,'(t)\|} = \dfrac{\dfrac{ab\omega}{a^2\sin^2(\omega t) + b^2\cos^2(\omega t)}}{\omega\sqrt{a^2\sin^2(\omega t) + b^2\cos^2(\omega t)}}$

$= \dfrac{ab}{[a^2\sin^2(\omega t) + b^2\cos^2(\omega t)]^{3/2}}$

30. $\mathbf{r}(t) = \langle a(\omega t - \sin \omega t),\ a(1 - \cos \omega t)\rangle$

From Exercise 22, Section 11.4, we have:

$\mathbf{a} \cdot \mathbf{N} = \dfrac{a\omega^2}{\sqrt{2}} \cdot \sqrt{1 - \cos \omega t}$

$K = \dfrac{\mathbf{a}(t) \cdot \mathbf{N}(t)}{\|\mathbf{v}(t)\|^2}$

$= \dfrac{\left(\dfrac{a\omega^2}{\sqrt{2}}\right)\sqrt{1 - \cos \omega t}}{2a^2\omega^2(1 - \cos \omega t)} = \dfrac{\sqrt{2}}{4a\sqrt{1 - \cos \omega t}}$

32. $\mathbf{r}(t) = 4t\mathbf{i} - 4t\mathbf{j} + 2t\mathbf{k}$

$\mathbf{r}\,'(t) = 4\mathbf{i} - 4\mathbf{j} + 2\mathbf{k}$

$\mathbf{T}(t) = \dfrac{1}{3}(2\mathbf{i} - 2\mathbf{j} + \mathbf{k})$

$\mathbf{T}\,'(t) = \mathbf{0}$

$K = \dfrac{\|\mathbf{T}\,'(t)\|}{\|\mathbf{r}\,'(t)\|} = 0$

34. $\mathbf{r}(t) = 2t^2\mathbf{i} + t\mathbf{j} + \dfrac{1}{2}t^2\mathbf{k}$

$\mathbf{r}\,'(t) = 4t\mathbf{i} + \mathbf{j} + t\mathbf{k}$

$\mathbf{T}(t) = \dfrac{4t\mathbf{i} + \mathbf{j} + t\mathbf{k}}{\sqrt{1 + 17t^2}}$

$\mathbf{T}\,'(t) = \dfrac{4\mathbf{i} - 17t\mathbf{j} + \mathbf{k}}{(1 + 17t^2)^{3/2}}$

$K = \dfrac{\|\mathbf{T}\,'(t)\|}{\|\mathbf{r}\,'(t)\|} = \dfrac{\sqrt{289t^2 + 17}}{(1 + 17t^2)^{3/2}} / (1 + 17t^2)^{1/2}$

$= \dfrac{\sqrt{17}}{(1 + 17t^2)^{3/2}}$

36. $\mathbf{r}(t) = e^t\cos t\mathbf{i} + e^t\sin t\mathbf{j} + e^t\mathbf{k}$

$\mathbf{r}\,'(t) = (-e^t\sin t + e^t\cos t)\mathbf{i} + (e^t\cos t + e^t\sin t)\mathbf{j} + e^t\mathbf{k}$

$\mathbf{T}(t) = \dfrac{1}{\sqrt{3}}[(-\sin t + \cos t)\mathbf{i} + (\cos t + \sin t)\mathbf{j} + \mathbf{k}]$

$\mathbf{T}\,'(t) = \dfrac{1}{\sqrt{3}}[(-\cos t - \sin t)\mathbf{i} + (-\sin t + \cos t)\mathbf{j}]$

$K = \dfrac{\|\mathbf{T}\,'(t)\|}{\|\mathbf{r}\,'(t)\|} = \dfrac{(1/\sqrt{3})\sqrt{(-\cos t - \sin t)^2 + (-\sin t + \cos t)^2}}{\sqrt{3}e^t} = \dfrac{\sqrt{2}}{3e^t}$

38. $y = mx + b$

Since $y'' = 0$, $K = 0$, and the radius of curvature is undefined.

40. $y = 2x + \dfrac{4}{x}$, $x = 1$

$y' = 2 - \dfrac{4}{x^2}$, $y'(1) = -2$

$y'' = \dfrac{8}{x^3}$, $y''(1) = 8$

$K = \dfrac{|y''|}{[1 + (y')^2]^{3/2}} = \dfrac{8}{(1 + 4)^{3/2}} = \dfrac{8}{5^{3/2}}$

$\dfrac{1}{K} = \dfrac{5^{3/2}}{8}$ (radius of curvature)

42. $y = \dfrac{3}{4}\sqrt{16 - x^2}$

$y' = \dfrac{-9x}{16y}$

$y'' = \dfrac{-[9 + (16y')^2]}{16y}$

At $x = 0$: $y' = 0$

$y'' = -\dfrac{3}{16}$

$K = \left|\dfrac{-3/16}{(1 + 0^2)^{3/2}}\right| = \dfrac{3}{16}$

$\dfrac{1}{K} = \dfrac{16}{3}$ (radius of curvature)

44. (a) $y = \dfrac{4x^2}{x^2 + 3}$

$y' = \dfrac{24x}{(x^2 + 3)^2}$

$y'' = \dfrac{72(1 - x^2)}{(x^2 + 3)^3}$

At $x = 0$: $y' = 0$

$y'' = \dfrac{72}{27} = \dfrac{8}{3}$

$K = \dfrac{8/3}{(1 + 0^2)^{3/2}} = \dfrac{8}{3}$

$r = \dfrac{1}{K} = \dfrac{3}{8}$

Center: $\left(0, \dfrac{3}{8}\right)$

Equation: $x^2 + \left(y - \dfrac{3}{8}\right)^2 = \dfrac{9}{64}$

(b) The circles have different radii since the curvature is different and

$r = \dfrac{1}{K}$.

46. $y = \ln x$, $x = 1$

$y' = \dfrac{1}{x}$, $y'' = -\dfrac{1}{x^2}$

$y'(1) = 1$, $y''(1) = -1$

$K = \dfrac{|-1|}{(1 + (1)^2)^{3/2}} = \dfrac{1}{2^{3/2}}$, $r = \dfrac{1}{K} = 2^{3/2} = 2\sqrt{2}$

The slope of the tangent line at $(1, 0)$ is $y'(1) = 1$.

The slope of the normal line is -1.

Equation of normal line: $y = -(x - 1) = -x + 1$

The center of the circle is on the normal line $2\sqrt{2}$ units away from the point $(1, 0)$.

$\sqrt{(1 - x)^2 + (0 - y)^2} = 2\sqrt{2}$

$(1 - x)^2 + (x - 1)^2 = 8$

$2x^2 - 4x + 2 = 8$

$2(x^2 - 2x - 3) = 0$

$2(x - 3)(x + 1) = 0$

$x = 3$ or $x = -1$

Since the circle is below the curve, $x = 3$ and $y = -2$.

Center of circle: $(3, -2)$

Equation of circle: $(x - 3)^2 + (y + 2)^2 = 8$

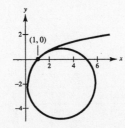

48. $y = \frac{1}{3}x^3$, $x = 1$

$y' = x^2$, $y''(1) = 2x$

$y'(1) = 1$, $y''(1) = 2$

$$K = \frac{2}{(1+1)^{3/2}} = \frac{1}{\sqrt{2}}, \; r = \frac{1}{K} = \sqrt{2}$$

The slope of the tangent line at $\left(1, \frac{1}{3}\right)$ is $y'(1) = 1$.

The slope of the normal line is -1.

Equation of normal line: $y - \frac{1}{3} = -(x-1)$ or $y = -x + \frac{4}{3}$

The center of the circle is on the normal line $\sqrt{2}$ units away from the point $\left(1, \frac{1}{3}\right)$.

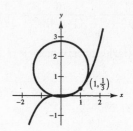

$$\sqrt{(1-x)^2 + \left(\frac{1}{3} - y\right)^2} = \sqrt{2}$$

$$(1-x)^2 + (x-1)^2 = 2$$

$$(x-1)^2 = 1$$

$$x = 0 \text{ or } x = 2$$

Since the circle is above the curve, $x = 0$ and $y = \frac{4}{3}$.

Center of circle: $\left(0, \frac{4}{3}\right)$

Equation of circle: $x^2 + \left(y - \frac{4}{3}\right)^2 = 2$

50.

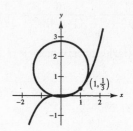

52. $y = x^3$, $y' = 3x^2$, $y'' = 6x$

$$K = \left| \frac{6x}{(1 + 9x^4)^{3/2}} \right|$$

(a) K is maximum at $\left(\frac{1}{\sqrt[4]{45}}, \frac{1}{\sqrt[4]{45^3}} \right)$, $\left(\frac{-1}{\sqrt[4]{45}}, \frac{-1}{\sqrt[4]{45^3}} \right)$.

(b) $\displaystyle\lim_{x \to \infty} K = 0$

54. $y = \ln x$, $y' = \frac{1}{x}$, $y'' = -\frac{1}{x^2}$

$$K = \left| \frac{-1/x^2}{[1 + (1/x)^2]^{3/2}} \right| = \frac{x}{(x^2 + 1)^{3/2}}$$

$$\frac{dK}{dx} = \frac{-2x^2 + 1}{(x^2 + 1)^{5/2}}$$

(a) K has a maximum when $x = \frac{1}{\sqrt{2}}$.

(b) $\displaystyle\lim_{x \to \infty} K = 0$

56. $y = \cos x$

$y' = -\sin x$

$y'' = -\cos x$

$$K = \frac{|y''|}{[1 + (y')^2]^{3/2}} = \frac{|-\cos x|}{(1 + \sin^2 x)^{3/2}} = 0 \text{ for } x = \frac{\pi}{2} + K\pi.$$

Curvature is 0 at $\left(\frac{\pi}{2} + K\pi, 0 \right)$.

58. $y = \cosh x = \frac{e^x + e^{-x}}{2}$

$$y' = \frac{e^x - e^{-x}}{2} = \sinh x$$

$$y'' = \frac{e^x + e^{-x}}{2} = \cosh x$$

$$K = \frac{|\cosh x|}{[1 + (\sinh x)^2]^{3/2}} = \frac{\cosh x}{(\cosh^2 x)^{3/2}} = \frac{1}{\cosh^2 x} = \frac{1}{y^2}$$

60. See page 828.

62. $K = \dfrac{|y''|}{[1 + (y')^2]^{3/2}}$

At the smooth relative extremum $y' = 0$, so $K = |y''|$. Yes, for example, $y = x^4$ has a curvature of 0 at its relative minimum $(0, 0)$. The curvature is positive for any other point of the curvature.

64. $y_1 = ax(b - x)$, $y_2 = \dfrac{x}{x + 2}$

We observe that $(0, 0)$ is a solution point to both equations. Therefore, the point P is the origin.

$$y_1 = ax(b - x), \quad y_1' = a(b - 2x), \quad y_1'' = -2a$$

$$y_2 = \frac{x}{x + 2}, \quad y_2' = \frac{2}{(x + 2)^2}, \quad y_2'' = \frac{-4}{(x + 2)^3}$$

At P,

$$y_1'(0) = ab \text{ and } y_2'(0) = \frac{2}{(0 + 2)^2} = \frac{1}{2}.$$

Since the curves have a common tangent at P, $y_1'(0) = y_2'(0)$ or $ab = \frac{1}{2}$. Therefore, $y_1'(0) = \frac{1}{2}$. Since the curves have the same curvature at P, $K_1(0) = K_2(0)$.

$$K_1(0) = \left| \frac{y_1''(0)}{[1 + (y_1(0))^2]^{3/2}} \right| = \left| \frac{-2a}{[1 + (1/2)^2]^{3/2}} \right|$$

$$K_2(0) = \left| \frac{y_2''(0)}{[1 + (y_2(0))^2]^{3/2}} \right| = \left| \frac{-1/2}{[1 + (1/2)^2]^{3/2}} \right|$$

Therefore, $2a = \pm\frac{1}{2}$ or $a = \pm\frac{1}{4}$. In order that the curves intersect at only one point, the parabola must be concave downward. Thus,

$$a = \frac{1}{4} \quad \text{and} \quad b = \frac{1}{2a} = 2.$$

$$y_1 = \frac{1}{4}x(2 - x) \quad \text{and} \quad y_2 = \frac{x}{x + 2}$$

66. $y = \dfrac{1}{4}x^{8/5}$, $0 \le x \le 5$

(a)

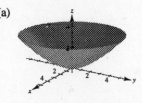

(rotated about y-axis)

(b) $V = \displaystyle\int_0^5 2\pi x \left(\frac{1}{4}x^{8/5}\right) dx$ (shells)

$$= \frac{\pi}{2}\int_0^5 x^{13/5}\, dx = \frac{\pi}{2}\left[\frac{x^{18/5}}{18/5}\right]_0^5$$

$$= \frac{5\pi}{36}5^{18/5} \approx 143.25 \text{ cm}^3$$

(c) $y' = \dfrac{2}{5}x^{3/5}$, $y'' = \dfrac{6}{25}x^{-2/5} = \dfrac{6}{25x^{2/5}}$

$$K = \frac{\dfrac{6}{25x^{2/5}}}{\left[1 + \dfrac{4}{25}x^{6/5}\right]^{3/2}} = \frac{6}{25x^{2/5}\left[1 + \dfrac{4}{25}x^{6/5}\right]^{3/2}}$$

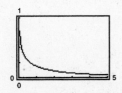

(d) No, the curvature approaches ∞ as $x \to 0^+$. Hence, any spherical object will hit the sides of the goblet before touching the bottom $(0, 0)$.

68. $s = \dfrac{c}{\sqrt{K}}$

$y = \dfrac{1}{3}x^3$

$y' = x^2$

$y'' = 2x$

$K = \left| \dfrac{2x}{(1 + x^4)^{3/2}} \right|$

When $x = 1$: $K = \dfrac{1}{\sqrt{2}}$

$$s = \dfrac{c}{\sqrt{1/\sqrt{2}}} = \sqrt[4]{2}\,c$$

$$30 = \sqrt[4]{2}\,c \implies c = \dfrac{30}{\sqrt[4]{2}}$$

At $x = \dfrac{3}{2}$, $K = \dfrac{3}{[1 + (81/16)]^{3/2}} \approx 0.201$

$$s = \left(\dfrac{3}{2} \right) = \dfrac{c}{\sqrt{K}} = \dfrac{30/\sqrt[4]{2}}{\sqrt{K}} \approx 56.27 \text{ mi/hr.}$$

70. $r(\theta) = r \cos \theta \mathbf{i} + r \sin \theta \mathbf{j} = f(\theta) \cos \theta \mathbf{i} + f(\theta) \sin \theta \mathbf{j}$

$x(\theta) = f(\theta) \cos \theta$

$y(\theta) = f(\theta) \sin \theta$

$x'(\theta) = -f(\theta) \sin \theta + f'(\theta) \cos \theta$

$y'(\theta) = f(\theta) \cos \theta + f'(\theta) \sin \theta$

$x''(\theta) = -f(\theta) \cos \theta - f'(\theta) \sin \theta - f'(\theta) \sin \theta + f''(\theta) \cos \theta = -f(\theta) \cos \theta - 2 f'(\theta) \sin \theta + f''(\theta) \cos \theta$

$y''(\theta) = -f(\theta) \sin \theta + f'(\theta) \cos \theta + f'(\theta) \cos \theta + f''(\theta) \sin \theta = -f(\theta) \sin \theta + 2 f'(\theta) \cos \theta + f''(\theta) \sin \theta$

$$K = \dfrac{|x'y'' - y'x''|}{[(x')^2 + (y')^2]^{3/2}} = \dfrac{|f^2(\theta) - f(\theta)f''(\theta) + 2(f'(\theta))^2|}{[f^2(\theta) + (f'(\theta))^2]^{3/2}} = \dfrac{|r^2 - rr'' + 2(r')^2|}{[r^2 + (r')^2]^{3/2}}$$

72. $r = \theta$

$r' = 1$

$r'' = 0$

$K = \dfrac{|2(r')^2 - rr'' + r^2|}{[(r')^2 + r^2]^{3/2}} = \dfrac{2 + \theta^2}{(1 + \theta^2)^{3/2}}$

74. $r = e^\theta$

$r' = e^\theta$

$r'' = e^\theta$

$K = \dfrac{|2(r')^2 - rr'' + r^2|}{[(r')^2 + r^2]^{3/2}} = \dfrac{2e^{2\theta}}{(2e^{2\theta})^{3/2}} = \dfrac{1}{\sqrt{2}\,e^\theta}$

76. At the pole, $r = 0$.

$$K = \dfrac{|2(r')^2 - rr'' + r^2|}{[(r')^2 + r^2]^{3/2}}$$

$$= \dfrac{|2(r')^2|}{|r'|^3} = \dfrac{2}{|r'|}$$

78. $r = 6 \cos 3\theta$

$r' = -18 \sin 3\theta$

At the pole,

$$\theta = \dfrac{\pi}{6}, \ r'\left(\dfrac{\pi}{6} \right) = -18,$$

and

$$K = \dfrac{2}{|r'(\pi/6)|} = \dfrac{2}{|-18|} = \dfrac{1}{9}.$$

80. $x(t) = t^3$, $x'(t) = 3t^2$, $x''(t) = 6t$

$y(t) = \dfrac{1}{2}t^2$, $y'(t) = t$, $y''(t) = 1$

$K = \dfrac{|(3t^2)(1) - (t)(6t)|}{[(3t^2)^2 + (t)^2]^{3/2}}$

$= \dfrac{3t^2}{|t^3|(9t^2 + 1)^{3/2}} = \dfrac{3}{|t|(9t^2 + 1)^{3/2}}$

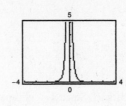

$K \to 0$ as $t \to \pm\infty$

82. (a) $\mathbf{r}(t) = 3t^2\mathbf{i} + (3t - t^3)\mathbf{j}$

$\mathbf{v}(t) = 6t\mathbf{i} + (3 - 3t^2)\mathbf{j}$

$\dfrac{ds}{dt} = \|\mathbf{v}(t)\| = 3(1 + t^2)$, $\dfrac{d^2s}{dt^2} = 6t$

$K = \dfrac{2}{3(1 + t^2)^2}$

$a_\mathbf{T} = \dfrac{d^2s}{dt^2} = 6t$

$a_\mathbf{N} = K\left(\dfrac{ds}{dt}\right)^2 = \dfrac{2}{3(1 + t^2)^2} \cdot 9(1 + t^2)^2 = 6$

(b) $\mathbf{r}(t) = t\mathbf{i} + t^2\mathbf{j} + \dfrac{1}{2}t^2\mathbf{k}$

$\mathbf{v}(t) = \mathbf{i} + 2t\mathbf{j} + t\mathbf{k}$

$\dfrac{ds}{dt} = \|\mathbf{v}(t)\| = \sqrt{5t^2 + 1}$

$\dfrac{d^2s}{dt^2} = \dfrac{5t}{\sqrt{5t^2 + 1}}$

$\mathbf{a}(t) = 2\mathbf{j} + \mathbf{k}$

$\mathbf{r}'(t) \times \mathbf{r}''(t) = \mathbf{v}(t) \times \mathbf{a}(t) = \begin{vmatrix} \mathbf{i} & \mathbf{j} & \mathbf{k} \\ 1 & 2t & t \\ 0 & 2 & 1 \end{vmatrix} = -\mathbf{j} + 2\mathbf{k}$

$K = \dfrac{\|\mathbf{r}'(t) \times \mathbf{r}''(t)\|}{\|\mathbf{r}'(t)\|^3} = \dfrac{\sqrt{5}}{(5t^2 + 1)^{3/2}}$

$a_\mathbf{T} = \dfrac{d^2s}{dt^2} = \dfrac{5t}{\sqrt{5t^2 + 1}}$

$a_\mathbf{N} = K\left(\dfrac{ds}{dt}\right)^2 = \dfrac{\sqrt{5}}{(5t^2 + 1)^{3/2}}(5t^2 + 1) = \dfrac{\sqrt{5}}{\sqrt{5t^2 + 1}}$

84. (a) $K = \|\mathbf{T}'(s)\| = \left\|\dfrac{d\mathbf{T}}{ds}\right\| = \left\|\dfrac{d\mathbf{T}}{dt} \cdot \dfrac{dt}{ds}\right\|$, by the Chain Rule

$= \left\|\dfrac{d\mathbf{T}/dt}{ds/dt}\right\| = \dfrac{\|\mathbf{T}'(t)\|}{\|\mathbf{v}(t)\|} = \dfrac{\|\mathbf{T}'(t)\|}{\|\mathbf{r}'(t)\|}$

(b) $\mathbf{T}(t) = \dfrac{\mathbf{r}'(t)}{\|\mathbf{r}'(t)\|} = \dfrac{\mathbf{r}'(t)}{ds/dt}$

$\mathbf{r}'(t) = \dfrac{ds}{dt}\mathbf{T}(t)$

$\mathbf{r}''(t) = \left(\dfrac{d^2s}{dt^2}\right)\mathbf{T}(t) + \dfrac{ds}{dt}\mathbf{T}'(t)$

$\mathbf{r}'(t) \times \mathbf{r}''(t) = \left(\dfrac{ds}{dt}\right)\left(\dfrac{d^2s}{dt^2}\right)[\mathbf{T}(t) \times \mathbf{T}(t)] + \left(\dfrac{ds}{dt}\right)^2[\mathbf{T}(t) \times \mathbf{T}'(t)]$

Since $\mathbf{T}(t) \times \mathbf{T}(t) = \mathbf{0}$ and $\dfrac{ds}{dt} = \|\mathbf{r}'(t)\|$, we have:

$\mathbf{r}'(t) \times \mathbf{r}''(t) = \|\mathbf{r}'(t)\|^2[\mathbf{T}(t) \times \mathbf{T}'(t)]$

$\|\mathbf{r}'(t) \times \mathbf{r}''(t)\| = \|\mathbf{r}'(t)\|^2\|\mathbf{T}(t) \times \mathbf{T}'(t)\| = \|\mathbf{r}'(t)\|^2\|\mathbf{T}(t)\|\,\|\mathbf{T}'(t)\| = \|\mathbf{r}'(t)\|^2(1)K\|\mathbf{r}'(t)\|$ from (a)

Therefore, $\dfrac{\|\mathbf{r}'(t) \times \mathbf{r}''(t)\|}{\|\mathbf{r}'(t)\|^3} = K$.

(c) $K = \dfrac{\|\mathbf{r}'(t) \times \mathbf{r}''(t)\|}{\|\mathbf{r}'(t)^3\|} = \dfrac{\dfrac{\|\mathbf{r}'(t) \times \mathbf{r}''(t)\|}{\|\mathbf{r}'(t)\|}}{\|\mathbf{r}'(t)\|^2} = \dfrac{\dfrac{\|\mathbf{v}(t) \times \mathbf{a}(t)\|}{\|\mathbf{v}(t)\|}}{\|\mathbf{r}'(t)\|^2} = \dfrac{\mathbf{a}(t) \cdot \mathbf{N}(t)}{\|\mathbf{r}'(t)\|^2}$

86. $\mathbf{F} = m\mathbf{a} \implies m\mathbf{a} = \dfrac{-GmM}{r^3}\mathbf{r}$

$$\mathbf{a} = -\dfrac{GM}{r^3}\mathbf{r}$$

Since $\mathbf{r}$ is a constant multiple of $\mathbf{a}$, they are parallel. Since $\mathbf{a} = \mathbf{r}''$ is parallel to $\mathbf{r}$, $\mathbf{r} \times \mathbf{r}'' = \mathbf{0}$. Also,

$$\left(\dfrac{d}{dt}\right)(\mathbf{r} \times \mathbf{r}') = \mathbf{r}' \times \mathbf{r}' + \mathbf{r} \times \mathbf{r}'' = \mathbf{0} + \mathbf{0} = \mathbf{0}.$$

Thus, $\mathbf{r} \times \mathbf{r}'$ is a constant vector which we will denote by $\mathbf{L}$.

88. $\dfrac{d}{dt}\left[\dfrac{\mathbf{r}'}{GM} \times \mathbf{L} - \dfrac{\mathbf{r}}{r}\right] = \dfrac{1}{GM}[\mathbf{r}' \times \mathbf{0} + \mathbf{r}'' \times \mathbf{L}] - \dfrac{1}{r^3}\{[\mathbf{r} \times \mathbf{r}'] \times \mathbf{r}\}$

$$= \dfrac{1}{GM}\left[\mathbf{0} + \left(\dfrac{-GM\mathbf{r}}{r^3}\right) \times [\mathbf{r} \times \mathbf{r}']\right] - \dfrac{1}{r^3}\{[\mathbf{r} \times \mathbf{r}'] \times \mathbf{r}\}$$

$$= -\dfrac{\mathbf{r}}{r^3} \times [\mathbf{r} \times \mathbf{r}'] - \dfrac{1}{r^3}\{[\mathbf{r} \times \mathbf{r}'] \times \mathbf{r}\}$$

$$= \dfrac{1}{r^3}\{[\mathbf{r} \times \mathbf{r}'] \times \mathbf{r} - [\mathbf{r} \times \mathbf{r}'] \times \mathbf{r}\} = \mathbf{0}$$

Thus, $\left(\dfrac{\mathbf{r}'}{GM}\right) \times \mathbf{L} - \left(\dfrac{\mathbf{r}}{r}\right)$ is a constant vector which we will denote by $\mathbf{e}$.

90. $\|\mathbf{L}\| = \|\mathbf{r} \times \mathbf{r}'\|$

Let: $\mathbf{r} = r(\cos\theta\mathbf{i} + \sin\theta\mathbf{j})$

$\mathbf{r}' = r(-\sin\theta\mathbf{i} + \cos\theta\mathbf{j})\dfrac{d\theta}{dt} \quad \left(\dfrac{d\mathbf{r}}{dt} = \dfrac{d\mathbf{r}}{d\theta} \cdot \dfrac{d\theta}{dt}\right)$

Then: $\mathbf{r} \times \mathbf{r}' = \begin{vmatrix} \mathbf{i} & \mathbf{j} & \mathbf{k} \\ r\cos\theta & r\sin\theta & 0 \\ -r\sin\theta\dfrac{d\theta}{dt} & r\cos\theta\dfrac{d\theta}{dt} & 0 \end{vmatrix}$

$$= r^2\dfrac{d\theta}{dt}\mathbf{k} \text{ and } \|\mathbf{L}\| = \|\mathbf{r} \times \mathbf{r}'\| = r^2\dfrac{d\theta}{dt}.$$

92. Let P denote the period. Then

$$A = \int_0^P \dfrac{dA}{dt}\,dt = \dfrac{1}{2}\|\mathbf{L}\|P.$$

Also, the area of an ellipse is πab where $2a$ and $2b$ are the lengths of the major and minor axes.

$$\pi ab = \dfrac{1}{2}\|\mathbf{L}\|P$$

$$P = \dfrac{2\pi ab}{\|\mathbf{L}\|}$$

$$P^2 = \dfrac{4\pi^2 a^2}{\|\mathbf{L}\|^2}(a^2 - c^2) = \dfrac{4\pi^2 a^2}{\|\mathbf{L}\|^2}a^2(1 - e^2)$$

$$= \dfrac{4\pi^2 a^4}{\|\mathbf{L}\|^2}\left(\dfrac{ed}{a}\right) = \dfrac{4\pi^2 ed}{\|\mathbf{L}\|^2}a^3$$

$$= \dfrac{4\pi^2(\|\mathbf{L}\|^2/GM)}{\|\mathbf{L}\|^2}a^3 = \dfrac{4\pi^2}{GM}a^3 = Ka^3$$

Review Exercises for Chapter 11

2. $\mathbf{r}(t) = \sqrt{t}\,\mathbf{i} + \dfrac{1}{t-4}\mathbf{j} + \mathbf{k}$

(a) Domain: $[0, 4)$ and $(4, \infty)$

(b) Continuous except at $t = 4$

4. $\mathbf{r}(t) = (2t + 1)\mathbf{i} + t^2\mathbf{j} + t\mathbf{k}$

(a) Domain: $(-\infty, \infty)$

(b) Continuous for all t

6. (a) $\mathbf{r}(0) = 3\mathbf{i} + \mathbf{j}$

(b) $\mathbf{r}\left(\dfrac{\pi}{2}\right) = -\dfrac{\pi}{2}\mathbf{k}$

(c) $\mathbf{r}(s - \pi) = 3\cos(s - \pi)\mathbf{i} + (1 - \sin(s - \pi))\mathbf{j} - (s - \pi)\mathbf{k}$

(d) $\mathbf{r}(\pi + \Delta t) - \mathbf{r}(\pi) = (3\cos(\pi + \Delta t)\mathbf{i} + (1 - \sin(\pi + \Delta t))\mathbf{j} - (\pi + \Delta t)\mathbf{k}) - (-3\mathbf{i} + \mathbf{j} - \pi\mathbf{k})$

$$= (-3\cos\Delta t + 3)\mathbf{i} + \sin\Delta t - \Delta t\mathbf{k}$$

8. $\mathbf{r}(t) = t\mathbf{i} + \dfrac{t}{t - 1}\mathbf{j}$

$x(t) = t,\ y(t) = \dfrac{t}{t - 1}$

$y = \dfrac{x}{x - 1}$

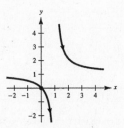

10. $\mathbf{r}(t) = 2t\mathbf{i} + t\mathbf{j} + t^2\mathbf{k}$

$x = 2t,\ y = t,\ z = t^2,$
$y = \frac{1}{2}x,\ z = y^2$

t	0	1	-1	2
x	0	2	-2	4
y	0	1	-1	2
z	0	1	1	4

12. $\mathbf{r}(t) = 2\cos t\mathbf{i} + t\mathbf{j} + 2\sin t\mathbf{k}$

$x = 2\cos t,\ y = t,\ z = 2\sin t$

$x^2 + z^2 = 4$

t	0	$\dfrac{\pi}{2}$	π	$\dfrac{3\pi}{2}$
x	2	0	-2	0
y	0	$\dfrac{\pi}{2}$	π	$\dfrac{3\pi}{2}$
z	0	2	0	-2

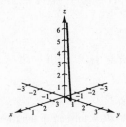

14. $\mathbf{r}(t) = \frac{1}{2}t\mathbf{i} + \sqrt{t}\mathbf{j} + \frac{1}{4}t^3\mathbf{k}$

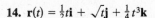

16. One possible answer is:

$\mathbf{r}_1(t) = 4t\mathbf{i},$ $\qquad 0 \le t \le 1$

$\mathbf{r}_2(t) = 4\cos t\mathbf{i} + 4\sin t\mathbf{j},$ $\qquad 0 \le t \le \dfrac{\pi}{2}$

$\mathbf{r}_3(t) = (4 - t)\mathbf{j},$ $\qquad 0 \le t \le 4$

18. The x- and y-components are $2\cos t$ and $2\sin t$. At

$$t = \dfrac{3\pi}{2},$$

the staircase has made $\frac{3}{4}$ of a revolution and is 2 meters high. Thus, one answer is

$$\mathbf{r}(t) = 2\cos t\mathbf{i} + 2\sin t\mathbf{j} + \dfrac{4}{3\pi}t\mathbf{k}.$$

20. $x^2 + z^2 = 4,\ x - y = 0,\ t = x$

$x = t,\ y = t,\ z = \pm\sqrt{4 - t^2}$

$\mathbf{r}(t) = t\mathbf{i} + t\mathbf{j} + \sqrt{4 - t^2}\mathbf{k}$

$\mathbf{r}(t) = t\mathbf{i} + t\mathbf{j} - \sqrt{4 - t^2}\mathbf{k}$

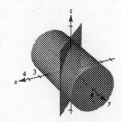

22. $\displaystyle\lim_{t \to 0}\left(\dfrac{\sin 2t}{t}\mathbf{i} + e^{-t}\mathbf{j} + e^t\mathbf{k}\right) = \left(\lim_{t \to 0}\dfrac{2\cos 2t}{1}\right)\mathbf{i} + \mathbf{j} + \mathbf{k}$

$$= 2\mathbf{i} + \mathbf{j} + \mathbf{k}$$

24. $\mathbf{r}(t) = \sin t\mathbf{i} + \cos t\mathbf{j} + t\mathbf{k}$, $\mathbf{u}(t) = \sin t\mathbf{i} + \cos t\mathbf{j} + \dfrac{1}{t}\mathbf{k}$

(a) $\mathbf{r}'(t) = \cos t\mathbf{i} - \sin t\mathbf{j} + \mathbf{k}$

(b) $\mathbf{r}''(t) = -\sin t\mathbf{i} - \cos t\mathbf{j}$

(c) $\mathbf{r}(t) \cdot \mathbf{u}(t) = 2$

$D_t[\mathbf{r}(t) \cdot \mathbf{u}(t)] = 0$

(d) $\mathbf{u}(t) - 2\mathbf{r}(t) = -\sin t\mathbf{i} - \cos t\mathbf{j} + \left(\dfrac{1}{t} - 2t\right)\mathbf{k}$

$D_t[\mathbf{u}(t) - 2\mathbf{r}(t)] = -\cos t\mathbf{i} + \sin t\mathbf{j} + \left(-\dfrac{1}{t^2} - 2\right)\mathbf{k}$

(e) $\|\mathbf{r}(t)\| = \sqrt{1 + t^2}$

$D_t[\|\mathbf{r}(t)\|] = \dfrac{t}{\sqrt{1 + t^2}}$

(f) $\mathbf{r}(t) \times \mathbf{u}(t) = \left(\dfrac{1}{t}\cos t - t\cos t\right)\mathbf{i} - \left(\dfrac{1}{t}\sin t - t\sin t\right)\mathbf{j}$

$D_t[\mathbf{r}(t) \times \mathbf{u}(t)] = \left(-\dfrac{1}{t}\sin t - \dfrac{1}{t^2}\cos t + t\sin t - \cos t\right)\mathbf{i} - \left(\dfrac{1}{t}\cos t - \dfrac{1}{t^2}\sin t - t\cos t - \sin t\right)\mathbf{j}$

26. The graph of $\mathbf{u}$ is parallel to the yz-plane.

28. $\displaystyle\int (\ln t\mathbf{i} + t\ln t\mathbf{j} + \mathbf{k})\,dt = (t\ln t - t)\mathbf{i} + \dfrac{t^2}{4}(-1 + 2\ln t)\mathbf{j} + t\mathbf{k} + \mathbf{C}$

30. $\displaystyle\int (t\mathbf{j} + t^2\mathbf{k}) \times (\mathbf{i} + t\mathbf{j} + t\mathbf{k})\,dt = \int [(t^2 - t^3)\mathbf{i} + t^2\mathbf{j} - t\mathbf{k}]\,dt = \left(\dfrac{t^3}{3} - \dfrac{t^4}{4}\right)\mathbf{i} + \dfrac{t^3}{3}\mathbf{j} - \dfrac{t^2}{2}\mathbf{k} + \mathbf{C}$

32. $\mathbf{r}(t) = \displaystyle\int (\sec t\mathbf{i} + \tan t\mathbf{j} + t^2\mathbf{k})\,dt = \ln|\sec t + \tan t|\mathbf{i} - \ln|\cos t|\mathbf{j} + \dfrac{t^3}{3}\mathbf{k} + \mathbf{C}$

$\mathbf{r}(0) = \mathbf{C} = 3\mathbf{k}$

$\mathbf{r}(t) = \ln|\sec t + \tan t|\mathbf{i} - \ln|\cos t|\mathbf{j} + \left(\dfrac{t^3}{3} + 3\right)\mathbf{k}$

34. $\displaystyle\int_0^1 \left(\sqrt{t}\mathbf{j} + t\sin t\,\mathbf{k}\right)dt = \left[\dfrac{2}{3}t^{3/2}\mathbf{j} + (\sin t - t\cos t)\mathbf{k}\right]_0^1 = \dfrac{2}{3}\mathbf{j} + (\sin 1 - \cos 1)\mathbf{k}$

36. $\displaystyle\int_{-1}^1 (t^3\mathbf{i} - \arcsin t\mathbf{j} - t^2\mathbf{k})\,dt = \left[\dfrac{t^4}{4}\mathbf{i} - \left(t\arcsin t + \sqrt{1 - t^2}\right)\mathbf{j} - \dfrac{t^3}{3}\mathbf{k}\right]_{-1}^1$

$= -\dfrac{2}{3}\mathbf{k}$

38. $\mathbf{r}(t) = \langle t, -\tan t, e^t\rangle$

$\mathbf{r}'(t) = \mathbf{v}(t) = \langle 1, -\sec^2 t, e^t\rangle$

$\|\mathbf{v}(t)\| = \sqrt{1 + \sec^4 t + e^{2t}}$

$\mathbf{r}''(t) = \mathbf{a}(t) = \langle 0, -2\sec^2 t \cdot \tan t, e^t\rangle$

40. $\mathbf{r}(t) = \langle 3\cosh t, \sinh t, -2t\rangle$, $t_0 = 0$

$\mathbf{r}'(t) = \langle 3\sinh t, \cosh t, -2\rangle$

$\mathbf{r}'(0) = \langle 0, 1, -2\rangle$ direction numbers

Since $\mathbf{r}(0) = \langle 3, 0, 0\rangle$, the parametric equations are $x = 3$, $y = t$, $z = -2t$.

$\mathbf{r}(t_0 + 0.1) = \mathbf{r}(0.1) \approx \langle 3, 0.1, -0.2\rangle$

42. Range $= 4 = \dfrac{v_0^2}{16} \sin\theta\cos\theta$

$= \dfrac{v_0^2}{16} \cdot \dfrac{6}{2\sqrt{13}} \cdot \dfrac{4}{2\sqrt{13}} = \dfrac{3v_0^2}{104}$

$\dfrac{416}{3} = v_0^2 \implies v_0 \approx 11.776$ ft/sec

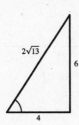

44. $\mathbf{r}(t) = [(v_0\cos\theta)t]\mathbf{i} + \left[(v_0\sin\theta)t - \tfrac{1}{2}(9.8)t^2\right]\mathbf{j}$

(a) $\mathbf{r}(t) = [(20\cos 30°)t]\mathbf{i} + [(20\sin 30°)t - 4.9t^2]\mathbf{j}$

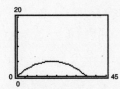

Maximum height ≈ 5.1 m; Range ≈ 35.3 m

(b) $\mathbf{r}(t) = [(20\cos 45°)t]\mathbf{i} + [(20\sin 45°)t - 4.9t^2]\mathbf{j}$

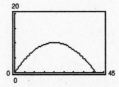

Maximum height ≈ 10.2 m; Range ≈ 40.8 m

(c) $\mathbf{r}(t) = [(20\cos 60°)t]\mathbf{i} + [(20\sin 60°)t - 4.9t^2]\mathbf{j}$

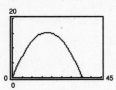

Maximum height ≈ 15.3 m; Range ≈ 35.3 m

(Note that 45° gives the longest range)

46. $\mathbf{r}(t) = (1 + 4t)\mathbf{i} + (2 - 3t)\mathbf{j}$

$\mathbf{v}(t) = 4\mathbf{i} - 3\mathbf{j}$

$\|\mathbf{v}\| = 5$

$\mathbf{a}(t) = \mathbf{0}$

$\mathbf{T}(t) = \dfrac{1}{5}(4\mathbf{i} - 3\mathbf{j})$

$\mathbf{N}(t)$ does not exist

$\mathbf{a}\cdot\mathbf{T} = 0$

$\mathbf{a}\cdot\mathbf{N}$ does not exist

48. $\mathbf{r}(t) = 2(t+1)\mathbf{i} + \dfrac{2}{t+1}\mathbf{j}$

$\mathbf{v}(t) = 2\mathbf{i} - \dfrac{2}{(t+1)^2}\mathbf{j}$

$\|\mathbf{v}(t)\| = \dfrac{2\sqrt{(t+1)^4 + 1}}{(t+1)^2}$

$\mathbf{a}(t) = \dfrac{4}{(t+1)^3}\mathbf{j}$

$\mathbf{T}(t) = \dfrac{(t+1)^2\mathbf{i} - \mathbf{j}}{\sqrt{(t+1)^4 + 1}}$

$\mathbf{N}(t) = \dfrac{\mathbf{i} + (t+1)^2\mathbf{j}}{\sqrt{(t+1)^4 + 1}}$

$\mathbf{a}\cdot\mathbf{T} = \dfrac{-4}{(t+1)^3\sqrt{(t+1)^4 + 1}}$

$\mathbf{a}\cdot\mathbf{N} = \dfrac{4(t+1)^2}{(t+1)^3\sqrt{(t+1)^4 + 1}}$

$= \dfrac{4}{(t+1)\sqrt{(t+1)^4 + 1}}$

50. $\mathbf{r}(t) = t \cos t \mathbf{i} + t \sin t \mathbf{j}$

$\mathbf{v}(t) = \mathbf{r}'(t) = (-t \sin t + \cos t)\mathbf{i} + (t \cos t + \sin t)\mathbf{j}$

$\|\mathbf{v}(t)\| = \text{speed} = \sqrt{(-t \sin t + \cos t)^2 + (t \cos t + \sin t)^2} = \sqrt{t^2 + 1}$

$\mathbf{a}(t) = \mathbf{r}''(t) = (-t \cos t - 2 \sin t)\mathbf{i} + (-t \sin t + 2 \cos t)\mathbf{j}$

$\mathbf{T}(t) = \dfrac{\mathbf{v}(t)}{\|\mathbf{v}(t)\|} = \dfrac{(-t \sin t + \cos t)\mathbf{i} + (t \cos t + \sin t)\mathbf{j}}{\sqrt{t^2 + 1}}$

$\mathbf{N}(t) = \dfrac{-(t \cos t + \sin t)\mathbf{i} + (-t \sin t + \cos t)\mathbf{j}}{\sqrt{t^2 + 1}}$

$\mathbf{a}(t) \cdot \mathbf{T}(t) = \dfrac{t}{\sqrt{t^2 + 1}}$

$\mathbf{a}(t) \cdot \mathbf{N}(t) = \dfrac{t^2 + 2}{\sqrt{t^2 + 1}}$

52. $\mathbf{r}(t) = (t - 1)\mathbf{i} + t\mathbf{j} + \dfrac{1}{t}\mathbf{k}$

$\mathbf{v}(t) = \mathbf{i} + \mathbf{j} - \dfrac{1}{t^2}\mathbf{k}$

$\|\mathbf{v}(t)\| = \dfrac{\sqrt{2t^4 + 1}}{t^2}$

$\mathbf{a}(t) = \dfrac{2}{t^3}\mathbf{k}$

$\mathbf{T}(t) = \dfrac{t^2\mathbf{i} + t^2\mathbf{j} - \mathbf{k}}{\sqrt{2t^4 + 1}}$

$\mathbf{N}(t) = \dfrac{\mathbf{i} + \mathbf{j} + 2t^2\mathbf{k}}{\sqrt{2}\sqrt{2t^4 + 1}}$

$\mathbf{a} \cdot \mathbf{T} = \dfrac{-2}{t^3 \sqrt{2t^4 + 1}}$

$\mathbf{a} \cdot \mathbf{N} = \dfrac{4}{t\sqrt{2}\sqrt{2t^4 + 1}}$

54. $\mathbf{r}(t) = t\mathbf{i} + t^2\mathbf{j} + \frac{2}{3}t^3\mathbf{k}$, $x = t$, $y = t^2$, $z = \frac{2}{3}t^3$

When $t = 2$, $x = 2$, $y = 4$, $z = \frac{16}{3}$.

$\mathbf{r}'(t) = \mathbf{i} + 2t\mathbf{j} + 2t^2\mathbf{k}$

Direction numbers when $t = 2$, $a = 1$, $b = 4$, $c = 8$

$x = t + 2$, $y = 4t + 4$, $z = 8t + \frac{16}{3}$

56. Factor of 4

58. $\mathbf{r}(t) = t^2\mathbf{i} + 2t\mathbf{k}$, $0 \le t \le 3$

$\mathbf{r}'(t) = 2t\mathbf{i} + 2\mathbf{k}$

$s = \displaystyle\int_a^b \|\mathbf{r}'(t)\| \, dt = \int_0^3 \sqrt{4t^2 + 4} \, dt$

$= \left[\ln\left| \sqrt{t^2 + 1} + t \right| + t\sqrt{t^2 + 1} \right]_0^3$

$= \ln\left(\sqrt{10} + 3 \right) + 3\sqrt{10} \approx 11.3053$

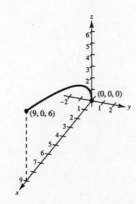

60. $\mathbf{r}(t) = 10 \cos t\mathbf{i} + 10 \sin t\mathbf{j}$

$\mathbf{r}'(t) = -10 \sin t\mathbf{i} + 10 \cos t\mathbf{j}$

$\|\mathbf{r}'(t)\| = 10$

$$s = \int_0^{2\pi} 10 \, dt = 20\pi$$

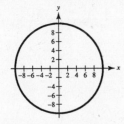

62. $\mathbf{r}(t) = t\mathbf{i} + t^2\mathbf{j} + 2t\mathbf{k}, 0 \le t \le 2$

$\mathbf{r}'(t) = \mathbf{i} + 2t\mathbf{j} + 2\mathbf{k}, \|\mathbf{r}'(t)\| = \sqrt{5 + 4t^2}$

$$s = \int_a^b \|\mathbf{r}'(t)\| \, dt = \int_0^2 \sqrt{5 + 4t^2} \, dt$$

$$= \sqrt{21} + \frac{5}{4} \ln 5 - \frac{5}{4} \ln\left(\sqrt{105} - 4\sqrt{5}\right) \approx 6.2638$$

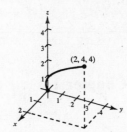

64. $\mathbf{r}(t) = \langle 2(\sin t - t \cos t), 2(\cos t + t \sin t), t\rangle, 0 \le t \le \dfrac{\pi}{2}$

$x'(t) = \langle 2t \sin t, 2t \cos t, 1\rangle, \|\mathbf{r}'(t)\| = \sqrt{4t^2 + 1}$

$$s = \int_a^b \|\mathbf{r}'(t)\| \, dt = \int_0^{\pi/2} \sqrt{4t^2 + 1} \, dt$$

$$= \sqrt{17} - \frac{1}{4} \ln\left(\sqrt{17} - 4\right) \approx 4.6468$$

66. $\mathbf{r}(t) = e^t \sin t\mathbf{i} + e^t \cos t\mathbf{k}, \ 0 \le t \le \pi$

$\mathbf{r}'(t) = (e^t \cos t + e^t \sin t)\mathbf{i} + (-e^t \sin t + e^t \cos t)\mathbf{k}$

$\|\mathbf{r}'(t)\| = \sqrt{(e^t \cos t + e^t \sin t)^2 + (-e^t \sin t + e^t \cos t)^2}$

$\quad = \sqrt{2} e^t$

$$s = \int_0^{\pi} \|\mathbf{r}'(t)\| \, dt$$

$$= \sqrt{2} \int_0^{\pi} e^t \, dt = \left[\sqrt{2} e^t\right]_0^{\pi} = \sqrt{2}(e^{\pi} - 1)$$

68. $\mathbf{r}(t) = 2\sqrt{t}\mathbf{i} + 3t\mathbf{j}$

$\mathbf{r}'(t) = \dfrac{1}{\sqrt{t}}\mathbf{i} + 3\mathbf{j}, \|\mathbf{r}'(t)\| = \sqrt{\dfrac{1}{t} + 9} = \sqrt{\dfrac{1 + 9t}{t}}$

$\mathbf{r}''(t) = -\dfrac{1}{2}t^{-3/2}\mathbf{i}$

$$\mathbf{r}' \times \mathbf{r}'' = \begin{vmatrix} \mathbf{i} & \mathbf{j} & \mathbf{k} \\ \dfrac{1}{\sqrt{t}} & 3 & 0 \\ -\dfrac{1}{2}t^{-3/2} & 0 & 0 \end{vmatrix} = \frac{3}{2}t^{-3/2}\mathbf{k}; \|\mathbf{r}' \times \mathbf{r}''\| = \frac{3}{2t^{3/2}}$$

$$K = \frac{\|\mathbf{r}'(t) \times \mathbf{r}''(t)\|}{\|\mathbf{r}'(t)\|^3} = \frac{3/2t^{3/2}}{(1 + 9t)^{3/2}/t^{3/2}} = \frac{3}{2(1 + 9t)^{3/2}}$$

70. $\mathbf{r}(t) = 2t\mathbf{i} + 5 \cos t\mathbf{j} + 5 \sin t\mathbf{k}$

$\mathbf{r}'(t) = 2\mathbf{i} - 5 \sin t\mathbf{j} + 5 \cos t\mathbf{k}, \|\mathbf{r}'(t)\| = \sqrt{29}$

$\mathbf{r}''(t) = 5 \cos t\mathbf{j} - 5 \sin t\mathbf{k}$

$$\mathbf{r}' \times \mathbf{r}'' = \begin{vmatrix} \mathbf{i} & \mathbf{j} & \mathbf{k} \\ 2 & -5 \sin t & 5 \cos t \\ 0 & -5 \cos t & -5 \sin t \end{vmatrix} = 25\mathbf{i} + 10 \sin t\mathbf{j} - 10 \cos t\mathbf{k}$$

$\|\mathbf{r}' \times \mathbf{r}''\| = \sqrt{725}$

$$K = \frac{\|\mathbf{r}' \times \mathbf{r}''\|}{\|\mathbf{r}'\|^3} = \frac{\sqrt{725}}{(29)^{3/2}} = \frac{\sqrt{25 \cdot 29}}{29\sqrt{29}} = \frac{5}{29}$$

72. $y = e^{-x/2}$

$y' = -\dfrac{1}{2}e^{-x/2}, y'' = \dfrac{1}{4}e^{-x/2}$

$K = \dfrac{|y''|}{[1 + (y')^2]^{3/2}} = \dfrac{\dfrac{1}{4}e^{-x/2}}{\left[1 + \dfrac{1}{4}e^{-x}\right]^{3/2}}$

At $x = 0$, $K = \dfrac{1/4}{(5/4)^{3/2}} = \dfrac{2}{5^{3/2}} = \dfrac{2}{5\sqrt{5}} = \dfrac{2\sqrt{5}}{25}, r = \dfrac{5\sqrt{5}}{2}$.

74. $y = \tan x$

$y' = \sec^2 x$

$y'' = 2\sec^2 x \tan x$

$K = \dfrac{|y''|}{[1 + (y')^2]^{3/2}} = \dfrac{|2\sec^2 x \tan x|}{[1 + \sec^4 x]^{3/2}}$

At $x = \dfrac{\pi}{4}$, $K = \dfrac{4}{5^{3/2}} = \dfrac{4}{5\sqrt{5}} = \dfrac{4\sqrt{5}}{25}$ and $r = \dfrac{5\sqrt{5}}{4}$.

Problem Solving for Chapter 11

2. $x^{2/3} + y^{2/3} = a^{2/3}$

$\dfrac{2}{3}x^{-1/3} + \dfrac{2}{3}y^{-1/3}y' = 0$

$y' = \dfrac{-y^{1/3}}{x^{1/3}}$ Slope at $P(x, y)$.

$\mathbf{r}(t) = \cos^3 t\mathbf{i} + \sin^3 t\mathbf{j}$

$\mathbf{r}'(t) = -3\cos^2 t \sin t\mathbf{i} + 3\sin^2 t \cos t\mathbf{j}$

$\|\mathbf{r}'(t)\mathbf{i} = |3\cos t \sin t|$

$\mathbf{T}(t) = \dfrac{\mathbf{r}'(t)}{\|\mathbf{r}'(t)\|} = -\cos t\mathbf{i} + \sin t\mathbf{j}$

$\mathbf{T}'(t) = \sin t\mathbf{i} + \cos t\mathbf{j}$

$Q(0, 0, 0)$ origin

$P = (\cos^3 t, \sin^3 t, 0)$ on curve.

$\overrightarrow{PQ} \times \mathbf{T} = \begin{vmatrix} \mathbf{i} & \mathbf{j} & \mathbf{k} \\ \cos^3 t & \sin^3 t & 0 \\ -\cos t & \sin t & 0 \end{vmatrix}$

$= (\cos^3 t \sin t - \sin^3 t \cos t)\mathbf{k}$

$D = \dfrac{\|\overrightarrow{PQ} \times \mathbf{T}\|}{\|\mathbf{T}\|} = |3\cos t \sin t|$

$K = \dfrac{\|\mathbf{T}'(t)\|}{\|\mathbf{r}'(t)\|} = \dfrac{1}{|3\cos t \sin t|}$

Thus, the radius of curvature, $\dfrac{1}{K}$, is three times the distance from the origin to the tangent line.

4. Bomb: $\mathbf{r}_1(t) = \langle 5000 + 400t, 3200 - 16t^2 \rangle$

Projectile: $\mathbf{r}_2(t) = \langle (v_0 \cos \theta)t, (v_0 \sin \theta)t - 16t^2 \rangle$

At 1600 feet: Bomb:

$3200 - 16t^2 = 1600 \Rightarrow t = 10$

Projectile will travel 5 seconds:

$5(v_0 \sin \theta) - 16(25) = 1600$

$v_0 \sin \theta = 400$.

Horizontal position:

At $t = 10$, bomb is at $5000 + 400(10) = 9000$.

At $t = 5$, projectile is at $(v_0 \cos \theta)5$.

Thus,

$5v_0 \cos \theta = 9000$

$v_0 \cos \theta = 1800$.

Combining, $\dfrac{v_0 \sin \theta}{v_0 \cos \theta} = \dfrac{400}{1800} \Rightarrow \tan \theta = \dfrac{2}{9} \Rightarrow \theta \approx 12.5°$.

$v_0 = \dfrac{1800}{\cos \theta} \approx 1843.9 \text{ ft/sec}$

6. $r = 1 - \cos \theta$

$r' = \sin \theta$

$$s(t) = \int_{\pi}^{t} \sqrt{(1 - \cos \theta)^2 + \sin^2 \theta} \, d\theta = \int_{\pi}^{t} \sqrt{2 - 2\cos \theta} \, d\theta$$

$$= \int_{\pi}^{t} 2 \sin \frac{\theta}{2} \, d\theta = \left[-4 \cos \frac{\theta}{2} \right]_{\pi}^{t} = -4 \cos \frac{t}{2}$$

$$K = \frac{|2(r')^2 - rr'' + r^2|}{[(r')^2 + r^2]^{3/2}}$$

$$= \frac{|2 \sin^2 \theta - (1 - \cos \theta)(\cos \theta) + (1 - \cos \theta)^2|}{8 \sin^3 \frac{\theta}{2}}$$

$$= \frac{|3 - 3\cos \theta|}{8 \sin^3 \frac{\theta}{2}}$$

$$= \frac{3}{4} \frac{\sin^2 \frac{\theta}{2}}{\sin^3 \frac{\theta}{2}} = \frac{3}{4 \sin \frac{\theta}{2}}$$

$$\rho = \frac{1}{K} = \frac{4 \sin \frac{\theta}{2}}{3}$$

$$s^2 + 9\rho^2 = 16 \cos^2 \frac{\theta}{2} + 16 \sin^2 \frac{\theta}{2} = 16$$

8. (a) $\mathbf{r} = x\mathbf{i} + y\mathbf{j}$ position vector

$\mathbf{r} = r \cos \theta \mathbf{i} + r \sin \theta \mathbf{j}$

$$\frac{d\mathbf{r}}{dt} = \left[\frac{dr}{dt} \cos \theta - r \sin \theta \frac{d\theta}{dt} \right] \mathbf{i} + \left[\frac{dr}{dt} \sin \theta + r \cos \theta \frac{d\theta}{dt} \right] \mathbf{j}$$

$$\mathbf{a} = \frac{d^2\mathbf{r}}{dt^2} = \left[\frac{d^2r}{dt^2} \cos \theta - \frac{dr}{dt} \sin \theta \frac{d\theta}{dt} - \frac{dr}{dt} \sin \theta \frac{d\theta}{dt} - r \cos \theta \left(\frac{d\theta}{dt} \right)^2 - r \sin \theta \frac{d^2\theta}{dt^2} \right] \mathbf{i}$$

$$+ \left[\frac{d^2r}{dt^2} \sin \theta + \frac{dr}{dt} \cos \theta \frac{d\theta}{dt} + \frac{dr}{dt} \cos \theta \frac{d\theta}{dt} - r \sin \theta \left(\frac{d\theta}{dt} \right)^2 + r \cos \theta \frac{d^2\theta}{dt^2} \right]$$

$$a_r = \mathbf{a} \cdot \mathbf{u}_r = \mathbf{a} \cdot (\cos \theta \mathbf{i} + \sin \theta \mathbf{j})$$

$$= \left[\frac{d^2r}{dt^2} \cos^2 \theta - 2 \frac{dr}{dt} \sin \theta \cos \theta \frac{d\theta}{dt} - r \cos^2 \theta \left(\frac{d\theta}{dt} \right)^2 - r \cos \theta \sin \theta \frac{d^2\theta}{dt^2} \right]$$

$$+ \left[\frac{d^2r}{dt^2} \sin^2 \theta + 2 \frac{dr}{dt} \sin \theta \cos \theta \frac{d\theta}{dt} - r \sin^2 \theta \left(\frac{d\theta}{dt} \right)^2 + r \cos \theta \sin \theta \frac{d^2\theta}{dt^2} \right]$$

$$= \frac{d^2r}{dt^2} - r \left(\frac{d\theta}{dt} \right)^2$$

$$a_\theta = \mathbf{a} \cdot u_\theta = \mathbf{a} \cdot (-\sin \theta \mathbf{i} + \cos \theta \mathbf{j}) = 2 \frac{dr}{dr} \frac{d\theta}{dt} + r \frac{d^2\theta}{dt^2}$$

$$\mathbf{a} = (\mathbf{a} \cdot \mathbf{u}_r)\mathbf{u}_r + (\mathbf{a} \cdot \mathbf{u}_\theta)u_\theta$$

$$= \left[\frac{d^2r}{dt^2} - r \left(\frac{d\theta}{dt} \right)^2 \right] \mathbf{u}_r + \left[2 \frac{dr}{dt} \frac{d\theta}{dt} + r \frac{d^2\theta}{dt^2} \right] \mathbf{u}_\theta$$

—CONTINUED—

8. —CONTINUED—

(b) $\mathbf{r} = 42{,}000 \cos\left(\dfrac{\pi t}{12}\right)\mathbf{i} + 42{,}000 \sin\left(\dfrac{\pi t}{12}\right)\mathbf{j}$

$\mathbf{r} = 42{,}000, \dfrac{dr}{dt} = 0, \dfrac{d^2 r}{dt^2} = 0$

$\dfrac{d\theta}{dt} = \dfrac{\pi}{12}, \dfrac{d^2\theta}{dt^2} = 0$

Therefore, $\mathbf{a} = -42000\left(\dfrac{\pi}{12}\right)^2\mathbf{u}_r = -\dfrac{875}{3}\pi^2\mathbf{u}_r$.

Radial component: $-\dfrac{875}{3}\pi^2$

Angular component: 0

10. $\mathbf{r}(t) = \cos t\mathbf{i} + \sin t\mathbf{j} - \mathbf{k}, t = \dfrac{\pi}{4}$

$\mathbf{r}'(t) = -\sin t\mathbf{i} + \cos t\mathbf{j}, \|\mathbf{r}'(t)\| = 1$

$\mathbf{T} = -\sin t\mathbf{i} + \cos t\mathbf{j}$

$\mathbf{T}' = -\cos t\mathbf{i} - \sin t\mathbf{j}$

$\mathbf{N} = -\cos t\mathbf{i} - \sin t\mathbf{j}$

$\mathbf{B} = \mathbf{T} \times \mathbf{N} = \mathbf{k}$

At $t = \dfrac{\pi}{4}$, $\mathbf{T}\left(\dfrac{\pi}{4}\right) = -\dfrac{\sqrt{2}}{2}\mathbf{i} + \dfrac{\sqrt{2}}{2}\mathbf{j}$

$\mathbf{N}\left(\dfrac{\pi}{4}\right) = -\dfrac{\sqrt{2}}{2}\mathbf{i} - \dfrac{\sqrt{2}}{2}\mathbf{j}$

$\mathbf{B}\left(\dfrac{\pi}{4}\right) = \mathbf{k}$

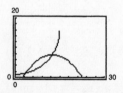

12. $y = \dfrac{1}{32}x^{5/2}$

$y' = \dfrac{5}{64}x^{3/2}$

$y'' = \dfrac{15}{128}x^{1/2}$

$K = \left|\dfrac{\dfrac{15}{128}x^{1/2}}{\left(1 + \dfrac{25}{4096}x^3\right)^{3/2}}\right|$

At the point $(4, 1)$, $K = \dfrac{120}{(89)^{3/2}} \Rightarrow r = \dfrac{1}{K} = \dfrac{(89)^{3/2}}{120} \approx 7$.

14. (a) Eliminate the parameter to see that the Ferris wheel has a radius of 15 meters and is centered at $16\mathbf{j}$. At $t = 0$, the friend is located at $\mathbf{r}_1(0) = \mathbf{j}$, which is the low point on the Ferris wheel.

(b) If a revolution takes Δt seconds, then

$$\dfrac{\pi(t + \Delta t)}{10} = \dfrac{\pi t}{10} + 2\pi$$

and so $\Delta t = 20$ seconds. The Ferris wheel makes three revolutions per minute.

(c) The initial velocity is $r'_2(t_0) = -8.03\mathbf{i} + 11.47\mathbf{j}$. The speed is $\sqrt{8.03^2 + 11.47^2} \approx 14$ m/sec. The angle of inclination is $\arctan(11.47/8.03) \approx 0.96$ radians or $55°$.

(d) Although you may start with other values, $t_0 = 0$ is a fine choice. The graph at the right shows two points of intersection. At $t = 3.15$ sec the friend is near the vertex of the parabola, which the object reaches when

$$t - t_0 = -\dfrac{11.47}{2(-4.9)} \approx 1.17 \text{ sec}.$$

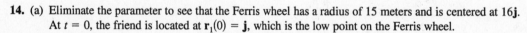

Thus, after the friend reaches the low point on the Ferris wheel, wait $t_0 = 2$ sec before throwing the object in order to allow it to be within reach.

(e) The approximate time is 3.15 seconds after starting to rise from the low point on the Ferris wheel. The friend has a constant speed of $\|\mathbf{r}'_1(t)\| = 15$ m/sec. The speed of the object at that time is

$$\|\mathbf{r}'_2(3.15)\| = \sqrt{8.03^2 + [11.47 - 9.8(3.15 - 2)]^2} \approx 8.03 \text{ m/sec}.$$

C H A P T E R   1 2
Functions of Several Variables

CHAPTER 12
Functions of Several Variables

Section 12.1   Introduction to Functions of Several Variables

Solutions to Even-Numbered Exercises

2. $xz^2 + 2xy - y^2 = 4$

No, z is not a function of x and y. For example, $(x, y) = (1, 0)$ corresponds to both $z = \pm 2$

4. $z + x \ln y - 8 = 0$

$z = 8 - x \ln y$

Yes, z is a function of x and y.

6. $f(x, y) = 4 - x^2 - 4y^2$

(a) $f(0, 0) = 4$

(b) $f(0, 1) = 4 - 0 - 4 = 0$

(c) $f(2, 3) = 4 - 4 - 36 = -36$

(d) $f(1, y) = 4 - 1 - 4y^2 = 3 - 4y^2$

(e) $f(x, 0) = 4 - x^2 - 0 = 4 - x^2$

(f) $f(t, 1) = 4 - t^2 - 4 = -t^2$

8. $g(x, y) = \ln|x + y|$

(a) $g(2, 3) = \ln|2 + 3| = \ln 5$

(b) $g(5, 6) = \ln|5 + 6| = \ln 11$

(c) $g(e, 0) = \ln|e + 0| = 1$

(d) $g(0, 1) = \ln|0 + 1| = 0$

(e) $g(2, -3) = \ln|2 - 3| = \ln 1 = 0$

(f) $g(e, e) = \ln|e + e| = \ln 2e$

$\qquad = \ln 2 + \ln e = (\ln 2) + 1$

10. $f(x, y, z) = \sqrt{x + y + z}$

(a) $f(0, 5, 4) = \sqrt{0 + 5 + 4} = 3$

(b) $f(6, 8, -3) = \sqrt{6 + 8 - 3} = \sqrt{11}$

12. $V(r, h) = \pi r^2 h$

(a) $V(3, 10) = \pi(3)^2(10) = 90\pi$

(b) $V(5, 2) = \pi(5)^2(2) = 50\pi$

14. $g(x, y) = \int_x^y \frac{1}{t}\, dt$

(a) $g(4, 1) = \int_4^1 \frac{1}{t}\, dt = \left[\ln|t|\right]_4^1 = -\ln 4$

(b) $g(6, 3) = \int_6^3 \frac{1}{t}\, dt = \left[\ln|t|\right]_6^3 = \ln 3 - \ln 6 = \ln\left(\frac{1}{2}\right)$

16. $f(x, y) = 3xy + y^2$

(a) $\dfrac{f(x + \Delta x, y) - f(x, y)}{\Delta x} = \dfrac{[3(x + \Delta x)y + y^2] - (3xy + y^2)}{\Delta x}$

$\qquad = \dfrac{3xy + 3(\Delta x)y + y^2 - 3xy - y^2}{\Delta x} = \dfrac{3(\Delta x)y}{\Delta x} = 3y,\ \Delta x \neq 0$

(b) $\dfrac{f(x, y + \Delta y) - f(x, y)}{\Delta y} = \dfrac{[3x(y + \Delta y) + (y + \Delta y)^2] - (3xy + y^2)}{\Delta y}$

$\qquad = \dfrac{3xy + 3x(\Delta y) + y^2 + 2y(\Delta y) + (\Delta y)^2 - 3xy - y^2}{\Delta y}$

$\qquad = \dfrac{\Delta y(3x + 2y + \Delta y)}{\Delta y} = 3x + 2y + \Delta y,\ \Delta y \neq 0$

18. $f(x, y) = \sqrt{4 - x^2 - 4y^2}$

Domain: $4 - x^2 - 4y^2 \geq 0$

$$x^2 + 4y^2 \leq 4$$

$$\frac{x^2}{4} + \frac{y^2}{1} \leq 1$$

$$\left\{(x, y): \frac{x^2}{4} + \frac{y^2}{1} \leq 1\right\}$$

Range: $0 \leq z \leq 2$

20. $f(x, y) = \arccos \dfrac{y}{x}$

Domain: $\left\{(x, y): -1 \leq \dfrac{y}{x} \leq 1\right\}$

Range: $0 \leq z \leq \pi$

22. $f(x, y) = \ln(xy - 6)$

Domain: $xy - 6 > 0$

$$xy > 6$$

$$\{(x, y): xy > 6\}$$

Range: all real numbers

24. $z = \dfrac{xy}{x - y}$

Domain: $\{(x, y): x \neq y\}$

Range: all real numbers

26. $f(x, y) = x^2 + y^2$

Domain: $\{(x, y): x$ is any real number,

y is any real number$\}$

Range: $z \geq 0$

28. $g(x, y) = x\sqrt{y}$

Domain: $\{(x, y): y \geq 0\}$

Range: all real numbers

30. (a) Domain: $\{(x, y): x$ is any real number,

y is any real number$\}$

Range: $-2 \leq z \leq 2$

(b) $z = 0$ when $x = 0$ which represents points on the y-axis.

(c) No. When x is positive, z is negative. When x is negative, z is positive. The surface does not pass through the first octant, the octant where y is negative and x and z are positive, the octant where y is positive and x and z are negative, and the octant where x, y and z are all negative.

32. $f(x, y) = 6 - 2x - 3y$

Plane

Domain: entire xy-plane

Range: $-\infty < z < \infty$

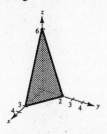

34. $g(x, y) = \frac{1}{2}x$

Plane: $z = \frac{1}{2}x$

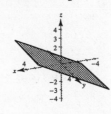

36. $z = \dfrac{1}{2}\sqrt{x^2 + y^2}$

Cone

Domain of f: entire xy-plane

Range: $z \geq 0$

38. $f(x, y) = \begin{cases} xy, & x \geq 0, \ y \geq 0 \\ 0, & \text{elsewhere} \end{cases}$

Domain of f: entire xy-plane

Range: $z \geq 0$

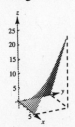

40. $f(x, y) = \frac{1}{12}\sqrt{144 - 16x^2 - 9y^2}$

Semi-ellipsoid

Domain: set of all points lying on or inside the ellipse $(x^2/9) + (y^2/16) = 1$

Range: $0 \leq z \leq 1$

42. $f(x, y) = x \sin y$

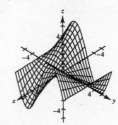

44. $f(x, y) = xy, x \geq 0, y \geq 0$

(a)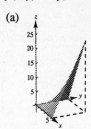

(b) g is a vertical translation of f 3 units downward

(c) g is a reflection of f in the xy-plane

(d) The graph of g is lower than the graph of f. If $z = f(x, y)$ is on the graph of f, then $\frac{1}{2}z$ is on the graph of g.

(e)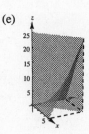

46. $z = e^{1-x^2+y^2}$

Level curves:

$$c = e^{1-x^2+y^2}$$

$$\ln c = 1 - x^2 + y^2$$

$$x^2 - y^2 = 1 - \ln c$$

Hyperbolas centered at $(0, 0)$

Matches (d)

48. $z = \cos\left(\dfrac{x + 2y^2}{4}\right)$

Level curves:

$$c = \cos\left(\frac{x^2 + 2y^2}{4}\right)$$

$$\cos^{-1} c = \frac{x^2 + 2y^2}{4}$$

$$x^2 + 2y^2 = 4 \cos^{-1} c$$

Ellipses

Matches (a)

50. $f(x, y) = 6 - 2x - 3y$

The level curves are of the form $6 - 2x - 3y = c$ or $2x + 3y = 6 - c$. Thus, the level curves are straight lines with a slope of $-\frac{2}{3}$.

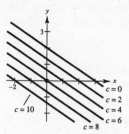

52. $f(x, y) = x^2 + 2y^2$

The level curves are ellipses of the form

$$x^2 + 2y^2 = c \quad (\text{except } x^2 + 2y^2 = 0 \text{ is the point } (0, 0)).$$

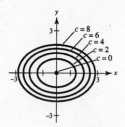

54. $f(x, y) = e^{xy/2}$

The level curves are of the form

$$e^{xy/2} = c, \text{ or } \ln c = \frac{xy}{2}.$$

Thus, the level curves are hyperbolas.

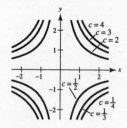

56. $f(x, y) = \ln(x - y)$

The level curves are of the form

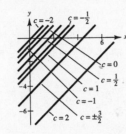

$$c = \ln(x - y)$$

$$e^c = x - y$$

$$y = x - e^c$$

Thus, the level curves are parallel lines of slope 1 passing through the fourth quadrant.

58. $f(x, y) = |xy|$

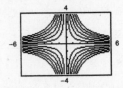

60. $h(x, y) = 3 \sin(|x| + |y|)$

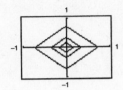

62. The graph of a function of two variables is the set of all points (x, y, z) for which $z = f(x, y)$ and (x, y) is in the domain of f. The graph can be interpreted as a surface in space. Level curves are the scalar fields $f(x, y) = c$, for c, a constant.

64. $f(x, y) = \dfrac{x}{y}$

The level curves are the lines

$$c = \frac{x}{y} \text{ or } y = \frac{1}{c}x$$

These lines all pass through the origin.

66. The surface could be an ellipsoid centered at $(0, 1, 0)$. One possible function is

$$f(x, y) = x^2 + \frac{(y - 1)^2}{4} = 1.$$

68. $A(r, t) = 1000e^{rt}$

Rate	Number of years			
	5	10	15	20
0.08	$1491.82	$2225.54	$3320.12	$4953.03
0.10	$1648.72	$2718.28	$4481.69	$7389.06
0.12	$1822.12	$3320.12	$6049.65	$11,023.18
0.14	$2013.75	$4055.20	$8166.17	$16,444.65

70. $f(x, y, z) = 4x + y + 2z$

$c = 4$

$4 = 4x + y + 2z$

Plane

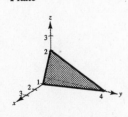

72. $f(x, y, z) = x^2 + \frac{1}{4}y^2 - z$

$c = 1$

$1 = x^2 + \frac{1}{4}y^2 - z$

Elliptic paraboloid

Vertex: $(0, 0, -1)$

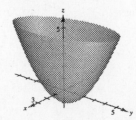

74. $f(x, y, z) = \sin x - z$

$c = 0$

$0 = \sin x - z$ or $z = \sin x$

76. $W(x, y) = \dfrac{1}{x - y}$, $y < x$

(a) $W(15, 10) = \dfrac{1}{15 - 10} = \dfrac{1}{5}$ hr = 12 min

(b) $W(12, 9) = \dfrac{1}{12 - 9} = \dfrac{1}{3}$ hr = 20 min

(c) $W(12, 6) = \dfrac{1}{12 - 6} = \dfrac{1}{6}$ hr = 10 min

(d) $W(4, 2) = \dfrac{1}{4 - 2} = \dfrac{1}{2}$ hr = 30 min

78. $f(x, y) = 100x^{0.6}y^{0.4}$

$f(2x, 2y) = 100(2x)^{0.6}(2y)^{0.4}$

$= 100(2)^{0.6}x^{0.6}(2)^{0.4}y^{0.4} = 100(2)^{0.6}(2)^{0.4}x^{0.6}y^{0.4} = 2[100x^{0.6}y^{0.4}] = 2f(x, y)$

80. $V = \pi r^2 l + \dfrac{4}{3}\pi r^3 = \dfrac{\pi r^2}{3}(3l + 4r)$

82. (a)

Year	1995	1996	1997	1998	1999	2000
z	12.7	14.8	17.1	18.5	21.1	25.8
Model	13.09	14.79	16.45	18.47	21.38	25.78

(b) x has the greater influence because its coefficient (0.143) is larger than that of y(0.024).

(c) $f(x, 25) = 0.143x + 0.024(25) + 0.502$

$= 0.143x + 1.102$

This function gives the shareholder's equity z in terms of net sales x and assumes constant assets of $y = 25$.

84. Southwest

86. Latitude and land versus ocean location have the greatest effect on temperature.

88. True

90. True

Section 12.2   Limits and Continuity

2. Let $\varepsilon > 0$ be given. We need to find $\delta > 0$ such that $|f(x, y) - L| = |x - 4| < \varepsilon$

whenever $0 < \sqrt{(x - a)^2 + (y - b)^2} = \sqrt{(x - 4)^2 + (y + 1)^2} < \delta$. Take $\delta = \varepsilon$.

Then if $0 < \sqrt{(x - 4)^2 + (y + 1)^2} < \delta = \varepsilon$, we have

$\sqrt{(x - 4)^2} < \varepsilon$

$|x - 4| < \varepsilon$.

4. $\displaystyle\lim_{(x, y)\to(a, b)}\left[\dfrac{4f(x, y)}{g(x, y)}\right] = \dfrac{4\left[\displaystyle\lim_{(x, y)\to(a, b)}f(x, y)\right]}{\displaystyle\lim_{(x, y)\to(a, b)}g(x, y)} = \dfrac{4(5)}{3} = \dfrac{20}{3}$

6. $\displaystyle\lim_{(x,\,y)\to(a,\,b)}\left[\frac{f(x,y)-g(x,y)}{f(x,y)}\right]=\frac{\displaystyle\lim_{(x,\,y)\to(a,\,b)}f(x,y)-\lim_{(x,\,y)\to(a,\,b)}g(x,y)}{\displaystyle\lim_{(x,\,y)\to(a,\,b)}f(x,y)}=\frac{5-3}{5}=\frac{2}{5}$

8. $\displaystyle\lim_{(x,\,y)\to(0,\,0)}(5x+y+1)=0+0+1=1$

Continuous everywhere

10. $\displaystyle\lim_{(x,\,y)\to(1,\,1)}\frac{x}{\sqrt{x+y}}=\frac{1}{\sqrt{1+1}}=\frac{\sqrt{2}}{2}$

Continuous for $x+y>0$

12. $\displaystyle\lim_{(x,\,y)\to(\pi/4,\,2)}y\cos(xy)=2\cos\frac{\pi}{2}=0$

Continuous everywhere

14. $\displaystyle\lim_{(x,\,y)\to(1,\,1)}\frac{xy}{x^2+y^2}=\frac{1}{2}$

Continuous except at $(0,0)$

16. $\displaystyle\lim_{(x,\,y,\,z)\to(2,\,0,\,1)}xe^{yz}=2e^0=2$

Continuous everywhere

18. $f(x,y)=\dfrac{x^2}{(x^2+1)(y^2+1)}$

$\displaystyle\lim_{(x,\,y)\to(0,\,0)}\frac{x^2}{(x^2+1)(y^2+1)}=\frac{0}{(0+1)(0+1)}=0$

Continuous everywhere

20. $\displaystyle\lim_{(x,\,y)\to(0,\,0)}\left[1-\frac{\cos(x^2+y^2)}{x^2+y^2}\right]=-\infty$

The limit does not exist.

Continuous except at $(0,0)$

22. $f(x,y)=\dfrac{y}{x^2+y^2}$

Continuous except at $(0,0)$

Path: $y=0$

(x,y)	$(1,1)$	$(0.5,0.5)$	$(0.1,0.1)$	$(0.01,0.01)$	$(0.001,0.001)$
$f(x,y)$	$\frac{1}{2}$	1	5	50	500

Path: $y=x$

(x,y)	$(1,0)$	$(0.5,0)$	$(0.1,0)$	$(0.01,0)$	$(0.001,0)$
$f(x,y)$	0	0	0	0	0

The limit does not exist because along the path $y=0$ the function equals 0, whereas along the path $y=x$ the function tends to infinity.

24. $f(x,y)=\dfrac{2x-y^2}{2x^2+y}$

Continuous except at $(0,0)$

Path: $y=0$

(x,y)	$(1,0)$	$(0.25,0)$	$(0.01,0)$	$(0.001,0)$	$(0.000001,0)$
$f(x,y)$	1	4	100	1000	$1{,}000{,}000$

Path: $y=x$

(x,y)	$(1,1)$	$(0.25,0.25)$	$(0.01,0.01)$	$(0.001,0.001)$	$(0.0001,0.0001)$
$f(x,y)$	$\frac{1}{3}$	1.17	1.95	1.995	2.0

The limit does not exist because along the line $y=0$ the function tends to infinity, whereas along the line $y=x$ the function tends to 2.

26. $\displaystyle\lim_{(x, y)\to(0, 0)} \frac{4x^2y^2}{(x^2 + y^2)} = 0$

Hence, $\displaystyle\lim_{(x, y)\to(0, 0)} f(x, y) = \lim_{(x, y)\to(0, 0)} g(x, y) = 0$.

f is continuous at $(0, 0)$, whereas g is not continuous at $(0, 0)$.

28. $\displaystyle\lim_{(x, y)\to(0, 0)} \left(\sin\frac{1}{x} + \cos\frac{1}{x} \right)$

Does not exist

30. $\displaystyle\lim_{(x, y)\to(0, 0)} \frac{x^2 + y^2}{x^2y}$

Does not exist

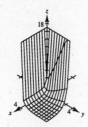

32. $f(x, y) = \dfrac{2xy}{x^2 + y^2 + 1}$

The limit equals 0.

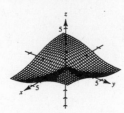

34. $\displaystyle\lim_{(x, y)\to(0, 0)} \frac{xy^2}{x^2 + y^2} = \lim_{r\to0} \frac{(r\cos\theta)(r^2\sin^2\theta)}{r^2} = \lim_{r\to0} (r\cos\theta\sin^2\theta) = 0$

36. $\displaystyle\lim_{(x, y)\to(0, 0)} \frac{x^2y^2}{x^2 + y^2} = \lim_{r\to0} \frac{r^4\cos^2\theta\sin^2\theta}{r^2} = \lim_{r\to0} r^2\cos^2\theta\sin^2\theta = 0$

38. $f(x, y, z) = \dfrac{z}{x^2 + y^2 - 9}$

Continuous for $x^2 + y^2 \neq 9$

40. $f(x, y, z) = xy\sin z$

Continuous everywhere

42. $\quad f(t) = \dfrac{1}{t}$

$g(x, y) = x^2 + y^2$

$f(g(x, y)) = f(x^2 + y^2)$

$\qquad = \dfrac{1}{x^2 + y^2}$

Continuous except at $(0, 0)$

44. $f(t) = \dfrac{1}{4 - t}$

$g(x, y) = x^2 + y^2$

$f(g(x, y)) = f(x^2 + y^2) = \dfrac{1}{4 - x^2 - y^2}$

Continuous for $x^2 + y^2 \neq 4$

46. $f(x, y) = x^2 + y^2$

(a) $\displaystyle\lim_{\Delta x\to0} \frac{f(x + \Delta x, y) - f(x, y)}{\Delta x} = \lim_{\Delta x\to0} \frac{[(x + \Delta x)^2 + y^2] - (x^2 + y^2)}{\Delta x}$

$\qquad = \displaystyle\lim_{\Delta x\to0} \frac{2x\Delta x + (\Delta x)^2}{\Delta x} = \lim_{\Delta x\to0} (2x + \Delta x) = 2x$

(b) $\displaystyle\lim_{\Delta y\to0} \frac{f(x, y + \Delta y) - f(x, y)}{\Delta y} = \lim_{\Delta y\to0} \frac{[x^2 + (y + \Delta y)^2] - (x^2 + y^2)}{\Delta y}$

$\qquad = \displaystyle\lim_{\Delta y\to0} \frac{2y\Delta y + (\Delta y)^2}{\Delta y} = \lim_{\Delta y\to0} (2y + \Delta y) = 2y$

48. $f(x, y) = \sqrt{y}(y + 1)$

(a) $\displaystyle\lim_{\Delta x \to 0} \frac{f(x + \Delta x, y) - f(x, y)}{\Delta x} = \lim_{\Delta x \to 0} \frac{\sqrt{y}(y + 1) - \sqrt{y}(y + 1)}{\Delta x} = 0$

(b) $\displaystyle\lim_{\Delta y \to 0} \frac{f(x, y + \Delta y) - f(x, y)}{\Delta y} = \lim_{\Delta y \to 0} \frac{(y + \Delta y)^{3/2} + (y + \Delta y)^{1/2} - (y^{3/2} + y^{1/2})}{\Delta y}$

$\displaystyle = \lim_{\Delta y \to 0} \frac{(y + \Delta y)^{3/2} - y^{3/2}}{\Delta y} + \lim_{\Delta y \to 0} \frac{(y + \Delta y)^{1/2} - y^{1/2}}{\Delta y}$

$\displaystyle = \frac{3}{2}y^{1/2} + \frac{1}{2}y^{-1/2}$ \qquad (L'Hôpital's Rule)

$\displaystyle = \frac{3y + 1}{2\sqrt{y}}$

50. See the definition on page 854.

52. $\displaystyle\lim_{(x, y) \to (0, 0)} \frac{x^2 + y^2}{xy}$

(a) Along $y = ax$: $\displaystyle\lim_{(x, ax) \to (0, 0)} \frac{x^2 + (ax)^2}{x(ax)}$

$\displaystyle = \lim_{x \to 0} \frac{x^2(1 + a^2)}{ax^2} = \frac{1 + a^2}{a}, \; a \neq 0$

If $a = 0$, then $y = 0$ and the limit does not exist.

(b) Along $y = x^2$: $\displaystyle\lim_{(x, x^2) \to (0, 0)} \frac{x^2 + (x^2)^2}{x(x^2)} = \lim_{x \to 0} \frac{1 + x^2}{x}$

limit does not exist

(c) No, the limit does not exist. Different paths result in different limits.

54. Given that $f(x, y)$ is continuous, then $\displaystyle\lim_{(x, y) \to (a, b)} f(x, y) = f(a, b) < 0$, which means that for each $\varepsilon > 0$, there corresponds

a $\delta > 0$ such that $|f(x, y) - f(a, b)| < \varepsilon$ whenever

$0 < \sqrt{(x - a)^2 + (y - b)^2} < \delta.$

Let $\varepsilon = |f(a, b)|/2$, then $f(x, y) < 0$ for every point in the corresponding δ neighborhood since

$\displaystyle |f(x, y) - f(a, b)| < \frac{|f(a, b)|}{2} \Rightarrow -\frac{|f(a, b)|}{2} < f(x, y) - f(a, b) < \frac{|f(a, b)|}{2}$

$\displaystyle \Rightarrow \frac{3}{2}f(a, b) < f(x, y) < \frac{1}{2}f(a, b) < 0.$

56. False. Let $f(x, y) = \dfrac{xy}{x^2 + y^2}$.

See Exercise 21.

58. True

Section 12.3   **Partial Derivatives**

2. $f_y(-1, -2) < 0$

4. $f_x(-1, -1) = 0$

6. $f(x, y) = x^2 - 3y^2 + 7$

$f_x(x, y) = 2x$

$f_y(x, y) = -6y$

8. $z = 2y^2\sqrt{x}$

$\dfrac{\partial z}{\partial x} = \dfrac{y^2}{\sqrt{x}}$

$\dfrac{\partial z}{\partial y} = 4y\sqrt{x}$

10. $z = y^3 - 4xy^2 - 1$

$\dfrac{\partial z}{\partial x} = -4y^2$

$\dfrac{\partial z}{\partial y} = 3y^2 - 8xy$

12. $z = xe^{x/y}$

$\dfrac{\partial z}{\partial x} = \dfrac{x}{y}e^{x/y} + e^{x/y} = e^{x/y}\left(\dfrac{x}{y} + 1\right)$

$\dfrac{\partial z}{\partial y} = xe^{x/y}\left(-\dfrac{x}{y^2}\right) = -\dfrac{x^2}{y^2}e^{x/y}$

14. $z = \ln\sqrt{xy} = \dfrac{1}{2}\ln(xy)$

$\dfrac{\partial z}{\partial x} = \dfrac{1}{2}\dfrac{y}{xy} = \dfrac{1}{2x}$

$\dfrac{\partial z}{\partial y} = \dfrac{1}{2}\dfrac{x}{xy} = \dfrac{1}{2y}$

16. $z = \ln(x^2 - y^2)$

$\dfrac{\partial z}{\partial x} = \dfrac{1}{x^2 - y^2}(2x) = \dfrac{2x}{x^2 - y^2}$

$\dfrac{\partial z}{\partial y} = \dfrac{-2y}{x^2 - y^2}$

18. $f(x, y) = \dfrac{xy}{x^2 + y^2}$

$f_x(x, y) = \dfrac{(x^2 + y^2)(y) - (xy)(2x)}{(x^2 + y^2)^2} = \dfrac{y^3 - x^2 y}{(x^2 + y^2)^2}$

$f_y(x, y) = \dfrac{(x^2 + y^2)(x) - (xy)(2y)}{(x^2 + y^2)^2} = \dfrac{x^3 - xy^2}{(x^2 + y^2)^2}$

20. $g(x, y) = \ln\sqrt{x^2 + y^2} = \dfrac{1}{2}\ln(x^2 + y^2)$

$g_x(x, y) = \dfrac{1}{2}\dfrac{2x}{x^2 + y^2} = \dfrac{x}{x^2 + y^2}$

$g_y(x, y) = \dfrac{1}{2}\dfrac{2y}{x^2 + y^2} = \dfrac{y}{x^2 + y^2}$

22. $f(x, y) = \sqrt{2x + y^3}$

$\dfrac{\partial f}{\partial x} = \dfrac{1}{2}(2x + y^3)^{-1/2}(2) = \dfrac{1}{\sqrt{2x + y^3}}$

$\dfrac{\partial f}{\partial y} = \dfrac{1}{2}(2x + y^3)^{-1/2}(3y^2) = \dfrac{3y^2}{2\sqrt{2x + y^3}}$

24. $z = \sin 3x \cos 3y$

$\dfrac{\partial z}{\partial x} = 3\cos 3x \cos 3y$

$\dfrac{\partial z}{\partial y} = -3\sin 3x \sin 3y$

26. $z = \cos(x^2 + y^2)$

$\dfrac{\partial z}{\partial x} = -2x\sin(x^2 + y^2)$

$\dfrac{\partial z}{\partial y} = -2y\sin(x^2 + y^2)$

28. $f(x, y) = \displaystyle\int_x^y (2t + 1)\, dt + \int_y^x (2t - 1)\, dt$

$= \displaystyle\int_x^y (2t + 1)\, dt - \int_x^y (2t - 1)\, dt$

$= \displaystyle\int_x^y 2\, dt = \Big[2t\Big]_x^y = 2y - 2x$

$f_x(x, y) = -2$

$f_y(x, y) = 2$

30. $f(x, y) = x^2 - 2xy + y^2 = (x - y)^2$

$\dfrac{\partial f}{\partial x} = \lim_{\Delta x \to 0} \dfrac{f(x + \Delta x, y) - f(x, y)}{\Delta x}$

$= \lim_{\Delta x \to 0} \dfrac{(x + \Delta x)^2 - 2(x + \Delta x)y + y^2 - x^2 + 2xy - y^2}{\Delta x} = \lim_{\Delta x \to 0}(2x + \Delta x - 2y) = 2(x - y)$

$\dfrac{\partial f}{\partial y} = \lim_{\Delta y \to 0} \dfrac{f(x, y + \Delta y) - f(x, y)}{\Delta y}$

$= \lim_{\Delta y \to 0} \dfrac{x^2 - 2x(y + \Delta y) + (y + \Delta y)^2 - x^2 + 2xy - y^2}{\Delta y} = \lim_{\Delta y \to 0}(-2x + 2y + \Delta y) = 2(y - x)$

32. $f(x, y) = \dfrac{1}{x + y}$

$$\frac{\partial f}{\partial x} = \lim_{\Delta x \to 0} \frac{f(x + \Delta x, y) - f(x, y)}{\Delta x} = \lim_{\Delta x \to 0} \frac{\dfrac{1}{x + \Delta x + y} - \dfrac{1}{x + y}}{\Delta x} = \lim_{\Delta x \to 0} \frac{-1}{(x + \Delta x + y)(x + y)} = \frac{-1}{(x + y)^2}$$

$$\frac{\partial f}{\partial y} = \lim_{\Delta y \to 0} \frac{f(x, y + \Delta y) - f(x, y)}{\Delta y} = \lim_{\Delta y \to 0} \frac{\dfrac{1}{x + y + \Delta y} - \dfrac{1}{x + y}}{\Delta y} = \lim_{\Delta y \to 0} \frac{-1}{(x + y + \Delta y)(x + y)} = \frac{-1}{(x + y)^2}$$

34. $h(x, y) = x^2 - y^2$

$h_x(x, y) = 2x$

At $(-2, 1)$: $h_x(-2, 1) = -4$

$h_y(x, y) = -2y$

At $(-2, 1)$: $h_y(-2, 1) = -2$

36. $z = \cos(2x - y)$

$\dfrac{\partial z}{\partial x} = -2 \sin(2x - y)$

At $\left(\dfrac{\pi}{4}, \dfrac{\pi}{3}\right)$, $\dfrac{\partial z}{\partial x} = -2 \sin\left(\dfrac{\pi}{6}\right) = -1$

$\dfrac{\partial z}{\partial y} = -\sin(2x - y)(-1) = \sin(2x - y)$

At $\left(\dfrac{\pi}{4}, \dfrac{\pi}{3}\right)$, $\dfrac{\partial z}{\partial y} = \sin\left(\dfrac{\pi}{6}\right) = \dfrac{1}{2}$

38. $f(x, y) = \arccos(xy)$

$f_x(x, y) = \dfrac{-y}{\sqrt{1 - x^2 y^2}}$

At $(1, 1)$, f_x is undefined.

$f_y(x, y) = \dfrac{-x}{\sqrt{1 - x^2 y^2}}$

At $(1, 1)$, f_y is undefined.

40. $f(x, y) = \dfrac{6xy}{\sqrt{4x^2 + 5y^2}}$

$f_x(x, y) = \dfrac{30y^3}{(4x^2 + 5y^2)^{3/2}}$

At $(1, 1)$, $f_x(1, 1) = \dfrac{30}{27} = \dfrac{10}{9}$

$f_y(x, y) = \dfrac{24x^3}{(4x^2 + 5y^2)^{3/2}}$

At $(1, 1)$, $f_y(1, 1) = \dfrac{8}{9}$

42. $z = x^2 + 4y^2$, $y = 1$, $(2, 1, 8)$

Intersecting curve: $z = x^2 + 4$

$\dfrac{\partial z}{\partial x} = 2x$

At $(2, 1, 8)$: $\dfrac{\partial z}{\partial x} = 2(2) = 4$

44. $z = 9x^2 - y^2$, $x = 1$, $(1, 3, 0)$

Intersecting curve: $z = 9 - y^2$

$\dfrac{\partial z}{\partial y} = -2y$

At $(1, 3, 0)$: $\dfrac{\partial z}{\partial y} = -2(3) = -6$

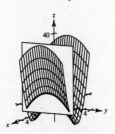

46. $f_x(x, y) = 9x^2 - 12y$, $f_y(x, y) = -12x + 3y^2$

$f_x = f_y = 0$: $9x^2 - 12y = 0 \implies 3x^2 = 4y$

$3y^2 - 12x = 0 \implies y^2 = 4x$

Solving for x in the second equation, $x = y^2/4$, you obtain $3(y^2/4)^2 = 4y$.

$3y^4 = 64y \implies y = 0$ or $y = \dfrac{4}{3^{1/3}}$

$\implies x = 0$ or $x = \dfrac{1}{4}\left(\dfrac{16}{3^{2/3}}\right)$

Points: $(0, 0)$, $\left(\dfrac{4}{3^{2/3}}, \dfrac{4}{3^{1/3}}\right)$

48. $f_x(x, y) = \dfrac{2x}{x^2 + y^2 + 1} = 0 \implies x = 0$

$f_y(x, y) = \dfrac{2y}{x^2 + y^2 + 1} = 0 \implies y = 0$

Points: $(0, 0)$

50. (a) The graph is that of f_x.

    (b) The graph is that of f_y.

52. $w = \dfrac{3xz}{x + y}$

$\dfrac{\partial w}{\partial x} = \dfrac{(x + y)(3z) - 3xz}{(x + y)^2} = \dfrac{3yz}{(x + y)^2}$

$\dfrac{\partial w}{\partial y} = \dfrac{-3xz}{(x + y)^2}$

$\dfrac{\partial w}{\partial z} = \dfrac{3x}{x + y}$

54. $G(x, y, z) = \dfrac{1}{\sqrt{1 - x^2 - y^2 - z^2}}$

$G_x(x, y, z) = \dfrac{x}{(1 - x^2 - y^2 - z^2)^{3/2}}$

$G_y(x, y, z) = \dfrac{y}{(1 - x^2 - y^2 - z^2)^{3/2}}$

$G_z(x, y, z) = \dfrac{z}{(1 - x^2 - y^2 - z^2)^{3/2}}$

56. $f(x, y, z) = 3x^2y - 5xyz + 10yz^2$

$f_x(x, y, z) = 6xy - 5yz$

$f_y(x, y, z) = 3x^2 - 5xz + 10z^2$

$f_z(x, y, z) = -5xy + 20yz$

58. $z = x^4 - 3x^2y^2 + y^4$

$\dfrac{\partial z}{\partial x} = 4x^3 - 6xy^2$

$\dfrac{\partial^2 z}{\partial x^2} = 12x^2 - 6y^2$

$\dfrac{\partial^2 z}{\partial y \partial x} = -12xy$

$\dfrac{\partial z}{\partial y} = -6x^2y + 4y^3$

$\dfrac{\partial^2 z}{\partial y^2} = -6x^2 + 12y^2$

$\dfrac{\partial^2 z}{\partial x \partial y} = -12xy$

60. $z = \ln(x - y)$

$\dfrac{\partial z}{\partial x} = \dfrac{1}{x - y}$

$\dfrac{\partial^2 z}{\partial x^2} = -\dfrac{1}{(x - y)^2}$

$\dfrac{\partial^2 z}{\partial y \partial x} = \dfrac{1}{(x - y)^2}$

$\dfrac{\partial z}{\partial y} = \dfrac{-1}{x - y} = \dfrac{1}{y - x}$

$\dfrac{\partial^2 z}{\partial y^2} = -\dfrac{1}{(x - y)^2}$

$\dfrac{\partial^2 z}{\partial x \partial y} = \dfrac{1}{(x - y)^2}$

Therefore, $\dfrac{\partial^2 z}{\partial y \partial x} = \dfrac{\partial^2 z}{\partial x \partial y}$.

62. $z = 2xe^y - 3ye^{-x}$

$\dfrac{\partial z}{\partial x} = 2e^y + 3ye^{-x}$

$\dfrac{\partial^2 z}{\partial x^2} = -3ye^{-x}$

$\dfrac{\partial^2 z}{\partial y \partial x} = 2e^y + 3ye^{-x}$

$\dfrac{\partial z}{\partial y} = 2xe^y - 3e^{-x}$

$\dfrac{\partial^2 z}{\partial y^2} = 2xe^y$

$\dfrac{\partial^2 z}{\partial x \partial y} = 2e^y + 3e^{-x}$

64. $z = \sin(x - 2y)$

$\dfrac{\partial z}{\partial x} = \cos(x - 2y)$

$\dfrac{\partial^2 z}{\partial x^2} = -\sin(x - 2y)$

$\dfrac{\partial^2 z}{\partial y \partial x} = 2\sin(x - 2y)$

$\dfrac{\partial z}{\partial y} = -2\cos(x - 2y)$

$\dfrac{\partial^2 z}{\partial y^2} = -4\sin(x - 2y)$

$\dfrac{\partial^2 z}{\partial x \partial y} = 2\sin(x - 2y)$

66. $z = \sqrt{9 - x^2 - y^2}$

$\dfrac{\partial z}{\partial x} = \dfrac{-x}{\sqrt{9 - x^2 - y^2}}$

$\dfrac{\partial^2 z}{\partial x^2} = \dfrac{y^2 - 9}{(9 - x^2 - y^2)^{3/2}}$

$\dfrac{\partial^2 z}{\partial y \partial x} = \dfrac{-xy}{(9 - x^2 - y^2)^{3/2}}$

$\dfrac{\partial z}{\partial y} = \dfrac{-y}{\sqrt{9 - x^2 - y^2}}$

$\dfrac{\partial^2 z}{\partial y^2} = \dfrac{x^2 - 9}{(9 - x^2 - y^2)^{3/2}}$

$\dfrac{\partial^2 z}{\partial x \partial y} = \dfrac{-xy}{(9 - x^2 - y^2)^{3/2}}$

Therefore, $\dfrac{\partial^2 z}{\partial y \partial x} = \dfrac{\partial^2 z}{\partial x \partial y}$.

$\dfrac{\partial z}{\partial x} = \dfrac{\partial z}{\partial y} = 0$ if $x = y = 0$

68. $z = \dfrac{xy}{x - y}$

$$\frac{\partial z}{\partial x} = \frac{y(x - y) - xy}{(x - y)^2} = \frac{-y^2}{(x - y)^2}$$

$$\frac{\partial^2 z}{\partial x^2} = \frac{2y^2}{(x - y)^3}$$

$$\frac{\partial^2 z}{\partial y \partial x} = \frac{(x - y)^2(-2y) + y^2(2)(x - y)(-1)}{(x - y)^4} = \frac{-2xy}{(x - y)^3}$$

$$\frac{\partial z}{\partial y} = -\frac{x(x - y) + xy}{(x - y)^2} = \frac{x^2}{(x - y)^2}$$

$$\frac{\partial^2 z}{\partial y^2} = \frac{2x^2}{(x - y)^3}$$

$$\frac{\partial^2 z}{\partial x \partial y} = \frac{(x - y)^2(2x) - x^2(2)(x - y)}{(x - y)^4} = \frac{-2xy}{(x - y)^3}$$

There are no points for which $z_x = z_y = 0$.

70. $f(x, y, z) = x^2 - 3xy + 4yz + z^3$

$f_x(x, y, z) = 2x - 3y$

$f_y(x, y, z) = -3x + 4z$

$f_{yy}(x, y, z) = 0$

$f_{xy}(x, y, z) = -3$

$f_{yx}(x, y, z) = -3$

$f_{yyx}(x, y, z) = 0$

$f_{xyy}(x, y, z) = 0$

$f_{yxy}(x, y, z) = 0$

Therefore, $f_{xyy} = f_{yxy} = f_{yyx} = 0$.

72. $f(x, y, z) = \dfrac{2z}{x + y}$

$f_x(x, y, z) = \dfrac{-2z}{(x + y)^2}$

$f_y(x, y, z) = \dfrac{-2z}{(x + y)^2}$

$f_{yy}(x, y, z) = \dfrac{4z}{(x + y)^3}$

$f_{xy}(x, y, z) = \dfrac{4z}{(x + y)^3}$

$f_{yx}(x, y, z) = \dfrac{4z}{(x + y)^3}$

$f_{yyx}(x, y, z) = \dfrac{-12z}{(x + y)^4}$

$f_{xyy}(x, y, z) = \dfrac{-12z}{(x + y)^4}$

$f_{yxy}(x, y, z) = \dfrac{-12z}{(x + y)^4}$

74. $z = \sin x\left(\dfrac{e^y - e^{-y}}{2}\right)$

$$\frac{\partial z}{\partial x} = \cos x\left(\frac{e^y - e^{-y}}{2}\right)$$

$$\frac{\partial^2 z}{\partial x^2} = -\sin x\left(\frac{e^y - e^{-y}}{2}\right)$$

$$\frac{\partial z}{\partial y} = \sin x\left(\frac{e^y + e^{-y}}{2}\right)$$

$$\frac{\partial^2 z}{\partial y^2} = \sin x\left(\frac{e^y - e^{-y}}{2}\right)$$

Therefore,

$$\frac{\partial^2 z}{\partial x^2} + \frac{\partial^2 z}{\partial y^2} = -\sin x\left(\frac{e^y - e^{-y}}{2}\right) + \sin x\left(\frac{e^y - e^{-y}}{2}\right)$$

$$= 0.$$

76. $z = \arctan \dfrac{y}{x}$

From Exercise 53, we have

$$\frac{\partial^2 z}{\partial x^2} + \frac{\partial^2 z}{\partial y^2} = \frac{2xy}{(x^2 + y^2)^2} + \frac{-2xy}{(x^2 + y^2)^2} = 0.$$

78. $z = \sin(wct) \sin(wx)$

$$\frac{\partial z}{\partial t} = wc \cos(wct) \sin(wx)$$

$$\frac{\partial^2 z}{\partial t^2} = -w^2c^2 \sin(wct) \sin(wx)$$

$$\frac{\partial z}{\partial x} = w \sin(wct) \cos(wx)$$

$$\frac{\partial^2 z}{\partial x^2} = -w^2 \sin(wct) \sin(wx)$$

Therefore, $\dfrac{\partial^2 z}{\partial t^2} = c^2\dfrac{\partial^2 z}{\partial x^2}$.

80. $z = e^{-t} \sin \dfrac{x}{c}$

$\dfrac{\partial z}{\partial t} = -e^{-t} \sin \dfrac{x}{c}$

$\dfrac{\partial z}{\partial x} = \dfrac{1}{c} e^{-t} \cos \dfrac{x}{c}$

$\dfrac{\partial^2 z}{\partial x^2} = -\dfrac{1}{c^2} e^{-t} \sin \dfrac{x}{c}$

Therefore, $\dfrac{\partial z}{\partial t} = c^2 \dfrac{\partial^2 z}{\partial x^2}$.

82. If $z = f(x, y)$, then to find f_x you consider y constant and differentiate with respect to x. Similarly, to find f_y, you consider x constant and differentiate with respect to y.

84. The plane $z = -x + y = f(x, y)$ satisfies

$$\dfrac{\partial f}{\partial x} < 0 \text{ and } \dfrac{\partial f}{\partial y} > 0.$$

86. In this case, the mixed partials are equal, $f_{xy} = f_{yx}$.

See Theorem 12.3.

88. $f(x, y) = 200x^{0.7}y^{0.3}$

(a) $\dfrac{\partial f}{\partial x} = 140x^{-0.3}y^{0.3} = 140\left(\dfrac{y}{x}\right)^{0.3}$

At $(x, y) = (1000, 500)$, $\dfrac{\partial f}{\partial x} = 140\left(\dfrac{500}{1000}\right)^{0.3} = 140\left(\dfrac{1}{2}\right)^{0.3} \approx 113.72$

(b) $\dfrac{\partial f}{\partial x} = 60x^{0.7}y^{-0.7} = 60\left(\dfrac{x}{y}\right)^{0.7}$

At $(x, y) = (1000, 500)$, $\dfrac{\partial f}{\partial x} = 60\left(\dfrac{1000}{500}\right)^{0.7} = 60(2)^{0.7} \approx 97.47$

90. $V(I, R) = 1000\left[\dfrac{1 + 0.10(1 - R)}{1 + I}\right]^{10}$

$V_I(I, R) = 10{,}000\left[\dfrac{1 + 0.10(1 - R)}{1 + I}\right]^{9}\left[-\dfrac{1 + 0.10(1 - R)}{(1 + I)^2}\right] = -10{,}000\dfrac{[1 + 0.10(1 - R)]^{10}}{(1 + I)^{11}}$

$V_I(0.03, 0.28) \approx -14{,}478.99$

$V_R(I, R) = 10{,}000\left[\dfrac{1 + 0.10(1 - R)}{1 + I}\right]^{9}\left[\dfrac{-0.10}{1 + I}\right] = -1000\dfrac{[1 + 0.10(1 - R)]^{9}}{(1 + I)^{10}}$

$V_R(0.03, 0.28) \approx -1391.17$

The rate of inflation has the greater negative influence on the growth of the investment. (See Exercise 61 in Section 12.1.)

92. $A = 0.885t - 22.4h + 1.20th - 0.544$

(a) $\dfrac{\partial A}{\partial t} = 0.885 + 1.20h$

$\dfrac{\partial A}{\partial t}(30°, 0.80) = 0.885 + 1.20(0.80) = 1.845$

$\dfrac{\partial A}{\partial h} = -22.4 + 1.20t$

$\dfrac{\partial A}{\partial h}(30°, 0.80) = -22.4 + 1.20(30°) = 13.6$

(b) The humidity has a greater effect on A since its coefficient -22.4 is larger than that of t.

94. $U = -5x^2 + xy - 3y^2$

(a) $U_x = -10x + y$

(b) $U_y = x - 6y$

(c) $U_x(2, 3) = -17$ and $U_y(2, 3) = -16$. The person should consume one more unit of y because the rate of decrease of satisfaction is less for y.

(d)

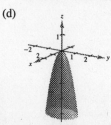

96. (a) $\dfrac{\partial z}{\partial x} = -1.55x + 22.15$ 　　(b) Concave downward $\left(\dfrac{\partial^2 z}{\partial x^2} < 0\right)$ 　　(c) Concave upward $\left(\dfrac{\partial^2 z}{\partial y^2} > 0\right)$

$\dfrac{\partial^2 z}{\partial x^2} = -1.55$

The rate of increase of Medicare expenses (z) is declining with respect to worker's compensation expenses (x).

The rate of increase of Medicare expenses (z) is increasing with respect to public assistance expenses (y).

$\dfrac{\partial z}{\partial y} = 0.014y - 0.54$

$\dfrac{\partial^2 z}{\partial y^2} = 0.014$

98. False

Let $z = x + y + 1$.

100. True

102. $f(x, y) = \displaystyle\int_x^y \sqrt{1 + t^3}\, dt$

By the Second Fundamental Theorem of Calculus,

$\dfrac{\partial f}{\partial x} = \dfrac{d}{dx}\displaystyle\int_x^y \sqrt{1 + t^3}\, dt = -\dfrac{d}{dx}\displaystyle\int_y^x \sqrt{1 + t^3}\, dt = -\sqrt{1 + x^3}$

$\dfrac{\partial f}{\partial y} = \dfrac{d}{dy}\displaystyle\int_x^y \sqrt{1 + t^3}\, dt = \sqrt{1 + y^3}.$

Section 12.4   Differentials

2. $z = \dfrac{x^2}{y}$

$dz = \dfrac{2x}{y}\, dx - \dfrac{x^2}{y^2}\, dy$

4. $w = \dfrac{x + y}{z - 2y}$

$dw = \dfrac{1}{z - 2y}\, dx + \dfrac{z + 2x}{(z - 2y)^2}\, dy - \dfrac{x + y}{(z - 2y)^2}\, dz$

6. $z = \left(\dfrac{1}{2}\right)\left(e^{x^2+y^2} - e^{-x^2-y^2}\right)$

$dz = 2x\left(\dfrac{e^{x^2+y^2} + e^{-x^2-y^2}}{2}\right) dx + 2y\left(\dfrac{e^{x^2+y^2} + e^{-x^2-y^2}}{2}\right) dy = \left(e^{x^2+y^2} + e^{-x^2-y^2}\right)(x\, dx + y\, dy)$

8. $w = e^y \cos x + z^2$

$dw = -e^y \sin x\, dx + e^y \cos x\, dy + 2z\, dz$

10. $w = x^2yz^2 + \sin yz$

$dw = 2xyz^2\, dx + (x^2z^2 + z\cos yz)\, dy +$
$\qquad (2x^2yz + y\cos yz)\, dz$

12. (a) $f(1, 2) = \sqrt{5} \approx 2.2361$

$f(1.05, 2.1) = \sqrt{5.5125} \approx 2.3479$

$\Delta z = 0.11180$

(b) $dz = \dfrac{x}{\sqrt{x^2 + y^2}}\, dx + \dfrac{y}{\sqrt{x^2 + y^2}}\, dy$

$\qquad = \dfrac{x\, dx + y\, dy}{\sqrt{x^2 + y^2}} = \dfrac{0.05 + 2(0.1)}{\sqrt{5}} \approx 0.11180$

14. (a) $f(1, 2) = e^2 \approx 7.3891$

$f(1.05, 2.1) = 1.05e^{2.1} \approx 8.5745$

$\Delta z = 1.1854$

(b) $dz = e^y\, dx + xe^y\, dy$

$\qquad = e^2(0.05) + e^2(0.1) \approx 1.1084$

16. (a) $f(1, 2) = \dfrac{1}{2} = 0.5$

$f(1.05, 2.1) = \dfrac{1.05}{2.1} = 0.5$

$\Delta z = 0$

(b) $dz = \dfrac{1}{y}\,dx - \dfrac{x}{y^2}\,dy$

$= \dfrac{1}{2}(0.05) - \dfrac{1}{4}(0.1) = 0$

18. Let $z = x^2(1 + y)^3$, $x = 2$, $y = 9$, $dx = 0.03$, $dy = -0.1$. Then: $dz = 2x(1 + y)^3\,dx + 3x^2(1 + y)^2\,dy$

$(2.03)^2(1 + 8.9)^3 - 2^2(1 + 9)^3 \approx 2(2)(1 + 9)^3(0.03) + 3(2)^2(1 + 9)^2(-0.1) = 0$

20. Let $z = \sin(x^2 + y^2)$, $x = y = 1$, $dx = 0.05$, $dy = -0.05$. Then: $dz = 2x\cos(x^2 + y^2)\,dx + 2y\cos(x^2 + y^2)\,dy$

$\sin[(1.05)^2 + (0.95)^2] - \sin 2 \approx 2(1)\cos(1^2 + 1^2)(0.05) + 2(1)\cos(1^2 + 1^2)(-0.05) = 0$

22. In general, the accuracy worsens as Δx and Δy increase.

24. If $z = f(x, y)$, then $\Delta z \approx dz$ is the propagated error, and $\dfrac{\Delta z}{z} \approx \dfrac{dz}{z}$ is the relative error.

26. $V = \pi r^2 h$

$dV = 2\pi rh\,dr + \pi r^2\,dh$

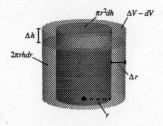

28. $S = \pi r\sqrt{r^2 + h^2}$

$r = 8$, $h = 20$

$\dfrac{dS}{dr} = \pi(r^2 + h^2)^{1/2} + \pi r^2(r^2 + h^2)^{-1/2}$

$= \dfrac{\pi(r^2 + h^2) + \pi r^2}{(r^2 + h^2)^{1/2}} = \pi\,\dfrac{2r^2 + h^2}{\sqrt{r^2 + h^2}}$

$\dfrac{dS}{dh} = \pi r(r^2 + h^2)^{-1/2}h = \pi\,\dfrac{rh}{\sqrt{r^2 + h^2}}$

$dS = \pi\,\dfrac{2r^2 + h^2}{\sqrt{r^2 + h^2}}\,dr + \pi\,\dfrac{rh}{\sqrt{r^2 + h^2}}\,dh$

$= \dfrac{\pi}{\sqrt{r^2 + h^2}}\left[(2r^2 + h^2)\,dr + (rh)\,dh\right]$

$S(8, 20) = 541.3758$

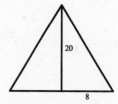

Δr	Δh	dS	ΔS	$\Delta S - dS$
0.1	0.1	10.0341	10.0768	0.0427
0.1	-0.1	5.3671	5.3596	-0.0075
0.001	0.002	0.12368	0.12368	0.683×10^{-5}
-0.0001	0.0002	-0.00303	-0.00303	-0.286×10^{-7}

30. $\dfrac{\partial C}{\partial v} = 0.0817\left[(3.71)\dfrac{1}{2}v^{-1/2} - 0.25\right](T - 91.4)$

$\qquad = \left[\dfrac{0.1516}{v^{1/2}} - 0.0204\right](T - 91.4)$

$\dfrac{\partial C}{\partial T} = 0.0817\left(3.71\sqrt{v} + 5.81 - 0.25v\right)$

$dC = C_v\,dv + C_T\,dT$

$\qquad = \left(\dfrac{0.1516}{23^{1/2}} - 0.0204\right)(8 - 91.4)(\pm 3) + 0.0817\left(3.71\sqrt{23} + 5.81 - 0.25(23)\right)(\pm 1)$

$\qquad = \pm 2.79 \pm 1.46 \doteq \pm 4.25$ Maximum propagated error

$\dfrac{dC}{C} = \dfrac{\pm 4.25}{-30.24} \approx \pm 0.14$

32. $(x, y) = (8.5, 3.2),\ |dx| \le 0.05,\ |dy| \le 0.05$

$r = \sqrt{x^2 + y^2} \Rightarrow dr = \dfrac{x}{\sqrt{x^2 + y^2}}\,dx + \dfrac{y}{\sqrt{x^2 + y^2}}\,dy$

$\qquad\qquad\qquad\quad = \dfrac{8.5}{\sqrt{8.5^2 + 3.2^2}}\,dx + \dfrac{3.2}{\sqrt{8.5^2 + 3.2^2}}\,dy \approx 0.9359\,dx + 0.3523\,dy$

$|dr| \le (1.288)(0.05) \approx 0.064$

$\theta = \arctan\left(\dfrac{y}{x}\right) \Rightarrow d\theta = \dfrac{-\dfrac{y}{x^2}}{1 + \left(\dfrac{y}{x}\right)^2}\,dx + \dfrac{\dfrac{1}{x}}{1 + \left(\dfrac{y}{x}\right)^2}\,dy$

$\qquad\qquad\qquad\quad = \dfrac{-y}{x^2 + y^2}\,dx + \dfrac{x}{x^2 + y^2}\,dy = \dfrac{-3.2}{8.5^2 + 3.2^2}\,dx + \dfrac{8.5}{8.5^2 + 3.2^2}\,dy$

Using the worst case scenario, $dx = -0.05$ and $dy = 0.05$, you see that

$\qquad |d\theta| \le 0.00194 + 0.00515 = 0.0071.$

34. $a = \dfrac{v^2}{r}$

$da = \dfrac{2v}{r}\,dv - \dfrac{v^2}{r^2}\,dr$

$\dfrac{da}{a} = 2\dfrac{dv}{v} - \dfrac{dr}{r} = 2(0.03) - (-0.02) = 0.08 = 8\%$

Note: The maximum error will occur when dv and dr differ in signs.

36. (a) Using the Law of Cosines:

$\qquad a^2 = b^2 + c^2 - 2bc\cos A$

$\qquad\quad = 330^2 + 420^2 - 2(330)(420)\cos 9°$

$\qquad a \approx 107.3$ ft.

(b) $a = \sqrt{b^2 + 420^2 - 2b(420)\cos\theta}$

$\quad da = \dfrac{1}{2}\left[b^2 + 420^2 - 840b\cos\theta\right]^{-1/2}\left[(2b - 840\cos\theta)\,db + 840b\sin\theta\,d\theta\right]$

$\qquad = \dfrac{1}{2}\left[330^2 + 420^2 - 840(330)\left(\cos\dfrac{\pi}{20}\right)\right]^{-1/2}\left[\left(2(330) - 840\cos\dfrac{\pi}{20}\right)(6) + 840(330)\left(\sin\dfrac{\pi}{20}\right)\left(\dfrac{\pi}{180}\right)\right]$

$\qquad \approx \dfrac{1}{2}[11512.79]^{-1/2}[\pm 1774.79] \approx \pm 8.27$ ft

38. $\dfrac{1}{R} = \dfrac{1}{R_1} + \dfrac{1}{R_2}$

$R = \dfrac{R_1 R_2}{R_1 + R_2}$

$dR_1 = \Delta R_1 = 0.5$

$dR_2 = \Delta R_2 = -2$

$\Delta R \approx dR = \dfrac{\partial R}{\partial R_1}\, dR + \dfrac{\partial R}{\partial R_2}\, dR_2 = \dfrac{R_2{}^2}{(R_1 + R_2)^2}\, \Delta R_1 + \dfrac{R_1{}^2}{(R_1 + R_2)^2}\, \Delta R_2$

When $R_1 = 10$ and $R_2 = 15$, we have $\Delta R \approx \dfrac{15^2}{(10 + 15)^2}(0.5) + \dfrac{10^2}{(10 + 15)^2}(-2) = -0.14$ ohm.

40. $T = 2\pi\sqrt{\dfrac{L}{g}}$

$dg = \Delta g = 32.24 - 32.09 = 0.15$

$dL = \Delta L = 2.48 - 2.5 = -0.02$

$\Delta T \approx dT = \dfrac{\partial T}{\partial g}\, dg + \dfrac{\partial T}{\partial L}\, dL = -\dfrac{\pi}{g}\sqrt{\dfrac{L}{g}}\,\Delta g + \dfrac{\pi}{\sqrt{Lg}}\,\Delta L$

When $g = 32.09$ and $L = 2.5$, we have $\Delta T \approx -\dfrac{\pi}{32.09}\sqrt{\dfrac{2.5}{32.09}}(0.15) + \dfrac{\pi}{\sqrt{(2.5)(32.09)}}(-0.02) \approx -0.0111$ sec.

42. $z = f(x, y) = x^2 + y^2$

$\Delta z = f(x + \Delta x,\ y + \Delta y) - f(x, y)$

$\quad = x^2 + 2x(\Delta x) + (\Delta x)^2 + y^2 + 2y(\Delta y) + (\Delta y)^2 - (x^2 + y^2)$

$\quad = 2x(\Delta x) + 2y(\Delta y) + \Delta x(\Delta x) + \Delta y(\Delta y)$

$\quad = f_x(x, y)\,\Delta x + f_y(x, y)\,\Delta y + \epsilon_1 \Delta x + \epsilon_2 \Delta y$ where $\epsilon_1 = \Delta x$ and $\epsilon_2 = \Delta y$.

As $(\Delta x, \Delta y) \to (0, 0)$, $\epsilon_1 \to 0$ and $\epsilon_2 \to 0$.

44. $z = f(x, y) = 5x - 10y + y^3$

$\Delta z = f(x + \Delta x,\ y + \Delta y) - f(x, y)$

$\quad = 5x + 5\Delta x - 10y - 10\Delta y + y^3 + 3y^2(\Delta y) + 3y(\Delta y)^2 + (\Delta y)^3 - (5x - 10y + y^3)$

$\quad = 5(\Delta x) + (3y^2 - 10)(\Delta y) + 0(\Delta x) + (3y(\Delta y) + (\Delta y)^2)\,\Delta y$

$\quad = f_x(x, y)\,\Delta x + f_y(x, y)\,\Delta y + \epsilon_1 \Delta x + \epsilon_2 \Delta y$ where $\epsilon_1 = 0$ and $\epsilon_2 = 3y(\Delta y) + (\Delta y)^2$.

As $(\Delta x, \Delta y) \to (0, 0)$, $\epsilon_1 \to 0$ and $\epsilon_2 \to 0$.

46. $f(x, y) = \begin{cases} \dfrac{5x^2 y}{x^3 + y^3}, & (x, y) \neq (0, 0) \\[2mm] 0, & (x, y) = (0, 0) \end{cases}$

(a) $f_x(0, 0) = \lim\limits_{\Delta x \to 0} \dfrac{f(\Delta x, 0) - f(0, 0)}{\Delta x} = \lim\limits_{\Delta x \to 0} \dfrac{0 - 0}{\Delta x} = 0$

$f_y(0, 0) = \lim\limits_{\Delta y \to 0} \dfrac{f(0, \Delta y) - f(0, 0)}{\Delta y} = \lim\limits_{\Delta y \to 0} \dfrac{0 - 0}{\Delta y} = 0$

Thus, the partial derivatives exist at $(0, 0)$.

(b) Along the line $y = x$: $\lim\limits_{(x,\,y) \to (0,\,0)} f(x, y) = \lim\limits_{x \to 0} \dfrac{5x^3}{2x^3} = \dfrac{5}{2}$.

Along the line $x = 0$, $\lim\limits_{(x,\,y) \to (0,\,0)} f(x, y) = 0$.

Thus, f is not continuous at $(0, 0)$. Therefore f is not differentiable at $(0, 0)$.

(See Theorem 12.5)

Section 12.5   Chain Rules for Functions of Several Variables

2. $w = \sqrt{x^2 + y^2}$

$x = \cos t, y = e^t$

$\dfrac{dw}{dt} = \dfrac{x}{\sqrt{x^2 + y^2}}(-\sin t) + \dfrac{y}{\sqrt{x^2 + y^2}}e^t$

$= \dfrac{-x \sin t + ye^t}{\sqrt{x^2 + y^2}} = \dfrac{-\cos t \sin t + e^{2t}}{\sqrt{\cos^2 t + e^{2t}}}$

4. $w = \ln \dfrac{y}{x}$

$x = \cos t$

$y = \sin t$

$\dfrac{dw}{dt} = \left(\dfrac{-1}{x}\right)(-\sin t) + \left(\dfrac{1}{y}\right)(\cos t)$

$= \tan t + \cot t = \dfrac{1}{\sin t \cos t}$

6. $w = \cos(x - y),\ x = t^2,\ y = 1$

(a) $\dfrac{dw}{dt} = -\sin(x - y)(2t) + \sin(x - y)(0)$

$= -2t \sin(x - y) = -2t \sin(t^2 - 1)$

(b) $w = \cos(t^2 - 1),\ \dfrac{dw}{dt} = -2t \sin(t^2 - 1)$

8. $w = xy \cos z$

$x = t$

$y = t^2$

$z = \arccos t$

(a) $\dfrac{dw}{dt} = (y \cos z)(1) + (x \cos z)(2t) + (-xy \sin z)\left(-\dfrac{1}{\sqrt{1 - t^2}}\right)$

$= t^2(t) + t(t)(2t) - t(t^2)\sqrt{1 - t^2}\left(\dfrac{-1}{\sqrt{1 - t^2}}\right) = t^3 + 2t^3 + t^3 = 4t^3$

(b) $w = t^4,\ \dfrac{dw}{dt} = 4t^3$

10. $w = xyz,\ x = t^2,\ y = 2t,\ z = e^{-t}$

(a) $\dfrac{dw}{dt} = yz(2t) + xz(2) + (xy)(-e^{-t})$

$= (2t)(e^{-t})(2t) + (t^2)(e^{-t})(2) + (t^2)(2t)(-e^{-t})$

$= 2t^2 e^{-t}(2 + 1 - t) = 2t^2 e^{-t}(3 - t)$

(b) $w = (t^2)(2t)(e^{-t}) = 2t^3 e^{-t}$

$\dfrac{dw}{dt} = (2t^3)(-e^{-t}) + (e^{-t})(6t^2) = 2t^2 e^{-t}(-t + 3)$

12. Distance $= f(t) = \sqrt{(x_2 - x_1)^2 + (y_2 - y_1)^2} = \sqrt{\left[48 + \left(\sqrt{3} - \sqrt{2}\right)\right]^2 + \left[48t\left(1 - \sqrt{2}\right)\right]^2}$

$= 48t\sqrt{8 - 2\sqrt{2} - 2\sqrt{6}}$

$f'(t) = 48\sqrt{8 - 2\sqrt{2} - 2\sqrt{6}} = f'(1)$

14. $w = \dfrac{x^2}{y}$,

     $x = t^2$,

     $y = t + 1$,

     $t = 1$

$$\frac{dw}{dt} = \frac{\partial w}{\partial x}\frac{dx}{dt} + \frac{\partial w}{\partial y}\frac{dy}{dt}$$

$$= \frac{2x}{y}(2t) + \frac{-x^2}{y^2}(1)$$

$$= \frac{2t^2(2t)}{t + 1} - \frac{t^4}{(t + 1)^2}$$

$$= \frac{(t + 1)(4t^3) - t^4}{(t + 1)^2}$$

$$= \frac{3t^4 + 4t^3}{(t + 1)^2}$$

$$\frac{d^2w}{dt^2} = \frac{(t + 1)^2(12t^3 + 12t^2) - (3t^4 + 4t^3)2(t + 1)}{(t + 1)^4}$$

At $t = 1$: $\dfrac{d^2w}{dt^2} = \dfrac{4(24) - (7)(4)}{16} = \dfrac{68}{16} = 4.25$

18. $w = \sin(2x + 3y)$

     $x = s + t$

     $y = s - t$

$$\frac{\partial w}{\partial s} = 2\cos(2x + 3y) + 3\cos(2x + 3y)$$

$$= 5\cos(2x + 3y) = 5\cos(5s - t)$$

$$\frac{\partial w}{\partial t} = 2\cos(2x + 3y) - 3\cos(2x + 3y)$$

$$= -\cos(2x + 3y) = -\cos(5s - t)$$

When $s = 0$ and $t = \dfrac{\pi}{2}$, $\dfrac{\partial w}{\partial s} = 0$ and $\dfrac{\partial w}{\partial t} = 0$.

20. $w = \sqrt{25 - 5x^2 - 5y^2}$, $x = r\cos\theta$, $y = r\sin\theta$

(a) $\dfrac{\partial w}{\partial r} = \dfrac{-5x}{\sqrt{25 - 5x^2 - 5y^2}}\cos\theta + \dfrac{-5y}{\sqrt{25 - 5x^2 - 5y^2}}\sin\theta$

$$= \frac{-5r\cos^2\theta - 5r\sin^2\theta}{\sqrt{25 - 5x^2 - 5y^2}} = \frac{-5r}{\sqrt{25 - 5r^2}}$$

$$\frac{\partial w}{\partial\theta} = \frac{-5x}{\sqrt{25 - 5x^2 - 5y^2}}(-r\sin\theta) + \frac{-5y}{\sqrt{25 - 5x^2 - 5y^2}}(r\cos\theta)$$

$$= \frac{-5r^2\sin^2\theta\cos\theta - 5r^2\sin\theta\cos\theta}{\sqrt{25 - 5x^2 - 5y^2}} = 0$$

(b) $w = \sqrt{25 - 5r^2}$

$$\frac{\partial w}{\partial r} = \frac{-5r}{\sqrt{25 - 5r^2}}; \frac{\partial w}{\partial\theta} = 0$$

16. $w = y^3 - 3x^2y$

     $x = e^s$

     $y = e^t$

$$\frac{\partial w}{\partial s} = -6xy(e^s) + (3y^2 - 3x^2)(0) = -6e^{2s+t}$$

$$\frac{\partial w}{\partial t} = -6xy(0) + (3y^2 - 3x^2)(e^t)$$

$$= 3e^t(e^{2t} - e^{2s})$$

When $s = 0$ and $t = 1$, $\dfrac{\partial w}{\partial s} = -6e$ and $\dfrac{\partial w}{\partial t} = 3e(e^2 - 1)$.

22. $w = \dfrac{yz}{x}, x = \theta^2, y = r + \theta, z = r - \theta$

(a) $\dfrac{\partial w}{\partial r} = \dfrac{-yz}{x^2}(0) + \dfrac{z}{x}(1) + \dfrac{y}{x}(1) = \dfrac{z + y}{x} = \dfrac{2r}{\theta^2}$

$\dfrac{\partial w}{\partial \theta} = \dfrac{-yz}{x^2}(2\theta) + \dfrac{z}{x}(1) + \dfrac{y}{x}(-1)$

$= \dfrac{-(r + \theta)(r - \theta)}{\theta^4}(2\theta) + \dfrac{(r - \theta) - (r + \theta)}{\theta^2}$

$= \dfrac{2(\theta^2 - r^2)}{\theta^3} - \dfrac{2}{\theta} = \dfrac{-2r^2}{\theta^3}$

(b) $w = \dfrac{yz}{x} = \dfrac{(r + \theta)(r - \theta)}{\theta^2} = \dfrac{r^2}{\theta^2} - 1$

$\dfrac{\partial w}{\partial r} = \dfrac{2r}{\theta^2}$

$\dfrac{\partial w}{\partial \theta} = \dfrac{-2r^2}{\theta^3}$

24. $w = x \cos yz, x = s^2, y = t^2, z = s - 2t$

$\dfrac{\partial w}{\partial s} = \cos(yz)(2s) - xz \sin(yz)(0) - xy \sin(yz)(1)$

$= \cos(st^2 - 2t^3)2s - s^2t^2 \sin(st^2 - 2t^3)$

$\dfrac{\partial w}{\partial t} = \cos(yz)(0) - xz \sin(yz)(2t) - xy \sin(yz)(-2)$

$= -2s^2t(s - 2t) \sin(st^2 - 2t^3) + 2s^2t^2 \sin(st^2 - 2t^3)$

$= (6s^2t^2 - 2s^3t) \sin(st^2 - 2t^3)$

26. $w = x^2 + y^2 + z^2, x = t \sin s, y = t \cos s, z = st^2$

$\dfrac{\partial w}{\partial s} = 2x + \cos s + 2y(-t \sin s) + 2z(t^2)$

$= 2t^2 \sin s \cos s - 2t^2 \sin s \cos s + 2st^4 = 2st^4$

$\dfrac{\partial w}{\partial t} = 2x \sin s + 2y \cos s + 2z(2st)$

$= 2t \sin^2 s + 2t \cos^2 s + 4s^2t^3 = 2t + 4s^2t^3$

28. $\cos x + \tan xy + 5 = 0$

$\dfrac{dy}{dx} = -\dfrac{F_x(x, y)}{F_y(x, y)} = -\dfrac{-\sin x + y \sec^2 xy}{x \sec^2 xy}$

30. $\dfrac{x}{x^2 + y^2} - y^2 - 6 = 0$

$\dfrac{dy}{dx} = -\dfrac{F_x(x, y)}{F_y(x, y)}$

$= -\dfrac{(y^2 - x^2)/(x^2 + y^2)^2}{(-2xy)/(x^2 + y^2)^2 - 2y}$

$= \dfrac{y^2 - x^2}{2xy + 2y(x^2 + y^2)^2}$

$= \dfrac{y^2 - x^2}{2xy + 2yx^4 + 4x^2y^3 + 2y^5}$

32. $F(x, y, z) = xz + yz + xy$

$F_x = z + y$

$F_y = z + x$

$F_z = x + y$

$\dfrac{\partial z}{\partial x} = -\dfrac{F_x}{F_z} = -\dfrac{y + z}{x + y}$

$\dfrac{\partial z}{\partial y} = -\dfrac{F_y}{F_z} = -\dfrac{x + z}{x + y}$

34. $F(x, y, z) = e^x \sin(y + z) - z$

$F_x = e^x \sin(y + z)$

$F_y = e^x \cos(y + z)$

$F_z = e^x \cos(y + z) - 1$

$\dfrac{\partial z}{\partial x} = -\dfrac{F_x}{F_z} = \dfrac{e^x \sin(y + z)}{1 - e^x \cos(y + x)}$

$\dfrac{\partial z}{\partial y} = -\dfrac{F_y}{F_z} = \dfrac{e^x \cos(y + z)}{1 - e^x \cos(y + z)}$

36. $x + \sin(y + z) = 0$

(i) $1 + \dfrac{\partial z}{\partial x} \cos(y + z) = 0$ implies

$\dfrac{\partial z}{\partial x} = -\dfrac{1}{\cos(y + z)} = -\sec(y + z).$

(ii) $\left(1 + \dfrac{\partial z}{\partial y}\right) \cos(y + z) = 0$ implies $\dfrac{\partial z}{\partial y} = -1.$

38. $x \ln y + y^2 z + z^2 - 8 = 0$

   (i) $\dfrac{\partial z}{\partial x} = \dfrac{-F_x(x, y, z)}{F_z(x, y, z)} = \dfrac{-\ln y}{y^2 + 2z}$

   (ii) $\dfrac{\partial z}{\partial y} = \dfrac{-F_y(x, y, z)}{F_z(x, y, z)} = -\dfrac{\dfrac{x}{y} + 2yz}{y^2 + 2z} = -\dfrac{x + 2y^2 z}{y^3 + 2yz}$

40. $x^2 + y^2 - z^2 - 5yw + 10w^2 - 2 = F(x, y, z, w)$

   $F_x = 2x, \ F_y = 2y - 5w, \ F_z = 2z, \ F_w = -5y + 20w$

   $\dfrac{\partial w}{\partial x} = -\dfrac{F_x}{F_w} = \dfrac{-2x}{-5y + 20w} = \dfrac{2x}{5y - 20w}$

   $\dfrac{\partial w}{\partial y} = -\dfrac{F_y}{F_w} = \dfrac{5w - 2y}{20w - 5y}$

   $\dfrac{\partial w}{\partial z} = -\dfrac{F_z}{F_w} = \dfrac{2z}{5y - 20w}$

42. $F(x, y, z, w) = w - \sqrt{x - y} - \sqrt{y - z} = 0$

   $\dfrac{\partial w}{\partial x} = \dfrac{-F_x}{F_w} = \dfrac{1}{2}\dfrac{(x - y)^{-1/2}}{1} = \dfrac{1}{2\sqrt{x - y}}$

   $\dfrac{\partial w}{\partial y} = \dfrac{-F_y}{F_w} = \dfrac{-1}{2}(x - y)^{-1/2} + \dfrac{1}{2}(y - z)^{-1/2}$

   $\qquad = \dfrac{-1}{2\sqrt{x - y}} + \dfrac{1}{2\sqrt{y - z}}$

   $\dfrac{\partial w}{\partial z} = \dfrac{-F_z}{F_w} = \dfrac{-1}{2\sqrt{y - z}}$

44. $f(x, y) = x^3 - 3xy^2 + y^3$

   $f(tx, ty) = (tx)^3 - 3(tx)(ty)^2 + (ty)^3$

   $\qquad = t^3(x^3 - 3xy^2 + y^3) = t^3 f(x, y)$

   Degree: 3

   $xf_x(x, y) + yf_y(x, y) = x(3x^2 - 3y^2) + y(-6xy + 3y^2)$

   $\qquad = 3x^3 - 9xy^2 + 3y^3 = 3f(x, y)$

46. $f(x, y) = \dfrac{x^2}{\sqrt{x^2 + y^2}}$

   $f(tx, ty) = \dfrac{(tx)^2}{\sqrt{(tx)^2 + (ty)^2}} = t\left(\dfrac{x^2}{\sqrt{x^2 + y^2}}\right) = tf(x, y)$

   Degree: 1

   $xf_x(x, y) + yf_y(x, y) = x\left[\dfrac{x^3 + 2xy^2}{(x^2 + y^2)^{3/2}}\right] + y\left[\dfrac{-x^2 y}{(x^2 + y^2)^{3/2}}\right]$

   $\qquad = \dfrac{x^4 + x^2 y^2}{(x^2 + y^2)^{3/2}} = \dfrac{x^2(x^2 + y^2)}{(x^2 + y^2)^{3/2}}$

   $\qquad = \dfrac{x^2}{\sqrt{x^2 + y^2}} = f(x, y)$

48. $\dfrac{\partial w}{\partial s} = \dfrac{\partial w}{\partial x}\dfrac{\partial x}{\partial s} + \dfrac{\partial w}{\partial y}\dfrac{\partial y}{\partial s}$

   $\dfrac{\partial w}{\partial t} = \dfrac{\partial w}{\partial x}\dfrac{\partial x}{\partial t} + \dfrac{\partial w}{\partial y}\dfrac{\partial y}{\partial t}$ (Page 878)

50. $\dfrac{dy}{dx} = -\dfrac{f_x(x, y)}{f_y(x, y)}$

   $\dfrac{\partial z}{\partial x} = -\dfrac{f_x(x, y, z)}{f_z(x, y, z)}$

   $\dfrac{\partial z}{\partial y} = -\dfrac{f_y(x, y, z)}{f_z(x, y, z)}$

52. (a) $V = \pi r^2 h$

   $\dfrac{dV}{dt} = \pi\left(2rh\dfrac{dr}{dt} + r^2\dfrac{dh}{dt}\right) = \pi r\left(2h\dfrac{dr}{dt} + r\dfrac{dh}{dt}\right) = \pi(12)[2(36)(6) + 12(-4)] = 4608\pi \ \text{in.}^3/\text{min}$

   (b) $S = 2\pi r(r + h)$

   $\dfrac{dS}{dt} = 2\pi\left[(2r + h)\dfrac{dr}{dt} + r\dfrac{dh}{dt}\right] = 2\pi[(24 + 36)(6) + 12(-4)] = 624\pi \ \text{in.}^2/\text{min}$

54. (a) $V = \dfrac{\pi}{3}(r^2 + rR + R^2)h$

$$\frac{dV}{dt} = \frac{\pi}{3}\left[(2r + R)h\frac{dr}{dt} + (r + 2R)h\frac{dR}{dt} + (r^2 + rR + R^2)\frac{dh}{dt}\right]$$

$$= \frac{\pi}{3}\left[[2(15) + 25](10)(4) + [15 + 2(25)](10)(4) + [(15)^2 + (15)(25) + (25)^2](12)\right]$$

$$= \frac{\pi}{3}(19{,}500) = 6{,}500\pi \text{ cm}^3/\text{min}$$

(b) $S = \pi(R + r)\sqrt{(R - r)^2 + h^2}$

$$\frac{dS}{dt} = \pi\left\{\left[\sqrt{(R - r)^2 + h^2} - (R + r)\frac{(R - r)}{\sqrt{(R - r)^2 + h^2}}\right]\frac{dr}{dt} + \left[\sqrt{(R - r)^2 + h^2} + (R + r)\frac{(R - r)}{\sqrt{(R - r)^2 + h^2}}\right]\frac{dR}{dt} + \right.$$

$$\left. (R + r)\frac{h}{\sqrt{(R - r)^2 + h^2}}\frac{dh}{dt}\right\}$$

$$= \pi\left\{\left[\sqrt{(25 - 15)^2 + 10^2} - (25 + 15)\frac{25 - 15}{\sqrt{(25 - 15)^2 + 10^2}}\right](4) + \right.$$

$$\left. \left[\sqrt{(25 - 15)^2 + 10^2} + (25 + 15)\frac{25 - 15}{\sqrt{(25 - 15)^2 + 10^2}}\right](4) + (25 + 15)\frac{10}{\sqrt{(25 - 15)^2 + 10^2}}(12)\right\}$$

$$= 320\sqrt{2}\pi \text{ cm}^2/\text{min}$$

56. $pV = mRT$

$$T = \frac{1}{mR}(pV)$$

$$\frac{dT}{dt} = \frac{1}{mR}\left[V\frac{dp}{dt} + p\frac{dV}{dt}\right]$$

58. $g(t) = f(xt, yt) = t^n f(x, y)$

Let $u = xt$, $v = yt$, then

$$g'(t) = \frac{\partial f}{\partial u}\cdot\frac{du}{dt} + \frac{\partial f}{\partial v}\cdot\frac{dv}{dt} = \frac{\partial f}{\partial u}x + \frac{\partial f}{\partial v}y$$

and $g'(t) = nt^{n-1}f(x, y)$.

Now, let $t = 1$ and we have $u = x$, $v = y$. Thus,

$$\frac{\partial f}{\partial x}x + \frac{\partial f}{\partial y}y = nf(x, y).$$

60. $w = (x - y)\sin(y - x)$

$$\frac{\partial w}{\partial x} = -(x - y)\cos(y - x) + \sin(y - x)$$

$$\frac{\partial w}{\partial y} = (x - y)\cos(y - x) - \sin(y - x)$$

$$\frac{\partial w}{\partial x} + \frac{\partial w}{\partial y} = 0$$

62. $w = \arctan\dfrac{y}{x}$, $x = r\cos\theta$, $y = r\sin\theta$

$$= \arctan\left(\frac{r\sin\theta}{r\cos\theta}\right) = \arctan(\tan\theta) = \theta \text{ for } -\frac{\pi}{2} < \theta < \frac{\pi}{2}$$

$$\frac{\partial w}{\partial x} = \frac{-y}{x^2 + y^2},\ \frac{\partial w}{\partial y} = \frac{x}{x^2 + y^2},\ \frac{\partial w}{\partial r} = 0,\ \frac{\partial w}{\partial \theta} = 1$$

$$\left(\frac{\partial w}{\partial x}\right)^2 + \left(\frac{\partial w}{\partial y}\right)^2 = \frac{y^2}{(x^2 + y^2)^2} + \frac{x^2}{(x^2 + y^2)^2} = \frac{1}{x^2 + y^2} = \frac{1}{r^2}$$

$$\left(\frac{\partial w}{\partial r}\right)^2 + \left(\frac{1}{r^2}\right)\left(\frac{\partial w}{\partial \theta}\right)^2 = 0 + \frac{1}{r^2}(1) = \frac{1}{r^2}$$

Therefore, $\left(\dfrac{\partial w}{\partial x}\right)^2 + \left(\dfrac{\partial w}{\partial y}\right)^2 = \left(\dfrac{\partial w}{\partial r}\right)^2 + \dfrac{1}{r^2}\left(\dfrac{\partial w}{\partial \theta}\right)^2.$

64. Note first that

$$\frac{\partial u}{\partial x} = \frac{\partial v}{\partial y} = \frac{x}{x^2 + y^2}$$

$$\frac{\partial u}{\partial y} = -\frac{\partial v}{\partial x} = \frac{y}{x^2 + y^2}.$$

$$\frac{\partial u}{\partial r} = \frac{x}{x^2 + y^2}\cos\theta + \frac{y}{x^2 + y^2}\sin\theta = \frac{r\cos^2\theta + r\sin^2\theta}{r^2} = \frac{1}{r}$$

$$\frac{\partial v}{\partial \theta} = \frac{-y}{x^2 + y^2}(-r\sin\theta) + \frac{x}{x^2 + y^2}(r\cos\theta) = \frac{r^2\sin^2\theta + r^2\cos^2\theta}{r^2} = 1$$

Thus, $\dfrac{\partial u}{\partial r} = \dfrac{1}{r}\dfrac{\partial v}{\partial \theta}.$

$$\frac{\partial v}{\partial r} = \frac{-y}{x^2 + y^2}\cos\theta + \frac{x}{x^2 + y^2}\sin\theta = \frac{-r\sin\theta\cos\theta + r\sin\theta\cos\theta}{r^2} = 0$$

$$\frac{\partial u}{\partial \theta} = \frac{x}{x^2 + y^2}(-r\sin\theta) + \frac{y}{x^2 + y^2}(r\cos\theta) = \frac{-r^2\sin\theta\cos\theta + r^2\sin\theta\cos\theta}{r^2} = 0$$

Thus, $\dfrac{\partial v}{\partial r} = -\dfrac{1}{r}\dfrac{\partial u}{\partial \theta}.$

Section 12.6   Directional Derivatives and Gradients

2. $f(x, y) = x^3 - y^3, \mathbf{v} = \dfrac{\sqrt{2}}{2}(\mathbf{i} + \mathbf{j})$

$\nabla f(x, y) = 3x^2\mathbf{i} - 3y^2\mathbf{j}$

$\nabla f(4, 3) = 48\mathbf{i} - 27\mathbf{j}$

$\mathbf{u} = \dfrac{\mathbf{v}}{\|\mathbf{v}\|} = \dfrac{\sqrt{2}}{2}\mathbf{i} + \dfrac{\sqrt{2}}{2}\mathbf{j}$

$D_{\mathbf{u}}f(4, 3) = \nabla f(4, 3) \cdot \mathbf{u} = 24\sqrt{2} - \dfrac{27}{2}\sqrt{2} = \dfrac{21}{2}\sqrt{2}$

4. $f(x, y) = \dfrac{x}{y}$

$\mathbf{v} = -\mathbf{j}$

$\nabla f(x, y) = \dfrac{1}{y}\mathbf{i} - \dfrac{x}{y^2}\mathbf{j}$

$\nabla f(1, 1) = \mathbf{i} - \mathbf{j}$

$\mathbf{u} = \dfrac{\mathbf{v}}{\|\mathbf{v}\|} = -\mathbf{j}$

$D_{\mathbf{u}}f(1, 1) = \nabla f(1, 1) \cdot \mathbf{u} = 1$

6. $g(x, y) = \arccos xy, \mathbf{v} = \mathbf{i} + 5\mathbf{j}$

$\nabla g(x, y) = \dfrac{-y}{\sqrt{1 - (xy)^2}}\mathbf{i} + \dfrac{-x}{\sqrt{1 - (xy)^2}}\mathbf{j}$

$\nabla g(1, 0) = -\mathbf{j}$

$\mathbf{u} = \dfrac{\mathbf{v}}{\|\mathbf{v}\|} = \dfrac{1}{\sqrt{26}}\mathbf{i} + \dfrac{5}{\sqrt{26}}\mathbf{j}$

$D_{\mathbf{u}}g(1, 0) = \nabla g(1, 0) \cdot \mathbf{u} = \dfrac{-5}{\sqrt{26}} = \dfrac{-5\sqrt{26}}{26}$

8. $h(x, y) = e^{-(x^2 + y^2)}$

$\mathbf{v} = \mathbf{i} + \mathbf{j}$

$\nabla h = -2xe^{-(x^2 + y^2)}\mathbf{i} - 2ye^{-(x^2 + y^2)}\mathbf{j}$

$\nabla h(0, 0) = \mathbf{0}$

$D_{\mathbf{u}}h(0, 0) = \nabla h(0, 0) \cdot \mathbf{u} = 0$

10. $f(x, y, z) = x^2 + y^2 + z^2$

$\mathbf{v} = \mathbf{i} - 2\mathbf{j} + 3\mathbf{k}$

$\nabla f = 2x\mathbf{i} + 2y\mathbf{j} + 2z\mathbf{k}$

$\nabla f(1, 2, -1) = 2\mathbf{i} + 4\mathbf{j} - 2\mathbf{k}$

$\mathbf{u} = \dfrac{\mathbf{v}}{\|\mathbf{v}\|} = \dfrac{1}{\sqrt{14}}\mathbf{i} - \dfrac{2}{\sqrt{14}}\mathbf{j} + \dfrac{3}{\sqrt{14}}\mathbf{k}$

$D_{\mathbf{u}}f(1, 2, -1) = \nabla f(1, 2, -1) \cdot \mathbf{u} = -\dfrac{6}{7}\sqrt{14}$

12. $h(x, y, z) = xyz$

$\mathbf{v} = \langle 2, 1, 2 \rangle$

$\nabla h = yz\mathbf{i} + xz\mathbf{j} + xy\mathbf{k}$

$\nabla h(2, 1, 1) = \mathbf{i} + 2\mathbf{j} + 2\mathbf{k}$

$\mathbf{u} = \dfrac{\mathbf{v}}{\|\mathbf{v}\|} = \dfrac{2}{3}\mathbf{i} + \dfrac{1}{3}\mathbf{j} + \dfrac{2}{3}\mathbf{k}$

$D_{\mathbf{u}}h(2, 1, 1) = \nabla h(2, 1, 1) \cdot \mathbf{u} = \dfrac{8}{3}$

14. $f(x, y) = \dfrac{y}{x + y}$

$$\mathbf{u} = \frac{\sqrt{3}}{2}\mathbf{i} - \frac{1}{2}\mathbf{j}$$

$$\nabla f = -\frac{y}{(x + y)^2}\mathbf{i} + \frac{x}{(x + y)^2}\mathbf{j}$$

$$D_{\mathbf{u}}f = \nabla f \cdot \mathbf{u} = -\frac{\sqrt{3}y}{2(x + y)^2} - \frac{x}{2(x + y)^2}$$

$$= -\frac{1}{2(x + y)^2}\left(\sqrt{3}y + x\right)$$

16. $g(x, y) = xe^y$

$$\mathbf{u} = -\frac{1}{2}\mathbf{i} + \frac{\sqrt{3}}{2}\mathbf{j}$$

$$\nabla g = e^y\mathbf{i} + xe^y\mathbf{j}$$

$$D_{\mathbf{u}}g = -\frac{1}{2}e^y + \frac{\sqrt{3}}{2}xe^y = \frac{e^y}{2}\left(\sqrt{3}x - 1\right)$$

18. $f(x, y) = \cos(x + y)$

$$\mathbf{v} = \frac{\pi}{2}\mathbf{i} - \pi\mathbf{j}$$

$$\nabla f = -\sin(x + y)\mathbf{i} - \sin(x + y)\mathbf{j}$$

$$\mathbf{u} = \frac{\mathbf{v}}{\|\mathbf{v}\|} = \frac{1}{\sqrt{5}}\mathbf{i} - \frac{2}{\sqrt{5}}\mathbf{j}$$

$$D_{\mathbf{u}}f = -\frac{1}{\sqrt{5}}\sin(x + y) + \frac{2}{\sqrt{5}}\sin(x + y)$$

$$= \frac{1}{\sqrt{5}}\sin(x + y) = \frac{\sqrt{5}}{5}\sin(x + y)$$

At $(0, \pi)$, $D_{\mathbf{u}}f = 0$.

20. $g(x, y, z) = xye^z$

$$\mathbf{v} = -2\mathbf{i} - 4\mathbf{j}$$

$$\nabla g = ye^z\mathbf{i} + xe^z\mathbf{j} + xye^z\mathbf{k}$$

At $(2, 4, 0)$, $\nabla g = 4\mathbf{i} + 2\mathbf{j} + 8\mathbf{k}$.

$$\mathbf{u} = \frac{\mathbf{v}}{\|\mathbf{v}\|} = -\frac{1}{\sqrt{5}}\mathbf{i} - \frac{2}{\sqrt{5}}\mathbf{j}$$

$$D_{\mathbf{u}}g = \nabla g \cdot \mathbf{u} = -\frac{4}{\sqrt{5}} - \frac{4}{\sqrt{5}} = -\frac{8}{\sqrt{5}}$$

22. $g(x, y) = 2xe^{y/x}$

$$\nabla g(x, y) = \left(-\frac{2y}{x}e^{y/x} + 2e^{y/x}\right)\mathbf{i} + 2e^{y/x}\mathbf{j}$$

$$\nabla g(2, 0) = 2\mathbf{i} + 2\mathbf{j}$$

24. $z = \ln(x^2 - y)$

$$\nabla z(x, y) = \frac{2x}{x^2 - y}\mathbf{i} - \frac{1}{x^2 - y}\mathbf{j}$$

$$\nabla z(2, 3) = 4\mathbf{i} - \mathbf{j}$$

26. $w = x\tan(y + z)$

$$\nabla w(x, y, z) = \tan(y + z)\mathbf{i} + x\sec^2(y + z)\mathbf{j} + x\sec^2(y + z)\mathbf{k}$$

$$\nabla w(4, 3, -1) = \tan 2\mathbf{i} + 4\sec^2 2\mathbf{j} + 4\sec^2 2\mathbf{k}$$

28. $\overrightarrow{PQ} = -2\mathbf{i} + 7\mathbf{j}$, $\mathbf{u} = -\dfrac{2}{\sqrt{53}}\mathbf{i} + \dfrac{7}{\sqrt{53}}\mathbf{j}$

$$\nabla f(x, y) = 6x\mathbf{i} - 2y\mathbf{j}, \quad \nabla f(3, 1) = 18\mathbf{i} - 2\mathbf{j}$$

$$D_{\mathbf{u}}f = \nabla f \cdot \mathbf{u} = -\frac{36}{\sqrt{53}} - \frac{14}{\sqrt{53}} = -\frac{50}{\sqrt{53}} = -\frac{50\sqrt{53}}{53}$$

30. $\overrightarrow{PQ} = \dfrac{\pi}{2}\mathbf{i} + \pi\mathbf{j}$, $\mathbf{u} = \dfrac{1}{\sqrt{5}}\mathbf{i} + \dfrac{2}{\sqrt{5}}\mathbf{j}$

$$\nabla f(x, y) = 2\cos 2x\cos y\mathbf{i} - \sin 2x\sin y\mathbf{j}$$

$$\nabla f(0, 0) = 2\mathbf{i}$$

$$D_{\mathbf{u}}f = \nabla f \cdot \mathbf{u} = \frac{2}{\sqrt{5}} = \frac{2\sqrt{5}}{5}$$

32. $h(x, y) = y \cos(x - y)$

$\nabla h(x, y) = -y \sin(x - y)\mathbf{i} + [\cos(x - y) + y \sin(x - y)]\mathbf{j}$

$\nabla h\left(0, \dfrac{\pi}{3}\right) = \dfrac{\sqrt{3}\pi}{6}\mathbf{i} + \left(\dfrac{3 - \sqrt{3}\pi}{6}\right)\mathbf{j}$

$\left\|\nabla h\left(0, \dfrac{\pi}{3}\right)\right\| = \sqrt{\dfrac{3\pi^2}{36} + \dfrac{9 - 6\sqrt{3}\pi + 3\pi^2}{36}} = \dfrac{\sqrt{3\left(2\pi^2 - 2\sqrt{3}\pi + 3\right)}}{6}$

34. $g(x, y) = ye^{-x^2}$

$\nabla g(x, y) = -2xye^{-x^2}\mathbf{i} + e^{-x^2}\mathbf{j}$

$\nabla g(0, 5) = \mathbf{j}$

$\|\nabla g(0, 5)\| = 1$

36. $w = \dfrac{1}{\sqrt{1 - x^2 - y^2 - z^2}}$

$\nabla w = \dfrac{1}{\left(\sqrt{1 - x^2 - y^2 - z^2}\right)^3}(x\mathbf{i} + y\mathbf{j} + z\mathbf{k})$

$\nabla w(0, 0, 0) = \mathbf{0}$

$\|\nabla w(0, 0, 0)\| = 0$

38. $w = xy^2z^2$

$\nabla w = y^2z^2\mathbf{i} + 2xyz^2\mathbf{j} + 2xy^2z\mathbf{k}$

$\nabla w(2, 1, 1) = \mathbf{i} + 4\mathbf{j} + 4\mathbf{k}$

$\|\nabla w(2, 1, 1)\| = \sqrt{33}$

For Exercises 40–46, $f(x, y) = 3 - \dfrac{x}{3} - \dfrac{y}{2}$ **and** $D_\theta f(x, y) = -\left(\dfrac{1}{3}\right)\cos\theta - \left(\dfrac{1}{2}\right)\sin\theta.$

40. (a) $D_{\pi/4}f(3, 2) = -\left(\dfrac{1}{3}\right)\dfrac{\sqrt{2}}{2} - \left(\dfrac{1}{2}\right)\dfrac{\sqrt{2}}{2} = -\dfrac{5\sqrt{2}}{12}$

(b) $D_{2\pi/3}f(3, 2) = -\left(\dfrac{1}{3}\right)\left(-\dfrac{1}{2}\right) - \left(\dfrac{1}{2}\right)\dfrac{\sqrt{3}}{2} = \dfrac{2 - 3\sqrt{3}}{12}$

42. (a) $\mathbf{u} = \left(\dfrac{1}{\sqrt{2}}\right)(\mathbf{i} + \mathbf{j})$

$D_\mathbf{u} f = \nabla f \cdot \mathbf{u}$

$= -\left(\dfrac{1}{3}\right)\dfrac{1}{\sqrt{2}} - \left(\dfrac{1}{2}\right)\dfrac{1}{\sqrt{2}} = -\dfrac{5\sqrt{2}}{12}$

(b) $\mathbf{v} = -3\mathbf{i} - 4\mathbf{j}$

$\|\mathbf{v}\| = \sqrt{9 + 16} = 5$

$\mathbf{u} = -\dfrac{3}{5}\mathbf{i} - \dfrac{4}{5}\mathbf{j}$

$D_\mathbf{u} f = \nabla f \cdot \mathbf{u} = \dfrac{1}{5} + \dfrac{2}{5} = \dfrac{3}{5}$

44. $\nabla f = -\left(\dfrac{1}{3}\right)\mathbf{i} - \left(\dfrac{1}{2}\right)\mathbf{j}$

46. $\nabla f = -\dfrac{1}{3}\mathbf{i} - \dfrac{1}{2}\mathbf{j}$

$\dfrac{\nabla f}{\|\nabla f\|} = \dfrac{1}{\sqrt{13}}(-2\mathbf{i} - 3\mathbf{j})$

Therefore, $\mathbf{u} = \left(1/\sqrt{13}\right)(3\mathbf{i} - 2\mathbf{j})$ and $D_\mathbf{u} f(3, 2) = \nabla f \cdot \mathbf{u} = 0.$ ∇f is the direction of greatest rate of change of $f.$ Hence, in a direction orthogonal to $\nabla f,$ the rate of change of f is 0.

For Exercises 48 and 50, $f(x, y) = 9 - x^2 - y^2$ **and** $D_\theta f(x, y) = -2x \cos \theta - 2y \sin \theta = -2(x \cos \theta + y \sin \theta)$.

48. (a) $D_{-\pi/4} f(1, 2) = -2\left(\dfrac{\sqrt{2}}{2} - \sqrt{2}\right) = \sqrt{2}$

(b) $D_{\pi/3} f(1, 2) = -2\left(\dfrac{1}{2} + \sqrt{3}\right) = -\left(1 + 2\sqrt{3}\right)$

50. $\nabla f(1, 2) = -2\mathbf{i} - 4\mathbf{j}$

$\dfrac{\nabla f(1, 2)}{\|\nabla f(1, 2)\|} = \dfrac{1}{\sqrt{5}}(-\mathbf{i} - 2\mathbf{j})$

Therefore,

$\mathbf{u} = \left(1/\sqrt{5}\right)(-2\mathbf{i} + \mathbf{j})$ and

$D_{\mathbf{u}} f(1, 2) = \nabla f(1, 2) \cdot \mathbf{u} = 0.$

52. (a) In the direction of the vector $\mathbf{i} + \mathbf{j}$.

(b) $\nabla f = \dfrac{1}{2} y \dfrac{1}{2\sqrt{x}} \mathbf{i} + \dfrac{1}{2} \sqrt{x} \mathbf{j} = \dfrac{y}{4\sqrt{x}} \mathbf{i} + \dfrac{1}{2} \sqrt{x} \mathbf{j}$

$\nabla f(1, 2) = \dfrac{1}{2} \mathbf{i} + \dfrac{1}{2} \mathbf{j}$

(Same direction as in part (a).)

(c) $-\nabla f = -\dfrac{1}{2} \mathbf{i} - \dfrac{1}{2} \mathbf{j}$, the direction opposite that of the gradient.

54. (a) $f(x, y) = \dfrac{8y}{1 + x^2 + y^2} = 2$

$\Rightarrow 4y = 1 + x^2 + y^2$

$4 = y^2 - 4y + 4 + x^2 + 1$

$(y - 2)^2 + x^2 = 3$

Circle: center: $(0, 2)$, radius: $\sqrt{3}$

(b) $\nabla f = \dfrac{-16xy}{(1 + x^2 + y^2)^2} \mathbf{i} + \dfrac{8 + 8x^2 - 8y^2}{(1 + x^2 + y^2)^2} \mathbf{j}$

$\nabla f\left(\sqrt{3}, 2\right) = \dfrac{-\sqrt{3}}{2} \mathbf{i}$

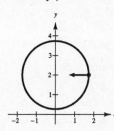

(c) The directional derivative of f is 0 in the directions $\pm\mathbf{j}$.

(d)

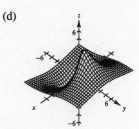

56. $f(x, y) = 6 - 2x - 3y$

$c = 6, \ P = (0, 0)$

$\nabla f(x, y) = -2\mathbf{i} - 3\mathbf{j}$

$6 - 2x - 3y = 6$

$0 = 2x + 3y$

$\nabla f(0, 0) = -2\mathbf{i} - 3\mathbf{j}$

58. $f(x, y) = xy$

$c = -3, \ P = (-1, 3)$

$\nabla f(x, y) = y\mathbf{i} + x\mathbf{j}$

$xy = -3$

$\nabla f(-1, 3) = 3\mathbf{i} - \mathbf{j}$

60. $3x^2 - 2y^2 = 1$

$f(x, y) = 3x^2 - 2y^2$

$\nabla f(x, y) = 6x\mathbf{i} - 4y\mathbf{j}$

$\nabla f(1, 1) = 6\mathbf{i} - 4\mathbf{j}$

$\dfrac{\nabla f(1, 1)}{\|\nabla f(1, 1)\|} = \dfrac{1}{\sqrt{13}}(3\mathbf{i} - 2\mathbf{j})$

$\qquad = \dfrac{\sqrt{13}}{13}(3\mathbf{i} - 2\mathbf{j})$

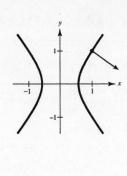

62. $xe^y - y = 5$

$f(x, y) = xe^y - y$

$\nabla f(x, y) = e^y\mathbf{i} + (xe^y - 1)\mathbf{j}$

$\nabla f(5, 0) = \mathbf{i} + 4\mathbf{j}$

$\dfrac{\nabla f(5, 0)}{\|\nabla f(5, 0)\|} = \dfrac{1}{\sqrt{17}}(\mathbf{i} + 4\mathbf{j})$

$\qquad = \dfrac{\sqrt{17}}{17}(\mathbf{i} + 4\mathbf{j})$

64. $h(x, y) = 5000 - 0.001x^2 - 0.004y^2$

$\nabla h = -0.002x\mathbf{i} - 0.008y\mathbf{j}$

$\nabla h(500, 300) = -\mathbf{i} - 2.4\mathbf{j}$ or

$5\nabla h = -(5\mathbf{i} + 12\mathbf{j})$

66. The directional derivative gives the slope of a surface at a point in an arbitrary direction $\mathbf{u} = \cos\theta\mathbf{i} + \sin\theta\mathbf{j}$.

68. See the definition, page 887.

70. The gradient vector is normal to the level curves.

See Theorem 12.12.

72. The wind speed is greatest at A.

74. $T(x, y) = 100 - x^2 - 2y^2,$ $\qquad P = (4, 3)$

$\dfrac{dx}{dt} = -2x$ $\qquad\qquad \dfrac{dy}{dt} = -4y$

$x(t) = C_1 e^{-2t}$ $\qquad\quad y(t) = C_2 e^{-4t}$

$4 = x(0) = C_1$ $\qquad\quad 3 = y(0) = C_2$

$x(t) = 4e^{-2t}$ $\qquad\qquad y(t) = 3e^{-4t}$

$\dfrac{3x^2}{16} = e^{-4t} = y \implies u = \dfrac{3}{16}x^2$

76. (a)

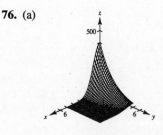

(b) $\nabla T(x, y) = 400e^{-(x^2 + y)/2}\left[(-x)\mathbf{i} - \frac{1}{2}\mathbf{j}\right]$

$\quad \nabla T(3, 5) = 400e^{-7}\left[-3\mathbf{i} - \frac{1}{2}\mathbf{j}\right]$

There will be no change in directions perpendicular to the gradient: $\pm(\mathbf{i} - 6\mathbf{j})$

(c) The greatest increase is in the direction of the gradient: $-3\mathbf{i} - \frac{1}{2}\mathbf{j}$

78. False

$D_\mathbf{u} f(x, y) = \sqrt{2} > 1$ when

$\mathbf{u} = \left(\cos\dfrac{\pi}{4}\right)\mathbf{i} + \left(\sin\dfrac{\pi}{4}\right)\mathbf{j}.$

80. True

Section 12.7   Tangent Planes and Normal Lines

2. $F(x, y, z) = x^2 + y^2 + z^2 - 25 = 0$

$\qquad\qquad\qquad x^2 + y^2 + z^2 = 25$

Sphere, radius 5, centered at origin.

4. $F(x, y, z) = 16x^2 - 9y^2 + 144z = 0$

$\qquad 16x^2 - 9y^2 + 144z = 0$ Hyperbolic paraboloid

6. $F(x, y, z) = x^2 + y^2 + z^2 - 11$

$\nabla F(x, y, z) = 2x\mathbf{i} + 2y\mathbf{j} + 2z\mathbf{k}$

$\nabla F(3, 1, 1) = 6\mathbf{i} + 2\mathbf{j} + 2\mathbf{k}$

$\mathbf{n} = \dfrac{\nabla F}{\|\nabla F\|} = \dfrac{1}{\sqrt{44}}(6\mathbf{i} + 2\mathbf{j} + 2\mathbf{k})$

$\qquad\qquad = \dfrac{1}{\sqrt{11}}(3\mathbf{i} + \mathbf{j} + \mathbf{k}) = \dfrac{\sqrt{11}}{11}(3\mathbf{i} + \mathbf{j} + \mathbf{k})$

8. $F(x, y, z) = x^3 - z$

$\nabla F(x, y, z) = 3x^2\mathbf{i} - \mathbf{k}$

$\nabla F(2, 1, 8) = 12\mathbf{i} - \mathbf{k}$

$\mathbf{n} = \dfrac{\nabla F}{\|\nabla F\|} = \dfrac{1}{\sqrt{145}}(12\mathbf{i} - \mathbf{k})$

$\qquad\qquad = \dfrac{\sqrt{145}}{145}(12\mathbf{i} - \mathbf{k})$

10. $F(x, y, z) = x^2 + 3y + z^3 - 9$

$\nabla F(x, y, z) = 2x\mathbf{i} + 3\mathbf{j} + 3z^2\mathbf{k}$

$\nabla F(2, -1, 2) = 4\mathbf{i} + 3\mathbf{j} + 12\mathbf{k}$

$\mathbf{n} = \dfrac{\nabla F}{\|\nabla F\|} = \dfrac{1}{13}(4\mathbf{i} + 3\mathbf{j} + 12\mathbf{k})$

12. $F(x, y, z) = ze^{x^2 - y^2} - 3$

$\nabla F(x, y, z) = 2xze^{x^2 - y^2}\mathbf{i} - 2yze^{x^2 - y^2}\mathbf{j} + e^{x^2 - y^2}\mathbf{k}$

$\nabla F(2, 2, 3) = 12\mathbf{i} - 12\mathbf{j} + \mathbf{k}$

$\mathbf{n} = \dfrac{\nabla F}{\|\nabla F\|} = \dfrac{1}{17}(12\mathbf{i} - 12\mathbf{j} + \mathbf{k})$

14. $F(x, y, z) = \sin(x - y) - z - 2$

$\nabla F(x, y, z) = \cos(x - y)\mathbf{i} - \cos(x - y)\mathbf{j} - \mathbf{k}$

$\nabla F\left(\dfrac{\pi}{3}, \dfrac{\pi}{6}, -\dfrac{3}{2}\right) = \dfrac{\sqrt{3}}{2}\mathbf{i} - \dfrac{\sqrt{3}}{2}\mathbf{j} - \mathbf{k}$

$\mathbf{n} = \dfrac{\nabla F}{\|\nabla F\|} = \dfrac{2}{\sqrt{10}}\left(\dfrac{\sqrt{3}}{2}\mathbf{i} - \dfrac{\sqrt{3}}{2}\mathbf{j} - \mathbf{k}\right)$

$\qquad\qquad = \dfrac{1}{\sqrt{10}}\left(\sqrt{3}\,\mathbf{i} - \sqrt{3}\,\mathbf{j} - 2\mathbf{k}\right)$

$\qquad\qquad = \dfrac{\sqrt{10}}{10}\left(\sqrt{3}\,\mathbf{i} - \sqrt{3}\,\mathbf{j} - 2\mathbf{k}\right)$

16. $f(x, y) = \dfrac{y}{x},\ (1, 2, 2)$

$F(x, y, z) = \dfrac{y}{x} - z$

$F_x(x, y, z) = -\dfrac{y}{x^2} \qquad F_y(x, y, z) = \dfrac{1}{x} \qquad F_z(x, y, z) = -1$

$F_x(1, 2, 2) = -2 \qquad F_y(1, 2, 2) = 1 \qquad F_z(1, 2, 2) = -1$

$-2(x - 1) + (y - 2) - (z - 2) = 0$

$\qquad\qquad -2x + y - z + 2 = 0$

$\qquad\qquad\qquad 2x - y + z = 2$

18. $g(x, y) = \arctan\dfrac{y}{x},\ (1, 0, 0)$

$G(x, y, z) = \arctan\dfrac{y}{x} - z$

$G_x(x, y, z) = \dfrac{-(y/x^2)}{1 + (y^2/x^2)} = \dfrac{-y}{x^2 + y^2} \qquad G_y(x, y, z) = \dfrac{1/x}{1 + (y^2/x^2)} = \dfrac{x}{x^2 + y^2} \qquad G_z(x, y, z) = -1$

$G_x(1, 0, 0) = 0 \qquad\qquad G_y(1, 0, 0) = 1 \qquad\qquad G_z(1, 0, 0) = -1$

$y - z = 0$

20. $f(x, y) = 2 - \frac{2}{3}x - y, \ (3, -1, 1)$

$F(x, y, z) = 2 - \frac{2}{3}x - y - z$

$F_x(x, y, z) = -\frac{2}{3}, \qquad F_y(x, y, z) = -1, \qquad F_z(x, y, z) = -1$

$-\frac{2}{3}(x - 3) - (y + 1) - (z - 1) = 0$

$-\frac{2}{3}x - y - z + 2 = 0$

$2x + 3y + 3z = 6$

22. $z = x^2 - 2xy + y^2, \ (1, 2, 1)$

$F(x, y, z) = x^2 - 2xy + y^2 - z$

$F_x(x, y, z) = 2x - 2y \qquad F_y(x, y, z) = -2x + 2y \qquad F_z(x, y, z) = -1$

$F_x(1, 2, 1) = -2 \qquad\qquad F_y(1, 2, 1) = 2 \qquad\qquad F_z(1, 2, 1) = -1$

$-2(x - 1) + 2(y - 2) - (z - 1) = 0$

$-2x + 2y - z - 1 = 0$

$2x - 2y + z = -1$

24. $h(x, y) = \cos y, \ \left(5, \dfrac{\pi}{4}, \dfrac{\sqrt{2}}{2}\right)$

$H(x, y, z) = \cos y - z$

$H_x(x, y, z) = 0 \qquad\qquad H_y(x, y, z) = -\sin y \qquad\qquad H_z(x, y, z) = -1$

$H_x\left(5, \dfrac{\pi}{4}, \dfrac{\sqrt{2}}{2}\right) = 0 \qquad H_y\left(5, \dfrac{\pi}{4}, \dfrac{\sqrt{2}}{2}\right) = -\dfrac{\sqrt{2}}{2} \qquad H_z\left(5, \dfrac{\pi}{4}, \dfrac{\sqrt{2}}{2}\right) = -1$

$-\dfrac{\sqrt{2}}{2}\left(y - \dfrac{\pi}{4}\right) - \left(z - \dfrac{\sqrt{2}}{2}\right) = 0$

$-\dfrac{\sqrt{2}}{2}y - z + \dfrac{\sqrt{2}\pi}{8} + \dfrac{\sqrt{2}}{2} = 0$

$4\sqrt{2}y + 8z = \sqrt{2}(\pi + 4)$

26. $x^2 + 2z^2 = y^2, \ (1, 3, -2)$

$F(x, y, z) = x^2 - y^2 + 2z^2$

$F_x(x, y, z) = 2x \qquad\qquad F_y(x, y, z) = -2y \qquad\qquad F_z(x, y, z) = 4z$

$F_x(1, 3, -2) = 2 \qquad\qquad F_y(1, 3, -2) = -6 \qquad\qquad F_z(1, 3, -2) = -8$

$2(x - 1) - 6(y - 3) - 8(z + 2) = 0$

$(x - 1) - 3(y - 3) - 4(z + 2) = 0$

$x - 3y - 4z = 0$

28. $x = y(2z - 3), \ (4, 4, 2)$

$F(x, y, z) = x - 2yz + 3y$

$F_x(x, y, z) = 1 \qquad\qquad F_y(x, y, z) = -2z + 3 \qquad\qquad F_z(x, y, z) = -2y$

$F_x(4, 4, 2) = 1 \qquad\qquad F_y(4, 4, 2) = -1 \qquad\qquad F_z(4, 4, 2) = -8$

$(x - 4) - 1(y - 4) - 8(z - 2) = 0$

$x - y - 8z = -16$

$-x + y + 8z = 16$

30. $x^2 + y^2 + z^2 = 9$, $(1, 2, 2)$

$F(x, y, z) = x^2 + y^2 + z^2 - 9$

$F_x(x, y, z) = 2x$ $F_y(x, y, z) = 2y$ $F_z(x, y, z) = 2z$

$F_x(1, 2, 2) = 2$ $F_y(1, 2, 2) = 4$ $F_z(1, 2, 2) = 4$

Direction numbers: 1, 2, 2

Plane: $(x - 1) + 2(y - 2) + 2(z - 2) = 0$, $x + 2y + 2z = 9$

Line: $\dfrac{x - 1}{1} = \dfrac{y - 2}{2} = \dfrac{z - 2}{2}$

32. $x^2 - y^2 + z^2 = 0$, $(5, 13, -12)$

$F(x, y, z) = x^2 - y^2 + z^2$

$F_x(x, y, z) = 2x$ $F_y(x, y, z) = -2y$ $F_z(x, y, z) = 2z$

$F_x(5, 13, -12) = 10$ $F_y(5, 13, -12) = -26$ $F_z(x, y, z) = -24$

Direction numbers: $5, -13, -12$

Plane   Line: $\dfrac{x - 5}{5} = \dfrac{y - 13}{-13} = \dfrac{z + 12}{-12}$

     $5(x - 5) - 13(y - 13) - 12(z + 12) = 0$

                    $5x - 13y - 12z = 0$

34. $xyz = 10$, $(1, 2, 5)$

$F(x, y, z) = xyz - 10$

$F_x(x, y, z) = yz$ $F_y(x, y, z) = xz$ $F_z(x, y, z) = xy$

$F_x(1, 2, 5) = 10$ $F_y(1, 2, 5) = 5$ $F_z(1, 2, 5) = 2$

Direction numbers: 10, 5, 2

Plane: $10(x - 1) + 5(y - 2) + 2(z - 5) = 0$, $10x + 5y + 2z = 30$

Line: $\dfrac{x - 1}{10} = \dfrac{y - 2}{5} = \dfrac{z - 5}{2}$

36. See the definition on page 897.

38. For a sphere, the common object is the center of the sphere. For a right circular cylinder, the common object is the axis of the cylinder.

40. $F(x, y, z) = x^2 + y^2 - z$ $G(x, y, z) = 4 - y - z$

     $\nabla F(x, y, z) = 2x\mathbf{i} + 2y\mathbf{j} - \mathbf{k}$ $\nabla G(x, y, z) = -\mathbf{j} - \mathbf{k}$

     $\nabla F(2, -1, 5) = 4\mathbf{i} - 2\mathbf{j} - \mathbf{k}$ $\nabla G(2, -1, 5) = -\mathbf{j} - \mathbf{k}$

(a) $\nabla F \times \nabla G = \begin{vmatrix} \mathbf{i} & \mathbf{j} & \mathbf{k} \\ 4 & -2 & -1 \\ 0 & -1 & -1 \end{vmatrix} = \mathbf{i} + 4\mathbf{j} - 4\mathbf{k}$

Direction numbers: $1, 4, -4$, $\dfrac{x - 2}{1} = \dfrac{y + 1}{4} = \dfrac{z - 5}{-4}$

(b) $\cos \theta = \dfrac{|\nabla F \cdot \nabla G|}{\|\nabla F\| \, \|\nabla G\|} = \dfrac{3}{\sqrt{21}\sqrt{2}} = \dfrac{3}{\sqrt{42}} = \dfrac{\sqrt{42}}{14}$; not orthogonal

42. $F(x, y, z) = \sqrt{x^2 + y^2} - z$ $\qquad\qquad$ $G(x, y, z) = 5x - 2y + 3z = 22$

$\nabla F(x, y, z) = \dfrac{x}{\sqrt{x^2 + y^2}}\mathbf{i} + \dfrac{y}{\sqrt{x^2 + y^2}}\mathbf{j} - \mathbf{k}$ $\qquad$ $\nabla G(x, y, z) = 5\mathbf{i} - 2\mathbf{j} + 3\mathbf{k}$

$\nabla F(3, 4, 5) = \dfrac{3}{5}\mathbf{i} + \dfrac{4}{5}\mathbf{j} - \mathbf{k}$ $\qquad\qquad$ $\nabla G(3, 4, 5) = 5\mathbf{i} - 2\mathbf{j} + 3\mathbf{k}$

$\nabla F \times \nabla G = \begin{vmatrix} \mathbf{i} & \mathbf{j} & \mathbf{k} \\ 3/5 & 4/5 & -1 \\ 5 & -2 & 3 \end{vmatrix} = \dfrac{2}{5}\mathbf{i} - \dfrac{34}{5}\mathbf{j} - \dfrac{26}{5}\mathbf{k}$

Direction numbers: $1, -17, -13$

$\dfrac{x - 3}{1} = \dfrac{y - 4}{-17} = \dfrac{z - 5}{-13}$ Tangent line

$\cos \theta = \dfrac{|\nabla F \cdot \nabla G|}{\|\nabla F\| \, \|\nabla G\|} = \dfrac{-(8/5)}{\sqrt{2}\sqrt{38}} = \dfrac{-8}{5\sqrt{76}}$ Not orthogonal

44. $F(x, y, z) = x^2 + y^2 - z$ $\qquad\qquad$ $G(x, y, z) = x + y + 6z - 33$

$\nabla F(x, y, z) = 2x\mathbf{i} + 2y\mathbf{j} - \mathbf{k}$ $\qquad$ $\nabla G(x, y, z) = \mathbf{i} + \mathbf{j} + 6\mathbf{k}$

$\nabla F(1, 2, 5) = 2\mathbf{i} + 4\mathbf{j} - \mathbf{k}$ $\qquad\qquad$ $\nabla G(1, 2, 5) = \mathbf{i} + \mathbf{j} + 6\mathbf{k}$

(a) $\nabla F \times \nabla G = \begin{vmatrix} \mathbf{i} & \mathbf{j} & \mathbf{k} \\ 2 & 4 & -1 \\ 1 & 1 & 6 \end{vmatrix} = 25\mathbf{i} - 13\mathbf{j} - 2\mathbf{k}$

$\qquad$ Direction numbers: $25, -13, -2, \; \dfrac{x - 1}{25} = \dfrac{y - 2}{-13} = \dfrac{z - 5}{-2}$

(b) $\cos \theta = \dfrac{|\nabla F \cdot \nabla G|}{\|\nabla F\| \, \|\nabla G\|} = 0;$ orthogonal

46.   (a) $f(x, y) = \sqrt{16 - x^2 - y^2 + 2x - 4y}$

$\qquad\qquad$ $g(x, y) = \dfrac{\sqrt{2}}{2}\sqrt{1 - 3x^2 + y^2 + 6x + 4y}$

$\qquad$ (b) $\qquad\qquad\qquad f(x, y) = g(x, y)$

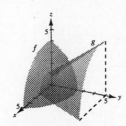

$16 - x^2 - y^2 + 2x - 4y = \dfrac{1}{2}(1 - 3x^2 + y^2 + 6x + 4y)$

$32 - 2x^2 - 2y^2 + 4x - 8y = 1 - 3x^2 + y^2 + 6x + 4y$

$\qquad\qquad\qquad x^2 - 2x + 31 = 3y^2 + 12y$

$\qquad\qquad (x^2 - 2x + 1) + 42 = 3(y^2 + 4y + 4)$

$\qquad\qquad\qquad\quad (x - 1)^2 + 42 = 3(y + 2)^2$

$\qquad$ To find points of intersection, let $x = 1$. Then

$\qquad\qquad 3(y + 2)^2 = 42$

$\qquad\qquad\quad (y + 2)^2 = 14$

$\qquad\qquad\qquad\quad y = -2 \pm \sqrt{14}$

$\qquad$ $\nabla f\left(1, -2 + \sqrt{14}\right) = -\sqrt{2}\mathbf{j}, \nabla g\left(1, -2 + \sqrt{14}\right) = \left(1/\sqrt{2}\right)\mathbf{j}.$ The normals to f and g at this point are $-\sqrt{2}\mathbf{j} - \mathbf{k}$ and $\left(1/\sqrt{2}\right)\mathbf{j} - \mathbf{k}$, which are orthogonal.

$\qquad$ Similarly, $\nabla f\left(1, -2 - \sqrt{14}\right) = \sqrt{2}\mathbf{j}$ and $\nabla g\left(1, -2 - \sqrt{14}\right) = \left(-1/\sqrt{2}\right)\mathbf{j}$ and the normals are $\sqrt{2}\mathbf{j} - \mathbf{k}$ and $\left(-1/\sqrt{2}\right)\mathbf{j} - \mathbf{k}$, which are also orthogonal.

(c)   No, showing that the surfaces are orthogonal at 2 points does not imply that they are orthogonal at every point of intersection.

48. $F(x, y, z) = 2xy - z^3, \ (2, 2, 2)$

$\nabla F = 2y\mathbf{i} + 2x\mathbf{j} - 3z^2\mathbf{k}$

$\nabla F(2, 2, 2) = 4\mathbf{i} + 4\mathbf{j} - 12\mathbf{k}$

$\cos \theta = \dfrac{|\nabla F(2, 2, 2) \cdot \mathbf{k}|}{\|\nabla F(2, 2, 2)\|} = \dfrac{|-12|}{\sqrt{176}} = \dfrac{3\sqrt{11}}{11}$

$\theta = \arccos\left(\dfrac{3\sqrt{11}}{11}\right) \approx 25.24°$

50. $F(x, y, z) = x^2 + y^2 - 5, \ (2, 1, 3)$

$\nabla F(x, y, z) = 2x\mathbf{i} + 2y\mathbf{j}$

$\nabla F(2, 1, 3) = 4\mathbf{i} + 2\mathbf{j}$

$\cos \theta = \dfrac{|\nabla F(2, 1, 3) \cdot \mathbf{k}|}{\|\nabla F(2, 1, 3)\|} = 0$

$\theta = \arccos 0 = 90°$

52. $F(x, y, z) = 3x^2 + 2y^2 - 3x + 4y - z - 5$

$\nabla F(x, y, z) = (6x - 3)\mathbf{i} + (4y + 4)\mathbf{j} - \mathbf{k}$

$6x - 3 = 0, \ x = \tfrac{1}{2}$

$4y + 4 = 0, \ y = -1$

$z = 3\left(\tfrac{1}{2}\right)^2 + 2(-1)^2 - 3\left(\tfrac{1}{2}\right) + 4(-1) - 5 = -\tfrac{31}{4}$

$\left(\tfrac{1}{2}, -1, -\tfrac{31}{4}\right)$

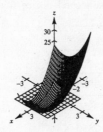

54. $T(x, y, z) = 100 - 3x - y - z^2, \ (2, 2, 5)$

$\dfrac{dx}{dt} = -3$	$\dfrac{dy}{dt} = -1$	$\dfrac{dz}{dt} = -2z$
$x(t) = -3t + C_1$	$y(t) = -t + C_2$	$z(t) = C_3 e^{-2t}$
$x(0) = C_1 = 2$	$y(0) = C_2 = 2$	$z(0) = C_3 = 5$
$x = -3t + 2$	$y = -t + 2$	$z = 5e^{-2t}$

56. $F(x, y, z) = \dfrac{x^2}{a^2} + \dfrac{y^2}{b^2} - \dfrac{z^2}{c^2} - 1$

$F_x(x, y, z) = \dfrac{2x}{a^2}$

$F_y(x, y, z) = \dfrac{2y}{b^2}$

$F_z(x, y, z) = \dfrac{-2z}{c^2}$

Plane: $\dfrac{2x_0}{a^2}(x - x_0) + \dfrac{2y_0}{b^2}(y - y_0) - \dfrac{2z_0}{c^2}(z - z_0) = 0$

$\dfrac{x_0 x}{a^2} + \dfrac{y_0 y}{b^2} - \dfrac{z_0 z}{c^2} = \dfrac{x_0^2}{a^2} + \dfrac{y_0^2}{b^2} - \dfrac{z_0^2}{c^2} = 1$

58. $z = xf\left(\dfrac{y}{x}\right)$

$F(x, y, z) = xf\left(\dfrac{y}{x}\right) - z$

$F_x(x, y, z) = f\left(\dfrac{y}{x}\right) + xf'\left(\dfrac{y}{x}\right)\left(-\dfrac{y}{x^2}\right) = f\left(\dfrac{y}{x}\right) - \dfrac{y}{x}f'\left(\dfrac{y}{x}\right)$

$F_y(x, y, z) = xf'\left(\dfrac{y}{x}\right)\left(\dfrac{1}{x}\right) = f'\left(\dfrac{y}{x}\right)$

$F_x(x, y, z) = -1$

Tangent plane at (x_0, y_0, z_0):

$$\left[f\left(\dfrac{y_0}{x_0}\right) - \dfrac{y_0}{x_0}f'\left(\dfrac{y_0}{x_0}\right)\right](x - x_0) + f'\left(\dfrac{y_0}{x_0}\right)(y - y_0) - (z - z_0) = 0$$

$$\left[f\left(\dfrac{y_0}{x_0}\right) - \dfrac{y_0}{x_0}f'\left(\dfrac{y_0}{x_0}\right)\right]x - x_0 f\left(\dfrac{y_0}{x_0}\right) + y_0 f'\left(\dfrac{y_0}{x_0}\right) + yf'\left(\dfrac{y_0}{x_0}\right) - y_0 f'\left(\dfrac{y_0}{x_0}\right) - z + x_0 f\left(\dfrac{y_0}{x_0}\right) = 0$$

$$\left[f\left(\dfrac{y_0}{x_0}\right) - \dfrac{y_0}{x_0}f'\left(\dfrac{y_0}{x_0}\right)\right]x + f'\left(\dfrac{y_0}{x_0}\right)y - z = 0$$

Therefore, the plane passes through the origin $(x, y, z) = (0, 0, 0)$.

60. $f(x, y) = \cos(x + y)$

$f_x(x, y) = -\sin(x + y)$ $\qquad$ $f_y(x, y) = -\sin(x + y)$

$f_{xx}(x, y) = -\cos(x + y),$ $\qquad$ $f_{yy}(x, y) = -\cos(x + y),$ $\qquad$ $f_{xy}(x, y) = -\cos(x + y)$

(a) $P_1(x, y) \approx f(0, 0) + f_x(0, 0)x + f_y(0, 0)y = 1$

(b) $P_2(x, y) \approx f(0, 0) + f_x(0, 0)x + f_y(0,0)y + \frac{1}{2}f_{xx}(0, 0)x^2 + f_{xy}(0, 0)xy + \frac{1}{2}f_{yy}(0, 0)y^2$

$\qquad = 1 - \frac{1}{2}x^2 - xy - \frac{1}{2}y^2$

(c) If $x = 0$, $P_2(0, y) = 1 - \frac{1}{2}y^2$. This is the second–degree Taylor polynomial for $\cos y$.

$\quad$ If $y = 0$, $P_2(x, 0) = 1 - \frac{1}{2}x^2$. This is the second–degree Taylor polynomial for $\cos x$.

(d)

x	y	$f(x, y)$	$P_1(x, y)$	$P_2(x, y)$
0	0	1	1	1
0	0.1	0.9950	1	0.9950
0.2	0.1	0.9553	1	0.9950
0.2	0.5	0.7648	1	0.7550
1	0.5	0.0707	1	-0.1250

(e)

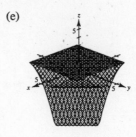

62. Given $z = f(x, y)$, then:

$\qquad F(x, y, z) = f(x, y) - z = 0$

$\qquad \nabla F(x_0, y_0, z_0) = f_x(x_0, y_0)\mathbf{i} + f_y(x_0, y_0)\mathbf{j} - \mathbf{k}$

$\qquad \qquad \cos \theta = \dfrac{|\nabla F(x_0, y_0, z_0) \cdot \mathbf{k}|}{\|\nabla F(x_0, y_0, z_0)\| \, \|\mathbf{k}\|}$

$\qquad \qquad \qquad = \dfrac{|-1|}{\sqrt{[f_x(x_0, y_0)]^2 + [f_y(x_0, y_0)]^2 + (-1)^2}}$

$\qquad \qquad \qquad = \dfrac{1}{\sqrt{[f_x(x_0, y_0)]^2 + [f_y(x_0, y_0)]^2 + 1}}$

Section 12.8 Extrema of Functions of Two Variables

2. $g(x, y) = 9 - (x - 3)^2 - (y + 2)^2 \le 9$

Relative maximum: $(3, -2, 9)$

$g_x = -2(x - 3) = 0 \implies x = 3$

$g_y = -2(y + 2) = 0 \implies y = -2$

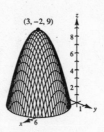

4. $f(x, y) = \sqrt{25 - (x - 2)^2 - y^2} \le 5$

Relative maximum: $(2, 0, 5)$

Check: $f_x = -\dfrac{x - 2}{\sqrt{25 - (x - 2)^2 - y^2}} = 0 \implies x = 2$

$\qquad \quad f_y = -\dfrac{y}{\sqrt{25 - (x - 2)^2 - y^2}} = 0 \implies y = 0$

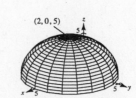

$\qquad \quad f_{xx} = -\dfrac{25 - y^2}{[25 - (x - 2)^2 - y^2]^{3/2}}, f_{yy} = -\dfrac{25 - (x - 2)^2}{[25 - (x - 2)^2 - y^2]^{3/2}}, f_{xy} = -\dfrac{y(x - 2)}{[25 - (x - 2)^2 - y^2]^{3/2}}$

At the critical point $(2, 0)$, $f_{xx} < 0$ and $f_{xx} f_{yy} - (f_{xy})^2 > 0$. Therefore, $(2, 0, 5)$ is a relative maximum.

6. $f(x, y) = -x^2 - y^2 + 4x + 8y - 11 = -(x - 2)^2 - (y - 4)^2 + 9 \leq 9$

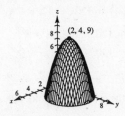

Relative maximum: $(2, 4, 9)$

Check: $f_x = -2x + 4 = 0 \implies x = 2$

$f_y = -2y + 8 = 0 \implies y = 4$

$f_{xx} = -2, f_{yy} = -2, f_{xy} = 0$

At the critical point $(2, 4), f_{xx} < 0$ and $f_{xx}f_{yy} - (f_{xy})^2 > 0$. Therefore, $(2, 4, 9)$ is a relative maximum.

8. $f(x, y) = -x^2 - 5y^2 + 10x - 30y - 62$

$\left. \begin{array}{l} f_x = -2x + 10 = 0 \\ f_y = -10y - 30 = 0 \end{array} \right\} x = 5, y = -3$

$f_{xx} = -2, f_{yy} = -10, f_{xy} = 0$

At the critical point $(5, -3), f_{xx} < 0$ and $f_{xx}f_{yy} - f_{xy}^2 > 0$.

Therefore, $(5, -3, 8)$ is a relative maximum.

10. $f(x, y) = x^2 + 6xy + 10y^2 - 4y + 4$

$\left. \begin{array}{l} f_x = 2x + 6y = 0 \\ f_y = 6x + 20y - 4 = 0 \end{array} \right\}$ Solving simultaneously yields $x = -6$ and $y = 2$.

$f_{xx} = 2, f_{yy} = 20, f_{xy} = 6$

At the critical point $(-6, 2), f_{xx} > 0$ and $f_{xx}f_{yy} - (f_{xy})^2 > 0$. Therefore, $(-6, 2, 0)$ is a relative minimum.

12. $f(x, y) = -3x^2 - 2y^2 + 3x - 4y + 5$

$f_x = -6x + 3 = 0$ when $x = \frac{1}{2}$.

$f_y = -4y - 4 = 0$ when $y = -1$.

$f_{xx} = -6, f_{yy} = -4, f_{xy} = 0$

At the critical point $\left(\frac{1}{2}, -1\right), f_{xx} < 0$ and $f_{xx}f_{yy} - (f_{xy})^2 > 0$. Therefore, $\left(\frac{1}{2}, -1, \frac{31}{4}\right)$ is a relative maximum.

14. $h(x, y) = (x^2 + y^2)^{1/3} + 2$

$\left. \begin{array}{l} h_x = \dfrac{2x}{3(x^2 + y^2)^{2/3}} = 0 \\[3mm] h_y = \dfrac{2y}{3(x^2 + y^2)^{2/3}} = 0 \end{array} \right\} x = 0, y = 0$

Since $h(x, y) \geq 2$ for all (x, y), $(0, 0, 2)$ is a relative minimum.

16. $f(x, y) = |x + y| - 2$

Since $f(x, y) \geq -2$ for all (x, y), the relative minima of f consist of all points (x, y) satisfying $x + y = 0$.

18. $f(x, y) = y^3 - 3yx^2 - 3y^2 - 3x^2 + 1$

Relative maximum: $(0, 0, 1)$

Saddle points: $(0, 2, -3), \left(\pm\sqrt{3}, -1, -3\right)$

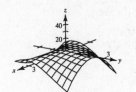

20. $z = e^{xy}$

Saddle point: $(0, 0, 1)$

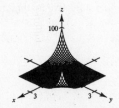

22. $g(x, y) = 120x + 120y - xy - x^2 - y^2$

$\left.\begin{array}{l} g_x = 120 - y - 2x = 0 \\ g_y = 120 - x - 2y = 0 \end{array}\right\}$ Solving simultaneously yields $x = 40$ and $y = 40$.

$g_{xx} = -2, \; g_{yy} = -2, \; g_{xy} = -1$

At the critical point $(40, 40)$, $g_{xx} < 0$ and $g_{xx} g_{yy} - (g_{xy})^2 > 0$. Therefore, $(40, 40, 4800)$ is a relative maximum.

24. $g(x, y) = xy$

$\left.\begin{array}{l} g_x = y \\ g_y = x \end{array}\right\} \quad x = 0 \text{ and } y = 0$

$g_{xx} = 0, \; g_{yy} = 0, \; g_{xy} = 1$

At the critical point $(0, 0)$, $g_{xx} g_{yy} - (g_{xy})^2 < 0$. Therefore, $(0, 0, 0)$ is a saddle point.

26. $f(x, y) = 2xy - \dfrac{1}{2}(x^4 + y^2) + 1$

$\left.\begin{array}{l} f_x = 2y - 2x^3 \\ f_y = 2x - 2y^3 \end{array}\right\}$ Solving by substitution yields 3 critical points: $(0, 0), (1, 1), (-1, -1)$

$f_{xx} = -6x^2, f_{yy} = -6y^2, f_{xy} = 2$

At $(0, 0), f_{xx}f_{yy} - (f_{xy})^2 < 0 \implies (0, 0, 1)$ saddle point.

At $(1, 1), f_{xx}f_{yy} - (f_{xy})^2 > 0$ and $f_{xx} < 0 \implies (1, 1, 2)$ relative maximum.

At $(-1, -1), f_{xx}f_{yy} - (f_{xy})^2 > 0$ and $f_{xx} < 0 \implies (-1, -1, 2)$ relative maximum.

28. $f(x, y) = \left(\dfrac{1}{2} - x^2 + y^2\right)e^{1-x^2-y^2}$

$\left.\begin{array}{l} f_x = (2x^3 - 2xy^2 - 3x)e^{1-x^2-y^2} = 0 \\ f_y = (2x^2y - 2y^3 + y)e^{1-x^2-y^2} = 0 \end{array}\right\}$ Solving yields the critical points $(0, 0), \left(0, \pm\dfrac{\sqrt{2}}{2}\right), \left(\pm\dfrac{\sqrt{6}}{2}, 0\right)$.

$f_{xx} = (-4x^4 + 4x^2y^2 + 12x^2 - 2y^2 - 3)e^{1-x^2-y^2}$

$f_{yy} = (4y^4 - 4x^2y^2 + 2x^2 - 8y^2 + 1)e^{1-x^2-y^2}$

$f_{xy} = (-4x^3y + 4xy^3 + 2xy)e^{1-x^2-y^2}$

At the critical point $(0, 0), f_{xx} f_{yy} - (f_{xy})^2 < 0$. Therefore, $(0, 0, e/2)$ is a saddle point. At the critical points $\left(0, \pm\sqrt{2}/2\right)$, $f_{xx} < 0$ and $f_{xx} f_{yy} - (f_{xy})^2 > 0$. Therefore, $\left(0, \pm\sqrt{2}/2, \sqrt{e}\right)$ are relative maxima. At the critical points $\left(\pm\sqrt{6}/2, 0\right), f_{xx} > 0$ and $f_{xx} f_{yy} - (f_{xy})^2 > 0$. Therefore, $\left(\pm\sqrt{6}/2, 0, -\sqrt{e}/e\right)$ are relative minima.

30. $z = \dfrac{(x^2 - y^2)^2}{x^2 + y^2} \geq 0.$ $z = 0$ if $x^2 = y^2 \neq 0$.

Relative minima at all points (x, x) and $(x, -x), x \neq 0$.

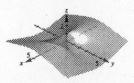

32. $f_{xx} < 0$ and $f_{xx} f_{yy} - (f_{xy})^2 = (-3)(-8) - 2^2 > 0$

f has a relative maximum at (x_0, y_0).

34. $f_{xx} > 0$ and $f_{xx} f_{yy} - (f_{xy})^2 = (25)(8) - 10^2 > 0$

f has a relative minimum at (x_0, y_0).

36. See Theorem 12.17.

38. 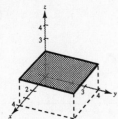   Extrema at all (x, y)

40. 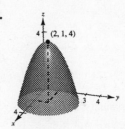   Relative maximum

42. A and B are relative extrema. C and D are saddle points.

44. $d = f_{xx} f_{yy} - f_{xy}^2 < 0$ if f_{xx} and f_{yy} have opposite signs. Hence, $(a, b, f(a, b))$ is a saddle point. For example, consider $f(x, y) = x^2 - y^2$ and $(a, b) = (0, 0)$.

46. $f(x, y) = x^3 + y^3 - 6x^2 + 9y^2 + 12x + 27y + 19$

$\left.\begin{array}{l} f_x = 3x^2 - 12x + 12 = 0 \\ f_y = 3y^2 + 18y + 27 = 0 \end{array}\right\}$ Solving yields $x = 2$ and $y = -3$.

$f_{xx} = 6x - 12, f_{yy} = 6y + 18, f_{xy} = 0$

At $(2, -3)$, $f_{xx} f_{yy} - (f_{xy})^2 = 0$ and the test fails. $(1, -2, 0)$ is a saddle point.

48. $f(x, y) = \sqrt{(x - 1)^2 + (y + 2)^2} \geq 0$

$\left.\begin{array}{l} f_x = \dfrac{x - 1}{\sqrt{(x - 1)^2 + (y + 2)^2}} = 0 \\[4mm] f_y = \dfrac{y + 2}{\sqrt{(x - 1)^2 + (y + 2)^2}} = 0 \end{array}\right\}$ Solving yields $x = 1$ and $y = -2$.

$f_{xx} = \dfrac{(y + 2)^2}{[(x - 1)^2 + (y + 2)^2]^{3/2}},\ f_{yy} = \dfrac{(x - 1)^2}{[(x - 1)^2 + (y + 2)^2]^{3/2}},\ f_{xy} = \dfrac{(x - 1)(y + 2)}{[(x - 1)^2 + (y + 2)^2]^{3/2}}$

At $(1, -2)$, $f_{xx} f_{yy} - (f_{xy})^2$ is undefined and the test fails.

Absolute minimum: $(1, -2, 0)$

50. $f(x, y) = (x^2 + y^2)^{2/3} \geq 0$

$\left.\begin{array}{l} f_x = \dfrac{4x}{3(x^2 + y^2)^{1/3}} \\[4mm] f_y = \dfrac{4y}{3(x^2 + y^2)^{1/3}} \end{array}\right\}$ f_x and f_y are undefined at $x = 0$, $y = 0$. The critical point is $(0, 0)$.

$f_{xx} = \dfrac{4(x^2 + 3y^2)}{9(x^2 + y^2)^{4/3}},\ f_{yy} = \dfrac{4(3x^2 + y^2)}{9(x^2 + y^2)^{4/3}},\ f_{xy} = \dfrac{-8xy}{9(x^2 + y^2)^{4/3}}$

At $(0, 0)$, $f_{xx} f_{yy} - (f_{xy})^2$ is undefined and the test fails.

Absolute minimum: $(0, 0, 0)$

52. $f(x, y, z) = 4 - [x(y - 1)(z + 2)]^2 \leq 4$

$\left.\begin{array}{l} f_x = -2x(y - 1)^2(z + 2)^2 = 0 \\ f_y = -2x^2(y - 1)(z + 2)^2 = 0 \\ f_z = -2x^2(y - 1)^2(z + 2) = 0 \end{array}\right\}$ Solving yields the critical points $(0, a, b)$, $(c, 1, d)$, $(e, f, -2)$. These points are all absolute maxima.

54. $f(x, y) = (2x - y)^2$

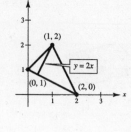

$f_x = 4(2x - y) = 0 \Rightarrow 2x = y$

$f_y = -2(2x - y) = 0 \Rightarrow 2x = y$

On the line $y = x + 1, 0 \leq x \leq 1$,

$\quad f(x, y) = f(x) = (2x - (x + 1))^2 = (x - 1)^2$

and the maximum is 1, the minimum is 0. On the line $y = -\frac{1}{2}x + 1, 0 \leq x \leq 2$,

$\quad f(x, y) = f(x) = \left(2x - \left(-\frac{1}{2}x + 1\right)\right)^2 = \left(\frac{5}{2}x - 1\right)^2$

and the maximum is 16, the minimum is 0. On the line $y = -2x + 4, 1 \leq x \leq 2$,

$\quad f(x, y) = f(x) = (2x - (-2x + 4))^2 = (4x - 4)^2$

and the maximum is 16, the minimum is 0.

Absolute maximum: 16 at $(2, 0)$

Absolute minimum: 0 at $(1, 2)$ and along the line $y = 2x$.

56. $f(x, y) = 2x - 2xy + y^2$

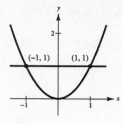

$f_x = 2 - 2y = 0 \Rightarrow y = 1$

$f_y = 2y - 2x = 0 \Rightarrow y = x \Rightarrow x = 1 \Bigg\} f(1, 1) = 1$

On the line $y = 1, -1 \leq x \leq 1$,

$\quad f(x, y) = f(x) = 2x - 2x + 1 = 1.$

On the curve $y = x^2, -1 \leq x \leq 1$

$\quad f(x, y) = f(x) = 2x - 2x(x^2) + (x^2)^2 = x^4 - 2x^3 + 2x$

and the maximum is 1, the minimum is $-\frac{11}{16}$.

Absolute maximum: 1 at $(1, 1)$ and on $y = 1$

Absolute minimum: $-\frac{11}{16} = -0.6875$ at $\left(-\frac{1}{2}, \frac{1}{4}\right)$

58. $f(x, y) = x^2 + 2xy + y^2, R = \{(x, y): |x| \leq 2, |y| \leq 1\}$

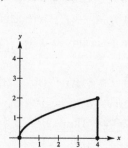

$f_x = 2x + 2y = 0 \Bigg\} y = -x$

$f_y = 2x + 2y = 0$

$f(x, -x) = x^2 - 2x^2 + x^2 = 0$

Along $y = 1, -2 \leq x \leq 2$,

$\quad f = x^2 + 2x + 1, f' = 2x + 2 = 0 \Rightarrow x = -1, f(-2, 1) = 1, f(-1, 1) = 0, f(2, 1) = 9.$

Along $y = -1, -2 \leq x \leq 2$,

$\quad f = x^2 - 2x + 1, f' = 2x - 2 = 0 \Rightarrow x = 1, f(-2, -1) = 9, f(1, -1) = 0, f(2, -1) = 1.$

Along $x = 2, -1 \leq y \leq 1, f = 4 + 4y + y^2, f' = 2y + 4 \neq 0.$

Along $x = -2, -1 \leq y \leq 1, f = 4 - 4y + y^2, f' = 2y - 4 \neq 0.$

Thus, the maxima are $f(-2, -1) = 9$ and $f(2, 1) = 9$, and the minima are $f(x, -x) = 0, -1 \leq x \leq 1.$

60. $f(x, y) = x^2 - 4xy + 5, R = \left\{(x, y): 0 \leq x \leq 4, 0 \leq y \leq \sqrt{x}\right\}$

$f_x = 2x - 4y = 0 \Bigg\} x = y = 0$

$f_y = -4x = 0$

$f(0, 0) = 5$

Along $y = 0, 0 \leq x \leq 4, f = x^2 + 5$ and $f(4, 0) = 21.$

Along $x = 4, 0 \leq y \leq 2, f = 16 - 16y + 5, f' = -16 \neq 0$ and $f(4, 2) = -11.$

Along $y = \sqrt{x}, 0 \leq x \leq 4, f = x^2 - 4x^{3/2} + 5, f' = 2x - 6x^{1/2} \neq 0$ on $[0, 4].$

Thus, the maximum is $f(4, 0) = 21$ and the minimum is $f(4, 2) = -11.$

62. $f(x, y) = \dfrac{4xy}{(x^2 + 1)(y^2 + 1)}$, $R = \{(x, y): x \geq 0, y \geq 0, x^2 + y^2 \leq 1\}$

$f_x = \dfrac{4(1 - x^2)y}{(y^2 + 1)(x^2 + 1)^2} = 0 \implies x = 1$ or $y = 0$

$f_y = \dfrac{4(1 - y^2)x}{(x^2 + 1)(y^2 + 1)^2} = 0 \implies y = 1$ or $x = 0$

For $x = 0$, $y = 0$, also, and $f(0, 0) = 0$.

For $x = 1$ and $y = 1$, the point $(1, 1)$ is outside R.

For $x^2 + y^2 = 1$, $f(x, y) = f\left(x, \sqrt{1 - x^2}\right) = \dfrac{4x\sqrt{1 - x^2}}{2 + x^2 - x^4}$, and the maximum occurs at $x = \dfrac{\sqrt{2}}{2}, y = \dfrac{\sqrt{2}}{2}$.

Absolute maximum is $\dfrac{8}{9} = f\left(\dfrac{\sqrt{2}}{2}, \dfrac{\sqrt{2}}{2}\right)$.

The absolute minimum is $0 = f(0, 0)$. (In fact, $f(0, y) = f(x, 0) = 0$)

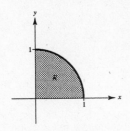

64. False

Let $f(x, y) = x^4 - 2x^2 + y^2$.

Relative minima: $(\pm 1, 0, -1)$

Saddle point: $(0, 0, 0)$

Section 12.9   Applications of Extrema of Functions of Two Variables

2. A point on the plane is given by $(x, y, 12 - 2x - 3y)$. The square of the distance from $(1, 2, 3)$ to a point on the plane is given by

$S = (x - 1)^2 + (y - 2)^2 + (9 - 2x - 3y)^2$

$S_x = 2(x - 1) + 2(9 - 2x - 3y)(-2)$

$S_y = 2(y - 2) + 2(9 - 2x - 3y)(-3)$.

From the equations $S_x = 0$ and $S_y = 0$, we obtain the system

$5x + 6y = 19$

$6x + 10y = 29$.

Solving simultaneously, we have $x = \frac{16}{14}$, $y = \frac{31}{14}$, $z = \frac{43}{14}$ and the distance is

$\sqrt{\left(\dfrac{16}{14} - 1\right)^2 + \left(\dfrac{31}{14} - 2\right)^2 + \left(\dfrac{43}{14} - 3\right)^2} = \dfrac{1}{\sqrt{14}}$.

4. A point on the paraboloid is given by $(x, y, x^2 + y^2)$. The square of the distance from $(5, 0, 0)$ to a point on the paraboloid is given by

$S = (x - 5)^2 + y^2 + (x^2 + y^2)^2$

$S_x = 2(x - 5) + 4x(x^2 + y^2) = 0$

$S_y = 2y + 4y(x^2 + y^2) = 0$.

From the equations $S_x = 0$ and $S_y = 0$, we obtain the system

$2x^3 + 2xy^2 + x - 5 = 0$

$2y^3 + 2x^2y + y = 0$.

Solving as in Exercise 3, we have $x \approx 1.235$, $y = 0$, $z \approx 1.525$ and the distance is

$\sqrt{(1.235 - 5)^2 + (1.525)^2} \approx 4.06$.

6. Since $x + y + z = 32$, $z = 32 - x - y$. Therefore,

$$P = xy^2z = 32xy^2 - x^2y^2 - xy^3$$

$$P_x = 32y^2 - 2xy^2 - y^3 = y^2(32 - 2x - y) = 0$$

$$P_y = 64xy - 2x^2y - 3xy^2 = y(64x - 2x^2 - 3xy) = 0.$$

Ignoring the solution $y = 0$ and substituting $y = 32 - 2x$ into $P_y = 0$, we have

$$64x - 2x^2 - 3x(32 - 2x) = 0$$

$$4x(x - 8) = 0.$$

Therefore, $x = 8$, $y = 16$, and $z = 8$.

8. Let x, y, and z be the numbers and let $S = x^2 + y^2 + z^2$. Since $x + y + z = 1$, we have

$$S = x^2 + y^2 + (1 - x - y)^2$$

$$\begin{aligned} S_x &= 2x - 2(1 - x - y) = 0 \\ S_y &= 2y - 2(1 - x - y) = 0 \end{aligned} \begin{aligned} 2x + y &= 1 \\ x + 2y &= 1. \end{aligned}$$

Solving simultaneously yields $x = \frac{1}{3}$, $y = \frac{1}{3}$, and $z = \frac{1}{3}$.

10. Let x, y, and z be the length, width, and height, respectively. Then $C_0 = 1.5xy + 2yz + 2xz$ and $z = \dfrac{C_0 - 1.5xy}{2(x + y)}$. The volume is given by

$$V = xyz = \frac{C_0xy - 1.5x^2y^2}{2(x + y)}$$

$$V_x = \frac{y^2(2C_0 - 3x^2 - 6xy)}{4(x + y)^2}$$

$$V_y = \frac{x^2(2C_0 - 3y^2 - 6xy)}{4(x + y)^2}.$$

In solving the system $V_x = 0$ and $V_y = 0$, we note by the symmetry of the equations that $y = x$. Substituting $y = x$ into $V_x = 0$ yields

$$\frac{x^2(2C_0 - 9x^2)}{16x^2} = 0, \ 2C_0 = 9x^2, \ x = \frac{1}{3}\sqrt{2C_0}, \ y = \frac{1}{3}\sqrt{2C_0}, \ \text{and } z = \frac{1}{4}\sqrt{2C_0}.$$

12. Consider the sphere given by $x^2 + y^2 + z^2 = r^2$ and let a vertex of the rectangular box be $\left(x, y, \sqrt{r^2 - x^2 - y^2}\right)$. Then the volume is given by

$$V = (2x)(2y)\left(2\sqrt{r^2 - x^2 - y^2}\right) = 8xy\sqrt{r^2 - x^2 - y^2}$$

$$V_x = 8\left(xy\frac{-x}{\sqrt{r^2 - x^2 - y^2}} + y\sqrt{r^2 - x^2 - y^2}\right) = \frac{8y}{\sqrt{r^2 - x^2 - y^2}}(r^2 - 2x^2 - y^2) = 0$$

$$V_y = 8\left(xy\frac{-y}{\sqrt{r^2 - x^2 - y^2}} + x\sqrt{r^2 - x^2 - y^2}\right) = \frac{8x}{\sqrt{r^2 - x^2 - y^2}}(r^2 - x^2 - 2y^2) = 0.$$

Solving the system

$$2x^2 + y^2 = r^2$$

$$x^2 + 2y^2 = r^2$$

yields the solution $x = y = z = r/\sqrt{3}$.

14. Let x, y, and z be the length, width, and height, respectively. Then the sum of the two perimeters of the two cross sections is given by

$$(2x + 2z) + (2y + 2z) = 144 \text{ or } x = 72 - y - 2z.$$

The volume is given by

$$V = xyz = 72yz - y^2z - 2yz^2$$

$$V_y = 72z - 2yz - 2z^2 = z(72 - 2y - 2z) = 0$$

$$V_z = 72y - y^2 - 4yz = y(72 - y - 4z) = 0.$$

Solving the system $2y + 2z = 72$ and $y + 4z = 72$, we obtain the solution

$$x = 24 \text{ inches}, \ y = 24 \text{ inches}, \text{ and } z = 18 \text{ inches}.$$

16. $A = \dfrac{1}{2}[(30 - 2x) + (30 - 2x) + 2x \cos \theta]x \sin \theta$

$\qquad = 30x \sin \theta - 2x^2 \sin \theta + x^2 \sin \theta \cos \theta$

$\dfrac{\partial A}{\partial x} = 30 \sin \theta - 4x \sin \theta + 2x \sin \theta \cos \theta = 0$

$\dfrac{\partial A}{\partial \theta} = 30 \cos \theta - 2x^2 \cos \theta + x^2(2 \cos^2 \theta - 1) = 0$

From $\dfrac{\partial A}{\partial x} = 0$ we have $15 - 2x + x \cos \theta = 0 \Rightarrow \cos \theta = \dfrac{2x - 15}{x}$.

From $\dfrac{\partial A}{\partial \theta} = 0$ we obtain

$$30x\left(\dfrac{2x - 15}{x}\right) - 2x^2\left(\dfrac{2x - 15}{x}\right) + x^2\left(2\left(\dfrac{2x - 15}{x}\right)^2 - 1\right) = 0$$

$$30(2x - 15) - 2x(2x - 15) + 2(2x - 15)^2 - x^2 = 0$$

$$3x^2 - 30x = 0$$

$$x = 10$$

Then $\cos \theta = \dfrac{1}{2} \Rightarrow \theta = 60°$.

18. $P(p, q, r) = 2pq + 2pr + 2qr$.

$p + q + r = 1$ implies that $r = 1 - p - q$.

$P(p, q) = 2pq + 2p(1 - p - q) + 2q(1 - p - q)$

$\qquad = 2pq + 2p - 2p^2 - 2pq + 2q - 2pq - 2q^2$

$\qquad = -2pq + 2p + 2q - 2p^2 - 2q^2$

$\dfrac{\partial P}{\partial p} = -2q + 2 - 4p; \ \dfrac{\partial P}{\partial q} = -2p + 2 - 4q$

Solving $\dfrac{\partial P}{\partial p} = \dfrac{\partial P}{\partial q} = 0$ gives

$q + 2p = 1$

$p + 2q = 1$

and hence $p = q = \dfrac{1}{3}$ and

$$P\left(\dfrac{1}{3}, \dfrac{1}{3}\right) = -2\left(\dfrac{1}{9}\right) + 2\left(\dfrac{1}{3}\right) + 2\left(\dfrac{1}{3}\right) - 2\left(\dfrac{1}{9}\right) - 2\left(\dfrac{1}{9}\right)$$

$$= \dfrac{6}{9} = \dfrac{2}{3}.$$

20. $R = 515p_1 + 805p_2 + 1.5p_1p_2 - 1.5p_1^2 - p_2^2$

$R_{p_1} = 515 + 1.5p_2 - 3p_1 = 0$

$R_{p_2} = 805 + 1.5p_1 - p_2 = 0$

$3p_1 - 1.5p_2 = 515$

$-1.5p_1 + p_2 = 805$

Solving this system yields $p_1 = \$2296.67, p_2 = \$4250$.

22. $S = d_1 + d_2 + d_3 = \sqrt{(0 - 0)^2 + (y - 0)^2} + \sqrt{(0 - 2)^2 + (y - 2)^2} + \sqrt{(0 + 2)^2 + (y - 2)^2}$

$\qquad = y + 2\sqrt{4 + (y - 2)^2}$

$\dfrac{dS}{dy} = 1 + \dfrac{2(y - 2)}{\sqrt{4 + (y - 2)^2}} = 0$ when $y = 2 - \dfrac{2\sqrt{3}}{3} = \dfrac{6 - 2\sqrt{3}}{3}$.

The sum of the distance is minimized when $y = \dfrac{2(3 - \sqrt{3})}{3} \approx 0.845$.

24. (a) $S = \sqrt{(x+4)^2 + y^2} + \sqrt{(x-1)^2 + (y-6)^2} + \sqrt{(x-12)^2 + (y-2)^2}$

The surface appears to have a minimum near $(x, y) = (1, 5)$.

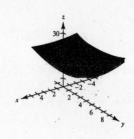

(b) $S_x = \dfrac{x+4}{\sqrt{(x+4)^2 + y^2}} + \dfrac{x-1}{\sqrt{(x-1)^2 + (y-6)^2}} + \dfrac{x-12}{\sqrt{(x-12)^2 + (y-2)^2}}$

$S_y = \dfrac{y}{\sqrt{(x+4)^2 + y^2}} + \dfrac{y-6}{\sqrt{(x-1)^2 + (y-6)^2}} + \dfrac{y-2}{\sqrt{(x-12)^2 + (y-2)^2}}$

(c) Let $(x_1, y_1) = (1, 5)$. Then

$-\nabla S(1, 5) = 0.258\mathbf{i} + 0.03\mathbf{j}$

Direction $\approx 6.6°$

(d) $t \approx 0.94$ $x_2 \approx 1.24$ $y_2 \approx 5.03$

(e) $t \approx 3.56,$ $x_3 \approx 1.24,$ $y_3 \approx 5.06,$

$t \approx 1.04,$ $x_4 \approx 1.23,$ $y_4 \approx 5.06$

Note: Minimum occurs at $(x, y) = (1.2335, 5.0694)$

(f) $-\nabla S(x, y)$ points in the direction that S *decreases* most rapidly.

26. See the last paragraph on page 915 and Theorem 12.18.

28. (a)

x	y	xy	x^2
-3	0	0	9
-1	1	-1	1
1	1	1	1
3	2	6	9
$\sum x_i = 0$	$\sum y_i = 4$	$\sum x_i y_i = 6$	$\sum x_i^2 = 20$

(b) $S = \left(\dfrac{1}{10} - 0\right)^2 + \left(\dfrac{7}{10} - 1\right)^2 + \left(\dfrac{13}{10} - 1\right)^2 + \left(\dfrac{19}{10} - 2\right)^2$

$= \dfrac{1}{5}$

$a = \dfrac{4(6) - 0(4)}{4(20) - (0)^2} = \dfrac{3}{10},\ b = \dfrac{1}{4}\left[4 - \dfrac{3}{10}(0)\right] = 1,$

$y = \dfrac{3}{10}x + 1$

30. (a)

x	y	xy	x^2
3	0	0	9
1	0	0	1
2	0	0	4
3	1	3	9
4	1	4	16
4	2	8	16
5	2	10	25
6	2	12	36
$\sum x_i = 28$	$\sum y_i = 8$	$\sum x_i y_i = 37$	$\sum x_i^2 = 116$

$a = \dfrac{8(37) - (28)(8)}{8(116) - (28)^2} = \dfrac{72}{144} = \dfrac{1}{2},\ b = \dfrac{1}{8}\left[8 - \dfrac{1}{2}(28)\right] = -\dfrac{3}{4},\ y = \dfrac{1}{2}x - \dfrac{3}{4}$

(b) $S = \left(\dfrac{3}{4} - 0\right)^2 + \left(-\dfrac{1}{4} - 0\right)^2 + \left(\dfrac{1}{4} - 0\right)^2 + \left(\dfrac{3}{4} - 1\right)^2 + \left(\dfrac{5}{4} - 1\right)^2 + \left(\dfrac{5}{4} - 2\right)^2 + \left(\dfrac{7}{4} - 2\right)^2 + \left(\dfrac{9}{4} - 2\right)^2 = \dfrac{3}{2}$

32. $(1, 0), (3, 3), (5, 6)$

$$\sum x_i = 9, \qquad \sum y_i = 9,$$

$$\sum x_i y_i = 39, \qquad \sum x_i^2 = 35$$

$$a = \frac{3(39) - 9(9)}{3(35) - (9)^2} = \frac{36}{24} = \frac{3}{2}$$

$$b = \frac{1}{3}\left[9 - \frac{3}{2}(9)\right] = -\frac{9}{6} = -\frac{3}{2}$$

$$y = \frac{3}{2}x - \frac{3}{2}$$

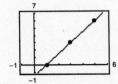

34. $(6, 4), (1, 2), (3, 3), (8, 6), (11, 8), (13, 8); n = 6$

$$\sum x_i = 42 \qquad \sum y_i = 31$$

$$\sum x_i y_i = 275 \qquad \sum x_i^2 = 400$$

$$a = \frac{6(275) - (42)(31)}{6(400) - (42)^2} = \frac{29}{53} \approx 0.5472$$

$$b = \frac{1}{6}\left(31 - \frac{29}{53}42\right) = \frac{425}{318} \approx 1.3365$$

$$y = \frac{29}{53}x + \frac{425}{318}$$

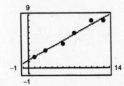

36. (a) $(1.00, 450), (1.25, 375), (1.50, 330)$

$$\sum x_i = 3.75, \sum y_i = 1{,}155, \sum x_i^2 = 4.8125,$$

$$\sum x_i y_i = 1{,}413.75$$

$$a = \frac{3(1{,}413.75) - (3.75)(1{,}155)}{3(4.8125) - (3.75)^2} = -240$$

$$b = \frac{1}{3}[1{,}155 - (-240)(3.75)] = 685$$

$$y = -240x + 685$$

(b) When $x = 1.40$, $y = -240(1.40) + 685 = 349$.

38. (a) $y = 1.8311x - 47.1067$

(b) For each 1 point increase in the percent (x), y increases by about 1.83 (slope of line).

40. $S(a, b) = \sum_{i=1}^{n}(ax_i + b - y_i)^2$

$$S_a(a, b) = 2a\sum_{i=1}^{n}x_i^2 + 2b\sum_{i=1}^{n}x_i - 2\sum_{i=1}^{n}x_i y_i$$

$$S_b(a, b) = 2a\sum_{i=1}^{n}x_i + 2nb - 2\sum_{i=1}^{n}y_i$$

$$S_{aa}(a, b) = 2\sum_{i=1}^{n}x_i^2$$

$$S_{bb}(a, b) = 2n$$

$$S_{ab}(a, b) = 2\sum_{i=1}^{n}x_i$$

$S_{aa}(a, b) > 0$ as long as $x_i \neq 0$ for all i. (**Note:** If $x_i = 0$ for all i, then $x = 0$ is the least squares regression line.)

$$d = S_{aa}S_{bb} - S_{ab}^2 = 4n\sum_{i=1}^{n}x_i^2 - 4\left(\sum_{i=1}^{n}x_i\right)^2 = 4\left[n\sum_{i=1}^{n}x_i^2 - \left(\sum_{i=1}^{n}x_i\right)^2\right] \geq 0 \text{ since } n\sum_{i=1}^{n}x_i^2 \geq \left(\sum_{i=1}^{n}x_i\right)^2.$$

As long as $d \neq 0$, the given values for a and b yield a minimum.

42. $(-4, 5)$, $(-2, 6)$, $(2, 6)$, $(4, 2)$

$$\sum x_i = 0$$

$$\sum y_i = 19$$

$$\sum x_i^2 = 40$$

$$\sum x_i^3 = 0$$

$$\sum x_i^4 = 544$$

$$\sum x_i y_i = -12$$

$$\sum x_i^2 y_i = 160$$

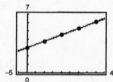

$544a + 40c = 160$, $40b = -12$, $40a + 4c = 19$

$a = -\frac{5}{24}$, $b = -\frac{3}{10}$, $c = \frac{41}{6}$, $y = -\frac{5}{24}x^2 - \frac{3}{10}x + \frac{41}{6}$

44. $(0, 10)$, $(1, 9)$, $(2, 6)$, $(3, 0)$

$$\sum x_i = 6$$

$$\sum y_i = 25$$

$$\sum x_i^2 = 14$$

$$\sum x_i^3 = 36$$

$$\sum x_i^4 = 98$$

$$\sum x_i y_i = 21$$

$$\sum x_i^2 y_i = 33$$

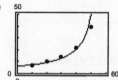

$98a + 36b + 14c = 33$

$36a + 14b + 6c = 21$

$14a + 6b + 4c = 25$

$a = -\frac{5}{4}$, $b = \frac{9}{20}$, $c = \frac{199}{20}$, $y = -\frac{5}{4}x^2 + \frac{9}{20}x + \frac{199}{20}$

46. (a) $y = 0.078x + 2.96$

(b) $y = 0.0001429x^2 + 0.07229x + 2.9886$

(c)

(d) For the linear model, $x = 50$ gives $y \approx 6.86$ billion.

For the quadratic model, $x = 50$ gives $y \approx 6.96$ billion.

As you extrapolate into the future, the quadratic model increases more rapidly.

48. (a) $\dfrac{1}{y} = ax + b = -0.0029x + 0.1640$

$$y = \frac{1}{-0.0029x + 0.1640}$$

(b)

(c) No. For $x = 60$, $y \approx -100$. Note that there is a vertical asymptote at $x \approx 56.6$.

Section 12.10   Lagrange Multipliers

2. Maximize $f(x, y) = xy$.

Constraint: $2x + y = 4$

$\nabla f = \lambda \nabla g$

$y\mathbf{i} + x\mathbf{j} = 2\lambda \mathbf{i} + \lambda \mathbf{j}$

$\qquad y = 2\lambda$

$\qquad x = \lambda$

$2x + y = 4 \implies 4\lambda = 4$

$\qquad\qquad \lambda = 1$, $x = 1$, $y = 2$

$f(1, 2) = 2$

4. Minimize $f(x, y) = x^2 + y^2$.

Constraint: $2x + 4y = 5$

$\nabla f = \lambda \nabla g$

$2x\mathbf{i} + 2y\mathbf{j} = 2\lambda \mathbf{i} + 4\lambda \mathbf{j}$

$\qquad 2x = 2\lambda \implies x = \lambda$

$\qquad 2y = 4\lambda \implies y = 2\lambda$

$\qquad 2x + 4y = 5 \implies 10\lambda = 5$

$\qquad\qquad \lambda = \frac{1}{2}$, $x = \frac{1}{2}$, $y = 1$

$f\left(\frac{1}{2}, 1\right) = \frac{5}{4}$

6. Maximize $f(x, y) = x^2 - y^2$.

Constraint: $2y - x^2 = 0$

$\nabla f = \lambda \nabla g$

$2x\mathbf{i} - 2y\mathbf{j} = -2x\lambda\mathbf{i} + 2\lambda\mathbf{j}$

$2x = -2x\lambda \implies x = 0$ or $\lambda = -1$

If $x = 0$, then $y = 0$ and $f(0, 0) = 0$.

If $\lambda = -1$,

$$-2y = 2\lambda = -2 \implies y = 1 \implies x^2 = 2 \implies x = \sqrt{2}.$$

$f(\sqrt{2}, 1) = 2 - 1 = 1$ Maximum.

8. Minimize $f(x, y) = 3x + y + 10$.

Constraint: $x^2 y = 6$

$\nabla f = \lambda \nabla g$

$3\mathbf{i} + \mathbf{j} = 2xy\lambda\mathbf{i} + x^2\lambda\mathbf{j}$

$$\left. \begin{array}{l} 3 = 2xy\lambda \implies \lambda = \dfrac{3}{2xy} \\[2mm] 1 = x^2\lambda \implies \lambda = \dfrac{1}{x^2} \end{array} \right\} 3x^2 = 2xy \implies y = \dfrac{3x}{2}$$
$$(x \neq 0)$$

$x^2 y = 6 \implies x^2\left(\dfrac{3x}{2}\right) = 6$

$$x^3 = 4$$

$$x = \sqrt[3]{4}, \quad y = \dfrac{3\sqrt[3]{4}}{2}$$

$$f\left(\sqrt[3]{4}, \dfrac{3\sqrt[3]{4}}{2}\right) = \dfrac{9\sqrt[3]{4} + 20}{2}$$

10. Note: $f(x, y) = \sqrt{x^2 + y^2}$ is minimum when $g(x, y)$ is minimum.

Minimize $g(x, y) = x^2 + y^2$.

Constraint: $2x + 4y = 15$

$$\left. \begin{array}{l} 2x = 2\lambda \\ 2y = 4\lambda \end{array} \right\} y = 2x$$

$2x + 4y = 15 \implies 10x = 15$

$$x = \dfrac{3}{2}, \ y = 3$$

$$f\left(\dfrac{3}{2}, 3\right) = \sqrt{g\left(\dfrac{3}{2}, 3\right)} = \dfrac{3\sqrt{5}}{2}$$

12. Minimize $f(x, y) = 2x + y$.

Constraint: $xy = 32$

$$\left. \begin{array}{l} 2 = y\lambda \\ 1 = x\lambda \end{array} \right\} y = 2x$$

$xy = 32 \implies 2x^2 = 32$

$$x = 4, y = 8$$

$$f(4, 8) = 16$$

14. Maximize or minimize $f(x, y) = e^{-xy/4}$.

Constraint: $x^2 + y^2 \leq 1$

Case 1: On the circle $x^2 + y^2 = 1$

$$\left. \begin{array}{l} -(y/4)e^{-xy/4} = 2x\lambda \\ -(x/4)e^{-xy/4} = 2y\lambda \end{array} \right\} \implies x^2 = y^2$$

$$x^2 + y^2 = 1 \implies x = \pm\dfrac{\sqrt{2}}{2}$$

Maxima: $f\left(\pm\dfrac{\sqrt{2}}{2}, \mp\dfrac{\sqrt{2}}{2}\right) = e^{1/8} \approx 1.1331$

Minima: $f\left(\pm\dfrac{\sqrt{2}}{2}, \pm\dfrac{\sqrt{2}}{2}\right) = e^{-1/8} \approx 0.8825$

Case 2: Inside the circle

$$\left. \begin{array}{l} f_x = -(y/4)e^{-xy/4} = 0 \\ f_y = -(x/4)e^{-xy/4} = 0 \end{array} \right\} \implies x = y = 0$$

$f_{xx} = \dfrac{y^2}{16}e^{-xy/4}, \ f_{yy} = \dfrac{x^2}{16}e^{-xy/4}, \ f_{xy} = e^{-xy}\left[\dfrac{1}{16}xy - \dfrac{1}{4}\right]$

At $(0, 0)$, $f_{xx}f_{yy} - (f_{xy})^2 < 0$.

Saddle point: $f(0, 0) = 1$

Combining the two cases, we have a maximum of $e^{1/8}$ at $\left(\pm\dfrac{\sqrt{2}}{2}, \mp\dfrac{\sqrt{2}}{2}\right)$ and a minimum of $e^{-1/8}$ at $\left(\pm\dfrac{\sqrt{2}}{2}, \pm\dfrac{\sqrt{2}}{2}\right)$.

16. Maximize $f(x, y, z) = xyz$.

Constraint: $x + y + z = 6$

$$\left. \begin{array}{r} yz = \lambda \\ xz = \lambda \\ xy = \lambda \end{array} \right\} x = y = z$$

$x + y + z = 6 \implies x = y = z = 2$

$f(2, 2, 2) = 8$

18. Minimize $x^2 - 10x + y^2 - 14y + 70$

Constraint: $x + y = 10$

$$\left. \begin{array}{r} 2x - 10 = \lambda \\ 2y - 14 = \lambda \\ x + y = 8 \end{array} \right\} \begin{array}{l} x = (1/2)(\lambda + 10) \\ y = (1/2)(\lambda + 14) \end{array}$$

$x + y = \dfrac{1}{2}(\lambda + 10) + \dfrac{1}{2}(\lambda + 14)$

$\quad\quad = \lambda + 12 = 8 \implies \lambda = -4$

Then $x = 3, y = 5$.

$f(3, 5) = 9 - 30 + 25 - 70 + 70 = 4$

20. Minimize $f(x, y, z) = x^2 + y^2 + z^2$.

Constraints: $x + 2z = 6$

$\quad\quad\quad\quad\quad x + y = 12$

$\nabla f = \lambda \nabla g + \mu \nabla h$

$2x\mathbf{i} + 2y\mathbf{j} + 2z\mathbf{k} = \lambda(\mathbf{i} + 2\mathbf{k}) + \mu(\mathbf{i} + \mathbf{j})$

$$\left. \begin{array}{r} 2x = \lambda + \mu \\ 2y = \mu \\ 2z = 2\lambda \end{array} \right\} 2x = 2y + z$$

$x + 2z = 6 \implies z = \dfrac{6 - x}{2} = 3 - \dfrac{x}{2}$

$x + y = 12 \implies y = 12 - x$

$2x = 2(12 - x) + \left(3 - \dfrac{x}{2}\right) \implies \dfrac{9}{2}x = 27 \implies x = 6$

$x = 6, z = 0$

$f(6, 6, 0) = 72$

22. Maximize $f(x, y, z) = xyz$.

Constraints: $x^2 + z^2 = 5$

$\quad\quad\quad\quad\quad x - 2y = 0$

$\nabla f = \lambda \nabla g + \mu \nabla h$

$yz\mathbf{i} + xz\mathbf{j} + xy\mathbf{k} = \lambda(2x\mathbf{i} + 2z\mathbf{k}) + \mu(\mathbf{i} - 2\mathbf{j})$

$yz = 2x\lambda + \mu$

$xz = -2\mu \implies \mu = -\dfrac{xy}{2}$

$xy = 2z\lambda \implies \lambda = \dfrac{xy}{2z}$

$x^2 + z^2 = 5 \implies z = \sqrt{5 - x^2}$

$x - 2y = 0 \implies y = \dfrac{x}{2}$

$yz = 2x\left(\dfrac{xy}{2z}\right) - \dfrac{xz}{2}$

$\dfrac{x\sqrt{5 - x^2}}{2} = \dfrac{x^3}{2\sqrt{5 - x^2}} - \dfrac{x\sqrt{5 - x^2}}{2}$

$x\sqrt{5 - x^2} = \dfrac{x^3}{2\sqrt{5 - x^2}}$

$2x(5 - x^2) = x^3$

$0 = 3x^3 - 10x = x(3x^2 - 10)$

$x = 0 \text{ or } x = \sqrt{\dfrac{10}{3}}, y = \dfrac{1}{2}\sqrt{\dfrac{10}{3}}, z = \sqrt{\dfrac{5}{3}}$

$f\left(\sqrt{\dfrac{10}{3}}, \dfrac{1}{2}\sqrt{\dfrac{10}{3}}, \sqrt{\dfrac{5}{3}}\right) = \dfrac{5\sqrt{15}}{9}$

Note: $f(0, 0, \sqrt{5}) = 0$ does not yield a maximum.

24. Minimize the square of the distance $f(x, y) = x^2 + (y - 10)^2$ subject to the constraint $(x - 4)^2 + y^2 = 4$.

$$\left. \begin{array}{r} 2x = 2(x - 4)\lambda \\ 2(y - 10) = 2y\lambda \end{array} \right\} \frac{x}{x - 4} = \frac{y - 10}{y} \implies y = -\frac{5}{2}x + 10$$

$$(x - 4)^2 + y^2 = 4 \implies (x^2 - 8x + 16) + \left(\frac{25}{4}x^2 - 50x + 100\right) = 4$$

$$\frac{29}{4}x^2 - 58x + 112 = 0$$

Using a graphing utility, we obtain $x \approx 3.2572$ and $x \approx 4.7428$ or, by the Quadratic Formula,

$$x = \frac{58 \pm \sqrt{58^2 - 4(29/4)(112)}}{2(29/4)} = \frac{58 \pm 2\sqrt{29}}{29/2} = 4 \pm \frac{4\sqrt{29}}{29}.$$

Using the smaller value, we have $x = 4\left(1 - \frac{\sqrt{29}}{29}\right)$ and $y = \frac{10\sqrt{29}}{29} \approx 1.8570$.

The point on the circle is $\left[4\left(1 - \frac{\sqrt{29}}{29}\right), \frac{10\sqrt{29}}{29} \right]$

and the desired distance is $d = \sqrt{16\left(1 - \frac{\sqrt{29}}{29}\right)^2 + \left(\frac{10\sqrt{29}}{29} - 10\right)^2} \approx 8.77$.

The larger x-value does not yield a minimum.

26. Minimize the square of the distance

$$f(x, y, z) = (x - 4)^2 + y^2 + z^2$$

subject to the constraint $\sqrt{x^2 + y^2} - z = 0$.

$$\left. \begin{array}{l} 2(x - 4) = \dfrac{x}{\sqrt{x^2 + y^2}}\lambda = \dfrac{x}{z}\lambda \\[2mm] 2y = \dfrac{y}{\sqrt{x^2 + y^2}}\lambda = \dfrac{y}{z}\lambda \\[2mm] 2z = -\lambda \end{array} \right\} \begin{array}{l} 2(x - 4) = -2x \\[2mm] 2y = -2y \end{array}$$

$$\sqrt{x^2 + y^2} - z = 0, \ x = 2, \ y = 0, \ z = 2$$

The point on the plane is $(2, 0, 2)$ and the desired distance is

$$d = \sqrt{(2 - 4)^2 + 0^2 + 2^2} = 2\sqrt{2}.$$

28. Maximize $f(x, y, z) = z$ subject to the constraints $x^2 + y^2 - z^2 = 0$ and $x + 2z = 4$.

$$0 = 2x\lambda + \mu$$

$$0 = 2y\lambda \implies y = 0$$

$$1 = -2z\lambda + 2\mu$$

$$x^2 + y^2 - z^2 = 0$$

$$x + 2z = 4 \implies x = 4 - 2z$$

$$(4 - 2z)^2 + 0^2 - z^2 = 0$$

$$3z^2 - 16z + 16 = 0$$

$$(3z - 4)(z - 4) = 0$$

$$z = \frac{4}{3} \text{ or } z = 4$$

The maximum value of f occurs when $z = 4$ at the point of $(-4, 0, 4)$.

30. See explanation at the bottom of page 922.

32. Maximize $V(x, y, z) = xyz$ subject to the constraint $1.5xy + 2xz + 2yz = C$.

$$\left. \begin{array}{l} yz = (1.5y + 2z)\lambda \\ xz = (1.5x + 2z)\lambda \\ xy = (2x + 2y)\lambda \end{array} \right\} x = y \text{ and } z = \frac{3}{4}x$$

$$1.5xy + 2xz + 2yz = C \implies 1.5x^2 + \frac{3}{2}x^2 + \frac{3}{2}x^2 = C$$

$$x = \frac{\sqrt{2C}}{3}$$

Volume is maximum when

$$x = y = \frac{\sqrt{2C}}{3} \quad \text{and} \quad z = \frac{\sqrt{2C}}{4}.$$

34. Minimize $A(\pi, r) = 2\pi rh + 2\pi r^2$ subject to the constraint $\pi r^2 h = V_0$.

$$\left. \begin{array}{r} 2\pi h + 4\pi r = 2\pi rh\lambda \\ 2\pi r = \pi r^2\lambda \end{array} \right\} h = 2r$$

$$\pi r^2 h = V_0 \implies 2\pi r^3 = V_0$$

Dimensions: $r = \sqrt[3]{\frac{V_0}{2\pi}}$ and $h = 2\sqrt[3]{\frac{V_0}{2\pi}}$

36. (a) Maximize $P(x, y, z) = xyz$ subject to the constraint

$$x + y + z = S.$$

$$\left.\begin{array}{l} yz = \lambda \\ xz = \lambda \\ xy = \lambda \end{array}\right\} x = y = z$$

$$x + y + z = S \implies x = y = z = \frac{S}{3}$$

Therefore,

$$xyz \le \left(\frac{S}{3}\right)\left(\frac{S}{3}\right)\left(\frac{S}{3}\right), \ x, y, z > 0$$

$$xyz \le \frac{S^3}{27}$$

$$\sqrt[3]{xyz} \le \frac{S}{3}$$

$$\sqrt[3]{xyz} \le \frac{x + y + z}{3}.$$

(b) Maximize $P = x_1 x_2 x_3 \ldots x_n$ subject to the constraint

$$\sum_{i=1}^{n} x_i = S.$$

$$\left.\begin{array}{l} x_2 x_3 \ldots x_n = \lambda \\ x_1 x_3 \ldots x_n = \lambda \\ x_1 x_2 \ldots x_n = \lambda \\ \vdots \\ x_1 x_2 x_3 \ldots x_{n-1} = \lambda \end{array}\right\} x_1 = x_2 = x_3 = \cdots = x_n$$

$$\sum_{i=1}^{n} x_i = S \implies x_1 = x_2 = x_3 = \cdots = x_n = \frac{S}{n}$$

Therefore,

$$x_1 x_2 x_3 \ldots x_n \le \left(\frac{S}{n}\right)\left(\frac{S}{n}\right)\left(\frac{S}{n}\right) \cdots \left(\frac{S}{n}\right), \ x_i \ge 0$$

$$x_1 x_2 x_3 \ldots x_n \le \left(\frac{S}{n}\right)^n$$

$$\sqrt[n]{x_1 x_2 x_3 \ldots x_n} \le \frac{S}{n}$$

$$\sqrt[n]{x_1 x_2 x_3 \ldots x_n} \le \frac{x_1 + x_2 + x_3 + \cdots + x_n}{n}.$$

38. Case 1: Minimize $P(l, h) = 2h + l + \left(\dfrac{\pi l}{2}\right)$ subject to the constraint $lh + \left(\dfrac{\pi l^2}{8}\right) = A.$

$$1 + \frac{\pi}{2} = \left(h + \frac{\pi l}{4}\right)\lambda$$

$$2 = l\lambda \implies \lambda = \frac{2}{l}, 1 + \frac{\pi}{2} = \frac{2h}{l} + \frac{\pi}{2}$$

$$l = 2h$$

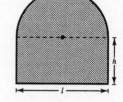

Case 2: Minimize $A(l, h) = lh + \left(\dfrac{\pi l^2}{8}\right)$ subject to the constraint $2h + l + \left(\dfrac{\pi l}{2}\right) = P.$

$$h + \frac{\pi l}{4} = \left(\perp + \frac{\pi}{2}\right)\lambda$$

$$l = 2\lambda \implies \lambda = \frac{l}{2}, h + \frac{\pi l}{4} = \frac{l}{2} + \frac{\pi l}{4}$$

$$h = \frac{l}{2} \text{ or } l = 2h$$

40. Maximize $T(x, y, z) = 100 + x^2 + y^2$ subject to the constraints $x^2 + y^2 + z^2 = 50$ and $x - z = 0.$

$$\left.\begin{array}{l} 2x = 2x\lambda + \mu \\ 2y = 2y\lambda \\ 0 = 2z\lambda - \mu \end{array}\right\}$$

If $y \ne 0$, then $\lambda = 1$ and $\mu = 0$, $z = 0$.

Thus, $x = z = 0$ and $y = \sqrt{50}$.

$$T\left(0, \sqrt{50}, 0\right) = 100 + 50 = 150$$

If $y = 0$, then $x^2 + z^2 = 2x^2 = 50$ and $x = z = \sqrt{50}/2.$

$$T\left(\frac{\sqrt{50}}{2}, 0, \frac{\sqrt{50}}{2}\right) = 100 + \frac{50}{4} = 112.5$$

Therefore, the maximum temperature is 150.

42. Maximize $P(x, y) = 100x^{0.4}y^{0.6}$

Constraint: $48x + 36y = 100,000.$

$$40x^{-0.6}y^{0.6} = 48\lambda \implies \left(\frac{y}{x}\right)^{0.6} = \frac{48\lambda}{40}$$

$$60x^{0.4}y^{-0.4} = 36\lambda \implies \left(\frac{x}{y}\right)^{0.4} = \frac{36\lambda}{60}$$

$$\left(\frac{y}{x}\right)^{0.6}\left(\frac{y}{x}\right)^{0.4} = \left(\frac{48\lambda}{40}\right)\left(\frac{60}{36\lambda}\right)$$

$$\frac{y}{x} = 2 \implies y = 2x$$

$$48x + 36y(2x) = 100,000 \implies x = \frac{2500}{3}, y = \frac{5000}{3}$$

$$P\left(\frac{2500}{3}, \frac{5000}{3}\right) \approx \$126,309.71.$$

44. Minimize $C(x, y) = 48x + 36y$ subject to the constraint $100x^{0.6}y^{0.4} = 20,000$.

$$48 = 60x^{-0.4}y^{0.4}\lambda \implies \left(\frac{y}{x}\right)^{0.4} = \frac{48}{60\lambda}$$

$$36 = 40x^{0.6}y^{-0.6}\lambda \implies \left(\frac{x}{y}\right)^{0.6} = \frac{36}{40\lambda}$$

$$\left(\frac{y}{x}\right)^{0.4}\left(\frac{y}{x}\right)^{0.6} = \left(\frac{48}{60\lambda}\right)\left(\frac{40\lambda}{36}\right)$$

$$\frac{y}{x} = \frac{8}{9} \implies y = \frac{8}{9}x$$

$$100x^{0.6}y^{0.4} = 20,000 \implies x^{0.6}\left(\frac{8}{9}x\right)^{0.4} = 200$$

$$x = \frac{200}{(8/9)^{0.4}} \approx 209.65$$

$$y = \frac{8}{9}\left[\frac{200}{(8/9)^{0.4}}\right] \approx 186.35$$

Therefore, $C(209.65, 186.35) = \$16,771.94$.

46. $f(x, y) = ax + by, \ x, y > 0$

Constraint: $\dfrac{x^2}{64} + \dfrac{y^2}{36} = 1$

(a) Level curves of $f(x, y) = 4x + 3y$ are lines of form

$$y = -\frac{4}{3}x + C.$$

Using $y = -\dfrac{4}{3}x + 12.3$, you obtain

$$x \approx 7, \ y \approx 3, \quad \text{and} \quad f(7, 3) = 28 + 9 = 37.$$

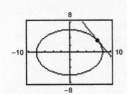

Constraint is an ellipse.

(b) Level curves of $f(x, y) = 4x + 9y$ are lines of form

$$y = -\frac{4}{9}x + C.$$

Using $y = -\dfrac{4}{9}x + 7$, you obtain

$$x \approx 4, \ y \approx 5.2, \ \text{and} \ f(4, 5.2) = 62.8.$$

Review Exercises for Chapter 12

2. Yes, it is the graph of a function.

4. $f(x, y) = \ln xy$

The level curves are of the form

$$c = \ln xy$$

$$e^c = xy.$$

The level curves are hyperbolas.

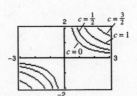

6. $f(x, y) = \dfrac{x}{x + y}$

The level curves are of the form

$$c = \frac{x}{x + y}$$

$$y = \left(\frac{1 - c}{c}\right)x.$$

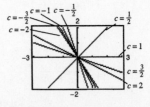

The level curves are passing through the origin with slope

$$\frac{1 - c}{c}.$$

8. $g(x, y) = |y|^{1 + |x|}$

10. $f(x, y, z) = 9x^2 - y^2 + 9z^2 = 0$

Elliptic cone

12. $\displaystyle\lim_{(x, y) \to (1, 1)} \frac{xy}{x^2 - y^2}$

Does not exist

Continuous except when $y = \pm x$.

14. $\displaystyle\lim_{(x, y) \to (0, 0)} \frac{y + xe^{-y^2}}{1 + x^2} = \frac{0 + 0}{1 + 0} = 0$

Continuous everywhere

16. $f(x, y) = \dfrac{xy}{x + y}$

$f_x = \dfrac{y(x + y) - xy}{(x + y)^2} = \dfrac{y^2}{(x + y)^2}$

$f_y = \dfrac{x^2}{(x + y)^2}$

18. $z = \ln(x^2 + y^2 + 1)$

$\dfrac{\partial z}{\partial x} = \dfrac{2x}{x^2 + y^2 + 1}$

$\dfrac{\partial z}{\partial y} = \dfrac{2y}{x^2 + y^2 + 1}$

20. $w = \sqrt{x^2 + y^2 + z^2}$

$\dfrac{\partial w}{\partial x} = \dfrac{1}{2}(x^2 + y^2 + z^2)^{-1/2}(2x) = \dfrac{x}{\sqrt{x^2 + y^2 + z^2}}$

$\dfrac{\partial w}{\partial y} = \dfrac{y}{\sqrt{x^2 + y^2 + z^2}}$

$\dfrac{\partial w}{\partial z} = \dfrac{z}{\sqrt{x^2 + y^2 + z^2}}$

22. $f(x, y, z) = \dfrac{1}{\sqrt{1 - x^2 - y^2 - z^2}}$

$f_x = -\dfrac{1}{2}(1 - x^2 - y^2 - z^2)^{-3/2}(-2x)$

$\quad = \dfrac{x}{(1 - x^2 - y^2 - z^2)^{3/2}}$

$f_y = \dfrac{y}{(1 - x^2 - y^2 - z^2)^{3/2}}$

$f_z = \dfrac{z}{(1 - x^2 - y^2 - z^2)^{3/2}}$

24. $u(x, t) = c(\sin akx) \cos kt$

$\dfrac{\partial u}{\partial x} = akc(\cos akx) \cos kt$

$\dfrac{\partial u}{\partial t} = -kc(\sin akx) \sin kt$

26. $z = x^2 \ln(y + 1)$

$\dfrac{\partial z}{\partial x} = 2x \ln(y + 1)$. At $(2, 0, 0)$, $\dfrac{\partial z}{\partial x} = 0$.

Slope in x-direction.

$\dfrac{\partial z}{\partial y} = \dfrac{x^2}{1 + y}$. At $(2, 0, 0)$, $\dfrac{\partial z}{\partial y} = 4$.

Slope in y-direction.

28. $h(x, y) = \dfrac{x}{x + y}$

$h_x = \dfrac{y}{(x + y)^2}$

$h_y = \dfrac{-x}{(x + y)^2}$

$h_{xx} = \dfrac{-2y}{(x + y)^3}$

$h_{yy} = \dfrac{2x}{(x + y)^3}$

$h_{xy} = \dfrac{(x + y)^2 - 2y(x + y)}{(x + y)^4} = \dfrac{x - y}{(x + y)^3}$

$h_{yx} = \dfrac{-(x + y)^2 + 2y(x + y)}{(x + y)^4} = \dfrac{x - y}{(x + y)^3}$

30. $g(x, y) = \cos(x - 2y)$

$g_x = -\sin(x - 2y)$

$g_y = 2 \sin(x - 2y)$

$g_{xx} = -\cos(x - 2y)$

$g_{yy} = -4 \cos(x - 2y)$

$g_{xy} = 2 \cos(x - 2y)$

$g_{yx} = 2 \cos(x - 2y)$

32. $z = x^3 - 3xy^2$

$\dfrac{\partial z}{\partial x} = 3x^2 - 3y^2$

$\dfrac{\partial^2 z}{\partial x^2} = 6x$

$\dfrac{\partial z}{\partial y} = -6xy$

$\dfrac{\partial^2 z}{\partial y^2} = -6x$

Therefore, $\dfrac{\partial^2 z}{\partial x^2} + \dfrac{\partial^2 z}{\partial y^2} = 0$.

34. $z = e^x \sin y$

$\dfrac{\partial z}{\partial x} = e^x \sin y$

$\dfrac{\partial^2 z}{\partial x^2} = e^x \sin y$

$\dfrac{\partial z}{\partial y} = e^x \cos y$

$\dfrac{\partial^2 z}{\partial y^2} = -e^x \sin y$

Therefore, $\dfrac{\partial^2 z}{\partial x^2} + \dfrac{\partial^2 z}{\partial y^2} = 0$.

36. $z = \dfrac{xy}{\sqrt{x^2 + y^2}}$

$dz = \dfrac{\partial z}{\partial x} dx + \dfrac{\partial z}{\partial y} dy$

$= \left[\dfrac{\sqrt{x^2 + y^2}\, y - xy\big(x/\sqrt{x^2 + y^2}\big)}{x^2 + y^2} \right] dx + \left[\dfrac{\sqrt{x^2 + y^2}\, x - xy\big(y/\sqrt{x^2 + y^2}\big)}{x^2 + y^2} \right] dy = \dfrac{y^3}{(x^2 + y^2)^{3/2}} dx + \dfrac{x^3}{(x^2 + y^2)^{3/2}} dy$

38. From the accompanying figure we observe

$\tan \theta = \dfrac{h}{x}$ or $h = x \tan \theta$

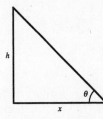

$dh = \dfrac{\partial h}{\partial x} dx + \dfrac{\partial h}{\partial \theta} d\theta = \tan \theta \, dx + x \sec^2 \theta \, d\theta.$

Letting $x = 100$, $dx = \pm\dfrac{1}{2}$, $\theta = \dfrac{11\pi}{60}$, and $d\theta = \pm\dfrac{\pi}{180}$.

(Note that we express the measurement of the angle in radians.) The maximum error is approximately

$dh = \tan\left(\dfrac{11\pi}{60}\right)\left(\pm\dfrac{1}{2}\right) + 100 \sec^2\left(\dfrac{11\pi}{60}\right)\left(\pm\dfrac{\pi}{180}\right) \approx \pm 0.3247 \pm 2.4814 \approx \pm 2.81$ feet.

40. $A = \pi r \sqrt{r^2 + h^2}$

$dA = \left(\pi\sqrt{r^2 + h^2} + \dfrac{\pi r^2}{\sqrt{r^2 + h^2}} \right) dr + \dfrac{\pi r h}{\sqrt{r^2 + h^2}} dh$

$= \dfrac{\pi(2r^2 + h^2)}{\sqrt{r^2 + h^2}} dr + \dfrac{\pi r h}{\sqrt{r^2 + h^2}} dh = \dfrac{\pi(8 + 25)}{\sqrt{29}}\left(\pm\dfrac{1}{8}\right) + \dfrac{10\pi}{\sqrt{29}}\left(\pm\dfrac{1}{8}\right) = \pm\dfrac{43\pi}{8\sqrt{29}}$

42. $u = y^2 - x$, $x = \cos t$, $y = \sin t$

Chain Rule: $\dfrac{du}{dt} = \dfrac{\partial u}{\partial x}\dfrac{\partial x}{\partial t} + \dfrac{\partial u}{\partial y}\dfrac{\partial y}{\partial t}$

$= -1(-\sin t) + 2y(\cos t)$

$= \sin t + 2(\sin t) \cos t$

$= \sin t(1 + 2\cos t)$

Substitution: $u = \sin^2 t - \cos t$

$\dfrac{du}{dt} = 2\sin t \cos t + \sin t = \sin t(1 + 2\cos t)$

44. $w = \dfrac{xy}{z}, x = 2r + t, y = rt, z = 2r - t$

Chain Rule: $\dfrac{\partial w}{\partial r} = \dfrac{\partial w}{\partial x}\dfrac{\partial x}{\partial r} + \dfrac{\partial w}{\partial y}\dfrac{\partial y}{\partial r} + \dfrac{\partial w}{\partial z}\dfrac{\partial z}{\partial r}$

$\qquad = \dfrac{y}{z}(2) + \dfrac{x}{z}(t) - \dfrac{xy}{z^2}(2)$

$\qquad = \dfrac{2rt}{2r - t} + \dfrac{(2r + t)t}{2r - t} - \dfrac{2(2r + t)(rt)}{(2r - t)^2}$

$\qquad = \dfrac{4r^2t - 4rt^2 - t^3}{(2r - t)^2}$

$\dfrac{\partial w}{\partial t} = \dfrac{\partial w}{\partial x}\dfrac{\partial x}{\partial t} + \dfrac{\partial w}{\partial y}\dfrac{\partial y}{\partial t} + \dfrac{\partial w}{\partial z}\dfrac{\partial z}{\partial t}$

$\qquad = \dfrac{y}{z}(1) + \dfrac{x}{z}(r) = \dfrac{xy}{z^2}(-1)$

$\qquad = \dfrac{4r^2t - rt^2 + 4r^3}{(2r - t)^2}$

Substitution: $w = \dfrac{xy}{z} = \dfrac{(2r + t)(rt)}{2r - t} = \dfrac{2r^2t + rt^2}{2r - t}$

$\dfrac{\partial w}{\partial r} = \dfrac{4r^2t - 4rt^2 - t^3}{(2r - t)^2}$

$\dfrac{\partial w}{\partial t} = \dfrac{4r^2t - rt^2 - 4r^3}{(2r - t)^2}$

46. $\qquad xz^2 - y\sin z = 0$

$2xz\dfrac{\partial z}{\partial x} + z^2 - y\cos z\dfrac{\partial z}{\partial x} = 0$

$\qquad\qquad \dfrac{\partial z}{\partial x} = \dfrac{z^2}{y\cos z - 2xz}$

$2xz\dfrac{\partial z}{\partial y} - y\cos z\dfrac{\partial z}{\partial y} - \sin z = 0$

$\qquad\qquad \dfrac{\partial z}{\partial y} = \dfrac{\sin z}{2xz - y\cos z}$

48. $f(x, y) = \dfrac{1}{4}y^2 - x^2$

$\nabla f = -2x\mathbf{i} + \dfrac{1}{2}y\mathbf{j}$

$\nabla f(1, 4) = -2\mathbf{i} + 2\mathbf{j}$

$\mathbf{u} = \dfrac{1}{\sqrt{5}}\mathbf{v} = \dfrac{2\sqrt{5}}{5}\mathbf{i} + \dfrac{\sqrt{5}}{5}\mathbf{j}$

$D_\mathbf{u}f(1, 4) = \nabla f(1, 4)\cdot\mathbf{u} = -\dfrac{4\sqrt{5}}{5} + \dfrac{2\sqrt{5}}{5} = -\dfrac{2\sqrt{5}}{5}$

50. $\qquad w = 6x^2 + 3xy - 4y^2z$

$\nabla w = (12x + 3y)\mathbf{i} + (3x - 8yz)\mathbf{j} + (-4y^2)\mathbf{k}$

$\nabla w(1, 0, 1) = 12\mathbf{i} + 3\mathbf{j}$

$\mathbf{u} = \dfrac{1}{\sqrt{3}}\mathbf{v} = \dfrac{\sqrt{3}}{3}\mathbf{i} + \dfrac{\sqrt{3}}{3}\mathbf{j} - \dfrac{\sqrt{3}}{3}\mathbf{k}$

$D_\mathbf{u}w(1, 0, 1) = \nabla w(1, 0, 1)\cdot\mathbf{u}$

$\qquad\qquad = 4\sqrt{3} + \sqrt{3} + 0 = 5\sqrt{3}$

52. $\qquad z = \dfrac{x^2}{x - y}$

$\nabla z = \dfrac{x^2 - 2xy}{(x - y)^2}\mathbf{i} + \dfrac{x^2}{(x - y)^2}\mathbf{j}$

$\nabla z(2, 1) = 4\mathbf{j}$

$\|\nabla z(2, 1)\| = 4$

54. $\qquad z = x^2y$

$\nabla z = 2xy\mathbf{i} + x^2\mathbf{j}$

$\nabla z(2, 1) = 4\mathbf{i} + 4\mathbf{j}$

$\|\nabla z(2, 1)\| = 4\sqrt{2}$

56. $4y\sin x - y^2 = 3$

$f(x, y) = 4y\sin x - y^2$

$\nabla f(x, y) = 4y\cos x\mathbf{i} + (4\sin x - 2y)\mathbf{j}$

$\nabla f\left(\dfrac{\pi}{2}, 1\right) = 2\mathbf{j}$

Normal vector: $\mathbf{j}$

58. $F(x, y, z) = y^2 + z^2 - 25 = 0$

$\nabla F = 2y\mathbf{j} + 2z\mathbf{k}$

$\nabla F(2, 3, 4) = 6\mathbf{j} + 8\mathbf{k} = 2(3\mathbf{j} + 4\mathbf{k})$

Therefore, the equation of the tangent plane is

$\qquad 3(y - 3) + 4(z - 4) = 0$ or $3y + 4z = 25,$

and the equation of the normal line is

$\qquad x = 2, \dfrac{y - 3}{3} = \dfrac{z - 4}{4}.$

60. $F(x, y, z) = x^2 + y^2 + z^2 - 9 = 0$

$\nabla F = 2x\mathbf{i} + 2y\mathbf{j} + 2z\mathbf{k}$

$\nabla F(1, 2, 2) = 2\mathbf{i} + 4\mathbf{j} + 4\mathbf{k} = 2(\mathbf{i} + 2\mathbf{j} + 2\mathbf{k})$

Therefore, the equation of the tangent plane is

$(x - 1) + 2(y - 2) + 2(z - 2) = 0$ or

$x + 2y + 2z = 9$,

and the equation of the normal line is

$$\frac{x - 1}{1} = \frac{y - 2}{2} = \frac{z - 2}{2}.$$

62. $F(x, y, z) = y^2 + z - 25 = 0$

$G(x, y, z) = x - y = 0$

$\nabla F = 2y\mathbf{i} + \mathbf{k}$

$\nabla G = \mathbf{i} - \mathbf{j}$

$\nabla F(4, 4, 9) = 8\mathbf{i} + \mathbf{k}$

$$\nabla F \times \nabla G = \begin{vmatrix} \mathbf{i} & \mathbf{j} & \mathbf{k} \\ 8 & 0 & 1 \\ 1 & -1 & 0 \end{vmatrix} = \mathbf{i} + \mathbf{j} - 8\mathbf{k}$$

Therefore, the equation of the tangent line is

$$\frac{x - 4}{1} = \frac{y - 4}{1} = \frac{z - 9}{-8}.$$

64. (a) $f(x, y) = \cos x + \sin y,$ $f(0, 0) = 1$

$f_x = -\sin x,$ $f_x(0, 0) = 0$

$f_y = \cos y,$ $f_y(0, 0) = 1$

$P_1(x, y) = 1 + y$

(b) $f_{xx} = -\cos x,$ $f_{xx}(0, 0) = -1$

$f_{yy} = -\sin y,$ $f_{yy}(0, 0) = 0$

$f_{xy} = 0,$ $f_{xy}(0, 0) = 0$

$P_2(x, y) = 1 + y - \frac{1}{2}x^2$

(c) If $y = 0$, you obtain the 2nd degree Taylor polynomial for $\cos x$.

(d)

x	y	$f(x, y)$	$P_1(x, y)$	$P_2(x, y)$
0	0	1.0	1.0	1.0
0	0.1	1.0998	1.1	1.1
0.2	0.1	1.0799	1.1	1.095
0.5	0.3	1.1731	1.3	1.175
1	0.5	1.0197	1.5	1.0

(e)

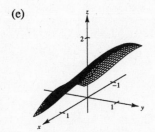 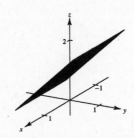 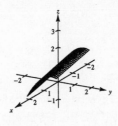

The accuracy lessens as the distance from $(0, 0)$ increases.

66. $f(x, y) = 2x^2 + 6xy + 9y^2 + 8x + 14$

$f_x = 4x + 6y + 8 = 0$

$f_y = 6x + 18y = 0,\ x = -3y$

$4(-3y) + 6y = -8 \implies y = \frac{4}{3},\ x = -4$

$f_{xx} = 4$

$f_{yy} = 18$

$f_{xy} = 6$

$f_{xx}f_{yy} - (f_{xy})^2 = 4(18) - (6)^2 = 36 > 0$ Therefore, $\left(-4, \frac{4}{3}, -2\right)$ is a relative minimum.

68. $z = 50(x + y) - (0.1x^3 + 20x + 150) - (0.05y^3 + 20.6y + 125)$

$z_x = 50 - 0.3x^2 - 20 = 0, \ x = \pm 10$

$z_y = 50 - 0.15y^2 - 20.6 = 0, \ y = \pm 14$

Critical Points: $(10, 14), \ (10, -14), \ (-10, 14), \ (-10, -14)$

$z_{xx} = -0.6x, \ z_{yy} = -0.3y, \ z_{xy} = 0$

At $(10, 14)$, $z_{xx}z_{yy} - (z_{xy})^2 = (-6)(-4.2) - 0^2 > 0$, $z_{xx} < 0$.

$(10, 14, 199.4)$ is a relative maximum.

At $(10, -14)$, $z_{xx}z_{yy} - (z_{xy})^2 = (-6)(4.2) - 0^2 < 0$.

$(10, -14, -349.4)$ is a saddle point.

At $(-10, 14)$, $z_{xx}z_{yy} - (z_{xy})^2 = (6)(-4.2) - 0^2 < 0$.

$(-10, 14, -200.6)$ is a saddle point.

At $(-10, -14)$, $z_{xx}z_{yy} - (x_{xy})^2 = (6)(4.2) - 0^2 > 0$, $z_{xx} < 0$.

$(-10, -14, -749.4)$ is a relative minimum.

70. The level curves indicate that there is a relative extremum at A, the center of the ellipse in the second quadrant, and that there is a saddle point at B, the origin.

72. Minimize $C(x_1, x_2) = 0.25x_1^2 + 10x_1 + 0.15x_2^2 + 12x_2$ subject to the constraint $x_1 + x_2 = 1000$.

$$\left. \begin{array}{l} 0.50x_1 + 10 = \lambda \\ 0.30x_2 + 12 = \lambda \end{array} \right\} 5x_1 - 3x_2 = 20$$

$$
\begin{aligned}
x_1 + x_2 = 1000 \implies 3x_1 + 3x_2 &= 3000 \\
\underline{5x_1 - 3x_2} &= \underline{20} \\
8x_1 &= 3020 \\
x_1 &= 377.5 \\
x_2 &= 622.5
\end{aligned}
$$

$C(377.5, 622.5) = 104{,}997.50$

74. Minimize the square of the distance:

$$f(x, y, z) = (x - 2)^2 + (y - 2)^2 + (x^2 + y^2 - 0)^2.$$

$$\left. \begin{array}{l} f_x = 2(x - 2) + 2(x^2 + y^2)2x = 0 \\ f_y = 2(y - 2) + 2(x^2 + y^2)2y = 0 \end{array} \right\} \begin{array}{l} x - 2 + 2x^3 + 2xy^2 = 0 \\ y - 2 + 2y^3 + 2x^2y = 0 \end{array}$$

Clearly $x = y$ and hence: $4x^3 + x - 2 = 0$. Using a computer algebra system, $x \approx 0.6894$.
Thus, (distance)$^2 = (0.6894 - 2)^2 + (0.6894 - 2)^2 + [2(0.6894)^2]^2 \approx 4.3389$.
distance ≈ 2.08

76. (a) $(25, 28), \ (50, 38), \ (75, 54), \ (100, 75), \ (125, 102)$

$$\sum x_i = 375, \qquad \sum y_i = 297, \qquad \sum x_i^2 = 34{,}375, \qquad \sum x_i^3 = 3{,}515{,}625$$

$$\sum x_i^4 = 382{,}421{,}875, \quad \sum x_i y_i = 26{,}900, \quad \sum x_i^2 y_i = 2{,}760{,}000,$$

$$382{,}421{,}875a + 3{,}515{,}625b + 34{,}375c = 2{,}760{,}000$$

$$3{,}515{,}625a + 34{,}375b + 375c = 26{,}900$$

$$34{,}375a + 375b + 5c = 297$$

$a \approx 0.0045, \ b \approx 0.0717, \ c \approx 23.2914, \ y \approx 0.0045x^2 + 0.0717x + 23.2914$

(b) When $x = 80$ km/hr, $y \approx 57.8$ km.

78. Optimize $f(x, y) = x^2y$ subject to the constraint $x + 2y = 2$.

$$\left.\begin{array}{r} 2xy = \lambda \\ x^2 = 2\lambda \end{array}\right\} x^2 = 4xy \implies x = 0 \text{ or } x = 4y$$

$x + 2y = 2$

If $x = 0$, $y = 1$. If $x = 4y$, then $y = \frac{1}{3}$, $x = \frac{4}{3}$.

Maximum: $f\left(\frac{4}{3}, \frac{1}{3}\right) = \frac{16}{27}$

Minimum: $f(0, 1) = 0$

Problem Solving for Chapter 12

2. $V = \dfrac{4}{3}\pi r^3 + \pi r^2 h$

Material $= M = 4\pi r^2 + 2\pi rh$

$V = 1000 \implies h = \dfrac{1000 - (4/3)\pi r^3}{\pi r^2}$

Hence,

$$M = 4\pi r^2 + 2\pi r\left(\dfrac{1000 - (4/3)\pi r^3}{\pi r^2}\right)$$

$$= 4\pi r^2 + \dfrac{2000}{r} - \dfrac{8}{3}\pi r^2$$

$$\dfrac{dM}{dr} = 8\pi r - \dfrac{2000}{r^2} - \dfrac{16}{3}\pi r = 0$$

$$8\pi r - \dfrac{16}{3}\pi r = \dfrac{2000}{r^2}$$

$$r^3\left(\dfrac{8}{3}\pi\right) = 2000$$

$$r^3 = \dfrac{750}{\pi} \implies r = 5\left(\dfrac{6}{\pi}\right)^{1/3}.$$

Then, $h = \dfrac{1000 - (4/3)\pi(750/\pi)}{\pi r^2} = 0.$

The tank is a sphere of radius $r = 5\left(\dfrac{6}{\pi}\right)^{1/3}$.

4. (a) As $x \to \pm\infty$, $f(x) = (x^3 - 1)^{1/3} \to x$ and hence

$$\lim_{x \to \infty} [f(x) - g(x)] = \lim_{x \to -\infty} [f(x) - g(x)] = 0.$$

(b) Let $(x_0, (x_0^3 - 1)^{1/3})$ be a point on the graph of f.

The line through this point perpendicular to g is

$$y = -x + x_0 + \sqrt[3]{x_0^3 - 1}.$$

This line intersects g at the point

$$\left(\frac{1}{2}\left[x_0 + \sqrt[3]{x_0^3 - 1}\right], \frac{1}{2}\left[x_0 + \sqrt[3]{x_0^3 - 1}\right]\right).$$

The square of the distance between these two points is

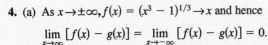

$$h(x_0) = \frac{1}{2}\left(x_0 - \sqrt[3]{x_0^3 - 1}\right)^2.$$

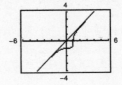

h is a maximum for $x_0 = \dfrac{1}{\sqrt[3]{2}}$. Hence, the point on f farthest from g is $\left(\dfrac{1}{\sqrt[3]{2}}, -\dfrac{1}{\sqrt[3]{2}}\right)$.

6. Heat Loss $= H = k(5xy + xy + 3xz + 3xz + 3yz + 3yz)$

$$= k(6xy + 6xz + 6yz)$$

$V = xyz = 1000 \implies z = \dfrac{1000}{xy}.$

Then $H = 6k\left(xy + \dfrac{1000}{y} + \dfrac{1000}{x}\right).$

Setting $H_x = H_y = 0$, you obtain $x = y = z = 10$.

8. (a) $T(x, y) = 2x^2 + y^2 - y + 10 = 10$

$$2x^2 + y^2 - y + \frac{1}{4} = \frac{1}{4}$$

$$2x^2 + \left(y - \frac{1}{2}\right)^2 = \frac{1}{4}$$

$$\frac{x^2}{1/8} + \frac{(y - (1/2))^2}{1/4} = 1 \quad \text{ellipse}$$

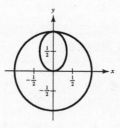

(b) On $x^2 + y^2 = 1$, $T(x, y) = T(y) = 2(1 - y^2) + y^2 - y + 10 = 12 - y^2 - y$

$$T'(y) = -2y - 1 = 0 \implies y = -\frac{1}{2}, x = \pm\frac{\sqrt{3}}{2}.$$

Inside: $T_x = 4x - 0, T_y = 2y - 1 = 0 \implies \left(0, \dfrac{1}{2}\right)$

$T\left(0, \dfrac{1}{2}\right) = \dfrac{39}{4}$ minimum

$T\left(\pm\dfrac{\sqrt{3}}{2}, -\dfrac{1}{2}\right) = \dfrac{49}{4}$ maximum

10. $x = r \cos \theta, y = r \sin \theta, z = z$

$$\frac{\partial u}{\partial \theta} = \frac{\partial u}{\partial x}\frac{\partial x}{\partial \theta} + \frac{\partial u}{\partial y}\frac{\partial y}{\partial \theta} + \frac{\partial u}{\partial z}\frac{\partial z}{\partial \theta}$$

$$= \frac{\partial u}{\partial x}(-r \sin \theta) + \frac{\partial u}{\partial y}r \cos \theta \quad \text{Similarly,}$$

$$\frac{\partial u}{\partial r} = \frac{\partial u}{\partial x}\cos \theta + \frac{\partial u}{\partial y}\sin \theta.$$

$$\frac{\partial^2 u}{\partial \theta^2} = (-r \sin \theta)\left[\frac{\partial^2 u}{\partial x^2}\frac{\partial x}{\partial \theta} + \frac{\partial^2 u}{\partial x \partial y}\frac{\partial y}{\partial \theta} + \frac{\partial^2 u}{\partial x \partial z}\frac{\partial z}{\partial \theta}\right] - r\frac{\partial u}{\partial x}\cos \theta$$

$$+ (r \cos \theta)\left[\frac{\partial^2 u}{\partial y \partial x}\frac{\partial x}{\partial \theta} + \frac{\partial^2 u}{\partial y^2}\frac{\partial y}{\partial \theta} + \frac{\partial^2 u}{\partial y \partial z}\frac{\partial z}{\partial \theta}\right] - r\frac{\partial u}{\partial y}\sin \theta$$

$$= \frac{\partial^2 u}{\partial x^2}r^2 \sin^2 \theta + \frac{\partial^2 u}{\partial y^2}r^2 \cos^2 \theta - 2\frac{\partial^2 u}{\partial x \partial y}r^2 \sin \theta \cos \theta - \frac{\partial u}{\partial x}r \cos \theta - \frac{\partial u}{\partial y}r \sin \theta$$

Similarly, $\dfrac{\partial^2 u}{\partial r^2} = \dfrac{\partial^2 u}{\partial x^2}\cos^2 \theta + \dfrac{\partial^2 u}{\partial y^2}\sin^2 \theta + 2\dfrac{\partial^2 u}{\partial x \partial y}\cos \theta \sin \theta.$

Now observe that

$$\frac{\partial^2 u}{\partial r^2} + \frac{1}{r}\frac{\partial u}{\partial r} + \frac{1}{r^2}\frac{\partial^2 u}{\partial \theta^2} + \frac{\partial^2 u}{\partial z^2} = \left[\frac{\partial^2 u}{\partial x^2}\cos^2 \theta + \frac{\partial^2 u}{\partial y^2}\sin^2 \theta + 2\frac{\partial^2 u}{\partial x \partial y}\cos \theta \sin \theta\right] + \frac{1}{r}\left[\frac{\partial u}{\partial x}\cos \theta + \frac{\partial u}{\partial y}\sin \theta\right]$$

$$+ \left[\frac{\partial^2 u}{\partial x^2}\sin^2 \theta + \frac{\partial^2 u}{\partial y^2}\cos^2 \theta - 2\frac{\partial^2 u}{\partial x \partial y}\sin \theta \cos \theta - \frac{1}{r}\frac{\partial u}{\partial x}\cos \theta - \frac{1}{r}\frac{\partial u}{\partial y}\sin \theta\right] + \frac{\partial^2 u}{\partial z^2}$$

$$= \frac{\partial^2 u}{\partial x^2} + \frac{\partial^2 u}{\partial y^2} + \frac{\partial^2 u}{\partial z^2}.$$

Thus, Laplaces equation in cylindrical coordinates, is $\dfrac{\partial^2 u}{\partial r^2} + \dfrac{1}{r}\dfrac{\partial u}{\partial r} + \dfrac{1}{r^2}\dfrac{\partial^2 u}{\partial \theta^2} + \dfrac{\partial^2 u}{\partial z^2} = 0.$

12. (a) $d = \sqrt{x^2 + y^2} = \sqrt{(32\sqrt{2}t)^2 + (32\sqrt{2}t - 16t^2)^2}$

$= \sqrt{4096t^2 - 1024\sqrt{2}t^3 + 256t^4}$

$= 16t\sqrt{t^2 - 4\sqrt{2}t + 16}$

(b) $\dfrac{dd}{dt} = \dfrac{32(t^2 - 3\sqrt{2}t + 8)}{\sqrt{t^2 - 4\sqrt{2}t + 16}}$

(c) When $t = 2$:

$\dfrac{dd}{dt} = \dfrac{32(12 - 6\sqrt{2})}{\sqrt{20 - 8\sqrt{2}}} \approx 38.16 \text{ ft/sec}$

(d) $\dfrac{d^2d}{dt^2} = \dfrac{32(t^3 - 6\sqrt{2}t^2 + 36t - 32\sqrt{12})}{(t^2 - 4\sqrt{2}t + 16)^{3/2}} = 0$

when $t \approx 1.943$ seconds. No. The projectile is at its maximum height when $t = \sqrt{2}$.

14. Given that f is a differentiable function such that $\nabla f(x_0, y_0) = \mathbf{0}$, then $f_x(x_0, y_0) = 0$ and $f_y(x_0, y_0) = 0$. Therefore, the tangent plane is $-(z - z_0) = 0$ or $z = z_0 = f(x_0, y_0)$ which is horizontal.

16. $(r, \theta) = \left(5, \dfrac{\pi}{18}\right)$

$dr = \pm 0.05, \; d\theta = \pm 0.05$

$x = r \cos \theta = 5 \cos \dfrac{\pi}{18} \approx 4.924$

$y = r \sin \theta = 5 \sin \dfrac{\pi}{18} \approx 0.868$

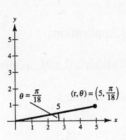

(a) dx should be more effected by changes in r.

$dx = (\cos \theta)dr + (-r \sin \theta)d\theta$

$\approx (0.985)dr - 0.868 \, d\theta$

dx is more effected by changes in r because $0.985 > 0.868$.

(b) dy should be more effected by changes in θ.

$dy = \sin \theta \, dr + r \cos \theta \, d\theta$

$\approx 0.174 \, dr + 4.924 \, d\theta$

dy is more effected by θ because $4.924 > 0.174$.

18. $\dfrac{\partial u}{\partial t} = \dfrac{1}{2}[-\cos(x - t) + \cos(x + t)]$

$\dfrac{\partial^2 u}{\partial t^2} = \dfrac{1}{2}[-\sin(x - t) - \sin(x + t)]$

$\dfrac{\partial u}{\partial x} = \dfrac{1}{2}[\cos(x - t) + \cos(x + t)]$

$\dfrac{\partial^2 u}{\partial x^2} = \dfrac{1}{2}[-\sin(x - t) - \sin(x + t)]$

Then, $\dfrac{\partial^2 u}{\partial t^2} = \dfrac{\partial^2 u}{\partial x^2}$.

C H A P T E R 13
Multiple Integration

CHAPTER 13
Multiple Integration

Section 13.1   Iterated Integrals and Area in the Plane

Solutions to Even-Numbered Exercises

2. $\displaystyle\int_{x}^{x^2} \frac{y}{x}\, dy = \left[\frac{1}{2}\frac{y^2}{x}\right]_{x}^{x^2} = \frac{1}{2}\left(\frac{x^4}{x} - \frac{x^2}{x}\right) = \frac{x}{2}(x^2 - 1)$

4. $\displaystyle\int_{0}^{\cos y} y\, dx = \left[yx\right]_{0}^{\cos y} = y\cos y$

6. $\displaystyle\int_{x^3}^{\sqrt{x}} (x^2 + 3y^2)\, dy = \left[x^2 y + y^3\right]_{x^3}^{\sqrt{x}} = \left(x^2\sqrt{x} + (\sqrt{x})^3\right) - (x^2 x^3 + (x^3)^3) = x^{5/2} + x^{3/2} - x^5 - x^9$

8. $\displaystyle\int_{-\sqrt{1-y^2}}^{\sqrt{1-y^2}} (x^2 + y^2)\, dx = \left[\frac{1}{3}x^3 + y^2 x\right]_{-\sqrt{1-y^2}}^{\sqrt{1-y^2}} = 2\left[\frac{1}{3}(1-y^2)^{3/2} + y^2(1-y^2)^{1/2}\right] = \frac{2\sqrt{1-y^2}}{3}(1 + 2y^2)$

10. $\displaystyle\int_{y}^{\pi/2} \sin^3 x \cos y\, dx = \int_{y}^{\pi/2} (1 - \cos^2 x)\sin x \cos y\, dx$

$$= \left[\left(-\cos x + \frac{1}{3}\cos^3 x\right)\cos y\right]_{y}^{\pi/2} = \left(\cos y - \frac{1}{3}\cos^3 y\right)\cos y$$

12. $\displaystyle\int_{-1}^{1}\int_{-2}^{2} (x^2 - y^2)\, dy\, dx = \int_{-1}^{1}\left[x^2 y - \frac{y^3}{3}\right]_{-2}^{2}\, dx = \int_{-1}^{1}\left[2x^2 - \frac{8}{3} + 2x^2 - \frac{8}{3}\right]\, dx$

$$= \int_{-1}^{1}\left(4x^2 - \frac{16}{3}\right)\, dx = \left[\frac{4x^3}{3} - \frac{16}{3}x\right]_{-1}^{1} = \left(\frac{4}{3} - \frac{16}{3}\right) - \left(-\frac{4}{3} + \frac{16}{3}\right) = -8$$

14. $\displaystyle\int_{-4}^{4}\int_{0}^{x^2} \sqrt{64 - x^3}\, dy\, dx = \int_{-4}^{4}\left[y\sqrt{64 - x^3}\right]_{0}^{x^2}\, dx$

$$= \int_{-4}^{4} \sqrt{64 - x^3}\, x^2\, dx = \left[-\frac{2}{9}(64 - x^3)^{3/2}\right]_{-4}^{4} = 0 + \frac{2}{9}(128)^{3/2} = \frac{2048}{9}\sqrt{2}$$

16. $\displaystyle\int_{0}^{2}\int_{y}^{2y} (10 + 2x^2 + 2y^2)\, dx\, dy = \int_{0}^{2}\left[10x + \frac{2x^3}{3} + 2y^2 x\right]_{y}^{2y}\, dy = \int_{0}^{2}\left[\left(20y + \frac{16}{3}y^3 + 4y^3\right) - \left(10y + \frac{2}{3}y^3 + 2y^3\right)\right]\, dy$

$$= \int_{0}^{2}\left[10y + \frac{14}{3}y^3 + 2y^3\right]\, dy = \left[5y^2 + \frac{7y^4}{6} + \frac{y^4}{2}\right]_{0}^{2} = 20 + \frac{56}{3} + 8 = \frac{140}{3}$$

18. $\displaystyle\int_{0}^{2}\int_{3y^2-6y}^{2y-y^2} 3y\, dx\, dy = \int_{0}^{2}\left[3xy\right]_{3y^2-6y}^{2y-y^2}\, dy = 3\int_{0}^{2}(8y^2 - 4y^3)\, dy = \left[3\left(\frac{8}{3}y^3 - y^4\right)\right]_{0}^{2} = 16$

20. $\displaystyle\int_{0}^{\pi/2}\int_{0}^{2\cos\theta} r\, dr\, d\theta = \int_{0}^{\pi/2}\left[\frac{r^2}{2}\right]_{0}^{2\cos\theta}\, d\theta = \int_{0}^{\pi/2} 2\cos^2\theta\, d\theta = \left[\theta - \frac{1}{2}\sin 2\theta\right]_{0}^{\pi/2} = \frac{\pi}{2}$

22. $\displaystyle\int_{0}^{\pi/4}\int_{0}^{\cos\theta} 3r^2 \sin\theta\, dr\, d\theta = \int_{0}^{\pi/4}\left[r^3 \sin\theta\right]_{0}^{\cos\theta}\, d\theta$

$$= \int_{0}^{\pi/4} \cos^3\theta \sin\theta\, d\theta = \left[-\frac{\cos^4\theta}{4}\right]_{0}^{\pi/4} = -\frac{1}{4}\left[\left(\frac{1}{\sqrt{2}}\right)^4 - 1\right] = \frac{3}{16}$$

24. $\displaystyle\int_0^3 \int_0^\infty \frac{x^2}{1+y^2}\,dy\,dx = \int_0^3 \Big[x^2 \arctan y\Big]_0^\infty\,dx = \int_0^3 x^2\Big(\frac{\pi}{2}\Big)\,dx = \Big[\frac{\pi}{2}\cdot\frac{x^3}{3}\Big]_0^3 = \frac{9\pi}{2}$

26. $\displaystyle\int_0^\infty \int_0^\infty xye^{-(x^2+y^2)}\,dx\,dy = \int_0^\infty \Big[-\frac{1}{2}ye^{-(x^2+y^2)}\Big]_0^\infty\,dy = \int_0^\infty \frac{1}{2}ye^{-y^2}\,dy = \Big[-\frac{1}{4}e^{-y^2}\Big]_0^\infty = \frac{1}{4}$

28. $\displaystyle A = \int_1^3 \int_1^3 dy\,dx = \int_1^3 \Big[y\Big]_1^3\,dx = \int_1^3 2\,dx = \Big[2x\Big]_1^3 = 4$

$\displaystyle A = \int_1^3 \int_1^3 dx\,dy = \int_1^3 \Big[x\Big]_1^3\,dy = \int_1^3 2\,dy = \Big[2y\Big]_1^3 = 4$

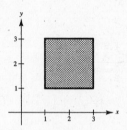

30. $\displaystyle A = \int_2^5 \int_0^{1/\sqrt{x-1}} dy\,dx = \int_2^5 \Big[y\Big]_0^{1/\sqrt{x-1}}\,dx = \int_2^5 \frac{1}{\sqrt{x-1}}\,dx = \Big[2\sqrt{x-1}\Big]_2^5 = 2$

$\displaystyle A = \int_0^{1/2} \int_2^5 dx\,dy + \int_{1/2}^1 \int_2^{1+(1/y^2)} dx\,dy$

$\displaystyle = \int_0^{1/2} \Big[x\Big]_2^5\,dy + \int_{1/2}^1 \Big[x\Big]_2^{1+(1/y^2)}\,dy$

$\displaystyle = \int_0^{1/2} 3\,dy + \int_{1/2}^1 \Big(\frac{1}{y^2}-1\Big)\,dy$

$\displaystyle = \Big[3y\Big]_0^{1/2} + \Big[-\frac{1}{y}-y\Big]_{1/2}^1 = 2$

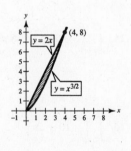

$y = \dfrac{1}{\sqrt{x-1}}$

32. $\displaystyle A = \int_0^2 \int_0^{\sqrt{4-x^2}} dy\,dx$

$\displaystyle = \int_0^2 \sqrt{4-x^2}\,dx$

$\displaystyle = 4\int_0^{\pi/2} \cos^2\theta\,d\theta$

$\displaystyle = 2\int_0^{\pi/2} (1+\cos 2\theta)\,d\theta$

$\displaystyle = \Big[2\Big(\theta+\frac{1}{2}\sin 2\theta\Big)\Big]_0^{\pi/2} = \pi$

$\big(x = 2\sin\theta,\ dx = 2\cos\theta\,d\theta,\ \sqrt{4-x^2} = 2\cos\theta\big)$

$\displaystyle A = \int_0^2 \int_0^{\sqrt{4-y^2}} dx\,dy = \int_0^2 \sqrt{4-y^2}\,dy$

$\displaystyle = 4\int_0^{\pi/2} \cos^2\theta\,d\theta = 2\int_0^{\pi/2} (1+\cos 2\theta)\,d\theta$

$\displaystyle = \Big[2\Big(\theta+\frac{1}{2}\sin 2\theta\Big)\Big]_0^{\pi/2} = \pi$

$\big(y = 2\sin\theta,\ dy = 2\cos\theta\,d\theta,\ \sqrt{4-y^2} = 2\cos\theta\big)$

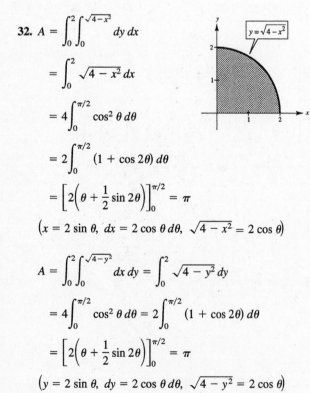

$y = \sqrt{4-x^2}$

34. $\displaystyle A = \int_0^4 \int_{x^{3/2}}^{2x} dy\,dx$

$\displaystyle = \int_0^4 \Big[y\Big]_{x^{3/2}}^{2x}\,dx$

$\displaystyle = \int_0^4 (2x - x^{3/2})\,dx$

$\displaystyle = \Big[x^2 - \frac{2}{5}x^{5/2}\Big]_0^4$

$\displaystyle = 16 - \frac{2}{5}(32) = \frac{16}{5}$

$\displaystyle A = \int_0^8 \int_{y/2}^{y^{2/3}} dx\,dy$

$\displaystyle = \int_0^8 \Big(y^{2/3} - \frac{y}{2}\Big)\,dy$

$\displaystyle = \Big[\frac{3}{5}y^{5/3} - \frac{y^2}{4}\Big]_0^8$

$\displaystyle = \frac{3}{5}(32) - 16 = \frac{16}{5}$

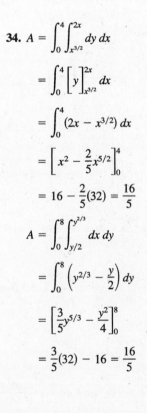

$y = 2x$ (4, 8) $y = x^{3/2}$

36. $A = \int_0^3 \int_0^x dy\, dx + \int_3^9 \int_0^{9/x} dy\, dx$

$= \int_0^3 \left[y \right]_0^x dx + \int_3^9 \left[y \right]_0^{9/x} dx = \int_0^3 x\, dx + \int_3^9 \frac{9}{x}\, dx$

$= \left[\frac{1}{2}x^2 \right]_0^3 + \left[9 \ln x \right]_3^9 = \frac{9}{2} + 9(\ln 9 - \ln 3)$

$= \frac{9}{2}(1 + \ln 9)$

$A = \int_0^1 \int_y^9 dx\, dy + \int_1^3 \int_y^{9/y} dx\, dy$

$= \int_0^1 \left[x \right]_y^9 dy + \int_1^3 \left[x \right]_y^{9/y} dy$

$= \int_0^1 (9 - y)\, dy + \int_1^3 \left(\frac{9}{y} - y \right) dy$

$= \left[9y - \frac{1}{2}y^2 \right]_0^1 + \left[9 \ln y - \frac{1}{2}y^2 \right]_1^3 = \frac{9}{2}(1 + \ln 9)$

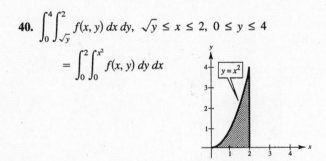

38. $A = \int_0^2 \int_{y/2}^y dx\, dy + \int_2^4 \int_{y/2}^2 dx\, dy$

$= \int_0^2 \frac{y}{2}\, dy + \int_2^4 \left(2 - \frac{y}{2} \right) dy$

$= \left[\frac{y^2}{4} \right]_0^2 + \left[2y - \frac{y^2}{4} \right]_2^4$

$= 1 + (4 - 3) = 2$

$A = \int_0^2 \int_x^{2x} dy\, dx = \int_0^2 (2x - x)\, dx = \left[\frac{x^2}{2} \right]_0^2 = 2$

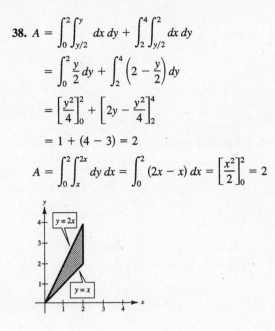

40. $\int_0^4 \int_{\sqrt{y}}^2 f(x, y)\, dx\, dy, \quad \sqrt{y} \le x \le 2, \ 0 \le y \le 4$

$= \int_0^2 \int_0^{x^2} f(x, y)\, dy\, dx$

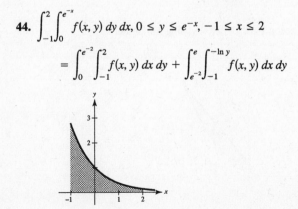

42. $\int_0^2 \int_0^{4-x^2} f(x, y)\, dy\, dx, \ 0 \le y \le 4 - x^2, \ 0 \le x \le 2$

$= \int_0^4 \int_0^{\sqrt{4-y}} f(x, y)\, dx\, dy$

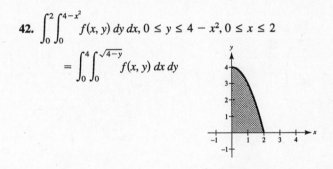

44. $\int_{-1}^2 \int_0^{e^{-x}} f(x, y)\, dy\, dx, \ 0 \le y \le e^{-x}, \ -1 \le x \le 2$

$= \int_0^{e^{-2}} \int_{-1}^2 f(x, y)\, dx\, dy + \int_{e^{-2}}^e \int_{-1}^{-\ln y} f(x, y)\, dx\, dy$

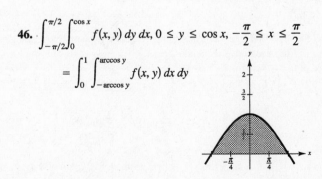

46. $\int_{-\pi/2}^{\pi/2} \int_0^{\cos x} f(x, y)\, dy\, dx, \ 0 \le y \le \cos x, \ -\frac{\pi}{2} \le x \le \frac{\pi}{2}$

$= \int_0^1 \int_{-\arccos y}^{\arccos y} f(x, y)\, dx\, dy$

48. $\int_1^2 \int_2^4 dx\, dy = \int_2^4 \int_1^2 dy\, dx = 2$

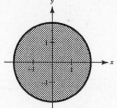

50. $\int_{-2}^2 \int_{-\sqrt{4-x^2}}^{\sqrt{4-x^2}} dy\, dx = \int_{-2}^2 \left(\sqrt{4-x^2} + \sqrt{4-x^2}\right) dx = 4\pi$

$\int_{-2}^2 \int_{-\sqrt{4-y^2}}^{\sqrt{4-y^2}} dx\, dy = 4\pi$

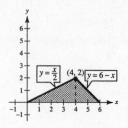

52. $\int_0^4 \int_0^{x/2} dy\, dx + \int_4^6 \int_0^{6-x} dy\, dx = \int_0^4 \frac{x}{2}\, dx + \int_4^6 (6-x)\, dx = 4 + 2 = 6$

$\int_0^2 \int_{2y}^{6-y} dx\, dy = \int_0^2 (6-3y)\, dy = \left[6y - \frac{3y^2}{2}\right]_0^2 = 6$

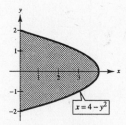

54. $\int_0^9 \int_{\sqrt{x}}^3 dy\, dx = \int_0^9 \left(3 - \sqrt{x}\right) dx = \left[3x - \frac{2}{3}x^{3/2}\right]_0^9 = 27 - 18 = 9$

$\int_0^3 \int_0^{y^2} dx\, dy = \int_0^3 y^2\, dy = \left[\frac{y^3}{3}\right]_0^3 = 9$

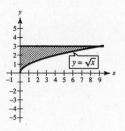

56. $\int_{-2}^2 \int_0^{4-y^2} dx\, dy = \int_0^4 \int_{-\sqrt{4-x}}^{\sqrt{4-x}} dy\, dx = \frac{32}{3}$

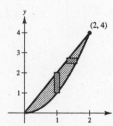

58. The first integral arises using vertical representative rectangles. The second integral arises using horizontal representative rectangles.

$\int_0^2 \int_{x^2}^{2x} x \sin y\, dy\, dx = \int_0^2 \left(-x\cos(2x) + x\cos(x^2)\right) dx$

$\qquad\qquad = -\frac{1}{4}\cos(4) - \frac{1}{2}\sin(4) + \frac{1}{4}$

$\int_0^4 \int_{y/2}^{\sqrt{y}} x \sin y\, dx\, dy = \int_0^4 \left(\frac{1}{2}y\sin(y) - \frac{1}{8}y^2\sin(y)\right) dy$

$\qquad\qquad = -\frac{1}{4}\cos(4) - \frac{1}{2}\sin(4) + \frac{1}{4}$

60. $\int_0^2 \int_x^2 e^{-y^2}\, dy\, dx = \int_0^2 \int_0^y e^{-y^2}\, dx\, dy$

$$= \int_0^2 \left[xe^{-y^2} \right]_0^y dy = \int_0^2 ye^{-y^2}\, dy = \left[-\frac{1}{2}e^{-y^2} \right]_0^2 = -\frac{1}{2}(e^{-4}) + \frac{1}{2}e^0 = \frac{1}{2}\left(1 - \frac{1}{e^4} \right) \approx 0.4908$$

62. $\int_0^2 \int_{y^2}^4 \sqrt{x}\, \sin x\, dx\, dy = \int_0^4 \int_0^{\sqrt{x}} \sqrt{x}\, \sin x\, dy\, dx$

$$= \int_0^4 \left[y\sqrt{x}\, \sin x \right]_0^{\sqrt{x}} dx = \int_0^4 x \sin x\, dx = \left[\sin x - x \cos x \right]_0^4 = \sin 4 - 4 \cos 4 \approx 1.858$$

64. $\int_0^1 \int_y^{2y} \sin (x + y)\, dx\, dy = \frac{\sin 2}{2} - \frac{\sin 3}{3} \approx 0.408$ **66.** $\int_0^a \int_0^{a-x} (x^2 + y^2)\, dy\, dx = \frac{a^4}{6}$

68. (a) $y = \sqrt{4 - x^2} \Leftrightarrow x = \sqrt{4 - y^2}$

$y = 4 - \dfrac{x^2}{4} \Leftrightarrow x = \sqrt{16 - 4y}$

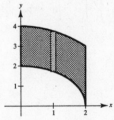

(b) $\int_0^2 \int_{\sqrt{4-y^2}}^2 \dfrac{xy}{x^2 + y^2 + 1}\, dx\, dy + \int_2^3 \int_0^2 \dfrac{xy}{x^2 + y^2 + 1}\, dx\, dy + \int_3^4 \int_0^{\sqrt{16-4y}} \dfrac{xy}{x^2 + y^2 + 1}\, dx\, dy$

(c) Both orders of integration yield 1.11899.

70. $\int_0^2 \int_x^2 \sqrt{16 - x^3 - y^3}\, dy\, dx \approx 6.8520$ **72.** $\int_0^{\pi/2} \int_0^{1+\sin \theta} 15 \theta r\, dr\, d\theta = \frac{45\pi^2}{32} + \frac{135}{8} \approx 30.7541$

74. A region is vertically simple if it is bounded on the left and right by vertical lines, and bounded on the top and bottom by functions of x. A region is horizontally simple if it is bounded on the top and bottom by horizontal lines, and bounded on the left and right by functions of y.

76. The integrations might be easier. See Exercise 59-62.

78. False, let $f(x, y) = x$.

Section 13.2   Double Integrals and Volume

For Exercises 2 and 4, $\Delta x_i = \Delta y_i = 1$ and the midpoints of the squares are

$$\left(\frac{1}{2}, \frac{1}{2} \right), \left(\frac{3}{2}, \frac{1}{2} \right), \left(\frac{5}{2}, \frac{1}{2} \right), \left(\frac{7}{2}, \frac{1}{2} \right), \left(\frac{1}{2}, \frac{3}{2} \right), \left(\frac{3}{2}, \frac{3}{2} \right), \left(\frac{5}{2}, \frac{3}{2} \right), \left(\frac{7}{2}, \frac{3}{2} \right).$$

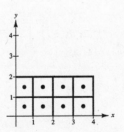

2. $f(x, y) = \frac{1}{2}x^2 y$

$$\sum_{i=1}^\infty f(x_i, y_i)\Delta x_i\, \Delta y_i = \frac{1}{16} + \frac{9}{16} + \frac{25}{16} + \frac{49}{16} + \frac{3}{16} + \frac{27}{16} + \frac{75}{16} + \frac{147}{16} = 21$$

$$\int_0^4 \int_0^2 \frac{1}{2}x^2 y\, dy\, dx = \int_0^4 \left[\frac{x^2 y^2}{4} \right]_0^2 dx = \int_0^4 x^2\, dx = \frac{x^3}{3}\Big]_0^4 = \frac{64}{3} \approx 21.3$$

4. $f(x, y) = \dfrac{1}{(x + 1)(y + 1)}$

$$\sum_{i=1}^{8} f(x_i, y_i) \, \Delta x_i \, \Delta y_i = \frac{4}{9} + \frac{4}{15} + \frac{4}{21} + \frac{4}{27} + \frac{4}{15} + \frac{4}{25} + \frac{4}{35} + \frac{4}{45} = \frac{7936}{4725} \approx 1.680$$

$$\int_0^4 \int_0^2 \frac{1}{(x + 1)(y + 1)} \, dy \, dx = \int_0^4 \left[\frac{1}{x + 1} \ln(y + 1) \right]_0^2 dx$$

$$= \int_0^4 \frac{\ln 3}{x + 1} \, dx = \left[\ln 3 \cdot \ln(x + 1) \right]_0^4 = (\ln 3)(\ln 5) \approx 1.768$$

6. $\displaystyle\int_0^2 \int_0^2 f(x, y) \, dy \, dx \approx 4 + 2 + 8 + 6 = 20$

8. $\displaystyle\int_0^\pi \int_0^{\pi/2} \sin^2 x \cos^2 y \, dy \, dx = \int_0^\pi \left[\frac{1}{2} \sin^2 x \left(y + \frac{1}{2} \sin 2y \right) \right]_0^{\pi/2} dx$

$$= \int_0^\pi \frac{1}{2} \sin^2 x \left(\frac{\pi}{2} \right) dx$$

$$= \frac{\pi}{8} \int_0^\pi (1 - \cos 2x) \, dx$$

$$= \left[\frac{\pi}{8} \left(x - \frac{1}{2} \sin 2x \right) \right]_0^\pi$$

$$= \frac{\pi^2}{8}$$

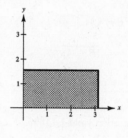

10. $\displaystyle\int_0^4 \int_{(1/2)y}^{\sqrt{y}} x^2 y^2 \, dx \, dy = \int_0^4 \left[\frac{x^3 y^2}{3} \right]_{(1/2)y}^{\sqrt{y}} dy$

$$= \int_0^4 \left(\frac{y^{7/2}}{3} - \frac{y^5}{24} \right) dy$$

$$= \left[\frac{2y^{9/2}}{27} - \frac{y^6}{144} \right]_0^4$$

$$= \frac{1024}{27} - \frac{256}{9} = \frac{256}{27}$$

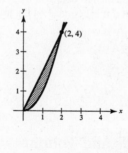

12. $\displaystyle\int_0^1 \int_{y-1}^0 e^{x+y} \, dx \, dy + \int_0^1 \int_0^{1-y} e^{x+y} \, dx \, dy = \int_0^1 \left[e^{x+y} \right]_{y-1}^0 dy + \int_0^1 \left[e^{x+y} \right]_0^{1-y} dy$

$$= \int_0^1 (e - e^{2y-1}) \, dy$$

$$= \left[ey - \frac{1}{2} e^{2y-1} \right]_0^1$$

$$= \frac{1}{2}(e + e^{-1})$$

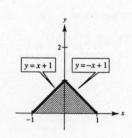

14. $\displaystyle\int_0^{\pi/2}\int_{-\pi}^{\pi} \sin x \sin y \, dx \, dy = \int_{-\pi}^{\pi}\int_0^{\pi/2} \sin x \sin y \, dy \, dx$

$$= \int_{-\pi}^{\pi}\Big[-\sin x \cos y\Big]_0^{\pi/2} dx$$

$$= \int_{-\pi}^{\pi} \sin x \, dx$$

$$= 0$$

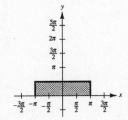

16. $\displaystyle\int_0^4\int_0^{4-x} xe^y \, dy \, dx = \int_0^4\int_0^{4-y} xe^y \, dx \, dy$

For the first integral, we obtain:

$$\int_0^4\Big[xe^y\Big]_0^{4-x} dx = \int_0^{4-x}(xe^4 - x)dx$$

$$= \Big[-e^{4-x}(1 + x) - \frac{x^2}{2}\Big]_0^4$$

$$= (-5 - 8) + e^4 = e^4 - 13.$$

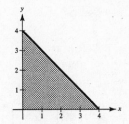

18. $\displaystyle\int_0^2\int_{y^2}^4 \frac{y}{1 + x^2} \, dx \, dy = \int_0^4\int_0^{\sqrt{x}} \frac{y}{1 + x^2} \, dy \, dx$

$$= \frac{1}{2}\int_0^4\Big[\frac{y^2}{1 + x^2}\Big]_0^{\sqrt{x}} dx$$

$$= \frac{1}{2}\int_0^4 \frac{x}{1 + x^2} \, dx$$

$$= \Big[\frac{1}{4}\ln(1 + x^2)\Big]_0^4 = \frac{1}{4}\ln(17)$$

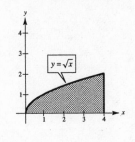

$y = \sqrt{x}$

20. $\displaystyle\int_0^2\int_{\sqrt{4-y^2}}^{\sqrt{4-y^2}} (x^2 + y^2) \, dx \, dy$

$$= \int_{-2}^2\int_0^{\sqrt{4-x^2}} (x^2 + y^2) \, dy \, dx$$

$$= \int_{-2}^2\Big[x^2 y + \frac{1}{3}y^3\Big]_0^{\sqrt{4-x^2}} dx$$

$$= \int_{-2}^2\Big[x^2\sqrt{4 - x^2} + \frac{1}{3}(4 - x^2)^{3/2}\Big] dx$$

$$= \Big[-\frac{x}{4}(4 - x^2)^{3/2} + \frac{1}{2}\Big(x\sqrt{4 - x^2} + 4 \arcsin\frac{x}{2}\Big) + \frac{1}{12}\Big[x(4 - x^2)^{3/2} + 6x\sqrt{4 - x^2} + 24 \arctan\frac{x}{2}\Big]\Big]_{-2}^2 = 4\pi$$

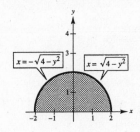

$x = -\sqrt{4-y^2}$ $\quad$ $x = \sqrt{4-y^2}$

22. $\displaystyle\int_0^4\int_0^2 (6 - 2y) \, dy \, dx = \int_0^4\Big[6y - y^2\Big]_0^2 dx$

$$= \int_0^4 8 \, dx = 32$$

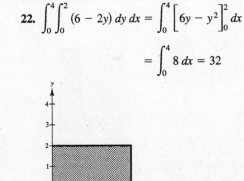

24. $\displaystyle\int_0^2\int_0^x 4 \, dy \, dx = \int_0^2 4x \, dx = 2x^2\Big]_0^2 = 8$

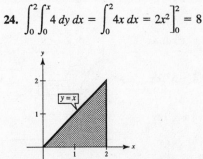

$y = x$

26. $\int_0^2 \int_0^{2-x} (2 - x - y)\, dy\, dx = \int_0^2 \left[2y - xy - \frac{y^2}{2} \right]_0^{2-x} dx$

$= \int_0^2 \frac{1}{2}(2 - x)^2\, dx$

$= -\frac{1}{6}(x - 2)^3 \Big]_0^2 = \frac{4}{3}$

28. $\int_0^2 \int_0^y (4 - y^2)\, dx\, dy = \int_0^2 (4y - y^3)\, dy$

$= \left[2y^2 - \frac{y^4}{4} \right]_0^2$

$= 4$

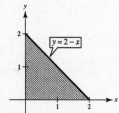

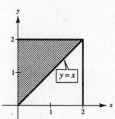

30. $\int_0^\infty \int_0^\infty e^{-(x+y)/2}\, dy\, dx = \int_0^\infty \left[-2e^{-(x+y)/2} \right]_0^\infty dx = \int_0^\infty 2e^{-x/2}\, dx = \left[-4e^{-x/2} \right]_0^\infty = 4$

32. $\int_0^1 \int_0^x \sqrt{1 - x^2}\, dy\, dx = \frac{1}{3}$

34. $V = \int_0^5 \int_0^x x\, dy\, dx$

$= \int_0^5 \left[xy \right]_0^x dx = \int_0^5 x^2\, dx$

$= \left[\frac{1}{3}x^3 \right]_0^5 = \frac{125}{3}$

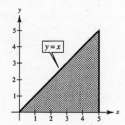

36. $V = 8 \int_0^r \int_0^{\sqrt{r^2 - x^2}} \sqrt{r^2 - x^2 - y^2}\, dy\, dx$

$= 4 \int_0^r \left[\left[y\sqrt{r^2 - x^2 - y^2} + (r^2 - x^2)\arcsin \frac{y}{\sqrt{r^2 - x^2}} \right] \right]_0^{\sqrt{r^2 - x^2}} dx$

$= 4 \left(\frac{\pi}{2} \right) \int_0^r (r^2 - x^2)\, dx$

$= \left[2\pi \left(r^2 x - \frac{1}{3}x^3 \right) \right]_0^r$

$= \frac{4\pi r^3}{3}$

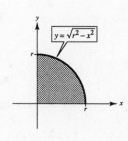

38. $V = \int_0^2 \int_0^{4-x^2} (4 - x^2)\, dy\, dx$

$= \int_0^2 (4 - x^2)(4 - x^2)\, dx$

$= \int_0^2 (16 - 8x^2 + x^4)\, dx$

$= \left[16x - 8\frac{x^3}{3} + \frac{x^5}{5} \right]_0^2$

$= 32 - \frac{64}{3} + \frac{32}{5} = \frac{256}{15}$

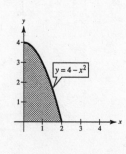

40. $V = \int_0^2 \int_0^\infty \frac{1}{1 + y^2}\, dy\, dx$

$= \int_0^2 \left[\arctan y \right]_0^\infty dx$

$= \int_0^2 \frac{\pi}{2}\, dx$

$= \left[\frac{\pi x}{2} \right]_0^2 = \pi$

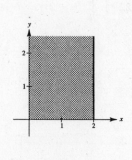

42. $V = \int_0^5 \int_0^\pi \sin^2 x \, dx \, dy$

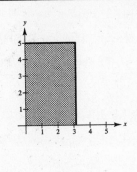

$= \int_0^5 \frac{\pi}{2} \, dy$

$= \left[\frac{\pi}{2} y \right]_0^5$

$= \frac{5\pi}{2}$

44. $V = \int_0^9 \int_0^{\sqrt{9-y}} \sqrt{9-y} \, dx \, dy = \frac{81}{2}$

46. $V = \int_0^{16} \int_0^{4-\sqrt{y}} \ln(1 + x + y) \, dx \, dy \approx 38.25$

48. $\frac{x}{a} + \frac{y}{b} + \frac{z}{c} = 1$

$z = c\left(1 - \frac{x}{a} - \frac{y}{b}\right)$

$V = \iint_R f(x, y) \, dA = \int_0^a \int_0^{b[1-(x/a)]} c\left(1 - \frac{x}{a} - \frac{y}{b}\right) dy \, dx$

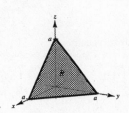

$= c \int_0^a \left[y - \frac{xy}{a} - \frac{y^2}{2b} \right]_0^{b[1-(x/a)]} dx$

$= c \int_0^a \left[b\left(1 - \frac{x}{a}\right) - \frac{xb}{a}\left(1 - \frac{x}{a}\right) - \frac{b^2}{2b}\left(1 - \frac{x}{a}\right)^2 \right] dx$

$= c \left[-\frac{ab}{2}\left(1 - \frac{x}{a}\right)^2 - \frac{x^2 b}{2a} + \frac{x^3 b}{3a^2} + \frac{ab}{6}\left(1 - \frac{x}{a}\right)^3 \right]_0^a$

$= c \left[\left(-\frac{ab}{2} + \frac{ab}{3}\right) - \left(-\frac{ab}{2} + \frac{ab}{6}\right) \right] = \frac{abc}{6}$

50. $\int_0^{\ln 10} \int_{e^x}^{10} \frac{1}{\ln y} \, dy \, dx = \int_1^{10} \int_0^{\ln y} \frac{1}{\ln y} \, dx \, dy$

$= \int_1^{10} \left[\frac{x}{\ln y} \right]_0^{\ln y} dy$

$= \int_1^{10} dy = \left[y \right]_1^{10} = 9$

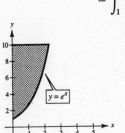

52. $\int_0^2 \int_{(1/2)x^2}^2 \sqrt{y} \cos y \, dy \, dx = \int_0^2 \int_0^{\sqrt{2y}} \sqrt{y} \cos y \, dx \, dy$

$= \int_0^2 \sqrt{y} \cos y \sqrt{2y} \, dy$

$= \sqrt{2} \int_0^2 y \cos y \, dy$

$= \sqrt{2} \left[\cos y + y \sin y \right]_0^2$

$= \sqrt{2} [\cos 2 + 2 \sin 2 - 1]$

54. Average $= \frac{1}{8} \int_0^4 \int_0^2 xy \, dy \, dx = \frac{1}{8} \int_0^4 2x \, dx = \left[\frac{x^2}{8} \right]_0^4 = 2$

56. Average $= \frac{1}{1/2} \int_0^1 \int_x^1 e^{x+y} \, dy \, dx = 2 \int_0^1 e^{x+1} - e^{2x} \, dx$

$= 2 \left[e^{x+1} - \frac{1}{2} e^{2x} \right]_0^1 = 2 \left[e^2 - \frac{1}{2} e^2 - e + \frac{1}{2} \right]$

$= e^2 - 2e + 1$

$= (e - 1)^2$

58. The second is integrable. The first contains $\int \sin y^2 \, dy$ which does not have an elementary antiderivation.

60. (a) The total snowfall in the county R.

(b) The average snowfall in R.

62. Average $= \dfrac{1}{150} \displaystyle\int_{45}^{60} \int_{40}^{50} [192x + 576y - x^2 - 5y^2 - 2xy - 5000] \, dx \, dy \approx 13{,}246.67$

64. $f(x, y) \geq 0$ for all (x, y) and

$$\int_{-\infty}^{\infty} \int_{-\infty}^{\infty} f(x, y) \, dA = \int_0^2 \int_0^2 \frac{1}{4} xy \, dy \, dx = \int_0^2 \frac{x}{2} \, dx = 1$$

$$P(0 \leq x \leq 1, 1 \leq y \leq 2) = \int_0^1 \int_1^2 \frac{1}{4} xy \, dy \, dx = \int_0^1 \frac{3x}{8} \, dx = \frac{3}{16}.$$

66. $f(x, y) \geq 0$ for all (x, y) and

$$\int_{-\infty}^{\infty} \int_{-\infty}^{\infty} f(x, y) \, dA = \int_0^{\infty} \int_0^{\infty} e^{-x-y} \, dy \, dx$$

$$= \int_0^{\infty} \lim_{b \to \infty} \left[-e^{-x-y} \right]_0^b \, dx = \int_0^{\infty} e^{-x} \, dx = \lim_{b \to \infty} \left[-e^{-x} \right]_0^b = 1$$

$$P(0 \leq x \leq 1, x \leq y \leq 1) = \int_0^1 \int_x^1 e^{-x-y} \, dy \, dx = \int_0^1 \left[e^{-x-y} \right]_x^1 \, dx = \int_0^1 (e^{-2x} - e^{-x-1}) \, dx$$

$$= \left[-\frac{1}{2} e^{-2x} + e^{-x-1} \right]_0^1 = \frac{1}{2} e^{-2} - e^{-1} + \frac{1}{2} = \frac{1}{2}(e^{-1} - 1)^2 \approx 0.1998.$$

68. Sample Program for TI-82:

Program: DOUBLE

```
: Input A
: Input B
: Input M
: Input C
: Input D
: Input N
: 0 → V
: (B − A)/M → G
: (D − C)/N → H
: For (I, 1, M, 1)
: For (J, 1, N, 1)
: A + 0.5G(2I − 1) → x
: C + 0.5H(2J − 1) → y
: V + sin (√x + y) × G × H → V
: End
: End
: Disp V
```

70. $\displaystyle\int_0^2 \int_0^4 20e^{-x^3/8} \, dy \, dx$ $m = 10, n = 20$

(a) 129.2018

(b) 129.2756

72. $\int_1^4 \int_1^2 \sqrt{x^3 + y^3}\, dx\, dy \quad m = 6, n = 4$

    (a) 13.956

    (b) 13.9022

74. $V \approx 50$

    Matches a.

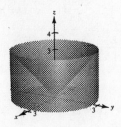

76. True

78. $\int_1^2 e^{-xy}\, dy = \left[-\frac{1}{x} e^{-xy} \right]_1^2 = \frac{e^{-x} - e^{-2x}}{x}$

Thus,

$$\int_0^\infty \frac{e^{-x} - e^{-2x}}{x}\, dx = \int_0^\infty \int_1^2 e^{-xy}\, dx\, dy$$

$$= \int_1^2 \int_0^\infty e^{-xy}\, dx\, dy$$

$$= \int_1^2 \left[-\frac{e^{-xy}}{y} \right]_0^\infty dy$$

$$= \int_1^2 \frac{1}{y}\, dy = \left[\ln y \right]_1^2 = \ln 2.$$

Section 13.3   Change of Variables: Polar Coordinates

2. Polar coordinates

4. Rectangular coordinates

6. $R = \{(r, \theta):\ 0 \le r \le 4 \sin \theta, 0 \le \theta \le \pi\}$

8. $R = \{(r, \theta):\ 0 \le r \le r \cos 3\theta, 0 \le \theta \le \pi\}$

10. $\int_0^{\pi/4} \int_0^4 r^2 \sin \theta \cos \theta\, dr\, d\theta = \int_0^{\pi/4} \left[\frac{r^3}{3} \sin \theta \cos \theta \right]_0^4 d\theta$

$$= \left[\left(\frac{64}{3} \right) \frac{\sin^2 \theta}{2} \right]_0^{\pi/4}$$

$$= \frac{16}{3}$$

12. $\int_0^{\pi/2} \int_0^3 r e^{-r^2}\, dr\, d\theta = \int_0^{\pi/2} \left[-\frac{1}{2} e^{-r^2} \right]_0^3 d\theta$

$$= \left[-\frac{1}{2}(e^{-9} - 1)\theta \right]_0^{\pi/2}$$

$$= \frac{\pi}{4}\left(1 - \frac{1}{e^9} \right)$$

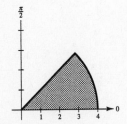

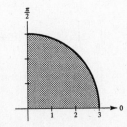

14. $\displaystyle\int_0^{\pi/2}\int_0^{1-\cos\theta}(\sin\theta)r\,dr\,d\theta = \int_0^{\pi/2}\left[(\sin\theta)\frac{r^2}{2}\right]_0^{1-\cos\theta}d\theta$

$$= \int_0^{\pi/2}\frac{\sin\theta}{2}(1-\cos\theta)^2\,d\theta$$

$$= \left[\frac{1}{6}(1-\cos(\theta))^3\right]_0^{\pi/2} = \frac{1}{6}$$

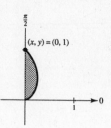

16. $\displaystyle\int_0^a\int_0^{\sqrt{a^2-x^2}}x\,dy\,dx = \int_0^{\pi/2}\int_0^a r^2\cos\theta\,dr\,d\theta = \frac{a^3}{3}\int_0^{\pi/2}\cos\theta\,d\theta = \left[\frac{a^3}{3}\sin\theta\right]_0^{\pi/2} = \frac{a^3}{3}$

18. $\displaystyle\int_0^2\int_y^{\sqrt{8-y^2}}\sqrt{x^2+y^2}\,dx\,dy = \int_0^{\pi/4}\int_0^{2\sqrt{2}}r^2\,dr\,d\theta$

$$= \int_0^{\pi/4}\frac{\left(2\sqrt{2}\right)^3}{3}\,d\theta = \left[\frac{\left(2\sqrt{2}\right)^3}{3}\theta\right]_0^{\pi/4} = \frac{\left(2\sqrt{2}\right)^3}{3}\cdot\frac{\pi}{4} = \frac{4\sqrt{2}\pi}{3}$$

20. $\displaystyle\int_0^4\int_0^{\sqrt{4y-y^2}}x^2\,dx\,dy = \int_0^{\pi/2}\int_0^{4\sin\theta}r^3\cos^2\theta\,dr\,d\theta = \int_0^{\pi/2}64\sin^4\theta\cos^2\theta\,d\theta$

$$= 64\int_0^{\pi/2}(\sin^4\theta - \sin^6\theta)\,d\theta = \frac{64}{6}\left[\sin^5\theta\cos\theta - \frac{\sin^3\theta\cos\theta}{4} + \frac{3}{8}(\theta-\sin\theta\cos\theta)\right]_0^{\pi/2} = 2\pi$$

22. $\displaystyle\int_0^{(5\sqrt{2})/2}\int_0^x xy\,dy\,dx + \int_{(5\sqrt{2})/2}^5\int_0^{\sqrt{25-x^2}}xy\,dy\,dx = \int_0^{\pi/4}\int_0^5 r^3\sin\theta\cos\theta\,dr\,d\theta$

$$= \int_0^{\pi/4}\frac{625}{4}\sin\theta\cos\theta\,d\theta$$

$$= \left[\frac{625}{8}\sin^2\theta\right]_0^{\pi/4}$$

$$= \frac{625}{16}$$

24. $\displaystyle\int_{-\pi/2}^{\pi/2}\int_0^5 e^{-r^2/2}r\,dr\,d\theta = \int_{-\pi/2}^{\pi/2}\left[-e^{-r^2/2}\right]_0^5 d\theta$

$$= \int_{-\pi/2}^{\pi/2}(1-e^{-25/2})\,d\theta$$

$$= \left[(1-e^{-25/2})\theta\right]_{-\pi/2}^{\pi/2} = \pi(1-e^{-25/2})$$

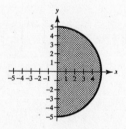

26. $\displaystyle\int_0^3\int_0^{\sqrt{9-x^2}}(9-x^2-y^2)\,dy\,dx = \int_0^{\pi/2}\int_0^3(9-r^2)r\,dr\,d\theta$

$$= \int_0^{\pi/2}\int_0^3(9r-r^3)\,dr\,d\theta = \int_0^{\pi/2}\left[\frac{9}{2}r^2-\frac{1}{4}r^4\right]_0^3 d\theta = \frac{81}{4}\int_0^{\pi/2}d\theta = \frac{81\pi}{8}$$

28. $V = 4\int_0^{\pi/2}\int_0^1 (r^2+3)r\,dr\,d\theta = 4\int_0^{\pi/2}\left(\frac{r^4}{4}+\frac{3r^2}{2}\right)_0^1 d\theta$

$$= 4\int_0^{\pi/4}\frac{7}{4}\,d\theta$$

$$= 7\left(\frac{\pi}{4}\right) = \frac{7\pi}{4}$$

30. $\int_R\int \ln(x^2+y^2)\,dA = \int_0^{2\pi}\int_1^2 (\ln r^2)r\,dr\,d\theta$

$$= 2\int_0^{2\pi}\int_1^2 r\ln r\,dr\,d\theta$$

$$= 2\int_0^{2\pi}\left[\frac{r^2}{4}(-1+2\ln r)\right]_1^2 d\theta$$

$$= 2\int_0^{2\pi}\left(\ln 4 - \frac{3}{4}\right)d\theta$$

$$= 4\pi\left(\ln 4 - \frac{3}{4}\right)$$

32. $V = \int_0^{2\pi}\int_1^4 \sqrt{16-r^2}\,r\,dr\,d\theta = \int_0^{2\pi}\left[-\frac{1}{3}\left(\sqrt{16-r^2}\right)^3\right]_1^4 d\theta = \int_0^{2\pi} 5\sqrt{15}\,d\theta = 10\sqrt{15}\,\pi$

34. $x^2+y^2+z^2 = a^2 \Rightarrow z = \sqrt{a^2-(x^2+y^2)} = \sqrt{a^2-r^2}$

$$V = 8\int_0^{\pi/2}\int_0^a \sqrt{a^2-r^2}\,r\,dr\,d\theta \qquad \text{(8 times the volume in the first octant)}$$

$$= 8\int_0^{\pi/2}\left[-\frac{1}{2}\cdot\frac{2}{3}(a^2-r^2)^{3/2}\right]_0^a d\theta$$

$$= 8\int_0^{\pi/2}\frac{a^3}{3}\,d\theta = \left[\frac{8a^3}{3}\theta\right]_0^{\pi/2} = \frac{4\pi a^3}{3}$$

36. $\dfrac{-9}{4(x^2+y^2+9)} \le z \le \dfrac{9}{4(x^2+y^2+9)}$; $\quad \dfrac{1}{4} \le r \le \dfrac{1}{2}(1+\cos^2\theta)$

(a) $\dfrac{-9}{4r^2+36} \le z \le \dfrac{9}{4r^2+36}$

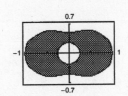

(b) Perimeter $= \displaystyle\int_\alpha^\beta \sqrt{r^2+\left(\frac{dr}{d\theta}\right)^2}\,d\theta$.

$r = \dfrac{1}{2}(1+\cos^2\theta) = \dfrac{1}{2}+\dfrac{1}{2}\cos^2\theta$

$\dfrac{dr}{d\theta} = -\cos\theta\sin\theta$

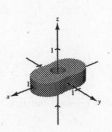

Perimeter $= 2\displaystyle\int_0^\pi \sqrt{\frac{1}{4}(1+\cos^2\theta)^2 + \cos^2\theta\sin^2\theta}\,d\theta \approx 5.21$

(c) $V = 2\displaystyle\int_0^{2\pi}\int_{1/4}^{1/2(1+\cos^2\theta)} \frac{9}{4r^2+36}\,r\,dr\,d\theta \approx 0.8000$

38. $A = \displaystyle\int_0^{2\pi}\int_2^4 r\,dr\,d\theta = \int_0^{2\pi} 6\,d\theta = 12\pi$

40. $\displaystyle\int_0^{2\pi}\int_0^{2+\sin\theta} r\,dr\,d\theta = \frac{1}{2}\int_0^{2\pi}(2+\sin\theta)^2\,d\theta = \frac{1}{2}\int_0^{2\pi}(4+4\sin\theta+\sin^2\theta)\,d\theta = \frac{1}{2}\int_0^{2\pi}\left(4+4\sin\theta+\frac{1-\cos 2\theta}{2}\right)d\theta$

$$= \frac{1}{2}\left[4\theta - 4\cos\theta + \frac{1}{2}\theta - \frac{1}{4}\sin 2\theta\right]_0^{2\pi} = \frac{1}{2}[8\pi - 4 + \pi + 4] = \frac{9\pi}{2}$$

42. $8\int_0^{\pi/4}\int_0^{3\cos 2\theta} r\,dr\,d\theta = 4\int_0^{\pi/4} 9\cos^2 2\theta\,d\theta = 18\int_0^{\pi/4}(1+\cos 4\theta)\,d\theta = 18\left[\theta + \frac{1}{4}\sin 4\theta\right]_0^{\pi/4} = \frac{9\pi}{2}$

44. See Theorem 13.3.

46. (a) Horizontal or polar representative elements

(b) Polar representative element

(c) Vertical or polar

48. (a) The volume of the subregion determined by the point $(5, \pi/16, 7)$ is base × height $= (5 \cdot 10 \cdot \pi/8)(7)$. Adding up the 20 volumes, ending with $(45 \cdot 10 \cdot \pi/8)(12)$, you obtain

$$V \approx 10 \cdot \frac{\pi}{8}[5(7 + 9 + 9 + 5) + 15(8 + 10 + 11 + 8) + 25(10 + 14 + 15 + 11)$$
$$+ 35(12 + 15 + 18 + 16) + 45(9 + 10 + 14 + 12)]$$
$$= \frac{5\pi}{4}[150 + 555 + 1250 + 2135 + 2025] \approx \frac{5\pi}{4}[6115] \approx 24013.5 \text{ ft}^3$$

(b) $(56)(24013.5) = 1{,}344{,}759$ pounds

(c) $(7.48)(24103.5) \approx 179{,}621$ gallons

50. $\int_0^{\pi/4}\int_0^4 5e^{\sqrt{r\theta}}\,r\,dr\,d\theta \approx 87.130$

52. Volume = base × height

$\approx \frac{9}{4}\pi \times 3 \approx 21$

Answer (a)

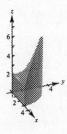

54. True

56. (a) Let $u = \sqrt{2}x$, then $\int_{-\infty}^{\infty} e^{-x^2}\,dx = \int_{-\infty}^{\infty} e^{-u^2/2}\frac{1}{\sqrt{2}}\,du = \frac{1}{\sqrt{2}}\left(\sqrt{2\pi}\right) = \sqrt{\pi}$.

(b) Let $u = 2x$, then $\int_{-\infty}^{\infty} e^{-4x^2}\,dx = \int_{-\infty}^{\infty} e^{-u^2}\frac{1}{2}\,du = \frac{1}{2}\sqrt{\pi}$.

58. $\int_0^{\infty}\int_0^{\infty} ke^{-(x^2+y^2)}\,dy\,dx = \int_0^{\pi/2}\int_0^{\infty} ke^{-r^2}r\,dr\,d\theta = \int_0^{\pi/2}\left[-\frac{k}{2}e^{-r^2}\right]_0^{\infty}\,d\theta = \int_0^{\pi/2}\frac{k}{2}\,d\theta = \frac{k\pi}{4}$

For $f(x, y)$ to be a probability density function,

$\frac{k\pi}{4} = 1$

$k = \frac{4}{\pi}$.

60. (a) $4\int_0^2\int_2^{2+\sqrt{4-y^2}} f\,dx\,dy$

(b) $4\int_0^2\int_0^{\sqrt{4-(x-2)^2}} f\,dy\,dx$

(c) $2\int_0^{\pi/2}\int_0^{4\cos\theta} fr\,dr\,d\theta$

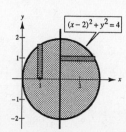

Section 13.4   Center of Mass and Moments of Inertia

2. $m = \int_0^3 \int_0^{9-x^2} xy \, dy \, dx = \int_0^3 \left[\frac{xy^2}{2} \right]_0^{9-x^2} dx$

$$= \int_0^3 \frac{x(9-x^2)^2}{2} \, dx$$

$$= \left[-\frac{1}{4} \frac{(9-x^2)^3}{3} \right]_0^3$$

$$= -\frac{1}{12}(0 - 9^3) = \frac{243}{4}$$

4. $m = \int_0^3 \int_3^{3+\sqrt{9-x^2}} xy \, dy \, dx = \int_0^3 \left[x \frac{y^2}{2} \right]_3^{3+\sqrt{9-x^2}} dx$

$$= \int_0^3 \frac{x}{2} \left(\left(3 + \sqrt{9-x^2}\right) - 9 \right) dx$$

$$= \frac{1}{2} \int_0^3 \left[6x\sqrt{9-x^2} + 9x - x^3 \right] dx$$

$$= \frac{1}{2} \left[-2(9-x^2)^{3/2} + \frac{9x^2}{2} - \frac{x^4}{4} \right]_0^3$$

$$= \frac{1}{2} \left[\frac{81}{2} - \frac{81}{4} + 54 \right] = \frac{297}{8}$$

6. (a) $m = \int_0^a \int_0^b kxy \, dy \, dx = \frac{ka^2b^2}{4}$

$M_x = \int_0^a \int_0^b kxy^2 \, dy \, dx = \frac{ka^2b^3}{6}$

$M_y = \int_0^a \int_0^b kx^2y \, dy \, dx = \frac{ka^3b^2}{6}$

$\bar{x} = \frac{M_y}{m} = \frac{ka^3b^2/6}{ka^2b^2/4} = \frac{2}{3}a$

$\bar{y} = \frac{M_x}{m} = \frac{ka^2b^3/6}{ka^2b^2/4} = \frac{2}{3}b$

(b) $m = \int_0^a \int_0^b k(x^2 + y^2) \, dy \, dx = \frac{kab}{3}(a^2 + b^2)$

$M_x = \int_0^a \int_0^b k(x^2y + y^3) \, dy \, dx = \frac{kab^2}{12}(2a^2 + 3b^2)$

$M_y = \int_0^a \int_0^b k(x^3 + xy^2) \, dy \, dx = \frac{ka^2b}{12}(3a^2 + 2b^2)$

$\bar{x} = \frac{M_y}{m} = \frac{(ka^2b/12)(3a^2 + 2b^2)}{(kab/3)(a^2 + b^2)} = \frac{a}{4}\left(\frac{3a^2 + 2b^2}{a^2 + b^2}\right)$

$\bar{y} = \frac{M_x}{m} = \frac{(kab^2/12)(2a^2 + 3b^2)}{(kab/3)(a^2 + b^2)} = \frac{b}{4}\left(\frac{2a^2 + 3b^2}{a^2 + b^2}\right)$

8. (a) $m = \frac{a^2k}{2}$

$M_x = \int_0^a \int_0^{a-x} ky \, dy \, dx = \frac{ka^3}{6}$

$M_y = M_x$ by symmetry

$\bar{x} = \bar{y} = \frac{M_x}{m} = \frac{ka^3/6}{ka^2/2} = \frac{a}{3}$

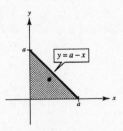

—CONTINUED—

8. —CONTINUED—

(b) $m = \int_0^a \int_0^{a-x} (x^2 + y^2) \, dy \, dx$

$\quad = \int_0^a \left[x^2 y + \dfrac{y^3}{3} \right]_0^{a-x} dx = \int_0^a \left[ax^2 - x^3 + \dfrac{1}{3}(a - x)^3 \right] dx = \dfrac{a^4}{6}$

$M_y = \int_0^a \int_0^{a-x} (x^3 + xy^2) \, dy \, dx$

$\quad = \int_0^a \left(ax^3 - x^4 + \dfrac{1}{3}a^3 x - a^2 x^2 + ax^3 - \dfrac{1}{3}x^4 \right) dx = \dfrac{1}{3} \int_0^a (a^3 x - 3a^2 x^2 + 6ax^3 - 4x^4) \, dx = \dfrac{a^5}{15}$

$\bar{x} = \dfrac{M_y}{m} = \dfrac{a^5/15}{a^4/6} = \dfrac{2a}{5}$

$\bar{y} = \dfrac{2a}{5}$ by symmetry

10. The x-coordinate changes by h units horizontally and k units vertically. This is not true for variable densities.

12. (a) $m = \int_0^a \int_0^{\sqrt{a^2 - x^2}} k \, dy \, dx = \dfrac{k\pi a^2}{4}$

$\quad M_y = \int_0^a \int_0^{\sqrt{a^2 - x^2}} kx \, dy \, dx$

$\quad\quad = k \int_0^a x\sqrt{a^2 - x^2} \, dx$

$\quad\quad = \left[-\dfrac{k}{3}(a^2 - x^2)^{3/2} \right]_0^a = \dfrac{ka^3}{3}$

$\quad \bar{x} = \dfrac{M_y}{m} = \dfrac{ka^3/3}{k\pi a^2/4} = \dfrac{4a}{3\pi}$

$\quad \bar{y} = \dfrac{4a}{3\pi}$ by symmetry

(b) $m = \int_0^a \int_0^{\sqrt{a^2 - x^2}} k(x^2 + y^2) \, dy \, dx$

$\quad = \int_0^{\pi/2} \int_0^a kr^3 \, dr \, d\theta = \dfrac{ka^4\pi}{8}$

$M_x = \int_0^a \int_0^{\sqrt{a^2 - x^2}} k(x^2 + y^2) y \, dy \, dx$

$\quad = \int_0^{\pi/2} \int_0^a kr^4 \sin\theta \, dr \, d\theta = \dfrac{ka^5}{5}$

$M_y = M_x$ by symmetry

$\bar{x} = \bar{y} = \dfrac{M_y}{m} = \dfrac{ka^5}{5} \cdot \dfrac{8}{ka^4\pi} = \dfrac{8a}{5\pi}$

14. $m = \int_0^2 \int_0^{x^3} kx \, dy \, dx = \int_0^2 kx^4 \, dx = \dfrac{32k}{5}$

$M_x = \int_0^2 \int_0^{x^3} kxy \, dy \, dx = 16k$

$M_y = \int_0^2 \int_0^{x^3} kx^2 \, dy \, dx = \dfrac{32k}{3}$

$\bar{x} = \dfrac{M_y}{m} = \dfrac{32k}{3} \cdot \dfrac{5}{32k} = \dfrac{5}{3}$

$\bar{y} = \dfrac{M_x}{m} = \dfrac{16k}{32k}(5) = \dfrac{5}{2}$

16. $m = \int_1^4 \int_0^{4/x} kx^2 \, dy \, dx = 30k$

$M_x = \int_1^4 \int_0^{4/x} kx^2 y \, dy \, dx = 24k$

$M_y = \int_1^4 \int_0^{4/x} kx^3 \, dy \, dx = 84k$

$\bar{x} = \dfrac{M_y}{m} = \dfrac{84k}{30k} = \dfrac{14}{5}$

$\bar{y} = \dfrac{M_y}{m} = \dfrac{24k}{30k} = \dfrac{4}{5}$

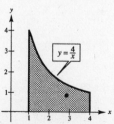

18. $\bar{x} = 0$ by symmetry

$$m = \int_{-3}^{3} \int_{0}^{9-x^2} ky^2 \, dy \, dx = \frac{23{,}328k}{35}$$

$$M_x = \int_{-3}^{3} \int_{0}^{9-x^2} ky^3 \, dy \, dx = \frac{139{,}968k}{35}$$

$$\bar{y} = \frac{M_x}{m} = \frac{139{,}968k}{35} \cdot \frac{35}{23{,}328k} = 6$$

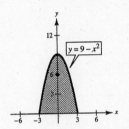

20. $m = \int_{0}^{L/2} \int_{0}^{\cos \pi x/L} k \, dy \, dx = \frac{kL}{\pi}$

$$M_x = \int_{0}^{L/2} \int_{0}^{\cos \pi x/L} ky \, dy \, dx = \frac{kL}{8}$$

$$M_y = \int_{0}^{L/2} \int_{0}^{\cos \pi x/L} kx \, dy \, dx = \frac{L^2(\pi - 2)k}{2\pi^2}$$

$$\bar{x} = \frac{M_y}{m} = \frac{L^2(\pi - 2)k}{2\pi^2} \cdot \frac{\pi}{kL} = \frac{L(\pi - 2)}{2\pi}$$

$$\bar{y} = \frac{M_x}{m} = \frac{kL}{8} \cdot \frac{\pi}{kL} = \frac{\pi}{8}$$

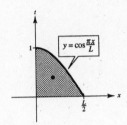

22. $m = \iint_R k\sqrt{x^2 + y^2} \, dA = \int_{0}^{\pi/4} \int_{0}^{a} kr^2 \, dr \, d\theta = \frac{ka^3\pi}{12}$

$$M_x = \iint_R k\sqrt{x^2 + y^2}\, y \, dA = \int_{0}^{\pi/4} \int_{0}^{a} kr^3 \sin\theta \, d\theta = \frac{ka^4(2 - \sqrt{2})}{8}$$

$$M_y = \iint_R k\sqrt{x^2 + y^2} \, dA = \int_{0}^{\pi/4} \int_{0}^{a} kr^3 \cos\theta \, d\theta = \frac{ka^4\sqrt{2}}{8}$$

$$\bar{x} = \frac{M_y}{m} = \frac{ka^4\sqrt{2}}{8} \cdot \frac{12}{ka^3\pi} = \frac{3\sqrt{2}a}{2\pi}$$

$$\bar{y} = \frac{M_x}{m} = \frac{ka^4(2 - \sqrt{2})}{8} \cdot \frac{12}{ka^3\pi} = \frac{3(2 - \sqrt{2})a}{2\pi}$$

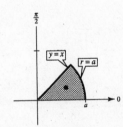

24. $m = \int_{1}^{e} \int_{0}^{\ln x} \frac{k}{x} \, dy \, dx = \frac{k}{2}$

$$M_x = \int_{1}^{e} \int_{0}^{\ln x} \frac{k}{x} y \, dy \, dx = \frac{k}{6}$$

$$M_y = \int_{1}^{e} \int_{0}^{\ln x} \frac{k}{x} x \, dy \, dx = k$$

$$\bar{x} = \frac{M_y}{m} = \frac{k}{1} \cdot \frac{2}{k} = 2$$

$$\bar{y} = \frac{M_x}{m} = \frac{k}{6} \cdot \frac{2}{k} = \frac{1}{3}$$

26. $\bar{y} = 0$ by symmetry

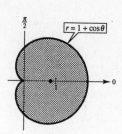

$$m = \iint_R k \, dA = \int_0^{2\pi} \int_0^{1+\cos\theta} kr \, dr \, d\theta = \frac{3\pi k}{2}$$

$$M_y = \iint_R kx \, dA = \int_0^{2\pi} \int_0^{1+\cos\theta} kr^2 \cos\theta \, dr \, d\theta$$

$$= \frac{k}{3} \int_0^{2\pi} \cos\theta(1 + 3\cos\theta + 3\cos^2\theta + \cos^3\theta) \, d\theta$$

$$= \frac{k}{3} \int_0^{2\pi} \left[\cos\theta + \frac{3}{2}(1 + \cos^2\theta) + 3\cos\theta(1 - \sin^2\theta) + \frac{1}{4}(1 + \cos 2\theta)^2 \right] d\theta$$

$$= \frac{5k\pi}{4}$$

$$\bar{x} = \frac{M_y}{m} = \frac{5k\pi}{4} \cdot \frac{2}{3k\pi} = \frac{5}{6}$$

28. $m = \int_0^b \int_0^{h-(hx/b)} dy \, dx = \dfrac{bh}{2}$

$$I_x = \int_0^b \int_0^{h-(hx/b)} y^2 \, dy \, dx = \frac{bh^3}{12}$$

$$I_y = \int_0^b \int_0^{h-(hx/b)} x^2 \, dy \, dx = \frac{b^3h}{12}$$

$$\bar{\bar{x}} = \sqrt{\frac{I_y}{m}} = \sqrt{\frac{b^3h/12}{bh/2}} = \frac{b}{\sqrt{6}} = \frac{\sqrt{6}}{6}b$$

$$\bar{\bar{y}} = \sqrt{\frac{I_x}{m}} = \sqrt{\frac{bh^3/12}{bh/2}} = \frac{h}{\sqrt{6}} = \frac{\sqrt{6}}{6}h$$

30. $m = \dfrac{\pi a^2}{2}$

$$I_x = \iint_R y^2 \, dA = \int_0^\pi \int_0^a r^3 \sin^2\theta \, dr \, d\theta = \frac{a^4\pi}{8}$$

$$I_y = \iint_R x^2 \, dA = \int_0^\pi \int_0^a r^3 \cos^2\theta \, dr \, d\theta = \frac{a^4\pi}{8}$$

$$I_0 = I_x + I_x = \frac{a^4\pi}{8} + \frac{a^4\pi}{8} = \frac{a^4\pi}{4}$$

$$\bar{\bar{x}} = \bar{\bar{y}} = \sqrt{\frac{I_x}{m}} = \sqrt{\frac{a^4\pi}{8} \cdot \frac{2}{\pi a^2}} = \frac{a}{2}$$

32. $m = \pi ab$

$$I_x = 4 \int_0^a \int_0^{(b/a)\sqrt{a^2-x^2}} y^2 \, dy \, dx$$

$$= 4 \int_0^a \frac{b^3}{3a^3}(a^2 - x^2)^{3/2} \, dx = \frac{4b^3}{3a^3} \int_0^a \left[a^2\sqrt{a^2 - x^2} - x^2\sqrt{a^2 - x^2} \right] dx$$

$$= \frac{4b^3}{3a^3} \left[\frac{a^2}{2}\left(x\sqrt{a^2 - x^2} + a^2 \arcsin\frac{x}{a} \right) - \frac{1}{8}\left[x(2x^2 - a^2)\sqrt{a^2 - x^2} + a^4 \arcsin\frac{x}{a} \right] \right]_0^a = \frac{ab^3\pi}{4}$$

$$I_y = 4 \int_0^b \int_0^{(a/b)\sqrt{b^2-y^2}} x^2 \, dx \, dy = \frac{a^3b\pi}{4}$$

$$I_0 = I_y + I_x = \frac{a^3b\pi}{4} + \frac{ab^3\pi}{4} = \frac{ab\pi}{4}(a^2 + b^2)$$

$$\bar{\bar{x}} = \sqrt{\frac{I_y}{m}} = \sqrt{\frac{a^3b\pi}{4} \cdot \frac{1}{\pi ab}} = \frac{a}{2}$$

$$\bar{\bar{y}} = \sqrt{\frac{I_x}{m}} = \sqrt{\frac{ab^3\pi}{4} \cdot \frac{1}{\pi ab}} = \frac{b}{2}$$

34. $\rho = ky$

$$m = 2k \int_0^a \int_0^{\sqrt{a^2-x^2}} y \, dy \, dx$$

$$= k \int_0^a (a^2 - x^2) \, dx = \frac{2ka^3}{3}$$

$$I_x = k \int_{-a}^a \int_0^{\sqrt{a^2-x^2}} y^3 \, dy \, dx = \frac{4ka^5}{15}$$

$$I_y = k \int_{-a}^a \int_0^{\sqrt{a^2-x^2}} x^2 y \, dy \, dx = \frac{2ka^5}{15}$$

$$I_0 = I_x + I_y = \frac{2ka^5}{5}$$

$$\bar{\bar{x}} = \sqrt{\frac{I_y}{m}} = \sqrt{\frac{2ka^5/15}{2ka^3/3}} = \sqrt{\frac{a^2}{5}} = \frac{a}{\sqrt{5}}$$

$$\bar{\bar{y}} = \sqrt{\frac{I_x}{m}} = \sqrt{\frac{4ka^5/15}{2ka^3/3}} = \sqrt{\frac{2a^2}{5}} = \frac{2a}{\sqrt{10}}$$

36. $\rho = kxy$

$$m = k \int_0^1 \int_{x^2}^x xy \, dy \, dx = \frac{k}{2} \int_0^1 (x^3 - x^5) \, dx = \frac{k}{24}$$

$$I_x = k \int_0^1 \int_{x^2}^x xy^3 \, dy \, dx = \frac{k}{4} \int_0^1 (x^5 - x^9) \, dx = \frac{k}{60}$$

$$I_y = k \int_0^1 \int_{x^2}^x x^3 y \, dy \, dx = \frac{k}{2} \int_0^1 (x^5 - x^7) \, dx = \frac{k}{48}$$

$$I_0 = I_x + I_y = \frac{9k}{240} = \frac{3k}{80}$$

$$\bar{\bar{x}} = \sqrt{\frac{I_y}{m}} = \sqrt{\frac{k/48}{k/24}} = \frac{1}{\sqrt{2}}$$

$$\bar{\bar{y}} = \sqrt{\frac{I_x}{m}} \sqrt{\frac{k/60}{k/24}} = \sqrt{\frac{2}{5}}$$

38. $\rho = x^2 + y^2$

$$m = \int_0^1 \int_{x^2}^{\sqrt{x}} (x^2 + y^2) \, dy \, dx = \frac{6}{35}$$

$$I_x = \int_0^1 \int_{x^2}^{\sqrt{x}} (x^2 + y^2) y^2 \, dy \, dx = \frac{158}{2079}$$

$$I_y = \int_0^1 \int_{x^2}^{\sqrt{x}} (x^2 + y^2) x^2 \, dy \, dx = \frac{158}{2079}$$

$$I_0 = I_x + I_y = \frac{316}{2079}$$

$$\bar{\bar{x}} = \sqrt{\frac{I_y}{m}} = \sqrt{\frac{158}{2079} \cdot \frac{35}{6}} = \sqrt{\frac{395}{891}}$$

$$\bar{\bar{y}} = \sqrt{\frac{I_x}{m}} = \bar{\bar{x}} = \sqrt{\frac{395}{891}}$$

40. $\rho = ky$

$$m = 2 \int_0^2 \int_{x^3}^{4x} ky \, dy \, dx = \frac{512k}{21}$$

$$I_x = 2 \int_0^2 \int_{x^3}^{4x} ky^3 \, dy \, dx = \frac{32{,}768k}{65}$$

$$I_y = 2 \int_0^2 \int_{x^3}^{4x} kx^2 y \, dy \, dx = \frac{2048k}{45}$$

$$I_0 = I_x + I_y = \frac{321{,}536k}{585}$$

$$\bar{\bar{x}} = \sqrt{\frac{I_y}{m}} = \sqrt{\frac{2048k}{45} \cdot \frac{21}{512k}} = \sqrt{\frac{28}{15}} = \frac{2\sqrt{105}}{15}$$

$$\bar{\bar{y}} = \sqrt{\frac{I_x}{m}} = \sqrt{\frac{32{,}768k}{65} \cdot \frac{21}{512k}} = \frac{8\sqrt{1365}}{65}$$

42. $I = \int_0^4 \int_0^2 k(x-6)^2 \, dy \, dx = \int_0^4 2k(x-6)^2 \, dx = \left[\frac{2k}{3}(x-6)^3\right]_0^4 = \frac{416k}{3}$

44. $I = \int_{-a}^a \int_0^{\sqrt{a^2-x^2}} ky(y-a)^2 \, dy \, dx$

$$= \int_{-a}^a k\left[\frac{y^4}{4} - \frac{2ay^3}{3} + \frac{a^2 y^2}{2}\right]_0^{\sqrt{a^2-x^2}} dx$$

$$= \int_{-a}^a k\left[\frac{1}{4}(a^4 - 2a^2 x^2 + x^4) - \frac{2a}{3}\left(a^2\sqrt{a^2-x^2} - x^2\sqrt{a^2-x^2}\right) + \frac{a^2}{2}(a^2 - x^2)\right] dx$$

$$= k\left[\frac{1}{4}\left(a^4 x - \frac{2a^2 x^3}{3} + \frac{x^5}{5}\right) - \frac{2a}{3}\left[\frac{a^2}{2}\left(x\sqrt{a^2-x^2} + a^2 \arcsin\frac{x}{a}\right)\right.\right.$$

$$\left.\left. - \frac{1}{8}\left(x(2x^2 - a^2)\sqrt{a^2-x^2} + a^4 \arcsin\frac{x}{a}\right)\right] + \frac{a^2}{2}\left(a^2 x - \frac{x^3}{3}\right)\right]_{-a}^a$$

$$= 2k\left[\frac{1}{4}\left(a^5 - \frac{2}{3}a^5 + \frac{1}{5}a^5\right) - \frac{2a}{3}\left(\frac{a^4\pi}{4} - \frac{a^4\pi}{16}\right) + \frac{a^2}{2}\left(a^3 - \frac{a^3}{3}\right)\right] = 2k\left(\frac{7a^5}{15} - \frac{a^5\pi}{8}\right) = ka^5\left(\frac{56 - 15\pi}{60}\right)$$

46. $I = \int_{-2}^{2}\int_{0}^{4-x^2} k(y-2)^2 \, dy \, dx = \int_{-2}^{2}\left[\frac{k}{3}(y-1)^3\right]_{0}^{4-x^2} dx = \int_{-2}^{2}\frac{k}{3}[(2-x^2)+8]\, dx$

$\qquad = \frac{k}{3}\int_{-2}^{2}(16-12x^2+6x^4-x^6)\, dx = \left[\frac{k}{3}\left(16x-4x^3+\frac{6}{5}x^5-\frac{1}{7}x^7\right)\right]_{-2}^{2}$

$\qquad = \frac{2k}{3}\left(32-32+\frac{192}{5}-\frac{128}{7}\right) = \frac{1408k}{105}$

48. $\rho(x,y) = k|2-x|$.

$(\bar{x}, \bar{y})$ will be the same.

50. $\rho(x,y) = k(4-x)(4-y)$. Both $\bar{x}$ and $\bar{y}$ will decrease

52. $I_x = \int_{R}\int y^2 \rho(x,y) \, dA$ Moment of inertia about x-axis.

$\quad I_y = \int_{R}\int x^2 \rho(x,y) \, dA$ Moment of inertia about y-axis.

54. Orient the xy-coordinate system so that L is along the y-axis and R is in the first quadrant. Then the volume of the solid is

$\qquad V = \int_{R}\int 2\pi x \, dA$

$\qquad\quad = 2\pi \int_{R}\int x \, dA$

$\qquad\quad = 2\pi \left(\dfrac{\int_{R}\int x \, dA}{\int_{R}\int dA}\right)\int_{R}\int dA$

$\qquad\quad = 2\pi \bar{x} A.$

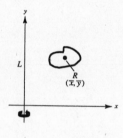

By our positioning, $\bar{x} = r$. Therefore, $V = 2\pi r A$.

56. $\bar{y} = \dfrac{a}{2}, A = ab, h = L - \dfrac{a}{2}$

$\quad I_{\bar{y}} = \int_{0}^{b}\int_{0}^{a}\left(y-\frac{a}{2}\right)^2 dy \, dx = \dfrac{a^3 b}{12}$

$\quad y_a = \dfrac{a}{2} - \dfrac{a^3 b/12}{[L-(a/2)]ab} = \dfrac{a(3L-2a)}{3(2L-a)}$

58. $\bar{y} = 0, A = \pi a^2, h = L$

$\quad I_{\bar{y}} = \int_{-a}^{a}\int_{-\sqrt{a^2-x^2}}^{\sqrt{a^2-x^2}} y^2 \, dy \, dx$

$\qquad = \int_{0}^{2\pi}\int_{0}^{a} r^3 \sin^2 \theta \, dr \, d\theta$

$\qquad = \int_{0}^{2\pi} \dfrac{a^4}{4}\sin^2 \theta \, d\theta$

$\qquad = \dfrac{a^4 \pi}{4}$

$\quad y_a = -\dfrac{(a^4 \pi/4)}{L\pi a^2} = -\dfrac{a^2}{4L}$

Section 13.5   Surface Area

2. $f(x, y) = 15 + 2x - 3y$

$f_x = 2, f_y = -3$

$\sqrt{1 + (f_x)^2 + (f_y)^2} = \sqrt{14}$

$S = \int_0^3 \int_0^3 \sqrt{14}\, dy\, dx = \int_0^3 3\sqrt{14}\, dx = 9\sqrt{14}$

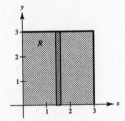

4. $f(x, y) = 10 + 2x - 3y$

$R = \{(x, y): x^2 + y^2 \le 9\}$

$f_x = 2, f_y = -3$

$\sqrt{1 + (f_x)^2 + (f_y)^2} = \sqrt{14}$

$S = \int_{-3}^3 \int_{-\sqrt{9-x^2}}^{\sqrt{9-x^2}} \sqrt{14}\, dy\, dx$

$= \int_0^{2\pi} \int_0^3 \sqrt{14}\, r\, dr\, d\theta = 9\sqrt{14}\pi$

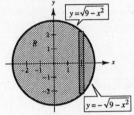

$y = \sqrt{9 - x^2}$

$y = -\sqrt{9 - x^2}$

6. $f(x, y) = y^2$

R = square with vertices $(0, 0), (3, 0), (0, 3), (3, 3)$

$f_x = 0, f_y = 2y$

$\sqrt{1 + (f_x)^2 + (f_y)^2} = \sqrt{1 + 4y^2}$

$S = \int_0^3 \int_0^3 \sqrt{1 + 4y^2}\, dx\, dy = \int_0^3 3\sqrt{1 + 4y^2}\, dy$

$= \left[\frac{3}{4}\left(2y\sqrt{1 + 4y^2} + \ln|2y + \sqrt{1 + 4y^2}|\right) \right]_0^3 = \frac{3}{4}\left(6\sqrt{37} + \ln|6 + \sqrt{37}|\right)$

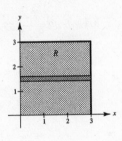

8. $f(x, y) = 2 + \frac{2}{3}y^{3/2}$

$f_x = 0, f_y = y^{1/2}$

$\sqrt{1 + f_x^2 + f_y^2} = \sqrt{1 + y}$

$S = \int_0^2 \int_0^{2-y} \sqrt{1 + y}\, dx\, dy = \int_0^2 \sqrt{1 + y}(2 - y)\, dy$

$= \left[2(1 + y)^{3/2} - \frac{2}{5}(1 + y)^{5/2} \right]_0^2$

$= 2 \cdot 3^{3/2} - \frac{2}{5} \cdot 3^{5/2} - 2 + \frac{2}{5}$

$= \frac{12}{5}\sqrt{3} - \frac{8}{5}$

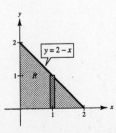

$y = 2 - x$

10. $f(x, y) = 9 + x^2 - y^2$

$f_x = 2x, f_y = -2y$

$\sqrt{1 + (f_x)^2 + (f_y)^2} = \sqrt{1 + 4x^2 + 4y^2}$

$S = \int_0^{2\pi} \int_0^2 \sqrt{1 + 4r^2}\, r\, dr\, d\theta$

$= \int_0^{2\pi} \left[\frac{1}{12}(1 + 4r^2)^{3/2} \right]_0^2 d\theta$

$= \int_0^{2\pi} \frac{1}{12}(17^{3/2} - 1)\, d\theta = \frac{\pi}{6}\left(17\sqrt{17} - 1\right)$

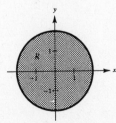

12. $f(x, y) = xy$

$R = \{(x, y): x^2 + y^2 \leq 16\}$

$f_x = y, f_y = x$

$\sqrt{1 + (f_x)^2 + (f_y)^2} = \sqrt{1 + y^2 + x^2}$

$S = \int_{-4}^{4} \int_{-\sqrt{16-x^2}}^{\sqrt{16-x^2}} \sqrt{1 + y^2 + x^2}\, dy\, dx$

$= \int_{0}^{2\pi} \int_{0}^{4} \sqrt{1 + r^2}\, r\, dr\, d\theta = \frac{2\pi}{3}\left(17\sqrt{17} - 1\right)$

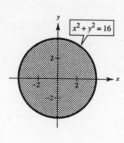

14. See Exercise 13.

$S = \int_{-a}^{a} \int_{-\sqrt{a^2-x^2}}^{\sqrt{a^2-x^2}} \frac{a}{\sqrt{a^2 - x^2 - y^2}}\, dy\, dx = \int_{0}^{2\pi} \int_{0}^{a} \frac{a}{\sqrt{a^2 - r^2}}\, r\, dr\, d\theta = 2\pi a^2$

16. $z = 16 - x^2 - y^2$

$\sqrt{1 + f_y^2 + f_y^2} = \sqrt{1 + 4x^2 + 4y^2}$

$S = \int_{0}^{4} \int_{0}^{\sqrt{16-x^2}} \sqrt{1 + 4(x^2 + y^2)}\, dy\, dx$

$= \int_{0}^{\pi/2} \int_{0}^{4} \sqrt{1 + 4r^2}\, r\, dr\, d\theta = \frac{\pi}{24}\left(65\sqrt{65} - 1\right)$

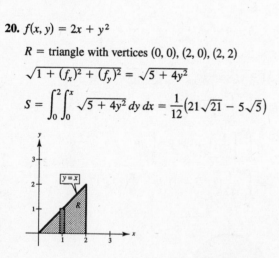

18. $z = 2\sqrt{x^2 + y^2}$

$\sqrt{1 + f_x^2 + f_y^2} = \sqrt{1 + \dfrac{4x^2}{x^2 + y^2} + \dfrac{4y^2}{x^2 + y^2}} = \sqrt{5}$

$S = \int_{0}^{2\pi} \int_{0}^{2} \sqrt{5}\, r\, dr\, d\theta = 4\pi\sqrt{5}$

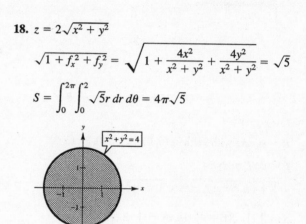

20. $f(x, y) = 2x + y^2$

$R = $ triangle with vertices $(0, 0), (2, 0), (2, 2)$

$\sqrt{1 + (f_x)^2 + (f_y)^2} = \sqrt{5 + 4y^2}$

$S = \int_{0}^{2} \int_{0}^{x} \sqrt{5 + 4y^2}\, dy\, dx = \frac{1}{12}\left(21\sqrt{21} - 5\sqrt{5}\right)$

22. $f(x, y) = x^2 + y^2$

$R = \{(x, y): 0 \leq f(x, y) \leq 16\}$

$0 \leq x^2 + y^2 \leq 16$

$f_x = 2x, f_y = 2y$

$\sqrt{1 + (f_x)^2 + (f_y)^2} = \sqrt{1 + 4x^2 + 4y^2}$

$S = \int_{-4}^{4} \int_{-\sqrt{16-x^2}}^{\sqrt{16-x^2}} \sqrt{1 + 4x^2 + 4y^2}\, dy\, dx$

$= \int_{0}^{2\pi} \int_{0}^{4} \sqrt{1 + 4r^2}\, dr\, d\theta = \frac{\left(65\sqrt{65} - 1\right)\pi}{6}$

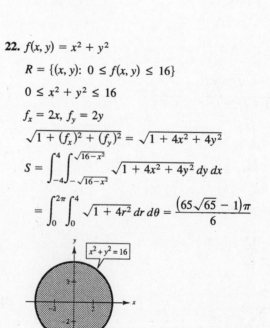

24. $f(x, y) = \frac{2}{3}x^{3/2} + \cos x$

$R = \{(x, y): 0 \le x \le 1, 0 \le y \le 1\}$

$f_x = x^{1/2} - \sin x, f_y = 0$

$\sqrt{1 + (f_x)^2 + (f_y)^2} = \sqrt{1 + (\sqrt{x} - \sin x)^2}$

$S = \int_0^1 \int_0^1 \sqrt{1 + (\sqrt{x} - \sin x)^2} \, dy \, dx \approx 1.02185$

26. Surface area $\approx (9\pi)$

Matches (c)

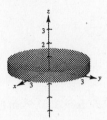

28. $f(x, y) = \frac{2}{5}y^{5/2}$

$R = \{(x, y): 0 \le x \le 1, 0 \le y \le 1\}$

$f_x = 0, f_y = y^{3/2}$

$\sqrt{1 + (f_x)^2 + (f_y)^2} = \sqrt{1 + y^3}$

$S = \int_0^1 \int_0^1 \sqrt{1 + y^3} \, dx \, dy$

$= \int_0^1 \sqrt{1 + y^3} \, dy \approx 1.1114$

30. $f(x, y) = x^2 - 3xy - y^2$

$R = \{(x, y): 0 \le x \le 4, 0 \le y \le x\}$

$f_x = 2x - 3y, f_y = -3x - 2y = -(3x + 2y)$

$\sqrt{1 + (f_x) + (f_y)^2} = \sqrt{1 + (2x - 3y)^2 + (3x + 2y)^2}$

$\qquad = \sqrt{1 + 13(x^2 + y^2)}$

$S = \int_0^4 \int_0^x \sqrt{1 + 13(x^2 + y^2)} \, dy \, dx$

32. $f(x, y) = \cos(x^2 + y^2)$

$R = \left\{(x, y): x^2 + y^2 \le \dfrac{\pi}{2}\right\}$

$f_x = -2x \sin(x^2 + y^2), f_y = -2y \sin(x^2 + y^2)$

$\sqrt{1 + (f_x)^2 + (f_y)^2} = \sqrt{1 + 4x^2 \sin^2(x^2 + y^2) + 4y^2 \sin^2(x^2 + y^2)} = \sqrt{1 + 4[\sin^2(x^2 + y^2)](x^2 + y^2)}$

$S = \int_{-\sqrt{\pi/2}}^{\sqrt{\pi/2}} \int_{-\sqrt{(\pi/2)-x^2}}^{\sqrt{(\pi/2)-x^2}} \sqrt{1 + 4(x^2 + y^2) \sin^2(x^2 + y^2)} \, dy \, dx$

34. $f(x, y) = e^{-x} \sin y$

$R = \{(x, y): 0 \le x \le 4, 0 \le y \le x\}$

$f_x = -e^{-x} \sin y, f_y = e^{-x} \cos y$

$\sqrt{1 + (f_x)^2 + (f_y)^2} = \sqrt{1 + e^{-2x} \sin^2 y + e^{-2x} \cos^2 y}$

$\qquad = \sqrt{1 + e^{-2x}}$

$S = \int_0^4 \int_0^x \sqrt{1 + e^{-2x}} \, dy \, dx$

36. (a) Yes. For example, let R be the square given by

$\qquad 0 \le x \le 1, 0 \le y \le 1,$

and S the square parallel to R given by

$\qquad 0 \le x \le 1, 0 \le y \le 1, z = 1.$

(b) Yes. Let R be the region in part (a) and S the surface given by $f(x, y) = xy$.

(c) No.

38. $f(x, y) = k\sqrt{x^2 + y^2}$

$\sqrt{1 + (f_x)^2 + (f_y)^2} = \sqrt{1 + \dfrac{k^2 x^2}{x^2 + y^2} + \dfrac{k^2 y^2}{x^2 + y^2}} = \sqrt{k^2 + 1}$

$S = \int\int_R \sqrt{1 + (f_x)^2 + (f_y)^2} \, dA = \int\int_R \sqrt{k^2 + 1} \, dA = \sqrt{k^2 + 1} \int\int_R dA = A\sqrt{k^2 + 1} = \pi r^2 \sqrt{k^2 + 1}$

40. (a) $z = \dfrac{-1}{75}y^3 + \dfrac{4}{25}y^2 - \dfrac{16}{15}y + 25$

(b) $V \approx 2(50)\displaystyle\int_0^{15}\left(-\dfrac{1}{75}y^3 + \dfrac{4}{25}y^2 - \dfrac{16}{15}y + 25\right)dy$

$= 100(266.25) = 26{,}625$ cubic feet

(c) $f(x, y) = -\dfrac{1}{75}y^3 + \dfrac{4}{25}y^2 - \dfrac{16}{15}y + 25$

$f_x = 0, f_y = -\dfrac{1}{25}y^2 + \dfrac{8}{25}y - \dfrac{16}{15}$

$S = 2\displaystyle\int_0^{50}\int_0^{15}\sqrt{1 + f_y^2 + f_x^2}\, dy\, dx \approx 3087.58$ sq ft

(d) Arc length ≈ 30.8758

Surface area of roof $\approx 2(50)(30.8758) = 3087.58$ sq ft

42. False. The surface area will remain the same for any vertical translation.

Section 13.6   Triple Integrals and Applications

2. $\displaystyle\int_{-1}^1\int_{-1}^1\int_{-1}^1 x^2y^2z^2\, dx\, dy\, dz = \dfrac{1}{3}\int_{-1}^1\int_{-1}^1\left[x^3y^2z^2\right]_{-1}^1 dy\, dz$

$= \dfrac{2}{3}\displaystyle\int_{-1}^1\int_{-1}^1 y^2z^2\, dy\, dz = \dfrac{2}{9}\int_{-1}^1\left[y^3z^2\right]_{-1}^1 dz = \dfrac{4}{9}\int_{-1}^1 z^2\, dz = \left[\dfrac{4}{27}z^3\right]_{-1}^1 = \dfrac{8}{27}$

4. $\displaystyle\int_0^9\int_0^{y/3}\int_0^{\sqrt{y^2-9x^2}} z\, dz\, dx\, dy = \dfrac{1}{2}\int_0^9\int_0^{y/3}(y^2 - 9x^2)\, dx\, dy$

$= \dfrac{1}{2}\displaystyle\int_0^9\left[xy^2 - 3x^3\right]_0^{y/3} dy = \dfrac{2}{18}\int_0^9 y^3\, dy = \left[\dfrac{1}{36}y^4\right]_0^9 = \dfrac{729}{4}$

6. $\displaystyle\int_1^4\int_1^{e^2}\int_0^{1/xz}\ln z\, dy\, dz\, dx = \int_1^4\int_1^{e^2}\left[(\ln z)y\right]_0^{1/xz} dz\, dx = \int_1^4\int_1^{e^2}\dfrac{\ln z}{xz}\, dz\, dx$

$= \displaystyle\int_1^4\left[\dfrac{1}{x}\dfrac{(\ln z)^2}{2}\right]_1^{e^2} dx = \int_1^4\dfrac{2}{x}\, dx = \left[2\ln|x|\right]_1^4 = 2\ln 4$

8. $\displaystyle\int_0^{\pi/2}\int_0^{y/2}\int_0^{1/y}\sin y\, dz\, dx\, dy = \int_0^{\pi/2}\int_0^{y/2}\dfrac{\sin y}{y}\, dx\, dy = \dfrac{1}{2}\int_0^{\pi/2}\sin y\, dy = \left[-\dfrac{1}{2}\cos y\right]_0^{\pi/2} = \dfrac{1}{2}$

10. $\displaystyle\int_0^{\sqrt2}\int_0^{\sqrt{2-x^2}}\int_{2x^2+y^2}^{4-y^2} y\, dz\, dy\, dx = \int_0^{\sqrt2}\int_0^{\sqrt{2-x^2}}(4y - 2x^2y - 2y^3)\, dy\, dx = \dfrac{16\sqrt2}{15}$

12. $\displaystyle\int_0^3\int_0^{2-(2y/3)}\int_0^{6-2y-3z} ze^{-x^2y^2}\, dx\, dz\, dy = \int_0^6\int_0^{(6-x)/2}\int_0^{(6-x-2y)/3} ze^{-x^2y^2}\, dz\, dy\, dx$

$= \displaystyle\int_0^6\int_0^{3-(x/2)}\dfrac{1}{2}\left(\dfrac{6-x-2y}{3}\right)^2 e^{-x^2y^2}\, dy\, dx \approx 2.118$

14. $\displaystyle\int_0^3\int_0^{2x}\int_0^{9-x^2} dz\, dy\, dx$

16. $z = \dfrac{1}{2}(x^2 + y^2) \implies 2z = x^2 + y^2$

$x^2 + y^2 + z^2 = 2z + z^2 = 80 \implies z^2 + 2z - 80 = 0 \implies (z - 8)(z + 10) = 0 \implies z = 8 \implies x^2 + y^2 = 2z = 16$

$$\int_{-4}^{4} \int_{-\sqrt{16-x^2}}^{\sqrt{16-x^2}} \int_{1/2(x^2+y^2)}^{\sqrt{80-x^2-y^2}} dz\, dy\, dx$$

18. $\displaystyle\int_{0}^{1}\int_{0}^{1}\int_{0}^{xy} dz\, dy\, dx = \int_{0}^{1}\int_{0}^{1} xy\, dy\, dx = \int_{0}^{1} \frac{x}{2}\, dx = \left[\frac{x^2}{4}\right]_{0}^{1} = \frac{1}{4}$

20. $4\displaystyle\int_{0}^{6}\int_{0}^{\sqrt{36-x^2}}\int_{0}^{36-x^2-y^2} dz\, dy\, dx = 4\int_{0}^{6}\int_{0}^{\sqrt{36-x^2}} (36 - x^2 - y^2)dy\, dx = 4\int_{0}^{6}\left[36y - x^2 y - \frac{y^3}{3}\right]_{0}^{\sqrt{36-x^2}} dx$

$$= 4\int_{0}^{6}\left[36\sqrt{36-x^2} - x^2\sqrt{36-x^2} - \frac{1}{3}(36-x^2)^{3/2}\right]dx$$

$$= 4\left[9x\sqrt{36-x^2} + 324\arcsin\!\left(\frac{x}{6}\right) + \frac{1}{6}x(36-x^2)^{3/2}\right]_{0}^{6} = 4(162\pi) = 648\pi$$

22. $\displaystyle\int_{0}^{2}\int_{0}^{2-x}\int_{0}^{9-x^2} dz\, dy\, dx = \int_{0}^{2}\int_{0}^{2-x} (9 - x^2)\, dy\, dx = \int_{0}^{2} (9 - x^2)(2 - x)\, dx$

$$= \int_{0}^{2} (18 - 9x - 2x^2 + x^3)\, dx = \left[18x - \frac{9}{2}x^2 - \frac{2}{3}x^3 + \frac{1}{4}x^4\right]_{0}^{2} = \frac{50}{3}$$

24. Top plane: $x + y + z = 6$

Side cylinder: $x^2 + y^2 = 9$

$$\int_{0}^{3}\int_{0}^{\sqrt{9-y^2}}\int_{0}^{6-x-y} dz\, dx\, dy$$

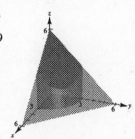

26. Elliptic cone: $4x^2 + z^2 = y^2$

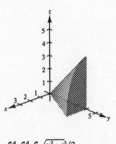

$$\int_{0}^{4}\int_{z}^{4}\int_{0}^{\sqrt{y^2-z^2}/2} dx\, dy\, dz$$

28. $Q = \{(x, y, z): 0 \le x \le 2, x^2 \le y \le 4, 0 \le z \le 2 - x\}$

$$\iiint\limits_{Q} xyz\, dV = \int_{0}^{2}\int_{x^2}^{4}\int_{0}^{2-x} xyz\, dz\, dy\, dx$$

$$= \int_{0}^{4}\int_{0}^{\sqrt{y}}\int_{0}^{2-x} xyz\, dz\, dx\, dy$$

$$= \int_{0}^{2}\int_{0}^{2-x}\int_{x^2}^{4} xyz\, dy\, dz\, dx$$

$$= \int_{0}^{2}\int_{0}^{2-z}\int_{x^2}^{4} xyz\, dy\, dx\, dz$$

$$= \int_{0}^{2}\int_{0}^{(2-z)^2}\int_{\sqrt{y}}^{\sqrt{y}} xyz\, dx\, dy\, dz + \int_{0}^{2}\int_{(2-z)^2}^{4}\int_{0}^{2-z} xyz\, dx\, dy\, dz$$

$$= \int_{0}^{4}\int_{0}^{2-\sqrt{y}}\int_{0}^{\sqrt{y}} xyz\, dx\, dz\, dy + \int_{0}^{4}\int_{2-\sqrt{y}}^{2}\int_{0}^{2-z} dx\, dz\, dy\left(\; = \frac{104}{21}\right)$$

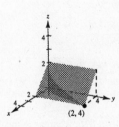

30. $Q = \{(x, y, z): 0 \le x \le 1, y \le 1 - x^2, 0 \le z \le 6\}$

$$\iiint_Q xyz \, dV = \int_0^1 \int_0^{\sqrt{1-x^2}} \int_0^6 xyz \, dz \, dy \, dx$$

$$= \int_0^1 \int_0^{\sqrt{1-y^2}} \int_0^6 xyz \, dz \, dx \, dy$$

$$= \int_0^1 \int_0^6 \int_0^{\sqrt{1-y^2}} xyz \, dx \, dz \, dy$$

$$= \int_0^6 \int_0^1 \int_0^{\sqrt{1-y^2}} xyz \, dx \, dy \, dz$$

$$= \int_0^1 \int_0^6 \int_0^{\sqrt{1-x^2}} xyz \, dy \, dz \, dx$$

$$= \int_0^6 \int_0^1 \int_0^{\sqrt{1-x^2}} xyz \, dy \, dx \, dz$$

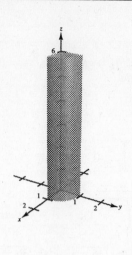

32. $m = k \int_0^5 \int_0^{5-x} \int_0^{1/5(15-3x-3y)} y \, dz \, dy \, dz = \dfrac{125}{8} k$

$M_{xz} = k \int_0^5 \int_0^{5-x} \int_0^{1/5(15-3x-3y)} y^2 \, dz \, dy \, dx = \dfrac{125}{4} k$

$\bar{y} = \dfrac{M_{xz}}{m} = 2$

34. $m = k \int_0^b \int_0^{a[1-(y/b)]} \int_0^{c[1-(y/b)-(x/a)]} dz \, dx \, dy = \dfrac{kabc}{6}$

$M_{xz} = k \int_0^b \int_0^{a[1-(y/b)]} \int_0^{c[1-(y/b)-(x/a)]} y \, dz \, dx \, dy = \dfrac{kab^2c}{24}$

$\bar{y} = \dfrac{M_{xz}}{m} = \dfrac{kab^2c/24}{kabc/6} = \dfrac{b}{4}$

36. $m = k \int_0^a \int_0^b \int_0^c z \, dz \, dy \, dx = \dfrac{kabc^2}{2}$

$M_{xy} = k \int_0^a \int_0^b \int_0^c z^2 \, dz \, dy \, dx = \dfrac{kabc^3}{3}$

$M_{yz} = k \int_0^a \int_0^b \int_0^c xz \, dz \, dy \, dx = \dfrac{ka^2bc^2}{4}$

$M_{xz} = k \int_0^a \int_0^b \int_0^c yz \, dz \, dy \, dx = \dfrac{kab^2c^2}{4}$

$\bar{x} = \dfrac{M_{yz}}{m} = \dfrac{ka^2bc^2/4}{kabc^2/2} = \dfrac{a}{2}$

$\bar{y} = \dfrac{M_{xz}}{m} = \dfrac{kab^2c^2/4}{kabc^2/2} = \dfrac{b}{2}$

$\bar{z} = \dfrac{M_{xy}}{m} = \dfrac{kabc^3/3}{kabc^2/2} = \dfrac{2c}{3}$

38. $\bar{z}$ will be greater than 8/5, whereas $\bar{x}$ and $\bar{y}$ will be unchanged.

40. $\bar{x}, \bar{y}$ and $\bar{z}$ will all be greater than their original values.

42. $m = 2k \displaystyle\int_0^2 \int_0^{\sqrt{4-x^2}} \int_0^y dz\, dy\, dx$

$\quad = k \displaystyle\int_0^2 (4 - x^2)\, dx = \dfrac{16k}{3}$

$M_{yz} = k \displaystyle\int_{-2}^2 \int_0^{\sqrt{4-x^2}} \int_0^y x\, dz\, dy\, dx = 0$

$M_{xz} = 2k \displaystyle\int_0^2 \int_0^{\sqrt{4-x^2}} \int_0^y y\, dz\, dy\, dx = 2k\pi$

$M_{xy} = 2k \displaystyle\int_0^2 \int_0^{\sqrt{4-x^2}} \int_0^y z\, dz\, dy\, dx = k\pi$

$\bar{x} = \dfrac{M_{yz}}{m} = \dfrac{0}{16k/3} = 0$

$\bar{y} = \dfrac{M_{xz}}{m} = \dfrac{2k\pi}{16k/3} = \dfrac{3\pi}{8}$

$\bar{z} = \dfrac{M_{xy}}{m} = \dfrac{k\pi}{16k/3} = \dfrac{3\pi}{16}$

44. $\bar{x} = 0$

$m = 2k \displaystyle\int_0^2 \int_0^1 \int_0^{1/(y^2+1)} dz\, dy\, dx = 2k \int_0^2 \int_0^1 \dfrac{1}{y^2+1}\, dy\, dx = 2k\left(\dfrac{\pi}{4}\right)\int_0^2 dx = k\pi$

$M_{xz} = 2k \displaystyle\int_0^2 \int_0^1 \int_0^{1/(y^2+1)} y\, dz\, dy\, dx = 2k \int_0^2 \int_0^1 \dfrac{y}{y^2+1}\, dy\, dx = k \int_0^2 (\ln 2)\, dx = k\ln 4$

$M_{xy} = 2k \displaystyle\int_0^2 \int_0^1 \int_0^{1/(y^2+1)} z\, dz\, dy\, dx$

$\quad = k \displaystyle\int_0^2 \int_0^1 \dfrac{1}{(y^2+1)^2}\, dy\, dx = k \int_0^2 \left[\dfrac{y}{2(y^2+1)} + \dfrac{1}{2}\arctan y \right]_0^1 dx = k\left(\dfrac{1}{4} + \dfrac{\pi}{8}\right)\int_0^2 dx = k\left(\dfrac{1}{2} + \dfrac{\pi}{4}\right)$

$\bar{y} = \dfrac{M_{xz}}{m} = \dfrac{k\ln 4}{k\pi} = \dfrac{\ln 4}{\pi}$

$\bar{z} = \dfrac{M_{xy}}{m} = k\left(\dfrac{1}{2} + \dfrac{\pi}{4}\right)\bigg/ k\pi = \dfrac{2+\pi}{4\pi}$

46. $f(x, y) = \dfrac{1}{15}(60 - 12x - 20y)$

$m = k \displaystyle\int_0^5 \int_0^{-(3/5)x+3} \int_0^{(1/15)(60-12x-20y)} dz\, dy\, dx = 10k$

$M_{yz} = k \displaystyle\int_0^5 \int_0^{-(3/5)x+3} \int_0^{(1/15)(60-12x-20y)} x\, dz\, dy\, dx = \dfrac{25k}{2}$

$M_{xz} = k \displaystyle\int_0^5 \int_0^{-(3/5)x+3} \int_0^{-(1/15)(60-12x-20y)} y\, dz\, dy\, dx = \dfrac{15k}{2}$

$M_{xy} = k \displaystyle\int_0^5 \int_0^{-(3/5)x+3} \int_0^{(1/15)(60-12x-20y)} z\, dz\, dy\, dx = 10k$

$\bar{x} = \dfrac{M_{yz}}{m} = \dfrac{25k/2}{10k} = \dfrac{5}{4}$

$\bar{y} = \dfrac{M_{xz}}{m} = \dfrac{15k/2}{10k} = \dfrac{3}{4}$

$\bar{z} = \dfrac{M_{xy}}{m} = \dfrac{10k}{10k} = 1$

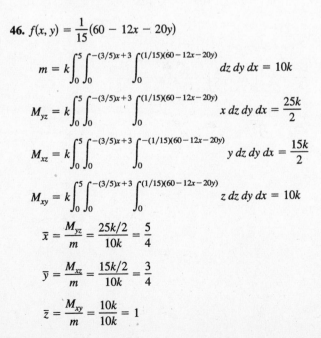

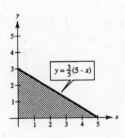

$y = \dfrac{3}{5}(5 - x)$

48. (a) $I_{xy} = k \int_{-a/2}^{a/2} \int_{-a/2}^{a/2} \int_{-a/2}^{a/2} z^2 \, dz \, dy \, dx = \dfrac{ka^5}{12}$

$I_{xz} = I_{yz} = \dfrac{ka^5}{12}$ by symmetry

$I_x = I_y = I_z = \dfrac{ka^5}{12} + \dfrac{ka^5}{12} = \dfrac{ka^5}{6}$

(b) $I_{xy} = k \int_{-a/2}^{a/2} \int_{-a/2}^{a/2} \int_{-a/2}^{a/2} z^2(x^2 + y^2) \, dz \, dy \, dx = \dfrac{a^3 k}{12} \int_{-a/2}^{a/2} \int_{-a/2}^{a/2} (x^2 + y^2) \, dy \, dx = \dfrac{a^7 k}{72}$

$I_{xz} = k \int_{-a/2}^{a/2} \int_{-a/2}^{a/2} \int_{-a/2}^{a/2} y^2(x^2 + y^2) \, dz \, dy \, dx = ka \int_{-a/2}^{a/2} \int_{-a/2}^{a/2} (x^2 y^2 + y^4) \, dy \, dx = \dfrac{7ka^7}{360}$

$I_{yz} = I_{xz}$ by symmetry

$I_x = I_{xy} + I_{xz} = \dfrac{a^7 k}{30}$

$I_y = I_{xy} + I_{yz} = \dfrac{a^7 k}{30}$

$I_z = I_{yz} + I_{xz} = \dfrac{7ka^7}{180}$

50. (a) $I_{xy} = k \int_0^4 \int_0^2 \int_0^{4-y^2} z^3 \, dz \, dy \, dx = k \int_0^4 \int_0^2 \dfrac{1}{4}(4 - y^2)^4 \, dy \, dx$

$\quad = \dfrac{k}{4} \int_0^4 \int_0^2 (256 - 256y^2 + 96y^4 - 16y^6 + y^8) \, dy \, dx$

$\quad = \dfrac{k}{4} \int_0^4 \left[256y - \dfrac{256y^3}{3} + \dfrac{96y^5}{5} - \dfrac{16y^7}{7} + \dfrac{y^9}{9} \right]_0^2 dx = k \int_0^4 \dfrac{16{,}384}{945} \, dx = \dfrac{65{,}536k}{315}$

$I_{xz} = k \int_0^4 \int_0^2 \int_0^{4-y^2} y^2 z \, dz \, dy \, dx = k \int_0^4 \int_0^2 \dfrac{1}{2} y^2 (4 - y^2)^2 \, dy \, dx$

$\quad = k \int_0^4 \int_0^2 \dfrac{1}{2}(16y^2 - 8y^4 + y^6) \, dy \, dx = \dfrac{k}{2} \int_0^4 \left[\dfrac{16y^3}{3} - \dfrac{8y^5}{5} + \dfrac{y^7}{7} \right]_0^2 dx = \dfrac{k}{2} \int_0^4 \dfrac{1024}{105} \, dx = \dfrac{2048k}{105}$

$I_{yz} = k \int_0^4 \int_0^2 \int_0^{4-y^2} x^2 z \, dz \, dy \, dx = k \int_0^4 \int_0^2 \dfrac{1}{2} x^2 (4 - y^2)^2 \, dy \, dx$

$\quad = k \int_0^4 \int_0^2 \dfrac{1}{2} x^2 (16 - 8y^2 + y^4) \, dy \, dx = \dfrac{k}{2} \int_0^4 \left[x^2 \left(16y - \dfrac{8y^3}{3} + \dfrac{y^5}{5} \right) \right]_0^2 dx = \dfrac{k}{2} \int_0^4 \dfrac{256}{15} x^2 \, dx = \dfrac{8192k}{45}$

$I_x = I_{xz} + I_{xy} = \dfrac{2048k}{9}, \; I_y = I_{yz} + I_{xy} = \dfrac{8192k}{21}, \; I_z = I_{yz} + I_{xz} = \dfrac{63{,}488k}{315}$

—CONTINUED—

50. —CONTINUED—

(b) $I_{xy} = \displaystyle\int_0^4 \int_0^2 \int_0^{4-y^2} z^2(4 - z)\, dz\, dy\, dx$

$= k\displaystyle\int_0^4 \int_0^2 \int_0^{4-y^2} 4z^2\, dz\, dy\, dx - k\int_0^4 \int_0^2 \int_0^{4-y^2} z^3\, dz\, dy\, dx = \dfrac{32{,}768k}{105} - \dfrac{65{,}536k}{315} = \dfrac{32{,}768k}{315}$

$I_{xz} = \displaystyle\int_0^4 \int_0^2 \int_0^{4-y^2} y^2(4 - z)\, dz\, dy\, dx$

$= k\displaystyle\int_0^4 \int_0^2 \int_0^{4-y^2} 4y^2\, dz\, dy\, dx - k\int_0^4 \int_0^2 \int_0^{4-y^2} y^2 z\, dz\, dy\, dx = \dfrac{1024k}{15} - \dfrac{2048k}{105} = \dfrac{1024k}{21}$

$I_{yz} = k\displaystyle\int_0^4 \int_0^2 \int_0^{4-y^2} x^2(4 - z)\, dz\, dy\, dx$

$= k\displaystyle\int_0^4 \int_0^2 \int_0^{4-y^2} 4x^2\, dz\, dy\, dx - k\int_0^4 \int_0^2 \int_0^{4-y^2} x^2 z\, dz\, dy\, dx = \dfrac{4096k}{9} - \dfrac{8192k}{45} = \dfrac{4096k}{15}$

$I_x = I_{xz} + I_{xy} = \dfrac{48{,}128k}{315}, \quad I_y = I_{yz} + I_{xy} = \dfrac{118{,}784k}{315}, \quad I_z = I_{xz} + I_{yz} = \dfrac{11{,}264k}{35}$

52. $I_{xy} = \displaystyle\int_{-c/2}^{c/2} \int_{-a/2}^{a/2} \int_{-b/2}^{b/2} z^2\, dz\, dy\, dx = \dfrac{b^3}{12}\int_{-c/2}^{c/2} \int_{-a/2}^{a/2} dy\, dx = \dfrac{1}{12}b^2(abc) = \dfrac{1}{12}mb^2$

$I_{xz} = \displaystyle\int_{-c/2}^{c/2} \int_{-a/2}^{a/2} \int_{-b/2}^{b/2} y^2\, dz\, dy\, dx = b\int_{-c/2}^{c/2} \int_{-a/2}^{a/2} y^2\, dy\, dx = \dfrac{ba^3}{12}\int_{-c/2}^{c/2} dx = \dfrac{ba^3 c}{12} = \dfrac{1}{12}a^2(abc) = \dfrac{1}{12}ma^2$

$I_{yz} = \displaystyle\int_{-c/2}^{c/2} \int_{-a/2}^{a/2} \int_{-b/2}^{b/2} x^2\, dz\, dy\, dx = ab\int_{-c/2}^{c/2} x^2\, dx = \dfrac{abc^3}{12} = \dfrac{1}{12}c^2(abc) = \dfrac{1}{12}mc^2$

$I_x = I_{xy} + I_{xz} = \dfrac{1}{12}m(a^2 + b^2)$

$I_y = I_{xy} + I_{yz} = \dfrac{1}{12}m(b^2 + c^2)$

$I_z = I_{xz} + I_{yz} = \dfrac{1}{12}m(a^2 + c^2)$

54. $\displaystyle\int_{-1}^{1} \int_{-\sqrt{1-x^2}}^{\sqrt{1-x^2}} \int_0^{4-x^2-y^2} kx^2(x^2 + y^2)\, dz\, dy\, dx$ **56.** 6

58. Because the density increases as you move away from the axis of symmetry, the moment of intertia will increase.

Section 13.7   Triple Integrals in Cylindrical and Spherical Coordinates

2. $\displaystyle\int_0^{\pi/4} \int_0^2 \int_0^{2-r} rz\, dz\, dr\, d\theta = \int_0^{\pi/4} \int_0^2 \left[\dfrac{rz^2}{2}\right]_0^{2-r} dr\, d\theta$

$= \dfrac{1}{2}\displaystyle\int_0^{\pi/4} \int_0^2 (4r - 4r^2 + r^3)\, dr\, d\theta = \dfrac{1}{2}\int_0^{\pi/4} \left[2r^2 - \dfrac{4r^3}{3} + \dfrac{r^4}{4}\right]_0^2 d\theta = \dfrac{2}{3}\int_0^{\pi/4} d\theta = \dfrac{\pi}{6}$

4. $\displaystyle\int_0^{\pi/2} \int_0^{\pi} \int_0^2 e^{-\rho^3}\rho^2\, d\rho\, d\theta\, d\phi = \int_0^{\pi/2} \int_0^{\pi} \left[-\dfrac{1}{3}e^{-\rho^3}\right]_0^2 d\theta\, d\phi = \int_0^{\pi/2} \int_0^{\pi} \dfrac{1}{3}(1 - e^{-8})\, d\theta\, d\phi = \dfrac{\pi^2}{6}(1 - e^{-8})$

6. $\displaystyle\int_0^{\pi/4}\int_0^{\pi/4}\int_0^{\cos\theta}\rho^2\sin\phi\cos\phi\,d\rho\,d\theta\,d\phi = \frac{1}{3}\int_0^{\pi/4}\int_0^{\pi/4}\cos^3\theta\sin\phi\cos\phi\,d\theta\,d\phi$

$\displaystyle\qquad\qquad = \frac{1}{3}\int_0^{\pi/4}\int_0^{\pi/4}\sin\phi\cos\phi[\cos\theta(1-\sin^2\theta)]d\theta\,d\phi$

$\displaystyle\qquad\qquad = \frac{1}{3}\int_0^{\pi/4}\sin\phi\cos\phi\left[\sin\theta - \frac{\sin^3\theta}{3}\right]_0^{\pi/4}d\phi$

$\displaystyle\qquad\qquad = \frac{5\sqrt{2}}{36}\int_0^{\pi/4}\sin\phi\cos\phi\,d\phi = \left[\frac{5\sqrt{2}}{36}\frac{\sin^2\phi}{2}\right]_0^{\pi/4} = \frac{5\sqrt{2}}{144}$

8. $\displaystyle\int_0^{\pi/2}\int_0^{\pi}\int_0^{\sin\theta}(2\cos\phi)\rho^2\,d\rho\,d\theta\,d\phi = \frac{8}{9}$

10. $\displaystyle\int_0^{2\pi}\int_0^{\sqrt{3}}\int_0^{3-r^2}r\,dz\,dr\,d\theta = \int_0^{2\pi}\int_0^{\sqrt{3}}r(3-r^2)dr\,d\theta$

$\displaystyle\qquad\qquad = \int_0^{2\pi}\left(\frac{3r^2}{2} - \frac{r^4}{4}\right)\Big]_0^{\sqrt{3}}d\theta$

$\displaystyle\qquad\qquad = \int_0^{2\pi}\frac{9}{4}d\theta = \frac{9\pi}{2}$

12. $\displaystyle\int_0^{2\pi}\int_0^{\pi}\int_2^5\rho^2\sin\phi\,d\rho\,d\phi\,d\theta = \frac{117}{3}\int_0^{2\pi}\int_0^{\pi}\sin\phi\,d\phi\,d\theta$

$\displaystyle\qquad\qquad = \frac{117}{3}\int_0^{2\pi}\Big[-\cos\phi\Big]_0^{\pi}d\theta$

$\displaystyle\qquad\qquad = \frac{468\pi}{3}$

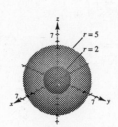

14. (a) $\displaystyle\int_0^{\pi/2}\int_0^2\int_0^{\sqrt{16-r^2}}r^2\,dz\,dr\,d\theta = \frac{8\pi^2}{3} - 2\pi\sqrt{3}$

(b) $\displaystyle\int_0^{\pi/2}\int_0^{\pi/6}\int_0^4\rho^3\sin^2\phi\,d\rho\,d\phi\,d\theta + \int_0^{\pi/2}\int_{\pi/6}^{\pi/2}\int_4^{2\csc\phi}\rho^3\sin^2\phi\,d\rho\,d\phi\,d\theta = \frac{8\pi^2}{3} - 2\pi\sqrt{3}$

16. (a) $\displaystyle\int_0^{\pi/2}\int_0^1\int_0^{\sqrt{1-r^2}}r\sqrt{r^2+z^2}\,dz\,dr\,d\theta = \frac{\pi}{8}$ (b) $\displaystyle\int_0^{\pi/2}\int_0^{\pi/2}\int_0^1\rho^3\sin\phi\,d\rho\,d\phi\,d\theta = \frac{\pi}{8}$

18. $\displaystyle V = \frac{2}{3}\pi(4)^3 + 4\left[\int_0^{\pi/2}\int_0^{2\sqrt{2}}\int_0^r r\,dz\,dr\,d\theta + \int_0^{\pi/2}\int_{2\sqrt{2}}^4\int_0^{\sqrt{16-r^2}}r\,dz\,dr\,d\theta\right]$

(Volume of lower hemisphere) + 4(Volume in the first octant)

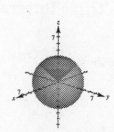

$\displaystyle V = \frac{128\pi}{3} + 4\left[\int_0^{\pi/2}\int_0^{2\sqrt{2}}r^2\,dr\,d\theta + \int_0^{\pi/2}\int_{2\sqrt{2}}^4 r\sqrt{16-r^2}\,dr\,d\theta\right]$

$\displaystyle\qquad = \frac{128\pi}{3} + 4\left[\frac{8\sqrt{2}\pi}{3} + \int_0^{\pi/2}\left[-\frac{1}{3}(16-r^2)^{3/2}\right]_{2\sqrt{2}}^4 d\theta\right]$

$\displaystyle\qquad = \frac{128\pi}{3} + 4\left[\frac{8\sqrt{2}\pi}{3} + \frac{8\sqrt{2}\pi}{3}\right]$

$\displaystyle\qquad = \frac{128\pi}{3} + \frac{64\sqrt{2}\pi}{3} = \frac{64\pi}{3}(2+\sqrt{2})$

20. $V = \int_0^{2\pi} \int_0^{\sqrt{2}} \int_r^{\sqrt{4-r^2}} r \, dz \, dr \, d\theta$

$= \int_0^{2\pi} \int_0^{\sqrt{2}} \left(r\sqrt{4-r^2} - r^2 \right) dr \, d\theta$

$= \int_0^{2\pi} \left[-\frac{1}{3}(4-r^2)^{3/2} - \frac{r^3}{3} \right]_0^{\sqrt{2}} d\theta$

$= \frac{8\pi}{3} \left(2 - \sqrt{2} \right)$

22. $\int_0^{\pi/2} \int_0^2 \int_0^{12e^{-r^2}} k \, r \, dz \, dr \, d\theta = \int_0^{\pi/2} \int_0^2 12ke^{-r^2} r \, dr \, d\theta$

$= \int_0^{\pi/2} \left[-6ke^{-r^2} \right]_0^2$

$= \int_0^{\pi/2} (-6ke^{-4} + 6k) \, d\theta$

$= 3k\pi(1 - e^{-4})$

24. $\bar{x} = \bar{y} = 0$ by symmetry

$m = \frac{1}{3}\pi r_0^2 hk$ from Exercise 23

$M_{xy} = 4k \int_0^{\pi/2} \int_0^{r_0} \int_0^{h(r_0-r)/r_0} z r \, dz \, dr \, d\theta$

$= \frac{2kh^2}{r_0^2} \int_0^{\pi/2} \int_0^{r_0} (r_0^2 r - 2r_0 r^2 + r^3) dr \, d\theta$

$= \frac{2kh^2}{r_0^2} \left(\frac{r_0^4}{12} \right) \left(\frac{\pi}{2} \right) = \frac{kr_0^2 h^2 \pi}{12}$

$\bar{z} = \frac{M_{xy}}{m} = \frac{kr_0^2 h^2 \pi}{12} \left(\frac{3}{\pi r_0^2 hk} \right) = \frac{h}{4}$

26. $\rho = kz$

$\bar{x} = \bar{y} = 0$ by symmetry

$m = 4k \int_0^{\pi/2} \int_0^{r_0} \int_0^{h(r_0-r)/r_0} z r \, dz \, dr \, d\theta$

$= \frac{1}{12}k\pi r_0^2 h^2$

$M_{xy} = 4k \int_0^{\pi/2} \int_0^{r_0} \int_0^{h(r_0-r)/r_0} z^2 r \, dz \, dr \, d\theta$

$= \frac{1}{30}k\pi r_0^2 h^3$

$\bar{z} = \frac{M_{xy}}{m} = \frac{k\pi r_0^2 h^3/30}{k\pi r_0^2 h^2/12} = \frac{2h}{5}$

28. $I_z = \iiint\limits_Q (x^2 + y^2)\rho(x,y,z) \, dV$

$= 4k \int_0^{\pi/2} \int_0^{r_0} \int_0^{h(r_0-r)/r_0} r^4 \, dz \, dr \, d\theta$

$= 4kh \int_0^{\pi/2} \int_0^{r_0} \frac{r_0-r}{r_0} r^4 \, dr \, d\theta$

$= 4kh \int_0^{\pi/2} \left[\frac{r^5}{5} - \frac{r^6}{6r_0} \right]_0^{r_0} d\theta$

$= 4kh \int_0^{\pi/2} \left[\frac{r_0^5}{5} - \frac{r_0^5}{6} \right] d\theta$

$= 4kh \int_0^{\pi/2} \frac{1}{30} r_0^5 \, d\theta$

$= 4kh \frac{1}{30} r_0^5 \frac{\pi}{2}$

$= \frac{1}{15} r_0^5 \pi kh$

30. $m = k\pi a^2 h$

$I_z = 2k \int_0^{\pi/2} \int_0^{2a\sin\theta} \int_0^h r^3 \, dz \, dr \, d\theta$

$= \frac{3}{2}k\pi a^4 h$

$= \frac{3}{2}ma^2$

32. $V = 8 \int_0^{\pi/4} \int_0^{\pi/2} \int_a^b \rho^2 \sin \phi \, d\rho \, d\theta \, d\phi$ (includes upper and lower cones)

$$= \frac{8}{3}(b^3 - a^3) \int_0^{\pi/4} \int_0^{\pi/2} \sin \phi \, d\theta \, d\phi$$

$$= \frac{4\pi}{3}(b^3 - a^3) \int_0^{\pi/4} \sin \phi \, d\phi$$

$$= \left[\frac{4\pi}{3}(b^3 - a^3)(-\cos \phi) \right]_0^{\pi/4}$$

$$= \left(1 - \frac{\sqrt{2}}{2} \right) \frac{4\pi}{3}(b^3 - a^3) = \frac{2\pi}{3}(2 - \sqrt{2})(b^3 - a^3)$$

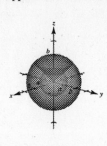

34. $m = 8k \int_0^{\pi/2} \int_0^{\pi/2} \int_0^a \rho^3 \sin^2 \phi \, d\rho \, d\theta \, d\phi$

$$= 2ka^4 \int_0^{\pi/2} \int_0^{\pi/2} \sin^2 \phi \, d\theta \, d\phi$$

$$= k\pi a^4 \int_0^{\pi/2} \sin^2 \phi \, d\phi$$

$$= \left[k\pi a^4 \left(\frac{1}{2}\phi - \frac{1}{4}\sin 2\phi \right) \right]_0^{\pi/2}$$

$$= k\pi a^4 \frac{\pi}{4} = \frac{1}{4}k\pi^2 a^4$$

36. $\bar{x} = \bar{y} = 0$ by symmetry

$$m = k\left(\frac{2}{3}\pi R^3 - \frac{2}{3}\pi r^3 \right) = \frac{2}{3}k\pi(R^3 - r^3)$$

$$M_{xy} = 4k \int_0^{\pi/2} \int_0^{\pi/2} \int_r^R \rho^3 \cos \phi \sin \phi \, d\rho \, d\theta \, d\phi$$

$$= \frac{1}{2}k(R^4 - r^4) \int_0^{\pi/2} \int_0^{\pi/2} \sin 2\phi \, d\theta \, d\phi$$

$$= \frac{1}{4}k\pi(R^4 - r^4) \int_0^{\pi/2} \sin 2\phi \, d\phi$$

$$= \left[-\frac{1}{8}k\pi(R^4 - r^4)\cos 2\phi \right]_0^{\pi/2} = \frac{1}{4}k\pi(R^4 - r^4)$$

$$\bar{z} = \frac{M_{xy}}{m} = \frac{k\pi(R^4 - r^4)/4}{2k\pi(R^3 - r^3)/3} = \frac{3(R^4 - r^4)}{8(R^3 - r^3)}$$

38. $I_z = 4k \int_0^{\pi/2} \int_0^{\pi/2} \int_r^R \rho^4 \sin^3 \phi \, d\rho \, d\theta \, d\phi$

$$= \frac{4k}{5}(R^5 - r^5) \int_0^{\pi/2} \int_0^{\pi/2} \sin^3 \phi \, d\theta \, d\phi$$

$$= \frac{2k\pi}{5}(R^5 - r^5) \int_0^{\pi/2} \sin \phi (1 - \cos^2 \phi) \, d\phi$$

$$= \left[\frac{2k\pi}{5}(R^5 - r^5)\left(-\cos \phi + \frac{\cos^3 \phi}{3} \right) \right]_0^{\pi/2}$$

$$= \frac{4k\pi}{15}(R^5 - r^5)$$

40. $x = \rho \sin \phi \cos \theta \qquad \rho^2 = x^2 + y^2 + z^2$

$y = \rho \sin \phi \sin \theta \qquad \tan \theta = \dfrac{y}{x}$

$z = \rho \cos \phi \qquad \cos \phi = \dfrac{z}{\sqrt{x^2 + y^2 + z^2}}$

42. $\displaystyle\int_{\theta_1}^{\theta_2} \int_{\phi_1}^{\phi_2} \int_{\rho_1}^{\rho_2} f(\rho \sin \phi \cos \theta, \rho \sin \phi \sin \theta, \rho \cos \phi)\rho^2 \sin \phi \, d\rho \, d\phi \, d\theta$

44. (a) You are integrating over a cylindrical wedge. (b) You are integrating over a spherical block.

46. The volume of this spherical block can be determined as follows. One side is length $\Delta\rho$. Another side is $\rho\Delta\phi$. Finally, the third side is given by the length of an arc of angle $\Delta\theta$ in a circle of radius $\rho \sin \phi$. Thus:

$$\Delta V \approx (\Delta\rho)(\rho\Delta\phi)(\Delta\theta\rho \sin \phi)$$

$$= \rho^2 \sin \phi \Delta\rho\Delta\phi\Delta\theta$$

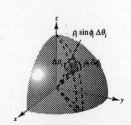

Section 13.8   Change of Variables: Jacobians

2. $x = au + bv$

$y = cu + dv$

$\dfrac{\partial x}{\partial u}\dfrac{\partial y}{\partial v} - \dfrac{\partial y}{\partial u}\dfrac{\partial x}{\partial v} = ad - cb$

4. $x = uv - 2u$

$y = uv$

$\dfrac{\partial x}{\partial u}\dfrac{\partial y}{\partial v} - \dfrac{\partial y}{\partial u}\dfrac{\partial x}{\partial v} = (v - 2)u - vu = -2u$

6. $x = u + a$

$y = v + a$

$\dfrac{\partial x}{\partial u}\dfrac{\partial y}{\partial v} - \dfrac{\partial y}{\partial u}\dfrac{\partial x}{\partial v} = (1)(1) - (0)(0) = 1$

8. $x = \dfrac{u}{v}$

$y = u + v$

$\dfrac{\partial x}{\partial u}\dfrac{\partial y}{\partial v} - \dfrac{\partial y}{\partial u}\dfrac{\partial x}{\partial v} = \left(\dfrac{1}{v}\right)(1) - (1)\left(-\dfrac{u}{v^2}\right) = \dfrac{1}{v} + \dfrac{u}{v^2} = \dfrac{u + v}{v^2}$

10. $x = \dfrac{1}{3}(4u - v)$

$y = \dfrac{1}{3}(u - v)$

$u = x - y$

$v = x - 4y$

(x, y)	(u, v)
$(0, 0)$	$(0, 0)$
$(4, 1)$	$(3, 0)$
$(2, 2)$	$(0, -6)$
$(6, 3)$	$(3, -6)$

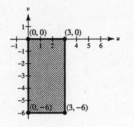

12. $x = \dfrac{1}{2}(u + v), \qquad u = x - y$

$y = -\dfrac{1}{2}(u - v), \qquad v = x + y$

$\dfrac{\partial x}{\partial u}\dfrac{\partial y}{\partial v} - \dfrac{\partial y}{\partial u}\dfrac{\partial x}{\partial v} = \dfrac{1}{2}\left(\dfrac{1}{2}\right) - \left(-\dfrac{1}{2}\right)\left(\dfrac{1}{2}\right) = \dfrac{1}{2}$

(x, y)	(u, v)
$(0, 1)$	$(-1, 1)$
$(2, 1)$	$(1, 3)$
$(1, 2)$	$(-1, 3)$
$(1, 0)$	$(1, 1)$

$\displaystyle\int_R\!\!\int 60xy\, dA$

$\displaystyle = \int_{-1}^{1}\int_{1}^{3} 60\left(\dfrac{1}{2}(u + v)\right)\left(-\dfrac{1}{2}(u - v)\right)\left(\dfrac{1}{2}\right) dv\, du$

$\displaystyle = \int_{-1}^{1}\int_{1}^{3} -\dfrac{15}{2}(v^2 - u^2)\, dv\, du$

$\displaystyle = \int_{-1}^{1}\left[-\dfrac{15}{2}\left(\dfrac{v^3}{3} - u^2v\right)\right]_{1}^{3} du$

$\displaystyle = \int_{-1}^{1}\dfrac{15}{2}\left(2u^2 - \dfrac{26}{3}\right) du$

$\displaystyle = \left[\dfrac{15}{2}\left(\dfrac{2}{3}u^3 - \dfrac{26}{3}u\right)\right]_{-1}^{1}$

$\displaystyle = 15\left(\dfrac{2}{3} - \dfrac{26}{3}\right) = -120$

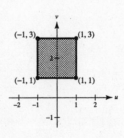

14. $x = \dfrac{1}{2}(u + v)$

$y = \dfrac{1}{2}(u - v)$

$\dfrac{\partial x}{\partial u}\dfrac{\partial y}{\partial v} - \dfrac{\partial y}{\partial u}\dfrac{\partial x}{\partial v} = -\dfrac{1}{2}$

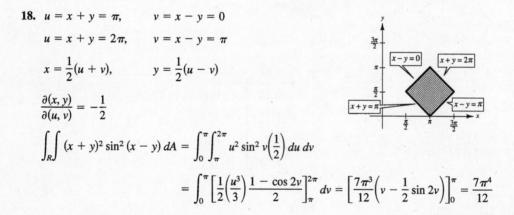

$\displaystyle\int_R\!\!\int 4(x + y)e^{x-y}\,dA = \int_0^2 \int_{u-2}^0 4ue^v\left(\dfrac{1}{2}\right) dv\,du$

$\displaystyle = \int_0^2 2u(1 - e^{u-2})\,du = 2\left[\dfrac{u^2}{2} - ue^{u-2} + e^{u-2}\right]_0^2 = 2(1 - e^{-2})$

16. $x = \dfrac{u}{v}$

$y = v$

$\dfrac{\partial x}{\partial u}\dfrac{\partial y}{\partial v} - \dfrac{\partial y}{\partial u}\dfrac{\partial x}{\partial v} = \dfrac{1}{v}$

$\displaystyle\int_R\!\!\int y\sin xy\,dA = \int_1^4 \int_1^4 v(\sin u)\dfrac{1}{v}\,dv\,du = \int_1^4 3\sin u\,du = \left[-3\cos u\right]_1^4 = 3(\cos 1 - \cos 4) \approx 3.5818$

18. $u = x + y = \pi, \qquad v = x - y = 0$

$u = x + y = 2\pi, \qquad v = x - y = \pi$

$x = \dfrac{1}{2}(u + v), \qquad y = \dfrac{1}{2}(u - v)$

$\dfrac{\partial(x, y)}{\partial(u, v)} = -\dfrac{1}{2}$

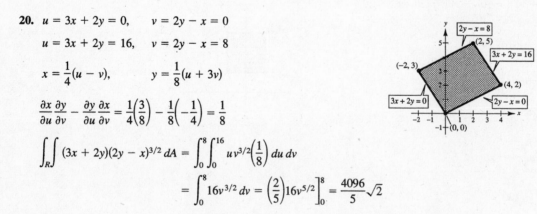

$\displaystyle\int_R\!\!\int (x + y)^2 \sin^2(x - y)\,dA = \int_0^\pi \int_\pi^{2\pi} u^2 \sin^2 v\left(\dfrac{1}{2}\right) du\,dv$

$\displaystyle = \int_0^\pi \left[\dfrac{1}{2}\left(\dfrac{u^3}{3}\right)\dfrac{1 - \cos 2v}{2}\right]_\pi^{2\pi} dv = \left[\dfrac{7\pi^3}{12}\left(v - \dfrac{1}{2}\sin 2v\right)\right]_0^\pi = \dfrac{7\pi^4}{12}$

20. $u = 3x + 2y = 0, \qquad v = 2y - x = 0$

$u = 3x + 2y = 16, \qquad v = 2y - x = 8$

$x = \dfrac{1}{4}(u - v), \qquad y = \dfrac{1}{8}(u + 3v)$

$\dfrac{\partial x}{\partial u}\dfrac{\partial y}{\partial v} - \dfrac{\partial y}{\partial u}\dfrac{\partial x}{\partial v} = \dfrac{1}{4}\left(\dfrac{3}{8}\right) - \dfrac{1}{8}\left(-\dfrac{1}{4}\right) = \dfrac{1}{8}$

$\displaystyle\int_R\!\!\int (3x + 2y)(2y - x)^{3/2}\,dA = \int_0^8 \int_0^{16} uv^{3/2}\left(\dfrac{1}{8}\right) du\,dv$

$\displaystyle = \int_0^8 16v^{3/2}\,dv = \left(\dfrac{2}{5}\right)16v^{5/2}\Big]_0^8 = \dfrac{4096}{5}\sqrt{2}$

22. $u = x = 1,$ $\qquad v = xy = 1$

$u = x = 4,$ $\qquad v = xy = 4$

$x = u,$ $\qquad\qquad y = \dfrac{v}{u}$

$\dfrac{\partial x}{\partial u}\dfrac{\partial y}{\partial v} - \dfrac{\partial y}{\partial u}\dfrac{\partial x}{\partial v} = \dfrac{1}{u}$

$\displaystyle\iint_R \frac{xy}{1 + x^2y^2}\, dA = \int_1^4\int_1^4 \frac{v}{1 + v^2}\left(\frac{1}{u}\right) dv\, du$

$\displaystyle\qquad = \int_1^4\left[\frac{1}{2}\ln(1 + v^2)\right]_1^4 \frac{1}{u}\, du = \left[\frac{1}{2}[\ln 17 - \ln 2]\ln u\right]_1^4 = \frac{1}{2}\left(\ln\frac{17}{2}\right)(\ln 4)$

24. (a) $f(x, y) = 16 - x^2 - y^2$

$R: \dfrac{x^2}{16} + \dfrac{y^2}{9} \le 1$

$V = \displaystyle\iint_R f(x, y)\, dA$

Let $x = 4u$ and $y = 3v$.

$\displaystyle\iint_R (16 - x^2 - y^2)\, dA = \int_{-1}^1\int_{-\sqrt{1-u^2}}^{\sqrt{1-u^2}} (16 - 16u^2 - 9v^2)\, 12dv\, du \qquad$ (Let $u = r\cos\theta$, $v = r\sin\theta$.)

$\displaystyle\qquad = \int_0^{2\pi}\int_0^1 (16 - 16r^2\cos^2\theta - 9r^2\sin^2\theta)\, 12r\, dr\, d\theta$

$\displaystyle\qquad = 12\int_0^{2\pi}\left[8r^2 - 4r^4\cos^2\theta - \frac{9}{4}r^4\sin^2\theta\right]_0^1 d\theta = 12\int_0^{2\pi}\left[8 - 4\cos^2\theta - \frac{9}{4}\sin^2\theta\right]d\theta$

$\displaystyle\qquad = 12\int_0^{2\pi}\left[8 - 4\left(\frac{1 + \cos 2\theta}{2}\right) - \frac{9}{4}\left(\frac{1 - \cos 2\theta}{2}\right)\right]d\theta = 12\int_0^{2\pi}\left[\frac{39}{8} - \frac{7}{8}\cos 2\theta\right]d\theta$

$\displaystyle\qquad = 12\left[\frac{39}{8}\theta - \frac{7}{16}\sin 2\theta\right]_0^{2\pi} = 12\left[\frac{39\pi}{4}\right] = 117\pi$

(b) $f(x, y) = A\cos\left[\dfrac{\pi}{2}\sqrt{\dfrac{x^2}{a^2} + \dfrac{y^2}{b^2}}\right]$

$R: \dfrac{x^2}{a^2} + \dfrac{y^2}{b^2} \le 1$

Let $x = au$ and $y = bv$.

$\displaystyle\iint_R f(x, y)\, dA = \int_{-1}^1\int_{-\sqrt{1-u^2}}^{\sqrt{1-u^2}} A\cos\left[\frac{\pi}{2}\sqrt{u^2 + v^2}\right] ab\, dv\, du$

Let $u = r\cos\theta$, $v = r\sin\theta$.

$\displaystyle Aab\int_0^{2\pi}\int_0^1 \cos\left[\frac{\pi}{2}r\right]r\, dr\, d\theta = Aab\left[\frac{2r}{\pi}\sin\left(\frac{\pi r}{2}\right) + \frac{4}{\pi^2}\cos\left(\frac{\pi r}{2}\right)\right]_0^1 (2\pi)$

$\displaystyle\qquad\qquad = 2\pi Aab\left[\left(\frac{2}{\pi} + 0\right) - \left(0 + \frac{4}{\pi^2}\right)\right] = \frac{4(\pi - 2)Aab}{\pi}$

26. See Theorem 13.5.

28. $x = 4u - v$, $y = 4v - w$, $z = u + w$

$$\frac{\partial(x, y, z)}{\partial(u, v, w)} = \begin{vmatrix} 4 & -1 & 0 \\ 0 & 4 & -1 \\ 1 & 0 & 1 \end{vmatrix} = 17$$

30. $x = r\cos\theta$, $y = r\sin\theta$, $z = z$

$$\frac{\partial(x, y, z)}{\partial(r, \theta, z)} = \begin{vmatrix} \cos\theta & -r\sin\theta & 0 \\ \sin\theta & r\cos\theta & 0 \\ 0 & 0 & 1 \end{vmatrix} = 1[r\cos^2\theta + r\sin^2\theta] = r$$

Review Exercises for Chapter 13

2. $\displaystyle\int_y^{2y} (x^2 + y^2)\, dx = \left[\frac{x^3}{3} + xy^2\right]_y^{2y} = \frac{10y^3}{3}$

4. $\displaystyle\int_0^2 \int_{x^2}^{2x} (x^2 + 2y)\, dy\, dx = \int_0^2 \left[x^2 y + y^2\right]_{x^2}^{2x} dx = \int_0^2 (4x^2 + 2x^3 - 2x^4)\, dx = \left[\frac{4}{3}x^3 + \frac{1}{2}x^4 - \frac{2}{5}x^5\right]_0^2 = \frac{88}{15}$

6. $\displaystyle\int_0^{\sqrt{3}} \int_{2-\sqrt{4-y^2}}^{2+\sqrt{4-y^2}} dx\, dy = 2\int_0^{\sqrt{3}} \sqrt{4 - y^2}\, dy = \left[y\sqrt{4 - y^2} + 4\arcsin\frac{y}{2}\right]_0^{\sqrt{3}} = \sqrt{3} + \frac{4\pi}{3}$

8. $\displaystyle\int_0^2 \int_0^x dy\, dx + \int_2^3 \int_0^{6-2x} dy\, dx = \int_0^2 \int_y^{(6-y)/2} dx\, dy$

$$A = \int_0^2 \int_y^{(6-y)/2} dx\, dy$$

$$= \frac{1}{2}\int_0^2 (6 - 3y)\, dy = \left[\frac{1}{2}\left(6y - \frac{3}{2}y^2\right)\right]_0^2 = 3$$

10. $\displaystyle\int_0^4 \int_{x^2-2x}^{6x-x^2} dy\, dx = \int_{-1}^0 \int_{1-\sqrt{1+y}}^{1+\sqrt{1+y}} dy\, dx + \int_0^8 \int_{3-\sqrt{9-y}}^{1+\sqrt{1+y}} dx\, dy + \int_8^9 \int_{3-\sqrt{9-y}}^{3+\sqrt{9-y}} dx\, dy$

$$A = \int_0^4 \int_{x^2-2x}^{6x-x^2} dy\, dx = \int_0^4 (8x - 2x^2)\, dx = \left[4x^2 - \frac{2}{3}x^3\right]_0^4 = \frac{64}{3}$$

12. $A = \displaystyle\int_0^2 \int_0^{y^2+1} dx\, dy = \int_0^1 \int_0^2 dy\, dx + \int_1^5 \int_{\sqrt{x-1}}^2 dy\, dx = \frac{14}{3}$

14. $A = \displaystyle\int_0^3 \int_{-y}^{2y-y^2} dx\, dy = \int_{-3}^0 \int_{-x}^{1+\sqrt{1-x}} dy\, dx + \int_0^1 \int_{1-\sqrt{1-x}}^{1+\sqrt{1-x}} dy\, dx = \frac{9}{2}$

16. Both integrations are over the common region R shown in the figure. Analytically,

$$\int_0^2 \int_{3y/2}^{5-y} e^{x+y}\, dx\, dy = \frac{2}{5} + \frac{8}{5}e^5$$

$$\int_0^3 \int_0^{2x/3} e^{x+y}\, dy\, dx + \int_3^5 \int_0^{5-x} e^{x+y}\, dy\, dx = \left(\frac{3}{5}e^5 - e^3 + \frac{2}{5}\right) + (e^5 + e^3) = \frac{8}{5}e^5 + \frac{2}{5}$$

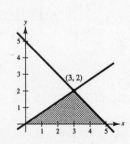

18. $V = \int_0^3 \int_0^x (x + y)\, dy\, dx$

$$= \int_0^3 \left[xy + \frac{1}{2}y^2 \right]_0^x dx$$

$$= \frac{3}{2}\int_0^3 x^2\, dx$$

$$= \left[\frac{1}{2}x^3 \right]_0^3 = \frac{27}{2}$$

20. Matches (c)

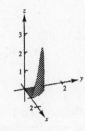

22. $\int_0^1 \int_0^x kxy\, dy\, dx = \int_0^1 \left[\frac{kxy^2}{2} \right]_0^x dx$

$$= \int_0^1 \frac{kx^3}{2}\, dx$$

$$= \left[\frac{kx^4}{8} \right]_0^1 = \frac{k}{8}$$

Since $k/8 = 1$, we have $k = 8$.

$$P = \int_0^{0.5} \int_0^{0.25} 8xy\, dy\, dx = 0.03125$$

24. False, $\int_0^1 \int_0^1 x\, dy\, dx \neq \int_1^2 \int_1^2 x\, dy\, dx$

26. True, $\int_0^1 \int_0^1 \dfrac{1}{1 + x^2 + y^2}\, dx\, dy < \int_0^1 \int_0^1 \dfrac{1}{1 + x^2}\, dx\, dy = \dfrac{\pi}{4}$

28. $\int_0^4 \int_0^{\sqrt{16-y^2}} (x^2 + y^2)\, dx\, dy = \int_0^{\pi/2} \int_0^4 r^3\, dr\, d\theta = \int_0^{\pi/2} \left[\dfrac{r^4}{4} \right]_0^4 d\theta = \int_0^{\pi/2} 64\, d\theta = 32\pi$

30. $V = 8 \int_0^{\pi/2} \int_b^R \sqrt{R^2 - r^2}\, r\, dr\, d\theta$

$$= -\frac{8}{3}\int_0^{\pi/2} \left[(R^2 - r^2)^{3/2} \right]_b^R d\theta$$

$$= \frac{8}{3}(R^2 - b^2)^{3/2} \int_0^{\pi/2} d\theta$$

$$= \frac{4}{3}\pi(R^2 - b^2)^{3/2}$$

32. $\tan\theta = \dfrac{12\sqrt{13}}{8\sqrt{13}} = \dfrac{3}{2} \implies \theta \approx 0.9828$

The polar region is given by $0 \le r \le 4$ and $0 \le \theta \le 0.9828$. Hence,

$$\int_0^{\arctan(3/2)} \int_0^4 (r\cos\theta)(r\sin\theta)r\, dr\, d\theta = \frac{288}{13}$$

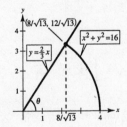

34. $m = k \int_0^L \int_0^{(h/2)[2-(x/L)-(x^2/L^2)]} dy \, dx = \frac{kh}{2} \int_0^L \left(2 - \frac{x}{L} - \frac{x^2}{L^2}\right) dx = \frac{7khL}{12}$

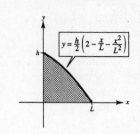

$y = \frac{h}{2}\left(2 - \frac{x}{L} - \frac{x^2}{L^2}\right)$

$M_x = k \int_0^L \int_0^{(h/2)[2-(x/L)-(x^2/L^2)]} y \, dy \, dx$

$= \frac{kh^2}{8} \int_0^L \left(2 - \frac{x}{L} - \frac{x^2}{L^2}\right)^2 dx$

$= \frac{kh^2}{8} \int_0^L \left[4 - \frac{4x}{L} - \frac{3x^2}{L^2} + \frac{2x^3}{L^3} + \frac{x^4}{L^4}\right] dx$

$= \frac{kh^2}{8} \left[4x - \frac{2x^2}{L} - \frac{x^3}{L^2} + \frac{x^4}{2L^3} + \frac{x^5}{5L^4}\right]_0^L = \frac{kh^2}{8} \cdot \frac{17L}{10} = \frac{17kh^2L}{80}$

$M_y = k \int_0^L \int_0^{(h/2)[2-(x/L)-(x^2/L^2)]} x \, dy \, dx$

$= \frac{kh}{2} \int_0^L \left(2x - \frac{x^2}{L} - \frac{x^3}{L^2}\right) dx = \frac{kh}{2} \left[x^2 - \frac{x^3}{3L} - \frac{x^4}{4L^2}\right]_0^L = \frac{kh}{2} \cdot \frac{5L^2}{12} = \frac{5khL^2}{24}$

$\bar{x} = \frac{M_y}{m} = \frac{5khL^2}{24} \cdot \frac{12}{7khL} = \frac{5L}{14}$

$\bar{y} = \frac{M_x}{m} = \frac{17kh^2L}{80} \cdot \frac{12}{7khL} = \frac{51h}{140}$

36. $I_x = \int_R \int y^2 \rho(x, y) \, dA = \int_0^2 \int_0^{4-x^2} ky^3 \, dy \, dx = \frac{16{,}384}{315}k$

$I_y = \int_R \int x^2 \rho(x, y) \, dA = \int_0^2 \int_0^{4-x^2} kx^2y \, dy \, dx = \frac{512}{105}k$

$I_0 = I_x + I_y = \frac{16{,}384k}{315} + \frac{512k}{105} = \frac{17{,}920}{315}k = \frac{512}{9}k$

$m = \int_R \int \rho(x, y) \, dA = \int_0^2 \int_0^{4-x^2} ky \, dy \, dx = \frac{128}{15}k$

$\bar{\bar{x}} = \sqrt{\frac{I_y}{m}} = \sqrt{\frac{512k/105}{128k/15}} = \sqrt{\frac{4}{7}}$

$\bar{\bar{y}} = \sqrt{\frac{I_x}{m}} = \sqrt{\frac{16{,}384k/315}{128k/15}} = \sqrt{\frac{128}{21}}$

38. $f(x, y) = 16 - x - y^2$

$R = \{(x, y) : 0 \leq x \leq 2, \ 0 \leq y \leq x\}$

$f_x = -1, f_y = -2y$

$\sqrt{1 + (f_x)^2 + (f_y)^2} = \sqrt{2 + 4y^2}$

$S = \int_0^2 \int_y^2 \sqrt{2 + 4y^2} \, dx \, dy = \int_0^2 \left[2\sqrt{2 + 4y^2} - y\sqrt{2 + 4y^2}\right] dy$

$= \left[\frac{1}{2}\left(2y\sqrt{2 + 4y^2} + 2\ln\left|2y + \sqrt{2 + 4y^2}\right|\right) - \frac{1}{12}(2 + 4y^2)^{3/2}\right]_0^2$

$= \left[\frac{1}{2}\left(4\sqrt{18} + 2\ln\left|4 + \sqrt{18}\right|\right) - \frac{1}{12}(18\sqrt{18})\right] - \left[\ln\sqrt{2} - \frac{2\sqrt{2}}{12}\right]$

$= 6\sqrt{2} + \ln\left|4 + 3\sqrt{2}\right| - \frac{9\sqrt{2}}{2} - \ln\sqrt{2} + \frac{\sqrt{2}}{6} = \frac{5\sqrt{2}}{3} + \ln\left|2\sqrt{2} + 3\right|$

40. (a) Graph of

$$f(x, y) = z$$

$$= 25\left[1 + e^{-(x^2+y^2)/1000} \cos^2\left(\frac{x^2+y^2}{1000}\right)\right]$$

over region R

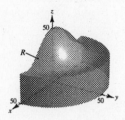

(b) Surface area $= \displaystyle\int_R\!\!\int \sqrt{1 + f_x(x, y)^2 + f_y(x, y)^2}\, dA$

Using a symbolic computer program, you obtain surface area $\approx 4{,}540$ sq. ft.

42. $\displaystyle\int_{-2}^{2}\int_{-\sqrt{4-x^2}}^{\sqrt{4-x^2}}\int_{0}^{(x^2+y^2)/2} (x^2+y^2)\, dz\, dy\, dx = \int_{0}^{2\pi}\int_{0}^{2}\int_{0}^{r^2/2} r^3\, dz\, dr\, d\theta = \frac{1}{2}\int_{0}^{2\pi}\int_{0}^{2} r^5\, dr\, d\theta = \frac{16}{3}\int_{0}^{2\pi} d\theta = \frac{32\pi}{3}$

44. $\displaystyle\int_{0}^{5}\int_{0}^{\sqrt{25-x^2}}\int_{0}^{\sqrt{25-x^2-y^2}} \frac{1}{1+x^2+y^2+z^2}\, dz\, dy\, dx = \int_{0}^{\pi/2}\int_{0}^{\pi/2}\int_{0}^{5} \frac{\rho^2}{1+\rho^2}\sin\phi\, d\rho\, d\phi\, d\theta$

$$= \int_{0}^{\pi/2}\int_{0}^{\pi/2}\Big[\rho - \arctan\rho\Big]_{0}^{5} \sin\phi\, d\phi\, d\theta$$

$$= \int_{0}^{\pi/2}\Big[(5 - \arctan 5)(-\cos\phi)\Big]_{0}^{\pi/2} d\theta = \frac{\pi}{2}(5 - \arctan 5)$$

46. $\displaystyle\int_{0}^{2}\int_{0}^{\sqrt{4-x^2}}\int_{0}^{\sqrt{4-x^2-y^2}} xyz\, dz\, dy\, dx = \frac{4}{3}$

48. $V = 2\displaystyle\int_{0}^{\pi/2}\int_{0}^{2\sin\theta}\int_{0}^{16-r^2} r\, dz\, dr\, d\theta = 2\int_{0}^{\pi/2}\int_{0}^{2\sin\theta} r(16-r^2)\, dr\, d\theta$

$$= 2\int_{0}^{\pi/2} (32\sin^2\theta - 4\sin^4\theta)\, d\theta = 8\int_{0}^{\pi/2} (8\sin^2\theta - \sin^4\theta)\, d\theta$$

$$= 8\left[4\theta - 2\sin 2\theta + \frac{1}{4}\sin^3\theta\cos\theta - \frac{3}{4}\left(\frac{1}{2}\theta - \frac{1}{4}\sin 2\theta\right)\right]_{0}^{\pi/2} = \frac{29\pi}{2}$$

50. $m = 2k\displaystyle\int_{0}^{\pi/2}\int_{0}^{a}\int_{0}^{cr\sin\theta} r\, dz\, dr\, d\theta = 2kc\int_{0}^{\pi/2}\int_{0}^{a} r^2\sin\theta\, dr\, d\theta = \frac{2}{3}kca^3\int_{0}^{\pi/2}\sin\theta\, d\theta = \frac{2}{3}kca^3$

$M_{xz} = 2k\displaystyle\int_{0}^{\pi/2}\int_{0}^{a}\int_{0}^{cr\sin\theta} r^2\sin\theta\, dz\, dr\, d\theta = 2kc\int_{0}^{\pi/2}\int_{0}^{a} r^3\sin^2\theta\, dr\, d\theta = \frac{1}{2}kca^4\int_{0}^{\pi/2}\sin^2\theta\, d\theta = \frac{1}{8}\pi kca^4$

$M_{xy} = 2k\displaystyle\int_{0}^{\pi/2}\int_{0}^{a}\int_{0}^{cr\sin\theta} rz\, dz\, dr\, d\theta = kc^2\int_{0}^{\pi/2}\int_{0}^{a} r^3\sin^2\theta\, dr\, d\theta = \frac{1}{4}kc^2a^4\int_{0}^{\pi/2}\sin^2\theta\, d\theta = \frac{1}{16}\pi kc^2a^4$

$\bar{x} = 0$

$\bar{y} = \dfrac{M_{xz}}{m} = \dfrac{\pi kca^4/8}{2kca^3/3} = \dfrac{3\pi a}{16}$

$\bar{z} = \dfrac{M_{xy}}{m} = \dfrac{\pi kc^2a^4/16}{2kca^3/3} = \dfrac{3\pi ca}{32}$

52. $m = \dfrac{500\pi}{3} - \displaystyle\int_0^3 \int_0^{2\pi} \int_4^{\sqrt{25-r^2}} r \, dz \, d\theta \, dr = \dfrac{500\pi}{3} - \displaystyle\int_0^3 \int_0^{2\pi} \left(r\sqrt{25 - r^2} - 4r \right) d\theta \, dr$

$\qquad = \dfrac{500\pi}{3} - 2\pi \left[-\dfrac{1}{3}(25 - r^2)^{3/2} - 2r^2 \right]_0^3 = \dfrac{500\pi}{3} - 2\pi \left[-\dfrac{64}{3} - 18 + \dfrac{125}{3} \right] = \dfrac{500\pi}{3} - \dfrac{14\pi}{3} = 162\pi$

$\qquad \bar{x} = \bar{y} = 0 \quad$ by symmetry

$\qquad M_{xy} = \displaystyle\int_0^{2\pi} \int_0^3 \int_{-\sqrt{25-r^2}}^4 zr \, dz \, dr \, d\theta + \displaystyle\int_0^{2\pi} \int_3^5 \int_{-\sqrt{25-r^2}}^{\sqrt{25-r^2}} zr \, dz \, dr \, d\theta = \displaystyle\int_0^{2\pi} \int_0^3 \left[8 - \dfrac{1}{2}(25 - r^2) \right] r \, dr \, d\theta + 0$

$\qquad = \displaystyle\int_0^{2\pi} \int_0^3 \left[\dfrac{1}{2}r^3 - \dfrac{9}{2}r \right] dr \, d\theta = \displaystyle\int_0^{2\pi} \left[\dfrac{1}{8}r^4 - \dfrac{9}{4}r^2 \right]_0^3 d\theta = \left[-\dfrac{81}{8}\theta \right]_0^{2\pi} = -\dfrac{81}{4}\pi$

$\qquad \bar{z} = \dfrac{M_{xy}}{m} = -\dfrac{81\pi}{4} \dfrac{1}{162\pi} = -\dfrac{1}{8}$

54. $I_z = k \displaystyle\int_0^{\pi} \int_0^{2\pi} \int_0^a \rho^2 \sin^2 \phi \, (\rho) \rho^2 \sin \phi \, d\rho \, d\theta \, d\phi$

$\qquad = \dfrac{4k\pi a^6}{9}$

56. $x^2 + y^2 + \dfrac{z^2}{a^2} = 1$

$\qquad I_z = \displaystyle\iiint_Q (x^2 + y^2) \, dV$

$\qquad = \displaystyle\int_{-a}^a \int_{-\sqrt{1-z^2-a^2}}^{\sqrt{1-z^2-a^2}} \int_{-\sqrt{1-y^2-z^2-a^2}}^{\sqrt{1-y^2-z^2-a^2}} (x^2 + y^2) \, dx \, dy \, dz$

$\qquad = \dfrac{8}{15}\pi a$

58. $\displaystyle\int_0^{\pi} \int_0^2 \int_0^{1+r^2} r \, dz \, dr \, d\theta$

Since $z = 1 + r^2$ represents a paraboloid with vertex $(0, 0, 1)$, this integral represents the volume of the solid below the paraboloid and above the semi-circle $y = \sqrt{4 - x^2}$ in the xy-plane.

60. $\dfrac{\partial(x, y)}{\partial(u, v)} = \dfrac{\partial x}{\partial u} \dfrac{\partial y}{\partial v} - \dfrac{\partial y}{\partial u} \dfrac{\partial x}{\partial v}$

$\qquad = (2u)(-2v) - (2u)(2v) = -8uv$

62. $\dfrac{\partial(x, y)}{\partial(u, v)} = \dfrac{\partial x}{\partial u} \dfrac{\partial y}{\partial v} - \dfrac{\partial x}{\partial v} \dfrac{\partial y}{\partial u} = 1\left(\dfrac{1}{u} \right) - 0 = \dfrac{1}{u}$

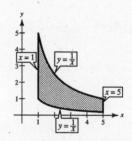

$x = u, y = \dfrac{v}{u} \implies u = x, v = xy$

Boundary in xy-plane	Boundary in uv-plane
$x = 1$	$u = 1$
$x = 5$	$u = 5$
$xy = 1$	$v = 1$
$xy = 5$	$v = 5$

$\displaystyle\iint_R \dfrac{x}{1 + x^2 y^2} \, dA = \displaystyle\int_1^5 \int_1^5 \dfrac{u}{1 + u^2(v/u)^2} \left(\dfrac{1}{u} \right) du \, dv = \displaystyle\int_1^5 \int_1^5 \dfrac{1}{1 + v^2} \, du \, dv = \displaystyle\int_1^5 \dfrac{4}{1 + v^2} \, dv$

$\qquad = 4 \arctan v \Big]_1^5 = 4 \arctan 5 - \pi$

Problem Solving for Chapter 13

2. $z = \dfrac{1}{c}(d - ax - by)$ Plane

$f_x = -\dfrac{a}{c},\ f_y = -\dfrac{b}{c}$

$\sqrt{1 + f_x^2 + f_y^2} = \sqrt{1 + \dfrac{a^2}{c^2} + \dfrac{b^2}{c^2}}$

$S = \displaystyle\int\!\!\!\int_R \sqrt{1 + \dfrac{a^2}{c^2} + \dfrac{b^2}{c^2}}\, dA$

$ = \dfrac{\sqrt{a^2 + b^2 + c^2}}{c}\displaystyle\int\!\!\!\int_R dA$

$ = \dfrac{\sqrt{a^2 + b^2 + c^2}}{c}\, A(R)$

6. (a) $V = \displaystyle\int_0^{2\pi}\!\!\int_0^2\!\!\int_2^{\sqrt{8-r^2}} r\, dz\, dr\, d\theta = \dfrac{8\pi}{3}\left(4\sqrt{2} - 5\right)$

   (b) $V = \displaystyle\int_0^{2\pi}\!\!\int_0^{\pi/4}\!\!\int_{2\sec\phi}^{2\sqrt{2}} \rho^2 \sin\phi\, d\rho\, d\phi\, d\theta = \dfrac{8\pi}{3}\left(4\sqrt{2} - 5\right)$

8. Volume $\approx [5 + 6 + 5 + 5]4 = 84\ \text{m}^3$

10. Let $v = \ln\!\left(\dfrac{1}{x}\right),\ dv = -\dfrac{dx}{x}$.

$e^v = \dfrac{1}{x},\ x = e^{-v},\ dx = -e^{-v}\, dv$

$\displaystyle\int_0^1 \sqrt{\ln(1/x)}\, dx = \int_\infty^0 \sqrt{v}\,(-e^{-v})\, dv = \int_0^\infty \sqrt{v}\, e^{-v}\, dv$

Let $u = \sqrt{v},\ u^2 = v,\ 2u\, du = dv$.

$\displaystyle\int_0^1 \sqrt{\ln(1/x)}\, dx = \int_0^\infty u\, e^{-u^2}(2u\, du) = 2\int_0^\infty u^2 e^{-u^2}\, du = 2\!\left(\dfrac{\sqrt{\pi}}{4}\right) = \dfrac{\sqrt{\pi}}{2}$ (PS #9)

12. Essay

4. $A:\ \displaystyle\int_0^{2\pi}\!\!\int_4^5 \left(\dfrac{r}{16} - \dfrac{r^2}{160}\right) r\, dr\, d\theta = \dfrac{1333\pi}{960} \approx 4.36\ \text{ft}^3$

$B = \displaystyle\int_0^{2\pi}\!\!\int_9^{10} \left(\dfrac{r}{16} - \dfrac{r^2}{160}\right) r\, dr\, d\theta = \dfrac{523\pi}{960} \approx 1.71\ \text{ft}^3$

The distribution is not uniform. Less water in region of greater area.

In one hour, the entire lawn receives

$\displaystyle\int_0^{2\pi}\!\!\int_0^{10} \left(\dfrac{r}{16} - \dfrac{r^2}{160}\right) r\, dr\, d\theta = \dfrac{125\pi}{12} \approx 32.72\ \text{ft}^3.$

14. The greater the angle between the given plane and the xy-plane, the greater the surface area. Hence:

$$z_2 < z_1 < z_4 < z_3$$

CHAPTER 14
Vector Analysis

CHAPTER 14
Vector Analysis

Section 14.1   Vector Fields

Solutions to Even-Numbered Exercises

2. All vectors are parallel to x-axis.

Matches (d)

4. Vectors are in rotational pattern.

Matches (e)

6. Vectors along x-axis have no x-component.

Matches (f)

8. $\mathbf{F}(x, y) = 2\mathbf{i}$

$\|\mathbf{F}\| = 2$

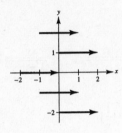

10. $\mathbf{F}(x, y) = x\mathbf{i} - y\mathbf{j}$

$\|\mathbf{F}\| = \sqrt{x^2 + y^2}$

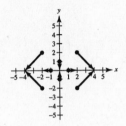

12. $\mathbf{F}(x, y) = x\mathbf{i}$

$\|\mathbf{F}\| = |x| = c$

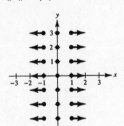

14. $\mathbf{F}(x, y) = (x^2 + y^2)\mathbf{i} + \mathbf{j}$

$\|\mathbf{F}\| = \sqrt{1 + (x^2 + y^2)^2}$

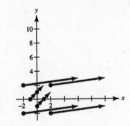

16. $\mathbf{F}(x, y, z) = x\mathbf{i} + y\mathbf{j} + z\mathbf{k}$

$\|\mathbf{F}\| = \sqrt{x^2 + y^2 + z^2} = c$

$x^2 + y^2 + z^2 = c^2$

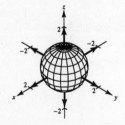

18. $\mathbf{F}(x, y) = (2y - 3x)\mathbf{i} + (2y + 3x)\mathbf{j}$

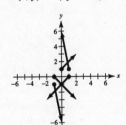

20. $\mathbf{F}(x, y, z) = x\mathbf{i} - y\mathbf{j} + z\mathbf{k}$

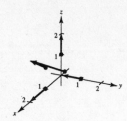

22. $f(x, y) = \sin 3x \cos 4y$

$f_x(x, y) = 3 \cos 3x \cos 4y$

$f_y(x, y) = -4 \sin 3x \sin 4y$

$\mathbf{F}(x, y) = 3 \cos 3x \cos 4y\mathbf{i} - 4 \sin 3x \sin 4y\mathbf{j}$

24. $f(x, y, z) = \dfrac{y}{z} + \dfrac{z}{x} - \dfrac{xz}{y}$

$f_x(x, y, z) = -\dfrac{z}{x^2} - \dfrac{z}{y}$

$f_y(x, y, z) = \dfrac{1}{z} + \dfrac{xz}{y^2}$

$f_z(x, y, z) = -\dfrac{y}{z^2} + \dfrac{1}{x} - \dfrac{x}{y}$

$\mathbf{F}(x, y, z) = \left(-\dfrac{z}{x^2} - \dfrac{z}{y}\right)\mathbf{i} + \left(\dfrac{1}{z} + \dfrac{xz}{y^2}\right)\mathbf{j} + \left(-\dfrac{y}{z^2} + \dfrac{1}{x} - \dfrac{x}{y}\right)\mathbf{k}$

26. $g(x, y, z) = x \arcsin yz$

$g_x(x, y, z) = \arcsin yz$

$g_y(x, y, z) = \dfrac{xz}{\sqrt{1 - y^2z^2}}$

$g_z(x, y, z) = \dfrac{xy}{\sqrt{1 - y^2z^2}}$

$\mathbf{G}(x, y, z) = (\arcsin yz)\mathbf{i} + \dfrac{xz}{\sqrt{1 - y^2z^2}}\mathbf{j} + \dfrac{xy}{\sqrt{1 - y^2z^2}}\mathbf{k}$

28. $\mathbf{F}(x, y) = \dfrac{1}{x^2}(y\mathbf{i} - x\mathbf{j}) = \dfrac{y}{x^2}\mathbf{i} - \dfrac{1}{x}\mathbf{j}$

$M = y/x^2$ and $N = -(1/x)$ have continuous first partial derivatives for all $x \neq 0$.

$\dfrac{\partial N}{\partial x} = \dfrac{1}{x^2} = \dfrac{\partial M}{\partial y} \implies \mathbf{F}$ is conservative.

30. $\mathbf{F}(x, y) = \dfrac{1}{xy}(y\mathbf{i} - x\mathbf{j}) = \dfrac{1}{x}\mathbf{i} - \dfrac{1}{y}\mathbf{j}$

$M = 1/x$ and $N = -1/y$ have continuous first partial derivatives for all $x, y \neq 0$.

$\dfrac{\partial N}{\partial x} = 0 = \dfrac{\partial M}{\partial y} \implies \mathbf{F}$ is conservative.

32. $M = \dfrac{x}{\sqrt{x^2 + y^2}}, N = \dfrac{y}{\sqrt{x^2 + y^2}}$

$\dfrac{\partial N}{\partial x} = + \dfrac{-xy}{(x^2 + y^2)^{3/2}} = \dfrac{\partial M}{\partial y} \implies$ Conservative

34. $M = \dfrac{y}{\sqrt{1 - x^2y^2}}, N = \dfrac{-x}{\sqrt{1 - x^2y^2}}$

$\dfrac{\partial N}{\partial x} = + \dfrac{-1}{(1 - x^2y^2)^{3/2}} \neq \dfrac{\partial M}{\partial y} = \dfrac{1}{(1 - x^2y^2)^{3/2}}$

$\implies$ Not conservative

36. $\mathbf{F}(x, y) = \dfrac{1}{y^2}(y\mathbf{i} - 2x\mathbf{j})$

$= \dfrac{1}{y}\mathbf{i} - \dfrac{2x}{y^2}\mathbf{j}$

$\dfrac{\partial}{\partial y}\left[\dfrac{1}{y}\right] = -\dfrac{1}{y^2}$

$\dfrac{\partial}{\partial x}\left[-\dfrac{2x}{y^2}\right] = -\dfrac{2}{y^2}$

Not conservative

38. $\mathbf{F}(x, y) = 3x^2y^2\mathbf{i} + 2x^3y\mathbf{j}$

$\dfrac{\partial}{\partial y}[3x^2y^2] = 6x^2y$

$\dfrac{\partial}{\partial x}[2x^3y] = 6x^2y$

Conservative

$f_x(x, y) = 3x^2y^2$

$f_y(x, y) = 2x^3y$

$f(x, y) = x^3y^2 + K$

40. $\mathbf{F}(x, y) = \dfrac{2y}{x}\mathbf{i} - \dfrac{x^2}{y^2}\mathbf{j}$

$\dfrac{\partial}{\partial y}\left[\dfrac{2y}{x}\right] = \dfrac{2}{x}$

$\dfrac{\partial}{\partial x}\left[-\dfrac{x^2}{y^2}\right] = -\dfrac{2x}{y^2}$

Not conservative

42. $F(x, y) = \dfrac{2x}{(x^2 + y^2)^2}\mathbf{i} + \dfrac{2y}{(x^2 + y^2)^2}\mathbf{j}$

$\dfrac{\partial}{\partial y}\left[\dfrac{2x}{(x^2 + y^2)^2}\right] = -\dfrac{8xy}{(x^2 + y^2)^3}$

$\dfrac{\partial}{\partial x}\left[\dfrac{2y}{(x^2 + y^2)^2}\right] = -\dfrac{8xy}{(x^2 + y^2)^3}$

Conservative

$f_x(x, y) = \dfrac{2x}{(x^2 + y^2)^2}$

$f_y(x, y) = \dfrac{2y}{(x^2 + y^2)^2}$

$f(x, y) = -\dfrac{1}{x^2 + y^2} + K$

44. $F(x, y, z) = x^2 z\mathbf{i} - 2xz\mathbf{j} + yz\mathbf{k}, \ (2, -1, 3)$

$\operatorname{curl} F = \begin{vmatrix} \mathbf{i} & \mathbf{j} & \mathbf{k} \\ \dfrac{\partial}{\partial x} & \dfrac{\partial}{\partial y} & \dfrac{\partial}{\partial z} \\ x^2 z & -2xz & yz \end{vmatrix}$

$= (z + 2x)\mathbf{i} - (0 - x^2)\mathbf{j} + (-2z - 0)\mathbf{k}$

$= (z + 2x)\mathbf{i} + x^2\mathbf{j} - 2z\mathbf{k}$

$\operatorname{curl} F\,(2, -1, 3) = 7\mathbf{i} + 4\mathbf{j} - 6\mathbf{k}$

46. $F(x, y, z) = e^{-xyz}(\mathbf{i} + \mathbf{j} + \mathbf{k}), \ (3, 2, 0)$

$\operatorname{curl} F = \begin{vmatrix} \mathbf{i} & \mathbf{j} & \mathbf{k} \\ \dfrac{\partial}{\partial x} & \dfrac{\partial}{\partial y} & \dfrac{\partial}{\partial z} \\ e^{-xyz} & e^{-xyz} & e^{-xyz} \end{vmatrix} = (-xz + xy)e^{-xyz}\mathbf{i} - (-yz + xy)e^{-xyz}\mathbf{j} + (-yz + xz)e^{-xyz}\mathbf{k}$

$\operatorname{curl} F\,(3, 2, 0) = 6\mathbf{i} - 6\mathbf{j}$

48. $F(x, y, z) = \dfrac{yz}{y - z}\mathbf{i} + \dfrac{xz}{x - z}\mathbf{j} + \dfrac{xy}{x - y}\mathbf{k}$

$\operatorname{curl} F = \begin{vmatrix} \mathbf{i} & \mathbf{j} & \mathbf{k} \\ \dfrac{\partial}{\partial x} & \dfrac{\partial}{\partial y} & \dfrac{\partial}{\partial z} \\ \dfrac{yz}{y - z} & \dfrac{xz}{x - z} & \dfrac{xy}{x - y} \end{vmatrix}$

$= \left[\dfrac{x^2}{(x - y)^2} - \dfrac{x^2}{(x - z)^2}\right]\mathbf{i} - \left[\dfrac{-y^2}{(x - y)^2} - \dfrac{y^2}{(y - z)^2}\right]\mathbf{j} + \left[\dfrac{-z^2}{(x - z)^2} - \dfrac{-z^2}{(y - z)^2}\right]\mathbf{k}$

$= x^2\left[\dfrac{1}{(x - y)^2} - \dfrac{1}{(x - z)^2}\right]\mathbf{i} + y^2\left[\dfrac{1}{(x - y)^2} + \dfrac{1}{(y - z)^2}\right]\mathbf{j} + z^2\left[\dfrac{1}{(y - z)^2} - \dfrac{1}{(x - z)^2}\right]\mathbf{k}$

50. $F(x, y, z) = \sqrt{x^2 + y^2 + z^2}(\mathbf{i} + \mathbf{j} + \mathbf{k})$

$\operatorname{curl} F = \begin{vmatrix} \mathbf{i} & \mathbf{j} & \mathbf{k} \\ \dfrac{\partial}{\partial x} & \dfrac{\partial}{\partial y} & \dfrac{\partial}{\partial z} \\ \sqrt{x^2 + y^2 + z^2} & \sqrt{x^2 + y^2 + z^2} & \sqrt{x^2 + y^2 + z^2} \end{vmatrix} = \dfrac{(y - z)\mathbf{i} + (z - x)\mathbf{j} + (x - y)\mathbf{k}}{\sqrt{x^2 + y^2 + z^2}}$

52. $F(x, y, z) = e^z(y\mathbf{i} + x\mathbf{j} + \mathbf{k})$

$\operatorname{curl} F = \begin{vmatrix} \mathbf{i} & \mathbf{j} & \mathbf{k} \\ \dfrac{\partial}{\partial x} & \dfrac{\partial}{\partial y} & \dfrac{\partial}{\partial z} \\ ye^z & xe^z & e^z \end{vmatrix} = -xe^z\mathbf{i} + ye^z\mathbf{j} \neq \mathbf{0}$

Not conservative

54. $F(x, y, z) = y^2 z^3\mathbf{i} + 2xyz^3\mathbf{j} + 3xy^2 z^2\mathbf{k}$

$\operatorname{curl} F = \begin{vmatrix} \mathbf{i} & \mathbf{j} & \mathbf{k} \\ \dfrac{\partial}{\partial x} & \dfrac{\partial}{\partial y} & \dfrac{\partial}{\partial z} \\ y^2 z^3 & 2xyz^3 & 3xy^2 z^2 \end{vmatrix} = \mathbf{0}$

Conservative

$f(x, y, z) = xy^2 z^3 + K$

56. $F(x, y, z) = \dfrac{x}{x^2 + y^2}\mathbf{i} + \dfrac{y}{x^2 + y^2}\mathbf{j} + \mathbf{k}$

$$\text{curl } F = \begin{vmatrix} \mathbf{i} & \mathbf{j} & \mathbf{k} \\ \dfrac{\partial}{\partial x} & \dfrac{\partial}{\partial y} & \dfrac{\partial}{\partial z} \\ \dfrac{x}{x^2 + y^2} & \dfrac{y}{x^2 + y^2} & 1 \end{vmatrix} = \mathbf{0}$$

Conservative

$$f_x(x, y, z) = \frac{x}{x^2 + y^2}$$

$$f_y(x, y, z) = \frac{y}{x^2 + y^2}$$

$$f_z(x, y, z) = 1$$

$$f(x, y, z) = \int \frac{x}{x^2 + y^2}\, dx$$

$$= \frac{1}{2}\ln(x^2 + y^2) + g(y, z) + K_1$$

$$f(x, y, z) = \int \frac{y}{x^2 + y^2}\, dy$$

$$= \frac{1}{2}\ln(x^2 + y^2) + h(x, z) + K_2$$

$$f(x, y, z) = \int dz = z + p(x, y) + K_3$$

$$f(x, y, z) = \frac{1}{2}\ln(x^2 + y^2) + z + K$$

58. $F(x, y) = xe^x\mathbf{i} + ye^y\mathbf{j}$

$$\text{div } F(x, y) = \frac{\partial}{\partial x}[xe^x] + \frac{\partial}{\partial y}[ye^y]$$

$$= xe^x + e^x + ye^y + e^y$$

$$= e^x(x + 1) + e^y(y + 1)$$

60. $F(x, y, z) = \ln(x^2 + y^2)\mathbf{i} + xy\mathbf{j} + \ln(y^2 + z^2)\mathbf{k}$

$$\text{div } F(x, y, z) = \frac{\partial}{\partial x}[\ln(x^2 + y^2)] + \frac{\partial}{\partial y}[xy] + \frac{\partial}{\partial z}[\ln(y^2 + z^2)] = \frac{2x}{x^2 + y^2} + x + \frac{2z}{y^2 + z^2}$$

62. $F(x, y, z) = x^2z\mathbf{i} - 2xz\mathbf{j} + yz\mathbf{k}$

$\text{div } F(x, y, z) = 2xz + y$

$\text{div } F(2, -1, 3) = 11$

64. $F(x, y, z) = \ln(xyz)(\mathbf{i} + \mathbf{j} + \mathbf{k})$

$\text{div } F(x, y, z) = \dfrac{1}{x} + \dfrac{1}{y} + \dfrac{1}{z}$

$\text{div } F(3, 2, 1) = \dfrac{1}{3} + \dfrac{1}{2} + 1 = \dfrac{11}{6}$

66. See the definition of Conservative Vector Field on page 1011. To test for a conservative vector field, see Theorem 14.1 and 14.2.

68. See the definition on page 1016.

70. $F(x, y, z) = x\mathbf{i} - z\mathbf{k}$

$G(x, y, z) = x^2\mathbf{i} + y\mathbf{j} + z^2\mathbf{k}$

$$F \times G = \begin{vmatrix} \mathbf{i} & \mathbf{j} & \mathbf{k} \\ x & 0 & -z \\ x^2 & y & z^2 \end{vmatrix} = yz\mathbf{i} - (xz^2 + x^2z)\mathbf{j} + xy\mathbf{k}$$

$$\text{curl}(F \times G) = \begin{vmatrix} \mathbf{i} & \mathbf{j} & \mathbf{k} \\ \dfrac{\partial}{\partial x} & \dfrac{\partial}{\partial y} & \dfrac{\partial}{\partial z} \\ yz & -xz^2 - x^2z & xy \end{vmatrix}$$

$$= (x + 2xz + x^2)\mathbf{i} - (y - y)\mathbf{j} + (-z^2 - 2xz - z)\mathbf{k}$$

$$= x(x + 2z + 1)\mathbf{i} - z(z + 2x + 1)\mathbf{k}$$

72. $\mathbf{F}(x, y, z) = x^2 z\mathbf{i} - 2xz\mathbf{j} + yz\mathbf{k}$

$$\text{curl } \mathbf{F} = \begin{vmatrix} \mathbf{i} & \mathbf{j} & \mathbf{k} \\ \dfrac{\partial}{\partial x} & \dfrac{\partial}{\partial y} & \dfrac{\partial}{\partial z} \\ x^2 z & -2xz & yz \end{vmatrix} = (z + 2x)\mathbf{i} + x^2\mathbf{j} - 2z\mathbf{k}$$

$$\text{curl(curl } \mathbf{F}) = \begin{vmatrix} \mathbf{i} & \mathbf{j} & \mathbf{k} \\ \dfrac{\partial}{\partial x} & \dfrac{\partial}{\partial y} & \dfrac{\partial}{\partial z} \\ z + 2x & x^2 & -2z \end{vmatrix} = \mathbf{j} + 2x\mathbf{k}$$

74. $\mathbf{F}(x, y, z) = x\mathbf{i} - z\mathbf{k}$

$\mathbf{G}(x, y, z) = x^2\mathbf{i} + y\mathbf{j} + z^2\mathbf{k}$

$$\mathbf{F} \times \mathbf{G} = \begin{vmatrix} \mathbf{i} & \mathbf{j} & \mathbf{k} \\ x & 0 & -z \\ x^2 & y & z^2 \end{vmatrix} = yz\mathbf{i} - (xz^2 + x^2 z)\mathbf{j} + xy\mathbf{k}$$

$$\text{div}(\mathbf{F} \times \mathbf{G}) = 0$$

76. $\mathbf{F}(x, y, z) = x^2 z\mathbf{i} - 2xz\mathbf{j} + yz\mathbf{k}$

$$\text{curl } \mathbf{F} = \begin{vmatrix} \mathbf{i} & \mathbf{j} & \mathbf{k} \\ \dfrac{\partial}{\partial x} & \dfrac{\partial}{\partial y} & \dfrac{\partial}{\partial z} \\ x^2 z & -2xz & yz \end{vmatrix} = (z + 2x)\mathbf{i} + x^2\mathbf{j} - 2z\mathbf{k}$$

$$\text{div(curl } \mathbf{F}) = 2 - 2 = 0$$

78. Let $f(x, y, z)$ be a scalar function whose second partial derivatives are continuous.

$$\nabla f = \frac{\partial f}{\partial x}\mathbf{i} + \frac{\partial f}{\partial y}\mathbf{j} + \frac{\partial f}{\partial z}\mathbf{k}$$

$$\text{curl}(\nabla f) = \begin{vmatrix} \mathbf{i} & \mathbf{j} & \mathbf{k} \\ \dfrac{\partial}{\partial x} & \dfrac{\partial}{\partial y} & \dfrac{\partial}{\partial z} \\ \dfrac{\partial f}{\partial x} & \dfrac{\partial f}{\partial y} & \dfrac{\partial f}{\partial z} \end{vmatrix} = \left(\frac{\partial^2 f}{\partial y \partial z} - \frac{\partial^2 f}{\partial z \partial y} \right)\mathbf{i} - \left(\frac{\partial^2 f}{\partial x \partial z} - \frac{\partial^2 f}{\partial z \partial x} \right)\mathbf{j} + \left(\frac{\partial^2 f}{\partial x \partial y} - \frac{\partial^2 f}{\partial y \partial x} \right)\mathbf{k} = \mathbf{0}$$

80. Let $\mathbf{F} = M\mathbf{i} + N\mathbf{j} + P\mathbf{k}$ and $\mathbf{G} = R\mathbf{i} + S\mathbf{j} + T\mathbf{k}$.

$$\mathbf{F} \times \mathbf{G} = \begin{vmatrix} \mathbf{i} & \mathbf{j} & \mathbf{k} \\ M & N & P \\ R & S & T \end{vmatrix} = (NT - PS)\mathbf{i} - (MT - PR)\mathbf{j} + (MS - NR)\mathbf{k}$$

$$\text{div}(\mathbf{F} \times \mathbf{G}) = \frac{\partial}{\partial x}(NT - PS) + \frac{\partial}{\partial y}(PR - MT) + \frac{\partial}{\partial z}(MS - NR)$$

$$= N\frac{\partial T}{\partial x} + T\frac{\partial N}{\partial x} - P\frac{\partial S}{\partial x} - S\frac{\partial P}{\partial x} + P\frac{\partial R}{\partial y} + R\frac{\partial P}{\partial y} - M\frac{\partial T}{\partial y} - T\frac{\partial M}{\partial y} + M\frac{\partial S}{\partial z} + S\frac{\partial M}{\partial z} - N\frac{\partial R}{\partial z} - R\frac{\partial N}{\partial z}$$

$$= \left[\left(\frac{\partial P}{\partial y} - \frac{\partial N}{\partial z} \right)R + \left(\frac{\partial M}{\partial z} - \frac{\partial P}{\partial x} \right)S + \left(\frac{\partial N}{\partial x} - \frac{\partial M}{\partial y} \right)T \right] - \left[M\left(\frac{\partial T}{\partial y} - \frac{\partial S}{\partial z} \right) + N\left(\frac{\partial R}{\partial z} - \frac{\partial T}{\partial x} \right) + P\left(\frac{\partial S}{\partial x} - \frac{\partial R}{\partial y} \right) \right]$$

$$= (\text{curl } \mathbf{F}) \cdot \mathbf{G} - \mathbf{F} \cdot (\text{curl } \mathbf{G})$$

82. Let $\mathbf{F} = M\mathbf{i} + N\mathbf{j} + P\mathbf{k}$.

$$\nabla \times (f\mathbf{F}) = \begin{vmatrix} \mathbf{i} & \mathbf{j} & \mathbf{k} \\ \dfrac{\partial}{\partial x} & \dfrac{\partial}{\partial y} & \dfrac{\partial}{\partial z} \\ fM & fN & fP \end{vmatrix}$$

$$= \left(\frac{\partial f}{\partial y}P + f\frac{\partial P}{\partial y} - \frac{\partial f}{\partial z}N - f\frac{\partial N}{\partial z} \right)\mathbf{i} - \left(\frac{\partial f}{\partial x}P + f\frac{\partial P}{\partial x} - \frac{\partial f}{\partial z}M - f\frac{\partial M}{\partial z} \right)\mathbf{j} + \left(\frac{\partial f}{\partial x}N + f\frac{\partial N}{\partial x} - \frac{\partial f}{\partial y}M - f\frac{\partial M}{\partial y} \right)\mathbf{k}$$

$$= f\left[\left(\frac{\partial P}{\partial y} - \frac{\partial N}{\partial z} \right)\mathbf{i} - \left(\frac{\partial P}{\partial x} - \frac{\partial M}{\partial z} \right)\mathbf{j} + \left(\frac{\partial N}{\partial x} - \frac{\partial M}{\partial y} \right)\mathbf{k} \right] + \begin{vmatrix} \mathbf{i} & \mathbf{j} & \mathbf{k} \\ \dfrac{\partial f}{\partial x} & \dfrac{\partial f}{\partial y} & \dfrac{\partial f}{\partial z} \\ M & N & P \end{vmatrix} = f[\nabla \times \mathbf{F}] + (\nabla f) \times \mathbf{F}$$

84. Let $\mathbf{F} = M\mathbf{i} + N\mathbf{j} + P\mathbf{k}$.

$$\text{curl } \mathbf{F} = \left(\frac{\partial P}{\partial y} - \frac{\partial N}{\partial z}\right)\mathbf{i} - \left(\frac{\partial P}{\partial x} - \frac{\partial M}{\partial z}\right)\mathbf{j} + \left(\frac{\partial N}{\partial x} - \frac{\partial M}{\partial y}\right)\mathbf{k}$$

$$\text{div}(\text{curl } \mathbf{F}) = \frac{\partial}{\partial x}\left[\frac{\partial P}{\partial y} - \frac{\partial N}{\partial z}\right] - \frac{\partial}{\partial y}\left[\frac{\partial P}{\partial x} - \frac{\partial M}{\partial z}\right] + \frac{\partial}{\partial z}\left[\frac{\partial N}{\partial x} - \frac{\partial M}{\partial y}\right]$$

$$= \frac{\partial^2 P}{\partial x \partial y} - \frac{\partial^2 N}{\partial x \partial z} - \frac{\partial^2 P}{\partial y \partial x} + \frac{\partial^2 M}{\partial y \partial z} + \frac{\partial^2 N}{\partial z \partial x} - \frac{\partial^2 M}{\partial z \partial y} = 0 \quad \text{(since the mixed partials are equal)}$$

In Exercises 86 and 88, $\mathbf{F}(x, y, z) = x\mathbf{i} + y\mathbf{j} + z\mathbf{k}$ and $f(x, y, z) = \|\mathbf{F}(x, y, z)\| = \sqrt{x^2 + y^2 + z^2}$.

86. $\dfrac{1}{f} = \dfrac{1}{\sqrt{x^2 + y^2 + z^2}}$

$$\nabla\left(\frac{1}{f}\right) = \frac{-x}{(x^2 + y^2 + z^2)^{3/2}}\mathbf{i} + \frac{-y}{(x^2 + y^2 + z^2)^{3/2}}\mathbf{j} + \frac{-z}{(x^2 + y^2 + z^2)^{3/2}}\mathbf{k} = \frac{-(x\mathbf{i} + y\mathbf{j} + z\mathbf{k})}{\left(\sqrt{x^2 + y^2 + z^2}\right)^3} = -\frac{\mathbf{F}}{f^3}$$

88. $w = \dfrac{1}{f} = \dfrac{1}{\sqrt{x^2 + y^2 + z^2}}$

$\dfrac{\partial w}{\partial x} = -\dfrac{x}{(x^2 + y^2 + z^2)^{3/2}}$

$\dfrac{\partial w}{\partial y} = -\dfrac{y}{(x^2 + y^2 + z^2)^{3/2}}$

$\dfrac{\partial w}{\partial z} = -\dfrac{z}{(x^2 + y^2 + z^2)^{3/2}}$

$\dfrac{\partial^2 w}{\partial x^2} = \dfrac{2x^2 - y^2 - z^2}{(x^2 + y^2 + z^2)^{5/2}}$

$\dfrac{\partial^2 w}{\partial y^2} = \dfrac{2y^2 - x^2 - z^2}{(x^2 + y^2 + z^2)^{5/2}}$

$\dfrac{\partial^2 w}{\partial z^2} = \dfrac{2z^2 - x^2 - y^2}{(x^2 + y^2 + z^2)^{5/2}}$

$\nabla^2 w = \dfrac{\partial^2 w}{\partial x^2} + \dfrac{\partial^2 w}{\partial y^2} + \dfrac{\partial^2 w}{\partial z^2} = 0$

Therefore $w = \dfrac{1}{f}$ is harmonic.

Section 14.2   Line Integrals

2. $\dfrac{x^2}{16} + \dfrac{y^2}{9} = 1$

$\cos^2 t + \sin^2 t = 1$

$\cos^2 t = \dfrac{x^2}{16}$

$\sin^2 t = \dfrac{y^2}{9}$

$x = 4\cos t$

$y = 3\sin t$

$\mathbf{r}(t) = 4\cos t\,\mathbf{i} + 3\sin t\,\mathbf{j}$

$0 \le t \le 2\pi$

4. $\mathbf{r}(t) = \begin{cases} t\mathbf{i} + \frac{4}{5}t\mathbf{j}, & 0 \le t \le 5 \\ 5\mathbf{i} + (9 - t)\mathbf{j}, & 5 \le t \le 9 \\ (14 - t)\mathbf{i}, & 9 \le t \le 14 \end{cases}$

6. $\mathbf{r}(t) = \begin{cases} t\mathbf{i} + t^2\mathbf{j}, & 0 \le t \le 2 \\ (4 - t)\mathbf{i} + 4\mathbf{j}, & 2 \le t \le 4 \\ (8 - t)\mathbf{j}, & 4 \le t \le 8 \end{cases}$

8. $\mathbf{r}(t) = t\mathbf{i} + (2 - t)\mathbf{j}$, $0 \le t \le 2$; $\mathbf{r}'(t) = \mathbf{i} - \mathbf{j}$

$$\int_C 4xy\,ds = \int_0^2 4t(2 - t)\sqrt{1 + 1}\,dt = 4\sqrt{2}\int_0^2 (2t - t^2)\,dt = 4\sqrt{2}\left[t^2 - \frac{t^3}{3}\right]_0^2 = 4\sqrt{2}\left(4 - \frac{8}{3}\right) = \frac{16\sqrt{2}}{3}$$

10. $\mathbf{r}(t) = 12t\mathbf{i} + 5t\mathbf{j} + 3\mathbf{k}, \ 0 \le t \le 2; \ \mathbf{r}'(t) = 12\mathbf{i} + 5\mathbf{j}$

$$\int_C 8xyz \, ds = \int_0^2 8(12t)(5t)(3)\sqrt{12^2 + 5^2 + 0^2} \, dt = \int_0^2 18{,}720t^2 \, dt = 18{,}720\left[\frac{t^3}{3}\right]_0^2 = 49{,}920$$

12. $\mathbf{r}(t) = t\mathbf{j}, \ 1 \le t \le 10$

$$\int_C (x^2 + y^2) \, ds = \int_1^{10} [0 + t^2]\sqrt{0 + 1} \, dt$$

$$= \int_1^{10} t^2 \, dt$$

$$= \left[\frac{1}{3}t^3\right]_1^{10} = 333$$

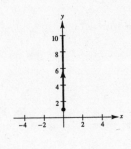

14. $\mathbf{r}(t) = 2\cos t\mathbf{i} + 2\sin t\mathbf{j}, \ 0 \le t \le \dfrac{\pi}{2}$

$$\int_C (x^2 + y^2) \, ds = \int_0^{\pi/2} [4\cos^2 t + 4\sin^2 t]\sqrt{(-2\sin t)^2 + (2\cos t)^2} \, dt$$

$$= \int_0^{\pi/2} 8 \, dt = 4\pi$$

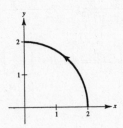

16. $\mathbf{r}(t) = t\mathbf{i} + 3t\mathbf{j}, \ 0 \le t \le 3$

$$\int_C (x + 4\sqrt{y}) \, ds = \int_0^3 \left(t + 4\sqrt{3t}\right)\sqrt{1 + 9} \, dt$$

$$= \left[\sqrt{10}\left(\frac{t^2}{2} + \frac{8\sqrt{3}}{3}t^{3/2}\right)\right]_0^3$$

$$= \frac{\sqrt{10}}{6}(27 + 144) = \frac{57\sqrt{10}}{2}$$

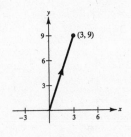

18. $\mathbf{r}(t) = \begin{cases} t\mathbf{i}, & 0 \le t \le 2 \\ 2\mathbf{i} + (t - 2)\mathbf{j}, & 2 \le t \le 4 \\ (6 - t)\mathbf{i} + 2\mathbf{j}, & 4 \le t \le 6 \\ (8 - t)\mathbf{j}, & 6 \le t \le 8 \end{cases}$

$$\int_{C_1} \left(x + 4\sqrt{y}\right) ds = \int_0^2 t \, dt = 2$$

$$\int_{C_2} \left(x + 4\sqrt{y}\right) ds = \int_2^4 \left(2 + 4\sqrt{t - 2}\right) ds = 4 + \frac{16\sqrt{2}}{3}$$

$$\int_{C_3} \left(x + 4\sqrt{y}\right) ds = \int_4^6 \left((6 - t) + 4\sqrt{2}\right)) ds = 2 + 8\sqrt{2}$$

$$\int_{C_4} \left(x + 4\sqrt{y}\right) ds = \int_6^8 4\sqrt{8 - t} \, ds = \frac{16\sqrt{2}}{3}$$

$$\int_C \left(x + 4\sqrt{y}\right) ds = 2 + 4 + \frac{16\sqrt{2}}{3} + 2 + 8\sqrt{2} + \frac{16\sqrt{2}}{3} = 8 + \frac{56}{3}\sqrt{2}$$

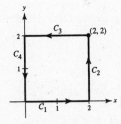

20. $\rho(x, y, z) = z$

$\mathbf{r}(t) = 3\cos t\mathbf{i} + 3\sin t\mathbf{j} + 2t\mathbf{k}, \ 0 \le t \le 4\pi$

$\mathbf{r}'(t) = -3\sin t\mathbf{i} + 3\cos t\mathbf{j} + 2\mathbf{k}$

$\|\mathbf{r}'(t)\| = \sqrt{(-3\sin t)^2 + (3\cos t)^2 + (2)^2} = \sqrt{13}$

$\text{Mass} = \int_C \rho(x, y, z) \, ds = \int_0^{4\pi} 2t\sqrt{13} \, dt = 16\pi^2\sqrt{13}$

22. $\mathbf{F}(x, y) = xy\mathbf{i} + y\mathbf{j}$

$C: \mathbf{r}(t) = 4\cos t\mathbf{i} + 4\sin t\mathbf{j}, \ 0 \le t \le \dfrac{\pi}{2}$

$\mathbf{F}(t) = 16\sin t\cos t\mathbf{i} + 4\sin t\mathbf{j}$

$\mathbf{r}'(t) = -4\sin t\mathbf{i} + 4\cos t\mathbf{j}$

$\int_C \mathbf{F} \cdot d\mathbf{r} = \int_0^{\pi/2} (-64\sin^2 t\cos t + 16\sin t\cos t) \, dt$

$= \left[-\dfrac{64}{3}\sin^3 t + 8\sin^2 t\right]_0^{\pi/2} = -\dfrac{40}{3}$

24. $\mathbf{F}(x, y) = 3x\mathbf{i} + 4y\mathbf{j}$

$C: \mathbf{r}(t) = t\mathbf{i} + \sqrt{4 - t^2}\mathbf{j}, \ -2 \le t \le 2$

$\mathbf{F}(t) = 3t\mathbf{i} + 4\sqrt{4 - t^2}\mathbf{j}$

$\mathbf{r}'(t) = \mathbf{i} - \dfrac{t}{\sqrt{4 - t^2}}\mathbf{j}$

$\int_C \mathbf{F} \cdot d\mathbf{r} = \int_{-2}^2 (3t - 4t) \, dt = \left[-\dfrac{t^2}{2}\right]_{-2}^2 = 0$

26. $\mathbf{F}(x, y, z) = x^2\mathbf{i} + y^2\mathbf{j} + z^2\mathbf{k}$

$C: \mathbf{r}(t) = 2\sin t\mathbf{i} + 2\cos t\mathbf{j} + \dfrac{1}{2}t^2\mathbf{k}, \ 0 \le t \le \pi$

$\mathbf{F}(t) = 4\sin^2 t\mathbf{i} + 4\cos^2 t\mathbf{j} + \dfrac{1}{4}t^4\mathbf{k}$

$\mathbf{r}'(t) = 2\cos t\mathbf{i} - 2\sin t\mathbf{j} + t\mathbf{k}$

$\int_C \mathbf{F} \cdot d\mathbf{r} = \int_0^\pi \left(8\sin^2 t\cos t - 8\cos^2 t\sin t + \dfrac{1}{4}t^5\right) dt$

$= \left[\dfrac{8}{3}\sin^3 t + \dfrac{8}{3}\cos^3 t + \dfrac{t^6}{24}\right]_0^\pi$

$= -\dfrac{8}{3} + \dfrac{\pi^6}{24} - \dfrac{8}{3} = \dfrac{\pi^6}{24} - \dfrac{16}{3}$

28. $\mathbf{F}(x, y, z) = \dfrac{x\mathbf{i} + y\mathbf{j} + z\mathbf{k}}{\sqrt{x^2 + y^2 + z^2}}$

$\mathbf{r}(t) = t\mathbf{i} + t\mathbf{j} + e^t\mathbf{k}, \ 0 \le t \le 2$

$\mathbf{F}(t) = \dfrac{t\mathbf{i} + t\mathbf{j} + e^t\mathbf{k}}{\sqrt{2t^2 + e^{2t}}}$

$d\mathbf{r} = (\mathbf{i} + \mathbf{j} + e^t\mathbf{k}) \, dt$

$\int_C \mathbf{F} \cdot d\mathbf{r} = \int_0^2 \dfrac{1}{\sqrt{2t^2 + e^{2t}}} (2t + e^{2t}) \, dt \approx 6.91$

30. $\mathbf{F}(x, y) = x^2\mathbf{i} - xy\mathbf{j}$

$C: x = \cos^3 t, \ y = \sin^3 t$ from $(1, 0)$ to $(0, 1)$

$\mathbf{r}(t) = \cos^3 t\mathbf{i} + \sin^3 t\mathbf{j}, \ 0 \le t \le \dfrac{\pi}{2}$

$\mathbf{r}'(t) = -3\cos^2 t\sin t\mathbf{i} + 3\sin^2 t\cos t\mathbf{j}$

$\mathbf{F}(t) = \cos^6 t\mathbf{i} - \cos^3 t\sin^3 t\mathbf{j}$

$\mathbf{F} \cdot \mathbf{r}' = -3\cos^8 t\sin t - 3\cos^4 t\sin^5 t$

$= -3\cos^4 t\sin t(\cos^4 t + \sin^4 t)$

$= -3\cos^4 t\sin t[\cos^4 t + (1 - \cos^2 t)^2]$

$= -3\cos^4 t\sin t(2\cos^4 t - 2\cos^2 t + 1)$

$= -6\cos^8 t\sin t + 6\cos^6 t\sin t - 3\cos^4 t\sin t$

$\text{Work} = \int_C \mathbf{F} \cdot d\mathbf{r} = \int_0^{\pi/2} [-6\cos^8 t\sin t + 6\cos^6 t\sin t - 3\cos^4 t\sin t] \, dt$

$= \left[\dfrac{2\cos^9 t}{3} - \dfrac{6\cos^7 t}{7} + \dfrac{3\cos^5 t}{5}\right]_0^{\pi/2} = -\dfrac{43}{105}$

32. $F(x, y) = -y\mathbf{i} - x\mathbf{j}$

    C: counterclockwise along the semicircle $y = \sqrt{4 - x^2}$
from $(2, 0)$ to $(-2, 0)$

$$\mathbf{r}(t) = 2\cos t\mathbf{i} + 2\sin t\mathbf{j}, \quad 0 \le t \le \pi$$

$$\mathbf{r}'(t) = -2\sin t\mathbf{i} + 2\cos t\mathbf{j}$$

$$\mathbf{F}(t) = -2\sin t\mathbf{i} - 2\cos t\mathbf{j}$$

$$\mathbf{F} \cdot \mathbf{r}' = 4\sin^2 t - 4\cos^2 t = -4\cos 2t$$

$$\text{Work} = \int_C \mathbf{F} \cdot d\mathbf{r} = -4\int_0^\pi \cos 2t\, dt = \left[-2\sin 2t\right]_0^\pi = 0$$

34. $F(x, y, z) = yz\mathbf{i} + xz\mathbf{j} + xy\mathbf{k}$

    C: line from $(0, 0, 0)$ to $(5, 3, 2)$

$$\mathbf{r}(t) = 5t\mathbf{i} + 3t\mathbf{j} + 2t\mathbf{k}, \quad 0 \le t \le 1$$

$$\mathbf{r}'(t) = 5\mathbf{i} + 3\mathbf{j} + 2\mathbf{k}$$

$$\mathbf{F}(t) = 6t^2\mathbf{i} + 10t^2\mathbf{j} + 15t^2\mathbf{k}$$

$$\mathbf{F} \cdot \mathbf{r}' = 90t^2$$

$$\text{Work} = \int_C \mathbf{F} \cdot d\mathbf{r} = \int_0^1 90t^2\, dt = 30$$

36. $\mathbf{r}(t) = t\mathbf{i} + t^2\mathbf{j},\ 0 \le t \le 1$

$$\mathbf{r}'(t) = \mathbf{i} + 2t\mathbf{j}$$

$$\int_C \mathbf{F} \cdot d\mathbf{r} \approx \frac{1-0}{3(4)}[5 + 4(4) + 2(4) + 4(6) + 11]$$

$$= \frac{16}{3}$$

(x, y)	$(0, 0)$	$\left(\frac{1}{4}, \frac{1}{16}\right)$	$\left(\frac{1}{2}, \frac{1}{4}\right)$	$\left(\frac{3}{4}, \frac{9}{16}\right)$	$(1, 1)$
$F(x, y)$	$5\mathbf{i}$	$3.5\mathbf{i} + \mathbf{j}$	$2\mathbf{i} + 2\mathbf{j}$	$1.5\mathbf{i} + 3\mathbf{j}$	$\mathbf{i} + 5\mathbf{j}$
$\mathbf{r}'(t)$	$\mathbf{i}$	$\mathbf{i} + 0.5\mathbf{j}$	$\mathbf{i} + \mathbf{j}$	$\mathbf{i} + 1.5\mathbf{j}$	$\mathbf{i} + 2\mathbf{j}$
$\mathbf{F} \cdot \mathbf{r}'$	5	4	4	6	11

38. $\mathbf{F}(x, y) = x^2 y\mathbf{i} + xy^{3/2}\mathbf{j}$

  (a) $\mathbf{r}_1(t) = (t + 1)\mathbf{i} + t^2\mathbf{j}, 0 \le t \le 2$

$$\mathbf{r}_1'(t) = \mathbf{i} + 2t\mathbf{j}$$

$$\mathbf{F}(t) = (t + 1)^2 t^2\mathbf{i} + (t + 1)t^3\mathbf{j}$$

$$\int_{C_1} \mathbf{F} \cdot d\mathbf{r} = \int_0^2 [(t + 1)^2 t^2 + 2t^4(t + 1)]\, dt = \frac{256}{3}$$

  (b) $\mathbf{r}_2(t) = (1 + 2\cos t)\mathbf{i} + 4\cos^2 t\mathbf{j}, 0 \le t \le \dfrac{\pi}{2}$

$$\mathbf{r}_2'(t) = -2\sin t\mathbf{i} - 8\cos t\sin t\mathbf{j}$$

$$\mathbf{F}(t) = (1 + 2\cos t)^2(4\cos^2 t)\mathbf{i} + (1 + 2\cos t)(8\cos^3 t)\mathbf{j}$$

$$\int_{C_2} \mathbf{F} \cdot d\mathbf{r} = \int_0^{\pi/2}\left[(1 + 2\cos t)^2(4\cos^2 t)(-2\sin t) - 8\cos t\sin t(1 + 2\cos t)(8\cos^3 t)\, dt = -\frac{256}{5}\right.$$

Both paths join $(1, 0)$ and $(3, 4)$. The integrals are negatives of each other because the orientations are different.

40. $\mathbf{F}(x, y) = -3y\mathbf{i} + x\mathbf{j}$

    C: $\mathbf{r}(t) = t\mathbf{i} - t^3\mathbf{j}$

$$\mathbf{r}'(t) = \mathbf{i} - 3t^2\mathbf{j}$$

$$\mathbf{F}(t) = 3t^3\mathbf{i} + t\mathbf{j}$$

$$\mathbf{F} \cdot \mathbf{r}' = 3t^3 - 3t^3 = 0$$

Thus, $\displaystyle\int_C \mathbf{F} \cdot d\mathbf{r} = 0$.

42. $\mathbf{F}(x, y) = x\mathbf{i} + y\mathbf{j}$

    C: $\mathbf{r}(t) = 3\sin t\mathbf{i} + 3\cos t\mathbf{j}$

$$\mathbf{r}'(t) = 3\cos t\mathbf{i} - 3\sin t\mathbf{j}$$

$$\mathbf{F}(t) = 3\sin t\mathbf{i} + 3\cos t\mathbf{j}$$

$$\mathbf{F} \cdot \mathbf{r}' = 9\sin t\cos t - 9\sin t\cos t = 0$$

Thus, $\displaystyle\int_C \mathbf{F} \cdot d\mathbf{r} = 0$.

44. $x = 2t,\ y = 10t,\ 0 \le t \le 1 \Rightarrow y = 5x,\ 0 \le x \le 2$

$$\int_C (x + 3y^2)\, dx = \int_0^2 (x + 75x^2)\, dx = \left[\frac{x^2}{2} + 25x^3\right]_0^2 = 202$$

46. $x = 2t$, $y = 10t$, $0 \le t \le 1 \Rightarrow y = 5x$, $dy = 5\,dx$, $0 \le x \le 2$

$$\int_C (3y - x)\,dx + y^2\,dy = \int_0^2 (3(5x) - x)\,dx + (5x)^2 5\,dx = \int_0^2 (14x + 125x^2)\,dx$$

$$= \left[7x^2 + \frac{125}{3}x^3 \right]_0^2 = 28 + \frac{125}{3}(8) = \frac{1084}{3}$$

48. $\mathbf{r}(t) = t\mathbf{j}$, $0 \le t \le 2$

$x(t) = 0$, $y(t) = t$

$dx = 0$, $dy = dt$

$$\int_C (2x - y)\,dx + (x + 3y)\,dy = \int_0^2 3t\,dt = \left[\frac{3}{2}t^2 \right]_0^2 = 6$$

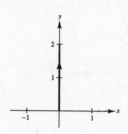

50. $\mathbf{r}(t) = \begin{cases} -t\mathbf{j}, & 0 \le t \le 3 \\ (t-3)\mathbf{i} - 3\mathbf{j}, & 3 \le t \le 5 \end{cases}$

C_1: $x(t) = 0$, $y(t) = -t$

$\quad\ dx = 0$, $dy = -dt$

$$\int_{C_1} (2x - y)\,dx + (x + 3y)\,dy = \int_0^3 3t\,dt = \frac{27}{2}$$

C_2: $x(t) = t - 3$, $y(t) = -3$

$\quad\ dx = dt$, $dy = 0$

$$\int_{C_2} (2x - y)\,dx + (x + 3y)\,dy = \int_3^5 [2(t-3) + 3]\,dt = \left[(t-3)^2 + 3t \right]_3^5 = 10$$

$$\int_C (2x - y)\,dx + (x + 3y)\,dy = \frac{27}{2} + 10 = \frac{47}{2}$$

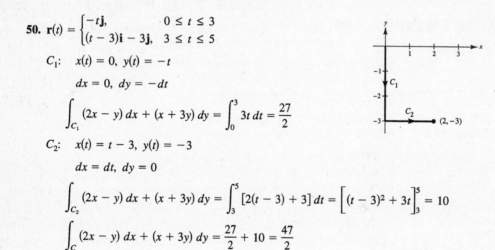

52. $x(t) = t$, $y(t) = t^{3/2}$, $0 \le t \le 4$, $dx = dt$, $dy = \frac{3}{2}t^{1/2}\,dt$

$$\int_C (2x - y)\,dx + (x + 3y)\,dy = \int_0^4 \left[(2t - t^{3/2}) + (t + 3t^{3/2})\left(\frac{3}{2}t^{1/2} \right) \right] dt$$

$$= \int_0^4 \left(\frac{9}{2}t^2 + \frac{1}{2}t^{3/2} + 2t \right) dt = \left[\frac{3}{2}t^3 + \frac{1}{5}t^{5/2} + t^2 \right]_0^4 = 96 + \frac{1}{5}(32) + 16 = \frac{592}{5}$$

54. $x(t) = 4\sin t$, $y(t) = 3\cos t$, $0 \le t \le \dfrac{\pi}{2}$

$dx = 4\cos t\,dt$, $dy = -3\sin t\,dt$

$$\int_C (2x - y)\,dx + (x + 3y)\,dy = \int_0^{\pi/2} (8\sin t - 3\cos t)(4\cos t)\,dt + (4\sin t + 9\cos t)(-3\sin t)\,dt$$

$$= \int_0^{\pi/2} (5\sin t \cos t - 12\cos^2 t - 12\sin^2 t)\,dt$$

$$= \left[\frac{5}{2}\sin^2 t - 12t \right]_0^{\pi/2} = \frac{5}{2} - 6\pi$$

56. $f(x, y) = y$

    C: line from $(0, 0)$ to $(4, 4)$

$$\mathbf{r}(t) = t\mathbf{i} + t\mathbf{j}, \ 0 \leq t \leq 4$$

$$\mathbf{r}'(t) = \mathbf{i} + \mathbf{j}$$

$$\|\mathbf{r}'(t)\| = \sqrt{2}$$

Lateral surface area:

$$\int_C f(x, y) \, ds = \int_0^4 t\left(\sqrt{2}\right) dt = 8\sqrt{2}$$

58. $f(x, y) = x + y$

    C: $x^2 + y^2 = 1$ from $(1, 0)$ to $(0, 1)$

$$\mathbf{r}(t) = \cos t\mathbf{i} + \sin t\mathbf{j}, \ 0 \leq t \leq \frac{\pi}{2}$$

$$\mathbf{r}'(t) = -\sin t\mathbf{i} + \cos t\mathbf{j}$$

$$\|\mathbf{r}'(t)\| = 1$$

Lateral surface area:

$$\int_C f(x, y) \, ds = \int_0^{\pi/2} (\cos t + \sin t) \, dt$$

$$= \left[\sin t - \cos t \right]_0^{\pi/2} = 2$$

60. $f(x, y) = y + 1$

    C: $y = 1 - x^2$ from $(1, 0)$ to $(0, 1)$

$$\mathbf{r}(t) = (1 - t)\mathbf{i} + [1 - (1 - t)^2]\mathbf{j}, \ 0 \leq t \leq 1$$

$$\mathbf{r}'(t) = -\mathbf{i} + 2(1 - t)\mathbf{j}$$

$$\|\mathbf{r}'(t)\| = \sqrt{1 + 4(1 - t)^2}$$

Lateral surface area:

$$\int_C f(x, y) \, ds = \int_0^1 [2 - (1 - t)^2]\sqrt{1 + 4(1 - t)^2} \, dt$$

$$= 2\int_0^1 \sqrt{1 + 4(1 - t)^2} \, dt - \int_0^1 (1 - t)^2\sqrt{1 + 4(1 - t)^2} \, dt$$

$$= -\frac{1}{2}\left[2(1 - t)\sqrt{1 + 4(1 - t)^2} + \ln|2(1 - t) + \sqrt{1 + 4(1 - t)^2}| \right]_0^1$$

$$+ \frac{1}{64}\left[2(1 - t)[2(4)(1 - t)^2 + 1]\sqrt{1 + 4(1 - t)^2} - \ln|2(1 - t) + \sqrt{1 + 4(1 - t)^2}| \right]_0^1$$

$$= \frac{1}{2}\left[2\sqrt{5} + \ln\left(2 + \sqrt{5}\right) \right] - \frac{1}{64}\left[18\sqrt{5} - \ln\left(2 + \sqrt{5}\right) \right]$$

$$= \frac{23}{32}\sqrt{5} + \frac{33}{64}\ln\left(2 + \sqrt{5}\right) = \frac{1}{64}\left[46\sqrt{5} + 33\ln\left(2 + \sqrt{5}\right) \right] \approx 2.3515$$

62. $f(x, y) = x^2 - y^2 + 4$

    C: $x^2 + y^2 = 4$

$$\mathbf{r}(t) = 2\cos t\mathbf{i} + 2\sin t\mathbf{j}, \ 0 \leq t \leq 2\pi$$

$$\mathbf{r}'(t) = -2\sin t\mathbf{i} + 2\cos t\mathbf{j}$$

$$\|\mathbf{r}'(t)\| = 2$$

Lateral surface area:

$$\int_C f(x, y) \, ds = \int_0^{2\pi} (4\cos^2 t - 4\sin^2 t + 4)(2) \, dt = 8\int_0^{2\pi} (1 + \cos 2t) \, dt = \left[8\left(t + \frac{1}{2}\sin 2t\right) \right]_0^{2\pi} = 16\pi$$

64. $f(x, y) = 20 + \frac{1}{4}x$

C: $y = x^{3/2}, \; 0 \le x \le 40$

$\mathbf{r}(t) = t\mathbf{i} + t^{3/2}\mathbf{j}, \; 0 \le t \le 40$

$\mathbf{r}'(t) = \mathbf{i} + \frac{3}{2}t^{1/2}\mathbf{j}$

$\|\mathbf{r}'(t)\| = \sqrt{1 + \left(\frac{9}{4}\right)t}$

Lateral surface area: $\displaystyle\int_C f(x, y)\, ds = \int_0^{40} \left(20 + \frac{1}{4}t\right)\sqrt{1 + \left(\frac{9}{4}\right)t}\; dt$

Let $u = \sqrt{1 + \left(\frac{9}{4}\right)t}$, then $t = \frac{4}{9}(u^2 - 1)$ and $dt = \frac{8}{9}u\, du$.

$$\int_0^{40} \left(20 + \frac{1}{4}t\right)\sqrt{1 + \left(\frac{9}{4}\right)t}\; dt = \int_1^{\sqrt{91}} \left[20 + \frac{1}{9}(u^2 - 1)\right](u)\left(\frac{8}{9}u\right) du = \frac{8}{81}\int_1^{\sqrt{91}} (u^4 + 179u^2)\, du$$

$$= \frac{8}{81}\left[\frac{u^5}{5} + \frac{179u^3}{3}\right]_1^{\sqrt{91}} = \frac{850{,}304\sqrt{91} - 7184}{1215} \approx 6670.12$$

66. $f(x, y) = y$

C: $y = x^2$ from $(0, 0)$ to $(2, 4)$

$S \approx 8$

Matches c.

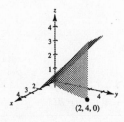

(2, 4, 0)

68. $W = \displaystyle\int_C \mathbf{F} \cdot d\mathbf{r} = \int_C M\, dx + N\, dy$

$M = 15(4 - x^2 y) = 60 - 15x^2(c - cx^2)$

$N = -15xy = -15x(c - cx^2)$

$dx = dx, \; dy = -2cx\, dx$

$W = \displaystyle\int_{-1}^{1} \left[60 - 15x^2(c - cx^2) + (-15x(c - cx^2))(-2\,cx)\right] dx$

$\quad = 120 - 4c + 8c^2 \quad \text{(parabola)}$

$w' = 16c - 4 = 0 \implies c = \frac{1}{4}$ yields the minimum work, 119.5. Along the straight line path, $y = 0$, the work is 120.

70. See the definition, page 1024.

72. (a) Work = 0

(b) Work is negative, since against force field.

(c) Work is positive, since with force field.

74. False, the orientation of C does not affect the form

$$\int_C f(x, y)\, ds.$$

76. False. For example, see Exercise 32.

Section 14.3   Conservative Vector Fields and Independence of Path

2. $F(x, y) = (x^2 + y^2)\mathbf{i} - x\mathbf{j}$

   (a) $\mathbf{r}_1(t) = t\mathbf{i} + \sqrt{t}\,\mathbf{j}, \; 0 \leq t \leq 4$

     $\mathbf{r}_1'(t) = \mathbf{i} + \dfrac{1}{2\sqrt{t}}\mathbf{j}$

     $\mathbf{F}(t) = (t^2 + t)\mathbf{i} - t\mathbf{j}$

     $\displaystyle \int_C \mathbf{F} \cdot d\mathbf{r} = \int_0^4 \left(t^2 + t - \frac{1}{2}\sqrt{t}\right) dt$

       $= \left[\dfrac{t^3}{3} + \dfrac{t^2}{2} - \dfrac{t^{3/2}}{3}\right]_0^4 = \dfrac{80}{3}$

   (b) $\mathbf{r}_2(w) = w^2\mathbf{i} + w\mathbf{j}, \; 0 \leq w \leq 2$

     $\mathbf{r}_2'(w) = 2w\mathbf{i} + \mathbf{j}$

     $\mathbf{F}(w) = (w^4 + w^2)\mathbf{i} - w^2\mathbf{j}$

     $\displaystyle \int_C \mathbf{F} \cdot d\mathbf{r} = \int_0^2 \left[2w(w^4 + w^2) - w^2\right] dw$

       $= \left[\dfrac{w^6}{3} + \dfrac{w^4}{2} - \dfrac{w^3}{3}\right]_0^2 = \dfrac{80}{3}$

4. $F(x, y) = y\mathbf{i} + x^2\mathbf{j}$

   (a) $\mathbf{r}_1(t) = (2 + t)\mathbf{i} + (3 - t)\mathbf{j}, \; 0 \leq t \leq 3$

     $\mathbf{r}_1'(t) = \mathbf{i} - \mathbf{j}$

     $\mathbf{F}(t) = (3 - t)\mathbf{i} + (2 + t)^2\mathbf{j}$

     $\displaystyle \int_C \mathbf{F} \cdot d\mathbf{r} = \int_0^3 \left[(3 - t) - (2 + t)^2\right] dt = \left[-\dfrac{(3 - t)^2}{2} - \dfrac{(2 + t)^3}{3}\right]_0^3 = -\dfrac{69}{2}$

   (b) $\mathbf{r}_2(w) = (2 + \ln w)\mathbf{i} + (3 - \ln w)\mathbf{j}, \; 1 \leq w \leq e^3$

     $\mathbf{r}_2'(w) = \dfrac{1}{w}\mathbf{i} - \dfrac{1}{w}\mathbf{j}$

     $\mathbf{F}(w) = (3 - \ln w)\mathbf{i} + (2 + \ln w)^2\mathbf{j}$

     $\displaystyle \int_C \mathbf{F} \cdot d\mathbf{r} = \int_1^{e^3} \left[(3 - \ln w)\left(\frac{1}{w}\right) - (2 + \ln w)^2\left(\frac{1}{w}\right)\right] dw = \left[-\dfrac{(3 - \ln w)^2}{2} - \dfrac{(2 + \ln w)^3}{3}\right]_1^{e^3} = -\dfrac{69}{2}$

6. $F(x, y) = 15x^2y^2\mathbf{i} + 10x^3y\mathbf{j}$

   $\dfrac{\partial N}{\partial x} = 30x^2y \qquad \dfrac{\partial M}{\partial y} = 30x^2y$

   Since $\dfrac{\partial N}{\partial x} = \dfrac{\partial M}{\partial y}$, $\mathbf{F}$ is conservative.

8. $F(x, y, z) = y \ln z\mathbf{i} - x \ln z\mathbf{j} + \dfrac{xy}{z}\mathbf{k}$

   curl $\mathbf{F} \neq \mathbf{0}$ so $\mathbf{F}$ is not conservative.

   $\left(\dfrac{\partial P}{\partial y} = \dfrac{x}{z} \neq -\dfrac{x}{z} = \dfrac{\partial N}{\partial z}\right)$

10. $F(x, y, z) = \sin(yz)\mathbf{i} + xz\cos(yz)\mathbf{j} + xy\sin(yz)\mathbf{k}$

   curl $\mathbf{F} \neq \mathbf{0}$, so $\mathbf{F}$ is not conservative.

12. $F(x, y) = ye^{xy}\mathbf{i} + xe^{xy}\mathbf{j}$

   (a) $\mathbf{r}_1(t) = t\mathbf{i} - (t - 3)\mathbf{j}, \; 0 \leq t \leq 3$

     $\mathbf{r}_1'(t) = \mathbf{i} - \mathbf{j}$

     $\mathbf{F}(t) = -(t - 3)e^{3t - t^2}\mathbf{i} + te^{3t - t^2}\mathbf{j}$

     $\displaystyle \int_C \mathbf{F} \cdot d\mathbf{r} = \int_0^3 \left[-(t - 3)e^{3t - t^2} - te^{3t - t^2}\right] dt$

       $= \displaystyle\int_0^3 e^{3t - t^2}(3 - 2t)\, dt$

       $= \left[e^{3t - t^2}\right]_0^3 = e^0 - e^0 = 0$

   (b) $F(x, y)$ is conservative since

     $\dfrac{\partial M}{\partial y} = \dfrac{\partial N}{\partial x} = xye^{xy} + e^{xy}.$

     The potential function is $f(x, y) = e^{xy} + k$.

14. $\mathbf{F}(x, y) = xy^2\mathbf{i} + 2x^2y\mathbf{j}$

(a) $\mathbf{r}_1(t) = t\mathbf{i} + \dfrac{1}{t}\mathbf{j}, \quad 1 \le t \le 3$

$\mathbf{r}_1'(t) = \mathbf{i} - \dfrac{1}{t^2}\mathbf{j}$

$\mathbf{F}(t) = \dfrac{1}{t}\mathbf{i} + 2t\mathbf{j}$

$\displaystyle \int_C \mathbf{F} \cdot d\mathbf{r} = \int_1^3 -\dfrac{1}{t}\,dt$

$\qquad = \Big[-\ln|t| \Big]_1^3 = -\ln 3$

(b) $\mathbf{r}_2(t) = (t + 1)\mathbf{i} - \dfrac{1}{3}(t - 3)\mathbf{j}, \quad 0 \le t \le 2$

$\mathbf{r}_2'(t) = \mathbf{i} - \dfrac{1}{3}\mathbf{j}$

$\mathbf{F}(t) = \dfrac{1}{9}(t + 1)(t - 3)^2\mathbf{i} - \dfrac{2}{3}(t + 1)^2(t - 3)\mathbf{j}$

$\displaystyle \int_C \mathbf{F} \cdot d\mathbf{r} = \int_0^2 \left[\dfrac{1}{9}(t + 1)(t - 3)^2 + \dfrac{2}{9}(t + 1)^2(t - 3) \right] dt$

$\qquad = \dfrac{1}{9}\int_0^2 (3t^3 - 7t^2 - 7t + 3)\,dt$

$\qquad = \dfrac{1}{9}\left[\dfrac{3t^4}{4} - \dfrac{7t^3}{3} - \dfrac{7t^2}{2} + 3t \right]_0^2 = -\dfrac{44}{27}$

16. $\displaystyle \int_C (2x - 3y + 1)\,dx - (3x + y - 5)\,dy$

Since $\partial M/\partial y = \partial N/\partial x = -3$, $\mathbf{F}(x, y) = (2x - 3y + 1)\mathbf{i} - (3x + y - 5)\mathbf{j}$ is conservative. The potential function is $f(x, y) = x^2 - 3xy - (y^2/2) + x + 5y + k$.

(a) and (d) Since C is a closed curve, $\displaystyle \int_C (2x - 3y + 1)\,dx - (3x + y - 5)\,dy = 0$.

(b) $\displaystyle \int_C (2x - 3y + 1)\,dx - (3x + y - 5)\,dy = \left[x^2 - 3xy - \dfrac{y^2}{2} + x + 5y \right]_{(0, -1)}^{(0, 1)} = 10$

(c) $\displaystyle \int_C (2x - 3y + 1)\,dx - (3x + y - 5)\,dy = \left[x^2 - 3xy - \dfrac{y^2}{2} + x + 5y \right]_{(0, 1)}^{(2, e^2)} = \dfrac{1}{2}(3 - 2e^2 - e^4)$

18. $\displaystyle \int_C (x^2 + y^2)\,dx + 2xy\,dy$

Since $\partial M/\partial y = \partial N/\partial x = 2y$,

$\mathbf{F}(x, y) = (x^2 + y^2)\mathbf{i} + 2xy\mathbf{j}$

is conservative. The potential function is

$f(x, y) = (x^3/3) + xy^2 + k$.

(a) $\displaystyle \int_C (x^2 + y^2)\,dx + 2xy\,dy = \left[\dfrac{x^3}{3} + xy^2 \right]_{(0, 0)}^{(8, 4)} = \dfrac{896}{3}$

(b) $\displaystyle \int_C (x^2 + y^2)\,dx + 2xy\,dy = \left[\dfrac{x^3}{3} + xy^2 \right]_{(2, 0)}^{(0, 2)} = -\dfrac{8}{3}$

20. $\mathbf{F}(x, y, z) = \mathbf{i} + z\mathbf{j} + y\mathbf{k}$

Since $\mathbf{curl\ F} = \mathbf{0}$, $\mathbf{F}(x, y, z)$ is conservative. The potential function is $f(x, y, z) = x + yz + k$.

(a) $\mathbf{r}_1(t) = \cos t\mathbf{i} + \sin t\mathbf{j} + t^2\mathbf{k}, \, 0 \le t \le \pi$

$\displaystyle \int_C \mathbf{F} \cdot d\mathbf{r} = \Big[x + yz \Big]_{(1, 0, 0)}^{(-1, 0, \pi^2)} = -2$

(b) $\mathbf{r}_2(t) = (1 - 2t)\mathbf{i} + \pi^2 t\mathbf{k}, \, 0 \le t \le 1$

$\displaystyle \int_C \mathbf{F} \cdot d\mathbf{r} = \Big[x + yz \Big]_{(1, 0, 0)}^{(-1, 0, \pi^2)} = -2$

22. $\mathbf{F}(x, y, z) = -y\mathbf{i} + x\mathbf{j} + 3xz^2\mathbf{k}$

$\mathbf{F}(x, y, z)$ is not conservative.

(a) $\mathbf{r}_1(t) = \cos t\mathbf{i} + \sin t\mathbf{j} + t\mathbf{k}, \, 0 \le t \le \pi$

$\mathbf{r}_1'(t) = -\sin t\mathbf{i} + \cos t\mathbf{j} + \mathbf{k}$

$\mathbf{F}(t) = -\sin t\mathbf{i} + \cos t\mathbf{j} + 3t^2\cos t\mathbf{k}$

$\displaystyle \int_C \mathbf{F} \cdot d\mathbf{r} = \int_0^\pi [\sin^2 t + \cos^2 t + 3t^2\cos t]\,dt = \int_0^\pi [1 + 3t^2\cos t]\,dt$

$\qquad = \Big[t \Big]_0^\pi + 3\Big[t^2\sin t \Big]_0^\pi - 6\int_0^\pi t\sin t\,dt = \Big[t + 3t^2\sin t - 6(\sin t - t\cos t) \Big]_0^\pi = -5\pi$

—**CONTINUED**—

22. —CONTINUED—

(b) $\mathbf{r}_2(t) = (1 - 2t)\mathbf{i} + \pi t\mathbf{k}, \ 0 \le t \le 1$

$\mathbf{r}_2{}'(t) = -2\mathbf{i} + \pi\mathbf{k}$

$\mathbf{F}(t) = (1 - 2t)\mathbf{j} + 3\pi^2 t^2(1 - 2t)\mathbf{k}$

$\displaystyle\int_C \mathbf{F} \cdot d\mathbf{r} = \int_0^1 3\pi^3 t^2(1 - 2t)\, dt = 3\pi^3 \int_0^1 (t^2 - 2t^3)\, dt = 3\pi^3 \left[\frac{t^3}{3} - \frac{t^4}{2}\right]_0^1 = -\frac{\pi^3}{2}$

24. $\mathbf{F}(x, y, z) = y \sin z\,\mathbf{i} + x \sin z\,\mathbf{j} + xy \cos x\,\mathbf{k}$

(a) $\mathbf{r}_1(t) = t^2\mathbf{i} + t^2\mathbf{j}, \ 0 \le t \le 2$

$\mathbf{r}_1{}'(t) = 2t\mathbf{i} + 2t\mathbf{j}$

$\mathbf{F}(t) = t^4 \cos t^2\,\mathbf{k}$

$\displaystyle\int_C \mathbf{F} \cdot d\mathbf{r} = \int_0^2 0\, dt = 0$

(b) $\mathbf{r}_2(t) = 4t\mathbf{i} + 4t\mathbf{j}, \ 0 \le t \le 1$

$\mathbf{r}_2{}'(t) = 4\mathbf{i} + 4\mathbf{j}$

$\mathbf{F}(t) = 16t^2 \cos(4t)\mathbf{k}$

$\displaystyle\int_C \mathbf{F} \cdot d\mathbf{r} = \int_0^1 0\, dt = 0$

26. $\displaystyle\int_C [2(x + y)\mathbf{i} + 2(x + y)\mathbf{j}] \cdot d\mathbf{r} = \left[(x + y)^2\right]_{(-3, 2)}^{(4, 3)}$

$= 49$

28. $\displaystyle\int_C \frac{y\, dx - x\, dy}{x^2 + y^2} = \left[\arctan\left(\frac{x}{y}\right)\right]_{(1, 1)}^{(2\sqrt{3}, 2)} = \frac{\pi}{3} - \frac{\pi}{4} = \frac{\pi}{12}$

30. $\displaystyle\int_C \frac{2x}{(x^2 + y^2)^2}\, dx + \frac{2y}{(x^2 + y^2)^2}\, dy = \left[-\frac{1}{x^2 + y^2}\right]_{(7, 5)}^{(1, 5)} = -\frac{1}{26} + \frac{1}{74} = \frac{-12}{481}$

32. $\displaystyle\int_C zy\, dx + xz\, dy + xy\, dz$

Note: Since $\mathbf{F}(x, y, z) = yz\mathbf{i} + xz\mathbf{j} + xy\mathbf{k}$ is conservative and the potential function is $f(x, y, z) = xyz + k$, the integral is independent of path as illustrated below.

(a) $\left[xyz\right]_{(0, 0, 0)}^{(1, 1, 1)} = 1$

(b) $\left[xyz\right]_{(0, 0, 0)}^{(0, 0, 1)} + \left[xyz\right]_{(0, 0, 1)}^{(1, 1, 1)} = 0 + 1 = 1$

(c) $\left[xyz\right]_{(0, 0, 0)}^{(1, 0, 0)} + \left[xyz\right]_{(1, 0, 0)}^{(1, 1, 0)} + \left[xyz\right]_{(1, 1, 0)}^{(1, 1, 1)} = 0 + 0 + 1 = 1$

34. $\displaystyle\int_C 6x\, dx - 4z\, dy - (4y - 20z)\, dz = \left[3x^2 - 4yz + 10z^2\right]_{(0, 0, 0)}^{(4, 3, 1)} = 46$

36. $\mathbf{F}(x, y) = \dfrac{2x}{y}\mathbf{i} - \dfrac{x^2}{y^2}\mathbf{j}$ is conservative.

$\text{Work} = \left[\dfrac{x^2}{y}\right]_{(-3, 2)}^{(1, 4)} = \dfrac{1}{4} - \dfrac{9}{2} = -\dfrac{17}{4}$

38. $\mathbf{F}(x, y, z) = a_1\mathbf{i} + a_2\mathbf{j} + a_3\mathbf{k}$

Since $\mathbf{F}(x, y, z)$ is conservative, the work done in moving a particle along any path from P to Q is

$$f(x, y, z) = \left[a_1x + a_2y + a_3z \right]_{P=(p_1, p_2, p_3)}^{Q=(q_1, q_2, q_3)}$$

$$= a_1(q_1 - p_1) + a_2(q_2 - p_2) + a_3(q_3 - p_3) = \mathbf{F} \cdot \overrightarrow{PQ}.$$

40. $\mathbf{F} = -150\mathbf{j}$

(a) $\mathbf{r}(t) = t\mathbf{i} + (50 - t)\mathbf{j}, \ 0 \le t \le 50$

$d\mathbf{r} = (\mathbf{i} - \mathbf{j}) \, dt$

$\displaystyle\int_C \mathbf{F} \cdot d\mathbf{r} = \int_0^{50} 150 \, dt = 7500 \ \text{ft} \cdot \text{lbs}$

(b) $\mathbf{r}(t) = t\mathbf{i} + \frac{1}{50}(50 - t)^2\mathbf{j}$

$d\mathbf{r} = \left(\mathbf{i} - \frac{1}{25}(50 - t)\mathbf{j}\right) dt$

$\displaystyle\int_C \mathbf{F} \cdot d\mathbf{r} = 6\int_0^{50} (50 - t) \, dt = 7500 \ \text{ft} \cdot \text{lbs}$

42. $\mathbf{F}(x, y) = \dfrac{y}{x^2 + y^2}\mathbf{i} - \dfrac{x}{x^2 + y^2}\mathbf{j}$

(a) $M = \dfrac{y}{x^2 + y^2}$

$\dfrac{\partial M}{\partial y} = \dfrac{(x^2 + y^2)(1) - y(2y)}{(x^2 + y^2)^2} = \dfrac{x^2 - y^2}{(x^2 + y^2)^2}$

$N = -\dfrac{x}{x^2 + y^2}$

$\dfrac{\partial N}{\partial x} = \dfrac{(x^2 + y^2)(-1) + x(2x)}{(x^2 + y^2)^2} = \dfrac{x^2 - y^2}{(x^2 + y^2)^2}$

Thus, $\dfrac{\partial N}{\partial x} = \dfrac{\partial M}{\partial y}$.

(c) $\mathbf{r}(t) = \cos t\mathbf{i} - \sin t\mathbf{j}, \ 0 \le t \le \pi$

$\mathbf{F} = -\sin t\mathbf{i} - \cos t\mathbf{j}$

$d\mathbf{r} = (-\sin t\mathbf{i} - \cos t\mathbf{j}) \, dt$

$\displaystyle\int_C \mathbf{F} \cdot d\mathbf{r} = \int_0^{\pi} (\sin^2 t + \cos^2 t) \, dt$

$= \left[t \right]_0^{\pi} = \pi$

(b) $\mathbf{r}(t) = \cos t\mathbf{i} + \sin t\mathbf{j}, \ 0 \le t \le \pi$

$\mathbf{F} = \sin t\mathbf{i} - \cos t\mathbf{j}$

$d\mathbf{r} = (-\sin t\mathbf{i} + \cos t\mathbf{j}) \, dt$

$\displaystyle\int_C \mathbf{F} \cdot d\mathbf{r} = \int_0^{\pi} (-\sin^2 t - \cos^2 t) \, dt = \left[-t \right]_0^{\pi} = -\pi$

(d) $\mathbf{r}(t) = \cos t\mathbf{i} + \sin t\mathbf{j}, \ 0 \le t \le 2\pi$

$\mathbf{F} = \sin t\mathbf{i} - \cos t\mathbf{j}$

$d\mathbf{r} = (-\sin t\mathbf{i} + \cos t\mathbf{j}) \, dt$

$\displaystyle\int_C \mathbf{F} \cdot d\mathbf{r} = \int_0^{2\pi} (-\sin^2 t - \cos^2 t) \, dt$

$= \left[-t \right]_0^{2\pi} = -2\pi$

This does not contradict Theorem 14.7 since $\mathbf{F}$ is not continuous at $(0, 0)$ in R enclosed by curve C.

(e) $\nabla\left(\arctan\dfrac{x}{y}\right) = \dfrac{1/y}{1 + (x/y)^2}\mathbf{i} + \dfrac{-x/y^2}{1 + (x/y)^2}\mathbf{j}$

$= \dfrac{y}{x^2 + y^2}\mathbf{i} - \dfrac{x}{x^2 + y^2}\mathbf{j} = \mathbf{F}$

44. A line integral is independent of path if $\displaystyle\int_C \mathbf{F} \cdot d\mathbf{r}$ does not depend on the curve joining P and Q. See Theorem 14.6

46. No, the amount of fuel required depends on the flight path. Fuel consumption is dependent on wind speed and direction. The vector field is not conservative.

48. True

50. False, the requirement is $\partial M/\partial y = \partial N/\partial x$.

Section 14.4   Green's Theorem

2. $\mathbf{r}(t) = \begin{cases} t\mathbf{i}, & 0 \le t \le 4 \\ 4\mathbf{i} + (t-4)\mathbf{j}, & 4 \le t \le 8 \\ (12-t)\mathbf{i} + (12-t)\mathbf{j}, & 8 \le t \le 12 \end{cases}$

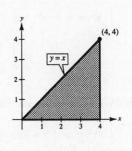

$$\int_C y^2\, dx + x^2\, dy = \int_0^4 [0\, dt + t^2(0)] + \int_4^8 [(t-4)^2(0) + 16\, dt]$$

$$+ \int_8^{12} [(12-t)^2(-dt) + (12-t)^2(-dt)] = 0 + 64 - \frac{128}{3} = \frac{64}{3}$$

4. $\mathbf{r}(t) = \cos t\mathbf{i} + \sin t\mathbf{j},\ 0 \le t \le 2\pi$

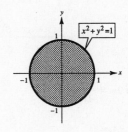

$$\int_C y^2\, dx + x^2\, dy = \int_0^{2\pi} [\sin^2 t(-\sin t\, dt) + \cos^2 t(\cos t\, dt)]$$

$$= \int_0^{2\pi} (\cos^3 t - \sin^3 t)\, dt$$

$$= \int_0^{2\pi} [\cos t(1 - \sin^2 t) - \sin t(1 - \cos^2 t)]\, dt$$

$$= \left[\sin t - \frac{\sin^3 t}{3} + \cos t - \frac{\cos^3 t}{3} \right]_0^{2\pi} = 0$$

By Green's Theorem,

$$\iint_R \left(\frac{\partial N}{\partial x} - \frac{\partial M}{\partial y} \right) dA = \int_{-1}^1 \int_{-\sqrt{1-x^2}}^{\sqrt{1-x^2}} (2x - 2y)\, dy\, dx$$

$$= \int_0^{2\pi} \int_0^1 (2r\cos\theta - 2r\sin\theta)r\, dr\, d\theta = \frac{2}{3} \int_0^{2\pi} (\cos\theta - \sin\theta)\, d\theta = \frac{2}{3}(0) = 0.$$

6. C: boundary of the region lying between the graphs of $y = x$ and $y = x^3$

$$\int_C xe^y\, dx + e^x\, dy = \int_0^1 (xe^{x^3} + 3x^2 e^x)\, dx + \int_1^0 (xe^x + e^x)\, dx \approx 2.936 - 2.718 \approx 0.22$$

$$\iint_R \left(\frac{\partial N}{\partial x} - \frac{\partial M}{\partial y} \right) dA = \int_0^1 \int_{x^3}^x (e^x - xe^y)\, dy\, dx = \int_0^1 (xe^{x^3} - x^3 e^x)\, dx \approx 0.22$$

In Exercises 8 and 10, $\dfrac{\partial N}{\partial x} - \dfrac{\partial M}{\partial y} = 1.$

8. Since C is an ellipse with $a = 2$ and $b = 1$, then R is an ellipse of area $\pi ab = 2\pi$. Thus, Green's Theorem yields

$$\int_C (y - x)\, dx + (2x - y)\, dy = \iint_R 1\, dA = \text{Area of ellipse} = 2\pi.$$

10. R is the shaded region of the accompanying figure.

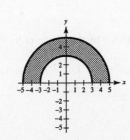

$$\int_C (y - x)\, dx + (2x - y)\, dy = \iint_R 1\, dA$$

$$= \text{Area of shaded region}$$

$$= \frac{1}{2}\pi[25 - 9] = 8\pi$$

12. The given curves intersect at $(0, 0)$ and $(9, 3)$. Thus, Green's Theorem yields

$$\int_C y^2\, dx + xy\, dy = \iint_R (y - 2y)\, dA$$

$$= \int_0^9 \int_0^{\sqrt{x}} -y\, dy\, dx = \int_0^9 \left[\frac{-y^2}{2}\right]_0^{\sqrt{x}}\, dx = \int_0^9 \frac{-x}{2}\, dx = \left[\frac{-x^2}{4}\right]_0^9 = -\frac{81}{4}$$

14. In this case, let $y = r\sin\theta$, $x = r\cos\theta$. Then $dA = r\, dr\, d\theta$ and Green's Theorem yields

$$\int_C (x^2 - y^2)\, dx + 2xy\, dy = \iint_R 4y\, dA = 4\int_0^{2\pi}\int_0^{1+\cos\theta} r\sin\theta r\, dr\, d\theta$$

$$= 4\int_0^{2\pi}\int_0^{1+\cos\theta} r^2\sin\theta\, dr\, d\theta$$

$$= \frac{4}{3}\int_0^{2\pi} \sin\theta(1 + \cos\theta)^3\, d\theta$$

$$= \left[-\frac{(1 + \cos\theta)^4}{3}\right]_0^{2\pi} = 0.$$

16. Since $\dfrac{\partial M}{\partial y} = -2e^x\sin 2y = \dfrac{\partial N}{\partial x}$ we have

$$\iint_R \left(\frac{\partial N}{\partial x} - \frac{\partial M}{\partial y}\right) dA = 0.$$

18. By Green's Theorem,

$$\int_C (e^{-x^2/2} - y)\, dx + (e^{-y^2/2} + x)\, dy = \iint_R 2\, dA = 2(\text{Area of } R) = 2[\pi(6)^2 - \pi(2)(3)] = 60\pi.$$

20. By Green's Theorem,

$$\int_C 3x^2\, e^y\, dx + e^y\, dy = \iint_R -3x^2 e^y\, dA$$

$$= \int_1^2\int_{-2}^2 -3x^2 e^y\, dy\, dx + \int_{-1}^1\int_1^2 -3x^2 e^y\, dy\, dx$$

$$+ \int_{-2}^{-1}\int_{-2}^2 -3x^2 e^y\, dy\, dx + \int_{-1}^1\int_{-2}^{-1} -3x^2 e^y\, dy\, dx$$

$$= -7(e^2 - e^{-2}) - 2(e^2 - e) - 7(e^2 - e^{-2}) - 2(e^{-1} - e^{-2})$$

$$= -16e^2 + 16e^{-2} + 2e - 2e^{-1}.$$

22. $\mathbf{F}(x, y) = (e^x - 3y)\mathbf{i} + (e^y + 6x)\mathbf{j}$

C: $r = 2\cos\theta$

$$\text{Work} = \int_C (e^x - 3y)\, dx + (e^y + 6x)\, dy = \iint_R 9\, dA = 9\pi \text{ since } r = 2\cos\theta \text{ is a circle with a radius of one.}$$

24. $\mathbf{F}(x, y) = (3x^2 + y)\mathbf{i} + 4xy^2\mathbf{j}$

C: boundary of the region bounded by the graphs of $y = \sqrt{x}$, $y = 0$, $x = 4$

$$\text{Work} = \int_C (3x^2 + y)\, dx + 4xy^2\, dy = \int_0^4\int_0^{\sqrt{x}} (4y^2 - 1)\, dy\, dx = \int_0^4 \left(\frac{4}{3}x^{3/2} - x^{1/2}\right) dx = \frac{176}{15}$$

26. From the figure we see that

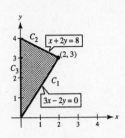

$$C_1: \ y = \frac{3}{2}x, \ dy = \frac{3}{2}dx, \ 0 \le x \le 2$$

$$C_2: \ y = -\frac{x}{2} + 4, \ dy = -\frac{1}{2}dx$$

$$C_3: \ x = 0, \ dx = 0.$$

$$A = \frac{1}{2}\int_0^2 \left(\frac{3}{2}x - \frac{3}{2}x\right) dx + \frac{1}{2}\int_2^0 \left(-\frac{1}{2}x + \frac{x}{2} - 4\right) dx + \frac{1}{2}(0)$$

$$= \frac{1}{2}\int_2^0 (-4) \, dx = 2\int_0^2 dx = 4$$

28. Since the loop of the folium is formed on the interval $0 \le t \le \infty$,

$$dx = \frac{3(1 - 2t^3)}{(t^3 + 1)^2} \, dt \text{ and } dy = \frac{3(2t - t^4)}{(t^3 + 1)^2} \, dt,$$

we have

$$A = \frac{1}{2}\int_0^\infty \left[\left(\frac{3t}{t^3 + 1}\right)\frac{3(2t - t^4)}{(t^3 + 1)^2} - \left(\frac{3t^2}{t^3 + 1}\right)\frac{3(1 - 2t^3)}{(t^3 + 1)^2}\right] dt$$

$$= \frac{9}{2}\int_0^\infty \frac{t^5 + t^2}{(t^3 + 1)^3} \, dt = \frac{9}{2}\int_0^\infty \frac{t^2(t^3 + 1)}{(t^3 + 1)^3} \, dt = \frac{3}{2}\int_0^\infty 3t^2(t^3 + 1)^{-2} \, dt = \left[\frac{-3}{2(t^3 + 1)}\right]_0^\infty = \frac{3}{2}.$$

30. See Theorem 14.9: $A = \dfrac{1}{2}\displaystyle\int_C x \, dy - y \, dx.$

32. (a) For the moment about the x-axis, $M_x = \displaystyle\int_R\!\!\int y \, dA$. Let $N = 0$ and $M = -y^2/2$. By Green's Theorem,

$$M_x = \int_C -\frac{y^2}{2} \, dx = -\frac{1}{2}\int_C y^2 \, dx \text{ and } \bar{y} = \frac{M_x}{2A} = -\frac{1}{2A}\int_C y^2 \, dx.$$

For the moment about the y-axis, $M_y = \displaystyle\int_R\!\!\int x \, dA$. Let $N = x^2/2$ and $M = 0$. By Green's Theorem,

$$M_y = \int_C \frac{x^2}{2} \, dy = \frac{1}{2}\int_C x^2 \, dy \text{ and } \bar{x} = \frac{M_y}{2A} = \frac{1}{2A}\int_C x^2 \, dy.$$

(b) By Theorem 14.9 and the fact that $x = r\cos\theta$, $y = r\sin\theta$, we have

$$A = \frac{1}{2}\int x \, dy - y \, dx = \frac{1}{2}\int (r\cos\theta)(r\cos\theta) \, d\theta - (r\sin\theta)(-r\sin\theta) \, d\theta = \frac{1}{2}\int_C r^2 \, d\theta.$$

34. Since $A = $ area of semicircle $= \dfrac{\pi a^2}{2}$, we have $\dfrac{1}{2A} = \dfrac{1}{\pi a^2}$. Note that $y = 0$ and $dy = 0$ along the boundary $y = 0$.

Let $x = a\cos t$, $y = a\sin t$, $0 \le t \le \pi$, then

$$\bar{x} = \frac{1}{\pi a^2}\int_0^\pi a^2\cos^2 t(a\cos t) \, dt = \frac{a}{\pi}\int_0^\pi \cos^3 t \, dt = \frac{a}{\pi}\int_0^\pi (1 - \sin^2 t)\cos t \, dt = \frac{a}{\pi}\left[\sin t - \frac{\sin^3 t}{3}\right]_0^\pi = 0$$

$$\bar{y} = \frac{-1}{\pi a^2}\int_0^\pi a^2\sin^2 t(-a\sin t \, dt) = \frac{a}{\pi}\int_0^\pi \sin^3 t \, dt = \frac{a}{\pi}\left[-\cos t + \frac{\cos^3 t}{3}\right]_0^\pi = \frac{4a}{3\pi}.$$

$$(\bar{x}, \bar{y}) = \left(0, \frac{4a}{3\pi}\right)$$

36. Since $A = \dfrac{1}{2}(2a)(c) = ac$, we have $\dfrac{1}{2A} = \dfrac{1}{2ac}$,

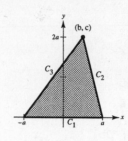

C_1: $y = 0$, $dy = 0$

C_2: $y = \dfrac{c}{b-a}(x-a)$, $dy = \dfrac{c}{b-a}dx$

C_3: $y = \dfrac{c}{b+a}(x+a)$, $dy = \dfrac{c}{b+a}dx$.

Thus,

$$\bar{x} = \frac{1}{2ac}\int_C x^2\,dy = \frac{1}{2ac}\left[\int_{-a}^a 0 + \int_a^b x^2\frac{c}{b-a}\,dx + \int_b^{-a} x^2\frac{c}{b+a}\,dx\right] = \frac{1}{2ac}\left[0 + \frac{2abc}{3}\right] = \frac{b}{3}$$

$$\bar{y} = \frac{-1}{2ac}\int_C y^2\,dx = \frac{-1}{2ac}\left[0 + \int_a^b \left(\frac{c}{b-a}\right)^2 (x-a)^2\,dx + \int_b^{-a}\left(\frac{c}{b+a}\right)^2 (x+a)^2\,dx\right]$$

$$= \frac{-1}{2ac}\left[\frac{c^2(b-a)}{3} - \frac{c^2(b+a)}{3}\right] = \frac{c}{3}.$$

$$(\bar{x}, \bar{y}) = \left(\frac{b}{3}, \frac{c}{3}\right)$$

38. $A = \dfrac{1}{2}\displaystyle\int_0^\pi a^2\cos^2 3\theta\,d\theta = \dfrac{a^2}{2}\int_0^\pi \dfrac{1+\cos 6\theta}{2}\,d\theta = \dfrac{a^2}{4}\left[\theta + \dfrac{\sin 6\theta}{6}\right]_0^\pi = \dfrac{\pi a^2}{4}$

Note: In this case R is enclosed by $r = a\cos 3\theta$ where $0 \le \theta \le \pi$.

40. In this case, $0 \le \theta \le 2\pi$ and we let

$$u = \frac{\sin\theta}{1+\cos\theta}, \quad \cos\theta = \frac{1-u^2}{1+u^2}, \quad d\theta = \frac{2\,du}{1+u^2}.$$

Now $u \Rightarrow \infty$ as $\theta \Rightarrow \pi$ and we have

$$A = 2\left(\frac{1}{2}\right)\int_0^\pi \frac{9}{(2-\cos\theta)^2}\,d\theta = 9\int_0^\infty \frac{\dfrac{2du}{1+u^2}}{4 - 4\left(\dfrac{1-u^2}{1+u^2}\right) + \dfrac{(1-u^2)^2}{(1+u^2)^2}} = 18\int_0^\infty \frac{1+u^2}{(1+3u^2)^2}\,du$$

$$= 18\int_0^\infty \frac{1/3}{1+3u^2}\,du + 18\int_0^\infty \frac{2/3}{(1+3u^2)^2}\,du = \left[\frac{6}{\sqrt{3}}\arctan\sqrt{3}\,u\right]_0^\infty + \frac{12}{\sqrt{3}}\left(\frac{1}{2}\right)\left[\frac{u}{1+3u^2} + \int\frac{\sqrt{3}}{1+3u^2}\,du\right]_0^\infty$$

$$= \frac{6}{\sqrt{3}}\left(\frac{\pi}{2}\right) + \frac{6}{\sqrt{3}}\left[\frac{u}{1+3u^2}\right]_0^\infty + \left[\frac{6}{\sqrt{3}}\arctan\sqrt{3}\,u\right]_0^\infty = \frac{3\pi}{\sqrt{3}} + 0 + \frac{3\pi}{\sqrt{3}} = 2\sqrt{3}\,\pi.$$

42. (a) Let C be the line segment joining (x_1, y_1) and (x_2, y_2).

$$y = \frac{y_2 - y_1}{x_2 - x_1}(x - x_1) + y_1$$

$$dy = \frac{y_2 - y_1}{x_2 - x_1}\,dx$$

$$\int_C -y\,dx + x\,dy = \int_{x_1}^{x_2}\left[-\frac{y_2-y_1}{x_2-x_1}(x-x_1) - y_1 + x\left(\frac{y_2-y_1}{x_2-x_1}\right)\right]dx = \int_{x_1}^{x_2}\left[x_1\left(\frac{y_2-y_1}{x_2-x_1}\right) - y_1\right]dx$$

$$= \left[\left[x_1\left(\frac{y_2-y_1}{x_2-x_1}\right) - y_1\right]x\right]_{x_1}^{x_2} = \left[x_1\left(\frac{y_2-y_1}{x_2-x_1}\right) - y_1\right](x_2 - x_1)$$

$$= x_1(y_2 - y_1) - y_1(x_2 - x_1) = x_1 y_2 - x_2 y_1$$

—CONTINUED—

42. —CONTINUED—

(b) Let C be the boundary of the region $A = \frac{1}{2} \int_C -y\, dx + x\, dy = \frac{1}{2} \int_R \int (1 - (-1))\, dA = \int_R \int dA.$

Therefore,

$$\int_R \int dA = \frac{1}{2}\left[\int_{C_1} -y\, dx + x\, dy + \int_{C_2} -y\, dx + x\, dy + \cdots + \int_{C_n} -y\, dx + x\, dy\right]$$

where C_1 is the line segment joining (x_1, y_1) and (x_2, y_2), C_2 is the line segment joining (x_2, y_2) and (x_3, y_3), . . . , and C_n is the line segment joining (x_n, y_n) and (x_1, y_1). Thus,

$$\int_R \int dA = \frac{1}{2}[(x_1 y_2 - x_2 y_1) + (x_2 y_3 - x_3 y_2) + \cdots + (x_{n-1}y_n - x_n y_{n-1}) + (x_n y_1 - x_1 y_n)].$$

44. Hexagon: $(0, 0), (2, 0), (3, 2), (2, 4), (0, 3), (-1, 1)$

$A = \frac{1}{2}[(0 - 0) + (4 - 0) + (12 - 4) + (6 - 0) + (0 + 3) + (0 - 0)] = \frac{21}{2}$

46. Since $\int_C \mathbf{F} \cdot \mathbf{N}\, ds = \int_R \int \operatorname{div} \mathbf{F}\, dA$, then

$$\int_C f D_{\mathbf{N}} g\, ds = \int_C f\nabla g \cdot \mathbf{N}\, ds$$

$$= \int_R \int \operatorname{div}(f\nabla g)\, dA = \int_R \int (f \operatorname{div}(\nabla g) + \nabla f \cdot \nabla g)\, dA = \int_R \int (f\nabla^2 g + \nabla f \cdot \nabla g)\, dA.$$

48. $\int_C f(x)\, dx + g(y)\, dy = \int_R \int \left[\frac{\partial}{\partial x}g(y) - \frac{\partial}{\partial y}f(x)\right] dA = \int_R \int (0 - 0)\, dA = 0$

Section 14.5   Parametric Surfaces

2. $\mathbf{r}(u, v) = u \cos v \mathbf{i} + u \sin v \mathbf{j} + u\mathbf{k}$

$x^2 + y^2 = z^2$

Matches d.

4. $\mathbf{r}(u, v) = 4 \cos u \mathbf{i} + 4 \sin u \mathbf{j} + v\mathbf{k}$

$x^2 + y^2 = 16$

Matches a.

6. $\mathbf{r}(u, v) = 2u \cos v \mathbf{i} + 2u \sin v \mathbf{j} + \frac{1}{2}u^2 \mathbf{k}$

$z = \frac{1}{2}u^2, \; x^2 + y^2 = 4u^2 \implies z = \frac{1}{8}(x^2 + y^2)$

Paraboloid

8. $\mathbf{r}(u, v) = 3 \cos v \cos u \mathbf{i} + 3 \cos v \sin u \mathbf{j} + 5 \sin v \mathbf{k}$

$x^2 + y^2 = 9 \cos^2 v \cos^2 u + 9 \cos^2 v \sin^2 u = 9 \cos^2 v$

$\dfrac{x^2 + y^2}{9} + \dfrac{z^2}{25} = \cos^2 v + \sin^2 v = 1$

$\dfrac{x^2}{9} + \dfrac{y^2}{9} + \dfrac{z^2}{25} = 1$

Ellipsoid

For Exercises 10 and 12,

$$\mathbf{r}(u, v) = u \cos v\mathbf{i} + u \sin v\mathbf{j} + u^2\mathbf{k}, \; 0 \le u \le 2, \; 0 \le v \le 2\pi.$$

Eliminating the parameter yields

$$z = x^2 + y^2, \; 0 \le z \le 4.$$

10. $\mathbf{s}(u, v) = u \cos v\mathbf{i} + u^2\mathbf{j} + u \sin v\mathbf{k}, \; 0 \le u \le 2, \; 0 \le v \le 2\pi$

$y = x^2 + z^2$

The paraboloid opens along the y-axis instead of the z-axis.

12. $\mathbf{s}(u, v) = 4u \cos v\mathbf{i} + 4u \sin v\mathbf{j} + u^2\mathbf{k}, \; 0 \le u \le 2, \; 0 \le v \le 2\pi$

$$z = \frac{x^2 + y^2}{16}$$

The paraboloid is "wider." The top is now the circle $x^2 + y^2 = 64$. It was $x^2 + y^2 = 4$.

14. $\mathbf{r}(u, v) = 2 \cos v \cos u\mathbf{i} + 4 \cos v \sin u\mathbf{j} + \sin v\mathbf{k},$

$0 \le u \le 2\pi, \; 0 \le v \le 2\pi$

$$\frac{x^2}{4} + \frac{y^2}{16} + \frac{z^2}{1} = 1$$

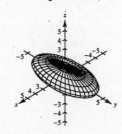

16. $\mathbf{r}(u, v) = 2u \cos v\mathbf{i} + 2u \sin v\mathbf{j} + v\mathbf{k},$

$0 \le u \le 1, \; 0 \le v \le 3\pi$

$$z = \arctan\left(\frac{y}{x}\right)$$

18. $\mathbf{r}(u, v) = \cos^3 u \cos v\mathbf{i} + \sin^3 u \sin v\mathbf{j} + u\mathbf{k},$

$0 \le u \le \dfrac{\pi}{2}, \; 0 \le v \le 2\pi$

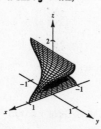

20. $z = 6 - x - y$

$\mathbf{r}(u, v) = u\mathbf{i} + v\mathbf{j} + (6 - u - v)\mathbf{k}$

22. $4x^2 + y^2 = 16$

$\mathbf{r}(u, v) = 2 \cos u\mathbf{i} + 4 \sin u\mathbf{j} + v\mathbf{k}$

24. $\dfrac{x^2}{9} + \dfrac{y^2}{4} + \dfrac{z^2}{1} = 1$

$\mathbf{r}(u, v) = 3 \cos v \cos u\mathbf{i} + 2 \cos v \sin u\mathbf{j} + \sin v\mathbf{k}$

26. $z = x^2 + y^2$ inside $x^2 + y^2 = 9$.

$\mathbf{r}(u, v) = v \cos u\mathbf{i} + v \sin u\mathbf{j} + v^2\mathbf{k}, \; 0 \le v \le 3$

28. Function: $y = x^{3/2}, \; 0 \le x \le 4$

Axis of revolution: x-axis

$x = u, \; y = u^{3/2} \cos v, \; z = u^{3/2} \sin v$

$0 \le u \le 4, \; 0 \le v \le 2\pi$

30. Function: $z = 4 - y^2, \; 0 \le y \le 2$

Axis of revolution: y-axis

$x = (4 - u^2) \cos v, \; y = u, \; z = (4 - u^2) \sin v$

$0 \le u \le 2, \; 0 \le v \le 2\pi$

32. $\mathbf{r}(u, v) = u\mathbf{i} + v\mathbf{j} + \sqrt{uv}\,\mathbf{k}, \ (1, 1, 1)$

$\mathbf{r}_u(u, v) = \mathbf{i} + \dfrac{v}{2\sqrt{uv}}\mathbf{k}, \ \mathbf{r}_v(u, v) = \mathbf{j} + \dfrac{u}{2\sqrt{uv}}\mathbf{k}$

At $(1, 1, 1)$, $u = 1$ and $v = 1$.

$\mathbf{r}_u(1, 1) = \mathbf{i} + \dfrac{1}{2}\mathbf{k}, \ \mathbf{r}_v(1, 1) = \mathbf{j} + \dfrac{1}{2}\mathbf{k}$

$\mathbf{N} = \mathbf{r}_u(1, 1) \times \mathbf{r}_v(1, 1) = \begin{vmatrix} \mathbf{i} & \mathbf{j} & \mathbf{k} \\ 1 & 0 & \frac{1}{2} \\ 0 & 1 & \frac{1}{2} \end{vmatrix} = -\tfrac{1}{2}\mathbf{i} - \tfrac{1}{2}\mathbf{j} + \mathbf{k}$

Direction numbers: $1, 1, -2$

Tangent plane: $(x - 1) + (y - 1) - 2(z - 1) = 0$

$\qquad\qquad x + y - 2z = 0$

34. $\mathbf{r}(u, v) = 2u \cosh v\,\mathbf{i} + 2u \sinh v\,\mathbf{j} + \dfrac{1}{2}u^2\mathbf{k}$,

$\mathbf{r}_u(u, v) = 2 \cosh v\,\mathbf{i} + 2 \sinh v\,\mathbf{j} + u\mathbf{k}$

$\mathbf{r}_v(u, v) = 2u \sinh v\,\mathbf{i} + 2u \cosh v\,\mathbf{j}$

At $(-4, 0, 2)$, $u = -2$ and $v = 0$.

$\mathbf{r}_u(-2, 0) = 2\mathbf{i} - 2\mathbf{k}, \ \mathbf{r}_v(-2, 0) = -4\mathbf{j}$

$\mathbf{N} = \mathbf{r}_u \times \mathbf{r}_v = -8\mathbf{i} - 8\mathbf{k}$

Direction numbers: $1, 0, 1$

Tangent plane: $(x + 4) + (z - 2) = 0$

$\qquad\qquad x + z = -2$

36. $\mathbf{r}(u, v) = 4u \cos v\,\mathbf{i} + 4u \sin v\,\mathbf{j} + u^2\mathbf{k}, \ 0 \le u \le 2, \ 0 \le v \le 2\pi$

$\mathbf{r}_u(u, v) = 4 \cos v\,\mathbf{i} + 4 \sin v\,\mathbf{j} + 2u\mathbf{k}$

$\mathbf{r}_v(u, v) = -4u \sin v\,\mathbf{i} + 4u \cos v\,\mathbf{j}$

$\mathbf{r}_u \times \mathbf{r}_v = \begin{vmatrix} \mathbf{i} & \mathbf{j} & \mathbf{k} \\ 4\cos v & 4\sin v & 2u \\ -4u\sin v & 4u\cos v & 0 \end{vmatrix} = -8u^2 \cos v\,\mathbf{i} - 8u^2 \sin v\,\mathbf{j} + 16u\mathbf{k}$

$\|\mathbf{r}_u \times \mathbf{r}_v\| = \sqrt{64u^4 + 256u^2} = 8u\sqrt{u^2 + 4}$

$A = \displaystyle\int_0^{2\pi}\int_0^2 8u\sqrt{u^2 + 4}\,du\,dv = \int_0^{2\pi}\left(\frac{128\sqrt{2}}{3} - \frac{64}{3}\right)dv = \frac{128\pi}{3}\left(2\sqrt{2} - 1\right)$

38. $\mathbf{r}(u, v) = a \sin u \cos v\,\mathbf{i} + a \sin u \sin v\,\mathbf{j} + a \cos u\,\mathbf{k}, \ 0 \le u \le \pi, \ 0 \le v \le 2\pi$

$\mathbf{r}_u(u, v) = a \cos u \cos v\,\mathbf{i} + a \cos u \sin v\,\mathbf{j} - a \sin u\,\mathbf{k}$

$\mathbf{r}_v(u, v) = -a \sin u \sin v\,\mathbf{i} + a \sin u \cos v\,\mathbf{j}$

$\mathbf{r}_u \times \mathbf{r}_v = \begin{vmatrix} \mathbf{i} & \mathbf{j} & \mathbf{k} \\ a\cos u\cos v & a\cos u\sin v & -a\sin u \\ -a\sin u\sin v & a\sin u\cos v & 0 \end{vmatrix} = a^2 \sin^2 u \cos v\,\mathbf{i} + a^2 \sin^2 u \sin v\,\mathbf{j} + a^2 \sin u \cos u\,\mathbf{k}$

$\|\mathbf{r}_u \times \mathbf{r}_v\| = a^2 \sin u$

$A = \displaystyle\int_0^{2\pi}\int_0^{\pi} a^2 \sin u\,du\,dv = 4\pi a^2$

40. $\mathbf{r}(u, v) = (a + b \cos v) \cos u\,\mathbf{i} + (a + b \cos v) \sin u\,\mathbf{j} + b \sin v\,\mathbf{k}, \ a > b, \ 0 \le u \le 2\pi, \ 0 \le v \le 2\pi$

$\mathbf{r}_u(u, v) = -(a + b \cos v) \sin u\,\mathbf{i} + (a + b \cos v) \cos u\,\mathbf{j}$

$\mathbf{r}_v(u, v) = -b \sin v \cos u\,\mathbf{i} - b \sin v \sin u\,\mathbf{j} + b \cos v\,\mathbf{k}$

$\mathbf{r}_u \times \mathbf{r}_v = \begin{vmatrix} \mathbf{i} & \mathbf{j} & \mathbf{k} \\ -(a + b\cos v)\sin u & (a + b\cos v)\cos u & 0 \\ -b\sin v\cos u & -b\sin v\sin u & b\cos v \end{vmatrix}$

$\qquad = b \cos u \cos v(a + b \cos v)\mathbf{i} + b \sin u \cos v(a + b \cos v)\mathbf{j} + b \sin v(a + b \cos v)\mathbf{k}$

$\|\mathbf{r}_u \times \mathbf{r}_v\| = b(a + b \cos v)$

$A = \displaystyle\int_0^{2\pi}\int_0^{2\pi} b(a + b \cos v)\,du\,dv = 4\pi^2 ab$

42. $\mathbf{r}(u, v) = \sin u \cos v\mathbf{i} + u\mathbf{j} + \sin u \sin v\mathbf{k}$, $0 \le u \le \pi$, $0 \le v \le 2\pi$

$\mathbf{r}_u(u, v) = \cos u \cos v\mathbf{i} + \mathbf{j} + \cos u \sin v\mathbf{k}$

$\mathbf{r}_v(u, v) = -\sin u \sin v\mathbf{i} + \sin u \cos v\mathbf{k}$

$\mathbf{r}_u \times \mathbf{r}_v = \sin u \cos v\mathbf{i} - \cos u \sin u\mathbf{j} + \sin u \sin v\mathbf{k}$

$\|\mathbf{r}_u \times \mathbf{r}_v\| = \sin u \sqrt{1 + \cos^2 u}$

$A = \int_0^{2\pi} \int_0^{\pi} \sin u \sqrt{1 + \cos^2 u}\, du\, dv = \pi\left[2\sqrt{2} + \ln\left|\frac{\sqrt{2} + 1}{\sqrt{2} - 1}\right|\right]$

44. See the definition, page 1055.

46. Graph of $\mathbf{r}(u, v) = u \cos v\mathbf{i} + u \sin v\mathbf{j} + v\mathbf{k}$

$0 \le u \le \pi$, $0 \le v \le \pi$ from

(a) $(10, 0, 0)$

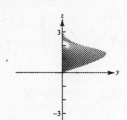

(b) $(0, 0, 10)$

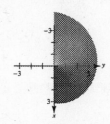

(c) $(10, 10, 10)$

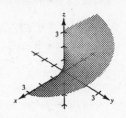

48. $\mathbf{r}(u, v) = 2u \cos v\mathbf{i} + 2u \sin v\mathbf{j} + v\mathbf{k}$, $0 \le u \le 1$, $0 \le v \le 3\pi$

(a) If $u = 1$:

$\mathbf{r}(1, v) = 2 \cos v\mathbf{i} + 2 \sin v\mathbf{j} + v\mathbf{k}$

$x^2 + y^2 = 4$

$0 \le z \le 3\pi$

Helix

(b) If $v = \dfrac{2\pi}{3}$:

$\mathbf{r}\left(u, \dfrac{2\pi}{3}\right) = -u\mathbf{i} + \sqrt{3}u\mathbf{j} + \dfrac{2\pi}{3}\mathbf{k}$

$y = -\sqrt{3}x$

$z = \dfrac{2\pi}{3}$

Line

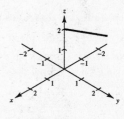

(c) If one parameter is held constant, the result is a **curve** in 3-space.

50. $x^2 + y^2 - z^2 = 1$

Let $x = u \cos v$, $y = u \sin v$, and $z = \sqrt{u^2 - 1}$. Then,

$\mathbf{r}_u(u, v) = \cos v\mathbf{i} + \sin v\mathbf{j} + \dfrac{u}{\sqrt{u^2 - 1}}\mathbf{k}$

$\mathbf{r}_v(u, v) = -u \sin v\mathbf{i} + u \cos v\mathbf{j}$.

At $(1, 0, 0)$, $u = 1$ and $v = 0$. $\mathbf{r}_u(1, 0)$ is undefined and $\mathbf{r}_v(1, 0) = \mathbf{j}$. The tangent plane at $(1, 0, 0)$ is $x = 1$.

52. $\mathbf{r}(u, v) = u\mathbf{i} + f(u) \cos v\mathbf{j} + f(u) \sin v\mathbf{k}, \ a \le u \le b, \ 0 \le v \le 2\pi$

$\mathbf{r}_u(u, v) = \mathbf{i} + f'(u) \cos v\mathbf{j} + f'(u) \sin v\mathbf{k}$

$\mathbf{r}_v(u, v) = -f(u) \sin v\mathbf{j} + f(u) \cos v\mathbf{k}$

$\mathbf{r}_u \times \mathbf{r}_v = \begin{vmatrix} \mathbf{i} & \mathbf{j} & \mathbf{k} \\ 1 & f'(u) \cos v & f'(u) \sin v \\ 0 & -f(u) \sin v & f(u) \cos v \end{vmatrix} = f(u)f'(u)\mathbf{i} - f(u) \cos v\mathbf{j} - f(u) \sin v\mathbf{k}$

$\|\mathbf{r}_u \times \mathbf{r}_v\| = f(u)\sqrt{1 + [f'(u)]^2}$

$$A = \int_0^{2\pi} \int_a^b f(u)\sqrt{1 + [f'(u)]^2} \, du \, dv$$

$$= 2\pi \int_a^b f(x)\sqrt{1 + [f'(x)]^2} \, dx \quad \text{(since } u = x)$$

Section 14.6   Surface Integrals

2. $S: z = 15 - 2x + 3y, \ 0 \le x \le 2, \ 0 \le y \le 4, \ \dfrac{\partial z}{\partial x} = -2, \ \dfrac{\partial z}{\partial y} = 3, \ dS = \sqrt{1 + 4 + 9} \, dy \, dx = \sqrt{14} \, dy \, dx$

$$\iint_S (x - 2y + z) \, dS = \int_0^2 \int_0^4 (x - 2y + 15 - 2x + 3y)\sqrt{14} \, dy \, dx$$

$$= \sqrt{14} \int_0^2 \int_0^4 (15 - x + y) \, dy \, dx = 128\sqrt{14}$$

4. $S: z = \dfrac{2}{3}x^{3/2}, \ 0 \le x \le 1, \ 0 \le y \le x, \ \dfrac{\partial z}{\partial x} = x^{1/2}, \ \dfrac{\partial z}{\partial y} = 0$

$$\iint_S (x - 2y + z) \, dS = \int_0^1 \int_0^x \left(x - 2y + \frac{2}{3}x^{3/2}\right)\sqrt{1 + (x^{1/2})^2 + (0)^2} \, dy \, dx$$

$$= \int_0^1 \int_0^x \left(x - 2y + \frac{2}{3}x^{3/2}\right)\sqrt{1 + x} \, dy \, dx$$

$$= \frac{2}{3} \int_0^1 x^{5/2}\sqrt{x + 1} \, dx$$

$$= \frac{2}{3}\left[\frac{1}{4}x^{5/2}(1 + x)^{3/2}\right]_0^1 - \frac{5}{12}\int_0^1 x^{3/2}\sqrt{1 + x} \, dx$$

$$= \left[\frac{1}{6}x^{5/2}(1 + x)^{3/2}\right]_0^1 - \frac{5}{12}\left(\frac{1}{3}\right)\left[x^{3/2}(1 + x)^{3/2}\right]_0^1 + \frac{5}{24}\int_0^1 x^{1/2}\sqrt{1 + x} \, dx$$

$$= \frac{\sqrt{2}}{3} - \frac{5\sqrt{2}}{18} + \frac{5}{24}\int_0^1 \sqrt{x + x^2} \, dx$$

$$= \frac{\sqrt{2}}{18} + \frac{5}{24}\int_0^1 \sqrt{\left(x + \frac{1}{2}\right)^2 - \frac{1}{4}} \, dx$$

$$= \frac{\sqrt{2}}{18} + \frac{5}{24}\left(\frac{1}{2}\right)\left[\left(x + \frac{1}{2}\right)\sqrt{x^2 + x} - \frac{1}{4}\ln\left|\left(x + \frac{1}{2}\right) + \sqrt{x^2 + x}\right|\right]_0^1$$

$$= \frac{\sqrt{2}}{18} + \frac{5}{48}\left[\frac{3}{2}\sqrt{2} - \frac{1}{4}\ln\left|\frac{3}{2} + \sqrt{2}\right| + \frac{1}{4}\ln\left|\frac{1}{2}\right|\right]$$

$$= \frac{\sqrt{2}}{18} + \frac{15\sqrt{2}}{96} + \frac{5}{192}\ln\left|\frac{1}{3 + 2\sqrt{2}}\right| = \frac{61\sqrt{2}}{288} - \frac{5}{192}\ln|3 + 2\sqrt{2}| \approx 0.2536$$

6. $S: z = h,\ 0 \le x \le 2,\ 0 \le y \le \sqrt{4 - x^2},\ \dfrac{\partial z}{\partial x} = \dfrac{\partial z}{\partial y} = 0$

$$\int\!\!\int_S dx\, dS = \int_0^2 \int_0^{\sqrt{4-x^2}} xy\, dy\, dx = \frac{1}{2}\int_0^2 x(4 - x^2)\, dx = \frac{1}{2}\left[\, 2x^2 - \frac{x^4}{4}\,\right]_0^2 = 2$$

8. $S:\ z = \dfrac{1}{2}xy,\ 0 \le x \le 4,\ 0 \le y \le 4,\ \dfrac{\partial z}{\partial x} = \dfrac{1}{2}y,\ \dfrac{\partial z}{\partial y} = \dfrac{1}{2}x$

$$\int\!\!\int_S xy\, dS = \int_0^4 \int_0^4 xy\sqrt{1 + \frac{y^2}{4} + \frac{x^2}{4}}\, dy\, dx = \frac{3904}{15} - \frac{160\sqrt{5}}{3}$$

10. $S:\ z = \cos x,\ 0 \le x \le \dfrac{\pi}{2},\ 0 \le y \le \dfrac{x}{2}$

$$\int\!\!\int_S (x^2 - 2xy)\, dS = \int_0^{\pi/2} \int_0^{x/2} (x^2 - 2xy)\sqrt{1 + \sin^2 x}\, dy\, dx = \int_0^{\pi/2} \frac{x^3}{4}\sqrt{1 + \sin^2 x}\, dx \approx 0.52$$

12. $S:\ z = \sqrt{a^2 - x^2 - y^2}$

$\rho(x, y, z) = kz$

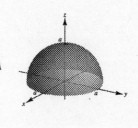

$$m = \int\!\!\int_S kz\, dS = \int\!\!\int_R k\sqrt{a^2 - x^2 - y^2}\sqrt{1 + \left(\frac{-x}{\sqrt{a^2 - x^2 - y^2}}\right)^2 + \left(\frac{-y}{\sqrt{a^2 - x^2 - y^2}}\right)^2}\, dA$$

$$= \int\!\!\int_R k\sqrt{a^2 - x^2 - y^2}\left(\frac{a}{\sqrt{a^2 - x^2 - y^2}}\right) dA$$

$$= \int\!\!\int_R ka\, dA = ka\int\!\!\int_R dA = ka(2\pi a^2) = 2ka^3\pi$$

14. $S:\ \mathbf{r}(u, v) = 2\cos u\mathbf{i} + 2\sin u\mathbf{j} + v\mathbf{k},\ 0 \le u \le \dfrac{\pi}{2},$

$\qquad 0 \le v \le 2$

$\|\mathbf{r}_u \times \mathbf{r}_v\| = \|2\cos u\mathbf{i} + 2\sin u\mathbf{j}\| = 2$

$$\int\!\!\int_S (x + y)\, dS = \int_0^2 \int_0^{\pi/2} (2\cos u + 2\sin u)2\, du\, dv = 16$$

16. $S:\ \mathbf{r}(u, v) = 4u\cos v\mathbf{i} + 4u\sin v\mathbf{j} + 3u\mathbf{k},\ 0 \le u \le 4,\ 0 \le v \le \pi$

$\|\mathbf{r}_u \times \mathbf{r}_v\| = \|-12u\cos v\mathbf{i} - 12u\sin v\mathbf{j} + 16u\mathbf{k}\| = 20u$

$$\int\!\!\int_S (x + y)\, dS = \int_0^\pi \int_0^4 (4u\cos v + 4u\sin v)20u\, du\, dv = \frac{10{,}240}{3}$$

18. $f(x, y, z) = \dfrac{xy}{z}$

$S:\ z = x^2 + y^2,\ 4 \le x^2 + y^2 \le 16$

$$\int\!\!\int_S f(x, y, z)\, dS = \int\!\!\int_S \frac{xy}{x^2 + y^2}\sqrt{1 + 4x^2 + 4y^2}\, dy\, dx = \int_0^{2\pi} \int_2^4 \frac{r^2 \sin\theta\cos\theta}{r^2}\sqrt{1 + 4r^2}\, r\, dr\, d\theta$$

$$= \int_0^{2\pi} \int_2^4 r\sqrt{1 + 4r^2}\, \sin\theta\cos\theta\, dr\, d\theta = \int_0^{2\pi} \left[\frac{1}{12}(1 + 4r^2)^{3/2}\right]_2^4 \sin\theta\cos\theta\, d\theta$$

$$= \left[\frac{65\sqrt{65} - 17\sqrt{17}}{12}\left(\frac{\sin^2\theta}{2}\right)\right]_0^{2\pi} = 0$$

20. $f(x, y, z) = \sqrt{x^2 + y^2 + z^2}$

    $S: z = \sqrt{x^2 + y^2}, \ (x - 1)^2 + y^2 \le 1$

$$\int\!\!\int_S f(x, y, z)\, dS = \int\!\!\int_S \sqrt{x^2 + y^2 + \left(\sqrt{x^2 + y^2}\right)^2} \sqrt{1 + \left(\frac{x}{\sqrt{x^2 + y^2}}\right)^2 + \left(\frac{y}{\sqrt{x^2 + y^2}}\right)^2}\, dy\, dx$$

$$= \int\!\!\int_S \sqrt{2(x^2 + y^2)} \sqrt{\frac{2(x^2 + y^2)}{x^2 + y^2}}\, dy\, dx$$

$$= 2\int\!\!\int_S \sqrt{x^2 + y^2}\, dy\, dx = 2\int_0^\pi \int_0^{2\cos\theta} r^2\, dr\, d\theta$$

$$= \frac{16}{3}\int_0^\pi \cos^3\theta\, d\theta = \frac{16}{3}\int_0^\pi (1 - \sin^2\theta)\cos\theta\, d\theta$$

$$= \left[\frac{16}{3}\left(\sin\theta - \frac{\sin^3\theta}{3}\right)\right]_0^\pi = 0$$

22. $f(x, y, z) = x^2 + y^2 + z^2$

    $S: x^2 + y^2 = 9, \ 0 \le x \le 3, \ 0 \le z \le x$

    Project the solid onto the xz-plane; $y = \sqrt{9 - x^2}$.

$$\int\!\!\int_S f(x, y, z)\, dS = \int_0^3 \int_0^x [x^2 + (9 - x^2) + z^2] \sqrt{1 + \left(\frac{-x}{\sqrt{9 - x^2}}\right)^2 + (0)^2}\, dz\, dx$$

$$= \int_0^3 \int_0^x (9 + z^2)\frac{3}{\sqrt{9 - x^2}}\, dz\, dx = \int_0^3 \left[\frac{3}{\sqrt{9 - x^2}}\left(9z + \frac{z^3}{3}\right)\right]_0^x dx$$

$$= \int_0^3 \frac{3}{\sqrt{9 - x^2}}\left(9x + \frac{x^3}{3}\right) dx = \int_0^3 27x(9 - x^2)^{-1/2}\, dx + \int_0^3 x^3(9 - x^2)^{-1/2}\, dx$$

    Let $u = x^2$, $dv = x(9 - x^2)^{-1/2}\, dx$, then $du = 2x\, dx$, $v = -\sqrt{9 - x^2}$.

$$= \left[-27\sqrt{9 - x^2}\right]_0^3 + \left[\left[-x^2\sqrt{9 - x^2}\right]_0^3 + \int_0^3 2x\sqrt{9 - x^2}\, dx\right]$$

$$= \left[81 - \frac{2}{3}(9 - x^2)^{3/2}\right]_0^3 = 81 + 18 = 99$$

24. $\mathbf{F}(x, y, z) = x\mathbf{i} + y\mathbf{j}$

    $S: 2x + 3y + z = 6$ (first octant)

    $G(x, y, z) = 2x + 3y + z - 6$

    $\nabla G(x, y, z) = 2\mathbf{i} + 3\mathbf{j} + \mathbf{k}$

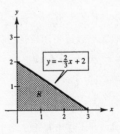

$$\int\!\!\int_S \mathbf{F} \cdot \mathbf{N}\, dS = \int\!\!\int_R \mathbf{F} \cdot \nabla G\, dA = \int_0^3 \int_0^{-(2x/3)+2} (2x + 3y)\, dy\, dx$$

$$= \int_0^3 \left[-\frac{4}{3}x^2 + 4x + \frac{3}{2}\left(-\frac{2}{3}x + 2\right)^2\right] dx$$

$$= \left[-\frac{4}{9}x^3 + 2x^2 - \frac{3}{4}\left(-\frac{2}{3}x + 2\right)^3\right]_0^3 = 12$$

26. $\mathbf{F}(x, y, z) = x\mathbf{i} + y\mathbf{j} + z\mathbf{k}$

$S: x^2 + y^2 + z^2 = 36$ (first octant)

$z = \sqrt{36 - x^2 - y^2}$

$G(x, y, z) = z - \sqrt{36 - x^2 - y^2}$

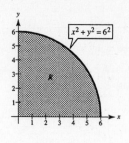

$\nabla G(x, y, z) = \dfrac{x}{\sqrt{36 - x^2 - y^2}}\mathbf{i} + \dfrac{y}{\sqrt{36 - x^2 - y^2}}\mathbf{j} + \mathbf{k}$

$\mathbf{F} \cdot \nabla G = \dfrac{x^2}{\sqrt{36 - x^2 - y^2}} + \dfrac{y^2}{\sqrt{36 - x^2 - y^2}} + z = \dfrac{36}{\sqrt{36 - x^2 - y^2}}$

$\displaystyle\iint_S \mathbf{F} \cdot \mathbf{N}\, dS = \iint_R \mathbf{F} \cdot \nabla G\, dA = \iint_R \dfrac{36}{\sqrt{36 - x^2 - y^2}}\, dA$

$\displaystyle\phantom{\iint_S \mathbf{F} \cdot \mathbf{N}\, dS} = \int_0^{\pi/2}\int_0^6 \dfrac{36}{\sqrt{36 - r^2}}\, r\, dr\, d\theta$ (improper)

$\displaystyle\phantom{\iint_S \mathbf{F} \cdot \mathbf{N}\, dS} = 108\pi$

28. $\mathbf{F}(x, y, z) = x\mathbf{i} + y\mathbf{j} - 2z\mathbf{k}$

$S: z = \sqrt{a^2 - x^2 - y^2}$

$G(x, y, z) = z - \sqrt{a^2 - x^2 - y^2}$

$\nabla G(x, y, z) = \dfrac{x}{\sqrt{a^2 - x^2 - y^2}}\mathbf{i} + \dfrac{y}{\sqrt{a^2 - x^2 - y^2}}\mathbf{j} + \mathbf{k}$

$\mathbf{F} \cdot \nabla G = \dfrac{x^2}{\sqrt{a^2 - x^2 - y^2}} + \dfrac{y^2}{\sqrt{a^2 - x^2 - y^2}} - 2\sqrt{a^2 - x^2 - y^2} = \dfrac{3x^2 + 3y^2 - 2a^2}{\sqrt{a^2 - x^2 - y^2}}$

$\displaystyle\iint_S \mathbf{F} \cdot \mathbf{N}\, dS = \iint_R \mathbf{F} \cdot \nabla G\, dA = \iint_R \dfrac{3x^2 + 3y^2 - 2a^2}{\sqrt{a^2 - x^2 - y^2}}\, dA$

$\displaystyle\phantom{\iint_S \mathbf{F} \cdot \mathbf{N}\, dS} = \int_0^{2\pi}\int_0^a \dfrac{3r^2 - 2a^2}{\sqrt{a^2 - r^2}}\, r\, dr\, d\theta$

$\displaystyle\phantom{\iint_S \mathbf{F} \cdot \mathbf{N}\, dS} = 3\int_0^{2\pi}\int_0^a \dfrac{r^3}{\sqrt{a^2 - r^2}}\, dr\, d\theta - 2a^2 \int_0^{2\pi}\int_0^a \dfrac{r}{\sqrt{a^2 - r^2}}\, dr\, d\theta$

$\displaystyle\phantom{\iint_S \mathbf{F} \cdot \mathbf{N}\, dS} = 3\left[\int_0^{2\pi}\left[-r^2\sqrt{a^2 - r^2} - \dfrac{2}{3}(a^2 - r^2)^{3/2}\right]_0^a d\theta\right] - 2a^2\int_0^{2\pi}\left[-\sqrt{a^2 - r^2}\right]_0^a d\theta$

$\displaystyle\phantom{\iint_S \mathbf{F} \cdot \mathbf{N}\, dS} = 3\int_0^{2\pi} \dfrac{2}{3}a^3\, d\theta - 2a^2\int_0^{2\pi} a\, d\theta = 0$

30. $\mathbf{F}(x, y, z) = (x + y)\mathbf{i} + y\mathbf{j} + z\mathbf{k}$

$S: z = 1 - x^2 - y^2,\ z = 0$

$G(x, y, z) = z + x^2 + y^2 - 1$

$\nabla G(x, y, z) = 2x\mathbf{i} + 2y\mathbf{j} + \mathbf{k}$

$\mathbf{F} \cdot \nabla G = 2x(x + y) + 2y(y) + (1 - x^2 - y^2) = x^2 + 2xy + y^2 + 1$

$\displaystyle\iint_S \mathbf{F} \cdot \mathbf{N}\, dS = \iint_R \mathbf{F} \cdot \nabla G\, dA = \iint_R (x^2 + 2xy + y^2 + 1)\, dA$

$\displaystyle\phantom{\iint_S \mathbf{F} \cdot \mathbf{N}\, dS} = \int_0^{2\pi}\int_0^1 (r^2 + 2r^2\cos\theta\sin\theta + 1)r\, dr\, d\theta$

$\displaystyle\phantom{\iint_S \mathbf{F} \cdot \mathbf{N}\, dS} = \int_0^{2\pi}\left(\dfrac{3}{4} + \dfrac{1}{2}\sin\theta\cos\theta\right)d\theta = \left[\dfrac{3}{4}\theta + \dfrac{\sin^2\theta}{4}\right]_0^{2\pi} = \dfrac{3\pi}{2}$

The flux across the bottom $z = 0$ is zero.

32. A surface is orientable if a unit normal vector N can be defined at every nonboundary point of S in such a way that the normal vectors vary continuously over the surface S.

34. Orientable

36. $\mathbf{E} = yz\mathbf{i} + xz\mathbf{j} + xy\mathbf{k}$

S: $z = \sqrt{1 - x^2 - y^2}$

$$\iint_S \mathbf{E} \cdot \mathbf{N} \, dS = \iint_R \mathbf{E} \cdot (-g_x(x, y)\mathbf{i} - g_y(x, y)\mathbf{j} + \mathbf{k}) \, dA$$

$$= \iint_R (yz\mathbf{i} + xz\mathbf{j} + xy\mathbf{k}) \cdot \left(\frac{x}{\sqrt{1 - x^2 - y^2}}\mathbf{i} + \frac{y}{\sqrt{1 - x^2 - y^2}}\mathbf{j} + \mathbf{k}\right) dA$$

$$= \iint_R \left(\frac{2xyz}{\sqrt{1 - x^2 - y^2}} + xy\right) dA = \iint_R 3xy \, dA = \int_{-1}^{1} \int_{-\sqrt{1-x^2}}^{\sqrt{1-x^2}} 3xy \, dy \, dx = 0$$

38. $x^2 + y^2 + z^2 = a^2$

$z = \pm\sqrt{a^2 - x^2 - y^2}$

$$m = 2\iint_S k \, dS = 2k \iint_R \sqrt{1 + \left(\frac{-x}{\sqrt{a^2 - x^2 - y^2}}\right)^2 + \left(\frac{-y}{\sqrt{a^2 - x^2 - y^2}}\right)^2} \, dA$$

$$= 2k \iint_R \frac{a}{\sqrt{a^2 - x^2 - y^2}} \, dA = 2ka \int_0^{2\pi} \int_0^a \frac{r}{\sqrt{a^2 - r^2}} \, dr \, d\theta$$

$$= 2ka\left[-\sqrt{a^2 - r^2}\right]_0^a (2\pi) = 4\pi ka^2$$

$$I_z = 2\iint_S k(x^2 + y^2) \, dS$$

$$= 2k \iint_R (x^2 + y^2)\frac{a}{\sqrt{a^2 - x^2 - y^2}} \, dA = 2ka \int_0^{2\pi} \int_0^a \frac{r^3}{\sqrt{a^2 - r^2}} \, dr \, d\theta \quad \text{(use integration by parts)}$$

$$= 2ka\left[-r^2\sqrt{a^2 - r^2} - \frac{2}{3}(a^2 - r^2)^{3/2}\right]_0^a (2\pi)$$

$$= 2ka\left(\frac{2}{3}a^3\right)(2\pi) = \frac{2}{3}a^2(4\pi ka^2) = \frac{2}{3}a^2 m$$

Let $u = r^2$, $dv = r(a^2 - r^2)^{-1/2} \, dr$, $du = 2r \, dr$, $v = -\sqrt{a^2 - r^2}$.

40. $z = x^2 + y^2$, $0 \le z \le h$

Project the solid onto the xy-plane.

$$I_z = \iint_S (x^2 + y^2)(1) \, dS$$

$$= \int_{-\sqrt{h}}^{\sqrt{h}} \int_{-\sqrt{h-x^2}}^{\sqrt{h-x^2}} (x^2 + y^2)\sqrt{1 + 4x^2 + 4y^2} \, dy \, dx$$

$$= \int_0^{2\pi} \int_0^{\sqrt{h}} r^2\sqrt{1 + 4r^2}\, r \, dr \, d\theta$$

$$= 2\pi\left[\frac{h}{12}(1 + 4h)^{3/2} - \frac{1}{120}(1 + 4h)^{5/2}\right] + \frac{2\pi}{120}$$

$$= \frac{(1 + 4h)^{3/2}\pi}{60}[10h - (1 + 4h)] + \frac{\pi}{60} = \frac{\pi}{60}[(1 + 4h)^{3/2}(6h - 1) + 1]$$

42. S: $z = \sqrt{16 - x^2 - y^2}$

$\mathbf{F}(x, y, z) = 0.5z\mathbf{k}$

$$\iint_S \rho \mathbf{F} \cdot \mathbf{N} \, dS = \iint_R \rho \mathbf{F} \cdot (-g_x(x, y)\mathbf{i} - g_y(x, y)\mathbf{j} + \mathbf{k}) \, dA$$

$$= \iint_R 0.5\rho z \mathbf{k} \cdot \left[\frac{x}{\sqrt{16 - x^2 - y^2}}\mathbf{i} + \frac{y}{\sqrt{16 - x^2 - y^2}}\mathbf{j} + \mathbf{k} \right] dA$$

$$= \iint_R 0.5 \, \rho z \, dA = \iint_R 0.5\rho\sqrt{16 - x^2 - y^2} \, dA$$

$$= 0.5\rho \int_0^{2\pi} \int_0^4 \sqrt{16 - r^2}\, r \, dr \, d\theta = 0.5\rho \int_0^{2\pi} \frac{64}{3} \, d\theta = \frac{64\pi\rho}{3}$$

Section 14.7   Divergence Theorem

2. Surface Integral: There are three surfaces to the cylinder.

Bottom: $z = 0$, $\mathbf{N} = -\mathbf{k}$, $\mathbf{F} \cdot \mathbf{N} = -z^2$

$$\iint_{S_1} 0 \, dS = 0$$

Top: $z = h$, $\mathbf{N} = \mathbf{k}$, $\mathbf{F} \cdot \mathbf{N} = z^2$

$$\iint_{S_2} h^2 \, dS = h^2 \, (\text{Area of circle}) = 4\pi h^2$$

Side: $\mathbf{r}(u, v) = 2 \cos u\mathbf{i} + 2 \sin u\mathbf{j} + v\mathbf{k}$, $0 \le u \le 2\pi$, $0 \le v \le h$

$\mathbf{r}_u = -2 \sin u\mathbf{i} + 2 \cos u\mathbf{j}$, $r_v = \mathbf{k}$

$\mathbf{r}_u \times \mathbf{r}_v = 2 \cos u\mathbf{i} + 2 \sin u\mathbf{j}$

$\mathbf{F} \cdot (\mathbf{r}_u \times \mathbf{r}_v) = 8 \cos^2 u - 8 \sin^2 u$

$$\iint_{S_3} \mathbf{F} \cdot \mathbf{N} \, dS = \int_0^h \int_0^{2\pi} (8 \cos^2 u - 8 \sin^2 u) \, du \, dv = 0$$

Therefore, $\displaystyle\iint_S \mathbf{F} \cdot \mathbf{N} \, dS = 0 + 4\pi h^2 + 0 = 4\pi h^2$.

Divergence Theorem: $\text{div } \mathbf{F} = 2 - 2 + 2z = 2z$

$$\iiint_Q 2z \, dV = \int_0^{2\pi} \int_0^2 \int_0^h 2zr \, dz \, dr \, d\theta = 4\pi h^2.$$

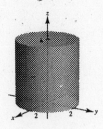

4. $\mathbf{F}(x, y, z) = xy\mathbf{i} + z\mathbf{j} + (x + y)\mathbf{k}$

S: surface bounded by the planes $y = 4$, $z = 4 - x$ and the coordinate planes

Surface Integral: There are five surfaces to this solid.

$z = 0$, $\mathbf{N} = -\mathbf{k}$, $\mathbf{F} \cdot \mathbf{N} = -(x + y)$

$$\iint_{S_1} -(x + y)\, dS = \int_0^4 \int_0^4 -(x + y)\, dy\, dx = -\int_0^4 (4x + 8)\, dx = -64$$

$y = 0$, $\mathbf{N} = -\mathbf{j}$, $\mathbf{F} \cdot \mathbf{N} = -z$

$$\iint_{S_2} -z\, dS = \int_0^4 \int_0^{4-x} -z\, dz\, dx = -\int_0^4 \frac{(4 - x)^2}{2}\, dx = -\frac{32}{3}$$

$y = 4$, $\mathbf{N} = \mathbf{j}$, $\mathbf{F} \cdot \mathbf{N} = z$

$$\iint_{S_3} z\, dS = \int_0^4 \int_0^{4-x} z\, dz\, dx = \int_0^4 \frac{(4 - x)^2}{2}\, dx = \frac{32}{3}$$

$x = 0$, $\mathbf{N} = -\mathbf{i}$, $\mathbf{F} \cdot \mathbf{N} = -xy$

$$\iint_{S_4} -xy\, dS = \int_0^4 \int_0^4 0\, dS = 0$$

$x + z = 4$, $\mathbf{N} = \dfrac{\mathbf{i} + \mathbf{k}}{\sqrt{2}}$, $\mathbf{F} \cdot \mathbf{N} = \dfrac{1}{\sqrt{2}}[xy + x + y]$, $dS = \sqrt{2}\, dA$

$$\iint_{S_5} \frac{1}{\sqrt{2}}[xy + x + y]\sqrt{2}\, dA = \int_0^4 \int_0^4 (xy + x + y)\, dy\, dx = 128$$

Therefore, $\displaystyle\iint_S \mathbf{F} \cdot \mathbf{N}\, dS = -64 - \frac{32}{3} + \frac{32}{3} + 0 + 128 = 64$.

Divergence Theorem: Since div $\mathbf{F} = y$, we have

$$\iiint_Q \operatorname{div} \mathbf{F}\, dV = \int_0^4 \int_0^4 \int_0^{4-x} y\, dz\, dy\, dx = 64.$$

6. Since div $\mathbf{F} = 2xz^2 - 2 + 3xy$ we have

$$\iiint_Q \operatorname{div} \mathbf{F}\, dV = \int_0^a \int_0^a \int_0^a (2xz^2 - 2 + 3xy)\, dz\, dy\, dx = \int_0^a \int_0^a \left(\frac{2}{3}xa^3 - 2a + 3xya\right) dy\, dx$$

$$= \int_0^a \left(\frac{2}{3}xa^4 - 2a^2 + \frac{3}{2}xa^3\right) dx$$

$$= \frac{1}{3}a^6 - 2a^3 + \frac{3}{4}a^5.$$

8. Since div $\mathbf{F} = y + z - y = z$, we have

$$\iiint_Q \operatorname{div} \mathbf{F}\, dV = \int_{-a}^a \int_{-\sqrt{a^2-x^2}}^{\sqrt{a^2-x^2}} \int_0^{\sqrt{a^2-x^2-y^2}} z\, dz\, dy\, dx = \int_0^{2\pi} \int_0^a \int_0^{\sqrt{a^2-r^2}} zr\, dz\, dr\, d\theta$$

$$= \int_0^{2\pi} \int_0^a \left[\frac{a^2 r}{2} - \frac{r^3}{2}\right] dr\, d\theta = \int_0^{2\pi} \left[\frac{a^2 r^2}{4} - \frac{r^4}{8}\right]_0^a d\theta = \int_0^{2\pi} \frac{a^4}{8}\, d\theta = \frac{\pi a^4}{4}.$$

10. Since div $\mathbf{F} = xz$, we have

$$\iiint_Q xz\, dV = \int_0^4 \int_{-3}^3 \int_{-\sqrt{9-y^2}}^{\sqrt{9-y^2}} xz\, dx\, dy\, dz = \int_0^4 \int_{-3}^3 \frac{z}{2}(0)\, dy\, dz = 0.$$

12. Since div $\mathbf{F} = y^2 + x^2 + e^z$, we have

$$\iiint_Q (x^2 + y^2 + e^z)\, dV = \int_0^{16} \int_{-\sqrt{256-x^2}}^{\sqrt{256-x^2}} \int_{(1/2)\sqrt{x^2+y^2}}^{8} (x^2 + y^2 + e^z)\, dz\, dy\, dx$$

$$= \int_0^{2\pi} \int_0^{16} \int_{r/2}^{8} (r^2 + e^z) r\, dz\, dr\, d\theta = \int_0^{2\pi} \int_0^{16} \left(8r^3 + re^8 - \frac{1}{2}r^4 - re^{r/2}\right) dr\, d\theta$$

$$= \int_0^{2\pi} \left(\frac{131{,}052}{5} + 100e^8\right) d\theta = \frac{262{,}104}{5}\pi + 200e^8\pi$$

14. Since div $\mathbf{F} = e^z + e^z + e^z = 3e^z$, we have

$$\iiint_Q 3e^z\, dV = \int_0^6 \int_0^4 \int_0^{4-y} 3e^z\, dz\, dy\, dx = \int_0^6 \int_0^4 3[e^{4-y} - 1]\, dy\, dx = \int_0^6 3(e^4 - 5)\, dx = 18(e^4 - 5).$$

16. div $\mathbf{F} = 2$

$$\iint_S \mathbf{F} \cdot \mathbf{N}\, dS = \iiint_Q \operatorname{div} \mathbf{F}\, dV = \iiint_Q 2\, dV.$$

The surface S is the upper half of a hemisphere of radius 2. Since the volume is $\frac{1}{2}\left(\frac{4}{3}\pi(2^3)\right) = 16\pi/3$, you have

$$\iint_S \mathbf{F} \cdot \mathbf{N}\, dS = 2(\text{Volume}) = \frac{32\pi}{3}.$$

18. Using the Divergence Theorem, we have

$$\iint_S \operatorname{\mathbf{curl}} \mathbf{F} \cdot \mathbf{N}\, dS = \iiint_Q \operatorname{div} (\operatorname{\mathbf{curl}} \mathbf{F})\, dV$$

$$\operatorname{\mathbf{curl}} \mathbf{F}(x, y, z) = \begin{vmatrix} \mathbf{i} & \mathbf{j} & \mathbf{k} \\ \dfrac{\partial}{\partial x} & \dfrac{\partial}{\partial y} & \dfrac{\partial}{\partial z} \\ xy\cos z & yz\sin x & xyz \end{vmatrix} = (xz - y\sin x)\mathbf{i} - (yz + xy\sin z)\mathbf{j} + (yz\cos x - x\cos z)\mathbf{k}.$$

Now, div $\operatorname{\mathbf{curl}} \mathbf{F}(x, y, z) = (z - y\cos x) - (z + x\sin z) + (y\cos x + x\sin z) = 0$. Therefore,

$$\iint_S \operatorname{\mathbf{curl}} \mathbf{F} \cdot \mathbf{N}\, dS = \iiint_Q \operatorname{div} (\operatorname{\mathbf{curl}} \mathbf{F})\, dV = 0.$$

20. If div $\mathbf{F}(x, y, z) > 0$, then source.

If div $\mathbf{F}(x, y, z) < 0$, then sink.

If div $\mathbf{F}(x, y, z) = 0$, then incompressible.

22. $v = \displaystyle\int_0^a \int_0^a x\, dy\, dz = \int_0^a \int_0^a a\, dy\, dz = \int_0^a a^2\, dz = a^3$

Similarly, $\displaystyle\int_0^a \int_0^a y\, dz\, dx = \int_0^a \int_0^a z\, dx\, dy = a^3.$

24. If $\mathbf{F}(x, y, z) = a_1\mathbf{i} + a_2\mathbf{j} + a_3\mathbf{k}$, then div $\mathbf{F} = 0$.
Therefore,

$$\iint_S \mathbf{F} \cdot \mathbf{N}\, dS = \iiint_Q \operatorname{div} \mathbf{F}\, dV = \iiint_Q 0\, dV = 0.$$

26. If $\mathbf{F}(x, y, z) = x\mathbf{i} + y\mathbf{j} + z\mathbf{k}$, then div $\mathbf{F} = 3$.

$$\frac{1}{\|\mathbf{F}\|} \iint_S \mathbf{F} \cdot \mathbf{N}\, dS = \frac{1}{\|\mathbf{F}\|} \iiint_Q \operatorname{div} \mathbf{F}\, dV = \frac{1}{\|\mathbf{F}\|} \iiint_Q 3\, dV = \frac{3}{\|\mathbf{F}\|} \iiint_Q dV$$

28. $\displaystyle\iint_S (fD_\mathbf{N} g - gD_\mathbf{N} f)\, dS = \iint_S fD_\mathbf{N} g\, dS - \iint_S gD_\mathbf{N} f\, dS$

$$= \iiint_Q (f\nabla^2 g + \nabla f \cdot \nabla g)\, dV - \iiint_Q (g\nabla^2 f + \nabla g \cdot \nabla f)\, dV = \iiint_Q (f\nabla^2 g - g\nabla^2 f)\, dV$$

Section 14.8   Stokes's Theorem

2. $\mathbf{F}(x, y, z) = x^2\mathbf{i} + y^2\mathbf{j} + x^2\mathbf{k}$

$$\text{curl } \mathbf{F} = \begin{vmatrix} \mathbf{i} & \mathbf{j} & \mathbf{k} \\ \dfrac{\partial}{\partial x} & \dfrac{\partial}{\partial y} & \dfrac{\partial}{\partial z} \\ x^2 & y^2 & x^2 \end{vmatrix} = -2x\mathbf{j}$$

4. $\mathbf{F}(x, y, z) = x \sin y\mathbf{i} - y \cos x\mathbf{j} + yz^2\mathbf{k}$

$$\text{curl } \mathbf{F} = \begin{vmatrix} \mathbf{i} & \mathbf{j} & \mathbf{k} \\ \dfrac{\partial}{\partial x} & \dfrac{\partial}{\partial y} & \dfrac{\partial}{\partial z} \\ x \sin y & -y \cos x & yz^2 \end{vmatrix}$$

$$= z^2\mathbf{i} + (y \sin x - x \cos y)\mathbf{k}$$

6. $\mathbf{F}(x, y, z) = \arcsin y\mathbf{i} + \sqrt{1 - x^2}\,\mathbf{j} + y^2\mathbf{k}$

$$\text{curl } \mathbf{F} = \begin{vmatrix} \mathbf{i} & \mathbf{j} & \mathbf{k} \\ \dfrac{\partial}{\partial x} & \dfrac{\partial}{\partial y} & \dfrac{\partial}{\partial z} \\ \arcsin y & \sqrt{1 - x^2} & y^2 \end{vmatrix}$$

$$= 2y\mathbf{i} + \left[\dfrac{-x}{\sqrt{1 - x^2}} - \dfrac{1}{\sqrt{1 - y^2}} \right]\mathbf{k}$$

$$= 2y\mathbf{i} - \left[\dfrac{x}{\sqrt{1 - x^2}} + \dfrac{1}{\sqrt{1 - y^2}} \right]\mathbf{k}$$

8. In this case C is the circle $x^2 + y^2 = 4$, $z = 0$, $dz = 0$.

Line Integral: $\displaystyle\int_C \mathbf{F} \cdot d\mathbf{r} = \int_C -y\, dx + x\, dy$

Let $x = 2 \cos t$, $y = 2 \sin t$, then $dx = -2 \sin t\, dt$, $dy = 2 \cos t\, dt$, and $\displaystyle\int_C -y\, dx + x\, dy = \int_0^{2\pi} 4\, dt = 8\pi$.

Double Integral: $F(x, y, z) = z + x^2 + y^2 - 4$, $\mathbf{N} = \dfrac{\nabla F}{\|\nabla F\|} = \dfrac{2x\mathbf{i} + 2y\mathbf{j} + \mathbf{k}}{\sqrt{1 + 4x^2 + 4y^2}}$, $dS = \sqrt{1 + 4x^2 + 4y^2}\, dA$

$\text{curl } \mathbf{F} = 2\mathbf{k}$, therefore

$$\iint (\text{curl } \mathbf{F}) \cdot \mathbf{N}\, dS = \int_R \int 2\, dA = \int_{-2}^{2} \int_{-\sqrt{4-x^2}}^{\sqrt{4-x^2}} 2\, dy\, dx = 2\int_{-2}^{2} 2\sqrt{4 - x^2}\, dx$$

$$= 4\int_{-2}^{2} \sqrt{4 - x^2}\, dx = 2\left[x\sqrt{4 - x^2} + 4 \arcsin\frac{x}{2} \right]_{-2}^{2} = 8\pi.$$

10. Line Integral: From the accompanying figure we see that for

C_1: $y = 0$, $z = 0$, $dy = dz = 0$

C_2: $z = y^2$, $x = 0$, $dx = 0$, $dz = 2y\, dy$

C_3: $y = a$, $z = a^2$, $dy = dz = 0$

C_4: $z = y^2$, $x = a$, $dx = 0$, $dz = 2y\, dy$.

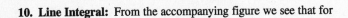

Hence,

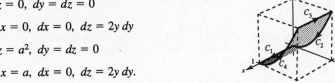

$$\int_C \mathbf{F} \cdot d\mathbf{r} = \int_C z^2\, dx + x^2\, dy + y^2\, dz$$

$$= \int_{C_1} 0 + \int_{C_2} 2y^3\, dy + \int_{C_3} a^4\, dx + \int_{C_4} a^2\, dy + y^2(2y)\, dy$$

$$= \int_0^a 2y^3\, dy + \int_0^a a^4\, dx + \int_a^0 a^2\, dy + \int_a^0 2y^3\, dy = \left[a^4 x \right]_0^a + \left[a^2 y \right]_a^0 = a^5 - a^3 = a^3(a^2 - 1).$$

—CONTINUED—

10. —CONTINUED—

Double Integral: Since $\mathbf{F}(x, y, z) = y^2 - z$, we have

$$\mathbf{N} = \frac{2y\mathbf{j} - \mathbf{k}}{\sqrt{1 + 4y^2}} \text{ and } dS = \sqrt{1 + 4y^2}\, dA.$$

Furthermore, **curl F** $= 2y\mathbf{i} + 2z\mathbf{j} + 2x\mathbf{k}$. Therefore,

$$\int_S\int (\text{curl }\mathbf{F}) \cdot \mathbf{N}\, dS = \int_R\int (4yz - 2x)\, dA = \int_0^a \int_0^a (4y^2 - 2x)\, dy\, dx = \int_0^a (a^4 - 2ax)\, dx = \left[a^4 x - ax^2\right]_0^a = a^3(a^2 - 1).$$

12. Let $A = (0, 0, 0)$, $B = (1, 1, 1)$, and $C = (0, 0, 2)$. Then $\mathbf{U} = \vec{AB} = \mathbf{i} + \mathbf{j} + \mathbf{k}$, and $\mathbf{V} = \vec{AC} = 2\mathbf{k}$, and

$$\mathbf{N} = \frac{\mathbf{U} \times \mathbf{V}}{\|\mathbf{U} \times \mathbf{V}\|} = \frac{2\mathbf{i} - 2\mathbf{j}}{2\sqrt{2}} = \frac{\mathbf{i} - \mathbf{j}}{\sqrt{2}}.$$

Hence, $F(x, y, z) = x - y$ and $dS = \sqrt{2}\, dA$. Since **curl F** $= \dfrac{2x}{x^2 + y^2}\mathbf{k}$, we have $\displaystyle\int_S\int (\text{curl }\mathbf{F}) \cdot \mathbf{N}\, dS = \int_R\int 0\, dS = 0.$

14. $\mathbf{F}(x, y, z) = 4xz\mathbf{i} + y\mathbf{j} + 4xy\mathbf{k}$, $S: 9 - x^2 - y^2$, $z \le 0$

$\text{curl }\mathbf{F} = 4x\mathbf{i} + (4x - 4y)\mathbf{j}$

$G(x, y, z) = x^2 + y^2 + z - 9$

$\nabla G(x, y, z) = 2x\mathbf{i} + 2y\mathbf{j} + \mathbf{k}$

$$\int_S\int (\text{curl }\mathbf{F}) \cdot \mathbf{N}\, dS = \int_R\int [8x^2 + 2y(4x - 4y)]\, dA$$

$$= \int_{-3}^3 \int_{-\sqrt{9-x^2}}^{\sqrt{9-x^2}} [8x^2 + 8xy - 8y^2]\, dy\, dx$$

$$= \int_{-3}^3 \left(16x^2\sqrt{9 - x^2} - \frac{16}{3}(9 - x^2)^{3/2}\right) dx = 0$$

16. $\mathbf{F}(x, y, z) = x^2\mathbf{i} + z^2\mathbf{j} - xyz\mathbf{k}$, $S: z = \sqrt{4 - x^2 - y^2}$

$$\text{curl }\mathbf{F} = \begin{vmatrix} \mathbf{i} & \mathbf{j} & \mathbf{k} \\ \dfrac{\partial}{\partial x} & \dfrac{\partial}{\partial y} & \dfrac{\partial}{\partial z} \\ x^2 & z^2 & -xyz \end{vmatrix} = (-xz - 2z)\mathbf{i} + yz\mathbf{j}$$

$G(x, y, z) = z - \sqrt{4 - x^2 - y^2}$

$$\nabla G(x, y, z) = \frac{x}{\sqrt{4 - x^2 - y^2}}\mathbf{i} + \frac{y}{\sqrt{4 - x^2 - y^2}}\mathbf{j} + \mathbf{k}$$

$$\int_S\int (\text{curl }\mathbf{F}) \cdot \mathbf{N}\, dS = \int_R\int \left[\frac{-z(x + 2)x}{\sqrt{4 - x^2 - y^2}} + \frac{y^2 z}{\sqrt{4 - x^2 - y^2}}\right] dA$$

$$= \int_R\int [-x(x + 2) + y^2]\, dA = \int_{-2}^2 \int_{-\sqrt{4-x^2}}^{\sqrt{4-x^2}} (-x^2 - 2x + y^2)\, dy\, dx$$

$$= \int_{-2}^2 \left[-x^2 y - 2xy + \frac{y^3}{3}\right]_{-\sqrt{4-x^2}}^{\sqrt{4-x^2}} dx$$

$$= \int_{-2}^2 \left[-2x^2\sqrt{4 - x^2} - 4x\sqrt{4 - x^2} + \frac{2}{3}(4 - x^2)\sqrt{4 - x^2}\right] dx$$

$$= \int_{-2}^2 \left[-\frac{8}{3}x^2\sqrt{4 - x^2} - 4x\sqrt{4 - x^2} + \frac{8}{3}\sqrt{4 - x^2}\right] dx$$

$$= \left[-\frac{8}{3}\left(\frac{1}{8}\right)\left[x(2x^2 - 4)\sqrt{4 - x^2} + 16\arcsin\frac{x}{2}\right] + \frac{4}{3}(4 - x^2)^{3/2} + \frac{8}{3}\left(\frac{1}{2}\right)\left[x\sqrt{4 - x^2} + 4\arcsin\frac{x}{2}\right]\right]_{-2}^2$$

$$= \left[\left(-\frac{1}{3}\right)(8\pi) + \frac{4}{3}(2\pi) + \frac{1}{3}(-8\pi) - \frac{4}{3}(-2\pi)\right] = 0$$

18. $\mathbf{F}(x, y, z) = yz\mathbf{i} + (2 - 3y)\mathbf{j} + (x^2 + y^2)\mathbf{k}$

$$\mathbf{curl\ F} = \begin{vmatrix} \mathbf{i} & \mathbf{j} & \mathbf{k} \\ \dfrac{\partial}{\partial x} & \dfrac{\partial}{\partial y} & \dfrac{\partial}{\partial z} \\ yz & 2 - 3y & x^2 + y^2 \end{vmatrix} = 2y\mathbf{i} + (y - 2x)\mathbf{j} - z\mathbf{k}$$

S: the first octant portion of $x^2 + z^2 = 16$ over $x^2 + y^2 = 16$

$G(x, y, z) = z - \sqrt{16 - x^2}$

$\nabla G(x, y, z) = \dfrac{x}{\sqrt{16 - x^2}}\mathbf{i} + \mathbf{k}$

$$\iint_S (\mathbf{curl\ F}) \cdot \mathbf{N}\, dS = \iint_R \left[\frac{2xy}{\sqrt{16 - x^2}} - z \right] dA$$

$$= \iint_R \left[\frac{2xy}{\sqrt{16 - x^2}} - \sqrt{16 - x^2} \right] dA$$

$$= \int_0^4 \int_0^{\sqrt{16 - x^2}} \left[\frac{2xy}{\sqrt{16 - x^2}} - \sqrt{16 - x^2} \right] dy\, dx$$

$$= \int_0^4 \left[\frac{x}{\sqrt{16 - x^2}} y^2 - \sqrt{16 - x^2}\, y \right]_0^{\sqrt{16 - x^2}} dx$$

$$= \int_0^4 \left[x\sqrt{16 - x^2} - (16 - x^2) \right] dx$$

$$= \left[-\frac{1}{3}(16 - x^2)^{3/2} - 16x + \frac{x^3}{3} \right]_0^4$$

$$= \left(-64 + \frac{64}{3} \right) - \left(-\frac{64}{3} \right) = -\frac{64}{3}$$

20. $\mathbf{F}(x, y, z) = xyz\mathbf{i} + y\mathbf{j} + z\mathbf{k}$

$$\mathbf{curl\ F} = \begin{vmatrix} \mathbf{i} & \mathbf{j} & \mathbf{k} \\ \dfrac{\partial}{\partial x} & \dfrac{\partial}{\partial y} & \dfrac{\partial}{\partial z} \\ xyz & y & z \end{vmatrix} = xy\mathbf{j} - xz\mathbf{k}$$

S: the first octant portion of $z = x^2$ over $x^2 + y^2 = a^2$. We have

$\mathbf{N} = \dfrac{2x\mathbf{i} - \mathbf{k}}{\sqrt{1 + 4x^2}}$ and $dS = \sqrt{1 + 4x^2}\, dA$.

$$\iint_S (\mathbf{curl\ F}) \cdot \mathbf{N}\, dS = \iint_R xz\, dA = \iint_R x^3\, dA$$

$$= \int_0^a \int_0^{\sqrt{a^2 - x^2}} x^3\, dy\, dx$$

$$= \int_0^a x^3 \sqrt{a^2 - x^2}\, dx$$

$$= \left[-\frac{1}{3}x^2(a^2 - x^2)^{3/2} - \frac{2}{15}(a^2 - x^2)^{5/2} \right]_0^a$$

$$= \frac{2}{15}a^5$$

22. $\mathbf{F}(x, y, z) = -z\mathbf{i} + y\mathbf{k}$

$S: x^2 + y^2 = 1$

$$\text{curl } \mathbf{F} = \begin{vmatrix} \mathbf{i} & \mathbf{j} & \mathbf{k} \\ \dfrac{\partial}{\partial x} & \dfrac{\partial}{\partial y} & \dfrac{\partial}{\partial z} \\ -z & 0 & y \end{vmatrix} = \mathbf{i} - \mathbf{j}$$

Letting $\mathbf{N} = \mathbf{k}$, $\text{curl } \mathbf{F} \cdot \mathbf{N} = 0$ and $\displaystyle\iint_S (\text{curl } \mathbf{F}) \cdot \mathbf{N} \, dS = 0$.

24. $\text{curl } \mathbf{F}$ measures the rotational tendency.

See page 1084.

26. $f(x, y, z) = xyz$, $g(x, y, z) = z$, $S: z = \sqrt{4 - x^2 - y^2}$

(a) $\nabla g(x, y, z) = \mathbf{k}$

$f(x, y, z)\nabla g(x, y, z) = xyz\mathbf{k}$

$\mathbf{r}(t) = 2\cos t\mathbf{i} + 2\sin t\mathbf{j} + 0\mathbf{k}$, $0 \le t \le 2\pi$

$\displaystyle\int_C [f(x, y, z)\nabla g(x, y, z)] \cdot d\mathbf{r} = 0$

(b) $\nabla f(x, y, z) = yz\mathbf{i} + xz\mathbf{j} + xy\mathbf{k}$

$\nabla g(x, y, z) = \mathbf{k}$

$$\nabla f \times \nabla g = \begin{vmatrix} \mathbf{i} & \mathbf{j} & \mathbf{k} \\ yz & xz & xy \\ 0 & 0 & 1 \end{vmatrix} = xz\mathbf{i} - yz\mathbf{j}$$

$$\mathbf{N} = \frac{x}{\sqrt{4 - x^2 - y^2}}\mathbf{i} + \frac{y}{\sqrt{4 - x^2 - y^2}}\mathbf{j} + \mathbf{k}$$

$$dS = \sqrt{1 + \left(\frac{-x}{\sqrt{4 - x^2 - y^2}}\right)^2 + \left(\frac{-y}{\sqrt{4 - x^2 - y^2}}\right)^2} \, dA = \frac{2}{\sqrt{4 - x^2 - y^2}} \, dA$$

$$\iint_S [\nabla f(x, y, z) \times \nabla g(x, y, z)] \cdot \mathbf{N} \, dS = \iint_S \left[\frac{x^2 z}{\sqrt{4 - x^2 - y^2}} - \frac{y^2 z}{\sqrt{4 - x^2 - y^2}}\right] \frac{2}{\sqrt{4 - x^2 - y^2}} \, dA$$

$$= \iint_S \frac{2(x^2 - y^2)}{\sqrt{4 - x^2 - y^2}} \, dA$$

$$= \int_0^2 \int_0^{2\pi} \frac{2r^2(\cos^2\theta - \sin^2\theta)}{\sqrt{4 - r^2}} r \, d\theta \, dr$$

$$= \int_0^2 \left[\frac{2r^3}{\sqrt{4 - r^2}}\left(\frac{1}{2}\sin 2\theta\right)\right]_0^{2\pi} dr = 0$$

Review Exercises for Chapter 14

2. $\mathbf{F}(x, y) = \mathbf{i} - 2y\mathbf{j}$

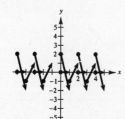

4. $f(x, y, z) = x^2 e^{yz}$

$\mathbf{F}(x, y, z) = 2xe^{yz}\,\mathbf{i} + x^2 z e^{yz}\mathbf{j} + x^2 y e^{yz}\,\mathbf{k}$

$= xe^{yz}(2\mathbf{i} + xz\mathbf{j} + xy\mathbf{k})$

6. Since $\partial M/\partial y = -1/x^2 = \partial N/\partial x$, **F** is conservative. From $M = \partial U/\partial x = -y/x^2$ and $N = \partial U/\partial y = 1/x$, partial integration yields $U = (y/x) + h(y)$ and $U = (y/x) + g(x)$ which suggests that $U(x, y) = (y/x) + C$.

8. Since $\partial M/\partial y = -6y^2 \sin 2x = \partial N/\partial x$, **F** is conservative. From $M = \partial U/\partial x = -2y^3 \sin 2x$ and $N = \partial U/\partial y = 3y^2(1 + \cos 2x)$, we obtain $U = y^3 \cos 2x + h(y)$ and $U = y^3(1 + \cos 2x) + g(x)$ which suggests that $h(y) = y^3$, $g(x) = C$, and $U(x, y) = y^3(1 + \cos 2x) + C$.

10. Since

$$\frac{\partial M}{\partial y} = 4x = \frac{\partial N}{\partial x},$$

$$\frac{\partial M}{\partial z} = 2z = \frac{\partial P}{\partial x},$$

$$\frac{\partial N}{\partial z} = 6y \neq \frac{\partial P}{\partial y}$$

F is not conservative.

12. Since

$$\frac{\partial M}{\partial y} = \sin z = \frac{\partial N}{\partial x}, \quad \frac{\partial M}{\partial z} = y \cos z \neq \frac{\partial P}{\partial x},$$

F is not conservative.

14. Since $\mathbf{F} = xy^2\mathbf{j} - zx^2\mathbf{k}$;

  (a) div $\mathbf{F} = 2xy - x^2$

  (b) curl $\mathbf{F} = 2xz\mathbf{j} + y^2\mathbf{k}$

16. Since $\mathbf{F} = (3x - y)\mathbf{i} + (y - 2z)\mathbf{j} + (z - 3x)\mathbf{k}$:

  (a) div $\mathbf{F} = 3 + 1 + 1 = 5$

  (b) curl $\mathbf{F} = 2\mathbf{i} + 3\mathbf{j} + \mathbf{k}$

18. Since $\mathbf{F} = (x^2 - y)\mathbf{i} - (x + \sin^2 y)\mathbf{j}$:

  (a) div $\mathbf{F} = 2x - 2\sin y \cos y$

  (b) curl $\mathbf{F} = 0$

20. Since $\mathbf{F} = \dfrac{z}{x}\mathbf{i} + \dfrac{z}{y}\mathbf{j} + z^2\mathbf{k}$:

  (a) div $\mathbf{F} = -\dfrac{z}{x^2} - \dfrac{z}{y^2} + 2z = z\left(2 - \dfrac{1}{x^2} - \dfrac{1}{y^2}\right)$

  (b) curl $\mathbf{F} = -\dfrac{1}{y}\mathbf{i} + \dfrac{1}{x}\mathbf{j}$

22. (a) Let $x = 5t, y = 4t, 0 \leq t \leq 1$, then $ds = \sqrt{41}\, dt$.

$$\int_C xy\, ds = \int_0^1 20t^2 \sqrt{41}\, dt = \frac{20\sqrt{41}}{3}$$

  (b) $C_1: x = t, y = 0, 0 \leq t \leq 4, ds = dt$

    $C_2: x = 4 - 4t, y = 2t, 0 \leq t \leq 1, ds = 2\sqrt{5}\, dt$

    $C_3: x = 0, y = 2 - t, 0 \leq t \leq 2, ds = dt$

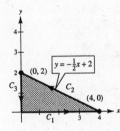

    Therefore, $\displaystyle\int_C xy\, ds = \int_0^4 0\, dt = \int_0^1 (8t - 8t^2)2\sqrt{5}\, dt + \int_0^2 0\, dt$

$$= 16\sqrt{5}\left[\frac{t^2}{2} - \frac{t^3}{3}\right]_0^1 = \frac{8\sqrt{5}}{3}.$$

24. $x = t - \sin t, y = 1 - \cos t, 0 \leq t \leq 2\pi, \dfrac{dx}{dt} = 1 - \cos t, \dfrac{dy}{dt} = \sin t$

$$\int_C x\, ds = \int_0^{2\pi} (t - \sin t)\sqrt{(1 - \cos t)^2 + (\sin t)^2}\, dt = \int_0^{2\pi} (t - \sin t)\sqrt{2 - 2\cos t}\, dt$$

$$= \sqrt{2}\int_0^{2\pi} \left[t\sqrt{1 - \cos t} - \sin t\sqrt{1 - \cos t}\right] dt = \sqrt{2}\left[-\frac{2}{3}(1 - \cos t)^{3/2}\right]_0^{2\pi} + \sqrt{2}\int_0^{2\pi} t\sqrt{1 - \cos t}\, dt$$

$$= \sqrt{2}\int_0^{2\pi} t\sqrt{1 - \cos t}\, dt$$

$$= 8\pi$$

26. $x = \cos t + t \sin t, y = \sin t - t \sin t, 0 \leq t \leq \dfrac{\pi}{2}, dx = t \cos t \, dt, dy = (\cos t - t \cos t - \sin t) \, dt$

$$\int_C (2x - y) \, dx + (x + 3y) \, dy = \int_0^{\pi/2} \left[\sin t \cos t(5t^2 - 6t + 2) + \cos^2 t(t + 1) + \sin^2 t(2t - 3) \right] dt \approx 1.01$$

28. $\mathbf{r}(t) = t\mathbf{i} + t^2\mathbf{j} + t^{3/2}\mathbf{k}, 0 \leq t \leq 4$

$x'(t) = 1, \; y'(t) = 2t, \; z'(t) = \dfrac{3}{2}t^{1/2}$

$$\int_C (x^2 + y^2 + z^2) \, ds = \int_0^4 (t^2 + t^4 + t^3)\sqrt{1 + 4t^2 + \dfrac{9}{4}t} \; dt \approx 2080.59$$

30. $f(x, y) = 12 - x - y$

$C: y = x^2$ from $(0, 0)$ to $(2, 4)$

$\mathbf{r}(t) = t\mathbf{i} + t^2\mathbf{j}, 0 \leq t \leq 2$

$\mathbf{r}'(t) = \mathbf{i} + 2t\mathbf{j}$

$\|\mathbf{r}'(t)\| = \sqrt{1 + 4t^2}$

Lateral surface area:

$$\int_C f(x, y) \, ds = \int_0^2 (12 - t - t^2)\sqrt{1 + 4t^2} \; dt \approx 41.532$$

32. $d\mathbf{r} = [(-4 \sin t)\mathbf{i} + 3 \cos t\mathbf{j}] \, dt$

$\mathbf{F} = (4 \cos t - 3 \sin t)\mathbf{i} + (4 \cos t + 3 \sin t)\mathbf{j}, 0 \leq t \leq 2\pi$

$$\int_C \mathbf{F} \cdot d\mathbf{r} = \int_0^{2\pi} (12 - 7 \sin t \cos t) \, dt = \left[12t - \dfrac{7 \sin^2 t}{2} \right]_0^{2\pi} = 24\pi$$

34. $x = 2 - t, y = 2 - t, z = \sqrt{4t - t^2}, 0 \leq t \leq 2$

$d\mathbf{r} = \left[-\mathbf{i} - \mathbf{j} + \dfrac{2 - t}{\sqrt{4t - t^2}}\mathbf{k} \right] dt$

$\mathbf{F} = \left(4 - 2t - \sqrt{4t - t^2} \right)\mathbf{i} + \left(\sqrt{4t - t^2} - 2 + t \right)\mathbf{j} + 0\mathbf{k}$

$$\int_C \mathbf{F} \cdot d\mathbf{r} = \int_0^2 (t - 2) \, dt = \left[\dfrac{t^2}{2} - 2t \right]_0^2 = -2$$

36. Let $x = 2 \sin t, y = -2 \cos t, z = 4 \sin^2 t, 0 \leq t \leq \pi$.

$d\mathbf{r} = [(2 \cos t)\mathbf{i} + (2 \sin t)\mathbf{j} + (8 \sin t \cos t)\mathbf{k}] \, dt$

$\mathbf{F} = 0\mathbf{i} + 4\mathbf{j} + (2 \sin t)\mathbf{k}$

$$\int_C \mathbf{F} \cdot d\mathbf{r} = \int_0^\pi (8 \sin t + 16 \sin^2 t \cos t) \, dt = \left[-8 \cos t + \dfrac{16}{3} \sin^3 t \right]_0^\pi = 16$$

38. $\displaystyle\int_C \mathbf{F} \cdot d\mathbf{r} = \int_C (2x - y) \, dx + (2y - x) \, dy$

$\mathbf{r}(t) = (2 \cos t + 2t \sin t)\mathbf{i} + (2 \sin t - 2t \cos t)\mathbf{j}, 0 \leq t \leq \pi$

$\displaystyle\int_C \mathbf{F} \cdot d\mathbf{r} = 4\pi^2 + 4\pi$

40. $\mathbf{r}(t) = 10 \sin t\mathbf{i} + 10 \cos t\mathbf{j} + \dfrac{2000/5280}{\pi/2}t\mathbf{k}, \quad 0 \le t \le \dfrac{\pi}{2}$

$= 10 \sin t\mathbf{i} + 10 \cos t\mathbf{j} + \dfrac{25}{33\pi}t\mathbf{k}$

$\mathbf{F} = 20\mathbf{k}$

$d\mathbf{r} = \left(10 \cos t\mathbf{i} - 10 \sin t\mathbf{j} + \dfrac{25}{33\pi}\mathbf{k}\right)$

$\displaystyle\int_C \mathbf{F} \cdot d\mathbf{r} = \int_0^{\pi/2} \dfrac{500}{33\pi}\, dt = \dfrac{250}{33}\, \text{mi} \cdot \text{ton}$

42. $\displaystyle\int_C y\, dx + x\, dy + \dfrac{1}{z}\, dz = \left[xy + \ln|z|\right]_{(0,0,1)}^{(4,4,4)} = 16 + \ln 4$

44. $x = a(\theta - \sin \theta), y = a(1 - \cos \theta), 0 \le \theta \le 2\pi$

(a) $A = \dfrac{1}{2}\displaystyle\int_C x\, dy - y\, dx.$

Since these equations orient the curve backwards, we will use

$A = \dfrac{1}{2}\displaystyle\int (y\, dx - x\, dy)$

$= \dfrac{1}{2}\displaystyle\int_0^{2\pi} [a^2(1 - \cos \theta)(1 - \cos \theta) - a^2(\theta - \sin \theta)(\sin \theta)]\, d\theta + \dfrac{1}{2}\displaystyle\int_0^{2\pi a} (0-0)\, d\theta$

$= \dfrac{a^2}{2}\displaystyle\int_0^{2\pi} [1 - 2\cos \theta + \cos^2 \theta - \theta \sin \theta + \sin^2 \theta]\, d\theta$

$= \dfrac{a^2}{2}\displaystyle\int_0^{2\pi} (2 - 2\cos \theta - \theta \sin \theta)\, d\theta = \dfrac{a^2}{2}(6\pi) = 3\pi a^2.$

(b) By symmetry, $\bar{x} = \pi a$. From Section 14.4,

$\bar{y} = -\dfrac{1}{2A}\displaystyle\int_C y^2\, dx = \dfrac{1}{2A}\displaystyle\int_0^{2\pi} a^3(1 - \cos \theta)^2(1 - \cos \theta)\, d\theta = \dfrac{1}{2(3\pi a^2)}a^3(5\pi) = \dfrac{5}{6}a$

46. $\displaystyle\int_C xy\, dx + (x^2 + y^2)\, dy = \int_0^2\int_0^2 (2x - x)\, dy\, dx$

$= \displaystyle\int_0^2 2x\, dx = 4$

48. $\displaystyle\int_C (x^2 - y^2)\, dx + 2xy\, dy = \int_{-a}^a\int_{-\sqrt{a^2-x^2}}^{\sqrt{a^2-x^2}} 4y\, dy\, dx$

$= \displaystyle\int_{-a}^a 0\, dx = 0$

50. $\displaystyle\int_C y^2\, dx + x^{4/3}\, dy = \int_{-1}^1\int_{-(1-x^{2/3})^{3/2}}^{(1-x^{2/3})^{3/2}} \left(\dfrac{4}{3}x^{1/3} - 2y\right)\, dy\, dx$

$= \displaystyle\int_{-1}^1 \left[\dfrac{4}{3}x^{1/3}y - y^2\right]_{-(1-x^{2/3})^{3/2}}^{(1-x^{2/3})^{3/2}}\, dx$

$= \displaystyle\int_{-1}^1 \dfrac{8}{3}x^{1/3}(1 - x^{2/3})^{3/2}\, dx$

$= \left[-\dfrac{8}{7}x^{2/3}(1 - x^{2/3})^{5/2} - \dfrac{16}{35}(1 - x^{2/3})^{5/2}\right]_{-1}^1$

$= 0$

52. $\mathbf{r}(u, v) = e^{-u/4} \cos v\mathbf{i} + e^{-u/4} \sin v\mathbf{j} + \dfrac{u}{6}\mathbf{k}$

$0 \le u \le 4, \quad 0 \le v \le 2\pi$

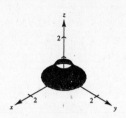

54. $S: \mathbf{r}(u, v) = (u + v)\mathbf{i} + (u - v)\mathbf{j} + \sin v\mathbf{k}, \quad 0 \le u \le 2, 0 \le v \le \pi$

$\mathbf{r}_u(u, v) = \mathbf{i} + \mathbf{j}$

$\mathbf{r}_u(u, v) = \mathbf{i} - \mathbf{j} + \cos v\mathbf{k}$

$\mathbf{r}_u \times \mathbf{r}_v = \begin{vmatrix} \mathbf{i} & \mathbf{j} & \mathbf{k} \\ 1 & 1 & 0 \\ 1 & -1 & \cos v \end{vmatrix} = \cos v\mathbf{i} - \cos v\mathbf{j} - 2\mathbf{k}$

$\|\mathbf{r}_u \times \mathbf{r}_v\| = \sqrt{2\cos^2 v + 4}$

$\displaystyle\iint_S z \, dS = \int_0^\pi \int_0^2 \sin v\sqrt{2\cos^2 v + 4} \, du \, dv = 2\left[\sqrt{6} + \sqrt{2}\ln\left(\dfrac{\sqrt{6} + \sqrt{2}}{\sqrt{6} - \sqrt{2}}\right)\right]$

56. (a) $z = a\left(a - \sqrt{x^2 + y^2}\right), 0 \le z \le a^2$

$z = 0 \Longrightarrow x^2 + y^2 = a^2$

(b) $S: g(x, y) = z = a^2 - a\sqrt{x^2 + y^2}$

$\rho(x, y) = k\sqrt{x^2 + y^2}$

$m = \displaystyle\iint_S e(x, y, z) \, dS$

$= \displaystyle\iint_R k\sqrt{x^2 + y^2} \sqrt{1 + g_x^2 + g_y^2} \, dA$

$= k\displaystyle\iint_R \sqrt{x^2 + y^2} \sqrt{1 + \dfrac{a^2 x^2}{x^2 + y^2} + \dfrac{a^2 y^2}{x^2 + y^2}} \, dA$

$= k\displaystyle\iint_R \sqrt{a^2 + 1}\left(\sqrt{x^2 + y^2}\right) dA$

$= k\sqrt{a^2 + 1} \displaystyle\int_0^{2\pi} \int_0^a r^2 \, dr \, d\theta$

$= k\sqrt{a^2 + 1} \displaystyle\int_0^{2\pi} \dfrac{a^3}{3} \, d\theta$

$= \dfrac{2}{3} k\sqrt{a^2 + 1} \, a^3 \pi$

58. $\mathbf{F}(x, y, z) = x\mathbf{i} + y\mathbf{j} + z\mathbf{k}$

Q: solid region bounded by the coordinate planes and the plane $2x + 3y + 4z = 12$

Surface Integral: There are four surfaces for this solid.

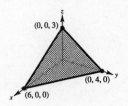
(0, 0, 3)
(0, 4, 0)
(6, 0, 0)

$z = 0 \quad \mathbf{N} = -\mathbf{k}, \quad \mathbf{F} \cdot \mathbf{N} = -z, \quad \int\int_{S_1} 0 \, dS = 0$

$y = 0, \quad \mathbf{N} = -\mathbf{j}, \quad \mathbf{F} \cdot \mathbf{N} = -y, \quad \int\int_{S_2} 0 \, dS = 0$

$x = 0, \quad \mathbf{N} = -\mathbf{i}, \quad \mathbf{F} \cdot \mathbf{N} = -x, \quad \int\int_{S_3} 0 \, dS = 0$

$2x + 3y + 4z = 12, \mathbf{N} = \dfrac{2\mathbf{i} + 3\mathbf{j} + 4\mathbf{k}}{\sqrt{29}}, dS = \sqrt{1 + \left(\dfrac{1}{4}\right) + \left(\dfrac{9}{16}\right)} dA = \dfrac{\sqrt{29}}{4} dA$

$\int\int_{S_4} \mathbf{N} \cdot \mathbf{F} \, dS = \dfrac{1}{4} \int\int_R (2x + 3y + 4z) \, dy \, dx$

$= \dfrac{1}{4} \int_0^6 \int_0^{(12-2x)/3} 12 \, dy \, dx = 3 \int_0^6 \left(4 - \dfrac{2x}{3}\right) dx = 3\left[4x - \dfrac{x^2}{3}\right]_0^6 = 36$

Triple Integral: Since div $\mathbf{F} = 3$, the Divergence Theorem yields.

$\iiint_Q \text{div } \mathbf{F} \, dV = \iiint_Q 3 \, dV = 3(\text{Volume of solid}) = 3\left[\dfrac{1}{3}(\text{Area of base})(\text{Height})\right] = \dfrac{1}{2}(6)(4)(3) = 36.$

60. $\mathbf{F}(x, y, z) = (x - z)\mathbf{i} + (y - z)\mathbf{j} + x^2\mathbf{k}$

S: first octant portion of the plane $3x + y + 2z = 12$

Line Integral:

(0, 0, 6)
(4, 0, 0)
(0, 12, 0)

$C_1: y = 0, \quad dy = 0, \quad z = \dfrac{12 - 3x}{2}, \quad dz = -\dfrac{3}{2} dx$

$C_2: x = 0, \quad dx = 0, \quad z = \dfrac{12 - y}{2}, \quad dz = -\dfrac{1}{2} dy$

$C_3: z = 0, \quad dz = 0, \quad y = 12 - 3x, \quad dy = -3 \, dx$

$\int_C \mathbf{F} \cdot d\mathbf{r} = \int_C (x - z) \, dx + (y - z) \, dy + x^2 \, dz$

$= \int_{C_1} \left[x - \dfrac{12 - 3x}{2} + x^2\left(-\dfrac{3}{2}\right)\right] dx + \int_{C_2} \left[y - \dfrac{12 - y}{2}\right] dy + \int_{C_3} [x + (12 - 3x)(-3)] \, dx$

$= \int_4^0 \left(-\dfrac{3}{2}x^2 + \dfrac{5}{2}x - 6\right) dx + \int_0^{12} \left(\dfrac{3}{2}y - 6\right) dy + \int_0^4 (10x - 36) \, dx = 8$

Double Integral: $G(x, y, z) = \dfrac{12 - 3x - y}{2} - z$

$\nabla G(x, y, z) = -\dfrac{3}{2}\mathbf{i} - \dfrac{1}{2}\mathbf{j} - \mathbf{k}$

$\text{curl } \mathbf{F} = \mathbf{i} - (2x + 1)\mathbf{j}$

$\int\int_S (\text{curl } \mathbf{F}) \cdot \mathbf{N} \, dS = \int_0^4 \int_0^{12 - 3x} (x - 1) \, dy \, dx = \int_0^4 (-3x^2 + 15x - 12) \, dx = 8$

Problem Solving for Chapter 14

2. (a) $z = \sqrt{1 - x^2 - y^2}, \dfrac{\partial z}{\partial x} = \dfrac{-x}{\sqrt{1 - x^2 - y^2}}, \dfrac{\partial z}{\partial y} = \dfrac{-y}{\sqrt{1 - x^2 - y^2}}$

$$dS = \sqrt{\left(\frac{\partial z}{\partial x}\right)^2 + \left(\frac{\partial z}{\partial y}\right)^2 + 1}\, dA = \frac{1}{\sqrt{1 - x^2 - y^2}}$$

$$\nabla T = \frac{-25}{(x^2 + y^2 + z^2)^{3/2}}(x\mathbf{i} + y\mathbf{i} + z\mathbf{k}) = -25(x\mathbf{i} + y\mathbf{j} + z\mathbf{k})$$

$$N = \frac{-\dfrac{\partial z}{\partial x}\mathbf{i} - \dfrac{\partial z}{\partial y}\mathbf{j} + \mathbf{k}}{\sqrt{\left(\dfrac{\partial z}{\partial x}\right)^2 + \left(\dfrac{\partial z}{\partial y}\right)^2 + 1}}$$

$$= \left(\frac{x}{\sqrt{1 - x^2 - y^2}}\mathbf{i} + \frac{y}{\sqrt{1 - x^2 - y^2}}\mathbf{j} + \mathbf{k}\right)\sqrt{1 - x^2 - y^2}$$

$$= x\mathbf{i} + y\mathbf{j} + \sqrt{1 - x^2 - y^2}\,\mathbf{k} = x\mathbf{i} + y\mathbf{j} + z\mathbf{k}$$

$$\text{Flux} = \iint_S -k\nabla T \cdot N\, dS$$

$$= k\iint_R 25(x\mathbf{i} + y\mathbf{j} + z\mathbf{k}) \cdot (x\mathbf{i} + y\mathbf{j} + z\mathbf{k})\frac{1}{\sqrt{1 - x^2 - y^2}}\, dA$$

$$= k\iint_R \frac{25}{\sqrt{1 - x^2 - y^2}}\, dA$$

$$= 25k\int_0^{2\pi}\int_0^1 \frac{1}{\sqrt{1 - r^2}}\, r\, dr\, d\theta = 50\pi k$$

(b) $\mathbf{r}(u, v) = \langle \sin u \cos v, \sin u \sin v, \cos u \rangle$

$\mathbf{r_u} = \langle \cos u \cos v, \cos u \sin v, -\sin u \rangle$

$\mathbf{r_v} = \langle -\sin u \sin v, \sin u \cos v, 0 \rangle$

$\mathbf{r_u} \times \mathbf{r_v} = \langle \sin^2 u \cos v, \sin^2 u \sin v, \sin u \cos u \sin^2 v + \sin u \cos u \cos^2 v \rangle$

$\|\mathbf{r_u} \times \mathbf{r_v}\| = \sin u$

$\text{Flux} = 25k\displaystyle\int_0^{2\pi}\int_0^{\pi/2} \sin u\, du\, dv = 50\pi k$

4. $\mathbf{r}(t) = \left\langle \dfrac{t^2}{2}, t, \dfrac{2\sqrt{2}t^{3/2}}{3} \right\rangle$

$\mathbf{r}'(t) = \left\langle t, 1, \sqrt{2}t^{1/2} \right\rangle, \|\mathbf{r}'(t)\| = t + 1$

$\rho\, ds = \dfrac{1}{1 + t}(t + 1)\, dt = 1$

$I_y = \displaystyle\int_C (x^2 + z^2)\rho\, ds = \int_0^1 \left(\frac{t^4}{4} + \frac{8}{9}t^3\right) dt = \frac{49}{180}$

$I_x = \displaystyle\int_C (y^2 + z^2)\rho\, ds = \int_0^1 \left(t^2 + \frac{8}{9}t^3\right) dt = \frac{5}{9}$

$I_z = \displaystyle\int_C (x^2 + y^2)\rho\, ds = \int_0^1 \left(\frac{t^4}{4} + t^2\right) dt = \frac{23}{60}$

6. $\dfrac{1}{2}\displaystyle\int_C x\,dy - y\,dx = 2\displaystyle\int_0^{\pi/2}\left[\dfrac{1}{2}\sin 2t\cos t - \sin t\cos 2t\right]dt = 2\left(\dfrac{2}{3}\right)$

Hence, the area is $4/3$.

8. $F(x, y) = 3x^2y^2\mathbf{i} + 2x^3y\mathbf{j}$ is conservative.

$f(x, y) = x^3y^2$ potential function.

Work $= f(2, 4) - f(1, 1) = 8(16) - 1 = 127$

10. Area $= \pi ab$

$\mathbf{r}(t) = a\cos t\mathbf{i} + b\sin t\mathbf{j},\ 0 \le t \le 2\pi$

$\mathbf{r}'(t) = -a\sin t\mathbf{i} + b\cos t\mathbf{j}$

$\mathbf{F} = -\dfrac{1}{2}b\sin t\mathbf{i} + \dfrac{1}{2}a\cos t\mathbf{j}$

$\mathbf{F}\cdot d\mathbf{r} = \left[\dfrac{1}{2}ab\sin^2 t + \dfrac{1}{2}ab\cos^2 t\right]dt = \dfrac{1}{2}ab$

$W = \displaystyle\int_0^{2\pi}\mathbf{F}\cdot d\mathbf{r} = \dfrac{1}{2}ab(2\pi) = \pi ab$

Same as area.

APPENDIX A

Appendix A.1   Additional Topics in Differential Equations

Solutions to Even-Numbered Exercises

2.

x	-4	-2	0	2	4	8
y	2	0	4	4	6	8
dy/dx	$-2\sqrt{2}$	-2	0	0	$-2\sqrt{2}$	-8

$\dfrac{dy}{dx} = x \cos \dfrac{\pi y}{8}$. For $(x, y) = (-4, 2)$, $\dfrac{dy}{dx} = -4 \cos \dfrac{\pi 2}{8} = -2\sqrt{2}$.

4. (a), (c)

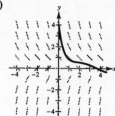

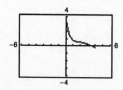

(b) $y' + 2y = \sin x$ Integrating factor: $e^{\int 2\,dx} = e^{2x}$

$e^{2x}y' + 2e^{2x}y = e^{2x} \sin x$

$(ye^{2x}) = \int e^{2x} \sin x \, dx$

$ye^{2x} = \dfrac{1}{5}e^{2x}(2 \sin x - \cos x) + C$

$y(0) = 4 \Rightarrow 4 = \dfrac{1}{5}(0 - 1) + C \Rightarrow 4 = \dfrac{-1}{5} + C \Rightarrow C = \dfrac{21}{5}$

$ye^{2x} = \dfrac{1}{5}e^{2x}(2 \sin x - \cos x) + \dfrac{21}{5}$

$y = \dfrac{1}{5}(2 \sin x - \cos x) + \dfrac{21}{5}e^{-2x}$

6. (a), (c)

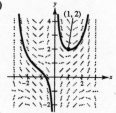

(b) $\dfrac{dy}{dx} = \csc x - y \cot x$

$\dfrac{dy}{dx} + (\cot x)y = \csc x$

Integrating factor: $e^{\int \cot x \, dx} = e^{\ln|\sin x|} = \sin x$

$\sin x \, y' + \cos x \, y = 1$

$(y \sin x)' = 1$

$y \sin x = x + C$

$y(1) = 2 \Rightarrow 2 \sin 1 = 1 + C \Rightarrow C = 2 \sin 1 - 1 \approx 0.683$

$y = x \csc x + C \csc x$

8.

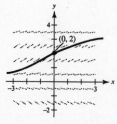

450

10. $y' = x + y$, $y(0) = 2$, $n = 20$, $h = 0.05$

$y_1 = y_0 + hF(x_0, y_0) = 2 + (0.05)(0 + 2) = 2.1$

$y_2 = y_1 + hF(x_1, y_1) = 2.1 + (0.05)(0.05 + 2.1) = 2.2075$, etc.

The table shows the values for $n = 0, 2, 4, \ldots, 20$.

n	0	2	4	6	8	10	12	14	16	18	20
x_n	0	0.1	0.2	0.3	0.4	0.5	0.6	0.7	0.8	0.9	1.0
y_n	2	2.208	2.447	2.720	3.032	3.387	3.788	4.240	4.749	5.320	5.960

12. $y' = 0.5x(3 - y)$, $y(0) = 1$, $n = 5$, $h = 0.4$

$y_1 = y_0 + hF(x_0, y_0) = 1 + (0.4)(0.5(0)(3 - 1)) = 1$

$y_2 = y_1 + hF(x_1, y_1) = 1 + (0.4)(0.5(0.4)(3 - 1)) = 1.16$, etc.

n	0	1	2	3	4	5
x_n	0	0.4	0.8	1.2	1.6	2.0
y_n	1	1	1.16	1.454	1.825	2.201

14. $y' = \cos x + \sin y$, $y(0) = 5$, $n = 10$, $h = 0.1$

$y_1 = y_0 + hF(x_0, y_0) = 5 + (0.1)(\cos 0 + \sin 5) \approx 5.0041$

$y_2 = y_1 + hF(x_1, y_1) = 5.0041 + (0.1)(\cos(0.1) + \sin(5.0041)) \approx 5.0078$, etc.

n	0	1	2	3	4	5	6	7	8	9	10
x_n	0	0.1	0.2	0.3	0.4	0.5	0.6	0.7	0.8	0.9	1.0
y_n	5	5.004	5.008	5.010	5.010	5.007	4.999	4.985	4.965	4.938	4.903

16. True

$y' + y(x - e^x) = 0$ is first-order linear.

18. $\dfrac{dy}{dx} + \left(\dfrac{2}{x}\right)y = 3x + 1$

Integrating factor: $e^{\int (2/x)\,dx} = e^{\ln x^2} = x^2$

$x^2 y = \displaystyle\int x^2(3x + 1)\,dx = \dfrac{3}{4}x^4 + \dfrac{1}{3}x^3 + C$

$y = \dfrac{3x^2}{4} + \dfrac{x}{3} + \dfrac{C}{x^2}$

20. $\dfrac{dy}{dx} - \dfrac{3y}{x^2} = \dfrac{1}{x^2}$

Integrating factor: $e^{-\int (3/x^2)\,dx} = e^{3/x}$

$ye^{3/x} = \displaystyle\int \dfrac{1}{x^2}e^{3/x}\,dx = -\dfrac{1}{3}e^{3/x} + C$

$y = -\dfrac{1}{3} + Ce^{-3/x}$

22. $y' + 2xy = 2x$

Integrating factor: $e^{\int 2x\,dx} = e^{x^2}$

$ye^{x^2} = \displaystyle\int 2xe^{x^2}\,dx = e^{x^2} + C$

$y = 1 + Ce^{-x^2}$

24. $\dfrac{dy}{dx} = \dfrac{e^x - 2y}{x} = \dfrac{-2}{x}y + \dfrac{e^x}{x}$

$y' + \dfrac{2}{x}y = \dfrac{e^x}{x}$

Integrating factor: $e^{\int 2/x\, dx} = e^{2\ln|x|} = x^2$

$x^2 y' + 2xy = xe^x$

$(x^2 y)' = xe^x$

$x^2 y = \displaystyle\int xe^x\, dx = xe^x - e^x + C$

$y = \dfrac{e^x}{x} - \dfrac{e^x}{x^2} + \dfrac{C}{x^2}$

26. $[(y - 1)\sin x]\,dx - dy = 0$

$y' - (\sin x)y = -\sin x$

Integrating factor: $e^{\int -\sin x\, dx} = e^{\cos x}$

$ye^{\cos x} = \displaystyle\int -\sin x e^{\cos x}\, dx = e^{\cos x} + C$

$y = 1 + Ce^{-\cos x}$

28. $y' + 5y = e^{5x}$

Integrating factor: $e^{\int 5\, dx} = e^{5x}$

$ye^{5x} = \displaystyle\int e^{10x}\, dx = \dfrac{1}{10}e^{10x} + C$

$y = \dfrac{1}{10}e^{5x} + Ce^{-5x}$

30. $xy' + y = \sin x$

$y' + \left(\dfrac{1}{x}\right)y = \dfrac{1}{x}\sin x$

Integrating factor: $e^{\int (1/x)\, dx} = e^{\ln x} = x$

$yx = \displaystyle\int \sin x\, dx = -\cos x + C$

$yx + \cos x = C$

32. $y' = y + 2x(y - e^x)$

$y' - (1 + 2x)y = -2xe^x$

Integrating factor: $e^{\int -(1 + 2x)\, dx} = e^{-(x + x^2)}$

$ye^{-(x + x^2)} = \displaystyle\int e^{-(x + x^2)}(-2xe^x)dx = e^{-x^2} + C$

$y = e^x(1 + Ce^{x^2})$

34. $x^3 y' + 2y = e^{1/x^2}$

$y' + \left(\dfrac{2}{x^3}\right)y = \dfrac{1}{x^3}e^{1/x^2}$

Integrating factor: $e^{\int (2/x^3)\, dx} = e^{-(1/x^2)}$

$ye^{-1/x^2} = \displaystyle\int \dfrac{1}{x^3}\, dx = -\dfrac{1}{2x^2} + C_1$

$y = e^{1/x^2}\left(\dfrac{Cx^2 - 1}{2x^2}\right)$

Initial condition: $y(1) = e,\ C = 3$

Particular solution: $y = e^{1/x^2}\left(\dfrac{3x^2 - 1}{2x^2}\right)$

36. $y' + y \sec x = \sec x$

Integrating factor: $e^{\int \sec x\, dx} = e^{\ln|\sec x + \tan x|} = \sec x + \tan x$

$y(\sec x + \tan x) = \displaystyle\int (\sec x + \tan x)\sec x\, dx = \sec x + \tan x + C$

$y = 1 + \dfrac{C}{\sec x + \tan x}$

Initial condition: $y(0) = 4,\ 4 = 1 + \dfrac{C}{1 + 0},\ C = 3$

Particular solution: $y = 1 + \dfrac{3}{\sec x + \tan x} = 1 + \dfrac{3\cos x}{1 + \sin x}$

38. $y' + (2x - 1)y = 0$

Integrating factor: $e^{\int (2x-1)\,dx} = e^{x^2 - x}$

$ye^{x^2 - x} = C$

$\quad\quad y = Ce^{x - x^2}$

Separation of variables:

$$\int \frac{1}{y}\,dy = \int (1 - 2x)\,dx$$

$\ln y + \ln C_1 = x - x^2$

$\quad\quad yC_1 = e^{x - x^2}$

$\quad\quad\quad y = Ce^{x - x^2}$

Initial condition: $y(1) = 2,\ 2 = C$

Particular solution: $y = 2e^{x - x^2}$

40. $2xy' - y = x^3 - x$

$y' - \left(\dfrac{1}{2x}\right)y = \dfrac{1}{2}(x^2 - 1)$

Integrating factor: $e^{\int -(1/2x)\,dx} = e^{\ln x^{-1/2}} = x^{-1/2}$

$yx^{-1/2} = \displaystyle\int \frac{1}{2}x^{-1/2}(x^2 - 1)\,dx$

$\quad\quad\quad = \dfrac{1}{5}x^{5/2} - x^{1/2} + C$

$\quad\quad y = \dfrac{1}{5}x^3 - x + C\sqrt{x}$

Initial condition: $y(4) = 2$

$\quad\quad 2 = \dfrac{64}{5} - 4 + 2C$

$\quad\quad C = -\dfrac{17}{5}$

Particular solution: $y = \dfrac{1}{5}x^3 - x - \dfrac{17}{5}\sqrt{x}$

42. (a)

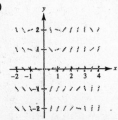

(b) $y' + (\cot x)y = x$

Integrating factor $e^{\int \cot x\,dx} = e^{\ln \sin x} = \sin x$

$y' \sin x + (\cos x)y = x \sin x$

$y \sin x = \displaystyle\int x \sin x\,dx = \sin x - x \cos x + C$

$\quad\quad y = 1 - x \cot x + C - \csc x$

$(1, 1)$: $1 = 1 - \cot(1) + C \csc(\perp) \implies C = \dfrac{\cot(1)}{\csc(1)} = \cos(1)$

$\quad\quad y = 1 - x \cot x + \cos(1) \csc x$

$(3, -1)$: $-1 = 1 - 3 \cot 3 + C \cdot \csc 3 \implies C \cdot \csc 3 = 3 \cot 3 - 2$

$\quad\quad C = \dfrac{3 \cot 3 - 2}{\csc 3} = 3 \cos 3 - 2 \sin 3$

(c)

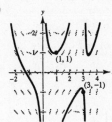

44. $I(0) = 0, E_0 = 110$ volts

$R = 550$ ohms, $L = 4$ henrys

$0 = \dfrac{110}{550} + Ce^o, C = -\dfrac{1}{5}$

$y = \dfrac{E_0}{R} - \dfrac{1}{5}e^{-Rt/L} = \dfrac{1}{5}(1 - e^{-137.5t})$

$\displaystyle\lim_{t\to\infty} \dfrac{1}{5}(1 - e^{-137.5t}) = \dfrac{1}{5}$ amp

$(0.90)\left(\dfrac{1}{5}\right) = 0.18$

$0.18 = \dfrac{1}{5}(1 - e^{-137.5t})$

$0.90 = 1 - e^{-137.5t}$

$-137.5t = \ln(0.10)$

$t = \dfrac{\ln(0.10)}{-137.5} \approx 0.0167$

46. $\sin(\omega t - \phi) = \sin \omega t \cos \phi - \cos \omega t \sin \phi$

$= \dfrac{R}{\sqrt{R^2 + \omega^2 L^2}} \sin \omega t - \dfrac{\omega L}{\sqrt{R^2 \omega^2 L^2}} \cos \omega t$

$= \dfrac{1}{\sqrt{R^2 + \omega^2 L^2}}(R \sin \omega t - \omega L \cos \omega t)$

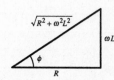

From Exercise 45, we have:

$I = Ce^{-Rt/L} + \dfrac{E_0}{\sqrt{R^2 + \omega^2 L^2}} \cdot \dfrac{1}{\sqrt{R^2 + \omega^2 L^2}}(R \sin \omega t - \omega L \cos \omega t) = Ce^{-kt/L} + \dfrac{E_0}{\sqrt{R^2 + \omega^2 L^2}}\sin(\omega t - \phi)$

48. $\dfrac{dA}{dt} = rA + P$

$\dfrac{dA}{rA + P} = dt$

$\displaystyle\int \dfrac{dA}{rA + P} = \int dt$

$\dfrac{1}{r}\ln(rA + P) = t + C_1$

$\ln(rA + P) = rt + C_2$

$rA + P = e^{rt + C_2}$

$A = \dfrac{C_3 e^{rt} - P}{r}$

$A = Ce^{rt} - \dfrac{P}{r}$

When $t = 0$: $A = 0$

$0 = C - \dfrac{P}{r} \Rightarrow C = \dfrac{P}{r}$

$A = \dfrac{P}{r}(e^{rt} - 1)$

50. $800,000 = \dfrac{75,000}{0.08}(e^{0.08t} - 1)$

$1.85333333 = e^{0.08t}$

$t = \dfrac{\ln(1.85333333)}{0.08} \approx 7.71$ years

52. $A_0 = 500,000$, $r = 0.10$

    (a) $P = 40,000$

$$A = \frac{40,000}{0.10} + \left(500,000 - \frac{40,000}{0.10}\right)e^{0.10t} = 100,000(4 + e^{0.10t})$$

    The balance continues to increase.

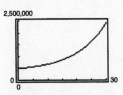

    (b) $P = 50,000$

$$A = \frac{50,000}{0.10} + \left(500,000 - \frac{50,000}{0.10}\right)e^{0.10t} = 500,000$$

    The balance remains at \$500,000.

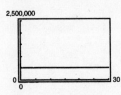

    (c) $P = 60,000$

$$A = \frac{60,000}{0.10} + \left(500,000 - \frac{60,000}{0.10}\right)e^{0.10t} = 100,000(6 - e^{0.10t})$$

    The balance decreases and is depleted in $t = (\ln 6)/0.10 \approx 17.9$ years.

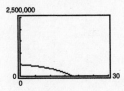

54. (a) $\dfrac{dN}{dt} = k(30 - N)$

    (b) $N' + kN = 30k$

      Let $P(t) = k$, $Q(t) = 30k$, then the integrating factor is $u(t) = e^{kt}$.

$$N = e^{-kt}\int 30ke^{kt}\, dt = e^{-kt}(30e^{kt} + C) = 30 + Ce^{-kt}$$

    (c) When $t = 1$: $N = 10$

$$10 = 30 + Ce^{-k} \text{ and when } t = 20\text{: } N = 19 \qquad 19 = 30 + Ce^{-20k}$$

$$C = -20e^{k} \qquad\qquad\qquad\qquad C = -11e^{20k}$$

$$-20e^{k} = -11e^{20k}$$

$$\frac{20}{11} = e^{19k}$$

$$k = \frac{\ln(20/11)}{19} \approx 0.0315$$

$$C = -20e^{[\ln(20/11)]/19} \approx -20.6393$$

$$N = 30 - 20.6393e^{-0.0315t}$$

56. $y' - 2y = 0$

$$\int \frac{dy}{y} = \int 2\, dx$$

$$\ln y = 2x + C_1$$

$$y = Ce^{2x}$$

Matches d.

58. $y' - 2xy = x$

$$\int \frac{dy}{2y + 1} = \int x\, dx$$

$$\frac{1}{2}\ln(2y + 1) = \frac{1}{2}x^2 + C_1$$

$$2y + 1 = C_2 e^{x^2}$$

$$y = -\frac{1}{2} + Ce^{x^2}$$

Matches b.